# Understanding Federal Courts and Jurisdiction

(2016–Pub.844)

# Understanding Federal Courts and Jurisdiction

## *Second Edition*

**Linda Mullenix**
*Rita and Morris Atlas Chair in Advocacy*
*University of Texas School of Law*

**Martin Redish**
*Louis and Harriet Ancel Professor of Law and Public Policy*
*Northwestern University School of Law*

**Georgene Vairo**
*Professor of Law*
*David P. Leonard Chair*
*Loyola Law School, Los Angeles*

Carolina Academic Press
Durham, North Carolina

ISBN: 978-1-5310-0254-1

**Library of Congress Cataloging-in-Publication Data**

**Mullenix, Linda S., 1950- author.**

**Understanding federal courts and jurisdiction / Linda Mullenix, Rita and Morris Atlas Chair in Advocacy, University of Texas School of Law; Martin Redish, Louis and Harriet Ancel Professor of Law and Public Policy, Northwestern University School of Law; Georgene Vairo, Professor of Law, David P. Leonard Chair Loyola Law School, Los Angeles. -- Second edition.**

**pages cm**

**Includes index.**

**ISBN 978-1-63044-792-2**

**1. Courts--United States. 2. Jurisdiction--United States. I. Redish, Martin H., author. II. Vairo, Georgene, author. III. Title.**

**KF8719.M85 2014**

**347.73'12--dc23**

2014025390

Carolina Academic Press, LLC
700 Kent Street
Durham, NC 27701
Telephone (919) 489-7486
Fax (919) 493-5668
www.caplaw.com

Printed in the United States of America

(2016–Pub.844)

# *Table of Contents*

# DIVISION I

# FEDERAL COURTS AND JURISDICTION

# Chapter 1

# THE STRUCTURE OF THE FEDERAL JUDICIAL SYSTEM

## § 1.01 ARTICLE III AND THE SCOPE OF FEDERAL JUDICIAL POWER

Article III, Section 1 of the Constitution of the United States vests the federal judicial power in a Supreme Court and in such inferior courts as Congress may from time to time ordain and establish. Judges of the courts established under the auspices of Article III are given special protections of their independence. In order to insulate them from undue political pressures, Article III judges have life tenure during "good behavior" and may not have their salaries reduced.

Article III, Section 2 extends the federal judicial power to a variety of cases and controversies.[1] That provision also gives the Supreme Court original jurisdiction over all cases affecting ambassadors, other public ministers and consuls, and cases in which a state is a party. The Supreme Court has appellate jurisdiction for all other cases to which the federal judicial power extends, subject to such exceptions and regulations as Congress may make.[2] Congress also possesses a limited power to create non-Article III courts that may exercise the federal judicial power.

## § 1.02 THE SALARY AND TENURE PROTECTIONS OF ARTICLE III JUDGES

Although it is widely thought that Article III provided Congress with the discretion whether or not to create lower federal courts, if inferior Article III courts are created, the judges of those courts must have certain protections. Specifically, Article III judges are afforded lifetime tenure during "good behavior" (the Tenure Clause) and are protected against salary reduction (the Compensation Clause).[3] These two attributes of Article III judges are designed to promote the independence of the judicial branch.[4] As Alexander Hamilton wrote in the Federalist Papers:[5]

---

[1] U.S. Const., art. III, § 2.

[2] U.S. Const., art. III, § 2.

[3] U.S. Const., art. III, § 1.

[4] Article III promotes independent judiciary. United States v. Will, 449 U.S. 200, 217–218 (1980).

[5] View of Alexander Hamilton. Hamilton, The Federalist Papers No. 78, at 508 (Bicentennial ed. 1976); *see also* Evans v. Gore, 253 U.S. 245, 253 (1920) (complete independence of court is particularly essential in limited Constitution).

> That inflexible and uniform adherence to the rights of the Constitution, and of individuals, which we perceive to be indispensable in the courts of justice, can certainly not be expected from judges who hold their offices by a temporary commission. Periodical appointments, however regulated, or by whomsoever made, would, in some way or other, be fatal to their necessary independence.

Article III proceeds on the assumption that judges may be the subject of congressional retribution because of their decisions while lacking the ability either to protect individual rights against majoritarian encroachment or to provide meaningful legitimacy to the decisions of the majoritarian branches. The insulation of federal judges from majoritarian political pressures is central both to the maintenance of judicial integrity and to the vital role performed by the judiciary as the ultimate interpreter and enforcer of the countermajoritarian Constitution. Absent protection and interpretation by independent judges, as Chief Justice John Marshall warned, "then written constitutions are absurd attempts, on the part of the people, to limit a power in its own nature illimitable."[6]

## § 1.03 LIFE TENURE OF ARTICLE III JUDGES DURING "GOOD BEHAVIOR"

Although there appears to have been no definitive ruling on the point, the better view is that impeachment is the sole means by which Congress may remove an Article III judge from office.[7] Such a conclusion makes a great deal of sense as a matter of both constitutional interpretation and political theory. If impeachment were merely one of multiple alternative means of removing federal judges from office, the process's special supermajoritarian limitations could be easily circumvented, rendering them useless for all practical purposes as a protection of judicial independence. For example, if Congress could, under its enumerated power to create inferior courts[8] combined with the Necessary and Proper Clause of Article I,[9] legislatively remove a federal judge from office, the requirements of a Senate trial and a two-thirds Senate vote for conviction could be easily avoided. Because the Constitution's extraordinary procedural limitations on the impeachment process were quite obviously included in order to avoid or reduce the danger of legislative harassment of civil officers,[10] it is most unlikely that the very document that contains the Impeachment Clause could be properly construed to enable Congress so easily to circumvent the clause's inherent procedural protections.

---

[6] View of John Marshall. Marbury v. Madison, 5 U.S. (1 Cranch) 137, 177 (1803). For a more detailed discussion of the countermajoritarian role of the federal judiciary, see Redish, The Federal Courts in the Political Order: Judicial Jurisdiction and American Political Theory, 75–85 (1991).

[7] Impeachment sole constitutional manner of removal of judges. *See* Bergen v. Edenfield, 701 F.2d 906, 908 (11th Cir. 1983) (no law authorizes private action for removal of federal judge and return of salary; only mechanism for removal provided in Constitution is impeachment).

[8] U.S. Const., art. I, § 8, cl. 9.

[9] U.S. Const., art. I, § 8, cl. 18.

[10] *See* Gerhardt, The Federal Impeachment Process: A Constitutional and Historical Analysis (1996).

Despite these compelling textual and policy arguments, the presence of the "good behavior" language in Article III gives rise to the potential for confusion concerning the exclusivity of impeachment as a means of removing federal judges from office. It might be argued that failure to maintain good behavior is an alternative basis for removal of federal judges, in addition to impeachment.[11] The apparent difference in the applicable substantive standards of the two provisions might be viewed as supporting such an interpretation; Article III refers to "good behavior," while the standard for impeachment under Article II is the commission of "treason, bribery, or other high crimes and misdemeanors."[12] This difference in language might be thought to imply the existence of two distinct — and therefore alternative — standards for removal.

Despite the superficially appealing nature of this argument, closer examination reveals flaws in this analysis. Most critical is the fact, previously noted, that construing the "good behavior" language to establish an alternative basis of removal effectively renders nugatory the supermajoritarian limitations contained in the impeachment provisions. Additionally, the absence of even the slightest textual reference to either *who* is to make the determination that the requirement of "good behavior" has been violated or *how* such a determination is to be made (either substantively or procedurally), makes it unlikely that the "good behavior" language was intended to establish a distinct, alternative basis for judicial removal. This point acquires increased force by contrasting the "good behavior" language to the Constitution's careful and detailed description of the procedures to be employed on impeachment.

Further, there is the enormous potential for confusion that inevitably results from such a broad interpretation of "good behavior." If the words, "good behavior" were actually construed to establish an independent basis for removal, do they authorize Congress to remove judges legislatively? Do they authorize the federal judiciary itself to remove its members? There are absolutely no textual or historical bases on which to provide coherent answers to these questions. Thus, while one member of the federal judicial branch has argued that the "good behavior" language is properly construed to vest removal power in the judicial branch,[13] and there has been no definitive construction of the phrase by the Supreme Court, the wisest interpretive course is to construe the words, "good behavior" in Article III as simply a cross-reference to the availability of impeachment. Such a construction would amount to an acknowledgment that the life tenure granted federal judges is qualified by the potential for impeachment, in accordance with the standards and procedures described in the Impeachment Clause.

---

11 *See* Edwards, *Regulating Judicial Misconduct and Divining "Good Behavior" for Federal Judges*, 87 Mich. L. Rev. 765 (1989).

12 U.S. Const., art. II, § 4.

13 *See* Edwards, *Regulating Judicial Misconduct and Divining "Good Behavior" for Federal Judges*, 87 Mich. L. Rev. 765 (1989).

## § 1.04 ARTICLE III JUDGES' PROTECTION AGAINST SALARY REDUCTIONS

### [1] Determining The Methodology of Compensation Clause Analysis

On first examination, the Compensation Clause appears to be as straightforward as virtually any constitutional provision. "The Judges, both of the supreme and inferior courts, shall . . . receive for their services a compensation, which shall not be diminished during their continuance in office."[14] Thus, the political branches may not reduce the salaries of judges protected by Article III.

The framers' obvious motivation in imposing this protection was to insulate the federal judiciary from pressure from the political branches. The framers recognized, in the words of Alexander Hamilton in Federalist No. 79, that "[i]n the general course of human nature, a power over a man's subsistence amounts to a power over his will."[15] The Supreme Court stated in *Evans v. Gore*:[16]

> [T]he prohibition against diminution was not to benefit the judges, but, like the clause in respect of tenure, to attract good and competent men to the bench and to promote that independence of action and judgment which is essential to the maintenance of the guaranties, limitations, and pervading principles of the Constitution and to the administration of justice without respect to persons and with equal concern for the poor and the rich.

Judicial interpretation of the clause, however, has been fraught with confusion. Before examining the specific issues of construction that have arisen in interpretation of the Compensation Clause, it is helpful to explore possible structural methods of analysis that could be applied to the clause. An understanding of these methodological approaches may help to shed light on the narrower doctrinal questions.

Basically, in shaping the Compensation Clause, two possible methodological alternatives were available to the framers. Both may be analogized to alternative methods for determining whether a suit should be dismissed because it is untimely: a "laches" analogy and a "statute of limitations" analogy.

Laches is an equitable doctrine that is designed to effect fundamental fairness in determining whether an action may proceed. Under laches, a court examines each case individually to determine whether, under the specific circumstances, the concerns that give rise to a limitation are present.[17] Thus, in deciding whether a suit is untimely under a laches approach, a court would decide whether, in light of all the relevant circumstances, it would be unfair or unreasonable to allow the plaintiff to

---

[14] U.S. Const., art. III, § 1.

[15] The Federalist No. 79, at 472 (Clinton Rossiter ed., 1961 (emphasis omitted)); *see* Hatter v. United States, 64 F.3d 647, 649 (Fed. Cir. 1995) (quoting Hamilton).

[16] Purpose of Compensation Clause. Evans v. Gore, 253 U.S. 245, 253 (1920).

[17] *See* Redish, *Federal Judicial Independence: Constitutional and Political Perspectives*, 46 Mercer L. Rev. 697, 701 (1995).

proceed. By analogy, a court employing a laches approach to Compensation Clause issues to ensure judicial independence would invalidate any congressional action that, under all of the relevant circumstances, was found to present real a threat to that independence.

By its terms, Article III's protection of judicial salaries appears to reject use of this laches (or equitable) methodology. The clause does not prohibit only those salary reductions that are either aimed at or have the effect of threatening judicial independence. Instead, the terms of Article III quite clearly indicate a methodology more analogous to a statute of limitations approach.

A statute of limitations is a rigid "line in the sand" that is drawn and applied regardless of the special needs or circumstances of the individual situation. In enforcing a statute of limitations, a court may not consider in any particular case that it would be inequitable to proceed even though it was filed a day *before* the expiration of the statutory period; nor may it consider that it would be equitable to allow the action to proceed even though it was filed a day *after* expiration. A statute of limitations is employed for the very purpose of avoiding the uncertainty inherent in the equitable approach to determining the timeliness of a lawsuit. Similarly, by its terms, Article III appears to impose a rigid line concerning federal judicial compensation. Salaries may not be reduced regardless of either congressional motivation or the actual impact of its actions on judicial independence.

Using the statute of limitations approach, as long as Congress does not go so far as to actually reduce judicial salaries, the Compensation Clause would provide no bar to congressional action, even action that may actually be intended to limit or have the effect of undermining judicial independence. On the other hand, if Congress acts to reduce judicial salaries, that action is unconstitutional, even if it is neither discriminatory against federal judges nor designed to undermine judicial independence.

Such an approach might appear clumsy and counterintuitive in the individual instance; however, when viewed from a broader perspective, the methodology — much like the statute of limitations to which it is analogous — makes sense. Both the difficulties in determining whether judicial independence has in fact been compromised in the individual instance and the political friction that could result from such an inquiry would be prohibitive.

Though on its face, the Compensation Clause appears quite clearly to have adopted the statute of limitations rather than the laches approach, the courts have not been consistent in recognizing this fact. In fact, judicial confusion on the issue has been substantial.

### [2] Prohibition of Direct Reduction in Salary of an Article III Judge

The one issue on which all decisions appear to agree is that Congress may not directly reduce judicial salaries, regardless of Congress's motivation or the effect of the reduction on judicial salaries. This is true even if Congress reduces judicial salaries as part cf an across-the-board reduction in federal employee salaries. It would be difficult to imagine how the result could be different, in light of the

Compensation Clause's unambiguous and unqualified prohibitions on such salary reductions.[18]

A decision illustrating this approach is *United States v. Will*, in which the Supreme Court invalidated congressional statutes revoking already vested annual cost-of-living adjustments in salary as violations of the Compensation Clause.[19] In so holding, the Court expressly rejected the argument that Congress could reduce judicial compensation as long as it did not single out judges during the process. The Court stated:[20]

> That the "freeze" applied to various officials in the Legislative and the Executive Branches, as well as judges, does not save the statute. . . . The inclusion in the freeze of other officials who are not protected by the Compensation Clause does not insulate a direct diminution in judges' salaries from the clear, mandate of that Clause; the Constitution makes no exceptions for "nondiscriminatory" reductions.

### [3] Indirect Reductions in Judicial Salaries: A State of Doctrinal Uncertainty

While the courts have uniformly employed an unbending "statute of limitations" approach to *direct* reductions in judicial salaries, the decisions are hopelessly confused on the question of the constitutionality of *indirect* salary reductions, such as the imposition of new taxes by Congress on judicial salaries. In *United States v. Will*, in which the Supreme Court rejected a case-by-case approach to direct reductions in vested salary benefits, it expressly left unresolved whether evidence of congressional intent to influence the judiciary would invalidate a statute that on its face did not directly reduce judicial compensation, citing its decision in *Evans v. Gore*.[21]

In *Evans*, the Court held that the Compensation Clause prohibited imposition of the newly enacted income tax on sitting judges. In so holding, the Court reasoned:[22]

> The prohibition [on judicial salary reduction] in general, contains no excepting words and appears to be directed against all diminution, whether for one purpose or another; and the reasons for its adoption . . . make with impelling force for the conclusion that the fathers of the Constitution intended to prohibit diminution by taxation as well as otherwise — that they regarded the independence of the judges as of far greater importance than any revenue that could come from taxing their salaries.

---

18 *See* U.S. Const., art. III, § 1.

19 Vested salary benefits may not be revoked. United States v. Will, 449 U.S. 200, 217–221 (1980).

20 Fact that judges are not targeted is insignificant. 449 U.S. at 226.

21 Indirect reductions left unresolved. United States v. Will, 449 U.S. 200, 226 n.30 (1980); *see* Evans v. Gore, 253 U.S. 245 (1920).

22 Sitting judges not subject to newly imposed income tax. Evans v. Gore, 253 U.S. 245, (1920).

The Court in *Evans* thus employed a statute-of-limitations methodology: Article III prohibits salary diminution, and imposition of a newly created tax on sitting judges is the equivalent of a diminution.[23] Such a conclusion makes perfect sense. To allow Congress to do indirectly what it is constitutionally prohibited from doing directly would place form over substance by ignoring the simple and obvious fact that both direct and indirect reductions have the same effect of reducing judicial salaries. Moreover, to do so would invite congressional attempts to circumvent an unambiguous constitutional prohibition.

Though *Evans* has never been overruled, both courts and commentators have questioned its modern vitality.[24] *Evans* was limited in the subsequent decision in *O'Malley v. Woodrough*, in which the Court held that judges appointed after adoption of the income tax could constitutionally be subjected to that tax.[25] This result, which is surely correct, in no way conflicts with the core holding in *Evans* because that decision applied solely to judges who were already sitting. However, in *O'Malley*, Justice Frankfurter, speaking for the Court, also did much to undermine *Evans's* historical foundation, stating:[26]

> The meaning which *Evans v. Gore* . . . imputed to the history which explains Article III, § 1 was contrary to the way in which it was read by other English-speaking courts. The decision met wide and steadily growing disfavor from legal scholarship and professional opinion.

He then added a statement, certainly not essential to the decision of the case before him, frontally assaulting *Evans*'s underlying rationale. "To subject [judges] to a general tax," Justice Frankfurter stated, "is merely to recognize that judges are also citizens, and that their particular function in government does not generate an immunity from sharing with their fellow citizens the material burden of the government whose Constitution and laws they are charged with administering."[27]

To the extent *O'Malley* is viewed as challenging the *Evans* rationale, it would seem that, for reasons already discussed, it is *Evans* that should logically prevail. The language of Article III, it should be recalled, speaks of salary reductions, and it would surely defy reality to suggest that such a reduction does not take place when the salaries are reduced indirectly, rather than directly. Moreover, while the courts might seek to strike down indirect reductions that actually threaten judicial independence, the difficulty and awkwardness of engaging in this equitable inquiry lies behind the prophylactically protective nature of separation of powers in general.[28] In any event, the text of Article III does not permit such a course. Either congressional action constitutes a salary reduction, in which case it is unconstitu-

---

[23] 253 U.S. at 255.

[24] Vitality of *Evans* questioned. *See, e.g.*, Atkins v. United States, 556 F.2d 1028, 1044–1045 (Ct. Cl. 1977); Beer v. Commissioner, 64 T.C. 879 (1975); Kornhauser, *The Constitutional Meaning of Income and the Income Taxation of Gifts*, 25 Conn. L. Rev. 1, 20 n.84 (1992).

[25] Later appointed judges subject to income tax. O'Malley v. Woodrough, 307 U.S. 277, 281–282 (1939).

[26] 307 U.S. at 281.

[27] 307 U.S. at 282.

[28] *See* Redish, The Constitution as Political Structure, 99–134 (1995).

tional regardless of its specific effect on judicial independence, or it is not a reduction, in which case, it does not violate the Compensation Clause regardless of its effects. By its terms, the provision does not countenance a case-by-case inquiry into a reduction's impact on judicial independence.

### [4] Provision of Cost of Living Adjustments Left to the Discretion of Congress

During periods of inflation, if Article III judges' salaries are not increased, their real income obviously declines. By inaction, Congress may thus effectively accomplish a diminution in real income, posing an arguable constitutional problem, especially if the salaries of other federal officials are being increased during the inflationary period. Despite substantial inflation, the salaries of Article III judges and a few other federal officials were not substantially increased between 1969 and 1977. Claiming that Congress's failure to grant salary increases constituted an unconstitutional diminution in salary, numerous Article III judges filed suit in the Court of Claims seeking additional compensation.[29]

The Court of Claims rejected the Article III judges' suit. It found that the history of the enactment of the Compensation Clause indicated that the framers were well acquainted with the problems of inflation and with the need to make periodic increases in the Article III judges' salaries.[30] A proposal to provide that Article III judges' salaries could not be *increased* during their term of office was defeated by arguments that increases might be necessary to maintain the attractiveness of judicial service in light of changing economic conditions and judicial workloads.[31] But the Compensation Clause would seem to leave the determination of when increases are warranted to the discretion of Congress. Congress's ability to raise the salaries of Article III judges as a result of inflation does not mean that Congress is *required* to raise them.[32]

Congress might abuse this discretion by raising all other federal salaries, but absent a substantial showing of clearly discriminatory treatment, protection of the Article III judges' real income is probably best left to Congress. One commentator has concluded that although the United States Constitution does leave the question of increases to Congress, Congress has a "moral obligation" to protect the Article III judges' real income, an obligation it has not fulfilled from time to time.[33]

---

[29] Claim that failure to grant salary increases was unconstitutional diminution in salary. *See* Atkins v. United States, 556 F.2d 1028 (Ct. Cl. 1977). After the suit was filed, the Article III judges and the other federal officials were given a substantial pay raise by Congress. *See* 5 U.S.C. § 5332.

[30] Rosenn, *The Constitutional Guaranty Against Diminution of Judicial Compensation*, 24 U.C.L.A. L. Rev. 308 (1976).

[31] 2 Farrand, Records of the Federal Convention 45 (1911).

[32] Adjustments for inflation are not required. Atkins v. United States, 556 F.2d 1028, 1045–1051 (Ct. Cl. 1977).

[33] Rosenn, *The Constitutional Guaranty Against Diminution of Judicial Compensation*, 24 U.C.L.A. L. Rev. 308 (1976).

## § 1.05 CONGRESSIONAL POWER TO CONTROL LOWER FEDERAL COURT JURISDICTION

### [1] The Madisonian Compromise: Congressional Discretion Not to Create Lower Federal Courts

Article III vests the judicial power of the United States in one Supreme Court and "in such inferior courts as the Congress may from time to time ordain and establish."[34] This language appears to give Congress the discretion to determine whether any "inferior courts" are to be created, and the history of the adoption of the United States Constitution strongly supports this interpretation of Congress's power.[35] Though the framers had agreed from the beginning that at least one national tribunal, a Supreme Court, would be necessary, there existed considerable controversy over the need for the creation of inferior federal courts.[36]

One group of framers favored the mandatory creation of lower federal courts because of their fear of state court parochialism and hostility to federal interests. Another group of framers insisted on the prohibition of the creation of lower federal courts, arguing that the state courts could effectively adjudicate claims arising under federal law and that the Supreme Court could adequately unify and oversee state court interpretations of federal law.[37] Ultimately, the framers entered into a compromise, engineered primarily by James Madison, in which the creation of lower federal courts was to be neither required nor prohibited in the body of the United States Constitution. Instead, under this "Madisonian Compromise," Congress was to have the power to create them if it so chose.[38] Nevertheless, from the nation's beginning, Congress did establish lower federal courts.[39]

---

[34] U.S. Const., art. III, § 1.

[35] Congressional discretion to create inferior courts. *See* Lockerty v. Phillips, 319 U.S. 182, 187 (1943) (Article III left Congress free to establish inferior federal courts as it deemed appropriate).

[36] For a complete discussion of this history, *see generally*, Farrand, Records of the Federal Convention (1911); *see also* Calabresi & Lawson, 2007 Colum. L. Rev. 1003; Clinton, *A Mandatory View of Federal Court Jurisdiction: Early Implementation of and Departures from the Constitutional Plan*, 86 Colum. L. Rev. 1515 (1986); Clinton, *A Mandatory View of Federal Court Jurisdiction: A Guided Quest for the Original Understanding of Article III*, 132 U. Pa. L. Rev. 741 (1984); Redish & Woods, *Congressional Power to Control the Jurisdiction of Lower Federal Courts: A Critical Review and a New Synthesis*, 124 U. Pa. L. Rev. 45, 52–55 (1975).

[37] Eisenberg, *Congressional Authority to Restrict Lower Federal Court Jurisdiction*, 83 Yale L.J. 498 (1974).

[38] *See* Redish & Woods, *Congressional Power to Control the Jurisdiction of Lower Federal Courts: A Critical Review and a New Synthesis*, 124 U. Pa. L. Rev. 45, (1975).

[39] *See* 1 Stat. 84 (1789) (Judiciary Act of 1789).

### [2] Congress's Broad Power to Control Lower Federal Court Jurisdiction

It has generally been understood that because Congress has discretion under Article III as to whether or not to create lower federal courts, it can abolish them once they have been created. It was also assumed that because Congress could abolish the lower federal courts completely, logically it could "abolish" them to a lesser extent by allowing them to exist but at the same time limiting their jurisdiction. Thus, although Congress may vest in the lower federal courts full power to hear all cases to which the federal judicial power extends under Article III, Section 2 of the Constitution, it is not required to do so. In other words, Congress's "greater" power to abolish the lower federal courts is widely thought logically to include the "lesser" power to limit the kinds or amount of cases that they can hear.

The leading Supreme Court decision expounding this view is the 1850 case of *Sheldon v. Sill*. Petitioners had challenged the validity of the assignment-of-claims clause of the Judiciary Act of 1789, which vested diversity jurisdiction in the lower federal courts, but excepted suits in which diversity was created by the assignment of promissory notes. Because under Article III the judicial power extends to *all* diversity cases, regardless of any assignment,[40] the issue was whether Congress could refuse to vest in the federal courts the full range of diversity jurisdiction authorized by the Constitution. In upholding the statute, the Supreme Court stated, "It must be admitted, that if the Constitution had ordained and established the inferior courts, and distributed to them their respective powers, they could not be restricted or divested by Congress."[41] But because the Constitution did not do this, the Court concluded that Congress may withhold from any court of its creation jurisdiction of any of the enumerated controversies. Courts created by statute can have no jurisdiction other than that which the statute confers.[42]

Since the inception of the lower federal courts, Congress has assumed that it possesses discretion to define or limit their jurisdiction. Indeed, Congress's power to impose the jurisdictional amount requirement in diversity cases derives ultimately from the terms of the Madisonian Compromise and its logical implications recognized in *Sheldon v. Sill*. For if Congress so desired, it could, under the terms of Article III, Section 2, vest power in the lower federal courts to hear *any* case arising under federal law or involving parties of diverse citizenship. Because of the history and logic surrounding Article III, however, it is generally assumed today that Congress may constitutionally impose a jurisdictional minimum amount as a prerequisite to entering federal court.[43]

---

[40] U.S. Const., art. III, § 2 (judicial power extends to cases between citizens of different states).

[41] Congress may withhold jurisdiction authorized by Article III. Sheldon v. Sill, 49 U.S. (8 How.) 441 (1850).

[42] Sheldon v. Sill, 49 U.S. (8 How.) 441, 449 (1850).

[43] For an argument against the "greater-includes-the-lesser" view, see Rotunda, *Congressional Power to Restrict the Jurisdiction of the Lower Federal Courts and the Problem of School Busing,* 64 Geo. L.J. 839, 842-844 (1976).

## [3] Congressional Power to Control Lower Federal Court Jurisdiction: A Brief Overview of the Scholarly Theories

### [a] *Martin v. Hunter's Lessee*: The View That Judicial Power Must Be Vested in Some Federal Court

Not everyone has agreed that the language of Article III was intended to — or does — provide Congress with discretion to refuse to create lower federal courts. And, of course, if Congress were required to create lower federal courts, then congressional power to limit lower federal court jurisdiction, premised as it is on the assumed congressional power to abolish those courts completely, would not be as broad as *Sheldon v. Sill* suggests.

Early in the nation's history, in *Martin v. Hunter's Lessee,* Justice Joseph Story argued that the framers' choice of language in the drafting of Article III indicated their intent to require the establishment of lower federal courts. He emphasized that Section 1 begins with the phrase, "The judicial power of the United States *shall be vested.*" "The language of the article throughout," he wrote, "is manifestly designed to be mandatory upon the legislature. Its obligatory force is so imperative, that Congress could not, without a violation of its duty, have refused to carry it into operation."[44]

There may be some question whether use of the words, "shall be vested" was intended to be imperative, as Justice Story contended it was. Justice Story did not argue, however, that Article III's language *directly* required the creation of lower federal courts. Rather, he contended that under Article III, Section 1, the "judicial power," as described in Article III, Section 2, must vest *somewhere* in the federal judicial system.[45] If the Supreme Court alone were to have jurisdiction over all of the enumerated jurisdictional areas, there presumably would be no requirement, under Justice Story's analysis, for the creation of lower federal courts.

Justice Story assumed, however, that state courts constitutionally lacked power to hear at least certain federal causes of action.[46] Because the Supreme Court's original jurisdiction is quite limited,[47] he reasoned that in the absence of lower federal courts, there would be no trial forum available for adjudication of federal causes of action. Hence, the Supreme Court could not hear the many cases limited to its appellate jurisdiction because there would be no court from which an appeal could be taken. Thus, the constitutional imperative that the judicial power "shall be vested" in the federal judiciary would not be fulfilled.

The problem with this view is that it disregards the documented and detailed debates of the framers, which seem to reject his conclusion that Congress must

---

[44] View that Congress must establish lower federal courts. *See* Martin v. Hunter's Lessee, 14 U.S. (1 Wheat.) 304, 328, 331 (1816); *see also* 3 Joseph Story Commentaries on the Constitution §§ 1584–1590 (1833).

[45] Martin v. Hunter's Lessee, 14 U.S. (1 Wheat.) 304 (1816).

[46] Martin v. Hunter's Lessee, 14 U.S. (1 Wheat.) 304, 338–340 (1816).

[47] *See* U.S. Const., art. III, § 2 (Supreme Court's original jurisdictional extends only to "all Cases affecting Ambassadors, other public Ministers and Consuls, and those in which a State shall be a Party").

create lower federal courts. Additionally, even if he were correct that the words "shall be vested" were intended to require that the cases within the federal judicial power must be heard at some point by *some* federal court, his assumption that state courts could not adjudicate federal cases, even at the time he wrote, seems to have been incorrect. As noted, many of the framers opposed the creation of lower federal courts precisely because they assumed that state courts could adequately adjudicate federal suits. Since that time, the power and obligation of state courts to hear federal cases has become well established.[48] Justice Story's dictate, then, could be met by vesting original jurisdiction over federal cases in state courts with provision for appellate review by the Supreme Court. Lower federal courts would still not be required.

Not surprisingly, Justice Story's theory has received little acceptance in the years since its inception. One lower court decision that did adopt it is *Eisentrager v. Forrestal*.[49] The overwhelming majority of decisions, however, have rejected the conclusion that Congress was obligated to create lower federal courts.[50] However, one commentator has suggested that the theory should be taken seriously.[51]

### [b] Theory of Mandatory Federal Judicial Review of State Court Constitutional Determinations

An alternative theory is premised on a construction of Article III that restricts Congress's power to regulate federal jurisdiction.[52] According to this view, the history and logic of Article III dictate that there must be at least one Article III forum in which to review assertions of constitutional right. The only meaningful way that the various provisions of Article III can function effectively together is if the adjudication of Article III business may be vested in the state courts, but with a right of review in some Article III court in cases involving claims of federal constitutional rights.[53] Congress may remove either Supreme Court or lower federal court review of state court determinations of constitutional claims, but not both. These seemingly separate provisions concerning congressional power are linked both by means of what is deemed to be the relevant history and by a creative use of the Salary and Tenure Clauses of Article III, Section 1.

---

[48] State courts may hear federal cases. *See, e.g.*, Yellow Freight System, Inc. v. Donnelly, 494 U.S. 820, 826 (1990); Testa v. Katt, 330 U.S. 386 (1947); *see* Ch. 120.

[49] Story's view adopted. Eisentrager v. Forrestal, 174 F.2d 961, 966 (D.C. Cir. 1949), *rev'd on other grounds sub nom.* Johnson v. Eisentrager, 339 U.S. 763 (1950) (if case arises under Constitution, laws, or treaties, of United States, jurisdiction is in district court by compulsion of Constitution itself).

[50] Story's view rejected. *See, e.g.*, Lockerty v. Phillips, 319 U.S. 182, 187 (1943) (Congress could have declined to create any inferior federal courts).

[51] *See* Amar, *A Neo-Federalist View of Article III: Separating the Two Tiers of Federal Jurisdiction*, 65 B.U. L. Rev. 205, 272 (1985).

[52] *See* Sager, *The Supreme Court, 1980 Term — Foreword: Constitutional Limitations on Congress' Authority to Regulate the Jurisdiction of the Federal Courts*, 95 Harv. L. Rev. 17 (1981); *cf.* Redish, *Constitutional Limitations on Congressional Power to Control Federal Jurisdiction: A Reaction to Professor Sager*, 77 Nw. U.L. Rev. 143 (1982).

[53] 95 Harv. L. Rev. at 66.

At no point, of course, does Article III expressly state that there exists a right to an Article III forum in constitutional cases. Indeed, the language appears to vest in Congress broad authority to regulate the jurisdiction of both the lower courts and the Supreme Court. To support the theory, therefore, the case is built in part on the history surrounding Article III's adoption.

It is argued that the drafters deemed federal judicial supervision over both state and federal compliance with the Constitution to be essential. As to the former, "the firm commitment to federal judicial supervision of the states reflected in the history and logic of the Constitution" is cited. Further, the framers put critical restraints on state autonomy into the Constitution itself and gave Congress legislative authority to direct a strong national government, as manifested ultimately in the Supremacy Clause.[54] The framers also concluded that federal judicial, rather than legislative, control should be the method of enforcing limitations on state autonomy.[55]

The most conspicuous aspect of this historical discussion, however, is that at no point does it undermine — and indeed at all times seems perfectly reconcilable with — Article III's language vesting virtually total authority over federal jurisdiction in Congress. The debates that are referred to appear to focus on the question of whether Congress will even have the power to employ the federal judiciary to ensure state compliance with federal law rather than on the issue of Congress's obligation to employ the federal judiciary in this manner.[56] This conclusion follows from the purpose that the framers apparently hoped to achieve in establishing a Supreme Court. According to the proposed evidence, that purpose was to assure state court compliance with federal law.[57] Their fear seems to have been that, absent policing by some branch of the federal government, state courts might undermine federal supremacy. Ultimately, the framers chose the judicial branch to perform this policing function. But the problem with the theory is that if the policy-making branches of the federal government — Congress and the executive — conclude in a particular instance that there is no need to worry about state court interference, there is, by definition, no possibility of interference with federal supremacy.

Perhaps an analogy may be drawn to the subject of substantive federal preemption of state law. To be sure, the constitutional scheme could not function if the states could enact legislation in conflict with relevant federal statutes. But simply because Congress necessarily has the authority to preempt state law does not mean that it cannot decide, in individual instances, to allow the states to legislate in an area subject to congressional control. Every historical reference noted above is at least consistent with, if not limited to, a similar view of congressional authority

---

[54] 95 Harv. L. Rev. at 45–49. The Supremacy Clause provides:

> This Constitution, and the Laws of the United States which shall be made in Pursuance thereof; and all Treaties made, or which shall be made, under the Authority of the United States, shall be the supreme Law of the Land; and the Judges in every State shall be bound thereby, any Thing in the Constitution or Laws of any State to the Contrary notwithstanding.

U.S. Const., art. VI, cl. 2.

[55] 95 Harv. L. Rev. at 46–48.

[56] 95 Harv. L. Rev. at 46–52.

[57] 95 Harv. L. Rev. at 46–52.

to employ the federal judiciary to ensure state compliance with federal law. Therefore, this theory fails to meet the burden of establishing a foundation in the historical context.

Finally, even if one were to accept that the historical case is proven, much more is proven than intended. If there is a need for an Article III court to police the states in cases involving assertions of constitutional rights, then these courts must also be policed on their interpretation and enforcement of *any* federal law if they are not to be allowed to undermine the establishment of national supremacy. The Supremacy Clause is not limited in its scope to matters of constitutional law, much less of constitutional right.

The corollary of the argument is that the language of Article III, when taken as a whole, dictates the availability of an Article III forum for the ultimate enforcement of constitutional rights. State judges need not, and often do not, have their independence protected by Article III's salary and tenure provisions.[58] Therefore, the ability of Congress to direct Article III adjudication to non-Article III entities (including state courts) must have limits; otherwise, the Article III tenure and salary requirements would be meaningless.[59] While this proposition is hardly startling when applied to federal entities, the extension of the proposition to state courts is a novel step.

It is presumably true that the framers did not intend to put in Article III two major premises at war with one another.[60] It therefore might seem reasonable to conclude that whatever else the other provisions of Article III allow Congress to do to federal jurisdiction, they cannot be read to do away with the explicit provision designed to guard judicial independence. On further reflection, however, it is clear that this thesis does not work. Under this analysis, the "whole" is considerably greater than the "sum of all its parts," a result that is no more logically permissible in law than it is in geometry. The difficulty is that the emphasis in attempting to reconcile possibly competing constitutional clauses is reversed. In reality, it is the salary and tenure provision that must not be read in a manner that undermines the explicit language and clear history of the other provisions.

Initially, the language of the salary and tenure provision presents no real dilemma. It states merely that judges of the federal courts created under Article III must retain the specified protections. It in no way posits that this requirement somehow rises above the remaining portions of Article III, which determine Congress's authority to control the jurisdiction of those courts and instead employ the state judiciaries as enforcers of federal law. So read, the salary and tenure provisions mean only that *if and when* Congress employs judges of the federal courts as interpreters and enforcers of federal law, it may not interfere with their independence. Moreover, even if the salary and tenure provisions were read to require the existence of at least some court whose judges retain these protections, such a requirement is fully satisfied by the constitutionally mandated — albeit quite limited — original jurisdiction of the Supreme Court.

---

[58] 95 HARV. L. REV. at 62–63.

[59] 95 HARV. L. REV. at 62.

[60] 95 HARV. L. REV. at 67.

This reading of the salary and tenure provisions is consistent with a traditional separation-of-powers analysis of Article III. Under the clear compromise of the framers and the equally clear language of the Exceptions Clause, Congress has broad discretion to circumvent the federal judiciary in favor of state courts. But Congress may not demean or undermine the integrity of the federal courts by using them for enforcement or interpretation of federal law while denying federal judges full independence.[61] The final balance struck is a form of quid pro quo. If Congress desires the stamp of legitimacy that Article III courts provide, it cannot simultaneously undermine that legitimacy by impeding the independence of those courts. None of this, however, requires that for all assertions of constitutional rights, an Article III federal court must be available. Indeed, if that had been the framers' intent, they quite easily could have said so. They did not, and the language that they did choose, if anything, leads to much the opposite conclusion. No greater weight may be placed on the shoulders of the salary and tenure provisions than they can bear.

One final point about this thesis should be made. Assuming for the moment that it is true that the framers believed that at least one Article III forum must be available to protect constitutional rights, it would seem that, as a practical matter, such a goal could not today be met by relying on the availability of Supreme Court review. As the most casual observer of current Supreme Court practice is well aware, the Court gives full review only to a minuscule percentage of the cases that contain constitutional issues. True, the Court will give at least minimal review to all cases, in that the Justices must make a decision on whether or not to proceed with full review by granting certiorari. But this form of review is cursory at best and, in any event, may fail to reach the merits. Since a *meaningful* review by an Article III forum is today impossible in the Supreme Court for all cases, the logic of the thesis would seem to lead to the conclusion that at least some lower federal court must exist to review assertions of constitutional right, lest the tenure and salary provision be circumvented. So described, the thesis transforms itself into something similar to the position that the jurisdiction of the lower courts cannot be regulated in a substantive manner.[62]

---

[61] Congress may not undermine integrity of federal courts. *See* United States v. Klein, 80 U.S. (13 Wall.) 128, 145–147 (1872) (Congress possesses constitutional authority to limit its appellate jurisdiction, but that power does not extend to congressional vesting of jurisdiction in a manner that undermines Court's independence); *see also* Yakus v. United States, 321 U.S. 414, 460–468 (1944) (Rutledge, J., dissenting; Congress may not confer jurisdiction then direct that it be exercised in unconstitutional manner).

[62] *See* Eisenberg, *Congressional Authority to Restrict Lower Federal Court Jurisdiction*, 83 Yale L.J. 498, (1974). *But see* Sager, *The Supreme Court, 1980 Term — Foreword: Constitutional Limitations on Congress's Authority to Regulate the Jurisdiction of the Federal Courts*, 95 Harv. L. Rev. 17, 35–36 (1981) (rejecting view of Professor Eisenberg). For other criticism of Professor Sager's theory, *see* Gunther, *Congressional Power to Curtail Federal Court Jurisdiction: An Opinionated Guide to the Ongoing Debate*, 36 Stan. L. Rev. 895, 914 (1984); Berger, *Insulation of Judicial Usurpation: A Comment on Lawrence Sager's "Court Stripping" Polemic*, 44 Ohio St. L.J. 611 (1983).

### [c] The View That Some, But Not All, Cases Must Be Heard in a Federal Forum

Another theory of congressional power to control federal jurisdiction finds Justice Story's reliance on the mandatory nature of Article III's "shall-be-vested" directive generally persuasive, but nevertheless rejects Story's conclusion that, as a result, lower federal courts must exist.[63] Rather, according to this theory, the dictates of Article III may be met by the vesting of jurisdiction in either the lower federal courts or the Supreme Court. More significantly, the mandatory reach of Article III's "shall be vested" language is limited to only certain categories of the cases entrusted to the federal judicial power under Article III, Section 2.

Under this view,[64]

> [T]he judicial power of the United States must, as an absolute minimum, comprehend the subject matter jurisdiction to decide finally all cases involving federal questions, admiralty, or public ambassadors. . . . [T]he judicial power may — but need not — extend to cases in the six other, party-defined, jurisdictional categories. The power to decide which of these party-defined cases shall be heard in Article III courts is given to Congress by virtue of its powers to create and regulate the jurisdiction of lower federal courts, to make exceptions to the Supreme Court's appellate jurisdiction, and to enact all laws necessary and proper for putting the judicial power into effect.

This dichotomy is textually premised on the presence of the word "all" as a modifier of the first three categories of cases enumerated in Section 2 and the absence of that modifier in the final three categories.[65]

Immediately, one can recognize an internal contradiction in this textual analysis. On the one hand, the conclusion that Article III imposes a duty on Congress to vest federal jurisdiction in *some* Article III court is premised on the mandatory nature of the words, "shall be vested" contained in Section 1 and the "shall extend" language in Section 2.[66] But those words precede *all* of the categories of cases enumerated in Section 2. Logically, then, the emphasis on the use of the word "shall" and its assumed mandatory nature should lead to the conclusion — as it did Justice Story — that the mandatory vesting of jurisdiction applies to all categories listed in Section 2. As already noted, however, under this theory it does not, because of the respective presence and absence of the word "all" before the various categories enumerated in Section 2. Yet if the mandatory nature of Article III jurisdiction — on which this entire theory is premised — derives from use of the word "shall" in Section 1, what possible difference does the presence or absence of

---

[63] *See* Amar, *A Neo-Federalist View of Article III: Separating the Two Tiers of Federal Jurisdiction*, 65 B.U. L. Rev. 205, 208–209, 212 (1985).

[64] 65 B.U. L. Rev. at 229–230.

[65] 65 B.U. L. Rev. at 218–219.

[66] *See* 65 B.U. L. Rev. at 215 ("[T]he text is clear: 'the judicial Power of the United States *shall* be vested' in a national judiciary. . . . These are words of obligation, paralleling the usage of 'shall' in myriad language of the Constitution. Unless clearly overruled or modified by other language of the Constitution, this mandatory language must be given effect"; footnote omitted, emphasis in original).

the word "all" in Section 2 make? The words "shall be vested" and "shall extend" establish the compulsory nature of Article III jurisdiction, and *those* words apply to all categories of cases listed in Section 2. For example, Section 2 provides that "the judicial power shall extend . . . to controversies to which the United States shall be a party." If the words "shall be vested" in Section 1 are to be construed as mandatory, there is no logical way that this language could reasonably be construed not to mandate jurisdiction in some Article III court for cases to which the United States is a party, despite the absence of the modifier "all."[67] Thus, either the words "shall be vested" in Section 1 give rise to mandatory jurisdiction, in which event *all* categories of cases listed in Section 2 must be heard in an Article III court, or the words do *not* give rise to mandatory jurisdiction, in which event *none* of section 2's jurisdiction is mandatory and the textual basis for the thesis collapses.

Even if one were to ignore this defect in textual construction, the theory cannot withstand analysis because the reliance on the "shall be vested" and "shall extend" language in Article III takes those phrases out of context. Their arguably mandatory nature is unambiguously qualified by Section 1's clear vesting of discretion in Congress not to create lower federal courts and Section 2's equally explicit and unqualified vesting of authority in Congress to make exceptions to the Supreme Court's appellate jurisdiction. It cannot be assumed that the framers intended to counter the clear textual implication derived from a synthesis of these two explicit congressional powers — namely, that Congress has virtually unlimited constitutional power to control Article III court jurisdiction — by the cryptic selective insertion and omission of the word "all" in Section 2. If such a sweeping limitation on congressional power to control federal court jurisdiction were in fact intended, is it reasonable to suppose that the framers would do so in such an indirect and tenuous manner, given the presence of explicit language to the contrary contained in the very same article? Moreover, there is no direct historical evidence to counter this common sense analysis of the framers' behavior. One cannot find a single contemporaneous comment by a framer explaining the meaning of Article III's selective use of the word "all."[68] Rendering this absence even more pertinent is the clear historical basis of the Madisonian Compromise.[69]

### [4] Congress May Impose Procedural Prerequisites to Federal Jurisdiction

Congress's power to regulate federal jurisdiction necessarily includes the power to establish specific procedures that a litigant must follow in order to obtain judicial relief. Thus, the fact that Congress requires litigants to proceed in a particular manner does not violate due process. However, those procedures must not be so

---

[67] It is interesting to note that use of the word "shall" in the clause extending the judicial power to cases to which the United States "shall be" a party establishes that use of the word in the constitutional text does not always imply imposition of a mandatory obligation. Rather, as used here, the word could simply imply the future tense.

[68] *See* Amar, *A Neo-Federalist View of Article III: Separating the Two Tiers of Federal Jurisdiction*, 65 B.U. L. Rev. 205, 242–245 (1985) (failing to note any such comment).

[69] *See* 65 B.U. L. Rev. at 212.

burdensome or inadequate as to deprive a litigant of a meaningful judicial remedy, at least if state courts are unavailable.[70]

The burdens imposed by special procedures established by Congress for obtaining judicial review may be quite substantial without violating the Constitution, at least when the governmental interest is compelling. Thus, in *Bob Jones University v. Simon*, the Supreme Court held that prohibiting the petitioner from seeking an injunction against the removal of its tax exemption by the Internal Revenue Service did not deny the petitioner due process of law. The Court noted that other means of challenging the loss of the exemption existed, including petitioning the Tax Court to review the assessment of income taxes that would accrue as a result of the loss of the exemption and suing for a refund after paying the taxes and exhausting IRS refund procedures. The Court acknowledged that these remedies were burdensome, stating:[71]

> We do not say that these avenues of review are the best that can be devised. They present serious problems of delay, during which the flow of donations to an organization will be impaired and in some cases perhaps even terminated. . . . [A]lthough the congressional restriction to postenforcement review may place an organization claiming tax-exempt status in a precarious financial position, the problems presented do not rise to the level of constitutional infirmities, in light of the powerful governmental interests in protecting the administration of the tax system from premature judicial interference.

The Court noted that its conclusion might have been different had there been no access to judicial review.[72]

## § 1.06 DUE PROCESS LIMITS ON CONGRESS'S POWER TO CONTROL LOWER FEDERAL COURT JURISDICTION

### [1] Must Congress Provide Federal Jurisdiction to Hear Constitutional Claims?

Although Congress's power to regulate lower federal court jurisdiction under Article III is broad, it does not necessarily follow that it is unlimited. Anything contained in the body of the Constitution is, of course, superseded by any conflicting subsequent amendment of the Constitution itself. Therefore, to the extent that the provisions of Article III are inconsistent with the Due Process Clause of the Fifth Amendment, Article III must be considered modified by the amendment.[73]

---

[70] Congress may impose nonburdensome conditions on access to federal court. Bob Jones Univ. v. Simon, 416 U.S. 725, 746–747 (1974).

[71] Substantial burdens on obtaining judicial review not unconstitutional. Bob Jones Univ. v. Simon, 416 U.S. 725, 746–747 (1974).

[72] Different result if no access to judicial review. 416 U.S. at 746.

[73] Due process confines Congress' power to limit federal court jurisdiction.

There is disagreement, however, about exactly how the Due Process Clause affects Congress's Article III power. One key issue for due process purposes is whether, if it exercises its Article III power to limit federal court jurisdiction, Congress deprives a litigant of an independent judicial forum. Courts have long recognized a due process right to have the scope of one's constitutional rights determined by an independent judicial body.[74] Unless the adjudicatory tribunal is sufficiently independent of the governmental unit that has allegedly violated constitutional rights, the individual cannot reasonably expect to receive a truly fair adjudication of rights.[75] Absent a fair adjudication of their scope, the rights are, for all practical purposes, worthless.

Federal judges shielded by the life tenure and salary protections included in Article III are deemed sufficiently independent of federal and state legislative and executive bodies to provide a fair adjudication of constitutional rights. If Congress then limits federal court jurisdiction in a manner that deprives a litigant of an independent forum for the adjudication of constitutional rights, the exercise of that power might possibly be unconstitutional, even though Congress's action represented an otherwise wholly proper exercise of its Article III power.[76]

It might be argued that by denying a litigant access to an original hearing on a constitutional claim in federal court, Congress is denying the independent tribunal that due process guarantees. But it is not clear that a congressional limitation of lower federal court jurisdiction, standing alone, could ever deprive a litigant of a sufficiently independent judicial forum. When the framers entered into the Madisonian Compromise, they apparently assumed that if Congress chose not to create lower federal courts, the state courts could adjudicate federal cases. Indeed, many of them believed that state courts could adequately perform the function of adjudicating federal causes of action. It is now firmly established that under the Supremacy Clause,[77] state courts have both the power and the obligation to hear federal cases. And it is usually assumed, rightly or wrongly, that state courts constitute an appropriate independent judicial forum to provide a fair adjudication of federal constitutional rights.

---

[74] Due process right to have constitutional rights determined by independent judiciary. Tumey v. Ohio, 273 U.S. 510, 523 (1927) (criminal defendant's due process rights are violated if judge has direct, personal, and substantial pecuniary interest in reaching particular result); Ng Fung Ho v. White, 259 U.S. 276, 283–285 (1922) (executive branch's summary deportation of person claiming to be United States citizen is violation of due process as deportation is judicial in nature).

[75] *See* Redish & Marshall, *Adjudicatory Independence and the Values of Procedural Due Process*, 95 Yale L.J. 455 (1986).

[76] Limitations on jurisdiction to adjudicate constitutional claims raise constitutional concerns. *See* Bartlett v. Bowen, 816 F.2d 695, 706 (D.C. Cir. 1987) (". . . courts and legal scholars routinely assume that there is a due process right to have the scope of constitutional rights determined by some independent judicial body — and the Supreme Court has never held otherwise").

[77] U.S. Const., art. VI, cl. 2.

## [2] The View That State Courts Provide Sufficient Independent Adjudication to Satisfy Due Process

Professor Henry Hart's famous "Dialogue"[78] seems to adopt the position that state court adjudication — except perhaps in exceptional circumstances — provides independent adjudication sufficient to satisfy the demands of due process. This view holds that in the scheme of the Constitution, the state courts are the primary guarantors of constitutional rights, and in many cases they may be the ultimate ones. Hence, it is unlikely that the Constitution provides a right to proceed or be proceeded against in the first instance in a federal rather than a state court. Congress seems to have plenary power to limit federal jurisdiction when the consequence is merely to force proceedings to be brought, if at all, in a state court.[79]

Later in the Dialogue, however, this earlier conclusion is undermined by the following example.[80] Suppose Congress authorizes a program of direct action by government officials against private persons or private property, and that it not only dispenses with judicial enforcement but either limits the jurisdiction of the federal courts to inquire into what the officials do or denies it altogether. The answer is that the validity of the jurisdictional limitation depends on the validity of the program itself. If the court finds that what is being done is invalid, its duty is simply to declare the jurisdictional limitation invalid also, and then proceed under the general grant of jurisdiction.[81]

Presumably, the argument is that the hypothetical congressional limitation on federal court jurisdiction to review legislation is somehow rendered unconstitutional if the substantive provisions of the legislation are themselves unconstitutional. However, because state courts may provide an independent judicial forum to test the constitutionality of substantive congressional statutes, it is not clear why the limitation is unconstitutional, apart from possible equal protection considerations. For if state courts remain open, a limitation of federal court jurisdiction has not deprived a litigant of an independent judicial forum; it has merely allocated the case to a state, instead of a federal forum.

## [3] Limits on Federal Jurisdiction May Violate Due Process if State Courts Are Unavailable or Inadequate

The better view is that certain congressional limitations on lower federal court jurisdiction may well violate the due process right to an independent judicial forum if the state courts are for some reason unavailable or inadequate to resolve constitutional claims. For example, suppose that an individual must seek direct judicial control of the actions of federal officers to vindicate the individual's

[78] *See* Hart, *The Power of Congress to Limit the Jurisdiction of Federal Courts: An Exercise in Dialectic,* Hart, *The Power of Congress to Limit the Jurisdiction of Federal Courts: An Exercise* 66 Harv. L. Rev. 1362 (1953).

[79] 66 Harv. L. Rev. at 1363–1364.

[80] 66 Harv. L. Rev. at 1387.

[81] 66 Harv. L. Rev. at 1387.

constitutional rights. A limit on federal court power to review this conduct may raise constitutional problems. A well-known line of cases holds that state courts lack the authority to issue against federal officers a writ of habeas corpus,[82] a writ of mandamus,[83] or an injunction.[84] Assuming that these cases are still good law, and that they would apply if no adequate federal forum existed (a conclusion that is far from clear),[85] a congressional limitation on federal court power to review the actions of federal officials, combined with the lack of state court power to do likewise, would seem to deprive a litigant of the independent judicial forum required by due process.

Several courts, noting the existence of possible limitations on state court power to control directly the actions of federal officials, have intimated that a congressional limitation on federal court jurisdiction — even one as seemingly innocuous as the now-repealed[86] jurisdictional minimum amount in federal question cases — may have to fall, if the effect of the limitation is to restrict the federal court's power to enjoin or issue writs of habeas corpus to federal officials.[87]

Though the Supreme Court has never directly addressed the question, it is likely that a limitation on the jurisdiction of *both* state and federal courts to review the constitutionality of federal legislation or the acts of federal or state officials would be held unconstitutional. Such a limitation would clearly deprive an individual of an independent forum for the adjudication of constitutional rights.

An example of an act that limited both federal and state court jurisdiction was the Portal-to-Portal Act,[88] which eliminated liabilities that the Supreme Court had earlier found to be required by the Fair Labor Standards Act of 1938. Section 2(d) of the Portal-to-Portal Act provided in part:

> No court of the United States, of any State, Territory, or possession of the United States, or of the District of Columbia, shall have jurisdiction of any action or proceeding . . . to enforce liability or impose punishment for or on account of the failure of the employer to pay minimum wages or overtime compensation under the Fair Labor Standards Act of 1938, as amended . . . to the extent that such action or proceeding seeks to enforce any

---

[82] State courts may not issue writ of habeas corpus directed at federal officer. Tarble's Case, 80 U.S. (13 Wall.) 397, 20 L. Ed. 597 (1871); Ableman v. Booth, 62 U.S. (21 How.) 506 (1859).

[83] State courts may not issue writ of mandamus directed at federal officer. M'Clung v. Silliman, 19 U.S. (6 Wheat.) 598 (1821); Armand Schmoll, Inc. v. Federal Reserve Bank of N.Y., 286 N.Y. 503 (1941).

[84] State courts may not enjoin act of federal officer. Alabama *ex rel.* Gallion v. Rogers, 187 F. Supp. 848 (M.D. Ala. 1960), *aff'd per curiam*, 285 F.2d 430 (5th Cir.). The issue of injunctive relief, however, has never been resolved by the Supreme Court, and some lower federal courts have chosen not to extend *Tarble's Case* to injunctions. *See, e.g.*, Lewis Pub. Co. v. Wyman, 152 F. 200, 205 (E.D. Mo. 1907).

[85] In *Tarble*, for example, the federal courts remained open to provide habeas corpus, a point noted in the Court's opinion. 80 U.S. (13 Wall.) at 411.

[86] *See* Pub. L. 96-486, 94 Stat. 2369 (1980).

[87] Jurisdictional amount is constitutionally questionable in suits to enforce constitutional rights. *See* Cortright v. Resor, 325 F. Supp. 797, 808–811 (E.D.N.Y. 1971), *rev'd on other grounds*, 447 F.2d 245 (2d Cir. 1971) (and cases cited therein: jurisdictional amount presents constitutional difficulties in suits against federal officers to protect constitutional rights).

[88] 29 U.S.C. § 252(d); *see* 61 Stat. 84, Ch. 52, § 52(d) (1947).

liability or impose any punishment with respect to an activity which was not compensable under subsections (a) and (b) of this section.

By its terms, the Act did not explicitly remove from the federal courts the power to review its constitutionality. All the Act did was to prohibit state, federal or territorial courts from enforcing certain liabilities under the Fair Labor Standards Act that the Supreme Court had previously held to be due. However, if Congress's Article III power to regulate lower federal court jurisdiction is deemed absolute, the fact that the result of the exercise of that power in this case may have been to deprive an individual of constitutionally-protected rights would have been irrelevant. Hence, although the lower federal courts universally rejected the employees' substantive claim that the Act deprived them of property without due process,[89] the fact that the decisions even reached the merits, despite the congressional limitation on the lower courts' jurisdiction, is significant. In doing so the federal courts asserted their authority to disregard an exercise by Congress of its Article III power if the result would have been to deprive a litigant of constitutional rights. The importance of the majority of lower court decisions under the Portal-to-Portal Act, then, is that they recognized the existence of a due process restraint on Congress's Article III power.

Perhaps the leading decision in this line of cases was the Second Circuit's opinion in *Battaglia v. General Motors Corp.*, in which the court explicitly stated: "We think . . . that the exercise by Congress of its control over jurisdiction is subject to compliance with at least the requirements of the Fifth Amendment." The court concluded that it had the power to determine whether the statute was depriving persons of constitutional rights.[90]The Second Circuit appears to have been on firm ground in recognizing that the Fifth Amendment limits Congress's Article III power, and in concluding, implicitly, at least, that the Fifth Amendment would be violated if Congress had prevented judicial enforcement of constitutional rights.

A similar conclusion was reached more recently, as dictum, by the District of Columbia Circuit in *Bartlett v. Bowen*. The case concerned a constitutional challenge to a portion of the Medicare Act on the ground that its partial ban on payment of benefits for use in a Christian Science care facility violated the right of free exercise of religion. In response to the argument that a provision of the Act was intended to preclude judicial review, Judge Edwards, writing for the majority, stated:[91]

> In our view, a statutory provision precluding *all* judicial review of constitutional issues removes from the courts an essential judicial function under our implied constitutional mandate of separation of powers, and deprives an

[89] Due process challenge rejected. *See, e.g.*, Thomas v. Carnegie-Illinois Steel Corp., 174 F.2d 711, 713 (3d Cir. 1949).

[90] Federal court may determine whether statute violates constitutional rights despite jurisdiction-limiting provision. Battaglia v. General Motors Corp., 169 F.2d 254, 257 (2d Cir. 1948).

[91] All review of constitutionality of conduct may not be denied. Bartlett v. Bowen, 816 F.2d 695, 703 (D.C. Cir. 1987) (emphasis in original); *see also* Bowen v. Michigan Academy of Family Physicians, 476 U.S. 667, 681 n.12, (1986) (strong presumption that Congress expects courts to grant relief if executive agency violates legislative command avoids serious constitutional question that would arise if statute were construed to deny judicial forum for constitutional claims).

> individual of an independent forum for the adjudication of a claim of constitutional right. We have little doubt that such a "limitation on the jurisdiction of *both* state and federal courts to review the constitutionality of federal legislation . . . would be [an] unconstitutional" infringement of due process

This statement was dictum because the court found that Congress had not in fact intended to preclude judicial review. The court conceded, however, that it had become something of a time-honored tradition for the Supreme Court and lower federal courts to find that Congress did not intend to preclude judicial review of constitutional claims altogether in light of the serious due process concerns that such a preclusion would raise.[92]

Judge Bork, in dissent, argued that the plaintiff was seeking a benefit from the government, not resisting a government or private enforcement action. He therefore concluded that sovereign immunity denied the district court jurisdiction to entertain the claim.[93] The obvious fallacy in Judge Bork's logic, however, was that the plaintiff was not merely challenging the government's refusal to provide a statutory benefit, she was alleging that the denial of a benefit was premised on a choice to use a Christian Science medical facility, and therefore constituted a violation of the constitutional right of free exercise of religion.

## § 1.07 CONGRESSIONAL POWER TO LIMIT FEDERAL COURT JURISDICTION AND SEPARATION OF POWERS

### [1] Separation of Powers and Due Process Are Separate and Distinct Limitations on Congressional Power over Federal Jurisdiction

Jurists and commentators have long maintained that Congress cannot employ its Article III power to make exceptions to the Supreme Court's appellate jurisdiction and to limit lower federal court jurisdiction in a manner that improperly abridges the implied constitutional mandate of separation of powers.[94] In other words, though Congress has the power to control jurisdiction, it cannot use that power to interfere improperly with the independence of the judiciary in the exercise of its functions. Interference could result if, rather than merely excluding certain cases from the courts' jurisdiction, Congress chose to vest those courts with the power to hear a case, but require that the case be decided in a

---

[92] Courts construe to find no congressional intent to preclude jurisdiction. Bartlett v. Bowen, 816 F.2d 695, 699 (D.C. Cir. 1987); *see* Webster v. Doe, 486 U.S. 592 (1988) (if Congress intends to preclude judicial review of constitutional claims, its intent to do so must be clear; heightened showing is required to avoid "serious constitutional question" that would arise if federal statute were construed to deny any judicial forum for colorable constitutional claim).

[93] 816 F.2d at 719–721 (Bork, J., dissenting).

[94] *See* Hart, *The Power of Congress to Limit the Jurisdiction of Federal Courts: An Exercise in Dialectic*, 66 Harv. L. Rev. 1362, 1365 (1953).

certain manner.[95] As noted by one commentator, the difficulty involved in asserting any judicial control in the face of a total denial of jurisdiction does not exist if Congress gives jurisdiction but puts strings on it. If Congress directs an Article III court to decide a case, there can be read into Article III a limitation on the power of Congress to tell the court *how* to decide it.[96]

There is obviously an overlap between this theory — based on a concept of separation of powers in Article III — and the theory that due process limits congressional power to regulate federal jurisdiction. For example, if Congress were to give lower federal courts exclusive jurisdiction over the prosecution of federal crimes but provided that these courts did not have jurisdiction to consider coerced confession claims, both due process and separation of powers would be offended. The individual litigant could legitimately complain that his Fifth Amendment rights were violated by the jurisdictional limitation. At the same time, the court could legitimately complain that its independence was being violated because it was being told to reach an outcome different from the one that it would otherwise have reached.

Of course, courts are often told "how to decide" cases through statutory directives. The directive in the above example to ignore Fifth Amendment claims is invalid, however, because it directs the court to reach an *unconstitutional* result, one that violates the constitutional rights of an individual. But could a jurisdictional limitation that told a court how to decide a case without abridging individual constitutional rights — and hence did not violate due process — nevertheless violate the separation of powers doctrine? In other words, are there any congressional restrictions on jurisdiction that would not offend due process but that nevertheless offend the separation of powers doctrine? The leading Supreme Court separation-of-powers cases suggest that the doctrine does in fact place a limit on congressional authority, above and beyond due process.

### [2] *Hayburn's Case*: First Recognition of Separation of Powers Limitation

The first case in which the Supreme Court recognized a separation-of-powers limitation on congressional power early in the nation's history was *Hayburn's Case*. In *Hayburn*, the Court invalidated, on separation-of-powers grounds, a congressional statute authorizing the Secretary of War to review decisions of the federal courts accepting or rejecting applications by Revolutionary War veterans for disability pensions. The Secretary had been authorized to deny pensions when he suspected impropriety or mistake. The Court found this procedure to violate separation of powers.[97] Thus, Congress cannot vest review of the decisions of

---

[95] Congress may not direct courts to decide particular case in particular manner. *See* Seattle Audubon Soc. v. Robertson, 914 F.2d 1311, 1315 (9th Cir. 1990), *rev'd on other grounds*, 503 U.S. 429 (1990) (Congress may amend or repeal any law, even for the purpose of ending pending litigation; but Congress may not prescribe a rule for a decision of a cause in a certain way if no new circumstances have been created by legislation).

[96] Hart, *The Power of Congress to Limit the Jurisdiction of Federal Courts: An Exercise in Dialectic*, 66 Harv. L. Rev. 1362, 1365, 1372–1373 (1953).

[97] Hayburn's Case, 2 U.S. (2 Dall.) 409, 410 (1792).

Article III courts in officials of the Executive Branch.[98]

### [3] *United States v. Klein*: Congress May Not Dictate the Result of a Particular Case

Perhaps the leading early separation-of-powers decision was *United States v. Klein*. Congress had provided that persons whose property had been seized during the Civil War could recover the property (or the proceeds from its sale) on proof that they had not given aid or comfort to the enemy during the war.[99] The Supreme Court had previously held that a presidential pardon for activities during the war constituted proof that the person had not given aid or comfort to the enemy. The Court's theory apparently was that the constitutional effect of a pardon, unless it is specifically limited by the President, is that the pardoned person is treated as if he had not committed the pardoned acts.

Klein, representing a pardoned decedent, sued in the Court of Claims to recover the proceeds of seized property. Following the Supreme Court's precedent, the Court of Claims awarded relief. The government appealed, and while the case was pending in the Supreme Court, Congress passed legislation providing that federal courts should treat a pardon as proof that a person had been disloyal, and that the lower courts and the Supreme Court should dismiss the case seeking return of the property for want of jurisdiction.

The Supreme Court held this limitation on its jurisdiction and the direction to treat pardons as proof of disloyalty to be unconstitutional.[100] The Court made it clear that it did not view the limitation on its jurisdiction as part of Congress's power to make exceptions and regulations to its appellate jurisdiction under the Exceptions Clause. It stated, "[T]he language of the proviso shows plainly that it does not intend to withhold appellate jurisdiction except as a means to an end . . . . It is evident from this statement that the denial of jurisdiction to this court, as well as to the Court of Claims, is founded solely on the application of a rule of decision . . . prescribed by Congress."[101]

The Court suggested that there were constitutional problems because Congress had attempted to change the result in a case already pending before the Supreme Court and because the government was attempting to alter the outcome of a case in which it was a party.[102] But given the well-established doctrine that courts are to

---

[98] Executive branch may not review judicial determinations. *See* Plaut v. Spendthrift Farm, Inc., 514 U.S. 211, 218, (1995); *see also* Gordon v. United States, 69 U.S. (2 Wall.) 561, 17 L. Ed. 921 (1865) (statute's grant of power to executive branch to revise decisions of Court of Claims held unconstitutional); United States v. Ferreira, 54 U.S. (13 How.) 40, 48 (1852) (statutory dictate that federal judges must make and report findings to Secretary of Treasury who would then make decision did not fall within judicial power of Article III); Lobue v. Christopher, 893 F. Supp. 65, 68 (D.D.C. 1995) (extradition statute giving Secretary of State authority to review legal findings of extradition judges held unconstitutional violation of separation of powers).

[99] United States v. Klein, 80 U.S. (13 Wall.) 128 (1872).

[100] 80 U.S. at 141–142.

[101] 80 U.S. at 145–146.

[102] 80 U.S. at 146.

apply the law as it exists at the time of the final judicial decision, neither of these factors can justify the Court's decision. Absent Fifth Amendment due process retroactivity or taking of "vested" property right problems, Congress is generally free to alter rules of decision while a case is pending, even if the suit is one in which the government is a party.

A possible reading of the Court's decision in *Klein* is that the rule of decision that the courts were in effect being directed to apply was unconstitutional because it denied to the presidential pardon — which the President was constitutionally authorized to issue — the effect that the Court had ruled it had. Congress might have been free to rescind the statute providing for recovery of seized property, but as long as it allowed for recovery on proof of loyalty, it had to consider pardoned persons loyal. *Klein* thus established a separation-of-powers restraint limiting Congress's power over federal court jurisdiction. It clearly affirms that there are limitations on Congress's power over jurisdiction.

### [4] *Yakus v. United States* and *Adamo Wrecking Company*: Foreclosing Review of Validity of Regulations

A separation-of-powers limitation was also discussed in the famous case of *Yakus v. United States*.[103] In the Emergency Price Control Act of 1942, Congress had created an Emergency Court of Appeals, consisting of three federal district or circuit judges, all of whom, of course, possessed the protections of Article III. The Emergency Court was designed to review protests of determinations made by the Price Administrator. The court had all the powers of a district court with respect to the jurisdiction given it by Congress, with the exception that it had no power to issue temporary restraining orders or interlocutory decrees staying the effectiveness of orders, regulations, or price schedules issued under the Act's authority. In *Lockerty v. Phillips*, the Supreme Court had upheld the constitutionality of the procedure set down by Congress.[104]

In *Yakus*, however, the Court was faced with the question of whether an individual who had been criminally prosecuted in federal district court for failure to comply with the Act's regulations could, consistent with due process, be barred from raising the invalidity of the regulation in question as a defense. Concluding that the protest procedure laid down by Congress was an adequate judicial remedy for a litigant challenging a regulation, the majority rejected the due process challenge.[105]

Justice Rutledge, in an opinion joined by Justice Murphy, dissented.[106] He first emphasized his agreement that Congress could constitutionally take all jurisdiction under the Act away from the federal district courts and place it exclusively in the Emergency Court. But it was not so clear to Justice Rutledge that Congress could

---

[103] Yakus v. United States, 321 U.S. 414 (1944).

[104] Lockerty v. Phillips, 319 U.S. 182, 187–188 (1943).

[105] Congress may provide alternate means to challenge validity of federal regulation. Yakus v. United States, 321 U.S. 414, 433 (1944).

[106] 321 U.S. at 460 (Rutledge, J., dissenting).

confer jurisdiction on federal and state courts in the enforcement proceedings, more particularly the criminal suit, and at the same time deny them jurisdiction or power to consider the validity of the regulations for which enforcement was sought.[107] To Justice Rutledge, it was one thing for Congress to withhold jurisdiction. It was entirely another to confer it and direct that it be exercised in a manner inconsistent with constitutional requirements or without regard to them. The thrust of his objection was not limited to the litigant's due process right. He noted that it is equally one of the separation and independence of the powers of government and of the constitutional integrity of the judicial process, more especially in criminal trials.[108]

Though Justice Rutledge's opinion was in dissent, the Court's majority opinion in *Yakus* did not seem to disagree on this broad point. It emphasized that even though the statute should be deemed to require it, any ruling at the criminal trial that would preclude the accused from showing that he had had no opportunity to establish the invalidity of the regulation by resort to the statutory procedure, would be reviewable on appeal on constitutional grounds.[109] The majority concluded, however, that there is no constitutional requirement that the test of the validity of a regulation be made in one tribunal rather than in another, as long as there is an opportunity to be heard and for judicial review that satisfies the demands of due process.[110]

As one commentator has reasoned, "[t]he alternative procedure for the decision of the questions of law [involved in *Yakus*] was in a court; and everybody assumed it had to be."[111] Hence, to the majority in *Yakus,* both due process and separation-of-powers requirements were satisfied by the fact that the federal judiciary, *as a whole,* had been given complete power to review constitutionality and legality, in addition to the obligation of enforcement. The federal courts thus had not been ordered to act in an unconstitutional manner.

The Court distinguished *Yakus* in *Adamo Wrecking Co. v. United States.*[112] The Clean Air Act authorizes the Administrator of the Environmental Protection Agency (EPA) to promulgate emission standards for certain pollutants and subjects a knowing violator of those standards to criminal penalties.[113] Section 307(b) of the Act provides for review of the Administrator's actions in promulgating the emission standards only in the United States Court of Appeals for the District of Columbia, usually within thirty days from the date of promulgation or approval of the standards.[114]

---

[107] 321 U.S. at 467 (Rutledge, J., dissenting).

[108] 321 U.S. at 468 (Rutledge, J., dissenting).

[109] Alternative means provided ultimately for judicial review. 321 U.S. at 447.

[110] 321 U.S. at 444.

[111] Hart, *The Power of Congress to Limit the Jurisdiction of Federal Courts: An Exercise in Dialectic,* 66 Harv. L. Rev. 1362, 1365, 1380 (1953).

[112] Adamo Wrecking Co. v. United States, 434 U.S. 275 (1978).

[113] 42 U.S.C. § 7412(b)(1)(B).

[114] 42 U.S.C. § 7607(b)(1).

Petitioner in *Adamo* was indicted for violating an emission standard by releasing asbestos in the course of a building demolition, in contravention of an asbestos "emission standard" promulgated by the EPA. The Sixth Circuit, reversing the district court, had concluded that the petitioner was barred by the statute from contending at trial that what he had violated was not an emission standard as described in the Act. Further, under *Yakus* this procedure did not create any separation-of-powers problems. The Supreme Court, in turn, reversed the Sixth Circuit, holding that Congress's jurisdiction-limiting provision was not intended to foreclose inquiry into whether the challenged conduct was within the purview of the Act. While in *Yakus,* there was no doubt that what was violated was a "price control," here, the petitioner was challenging, in fact, whether the regulation that he was accused of violating constituted an "emission standard," as contemplated by Congress in enacting the Clean Air Act.[115]

### [5] *United States v. Sioux Nation*: Congress May Waive Defense of Res Judicata in Cases Against Federal Government

In *United States v. Sioux Nation,* the act of Congress at issue required the Court of Claims to review on the merits, without regard to the defenses of res judicata or collateral estoppel, a Sioux claim for just compensation from the United States for the taking of the Black Hills, even though the Court of Claims had previously heard and rejected that very claim.[116] The Court held this provision was not an unconstitutional congressional incursion into matters reserved to the judiciary. Rather, Congress was deemed to have the right, under its broad powers to recognize and pay the nation's debts, to waive the defense of res judicata as to the effect of a prior judgment entered in the government's favor on a claim against the United States.[117]

In so holding, the Court described the rationale of *Klein* in the following manner: "[T]he [congressionally enacted] proviso was unconstitutional in two respects: First, it prescribed a rule of decision in a case pending before the courts, and did so in a manner that required the courts to decide a controversy in the Government's favor.[118] Under this reading of *Klein,* which is somewhat broader than the one presented above, the rule prescribed by Congress apparently does not itself need to be unconstitutional for the prescription to be invalid.

---

[115] Criminal defendant not foreclosed from challenging applicability of law to conduct. Adamo Wrecking Co. v. United States, 434 U.S. 275, 278–285 (1978).

[116] United States v. Sioux Nation of Indians, 448 U.S. 371, 391 (1980).

[117] Congress may waive defenses related to finality of judgment in claims against United States. 448 U.S. at 397–407.

[118] 448 U.S. at 404.

### [6] *Plaut v. Spendthrift Farm*: Congress May Not Reopen Final Judgments

The Supreme Court's most recent statement on the separation-of-powers limitation came in *Plaut v. Spendthrift Farm, Inc.*[119] The case concerned the constitutionality of congressional efforts simultaneously to amend governing substantive law and to reopen final judgments of the federal courts in order to revise them in accordance with those amendments. Section 27A(b) of the Securities and Exchange Act of 1934,[120] a provision added to the Act by amendment in 1991, was enacted in response to a Supreme Court decision construing the 1934 Act to establish a uniform rule that litigation instituted under § 10(b) of the Act[121] must be commenced within one year after the discovery of the facts constituting the violation and within three years after the violation.[122] In a separate decision made the same day, the Court held that this statute of limitations was to be applied to pending claims brought under Section 10(b).[123] As a result, various district courts dismissed pending suits. In response, Congress enacted Section 27A, which provided for the reinstitution of cases that had been dismissed under the Court's statute of limitations.

In *Pacific Mutual Life Insurance Co. v. First Republicbank Corp.*, a decision subsequently affirmed without opinion by an equally divided Supreme Court, the Fifth Circuit rejected a challenge to section 27A(b) as a violation of Article III.[124] The Fifth Circuit reasoned that Section 27A(b) satisfied the principle of *Klein* because it actually changed the governing general substantive law. The court assured that "[i]f we understood a statute's purpose to be the reversal of results in particular controversies between private individuals, we would strike the statute as violative of our authority to decide cases."[125]

In *Plaut*, the United States Supreme Court finally reached the merits and held the statute unconstitutional. The Court acknowledged that the provision violated neither *Klein* nor *Hayburn*, stating that: "[U]nder any application of Section 27A(b) only courts are involved; no officials of other departments sit in direct review of their decisions. Section 27A(b) therefore offends neither of these previously established prohibitions."[126] Nevertheless, the statute was unconstitutional, because, in the Court's view, it offended a postulate of Article III just as deeply rooted in the law, namely that the federal judiciary has the power not merely to rule on cases, but to decide them, subject to review only by superior courts in the Article III hierarchy. By retroactively commanding the federal courts

---

119 Plaut v. Spendthrift Farm, Inc., 514 U.S. 211 (1995).

120 15 U.S.C. § 78aa-1.

121 15 U.S.C. § 78j(b).

122 *See* Lampf, Pleva, Lipkind, Prupis & Petigrow v. Gilbertson, 501 U.S. 350, 364 (1991).

123 James B. Beam Distilling Co. v. Georgia, 501 U.S. 529, 544 (1991).

124 Pacific Mutual Life Insurance Co. v. First Republicbank Corp., 997 F.2d 39, 52–54 (5th Cir. 1993), *aff'd*, 511 U.S. 658 (1994).

125 997 F.2d at 54.

126 Plaut v. Spendthrift Farm, Inc., 514 U.S. 211, 218 (1995).

to reopen final judgments, Congress had violated this fundamental principle.[127]

The Court conceded that Congress can always revise the judgments of Article III courts in one sense. If a new law makes clear that it is retroactive, an appellate court must apply that law in reviewing judgments still on appeal that were rendered before the law was enacted, and must alter the outcome accordingly.[128] However, the Court found the impact of section 27A(b) to be very different because of its impact on final decisions. Having achieved finality, a judicial decision becomes the last word of the judicial department with regard to a particular case or controversy, and Congress may not declare by retroactive legislation that the law applicable *to that very case* was something other than what the courts said it was.[129] The Court acknowledged that section 27A(b) directs the reopening of final judgments in a whole class of cases rather than in a particular suit. The Court, however, found that fact to be of no import.[130]

The one case that gave the Court in *Plaut* the most difficulty was *United States v. Sioux Nation*. The Court read *Sioux Nation* narrowly, and essentially limited it to its facts. It accepted the proposition that the United States may waive the defense of res judicata in any action on a claim against it, but refused to extend this proposition to afford to Congress the power to otherwise reopen final judgments.[131] Thus, the result is that Congress may waive the defense of res judicata in claims against the United States, but may not waive other defenses applicable to other litigants, such as the bar of a statute of limitations, if the effect of the waiver is to reopen final judgments.

The Court in *Plaut* consciously chose to apply an unbending rule of separation of powers rather than a more flexible case-by-case analysis. It did so by reasoning that separation of powers "is a prophylactic device, establishing high walls and clear distinctions because low walls and vague distinctions will not be judicially defensible in the heat of interbranch conflict."[132]

## § 1.08 CONGRESSIONAL POWER TO VEST ARTICLE III COURTS WITH NON-ARTICLE III POWER

### [1] Congressional Power to Assign Non-Article III Cases to Article III Courts

Article III, Section 2, enumerates various categories of cases to which the judicial power of the United States extends. The question has arisen whether this enumeration sets the outer limits of the jurisdiction of Article III courts, or whether Congress may give these courts jurisdiction over other cases as well. The

---

[127] Congress may not retroactively require courts to reopen final judgments. 514 U.S. at 218–219.

[128] Congress may amend statutes and apply amendment to pending cases. 514 U.S. at 226.

[129] 514 U.S. at 227.

[130] 514 U.S. at 227.

[131] 514 U.S. at 230–231.

[132] Separation of powers given broad reach. 514 U.S. at 239.

issue was presented in the well-known case of *National Mutual Insurance v. Tidewater Transfer*.[133]

Congress had authorized federal courts to entertain suits between citizens of the District of Columbia and citizens of other states. Under this statute, a District of Columbia corporation sued a Virginia corporation in Maryland district court on a claim arising out of an insurance contract. The district court dismissed the suit, however, finding that the statute authorizing district court jurisdiction was unconstitutional. The court based its ruling on *Hepburn & Dundas v. Elizey*, an 1804 decision written by Chief Justice Marshall, which had held that the District of Columbia was not a "state" as that term is used in Article III.[134] Therefore, the district court ruled, suits between citizens of a state and citizens of the District of Columbia were not "suits between citizens of different states" authorized by Article III, Section 2 to be heard by federal courts, and Congress had exceeded its authority by authorizing Article III courts to take jurisdiction over cases not enumerated in Article III.

The Supreme Court reversed without a majority opinion. Justice Jackson, writing the plurality opinion joined only by Justices Black and Burton, agreed that the case was not one of those enumerated in Article III, Section 2. However, he believed Article III allowed Congress to extend federal jurisdiction to cases other than those enumerated in Article III if such an extension of jurisdiction was "necessary and proper" to effectuate one of its powers enumerated in Article I.[135] Justices Rutledge and Murphy concurred separately, solely on the grounds that *Hepburn*, finding that the District of Columbia is not a "state" within the meaning of Article III, should be overruled. Justice Rutledge's opinion vigorously rejected Justice Jackson's reasoning.[136] Chief Justice Vinson dissented in an opinion joined by Justice Douglas,[137] and Justice Frankfurter, joined by Justice Reed, wrote a separate dissenting opinion.[138]

Justice Jackson believed that Congress had the power to confer jurisdiction over suits between citizens of a state and citizens of the District of Columbia as a necessary and proper means of implementing its power under Article I, Section 8 to establish the District.[139] But six Justices rejected this interpretation of Article III, reading that provision to confine the jurisdiction of Article III courts to the cases enumerated in Article III, Section 2. This rejection by a majority of the Court of Justice Jackson's opinion in *Tidewater* demonstrates the prevailing view that Article III prohibits Article III courts from assuming jurisdiction of cases not enumerated in Article III. It is not immediately clear, however, what policy lies behind this doctrine.

---

133 National Mutual Ins. Co. v. Tidewater Transfer Co., 337 U.S. 582 (1949).

134 Hepburn & Dundas v. Ellzey, 6 U.S. (2 Cranch) 445 (1804).

135 Plurality: Congress may extend federal jurisdiction beyond parameters of Article III (plurality opinion). National Mutual Ins. Co. v. Tidewater Transfer Co., 337 U.S. 582, 588–589 (1949).

136 337 U.S. at 604 (Rutledge, J., concurring).

137 337 U.S. at 626 (Vinson, C.J., dissenting).

138 337 U.S. at 646 (Frankfurter, J., dissenting).

139 337 U.S. at 600.

It could be argued that it is the basic policy of federalism; the Constitution limits the instances in which federal courts, as opposed to state courts, can exercise jurisdiction. Unless Congress demonstrates sufficient interest in a class of cases by passing legislation that brings them within the "arising under federal law" head of Article III jurisdiction, or unless the parties are diverse in one of the ways specified in Article III, state, not federal courts, must be the forum. The problem with this argument is that the doctrine that Article III courts may decide only Article III cases does not seem to prevent Congress from assigning jurisdiction of non-Article III "federal" cases to so-called Article I or "legislative" courts thus depriving state courts of jurisdiction over them. This power was explicitly recognized by the dissenting Justices in *Tidewater* itself.[140] From the perspective of the federal system, it is difficult to see how the power of the states to adjudicate non-Article III cases is infringed less when those cases are allocated to Article I courts (courts whose judges lack Article III protections) instead of to Article III federal courts.

In his dissenting opinion in *Tidewater*, Justice Frankfurter suggested a separation-of-powers rationale for the doctrine. Justice Frankfurter asked, "[I]f the precise enumeration of cases as to which Article III authorized Congress to grant jurisdiction to [Article III courts] does not preclude Congress from vesting these courts with authority which Article III disallows, by what rule of reason is Congress to be precluded from bringing to its aid the advisory opinions of this Court . . . ?"[141] Justice Frankfurter was suggesting that if Congress could give Article III courts jurisdiction over cases not enumerated in Article III, it could also give those courts jurisdiction over disputes that were not "cases." Yet the limitation of the federal judicial power to "cases" has usually been thought essential to the independence and integrity of the federal courts.

Justice Frankfurter's suggestion is not convincing, however, because the power to extend federal jurisdiction to non-Article III cases in no way logically implies a power to extend jurisdiction to disputes that are not "cases." Whatever one thinks of the historical support or policy arguments for Justice Jackson's approach, it can be adopted without calling into question the doctrine that Article III must be read as if it said, "The judicial power shall extend *only* to cases." The limitation of the judicial power to "cases" serves to ensure the legitimacy and independence of judicial judgments; it is difficult to see how the doctrine that Article III courts may decide only *Article III* cases is required by these same interests.

Perhaps the strongest argument in support of the rejection of Justice Jackson's approach is a textual one. The enumeration of categories in Article III, Section 2 is effectively rendered meaningless unless it is construed to provide a ceiling on congressional power to vest the Article III courts with jurisdiction because it is clear that the enumeration was not intended to provide a floor. This is true, because it is well established that Congress need not vest the full judicial power described in Article III in the federal courts. Thus, if the enumeration is not intended to

---

140 337 U.S. at 641–645 (Vinson, C.J., dissenting).

141 337 U.S. at 648 (Frankfurter, J., dissenting).

provide an outer limit, it would serve no function at all.[142]

### [2] Allocation of Non-Article III Functions to Article III Courts and Judges Is Generally Unconstitutional

#### [a] The Unique Role of the Judiciary Precludes Performance of Nonjudicial Functions

The Supreme Court has traditionally resisted direct validation of the use of the Article III courts for the performance of functions outside the scope of Article III. As it has said, "The constitutional power of federal courts cannot be defined, and indeed has no substance, without reference to the necessity 'to adjudge the legal rights of litigants in actual controversies.' The requirements of Art. III are not satisfied merely because a party requests a court of the United States to declare its legal rights. . . . "[143] Indeed, several Justices have strongly resisted the vesting of authority in the Article III courts to adjudicate cases falling outside the bounds of the categories enumerated in Article III, Section 2, for fear that the performance of nonjudicial functions might logically follow.

It is reasonable to inquire whether allowing Article III courts to perform nonjudicial functions — in other words, tasks not directly involving the adjudication of live disputes — would truly undermine the constitutional structure. First, the complete absence of any textual authorization for the judicial performance of nonjudicial functions must be noted. Ours is supposedly a government of both separated and limited powers. With only one limited and arcane exception,[144] constitutional authorization for federal judicial action is confined to the vesting of the judicial power in the federal courts and the extension of that power only to the adjudication of specified "cases" and "controversies." There appears to be no textual authorization in Article III for the performance of functions not tied to adjudication of cases or controversies.

In most cases of constitutional analysis, however, resort to a purely linguistic examination of text has not been dispositive in judicial construction. Whether Congress may authorize or direct the Article III courts to perform nonjudicial functions, then, is likely to be resolved by considerations that go beyond examination of constitutional language. Rather, it will probably be resolved by examination of structural, theoretical and political underpinnings of the concept of separation of powers, particularly with regard to the judiciary, as well as by textual examination.

---

[142] *See* 337 U.S. at 607 (Rutledge, J., concurring).

[143] Judicial power limited to adjudging rights of actual litigants in actual controversies. Valley Forge Christian College v. Americans United for Separation of Church and State, Inc., 454 U.S. 464, 471 (1982); *see also* National Mut. Ins. Co. v. Tidewater Transfer Co., 337 U.S. 582, 647 (1949) (Frankfurter, J., dissenting) ("According to Article III only 'judicial power' can be 'vested' in the courts established under it.").

[144] *See* O'Donoghue v. United States, 289 U.S. 516 (1933), in which the Court validated use of Article III courts for nonadjudicatory purposes. However, that case concerned federal courts within District of Columbia, which, rightly or wrongly, are often considered unique; *see, e.g.*, Palmore v. United States, 411 U.S. 389 (1973).

Among the three distinct branches of the federal government, the judiciary is, of course, unique because of its consciously chosen, carefully protected, unrepresentativeness. This characteristic in the constitutional democracy simultaneously dictates both powers and limitations. On the one hand, if the judiciary is to serve as an enforcer of countermajoritarian constitutional norms and as an effective check against the representative branches, its integrity and independence must be shielded from undermining by those branches. On the other hand, because the judiciary is unrepresentative, it is important that its functioning be confined to the performance of the traditional judicial function of adjudication, lest it be placed in a position to usurp the function and authority of the representative branches.

Paradoxically, vesting authority in the judiciary to perform tasks that are wholly legislative, executive, or administrative in nature simultaneously endangers both political values served by the judicial separation of powers. Requiring the judiciary to perform tasks beyond the scope of case adjudication may threaten its integrity by blurring its special place within the governmental structure. An Article III court reduced to acting as a mere administrative functionary assisting or serving the political branches may have difficulty commanding the prestige necessary to check the exercise of majoritarian will found to conflict with constitutionalized values. Yet ironically, the judicial exercise of purely legislative or executive power, disconnected from the adjudicatory function, may threaten fundamental democratic values by effectively allowing the one unrepresentative branch of government to perform the starkly political functions reserved for those branches most directly responsible to public will.

Of course, it will often be impossible to predict, with any degree of certainty, that exercise of a particular nonjudicial function by the Article III judiciary will significantly undermine the fundamental political values of self-determination or constitutionalism. Generally, the danger is an incremental one. Eventually, the judicial branch will either have acquired an excess of authority, or will have lost much of its requisite integrity, though responsibility for the overall harm might not be attributed to any single breach. But it is presumably for that very reason that separation-of-powers protections are largely prophylactic in nature. They are designed to prevent damage to the political framework before the truly serious harm intended to be avoided can occur. Largely for these reasons, the Supreme Court's doctrines of justiciability have policed the work of the Article III federal judiciary in order to ensure that the courts perform only truly adjudicatory functions.

Despite both these strong justifications for prohibiting the exercise of non-Article III power by non-Article III courts, and the well-established doctrines of justiciability, in two major decisions from the late 1980s, the Supreme Court appears to have authorized the exercise of nonadjudicatory power by both Article III courts and judges.

### [b] *Morrison v. Olsen*: Judiciary May Appoint, Administer, and Terminate Special Counsel

*Morrison v. Olsen* involved a constitutional challenge to Title VI of the independent-counsel provisions of the Ethics in Government Act of 1978[145] The challenged enactment authorized appointment of an independent counsel to investigate, and if appropriate, to prosecute certain high-ranking government officials for violations of federal criminal laws. The Attorney General was required, under appropriate circumstances, to conduct a preliminary investigation and to report to a "Special Division," a specially created Article III court established for the purpose of appointing independent counsel. The Court upheld the Special Division's authority to appoint the independent counsel, because it found that Article II's express authorization of such a power constituted a supplement to the judiciary's adjudicatory power under Article III.[146]

More questionable, however, was the vesting in the Special Division of various powers and duties in relation to the independent counsel that, because they did not involve appointing the counsel or defining jurisdiction, could not be said to derive from the Division's Article II Appointments Clause authority.[147] These included activities such as the power to grant extensions for the Attorney General's preliminary investigation, the power to receive the Attorney General's report, and the authority to receive the independent counsel's report on expenses. But the Court nevertheless upheld these powers, ruling:[148]

> The Act simply does not give the Division power to "supervise" the independent counsel in the exercise of her investigative or prosecutorial authority. And, the functions that the Special Division is empowered to perform are not inherently "Executive"; indeed, they are directly analogous to functions that federal judges perform in other contexts.

More difficult to justify was the Special Division's statutory power to terminate the office of independent counsel. While the Court conceded that such a power is "administrative" and "not a power that could be considered typically 'judicial,' " it ultimately chose not to view this provision as a significant judicial encroachment on executive power or on the prosecutorial discretion of the independent counsel. The Court explained its conclusion in the following manner:[149]

> [I]t is the duty of federal courts to construe a statute in order to save it from constitutional infirmities. . . . The termination provisions of the Act do not give the Special Division anything approaching the power to *remove* the counsel while an investigation or court proceeding is still underway. . . . "[T]ermination" may occur only when the duties of the counsel are truly "completed." . . . It is basically a device for removing from the public payroll an independent counsel who has served his or her purpose,

---

[145] 28 U.S.C. § 591 *et seq.*

[146] Article III court may appoint special counsel. Morrison v. Olson, 487 U.S. 654, 670–677 (1988).

[147] 487 U.S. at 680.

[148] 487 U.S. at 681.

[149] 487 U.S. at 682–683.

> but is unwilling to acknowledge the fact. So construed, the Special Division's power to terminate does not pose a sufficient threat of judicial intervention into matters that are more properly within the Executive's authority.

There can be little doubt that the Court's approach in *Morrison* departs dramatically from a formalist model of separation of powers. In its place, the Court employed a type of *ad hoc* balancing analysis.

### [c] *Mistretta v. United States*: Members of the Judiciary May Be Required to Sit on Sentencing Commission

In *Mistretta v. United States*, the Supreme Court also employed a form of *ad hoc* balancing analysis in order to resolve the issue of judicial separation of powers. The separation-of-powers challenge in *Mistretta* was to the statutory requirement that three Article III judges sit on the United States Sentencing Commission, an administrative body that was placed by Congress within the judiciary, whose task is to promulgate criminal sentencing guidelines. Rather than draw a strict demarcation between performance of judicial and nonjudicial functions, the Court in *Mistretta* expressed a willingness to invalidate separation-of-powers breaches only if they either accreted powers more appropriately diffused among separate branches to a single branch, or undermined the authority and independence of another coordinate branch.[150]

The Court noted several specific factors concerning the use of Article III judges on the Sentencing Commission that arguably distinguished the situation from the performance by Article III judges of other nonjudicial functions. These factors conceivably limit the decision's reach. Careful analysis reveals, however, that none of these specific factors justifies the upholding of the Sentencing Commission's breach of the case-or-controversy requirement.

The most important of the factors cited by the Court is also the most dubious. The Court noted:[151]

> Prior to the passage of the Act, the Judicial Branch, as an aggregate, decided precisely the questions assigned to the Commission: what sentence is appropriate to what criminal conduct under what circumstances. It was the everyday business of judges, taken collectively, to evaluate and weigh the various aims of sentencing and to apply those aims to the individual cases that came before them. The Sentencing Commission does no more than this, albeit basically through the methodology of sentencing guidelines, rather than individualized sentencing determinations.

The obvious fallacy in the Court's reasoning can be seen when its argument is paraphrased: "Use of federal judges on the Sentencing Commission does not violate the case-or-controversy requirement, because the tasks of the Commission and of the federal courts are identical, except for the absence of a case or controversy in

---

150 Performance of nonjudicial functions prohibited only if it involves accretion of power. Mistretta v. United States, 488 U.S. 361, 382 (1989).

151 488 U.S. at 395.

the work of the Commission." The key difference between the two situations, of course, is that before the Commission's creation, judges performed the sentencing task *in the context of live, individualized cases.* The Commission, on the other hand, promulgates binding, generalized guidelines, divorced from the setting of a specific case, much as a legislature would.

The essential point that seems to have been ignored by the Court is that the case-or-controversy requirement does not turn on the substance of the judiciary's task, but rather on the presence of the adjudicatory form — the very difference between judicial sentencing and the commission's work. To underscore the point, it is unimaginable that a law directing the federal judiciary to promulgate binding regulations enforcing the First Amendment right of free speech could survive examination under the case-or-controversy requirement, on the grounds that the judiciary has traditionally developed the substance of First Amendment law in the context of live cases. This logic would, of course, be rejected, if the case-or-controversy requirement is not to be rendered a dead letter. Yet the Court's reasoning in *Mistretta* effectively amounts to the very same questionable logic.

A second argument relied on by the Court in *Mistretta* was that no specific court had been delegated the power to promulgate sentencing guidelines. Rather, the law directed that individual Article III judges were to be made members of the Commission. The Court emphasized this distinction, citing the long tradition of Supreme Court Justices' service in nonjudicial capacities (for example, Chief Justice Warren's chairmanship of the commission investigating President Kennedy's assassination). It noted that the text of the Constitution contained no prohibition against the service of active federal judges on independent commissions such as the Sentencing Commission.[152] The difference between the examples cited by the Court and the use of Article III judges on the Sentencing Commission, however, is that in the former situations the posts are not *required* to be filled by Article III judges *as a matter of law.*

Ultimately, the Court's argument fails, because it ignores the primary values served by the case-or-controversy requirement, and thus effectively amounts to a preference for form over substance. If we assume that the vesting of nonjudicial authority in a particular Article III court would be held to violate the case-or-controversy requirement, it is difficult to imagine that the Article III problem would disappear if the legislation were instead to create a nonjudicial commission whose membership happened to consist of all the judges of that Article III court. Burdening Article III judges with administrative tasks could simultaneously undermine the prestige of those judges and distract them from the effective performance of their adjudicatory task. It is presumably in part for these reasons that the case-or-controversy requirement was imposed in the first place. Thus, it should matter little, for Article III purposes, whether the nonjudicial authority is vested directly in an Article III court or in a non-Article III body whose membership by law consists, at least in part, of Article III judges.

The Court in *Mistretta* itself acknowledged that the fact "[t]hat the Constitution does not absolutely prohibit a federal judge from assuming extrajudicial duties does

---

[152] 488 U.S. at 397.

not mean that every extrajudicial service would be compatible with, or appropriate to, continuing service on the bench. . . . The ultimate inquiry remains whether a particular extrajudicial assignment undermines the integrity of the Judicial Branch."[153] Ultimately, then, the Court appears to have abandoned its own suggested distinction between nonjudicial activities by courts on the one hand and by individual judges on the other because the Court tests both by much the same nebulous functional balancing analysis. But the Court's failure to provide any principled basis for application of this test underscores the probable reasons why the text of Article III provides for no exceptions to its case-or-controversy requirement. It is simply impossible to discern, on a case-by-case basis, whether a particular breach of the case-or-controversy requirement substantially undermines the values served by judicial separation of powers.

## § 1.09 ARTICLE III COURTS HAVE ULTIMATE POWER TO RESOLVE QUESTIONS OF "CONSTITUTIONAL FACT"

In its well-known and controversial decision in *Crowell v. Benson,* the Supreme Court held that Article III separation-of-powers concerns require that an Article III court be given jurisdiction to inquire, *de novo,* into certain factual findings in order to ensure that the Constitution had not been violated. The findings that fall within this category are described as "constitutional facts;" factual issues that if resolved one way would render the administrative rulings constitutional, and if resolved another way would render that ruling unconstitutional.[154] In *Crowell,* the specific factual questions concerned whether an injury claimed to be compensable under a federal statute had occurred on navigable waters and whether the injured individual was in the employ of the defendant. The former factual question was of constitutional magnitude because of the limits of federal power precluding federal maritime action on other than navigable waters. The latter was of constitutional magnitude because of substantive economic due process concerns (argued to preclude governmental power to impose liability absent the existence of an employment relationship).

In explaining the "constitutional fact" doctrine, Chief Justice Hughes, writing for the majority, stated: "In cases brought to enforce constitutional rights, the judicial power of the United States necessarily extends to the independent determination of all questions, both of fact and law, necessary to the performance of that supreme function."[155] He emphasized that the issue involved a question of the appropriate maintenance of the federal judicial power in requiring the observance of constitutional restrictions. It is the question whether the Congress may substitute an administrative agency for the judiciary for the final determination of the existence of the facts on which the enforcement of the constitutional rights depends.[156] Any other result, the opinion concluded, "would be to sap the judicial power as it exists

153 488 U.S. at 404 (footnote omitted).

154 Right to review constitutional facts de novo. Crowell v. Benson, 285 U.S. 22 (1932).

155 285 U.S. at 60.

156 285 U.S. at 56.

under the Federal Constitution, and to establish a government of a bureaucratic character alien to our system, wherever fundamental rights depend . . . upon the facts."[157]

While *Crowell* was merely one decision in an extended line of Supreme Court cases,[158] from the outset its holding was controversial. Justice Brandeis, dissenting in *Crowell*, rejected any distinct separation-of-powers limitation on congressional power to remove the task of fact-finding from the federal courts, stating:[159]

> If there be any controversy to which the judicial power extends that may not be subjected to the conclusive determination of administrative bodies or federal legislative courts, it is not because of any prohibition against the diminution of the jurisdiction of the federal district courts as such, but because, under certain circumstances, the constitutional requirement of due process is a requirement of judicial process.

Justice Brandeis supported this view by noting that Congress could give state courts the power to determine the issues delegated to the administrator, even though their judges lack protections of salary and tenure.[160] His argument, however, fails to distinguish between restrictions on federal court power in favor of the state courts, whose judges (though they may lack independence from the political branches of the *state* government) are formally independent of the political branches of the federal government, and restrictions that transfer power to organs directly under the control of the federal political branches.

Justice Brandeis, it should be noted, had himself authored the opinion of the Court in *Ng Fung Ho v. White*, another in the *Crowell* line of cases. There the Court held that individuals deported by the Department of Labor were entitled to a judicial determination of their claim of United States citizenship because the issue of citizenship presented a question of "constitutional fact" to be decided by the courts. Justice Brandeis reached this conclusion, however, exclusively on grounds of procedural due process, because of the importance of the liberty interest involved.[161] He did not believe that the economic constitutional interests asserted in *Crowell* required similar treatment.

Several courts and commentators have expressed the view that the constitutional fact doctrine of *Crowell* is no longer good law.[162] But the decision has never formally been overruled, and, at least in regard to issues of personal liberty rather than

---

157 285 U.S. at 57.

158 Line of cases. *See* St. Joseph Stock Yards Co. v. United States, 298 U.S. 38 (1936); Ng Fung Ho v. White, 259 U.S. 276 (1922); Ohio Valley Water Co. v. Ben Avon Borough, 253 U.S. 287 (1920).

159 Dissent: fact finding may be removed from federal courts. Crowell v. Benson, 285 U.S. 22, 87 (1932) (Brandeis, J., dissenting).

160 285 U.S. at 86–87 (Brandeis, J., dissenting).

161 Constitutional-fact doctrine may be rooted in due process. Ng Fung Ho v. White, 259 U.S. 276, 284–285 (1922).

162 Continuing validity of constitutional-fact doctrine questioned. *See, e.g.*, Estep v. United States, 327 U.S. 114, 142 (1946), (suggesting that "one had supposed that the doctrine had earned a deserved repose"); Associated Indemnity Corp. v. Shea, 455 F.2d 913, 914 n.2 (5th Cir. 1972) (per curiam) ("whether any vestige of validity remains of the extensively criticized *Crowell* doctrine is extremely

property rights, it appears that the constitutional fact doctrine retains force.[163] In more modern decisions, several lower courts have cited at least the broad implications of *Crowell's* constitutional fact doctrine favorably.[164]

## § 1.10 CONGRESS HAS POWER TO MAKE EXCEPTIONS TO THE SUPREME COURT'S APPELLATE JURISDICTION

### [1] The Exceptions Clause Allows Congress to Limit the Supreme Court's Appellate Jurisdiction

Article III, Section 2, Clause 2 of the Constitution gives the Supreme Court original jurisdiction over enumerated categories of cases.[165] In all other cases, the Supreme Court is given appellate jurisdiction, both as to law and fact, *"with such exceptions, and under such regulations as the Congress shall make."*[166] This last provision is the so-called "Exceptions Clause."

It is generally assumed that the Constitution's grant of *original* jurisdiction to the Supreme Court is both self-executing and immune from limitation by Congress. There is, however, significant case law indicating that even though the Constitution's grant of cases to the Court's appellate jurisdiction may on its face also appear to be self-executing, Congress has significant power to prohibit the Supreme Court from taking jurisdiction over cases allocated to its appellate jurisdiction.[167] The textual support for congressional power to restrict the scope of the Court's appellate jurisdiction is the Exceptions Clause.

### [2] *Ex parte McCardle*: The Supreme Court Gives the Exceptions Clause Broad Scope

In the famous case of *Ex parte McCardle,* the Supreme Court gave a broad reading to Congress's power under the Exceptions Clause. McCardle was a newspaper publisher who had been taken into custody by military authorities in the south shortly after the close of the Civil War. He was charged with printing

---

doubtful"); *see also* Schwartz, *Does the Ghost of* Crowell v. Benson *Still Walk?*, 98 U. PA. L. REV. 163 (1949).

163 Constitutional fact doctrine may still be valid. *See* Jacobellis v. Ohio, 378 U.S. 184, 190 n.6 (1964) (recognizing *Crowell's* relevance in the area of obscenity regulation and the First Amendment guarantee of free expression).

164 *Crowell* cited favorably. *4th Circuit See* Cross v. United States, 512 F.2d 1212, 1217 (4th Cir. 1975) (en banc) (retailer disqualified from participation in food stamp program has been deprived of property right and is entitled to due process). *D.C. Circuit See* Feinberg v. Federal Deposit Ins. Corp., 522 F.2d 1335, 1342 (D.C. Cir. 1975) (Congress may not use power to create courts' jurisdiction to deprive person of life, liberty, and property without due process).

165 U.S. Const., art. III, § 2, cl. 2 (in all cases affecting ambassadors, other public ministers, and consuls, and those in which a state is a party).

166 U.S. Const., art. III, § 2, cl. 2 (emphasis added).

167 Congress may limit Supreme Court's appellate jurisdiction. *See Ex parte* McCardle, 74 U.S. (7 Wall.) 506 (1869).

articles that were libelous and that "impeded reconstruction" in violation of the Military Reconstruction Act, a federal statute. While awaiting trial before a military commission, McCardle filed a petition for habeas corpus in the federal circuit court, under the Act of February 5, 1867, which authorized federal courts to grant habeas corpus "in all cases where any person may be restrained of his or her liberty in violation of the Constitution, or of any treaty or law of the United States."[168] The Act of February 5 had been passed so that federal courts could entertain writs of habeas corpus from persons held in *state* custody, something they could not generally do before the Civil War. The Act was cast in broad terms, however, and it was interpreted to apply to persons in federal custody as well, although persons in federal custody had always been able to seek writs in the federal courts.[169]

The circuit court dismissed McCardle's petition, and he sought review in the Supreme Court, again under the Act of February 5, 1867, which provided that cases brought under that Act could be appealed to the Supreme Court. After the case had been argued before the Court, Congress passed, over President Johnson's veto, a repeal of the appeals provision of the Act of February 5, 1867: "[t]hat so much of the act approved February 5, 1867 . . . as authorized an appeal from the judgment of the circuit court to the Supreme Court of the United States, or the exercise of any such jurisdiction by said Supreme Court, on appeals which have been, or may hereafter be taken, be, and the same is, hereby repealed."[170] The effect of this repealer was argued to the Court, and the Court subsequently dismissed the appeal of McCardle's case for want of jurisdiction.

First, citing an earlier decision by Chief Justice Marshall,[171] the Court reiterated that the Supreme Court can exercise only that appellate jurisdiction that has been conveyed to it by Congress.[172] Although the appellate jurisdiction is conferred by the Constitution, Congress is authorized by the Exceptions Clause to make exceptions and regulations to that jurisdiction. When Congress grants the Court appellate jurisdiction in some classes of cases, it impliedly prohibits its exercise in those not mentioned. In other words, the affirmative description of the Court's appellate jurisdiction by Congress "has been understood to imply a negation of the exercise of such appellate power as is not comprehended within [the affirmative description]."[173] But Congress had not merely been silent about McCardle's right to appeal; Congress specifically excepted a class of cases from review by appeal from the circuit court. The Court stated that it is hardly possible to imagine a plainer instance of positive exception. Because McCardle's case was in the Supreme Court on appeal solely under the 1867 Act, the Supreme Court no longer possessed jurisdiction over it.[174]

---

[168] Ex parte McCardle, 74 U.S. (7 Wall.) 506 (1869).

[169] *See* Van Alstyne, *A Critical Guide to Ex parte McCardle,* 15 Ariz. L. Rev. 229, 233–234 (1973).

[170] Act of March 27, 1868, ch. 34, § 2, 15 Stat. 44 (1868).

[171] Durousseau v. United States, 10 U.S. (6 Cranch) 307 (1810).

[172] Ex parte McCardle, 74 U.S. (7 Wall.) 506, 515 (1869).

[173] 74 U.S. (7 Wall.) at 513.

[174] 74 U.S. (7 Wall.) at 514; *see* U.S. Const., art. VI, cl. 2.

### [3] Possible Limits on Congress's Broad Powers Under *McCardle* and the Exceptions Clause

Read "for all it might be worth,"[175] *McCardle* seems to give Congress broad power to preclude Supreme Court appellate review. The language of *McCardle* and of other cases interpreting Congress's power seems to give Congress plenary power over the Court's appellate jurisdiction, allowing Congress to prevent review of all or part of the cases allocated to the Court's appellate jurisdiction. Such a broad power could substantially nullify the Court's power of judicial review established in *Marbury v. Madison*.[176]

*Ex parte McCardle* and cases containing similar language recognizing broad congressional power over the Supreme Court's appellate jurisdiction pose a seemingly significant problem to those who argue that the Exceptions Clause itself contains limits on Congress's power to restrict the Supreme Court's appellate jurisdiction. In accepting Congress's withdrawal of a case already argued before it, the Supreme Court mentioned no limitation in Article III, and the statute upheld in *McCardle* seems to be a most intrusive restriction on the Court's jurisdiction. But those who find limitations within the Exceptions Clause itself urge that *McCardle* should not be "read for all it might be worth." They further argue that although *McCardle* and other cases have used broad language in describing Congress's power, this language is not dispositive because the Court has never been faced with a truly significant restriction on its appellate jurisdiction. For example, all that Congress did in *McCardle* was to eliminate *one route* that McCardle could take to the Supreme Court. Even after the repealer, McCardle himself could have taken his case to the Supreme Court by filing a writ of habeas corpus directly in the Supreme Court, as a collateral proceeding, under a preexisting alternative statutory method of review. The Supreme Court had previously ruled that these writs were within the appellate jurisdiction conferred by the Judiciary Act of 1789 and were also within the scope of Article III appellate jurisdiction because they sought review of the actions of a lower court.[177] Thus, the argument runs, the repealer did not "except" a case or class of cases from the Court's appellate jurisdiction. Rather, it merely rescinded a statutory right of appeal — one of the two procedures through which the Court could assert appellate jurisdiction in such a case. The Court's broad language in *McCardle* is, according to this view, unfortunate, but certainly not conclusive of Congress's power to preclude totally appellate review in one of the cases within the Court's appellate jurisdiction.

This argument is supported by the Court's action in the subsequent case of *Ex parte Yerger*. Yerger, another Southern newspaper editor held in military custody, filed a writ of habeas corpus in the Supreme Court. And the Court, less than one year after its decision in *McCardle* unanimously upheld its jurisdiction to consider his case on the merits. In so holding, the Court found that the 1868 act had

---

[175] *See* Hart, *The Power of Congress to Limit the Jurisdiction of Federal Courts: An Exercise in Dialectic*, 66 Harv. L. Rev. 1362, 1364 (1953).

[176] Marbury v. Madison, 5 U.S. (1 Cranch) 137 (1803).

[177] Alternative route to review in Supreme Court. *See* Ex parte Bollman & Swartwout, 8 U.S. (4 Cranch) 75, 100–101 (1807).

repealed only the form of habeas corpus review provided for in the 1867 act, and therefore had no effect on the alternative, preexisting method of obtaining habeas corpus review provided for in the Judiciary Act of 1789.[178] The Court was thus able to avoid the difficult constitutional question of the scope of the Exceptions Clause.

The Supreme Court relied on its analysis in *Yerger* to avoid having to determine the scope of the Exceptions Clause. In *Felker v. Turpin*, the Court construed the limit imposed on Supreme Court jurisdiction to review certain denials of habeas corpus by Title I of the Antiterrorism and Effective Death Penalty Act of 1996[179] not to have repealed alternative original habeas petitions in the Supreme Court "for reasons similar to those stated in *Yerger*." The Court openly acknowledged that this interpretation obviated the need to reach the Exceptions Clause issue.[180]

One scholar, who admits that the Court's ruling in *McCardle* did not deprive McCardle of access to the Supreme Court, nevertheless find it "more precious than useful" to conclude from this that the Supreme Court thought that the Exceptions Clause itself limits Congress's power. He emphasizes that the Court's statements in *McCardle* and similar statements in other cases recognize no limitation in the clauses.[181] Under this view, the natural reading of the clause is consistent with the Court's descriptions of it in *McCardle*, and any limitation on Congress's power to make exceptions must come from *outside* the clause itself. But assuming that *McCardle* and other cases containing similarly broad statements about Congress's "plenary" power to make exceptions to the Court's appellate jurisdiction are not conclusive, what implicit limitations does the Exceptions Clause even arguably impose on Congress's power? Commentators have expressed two different views.

First, building on the argument that the common understanding of power to *make exceptions* to jurisdiction does not include the power totally to abolish the jurisdiction, it has been vigorously argued that Congress's power to make exceptions to the Supreme Court's appellate jurisdiction does not extend to the power to prevent the Court from performing its "essential role" or "essential functions" in the constitutional scheme.[182] These functions are to resolve conflicting interpretations of the federal law and to maintain the supremacy of that law when it conflicts with state law or is challenged by state authority.[183] Under this view, any attempt by Congress to preclude appellate review in every case involving a particular subject would be unconstitutional. Although there is no significant judicial authority to support this view, Congress has not enacted legislation that would test the theory. None of the cases in which the Court has approved congressional restriction of its jurisdiction has involved what would be termed an "essential function" of the Court.

---

178 Habeas Corpus review found still to be available. Ex parte Yerger, 75 U.S. (8 Wall.) 85, 105 (1869).

179 Pub. L. 104–132, 110 Stats. 1214.

180 Exceptions Clause issue avoided. Felker v. Turpin, 518 U.S. 651, 660–662 (1996).

181 Van Alstyne, *A Critical Guide to Ex parte McCardle*, 15 Ariz. L. Rev. 229, 255 (1973).

182 *See* Hart, *The Power of Congress to Limit the Jurisdiction of Federal Courts: An Exercise in Dialectic*, 66 Harv. L. Rev. 1362, 1365 (1953); Ratner, *Congressional Power Over the Appellate Jurisdiction of the Supreme Court*, 109 U. Pa. L. Rev. 157, 201–202 (1960).

183 Ratner, *Congressional Power Over the Appellate Jurisdiction of the Supreme Court*, 109 U. Pa. L. Rev. 157, 166 (1960).

This theory, if accepted, ensures appellate jurisdiction to a greater extent than do some of the theories that rely on limitations outside the Exceptions Clause, most notably the Due Process Clause. So far at least, the Supreme Court has held that due process does not guarantee the right to an appeal in either civil or criminal cases.[184] Thus, a litigant who has received a hearing in a state court would not appear to have a due process objection if the case could not be heard in the Supreme Court. However, if the case involved a conflict over the supremacy of federally guaranteed rights, and Congress had purported to preclude all Supreme Court review over that class of cases, it might be successfully argued that congressional preclusion of Supreme Court review unconstitutionally prevented the Court from exercising one of its "essential functions." As appealing as the "essential functions" thesis may seem purely as a matter of political or social policy, it finds no support in either the text or history of the Constitution. Ultimately, it amounts to little more than constitutional "wishful thinking."[185]

It might be argued that it is fortunate that the Court has never explicitly ruled on the validity of the "essential functions" theory, thereby leaving a desirable tension between the Court and the Congress; a tension that makes the Court sensitive to public concern about what some view as overreaching. It is, of course, fortunate that the Court has never had to decide whether the "essential functions" theory is valid because the necessity for such a decision would reflect the existence of a serious political upheaval. However, the extent to which the "essential functions" theory has actually influenced the political debates that have accompanied some of the attempts to pass jurisdiction-curbing legislation through Congress is uncertain.

The second view restricts congressional power to an even greater degree than does the "essential functions" thesis. Based primarily on historical research into the framing and ratification of the Constitution, this view is that the Exceptions Clause refers only to Supreme Court review of questions of fact and not to questions of law. In effect, this theory asserts that the comma in the clause that follows "law and fact" should actually be placed after "law," so that the clause reads, "the Supreme Court shall have appellate jurisdiction, both as to law, and fact with such exceptions, and under such regulations as the Congress shall make."[186] According to this theory, the Exceptions Clause was placed in Article III because the framers could not agree about whether the Supreme Court should be able to redetermine questions of fact decided by lower courts. At the time of ratification, the practice in the various states concerning the power of appellate courts to review the findings of juries and the findings of lower courts in equity and admiralty cases apparently differed significantly. Rather than specifying which of these varying practices the Supreme Court should follow, the framers decided, according to this view, to leave the matter to Congress. The misplacing of a comma

---

[184] Due process does not guarantee right of appeal. Lindsey v. Normet, 405 U.S. 56, 77 (1972); Griffin v. Illinois, 351 U.S. 12, 18 (1956).

[185] *See* Redish, *Congressional Power to Limit Supreme Court Appellate Jurisdiction Under the Exceptions Clause: An Internal and External Examination,* 27 VILL. L. REV. 900 (1982).

[186] *See* Berger, Congress v. The Supreme Court 285–296 (1969); Merryman, *Scope of the Supreme Court's Appellate Jurisdiction: Historical Basis,* 47 MINN. L. REV. 53 (1962).

in Article III has, according to this argument, led to a completely erroneous view of congressional power.

Most, if not all, of those who have studied the relevant historical materials agree that concern over the review of facts influenced the adoption of the Exceptions Clause.[187] There is disagreement, however, as to whether this was the sole concern, because there are relevant statements indicating the desirability of a broader scope for the Exceptions Clause. But perhaps the greatest obstacle to this very limited view of the scope of the Exceptions Clause is the appellate jurisdiction authorized by the Judiciary Act passed just after ratification. While it arguably did not prohibit the Court from performing its "essential functions," it did limit appellate jurisdiction to a far greater extent than the review-of-questions-of-fact view would allow.

## § 1.11 CONGRESS POSSESSES LIMITED AUTHORITY TO VEST THE JUDICIAL POWER IN NON-ARTICLE III ADJUDICATORS

The essential characteristic of the Article III courts is the independence that their judges possess with respect to the executive and legislative branches of the federal government. However, Congress's power to create at least certain types of adjudicatory bodies not subject to these protections has long been recognized.

Congressional authority to establish non-Article III courts does not derive from any explicit constitutional power. The Supreme Court has stated that the power given Congress in Article I, Section 8, Clause 9 of the Constitution, to constitute tribunals inferior to the Supreme Court, plainly refers to the inferior courts provided for in Article III, Section 1; it has never been relied on for establishment of any other tribunals.[188] Rather, the power derives from the conclusion that Congress may create certain non-Article III courts under its enumerated powers in Article I, in combination with the Necessary and Proper Clause.[189] For example, Congress has employed its Article I power to make rules for the government and regulation of the land and naval forces[190] to establish military tribunals whose judges do not have Article III protections.[191] Similarly, Congress has used its Article IV power to govern territories[192] to establish territorial courts and its Article I power to lay and collect taxes[193] to establish the Tax Court. Courts established in this manner have been referred to as "Article I" or "legislative" courts.

---

[187] *See* Van Alstyne, *A Critical Guide to Ex parte McCardle*, 15 ARIZ. L. REV. 229, 260 (1973).

[188] Article I does not support creation of non-Article III tribunals. Glidden Co. v. Zdanok, 370 U.S. 530, 543 (1962).

[189] U.S. Const., art. I, § 8, cl. 18.

[190] U.S. Const., art. I, § 8, cl. 14.

[191] Congress may create military courts. *See* Dynes v. Hoover, 61 U.S. (20 How.) 65, 79 (1858).

[192] U.S. Const., art. IV, § 3, cl. 2.

[193] U.S. Const., art. I, § 8, cl. 1.

While it has not always been clear whether certain courts are of the Article I or Article III variety, the distinction has significant consequences. One distinguishing factor is the vast difference in the degree of independence possessed by the judges of the two types of courts. The business of the judiciary is often to review the constitutional legitimacy of the actions of the legislative or executive branches. To the extent that these branches retain power to retaliate against judges who displease them, courts might conceivably be unable to review the activities of those branches with proper neutrality. It was for this very reason that the framers inserted the salary and tenure protections in Article III. Another important consequence that flows from the distinction between Article I and Article III courts is that the former may be made to perform nonjudicial functions, while the latter, on the, may not. For example, legislative courts may be required to give advisory opinions free from the "case or controversy" requirement imposed on Article III courts.[194]

Though Congress's power to establish Article I courts in certain areas is well established, the parameters, if any, of this power remain shrouded in uncertainty. The primary question concerns the extent to which Congress may invest Article I courts with the "judicial power" of the United States. In other words, to what extent may Congress delegate to Article I courts authority to adjudicate the categories of cases described in Article III, Section 2 of the Constitution? If it were to be held that Article I bodies (which, in addition to legislative courts, include administrative agencies) could hear no case falling within the "judicial power," Congress's ability to make use of these institutions would be severely limited. Virtually all the controversies given for determination to these bodies could be deemed cases "arising under the laws of the United States," a central category of the judicial power described in Article III, Section 2. On the other hand, if the authority of Article I courts to adjudicate controversies within the judicial power were unlimited, Congress could easily circumvent the independence protections of Article III by simply vesting all judicial power in Article I courts. Any attempt to deal with these issues, however, must be preceded by an examination of the historical development of the concept of legislative courts.

## § 1.12 THE ORIGINS OF LEGISLATIVE COURTS

### [1] Territorial Courts

The first decision recognizing the existence of legislative courts was *American Insurance Co. v. Canter*, in which Chief Justice Marshall found that the judges of the territorial courts created by Congress for the territory of Florida did not have the protections of Article III because those courts were not created under its provisions. Chief Justice Marshall concluded that the power that they exercised was not the judicial power described in Article III, Section 2. Indeed, they were incapable of receiving it. He wrote:[195]

---

[194] Article I courts may give advisory opinions. Ex parte Bakelite Corp., 279 U.S. 438, 454 (1929).

[195] Territorial courts do not exercise Article III judicial power. American Ins. Co. v. Canter, 1 Peters 516, 1 F. Cas. 658 (1828).

> They are legislative Courts, created in virtue of the general right of sovereignty which exists in the government, or in virtue of that clause which enables Congress to make all needful rules and regulations, respecting the territory belonging to the United States. The jurisdiction with which they are invested, is not a part of that judicial power which is defined in the 3d article of the Constitution, but is conferred by Congress, in the execution of those general powers which that body possesses over the territories of the United States

Since the *Canter* decision, it has been well established that territorial courts are legislative courts.[196] It has, therefore, been held that the salary of a territorial judge may be reduced,[197] and that he or she may be appointed for a limited term or removed from office.[198]

More recently, the Supreme Court has held that a judge of a territorial district court, an Article IV judge, does not qualify as a "district judge" who may be designated to sit on a panel of the court of appeals.[199] In *Nguyen v. United States*, the Court reversed a court of appeals judgment in a criminal case because the appellate panel consisted of two Article III judges and an Article IV judge. The Article IV judge was a district judge of a territorial court created by Congress pursuant to Article IV, Section 3, of the Constitution. However, the Court concluded that Article IV judges are not "district judges" for this purpose: unlike an Article III judge, an Article IV judge does not have life tenure and is not qualified to exercise the judicial power of an Article III judge. Accordingly, an appellate panel that includes an Article IV judge is improperly constituted and lacks authority to act.[200]

The reasons for considering territorial courts to be non-Article III bodies were historically pragmatic in nature. Judges in the territories performed functions that were traditionally within the purview of both state and federal courts. When a territory became a state, a significant portion of the duties performed by its courts was to be assumed by a newly established state judiciary. If the judges of the territorial courts had the life tenure protections of Article III, Congress would have been hard pressed to know what to do with many of them.[201]

---

[196] Territorial courts are legislative courts. McAllister v. United States, 141 U.S. 174, 185 (1891).

[197] Salary of judge of territorial court may be reduced. United States v. Fisher, 109 U.S. 143, 145 (1883).

[198] Territorial judge may be appointed for limited term or removed. McAllister v. United States, 141 U.S. 174, 185–186 (1891).

[199] Article IV judge not district judge. Nguyen v. United States, 539 U.S. 69, 72–73 (2003).

[200] Appellate panel with Article IV judge lacks authority. Nguyen v. United States, 539 U.S. 69, 70, 82–83 (2003).

[201] Difficulties on obtaining statehood. *See* Glidden Co. v. Zdanok, 370 U.S. 530, 545–546 (1962) It is interesting to note, however, the view of one commentator that "[t]hese grounds, whatever their strength in 1829, have a decidedly false ring today. The small number of remaining territories are not apt to become states in the near future and even if they did, their judges could easily be absorbed into the relatively large federal judiciary." Note, *Legislative and Constitutional Courts: What Lurks Ahead for Bifurcation?*, 71 Yale L.J. 979, 982 (1962) (footnote omitted).

Though the status of territorial courts as Article I institutions appears to be beyond question, the supporting policy and constitutional arguments are far from settled. First, it is questionable whether practical considerations actually justified the sweeping conclusion that territorial courts were not part of the Article III judiciary. The problem might well have been solved by the creation of two court systems in the territories, one acting as federal district courts (with all the protections of Article III) and one acting in a manner analogous to a state court. When the territory became a state, the Article III court could have simply continued to function as it had previously. More importantly, the result of the doctrine that territorial courts are Article I bodies is that individuals in the territories may be deprived of their personal liberty by a judge who is not independent — at least in the sense contemplated in Article III — of the government that is prosecuting them. The Supreme Court has concluded that traditionally,[202]

> the realities of territorial government typically made it less urgent that judges there enjoy the independence from Congress and the President envisioned by . . . article [III]. For the territories were not ruled immediately from Washington; in a day of poor roads and slow mails, it was unthinkable that they should be.

But the historical accuracy of this assumption is open to some question,[203] and in any event, it is surely not the case today. Yet the courts of our remaining territories are still deemed to be Article I bodies. Furthermore, it is likely that the framers' primary purpose in inserting the independence protections into Article III was to avoid the need for the very kind of speculation about judicial independence in which the Supreme Court has engaged in excluding the territorial courts from the scope of Article III protections.

This points to a broader difficulty with the description of territorial courts as legislative courts. The language of Article III seems to make clear that judges of courts created by Congress are to enjoy the guarantees of independence. It makes no mention of exceptions for which the use of independent judges would be "burdensome" or "inconvenient." Yet, if we are to accept the asserted rationale for exempting territorial courts form the protections of Article III, are we not simply concluding that the guarantees of the Constitution apply only if they cause no undue inconvenience?

If the decision to categorize territorial courts as Article I bodies is not to lead to such an unacceptable conclusion, a principled basis must be found on which to conclude that the territorial courts present a unique situation. One possible rationale is that in Article IV of the Constitution, the framers gave Congress plenary power to govern the territories.[204] But this, in and of itself, is surely no

---

202 Territorial courts have less need for Article III protection. Glidden Co. v. Zdanok, 370 U.S. 530, 546 (1962).

203 *See* Watson, *The Concept of the Legislative Court: A Constitutional Fiction,* 10 Geo. Wash. L. Rev. 799, 803 (1942) (noting complete absence in records of framers' debates of any mention of territorial judiciary).

204 U.S. Const., art. IV, § 3, cl. 2.

basis on which to conclude that the framers intended the power to be so broad as to supersede the limits imposed by other constitutional provisions. One commentator has made the following argument to support the contention that Article III does not limit Congress's power to regulate the territories:[205]

> The Constitution is a document that was designed to meet the needs of a body of people with a more or less common social, political, and cultural background. It is not realistic to assume that the institutions there provided are necessarily the best for the government of any piece of territory that may come under the control of the United States, and it does not seem unlikely that the framers intended to give Congress a great deal of flexibility in its government of the territories.

This total speculation, however, provides a weak basis on which to reject a seemingly absolute constitutional guarantee.

Another possible justification for special treatment of territorial courts is that it has been held, for some unknown reason, that only "fundamental" constitutional protections apply in the territories.[206] It might be thought, then, that the limited applicability of the Constitution to the territories explains the absence of Article III protections for territorial judges.

Finally, and perhaps most persuasively, it might be argued that territorial courts deserve unique treatment because in creating them, Congress is actually acting in a manner analogous to a state legislature. As already noted, in the territories, the courts may function as state courts, as well as federal district courts.[207] It could be argued that, when acting in a manner analogous to a state legislature, Congress is no more bound to adhere to the requirements of Article III than is a state legislature itself. While this view has the benefit of providing a fairly narrow principle on which to limit the extension of legislative courts, it fails to recognize that Congress is always limited by the terms of Article III, while a state legislature is not. Ultimately, then, none of the bases for distinguishing territorial courts provides adequate justification for the sweeping exclusion of territorial courts from the Article III judiciary.

### [2] Military Courts

Also troubling is the equally well established principle that military courts are not part of the Article III judiciary.[208] Despite the long and accepted history of this practice, it is fraught with serious dangers. As the Supreme Court has itself

---

[205] Note, *The Distinction Between Legislative and Constitutional Courts and Its Effect on Judicial Assignment*, 62 Colum. L. Rev. 133, 150 (1962) (footnote omitted).

[206] Constitutional protections are limited in the territories. Soto v. United States, 273 F. 628, 633 (3d Cir. 1921); Government of Virgin Islands v. Rijos, 285 F. Supp. 126, 129 (D.V.I. 1968).

[207] Territorial courts function as state courts. *See* Palmore v. United States, 411 U.S. 389, 402–403 (1973).

[208] Military courts are not Article III courts. *See* Dynes v. Hoover, 61 U.S. (20 How.) 65, 79, 15 L. Ed. 838 (1858) ("Congress has the power to provide for the trial and punishment of military and naval offenses in the manner then and now practiced by civilized nations. . . . [T]he power to do so is given

recognized:[209]

> [C]onceding to military personnel that high degree of honesty and sense of justice which nearly all of them undoubtedly have, it still remains true that military tribunals have not been and probably never can be constituted in such way that they can have the same kind of qualifications that the Constitution has deemed essential to fair trials of civilians in federal courts.

Military courts have the power to deprive military personnel of their personal liberty, yet the individuals who exercise this power are not truly independent of the prosecution. Recognizing this danger, the Supreme Court has significantly reduced the jurisdiction of the military courts to deal with crimes alleged to have been committed by civilians, former service members, or service members in a nonservice-related context.[210] The Court, however, has not raised any question about the legitimacy of the Article I military courts' performance of their central functions.

As in the case of the territorial courts, it is necessary to determine the reasons for the special exception of the military courts from the guarantees of Article III. Courts and commentators have often suggested that practical considerations inherent in the operations of the military justify the Article I status of military courts.[211] They believe that the exercise of control by federal judges is incompatible with the proper functioning of the military system. But the choice is not between judges who sit at the whim of the government on the one hand, and direct control by federal judges, on the other. The issue is, simply, whether those personnel who do hear military cases will have their salary and tenure protected by Article III. Therefore, it is difficult to understand how the exigencies of military discipline in any way require nonindependent adjudicators. Accepting as given that the military system requires firm discipline, and that on the battlefield, the right to all the trappings of due process may be forced to give way, it does not necessarily follow that individual judges who hear military cases need not be independent of the prosecution. More importantly, even if convenience factors might be thought to justify the Article I status of military courts, the argument described above may set the dangerous precedent that constitutional guarantees (such as the independence protections of Article III) may be forced to give way when it is "inconvenient" to enforce them.

---

without any connection between it and the 3d article of the Constitution"); *see also* United States *ex rel.* Toth v. Quarles, 350 U.S. 11, 17 (1955).

[209] Military courts cannot function with full constitutional protections. United States ex rel. Toth v. Quarles, 350 U.S. 11, 17 (1955).

[210] Criminal jurisdiction of military courts is limited. *See* Reid v. Covert, 354 U.S. 1, 21 (1957) (military jurisdiction is very limited and extraordinary and is intended to be only narrow exception to normal method of trial in courts of law); United States ex rel. Toth v. Quarles, 350 U.S. 11, 22 (1955) (free countries have tried to restrict military tribunals to narrowest jurisdiction deemed absolutely essential to maintaining discipline among troops in active service).

[211] View that practical considerations justify Article I status of military courts. *See* United States *ex rel.* Toth v. Quarles, 350 U.S. 11, 17 (1955) ("it is the primary business of armies and navies to fight or be ready to fight wars should the occasion arise").

Stronger arguments, however, might be made to justify the special treatment given military courts. If it could be established that the framers specifically intended to exclude the military courts from the requirements of Article III, there might be a more principled means of excepting the military from the traditional protections afforded the judicial branch. Whether such an historical conclusion can be reached is not altogether clear. It is true that Article I empowers Congress to make rules for the government and regulation of the land and naval forces.[212] But, as already noted, the mere fact that Congress has power to act under the Constitution does not necessarily imply that this power was intended to be exercised in a manner inconsistent with limitations imposed by other constitutional provisions.

Stronger evidence can be found in the Fifth Amendment's explicit exemption from the requirement of a grand jury indictment of cases "arising in the land or naval forces, or in the militia, when in actual service in time of war or public danger."[213] In addition, the Sixth Amendment right to jury trial in criminal cases has been construed to be inapplicable to the military.[214] It might, therefore, be argued that from the outset, the framers recognized the special role of military justice. Of course, this argument can be reversed; the specific insertion in the Fifth Amendment of an exception for the military demonstrates that when the framers desired to make a special rule for the military, they did so explicitly. Therefore, their failure to make an explicit exception for the military courts from Article III demonstrates their understanding that the military courts were to be governed by its terms. Ultimately, neither version of the argument is conclusive. In any event, while the pressing necessities of battlefield justice make clear why the use of grand or petit juries would be impractical, it is not equally clear why the military could not have a corps of judges afforded the protections of Article III.

### [3] Other Legislative Courts

While the territorial and military courts constitute the classic illustrations of legislative courts, a number of others have existed over the years. One well established current example is the Tax Court.[215] Another is the United States Court of Appeals for Veterans Claims, which has responsibility for reviewing decisions made by Veterans' Administration Region Offices and the Board of Veterans' Appeals.[216] In *Ex parte Bakelite Corp.*,[217] the Supreme Court noted several other courts that had been deemed legislative, including the Courts of

---

[212] U.S. Const., art. I, § 8, cl. 14.

[213] U.S. Const., amend. V.

[214] No right to jury trial in military court. *Ex parte* Quirin, 317 U.S. 1, 40 (1942).

[215] *See* 26 U.S.C. § 7441, as amended by Act of December 30, 1969, Pub. L. No. 91-172, § 951, 83 Stat. 487 (1969).

[216] Court of Appeals for Veterans Claims. 38 U.S.C. § 7251 ("There is hereby established, under Article I of the Constitution of the United States, a court of record to be known as the United States Court of Appeals for Veterans Claims."); 38 U.S.C. § 7261 (scope of review of Court of Appeals for Veterans Claims); *see also* 38 U.S.C. § 7252 (conferring exclusive jurisdiction to review decisions of Board of Veterans' Appeals on Court of Appeals for Veterans Claims); 38 U.S.C. § 7292 (conferring exclusive jurisdiction to review decisions of Court of Appeals for Veterans Claims on Federal Circuit Court of Appeals).

Private Land Claims.[218] and the Choctaw and Chickasaw Citizenship Court. Following two major Supreme Court decisions,[219] both the Court of Claims and the Court of Customs Appeals (later called the Court of Customs and Patent Appeals and subsequently merged into the Federal Circuit) were also considered to be legislative courts. These conclusions were expressly rejected by the Supreme Court in its 1962 decision in *Glidden Co. v. Zdanok*.[220] It is now accepted that these are Article III courts, and that as a result, their judges have both tenure and salary protections. For further information regarding these courts, see the Historical Appendix to this chapter.

### [4] Administrative Agencies

Congress may vest administrative agencies with the authority to perform adjudicatory functions regarding matters within the purview of the agency. In so doing, Congress may withhold from the federal courts the jurisdiction to review the final determinations of the agency as to matters within its jurisdiction.[221] In this regard, administrative agencies have the character of Article I legislative courts, and the discussion in the subsequent sections may be applicable to the adjudicatory functions of agencies.[222]

## § 1.13 *PALMORE v. UNITED STATES*: CONGRESS MAY CREATE NON-ARTICLE III COURTS IN THE DISTRICT OF COLUMBIA

In the District of Columbia Court Reform and Criminal Procedure Act of 1970,[223] Congress vested all authority to adjudicate local District of Columbia cases in a newly created Superior Court. Judges of the Superior Court were to serve 15-year terms, and were subject to removal or suspension by a judicial commission. In establishing the Superior Courts, Congress expressly stated that these bodies were Article I courts.

In *Palmore v. United States*, the Supreme Court held that a defendant who was charged with a felony under the District of Columbia Code could be tried by a judge who did not have the protections with respect to tenure and salary provided by

---

[217] Other legislative courts noted. *Ex parte* Bakelite Corp., 279 U.S. 438, 456–457 (1929).

[218] Court of Private Land Claims. *See* United States v. Coe, 155 U.S. 76 (1894).

[219] Two major Supreme Court decisions. *See* Williams v. United States, 289 U.S. 553 (1933); *Ex parte* Bakelite Corp., 279 U.S. 438 (1929).

[220] Court of Claims and Court of Customs and Patent Appeals are not legislative courts. Glidden Co. v. Zdanok, 370 U.S. 530 (1962).

[221] Congress may make agency adjudicatory determinations nonreviewable. Butte, A. & P. R. Co. v. United States, 290 U.S. 127, 143 (1933) (determinations of Interstate Commerce Commission are not reviewable in federal court for errors of fact or law).

[222] Administrative agencies may have legislative court functions. *See, e.g.*, Commodities Futures Trading Commission v. Schor, 478 U.S. 833, 847–848 (1986) (discussed in detail in § 100.44[2]).

[223] Pub. L. No. 91-358, 84 Stat. 473 (1970).

Article III of the Constitution.[224] The defendant, who had been convicted in the Superior Court, argued that because his prosecution was a case "arising under the laws of the United States," a category of cases included in the judicial power described in Article III, he had the right to be judged by an individual who had the independence guarantees of that Article.[225] Such a broadly phrased argument was doomed to fail because it effectively reasserted the discredited theory that an Article I court could not hear any matter falling within Article III, Section 2. However, even the narrower argument, that no Article I court could deprive an individual of his personal liberty, would have been equally unsuccessful.

The Court in *Palmore* cited three situations in which Congress had been allowed to invest judges lacking the independence protections of Article III with power to deprive individuals of personal liberty. Two of these have already been considered; the territorial and military courts. It is questionable, however, whether these traditional exceptions to the requirements of Article III support the *Palmore* decision. Rightly or wrongly, it has long been thought that citizens of the territories and military personnel are not entitled to all constitutional protections, but no such exclusion has been reached for citizens of the District of Columbia.

The Court's third category was the state courts. The Court noted that Congress, if it so chooses, may vest power in the state courts to adjudicate federal criminal cases,[226] yet state judges lack the guarantees of independence provided by Article III. Once again, the court's analogy is dubious. While it is true that Congress may circumvent the lower federal judiciary by vesting federal judicial power in the state courts, and that state judges may lack the protections of salary and tenure afforded Article III judges, Congress lacks power to control either the salary of tenure of state judges. Although state judges may not be independent of their own legislature, they are independent of Congress and the President. It is, then, one thing to say that state courts may adjudicate federal criminal cases; it is quite another to hold that individuals directly subject to the control of the federal government may do so.

Perhaps the strongest argument in support of the *Palmore* decision — and the most limiting — is that in establishing courts to handle the local affairs of the District of Columbia, Congress acts in a manner analogous to a state legislature. The argument is that while Congress may be bound to vest jurisdiction over criminal cases of a traditional federal nature in Article III courts (or in state courts equally independent of the federal government), when acting in the capacity of a state legislature, Congress is no more bound to adhere to the independence requirements of Article III than is a state legislature. The Court in *Palmore* relied, at least in part, on this rationale. It noted that Congress intended to establish an entirely new court system with functions essentially similar to those of the local courts found in the 50 states. These courts have the responsibility for trying and deciding those distinctively local controversies that arise under local law, including

224 D.C. courts need not have Article III protections. Palmore v. United States, 411 U.S. 389, 390 (1973).

225 411 U.S. at 400.

226 411 U.S. at 402.

local criminal laws, that have little, if any, impact beyond the local jurisdiction.[227] The Court also noted that the defendant was no more disadvantaged and no more entitled to an Article III judge than any other citizen of any other state who is tried for a strictly local crime.[228] Subsequent statements of both the Supreme Court[229] and lower federal courts[230] have underscored the importance of the state court analogy as a basis for the non-Article III status of District of Columbia judges. This argument might be employed to justify the exception of territorial courts from the requirements of Article III, and to this extent, the Court's reliance in *Palmore* on the territorial court precedents may be valid. Once again, however, it is necessary to point out the fallacy of this argument; while Article III does not limit state legislatures, it does limit Congress in all of its actions.

Although congressional regulation of the District of Columbia judiciary has always been viewed as *sui generis*,[231] certain language in the Court's opinion arguably extends its holding well beyond this limited factual situation. As partial justification for its conclusion that Congress may vest criminal jurisdiction in the District of Columbia Superior Courts, the Court stated:[232]

> From its own studies, Congress had concluded that there was a crisis in the judicial system of the District of Columbia, that case loads had become unmanageable, and that neither those matters of national concern nor those of strictly local cognizance were being promptly tried and disposed of by the existing court system.

The Court also noted:[233]

> Congress made a deliberate choice to create judgeships with terms of 15 years . . . and to subject judges in those positions to removal or suspension by a judicial commission under certain established circumstances. . . . It was thought that such a system would be more workable and efficient in administering and discharging the work of a multifaceted metropolitan court system.

This reasoning would seem to justify Congress's circumvention of the requirements of Article III any time it is determined that its requirements would be unduly burdensome. It is true that such an argument could be — and has been — used to justify the Article I status of both territorial and military courts. But acceptance of inconvenience as a general rationale for the use of legislative courts to adjudicate fundamental constitutional rights could extend this practice well beyond the

---

227 Congress acts like a legislature in government of D.C. 411 U.S. at 409.

228 411 U.S. at 410.

229 *See* Swain v. Pressley, 430 U.S. 372, 382 (1977); *but see* Key v. Doyle, 434 U.S. 59, 64 (1977) (analogy between District of Columbia local courts and state courts is "not perfect").

230 *See, e.g.*, Halleck v. Berliner, 427 F. Supp. 1225, 1233 (D.D.C. 1977) (Congress may exercise within the District of Columbia all legislative powers that a state legislature may exercise over a state's affairs).

231 *See* O'Donoghue v. United States, 289 U.S. 516, 538 (1933) (Congress has exclusive power to enact legislation over seat of United States government).

232 Palmore v. United States, 411 U.S. 389, 408 (1973).

233 411 U.S. at 409.

narrowly defined instances in which it has been accepted to date, perhaps threatening the continued vitality of the Article III protections. As will be seen in subsequent sections, in many ways the Court has in fact moved toward this end.

## § 1.14 THE EVOLUTION OF MODERN LEGISLATIVE COURT DOCTRINE: THE BANKRUPTCY COURTS AND THE *NORTHERN PIPELINE* DECISION

In 1982, the Supreme Court spoke again on the issue of legislative courts in *Northern Pipeline Construction Co. v. Marathon Pipe Line Co.* In *Northern Pipeline*, a sharply divided Court[234] held that the non-Article III judges of the bankruptcy courts, which Congress had established in the Bankruptcy Reform Act of 1978,[235] could not constitutionally exercise at least a part of the jurisdiction vested in them under that Act.[236]

The decision created serious and immediate problems for Congress by forcing it to restructure the method of bankruptcy adjudication. It responded by enacting the Bankruptcy Amendments and Federal Judgeship Act of 1984[237] after the Supreme Court's final stay of the effect of its decision. In effect, the amendments purported to transform the bankruptcy courts into "adjuncts" of the federal district courts, thereby avoiding Article III difficulties. The Supreme Court later rejected this characterization of the bankruptcy courts under the 1984 act.[238] In any event, the ramifications of *Northern Pipeline* extended far beyond the case's immediate impact on the exercise of bankruptcy jurisdiction.

The case actually involved only the question of whether bankruptcy courts may adjudicate state-created common law rights that involve the bankrupt.[239] Justice Brennan's opinion nevertheless began as if he were deciding much more. He stated:[240]

---

[234] Justice Brennan, speaking for a plurality of four Justices, announced the judgment of the Court. Justice Rehnquist, joined by Justice O'Connor, concurred separately. Justices White and Powell, and Chief Justice Burger, dissented.

[235] Pub. L. No. 95-598, 92 Stat. 2549.

[236] Bankruptcy courts must be afforded Article III status for some exercises of jurisdiction. Northern Pipeline Construction Co. v. Marathon Pipe Line Co., 458 U.S. 50, 87 (1982).

[237] Pub. L. No. 98-353 (98th Cong. 2d Sess. 1984).

[238] Bankruptcy courts not adjuncts of district courts. Stern v. Marshall, 131 S. Ct. 2594, 180 L. Ed. 2d 475, 505 (2011) (majority rejected argument that bankruptcy courts are adjuncts of district courts under 1984 law because they resolve all matters of fact and law in whatever domain of law to which parties' claims might lead and have power to enter final judgments, subject to review only if party chooses to appeal).

[239] *See* Northern Pipeline Construction Co. v. Marathon Pipe Line Co., 458 U.S. 50 (1982). Justice Brennan's decision left open the question whether Congress may have the traditional issues of bankruptcy and the division of the debtor's assets decided by non-Article III judges. However, the Court found that the jurisdictional grants were not severable and therefore invalidated the entire jurisdictional provision.

[240] 458 U.S. at 52.

> The question presented is whether the assignment by Congress to bankruptcy judges of the jurisdiction granted in § 241(a) of the Bankruptcy Act of 1978 . . . violated Article III of the Constitution.

The jurisdictional provision to which Justice Brennan referred encompassed the entire jurisdiction of the bankruptcy courts. The reasoning in his opinion demonstrates, however, that Justice Brennan's ultimate conclusion is not as broad as his initial question.

Justice Brennan initially stated that *Northern Pipeline* differed from cases upholding the use of legislative courts and administrative agencies to adjudicate cases involving public rights because *Northern Pipeline* involved adjudication of only so-called "private rights."[241] He asserted that although the restructuring of debtor-creditor relations might be a public right, the type of common law adjudication involved in *Northern Pipeline* was not.[242] Drawing on Chief Justice Hughes' famed opinion in *Crowell v. Benson,* Brennan concluded that cases adjudicating so-called "public rights" are those arising between the Government and persons subject to its authority in connection with the performance of the constitutional functions of the executive or legislative departments.[243] The adjudication of these rights, Justice Brennan wrote, is not "inherently judicial;" therefore, they may be adjudicated by an Article III court if Congress so desires, but need not be. "Inherently judicial" cases, on the other hand, are disputes between private litigants of private rights disputes. According to Justice Brennan, these cases lie at the core of the historically recognized judicial power, and must, therefore, be heard by an Article III court.[244]

Thus, despite his broad opening statement, Justice Brennan never decided whether a non-Article III bankruptcy court could constitutionally perform the traditional functions of dividing a bankrupt debtor's assets among its creditors and discharging the bankrupt.[245] As Chief Justice Burger accurately remarked in dissent:[246]

> [T]he Court's holding is limited to the proposition . . . that a "traditional" state common law action, not made subject to a federal rule of decision, and related only peripherally to an adjudication of bankruptcy under federal law, must, absent the consent of the litigants, be heard by an "article III court" if it is to be heard by any court or agency of the United States.

Under Justice Brennan's opinion, then, the public-private right dichotomy was to serve as the standard for determining the division of authority between Article III

---

241 458 U.S. at 67.

242 458 U.S. at 71.

243 458 U.S. at 67–68 (quoting Crowell v. Benson, 285 U.S. 22, 50 (1932)); *see* § 100.24.

244 458 U.S. at 68–70.

245 *See* Granfinanciera, S.A. v. Nordberg, 492 U.S. 33, 56 n.11 (1989), in which the Court, in an opinion by Justice Brennan, stated, "[w]e do not suggest that the restructuring of debtor-creditor relations is in fact a public right," and acknowledged that "[t]his thesis has met with substantial scholarly criticism . . . ."

246 Northern Pipeline Construction Co. v. Marathon Pipe Line Co., 458 U.S. 50, 92 (1982) (Burger, C.J., dissenting).

and Article I courts.[247] The origin of the dichotomy appears to be the following mid-nineteenth century statement by Justice Curtis in *Murray's Lessee v. Hoboken Land & Improvement Co.*:[248]

> [W]e do not consider [whether] Congress can either withdraw from judicial cognizance any matter which, from its nature, is the subject of a suit at the common law, or in equity, or admiralty; nor, on the other hand, can it bring under the judicial power, a matter which, from its nature, is not a subject for judicial determination. At the same time there are matters, involving public rights, which may be presented in such form that the judicial power is capable of acting on them, and which are susceptible of judicial determination, but which Congress may or may not bring within the cognizance of the courts of the United States, as it may deem proper.

Notably, Justice Curtis made no reference to the language, history, or policies of Article III to support his suggested dichotomy.

What makes the approval of the exercise of Article I court authority over so-called "public rights" cases puzzling is the contrast to the type of case that the dichotomy dictates must be heard in Article III courts; that is, suits between private individuals involving state-created common law rights. These cases barely fall within the categories of cases to which the judicial power is extended in Article III, Section 2. Most of these cases fall only within the diversity jurisdiction,[249] although the Supreme Court has upheld, albeit cryptically, the exercise of Article III court power over nondiverse common law disputes involving a bankrupt even though no issue of substantive federal law is involved in the dispute.[250] Such a strained use of the "arising under" jurisdiction, however, can be strongly criticized, and is, at most, a peripheral exercise of it. Thus, the cases that, according to Justice Brennan, make up the "core" of the federal judicial power, and therefore comprise the category of cases that may not be given for final resolution to an Article I body, are those that barely fall within the judicial power in the first place.

Further, the public-private right dichotomy effectively frustrates the purposes served by the constitutional protections of judicial independence. The dangers of both potential federal governmental domination of the federal judiciary and potential governmental displeasure with judicial decisions is at a minimum in suits between private individuals involving state-created common law rights. In contrast, the types of cases in which the dangers are greatest, those involving a dispute between private individuals and the federal government, are the very cases that Justice Brennan permits Article I bodies to adjudicate. Thus, as a matter of

---

[247] 458 U.S. at 70.

[248] Origin of public-private right dichotomy. Murray's Lessee v. Hoboken Land & Improvement Co., 59 U.S. (18 How.) 272, 284 (1856).

[249] U.S. Const., art. III, § 2; *see* Mishkin, *The Federal "Question" in the District Courts*, 53 Colum. L. Rev. 157, 190 (1953).

[250] Federal jurisdiction over nondiverse parties within bankruptcy proceeding. Williams v. Austrian, 331 U.S. 642, 658 (1947) (Congress intended to establish jurisdiction of federal courts to hear suits by reorganization trustee, even though diversity is not present); Schumacher v. Beeler, 293 U.S. 367, 377 (1934) (by virtue of Congress's power of bankruptcies, it may confer or withhold jurisdiction over such suits, and can prescribe conditions on which it may be exercised).

constitutional language and policy, this dichotomy is a questionable basis on which to erect a standard to determine the proper division of authority between Article III and Article I adjudicatory bodies.

In a separate concurring opinion, Justice Rehnquist, explicitly left open the question whether "public" rights could be adjudicated by non-Article III bodies.[251]He concluded that only an Article III court could hear the *Northern Pipeline* dispute because the lawsuit sought damages for breach of contract, misrepresentation, and other counts that "are the stuff of the traditional actions at common law tried by the courts at Westminster in 1789."[252] His point is that at the time the Constitution was written, common law disputes constituted the heart of the English judiciary's work, making it reasonable to conclude that the framers referred to this traditional judicial activity when they employed the term "judicial power" and vested that "judicial power" in the Article III judiciary.

In his dissent in *Northern Pipeline,* Justice White drew on the analysis contained in his opinion for the Court in *Palmore v. United States.*[253] Justice Brennan had distinguished *Palmore* on the ground that the decision's reach was limited to the District of Columbia, and therefore did not justify use of Article I courts that are not geographically defined.[254] Justice White, however, rejected this suggestion, arguing that the Court's decision to uphold the use of Article I courts in *Palmore* rested on "an evaluation of the strength of the legislative interest in pursuing in this manner one of its constitutionally assigned responsibilities — a responsibility not different in kind from numerous other legislative responsibilities."[255] Thus, according to Justice White, although "Article III is not to be read out of the Constitution . . . it should be read as expressing one value that must be balanced against competing constitutional values and legislative responsibilities."[256]

Justice White was probably correct in his assertion that such a balancing approach stands behind many of the decisions upholding Article I courts.[257] Although Justice Brennan's opinion purported to distinguish the Article I status of both the territorial and military courts on other grounds,[258] ultimately no grounds, other than a desire not to impose undue burdens on legislative and executive policies, can justify these results. Nevertheless, it does not follow that a balancing analysis — at least one so unprincipled as the *ad hoc* balance suggested by Justice White — provides the proper scope of authority of an Article I body.

---

[251] Concurrence: no reliance on public-private rights dichotomy. Northern Pipeline Construction Co. v. Marathon Pipe Line Co., 458 U.S. 50, 91 (1982) (Rehnquist, J., concurring; "To whatever extent different powers granted under [the 1978] Act might be sustained under the 'public rights' doctrine . . ., I am satisfied that the adjudication of Northern's lawsuit cannot be so sustained.").

[252] Northern Pipeline Construction Co. v. Marathon Pipe Line Co., 458 U.S. 50, 90 (1982) (Rehnquist, J., concurring).

[253] Palmore v. United States, 411 U.S. 389 (1973); *see* § 100.42.

[254] Northern Pipeline Construction Co. v. Marathon Pipe Line Co., 458 U.S. 50, 75–76 (1982).

[255] 458 U.S. at 114 (White, J., dissenting).

[256] 458 U.S. at 113 (White, J., dissenting).

[257] 458 U.S. at 113–114 (White, J., dissenting).

[258] 458 U.S. at 64–66.

The most obvious difficulty with the balancing analysis is that it does not appear to be authorized by the language of Article III. The framers did not provide for an exception to the federal judges' salary and tenure protections should Congress find application of these protections burdensome or inconvenient. Indeed, it is likely that it is just such an approach that the framers attempted to avoid. The framers apparently decided that such a burden was justified by the need to preserve an independent judiciary.

An equally significant problem with Justice White's analysis is that the Salary and Tenure Clause of Article III, Section 1 is one of the constitutional provisions least adaptable to a case-by-case balancing approach. A balancing approach requires the Court to weigh the legislative interest in freeing the government from the constraints of the salary and tenure protections against the competing interest in guaranteeing judicial independence. Such a balance will invariably favor the legislative interest because there is an inherent inequality in the weighing process. An immediately recognizable, concrete interest is balanced against an interest wholly prophylactic in nature, and therefore one whose benefits will never be immediately recognizable. Without the salary and tenure protections, it is unlikely that there would be open and heavy-handed legislative and executive pressure on or threats against the judiciary. Indeed, there is little documented evidence of this kind of pressure or threats in the state courts, where constitutional protections of salary and tenure rarely exist. Rather, salary and tenure provisions protect against subtle or unstated pressure on the judiciary. Presumably, it was because it would be virtually impossible to detect undue pressure that the framers chose to insert these prophylactic protections. Thus, any case-by-case balancing process will always tend to find the benefit of maintaining these protections illusory.

## § 1.15 THE RISE OF THE BALANCING TEST AS THE LEGISLATIVE COURT STANDARD

### [1] *Thomas v. Union Carbide*: Retreat from the Public-Private Rights Dichotomy

After the decision in *Northern Pipeline*, the Supreme Court has issued two major opinions dealing with the general question of the constitutional parameters of the use of Article I bodies. Though neither fully clarified the Court's position on that question, both tended to illustrate a dramatic shift away from Justice Brennan's plurality position in *Northern Pipeline* in the direction of the more flexible balancing approach advocated by Justice White dissenting in that decision.[259]

The first of these two opinions came in the 1985 case of *Thomas v. Union Carbide Agricultural Products Co.* The case concerned the constitutionality of a provision of the Federal Insecticide, Fungicide and Rodenticide Act [FIFRA] that

[259] *But see* Granfinanciera, S.A. v. Nordberg, 492 U.S. 33 (1989), in which the Court returned to the language of the "public rights" doctrine in referring to the constitutional division of authority between the Article III judiciary and executive agencies. The specific issue in that case concerned the Seventh Amendment right to jury trial, rather than the constitutionality of an allocation of adjudicatory authority.

provided for binding arbitration with only limited judicial review as the mechanism for resolving disputes among participants in FIFRA's pesticide registration scheme. The need for that provision arose because of Congress's decision to establish data-sharing provisions among registrants, in order to streamline pesticide registration procedures, increase competition, and avoid unnecessary duplication of data-generation costs.[260]

Originally, the Act provided that registrants whose data was relied on by subsequent registrants would be compensated by negotiation of the parties, or if those efforts failed, by the Environmental Protection Agency (EPA), subject to judicial review. Six years later, in response to the "logjam of litigation" that resulted from controversies over data compensation and trade secret protection, Congress relieved the EPA of the task of valuation and substituted binding arbitration. The arbitrator's decision was subject to judicial review only for fraud, misrepresentation, or other misconduct.[261] The scheme provided for no judicial enforcement of the arbitrator's decisions. Instead, if the arbitrator's award was ignored, the administrator was required to cancel the new registration or to consider the data without compensation to the original submitter.[262]

This statutory scheme was challenged on the ground that Article III bars Congress from requiring arbitration of disputes among registrants concerning compensation under FIFRA without also affording substantial review of the arbitrator's decision by a tenured Article III judge.[263] Justice O'Connor, writing for a five-member majority, immediately eschewed the rigid formalism of Justice Brennan's plurality opinion in *Northern Pipeline*. Rather, she began her legal analysis by asserting that "Article III, Section 1, establishes a broad *policy* that federal judicial power shall be vested in courts whose judges enjoy life tenure and fixed compensation."[264] A "policy," of course, generally implies something considerably more politically malleable than a rigid constitutional "doctrine" or "rule." Then in the next paragraph, Justice O'Connor cited Justice Rehnquist's concurring opinion in *Northern Pipeline* for the proposition that "[a]n absolute construction of Article III is not possible in this area of 'frequently arcane distinctions and confusing precedents.' "[265]

Nevertheless, Justice O'Connor managed to uphold FIFRA's scheme without directly rejecting *Northern Pipeline's* plurality opinion. She rejected the argument that claims to compensation under FIFRA are a matter of state law, and thus are encompassed by the holding of *Northern Pipeline,* because "[a]ny right to compensation from follow-on registrants . . . for EPA's use of data results from FIFRA and does not depend on or replace a right to such compensation under state law." This was because "[a]s a matter of state law, property rights in its trade secret are extinguished when a company discloses a trade secret to persons not

---

260 *See* Thomas v. Union Carbide Agricultural Products Co., 473 U.S. 568, 571 (1985).

261 7 U.S.C. § 136a(c)(1)(F)(ii).

262 *See* 7 U.S.C. § 136a(c)(1)(F).

263 *See* Thomas v. Union Carbide Agricultural Products Co., 473 U.S. 568, 582 (1985).

264 473 U.S. at 582 (emphasis added).

265 473 U.S. at 583.

obligated to protect the confidentiality of the information."[266]

But as a result of this approach, Justice O'Connor was forced to deal with an issue left ambiguous in *Northern Pipeline*: whether a statutory right granted by the federal government, to be exercised not against the government but rather against another private party, constitutes a "private right" that, according to *Northern Pipeline*, must be adjudicated by an Article III court. Effectively undercutting much of Justice Brennan's *Northern Pipeline* opinion, Justice O'Connor responded:[267]

> This theory that the public rights/private rights dichotomy . . . provides a bright line test for determining the requirements of Article III did not command a majority of the Court in *Northern Pipeline*. Insofar as appellees interpret that case . . . as establishing that the right to an Article III forum is absolute unless the federal government is party of record, we cannot agree.

After attempting — largely unsuccessfully — to escape without rejecting the underlying premise of *Northern Pipeline* on the basis of both practical and historical considerations, Justice O'Connor continued, "Given the nature of the right at issue and the concerns motivating the legislature, we do not think this system threatens the independent role of the judiciary in our constitutional scheme." She then followed with a reference to Justice White's opinion in *Palmore v. United States* for the proposition that "the requirements of Article III must, in proper circumstances, give way to accommodate plenary grants of power to Congress to legislate with respect to specialized areas."[268] Finally, somewhat illogically combining White's balancing approach with Brennan's public-private rights dichotomy, she concluded:[269]

> Congress, acting for a valid legislative purpose pursuant to its constitutional powers under Article I, may create a seemingly "private" right that is so closely integrated into a public regulatory scheme as to be a matter appropriate for agency resolution with limited involvement by the Article III judiciary.[270]

Not surprisingly, Justice Brennan (joined by Justices Marshall and Blackmun) filed a separate opinion, concurring only in the judgment. Adhering to his formalistic dichotomy adopted in *Northern Pipeline*, Justice Brennan asserted that "the question for decision here is whether fixing the amount of compensation for test data under FIFRA can be characterized as a public rights dispute . . . should it be concluded that this is such a dispute, the further issue must be confronted of

---

[266] 473 U.S. at 584.

[267] 473 U.S. at 585–586.

[268] 473 U.S. at 590.

[269] 473 U.S. at 593–594.

[270] *See also* Granfinanciera, S.A. v. Nordberg, 492 U.S. 33, 52 (1989), in which the Court reiterated its conclusion that the federal government need not be a party for a case to revolve around "public rights." It also reaffirmed the *Thomas* standard. Justice Scalia, however, concluded that such an approach contravened the essential premise of waiver of sovereign immunity implicit in the public-rights doctrine. 492 U.S. at 67 (Scalia, J., concurring in part and concurring in the judgment).

whether some form of appellate oversight by an Article III court is nonetheless required." Retreating from the strict definitional model he had adopted in *Northern Pipeline,* he conceded that the determinative factor with respect to the proper characterization of the nature of the dispute in the case should not be the presence or absence of the government as a party.[271] Brennan ultimately concluded that the FIFRA compensation scheme challenged in the case should be viewed as involving a matter of public rights "as that term is understood in the line of cases culminating in *Northern Pipeline*."[272] Though nothing in his *Northern Pipeline* opinion in any way indicated such a conclusion, the obvious consequence of Justice Brennan's characterization, under the logic of *Northern Pipeline,* was the upholding of the administrative program.

### [2] *Commodities Futures Trading Commission v. Schor*: The All-But-Total Departure

The Supreme Court faced much the same type of issue as raised in *Thomas v. Union Carbide* in the subsequent case of *Commodities Futures Trading Commission v. Schor*.[273] The decision involved a regulation promulgated by the Commodities Futures Trading Commission (CFTC) allowing it to adjudicate counterclaims "[arising] out of the transaction or occurrence of series of transactions or occurrences set forth" in a complaint filed with the Commission alleging a violation of the Commodities Futures Trading Act.[274] Though the counterclaim rule authorized the CFTC to adjudicate claims falling outside its statutorily defined subject matter jurisdiction, the counterclaims were permissive in nature. The CFTC's counterclaim jurisdiction was alleged to violate Article III on the grounds that the Article prohibits Congress from authorizing the initial adjudication of common law counterclaims by an administrative agency whose adjudicatory officers do not enjoy the tenure and salary protections of Article III.[275]

The Court, again in a majority opinion by Justice O'Connor, upheld the constitutionality of the agency's counterclaim jurisdiction.[276] Justice Brennan, joined by Justice Marshall, dissented.[277] The majority opinion initially noted that the original complainant and defendant on the counterclaim indisputably waived any right that he may have possessed to the full trial of the counterclaim before an Article III court by demanding that the defendant proceed on its counterclaim in the reparations preceding rather than before the District Court.[278] The Court conceded that when the structural principle of separation of powers is implicated in

---

[271] Thomas v. Union Carbide Agricultural Products Co., 473 U.S. 568, 598 (1985) (Brennan, J. concurring).

[272] 473 U.S. at 600 (Brennan, J. concurring).

[273] Commodities Futures Trading Commission v. Schor, 478 U.S. 833 (1986).

[274] 17 C.F.R. § 12.23(b)(2).

[275] Commodities Futures Trading Commission v. Schor, 478 U.S. 833, 839 (1986).

[276] 478 U.S. at 857.

[277] 478 U.S. at 859 (Brennan, J., dissenting).

[278] 478 U.S. at 849.

a given case, the parties cannot by consent cure the constitutional difficulty because the limitations serve institutional interests that the parties cannot be expected to protect.[279] However, the Court found that the congressional scheme did not impermissibly intrude on the province of the judiciary.[280] The single deviation from the "agency model" — namely, the counterclaim jurisdiction — was not fatal, because the Commodities Exchange Act left far more of the essential attributes of judicial power to Article III courts than did that portion of the Bankruptcy Act found unconstitutional in *Northern Pipeline*.[281]

Though, as in *Northern Pipeline*, the issues decided by the agency in the exercise of its counterclaim jurisdiction included state common law rights, the Court correctly noted that CFTC orders were reviewed by an Article III court under a standard more strict than the deferential evidentiary standard struck down in *Northern Pipeline*.[282] In short, the CFTC fit well within the contours of the "adjunct" concept, relied on, in part, in *Northern Pipeline* as a method of rationalizing the work of administrative agencies. Thus, despite the argument of dissenting Justice Brennan to the contrary, it appears that the Court properly fit the CFTC's counterclaim within the analytic framework established in *Northern Pipeline*.

The fact that the case was, at least potentially, so easily resolvable on the basis of the plurality opinion in *Northern Pipeline*, however, makes the remainder of the *Schor* opinion especially interesting. The Court's underlying tone in the remaining portion of its opinion quite clearly represented an all-but-total departure from the analysis of the *Northern Pipeline* plurality toward complete acceptance of Justice White's balancing test in the case.[283]

## § 1.16 REASSERTION OF THE PUBLIC-PRIVATE RIGHTS DICHOTOMY

In *Stern v. Marshall*, the Court again relied on the public-private rights dichotomy in considering Article III limitations on the jurisdiction of "legislative" courts. At issue in that case was a bankruptcy court's authority to adjudicate a debtor's state law counterclaim for tortious interference, filed against a man who had brought a defamation claim against the estate. In a 5-4 decision, the Court held that a bankruptcy court does not have constitutional authority to enter a final judgment on a state law counterclaim that is not resolved in the process of ruling on a creditor's proof of claim. Writing for the Court, Chief Justice Roberts reasoned that the bankruptcy court's entry of final judgment on the debtor's state common law counterclaim was an exercise of the judicial power of the United States purporting to resolve and enter final judgment on a state common law claim, just as

---

[279] 478 U.S. at 850–851.

[280] 478 U.S. at 851–852.

[281] 478 U.S. at 852.

[282] 478 U.S. at 852–853.

[283] 478 U.S. at 852.

in *Northern Pipeline*. And, just as in *Northern Pipeline*, such exercise was a violation of Article III.[284]

The counterclaim in *Stern* did not fall within any public rights exception to Article III limitations on the authority of bankruptcy courts, the Court held, because it was a state law action independent of the federal bankruptcy law and not necessarily resolvable by a ruling on the creditor's proof of claim in bankruptcy. The Court acknowledged that in post-*Northern Pipeline* decisions, it had held that the public rights exception is not limited to actions in which the government is a party. However, the exception had been limited to cases in which the claim at issue derived from a federal regulatory scheme or in which resolution of the claim by an expert government agency was deemed essential to a limited regulatory objective within the agency's authority. In other words, what makes a right "public" rather than private is its integral relationship to particular federal government action, according to the majority.[285] The Court concluded that the debtor's counterclaim did not fall within the public rights exception because it was not a matter that could be pursued only by the grace of the other branches of government or one that historically could have been determined exclusively by those branches. Nor did it flow from a federal statutory scheme or depend completely on adjudication of a claim created by federal law. It was merely a state common law claim between two private parties.[286]

Justice Scalia concurred in the Court's opinion in *Stern*, agreeing with the Court's interpretation of Article III precedents. However, he adhered to his view contrary precedents notwithstanding, that a matter of public rights must, at a minimum, arise between the government and others. He argued that apart from certain adjudications by federal administrative agencies, an Article III judge is required in *all* federal adjudications, unless there is a firmly established historical practice to the contrary.[287]

Justice Breyer, joined by Justices Ginsburg, Sotomayor, and Kagan, dissented, taking particular issue with the Court's emphasis on "an analysis that did not command a Court majority in *Northern Pipeline* . . . and that was subsequently disavowed." The dissent noted that three years after *Northern Pipeline*, the Court stated that the decision establishes only that Congress may not vest in a non-Article III court the power to adjudicate, render final judgment, and issue binding orders

---

[284] No jurisdiction over counterclaim. Stern v. Marshall, 131 S. Ct. 2594, 180 L. Ed. 2d 475, 507 (2011) (bankruptcy court does not have constitutional authority to enter final judgment on state law counterclaim that is not resolved in process of ruling on creditor's proof of claim).

[285] Limits on public rights exception. Stern v. Marshall, 131 S. Ct. 2594, 180 L. Ed. 2d 475, 498 (2011) (public rights exception limited to cases in which claim derives from federal regulatory scheme or in which resolution of claim by expert government agency is deemed essential to limited regulatory objective within agency's authority).

[286] State common law claim not within public rights exception. Stern v. Marshall, 131 S. Ct. 2594, 180 L. Ed. 2d 475, 500–501 (2011) (state law counterclaim for tortious interference did not fall within public rights exception).

[287] Concurrence: public rights must arise between government and others. Stern v. Marshall, 131 S. Ct. 2594, 180 L. Ed. 2d 475, 507–508 (2011) (Scalia, J., concurring: quoting *Granfinanciera, S.A. v. Nordberg*, 492 U.S. 33, 65(1989), "a matter of public rights . . . must at a minimum arise between the government and others").

in a traditional contract action arising under state law, without consent of the litigants, and subject only to ordinary appellate review.[288]

Justice Breyer also considered the majority to have understated the importance of *Crowell v. Benson*, an opinion "widely thought to demonstrate the constitutional basis for the current authority of administrative agencies to adjudicate private disputes," and to have failed to follow the analysis in *Thomas v. Union Carbide* and *Commodities Futures Trading Comm'n v. Schor*. The Court took a more pragmatic approach in these later cases, according to Justice Breyer, seeking to determine whether, in the particular instance, the challenged delegation of adjudicatory authority posed a genuine and serious threat that one branch of Government sought to aggrandize its own constitutionally delegated authority by encroaching upon a field of authority that the Constitution assigns exclusively to another branch.[289]

In applying that pragmatic approach, Justice Breyer stated, the Court must examine relevant factors to determine whether the delegation of adjudicatory authority to the bankruptcy courts constitutes a significant encroachment by the legislative or executive branch of government on the realm of authority that Article III reserves for exercise by the judicial branch. Those factors include (1) the nature of the claim to be adjudicated; (2) the nature of the non-Article III tribunal; (3) the extent to which Article III courts exercise control over the proceeding; (4) the presence or absence of the parties' consent; and (5) the nature and importance of the legislative purpose served by the grant of adjudicatory authority to a tribunal with judges who lack Article III's tenure and compensation protections. Under this analysis, the presence of "private rights" does not automatically determine the outcome of the question, but merely requires a more searching examination of the relevant factors. Considering these factors, Justice Breyer concluded that the magnitude of any intrusion on the judicial branch in the grant of authority to a bankruptcy court to adjudicate compulsory counterclaims is de minimis, and that the delegation does not violate any constitutional separation-of-powers principle related to Article III.[290]

The dissent also expressed concern that, as a practical matter, restrictions on a bankruptcy court's ability to resolve compulsory counterclaims will create significant delays and impose additional costs on the bankruptcy process.[291] The Court

---

[288] Dissent: *Northern Pipeline* limited by later decisions. Stern v. Marshall, 131 S. Ct. 2594, 180 L. Ed. 2d 475, 508–509 (2011) (Breyer, J., dissenting, taking issue with majority's interpretation and emphasis of precedents); *see* Thomas v. Union Carbide Agric. Prods. Co., 473 U.S. 568, 584 (1985) (limit on *Northern Pipeline*).

[289] Dissent: Court ignored post-*Northern Pipeline* precedents. Stern v. Marshall, 131 S. Ct. 2594, 180 L. Ed. 2d 475, 508–509 (2011) (Breyer, J., dissenting, citing *Crowell v. Benson*, 285 U.S. 22 (1932) as demonstrating constitutional basis for administrative agencies' authority to adjudicate private disputes and *Commodity Futures Trading Comm'n v. Schor*, 478 U.S. 833 (1986) and *Thomas v. Union Carbide Agric. Prods. Co.*, 473 U.S. 568 (1985) for recent analysis of congressional delegation of adjudicatory authority).

[290] Dissent: balance of factors. Stern v. Marshall, 131 S. Ct. 2594, 180 L. Ed. 2d 475, 513–517 (2011) (Breyer, J., dissenting, undertaking pragmatic consideration of relevant factors and concluding bankruptcy courts' adjudication of compulsory counterclaims does not violate Article III).

[291] Dissent's concern with practical effect. Stern v. Marshall, 131 S. Ct. 2594, 180 L. Ed. 2d 475, 517–518 (2011) (Breyer, J., dissenting; compulsory counterclaims arise frequently in "staggering"

was not particularly moved by this concern, observing that the efficiency, convenience, and usefulness of a law or procedure will not, by themselves, preserve the law or procedure if it is unconstitutional. Moreover, the Court was not convinced that the practical consequences would be as significant as the dissent suggested. Emphasizing the narrowness of its ruling, the Court stated that the Bankruptcy Act of 1984 exceeded the Article III limitations "in one isolated respect," concluding that "[t]he Bankruptcy Court below lacked the constitutional authority to enter a final judgment on a state law counterclaim that is not resolved in the process of ruling on a creditor's proof of claim."[292]

One may question whether the line in the sand drawn by the *Stern* majority is the appropriate one. It is hard to believe that the area in which the independence of Article III judges is most vital involves adjudication of state-created claims between private litigants. Far more dangerous, however, would be a vague and flexible pragmatic approach like the one suggested by Justice Breyer. It is far too easy under such an approach to balance away core protections of judicial independence.

## § 1.17 THE USE OF MAGISTRATE JUDGES UNDER 28 U.S.C. § 636 DOES NOT VIOLATE ARTICLE III

### [1] The Role of Magistrate Judges in Federal Adjudication

Although magistrate judges lack Article III's protections of salary and tenure, they are nevertheless members of the judicial branch who exercise an ever-growing role in federal adjudication. Congress initially provided a role for magistrate judges in the Federal Magistrates Act of 1968,[293] and expanded their role in both 1976[294] and 1979.[295]

The primary statute setting forth the powers of magistrate judges is 28 United States Code Section 636. Among the powers granted to magistrate judges by this statute are the following:[296]

- Power to hear and rule on nondispositive pretrial motions, such as discovery motions;[297]
- Power to hear dispositive pretrial motions, such as a motion to dismiss, and to file a report containing findings of fact and recommendations to the

volume of bankruptcy cases; "constitutionally required game of jurisdictional ping-pong between courts [with respect to compulsory counterclaims] would lead to inefficiency, increased cost, delay, and needless additional suffering among those faced with bankruptcy").

292 Court not concerned about practical implications. Stern v. Marshall, 131 S. Ct. 2594, 180 L. Ed. 2d 475, 505–507 (2011) (practical concerns do not save unconstitutional law and, in any event, will not be as severe as suggested by dissent).

293 28 U.S.C. § 631.

294 Act of Oct. 21, 1976, Pub. L. No. 94-577, 90 Stat. 2729 (1976).

295 Federal Magistrates Act of 1979, Pub. L. No. 96-82, 93 Stat. 643–645 (1979).

296 Statutory powers of magistrates. *See* Brown v. Wesley's Quaker Maid, Inc., 771 F.2d 952, 954 (6th Cir. 1985).

297 28 U.S.C. § 636(b)(1)(A).

district judge, who then makes the ruling;[298]

- Power to serve as a special master for a nonjury trial on a showing that some exceptional condition requires it, or without such a showing if the parties consent;[299]
- Only on the consent of all parties, power to conduct civil jury or nonjury trials and to enter a final judgment.[300]

## [2] Magistrate Judges May Conduct Suppression Hearings in Criminal Cases

Because the Magistrate Act vested broad power in non-Article III officials, concern was expressed, both before and after passage of the original act in 1968, as to its constitutionality.[301] In *United States v. Raddatz,* the Supreme Court upheld the use of Section 636(b) of the Federal Magistrates Act of 1979[302] to permit a magistrate to make factual findings at a suppression hearing in a criminal case, in which the district judge exercises ultimate review and control. The Court did not reach the issue of whether Congress could constitutionally have delegated the task of rendering a final decision on a suppression motion to a non-Article III officer. Rather, it found that the provision for de novo review by the district court was sufficient to meet any objection based on Article III.[303] Justice Blackmun, concurring, reasoned that the court was not facing a procedure under which Congress had delegated to a non-Article III judge the authority to make final determinations on issues of fact. Rather, Congress had vested in Article III judges the discretionary power to delegate certain functions to competent and impartial assistants, while ensuring that the judges retained complete supervisory control over the assistants' activities.[304]

However, Justice Marshall, dissenting, argued that if the motion to suppress turns on issues of credibility that cannot be resolved on the basis of the record, and if the district judge does not hear the witnesses, the magistrate's report is no mere recommendation. Unless the district judge ventures a blind guess, the report is effectively the final determination of the facts underlying the suppression motion.[305]

---

[298] 28 U.S.C. § 636(b)(1)(B).

[299] 28 U.S.C. § 636(b)(2); Fed. R. Civ. P. 53(b).

[300] 28 U.S.C. § 636(c).

[301] Constitutionality of Magistrate Act questioned. *See* Mathews v. Weber, 423 U.S. 261, 269 (1976); TPO, Inc. v. McMillen, 460 F.2d 348, 352–354 (7th Cir. 1972).

[302] 28 U.S.C. § 636(b)(1)(B).

[303] Reference of motion to suppress to magistrate for findings and recommendation found constitutional. United States v. Raddatz, 447 U.S. 667, 681–685 (1980).

[304] 447 U.S. at 686 (Blackmun, J., concurring).

[305] Dissent points out that magistrate judge's report is final determination of underlying facts. United States v. Raddatz, 447 U.S. 667, 703 (1980) (Marshall, J., dissenting).

## [3] Magistrate Judges May Conduct Full Trials with the Consent of All Parties

### [a] Consent Required

Section 636(c) of the Act of allows magistrate judges to conduct civil trials, without review in the district court, with the consent of all the parties.[306] Unlike Section 636(b) upheld in *Raddatz*, Section 636(c) does not provide for de novo review in the district court. However, Section 636(c)'s consent requirement is absent from Section 636(b).

One might question whether even fully informed consent of the litigants should be allowed to authorize waiver of the Article III protections. It might reasonably be argued that the protections of the separation of powers are not solely for the benefit of the individual litigants, but rather primarily for the systemic benefits of the nation's political structure.

However, in *Commodities Futures Trading Commission v. Schor*, the Supreme Court found that while the Article III protections are designed at least in part to protect the role of the independent judiciary within the constitutional scheme of tripartite government,[307] Article III's guarantee of an impartial and independent federal adjudication is subject to waiver as a personal right, just as are other personal constitutional rights that dictate the procedures by which civil and criminal matters must be tried.[308]

### [b] Consent May Be Inferred From Conduct

The parties' consent to the designation of a magistrate judge may be oral or written, but must be unambiguous. The Supreme Court has held that the requisite consent may be inferred from the parties' conduct during the litigation.[309] In *Roell v. Withrow*, the referral to the magistrate judge to determine whether the suit could proceed in forma pauperis was made before two of the defendants gave their express consent. However, these defendants clearly implied their consent by appearing before the magistrate judge, without expressing any reservation, after being notified of their right to refuse and after being told that she intended to exercise case-dispositive authority. On plaintiff's appeal, the Fifth Circuit sua sponte remanded the case to determine whether the parties had consented, orally or in writing, to proceed before the magistrate judge. On remand, these two defendants filed a formal letter of consent with the district court, which then referred the remanded proceedings to the same magistrate judge who had

---

306 Magistrate judge may conduct trial with parties' consent. 28 U.S.C. § 636(c). Roell v. Withrow, 538 U.S. 580, (2003) (upholding constitutionality of Section 636(c) and holding that magistrate judges may conduct civil trials with consent of parties).

307 Commodities Futures Trading Commission v. Schor, 478 U.S. 833, 848 (1986) (quoting Thomas v. Union Carbide Agricultural Products Co., 473 U.S. 568, 600 (1985)).

308 Article III protections are subject to waiver by private litigants. 478 U.S. at 848–849.

309 Consent may be implied from conduct. Roell v. Withrow, 538 U.S. 580, 589–591 (2003) (defendants' general appearances before magistrate judge after being told of their right to trial by district judge sufficient for magistrate judge's exercise of jurisdiction).

conducted the trial. The magistrate judge reported that these two defendants had clearly implied their consent by their actions at trial. The record showed that these defendants voluntarily participated in the entire course of proceedings and voiced no objection when, at several points, the magistrate judge indicated that she believed they had consented. Nevertheless, circuit precedent compelled the magistrate judge to hold that the failure to give express pretrial consent meant that she had lacked jurisdiction. The district court adopted the report and the Fifth Circuit affirmed. Reversing, the Supreme Court held that consent to the designation of a magistrate judge may be inferred from the parties' conduct during the litigation.[310]

The defendants' general appearances before the magistrate judge, after they had been told of their right to trial by a district judge, supplied the consent necessary for the magistrate judge's exercise of jurisdiction.[311] On a textual level, the Court found significant the fact that the Act's provision concerning full-time magistrates' jurisdiction speaks only of "the consent of the parties," without qualification as to form, and provides that "[t]he consent of the parties allows" a full-time magistrate to enter a final, appealable judgment of the district court.[312] In contrast, the Act's provision concerning referral to part-time magistrates requires the parties' "specific written request."[313] The statute thus distinguishes between consent and consent expressed in a "specific written request." Reading the statute as a whole, the Court concluded that a defect in the referral to a full-time magistrate judge under the Act and Rule 73 does not eliminate that magistrate judge's jurisdiction so long as the parties have in fact voluntarily consented.[314]

On a policy level, the Court framed the issue to be the determination of which outcome better serves the mix of congressional objectives. A bright-line rule — strict insistence on express consent — would minimize the risk of compromising the right to an Article III judge, but it would also raise the risk (present in this case) of a full and complicated trial wasted at the option of an undeserving and possibly opportunistic litigant. Such a bright-line rule would create a potential for parties to litigate before a magistrate judge without expressly consenting, and then to vacate any judgment that turned out not to their liking.[315] The better rule, the Court reasoned, is to accept implied consent when, as here, the litigant or counsel was made aware of the need for consent and the right to refuse it, and still voluntarily appeared to try the case before the magistrate judge. Inferring consent in these circumstances minimizes gamesmanship by depriving parties of the luxury of waiting for the outcome before denying the magistrate judge's authority. Recognizing implied consent serves judicial efficiency while substantially honoring the

---

[310] Consent may be implied from litigation conduct. Roell v. Withrow, 538 U.S. 580, 589–591 (2003).

[311] General appearance after notice of right to district court trial sufficient consent. Roell v. Withrow, 538 U.S. 580, 586–588 (2003).

[312] *See* 28 U.S.C. § 636(c)(1), (3).

[313] *See* 28 U.S.C. § 636(c)(1).

[314] Referral defect does not destroy jurisdiction in parties in fact voluntarily consent. Roell v. Withrow, 538 U.S. 580, 586–588 (2003) (legislative history supports notion that Congress intended to permit implied consent).

[315] Court rejects bright-line rule requiring express consent. Roell v. Withrow, 538 U.S. 580, 589–591 (2003) (benefit of bright-line rule outweighed by its inherent risks).

right to an Article III judge.[316] The *Roell* Court noted that its conclusion obviated the need to address two open issues: (1) whether express postjudgment consent may be sufficient in a case when there was no prior implied consent and (2) whether a lack of consent is a jurisdictional defect that can be raised for the first time on appeal.[317]

---

316 Recognizing implied consent serves judicial efficiency. Roell v. Withrow, 538 U.S. 580, 589–591 (2003).

317 Open questions remaining. Roell v. Withrow, 538 U.S. 580, 589–591 (2003).

# Chapter 2

# ISSUES OF JUSTICIABILITY

## § 2.01 NATURE OF JUSTICIABILITY

The doctrines of standing, mootness, ripeness, and political question are devices used by the courts to determine whether an issue that has been presented for resolution is *justiciable*. These doctrines aid the court in determining which cases are appropriate to hear and decide, both from the standpoint of the constitutional requirement that the jurisdiction of the federal courts extend only to actual cases or controversies,[1] and from a prudential viewpoint, considering policy factors such as political concerns and separation of powers.

At least until very recently, concerns of justiciability have gone both to the power of the federal courts to entertain disputes and to the wisdom of their doing so.[2] In more recent decisions, however, the Court has seriously questioned its authority to allow the federal courts to decline federal jurisdiction solely on the basis of prudential considerations. On the whole, justiciability is a concept of uncertain meaning and scope. Its reach is illustrated by the various grounds on which questions sought to be adjudicated in federal courts have been held not to be justiciable. Thus, no justiciable controversy is presented if the parties seek adjudication of only a political question, if the parties are asking for an advisory opinion if the question sought to be adjudicated has been mooted by subsequent developments, or if there is no standing to maintain the action. Yet it remains true that justiciability is not a legal concept with a fixed content susceptible of scientific verification. Its use is the result of many subtle pressures.[3]

The justiciability doctrines for the most part grow out of the so-called "private rights" model of adjudication, which posits that the exclusive role of the federal judiciary is to adjudicate live disputes, and any judicial pronouncements of law must come as an incident to performance of that adjudicatory function. Thus, there must be a tangible dispute that is capable of resolution in a manner that will have a concrete impact on the parties to the dispute.[4]

---

[1] *See* U.S. Const., art. III, § 2.

[2] Power of courts to hear disputes and wisdom of doing so. Renne v. Geary, 501 U.S. 312, 316 (1991); Bender v. Williamsport Area Sch. Dist., 475 U.S. 534, 546 (1986); King Bridge Co. v. Otoe County, 120 U.S. 225, 226 (1887).

[3] No precise definition or scope of justiciability. Flast v. Cohen, 392 U.S. 83, 95 (1968) (quoting Poe v. Ullman, 367 U.S. 497, 508 (1961); *see also* Vander Jagt v. O'Neill, 699 F.2d 1166, 1178–1179 (D.C. Cir. 1982) (doctrines of justiciability are more an intuition than a rigorous and explicit theory).

[4] Tangible dispute is required. *See* Church of Scientology v. United States, 506 U.S. 9, 12 (1992) (if

## § 2.02 THE CONSTITUTIONAL REQUIREMENT OF ACTUAL CASE OR CONTROVERSY

The justiciability doctrines are grounded in the constitutional provision that the judicial power of the United States extends to specified *cases and controversies.*[5] Although it is theoretically possible to parse distinctions between a "controversy" and a "case," the record of the framers supports the more common modern practice of merging the terms.[6]

Article III's reference to "cases" and "controversies" represents the first critical threshold to federal court jurisdiction.[7] Because Article III is a limit on judicial power, a court will not have subject matter jurisdiction over an action absent the requisite case or controversy.[8]

As stated by the United States Supreme Court in *Flast v. Cohen*, the words "case or controversy" have "an iceberg quality, containing beneath their surface simplicity, submerged complexities that go to the very heart of the constitutional form of government."[9] Embodied in them are two complementary but somewhat different limitations on federal judicial power. In part, those words limit the business of federal courts to questions presented in an adversary context and in a form historically viewed as capable of resolution through the judicial process, as opposed to those presenting purely hypothetical[10] or abstract issues.[11] And in part, those words define the role assigned to the judiciary in a tripartite allocation of power to assure that the federal courts will not intrude into areas committed to the other branches of government. Justiciability is the term of art employed to give expression to this dual limitation placed on federal courts by the case-and-controversy doctrine.[12] The test for determining the existence of a justiciable case or controversy in an intrabranch dispute between government agencies is whether the issue is traditionally justiciable and the setting of the dispute shows true adversity between the parties.[13]

---

something occurs while appeal is pending that makes it impossible for court to grant effective relief, appeal must be dismissed).

[5] U.S. Const., art. III, § 2.

[6] No distinction between "case" and "controversy." New Jersey v. Heldor Indus., Inc., 989 F.2d 702, 706 (3d Cir. 1993); *see also* Joint Anti-Fascist Refugee Comm. v. McGrath, 341 U.S. 123, 150 (1951) (Frankfurter, J., concurring, and finding no distinction between two terms as used in Article III).

[7] Critical threshold to federal jurisdiction. New Jersey v. Heldor Indus., Inc., 989 F.2d 702, 706 (3d Cir. 1993).

[8] No subject matter jurisdiction absent proper case or controversy.

[9] Iceberg quality. Flast v. Cohen, 392 U.S. 83, 94 (1968).

[10] Hypothetical claim insufficient. Ashcroft v. Mattis, 431 U.S. 171, 172 (1977) (hypothetical question of whether police officers would be liable for shooting plaintiff's son if they had not acted in good faith did not present live case or controversy).

[11] True adversarial matter required. Flast v. Cohen, 392 U.S. 83, 95 (1968); *see also* Cardinal Chem. Co. v. Morton Int'l, Inc., 508 U.S. 83, 98–99 (1993) (existence of case and controversy is prerequisite to all federal actions).

[12] Term of art expressing dual limitation. Flast v. Cohen, 392 U.S. 83, 95 (1968).

[13] Test for intrabranch governmental dispute. TVA v. United States EPA, 278 F.3d 1184, 1193–1197 (11th Cir. 2002) (TVA's challenge to EPA's finding of Clear Air Act violations is justiciable case or

## § 2.03 HISTORICAL ROOTS OF THE JUSTICIABILITY DOCTRINE: THE PROHIBITION ON ADVISORY OPINIONS

Part of the difficulty in giving precise meaning and form to the concept of justiciability stems from the uncertain historical antecedents of the case-and-controversy doctrine.[14] For example, Justice Frankfurter twice suggested that historical meaning could be imparted to the concepts of justiciability and case and controversy by reference to the practices of the courts of Westminster when the Constitution was adopted.[15] However, the power of English judges to deliver advisory opinions was well established at the time the Constitution was drafted,[16] while the prohibition on advisory opinions in the federal judiciary was established in the early days of the republic.[17]

Thus, the policies embodied in Article III, and not history alone, impose the rule against advisory opinions on the federal courts. When the federal judicial power is invoked to pass on the validity of actions by the legislative and executive branches of the government, the rule against advisory opinions implements the separation of powers prescribed by the Constitution and confines federal courts to the role assigned them by Article III.[18] However, the rule against advisory opinions also recognizes that these suits often "are not pressed before the Court with that clear concreteness provided in cases in which a question emerges precisely framed and necessary for decision from a clash of adversary argument exploring every aspect of a multifaceted situation embracing conflicting and demanding interests."[19] Consequently, the Article III prohibition against advisory opinions reflects the complementary constitutional considerations expressed by the justiciability doctrine. Federal judicial power is limited to those disputes that confine federal courts to a role consistent with a system of separated powers and that are traditionally thought to be capable of resolution through the judicial process.[20]

---

controversy, even though both are executive branch agencies serving at pleasure of president, because issue was traditionally justiciable and parties advocated actually conflicting views).

[14] Uncertain historical antecedents. Flast v. Cohen, 392 U.S. 83, 95–96 (1968).

[15] Justice Frankfurter's view. Joint Anti-Fascist Refugee Committee v. McGrath, 341 U.S. 123, 150 (1951) (Frankfurter, J., concurring); Coleman v. Miller, 307 U.S. 433, 460 (1939) (separate opinion).

[16] *See* 3 K. Davis, Administrative Law Treatise 127–128 (1958).

[17] Advisory opinions prohibited. *See* Flast v. Cohen, 392 U.S. 83, 96 n.14 (1968) (rule against advisory opinions was established as early as 1793, and rule has been adhered to without deviation); *see also* New Jersey v. Heldor Indus., Inc., 989 F.2d 702, 706 (3d Cir. 1993) (tracing rejection of advisory opinion role in Constitutional Convention of 1787 and celebrated Correspondence of the Justices six years later, in which Chief Justice Jay politely declined request of Secretary of State Jefferson to issue opinions on 29 questions pertaining to extant treaties between United States and France).

[18] Rule against advisory opinions invokes separation of powers. 392 U.S. at 96; *see* Muskrat v. United States, 219 U.S. 346, 357–360 (1911); 3 H. Johnston, Correspondence and Public Papers of John Jay 486–489 (1891) (correspondence between Secretary of State Jefferson and Chief Justice Jay).

[19] Advisory opinion cases not precisely framed. Flast v. Cohen, 392 U.S. 83, 96–97 (1968) (citing *United States v. Fruehauf*, 365 U.S. 146, 157 (1961)).

[20] 392 U.S. at 97.

## § 2.04 JUSTICIABILITY AS A BLEND OF CONSTITUTIONAL REQUIREMENTS AND POLICY CONSIDERATIONS

Additional uncertainty has long existed in the doctrine of justiciability because the doctrine became a blend of constitutional requirements and policy considerations.[21] For example, in his concurring opinion in *Ashwander v. Tennessee Valley Authority*, Justice Brandeis listed seven rules developed by the Supreme Court for its own governance to avoid passing prematurely on constitutional questions. Because the rules operate in cases admittedly within the Court's jurisdiction, he noted, they find their source in policy, rather than purely in constitutional, considerations.[22] However, several of the cases cited by Justice Brandeis in illustrating the rules of self-governance articulated purely constitutional grounds for decision.[23] The many subtle pressures that cause policy considerations to blend into the constitutional limitations of Article III make the justiciability doctrine one of uncertain and shifting contours.[24] More recently, the Supreme Court has intimated that the federal judiciary lacks authority to decline to adjudicate cases solely on policy grounds,[25] though it is unclear how far the Court will ultimately abandon its sub-constitutional limits on justiciability.

## § 2.05 STANDING

### [1] Nature of Standing Doctrine

Standing addresses *who* may bring the suit. The standing inquiry requires careful judicial examination of a complaint's allegations to ascertain whether the particular plaintiff is entitled to an adjudication of the particular claims asserted.[26]

The Supreme Court has noted that "standing has not been defined with complete consistency in all of the various cases decided by this Court which have discussed it," and that "the concept cannot be reduced to a one-sentence or one paragraph definition."[27] Justice O'Connor pointed out that in many cases, the standing question can be answered chiefly by comparing the allegations of the

---

[21] Uncertainty in justiciability. Flast v. Cohen, 392 U.S. 83, 97 (1968); see Barrows v. Jackson, 346 U.S. 249, 255 (1953) (policy limitation is not always clearly distinguished from constitutional limitation).

[22] Rules based on policy rather than on Constitution. Ashwander v. Tennessee Valley Auth., 297 U.S. 288, 346–348 (1936) (Brandeis, J., concurring).

[23] Cases articulated constitutional grounds. Flast v. Cohen, 392 U.S. 83, 97 (1968) (noting *Massachusetts v. Mellon*, 262 U.S. 447, 485 (1923), *Fairchild v. Hughes*, 258 U.S. 126, 129 (1922), and *Chicago & Grand Trunk Ry. Co. v. Wellman*, 143 U.S. 339, 344–345 (1892)).

[24] Uncertain and shifting contours. Flast v. Cohen, 392 U.S. 83, 97 (1968).

[25] Lexmark International, Inc. v. Static Control Components, Inc., 134 S. Ct. 1377 (2014).

[26] Particular plaintiff. Allen v. Wright, 468 U.S. 737, 752 (1984) (parents of Afro-American public school students did not have standing to challenge tax exemption for segregated private schools).

[27] Definition. Valley Forge Christian College v. Americans United for Separation of Church and State, Inc., 454 U.S. 464, 475 (1982) (finding organization devoted to separation of church and state lacked standing to challenge transfer of surplus federal property to religious college).

particular complaint to those made in prior standing cases.[28]

Because States are not bound by the directives of Article III, state courts are not bound by the limitations of a case or controversy or other federal rules of justiciability, even when they address issues of substantive federal law.[29] In *Virginia v. Hicks*, the plaintiff had been convicted of trespass under state law, after violating a notice from the local police forbidding him from returning to a particular neighborhood. The plaintiff then filed suit against the state, in state court, challenging the constitutionality of the local political subdivision's trespass policy under which the notice had been issued. The state supreme court upheld the plaintiff's challenge, finding that the trespass policy was unconstitutionally overbroad, because it authorized the prohibition of speech and conduct protected by the First Amendment. The state then sought review in the United States Supreme Court, arguing that the plaintiff's action should be dismissed because he lacked standing to challenge the constitutionality of the trespass policy. Specifically, the state argued that since the plaintiff's own conduct did not involve any expressive activity, he lacked standing to claim that the trespass policy infringed First Amendment rights. The Supreme Court rejected this argument, finding it significant that a *state court* decision was under review. Whether the state's courts should have entertained the plaintiff's overbreadth challenge was entirely a matter of state law because state courts are not bound by the limitations of a case or controversy or other federal rules of justiciability.[30]

The Court clearly had jurisdiction to review the First Amendment merits question because it was the state, rather than the plaintiff, that invoked the authority of the federal courts by petitioning for a writ of certiorari. As a consequence of the state court's judgment, the state had suffered an actual injury in fact: an inability to prosecute the plaintiff for trespass. That injury was sufficiently distinct and palpable to confer standing under Article III. Accordingly, the Supreme Court proceeded to consider the merits of the case.[31]

The Supreme Court has stated that of the several doctrines that courts have recognized as manifestations of the case-or-controversy requirement, the requirement that a litigant have standing to invoke the power of a federal court is perhaps the most important.[32] Although for many years standing at the margins was considered a prudential concept to be shaped by the decisions of the courts as a matter of sound judicial policy and subject to the control of Congress, in the

---

[28] Prior cases. Allen v. Wright, 468 U.S. 737, 752 (1984) (parents of Afro-American public school students did not have standing to challenge tax exemption for segregated private schools).

[29] State courts not bound by case or controversy or other federal rules of justiciability. Virginia v. Hicks, 539 U.S. 113, 120 (2003); *see also* ASARCO v. Kadish, 490 U.S. 605 (1989) (adverse state court decision creates requisite injury in fact for Article III).

[30] Whether state courts should entertain constitutional challenge to state law is matter of state law. Virginia v. Hicks, 539 U.S. 113, 120 (2003).

[31] Supreme Court has jurisdiction to review First Amendment decision because state requested review and had standing. Virginia v. Hicks, 539 U.S. 113, 120 (2003) (expressly leaving open question whether ordinary rule that litigant may not rest claim to relief on legal rights or interests of third parties would exclude case such as this from being commenced in federal court).

[32] Standing most important. *See* Allen v. Wright, 468 U.S. 737, 750 (1984) (parents of Afro-American public school students did not have standing to challenge tax exemption for segregated private schools).

Court's recent decision in *Lexmark*, it seemed to reject the idea of any prudentially derived limits on standing.[33] In any event, the Court has stated, at its core standing is a constitutional question.[34] The standing inquiry has been especially rigorous when reaching the merits of the dispute would force the Court to decide whether an action taken by one of the other two branches of the Federal Government is unconstitutional.[35]

Until recently, in analyzing the standing requirement the Supreme Court formulated a two-component framework, consisting of "irreducible" constitutional requirements and sub-constitutional prudential, that is, judge-made, considerations.[36] The two branches of the standing requirement differed in both analytical and consequential terms. Constitutional standing is grounded in Article III's provision that limits the jurisdiction of federal courts to cases and controversies.[37] In contrast, prudential limitations on standing were judge-made and designed to limit access to the federal courts to those litigants best suited to assert a particular claim. Thus, because prudential limits were not dictated by the Constitution, they were subject to reversal by Congress. Standing limits derived from Article III, on the other hand, of course are not subject to congressional repeal.[38]

But in *Lexmark International, Inc. v. Static Control Components, Inc.*,[39] Justice Scalia, writing for the Court, found that the concept of prudential limits on standing "is in some tension with our recent reaffirmation of the principle that 'a federal court's "obligation" to hear and decide' cases within its jurisdiction is 'virtually unflagging.'"[40]

In *Warth v. Seldin*,[41] a non-profit corporation seeking to alleviate the housing shortage for low- and moderate-income persons (as well as several racial and ethnic minorities) brought suit against a municipality, alleging that its zoning ordinance effectively excluded low and moderate income persons from living in the town in

---

[33] No prudential limits on standing. Lexmark International, Inc. v. Static Control Components, Inc., 134 S. Ct. 1377 (2014).

[34] Controlling element. Asarco Inc. v. Kadish, 490 U.S. 605, 613 (1989); *see* Valley Forge Christian College v. Americans United for Separation of Church and State, Inc., 454 U.S. 464, 471–476 (1982).

[35] Rigorous inquiry when action of other branches involved. Clapper v. Amnesty Int'l USA, 133 S. Ct. 1138, 185 L. Ed. 2d 264, 275 (2013) (citing cases in which Court found plaintiff did not have standing to challenge actions of political branches in fields of intelligence gathering and foreign affairs and holding that plaintiff attorneys and human rights, labor, legal, and media organizations did not have standing to challenge constitutionality of Section 702 of Foreign Intelligence Surveillance Act).

[36] Two-component test. United States v. Windsor, 133 S. Ct. 2675, 186 L. Ed. 2d 808, 819 (2013) (Article III standing, which enforces Constitution's case-or-controversy requirement, and prudential standing, which embodies judicially self-imposed limits on exercise of federal jurisdiction, are two separate strands of standing); Caplin & Drysdale v. United States, 491 U.S. 617, 624 n.3 (1989) (court asks both constitutional and prudential standing questions).

[37] Constitutional standing is grounded in Article III. Warth v. Seldin, 422 U.S. 490, 498 (1975).

[38] Congress may affect prudential, but not constitutional limitations. Warth v. Seldin, 422 U.S. 490, 501 (1975).

[39] 134 S. Ct. 1377 (2014).

[40] 134 S. Ct. at 1386 (quoting Sprint Communications, Inc. v. Jacobs, 134 S. Ct. 584, 591 (2014)).

[41] *Warth v. Seldin*. Warth v. Seldin, 422 U.S. 490, 499 (1975).

contravention of the Fourteenth Amendment[42] and civil rights statutes.[43] In ruling on plaintiffs' claims, the Supreme Court explained the different branches of the standing doctrine dictated by Article III's "case or controversy" requirement. The court must determine whether a plaintiff has suffered some threatened or actual injury resulting from the putatively illegal action by the defendant that is judicially redressable.[44]

Only one plaintiff needs to have standing to assert a claim. Therefore, once a court determines the existence of one plaintiff with standing, at least when generalized equitable relief is sought, it need not consider whether other plaintiffs also have standing to assert that claim.[45] Of course, in order to qualify for the award of damages each plaintiff must establish injury.

### [2] The Injury-in-Fact Requirement

The first of the three prongs of the constitutional test for standing is the injury-in-fact requirement. To have an injury-in-fact, the plaintiff must have a "personal stake" in the matter to be adjudicated.[46] At an "irreducible minimum," the party who invokes the court's authority must show that he or she has personally suffered some actual or threatened injury as a result of the putatively illegal conduct of the defendant.[47] One rationale for the injury-in-fact requirement is to ensure that the court will have the benefit of an adversary presentation with full development of the relevant facts.[48] Combined with the redressability requirement, it tends to assure that the legal questions presented to the court will be resolved in a concrete,

---

[42] U.S. Const., Amend. XIV.

[43] 42 U.S.C. § 1983.

[44] Prudential concerns. Warth v. Seldin, 422 U.S. 490, 499, 518 (1975) (civic organization, individual taxpayers, and low-income residents lacked standing to challenge nearby town's zoning ordinance, which effectively excluded low-income persons from living there).

[45] One plaintiff with standing required. Massachusetts v. EPA, 549 U.S. 497, 518 (2007) ("Only one of the petitioners needs to have standing to permit us to consider the petition for review"; because it was clear that union members had standing, Court did not have to consider standing of union or members of Congress); Arlington Heights v. Metropolitan Housing Development Corp., 429 U.S. 252, 264 (1977) ("[W]e have at least one individual plaintiff who has demonstrated standing . . . . Because of the presence of this plaintiff, we need not consider whether the other individual and corporate plaintiffs have standing to maintain the suit."; Court declined to decide whether nonprofit developer had standing to assert constitutional rights of prospective minority tenants because there was one individual plaintiff who demonstrated standing to assert rights on his own); *see also* Horne v. Flores, 557 U.S. 433, 445–446 (2009) (because state superintendent of public instruction had standing to challenge lower courts' decisions concerning funding for English Language Learner instruction, Court did not consider whether legislators also had standing).

[46] Personal stake. Lujan v. Defenders of Wildlife, 504 U.S. 555, 560 n.1 (1992) (injury must affect plaintiff in personal and individual way).

[47] Personal suffering of injury. Lujan v. Defenders of Wildlife, 504 U.S. 555, 560 (1992) (environmental organization lacked standing to challenge endangered species regulations); Valley Forge Christian College v. Americans United for Separation of Church and State, Inc., 454 U.S. 464, 472 (1982) (citizens and taxpayers had no standing to challenge government's conveyance of property to church-related college).

[48] Adversary presentation; full development of facts. Bender v. Williamsport Area Sch. Dist., 475 U.S. 534, 542 (1986).

factual context conducive to a realistic appreciation of the consequences of judicial action, rather than in the rarified atmosphere of a debating society.[49] Put more colloquially, it prevents "kibitzers, bureaucrats, publicity seekers, and 'cause' mongers from wresting control of litigation from the people directly affected."[50]

One scholar has argued that viewing the injury-in-fact requirement as part of the standing doctrine is necessary to ensure the fairness and accuracy of the litigation process. She asserts that the requirement fosters three policies underlying Article III: "the smooth allocation of power among courts over time; the unfairness of holding later litigants to an adverse judgment in which they may not have been properly represented; and the importance of placing control over political processes in the hands of the people most closely involved." She labels these values "restraint," "representation," and "self-determination."[51] Whether the injury in fact requirement actually fosters efficiency and accuracy, however, may be questioned. Such a rationale assumes that a party will have a sufficient incentive to litigate an issue to the fullest only when that party has a concrete stake in the outcome of the case. However, neither empirical, psychological, nor anthropological evidence has ever been cited to support this assumption, and it is doubtful that it can be intuitively derived. It is certainly conceivable that litigants motivated out of purely ideological concern would mount an elaborate and effective case, even if they themselves had suffered no direct financial or personal harm.[52] Nevertheless, the Supreme Court has concluded that the decision to seek review should not be placed in the hands of "concerned bystanders."[53]

In *United States v. Windsor*, the Court took a position that appears to be somewhat at odds with the idea that the requirement of an injury-in-fact ensures an adversary presentation of the issues. The Court held that the United States suffered an injury sufficient to support Article III jurisdiction even though the government actually agreed with the position of the opposing party.[54] The plaintiff in that case sued the United States for a refund of an estate tax she was required to pay because Section 3 of the Defense of Marriage Act (DOMA) denied recognition to same-sex spouses.[55] The President took a bifurcated stance in the

---

[49] Realistic appreciation of consequences. Bender v. Williamsport Area Sch. Dist., 475 U.S. 534, 542 (1986); Valley Forge Christian College v. Americans United for Separation of Church and State, Inc., 454 U.S. 464, 472 (1982).

[50] Prevention. Illinois Dep't of Transp. v. Hinson, 122 F.3d 370, 373 (7th Cir. 1997).

[51] Restraint, representation, and self-determination. Brilmayer, *The Jurisprudence of Article III: Perspectives on the "Case or Controversy" Requirement*, 93 HARV. L. REV. 297, 302 (1979).

[52] Further criticism of injury-in-fact requirement. *See* Tushnet, *The Sociology of Article III: A Response to Professor Brilmayer*, 93 HARV. L. REV. 1698 (1980); Nichol, *Rethinking Standing*, 72 CAL. L. REV. 68 (1984); *see also* Berger, *Standing to Sue in Public Actions: Is It a Constitutional Requirement?* 78 YALE L.J. 816 (1969).

[53] No standing for "concerned bystanders." Diamond v. Charles, 476 U.S. 54, 62 (1986); United States v. SCRAP, 412 U.S. 669, 687 (1973).

[54] Injury despite agreement. United States v. Windsor, 133 S. Ct. 2675, 186 L. Ed. 2d 808, 819 (2013) ("The Government of the United States has a valid legal argument that it is injured even if the Executive disagrees with § 3 of DOMA, which results in Windsor's liability for the tax.").

[55] Defense of Marriage Act. 1 U.S.C. § 7 ("In determining the meaning of any Act of Congress, or of any ruling, regulation, or interpretation of the various administrative bureaus and agencies of the United

case, declining to defend the constitutionality of DOMA but continuing to enforce it in recognition of the judiciary as the final arbiter of the constitutional issue. The district court ruled against the United States and ordered it to refund the tax payment to the plaintiff. The Court concluded that the United States had standing to appeal the district court's order because payment of the refund would inflict a real and immediate economic injury on the United States Treasury, despite the fact that the President might welcome the order to pay the refund if it were accompanied by a ruling that Section 3 of DOMA was unconstitutional.[56]

In *Windsor*, the Court — dubiously — relegated the requirement of adverseness to the prudential realm.[57] The Court acknowledged that the Executive's agreement with the plaintiff's legal argument raised the risk of a friendly, non-adversary proceeding. However, the Court concluded that the adversarial presentation of issues by the Bipartisan Legal Advisory Group of the House of Representatives (BLAG) as an amici curiae was sufficient to satisfy the prudential adverseness concern.[58]

The *Windsor* Court also noted that if prudential rules concerning adverseness required dismissal, extensive litigation would ensue. District courts throughout the country would be without precedential guidance in cases involving the whole of DOMA's sweep, involving over 1,000 federal statutes and a myriad of federal regulations, and adversely affecting the rights and privileges of hundreds of thousands of persons pending a case in which all prudential concerns about justiciability were absent. The cost in judicial resources and litigation expenses would be immense. The Court concluded, "In these unusual and urgent circumstances, the very term 'prudential' counsels that it is a proper exercise of the Court's responsibility to take jurisdiction."[59]

---

States, the word 'marriage' means only a legal union between one man and one woman as husband and wife, and the word 'spouse' refers only to a person of the opposite sex who is a husband or a wife."); *see also* 26 U.S.C. § 2056(a) (marital exemption from federal estate tax).

[56] Injury to U.S. Treasury. United States v. Windsor, 133 S. Ct. 2675, 186 L. Ed. 2d 808, 819 (2013) ("An order directing the Treasury to pay money is a real and immediate economic injury, indeed as real and immediate as an order directing an individual to pay a tax. That the Executive may welcome this order to pay the refund if it is accompanied by the constitutional ruling it wants does not eliminate the injury to the national Treasury if payment is made, or to the taxpayer if it is not." [citations and internal quotation marks omitted]).

[57] Adverseness as prudential element. United States v. Windsor, 133 S. Ct. 2675, 186 L. Ed. 2d 808, 820–821 (2013) ("Even when Article III permits the exercise of federal jurisdiction, prudential considerations demand that the Court insist upon that concrete adverseness which sharpens the presentation of issues upon which the court so largely depends for illumination of difficult constitutional questions." [citations and internal quotations marks omitted]).

[58] Defense provided by BLAG. United States v. Windsor, 133 S. Ct. 2675, 186 L. Ed. 2d 808, 820–821 (2013) ("BLAG's sharp adversarial presentation of the issues satisfies the prudential concerns that otherwise might counsel against hearing an appeal from a decision with which the principal parties agree.").

[59] Dismissal would have resulted in extensive litigation. United States v. Windsor, 133 S. Ct. 2675, 186 L. Ed. 2d 808, 821–822 (2013) ("Were this Court to hold that prudential rules require it to dismiss the case, and, in consequence, that the Court of Appeals erred in failing to dismiss it as well, extensive litigation would ensue.").

In a dissenting opinion, Justice Scalia objected most vigorously to the *Windsor* Court's treatment of the adverseness requirement as a prudential aspect of standing rather than as a separate and essential Article III requirement. Article III requires not just a plaintiff or appellant with standing, he argued, but also an opposing party who denies the validity of the complaint. He rejected the idea that a suit between friendly parties may be maintained as long as the participation of amici curiae ensures the adversarial presentation of issues.[60] On this point Justice Scalia quite clearly has the better of the argument. Absent true adverseness between the parties, it is inconceivable that an adjudication satisfies the requirements of case or controversy inherent in Article III.

Justice Scalia argued that the Court did not have authority to decide *Windsor* because there was no injured party seeking redress before the Court. The plaintiff's injury had been cured when the district court ordered the government to refund her estate tax, and any injury the Government suffered would not be redressed by affirmance of the Second Circuit's judgment, which is what the United States had asked the Court to do. Therefore, the suit should have been dismissed by the Second Circuit for lack of jurisdiction, and because that did not happen, it should have been dismissed by the Supreme Court for the same reason, according to Justice Scalia.[61]

The injury-in-fact requirement also plays a role in the separation of powers between the three branches of the government. As Justice Scalia explained in *Lewis v. Casey*, in which prison inmates alleged that they were deprived of access to the courts in violation of *Bounds v. Smith*,[62] the role of courts is to provide relief to claimants who have suffered, or will imminently suffer, actual harm. It is the role of the political branches to shape the institutions of government in such a fashion as to comply with the laws and the Constitution. "[T]he distinction between the two roles would be obliterated if, to invoke intervention of the courts, no actual or imminent harm were needed, but merely the status of being subject to a governmental institution that was not organized or managed properly."[63]

In *Mellon v. Massachusetts*, in the context of a challenge to the constitutionality of a federal statute, the Court expressed the connection between the injury-in-fact requirement and separation of powers as follows:[64]

> We have no power per se to review and annul acts of Congress on the ground that they are unconstitutional. That question may be considered

---

[60] Adverseness is separate Article III requirement. United States v. Windsor, 133 S. Ct. 2675, 186 L. Ed. 2d 808, 836–837 (2013) (Scalia, J., dissenting; "The majority's notion that a case between friendly parties can be entertained so long as 'adversarial presentation of the issues is assured by the participation of amici curiae prepared to defend with vigor' the other side of the issue [citation omitted] effects a breathtaking revolution in our Article III jurisprudence.").

[61] Justice Scalia's argument. United States v. Windsor, 133 S. Ct. 2675, 186 L. Ed. 2d 808, 834–835 (2013) (Scalia, J., dissenting; suit should have been dismissed by Second Circuit or Court, because there was no injured party seeking redress).

[62] Prisoners' right to court access. Bounds v. Smith, 430 U.S. 817, 821, 828 (1977).

[63] Actual or imminent harm preserves distinction between judicial and political branches. Lewis v. Casey, 518 U.S. 343, 349–350 (1996).

[64] Constitutional challenge to federal statute. Massachusetts v. Mellon, 262 U.S. 447, 488–489 (1923).

> only when the justification for some direct injury suffered or threatened, presenting a justiciable issue, is made to rest upon such an act. . . . The party who invokes the power [of the judiciary] must be able to show not only that the statute is invalid but that he has sustained or is immediately in danger of sustaining some direct injury as the result of its enforcement, and not merely that he suffers in some indefinite way in common with people generally. If a case for preventive relief be presented the court enjoins, in effect, not the execution of the statute, but the acts of the official, the statute notwithstanding. . . . To [merely prevent officials of the executive department from executing a law asserted to be unconstitutional] would be not to decide a judicial controversy, but to assume a position of authority over the governmental acts of another and co-equal department, an authority which plainly we do not possess.

Thus, the requirement of standing helps to preserve the separation of powers and to demarcate the limited role of the courts by differentiating disputes that are appropriately resolved through the judicial process from policy disputes that are appropriately addressed by the elected branches. Citizens are required to express their generalized dissatisfaction with government policy through their elected representatives, not through the courts.[65]

The relationship between the injury-in-fact requirement and the separation-of-powers doctrine also played a role in *United States v. Windsor*.[66] In that case, the Court held that even though the United States agreed with the plaintiff that the statute she challenged was unconstitutional, the government nevertheless suffered an injury in fact sufficient to support standing because if the plaintiff prevailed, the government would be required to refund estate taxes the plaintiff had paid.[67] Writing for the Court, Justice Kennedy opined that the principles of separation of powers would be undermined if the President's agreement with a plaintiff that a law was unconstitutional precluded judicial review. This would undercut what Justice Kennedy saw as the judiciary's primary role in determining the constitutionality of a law that has injured a plaintiff who has brought a justiciable legal claim, rendering the judiciary's role secondary to the President's. Similarly, it would pose a challenge to the allocation of powers between the legislative and executive branches if the executive branch were able to nullify a law on its own initiative, without any

---

[65] Generalized dissatisfaction properly addressed to elected representatives. Coalition for Mercury-Free Drugs v. Sebelius, 671 F.3d 1275, 1278–1279 (D.C. Cir. 2012) ("Standing protects democratic government by requiring citizens to express their generalized dissatisfaction with government policy through the Constitution's representative institutions, not the courts."; plaintiffs did not have standing to challenge FDA's approval of thimerosal-preserved vaccines, because they were not injured by that approval).

[66] *Windsor* case. United States v. Windsor, 133 S. Ct. 2675, 186 L. Ed. 2d 808 (2013).

[67] Government suffered injury in fact. United States v. Windsor, 133 S. Ct. 2675, 186 L. Ed. 2d 808, 819 (2013) ("An order directing the Treasury to pay money is a real and immediate economic injury, indeed as real and immediate as an order directing an individual to pay a tax. That the Executive may welcome this order to pay the refund if it is accompanied by the constitutional ruling it wants does not eliminate the injury to the national Treasury if payment is made, or to the taxpayer if it is not." [citations and internal quotation marks omitted]).

determination from the Court.[68] Justice Scalia took a very different view in his dissent, arguing that the Court's decision actually did violence to separation of powers principles by aggrandizing the power of the judiciary while diminishing the power of the legislative and executive branches.[69] When the dust settles, it is difficult to accept Justice Kennedy's logic, which leads him to conclude that deciding a case even though both sides are in agreement somehow advances the interests of separation of powers. To perform its limited function in a constitutional democracy, the judiciary must be restricted to the adjudication of truly adversary disputes.

The logic behind the asserted connection between injury-in-fact and separation of powers flows from the premises of the "private rights" model of adjudication. Under this model, the judiciary's sole justification for action is to resolve real disputes. Whatever lawmaking a court engages in, then, must be solely incidental to its power to resolve such disputes. Injury-in-fact thus derives from principles of judicial restraint. The requirement reduces the number of instances in which the judiciary will be given the opportunity to strike down the actions of the majoritarian branches, arguably limiting the situations in which fundamental democratic principles will be undermined to the extraordinary case.[70]

It is true, of course, that use of an injury-in-fact requirement reduces the sum total of constitutional challenges to majoritarian action. On the other hand, in certain instances rigid adherence to the injury-in-fact requirement can substantially interfere with the judiciary's performance of its role as constitutional check on both the other branches of government and the states. This will be true when another branch has violated a constitutional dictate, but no single individual possesses a sufficiently distinguishable injury to support a finding of injury-in-fact.[71] Several scholars have criticized the injury-in-fact requirement and the "private rights" model from which it derives.[72]

Even in cases of widespread injury, the person bringing suit must have suffered a distinct and concrete harm particular to that person.[73] An injury is sufficiently

---

68 Court's role in determining constitutionality. United States v. Windsor, 133 S. Ct. 2675, 186 L. Ed. 2d 808, 822 (2013) (separation of powers would be undermined if executive branch were able to nullify law by declaring it unconstitutional without any input from judiciary).

69 Dissent: power of judiciary aggrandized. United States v. Windsor, 133 S. Ct. 2675, 186 L. Ed. 2d 808, 832–833 (2013) (Scalia, J., dissenting: in declaring that it is province and duty of judicial department to say what law is when act of Congress is alleged to conflict with Constitution, Court asserted judicial supremacy over Congress and executive branch).

70 *See* Redish, The Federal Courts in the Political Order 88–97 (1991) (detailed analysis of "private rights" model).

71 Interference with court's role as constitutional check on other branches of government and states. *See, e.g.*, City of Los Angeles v. Lyons, 461 U.S. 95, 101–102 (1983) (victim of allegedly unconstitutional "chokehold" during routine traffic stop did not have injury-in-fact required to seek injunctive relief; there was no reason to believe he was more likely to face chokehold in future than any other individual).

72 Criticism of injury-in-fact requirement and "private rights" model. *See* Redish, The Federal Courts in the Political Order 94–95 (1991) (criticizing rationale of private rights model); Sunstein, *Standing and the Privatization of Public Law*, 88 Colum. L. Rev. 1432 (1988) (criticizing injury-in-fact requirement and private rights model); *see also* Sunstein, *What's Standing After* Lujan? *Citizen Suits, "Injuries," and Article III*, 91 Mich. L. Rev. 163 (1992).

73 Particular harm. Michel v. Anderson, 14 F.3d 623, 626 (D.C. Cir. 1994) (plaintiff voters had standing

"particular" to satisfy the injury-in-fact requirement as long as it affects the plaintiff in a personal and individual way.[74]

The assignee of a claim has standing to assert the injury-in-fact suffered by the assignor.[75] As long as the assignment properly transfers ownership of the claim, it does not matter that it was the assignor, not the assignee, who originally suffered the injury.[76] Nor does it matter if the assignee has agreed to return all or part of the proceeds of the suit to the assignor.[77]

Several federal statutes give private individuals the right to pursue actions on behalf of the federal government and to receive a share of the recovery, even though the individuals have not themselves suffered any injury.[78] Under statutes invoking the venerable qui tam form of litigation, private individuals may sue for redress of an injury suffered by the government itself. The government employs the qui tam device to induce private individuals to ferret out and legally pursue those who have injured the government. Statutes authorizing qui tam actions are uncommon.[79]

The most frequently used of the qui tam statutes is the False Claims Act (FCA), under which a private person (the "relator") may bring a qui tam civil action in the

---

to challenge rule granting delegates right to vote in House Committee of the Whole; fact that all voters in states suffered same injury did not deprive plaintiff voters of standing).

[74] Individual effect on plaintiff. Lac Du Flambeau Band of Lake Superior v. Norton, 422 F.3d 490, 496–497 (7th Cir. 2005) (Indian tribes put at competitive disadvantage by Secretary of Interior's approval of gaming pact between another tribe and state had standing even though other tribes were similarly disadvantaged). *9th Circuit* Jewel v. NSA, 673 F.3d 902, 910 (9th Cir. 2011) (plaintiffs challenging allegedly illegal and unconstitutional interception of their telephone, internet, and electronic communications by government agencies and officers alleged sufficiently concrete and particularized injury; allegations were highly specific and laid out concrete harms arising from warrantless searches); Newdow v. Lefevre, 598 F.3d 638, 642 (9th Cir. 2010) (injury suffered by atheist plaintiff who was forced to encounter national motto, "In God We Trust," on coins and currency was sufficient to confer Article III standing even though encounters were common to all United States citizens, because plaintiff alleged "concrete, particularized, and personal injury resulting from his frequent, unwelcome contact with the motto").

[75] Assignee asserts assignor's injury. Vermont Agency of Natural Resources v. United States, 529 U.S. 765, 773 (2000) (position of qui tam plaintiff under False Claims Act analogized to that of assignee or subrogee of claim).

[76] Injury originally suffered by assignor. Sprint Commc'ns Co., L.P. v. APCC Servs., 554 U.S. 269, 286 (2008) (assignee has standing to assert injury-in-fact suffered by assignor).

[77] Agreement to return proceeds to assignor. Sprint Commc'ns Co., L.P. v. APCC Servs., 554 U.S. 269, 287 (2008) (if plaintiffs prevail, defendants will write a check to them for the amount of compensation owed; "What does it matter what [plaintiffs] do with the money afterward?").

[78] Qui tam statutes. 31 U.S.C. § 3729 *et seq.* (action against person who knowingly presents false or fraudulent claim for payment to federal government); 25 U.S.C. §§ 81, 201 (actions against persons contracting with Indians in unlawful manner or violating Indian protection laws); 35 U.S.C. § 292(b) (action against person who falsely marks patented articles); *cf.* 18 U.S.C. § 962 (forfeiture to informer of share of vessels privately armed against friendly nations, but not expressly authorizing suit by informer); 46 U.S.C. § 723 (forfeiture to informer of share of vessels removing undersea treasure from Florida coast to foreign nations, but not expressly authorizing suit by informer).

[79] Qui tam statutes uncommon. Woods v. Empire Health Choice, Inc., 574 F.3d 92, 98–100 (2d Cir. 2009) (noting that in *Vermont Agency of Natural Resources v. United States*, 529 U.S. 765, 768 & n.1 (2000), Supreme Court recognized fewer than five clear qui tam statutes in entire U.S. Code; joining other circuits in holding that Medicare Secondary Payer Statute, 42 U.S.C. § 1395y(b), does not authorize qui tam action).

name of the federal government against any person who, inter alia, knowingly presents a false or fraudulent claim for payment to the federal government. The relator in such a suit receives a share of any proceeds from the action.[80] In *Vermont Agency of Natural Resources v. United States*, the Supreme Court held that as an assignee of the government's claim, an individual bringing suit on behalf of the government under the FCA has standing to assert the injury in fact suffered by the assignor.[81] The Federal Circuit applied the same reasoning to a suit under the false patent marking statute.[82] Presumably the Court's reasoning would apply to an individual's standing under the other qui tam statutes as well.[83]

In *Vermont Agency*, the Court rejected the theory that an FCA relator has standing as a statutorily designated agent bringing suit in the name of the United States, because the statute gives the relator an actual interest in the lawsuit, not merely the right to retain a fee out of the recovery. Specifically, the FCA provides that a person may bring a civil action for a violation of the FCA both for the person himself or herself and for the United States government.[84] The Act (1) gives the relator the right to continue as a party to the action even after the government itself has assumed primary responsibility for prosecuting it, (2) entitles the relator to a hearing if the government seeks to dismiss the suit voluntarily, and (3) prohibits the government from settling the suit over the relator's objection without a judicial determination of fairness, adequacy, and reasonableness.[85] For the portion of the recovery retained by the relator, therefore, something more than mere agency for the government was required to support the relator's standing.[86]

Nor was it sufficient, the Court explained, that the relator had been given a concrete interest in the bounty he would receive if the suit proved successful. The interest must be in obtaining compensation for, or preventing, the violation of a legally protected right. A qui tam relator has not suffered any such violation.[87] Otherwise, Congress could easily circumvent the injury-in-fact requirement simply by circularly creating a right to sue.

Instead, the Court relied on the doctrine that the assignee of a claim has standing to assert the injury in fact suffered by the assignor. The Court reasoned that the FCA can reasonably be regarded as effecting a partial assignment of the

---

80 31 U.S.C. §§ 3729(a), 3730(b), (d)(1)–(2).

81 FCA relator may assert government's injury as assignee. Vermont Agency of Natural Resources v. United States, 529 U.S. 765, 773–774 (2000).

82 Plaintiff is government assignee under false marking statute. Stauffer v. Brooks Brothers, Inc., 619 F.3d 1321, 1325–1326 (Fed. Cir. 2010) (plaintiff had standing as government assignee under false marking statute).

83 Presumed application to other qui tam statutes. *See* Vermont Agency of Natural Resources v. United States, 529 U.S. 765, 774–778 (2000) (noting that standing for qui tam plaintiffs is supported by long tradition of qui tam actions in England and in American colonies).

84 31 U.S.C. § 3730(b).

85 31 U.S.C. § 3730(c)(2)(B).

86 Agency theory rejected. Vermont Agency of Natural Resources v. United States, 529 U.S. 765, 771–772 (2000).

87 Interest in bounty insufficient. Vermont Agency of Natural Resources v. United States, 529 U.S. 765, 772–773 (2000).

government's damages claim to the qui tam relator. Although the Court had not previously expressly recognized "representational standing" on the part of assignees, it had routinely entertained assignees' suits. The Court concluded the relator had standing to assert the government's injury-in-fact as an assignee.[88]

The Court's interpretation of the FCA as assigning the federal government's claim to the relator is questionable. Under the Act, the government may initially exercise the option to assume control of the action, which does not seem possible if the Act truly assigns the government's claim to the relator. Moreover, on its face, the FCA actually "assigns" nothing to any particular individual or group of individuals. It merely provides that individuals who take certain actions will be benefited. Thus, while the Court was correct that an assignee has the right to assert the assignor's injury, it is doubtful that rule can properly be applied to qui tam actions. The Court's assignment rationale, then, appears to be little more than an after-the-fact rationalization.

The injury component of the standing doctrine requires an "actual or imminent" injury. This means that the injury must have already been inflicted or it must be likely to occur "imminently."[89] "Imminence" is a somewhat elastic concept, the purpose of which is to ensure that the alleged injury is not too speculative for purposes of standing, i.e., that the injury is "certainly impending."[90] A threatened injury will qualify if it is sufficiently probable.[91]

Contingent liability may cause an injury that is sufficiently actual or imminent for standing purposes even though actual liability may not arise for some time or at all.[92] The fact that the injury is "threatened" rather than "actual" does not, by itself, defeat the claim. Thus, threats of harm have been held to satisfy the injury-in-fact

---

[88] FCA relator has standing to assert government's injury. Vermont Agency of Natural Resources v. United States, 529 U.S. 765, 774–775 (2000).

[89] Injury already inflicted or will be soon. Lujan v. Defenders of Wildlife, 504 U.S. 555, 560 (1992); *see* Summers v. Earth Island Institute, 555 U.S. 488, 499–500 (2009) (refusing to replace requirement of "imminent" harm with requirement of "realistic threat" that reoccurrence of challenged activity would cause plaintiff harm in reasonably near future); *but see* Summers v. Earth Island Institute, 555 U.S. 488, 505 (2009) (Breyer, J., dissenting) ("imminence" more appropriately considered in context of ripeness or necessity of injunctive relief; in context of standing, "imminence" used to emphasize that harm in question was merely hypothetical or conjectural).

[90] "Imminence" requirement ensures injury is not speculative. Clapper v. Amnesty Int'l USA, 133 S. Ct. 1138, 185 L. Ed. 2d 264, 275–276 (2013) (imminence is somewhat elastic concept, but it cannot be stretched beyond purpose of ensuring alleged injury is not too speculative; plaintiffs' alleged injuries relating to foreign intelligence surveillance were too speculative to support standing, i.e., they were not imminent); Lujan v. Defenders of Wildlife, 504 U.S. 555, 564 n.2 (1992) ("Although 'imminence' is concededly a somewhat elastic concept, it cannot be stretched beyond its purpose, which is to ensure that the alleged injury is not too speculative for Article III purposes—that the injury is '*certainly impending*' " [Court's emphasis; citation and internal quotation marks omitted]).

[91] Sufficiently probable threatened injury. Pennell v. San Jose, 485 U.S. 1, 8 (1988) (likelihood of enforcement of rent control ordinance, with concomitant probability that landlord's rent would be reduced below what he or she would otherwise be able to obtain, was sufficient threat of actual injury to satisfy requirement that plaintiff who challenges statute must demonstrate realistic danger of sustaining direct injury as result of statute's operation or enforcement).

[92] Contingent liability may cause immediate injury. Clinton v. City of New York, 524 U.S. 417, 430–431 (1998).

requirement of standing on numerous occasions.[93]

The immediacy of an alleged harm may be a factor in determining whether an arguably speculative injury constitutes a sufficient injury-in-fact to confer standing.[94] In *United States v. Students Challenging Regulatory Agency Procedures (SCRAP)*, which was later described as going "to the very outer limit of the law" with respect to an arguably speculative injury,[95] the Court held that an environmental group alleged a sufficient injury-in-fact in its challenge to the approval of a surcharge on railroad freight rates by the Interstate Commerce Commission (ICC). The plaintiff claimed that the adverse environmental impact of the ICC's action on the Washington metropolitan area would cause the group's members to suffer economic, recreational and aesthetic harm because a general rate increase would cause increased use of nonrecyclable commodities, resulting in the need to use more natural resources to produce such goods, some of which resources might be taken from the Washington area, and resulting in more refuse that might be discarded in national parks in the Washington area. The Court held that those pleadings alleged a specific and perceptible harm sufficient to survive a motion to dismiss for lack of standing.[96] The Court later emphasized that the *SCRAP* plaintiffs alleged specific and perceptible harms that would befall its members *imminently* if the ICC orders were not reversed.[97]

An injury that is merely conjectural, speculative, or hypothetical will not satisfy the injury-in fact component of standing.[98] There is significant overlap among these terms. Thus, while claims of injury that are deemed insufficient to support standing under this rubric are usually described as being too "speculative" or "conjectural," injuries that are deemed "hypothetical" can often also be described as "speculative" or "conjectural." However it is denominated, the mere possibility of future injury is insufficient to establish injury-in-fact. Standing may also be denied on the ground that the injury is only hypothetical in the sense that the plaintiff *could* have been injured, but was not.

Claims that are deemed too speculative to support the injury component of standing often depend on a chain of speculative contingencies that must occur for

---

[93] Immediate threat. Blum v. Yaretsky, 457 U.S. 991, 1000–1002 (1982) (nursing home residents had standing to challenge procedural adequacy of discharges and transfers to *lower* levels of care despite consent judgment halting transfers based on utility review committee recommendations, because threat that nursing homes might determine independently that plaintiffs' continued stay at current levels of care was not medically necessary was not imaginary or speculative; in contrast, plaintiffs had no standing to challenge procedures concerning transfers to *higher* levels of care, because no such transfers were threatened).

[94] Immediacy as factor. *See* United States v. Students Challenging Regulatory Agency Procedures (SCRAP), 412 U.S. 669, 684–690 (1973).

[95] *SCRAP* at outer limit of law. *See* Whitmore v. Arkansas, 495 U.S. 149, 158–159 (1990).

[96] Alleged adverse environmental impact sufficient injury-in-fact. United States v. Students Challenging Regulatory Agency Procedures (SCRAP), 412 U.S. 669, 684–690 (1973).

[97] Allegation of imminent harm in *SCRAP.* Whitmore v. Arkansas, 495 U.S. 149, 159–160 (1990).

[98] Conjectural, speculative, or hypothetical injury insufficient. Whitmore v. Arkansas, 495 U.S. 149, 155, 157 (1990).

the alleged injury to manifest itself.[99] For example, in *Clapper v. Amnesty International*, several attorneys and human rights, labor, legal, and media organizations challenged the constitutionality of Section 702 of the Foreign Intelligence Surveillance Act, which allowed the U.S. Attorney General and the Director of National Intelligence to acquire foreign intelligence information by jointly authorizing the surveillance of individuals who were not "United States persons" and were reasonably believed to be located outside the U.S.[100] The plaintiffs alleged that the statute compromised their ability to locate witnesses, cultivate sources, obtain information, and communicate confidential information to their clients. A five-member majority of the Court held that the plaintiffs did not have standing to challenge the statute, because their alleged injury was dependent on their "highly speculative fear" that (1) the government would target the communications of non-U.S. persons with whom the plaintiffs communicated; (2) the surveillance would be proposed under Section 702; (3) the Foreign Intelligence Surveillance Court judges would conclude that the proposed surveillance satisfied Section 702's safeguards and was consistent with the Fourth Amendment; (4) the government would successfully intercept communications of the plaintiffs' contacts; and (5) the plaintiffs would be parties to the intercepted communications. The Court concluded that an injury based on this "highly attenuated chain of possibilities" does not satisfy the "certainly impending" requirement for standing.[101] The four dissenting Justices argued that there was a very high likelihood that the government, acting under the authority of Section 702, would intercept at least some of the plaintiffs' communications and, therefore, the harm with which the plaintiffs was threatened was not speculative.[102]

In *Whitmore v. Arkansas*, the Supreme Court held that a death row inmate had no standing to intervene in a proceeding to review a determination that a different death row inmate was competent to waive his right to appeal his death sentence. The plaintiff claimed that he would be injured by the failure of the Arkansas Supreme Court to review the other inmate's death sentence because Arkansas had a system of comparative review in death penalty cases. Under that system, the plaintiff inmate claimed a direct and substantial interest in having the data base against which his crime would be compared include the heinous crime of the inmate who had waived his right to appeal. The Court noted that the plaintiff inmate had already been convicted of murder and sentenced to death. He had exhausted his direct appellate review and been denied state post-conviction relief. For him to be injured by the failure to review the other inmate's death sentence, he would have to

---

[99] Chain of events too speculative. Clapper v. Amnesty Int'l USA, 133 S. Ct. 1138, 185 L. Ed. 2d 264, 276–279 (2013) (plaintiffs' "speculative chain of possibilities" did not establish standing to challenge statute relating to foreign intelligence surveillance); Whitmore v. Arkansas, 495 U.S. 149, 155, 157 (1990).

[100] Section 702 of Foreign Intelligence Surveillance Act. 50 U.S.C. § 1881.

[101] Possible surveillance injury too speculative. Clapper v. Amnesty Int'l USA, 133 S. Ct. 1138, 185 L. Ed. 2d 264, 276–279 (2013) (no standing to challenge intelligence-gathering statute, because speculative chain of possibilities with regard to surveillance did not establish that injury based on potential future surveillance was certainly impending).

[102] High probability of surveillance. Clapper v. Amnesty Int'l USA, 133 S. Ct. 1138, 185 L. Ed. 2d 264, 287–289 (2013) (Breyer, J., dissenting; "[W]e need only assume that the Government is doing its job . . . in order to conclude that there is a high probability that the Government will intercept at least some electronic communication to which at least some of the plaintiffs are parties.").

obtain federal habeas relief and then be retried, convicted, and sentenced to death. Even if all of those things happened, it would still be no more than conjecture to believe that adding the other inmate's crimes to a comparative review data base would cause the Arkansas Supreme Court to set aside the plaintiff's death sentence. In fact, there was no factual basis to conclude that the sentence imposed on the other inmate for mass murder would even be relevant to a future comparative review of the sentence of the plaintiff. The Court concluded that the claim of injury from the failure to review the other inmate's sentence was too speculative to support standing.[103]

In *Diamond v. Charles*, the Court held that a pediatrician's interest in defending a state law restricting abortions was too speculative to support standing. The plaintiff claimed that if the law were enforced, more children would be born, enlarging the pool of potential fee-paying clients. The Court reasoned that the possibility that more fetuses would survive and would then find their way to the plaintiff's office to become patients was too speculative to constitute an injury-in-fact. The Court distinguished cases brought by doctors on whose income abortion funding regulations would have a direct financial impact or who were threatened with criminal prosecution under a law restricting abortion.[104]

Injuries that are dependent on the plaintiff either committing or being charged with a crime in the future or otherwise coming into contact with the law enforcement system have generally been held to be too speculative to support standing.[105] For example, in *O'Shea v. Littleton*, the Court held that residents of an Illinois town did not allege an injury sufficient to confer standing to obtain injunctive relief against a magistrate and a circuit court judge whom the plaintiffs claimed were engaged in a pattern and practice of illegal bond setting, sentencing, and jury-fee practices in criminal cases. The Court noted that the plaintiffs would not be subject to the alleged discriminatory practices unless they violated an unchallenged law and were charged, held to answer, and tried in proceedings before the defendants. "[A]ttempting to anticipate whether and when these respondents will be charged with crime and will be made to appear before either petitioner takes us into the area of speculation and conjecture," the Court stated.[106] In contrast, the Ninth Circuit held that Latino plaintiffs did have standing to seek an injunction barring county sheriffs from detaining individuals based solely on reasonable

---

[103] Injury from failure to review other inmate's death sentence too speculative. Whitmore v. Arkansas, 495 U.S. 149, 157 (1990).

[104] Possibility of more patients as result of fewer abortions too speculative. Diamond v. Charles, 476 U.S. 54, 65–66 (1986) (distinguishing *Singleton v. Wulff*, 428 U.S. 106, 113 (1976) (doctor had standing to challenge abortion funding regulations that had direct financial impact on his practice) and *Doe v. Bolton*, 410 U.S.179, 188 (1973) (doctor had standing to challenge abortion law that posed threat of his criminal prosecution).

[105] Injury dependent on future contact with law enforcement too speculative. City of Los Angeles v. Lyons, 461 U.S. 95, 105 (1983) (allegation of future injury contingent on plaintiff having encounter with police in which police would administer allegedly illegal chokehold too speculative to establish injury-in-fact); Ashcroft v. Mattis, 431 U.S. 171, 173 n.2 (1977) (claim that brother of boy who was shot and killed by police while attempting to escape arrest might also flee if arrested and would be in danger of being killed by defendants or other police officers too speculative to support standing).

[106] Injury dependent on commission of crime and trial before defendants too speculative. O'Shea v. Littleton, 414 U.S. 488, 497 (1974).

suspicion or knowledge that the individual was unlawfully present in the country. In that case, the district court found that the plaintiffs were sufficiently likely to be seized in violation of the Fourth Amendment because the defendants claimed authority to detain persons they believed were not authorized to be in the country based only on a reasonable suspicion that the person was not legally present in the U.S. In addition, there was evidence defendants had engaged in a pattern or practice of conducting traffic stops as part of "saturation patrols" or "sweeps" targeting Latinos suspected of being illegally present in the country. The district court determined that exposure to this policy constituted ongoing harm and that there was a sufficient likelihood the plaintiffs' rights would be violated again. Under these circumstances, even though the likelihood of a future stop of a particular individual plaintiff might not be high, the district court did not err in determining that future injury was sufficiently likely to support standing. The Ninth Circuit noted that under the defendants' policy and practice, the plaintiffs could not avoid unlawful detention merely by avoiding illegal conduct or obeying all traffic laws.

The fact that the potential injury would be the result of a chain of events does not always preclude standing. For example, in *United States v. Students Challenging Regulatory Agency Procedures (SCRAP)*, the Supreme Court held that an organization that alleged that its members' use of natural resources would be affected by a chain of third-party responses to an Interstate Commerce Commission rate decision satisfied the injury-in-fact component of standing.[107] *SCRAP* was later described by the Court as going "to the very outer limit of the law" with respect to an arguably speculative injury.[108]

The likelihood of a future injury cannot be based solely on the defendant's conduct in the past. A plaintiff seeking equitable relief against the defendants' future conduct must show that he or she faces a real and immediate threat of a similar injury in the future.[109] For example, an allegation that the plaintiff was illegally choked while being arrested might have given the plaintiff standing to sue for damages, but it did not give him standing to seek an injunction barring the police from using the chokehold in the future. Even allegations that police officers in that area routinely applied chokeholds regardless of whether the officers were threatened by the use of deadly force were insufficient to prove a future injury.[110] On the other hand, evidence of past wrongs is by no means irrelevant to whether there is a real and immediate threat of repeated injury.[111]

---

[107] Third party responses to rate increase would injure plaintiffs. United States v. SCRAP, 412 U.S. 669, 688–690 (1973) (allegations that rate increase would cause increased use of nonrecyclable commodities, resulting in use of more natural resources to produce such goods, some of which might be taken from area in which plaintiff's members lived, and resulting in more refuse that might be discarded in national parks in area, "if proved, would place [plaintiff's members] squarely among those persons injured in fact by the Commission's action").

[108] *SCRAP* at outer limit of law. Whitmore v. Arkansas, 495 U.S. 149, 159 (1990).

[109] Past conduct insufficient to establish future injury. Los Angeles v. Lyons, 461 U.S. 95, 109–111 (1983).

[110] No standing to enjoin use of chokehold. Los Angeles v. Lyons, 461 U.S. 95, 101–102, 105, 107 (1983).

[111] Past wrongs bear on threat of repeated injury. O'Shea v. Littleton, 414 U.S. 488, 496 (1974) (although evidence of past wrongs bears on whether there is real and immediate threat of repeated

The likelihood of injury-causing conduct being repeated, causing future injury to the plaintiff, depends in part on whether the conduct was random and who committed it. An allegation of future injury based on a predicted repetition of random or unauthorized acts of a third party that caused injury in the past will probably be deemed too speculative to satisfy the injury-in-fact requirements. In contrast, when the acts that caused the past injury were authorized as a result of an established policy of the defendant, it is significantly more likely that the actions, and thus the injury, will recur.

It is often stated that to support standing, the alleged injury must be concrete, distinct, and palpable, as opposed to abstract.[112] These terms are not clearly defined in the case law or even consistently differentiated from the requirement that the injury not be conjectural, speculative, or hypothetical. Their meaning must be gleaned from an examination of the types of injuries that have been held sufficient to meet this somewhat ambiguous standard and those that have not.[113]

The injury-in-fact necessary to support standing may come in the form of an economic injury.[114] Economic injury can take many forms. For example, loss of profits,[115] loss of revenue, loss of the use of money for a period of time, payment of an inflated price for goods or services, an obligation to pay the costs of complying with environmental regulations, an obligation to purchase medical insurance, loss of value or usefulness of property, or of government funds to which the plaintiff would otherwise be entitled have all been held to satisfy the injury-in-fact requirement.

Of course, the economic injury must also satisfy the other requirements for injury-in-fact, such as immediacy and concreteness. Non-economic injuries may also be sufficient to satisfy the injury-in-fact component of standing.[116] Some conduct may cause both economic and non-economic injuries. For example, in *Gladstone, Realtors v. Village of Bellwood*, a village and some of its residents sued real estate brokerage firms, alleging that the defendants were violating the Fair Housing Act by steering prospective African-American homeowners toward a specific "target"

---

injury, threat of future injury in this case was too speculative because it depended on likelihood that plaintiffs would again be charged with violations of criminal law and subject to challenged activities of defendants).

112 Concrete, distinct, and palpable. Whitmore v. Arkansas, 495 U.S. 149, 155 (1990) (death row inmate's claim of future injury based on lack of review of other death row inmate's sentence too speculative to support standing); O'Shea v. Littleton, 414 U.S. 488, 494 (1974) (claim of future injury as result of allegedly discriminatory bail-setting, jury selection, and sentencing practices too speculative to support standing).

113 Look to case law to determine standing. *See* Allen v. Wright, 468 U.S. 737, 751–752 (1984) ("In many cases the standing question can be answered chiefly by comparing the allegations of the particular complaint to those made in prior standing cases.").

114 Economic injury may support standing. Association of Data Processing Serv. Orgs., Inc. v. Camp, 397 U.S. 150, 152 (1970) ("The first question [in determining whether the plaintiff has standing] is whether the plaintiff alleges that the challenged action has caused him injury in fact, economic or otherwise.").

115 Lost profits. Association of Data Processing Serv. Orgs., Inc. v. Camp, 397 U.S. 150, 152 (1970).

116 Non-economic injuries sufficient. *See* Association of Data Processing Serv. Orgs., Inc. v. Camp, 397 U.S. 150, 153–154 (1970) ("The first question [in determining whether the plaintiff has standing] is whether the plaintiff alleges that the challenged action has caused him injury in fact, economic or otherwise.").

area and steering prospective white customers away from that area. The Court held that the village had standing to challenge the legality of conduct that robbed the village of its racial balance and stability, which can cause both economic and non-economic injuries. The village residents had standing based on the alleged deprivation of the social and professional benefits of living in an integrated society and the economic injury of declining property values.[117]

Harm to the plaintiff's aesthetic, environmental, or recreational interests may constitute a sufficient injury in fact to support standing. In cases involving such injuries, the standing inquiry focuses on the injury to the plaintiff rather than the injury to the environment.[118]

Injury caused by a violation of a required procedure can satisfy the injury-in-fact component of standing.[119] To give rise to a procedural injury for standing purposes, the procedural requirement that has allegedly been violated must be designed to protect some threatened concrete interest of the plaintiff.[120] Moreover, the plaintiff asserting standing on the basis of the procedural violation must have personally suffered an injury as a result of the claimed procedural error or omission.[121]

The intensity of the litigant's interest or motivation or the fervor of his or her advocacy is not a substitute for a showing of injury.[122] For example, in *Valley Forge Christian College v. Americans United for Separation of Church and State, Inc.*, an organization dedicated to the separation of church and state and several of its employees challenged a transfer of a valuable piece of property to a church-related college on the ground that it violated the Establishment Clause of the First Amendment. The plaintiffs were denied standing because they failed to allege any actual injury beyond a generalized grievance common to all taxpayers. The Court acknowledged that the plaintiffs were firmly committed to the constitutional principle of separation of church and state. Nevertheless, they had no standing in

---

[117] Economic and non-economic injuries from "steering" practices. Gladstone, Realtors v. Village of Bellwood, 441 U.S. 91, 110–115 & n. 30 (1979) (defendants alleged to have manipulated housing market of village "to the economic and social detriment" of plaintiffs).

[118] Aesthetic, environmental, or recreational interest. Friends of the Earth, Inc. v. Laidlaw Envtl. Servs. (TOC), Inc., 528 U.S. 167, 183 (2000) (plaintiffs' recreational, aesthetic, and economic interests were directly affected by discharge of pollutants into water).

[119] Procedural injuries sufficient. *See* Lujan v. Defenders of Wildlife, 504 U.S. 555, 571–573 & n.8 (1992) (validity of procedural injuries acknowledged, but procedural violation did not suffice for standing in this case because no concrete interest of plaintiff was injured by violation).

[120] Concrete interest of plaintiff. *See* Summers v. Earth Island Inst., 555 U.S. 488, 497 (2009) (requirement of threatened concrete interest not affected by procedural nature of injury; environmental groups did not have standing to challenge U.S. Forest Service regulations in absence of live dispute over concrete application of regulations); Lujan v. Defenders of Wildlife, 504 U.S. 555, 573 n. 8 (1992).

[121] Injury must be personal to plaintiff. Lujan v. Defenders of Wildlife, 504 U.S. 555, 571–573 & n.8 (1992) (validity of procedural injuries acknowledged, but procedural violation did not suffice for standing in this case because no concrete interest of plaintiff was injured by violation).

[122] Interest or fervor no substitute for injury. Valley Forge Christian College v. Americans United for Separation of Church and State, Inc., 454 U.S. 464, 485–486 (1982); Sierra Club v. Morton, 405 U.S. 727, 739 (1972) (environmental organization had no standing to sue to restrain federal official from approving extensive skiing development because development would not affect organization or its members; organization's historic commitment to cause of protecting nation's natural heritage from man's depredations insufficient substitute for injury-in-fact).

the absence of an allegation of an injury suffered by them personally as a consequence of the alleged constitutional violation.

## [3] Traceability

The second prong of the standing criteria under Article III's case-or-controversy requirement constitutes the traceability or "causation" component of the doctrine. A litigant must satisfy the traceability prong of the Article III prerequisites by showing that the injury "fairly can be traced to the challenged action."[123] Standing requires that there be a causal connection between plaintiff's asserted injury and defendant's challenged action. The fact that a plaintiff in some sense contributed to the injury does not necessarily break the causal connection between the injury and the defendants' conduct to defeat standing. Similarly, some courts have held that the fact that the defendant's actions were not the only cause of the plaintiff's harm does not preclude a finding of causation sufficient to support standing. But while that is correct in the abstract, a court should be careful not to rely on this dictate to ignore the traceability and redressability prerequisites of Article III. Where defendant's conduct is not a necessary element for plaintiff's injury, i.e., the exact same injury would have occurred even absent defendant's conduct, it is questionable whether either of these core constitutional requirements has been satisfied.

In order to establish the link between the injury and the defendant's conduct, the plaintiff need not establish proximate cause. Proximate cause has been defined as the dominant or effective cause that necessarily sets the other causes in operation; an act or omission occurring with another, without which injury would not have been inflicted. However, some causal connection between the injury and the defendant's conduct must be shown.

To the extent that an injury is self-inflicted or is due to the plaintiff's own fault, the causal chain is broken. In *Clapper v. Amnesty International*, several attorneys and human rights, labor, legal, and media organizations challenged the constitutionality of Section 702 of the Foreign Intelligence Surveillance Act, which allowed the U.S. Attorney General and the Director of National Intelligence to acquire foreign intelligence information by jointly authorizing the surveillance of individuals who were not "United States persons" and were reasonably believed to be located outside the U.S.[124] The plaintiffs alleged that, because of the threat of surveillance under the act, they had undertaken costly and burdensome measures to protect the confidentiality of sensitive communications. The Court held that the plaintiffs did not face a threat of certainly impending interception of their communications under Section 702, and therefore any costs they incurred to avoid such interception were simply the product of their fear of surveillance and were not traceable to Section 702.[125] However, the fact that the plaintiff is partly to blame

---

[123] Fairly traceable. Whitmore v. Arkansas, 495 U.S. 149, 155 (1990); Valley Forge Christian College v. Americans United for Separation of Church and State, Inc., 454 U.S. 464, 472 (1982); Simon v. Eastern Ky. Welfare Rights Org., 426 U.S. 26, 38, 41 (1976).

[124] Section 702 of Foreign Intelligence Surveillance Act. 50 U.S.C. § 1881.

[125] Costs incurred to avoid surveillance not traceable to statute. Clapper v. Amnesty Int'l USA, 133

for his or her alleged injury will not necessarily deprive the plaintiff of standing if the defendant's conduct is also partly to blame.

### [4] Redressability

The third prong of the requirement of constitutional standing is that the plaintiff's injury likely will be redressed by a favorable decision. This requirement has been described as the "redressability" prong of Article III.[126] Redressability does not require that the plaintiff actually be entitled to the relief sought; it is enough that the requested relief, if granted, would redress the plaintiff's injury. The fact that there might be some other way in which the plaintiff could rectify the injury does not affect the redressability analysis.

The redressability requirement is satisfied if a favorable decision would relieve or reduce a discrete injury to the plaintiff. It is not necessary that a favorable decision would relieve *every* injury.[127] At least in cases in which Congress has legislatively vested enforcement power in an administrative agency, it is not necessary that the injury be completely eliminated; a reduction in the injury will suffice.[128] However, where the reduction in the injury will likely be no better than negligible, the injury-in-fact requirement should not be deemed satisfied. For all practical purposes, a decision in such a case would differ not at all from an advisory opinion.

The requirement of "actual injury redressable by the court" serves several of the implicit policies embodied in Article III.[129] The redressability requirement prerequisite tends to ensure that the legal questions presented to the court will be resolved in a concrete factual context conducive to a realistic appreciation of the consequences of judicial action.[130]

The redressability requirement enforces Article III's limitation of the federal judicial power "to those disputes which confine federal courts to a role consistent

---

S. Ct. 1138, 185 L. Ed. 2d 264, 279–281 (2013) (costs incurred to avoid surveillance were not traceable to challenged statute, because plaintiffs did not face threat of imminent surveillance under that statute).

[126] Redressability prong. Whitmore v. Arkansas, 495 U.S. 149, 155 (1990); Valley Forge Christian College v. Americans United for Separation of Church and State, Inc., 454 U.S. 464, 472 (1982); Simon v. Eastern Ky. Welfare Rights Org., 426 U.S. 26, 38, 41 (1976).

[127] Not every injury need be redressed. Larson v. Valente, 456 U.S. 228, 243 n.15 (1982) (plaintiff not required to show that favorable decision would definitely result in its receiving religious organization exemption from registration and reporting requirements of state charitable solicitations act; redressability requirement satisfied because favorable decision would make it easier to secure exemption).

[128] Reduction of injury is enough. *See* Massachusetts v. Environmental Protection Agency, 549 U.S. 497 (2007) ("While it may be true that regulating motor-vehicle emissions will not by itself *reverse* global warming, it by no means follows that we lack jurisdiction to decide whether EPA has a duty to take steps to *slow* or *reduce* it.").

[129] Implicit policies. Bender v. Williamsport Area Sch. Dist., 475 U.S. 534, 542 (1986); Valley Forge Christian College v. Americans United for Separation of Church and State, Inc., 454 U.S. 464, 472 (1982); Flast v. Cohen, 392 U.S. 83, 96 (1968).

[130] Conducive to judicial action. Valley Forge Christian College v. Americans United for Separation of Church and State, Inc., 454 U.S. 464, 472 (1982); *see also* Bender v. Williamsport Area Sch. Dist., 475 U.S. 534, 542–543 (1986); Director v. Perini N. River Assocs., 459 U.S. 297, 305 (1983); Simon v. Eastern Ky. Welfare Rights Org., 426 U.S. 26, 39 (1976).

with a system of separated powers and which are traditionally thought to be capable of resolution through the judicial process."[131] It is designed to bar disputes that will not be resolved by judicial action.

The redressability component has on occasion been described as the causal connection between the alleged injury and the relief sought.[132] The question relevant to redressability is whether the prospect of obtaining relief from the injury as a result of a favorable ruling is unduly speculative. If the relief sought by the plaintiff would not likely remedy the injury of which the plaintiff complains, the suit will not satisfy the redressability element of standing.[133]

To demonstrate redressability, a plaintiff need not show beyond question that a favorable judgment would redress his or her injury. For example, the Supreme Court held that the plaintiffs met their burden of alleging that their injury — lack of irrigation water — would be redressed if a Fish and Wildlife Service biological opinion were set aside because the Bureau of Reclamation would be unlikely to impose minimum water restrictions in the absence of a biological opinion.[134] Further, the Supreme Court has held that the deterrent effect of civil penalties paid to the government satisfies the redressability requirement even though the penalties are paid to the public coffers.[135]

Redressability is harder to establish if relief for the plaintiff depends on actions by a third party not before the court. Redressability cannot rest on the mere assumption that a nonparty will act in a certain way on the basis of a judicial decision in the plaintiff's favor, and that such action would ultimately redress plaintiff's injury. If any prospective benefit to the plaintiff depends on the actions of independent actors who retain broad and legitimate discretion over which the court has no control, the redressability element of standing is not met.[136]

When redress depends on the actions of a third party, redressability may turn on the scope of the defendant's authority over the third party. However, if there is sufficient evidence that the third party will act in such a way as to redress the injury if the prevails in court, the redressability prong will be satisfied.

---

[131] Limitation on federal judiciary. Flast v. Cohen, 392 U.S. 83, 97 (1968).

[132] Causal connection. Allen v. Wright, 468 U.S. 737, 751 (1984) (parents of Afro-American public school students did not have standing to challenge tax exemption for segregated private schools).

[133] Striking challenged law would not remedy alleged injury. McConnell v. FEC, 540 U.S. 93, 228–229 (2003), *overruled on other grounds*, Citizens United v. FEC, 130 S. Ct. 876, 175 L. Ed. 2d 753 (2010).

[134] Set aside of biological opinion would likely redress injury. Bennett v. Spear, 520 U.S. 154, 168–171 (1997).

[135] Redressability satisfied even though penalties paid to government. Friends of the Earth, Inc. v. Laidlaw Envtl. Servs (TOC), Inc., 528 U.S. 167, 185–186 (2000) (plaintiffs had standing to seek civil penalties because sanction that effectively abated challenged conduct and prevented its recurrence provided form of redress even though plaintiff received no money).

[136] Action of nonparty. ASARCO, Inc. v. Kadish, 490 U.S. 605, 615 (1989) (teachers' association would not have standing to challenge law that allegedly imposed adverse economic impact on association and its members because invalidation of state law would not require state to devote more money to schools or necessarily result in increase in teacher salaries or benefits).

## [5] Prudential Standing Limitations

Traditionally, the standing requirement has been composed of two separate categories: the constitutional branch and the so-called "prudential" branch. The latter category consisted exclusively of subconstitutional, judge-made limitations on standing, designed to foster considerations of litigation effectiveness and judicial restraint. These prudential limitations, unlike the constitutionally dictated standing rules, could be modified or abrogated by Congress.[137] Thus, a federal statute may afford a plaintiff the express right to bring a suit, extending the plaintiff's standing to the limits permitted by the Constitution and relieving the plaintiff of the judicially created prudential standing requirements. However as a general matter, the prudential standing requirements applied unless expressly negated by Congress.[138]

However, in *Lexmark International, Inc. v. Static Control Components, Inc.*, the Supreme Court appeared to abandon any form of sub-constitutional prudential limit on standing.[139]

In deciding whether standing exists, a court traditionally considered three prudential concerns:[140]

1. Whether the alleged injury to plaintiff falls within the "zone of interests"

2. Whether the complaint raises nothing more than abstract questions, amounting to generalized grievances that are more appropriately resolved by the legislative and executive branches, and

3. Whether the plaintiff is asserting his or her own legal rights and interests, rather than those of third parties. The judiciary seeks to avoid deciding questions of broad social import if no individual rights would be vindicated, and to limit access to the federal courts to those litigants best suited to assert a particular claim.[141]

Under the zone of interests test, the interest the complaining party seeks to protect must be arguably within the zone of interests to be protected or regulated by the statute or constitutional guarantee in question.[142] In determining whether the zone of interests requirement is satisfied, the court must examine the interest

---

[137] Judge-made rules that Congress may abrogate. Bennett v. Spear, 520 U.S. 154, 162 (1997).

[138] Prudential requirements apply unless expressly negated. Bennett v. Spear, 520 U.S. 154, 163 (1997) ("Congress legislates against the background of our prudential standing doctrine, which applies unless it is expressly negated.").

[139] 134 S. Ct. 1377 (2014).

[140] Prudential factors. E.F. Hutton & Co., Inc. v. Hadley, 901 F.2d 979, 984–985 (11th Cir. 1990) (party alleging standing must surmount all of these prudential considerations).

[141] Limitation to court access. Phillips Petroleum Co. v. Shutts, 472 U.S. 797, 804 (1985); Gladstone, Realtors v. Village of Bellwood, 441 U.S. 91, 99–100 (1979).

[142] Zone of interest test. Association of Data Processing Serv. Orgs., Inc. v. Camp, 397 U.S. 150, 153 (1970) (in addition to case or controversy test, standing concerns "question whether the interest sought to be protected by the complainant is arguably within the zone of interests to be protected or regulated by the statute or constitutional guarantee in question.").

the plaintiff seeks to protect, not the identity of the plaintiff.[143]

The "zone of interests" test derived from the Supreme Court's decision in *Association of Data Processing Service Organizations, Inc. v. Camp.*[144] The case involved a suit by sellers of data processing services to businesses challenging a ruling by the Comptroller of the Currency that national banks may make data processing services available to other banks and bank customers. After articulating the "zone of interests" test, the Court held that Section 4 of the Bank Service Corporation Act of 1962, which provides that bank service corporations may not engage in any activity other than the performance of bank services for banks, brought a bank's competitor within the zone of interests protected by it.[145] Before *Camp*, the Supreme Court had generally demanded that the plaintiff demonstrate the abrogation of a "legal interest" in order to obtain standing.[146] Concluding that the "legal interest" test goes to the merits of the case rather than to standing, the Court in *Camp* substituted the liberalized "zone of interests" test.

In *Lexmark*, the Supreme Court adopted the position that "prudential standing" is a misnomer as applied to the zone-of-interests analysis, because it "is an issue that requires us to determine, using traditional tools of statutory interpretation, whether a legislatively conferred cause of action encompasses a particular plaintiff's claim.[147]

Another consideration that has sometimes been thought to be prudential is that the exercise of federal jurisdiction is not warranted if the harm asserted is merely a generalized grievance that is shared equally by a large class of citizens.[148] A claim of generalized or amorphous harm does not constitute an injury sufficient to afford standing. It is not entirely clear whether this limit on standing is appropriately viewed as a prudential or a constitutional limit.[149] In *Lexmark*, however, the Court viewed this standing limitation as constitutional.

A concrete injury is not considered a generalized grievance merely because it is suffered by many people. For example, the injury inflicted by a mass tort is widely shared, but it is not considered a generalized grievance if each victim suffers a

---

[143] Plaintiff's interest must be considered. National Credit Union Admin. v. First Nat'l Bank & Trust Co., 522 U.S. 479, 492 (1998) (issue is whether interest is arguably protected by statutory provision at issue, not whether Congress specifically intended to benefit plaintiff).

[144] Association of Data Processing Serv. Orgs., Inc. v. Camp, 397 U.S. 150 (1970).

[145] Statute barring non-bank activities brought competitor's suit within zone of interests. Association of Data Processing Serv. Orgs., Inc. v. Camp, 397 U.S. 150, 156 (1970).

[146] *See* VINING, THE LEGAL IDENTITY: THE COMING AGE OF PUBLIC LAW 20–33 (1978).

[147] 134 S. Ct. at 1387.

[148] Generalized grievance. Hollingsworth v. Perry, 133 S. Ct. 2652, 186 L. Ed. 2d 768, 779 (2013) (generalized interest in vindicating constitutional validity of California law prohibiting same-sex marriage was sort of "generalized grievance" that, "no matter how sincere, is insufficient to confer standing"); Gladstone, Realtors v. Village of Bellwood, 441 U.S. 91, 100 (1979); Schlesinger v. Reservists Comm. to Stop the War, 418 U.S. 208, 220 (1974).

[149] Prudential or constitutional. *See* FEC v. Akins, 524 U.S. 11, 23 (1998) ("Whether styled as a constitutional or prudential limit on standing, the Court has sometimes determined that where large numbers of Americans suffer alike, the political process, rather than the judicial process, may provide the more appropriate remedy for a widely shared grievance.").

particularized and differentiated harm, such as a burnt leg or a burnt arm. To be considered a generalized grievance, the injury must be undifferentiated as well as widely shared.[150]

The distinction between the two types of grievances can be seen in cases concerning voting rights. In *Baker v. Carr*, the Supreme Court held that voters had standing to challenge a state statute that allegedly apportioned seats in the state legislature arbitrarily and capriciously among the state's 95 counties. The plaintiffs argued that the statute denied equal protection to voters in the counties in which they resided because it effectively debased the value of votes from those counties. The Court concluded that the plaintiffs had a sufficiently personal stake in the outcome of the controversy to have standing.[151] In contrast, in *Lance v. Coffman*, the Court held that four Colorado citizens did not have standing to challenge a Colorado Supreme Court injunction prohibiting Colorado's secretary of state from implementing a redistricting plan passed by the Colorado legislature. The citizens argued that as interpreted by the Colorado Supreme Court, the provision of the Colorado Constitution that limited redistricting to once per census violated their rights under the Elections Clause of the United States Constitution. In denying these plaintiffs standing, the Court reasoned that the only injury alleged was that the law, in this case the Elections Clause, had not been followed, which is "precisely the kind of undifferentiated, generalized grievance about the conduct of government" that the Court had refused to countenance in the past. Unlike the plaintiffs in *Baker v. Carr*, these plaintiffs did not assert "a particularized stake in the litigation."[152] The real difference between *Baker* and *Lance* was not the number of people affected in each case, but rather the nature of the constitutional right asserted. The equal protection right asserted in *Baker* is personal in nature, while any right under the Elections Clause is held by the electorate as a whole.

Among the reasons underlying the rule barring adjudication of generalized grievances is said to be the recognition that other governmental institutions may be more competent to address questions of wide public significance.[153] Vindicating the public interest (including the public interest in government observance of the Constitution and laws) is said to be the function of Congress and the Chief Executive.[154] Such an argument, however, ignores the fact that matters of public interest may well rise to the level of constitutional violation, in which event the judiciary's proper rule is clearly implicated.

---

[150] Generalized grievance must be undifferentiated. Lujan v. Defenders of Wildlife, 504 U.S. 555, 572 (1992) (no generalized grievance when concrete injury has been suffered by many persons, as in mass fraud or mass tort situations); *see* FEC v. Akins, 524 U.S. 11, 35 (1998) (Scalia, J., dissenting).

[151] Voters in particular counties disadvantaged. Baker v. Carr, 369 U.S. 186, 203–208 (1962).

[152] Suit under Elections Clause held to be generalized grievance. Lance v. Coffman, 549 U.S. 437, 441–442 (2007) (plaintiffs whose only injury was that Elections Clause was not followed did not have standing; injury was "precisely the kind of undifferentiated, generalized grievance about the conduct of government" Court has refused to consider).

[153] Governmental domain. Lujan v. Defenders of Wildlife, 504 U.S. 555, 563 (1992) (environmental organization lacked standing to challenge endangered species regulations); Apache Bend Apartments, Ltd. v. United States, 987 F.2d 1174, 1179 (5th Cir. 1993).

[154] Other branches of government. Lujan v. Defenders of Wildlife, 504 U.S. 555, 563 (1992) (environmental organization lacked standing to challenge endangered species regulations).

The final category of traditionally recognized prudential standing concerns so-called "third party" standing. The well-established rule of third-party standing has been that in the ordinary course, a litigant must assert his or her own legal rights and interests and cannot rest a claim to relief on the legal rights or interests of third parties.

In *Lexmark*, the Supreme Court left open the issue of whether the limit on third-party standing should be deemed constitutionally dictated, now that it has rejected the concept of prudential standing. Generally, the third party whose rights or interests are at stake will be the best advocate of its own position. The Supreme Court has reasoned that if the claim is brought by someone other than the holder of the right, courts might be called on to decide abstract questions of wide public significance even though other governmental institutions may be more competent to address the questions and even though judicial intervention may be unnecessary to protect individual rights.[155] However, this general rule against third-party standing is not ironclad.

In special circumstances, the Supreme Court has authorized third party standing.[156] For example, in the context of the First Amendment, the Supreme Court has enunciated other concerns that, under very limited circumstances, may justify a lessening of prudential limitations on standing.[157] Also, the Court has allowed a litigant to assert the rights of others when enforcement of a challenged restriction *against the litigant* would result indirectly in the violation of third parties' rights.[158]

For a litigant to be able to assert the rights of third parties, three criteria must be met first, the litigant must have suffered an injury in fact, thus giving him or her a sufficiently concrete interest in the outcome of the litigation.[159] The litigant must have a close relationship to the third party whose rights are being asserted.[160] The

---

155 Third-party standing rule limits adjudication of abstract significant public issues. Kowalski v. Tesmer, 543 U.S. 125, 129 (2004); *see* Warth v. Seldin, 422 U.S. 490, 500 (1975).

156 Court lenient as to third party standing only in limited circumstances. Kowalski v. Tesmer, 543 U.S. 125, 129–130 (2004) (outside special circumstances, third-party standing is disfavored).

157 First Amendment cases. *See* Secretary of State of Md. v. Joseph H. Munson Co., 467 U.S. 947, 956 (1984) (failure to establish hindrance to right-holder's ability to protect his or her interests is not dispositive in determining whether standing exists to challenge statute that allegedly chills free speech).

158 Enforcement against litigant would indirectly violate others' rights. *See, e.g.*, Warth v. Seldin, 422 U.S. 490, 510 (1975).

159 Concrete interest. Hollingsworth v. Perry, 133 S. Ct. 2652, 186 L. Ed. 2d 768, 780–781 (2013) (proponents of Proposition 8, which amended California Constitution to bar same-sex marriages in California, did not have standing to assert State of California's interest in constitutionality of measure, because proponents did not themselves suffer injury in fact); Powers v. Ohio, 499 U.S. 400, 411 (1991) (criminal defendant has standing to challenge racial composition of jury); Caplin & Drysdale, Chartered v. United States, 491 U.S. 617, 623 n.3 (1989) (law firm had standing to challenge forfeiture law's alleged infringement of criminal defendants' Sixth Amendment right to counsel of choice); Craig v. Boren, 429 U.S. 190, 195–197 (1976) (vendors and the like are uniformly permitted to resist efforts to restrict business; because bartender could be sanctioned for serving beer to males under age 21 and females under 18, bartender had standing to assert equal protection claims of male plaintiff who attained age 21 during appeal and whose claims became moot).

160 Close relationship. Kowalski v. Tesmer, 543 U.S. 125, 129 (2004); Powers v. Ohio, 499 U.S. 400, 411 (1991) (bond of trust between defendant and jurors); Caplin & Drysdale, Chartered v. United States, 491

purpose of the close relationship requirement is to ensure that the plaintiff will act as an effective advocate for the third party. If rights holders are unable to raise their own rights, and their relationship with the plaintiff suggests an identity of interests, courts can be certain that the litigation is necessary and the issues will be framed clearly and effectively.[161] The interests of the plaintiff and the third party need not be identical; it is enough that the relationship is sufficiently close that the plaintiff will be a zealous advocate of the legal rights at issue.

A confidential relationship between the plaintiff and third parties may be sufficient. For example, in *Griswold v. Connecticut*, two persons had been convicted of illegally giving advice about contraception. The Supreme Court permitted the defendants, one of whom was a licensed physician, to assert the privacy rights of the married individuals whom they had advised. The Court pointed to the confidential nature of the relationship between the defendants and the married individuals, and reasoned that the married individuals' rights were "likely to be diluted or adversely affected" if they could not be asserted in that case.[162] A doctor-patient relationship similar to that in *Griswold* was found to exist in *Doe v. Bolton*, in which the Supreme Court also permitted physicians to assert the rights of their patients.[163]

Similarly, the parent-child relationship has been found to be sufficiently close to establish the requisite relationship between the litigant and the third party whose rights are being asserted. The nature of this relationship ensures that the parent is an effective advocate for the minor litigants' interests.[164]

The Supreme Court has also recognized that an attorney-client relationship may be sufficient to confer third-party standing.[165] For example, in *Caplin & Drysdale v. United States*, the Court granted a law firm third-party standing to challenge a drug forfeiture statute by invoking the rights of an existing client.[166]

---

U.S. 617, 623 n.3 (1989) (attorney-client relationship is one of special consequence); Singleton v. Wulff, 428 U.S. 106, 117–118 (1976) (relationship between litigant and third party may be such that litigant is as effective proponent of right as third party would be).

[161] Identity of interest. Powers v. Ohio, 499 U.S. 400, 411 (1991) (excluded juror and criminal defendant have common interest in eliminating racial discrimination from courtroom).

[162] Confidential relationship. Griswold v. Connecticut, 381 U.S. 479, 481 (1965); *see also* Eisenstadt v. Baird, 405 U.S. 438, 445–446 (1972) (stressing "advocate" relationship and impact of litigation on third-party interests); Barrows v. Jackson, 346 U.S. 249, 259 (1953) (owner of real estate subject to racial covenant granted standing to challenge covenant in part because she was "the one in whose charge and keeping repose[d] the power to continue to use her property to discriminate or to discontinue such use").

[163] Physician standing. Doe v. Bolton, 410 U.S. 179, 188–189 (1973); *see also* Singleton v. Wulff, 428 U.S. 106, 117–118 (1976); Planned Parenthood of Cent. Mo. v. Danforth, 428 U.S. 52, 62 (1976).

[164] Parent-child relationship provides basis for third-party standing. Dayton Bd. of Educ. v. Brinkman, 433 U.S. 406, 408–409 n.1 (1977) (parents had standing to raise equal protection and First Amendment claims on behalf of themselves and their children in school desegregation and school prayer cases).

[165] Attorney standing. *See* Kowalski v. Tesmer, 543 U.S. 125, 130–131 (2004); United States Dep't of Labor v. Triplett, 494 U.S. 715, 720–721 (1990); Caplin & Drysdale v. United States, 491 U.S. 617, 622–623 (1989).

[166] Invoking rights of existing client. Caplin & Drysdale v. United States, 491 U.S. 617, 622–623 (1989).

Finally, some hindrance must exist to the third party's ability to protect his or her own interests.[167] For example in *NAACP v. Alabama*, the Supreme Court held that the National Association for the Advancement of Colored People, in resisting a court order to divulge the names of its members, could assert the First and Fourteenth Amendment rights[168] of those members to remain anonymous. The Court reasoned that to require that the right be claimed by the members themselves would result in nullification of the right at the very moment of its assertion.[169]

A legal or physical inability to bring suit qualifies as an obstacle that might permit a plaintiff to bring suit on behalf of a third party. For example, in *Hodel v. Irving*, the Supreme Court ruled that Indian plaintiffs had standing to assert that their decedents' right to pass property at death had been statutorily taken without just compensation. The Court noted that because the statutory executor (i.e., the Secretary of the Interior) was charged with enforcing the statute, he could "hardly be expected to assert [plaintiffs'] rights."[170]

The cases do not demand an absolute impossibility of suit in order to fall within this exception. At the other end of the spectrum, a practical disincentive to sue may suffice, although a mere disincentive is less compelling than a concrete impediment. Moreover, if the disincentive is such that the person whose right is being asserted does not *want* it asserted, standing will probably be denied.

In *Kowalski v. Tesmer*, the Supreme Court concluded that the lack of an attorney was not the kind of hindrance necessary to allow attorney plaintiffs to assert indigent criminal defendants' constitutional rights against a challenged Michigan statute. The attorney plaintiffs conceded that an indigent denied appellate counsel has other avenues to argue that the denial is a deprivation of his or her constitutional rights. He or she could seek leave to challenge that denial in a Michigan appellate court, seek review in Michigan's highest court, and then seek a writ of certiorari in the Supreme Court. Beyond that, both state and federal collateral (habeas corpus) review would be available. The attorney plaintiffs argued that these avenues would effectively be foreclosed to indigents who did not have attorneys, but the Court noted that pro se indigents had pursued constitutional claims in both Michigan courts and in the Supreme Court.[171] Moreover, the Court inferred from the attorneys' failure to assist the indigents in pursuing their own challenge in state court that the plaintiffs wanted a federal court to short-circuit the state's adjudication of the constitutional question. The Court concluded that to permit the attorney plaintiffs to assert their claims in federal court after the indigent plaintiffs were appropriately dismissed under *Younger* abstention

---

[167] Hindrance. Kowalski v. Tesmer, 543 U.S. 125, 130 (2004); Powers v. Ohio, 499 U.S. 400, 414 (1991) ("barriers to a suit by an excluded juror are daunting."); Caplin & Drysdale, Chartered v. United States, 491 U.S. 617, 623 n.3 (1989) (attorneys had standing to raise criminal defendants' Sixth Amendment rights, even though criminal defendants faced no obstacles to raising issue).

[168] U.S. Const., Amends. I, XIV.

[169] Anonymity necessary. NAACP v. Alabama, 357 U.S. 449, 459 (1958).

[170] Statutory executor would not sue. Hodel v. Irving, 481 U.S. 704, 711 (1987).

[171] Lack of attorney insufficient hindrance. Kowalski v. Tesmer, 543 U.S. 125, 131–132 (2004).

principles because of the ongoing state proceedings would circumvent the *Younger* doctrine.[172]

In *Powers v. Ohio*, the Supreme Court noted that although a juror who has been unconstitutionally excluded from a venire has the legal right to sue on his or her own behalf, practical obstacles will render such challenges rare. Declaratory or injunctive relief against a particular prosecutor is unlikely because the violation is unlikely to recur, and the juror's financial stake in the litigation is small, relative to the costs of litigation. The Supreme Court concluded that a criminal defendant has third-party standing to raise an excluded venireperson's rights, in part because the juror possesses little incentive to set in motion the arduous process needed to vindicate his or her own rights.[173]

In *Singleton v. Wulff*, a plurality of the Supreme Court concluded that doctors had standing to raise their patients' constitutional rights in challenging a statute restricting abortion-funding. Justice Blackmun's opinion noted that a woman's concern for privacy might deter her from suing, thereby mooting her claim from a practical, if not legal, standpoint. The plurality conceded the dissent's point that those obstacles were not insurmountable (a pseudonymous or class action suit was possible, and a woman who gave birth might press her claim as "capable of repetition yet evading review"), but nevertheless held that the doctors had standing.[174]

If the third party cannot sue because it did not suffer any injury, the plaintiff will not be able to sue on the third party's behalf. The requirement that the third party actually suffered an injury is implicit in the requirements for third party standing.

Confusion exists as to whether the three factors constitute individual prerequisites to third-party standing or are, instead to be balanced. In some cases, the Supreme Court has either explicitly or implicitly held that an obstacle to the rightholder's suit is not necessarily a prerequisite for third-party standing. In *Caplin & Drysdale, Chartered v. United States*, the Court held that a lawyer had third-party standing to raise the Sixth Amendment rights of a client when challenging a statute that might have inhibited the client from paying attorney's fees. The Court concluded that even though a criminal defendant suffers no serious obstacles to advancing his or her own claim, the other two factors weighed strongly enough that the lawyer had standing.[175] Similarly, the Court has held that in First Amendment[176] overbreadth challenges, the danger of chilling expression is so

---

[172] Federalism concerns. Kowalski v. Tesmer, 543 U.S. 125, 132–133 (2004) (case had already caused unnecessary conflict between federal and state courts and confusion among state judges trying to implement conflicting commands of state's highest court, holding prestatutory practice constitutional, and Sixth Circuit, holding statute unconstitutional).

[173] Juror would not sue. Powers v. Ohio, 499 U.S. 400, 414 (1991) (criminal defendant has standing to challenge racial composition of jury).

[174] Abortion funding. Singleton v. Wulff, 428 U.S. 106, 115–118 (1976).

[175] Lawyer standing. Caplin & Drysdale, Chartered v. United States, 491 U.S. 617, 623 n.3 (1989).

[176] U.S. Const., Amend. I.

important that the showing of an obstacle is not required.[177]

On the other hand, in *Powers v. Ohio*, which upheld a litigant's standing to raise the equal protection claims of jurors peremptorily challenged due to their race, the Court's language seemed to require specific showings from would-be third-party claimants:[178]

> We have recognized the right of litigants to bring actions on behalf of third parties, provided three important criteria are satisfied: the litigant must have suffered an "injury in fact," thus giving him a "sufficiently concrete interest" in the outcome of the issue in dispute . . . ; the litigant must have a close relationship to the third party . . . ; and there must exist some hindrance to the third party's ability to protect his own interests. . . .

## [6] Associational Standing

An association has standing to sue in federal court based on either an injury to the organization in its own right or its status as the representative of its members who have been injured.[179]

The doctrine of "associational" or "representational" standing permits an organization, in certain circumstances, to premise standing entirely on injuries suffered by its members, even absent a distinct injury to itself. This doctrine does not eliminate the constitutional requirement of a live case or controversy between the parties, but it recognizes that injury to an organization's members may satisfy the requirements of Article III and allow the organization to litigate in federal court on their behalf.[180]

The test for associational standing is, much like the basic standing inquiry, composed of three parts. The plaintiff association must show all of the following:[181]

1. At least one of its members possesses standing to sue in his or her own

---

[177] First Amendment rights. Secretary of State of Md. v. Joseph H. Munson Co., 467 U.S. 947, 957 (1984) ("Although [failure to show an obstacle] might defeat a party's standing outside the First Amendment context, this Court has not found the argument dispositive in determining whether standing exists to challenge a statute that allegedly chills free speech."); *see also* Virginia v. American Booksellers Ass'n, Inc., 484 U.S. 383, 392–393 (1988) (no inquiry into obstacle in summarily upholding booksellers' standing to raise book buyers' First Amendment rights in facial challenge to statute); *see also* Amato v. Wilentz, 952 F.2d 742, 749 (3d Cir. 1991) (discussing Supreme Court cases).

[178] Peremptory challenges. Powers v. Ohio, 499 U.S. 400, 410–411 (1991).

[179] Suit in own right or representational. Warth v. Seldin, 422 U.S. 490, 511 (1975) ("There is no question that an association may have standing in its own right to seek judicial relief from injury to itself and to vindicate whatever rights and immunities the association itself may enjoy . . . . Even in the absence of injury to itself, an association may have standing solely as the representative of its members.").

[180] Live case or controversy. Automobile Workers v. Brock, 477 U.S. 274, 281 (1986).

[181] Tripartite test. United Food & Commercial Workers Union Local 751 v. Brown Group, 517 U.S. 544, 556–558 (1996) (labor union had standing to sue employer on behalf of its members for damages resulting from employer's violation of Worker Adjustment and Retraining Notification Act [WARN], 29 U.S.C. § 2101 *et seq.*); Pennell v. City of San Jose, 485 U.S. 1, 7 n.3 (1988); Automobile Workers v. Brock, 477 U.S. 274, 282 (1986) (labor union had standing to challenge guidelines for laid off workers' benefits); Hunt v. Washington State Apple Adver. Comm'n, 432 U.S. 333, 343 (1977).

right,[182] i.e., the member can satisfy the three requirements of injury traceability, and redressability.

2. The interests the suit seeks to vindicate are germane to the association's purpose; and

3. Neither the claim asserted nor the relief requested requires the participation of individual members in the lawsuit.

The first two prongs are based on Article III constitutional requirements, while the third prong is solely prudential.[183]

## [7] Taxpayer Standing

Federal taxpayers ordinarily do not have standing to challenge laws of general application if their own injury is not distinct from that suffered by other taxpayers and citizens.[184] One may not utilize the courts to challenge government taxation or expenditures as a representative of the people merely because one is a taxpayer or a citizen.

The Supreme Court in *Frothingham v. Mellon*[185] established a general rule barring federal taxpayer standing to challenge federal action. This did not mean, however, that the Court would never countenance any form of taxpayer action. In *Doremus v. Board of Education*,[186] Justice Jackson, writing for the Court, recognized the possibility of municipal taxpayer actions, "but only when it is a good-faith pocketbook action."

The Court appeared to take a different view of the federal courts' role in its subsequent decision in *Flast v. Cohen*.[187] The Court in *Flast*, however, did not overtly reject the framework established in *Frothingham*. Rather, it purported to adhere to that general framework, and merely to recognize certain limited exceptions to it.

*Flast* involved an allegation that federally appropriated funds were being used to finance instruction and purchase textbooks in religious schools, in violation of the

---

[182] Standing of one member.

[183] First two requirements constitutional; third prudential. *See* United Food & Commercial Workers Union Local 751 v. Brown Group, 517 U.S. 544, 555 (1996) (first requirement "can only be seen as itself an Article III necessity for an association's representative suit," second requirement is complementary to first, but third requirement is not constitutional necessity).

[184] No taxpayer standing. Asarco Inc. v. Kadish, 490 U.S. 605, 613–614 (1989).

[185] No taxpayer standing. Massachusetts v. Mellon, 262 U.S. 447, 486–488 (1923) (Court denied standing to taxpayer seeking to raise constitutional challenge to federal statute that provided for appropriations to states for purposes of reducing infant mortality and protecting health of mothers and infants).

[186] Financial interest. Doremus v. Board of Educ., 342 U.S. 429, 435 (1952) ("It is not a question of motivation but of possession of the requisite financial interest that is, or is threatened to be, injured by the unconstitutional conduct.").

[187] Different view. Flast v. Cohen, 392 U.S. 83, 87 (1968) (plaintiffs had standing to challenge federal funding of textbooks for religious schools).

Establishment and Free Exercise Clauses of the First Amendment.[188] In finding taxpayer standing to be proper, the Court established two elements of its "nexus" requirement for taxpayers' suits: (1) the taxpayer must be challenging a direct, rather than an incidental, expenditure of federal funds; and (2) the substantive constitutional challenge cannot be merely that the enactment exceeds congressional authority under Article I. Why either factor has any relevance whatsoever to the level of actual injury suffered by a taxpayer for purposes of standing remains a total mystery. The federal treasury can be affected as much or more by expenditures that are incidental to federal regulatory programs as by direct congressionally appropriated expenditures. In any event, in neither case is it clear that if the challenged expenditure were not to be made, the taxpayer's tax bill would be reduced.[189] Yet the Court was willing to assume that in the case of a direct expenditure, a taxpayer could satisfy the injury-in-fact requirement but would not make such an assumption for incidental expenditures.

Even more difficult to comprehend is the requirement that the taxpayer's constitutional challenge not be premised on an allegation Congress exceeded its Article I authority. It is impossible to see how this fact could in any manner affect the nature of the taxpayer's injury. The Court in *Flast* thus effectively established a constitutional non sequitur. The Court appears to have been implicitly creating an unprincipled and result-oriented exception to the injury-in-fact requirement for suits challenging federal expenditures under the Establishment Clause.

In what appears to be a type of poetic justice, some 14 years later the Court dramatically confined the reach of *Flast* by adhering literally to the contours of the *Flast* exception, even though those contours made little practical sense in the first place. In *Valley Forge Christian College v. Americans United for Separation of Church & State, Inc.*,[190] the Court denied standing to taxpayers seeking to challenge, on Establishment Clause grounds, the transfer by an executive official of government property to a Christian college. "Unlike the plaintiffs in *Flast*," the Court noted, the plaintiffs in *Valley Forge* "fail the first prong of the test for taxpayer standing" because the source of their complaint was not a congressional action, but a decision by the executive branch. Moreover, the congressional action authorizing the challenged transfer did not involve a direct expenditure of funds under the congressional spending power of Article I, section 8, but rather an exercise of Congress's power under the Property Clause of Article IV.[191] More importantly, the entire tenor of the Court's opinion in *Valley Forge* reflected a much more restrictive view towards standing than had been evinced in *Flast*. Thus, as a result of *Valley Forge*, while *Flast* has not been overruled, its reach has been severely confined.

---

[188] U.S. Const., Amend. I.

[189] Dissent. *See* Flast v. Cohen, 392 U.S. 83, 117 (1968) (Harlan, J., dissenting) ("The complaint in this case . . . contains no allegation that the contested expenditures will in any fashion affect the amount of these taxpayers' own existing or foreseeable tax obligations.").

[190] Confining reach of *Flast*. Valley Forge Christian College v. Americans United for Separation of Church and State, Inc., 454 U.S. 464, 485 (1982) (federal taxpayers lacked standing to challenge transfer of federal property to religious college).

[191] U.S. Const., Art. IV, § 3, cl. 2.

Even before *Valley Forge*, the Supreme Court seemed to confine the scope of *Flast's* allowance of federal taxpayer suits. For example, in *United States v. Richardson*, a federal taxpayer sued to have declared unconstitutional the Central Intelligence Act, which permits the CIA to account for its expenditures solely on the certificate of the CIA director, on the ground that it violates Article I, § 9, cl. 7 of the Constitution.[192] Plaintiff alleged that without detailed information on CIA expenditures (and activities), he could not intelligently follow the actions of Congress or the Executive, nor fulfill his obligations as a member of the electorate in voting for candidates seeking national office. The Supreme Court found that plaintiff had no standing, describing his injury as a generalized grievance, in that it is "plainly undifferentiated and common to all members of the public." The Court noted that the plaintiff was not "in danger of suffering any particular concrete injury as a result of the operation of the statute."[193]

In *Schlesinger v. Reservists Comm. to Stop the War*, citizens and taxpayers (among others) challenged the reserve membership of certain members of Congress as violative of Article I, § 6, cl. 2 of the Constitution,[194] which prohibits members of Congress from eligibility for appointment to certain offices, and from holding other offices. Plaintiffs sought to remove from Congress all members of the military reserve. Plaintiffs alleged that they suffered injury because members of Congress holding a reserve position in the executive branch were subject to possible undue influence by the executive branch, in violation of the concept of the independence of Congress implicit in Article I of the Constitution. The Supreme Court denied citizen standing on the ground that plaintiffs had no personal stake in the outcome of the controversy, that they failed to allege a concrete injury, and that the injury alleged constituted a generalized grievance about the conduct of the government.[195]

In *Daimlerchrysler Corp. v. Cuno*, the Supreme Court again refused to extend the scope of the *Flast* exception beyond alleged violations of the Establishment Clause. In *Daimlerchrysler*, the taxpayers complained that state franchise tax credits and city property tax exemptions given to a manufacturer violated the Commerce Clause of the U.S. Constitution and injured the plaintiffs by diminishing the funds available to the city and the state, imposing a "disproportionate burden" on the plaintiffs. The Court characterized "whatever rights plaintiffs have under the Commerce Clause" as fundamentally different from the right not to contribute to the support of any one religious establishment. The "injury" alleged in an Establishment Clause challenge to federal spending is the very extraction and spending of tax money in aid of religion, the court reasoned. An injunction against that spending would redress that injury, regardless of whether lawmakers would dispose of the savings in a way that would benefit taxpayer-

---

[192] U.S. Const., Art. I § 9, cl. 7.

[193] No concrete injury. United States v. Richardson, 418 U.S. 166, 176–185 (1974).

[194] U.S. Const., Art. I, § 6, cl. 2.

[195] No personal stake. Schlesinger v. Reservists Comm. to Stop the War, 418 U.S. 208, 217–227 (1974) (plaintiffs failed to show a "logical nexus" between the taxpayer status asserted and the claim sought to be adjudicated).

plaintiffs personally.[196] It is difficult to justify this conclusion, however, as a matter of either logic or principle. The fact that the "injury" is supposed to be the very fact of government spending for religion cannot disguise the simple fact that no true injury in fact has been suffered; the harm is purely ideological. This fact tends to confirm the very reasonable suspicion that *Flast's* authorization of taxpayer standing in Establishment Clause cases is nothing more than a result-oriented, unprincipled exception to the injury-in-fact requirement.

Although quite restricted, the *Flast* exception has not been entirely eliminated. In *Bowen v. Kendrick*, the Supreme Court applied the exception to federal taxpayers who raised an Establishment Clause challenge to the Adolescent Family Life Act, a congressional spending program, as applied by the Secretary of Health and Human Services. The Court held that the plaintiffs had standing, reasoning that their claim that AFLA funds were being used improperly by individual grantees was no less a challenge to congressional taxing and spending power simply because the congressionally authorized funding had flowed through and been administered by the Secretary.[197] Subsequently, in *Hein v. Freedom From Religion Foundation*, five justices (including four dissenters) indicated that *Flast* was correctly decided,[198] while two concurring justices argued that it should be overturned.[199]

## § 2.06 RIPENESS

The question of ripeness generally goes to whether the district court has subject matter jurisdiction.[200] However, traditionally there was also a prudential element to ripeness.

Whether that prudential element will continue following the Supreme Court's rejection of prudential limitations on standing in *Lexmark*, discussed in the prior section, remains to be seen. The ripeness doctrine concerns the timing of the suit.[201] It asks whether the case has been brought at a point so early that it is not yet clear whether a real dispute to be resolved exists between the parties. In this sense, the ripeness requirement furthers the interests of judicial restraint by avoiding

---

[196] Limit on scope of *Flast* exception. Daimlerchrysler Corp. v. Cuno, 547 U.S. 332, 346–349 (2006).

[197] Standing in Establishment Clause challenge to congressional spending program administered by executive branch. Bowen v. Kendrick, 487 U.S. 589, 618–620 (1988) ("[W]e have not questioned the standing of taxpayer plaintiffs to raise Establishment Clause challenges, even when their claims raised questions about the administratively made grants.").

[198] *Flast* correctly decided. Hein v. Freedom From Religion Foundation, Inc., 551 U.S. 587, 615–616, 643, (2007) (Kennedy, J., concurring, and Souter, J, joined by Stevens, J., Ginsburg, J., and Breyer, J., dissenting).

[199] *Flast* should be overturned. Hein v. Freedom From Religion Foundation, Inc., 551 U.S. 587, 618 (2007) (Scalia, J., joined by Thomas, J., concurring in judgment).

[200] Jurisdiction. Tari v. Collier County, 56 F.3d 1533, 1535–1536 (11th Cir. 1995) (property owners' due process and taking claims were unripe because county zoning decision was not final).

[201] Timing. Anderson v. Green, 513 U.S. 557, 559 (1995) (quoting *Regional Rail Reorganization Act, Cases*, 419 U.S. 102, 139–140) (1974) ("ripeness is peculiarly a question of timing" and "it is the situation now rather than the situation at the time of the [decision under review] that must govern"); Renne v. Geary, 501 U.S. 312, 320 (1991) (justiciability concerns appropriate timing of judicial intervention).

possible judicial interference with the other branches of government that would ultimately prove unnecessary if a live dispute were never to develop. Moreover, unless a case is ripe, a court cannot be assured that the facts have been sufficiently developed and the matter is sufficiently concrete for the court to render a decision that will resolve the dispute and affect the conduct of the parties. The ripeness doctrine therefore prevents the courts from becoming entangled in purely abstract or theoretical disagreements.[202]

The ripeness doctrine is often confused with the standing doctrine.[203] While ripeness addresses *when* the suit should be brought, standing addresses *who* may bring the suit. Determining whether a case is sufficiently ripe for adjudication often bears close affinity to questions of standing, but the two doctrines are not identical.

The doctrines of ripeness and standing are intertwined in another sense, as well. If a plaintiff has not yet suffered a concrete injury-in-fact, he or she lacks standing, even though it is possible that in the future such an injury will occur.[204] Yet such a suit could also be said to suffer from a lack of ripeness because the circumstances have not yet developed to the point where the court can be assured that a live controversy exists. On the other hand, some courts have stated that if a threatened injury is sufficiently "imminent" to establish standing, the constitutional requirements of the ripeness doctrine will necessarily be satisfied. Thus, courts may employ a mixed standing/ripeness analysis in cases involving possible injuries contingent on future events.

The ripeness and mootness doctrines are both based in part on the Article III requirement that courts decide only cases or controversies.[205] The ripeness inquiry asks whether there is a present need for the court to act, while the mootness inquiry asks whether there is anything left for the court to do. However, there is considerable confusion between the two concepts.

The burden is on the plaintiff to allege in the complaint sufficient facts to establish the court's jurisdiction. The court will review the issue for ripeness as of the time the litigation is commenced. The matter must have been ripe for review at that time; subsequent ripening of the issue while the matter is under the court's consideration on a jurisdictional motion to dismiss is not sufficient to confer jurisdiction that did not originally exist when the action was initiated.

While the court will determine whether the matter is ripe for judicial review as of the time the case is commenced, the matter must remain live throughout the course of the litigation. The threat of harm must be extant throughout the course of the litigation. If an intervening event occurs that removes the threat of harm, the

---

[202] Avoids premature adjudication. Abbott Labs. v. Gardner, 387 U.S. 136, 148 (1967) (ripeness prevents courts from entangling themselves in abstract disagreements).

[203] Confusion. Wilderness Soc'y. v. Alcock, 83 F.3d 386, 390 (11th Cir. 1996) (confusion in law of standing and ripeness is hardly surprising).

[204] Standing. Lujan v. Defenders of Wildlife, 504 U.S. 555, 560–561 (1992) (plaintiff lacks standing when it is purely speculative whether he or she will suffer injury in future); *see* § 101.40.

[205] Case or controversy. Regional Rail Reorganization Act, Cases, 419 U.S. 102, 138 (1974). For a comprehensive discussion of mootness, see Pt. D. For discussion of the case-or-controversy requirement, see Pt. A.

controversy becomes speculative, and the court should refrain from addressing the issue.[206]

This requirement is another example of the interrelation of the various doctrines of justiciability — in this instance, a blending of the concepts of ripeness and mootness. A case will be deemed moot if there is no longer a live controversy between the parties. An injury that seemed to be imminent and likely to occur at the time the case was commenced may be rendered speculative, contingent, or remote because of an intervening event.[207]

To satisfy the ripeness requirement, the issue involved must be "fit" for review.[208] The critical question concerning fitness for review is whether the claim involves uncertain and contingent events that may not occur as anticipated or may not occur at all. Encompassed within the fitness inquiry are sub-issues concerning determinations such as finality of the issue presented for review, definiteness of the threat of harm, and the extent to which resolution of the matter depends on facts not yet developed.[209] An underlying consideration is whether putting off a decision may avoid the need to make a decision altogether, preserving judicial resources and comporting with the court's role as the governmental branch of last resort, which should not make unnecessary decisions.

If further factual development of the issues before the court is unlikely to have a significant effect on the legal issue before the court, then the likelihood increases that the court can render a definitive decision on the issue.[210] Thus, a case will more likely be found to satisfy the fitness requirement for ripeness if the remaining questions are purely legal ones, and less likely to be found ripe if further factual development is required.[211]

Ordinarily, a claim involving the action of an administrative agency is fit for review only when the agency action is final. The ripeness doctrine prevents judicial

---

[206] Threat of harm must remain extant. Steffel v. Thompson, 415 U.S. 452, 459 n.10 (1974) (whether controversy remains substantial and continuing in light of changing political events must be resolved by district court on remand).

[207] Intervening event. Powell v. McCormack, 395 U.S. 486, 496 (1969) (ripe controversy can become moot).

[208] Issue must be fit for review. Abbott Labs. v. Gardner, 387 U.S. 136, 149 (1967), *overruled on other grounds by Califano v. Sanders*, 430 U.S. 99, 105 (1977) (ripeness determination evaluates both fitness of issues for judicial decision and hardship to parties of withholding court consideration).

[209] Finality, definiteness, and developed facts. Ohio Forestry Ass'n, Inc. v. Sierra Club, 523 U.S. 726, 733–737 (1998) (case not ripe for review as no significant hardship in delay and further factual development and agency refining of policy required).

[210] Legal issues unaffected by further factual development. Pacific Gas & Elec. Co. v. State Energy Resources Conservation and Dev. Comm'n, 461 U.S. 190, 201 (1983) (finding fitness for judicial review supported by "predominantly legal" nature of question presented); Duke Power Co. v. Carolina Envtl. Study Group, Inc., 438 U.S. 59, 81–82 (1978) (finding fitness for judicial review supported by fact that further factual development would neither significantly advance judiciary's ability to deal with legal issues presented nor aid in resolution).

[211] Issues presented purely legal. Thomas v. Union Carbide Agric. Prods. Co., 473 U.S. 568 (1985) (case is generally ripe if any remaining questions are purely legal ones); *see* Ohio Forestry Ass'n, Inc. v. Sierra Club, 523 U.S. 726, 733–737 (1998) (withholding review would not cause plaintiffs significant hardship as challenged plan provisions did not create adverse effects of strictly legal kind).

interference until an administrative decision has been formalized and finalized and its effects felt in a concrete way by the parties. Generally, two conditions must be satisfied for agency action to be considered final: (1) the action must mark the consummation of the agency's decisionmaking process rather than merely a tentative or interlocutory step in the process; and (2) the action must be one by which rights or obligations have been determined or from which legal consequences will flow.[212]

The purpose of the finality rule is to ensure that the issues are based on particular facts and are concrete and ripe for judicial review, and that the agency is not precluded from correcting any errors before rendering a final decision. The rule is designed to enforce this doctrine, not to require the exhaustion of administrative remedies. Thus, the finality rule allows a suit whenever a decision has been made that inflicts an actual, concrete injury. However, a case may be considered ripe for judicial review even in the absence of final agency action, when no compelling judicial interest exists to defer review.

In making a ripeness determination, courts have traditionally examined the hardship that the parties would endure if consideration of the issue were withheld on grounds that the controversy was not ripe.[213] "Hardship" means something that violates a legal right or harms the plaintiff in a practical way. The court must inquire whether the subject of the challenge presents a true dilemma for the parties, or whether their course of action would be unlikely to be altered regardless of any decision that the court could render.

Because the hardship factor requires a threat of direct and immediate harm, a mere uneasiness on the part of the plaintiff about potential implications of an anticipated action is not sufficient to establish a ripe controversy. The fact that an action, if taken, could possibly produce a harm, or that a regulation or ordinance could be interpreted in such a way as to cause hardship is insufficient to warrant judicial review if there is no indication that the action is, in fact, about to be taken, or that the regulation will be interpreted or implemented in the manner feared by the plaintiff.[214]

Ordinarily, a determination of the ripeness of a controversy for judicial review requires federal courts to evaluate both the fitness for review and the hardship of withholding federal court consideration. However, when the fitness prong of the ripeness test is satisfied and Congress has emphatically declared a preference for immediate review, no purpose is served by proceeding to, and federal courts need not address, the hardship factor.

---

[212] Two conditions for finality. Bennett v. Spear, 520 U.S. 154, 177–178 (1997).

[213] Hardship considered. Babbitt v. United Farm Workers Nat'l Union, 442 U.S. 289, 298 (1979) (dispute is ripe when there is real, substantial controversy, that is definite and concrete, not hypothetical or abstract); Abbott Labs. v. Gardner, 387 U.S. 136, 149 (1967) (discussing criteria); *see* Ohio Forestry Ass'n, Inc. v. Sierra Club, 523 U.S. 726, 732–737 (1998) (withholding review would not cause plaintiffs significant hardship as challenged plan provisions do not create adverse effects of strictly legal kind).

[214] Possibility of harm insufficient. Younger v. Harris, 401 U.S. 37, 41–42 (1971) (no live controversy existed between certain plaintiffs and state attorney general because "[n]o one has been indicted, arrested, or even threatened by the prosecutor.").

In order for an issue to be ripe for litigation, it is necessary that the court be able to grant relief or fashion a remedy in a manner that would have a conclusive effect on the dispute. This requires the existence of a real and substantial controversy, as opposed to hypothetical or abstract issues that could result in nothing more than the issuance of an advisory opinion. If the dispute concerns events that have not yet occurred, the plaintiff must show that the probability of the future event occurring is of "sufficient immediacy and reality" to have a current effect on the actions of the parties, and to provide a concrete set of circumstances on which the court can base a ruling.[215]

The "conclusiveness" test for ripeness helps to ensure that there is a live controversy for the court to review. If the court cannot render a decision that would have a conclusive effect on the issue, it means that either the likelihood of a particular event occurring is too speculative, or that the threat of harm is not real and immediate. This would violate the constitutional prohibition on the rendering of advisory opinions, as well as the prudential grounds for the ripeness doctrine. Judicial resources would be wasted rendering decisions that never take effect because the scenarios on which they were based would never come to pass. Moreover, the legal rights of the parties would not be finally determined in any helpful matter that would put an end to the dispute.

Courts are particularly vigilant to ensure that cases are ripe when constitutional questions are at issue. However, the doctrine of ripeness is more loosely applied in the First Amendment context. The broader the First Amendment right at issue, the more likely the court will find a justiciable case. In that context, in addition to hardship to the parties and fitness for judicial review, courts consider the chilling effect the challenged law may have on First Amendment liberties.

The ripeness doctrine applies differently to facial and as-applied challenges to statutes. A facial challenge asserts that a law *always* operates unconstitutionally. Therefore, in the context of a facial challenge, a purely legal claim is presumptively ripe for judicial review, because it does not require a developed factual record. An as-applied challenge, on the other hand, asserts that a statute is unconstitutional on the facts of a particular case or to a particular party. Therefore, a factual record must be developed.[216]

The ripeness doctrine limits the availability of declaratory judgments. In enacting the Declaratory Judgment Act,[217] Congress allowed parties to ascertain the potential legal consequences of their actions before taking those actions. In this sense, a declaratory judgment action enables parties to avoid potentially harmful legal results.[218] In essence, a request for declaratory relief is a request that the

---

215 Real and substantial probability. Steffel v. Thompson, 415 U.S. 452, 460 (1974).

216 Facial and as-applied challenges distinguished. *See* Suitum v. Tahoe Regional Planning Agency, 520 U.S. 725, 736 n. 10 (1997) (facial challenges to regulation are generally ripe as soon as regulation is passed, but they face uphill battle because it is difficult to demonstrate that mere enactment of regulation deprived owner of economically viable use of property).

217 28 U.S.C. § 2201; *see* Fed. R. Civ. P. 57.

218 *See* Redish, Federal Jurisdiction: Tensions in the Allocation of Judicial Power 109–110 (2d ed. 1990).

court delineate the rights, obligations, or relations of the parties so that any future action undertaken by the parties, in respect of the subject dispute, will be pre-approved by the court and will not subject the parties to additional liability. The benefits of such relief are readily apparent. Relief is generally quicker and less expensive, it may avoid the need to invoke coercive remedies, it removes uncertainty from legal relationships, and it is judicially economical to resolve controversies at an earlier stage because there are fewer facts to determine and less damages, if any, to be proven. Thus, a real and legitimate need is served by the availability of declaratory relief. For example, a party to a contract who believes that the other party's failure to comply with certain contractual requirements legally authorizes it to ignore its obligations under the contract may, before actually ignoring those obligations, seek a declaratory judgment against the other party to the effect that it now has the legal right to ignore its contractual obligations, thereby avoiding liability for breach of contract.

Like any suit filed in federal court, federal declaratory judgment actions are limited by the case-or-controversy requirement in general and the ripeness doctrine in particular. Thus, to be heard in federal court, a suit seeking a declaratory judgment cannot present a controversy that is uncertain or speculative. A tension thus exists between the declaratory judgment remedy and the doctrine of ripeness. On the one hand, a party seeking a declaratory judgment generally does so in anticipation of a future injury; on the other hand, the ripeness doctrine prevents courts from becoming involved in premature adjudication of disputes that are uncertain to occur or contingent in nature. In order to ensure that declaratory relief is not granted absent an actual case or controversy, a party requesting such relief must allege an immediate danger of sustaining an injury as a result of the adversary's conduct.

## § 2.07 MOOTNESS

The *mootness* doctrine provides that although there may be an actual and justiciable controversy at the time the litigation is commenced, once that controversy ceases to exist, the federal court must dismiss the action for want of jurisdiction.[219] The constitutional case or controversy requirement of Article III, as well as the prudential considerations underlying justiciability, are related to the mootness doctrine because each of these concepts requires that any case or dispute that is presented to a federal court be definite, concrete, and amenable to specific relief. The mootness doctrine focuses on an important and practical aspect of this requirement, namely, whether a definite controversy exists throughout the litigation and whether conclusive relief may still be conferred by the court despite the lapse of time and any change of circumstances that may have occurred since the commencement of the action.

A controversy ceases to be real or definite when the issues presented are no longer "live," or the parties lack a legally cognizable interest in the outcome. In

[219] Courts will dismiss moot cases for lack of jurisdiction. Aetna Life Ins. Co. v. Haworth, 300 U.S. 227, 240–241 (1937) (action will be dismissed if there is not a definite and concrete controversy between the parties).

other words, if the controversy initially presented to the court has been resolved during the pendency of the action, if either of the parties experiences a change in his or her legal status while the case is pending, or if the dispute has lost its adverse character due to any other reason, the court will not be able to grant effective relief unless it appears that the precise conditions of the case are likely to recur.

In contrast to the doctrine of ripeness, which refers to whether an action is unfit for review due to its prematurity, the mootness doctrine focuses on what has happened *since* the action was initiated. Whether the event that triggers a change in circumstances is the result of some factual incident that affects a party, whether it is caused by a change in the legal relations of the parties, or whether it is a consequence of action taken by a higher court or the legislature that alters the state of the law, a pending claim may be declared moot if, in the court's opinion, the relief requested would no longer serve any purpose.

In sum, the mooting of a case can occur in one of two ways. It may occur because the legal issue in dispute is no longer amenable to review and judicial relief would serve no purpose, or it may occur because a party no longer has a personal stake in the controversy and has, in essence, been divested of standing.

The Supreme Court has long held that "federal courts are without power to decide question that cannot affect the rights of litigants in the case before them."[220] If a case is found to be moot, it is assumed that the rights of the litigants can no longer be affected by a judicial decision.

To a certain extent, the theoretical foundation of the concept of mootness stems from constitutional precepts. The federal judiciary's inability to review moot cases has been said to derive from the case-or-controversy requirement of Article III of the Constitution.[221] If a case is moot, the plaintiff can no longer have a "personal stake" in the outcome.[222] The mootness doctrine thus reflects the assumptions of the "private rights" model of adjudication, under which the courts' function is confined to the resolution of concrete private controversies and their lawmaking authority is only incidental to the performance of the adjudicatory function.[223] Under this model, legal pronouncements by the judiciary that are untied to the resolution of a live controversy constitute an invasion of the legislative lawmaking power and thus a violation of separation of powers.

Not all observers have agreed, however, that the mootness doctrine can properly be grounded in the case-or-controversy requirement of Article III. Chief Justice

---

220 Supreme Court statement. North Carolina v. Rice, 404 U.S. 244, 246 (1971); *see also* DeFunis v. Odegaard, 416 U.S. 312, 316 (1974) (quoting *North Carolina v. Rice*, 404 U.S. 244, 246 (1971)).

221 Case-or-controversy requirement. U.S. Const., art. III, § 2 (extending the judicial power only to "cases" or "controversies"); *see* Liner v. Jafco, Inc., 375 U.S. 301, 306 n.3 (1964) (case or controversy requirement derives from Article III). On the general issue of the rationale underlying mootness, *see* Note, *The Mootness Doctrine in the Supreme Court*, 88 Harv. L. Rev. 373 (1974).

222 Personal stake in outcome required. Lewis v. Continental Bank Corp., 494 U.S. 472, 477–478 (1990) (parties must continue to have "a personal stake in the outcome" of the case); Franks v. Bowman Transp. Co., 424 U.S. 747, 755 (1976) (personal stake in outcome required).

223 Private rights model of adjudication. *See* Redish, The Federal Courts in the Political Order (1991).

Rehnquist, for example, has suggested that while an unwillingness to decide moot cases may be connected to the case-or-controversy requirement of Article III, it is an attenuated connection that may be overridden if there are strong reasons to override it.[224] He pointed to the so-called "capable of repetition, yet evading review" exception to the mootness requirement. A number of scholars have agreed.[225] It is certainly true that the numerous exceptions to the mootness doctrine that have been recognized are difficult to reconcile with the doctrine's supposed constitutional underpinnings in Article III. Either a particular litigation is or is not properly conceptualized as a case or controversy; the Constitution contemplates no exceptions to the requirement. Thus, it is arguable that unless the widely recognized exceptions are improper, the mootness doctrine is grounded at least in part on subconstitutional prudential notions.

While the dichotomy between constitutionally dictated limits on justiciability and prudentially dictated limits was, at least until the decision in *Lexmark*, well established in the law of standing, its application in the mootness area runs serious risks. The main problem — one that does not affect the constitutional-prudential dichotomy with respect to standing — is the inherent vagueness of the criteria for invoking prudential mootness. Courts have suggested that it applies when the case is "so 'attenuated that considerations of prudence and comity for coordinate branches of government counsel the court to stay its hand, and to withhold relief it has the power to grant.' "[226] This standard is so vague and so circular that it would seem to justify abdication of the judicial function in almost any case. Moreover, to the extent one is actually able to glean any substance from the language of the test, it would appear to redundantly perform the function already performed by the political question doctrine — namely, deference to the other branches of government.

To the extent the mootness doctrine is not constitutionally based, potentially significant consequences may result. For example, the Supreme Court could conceivably recognize an exception to mootness for cases that become moot after certiorari is granted.[227] Moreover, if not constitutionally dictated, Congress could overrule the requirement by statute. Nevertheless, a majority of the Supreme Court has never accepted Chief Justice Rehnquist's suggestion, and courts generally still deem the mootness doctrine to have ultimate grounding in Article III's case-or-controversy requirement.

---

224 Requirement of Article III. Honig v. Doe, 484 U.S. 305, 329–333 (1988) (Rehnquist, C.J., concurring, arguing for reconsideration of "our mootness jurisprudence").

225 Mootness doctrine need not be based on Constitution. *See* Lee, *Deconstitutionalizing Justiciability: The Example of Mootness*, 105 Harv. L. Rev. 605 (1992); Nichol, *Moot Cases, Chief Justice Rehnquist, and the Supreme Court*, 22 U. Conn. L. Rev. 703 (1990).

226 Prudential mootness standard based on prudence and comity for coordinate branches of government. Fletcher v. United States, 116 F.3d 1315, 1321 (10th Cir. 1997) (quoting *Building & Constr. Dep't v. Rockwell Int'l Corp.*, 7 F.3d 1487, 1491–1492 (10th Cir. 1993)).

227 Exception after certiorari is granted. *See* Honig v. Doe, 484 U.S. 305, 330 (1988) (Rehnquist, C.J. concurring, and calling for relaxing mootness test in cases in which certiorari has been granted and suggesting recognition of such an exception).

Under the mootness doctrine, the legal issues that are sought to be litigated must remain live or extant throughout the entire course of the action. Thus, a case will be considered moot when a court is no longer in a position to grant effective relief because the dispute has been resolved through other means, or the passage of time has made the claim stale and it is unlikely that the precise conditions of the case will ever recur. The clearest examples of cases in which the passage of time may render a claim moot are those in which the claim arose out of a transitory event or condition.

Just as the mere passage of time may affect the justiciability of a claim involving a transitory condition or conduct, an intervening factual event may render a case moot, thereby divesting the court of jurisdiction. Article III notions of justiciability require that the plaintiff have a personal stake in the outcome of the controversy throughout the pendency of the action. A claim may therefore be rendered moot because the plaintiff, as a result of some intervening factual event, has lost a present right to be vindicated or no longer has a stake or interest in the outcome of the litigation.

The intervening event will render the case moot only if the plaintiff is wholly divested of all personal interest in the outcome of the controversy or if the event completely eliminates the effect of the alleged violation and there is no reason to believe that the alleged violation will recur.[228] If, however, the plaintiff retains some personal stake in the controversy and there are some outstanding issues that are amenable to judicial resolution, those claims may proceed for review even though an intervening event might render other issues moot.[229]

The existence of a claim for attorney's fees does not prevent the underlying claim from becoming moot.[230] This is because the claim for attorney's fees is collateral to, and separate from, the merits decision.[231] However, the claim for attorney's fees itself may still be justiciable. When the merits of the underlying claim cannot be

---

[228] Intervening event divests plaintiff of all interest. Honig v. Students of Cal. Sch. for the Blind, 471 U.S. 148, 149 (1985) (claim by students seeking to compel their school to conduct seismic safety tests rendered moot once tests were completed); *see* City News & Novelty, Inc. v. City of Waukesha, 531 U.S. 278, 283–284 (2001) (appeal is moot when party that lost in proceedings below voluntarily ceases regulated conduct and can gain nothing from dismissal of its own petition for review).

[229] Case not moot if plaintiff retains some personal stake. *See* Pac. Bell Tel. Co. v. linkLine Communs., Inc., 555 U.S. 438, 446–447 (2009) (case was not rendered moot by plaintiffs' agreement with dissent to lower court's decision in plaintiffs' favor after Supreme Court granted certiorari, because parties continued to seek different relief; it was not clear plaintiffs had abandoned claims validity of which Court had granted certiorari to determine; parties had invested considerable time, money, and effort arguing merits of case; adversarial positions had been adequately briefed and would be adequately argued; and circuit conflict Court had granted certiorari to resolve would remain if Court did not decide case on merits).

[230] Underlying claim moot despite attorney's fee claim. *See* Lewis v. Continental Bank Corp., 494 U.S. 472, 480 (1990) (interest in attorney's fees is insufficient to create Article III case or controversy where none exists on merits of underlying claim; "Where on the face of the record it appears that the only concrete interest in the controversy has terminated, reasonable caution is needed to be sure that mooted litigation is not pressed forward, and unnecessary judicial pronouncements on even constitutional issues obtained, solely in order to obtain reimbursement of sunk costs.").

[231] Attorney's fee claim collateral to merits. *See* Budinich v. Becton Dickinson & Co., 486 U.S. 196, 200 (1988).

reviewed because the claim is moot, a court reviewing an award of attorney's fees may consider only whether the plaintiff prevailed in the lower court. It may not review or in any way reconsider the merits of the case.

Voluntary agreement between the parties to resolve the controversy by means of a defendant's promise to refrain from continuing the allegedly unlawful activity will not necessarily render the pending litigation moot if the promise has not been fully executed or there is a reasonable likelihood that the defendant will resume the unlawful activity. In such circumstances, the court will consider whether the parties' agreement fully resolves all outstanding issues and whether there remains a need for a judicial remedy if the promise or agreement goes unfulfilled.

When a large number of individuals are affected by the conduct or activity of a defendant, the concept of mootness takes on more flexible dimensions. If the claims of the named plaintiffs in a class action become moot after the class is certified, mootness has no effect on the suit or on the named plaintiffs' status as class representatives.[232]

When the claims of the named plaintiffs become moot before the class is certified, the claims of the entire class may become moot as well. However, if the nature of the claims is inherently transitory, the termination of the representative's claim prior to class certification may not moot the claims of the unnamed members of the class.[233] In such instances, certification may be deemed to relate back to the filing of the complaint if the claim is of such a transitory nature that the court cannot be expected to rule on the class certification motion before the claim expires, and the relation back doctrine will work to avoid the mooting of the entire controversy.[234] When a court is presented with a motion for class certification after the class representatives' claims have become moot, the court will usually consider the importance of the issue to be litigated in determining whether to keep the litigation alive by relating certification back to the filing of the complaint.

When a statute, regulation, or any other type of legislation is passed while litigation is pending and the new legislation corrects or cures the condition complained of, the underlying claim may be rendered moot. In such a case, there is no longer an actual controversy for the court to address and a judicial remedy is no longer needed. If a law is amended so as to remove the challenged features, a claim

---

[232] Mootness after class certification. Franks v. Bowman Transp. Co., 424 U.S. 747, 752–756 (1976) (fact that named plaintiff no longer had personal stake in outcome of certified class action does not moot class action); Sosna v. Iowa, 419 U.S. 393, 401–402 (1975) (constitutional justiciability requires that named plaintiff have case or controversy when suit filed and class is certified and live controversy throughout; controversy may be between named defendant and class member, even though named plaintiff's claim is moot).

[233] If underlying claims transitory. Gerstein v. Pugh, 420 U.S. 103, 110 n.11 (1975) (pretrial detention claim survived because of temporary nature of detention); Sosna v. Iowa, 419 U.S. 393, 401–402 (1975) (residency requirement shorter than appellate process).

[234] Certification of class relates back. County of Riverside v. McLaughlin, 500 U.S. 44, 50–52 (1991) (plaintiff's assertion that county had failed to provide prompt judicial determinations of probable cause was not rendered moot, even though claims of named plaintiffs had expired, because other remaining plaintiffs were in need of such determination before they could be released from detention).

seeking injunctive relief becomes moot as to those features.[235] New legislation may also moot a case by making it impossible for the court to grant any effective relief. At every stage in the proceedings, the court must "stop, look, and listen" in order to determine the effect of changes in law on the case before it.[236]

These principles also apply to cases in which legislation is challenged by means of a court action, but the legislation has been repealed or has expired before a judicial declaration as to its validity.[237] The repeal of a challenged statute is one of those events that makes it absolutely clear that the allegedly wrongful behavior, the threat of prosecution under the repealed statute, cannot be reasonably expected to recur.[238] The rule that a suit challenging the constitutionality of a statute is mooted by the statute's repeal absent evidence that it will likely be reenacted also applies to statutes that are repealed by implication under state law.

In the context of a declaratory relief action, the test for mootness is whether the facts alleged, under all the circumstances, show that a substantial controversy remains between parties with adverse legal interests of sufficient immediacy and reality to warrant the issuance of a declaratory judgment.[239] Because the doctrine of mootness is "the doctrine of standing set in a time frame,"[240] this test is the same as the test for standing in declaratory relief actions.[241] The claim for declaratory relief may remain live even though requests for other forms of relief have been mooted.[242]

Applying this test in *Super Tire Engineering Co. v. McCorkle*, the Supreme Court held that a request for declaratory relief with respect to the legality of state regulations that made striking workers eligible for public assistance was not moot, even though the strike that had been in progress when the suit was filed had been settled. The conclusion of the strike mooted the employer's request for injunctive

---

[235] Law amended. Lewis v. Continental Bank Corp., 494 U.S. 472, 478 (1990) (stake represented by applicant rendered moot by amendment of law).

[236] Effect of changes in law. Kremens v. Bartley, 431 U.S. 119, 135 (1977) (impact of changes in challenged statute on composition of certified plaintiffs' class).

[237] Challenged legislation repealed or expires. Friends of the Earth, Inc. v. Laidlaw Envtl. Servs., Inc., 528 U.S. 167, 189 (2000) (repeal of challenged statute makes it absolutely clear that allegedly wrongful behavior, threat of prosecution under repealed statute, cannot be reasonably expected to recur).

[238] Repeal of challenged legislation moots challenge to its validity. Friends of the Earth, Inc. v. Laidlaw Envtl. Servs., Inc., 528 U.S. 167, 189 (2000).

[239] Test for mootness in declaratory relief actions. Super Tire Eng'g Co. v. McCorkle, 416 U.S. 115, 121–122 (1974) (substantial controversy of sufficient immediacy and reality to warrant issuance of declaratory judgment remained between union and employer even after strike had been settled and workers returned to work).

[240] Standing set in time frame. *See* United States Parole Comm'n v. Geraghty, 445 U.S. 388, 397 (1980) (quoting Monaghan, Constitutional Adjudication: The Who and When, 82 Yale L. J. 1363, 1384 (1973).

[241] Same test as for standing. Biodiversity Legal Found. v. Badgley, 284 F.3d 1046, 1054 (9th Cir. 2002) (in declaratory judgment action, test for mootness is same as test for standing).

[242] Mootness of other claims irrelevant. Super Tire Eng'g Co. v. McCorkle, 416 U.S. 115, 121–122 (1974) (request for injunctive relief concerning payment of public assistance benefits to striking workers was mooted by settlement of strike, but request for declaratory relief remained live).

relief. In contrast, the request for declaratory relief was not moot, because the availability of public assistance benefits to striking employees had an effect on the ongoing collective bargaining relationship.[243]

Although a lawsuit may be technically moot, an exception to the mootness doctrine will be found if the defendant's conduct is capable of repetition, yet will evade review. The exception applies under the following circumstances:[244]

- If the challenged action is inherently too short in duration to be fully litigated before its cessation or expiration, and
- If there is a reasonable expectation that the plaintiff will again be subjected to the same action unless court intervention occurs.

This "capable of repetition, yet evading review" exception to mootness is narrow, applying only in exceptional situations and when both factors are simultaneously present.

The Supreme Court invoked the "capable of repetition, yet evading review" exception in *Roe v. Wade*, in which the Court initially recognized the constitutional right to an abortion. By the time the case reached the Supreme Court, the woman seeking to assert that right had already had her baby, arguably mooting her constitutional challenge. The Court nevertheless reasoned that when "pregnancy is a significant fact in the litigation, the normal 266-day human gestation period is so short that the pregnancy will come to term before the usual appellate process is complete. If that termination makes a case moot, pregnancy litigation seldom will survive much beyond the trial stage, and appellate review will be effectively denied. Our law should not be that rigid."[245]

One may wonder whether the "capable of repetition, yet evading review" exception fits within the logic of the mootness doctrine. Basically, the rationale for the exception appears to be that absent the exception, the court could never adjudicate the claim. But as long as the court's holding will have no impact on the immediate rights of the litigants in the case before it, why *should* the court adjudicate the claim? To be sure, if one were to reject the precepts of the "private rights" adjudicatory model in favor of one that openly recognized the value of judicial law interpretation for its own value, then recognition of such an exception to the mootness doctrine might arguably make sense.[246] But the whole point of the

---

[243] Availability of benefits had continuing effect. Super Tire Eng'g Co. v. McCorkle, 416 U.S. 115, 124–125 (1974) (dispute as to legality of making public assistance available to striking workers was not moot, despite conclusion of strike, because availability of public assistance to striking workers had continuing effect on ongoing collective bargaining relationship).

[244] Exception for conduct capable of repetition. Turner v. Rogers, 131 S. Ct. 2507, 180 L. Ed. 2d 452, 460 (2011) (appeal of state court civil contempt order for failure to pay child support was not moot because it fell within capable of repetition yet evading review exception); Spencer v. Kemna, 523 U.S. 1, 18 (1998); Murphy v. Hunt, 455 U.S. 478, 482 (1982); Weinstein v. Bradford, 423 U.S. 147, 149 (1975); Southern Pac. Terminal Co. v. Interstate Commerce Comm'n, 219 U.S. 498, 515 (1911) (exception exists for cases capable of repetition yet evading review).

[245] Abortion case. Roe v. Wade, 410 U.S. 113, 125 (1973) (since pregnancy is significant fact in litigation and appellate process outlasts period of pregnancy, case not mooted).

[246] Model favoring judicial lawmaking authority. *See* Redish, The Federal Courts in the Political Order 90–97 (1991).

mootness doctrine in the first place is to avoid such judicial lawmaking, unless it is inherently incidental to performance of its function of resolving live disputes that are before it.

By "evading review," the Supreme Court means evading Supreme Court review.[247] In other words, for an action to be fully litigable, there must be time for it to be decided by the Supreme Court before it ceases or expires. The Supreme Court has held periods of one year,[248] 18 months,[249] and two years[250] to be too short for full litigation.

The Supreme Court has made it clear that the "capable of repetition, yet evading review" exception applies only if the claim of the *very same litigant* will evade review. It is not sufficient that other, similarly situated litigants will face the same issue under similar time constraints.[251] However, this standard has been relaxed in some cases involving elections or challenges to ongoing government policies, which are discussed later in this subsection.

On occasion, it is not immediately clear whether the litigant will, in fact, face the same problem in the future. One example is *Honig v. Doe*, in which the Court applied the exception to a suit by an emotionally disturbed student seeking injunctive relief against school district officials who had suspended him indefinitely for disruptive conduct related to his disability, allegedly in violation of his rights under the federal Education of the Handicapped Act. The Act's protections terminate when the student reaches the age of 21. The plaintiff was 20 and had not yet completed high school. The Court reasoned that "[a]lthough at present he is not faced with any proposed expulsion or suspension proceedings, and indeed no longer even resides within the [same school district], he remains a resident of California and is entitled to a 'free-appropriate public education' within that State." The Court therefore concluded that there was a "reasonable expectation" that the plaintiff

---

[247] Evading Supreme Court review. *See* Nebraska Press Ass'n v. Stuart, 427 U.S. 539, 546–547 (1976) (controversy over state court orders restricting reporting of criminal trials "will evade review, or at least considered plenary review in this Court, since these orders are by nature short-lived").

[248] One year too short. Turner v. Rogers, 131 S. Ct. 2507, 180 L. Ed. 2d 452, 460–461 (2011) (12 months imprisonment for failure to pay child support was too short in duration to be fully litigated).

[249] Eighteen months too short. First Nat'l Bank of Boston v. Bellotti, 435 U.S. 765, 774 (1978) (challenge to constitutionality of state statute prohibiting plaintiffs from making campaign contributions with respect to referendum proposal was not moot even though referendum had already occurred; 18-month interval between legislative authorization of proposal and submission to voters was too short to obtain complete judicial review).

[250] Two years too short. Southern Pac. Terminal Co. v. ICC, 219 U.S. 498, 514–516 (1911) (challenge to two-year cease and desist order that had expired was not moot).

[251] Exception for same litigant. City of Los Angeles v. Lyons, 461 U.S. 95, 106 n. 7 (1983) (exception does not apply to suit by victim of police choke hold for injunction against future use of choke holds, unless it can be shown that victim faces likelihood of choke hold in future); DeFunis v. Odegaard, 416 U.S. 312, 315–317 (1974) ("capable of repetition, yet evading review" exception does not apply in suit by law student challenging constitutionality of affirmative action program in law school's admissions because that student will graduate, regardless of court's decision); *but see* Honig v. Doe, 484 U.S. 305, 335–336 (1988) (Scalia, J., dissenting, some abortion and election law decisions dispense with same party requirement, focusing on likelihood issue will recur between defendant and other members of public). Application of the exception in election cases and ongoing government policy cases is discussed further *below*.

would once again suffer a similar injury in the future.[252] Justice Scalia vigorously dissented from both the Court's holding in *Honig* and its analysis. He found it extremely unlikely that the plaintiff would ever again be placed in an identical situation, rejecting what he considered the majority's overly lenient approach to the "capable of repetition yet will evade review" exception. Justice Scalia was surely correct in suggesting that the majority had bent over backwards to find the case capable of repetition. The majority's analysis in *Honig* therefore appears to signal the Supreme Court's willingness to resolve uncertainties about the future in favor of finding a case capable of repetition.

As a general proposition, the voluntary cessation of challenged conduct by a defendant does not render the underlying controversy moot unless there is no reasonable possibility that the challenged conduct will resume.[253] The party asserting mootness bears the burden of showing that the challenged conduct is unlikely to recur.[254] Whether the voluntary cessation of activity by a defendant can provide a basis for dismissing a case on mootness grounds turns on two key questions: (1) whether the defendant is free to return to its "old ways,"[255] and (2) whether it is likely that the defendant will do so. These questions require that the court evaluate the history, pattern, and duration of the conduct engaged in by the defendant. A defendant's continued assertion of a right to engage in the allegedly wrongful conduct, despite having ceased to do so, will generally preclude a finding of mootness.[256] The court will also assess the enforceability of a defendant's promise or representation that it will not resume the allegedly impermissible conduct. This test for mootness is a stringent one.[257]

---

[252] Plaintiff might suffer similar injury in future. Honig v. Doe, 484 U.S. 305, 318 (1988) (case not moot because students still eligible for benefits program in question).

[253] Voluntary cessation does not generally moot controversy. Adarand Constructors, Inc. v. Slater, 528 U.S. 216, 221–224 (2000) (state's voluntary cessation of conduct that allegedly harmed plaintiff, in response to judgment rendered in suit to which state was not party, does not justify vacatur of that judgment, especially when that judgment was only basis for change in state's conduct); Friends of the Earth, Inc. v. Laidlaw Envtl. Servs. (TOC), Inc., 528 U.S. 167, 189 (2000) (disputed factual issues prevented determination of whether defendant's permit compliance and facility closure made it absolutely clear no violations could reasonably be expected to recur).

[254] Party asserting mootness bears burden. Friends of the Earth, Inc. v. Laidlaw Envtl. Servs. (TOC), Inc., 528 U.S. 167, 189 (2000) ("The 'heavy burden of persuading' the court that the challenged conduct cannot reasonably be expected to start up again lies with the party asserting mootness." [citation omitted]).

[255] Return to "old ways." Adarand Constructors, Inc. v. Slater, 528 U.S. 216, 221–224 (2000) (state's voluntary cessation of conduct that allegedly harmed plaintiff, in response to judgment rendered in suit to which state was not party, does not justify vacatur of that judgment, especially when that judgment was only basis for change in state's conduct); United States v W.T. Grant Co., 345 U.S. 629, 632 (1953) (voluntary cessation does not deprive court of power to hear case).

[256] Assertion of right to engage in conduct generally precludes mootness. *See* Knox v. SEIU, Local 1000, 132 S. Ct. 2277, 183 L. Ed. 2d 281, 295 (2012) (union's post-certiorari notice to non-union member employees concerning their right to refund of certain assessed fees did not moot employees' claim concerning need to provide notice; because union continued to defend legality of fee, "it is not clear why the union would necessarily refrain from collecting similar fees in the future").

[257] Stringent test. Friends of the Earth, Inc. v. Laidlaw Envtl. Servs. (TOC), Inc., 528 U.S. 167, 189 (2000) (disputed factual issues prevent determination of whether stringent standard can be met).

Cessation of the complained-of conduct by government officials has been treated with more solicitude by the courts than similar action by private parties. Some courts apply a presumption that the government officials are acting in good faith.

In order to obtain a dismissal of the case on mootness grounds, the party asserting mootness (normally the defendant) bears the burden of establishing that its voluntary cessation of objectionable conduct is permanent in nature.[258] The plaintiff's failure to offer admissible evidence that the defendants are likely to repeat the wrongful conduct is not enough to satisfy the burden. In the final analysis, the determination as to whether the voluntary cessation exception should be applied will be based on a balancing of factors, namely, the facts presented by the defendant to establish that it has ceased and will not resume the conduct, as measured against the possibility of recurrence and the public interest in having the case decided on its merits.

## § 2.08 POLITICAL QUESTION DOCTRINE

The political question doctrine presents issues of justiciability distinct from those implicated by the concepts of standing, mootness, and ripeness. As a general matter, the doctrine requires federal courts to abstain from the review of constitutional claims that are more amenable to resolution by other branches of the federal government instead of rendering a judgment on the merits.[259] But the precise nature of the doctrine is difficult to define, not only because the various elements that characterize a political question may differ depending on the context of each case, but also because the courts have not always made clear whether their decisions were based on the political question doctrine or on some other legal principle. The confusion that has resulted from seemingly inconsistent decisions has led commentators to disagree about the scope and rationale of the doctrine, and even to question whether a political question doctrine actually exists.[260] Perhaps the most that can be definitively said is that application of the political question doctrine requires a case-by-case analysis ,in order to determine whether the doctrine's broad criteria have been met.[261] for a discussion of application of the political question

---

[258] Defendant's burden. Friends of the Earth, Inc. v. Laidlaw Envtl. Servs. (TOC), 528 U.S. 167, 189 (2000) ("The 'heavy burden of persuading' the court that the challenged conduct cannot reasonably be expected to start up again lies with the party asserting mootness" (citation omitted)).

[259] Political question doctrine. Baker v. Carr, 369 U.S. 186, 217 (1962); (political question doctrine did not bar former state justice's 42 U.S.C. § 1983 federal civil rights suit against state senators asserting constitutional claims arising from impeachment and removal and seeking damages and declaratory and injunctive relief merely because case required court to review actions of state legislature).

[260] Existence of doctrine questioned. *Compare* Henkin, *Is There a "Political Question" Doctrine?* 85 Yale L.J. 597, 600–601 (1976) (cases that are supposed to have established political question doctrine required no extraordinary abstention from judicial review, only ordinary respect of courts for authority of President or Congress), *with* Redish, *Judicial Review and the "Political Question,"* 79 Nw. U. L. Rev. 1031, 1033–1039 (1985) (doctrine has been recognized and employed by Supreme Court, though it is based on incorrect understanding of judicial review theory); *see also* Nagel, *Political Law, Legalistic Politics: A Recent History of the Political Question Doctrine,* 56 U. Chi. L. Rev. 643, 668 (1989) (political question doctrine is largely incomprehensible).

[261] Case-by-case analysis. Baker v. Carr, 369 U.S. 186, 210–211 (1962) (much confusion results from capacity of political question label to obscure need for case-by-case analysis).

doctrine to specific situations.

### [1] Theoretical Underpinnings of Political Question Doctrine

The political question doctrine is thought to derive from the separation of powers principles inherent in the Constitution.[262] In reality, however, the doctrine represents a perversion of the concept of separation of powers because it dictates that the one truly countermajoritarian branch of government — the judiciary — abdicate its function as the final arbiter and enforcer of the countermajoritarian Constitution. As a result, it makes the very majoritarian branches sought to be regulated by that document the final arbiters of the constitutional limits on their own power.[263] While the doctrine purports to limit judicial abdication to a relatively narrow group of circumstances, careful analysis demonstrates that no logical basis exists on which to distinguish these situations from all other instances of judicial review.[264]

It is true that when the Supreme Court first established the power of the judicial branch of government to review determinations of the legislative and executive branches in *Marbury v. Madison*,[265] it recognized the existence of some questions that it could not decide because they were political in nature or were committed by the Constitution to another branch of government.[266] However, Chief Justice Marshall's reference in *Marbury* to "political questions" possessed a very different meaning from the one attributed to it by the modern version of the doctrine. In context, Marshall's reference was solely to constitutional challenges that had no validity on the merits because the Constitution itself provided no guidelines for the exercise of the governmental power in question. Far from constituting an abdication of judicial power, then, Chief Justice Marshall's statement represented an indication of the Court's views on the merits of the substantive constitutional issue.

In order to understand both the theoretical and practical ramifications of the modern political question doctrine, it is necessary initially to examine the doctrine's alternative structural frameworks. A formulation of the political question doctrine in terms of a constitutional commitment to another branch of government is commonly referred to as the "classical" version of the doctrine. Structuring the doctrine in terms of factors other than a constitutional commitment to another branch of government is commonly referred to as the "prudential" version of the doctrine. Although some commentators have expressed a preference for either the

---

[262] Separation of powers. Baker v. Carr, 369 U.S. 186, 210 (1962) (nonjusticiability of political question doctrine is primarily function of separation of powers); *see* U.S. Const., arts. I–III.

[263] *See* Redish, *Judicial Review and the "Political Question"*, 79 Nw. U. L. Rev. 1031 (1985). For a contrary theoretical approach, *see* Nagel, *Political Law, Legalistic Politics: A Recent History of the Political Question Doctrine*, 56 U. Chi. L. Rev. 643 (1989).

[264] *See* Redish, The Federal Courts in the Political Order 111–139 (1991).

[265] Power of judicial review. *See* Marbury v. Madison, 5 U.S. (1 Cranch) 137, 177 (1803) (judiciary possesses judicial review power).

[266] Existence of political questions. *See* Marbury v. Madison, 5 U.S. (1 Cranch) 137, 170 (1803) (certain questions cannot be decided by Court).

narrow, classical version or the broad, prudential version of the doctrine,[267] both versions may be criticized as in conflict with the constitutional duty of courts — dictated by the nature and logic of a countermajoritarian Constitution — to conduct judicial review of the actions of the majoritarian branches of government.[268]

It should be noted that the political question doctrine is purely a matter of separation of powers; it in no way implicates federalism concerns. It is the relationship between the federal judiciary and other branches of the *federal* government, not the relationship between the federal judiciary and the states, that gives rise to the political question doctrine.[269]

The political question doctrine precludes judicial review of "political questions," not "political cases."[270] The mere fact that a lawsuit seeks the protection of a political right does not mean that it presents a political question.[271] The courts cannot abstain from reviewing a bona fide controversy as to whether an action deemed "political" exceeds constitutional authority.[272] For example, a right to relief from discrimination under the Equal Protection Clause is not limited by the fact that the discrimination relates to political rights.[273] Similarly, the fact that a decision will have political implications does not render it non-justiciable under the political question doctrine.

The issue of what constitutes a political question has been complicated by the fact that the courts have formulated the doctrine in different terms, depending on the context in which the doctrine has been applied.[274] The elements of a political question that are applied in a case involving foreign relations may not be the same as those applied in a case involving the electoral process or in a case involving the validity of enactments.

In the landmark case of *Baker v. Carr*, the Supreme Court undertook a detailed analysis of the preceding cases to trace the contours of the political question

---

[267] Classical version versus prudential version. *Compare* Wechsler, *Toward Neutral Principles of Constitutional Law*, 73 HARV. L. REV. 1, 6–9 (1959), *with* Bickel, *The Supreme Court, 1960 Term — Foreword: The Passive Virtues*, 75 HARV. L. REV. 40, 75 (1961).

[268] Duty of judicial review. *See* Redish, *Judicial Review and the "Political Question,"* 79 NW. U. L. REV. 1031, 1059, 1060 (1985) (once we make initial assumption that judicial review plays legitimate role in constitutional democracy, we must abandon political question doctrine in all of its manifestations); *see* Marbury v. Madison, 5 U.S. (1 Cranch) 137, 177 (1803) (it is province and duty of judicial branch to say what law is).

[269] Relationship between federal and state governments does not implicate political question doctrine. Baker v. Carr, 369 U.S. 186, 210 (1962).

[270] Political question doctrine. Baker v. Carr, 369 U.S. 186, 217 (1962).

[271] Political right versus political question. Baker v. Carr, 369 U.S. 186, 209 (1962); Nixon v. Herndon, 273 U.S. 536, 540 (1927) (such a suggestion represents little more than play on words).

[272] Review of actions deemed political. Baker v. Carr, 369 U.S. 186, 217 (1962).

[273] Right to relief not diminished. Baker v. Carr, 369 U.S. 186, 210 (1962); Snowden v. Hughes, 321 U.S. 1, 11 (1944).

[274] Formulation of doctrine in different terms. Baker v. Carr, 369 U.S. 186, 210 (1962) (attributes of political question doctrine, in various settings, diverge, combine, appear, and disappear in seeming disorderliness).

doctrine.[275] Emphasizing that several formulations that vary according to context may describe a political question, the Court in *Baker v. Carr* summarized the elements of a political question that may be present within alternative formulations. Prominent on the surface of any case held to involve a political question, the Court found at least one of the following:[276]

1. A textually demonstrable constitutional commitment of the issue to a coordinate political department; or
2. A lack of judicially discoverable and manageable standards for resolving the issue; or
3. The impossibility of deciding the issue without an initial policy determination of a kind clearly for nonjudicial discretion; or
4. The impossibility of a court's undertaking independent resolution of the issue without expressing lack of the respect due coordinate branches of government; or
5. An unusual need for unquestioning adherence to a political decision already made; or
6. The potentiality of embarrassment from multifarious pronouncements by various departments on one question.

The majority in *Baker v. Carr* concluded that a federal constitutional challenge to the method of apportioning members of a state legislature among counties presented no nonjusticiable political question because none of the elements of a political question that it had identified were present in that case. There was no question to be decided by a branch of government coequal with the Court. Nor did the Court risk embarrassment of the government abroad or a grave disturbance at home. The Court believed that it had not been asked to render policy determinations for which judicially manageable standards were lacking because judicial standards under the Equal Protection Clause of the Fourteenth Amendment[277] were both well developed and familiar.[278]

The Supreme Court has expressed continuing approval of the analysis contained in *Baker v. Carr*.[279] Although its holding was limited to the context of the case,[280] the decision has been cited with approval in cases involving different contexts.[281] But because *Baker v. Carr* leaves room for different formulations of the political

---

[275] Detailed analysis of cases. Baker v. Carr, 369 U.S. 186, 211–226 (1962).

[276] Elements of political question. Baker v. Carr, 369 U.S. 186, 217 (1962).

[277] Equal Protection Clause. *See* U.S. Const., Amend. XIV, § 1.

[278] *Baker v. Carr*. Baker v. Carr, 369 U.S. 186, 226 (1962).

[279] Continuing approval. *See, e.g.*, Vieth v. Jubelirer, 541 U.S. 267, 277 (2004) (plurality refers to *Baker v. Carr* criteria as six separate tests); Nixon v. United States, 506 U.S. 224, 228 (1993) (controversy involves political question when elements identified in *Baker v. Carr* are present); Davis v. Bandemer, 478 U.S. 109, 121–127 (1986) (majority declined implicit invitation of minority to rethink approach of *Baker v. Carr*); Powell v. McCormack, 395 U.S. 486, 518–519 (1969) (elements identified in *Baker v. Carr* are reiterated).

[280] Holding limited to context. Baker v. Carr, 369 U.S. 186, 210 (1962) ("[w]e do not explore implications of cases being reviewed in contexts other than this apportionment case").

[281] Different contexts. *See* Nixon v. United States, 506 U.S. 224 (1993) (impeachment); Powell v.

question doctrine within different contexts, it is impossible to predict which elements of a political question may be considered relevant in a particular context without analyzing cases that have already been decided in the same context. The Supreme Court has suggested that the *Baker v. Carr* tests are listed in descending order of importance and certainty.[282] The import of the first two tests is borne out in Supreme Court and lower court cases.[283]

In a concurring opinion in *Zivotofsky v. Clinton*, Justice Sotomayor distilled the six *Baker* factors into three distinct justifications for withholding judgment on the merits: (1) the court lacks authority to resolve the issue (factor 1); (2) the decision is beyond the courts' competence to make (factors 2 and 3); and (3) prudential considerations (factors 4–6). Courts should be particularly cautious in abstaining on the basis of the last three circumstances, she opined. However, she acknowledged that there are rare occasions in which such abstention will be appropriate to accommodate considerations inherent in the separation of powers and Article III limitations on the courts.[284]

It is unclear the extent to which the elements of the political question doctrine intersect. While the Supreme Court has stated that a single element may be sufficient to trigger the doctrine's application in at least some contexts,[285] the decisions in cases in which the courts have held a nonjusticiable political question to be present have often rested on findings of multiple elements. In *Nixon v. United States*, for example, the Court intimated that some elements of a political question may be inextricably bound together, stating:[286]

> [T]he concept of a textual commitment to a coordinate political department is not completely separate from the concept of judicially discoverable and manageable standards for resolving it; the lack of judicially manageable standards may strengthen the conclusion that there is a textually demonstrable commitment to a coordinate branch.

---

McCormack, 395 U.S. 486 (1969) (exclusion from Congress).

[282] Factors listed in descending order of importance. Vieth v. Jubelirer, 541 U.S. 267, 278 (2004); *but see* United States v. Munoz-Flores, 495 U.S. 385, 390–393 (1990) (briefly dismissing other *Baker* formulations after explaining that mere judicial scrutiny of congressional enactment does not show lack of respect for Congress under fourth *Baker* formulation).

[283] First two tests are most important. *See, e.g.*, Zivotofsky v. Clinton, 132 S. Ct. 1421, 182 L. Ed. 2d 423, 429 (2012) (controversy involves political question "where there is a textually demonstrable constitutional commitment of the issue to a coordinate political department; or a lack of judicially discoverable and manageable standards for resolving it" [internal quotation marks and citations omitted]; political question doctrine did not bar review of claim that United States citizen born in Jerusalem was entitled to have "Israel" recorded on his passport as his birthplace); Powell v. McCormack, 395 U.S. 486, 548–549 (1969) (dismissing five *Baker* formulations as inapplicable after extensive discussion of first formulation).

[284] Three justifications for withholding judgment on merits. Zivotofsky v. Clinton, 132 S. Ct. 1421, 182 L. Ed. 2d 423, 434–436 (2012) (Sotomayor, J., concurring; *Baker* factors reflect three distinct justifications for withholding judgment on merits).

[285] Single element may be sufficient. Baker v. Carr, 369 U.S. 186, 217 (1962) (each formulation has one or more elements of political question).

[286] Elements may be bound together. Nixon v. United States, 506 U.S. 224, 228–229 (1993).

The majority in *Nixon* held that a nonjusticiable political question was presented by a claim that the U.S. Senate violated the Impeachment Trial Clause of the U.S. Constitution[287] by permitting a committee of Senators to hear evidence against a federal judge who had been impeached and to report that evidence to the full Senate. In addition to finding a textual commitment of the trial of impeachments to the Senate, the Court was persuaded that the lack of finality and the difficulty of fashioning relief counseled against justiciability.[288] On the other hand, if *none* of the *Baker* elements is present, the case cannot be dismissed under the political question doctrine.[289]

Much confusion has resulted from the fact that the courts have not always made clear whether their decisions are based on the political question doctrine or on some other constitutional or jurisdictional principle. In many cases, it is difficult to determine whether the court is applying the political question doctrine or making a judgment on the merits of the constitutional issue.[290] Contributing to this difficulty is the practical consideration that there may be no immediate difference in the outcome of a case as a result of either (1) declining judicial review by invoking the political question doctrine in deference to a constitutional commitment of the matter to the legislative or executive branch of government, or (2) affirming on the merits the action taken by the legislative or executive branch out of respect for the discretion and expertise possessed by that branch.[291] In fact, the words "deference to" and "respect for" are sometimes used interchangeably without regard to whether the political question doctrine is being invoked or judgment is being made on the merits. Some cases that the courts have purported to decide on the merits have constituted "exercises of the political question doctrine in everything but name."[292] The one clear difference between invocation of the political question doctrine and an invocation of deference on the substantive merits, however, is that at least as a technical matter, the former does not constitute a judicial affirmation

---

[287] Impeachment Trial Clause. *See* U.S. Const., art. I, § 3, cl. 6.

[288] Lack of finality and difficulty in fashioning relief. Nixon v. United States, 506 U.S. 224, 236 (1993).

[289] At least one element required. Baker v. Carr, 369 U.S. 186, 217 (1962) ("Unless one of these formulations is inextricable from the case at bar, there should be no dismissal for nonjusticiability on the ground of a political question's presence.").

[290] Political question doctrine versus decision on merits. *See, e.g.*, Shaughnessy v. United States ex rel Mezei, 345 U.S. 206, 210–216 (1953) (Court accepted executive branch determination to exclude without hearing alien who traveled abroad after 20 years as legal resident); United States *ex rel.* Knauff v. Shaughnessy, 338 U.S. 537, 542–547 (1950) (whatever procedure for exclusion was authorized by Congress, it was due process as far as alien was concerned).

[291] No substantive difference. *See* Henkin, *Is There a "Political Question" Doctrine?*, 85 Yale L.J. 597, 598–600 (1976) (failure to maintain distinction between ordinary respect for substantive decisions of political branches and extraordinary deference to those decisions has aggravated confusion and controversy).

[292] Exercise of doctrine in everything but name. *See* Redish, *Judicial Review and the "Political Question,"* 79 Nw. U.L. Rev. 1031, 1037–1039 (1985); *see also* Korematsu v. United States, 323 U.S. 214, 217–225 (1944) (authority to exclude all persons of Japanese ancestry from west coast military areas was not beyond war powers of Congress and executive branch); Hirabayashi v. United States, 320 U.S. 81, 92–105 (1943) (authority to prescribe curfew for all persons of Japanese ancestry was within constitutional authority of Congress and executive branch to prescribe emergency war measures); *see also* Weisselberg, *The Exclusion and Detention of Aliens: Lessons From the Lives of Ellen Knauf and Ignatz Mezei*, 143 U. Pa. L. Rev. 933 (1995).

of the constitutionality of the challenged governmental action, while the latter does.

Even when it is evident from the context of a case that the court is applying the political question doctrine, the term "political question" may not actually appear in the opinion. After discussing matters that are recognizable as elements of a political question, the court may simply conclude that the issue in question is either "justiciable" or "nonjusticiable." Or the court may state that a determination of the legislative or executive branch of government is "conclusive" or "binding" on the court.[293] Or a court may use a term such as "separation of powers concerns" in place of the term, "political question."[294] In at least one case, the Supreme Court used both "separation of powers" and "political question" as if they referred to two different legal concepts.[295]

Another consideration that may muddy the waters in cases involving the political question doctrine is that a court may find it necessary to delve into the merits of a case in some detail before determining whether a political question is present.[296] In these cases, the courts do appear to be interpreting constitutional text and thus rendering a decision on the constitutional merits, despite their subsequent invocation of the political question doctrine.

Moreover, the political question doctrine has difficulty commanding a working majority on the courts A fundamental disagreement among the justices regarding application of the political question doctrine, with only a plurality of justices joining in the opinion of the Court or the delivery of multiple contradictory opinions, is not uncommon.[297]

There is no bright-line test for what constitutes a political question.[298] Different elements of a political, or different combinations of elements, may be relevant in different contexts.[299] Deciding whether a matter has been constitutionally commit-

---

[293] Conclusive or binding on court. *See, e.g.*, Ex parte Republic of Peru, 318 U.S. 578, 589 (1943) (certification by executive branch of foreign government's claim of sovereign immunity must be accepted by courts as "conclusive" determination); Oetjen v. Central Leather Co., 246 U.S. 297, 302 (1918) (determination by executive branch of sovereignty over territory "conclusively binds" courts).

[294] Separation of powers concerns. *See, e.g.*, Vander Jagt v. O'Neill, 699 F.2d 1166, 1173–1174 (D.C. Cir. 1982) (though political question doctrine is useful as checklist of separation-of-powers concerns, court should avoid reliance on it as talismanic label); Riegle v. Federal Open Mkt. Comm., 656 F.2d 873, 881 (D.C. Cir. 1981) (political question doctrine is not sufficiently catholic in formulation or flexible in application to resolve prudential issues arising in congressional plaintiff cases).

[295] Two different legal concepts. *See* Elrod v. Burns, 427 U.S. 347, 352 (1976) (separation of powers principle, like political question doctrine, has no applicability to relationship of federal judiciary to states).

[296] Need to delve into merits of case. *See* Baker v. Carr, 369 U.S. 186, 217 (1962) (decided cases show necessity for discriminating inquiry into precise facts and circumstances of particular case); *see also* Nixon v. United States, 506 U.S. 224, 228 (1993) (courts must, in first instance, interpret text of Constitution to determine whether and to what extent issue is textually committed to coordinate political department).

[297] Disagreement among justices. *See, e.g.*, Goldwater v. Carter, 444 U.S. 996 (1979) (plurality of four justices found presence of nonjusticiable political question).

[298] No bright-line test. Baker v. Carr, 369 U.S. 186, 217 (1962) (impossibility of achieving successful resolution by semantic cataloguing).

[299] Different elements in different contexts. *See* Baker v. Carr, 369 U.S. 186, 217 (1962) (several

ted to another branch of government, or whether that branch has exceeded its authority, is invariably a delicate exercise in constitutional interpretation.[300]

For all of these reasons, application of the political question doctrine requires a case-by-case analysis.[301] When deciding whether issues present political questions, courts must make a discriminating inquiry into the precise facts and posture of the particular case because the doctrine resists resolution by any semantic cataloguing.

The Guaranty Clause provides that the United States shall guarantee to every state a republican form of government and shall protect each state against invasion. On application of the legislature of a state, or the executive of the state when the legislature cannot be convened, the United States shall protect the state against domestic violence.[302] One branch of political question cases has established that enforcement of the Guaranty Clause belongs to the political departments of the federal government and not to the judiciary.[303]

In *Luther v. Borden*, the Supreme Court affirmed the refusal of a state court to receive evidence concerning which of two competing groups represented the lawful government of Rhode Island during an armed insurrection. When the state court ruled that the earlier established charter government was the lawful government of the state, the appellant claimed that recognition of the charter government violated the Guaranty Clause of the Constitution. Refusing to review the Guaranty Clause claim, the Supreme Court held that the power to decide what government was established in a state rested with Congress, whose decision was binding on the courts. Congress had enacted legislation authorizing the President to activate the militia on application of the legislature or the executive of a state in the event of an insurrection, and the President had recognized the governor of the charter government as the executive of Rhode Island. Under the circumstances, no court would be justified in recognizing the opposing party as the lawful government of the state.[304]

After *Luther v. Borden*, the Supreme Court invoked the political question doctrine to deny judicial review of such issues as whether the federal Reconstruction Act of 1867 violated the Guaranty Clause,[305] whether the power of a state legislature to decide the outcome of a gubernatorial election contest violated the

---

formulations that vary according to context may describe political question).

[300] Delicate exercise in constitutional interpretation. Baker v. Carr, 369 U.S. 186, 211 (1962).

[301] Case-by-case analysis. Baker v. Carr, 369 U.S. 186, 211 (1962) (court must analyze representative cases to decipher analytical threads that make up political question doctrine); *see* Regan v. Wald, 468 U.S. 222 (1984) (case-by-case analysis applied to issue of freedom to travel); Dames & Moore v. Regan, 453 U.S. 654 (1981) (case-by-case analysis applied to issue of freezing foreign assets and suspending claims).

[302] Guaranty Clause. U.S. Const., art. IV, § 4.

[303] No judicial enforcement. *See* Taylor v. Beckham (No. 1), 178 U.S. 548, 578–581 (1900).

[304] Luther v. Borden. Luther v. Borden, 48 U.S. (7 How.) 1, 39–47 (1849); *cf.* Moyer v. Peabody, 212 U.S. 78, 81–82 (1909) (Court accepted as conclusive, without action by President, determination by governor of Colorado, confirmed by state supreme court, that existence of insurrection justified imprisonment without trial); Scharpf, *Judicial Review and the Political Question: A Functional Analysis*, 75 Yale L.J. 517, 538–539 (1966).

[305] Federal reconstruction. Georgia v. Stanton, 73 U.S. (6 Wall.) 50, 71–77 (1867) (Court lacked subject matter jurisdiction over case involving merely political rights).

Guaranty Clause,[306] whether state laws permitting initiative and referendum elections violated the Guaranty Clause,[307] whether procedures for amending a state constitution violated the Guaranty Clause,[308] and whether a supermajority voting requirement for state supreme court judges violated the Guaranty Clause.[309] In each case, claims grounded in the Guaranty Clause were held nonjusticiable because they implicated one or more traditional elements of a political question, not because they involved matters of state government organization.[310] The presence of nonjusticiable claims based on the Guaranty Clause, however, has not prevented the Court from rendering a judgment based on distinct constitutional claims presented in the same case.[311]

In *New York v. United States*, the Supreme Court raised questions concerning the continued viability of the political question doctrine as a bar to judicial review of Guaranty Clause claims. The Court held that Congress had the power to enact a statute requiring the states to provide for disposal of low-level radioactive waste. In response to a claim that the statute violated the Guaranty Clause, the Court stated that even assuming the claim to be justiciable, the statute could not reasonably be said to deny any state a republican form of government.[312]

The Court commented that in most cases, it had found Guaranty Clause claims to be nonjusticiable under the political question doctrine. But this view had not always been accepted by the Court. Before the limited holding of *Luther v. Borden* was elevated into a general rule of nonjusticiability, the Court had addressed the merits of claims based on the Guaranty Clause without any suggestion that the claims were nonjusticiable. The Court noted that more recently, it had suggested that perhaps not all claims under the Guaranty Clause presented nonjusticiable political questions.[313] In the absence of a reasonable Guaranty Clause claim, the

---

306 Gubernatorial election contest. Taylor v. Beckham (No. 1), 178 U.S. 548, 578–581 (1900) (it was long ago settled that enforcement of Guaranty Clause belongs to political department).

307 Initiative and referendum. Pacific States Tel. & Tel. Co. v. Oregon, 223 U.S. 118, 141–151 (1912) (Court lacked jurisdiction over Guaranty Clause issues that were committed to Congress and therefore not within reach of judicial power).

308 Amendment of state constitution. Marshall v. Dye, 231 U.S. 250, 256–257 (1913) (claim under Guaranty Clause presented no justiciable controversy).

309 Voting requirement for judges. Ohio *ex rel.* Bryant v. Akron Metro. Park Dist., 281 U.S. 74, 79–80 (1930) (questions arising under Guaranty Clause were political, not judicial, in character); *see* Bonfield, *The Guarantee Clause of Article IV, Section 4: A Study in Constitutional Desuetude*, 46 Minn. L. Rev. 513 (1962).

310 Political question doctrine does not apply to matters of state government organization. *See* Baker v. Carr, 369 U.S. 186, 228–229 (1962) (presence of matter affecting state government organization does not render case nonjusticiable).

311 Separate constitutional claims. *See* Baker v. Carr, 369 U.S. 186, 228 (1962) (nonjusticiability of claims based on Guaranty Clause has no bearing on justiciability of claim based on Equal Protection Clause of Fourteenth Amendment); *see also* Mountain Timber Co. v. Washington, 243 U.S. 219, 234–235 (1917) (due process and equal protection challenges to workers' compensation law were reviewed on merits after Guaranty Clause claim was denied judicial review).

312 Guaranty Clause not violated. New York v. United States, 505 U.S. 144, 183–186 (1992).

313 Some claims under Guaranty Clause may be justiciable. New York v. United States, 505 U.S. 144, 184–186 (1992); *see* Reynolds v. Sims, 377 U.S. 533, 582 (1964) ("some" questions raised under Guaranty Clause are nonjusticiable).

Court considered it unnecessary to resolve this difficult question in the case before it.[314]

*New York v. United States* also involved a claim under the Tenth Amendment, which provides that powers not delegated to the United States by the Constitution, nor prohibited by it to the states, are reserved to the states, respectively, or to the people.[315] Because of the absence of federal separation of powers concerns, the political question doctrine has traditionally failed to play the same role in barring Tenth Amendment claims as it has in precluding Guaranty Clause claims.[316]

The courts have traditionally recognized foreign relations as an activity best suited to control by the legislative and executive branches of government. As stated by the Supreme Court in *Baker v. Carr:*

> Not only does resolution of [questions touching foreign relations] frequently turn on standards that defy judicial application, or involve the exercise of a discretion demonstrably committed to the executive or legislature; but many such questions uniquely demand single-voiced statement of the Government's views.[317]

Even in the area of foreign relations, however, a role for the judiciary remains. The cases generally employ a careful analysis of the particular question posed in terms of the history of its management by the legislative and executive branches, its susceptibility to judicial handling in the specific case, and the possible consequences of judicial action.

Most fundamental to the conduct of foreign relations is the recognition of foreign governments. The courts adhere to the decision of the executive branch as to which government has sovereignty over disputed territory.[318] But once the question of

---

[314] Unnecessary to resolve difficult question. New York v. United States, 505 U.S. 144, 183–186 (1992); *see* Chemerinsky, *Cases Under the Guarantee Clause Should Be Justiciable*, 65 U. Colo. L. Rev. 849 (1994); Althouse, *Time for the Federal Courts to Enforce the Guarantee Clause? — A Response to Professor Chemerinsky*, 65 U. Colo. L. Rev. 881 (1994); Weinberg, *Political Questions and the Guarantee Clause*, 65 U. Colo. L. Rev. 887 (1994).

[315] Tenth Amendment. *See* U.S. Const., Amend. X.

[316] No traditional role for political question doctrine in Tenth Amendment claims. *See, e.g.*, New York v. United States, 505 U.S. 144, 155–159 (1992) (Court must determine whether challenged provisions of federal statute overstep boundaries between federal and state authority); Garcia v. San Antonio Metro. Transit Auth., 469 U.S. 528, 537–557 (1985) (Court decided on merits that there was no constitutional limitation on Commerce Clause powers over states, overruling *National League of Cities v. Usery*); National League of Cities v. Usery, 426 U.S. 833, 840–856 (1976) (Court decided on merits that Commerce Clause powers did not extend to traditional governmental functions performed by states); *but see* Massachusetts v. Mellon, 262 U.S. 447, 479–485 (1923) (claim that act of Congress usurped powers reserved to states presented question that was political and not judicial in character); Nagel, *Separation of Powers and the Scope of Federal Equitable Remedies*, 30 Stan. L. Rev. 661 (1978) (discussion of federal-state separation of powers concerns).

[317] Foreign relations. Baker v. Carr, 369 U.S. 186, 211 (1962); *see* Doe v. Braden, 57 U.S. (16 How.) 635, 657 (1853) (it would be impossible for executive branch to conduct foreign relations if courts were authorized to inquire into authority of persons acting on behalf of foreign governments).

[318] Sovereignty over disputed territory. *See* Baker v. Carr, 369 U.S. 186, 212 (1962); *see also* National City Bank v. Republic of China, 348 U.S. 356, 358 (1955) (official recognition of foreign sovereign is solely for President to determine and outside competence of courts); United States v. Pink, 315 U.S. 203,

sovereignty has been determined, the courts may decide for themselves the legal consequences of that determination, such as whether a particular statute applies to the territory in question.[319]

In *Zivotofsky v. Clinton*, the courts were faced with a case that appeared to the lower courts to raise a question concerning Israel's sovereignty over Jerusalem, which the courts would be barred from deciding by the political question doctrine. The plaintiffs' son was born in Jerusalem, and they sought to have "Israel" recorded on his passport as his birthplace, in accordance with Section 214(d) of the Foreign Relations Authorization Act.[320] However, the policy of the State Department was to record the birthplace of United States citizens born in Jerusalem as "Jerusalem," and not to include "Israel." The Supreme Court held that judicial resolution of the case was not barred by the political question doctrine, because the only question presented was whether the plaintiffs could vindicate their statutory right to have "Israel" recorded on their son's passport, which depended on whether the statute was constitutional, a matter well within the authority of the courts to decide. The courts were not being asked to resolve the political issue of Israeli sovereignty over Jerusalem.[321]

Closely related to the recognition of foreign governments is the act of state doctrine. Under the act of state doctrine, United States courts will refrain from judging the validity of a foreign state's governmental acts in regard to matters within that country's borders.[322] The act of state doctrine commonly arises as a foreign sovereign's defense in an action under the Foreign Sovereign Immunities Act[323] or under the alien tort statute.[324] The jurisprudential foundations of the act of state doctrine have evolved over the years. The doctrine originated as an

---

229–230 (1942) (recognition of Soviet government by executive and acceptance of assignment of claims was final and conclusive on courts); Guaranty Trust Co. v. United States, 304 U.S. 126, 137–138 (1938) (action of executive in recognizing foreign government and receiving diplomatic representatives is conclusive on courts); Foster v. Neilson, 27 U.S. (2 Pet.) 253, 307–309 (1829) (questions regarding boundaries of nations are political questions for which courts must respect pronounced will of legislatures); United States v. Palmer, 16 U.S. (3 Wheat.) 610, 634–635 (1818) (questions regarding sovereignty over territory are political rather than legal in character).

[319] Consequences of determination. *See* Baker v. Carr, 369 U.S. 186, 212 (1962).

[320] Foreign Relations Authorization Act provision. 107 Pub. L. 228, § 214(d) ("For purposes of the registration of birth, certification of nationality, or issuance of a passport of a United States citizen born in the city of Jerusalem, the Secretary [of State] shall, upon the request of the citizen or the citizen's legal guardian, record the place of birth as Israel").

[321] Constitutionality of statute not political question. Zivotofsky v. Clinton, 132 S. Ct. 1421, 182 L. Ed. 2d 423, 429–433 (2012) ("Resolution of Zivotofsky's claim demands careful examination of the textual, structural, and historical evidence put forward by the parties regarding the nature of the statute and of the passport and recognition powers. This is what courts do."; political question doctrine did not bar review of claim that United States citizen born in Jerusalem was entitled to have "Israel" recorded on his passport as his birthplace).

[322] Act of state doctrine. Underhill v. Hernandez, 168 U.S. 250, 252 (1897) (under act of state doctrine, "the courts of one country will not sit in judgment on the acts of the government of another, done within its own territory."

[323] *See* 28 U.S.C. §§ 1330, 1601 *et seq.*

[324] *See* 28 U.S.C. § 1350.

expression of international law,[325] but has been described more recently as "a consequence of domestic separation of powers."[326]

In *Banco Nacional de Cuba v. Sabbatino*, the Supreme Court declined to review a claim that an expropriation of foreign-owned property by the revolutionary government of Cuba violated international law, concluding that judicial review was precluded by the act of state doctrine. In discussing the foundations on which the doctrine rests, the Court stated that it was not compelled by the inherent nature of sovereign authority or by principles of international law. Although not required by the Constitution, the doctrine does have constitutional underpinnings. It arose out of the basic relationships between branches of government in a system of separation of powers, and it expresses the strong sense of the judicial branch that engaging in the task of passing on the validity of foreign acts of state could hinder rather than further the conduct of foreign relations.[327] The Court went on to describe the doctrine as a flexible rule involving a balance of relevant considerations, stating:[328]

> [I]ts continuing validity depends on its capacity to reflect the proper distribution of functions between the judicial and political branches of the Government on matters bearing on foreign affairs. It should be apparent that the greater the degree of codification or consensus concerning a particular area of international law, the more appropriate it is for the judiciary to render decisions regarding it, since the courts can then focus on the application of an agreed principle to circumstance of fact rather than on the sensitive task of establishing a principle not inconsistent with the national interest or with international justice. It is also evident that some aspects of international law touch more sharply on national nerves than do others; the less important the implications of an issue are for our foreign relations, the weaker the justification for exclusivity in the political branches.

In reaction to *Banco Nacional de Cuba v. Sabbatino*, Congress enacted legislation, commonly known as the Hickenlooper Amendment, that authorizes federal courts to review issues relating to expropriation of property by foreign governments in violation of international law in the absence of a presidential request to withhold review for reasons of foreign policy.[329] The Hickenlooper Amendment has been held to be constitutional and not an improper legislative interference with judicial power because it was proper for Congress to provide guidance to the courts in the area of foreign relations. The Hickenlooper Amendment is not a grant of jurisdiction and does not create a cause of action, but merely countered the Supreme Court's decision in *Sabbatino* by limiting the act of state

---

[325] Expression of international law. W.S. Kirkpatrick & Co. v. Environmental Tectonics Corp., Int'l, 493 U.S. 400, 404 (1990).

[326] Consequence of separation of powers. W.S. Kirkpatrick & Co. v. Environmental Tectonics Corp., Int'l, 493 U.S. 400, 404 (1990); *see* Banco Nacional de Cuba v. Sabbatino, 376 U.S. 398, 423 (1964) (act of state doctrine arose out of basic relationships between branches of government in system of separation of powers).

[327] Conduct of foreign relations. Banco Nacional de Cuba v. Sabbatino, 376 U.S. 398, 421–423 (1964).

[328] 376 U.S. at 427–428.

[329] Hickenlooper Amendment. 22 U.S.C. § 2370(e)(2).

doctrine to certain claims of expropriation.

Negotiation, ratification, and termination of treaties are governmental actions to be performed by the legislative and executive branches of government. However, the courts may interpret treaties in the absence of conclusive governmental action.[330] In interpreting treaties, the courts usually respect the position of the executive branch on the question under consideration.[331] But disagreement with the position of the executive branch is not unknown.[332]

A leading case in the area of treaties indicates a lack of consensus on the issue of what constitutes a political question. In *Goldwater v. Carter*, the Supreme Court dismissed a case challenging the power of the President to terminate a mutual defense treaty with the Republic of China without congressional approval. A clause in the treaty provided that either party could terminate the treaty on one year's notice, but did not delineate the procedure by which a termination might be effected. A plurality of four justices concluded that the case presented a nonjusticiable political question because it involved a conflict between the authority of the President and the authority of Congress. Of the five remaining justices, one concurred in the result without opinion, one concurred in the result on other grounds while denying the presence of a political question, one argued that no political question was present because the issue to be decided was a question of constitutional decision-making authority rather than a question of foreign relations, and two argued that the political question issue should not be decided without oral argument and full consideration by the Court.[333] Although the term "treaty" has a restrictive definition in the Constitution, executive agreements lacking the formalities of the treaty clause may in appropriate circumstances have an effect similar to treaties. An international compact is not always a treaty that requires the participation of the senate. Although not treaties, "executive agreements" between the United States and another sovereign have been tested by treaty principles.[334] When the foundation document is an agreement between governments, non-governmental entities may not ordinarily challenge either the interpretation or implementation of the agreement absent an express authorization for private

---

[330] Courts may interpret treaties. *See* Baker v. Carr, 369 U.S. 186, 212 (1962).

[331] Respect for position of executive branch. *See* New York Chinese TV Programs, Inc. v. U.E. Enters., Inc., 954 F.2d 847, 852 (2d Cir. 1992) (court owed deference to determinations of Congress and President that treaty with Republic of China remained valid and enforceable after U.S. recognition of Peoples Republic of China); Sullivan v. Kidd, 254 U.S. 433, 442 (1921) (construction pla ced on treaty and consistently adhered to by executive branch of government should be given much weight).

[332] Disagreement with executive branch. *See* Perkins v. Elg, 307 U.S. 325, 338–339 (1939) (naturalization treaty with Sweden did not abrogate right of child born in United States and removed to Sweden by parent to elect citizenship at maturity).

[333] Lack of consensus on issue. Goldwater v. Carter, 444 U.S. 996 (1979); *see* Berger, *The President's Unilateral Termination of the Taiwan Treaty*, 75 Nw. U.L. Rev. 577 (1980); *see also* Dole v. Carter, 569 F.2d 1109, 1110 (10th Cir. 1977) (action to prevent President from returning crown of St. Stephen to Hungary under treaty or executive agreement presented nonjusticiable political question).

[334] Executive agreements may have similar effect to treaties and treaty principles generally apply. Weinberger v. Rossi, 456 U.S. 25, 30 n.6 (1982); United States v. Belmont, 301 U.S. 324, 330–331 (1937) (analyzing executive agreement on treaty principles).

actions.[335]

The constitutional division of authority between Congress and the President with respect to the declaration and conduct of war[336] has been the source of a number of cases indicating the political question doctrine. The Supreme Court has generally avoided making decisions in this controversial area by denying certiorari rather than by granting certiorari and invoking the political question doctrine, leaving the lower federal courts to decide whether the doctrine is applicable to particular cases.[337] In one case in which certiorari was granted, the Supreme Court affirmed without opinion a lower court's conclusion that a political question was presented by the deployment of troops in Southeast Asia without a formal declaration of war.[338]

In most of the cases involving constitutional challenges to the war in Southeast Asia, the lower courts found a nonjusticiable political question to be present.[339] In other cases, the courts found that the absence of a dispute between the legislative and executive branches of government permitted them to review on the merits.[340] The same pattern has continued in later cases involving war powers.[341] However, actions for damages resulting from military activities have been held to be justiciable.

---

[335] Governmental agreements not subject to private party suit absent express private right of action. Edye v. Robertson (Head Money Cases), 112 U.S. 580 (1884) (treaty is primarily compact between independent nations depending on interest and honor of signatories for enforcement; judicial courts can give no redress); *see* Chicago & Southern Air Lines, Inc. v. Waterman S.S. Corp., 333 U.S. 103, 111 (1948) (foreign policy decisions are of kind for which judiciary has neither aptitude nor responsibility and has long been held to belong to domain of political power not subject to judicial intrusion or inquiry); *see also* Kwan v. United States, 272 F.3d 1360, 1362–1363 (Fed. Cir. 2001).

[336] Declaration and conduct of war. *See* U.S. Const., art. I, § 8, art. II, § 2.

[337] Certiorari denied. *See, e.g.*, Holtzman v. Schlesinger, 484 F.2d 1307 (2d Cir. 1973); Da Costa v. Laird, 448 F.2d 1368 (2d Cir. 1971); Mora v. McNamara, 387 F.2d 862 (D.C. Cir. 1967); Luftig v. McNamara, 373 F.2d 664 (D.C. Cir. 1967).

[338] Affirmed without opinion. *See* Atlee v. Laird, 347 F. Supp. 689, 691–709 (E.D. Pa. 1972), *aff'd sub nom.*, Atlee v. Richardson, 411 U.S. 911 (1973) (issue of constitutionality of undeclared war in Southeast Asia presented nonjusticiable political question); *see also* Firmage, *The War Powers and the Political Question Doctrine*, 49 U. Colo. L. Rev. 65 (1977); Schwartz & McCormack, *The Justiciability of Legal Objections to the American Military Effort in Vietnam*, 46 Tex. L. Rev. 1033 (1968).

[339] Presence of nonjusticiable political question. *See* Holtzman v. Schlesinger, 484 F.2d 1307, 1308–1312 (2d Cir. 1973) (issue of legality of bombing and other military activities in Cambodia presented nonjusticiable political question); Orlando v. Laird, 443 F.2d 1039, 1043 (2d Cir. 1971) (constitutional propriety of means by which Congress chose to approve protracted military operations in Southeast Asia was nonjusticiable political question); Da Costa v. Laird, 448 F.2d 1368, 1370 (2d Cir. 1971) (issue of constitutionality of means by which executive and legislative branches prosecuted and disengaged from military operations in Southeast Asia presented nonjusticiable political question); *see also* Shattuck, *The "Political Question" Quagmire: War and Peace in the Second Circuit*, 40 Brooklyn L. Rev. 1031 (1974).

[340] Absence of dispute permitted review on merits. *See* Massachusetts v. Laird, 451 F.2d 26, 30–34 (1st Cir. 1971) (military involvement in Vietnam did not violate Constitution because President acted with continuous congressional support); Drinan v. Nixon, 364 F. Supp. 854, 856–859 (D. Mass. 1973) (political question presented by issue of whether air combat operations in Cambodia violated domestic and international laws was resolved by political branches).

[341] Same pattern in later cases. *See* Cole, *Challenging Covert War: The Politics of the Political Question Doctrine*, 26 Harv. Int'l L.J. 155 (1985).

The private rights of individuals are often affected by the declaration or conduct of war or by legislation that regulates the activities of citizens at home or abroad for the duration of the hostilities. If the issue to be decided requires a determination of the date of cessation of hostilities for a particular purpose, the courts usually defer to a determination made by the legislative or executive branch. The power to declare war includes the power to establish the date of cessation of hostilities for private as well as public purposes.[342] A political question is present because of the need for finality in determinations involving emergencies.[343] If a need for finality due to an emergency is not manifest in a particular case, the courts may decide a case on the merits if definable criteria exist for the decision.[344]

In addition, the political question doctrine does not prevent the courts from interpreting legislation that contains provisions conditioned on the duration of hostilities. The courts are competent to decide, for example, whether a statute contemplates a formal or informal termination of hostilities.[345]

In analyzing political question cases, courts have been more willing to address the merits of cases that involve the private rights of individuals than cases that involve only the political authority of the legislative and executive branches of government. In *Harisiades v. Shaughnessy*, the Supreme Court was asked to review a claim that the deportation of an alien violated the Due Process Clause of the Fifth Amendment and other provisions of the Constitution. Although the Court upheld the deportation, it made its decision on the merits rather than invoking the political question doctrine.[346] In *Immigration & Naturalization Service v. Chadha*, the Court held that a statute authorizing the House of Representatives to veto a suspension by the U.S. Immigration and Naturalization Service of the deportation of an alien violated the constitutional separation of powers. The case did not present

---

342 Date of cessation of hostilities. Commercial Trust Co. v. Miller, 262 U.S. 51, 57 (1923) (Congress has power to provide for continuing seizure of property of enemy aliens after formal termination of war); *see also* Fleming v. Mohawk Wrecking & Lumber Co., 331 U.S. 111, 116 (1947) (war power may deal with problems of law enforcement that do not end with cessation of hostilities); Hamilton v. Kentucky Distilleries & Warehouse Co., 251 U.S. 146, 161 (1919) (war power includes power to remedy evils that arise during period of emergency).

343 Need for finality in emergencies. *See* Baker v. Carr, 369 U.S. 186, 213 (1962); Martin v. Mott, 25 U.S. (12 Wheat.) 19, 30 (1827) (nature of emergency demands prompt and unhesitating obedience).

344 Need for finality not manifest. Baker v. Carr, 369 U.S. 186, 214 (1962); Chastleton Corp. v. Sinclair, 264 U.S. 543, 547–548 (1924) (court could inquire as to continuing existence of emergency justifying regulation of rents after cessation of hostilities).

345 Power to interpret legislation. *Compare* Ludecke v. Watkins, 335 U.S. 160, 166–170 (1948) (Alien Enemy Act permitted removal of alien enemies after cessation of hostilities until formal termination of war) *with* Lee v. Madigan, 358 U.S. 228, 229–236 (1959) (soldier could not be tried for murder by court martial under Articles of War after cessation of hostilities).

346 Due process challenge to deportation. Harisiades v. Shaughnessy, 342 U.S. 580, 588–590 (1952) (political question restrictions on judiciary do not control decision concerning deportation); *see also* Hampton v. Mow Sun Wong, 426 U.S. 88, 99–105 (1976) (Civil Service Commission regulation that excluded aliens from federal government employment violated Due Process Clause of Fifth Amendment); *but see* Shaughnessy v. United States ex rel Mezei, 345 U.S. 206, 210–216 (1953) (power to exclude or expel alien is fundamental attribute of sovereignty exercised by political departments and largely immune from judicial control); United States *ex rel.* Knauff v. Shaughnessy, 338 U.S. 537, 542–547 (1950) (it is not within province of any court, unless expressly authorized by law, to review determination of political branch of government to exclude particular alien).

a political question, the Court found, merely because it challenged the constitutional authority of Congress.[347]

Immigration cases that are decided on the merits frequently contain an analysis of the issues resembling a political question rationale, including references to a need to provide "deference" to the legislative and executive branches of government.[348] The same reasons that preclude judicial review of political questions dictate a narrow standard of review on the merits of decisions made by Congress or the President in the area of immigration and naturalization.[349] The key difference between the two forms of judicial action, however, is that when a court invokes the political question doctrine, it is making no statement on the constitutional merits. When, on the other hand, a court affirms the constitutionality of executive or legislative action because of deference, whatever legal or political force a judicial decision may have is invoked.

In *Baker v. Carr*, the Supreme Court held that the political question doctrine did not bar judicial review of a federal constitutional challenge to the apportionment of state legislative districts.[350] In reaching its decision, the Court relied, in part, on earlier decisions relating to the apportionment of congressional districts.[351]

In *Colegrove v. Green*, the Court had refused to intervene in an election of members of the U.S. House of Representatives on behalf of Illinois voters who alleged that they had been disadvantaged by a state redistricting scheme that was alleged to violate various provisions of the Constitution and federal reapportionment statutes. But the Court's refusal to intervene reflected an exercise of discretion in an action seeking equitable relief. The shortness of time remaining before the election made it doubtful whether remedial action could be taken in time to secure effective relief.[352] A majority of the Court, including three dissenting justices who favored intervention, found the issue to be justiciable[353] in spite of

---

347 Separation of powers issues are justiciable. Immigration and Naturalization Serv. v. Chadha, 462 U.S. 919, 940–943 (1983) (presence of constitutional issues with significant political overtones does not automatically invoke political question doctrine); *see also* Massieu v. Reno, 915 F. Supp. 681, 697–698 (D.N.J. 1996) (statute giving Secretary of State exclusive authority to declare lawfully admitted alien deportable if presence is adverse to U.S. foreign policy interests was both justiciable and unconstitutional).

348 Deference to legislative and executive branches. *See, e.g.*, Fiallo v. Bell, 430 U.S. 787, 793 (1977) (statute granting immigration preference to illegitimate child by reason of relationship to mother rather than father was not unconstitutional); Mathews v. Diaz, 426 U.S. 67, 81–82 (1976) (statute limiting Medicare benefits to aliens who satisfied specific residence requirements did not violate Due Process Clause of Fifth Amendment).

349 Narrow standard of review on merits. Mathews v. Diaz, 426 U.S. 67, 81–82 (1976); *see* Narenji v. Civiletti, 617 F.2d 745, 747–748 (D.C. Cir. 1979) (regulation requiring nonimmigrant alien students from Iran to report residence and nonimmigrant status information to local INS office did not violate constitutional rights to due process and equal protection).

350 Challenge to legislative apportionment not barred. Baker v. Carr, 369 U.S. 186, 226 (1962).

351 Earlier apportionment decisions. *See* Baker v. Carr, 369 U.S. 186, 232–234 (1962).

352 Exercise of equitable discretion. *See* Colegrove v. Green, 328 U.S. 549, 564–566 (1946) (Rutledge, J., concurring; court of equity should interfere with enforcement of state laws only to prevent irreparable injury that is clear and imminent).

353 Issue is justiciable. *See* Colegrove v. Green, 328 U.S. 549, 564–566 (1946) (Rutledge, J., concurring;

constitutional provisions vesting in Congress the duty to apportion representatives among the states according to their respective numbers, the power to alter state laws prescribing the time, place, and manner of holding elections, and the power to judge the elections, returns, and qualifications of its members.[354]

The decision in *Baker v. Carr* cleared the path for a variety of subsequent cases reviewing the constitutionality of the electoral process at the federal, state, and local levels.[355] For the most part, these cases have concentrated on the application of specific constitutional or statutory provisions to particular electoral circumstances, rather than on the applicability of the political question doctrine. The cases involving apportionment at the federal level have focused on the constitutional duty of Congress to apportion representatives among the states,[356] which has been held to require a high degree of mathematical equality among congressional districts.[357] This requirement leaves open the question of gerrymandering, which can be accomplished in spite of numerical equality.[358]

In *Davis v. Bandemer*, the Supreme Court considered a claim by Indiana Democrats that a Republican plan to reapportion the state legislature by redrawing district lines and mixing single and multimember districts to disadvantage Democrats violated the Equal Protection Clause of the Fourteenth Amendment. Before upholding the reapportionment plan on the merits, the Court held that the issue to be decided did not present a nonjusticiable political question, stating:[359]

---

Court had power to afford relief against objection that issues were not justiciable).

354 Constitutional provisions. Colegrove v. Green, 328 U.S. 549, 553–555 (1946); *see* U.S. Const., art. I, §§ 2, 4, 5; *see also* Carroll v. Becker, 285 U.S. 380, 381–382 (1932) (Constitution did not give Missouri legislature power to disregard veto of governor in prescribing congressional districts); Koenig v. Flynn, 285 U.S. 375, 379 (1932) (Constitution did not give New York legislature power to prescribe congressional districts without approval of governor); Smiley v. Holm, 285 U.S. 355, 367–375 (1932) (U.S. Constitution did not give Minnesota legislature power to disregard veto of governor in prescribing congressional districts).

355 Cases after *Baker v. Carr. See, e.g.*, Department of Commerce v. Montana, 503 U.S. 442, 456–459 (1992) (claim that apportionment formula contained in federal statute violated constitutional duty of Congress to apportion representatives among states according to their respective numbers did not present nonjusticiable political question); Wesberry v. Sanders, 376 U.S. 1, 5–7 (1964) (claim that method of apportionment of Georgia congressional districts violated Article I of Constitution and Fourteenth Amendment did not present nonjusticiable political question).

356 Duty of Congress to apportion representatives. *See* U.S. Const., art. I, § 2.

357 High degree of mathematical equality. *See* Karcher v. Daggett, 462 U.S. 725, 730–731 (1983) (if population differences among districts could have been reduced or eliminated by good-faith effort to draw districts of equal population, state must prove that each significant variance between districts was necessary to achieve some legitimate goal); Kirkpatrick v. Preisler, 394 U.S. 526, 530–532, *reh'g denied*, 395 U.S. 917 (1969) (unless population variance among districts resulted in spite of good-faith effort to achieve precise mathematical equality, state must justify each variance no matter how small).

358 Question of gerrymandering. *See* Shaw v. Reno, 509 U.S. 630, 641–658 (1993) (redistricting legislation that is so bizarre on its face that it is unexplainable on grounds other than race demands close scrutiny even when designed to enhance voting power of racial minority); Karcher v. Daggett, 462 U.S. 725, 774–780 (1983) (White, J., dissenting; rule of absolute equality offers legislators ready justification for disregarding geographical and political boundaries).

359 Challenge to justiciability as political question rejected. Davis v. Bandemer, 478 U.S. 109, 123 (1986); *see also* Republican Party of North Carolina v. Martin, 980 F.2d 943, 950–952 (4th Cir. 1992)

> [The analysis contained in *Baker v. Carr*] applies equally to the question now before us. Disposition of this question does not involve us in a matter more properly decided by the coequal branch of our Government. There is no risk of foreign or domestic disturbance, and in the light of our cases since *Baker* we are not persuaded that there are no judicially discernable and manageable standards by which political gerrymander cases are to be decided.

A plurality of four justices in *Davis v. Bandemer* rejected the argument made by three concurring justices that the protection of individual rights afforded by *Baker v. Carr* should not be extended to group rights.[360] The plurality reasoned that the concurring justices failed to explain how the standards for adjudicating the political gerrymandering claim were less manageable than the standards that had been developed for adjudicating racial gerrymandering claims.[361]

At an early date, the Supreme Court assumed for itself a limited power to review the procedural validity (as opposed to the constitutionality) of congressional enactments. For example, in order to preserve the validity of a statute, it has looked behind the formalities of enactment to find a missing effective date in the legislative journals.[362] For the most part, however, the Court has been reluctant to inquire into the question of whether a statute has complied with all of the required legislative formalities.[363]

In *Marshall Field & Co. v. Clark*, the Court refused to review a claim that a statute omitted a section that had been included in the bill that was passed by Congress. Judicial review was precluded by the respect due to coequal and independent departments and the need for finality and certainty with respect to the status of a statute.[364] But in *United States v. Munoz-Flores*, the Court reviewed on the merits a challenge to the validity of a statute based on the Origination Clause of the Constitution,[365] which requires all revenue legislation to originate in the House of Representatives. The claim that a special assessment levied against persons who were convicted of certain misdemeanors was a revenue measure that was required to originate in the House of Representatives was held not to present

---

(claim of political gerrymandering in election of state trial court judges did not present nonjusticiable political question).

360 Argument against group rights. Davis v. Bandemer, 478 U.S. 109, 147 (1986) (O'Connor, J. concurring; otherwise courts will have no alternative but to reconcile competing claims of political, religious, ethnic, racial, occupational, and socioeconomic groups).

361 No distinction between political and racial gerrymandering. Davis v. Bandemer, 478 U.S. 109, 125 (1986); *see* Polsby & Popper, *The Third Criterion: Compactness as a Procedural Safeguard Against Partisan Gerrymandering*, 9 Yale L. & Pol'y Rev. 301 (1991); Schuck, *The Thickest Thicket: Partisan Gerrymandering and Judicial Regulation of Politics*, 87 Colum. L. Rev. 1325 (1987).

362 Limited power to review congressional enactments. Gardner v. Collector, 73 U.S. (6 Wall.) 499, 511 (1868) (whenever question arises as to existence of statute, time when statute takes effect, or precise terms of statute, court may resort to any source of information capable of conveying clear and satisfactory answer).

363 Reluctance to inquire into compliance with formalities. *See* Baker v. Carr, 369 U.S. 186, 215 (1962).

364 Review of statute for alleged omission rejected. Marshall Field & Co. v. Clark, 143 U.S. 649, 672–680 (1892).

365 U.S. Const., art. I, § 7.

a political question. An individual litigant had a legitimate interest in enforcing the proper operation of the federal government, and the issue of validity was capable of being determined by judicially manageable standards.[366]

The power to amend the United States Constitution is divided between Congress and the legislatures or given to constitutional conventions called by the several states.[367] The Supreme Court has refused to review a number of issues relating to the validity of constitutional amendments. In *Leser v. Garnett*, the Court held, without resorting to political question language, that certification by Tennessee and West Virginia that they had ratified the Nineteenth Amendment was conclusive on the Secretary of State, and when certified by his proclamation was conclusive on the courts.[368]

In *Coleman v. Miller*, the Court was asked to determine whether the legislature of Kansas had ratified a proposed Child Labor Amendment when the lieutenant governor resolved a tie vote of the state senate in favor of ratification. Twelve years earlier, the legislature had voted to reject the same amendment. The Court was divided as to whether a political question was presented by claims of invalidity relating to involvement of the lieutenant governor in the ratification process, but agreed that claims relating to the prior rejection and the long delay before reconsideration did present a nonjusticiable political question. Individual justices disagreed on the rationale of the decision, some emphasizing constitutional commitment of the issue to Congressional resolution, and others stressing the impracticality of judicial review.[369]

In *Nixon v. United States*, the Supreme Court held that the political question doctrine bars judicial review of a constitutional challenge to procedures adopted by the United States Senate for trial of impeachment cases.[370] The procedures in question permitted a committee of Senators to hear evidence against a person who had been impeached and to report that evidence to the full Senate. A federal judge who had been convicted by the Senate claimed that these procedures violated the Impeachment Trial Clause of the U.S. Constitution.[371] Specifically, he argued that failure of the whole Senate to hear the evidence contravened the provision giving the Senate "the sole power to try all impeachments." This provision, it was argued, implied that the proceedings must be in the nature of a judicial trial rather than a vote based on a cold record.[372]

---

[366] Origination Clause challenge was not political question. United States v. Munoz-Flores, 495 U.S. 385, 389–396 (1990) (provisions for separation of powers within legislative branch are not different in kind from provisions for separation of powers between legislative, executive, and judicial branches).

[367] Power to amend Constitution. *See* U.S. Const., art. V.

[368] Nineteenth Amendment. Leser v. Garnett, 258 U.S. 130, 137 (1922).

[369] Court divided. Coleman v. Miller, 307 U.S. 433, 446–456 (1939); *cf.* Dellinger, *The Legitimacy of Constitutional Change: Rethinking the Amendment Process*, 97 Harv. L. Rev. 386 (1983) (discussion of other issues relating to constitutional amendments that have been reviewed on merits).

[370] Political question doctrine barred judicial review. Nixon v. United States, 506 U.S. 224, 228–238 (1993).

[371] Impeachment Trial Clause. *See* U.S. Const., art. I, § 3, cl. 6.

[372] Argument that judicial trial was required. Nixon v. United States, 506 U.S. 224, 226–228 (1993).

Rejecting this argument, the Supreme Court concluded that use of the word "try" lacked sufficient precision to afford any judicially manageable standard of review. The greater precision of three very specific requirements relating to an oath, a two-thirds vote, and participation of the Chief Justice if the President is tried suggested that there was no intention to impose additional limitations by use of the word "try." The Court emphasized the greater significance of the word "sole," which appears nowhere else in the Constitution except in the parallel Power of Impeachment Clause.[373]

In determining whether a political question was present, the Supreme Court examined not only the precise language of the Constitution but also the sources documenting the history of the Constitutional Convention, stating:[374]

> The history and contemporary understanding of the impeachment provisions support our reading of the constitutional language. The parties do not offer even a single word in the history of the Constitutional Convention or in contemporary commentary that even alludes to the possibility of judicial review in the context of the impeachment powers. This silence is quite meaningful in light of the several explicit references to the availability of judicial review as a check on the Legislature's power with respect to bills of attainder, *ex post facto* laws, and statutes. See The Federalist No. 78, p. 524 (J. Cooke ed. 1961).

In reviewing the reasons why the judiciary was not chosen to have any role in impeachments, the Court noted that judicial review would be inconsistent with the constitutional system of checks and balances. In that system, impeachment was designed to be the only check on the judicial branch by the legislature. Judicial involvement in impeachment proceedings would eviscerate this important constitutional check on the judiciary. The risk that judicial power might be usurped by the Senate was averted by constitutional safeguards in the form of the division of impeachment power between the two legislative bodies and the two-thirds supermajority vote requirement.[375]

The Court concluded that the claim of violation of the Impeachment Trial Clause was not justiciable because of the presence of various elements of a political question, including a constitutional commitment of the issue to a coordinate branch of government, the lack of finality, and the difficulty of fashioning relief.[376] The Court distinguished this holding from its earlier decision in *Powell v. McCormack* on grounds that the Impeachment Trial Clause contained no separate provision that could be defeated by allowing the Senate final authority to determine the meaning of the word "try."[377]

---

[373] 506 U.S. at 229–231; *see* U.S. Const., art. I, § 2, cl. 5.

[374] 506 U.S. at 233.

[375] 506 U.S. at 234–236.

[376] 506 U.S. at 236.

[377] 506 U.S. at 236–238; *see* Powell v. McCormack, 395 U.S. 486 (1969); *see also* Gerhardt, *Rediscovering Nonjusticiability: Judicial Review of Impeachments After Nixon*, 44 Duke L.J. 231 (1994).

Despite the Court's detailed analysis in *Nixon*, its conclusion appears flawed. It is certainly true that impeachment was designed to be the only legislative check on the judicial branch. But that check was carefully circumscribed, both procedurally and substantively, by the text of the Constitution. Judges and executive officers, for example, may be impeached solely for the commission of "high crimes and misdemeanors."[378] If Congress were enabled to employ its enormous impeachment power unconfined by these constitutionally imposed requirements, that power could easily turn into an abusive and harassing device that itself seriously compromises the judicial independence guaranteed by Article III of the Constitution.[379] Unless the judiciary, as a whole, is able to assure that Congress has stayed within its constitutionally imposed restraints, threats to judicial independence — both to judges actually impeached and those merely chilled by the threat — will be very real. Application of the political question doctrine to the impeachment context will thus potentially give rise to serious dangers to the interests of judicial independence and separation of powers.

In *Powell v. McCormack*, the Supreme Court reviewed on the merits a claim that exclusion of a Congressman from the United States House of Representatives by a majority vote rather than the two-thirds vote required for expulsion[380] exceeded the constitutional authority of the House. The House based its action on the conclusion that the Congressman was unqualified because he had been accused of misappropriating public funds and abusing the process of the courts. The Constitution gives the House of Representatives the power to judge the elections, returns, and qualifications of its members.[381] However, a separate provision specifies three qualifications for membership in the House. A member must be at least 25 years of age, a citizen of the United States for no fewer than seven years, and an inhabitant of the state in which he or she was elected.[382] The Supreme Court held that the House could decide only whether the qualifications had been satisfied, not what the qualifications were. The political question doctrine did not bar judicial review of the Congressman's claims.[383]

In cases involving challenges to acts of the executive branch, the courts have been willing to review on the merits most issues relating to the scope of executive power. The fact that many of these issues involve conflicts between legislative and executive powers has not rendered them nonjusticiable. The refusal to review specific executive decisions has been based not on the political question doctrine but on a finding that those decisions fall within the scope of discretion conferred on the

---

[378] U.S. Const., art. II, § 4.

[379] U.S. Const., art. III, § 1; *see* Ch. 100.

[380] Vote required for expulsion. *See* U.S. Const., art. I, § 5, cl. 2.

[381] Power to judge qualifications of members. *See* U.S. Const., art. I, § 5, cl. 1.

[382] Qualifications specified by Constitution. *See* U.S. Const., art. I, § 2, cl. 2.

[383] Expulsion of representative was not political question. Powell v. McCormack, 395 U.S. 486, 518–548 (1969); *see also* Bond v. Floyd, 385 U.S. 116, 128–137 (1966) (claim that exclusion of member from state legislature for statements made in press interview violated First Amendment was reviewed on merits); Kucinich v. Forbes, 432 F. Supp. 1101, 1108–1110 (N.D. Ohio 1977) (claim that suspension of city councilman for remarks made in violation of rules of decorum during council deliberations violated First Amendment did not present political question).

executive by a statute or the Constitution.

Challenges to executive power commonly allege a failure to comply with the terms of a statute. A number of cases have involved impoundment by the President of funds appropriated by Congress for expenditure under specific statutory programs, suspension or termination of programs, or other matters relating to government expenditures.[384] In *Train v. City of New York*, the Supreme Court reviewed on the merits a claim by the City of New York that the Administrator of the Environmental Protection Agency had violated the Federal Water Pollution Control Act Amendments of 1972 by refusing to allot funds appropriated by Congress for sewers and sewage treatment plants. The Court held that the Act did not permit the Administrator to allot less than the entire amount appropriated by Congress.[385]

In considering the scope of executive power,[386] the courts have invoked the political question doctrine most consistently in cases involving military operations. They have extended this practice to cases challenging the use of military forces in domestic situations. In *Gilligan v. Morgan*, the Supreme Court refused to review an action, filed after the shooting tragedy at Kent State University, seeking limitations on use of the Ohio National Guard in the suppression of civil disorders. In addition to other relief, the plaintiffs had requested an evaluation of the training, weaponry, and orders of the National Guard and the establishment of standards to control its actions. The Supreme Court held that the case presented a nonjusticiable political question. The Constitution granted Congress the power to provide for organizing, arming, and disciplining the militia, reserving to the states the appointment of officers and the authority for training the militia according to the discipline prescribed by Congress.[387] Decisions as to the composition, training, equipping, and control of military forces were professional military judgments subject to civilian control of the legislative and executive branches of government.[388] But in *Scheuer v. Rhodes*, the Supreme Court reviewed on the merits an action against state officials for damages arising from the same activities of the Ohio National Guard. The Court held that nothing in *Gilligan v. Morgan* implied that the conduct of the National Guard was always beyond judicial review or that there may not be accountability in a judicial forum for unlawful conduct by military personnel.[389]

Even if individual rights are involved, the courts generally refuse to review claims arising from internal military decisions. They review these claims only if the claimant alleges deprivation of a constitutional right, violation of a statute, or violation of military regulations, and all administrative remedies have been ex-

---

[384] Impoundment of funds. *See* Mills & Munselle, *Unimpoundment: Politics and the Courts in the Release of Impounded Funds*, 24 Emory L.J. 313 (1974); Mikva & Hertz, *Impoundment of Funds — The Courts, The Congress, and The President: A Constitutional Triangle*, 69 Nw. U.L. Rev. 335 (1974).

[385] Train v. City of New York. Train v. City of New York, 420 U.S. 35, 41–49 (1975).

[386] *See* U.S. Const., art. II, § 1.

[387] Power of Congress over militia. *See* U.S. Const., art. I, § 8, cl. 16.

[388] Noninterference in use of National Guard. Gilligan v. Morgan, 413 U.S. 1, 5–12 (1973).

[389] Conduct of National Guard is reviewable. Scheuer v. Rhodes, 416 U.S. 232, 249 (1974).

hausted.[390] Most claims based on decisions relating to induction, assignment, promotion, and discharge are dismissed as nonjusticiable.

The courts have not been reluctant to review on the merits issues that define the scope of judicial power,[391] even if judicial power conflicts with legislative or executive powers. In *United States v. Nixon*, the Supreme Court held that a judicial subpoena directed to the President of the United States in connection with a grand jury proceeding could not be defeated by a claim of executive privilege. Because the dispute arose in the ordinary course of a federal criminal prosecution, it was subject to the judicial power of the Court under Article III of the U.S. Constitution. The Court stated that it could not share judicial power with the executive branch of government any more than the executive or legislative branches could share with the Court the power to veto legislation or the power to override a veto. Any other conclusion would be contrary to the basic concept of separation of powers and the checks and balances that flow from a tripartite form of government.[392]

In *Whalen v. United States*, the Supreme Court held that it was not prevented from reviewing a District of Columbia Court of Appeals decision interpreting a District of Columbia statute in the same way that it was barred from reviewing a state court decision interpreting a state statute. Acts of Congress affecting only the District of Columbia are subject to the judicial power of the Court under Article III of the Constitution.[393]

The Compensation Clause of Article III provides that the compensation of federal judges shall not be diminished while they remain in office.[394] In *United States v. Will*, the U.S. Supreme Court held that it was not necessary for federal judges to disqualify themselves from hearing a case challenging the validity of federal statutes under the Compensation Clause. Disqualification would jeopardize the independence of the judiciary that is protected by the Compensation Clause.[395]

---

[390] Violation of Constitution, statute, or regulations. *See, e.g.*, Goldman v. Weinberger, 475 U.S. 503, 506–510 (1986) (First Amendment challenge to Air Force dress code regulation was reviewed on merits); Rostker v. Goldberg, 453 U.S. 57, 64–83 (1981) (equal protection challenge to all-male draft registration statute was reviewed on merits); Brown v. Glines, 444 U.S. 348, 353–361 (1980) (First Amendment challenge to regulation limiting circulation of petitions at Air Force bases was reviewed on merits); Parker v. Levy, 417 U.S. 733, 743–762 (1974) (due process challenge to various provisions of Uniform Code of Military Justice was decided on merits); Frontiero v. Richardson, 411 U.S. 677, 682–691 (1973) (equal protection challenge to statutes discriminating against women in granting military benefits was reviewed on merits); *cf.* Chappell v. Wallace, 462 U.S. 296, 298–305 (1983) (unique disciplinary structure of military and activities of Congress constitute special factors that dictate impropriety of providing enlisted military personnel with remedy against superior officers).

[391] Scope of judicial power. *See* U.S. Const., art. III, § 1.

[392] Enforcement of judicial subpoena against President. United States v. Nixon, 418 U.S. 683, 703–705 (1974); *see also* United States v. Durenberger, 48 F.3d 1239, 1243–1246 (D.C. Cir. 1995) (criminal prosecution of U.S. Senator for submitting false claims for reimbursement of travel expenses did not violate separation of powers); *but see* United States v. Rostenkowski, 59 F.3d 1291, 1304–1312 (D.C. Cir. 1995) (portions of various counts of criminal indictment against Congressman for misappropriation of congressional funds were nonjusticiable under doctrine of separation of powers and Rulemaking Clause of Constitution).

[393] *Whalen v. United States.* Whalen v. United States, 445 U.S. 684, 687–688 (1980).

[394] Compensation Clause. *See* U.S. Const., art. III, § 1.

[395] *United States v. Will.* United States v. Will, 449 U.S. 200, 211–217 (1980) (common law rule of

In *Atkins v. United States*, the United States Court of Claims considered a claim by federal judges that a failure of Congress to increase judicial salaries to keep pace with inflation violated the Compensation Clause. After reviewing the elements of a political question identified in *Baker v. Carr*, the court concluded that the claim did not present a nonjusticiable political question.[396]

---

necessity prevailed over statute requiring disqualification to permit interpretation of statute granting cost-of-living increases to all federal judges).

[396] *Atkins v. United States.* Atkins v. United States, 556 F.2d 1028, 1051–1054 (Ct. Cl. 1977).

# Chapter 3

# DIVERSITY JURISDICTION

## § 3.01 HISTORICAL BASIS OF DIVERSITY JURISDICTION

Although the modern statutory basis for the diversity jurisdiction is embodied in 28 U.S.C. § 1332, the federal courts may adjudicate diversity cases only because Article III, Section 2, of the Constitution extends federal judicial power to controversies between citizens of different states and to controversies between citizens of a state and foreign states, citizens, or subjects. There exists some debate over the reason for the framers' original inclusion of the diversity jurisdiction in Article III, Section 2. It has often been suggested that the provision's purpose was to avoid potential prejudice against citizens of one state in another state's courts. As stated by Chief Justice Marshall in an early case:[1]

> However true the fact may be, that the tribunals of the states will administer justice as impartially as those of the nation, to parties of every description, it is not less true that the constitution itself either entertains apprehensions on this subject, or views with such indulgence the possible fears and apprehensions of suitors, that it has established national tribunals for the decision of controversies between aliens and a citizen, or between citizens of different states.

However, Judge Henry Friendly concluded that there was little cause to fear that the state tribunals would be hostile to litigants from other states.[2] Judge Friendly noted the absence of substantial debate over the diversity issue among the drafters of Article III and only a lackluster defense of the diversity jurisdiction against attack in the state ratifying conventions. He asserted, nevertheless, that the desire to protect creditors against legislation favorable to debtors was a principal reason for the grant of diversity jurisdiction, and that "as a reason it was by no means without validity." This was because of the reasonable fear that state courts in states with more favorable laws to debtors would apply the laws in favor of their own residents, even though the debt was payable in another state. He further pointed to the close ties between many state legislatures and state judges.[3] Congress first authorized federal courts to exercise diversity jurisdiction in the Judiciary Act of 1789.[4]

---

[1] Justice Marshall on diversity. United States v. Deveaux, 9 U.S. (5 Cranch) 61, 87 (1809); *see also* Frank, *Historical Bases of the Federal Judicial System*, 13 Law & Contemp. Prob. 1 (1948); Yntema & Jaffin, *Preliminary Analysis of Concurrent Jurisdiction*, 79 U. Pa. L. Rev. 869 (1931).

[2] Friendly, *The Historic Basis of Diversity Jurisdiction*, 41 Harv. L. Rev. 483, 497 (1928).

[3] Friendly, *The Historic Basis of Diversity Jurisdiction*, 41 Harv. L. Rev. 483, 496–498 (1928).

[4] Judiciary Act of 1789, ch. 20, § 11, 1 Stat. 78.

## § 3.02 THE MODERN VIABILITY OF THE DIVERSITY JURISDICTION

The modern utility of the diversity jurisdiction has long been the subject of scholarly dispute. On the one hand, it has been argued that in light of the serious burdens on the courts imposed by the diversity jurisdiction,[5] the result is a diversion of federal judicial power away from more pressing needs.[6] Moreover, since the Supreme Court's decision in *Erie R. Co. v. Tompkins*,[7] it is well established that a federal court must apply the substantive law of the state in which it sits. State law often involves issues about which federal judges lack expertise and over which they have no ultimate control. Their decisions in diversity cases, it is therefore argued, can serve little purpose and can actually be counterproductive to the interests of federalism.[8] In addition, it has been argued that the abolition of diversity would result in a beneficial simplification of federal practice.[9]

On the other hand, defenders of diversity jurisdiction have argued that the danger of prejudice to out-of-state residents in the state courts remains a serious concern.[10] According to a number of decisions, the main contemporary rationale for diversity jurisdiction remains the protection of nonresidents from the possibility of prejudice that they might otherwise encounter in local courts. To this end, diversity jurisdiction is said to provide a neutral forum for citizens from another state or country. The continuing viability of the anti-prejudice rationale is evidenced by the Class Action Fairness Act of 2005, which significantly expanded federal diversity jurisdiction over class actions; in the findings supporting the Act, Congress noted that, with respect to class actions, state and local courts were "sometimes acting in ways that demonstrate bias against out-of-State defendants."[11]

It might be responded that the concern over prejudice is today exaggerated because improvements in travel and communication have unified the nation and reduced the interstate xenophobia that arguably plagued the nation in its early years. The fact remains, however, that state judges are often elected, and therefore are generally more directly tied to the community and its political structures than are their federal counterparts.[12] The possibility of prejudice in favor of powerful or important in-state interests, then, is at least more than fanciful. Thus, one might still arguably justify the continuation of some form of diversity jurisdiction.

---

[5] *See* Federal Courts Study Comm., Judicial Conference of the U.S., Report of the Federal Courts Study Committee (1990); reprinted in 22 Conn. L. Rev. 733 (1990) (estimating that diversity accounts for almost one in every four cases in the district courts, about one of every two civil trials, about one of every ten from more pressing needs.

[6] *See* Friendly, Federal Jurisdiction: A General View, 139–152 (1973).

[7] *Erie* case. Erie R.R. v. Tompkins, 304 U.S. 64, 69–78 (1938).

[8] *See* Sloviter, *A Federal Judge Views Diversity Jurisdiction Through the Lens of Federalism*, 78 Va. L. Rev. 1671, 1675 (1992).

[9] Rowe, *Abolishing Diversity Jurisdiction: Positive Side Effects and Potential for Further Reforms*, 92 Harv. L. Rev. 963 (1979).

[10] *See* Frank, *For Maintaining Diversity Jurisdiction*, 73 Yale L. J. 7, 10–12 (1963); *see also* Frank, *The Case for Diversity Jurisdiction*, 16 Harv. J. Legis. 403 (1979).

[11] *See* P.L. No. 109-2, § 2(a)(4)(B), 119 Stat. 4, 5.

[12] *See* Neely, Why Courts Don't Work, 27–28 (1982).

Although this argument supports giving recourse in federal court to an out-of-state plaintiff who would otherwise have to proceed in the defendant's state court, it does not justify continuation of the provision that puzzlingly allows in-state plaintiffs to proceed initially in federal court under the diversity jurisdiction.[13] In such a case, whatever prejudice that might exist in the state court would actually favor the plaintiff. In the case of removal, it should be noted, an in-state defendant is not permitted by the governing statute to remove a case to federal court on grounds of diversity jurisdiction.[14] This inconsistency between the practices employed on original jurisdictional and removal remains unexplained, and appears indefensible on either logical or practical grounds.

Another argument possibly supporting the continuation of diversity jurisdiction is the widespread belief among many litigators that they receive a better quality of justice in terms of shorter dockets, better judges, and more streamlined procedures in federal court, even in the enforcement of state law.[15] Finally, it has been argued in defense of diversity jurisdiction that the educational value of having two systems in interaction benefits both state and federal systems.[16]

## § 3.03 SUGGESTED MODIFICATIONS OF DIVERSITY

Several commentaries have suggested modifications of diversity jurisdiction short of total abolition, in an attempt to satisfy the competing arguments both for and against diversity. One scholar, on the basis of responses to a questionnaire he submitted to all active federal district and appellate judges at the time, concluded that diversity jurisdiction may be more warranted in some districts than in others.[17] He based this conclusion on the fact that there exist different perceptions among judges in different districts about both the quality of state court justice and the extent to which courts regard the contribution of federal judges to the development of state law to be useful.[18] On the basis of this information, the same commentator suggested that each district be given a choice, to be exercised by a majority of that district's active judges, after notice and opportunity for comment, between retention of the present scheme, abolition of diversity jurisdiction within its borders, or a compromise modification of diversity.[19] It is questionable, however, whether such a proposed system would be workable. At the very least, it would likely give rise to substantial administrative costs and lead to confusion and intrasystemic forum shopping among litigants. Moreover, it would seriously undermine the national coherence of the federal jurisdictional framework.

---

[13] *See* 28 U.S.C. § 1332(a).

[14] 28 U.S.C. § 1441(b).

[15] *See* Redish, *Reassessing the Allocation of Judicial Business Between State and Federal Courts: Federal Jurisdiction and "The Martian Chronicles,"* 78 Va. L. Rev. 1769, 1800 (1992).

[16] Frank, *For Maintaining Diversity Jurisdiction*, 73 Yale L. J. 7, 11 (1963) (described as "cross-pollination" theory); *see* Redish, *Reassessing the Allocation of Judicial Business Between State and Federal Courts: Federal Jurisdiction and "The Martian Chronicles,"* 78 Va. L. Rev. 1769, 1802 (1992).

[17] Shapiro, *Federal Diversity Jurisdiction: A Survey and a Proposal*, 91 Harv. L. Rev. 317, 339 (1977).

[18] 91 Harv. L. Rev. at 339.

[19] 91 Harv. L. Rev. at 340.

In 1969, the American Law Institute proposed adoption of a new section of the Judicial Code, providing that "[n]o person can invoke [diversity] jurisdiction, either originally or on removal, in any district in a State of which he is a citizen."[20] Although current law is similar to this proposed provision as to removal,[21] adoption of the section would represent a significant change in the current structure of original diversity jurisdiction.[22] Such an alteration would wisely confine diversity jurisdiction to cases that actually serve the statutory purpose of preventing prejudice against out-of-state residents in the state courts.

The American Law Institute also proposed a provision stating that "[n]o corporation incorporated or having its principal place of business in the United States, and no partnership, unincorporated association, or sole proprietorship having its principal place of business in the United States, that has and for a period of more than two years has maintained a local establishment in a State, can invoke [the diversity] jurisdiction . . . in any district in that State in any action arising out of the activities of that establishment."[23]

In 1990, the Federal Courts Study Committee submitted to Congress a proposal to revise federal court jurisdiction, including the recommendation that the diversity jurisdiction be substantially reduced. The Committee recommended that Congress limit diversity jurisdiction to complex multistate litigation, interpleader, and suits involving aliens.[24] However, Congress not only failed to reduce the current scope of the diversity jurisdiction, it actually expanded diversity jurisdiction in large class actions under the Class Action Fairness Act of 2005.[25]

## § 3.04 PARTIES OVER WHOM DIVERSITY JURISDICTION MAY BE EXERCISED

Congress has vested the district courts with original jurisdiction of all civil actions in which the matter in controversy exceeds the sum or value of $75,000, exclusive of interests and costs, and is between the following parties:

- Citizens of different states;[26]
- Citizens of a state and citizens or subjects of a foreign state;[27]

---

[20] American Law Institute, Study of the Division of Jurisdiction Between State and Federal Courts, Proposed Section 1302(a) (1969).

[21] 28 U.S.C. § 1441(b) (prohibiting removal of suit under diversity jurisdiction if at least one of defendants is citizen of state in which suit had been brought).

[22] 28 U.S.C. § 1332(a)(1).

[23] American Law Institute, Proposed Section 1302(b). Subsection (c) of the proposal applies the same rule to individuals.

[24] Federal Courts Study Comm., Judicial Conference of the U.S., Report of the Federal Courts Study Committee 38 (1990); *see* Kramer, *Diversity Jurisdiction*, 1990 B.Y.U. L. Rev. 97. Professor Kramer served as reporter for the Study Committee.

[25] *See* P.L. 109-2, 119 Stat. 4.

[26] 28 U.S.C. § 1332(a)(1).

[27] 28 U.S.C. § 1332(a)(2).

- Citizens of different states and in which citizens or subjects of a foreign state are additional parties;[28] or
- A foreign state as plaintiff and citizens of a state or different states.[29]

Diversity jurisdiction presumptively applies to all causes of action for which its requirements are met, whether created by state or federal law. The presumption applies unless Congress explicitly expressed an intent to strip federal courts of diversity jurisdiction or such jurisdiction is irreconcilable with a federal statute.

## § 3.05 "STATES" INCLUDES TERRITORIES, DISTRICT OF COLUMBIA, AND PUERTO RICO

The term "states" for diversity purposes includes the territories, the District of Columbia, and the Commonwealth of Puerto Rico.[30] In *Hepburn & Dundas v. Ellzey*, the Supreme Court held that the term "states" in Article III of the Constitution did not include the District of Columbia.[31] Such a construction, of course, would normally render Congress's extension of the diversity jurisdiction to the District of Columbia unconstitutional. However, in *National Mutual Insurance Co. v. Tidewater Transfer Co.*, the Court upheld this jurisdictional extension without having a majority overrule *Hepburn v. Dundas*.[32] Although two Justices did wish to overrule *Hepburn*,[33] three other Justices upheld the extension of federal court jurisdiction over suits between citizens of a state and citizens of the District of Columbia as a congressional vesting of Article I power in the Article III courts.[34]

A corporation that is chartered under one of the above-listed governments is properly treated as both a citizen of its jurisdiction of incorporation and of the place (if different) where it has its principal place of business.

## § 3.06 THE COMPLETE DIVERSITY REQUIREMENT

In supposed accordance with both the asserted purposes of the diversity jurisdiction and the concern over the undue expenditure of federal judicial resources, diversity jurisdiction has been confined to cases of so-called "complete diversity." Under this principle, diversity jurisdiction is confined to suits in which *all* plaintiffs are from different states from *all* defendants.[35] The complete diversity

---

[28] 28 U.S.C. § 1332(a)(3).

[29] 28 U.S.C. § 1332(a)(4).

[30] 28 U.S.C. § 1332(e).

[31] Hepburn & Dundas v. Ellzey, 6 U.S. (2 Cranch) 445 (1805).

[32] National Mut. Ins. Co. v. Tidewater Transfer Co., 337 U.S. 582, 603–604 (1949).

[33] National Mut. Ins. Co. v. Tidewater Transfer Co., 337 U.S. 582, 604 (1949) (Rutledge, J. concurring, joined by Murphy, J.).

[34] National Mut. Ins. Co. v. Tidewater Transfer Co., 337 U.S. 582, 600 (1949) (opinion of Jackson, J., joined by Black and Burton, JJ.).

[35] Strawbridge v. Curtiss, 7 U.S. (3 Cranch) 267 (1806); Tapscott v. MS Dealer Serv. Corp, 77 F.3d 1353, 1359 (11th Cir. 1996) (action may remain removable despite fraudulent joinder of nondiverse parties).

rule should be contrasted with the alternative of "minimal diversity," which would require that only one plaintiff be a citizen of a different state from that of at least one defendant. Under a requirement of minimal diversity, an overlap of citizenship could exist among some plaintiffs and defendant without defeating jurisdiction, while in complete diversity, no such overlap may exist.

Although neither the constitutional nor statutory provisions of diversity jurisdiction expressly impose the complete diversity requirement,[36] the dictate was first recognized by Chief Justice Marshall in *Strawbridge v. Curtiss*.[37] What remained unclear for many years, however, was whether the complete diversity requirement represented an inference from the constitutional provision or from the statutory provision.

Chief Justice Marshall's opinion in *Strawbridge* failed to resolve this issue, and the text of neither provision provides any clue, since neither makes any explicit reference to the complete diversity requirement. The answer to this question can have potentially significant practical consequences. If the complete diversity requirement is deemed to have constitutional status, then alteration or repeal of the requirement would be beyond congressional power. If, on the other hand, the complete diversity standard is found merely to constitute an inference of congressional intent from congressional silence in the diversity statute, then Congress would be empowered to alter the complete diversity requirement.

The Supreme Court finally resolved this issue in *State Farm Fire & Casualty Co. v. Tashire*. There, the Court interpreted the federal interpleader statute[38] to require only minimal diversity among claimants, and upheld the constitutionality of the statute as a proper exercise of Article III's diversity jurisdiction.[39] In so holding, the Court finally established that the complete diversity requirement derives from the statutory grant of diversity jurisdiction, rather than from Article III of the Constitution.

The uncertainty about the textual source of the complete diversity requirement raises questions about the institutional appropriateness of the judiciary's recognition of that requirement in the first place. In *Strawbridge*, Chief Justice Marshall made absolutely no effort to glean the complete diversity requirement from either the text or policies of the diversity statute. Although the complete diversity requirement does not contradict explicit statutory text, the silence of the text at the very least imposes a burden on an interpreting court to discern the requirement from the normative legislative policies implicit in the statute. The Supreme Court has never undertaken this task.

Today, one might reasonably respond, complete diversity's historical pedigree is so strong that it would undoubtedly violate congressional understanding, if not explicit intent, for the Court to abandon it. As a purely practical matter, this

---

36 *See* U.S. Const., art. III, § 2; 28 U.S.C. § 1332.

37 Origin of complete diversity requirement. Strawbridge v. Curtiss, 7 U.S. (3 Cranch) 267, (1806).

38 28 U.S.C. § 1335.

39 Complete diversity requirement is not grounded in Article III. State Farm Fire & Cas. Co. v. Tashire, 386 U.S. 523, 530–531 (1967).

argument is undoubtedly correct. The fact that, over the years, Congress has made efforts to curb diversity jurisdiction[40] tends to demonstrate Congress's awareness and acceptance of the complete diversity requirement. Indeed, in enacting the Supplemental Jurisdiction Statute,[41] Congress indirectly expressed approval of the complete diversity requirement by declining to extend supplemental jurisdiction to most cases barred by the complete diversity requirement. Thus, today, if not at the time it was originally recognized, the complete diversity requirement represents a proper construction of congressional intent, though the principle is nowhere expressly embodied in the text of Section 1332.

The wisdom of the complete diversity requirement may be challenged purely on normative policy grounds, wholly apart from its validity as a matter of the construction of statutory text.[42] If one were to attempt to justify the complete diversity requirement in terms of the policies underlying diversity jurisdiction, the argument presumably would be that the presence of a citizen of the same state on both sides of the case effectively neutralizes any danger of state court prejudice. This may not be a valid assumption, however. Consider the following hypothetical: A, a resident of Illinois, and B, a resident of New York, sue C, a resident of Illinois, in Illinois state court. Clearly, the case could not be brought in federal court because it fails the complete diversity requirement. If one begins with the assumption that the purpose of diversity jurisdiction is to avoid state court prejudice against out-of-staters, however, it is by no means clear that this is a case in which diversity jurisdiction should be precluded. An Illinois state court bent on prejudicing the New York plaintiff is provided with little disincentive toward that end by the additional presence of the Illinois plaintiff. With an Illinois litigant on each side of the case, any state court protectiveness toward its own residents is neutralized. Thus, if the danger of prejudice is assumed to be real, the asserted rationale for the complete diversity requirement breaks down. This problem is even greater when a citizen of New York and a citizen of Illinois sue a citizen of Illinois in New York state court. In such a situation, the state court would have even less disincentive to avoid prejudicing the Illinois defendant.

One might reasonably respond that despite the arguably tenuous nature of the connection between the complete diversity requirement and the policies underlying diversity jurisdiction, the requirement may nevertheless today be defended on the grounds that it effectively controls the number of diversity cases that can be brought in federal court. However, a rule forbidding the assertion of diversity jurisdiction by persons born under specified astrological signs would have the same effect. Yet, such a method of limitation would be deemed so irrational as to be clearly unacceptable. Apart from its obvious historical pedigree, it is unclear that the complete diversity requirement is any more rational a means of curbing diversity

---

[40] *See, e.g.*, Act of July 25, 1958, Pub. L. 85-554, § 2, 72 Stat. 415, amending 28 U.S.C. § 1332 to classify a corporation as a resident not only of its state of incorporation but also of the state in which its principal place of business is located. As a result, suits between a corporation and a citizen of the state where that corporation's principal place of business is located no longer fell within the diversity jurisdiction, due to the complete diversity requirement.

[41] 28 U.S.C. § 1367.

[42] *See* Currie, *The Federal Courts and the American Law Institute, Part I*, 36 U. Chi. L. Rev. 1, 19 (1968).

jurisdiction than an approach premised on the basis of a litigant's astrological sign.

Because the complete diversity requirement derives from the statutory grant of diversity jurisdiction, Congress may extend federal diversity jurisdiction to cases involving less than complete diversity without running afoul of Article III of the Constitution. The following statutes require less than complete diversity for a federal court to have original jurisdiction over the action:

- The federal interpleader statute;[43]
- The Multiparty, Multiforum Trial Jurisdiction Act of 2002[44] and
- The Class Action Fairness Act of 2005.[45]

## § 3.07 TIME OF DETERMINATION OF DIVERSITY

Diversity is generally determined on the basis of the citizenship of the parties at the time suit is filed. This stems from the long-standing rule that a court's jurisdiction depends on the state of things when the action is brought.[46] Thus, a party's post-filing change in citizenship cannot cure an absence of diversity that existed when the suit was filed.[47] Nor can such a change *defeat* jurisdiction if diversity *did* exist when suit was filed.

The Supreme Court has indicated a strong disinclination to recognize exceptions to the rule that post-filing changes in the parties' citizenship do not affect jurisdiction. The Court reasoned that uncertainty regarding the question of jurisdiction is particularly undesirable, and collateral litigation on the point is especially wasteful.[48] However, a change in the *identity* of the parties will, in some cases, confer or defeat jurisdiction.

If a state-court case is removed to federal court, diversity generally must exist both when the state suit is filed and when the petition for removal is filed.[49] However, there are exceptions to this rule.[50]

---

[43] 28 U.S.C. § 1335.

[44] *See* P.L. No. 107-273, 116 Stat. 1758; *see also* 28 U.S.C. §§ 1369, 1391(g), 1441(e), (f), 1697, 1785.

[45] *See* P.L. No. 109-2, 119 Stat. 4; *see also* 28 U.S.C. §§ 1332(d), 1453.

[46] Jurisdiction depends on state of things when suit filed. Grupo Dataflux v. Atlas Global Group, L.P., 541 U.S. 567, 570–571 (2004) (citing *Mollan v. Torrance*, 22 U.S. 537,539 (1824)).

[47] Post-filing change cannot confer jurisdiction. Grupo Dataflux v. Atlas Global Group, L.P., 541 U.S. 567, 575 (2004) (departure of non-diverse partners from plaintiff partnership after suit was filed but before trial did not cure lack of diversity at time suit was filed).

[48] Exceptions disfavored. Grupo Dataflux v. Atlas Global Group, L.P., 541 U.S. 567, 582 (2004); *but see* Grupo Dataflux v. Atlas Global Group, L.P., 541 U.S. 567, 582–599 (2004) (Ginsburg, J., dissenting, arguing that departure of non-diverse partners from plaintiff partnership before trial conferred jurisdiction in case in which defendant did not raise jurisdictional defect until after jury returned verdict for plaintiff).

[49] Diversity when suit and removal petition filed. *See* Pullman Co. v. Jenkins, 305 U.S. 534, 540–541 (1939); Koenigsberger v. Richmond Silver Mining Co., 158 U.S. 41, 49–50 (1895).

[50] Exceptions. *See, e.g.*, 28 U.S.C. § 1446(b) (authorizing removal after filing of amended complaint from which it may be determined for first time that complete diversity exists).

## § 3.08 28 U.S.C. § 1359 PROHIBITS DISTRICT COURT JURISDICTION IF JOINDER IS COLLUSIVE

Under 28 U.S.C. § 1359, a federal district court lacks jurisdiction over a civil action in which any party, by assignment or otherwise, has been improperly or collusively made or joined in order to invoke the court's jurisdiction.[51] The phrase, "improper or collusive" joinder in Section 1359 has been construed to include those joinders that "confer jurisdiction not justified by aims of diversity."[52] By enacting Section 1359, Congress sought to assure that ordinary contract and tort litigation would not be diverted to federal courts by litigants using collusive or improper devices to create the appearance, but not the substance, of federal diversity jurisdiction.[53]

Federal courts are required by Section 1359 to determine if a party has been artificially brought into a suit solely to invoke federal jurisdiction.[54] The goal of the statute is to limit consideration of actions by federal courts to cases that truly and substantially involve a dispute within the proper jurisdiction of the federal court system. Under Section 1359, courts give careful scrutiny to assignments that might operate to manufacture diversity jurisdiction.

Section 1359 was enacted as part of the revision of the Judicial Code of 1948. Before that time, two federal statutes — now superseded by Section 1359 — regulated the use of devices to create diversity jurisdiction.[55] One, the so-called "assignee clause," with minor exceptions, prohibited diversity jurisdiction in any case to recover on a promissory note or other chose in action in favor of an assignee unless the suit could have been brought had no assignment been made.[56] The other provision stated that a district court must dismiss an action if it appears to the court's satisfaction that the suit does not really and substantially involve a dispute or controversy properly within the jurisdiction of the court, or that the parties to the suit have been improperly or collusively made or joined for the purpose of creating federal jurisdiction.[57] By framing Section 1359 in this latter, subjective, case-by-case approach, Congress abandoned the more objective and easily applied — although more clumsy and overly broad — methodology of the Assignee Clause.

Agreement of the parties to a suit may not be used to confer federal court jurisdiction.[58] Because an agreement of the parties to the assertion of federal jurisdiction is nothing more than a contrivance designed solely to place the litigation

---

[51] 28 U.S.C. § 1359.

[52] "Improper or collusive joinder" defined.

[53] Purpose of 28 U.S.C. § 1359. *See* Gross v. Hougland, 712 F.2d 1034, 1037 (6th Cir. 1983).

[54] Under 28 U.S.C. § 1359, courts determine bona fides of suit. U.S.I. Props. Corp. v. M.D. Constr. Co., 860 F.2d 1, 7 (1st Cir. 1988) (legitimate multilateral agreements were designed to lead to construction of housing project, not create diversity).

[55] 28 U.S.C. § 1359 superseded two statutes. *See* Kramer v. Caribbean Mills, Inc., 394 U.S. 823, 828–829 (1969).

[56] *See* former 28 U.S.C. § 41(1).

[57] Former 28 U.S.C. § 80, originally enacted in 1875; *see* 18 Stat. 470.

[58] Agreement does not confer federal jurisdiction. *See* City of Indianapolis v. Chase Nat'l Bank, 314 U.S. 63, 67 (1941).

within the federal court system, the agreement constitutes a collusive joinder under Section 1359 and may not be used to invoke federal district court jurisdiction.

The assignment or transfer of a claim that is feigned or merely colorable, rather than absolute or genuine, and made for the sole purpose of creating diversity jurisdiction violates Section 1359 as improper or collusive and does not create federal diversity jurisdiction.[59] The case-by-case approach taken in Section 1359 differs significantly from the more easily applied, but also more clumsy, objective standard employed in the so-called "assignee clause," which was superseded by the adoption of Section 1359 in 1948. Under the assignee clause, it should be recalled, district courts were prohibited from asserting diversity jurisdiction over any suit on a promissory note or chose in action in favor of an assignee unless the suit might have been prosecuted in that court had no assignment been made.[60]

The leading Supreme Court decision on the subject is *Kramer v. Caribbean Mills, Inc.* Caribbean Mills, a Haitian corporation, had entered into a contract with a Panamanian corporation to purchase shares of the Panamanian corporation's corporate stock. When Caribbean Mills failed to make the required installment payments, the Panamanian corporation assigned its entire interest in the contract to Kramer, a Texas attorney. By a separate agreement dated the same day, Kramer promised to pay back to the Panamanian corporation 95 percent of any net recovery on the assigned cause of action, "solely as a bonus." Kramer then brought suit against Caribbean in the Northern District of Texas.[61]

The Supreme Court affirmed the Fifth Circuit's decision dismissing the case because the assignment was improperly or collusively made under Section 1359. The Court found the assignment collusive by examination of the totality of the circumstances:[62]

> When the assignment to Kramer is considered together with his total lack of previous connection with the matter and his simultaneous reassignment of a 95% interest back to Panama, there can be little doubt that the assignment was for purposes of collection, with Kramer to retain 5% of the net proceeds "for the use of his name and his trouble in collecting."

The Court found its conclusion supported by examination of Section 1359's purpose, because if federal jurisdiction could be so easily created by assignment, then a substantial body of ordinary litigation could be channeled into federal court, in contravention of the congressional intent clearly manifested in section 1359.[63] Further, the court found that the fact that the assignment was legal under Texas law did not necessarily preclude a finding that it was improper under Section 1359.

---

59 Merely colorable assignment is collusive. Kramer v. Caribbean Mills, Inc., 394 U.S. 823, 829–830 (1969) (legality under Texas law of assignment to Texas attorney of Panamanian corporation's cause of action against Haitian corporation does not necessarily render assignment valid for purposes of federal jurisdiction).

60 Former 28 U.S.C. § 41(1). The clause appeared originally as Section 11 of the Judiciary Act of 1789, Stat. 79; *see* Kramer v. Caribbean Mills, Inc., 394 U.S. 823, 825–826 (1969).

61 Facts of *Kramer*. Kramer v. Caribbean Mills, Inc., 394 U.S. 823, 824–825 (1969).

62 394 U.S. at 827–828.

63 394 U.S. at 828–829.

This is due to the fact that state law does not take account of the interests of the federal judicial system in avoiding collusive diversity cases.[64]

In construing *Kramer* to determine if an assignment has been collusively or improperly made under Section 1359, the federal courts consider a variety of factors. In searching for a bona fide business interest, the adequacy of consideration for the assignment, coupled with the nature of any retained interest by the assignor, is a major factor. It may be deemed proper for purposes of diversity if the assignee fully pays the assignor and the transfer is made without recourse, but collusive if the assignee pays no consideration and the assignor retains an interest in the outcome of the litigation with the assignment intended solely to obtain diversity.

Another factor is whether the assignee is the real party in interest. Diversity is deemed proper if the plaintiff assignee has a real and substantial interest in the outcome of the litigation, and denied as collusive if the plaintiff lacks a true interest. The assignment and aggregation of several smaller claims in order to reach the jurisdictional amount is often considered collusive.

Some federal courts have adopted a two-pronged test for determining whether an assignment or transfer is collusive or improper under Section 1359. These prongs are as follows:

1. An objective determination as to whether the assignment is of a type that places the nominal plaintiffs in a position to assert the real interest of another; and, if so,
2. A subjective determination as to whether the transaction was manufactured solely to obtain federal diversity jurisdiction or was made for a bona fide business purpose wholly apart from acquiring federal jurisdiction.

There is also a view that motive is entirely irrelevant if the assignment is bona fide, even though its sole purpose is to create diversity. Before *Kramer*, a line of Supreme Court cases had held that if the transfer of a claim is absolute, with the transferor retaining no interest in the subject matter, the transfer is deemed not to be improper or collusive, regardless of the transferor's motive.[65] In *Kramer*, the Court noted that it had no occasion to reexamine those cases because they were distinguishable from the facts of the case before it, which involved only a partial assignment with the assignor retaining a substantial portion of the subject of the assignment.[66] This statement suggests that perhaps the continuing validity of the rule is subject to some doubt.

Because of the close relationship between parent corporations and their wholly owned subsidiaries, assignments between these business entities are subjected to a heightened scrutiny in determining if the assignment is collusive under Section 1359. In fact, some courts impose a rebuttable presumption that these assignments

---

[64] 394 U.S. at 829.

[65] Supreme Court cases holding that intent is irrelevant if transfer is absolute. Cross v. Allen, 141 U.S. 528 (1891); South Dakota v. North Carolina, 192 U.S. 286 (1904); Black & White Taxicab Co. v. Brown & Yellow Taxicab Co., 276 U.S. 518 (1928).

[66] Court in *Kramer* did not reexamine issue. Kramer v. Caribbean Mills, Inc., 394 U.S. 823, 828 n.9 (1969).

are made collusively in order to manufacture federal diversity jurisdiction. Assignments between a corporation and its corporate officers are also subject to this presumption of collusion in some circuits. When the presumption applies, the assignee must rebut it by establishing that the assignment was motivated by a bona fide business reason, not simply to manufacture federal jurisdiction.

By its terms, Section 1359 prohibits only the collusive *manufacture* of diversity jurisdiction, and, before the Supreme Court's decision in *Kramer v. Caribbean Mills, Inc.*,[67] the federal courts almost uniformly declined to inquire into the motives behind the collusive *destruction* of diversity.[68] However, the modern trend is toward applying parallel logic to reject the collusive destruction of diversity.

The court is responsible for realigning the parties in a diversity suit according to their interests. The leading decision on the realignment of parties in order to determine the existence of diversity is *City of Indianapolis v. Chase National Bank*. In that case, the Supreme Court held that to sustain diversity jurisdiction, there must be an "actual, substantial controversy" between citizens of different states.[69] The Supreme Court therefore directed the lower courts to examine the realities of the record in order to ascertain the real interests of the parties.[70] Whether the necessary "collision of interests" is present among parties pleaded as adverse must be ascertained from an assessment of the principal purpose of the suit and the primary and controlling matter in dispute.

In *City of Indianapolis*, the Supreme Court found that the principal matter in dispute was whether a lease was valid. Because both the plaintiff bank and the city, a named defendant, wanted the lease enforced, the city was realigned as a plaintiff with the bank. As a result, citizens of one state were on both sides of the dispute, and therefore diversity jurisdiction did not exist.

The initial difficulty courts have faced in attempting to apply the *City of Indianapolis* test is in deciding whether the existence of a colliding controversy between parties pleaded as adverse must be determined on the basis of only the principal purpose of the suit ("primary and controlling matter in dispute") or whether it is sufficient to find an "actual and substantial controversy" between the parties, regardless of whether or not that controversy concerns the principal purpose of the suit.

In *City of Indianapolis*, the Supreme Court stated that the finding of collision must concern the "primary and controlling matter in dispute."[71] In that case, there was an identifiable primary and controlling matter in dispute, the validity of a lease, as to which parties on each side had the same interests. The Supreme Court noted

---

[67] Kramer v. Caribbean Mills, Inc., 394 U.S. 823 (1969).

[68] Prior practice of nonscrutiny. *See* Provident Savings Life Assurance Society v. Ford, 114 U.S. 635, 641 (1885).

[69] Actual, substantial controversy is required. City of Indianapolis v. Chase Nat'l Bank, 314 U.S. 63, 69 (1941).

[70] Real interests of parties must be determined. City of Indianapolis v. Chase Nat'l Bank, 314 U.S. 63, 69 (1941); Maryland Cas. Co. v. W.R. Grace & Co., 23 F.3d 617, 623 (2d Cir. 1993).

[71] Primary and controlling matter in dispute. City of Indianapolis v. Chase Nat'l Bank, 314 U.S. 63, 69 (1941).

that the interests of two parties (although they were pleaded on adverse sides) turned identically on the validity of the lease.[72]

Under the "primary purpose" test, which reads *City of Indianapolis* literally, the parties must be realigned if there is no adverseness with regard to the primary issue in dispute. Use of this "primary purpose" test often requires realignment. For example, the parties may be in conflict over any number of matters, but they will be realigned if there is no conflict with regard to what the court determines the primary purpose of the suit to be. Courts rejecting the "primary purpose" test have reasoned that if the primary purpose of the suit were the sole controlling standard, that discussion in *City of Indianapolis* would have been wholly unnecessary. Courts declining to apply the "primary purpose" test often choose in its place the "substantial conflict" test. Under this standard, realignment of parties is not required if there is any "actual and substantial conflict" between the parties. Realignment is proper only if the court finds that no actual, substantial controversy exists between a party on one side of the dispute and a named opponent.

Yet another alternative is the "collision of interests" test. Under this approach, courts require the existence of an actual, substantial controversy, or a collision of interests, but the conflict may, in some cases, concern an issue other than the "primary issue" in dispute. The Second Circuit has followed the "collision of interests" test, holding that the approach is consistent with the Supreme Court's chief concern in *City of Indianapolis*, that is, that parties not manipulate alignment to manufacture diversity jurisdiction. The court also found this approach more flexible because it permits the court to consider the multiple interests and issues involved in the litigation.

In applying the "collision of interests" test, the court must determine that actual and substantial conflicts existed at the initiation of the suit. Hypothetical conflicts manufactured by skillful counsel must not control because that approach would reintroduce the notion of gamesmanship, which the Supreme Court has disparaged.

Subsequent events do not deprive a court of jurisdiction over parties who were properly aligned in the first instance. Any change of the parties by addition, substitution, or elimination will not divest a federal court of diversity jurisdiction, provided that the action remains the same and there is no evidence of collusion to create jurisdiction. A defendant's claim against a third-party defendant is within a federal court's supplemental jurisdiction.

## § 3.09 DIVERSITY AND REMOVAL

If a case is filed in state court and a defendant seeks removal to federal court, diversity of citizenship generally must exist both at the time the original action is filed and at the time the removal petition is filed.[73] Therefore, whether a defendant

---

[72] Identifiable primary matter. *See* Travelers Indem. Co. v. Metropolitan Life Ins. Co., 798 F. Supp. 156, 158 (S.D.N.Y. 1992).

[73] Diversity when suit filed and removal petition filed. Pullman Co. v. Jenkins, 305 U.S. 534, 537 (1939) (diversity required when action commenced and at time of removal); Koenigsberger v. Richmond Silver Mining Co., 158 U.S. 41, 49–50 (1895).

has the right to remove a case must be determined from the allegations in the complaint at the time of removal.[74] Jurisdiction that is present at the time a suit is both filed and removed is usually unaffected by subsequent acts.[75]

However, this rule is subject to exceptions. Title 28 U.S.C. § 1446(b) authorizes removal after the filing of an amended complaint from which it may be determined that the case is one that is or has become removable. This statute has been construed as providing that an amended complaint from which it may be determined for the first time that complete diversity exists is removable, even if the action was not removable at the time when it was filed in state court, subject to the one-year from filing limitation. However, the amendment must be on account of some voluntary action by the plaintiff that creates diversity, such as by dismissing a nondiverse defendant. A case may not be removed if the removability is a result of some development other than a voluntary act of plaintiff. For example, it may not be removed as a result of evidence from the defendant or because of a court order rendered on the merits of the case.

Further, the Class Action Fairness Act of 2005 (CAFA)[76] authorizes the removal of certain multistate class actions.[77] A class action involving multistate parties in state court that is not initially removable may become removable as the case progresses. For example, some state court plaintiffs may settle or otherwise drop out of the case, reducing the percentage of local plaintiffs so as to permit removal to federal court.[78] However, under CAFA, there is no overall one-year time limitation on removal as under the general removal statute.

Another evidentiary exception to the rule that removal diversity jurisdiction is determined at the time of the complaint applies if the complaint does not state a specific amount of damages. In that case, removal is proper if it is facially apparent from the complaint that the amount in controversy exceeds the jurisdictional minimum. If the jurisdictional amount is not facially apparent, the court should look to the removal notice and may require post-removal evidence relevant to the amount in controversy at the time of removal.

There is another exception based on principles of estoppel and judicial economy, referred to as the "*Caterpillar* rule." If, after removal, a case is tried on the merits without objection and the federal court enters judgment, the issue in subsequent proceedings on appeal is not whether the case was properly removed, but whether the federal district court would have had original jurisdiction of the case had it been filed in that court.[79] The *Caterpillar* rule extends to cases in which the district court

---

[74] Determine from allegations at time of removal. Pullman Co. v. Jenkins, 305 U.S. 534, 537 (1939).

[75] Subsequent acts irrelevant. Wichita R.R. & Light Co. v. Public Util. Comm'n, 260 U.S. 48, 54 (1922) (diverse when breach of contract action arose and when federal proceedings commenced); Mollan v. Torrance, 22 U.S. (9 Wheat.) 537, 539 (1824); *In re* Shell Oil Co., 966 F.2d 1130, 1133 (7th Cir. 1992) (general rule subject to exception under *Newman-Green, Inc. v. Alfonzo-Larrain*, 490 U.S. 826, 830 (1989)).

[76] P.L. No. 109-2, 119 Stat. 4.

[77] 28 U.S.C. §§ 1332(d)(10), 1453(b).

[78] *See, e.g.*, 28 U.S.C. § 1332(d)(4).

[79] Exception based on estoppel and judicial economy. Grubbs v. General Elec. Credit Corp., 405 U.S.

lacked diversity jurisdiction at the time of removal, if the defect subsequently is cured before it is noticed, and before trial and judgment.[80] This rule is strictly limited, however, and is not a general principle that lack of diversity can be ignored if substantial judicial resources have been invested before it is discovered. If there has been a lack of diversity between the parties throughout the proceedings in the trial court, the judgment must be vacated and the case remanded to state court.

The Supreme Court has clarified that the "*Caterpillar* rule" relates not to the cure of a *jurisdictional* defect, but rather to the cure of a *statutory* defect — the requirement that there be complete diversity at the time of removal.[81] The Court expressly rejected the application of the *Caterpillar* rule to diversity cases originally filed in federal court, at least when there is no change in parties. In other words, a party's post-filing change of citizenship does not cure a lack of subject-matter jurisdiction that existed at the time of filing the complaint because that is when federal diversity jurisdiction is determined.[82]

## § 3.10 FRAUDULENT JOINDER

In determining whether there is diversity of citizenship, the court must disregard parties fraudulently joined. The removing party bears a heavy burden of persuasion to demonstrate fraudulent joinder. Such a claim must be pled with particularity and supported by clear and convincing evidence.

Joinder will not be deemed fraudulent unless there clearly can be no recovery under state law on the cause alleged or on the facts as they exist when the petition to remand is heard. Impossibility of recovery must be established in order to show that the plaintiff had no real intention of obtaining a joint judgment, and that there was no colorable ground for the claim.

The court must determine whether there is "arguably a reasonable basis" for predicting that the state law might impose liability on the facts involved. If that possibility exists, an assertion of the expectancy is not a sham, and is not fraudulent in fact or in law. Under this standard, if there is any possibility of a valid claim against the nondiverse defendant, there is no diversity and the case is properly cognizable only in the state courts. It should be emphasized that this does not mean that the plaintiff must be able to demonstrate that he or she will, in fact, prevail, or even that the plaintiff could show that he or she could survive a motion for summary judgment filed by the in-state defendant.

---

699, 702 (1972) (jurisdiction must exist at time of judgment); *see* Caterpillar, Inc. v. Lewis, 519 U.S. 61, 75 n.13 (1996) (after motion to remand, all claims involving nondiverse defendant were settled and defendant was dismissed as party to action).

[80] Defect must be cured before judgment. *See* Caterpillar, Inc. v. Lewis, 519 U.S. 61, 70–73, 75 n.13 (1996) (after motion to remand, all claims involving nondiverse defendant were settled and defendant was dismissed as party to action before judgment).

[81] *Caterpillar* rule relates to statutory defect. Grupo Dataflux v. Atlas Global Group, L.P., 541 U.S. 567, 574 (2004) (final judgment was between diverse parties after diversity-destroying defendant was dismissed after pretrial settlement).

[82] Post-filing change in citizenship does not cure jurisdictional defect existing when suit filed in federal court. Grupo Dataflux v. Atlas Global Group, L.P., 541 U.S. 567, 574–575 (2004).

The federal court's review for fraud must be based on the plaintiff's pleadings at the time of removal, supplemented by any affidavits and deposition transcripts submitted by the parties.[83] The court must assume all the facts alleged by plaintiff to be true and resolve all uncertainties regarding state substantive law against defendants. Only if it finds that there is no possibility that a valid cause of action has been pleaded against the nondiverse defendant will fraudulent joinder be found to exist. Federal law controls joinder issues, including whether the court should proceed.

## § 3.11 JURISDICTION OF DISTRICT COURTS UNDER CLASS ACTION FAIRNESS ACT OF 2005 (CAFA)

The Class Action Fairness Act of 2005 (CAFA)[84] greatly expanded the scope of diversity jurisdiction in large, multistate class actions. CAFA includes special jurisdictional and procedural provisions that permit district courts to exercise original subject matter jurisdiction over multistate class actions based on minimal diversity.[85] Further, although Congress raised the amount in controversy required to exercise subject matter jurisdiction over a class action based on minimal diversity, the statute requires that the claims of all class members be aggregated in measuring whether the required amount is in controversy.[86] This aggregation requirement greatly increases the possibility that a federal court will have subject matter jurisdiction over large class actions involving a number of small monetary claims.

CAFA's jurisdictional provisions apply to any action brought as a class action, that is, any civil action filed under Rule 23 of the Federal Rules of Civil Procedure or similar state statute or rule of judicial procedure authorizing an action to be brought by one or more representative persons as a class action, both before and after the entry of a class certification order by the court.[87]

CAFA permits district courts to exercise federal subject matter jurisdiction over multistate class actions in which the amount in controversy requirement is met and either:[88]

- Any member of a class of plaintiffs is a citizen of a state different from any defendant;
- Any member of a class of plaintiffs is a foreign state or a citizen or subject of a foreign state and any defendant is a citizen of a state; or
- Any member of a class of plaintiffs is a citizen of a state and any defendant is a foreign state or a citizen or subject of a foreign state.

---

[83] Fraudulent joinder determined as of time of removal. Pacheco de Perez v. AT&T Co., 139 F.3d 1368, 1380 (11th Cir. 1998).

[84] Pub. L. 109-2; *see* 28 U.S.C. § 1332(d).

[85] Pub. L. 109-2, § 4; *see* 28 U.S.C. §§ 1332(d), 1453.

[86] *See* 28 U.S.C. § 1332(d).

[87] 28 U.S.C. § 1332(d)(1)(B), (8).

[88] 28 U.S.C. § 1332(d)(2).

Because complete diversity is not required under CAFA, a suit in which a state is a plaintiff may satisfy the minimal diversity requirement if the suit includes a plaintiff class of state citizens. Even without a class of citizen plaintiffs, a state attorney general's suit may be considered a "mass action" within the scope of CAFA if the suit seeks recovery on behalf of a group of individual citizens.[89]

Federal district courts have original jurisdiction over any class action governed by CAFA in which the matter in controversy exceeds the sum or value of $5,000,000, exclusive of interest and costs,[90] provided CAFA's minimal diversity requirements are met. Class members' claims must be aggregated to determine the requisite amount in controversy.[91] CAFA does not otherwise change the assessment of the amount in controversy.

Class actions that do not exceed the $5,000,000 threshold are not entitled to be brought in or removed to federal court under the provisions of CAFA. Nevertheless, they are not excluded from federal jurisdiction if they meet the requirements of some other basis of jurisdiction, such as federal question jurisdiction or traditional diversity jurisdiction under 28 U.S.C. § 1332(a). The latter jurisdictional requirement could, for example, be satisfied if the named plaintiff is diverse from the defendant[92] and each class member's claim exceeded the $75,000 jurisdictional minimum in the general diversity statute.[93] This scenario is conceivable, even when CAFA's aggregate $5 million dollar minimum is not satisfied or one of CAFA's other requirements is not satisfied.

The claims of all class members must be aggregated to determine whether CAFA's amount-in-controversy requirement is met in any case.[94] Thus, while the amount-in-controversy minimum of $5,000,000[95] seems quite high compared to the normal diversity jurisdiction minimum of only $75,000,[96] the aggregation rule makes the Act's $5,000,000 minimum easier to meet in many cases. The aggregation requirement is a major departure from the diversity requirements in situations not controlled by CAFA, under which either every class member must have a claim worth more than $75,000 or at least one named class member must have an individual claim worth more than $75,000 and the claims of every other class

---

[89] State attorney general's action deemed "mass action." *See* Louisiana *ex rel.* Caldwell v. Allstate Ins. Co., 536 F.3d 418, 429–430 (5th Cir. 2008) (state attorney general's suit on behalf of Louisiana policyholders considered "mass action").

[90] 28 U.S.C. § 1332(d)(2).

[91] 28 U.S.C. § 1332(d)(6).

[92] Diversity jurisdiction in case not controlled by CAFA. In a diversity class action not controlled by CAFA, there need not be complete diversity between the defendant and all class members. It is sufficient that the named plaintiff and the defendant be of diverse citizenship. Supreme Tribe of Ben-Hur v. Cauble, 255 U.S. 356, 365 (1921).

[93] Claims exceeding jurisdictional minimum. Each class member in a non-CAFA diversity class must have a claim worth in excess of the jurisdictional minimum. Snyder v. Harris 394 U.S. 332, 336 (1969).

[94] 28 U.S.C. § 1332(d)(6).

[95] 28 U.S.C. § 1332(d)(2).

[96] *See* 28 U.S.C. § 1332(a).

member must satisfy the requirements for supplemental jurisdiction.[97]

CAFA's expansive grant of minimal diversity of citizenship subject matter jurisdiction is unusual. If a party establishes the minimal diversity of citizenship and the minimum amount in controversy, the court has jurisdiction — but that jurisdiction is subject to a later rejection by the court.[98] CAFA requires federal courts to decline to exercise jurisdiction when more than two-thirds of the plaintiff class members are citizens of the forum state and it allows a federal court to decline to exercise jurisdiction when more than one-third and less than two-thirds of the plaintiff class members are citizens of the forum. Federal courts lack the discretion to decline jurisdiction *only* when one-third or fewer of the class members are citizens of the forum state. Thus, CAFA's jurisdictional grant creates a state of affairs contrary to the normal rule compelling a federal court to exercise its jurisdiction unless there are specific, limited grounds for its abstention.

In general, when one-third or fewer of the class members are citizens of the original forum state, federal courts must exercise jurisdiction over the class action.[99] CAFA does not permit federal courts to decline to exercise jurisdiction in this situation.

Although CAFA significantly expands federal diversity jurisdiction over class actions, it also limits this jurisdiction with respect to classes composed largely of citizens of the forum state. Specifically, CAFA establishes two situations in which the district court *must* decline jurisdiction:[100] (1) the "local controversy exception" and (2) the "home state exception". When the complex requirements of these exceptions are satisfied, the district court must dismiss the action or, if the action was removed to federal court from state court, remand the action to state court, absent some other basis for federal court jurisdiction, such as either federal question jurisdiction or traditional, "complete" diversity jurisdiction. Whether the exceptions apply is determined based on the class the plaintiff proposed when the suit was filed.

The local controversy and home state exceptions are not jurisdictional. Section 1332(d) gives the district courts broad subject matter jurisdiction over cases that fall within its parameters. District courts "shall decline to exercise [this] jurisdiction" when the requirements for the local controversy and home state rules are satisfied. Thus, the exceptions operate like abstention doctrines rather than as restrictions on jurisdiction. As non-jurisdictional provisions, the exceptions may be waived if not invoked within a reasonable time. It appears that if the other requirements of the local controversy or home state exception are met, the plaintiffs may ensure that the exception applies by defining the class in such a way that only citizens of the state in which the suit is filed are members.

---

[97] CAFA's aggregation requirement as departure from general diversity requirements. *See* 28 U.S.C. §§ 1332(a), 1367.

[98] *See* 28 U.S.C. § 1332(d)(3), (4); *see also* Graphic Commc'ns. Local 1B v. CVS Caremark, 636 F.3d 971, 973 (8th Cir. 2011) (local controversy provision operates as abstention doctrine, which does not divest district court of subject matter jurisdiction).

[99] 28 U.S.C. § 1332(d)(2)–(4).

[100] Mandatory declination of CAFA jurisdiction. 28 U.S.C. § 1332(d)(4).

CAFA affords federal district courts the discretion to decline jurisdiction under specified circumstances. Under CAFA, district courts may, in the interests of justice and looking at the totality of the circumstances, decline to exercise minimal diversity jurisdiction over a class action in which all of the following are true:[101]

- More than one-third of the members of all proposed plaintiff classes, in the aggregate, are citizens of the state in which the action was originally filed; *and*
- Fewer than two-thirds of the members of all proposed plaintiff classes, in the aggregate, are citizens of the state in which the action was originally filed; *and*
- The "primary" defendants are citizens of the state in which the action was originally filed.

The phrase "the primary defendants" means *all* the primary defendants. The term "primary defendant," which is used in both the discretionary declination of jurisdiction provision and the home state exception, is not defined in CAFA.[102]

CAFA provides considerable guidance as to the factors federal courts must consider in measuring "the interests of justice" and considering "the totality of the circumstances." In exercising its discretion, the court must consider all of the following six factors:[103]

- Whether the claims involve matters of national or interstate interest.[104] These interests presumably weigh in favor of a federal forum.
- Whether the claims will be governed by laws of the state in which the action was originally filed or by the laws of other states.[105] If the action is governed by the law of the forum state, then state court may be preferable to federal.
- Whether the class action has been pleaded in a manner that seeks to avoid federal jurisdiction.[106]
- Whether the action was brought in a forum with a distinct nexus with the class members, the alleged harm, or the defendants.[107] Presumably if the action has a strong connection with the forum state, state court is preferred.
- Whether the number of citizens of the state in which the action was originally filed in all proposed plaintiff classes, in the aggregate, is substantially larger than the number of citizens from any other state, and the citizenship of the other members of the proposed class is dispersed

---

[101] 28 U.S.C. § 1332(d)(3).

[102] "Primary defendant" not defined. *See* 28 U.S.C. § 1332(d)(3), (4)(B).

[103] 28 U.S.C. § 1332(d)(3).

[104] 28 U.S.C. § 1332(d)(3)(A).

[105] 28 U.S.C. § 1332(d)(3)(B).

[106] 28 U.S.C. § 1332(d)(3)(C).

[107] 28 U.S.C. § 1332(d)(3)(D).

among a substantial number of states.[108] This factor would also favor state court.

- Whether, during the three-year period preceding the filing of that class action, one or more other class actions asserting the same or similar claims on behalf of the same or other persons have been filed.[109] If there are multiple prior actions with similar claims, especially if filed in various states, a federal forum is indicated.

If the requirements for exercising discretion are met, and if the factors favor a state court proceeding rather than a federal one, the court may, in its discretion, "decline to exercise" the minimal diversity subject matter jurisdiction provided by CAFA.[110] However, the court may dismiss the action or, if the action was removed to federal court from the state court, remand the action to state court, only if there is no other basis for federal court jurisdiction. The discretion to decline jurisdiction under CAFA is limited to the minimal diversity jurisdiction established by CAFA.[111] CAFA does not authorize a district court to decline to exercise jurisdiction over a class action if that jurisdiction is based on either a federal question[112] or traditional, "complete" diversity of citizenship.[113]

The jurisdictional provisions of CAFA also apply to "mass actions."[114] A "mass action" is any civil action, other than a class action, in which monetary relief claims of 100 or more persons are proposed to be tried jointly on the ground that the plaintiffs' claims involve common questions of law or fact.[115] The ambiguous terms "claims of . . . persons" and "proposed to be tried jointly" have given rise to a number of different interpretations of the numerosity requirement).[116] Whether the claims actually proceed to a joint trial is irrelevant.[117]

A "mass action" does *not* include the following:[118]

- Any civil action in which all the claims arise from an event or occurrence in the state in which the action was filed, and that allegedly resulted in injuries in that state or in states contiguous to that state;
- Any civil action in which the claims are joined on motion of a defendant;
- Any civil action in which all the claims are asserted on behalf of the general

[108] 28 U.S.C. § 1332(d)(3)(E).

[109] 28 U.S.C. § 1332(d)(3)(F).

[110] 28 U.S.C. § 1332(d)(3).

[111] *See* 28 U.S.C. § 1332(d)(3) ("court may . . . decline to exercise jurisdiction under paragraph (2)").

[112] *See* 28 U.S.C. § 1331.

[113] *See* 28 U.S.C. § 1332(a); *see also* § 102.12 (complete diversity requirement).

[114] 28 U.S.C. § 1332(d)(11)(A).

[115] 28 U.S.C. § 1332(d)(11)(B)(i).

[116] Conflicting interpretations of numerosity requirement. Knight, *The CAFA Mass Action Numerosity Requirement: Three Problems With Counting to 100,* 78 FORDHAM L. REV. 1875 (2010).

[117] Actual joint trial irrelevant. Visendi v. Bank of Am., N.A., 733 F.3d 863, 868 (9th Cir. 2013) (district court's post-removal conclusion that plaintiff's claims were improperly joined did not affect court's jurisdiction, because at time of removal, plaintiffs proposed joint trial).

[118] 28 U.S.C. § 1332(d)(11)(B)(ii).

public (and not on behalf of individual claimants or members of a purported class) pursuant to a state statute specifically authorizing this type of action; or

- Any civil action in which the claims have been consolidated or coordinated solely for pretrial proceedings.

Thus, a federal district court may exercise subject matter jurisdiction over a "mass action" based on the same sort of minimal diversity of citizenship as applies to class actions.

When a class action is not subject to CAFA the action may nonetheless be brought in federal court under federal question jurisdiction or under traditional diversity principles if applicable. However, federal courts have experienced a number of problems applying the requirements of traditional, "complete" diversity jurisdiction to class actions.

## § 3.12 DETERMINING CITIZENSHIP OF INDIVIDUALS

There is no statutory definition of an individual's citizenship for diversity purposes. Under the Constitution, "[a]ll persons born or naturalized in the United States, and subject to the jurisdiction thereof, are citizens of the United States and of the State wherein they reside."[119]

To be a citizen of a state within the meaning of the diversity statute, a natural person must be both a citizen of the United States and *domiciled* within that state.[120] Thus, there are two necessary inquiries with regard to citizenship for diversity purposes; whether the person is a citizen of the United States, which is a relatively simple inquiry into the citizenship statutes and whether the person is domiciled in a particular state, a far more difficult inquiry.

The citizenship of a party is determined as of the time a suit is filed, based on circumstances as they existed at that time.[121] It is of no significance whether diversity existed at the time the facts giving rise to the cause of action occurred.

A person's domicile is the place where the person has his or her true, fixed home and principal establishment, and to which he or she has the intention of returning whenever absent. Domicile generally requires two elements: (1) physical presence in a state and (2) the intent to make the state a home.[122] Domicile therefore has both a physical and a subjective component, and is more than an individual's residence, although the two typically coincide.

Citizenship is not necessarily lost by protracted absence from home, if the intention to return remains. However, mere "mental fixing" of citizenship, without

---

[119] U.S. Const., amend. XIV.

[120] Citizen of state. Newman-Green, Inc. v. Alfonzo-Larrain, 490 U.S. 826, 828 (1989).

[121] Citizenship determined on circumstances at time suit was filed. Navarro Sav. Ass'n v. Lee, 446 U.S. 458, 459 (1980).

[122] Elements of domicile. Mississippi Band of Choctaw Indians v. Holyfield, 490 U.S. 30, 48 (1989) ("For adults, domicile is established by physical presence in a place in connection with a certain state of mind concerning one's intent to remain there.").

physical presence, is not sufficient to establish citizenship. At any given time, a person has but one domicile.[123]

The determination of a person's domicile is a mixed question of law and fact. Some courts have noted that it is mainly a question of fact, which may not be set aside by an appellate court unless clearly erroneous. Questions as to a person's intent to change or not change domicile from one state to another are factual questions.[124] Courts look to the "totality of the evidence" to determine a party's domicile. Under this standard, no single factor is conclusive.

In the context of diversity jurisdiction, domicile and residence are not necessarily synonymous. The fact that a person resides in a particular state is not, by itself, determinative of citizenship for the purpose of federal court jurisdiction because one can reside in one place but be domiciled in another if the person intends to return to a prior residence. A domicile is thus not the place where a party was residing temporarily when the action was filed.

For purposes of diversity jurisdiction, a citizen has only one domicile, regardless of the number of residences maintained.[125] In determining which of the person's residences is his or her domicile, the court must focus on the intent of the party, which requires an examination of the entire course of a person's conduct.

One court has noted that in this age of second homes and speedy transportation, choosing a single state as an individual's domicile can be a difficult, even a rather arbitrary undertaking. If a person has homes in different states, "domicile" is a legal conclusion, not a thing, "like a rabbit or a carrot," although treated as a factual determination for purposes of defining the scope of appellate review. In the case, a defendant who was originally domiciled in Illinois, bought a second home in Florida, which he used a few months each year as a vacation home, then more frequently after he retired. He was held to still be a domiciliary of Illinois because he intended to spend most of each year there. His voter registration in Florida and his choice of Florida as his permanent residence for tax-shelter purposes did not affect his citizenship for purposes of diversity jurisdiction.

There is no durational, or minimum period of residence that is required to establish domicile. Once the requisite elements of physical presence and intent to remain are met, a new domicile is established instantaneously. A person may change domiciles only by taking up residence in a different state either with the intention to remain there, or at least without any specific intention to live anywhere else.[126] This requirement has also been described as residence in fact, coupled with the purpose to make the place of residence one's home.

---

[123] Only one domicile at any time. Palazzo v. Corio, 232 F.3d 38, 42 (2d Cir. 2000).

[124] Intent to change domicile is question of fact. Palazzo v. Corio, 232 F.3d 38, 42 (2d Cir. 2000).

[125] Person may not have multiple domiciles. Williamson v. Osenton, 232 U.S. 619 (1914) (person may have only one domicile at a time); *see* Restatement (Second) of Conflict of Laws § 20 (if person with capacity to acquire domicile of choice has more than one dwelling, domicile is in earlier dwelling unless second one is principal home).

[126] Change of domicile requires change of residence plus intent. Williamson v. Osenton, 232 U.S. 619 (1914); Sun Printing & Pub. Assoc. v. Edwards, 194 U.S. 377, 383 (1904); Morris v. Gilmer, 129 U.S. 315 (1889) (finding that plaintiff's only motive in moving to Tennessee was to invoke federal jurisdiction).

The intention and the act must concur to effect the change of domicile.[127] Neither the physical presence nor the intention to change domicile, standing alone, is sufficient to effect the change. Thus, a domicile is not lost by mere absence from the domicile state.

It is difficult to set a rule establishing at exactly what point a residence becomes a domicile of choice. However, the court need not find a specific date on which the intent was formulated, as long as it finds that the intent was formed on a day before the filing of the suit and that the intent existed on the date the action was filed.

Questions as to a person's intent to change, or not to change, domicile from one state to another are factual questions. The party alleging that domicile has changed has the burden of proving the requisite intent to cede the old domicile and take up the new domicile, coupled with an actual acquisition of a residence in a new locality.

Because physical presence is easily determined but alone is insufficient to establish change of domicile, the intent element is the crux of the test.[128] There is no requirement that a person state an intention to live in a particular state permanently. It is the absence of an intention to go elsewhere that is controlling. One court has noted that a requirement that a person intend to remain permanently in the new domicile would prevent a significant portion of our mobile population from ever acquiring a new domicile.

To establish a new domicile, a person must have no fixed and definite intent to return to the place where he or she was formerly domiciled. It is sufficient as long as the individual intends to remain at the new home for an indefinite period.

Once a party has established a domicile, the burden of demonstrating that a new domicile has been established lies with the person seeking to establish the change. A plaintiff who claims to have changed his or her domicile in favor of a new one bears a heavy burden of establishing the new domicile. Even more evidence is required to establish a change of domicile from one nation to another than from one state to another.

The legal representative of the estate of a decedent is deemed to be a citizen only of the same state as the decedent for purposes of diversity. The legal representative of an infant or incompetent is deemed to be a citizen only of the same state as the infant or incompetent.[129] This provision was added under the Judicial Improvements Act of 1988 and resolved years of confusion over whose domicile was to be considered in an action by or against an estate.[130]

When an American citizen is residing abroad, the availability of diversity jurisdiction turns on whether the citizen is residing abroad temporarily or permanently. If the citizen is traveling or temporarily residing abroad with no intention to permanently change his or her existing domicile, the citizen's domicile

---

[127] Concurrence of intention and act. Morris v. Gilmer, 129 U.S. 315 (1889).

[128] Intent element is crux of test. Boston Safe Deposit & Trust Co. v. Morse, 779 F. Supp. 347, 349 (S.D.N.Y. 1991).

[129] 28 U.S.C. § 1332(c)(2).

[130] *See* Pub. L. 100-702, 102 Stat. 4646.

is unchanged for purposes of diversity jurisdiction.[131] However, if an American citizen is residing abroad permanently, the citizen cannot sue or be sued in federal court on the basis of diversity of citizenship.[132] The term "citizen of a state" in Section 1332(a)(1) of the diversity jurisdiction statute requires that the individual be a United States citizen and domiciled in one particular state.[133]

An American citizen residing abroad cannot avoid this problem by claiming alienage jurisdiction under 28 U.S.C. § 1332(a)(2), because American citizens will not be considered "citizens or subjects of a foreign state." This is true even if the American citizen has dual citizenship in the country of residence. Courts have reasoned that the dual citizen should not be allowed to invoke alienage jurisdiction, because that would give the dual citizen an advantage not enjoyed by those with only American citizenship.

## § 3.13 DETERMINING CITIZENSHIP OF CORPORATIONS AND OTHER ENTITIES

Under 28 U.S.C. § 1332(c)(1), for purposes of diversity jurisdiction a corporation is deemed to be a citizen of any state by which it has been incorporated and of the state where it has its principal place of business.[134] For complete diversity to exist, therefore, no adversary of a corporation may be a citizen of any state in which the corporation is incorporated or of the state in which it has its principal place of business. Section 1332(c) does not give a party the option of treating a corporation as a citizen of *either* the state of incorporation *or* the state where its principal place of business is located. Rather, the statute treats a corporation as a citizen of *both* states. Note further that a corporation is a citizen of *any* state in which it is incorporated, meaning that it may have more than one state of citizenship on account of incorporation. On the other hand, a corporation is not a citizen of every state in which it has an affiliate[135] or in which it does business. A corporation has only one principal place of business.

The purpose of Section 1332(c) in making a corporation a citizen of the state where it has its principal place of business as well as the state of incorporation is to exclude from the federal diversity jurisdiction cases between a citizen of a state and a corporation whose principal place of business is in the same state, even though it may be incorporated elsewhere. Stated differently, the "principal place of business" requirement was intended to prevent local businesses from avoiding local trials

---

[131] Temporary absence does not affect domicile. *See, e.g.*, Anderson v. Watt, 138 U.S. 694, 706 (1891) (presumption of continuing domicile).

[132] No diversity jurisdiction for American citizen permanently residing abroad. Newman-Green, Inc. v. Alfonzo-Larrain, 490 U.S. 826, 828 (1989) (United States citizen permanently residing abroad is not citizen of particular state for diversity purposes and cannot sue or be sued in federal court).

[133] Domicile in one particular state required. Newman-Green, Inc. v. Alfonzo-Larrain, 490 U.S. 826, 828 (1989) (United States citizen permanently residing abroad is not citizen of particular state for diversity purposes); *see* 28 U.S.C. § 1332(a)(1).

[134] Corporation is citizen of state of incorporation and principal place of business. 28 U.S.C. § 1332(c)(1); Lincoln Prop. Co. v. Roche, 546 U.S. 81, 94 (2005).

[135] Corporate citizenship not determined by citizenship of affiliates. Lincoln Prop. Co. v. Roche, 546 U.S. 81, 94 (2005).

based solely on foreign incorporation and to reserve diversity jurisdiction for those parties that are sufficiently unconnected to the forum state to have a legitimate fear of local prejudice. Before 1958, a corporation was deemed to be a citizen only of the state of incorporation. The addition of Section 1332(c) in 1958 was motivated by Congress's recognition that a corporation is not likely to be the victim of prejudice aimed towards out-of-state residents in the courts of a state in which its principal place of business is located.[136] A corporation may have its principal place of business for purposes of diversity jurisdiction in a state in which the corporation has not obtained a certificate of authority to transact state business and is thus not authorized by state law to transact business in that state.

Under Section 1332(c)(1), a corporation is a citizen of every state and foreign state by which it has been incorporated. Thus, a corporation may have multiple citizenships based on incorporation. This may include both domestic and foreign citizenship.[137]

To find diversity jurisdiction, a federal court must identify the principal place of business of a corporation, regardless of whether the corporation has ever made that identification for itself.[138] If the matter is contested, the burden of proving a corporation's principal place of business, based on the location of corporate activities at the time the suit is instituted, rests on the party asserting the existence of diversity jurisdiction.[139] The principal place of business may be in a state or in a foreign country.[140]

For purposes of diversity jurisdiction, a corporation's "principal place of business" is the place where the corporation's high level officers direct, control, and coordinate the corporation's activities, often referred to as the corporation's "nerve center."[141] The Supreme Court adopted the "nerve center" test in *Hertz Corp. v. Friend*, resolving conflicting interpretations of "principal place of business" that had been used in the circuit courts of appeals.[142]

*Hertz* was a class action filed in California state court by California citizens claiming violations of California labor laws. The defendant removed the case on the basis of diversity jurisdiction, claiming that its principal place of business was New Jersey, where its leadership was located and where most of its core executive and

---

[136] Legislative history. *See* S. Rep. No. 1830, 85th Cong., 2d Sess. 4, reprinted in 1958 U.S. Code Cong. & Admin. News 3099, 3103 (amendment was designed to remedy "the evil whereby a local institution, engaged in a local business and in many cases locally owned, is enabled to bring its litigation into the Federal courts simply because it has obtained a corporate charter from another state").

[137] *See* 28 U.S.C. § 1332(c)(1).

[138] Court must ascertain principal place of business. Media Duplication Servs. v. HDG Software, 928 F.2d 1228, 1236 (1st Cir. 1991).

[139] Burden on party asserting jurisdiction. Media Duplication Servs. v. HDG Software, 928 F.2d 1228, 1236 (1st Cir. 1991).

[140] *See* 28 U.S.C. § 1332(c)(1).

[141] Nerve center is principal place of business. Hertz Corp. v. Friend, 559 U.S. 77, 79–80 (2010) ("nerve center" test adopted for determining corporation's principal place of business).

[142] Nerve center test adopted. Hertz Corp. v. Friend, 559 U.S. 77, 79–80 (2010) (nerve center test adopted to resolve conflicting interpretations given phrase "principal place of business" by circuit courts of appeals).

administrative functions were carried out.

The Court reviewed the history of corporate citizenship for diversity purposes. The Court noted when Congress incorporated the "principal place of business" language into the diversity statute in 1958, courts of appeals were uncertain how to apply it. If the corporation's headquarters and executive offices were in the same state in which it did most of its business, it was a straightforward matter to identify that state as the principal place of business. Things were not so clear when corporate headquarters were in one state and the centers of business activity were in another, or in several other states. Various tests emerged, including the nerve center test ultimately adopted by the Court and tests based on the locus of operations or the center of corporate activities.[143]

Over time, the tests for determining principal place of business became more complex, possibly reflecting an effort by the courts to apply the statutory phrase in light of the general purpose of diversity jurisdiction, to avoid prejudice against an out-of-state corporation sued in state court. The Court described this effort as doomed to failure in light of the fact that such prejudice will often depend on factors that are not easily measured, such as the corporation's image, history, and advertising, while factors that are more easily measured, such as the location of an office or plant, the corporation's sales or employment, or the nature of the goods or services it supplies, may bear little relation to the likelihood of prejudice. Moreover, the increasingly complex approach to determining principal places of business was "at war with administrative simplicity" and "failed to achieve a nationally uniform interpretation of federal law, an unfortunate consequence in a federal legal system."[144]

In *Hertz*, in an effort to find a single, more uniform interpretation of "principal place of business," the Court adopted and expanded on the nerve center test. The Court concluded that "principal place of business" is best read as referring to the place where a corporation's officers direct, control, and coordinate the corporation's activities.[145] In practice, it will usually be the place where the corporation maintains its headquarters, as long as the headquarters is the actual center of direction, control, and coordination, i.e., the "nerve center," and not simply an office where the corporation holds its board meetings.[146] However, if the record reveals attempts at manipulation, such as an alleged "nerve center" that "is nothing more than a mail drop box, a bare office with a computer, or the location of an annual executive retreat," the place of actual direction, control, and coordination should be taken as the nerve center.[147]

---

[143] Various tests emerged. Hertz Corp. v. Friend, 559 U.S. 77, 91–93 (2010).

[144] Complexity. Hertz Corp. v. Friend, 559 U.S. 77, 92 (2010) (tests for determining principal place of business became increasingly complex, but neither advanced purpose of diversity jurisdiction nor led to administrative simplicity or federal uniformity).

[145] Nerve center test adopted. Hertz Corp. v. Friend, 559 U.S. 77, 92–93 (2010).

[146] Nerve center will ordinarily be corporate headquarters. Hertz Corp. v. Friend, 559 U.S. 77, 93 (2010).

[147] Actual place of direction, control and coordination is nerve center. Hertz Corp. v. Friend, 559 U.S. 77, 93 (2010).

The Court settled on the "nerve center" approach to determine principal place of business for three reasons. First, it is supported by the language of the statute, which refers to "place" in the singular and indicates a place *within* a state rather than the state itself. Second, the approach is relatively simple. Third, it is supported by the legislative history, which suggests that "principal place of business" should be interpreted to be no more complex than "half of gross income."[148]

The Court acknowledged that although the nerve center test is relatively easy to apply, there will still be hard cases, such as telecommuting situations. The Court also recognized that the test may produce some results that seem to cut against the basic rationale for diversity jurisdiction, such as when the bulk of a company's business activities that are visible to the public take place in one state, while its top officers direct those activities from across the border in another state. The Court concluded that such anomalous results must be accepted as "the price the legal system must pay to avoid overly complex jurisdictional administration while producing the benefits that accompany a more uniform legal system."[149]

*Hertz* provided a uniform test for courts to apply when determining the principal place of business for federal diversity jurisdiction purposes. It did not, however, impose a heightened pleading requirement or dictate a precise manner for pleading subject matter jurisdiction.

The citizenship rules for purposes of diversity apply to alien corporations just as they do to domestic corporations. In other words, an alien corporation is a citizen of every state and foreign country by which it was incorporated and of the state or foreign country in which its principal place of business is located.[150] Thus, an entity that was incorporated in a foreign country but has a principal place of business in the United States will be deemed a citizen of both the country of incorporation and the state in which the principal place of business is located.

The possibility of dual citizenship for alien corporations was made explicit in the amendment of Section 1332(c) effective January 6, 2012.[151] This was in line with the law in most circuits, which held that an alien corporation that had a principal place of business in the United States was deemed a citizen of both the country of incorporation and the state in which the principal place of business was located, with both citizenships considered when determining the existence of diversity jurisdiction.

The presence of an alien corporation with dual citizenship as a party can destroy diversity jurisdiction in two ways. The state citizenship based on the principal place

---

[148] Three reasons for nerve center test. Hertz Corp. v. Friend, 559 U.S. 77, 93–95 (2010) (statutory language, virtue of simplicity and legislative history support nerve center test).

[149] Hard cases and anomalies must be accepted. Hertz Corp. v. Friend, 559 U.S. 77, 95–96 (2010) (acknowledging and accepting imperfections in nerve center test).

[150] Dual citizenship for alien corporations. 28 U.S.C. § 1332(c)(1) ("a corporation shall be deemed to be a citizen of every State and foreign state by which it has been incorporated and of the State or foreign state where it has its principal place of business").

[151] *See* Pub. L. No. 112-63, § 102, 125 Stat. 758 (2011) ("any State" replaced with "every State and Foreign state" and "the State" replaced with "the State or foreign state").

of business destroys diversity if a citizen of the same state is on the other side.[152] The alien citizenship destroys diversity if there is an alien on the other side of the case and there are not citizens of states on both sides.[153]

As a general rule for purposes of diversity jurisdiction, a subsidiary maintains a separate corporate character and does not adopt the citizenship of its parent corporation. Therefore, in a suit involving a subsidiary corporation, the court looks to the states of incorporation and principal place of business of the subsidiary itself, rather than those of the parent corporation.

As long as the corporate separation between a parent and subsidiary, though perhaps merely formal, is nevertheless "real" and carefully maintained, the separate place of business of the subsidiary is recognized in determining jurisdiction. This is true, even though the parent corporation exerts a high degree of control through ownership or otherwise. The question of separation will turn on an individualized determination.[154]

The only recognized exception to the treatment of parent and subsidiary corporations as separate is if the subsidiary is deemed to be the alter ego of the parent corporation. In such a case, courts may view the formal separateness between the two corporations as merely a legal fiction and attribute the citizenship of the parent corporation to the subsidiary.[155]

For the alter ego doctrine to come into play, it must be shown that the parent's disregard of the subsidiary's corporate entity made it a mere instrumentality for the transaction of its own affairs; that there is such unity of interest and ownership that the separate personalities of the parent and the subsidiary no longer exist; and that to adhere to the fiction of a separate corporate entity would promote injustice or protect fraud.

## § 3.14 CITIZENSHIP OF NONCORPORATE ENTITIES IN ALL OTHER ACTIONS

There is no statutory authority that provides any special rule for partnerships with regard to diversity, as Section 1332(c) does for corporations. Therefore, a partnership is not a "citizen" of any state within the meaning of the statutes regulating jurisdiction, and its citizenship must be determined with reference to each of its partners.[156] Similarly, the citizenship of a joint venture is the citizenship of each member regardless of whether the member has an interest in the suit.[157]

---

[152] State citizenship. *See* 28 U.S.C. § 1332(a)(1).

[153] Alien citizenship. *See* 28 U.S.C. § 1332(a)(2)–(4).

[154] Individualized factual determination. U.S.I. Props. Corp. v. M.D. Constr. Co., 860 F.2d 1, 7 (1st Cir. 1988) (finding defendant subsidiary was not alter ego of parent corporation for diversity jurisdiction purposes).

[155] Alter ego exception. *See, e.g.,* Danjaq, S.A. v. Pathe Communications Corp., 979 F.2d 772, 775 (9th Cir. 1992).

[156] Partnership is not "citizen." Chapman v. Barney, 129 U.S. 677, 682 (1889).

[157] Joint ventures. Schiavone Constr. Co. v. City of New York, 99 F.3d 546, 548 (2d Cir. 1996).

Nor is there any liberalized rule with regard to limited partnerships. In *Carden v. Arkoma Associates*, the Supreme Court held that the citizenship of all partners in a limited partnership, rather than only the citizenship of the general partners or the state where the partnership is created, governs the determination of citizenship for jurisdictional purposes. Any alteration in this practice, the Court stated, must come from Congress.[158]

In so holding, the Court distinguished its earlier decision in *Navarro Savings Association v. Lee*. In *Navarro*, the Court had held that individual trustees of a business trust may invoke diversity jurisdiction on the basis of their own citizenship, without regard to the citizenship of the trust beneficiaries.[159] *Navarro*, said the Court in *Carden*, "did not involve the question whether a party that is an artificial entity other than a corporation can be considered a 'citizen' of a State, but the quite separate question whether parties that were undoubted 'citizens' were the real parties to the controversy."[160] A person's status as a partner is determined under the law of the state that governs the partnership agreement.

Similar to a partnership and unlike a corporation, an unincorporated association is deemed to have the citizenship of each of its members.[161] As a result, it will be highly unlikely that a nationally based association will meet the complete diversity requirement because it is likely that some members will share the citizenship of a party on the other side of the action.

The Puerto Rican entity known as the *sociedad en comandita* is the single exception to the Supreme Court's unwillingness to extend corporate treatment for diversity purposes to entities that are not formally incorporated.[162] A *sociedad en comandita* is treated as a corporation for purposes of determining diversity jurisdiction.[163] That entity was created under the civil law of Puerto Rico, and for diversity, is deemed to be a citizen of Puerto Rico only. The Supreme Court has held that the entity's juridical personality is so complete in contemplation of the law of Puerto Rico that it could find no adequate reason to hold that the *sociedad* has a different status for purposes of federal jurisdiction from a corporation organized under that law.[164]

For purposes of diversity jurisdiction, the citizenship of a limited liability company is determined by the citizenship of its members.[165]

---

[158] Same rule for limited partnership. Carden v. Arkoma Assocs., 494 U.S. 185, 197 (1990); *see* Grupo Dataflux v. Atlas Global Group, L.P., 541 U.S. 567, 569–570 (2004).

[159] *Navarro* holds trustee citizenship determines diversity. Navarro Sav. Ass'n v. Lee, 446 U.S. 458, 465–466 (1980).

[160] *Navarro* distinguished. Carden v. Arkoma Assocs., 494 U.S. 185, 191 (1990).

[161] Unincorporated associations have citizenship of members. United Steelworkers of America, AFL-CIO v. R.H. Bouligny, Inc., 382 U.S. 145, 146–150 (1965).

[162] Single exception. *See* Carden v. Arkoma Assocs., 494 U.S. 185, 189 (1990) (*sociedad en comandita* is "one exception to the admirable consistency of our jurisprudence on this matter").

[163] *Sociedad en comandita* is treated as corporation. Puerto Rico v. Russell & Co., 288 U.S. 476, 482 (1933).

[164] Entity resembles corporation. Puerto Rico v. Russell & Co., 288 U.S. 476, 482 (1933).

[165] Citizenship of LLCs determined by citizenship of members. *See* Grupo Dataflux v. Atlas Global

## § 3.15 DIVERSITY ACTIONS INVOLVING ALIENS

The federal district courts have original jurisdiction of all civil actions in which the amount in controversy requirement is met and the action is between citizens of a state and citizens or subjects of a foreign state, unless the citizen or subject of a foreign state is a permanent resident of the United States and is domiciled in the same state as the U.S. citizen.[166] This judicial power has often been referred to as alienage jurisdiction.

Alienage jurisdiction is strictly a component of diversity jurisdiction, and should not be confused with jurisdiction over an action against a foreign state under the Foreign Sovereign Immunities Act[167] or an action by an alien under the alien tort statute.[168] Those actions are within the constitutional "arising under" clause and are, therefore, manifestations of federal question jurisdiction.

The federal district courts also have original jurisdiction of all civil actions in which the amount in controversy requirement is met and the action is between citizens of different states, with citizens or subjects of a foreign state as additional parties.[169] Section 1332(a)(3) establishes a requirement of complete diversity between United States citizens, but permits aliens on each side of the dispute as additional parties.

The diverse citizens need not be the principal adversaries in the suit. As long as the diverse citizens have a legitimate dispute, Section 1332(a)(3) confers jurisdiction even when the main suit involves one or more alien parties.[170] It is irrelevant for diversity purposes that the aliens on both sides of the dispute come from the same country.

The diversity statute confers diversity jurisdiction over suits between a foreign state, as plaintiff, and citizens of a state or different states.[171] Because federal jurisdiction in actions brought *against* foreign states is comprehensively treated by the Foreign Sovereign Immunities Act,[172] a similar jurisdictional basis under diversity would be superfluous.[173]

Alienage jurisdiction was intended to provide the federal courts with a form of protective jurisdiction over matters implicating international relations, in which the

Group, L.P., 541 U.S. 567, 586 n. 1 (2004) ("Although the Court has never ruled on the issue, Courts of Appeals have held the citizenship of each member of an LLC counts for diversity purposes." (citations omitted)).

[166] Citizens of state v. citizens/subjects of foreign state. *See* 28 U.S.C. § 1332(a)(2).

[167] *See* 28 U.S.C. § 1330.

[168] *See* 28 U.S.C. § 1350.

[169] 28 U.S.C. § 1332(a)(3).

[170] Diverse citizens need not be principal adversaries. Dresser Indus. v. Underwriters at Lloyd's of London, 106 F.3d 494, 496–500 (3d Cir. 1997) (court had diversity jurisdiction over suit between diverse citizens in which aliens also appeared as both plaintiffs and defendants).

[171] 28 U.S.C. § 1332(a)(4).

[172] 28 U.S.C. § 1330.

[173] No diversity jurisdiction over foreign state as defendant. Argentine Republic v. Amerada Hess Shipping Corp., 488 U.S. 428, 437 n.5 (1989).

national interest is paramount. The dominant considerations prompting the provision for this type of jurisdiction appear to have been the following:

1. Failure of individual states to protect foreign citizens under treaties; and
2. Apprehension of entanglements with other sovereigns that might ensue from failure to treat the legal controversies of aliens on a national level.

The generally accepted test for determining whether a person is a foreign citizen for purposes of Section 1332(a)(2) is whether the country in which citizenship is claimed would recognize that status. This approach is in accord with the principle of international law that it is the inherent right of every independent nation to determine for itself, and according to its own constitution and laws, what classes of persons shall be entitled to citizenship. Under this rule, it does not matter whether the entity most closely resembles a corporation or any other common law entity, but only whether the entity is considered a "juridical person" under the law that created it.

Under the complete diversity requirement of alienage jurisdiction, diversity jurisdiction does not encompass suits by foreign plaintiffs against foreign defendants.[174] This exclusion extends to cases involving an alien on one side and an alien plus a U.S. citizen on the other.[175] However, the presence of diverse U.S. citizens on both sides preserves diversity.[176] It is not necessary that the diverse U.S. citizens be the principal adversaries as long as they have a legitimate dispute.[177]

The reason for these somewhat puzzling rules is found in the details of the statutory framework. Cases in which only foreign parties are on one side and a mixture of foreign and domestic parties are on the other do not fit within Section 1332 (a)(2) or (a)(3). Section 1332(a)(2) confers jurisdiction over suits between "citizens of a State and citizens or subjects of a foreign state."[178] Section 1332(a)(3) confers jurisdiction over suits between "citizens of different States and in which citizens or subjects of a foreign state are additional parties."[179] Thus, the jurisdictional problem when there is a foreigner on one side and both a domestic and a foreign party on the other is not that there are foreigners on both sides, but that there are not citizens on both sides.[180]

---

[174] Aliens suing aliens. Hodgson v. Bowerbank, 9 U.S. (5 Cranch) 303 (1809) (alien v. alien); *see* Romero v. International Terminal Operating Co., 358 U.S. 354, 381 (1959) (dictum states that diversity is lacking when only parties are foreign entities, or on one side there are citizens and aliens and only aliens on other side).

[175] Alien v. alien plus citizen. *See* 28 U.S.C. § 1332(a)(2).

[176] Diverse citizens on both sides preserves diversity. *See* 28 U.S.C. § 1332(a)(3) (diversity jurisdiction in suits between "citizens of different States and in which citizens or subjects of a foreign state are additional parties").

[177] U.S. citizens need not be principal parties. Dresser Indus., Inc. v. Underwriters at Lloyd's of London, 106 F.3d 494, 496–500 (3d Cir. 1997).

[178] 28 U.S.C. § 1332(a)(2).

[179] 28 U.S.C. § 1332(a)(3).

[180] Analyzing statutory framework. Allendale Mut. Ins. Co. v. Bull Data Sys., 10 F.3d 425, 428 (7th Cir. 1993).

Federal courts do not have original diversity jurisdiction of any civil action between citizens of a state and citizens or subjects of a foreign state who are lawfully admitted for permanent residence in the United States and are domiciled in the same state as the U.S. citizen. As of January 6, 2012, this is stated clearly in Section 1332(a)(2).[181] Prior to that time, the same result was accomplished through a statutory provision that permanent resident aliens were deemed citizens of the state in which they were domiciled.[182]

## § 3.16 JUDICIALLY CREATED EXCEPTIONS TO THE DIVERSITY JURISDICTION

Although the diversity statutes nowhere expressly so provide, the federal courts have long held that they lack jurisdiction in probate proceedings and most domestic relations matters, even if the parties are of diverse citizenship. Whether these exceptions constitute appropriate exercises of the judiciary's power, in light of Congress's failure to provide for them statutorily, is open to question.[183] However, courts have defended them as proper exercises of judicial discretion and as applications of the historical bases from which diversity jurisdiction stemmed.

Moreover, the Supreme Court reasoned in *Ankenbrandt v. Richards,* Congress's recodification of the diversity jurisdiction in 1948 without affirmatively revoking the exception manifested congressional acceptance of the principle.[184] The flaw in this logic however, is that it effectively transforms the failure to legislate as the equivalent of legislation. In a separate opinion in that case, Justice Blackmun rejected the view that Section 1332 can be properly construed to contain an exception for domestic relations cases. He also questioned the evolution of the exception, asserting misunderstood judicial precedent and legislative acquiescence to that misunderstanding.[185]

### [1] Domestic Relations Exception

The federal courts have been held to lack diversity jurisdiction to grant divorces, determine alimony and support obligations, or resolve the conflicting claims of divorced parents to the custody of their children.[186] First recognized by the

---

181 28 U.S.C. § 1332(a)(2) (district court has original diversity jurisdiction in cases between "citizens of a State and citizens or subjects of a foreign state, except that the district courts shall not have original jurisdiction under this subsection of an action between citizens of a State and citizens or subjects of a foreign state who are lawfully admitted for permanent residence in the United States and are domiciled in the same State.").

182 Former 28 U.S.C. § 1332(a) (amended effective Jan. 6, 2012).

183 *See* Redish, *Abstention, Separation of Powers, and the Limits of the Judicial Function,* 94 YALE L. J. 71 (1984).

184 Congressional inaction indicates assent. Ankenbrandt v. Richards, 504 U.S. 689, 700 (1992).

185 Exception questioned. *See* Ankenbrandt v. Richards, 504 U.S. 689, 707–717 (1992) (Blackmun, J., concurring in judgment).

186 Domestic relations exception to diversity jurisdiction. Sutter v. Pitts, 639 F.2d 842, 843 (1st Cir. 1981).

Supreme Court in *Barber v. Barber,*[187] the exception retains its full force today.[188] As a result, federal courts generally dismiss diversity cases involving divorce and alimony, child custody, visitation rights, establishment of paternity, child support, and enforcement of separation or divorce decrees still subject to state court modification. As stated by the Ninth Circuit, federal courts should decline jurisdiction of cases concerning domestic relations if the primary issue concerns the status of parent and child or husband and wife.

Further, the Supreme Court has acknowledged that it might be appropriate for federal courts to decline to hear cases involving elements of the domestic relationship even when divorce, alimony, or child custody is not strictly at issue.[189] The Court has opined that it is improper for federal courts to entertain a claim by a plaintiff whose standing to sue is founded on family law rights that are in dispute, when prosecution of the lawsuit may have an adverse effect on the person who is the source of the plaintiff's claimed standing. When hard questions of domestic relations are sure to affect the outcome, the Court has reasoned, the prudent course is for the federal court to stay its hand rather than reach out to resolve a weighty question of federal constitutional law.[190]

Among the general considerations underlying the domestic relations exception are said to be the strong state interest and the relative expertise of state courts in the area of family law, the ability of the state courts to provide ongoing supervision, the availability in state court of professional support services, and the undesirability of potentially incompatible federal and state decrees in this area. The domestic relations exception, then, is based on the premise that the states have traditionally adjudicated marital and child custody disputes and, therefore, have developed competence and expertise in those matters that federal courts lack.

Though the existence of the domestic relations exception is firmly established, viewed on a clean slate one may wonder whether the exception's supposed justifications are legitimate. After all, the entire concept of diversity jurisdiction presumes that the federal courts are qualified to interpret and enforce state law. Why matters of domestic relations fall more within state court expertise than most other areas of substantive state law is not readily apparent.

Nevertheless, the typical divorce decree provides for alimony payable in installments until the spouse receiving alimony remarries. If there are children, it provides for custody, visitation rights, and child support payments as well. These remedies often entail continuing judicial supervision of a volatile family situation. It has been assumed that the federal courts are not well suited to these tasks.

---

[187] First judicial recognition of exception. Barber v. Barber, 62 U.S. (21 How.) 582 (1859).

[188] Domestic relations exception. Ankenbrandt v. Richards, 504 U.S. 689, 693–707 (1992) (exception reaffirmed by Supreme Court); *see* Elk Grove Unified Sch. Dist. v. Newdow, 542 U.S. 1, 12–13 (2004) (discussing continued efficacy of exception).

[189] Exception may extend beyond divorce, alimony, and child custody. Elk Grove Unified Sch. Dist. v. Newdow, 542 U.S. 1, 12–13 (2004) (discussing continued efficacy of exception); *see* Ankenbrandt v. Richards, 504 U.S. 689, 703–706 (1992).

[190] Federal courts should stay rather than entertain important constitutional issues. Elk Grove Unified Sch. Dist. v. Newdow, 542 U.S. 1, 17 (2004).

It is often stated that the scope of the exception relating to matrimonial actions has been rather narrowly confined to the traditional family law remedies of divorce, support, and custody.[191] It does not apply to suits that are actually tort or contract claims having only domestic relations overtones. Nor does it usually apply to claims against third parties.[192]

The Supreme Court has indicated that federal courts may be required to abstain in a case involving elements of the domestic relationship even if the parties do not seek divorce, alimony, or child custody. This is so if a case presents "difficult questions of state law" bearing on policy problems of substantial public import that transcends the result in the case.[193]

The Supreme Court has held that the domestic relations exception to diversity jurisdiction does not apply to a suit based on diversity jurisdiction alleging that the plaintiff's former husband and his female companion committed tortious acts of sexual and physical abuse against the children.[194] The Court emphasized that the domestic relations exception "has no place in a suit such as this one, in which a former spouse sues another on behalf of children alleged to have been abused." Inasmuch as the allegations of the complaint did not request the district court to issue a divorce, alimony, or child custody decree, the Court held that the suit was appropriate for the exercise of jurisdiction under Section 1332, given the existence of diverse citizenship between petitioner and respondents and the pleading of the relevant amount in controversy.[195]

## [2] The Probate Exception

A federal court may not exercise diversity jurisdiction to probate a will, to administer an estate, or to dispose of property in the custody of a state probate court.[196] This is a common-law exception to the federal court's diversity jurisdiction. In the typical case, the probate exception disables a federal court from exercising diversity jurisdiction under Section 1332.

A determination that the probate exception does not apply to a particular case is reviewed under the de novo standard because a finding that the probate exception is applicable deprives a federal court of subject matter jurisdiction.[197]

---

[191] No jurisdiction if traditional family law relief is requested. Ankenbrandt v. Richards, 504 U.S. 689, 704 (1992).

[192] Inapplicable to claims against third parties. *See* Ankenbrandt v. Richards, 504 U.S. 689, 704 n. 7 (1992) (lower courts did not explain why domestic relations exception applies to third party).

[193] Difficult questions of state law. Ankenbrandt v. Richards, 504 U.S. 689, 704–705 (1992); *see* Burford v. Sun Oil Co., 319 U.S. 315, 320–324 (1943).

[194] Tortious acts by former spouse and another. Ankenbrandt v. Richards, 504 U.S. 689, 705 (1992) (also rejecting application of abstention doctrine under Younger v. Harris, 401 U.S. 37 (1971)).

[195] Child abuse not within exception. Ankenbrandt v. Richards, 504 U.S. 689, 706–707 (1992).

[196] Probate exception. Marshall v. Marshall, 547 U.S. 293, 311 (2006) (limiting scope of exception, superseding broader interpretations based on language in *Markham v. Allen*, 326 U.S. 490, 494 (1946)).

[197] De novo review. *See* Markham v. Allen, 326 U.S. 490, 494 (1946) (federal court lacks jurisdiction to probate will or administer estate); Rienhardt v. Kelly, 164 F.3d 1296, 1299 (10th Cir. 1999).

The rationale for the probate exception has been premised on the following factors:

1. The need for legal certainty concerning whether probate matters and will contests should be in state rather than federal courts; that is, the relative expertise of state courts with respect to their own probate law.
2. Judicial economy: restricting probate matters and will contests to state courts will ensure that questions regarding a will's validity can be resolved concurrently with the task of estate administration.
3. Avoidance of unnecessary interference with matters of important state probate concerns.

Federal courts construe the meaning of "probate" quite narrowly, thus limiting the scope of the exception. The probate exception is not a "hard and fast" jurisdictional rule. Rather, federal courts have manifested a certain degree of willingness to find the exception inapplicable. Moreover, a state cannot expand the application of the probate exception by declaring that an action falls within the exclusive jurisdiction of the state's probate courts.[198]

In *Marshall v. Marshall*, the Supreme Court stated that the probate exception reserves to state probate courts the probate or annulment of a will and the administration of a decedent's estate and prohibits federal courts from disposing of property in the custody of a state probate court, but it does not bar federal courts from adjudicating matters outside those confines and otherwise within federal jurisdiction.[199] The Court held that a widow's claim against her husband's son for tortious interference with a gift the widow expected to receive from her husband was not within the exception and could be adjudicated in federal court. The Court noted that the claim did not involve the administration of an estate, the probate of a will, or any other purely probate matter. Rather, the widow alleged a widely recognized tort and sought an in personam judgment against the son, not the probate or annulment of a will; the widow did not seek to reach a res in the custody of a state court. Moreover, no sound policy considerations militated in favor of extending the probate exception to cover the case, and state probate courts do not possess any special proficiency in handling such cases.[200]

In upholding the widow's right to access to the federal courts in *Marshall*, the Supreme Court revisited vague language in an earlier opinion concerning the scope of the exception. In *Markham v. Allen*, the Court had stated that federal courts of equity have jurisdiction to entertain claims against a decedent's estate "so long as the federal court does not *interfere with the probate proceedings* or assume general jurisdiction of the probate or control of the property in the custody of the state court" (emphasis added).[201] Some courts had read the italicized portion of the statement to block federal jurisdiction over a range of matters well beyond the

---

[198] State cannot expand application of exception. Marshall v. Marshall, 547 U.S. 293, 312–314 (2006).

[199] Scope of probate exception limited. Marshall v. Marshall, 547 U.S. 293, 311–312 (2006).

[200] Claim not subject to probate exception. Marshall v. Marshall, 547 U.S. 293, 311–312 (2006) (widow's claim against husband's son for tortious interference with gift widow expected to receive from husband was not within probate exception).

[201] *Markham* rule. Markham v. Allen, 326 U.S. 490, 494 (1946).

actual probate of a will or administration of a decedent's estate.[202] However, the *Markham* court had described a limited probate exception as follows: "[W]hile a federal court may not exercise its jurisdiction to disturb or affect the possession of property in the custody of a state court . . . , it may exercise its jurisdiction to adjudicate rights in such property where the final judgment does not undertake to interfere with the state court's possession save to the extent that the state court is bound by the judgment to recognize the right adjudicated by the federal court."[203] In *Marshall*, the Court read the "enigmatic" words in the first quoted passage as merely reiterating the general principle that when one court is exercising in rem jurisdiction over a res, a second court will not assume in rem jurisdiction over the same res. The Court acknowledged that this interpretation renders the passage in part redundant, but opined that in this context, redundancy "is preferable to incoherence."[204] Some circuits have explicitly acknowledged that *Marshall's* narrow interpretation of the probate exception superseded their previous overly broad interpretations.

## § 3.17 JURISDICTIONAL AMOUNT IN CONTROVERSY

There is diversity jurisdiction only if the matter in controversy exceeds the sum or value of $75,000, exclusive of interest and costs.[205] The origin of the modern jurisdictional amount requirement is the Judiciary Act of 1789, which set the requirement, for cases in which it was imposed, at $500.[206] By 1958, Congress had raised the minimum to an amount in excess of $10,000, exclusive of interests and costs. The modification under the Judicial Improvements and Access to Justice Act[207] raised the jurisdictional amount from $10,000 to $50,000. Then, in 1996, Congress once again raised the jurisdictional amount in controversy to $75,000.[208]

Between 1875 and 1980, some form of jurisdictional amount requirement applied to cases brought under the general federal question statutes as well. The requirement was completely removed in 1980.[209] Congress, in amending Section 1332 to raise the amount in controversy limit, sought to stem the tide of diversity litigation in the federal courts.[210] Of course, caseloads could be restricted in a variety of ways. The decision to control caseloads by means of a jurisdictional minimum, then, reflects a congressional decision to arrange priorities according to a case's financial

---

202 Expansive reading of exception. The expansive reading of the probate exception has been superseded by *Marshall v. Marshall*, 547 U.S. 293, 311 (2006).

203 *Markham* description of limited exception. Markham v. Allen, 326 U.S. 490, 494 (1946).

204 Interpretation of *Markham* in *Marshall* case. Marshall v. Marshall, 547 U.S. 293, 311 (2006).

205 28 U.S.C. § 1332(a).

206 *See* Baker, *The History and Tradition of the Amount in Controversy Requirement: A Proposal to "Up the Ante" in Diversity Jurisdiction*, 102 F.R.D. 299 (1985).

207 Pub. L. 100-702, 102 Stat. 4642 (1988).

208 Amount raised again. *See* Federal Courts Improvement Act of 1996, Pub. L. 104-317, 110 Stat. 3847 (1996).

209 *See* Pub. L. 96-486, 94 Stat. 2369.

210 Stem tide of diversity litigation. *See* Rosenboro v. Kim, 994 F.2d 13, 19 (D.C. Cir. 1993); *see also* H.R. Rep. No. 889, 100th Cong., 2d Sess. 45 (1988), reprinted in 1988 U.S. Code Cong. & Admin. News 5982, 6005.

worth. Simply put, Congress's decision to impose a jurisdictional minimum in diversity cases reflects its judgment that the federal courts should not expend resources on cases of only limited financial worth.

Determination of the value of the matter in controversy for purposes of federal jurisdiction is determined by application of federal standards.[211] This conclusion derives from the fact that in establishing the standards for determining jurisdictional amount, a court is in actuality interpreting a federal statute, Section 1332(a). However, in a diversity case, the court must look to state law to determine the nature and extent of the damages to be awarded.[212]

This conclusion is in no way inconsistent with the rule that the methodology for determining jurisdictional amount is purely a matter of federal law. The rule refers solely to the standards employed to determine whether the amount in controversy actually exceeds the jurisdictional minimum. However, in a diversity case, the substantive questions surrounding the measure of damages are purely a matter of state law. Hence, state law will dictate what is actually financially at stake in the case; federal standards will determine whether those financial stakes are sufficient to satisfy the statutory requirement.

The jurisdictional minimum is a requirement of federal subject matter jurisdiction. As such, it is not waivable by the parties. The issue may be raised by either party at any time, and if not raised by the parties, it is to be raised by the court on its own initiative.[213] As with the determination of citizenship, the relevant time for establishing the amount in controversy is at the commencement of the action.[214] The amount in controversy is therefore determined as of the time the complaint is filed.

Because jurisdiction is determined at the outset of litigation, if the requisite amount in controversy is satisfied at that time subsequent events that reduce the amount below the statutory requirement generally will not divest the court of jurisdiction.[215] For example, the mere fact that the plaintiff ultimately recovers a sum less than the jurisdictional amount will not divest the court of jurisdiction.[216] Similarly, the fact that a plaintiff ultimately settles the claim for less than the jurisdictional amount does not deprive a federal court of jurisdiction.

Courts have appropriately distinguished between subsequent events that change the amount in controversy and subsequent revelations that the required amount

---

[211] Stem tide of diversity litigation. *See* Rosenboro v. Kim, 994 F.2d 13, 19 (D.C. Cir. 1993); *see also* H.R. Rep. No. 889, 100th Cong., 2d Sess. 45 (1988), reprinted in 1988 U.S. Code Cong. & Admin. News 5982, 6005.

[212] State law determines damages. Horton v. Liberty Mut. Ins. Co., 367 U.S. 348, 352–353 (1961).

[213] Court may raise issue sua sponte. Fed. R. Civ. P. 12(h)(3).

[214] Commencement of action. Freeport-McMoRan, Inc. v. K N Energy, 498 U.S. 426, 428 (1991).

[215] Subsequent events. St. Paul Mercury Indem. Co. v. Red Cab. Co., 303 U.S. 283, 289–290 (1938) (subsequent events do not oust jurisdiction).

[216] Ultimate recovery. *See* Mt. Healthy City Sch. Dist. Bd. of Educ. v. Doyle, 429 U.S. 274, 277 (1977); Rosado v. Wyman, 397 U.S. 397, 405 n. 6 (1970) (well-settled rule that federal court does not lose jurisdiction over diversity suit well-founded at outset even though party later changes domicile or amount recovered is less than jurisdictional minimum). *See* 28 U.S.C. § 1332(b).

was not in controversy even when the suit was filed. The former do not defeat diversity jurisdiction. However, if the underlying facts remain the same and it is subsequently determined that the jurisdictional minimum was not met even at the time the complaint was filed, there is no diversity jurisdiction. The subsequent revelation that the jurisdictional minimum was not originally met is not a subsequent change that can be ignored.

In general, dismissal of part of the case at an early stage, thereby reducing the amount of recovery, does not necessarily destroy jurisdiction or prove that the plaintiff acted in bad faith. If diversity jurisdiction existed at the time the case was filed, it is not affected by the dismissal of one of the claims, whether on motion to dismiss or summary judgment, even though the amount recoverable on the remaining claim is less than the required amount. And, this is true even if the action is reduced by dismissal because part of the action was found to be time-barred by the applicable statute of limitation.

However, if the proofs adduced at trial conclusively show that the plaintiff never had a claim even arguably within the required range, a diversity action must be dismissed. Failure to satisfy the jurisdictional amount from the outset, although not recognized until later, is not a subsequent change that can be ignored. Thus, if the defendant establishes during the course of litigation that from the outset, the maximum conceivable amount in controversy was less than the jurisdictional minimum, the court must dismiss the case for lack of subject matter jurisdiction.

If a plaintiff who originally filed in federal court is finally adjudged to be entitled to recover less than the jurisdictional minimum, computed without regard to any set-off or counterclaim and exclusive of interests and costs, the trial court may both deny costs to the plaintiff and impose costs on the plaintiff.[217] Note that the penalty is discretionary. Courts have generally fashioned a bad-faith test to determine whether costs will be assessed.

In 1938, in *St. Paul Mercury Indemnity Co. v. Red Cab Co.*, the Supreme Court established a standard for determining whether the jurisdictional minimum has been met. Under this rule, the sum claimed by the plaintiff controls if the claim is apparently made in good faith.[218] A rebuttable presumption exists that the face of the complaint is a good faith representation of the actual amount in controversy. Thus, it must appear to a *legal certainty* that the claim is really for less than the jurisdictional amount to justify dismissal.[219] This test continues to control. The Court in *St. Paul* emphasized that the inability of plaintiff to recover an amount adequate to give the court jurisdiction neither shows bad faith nor ousts the court's jurisdiction. Nor does the fact that the complaint discloses the existence of a valid defense to the claims defeat jurisdiction.[220]

---

[217] Assessment of costs. 28 U.S.C. § 1332(b).

[218] Amount stated in complaint controls if made in good faith. *See* St. Paul Mercury Indem. Co. v. Red Cab Co., 303 U.S. 283, 288–289 (1938).

[219] Origin of "legal certainty" test. St. Paul Mercury Indem. Co. v. Red Cab Co., 303 U.S. 283, 288–289 (1938); *see also* Bell v. Preferred Life Assur. Soc., Etc., 320 U.S. 238, 240 (1943).

[220] Inability to recover or existence of valid defense. St. Paul Mercury Indem. Co. v. Red Cab Co., 303 U.S. 283, 289 (1938).

On its face, the Supreme Court opinion in *St. Paul* appears to give rise to two distinct jurisdictional principles. On the one hand, the Court referred to a subjective factor: the good faith of the plaintiff. On the other hand, the Court also made reference to an objective factor — the "legal certainty" standard. As an abstract matter, it is at least theoretically possible that a plaintiff could be making his claim in good faith, yet his claim nevertheless fails the "legal certainty" test. Moreover, it is also possible that a plaintiff files although believing that the claim is below the jurisdictional minimum (i.e., in bad faith), yet in reality the claim could, in fact, meet the "legal certainty" standard. The Court in *St. Paul* failed to make clear whether the two factors are to be treated as necessary conditions, sufficient conditions, or merely alternative methods of describing the same standard. As a practical matter, the judicial focus has been on the more objective "legal certainty" standard. However, reference is also on occasion made to a plaintiff's good faith in claiming an amount in controversy.

Under the "legal certainty" test, it should be emphasized, the plaintiff must establish merely that it does *not* appear to a legal certainty that the claim is *below* the jurisdictional minimum. Thus, under this standard, courts must be very confident that a party cannot recover the jurisdictional amount before dismissing the case for want of jurisdiction.

The clearest example of a case in which the damage claim fails to meet the "legal certainty" test is one in which by law, the allowable damages are capped at an amount below the jurisdictional minimum. Such a legally imposed limitation may derive either from a statute or a contractual agreement. Thus, a number of cases have indicated that a court has the power to dismiss for want of jurisdiction after deciding that a limitation-of-liability clause in a contract (or a state statute) caps damages at less than the jurisdictional amount.

The mere fact that a valid defense to plaintiff's claim on the merits may exist does not deprive a federal court of jurisdiction on the ground that the requisite amount was never in controversy.[221] Were the rule otherwise, any dismissal of a diversity case would raise a jurisdictional bar based on lack of jurisdictional amount, obfuscating the question of whether the dismissal was on the merits, and thus barred by res judicata, or on jurisdictional grounds, in which case, it could still be brought it state court.

Punitive and actual damages may be aggregated to meet the amount in controversy requirement.[222] In considering punitive damages, a two-part inquiry is necessary. The first question is whether punitive damages are recoverable as a matter of governing substantive law.[223] If so, the court has subject matter jurisdiction unless it is clear beyond a legal certainty that the plaintiff would under no circumstances be entitled to recover the jurisdictional amount. In this second

[221] Existence of valid defense does not deprive court of jurisdiction. St. Paul Mercury Indem. Co. v. Red Cab Co., 303 U.S. 283, 289 (1938).

[222] Punitive and actual damages may be aggregated. Bell v. Preferred Life Assur. Soc., Etc., 320 U.S. 238, 240 (1943).

[223] Governing substantive law. Bell v. Preferred Life Assur. Soc., Etc., 320 U.S. 238, 240 (1943) (noting that, under California law, punitive damages are recoverable against insurance company for bad faith breach of contract).

step, the plaintiff must present some factual evidence of entitlement to punitive damages. It is a question of law for the court, not for the jury, to decide whether a plaintiff has established that punitive damages are available.

Claims for punitive damages are to be subjected to closer scrutiny than claims for actual damages. This is particularly true if the claim for punitive damages comprises the bulk of the amount in controversy and may have been asserted solely or primarily for the purpose of conferring jurisdiction. Thus, the plaintiff's good faith in seeking punitive damages is an important consideration in determining entitlement under the "legal certainty" test. As a general rule, the jurisdictional amount requirement must be met "exclusive of interest and costs."[224] The purpose of excluding interest is to prevent the creation of federal jurisdiction by the deferral of a lawsuit for the sole purpose of accumulating the necessary amount for federal jurisdiction. The phrase "exclusive of interest or costs," however, refers to interest or costs that might be awarded in connection with the federal diversity proceedings. "Costs" that are allegedly incurred as a result of defendant's allegedly wrongful conduct as an element of the damage claim are not the type of costs that are excluded in determining the amount in controversy.

For purposes of calculating the jurisdictional amount, a federal court may not look to any amount claimed as interest by the plaintiff that is attributable solely to a delay in payment or to a wrongful deprivation of funds. This type of moratory interest, if not an essential ingredient of plaintiff's claim, is interest that has accrued before the filing of the complaint and is excluded from calculations of the jurisdictional amount.

Interest is includable in computing the jurisdictional amount if the interest is not merely incidental or accessory to the principal amount demanded, but constitutes an integral part of the aggregate amount of damages claimed[225] or is itself a principal obligation.[226] For example, interest that accrues on an instrument before its maturity is part of the amount of the claim and is included in the calculation of the jurisdictional amount. Further, many states impose statutory damages for failure to timely pay insurance claims, often expressed in terms of interest, designed to be in the nature of a coercive penalty to prompt settlement. Statutory damages that have accrued as of the time that the federal suit is filed are included in the amount in controversy calculation.

As a general matter, attorney's fees do not constitute part of the matter in controversy because the successful party typically does not collect attorney's fees from the opponent in addition to, or as a part of, the judgment. However, two exceptions to this rule exist: (1) if the fees are provided for by contract; or (2) if a statute mandates or allows payment of attorney's fees.

If the existence of the jurisdictional amount in controversy is disputed, the person asserting jurisdiction bears the burden of proof on the issue. Thus, a plaintiff who files in federal court bears the burden, and a defendant who seeks removal to

---

224 Interest and costs excluded. 28 U.S.C. § 1332(a).

225 Integral part. Brown v. Webster, 156 U.S. 328, 330 (1895).

226 Principal obligation. Edwards v. Bates County, 163 U.S. 269, 272 (1896).

federal court bears the burden.[227] But if the plaintiff bears the burden, it is not a heavy one. A plaintiff need demonstrate only that it is not legally impossible that he or she will recover more than the jurisdictional amount. A plaintiff's general allegation of damages that meet the requirement suffices unless questioned by the opposing party or the court. Once the alleged amount has been questioned, the plaintiff must allege with sufficient particularity facts indicating that it is not a legal certainty that the claim involves less than the jurisdictional amount. This burden may be met by amending pleadings or submitting affidavits. If a defendant or the court challenges the plaintiff's allegations, and if either asserts a credible argument that there is a "legal certainty" that plaintiff's recovery *must* be less than the jurisdictional minimum, the plaintiff must demonstrate that there is a *possibility* of recovering more than the jurisdictional minimum, and must do so by a preponderance of the evidence supported by competent proof.[228] Absolute certainty in valuation of the rights involved is not required if an amount in controversy exceeding the jurisdictional minimum can be ascertained according to some realistic formula.

A complaint is fatally defective if it fails to contain a proper allegation of the amount in controversy.[229] In applying the "legal certainty" test, however, resort to matters outside the pleadings may be relied on in order to amplify the meaning of the complaint's allegations.

Under Rule 18(a), a party asserting a claim to relief as an original claim, counterclaim, crossclaim, or third-party claim may join, either as independent or as alternate claims, as many claims as the party has against an opposing party.[230] A single plaintiff may aggregate all claims joined under Rule 18, related and unrelated, against a single defendant in calculating the amount in controversy. A plaintiff may aggregate otherwise insufficient claims in order to reach the threshold amount in excess of the jurisdictional amount.

However, a single plaintiff may not aggregate claims against unrelated defendants. A plaintiff must allege that the amount in controversy is in excess of the jurisdictional amount against each defendant unless the plaintiff's claims against the defendants are common and undivided so that the defendant's liability is properly characterized as joint and not several.[231] The same rule applies in a declaratory judgment action in which the plaintiff's potential liability to multiple claimants is at issue; the claims of the defendants may not be aggregated unless they are common and undivided. If all but one of the defendants are alter egos of another defendant on a claim that satisfies the jurisdictional minimum, the amount in controversy is satisfied as to those defendants.

---

[227] Burden of proof is on party seeking federal forum. McNutt v. General Motors Acceptance Corp. of Ind., Inc., 298 U.S. 178, 189 (1936).

[228] Competent proof. McNutt v. General Motors Acceptance Corp. of Ind., Inc., 298 U.S. 178, 189 (1936).

[229] Complaint must contain allegations regarding amount in controversy. Schlesinger v. Councilman, 420 U.S. 738, 744, 744 n.9 (1975).

[230] Fed. R. Civ. P. 18(a).

[231] Claim against each defendant. Sovereign Camp, Woodmen of the World v. O'Neill, 266 U.S. 292, 295–296 (1924).

Supplemental jurisdiction may extend over other plaintiffs' claims that are part of the same case or controversy. Rule 20 of the Federal Rules of Civil Procedure allows for joinder of parties with claims against a common defendant if the claims arise from the same transaction or occurrence.[232]

The Supreme Court has held that when at least one named plaintiff satisfies the amount-in-controversy requirement (and the other elements of jurisdiction are present), a district court may exercise supplemental jurisdiction over the claims of other plaintiffs in the same Article III case or controversy, even if those claims are for less than the jurisdictional minimum for diversity jurisdiction.[233] The Court held that when one plaintiff's claim or claims meet the jurisdictional amount, there is a "civil action of which the district courts have original jurisdiction" within the meaning of 28 U.S.C. § 1367. The court then has supplemental jurisdiction over other diverse plaintiffs' whose claims fail to meet the amount in controversy. In other words, as long as one claim in the plaintiff's well-pleaded complaint meets the test for original jurisdiction, the district court has supplemental jurisdiction, subject only to specified exceptions, over all other claims that form part of the same case and controversy.[234] Thus, Section 1367 confers supplemental jurisdiction over the claims of plaintiffs permissively joined under Rule 20 who do not individually meet the amount-in-controversy requirement, provided that there is complete diversity of citizenship between the parties under 28 U.S.C. § 1332.[235] The complete diversity requirement remains an element of original jurisdiction.[236]

When none of the plaintiffs' claims in a multi-plaintiff case individually satisfies the amount-in-controversy requirement, the question arises whether the plaintiffs' claims can be aggregated to meet the amount-in-controversy requirement. If several plaintiffs assert claims in a single action against a single defendant that are "separate and distinct," rather than "joint," the amount involved in each claim must meet the requisite amount in order to be within the jurisdiction of the district court. Those amounts cannot be aggregated in order to satisfy jurisdictional requirements.[237] Because very few claims will be deemed joint, it is not surprising that multiple plaintiffs will not often be permitted to aggregate their claims.

One may properly ask whether such an abstract and formalistic dichotomy is anything more than a historical vestige of a very different era. Today, asking whether rights are properly characterized as joint or several rivals the question of how many angels dance on the head of a pin for both difficulty and practical

---

232 Fed. R. Civ. P. 20(a)(1). *See* Chapter 5 for a discussion of supplemental jurisdiction.

233 Supplemental jurisdiction extends to members' claims below jurisdictional minimum. Exxon Mobil Corp. v. Allapattah Servs., Inc., 545 U.S. 546, 549 (2005).

234 If one claim meets test for original jurisdiction, supplemental jurisdiction extends to claims from same case or controversy. Exxon Mobil Corp. v. Allapattah Servs., Inc., 545 U.S. 546, 566 (2005).

235 Permissively joined plaintiffs need not meet amount-in-controversy requirement. Exxon Mobil Corp. v. Allapattah Servs., Inc., 545 U.S. 546, 559 (2005).

236 Complete diversity still required. Exxon Mobil Corp. v. Allapattah Servs., Inc., 545 U.S. 546, 554 (2005) ("[i]ncomplete diversity destroys original jurisdiction with respect to all claims, so there is nothing to which supplemental jurisdiction can adhere").

237 Separate claims in single suit. Clark v. Paul Gray, Inc., 306 U.S. 583, 589 (1939), *overruled on other grounds*, Exxon Mobil Corp. v. Allapattah Servs., Inc., 545 U.S. 546 (2005).

significance. Yet the Supreme Court has steadfastly refused to alter the aggregation rule. It has done so on the grounds that the rule is the product of statutory construction, and therefore if it is to be changed, the change must come from Congress.[238] But it is important to note that the diversity statute, by its terms, never has — nor does it now — make any reference to rules of aggregation. Rather, it refers only to "matter in controversy." The aggregation rule was, for all practical purposes, judge-made at its inception, and therefore should logically be subject to alteration by the Court in light of dramatically changed modern realities and perceptions.

Nevertheless, the current law continues to reflect the antiquated and formalistic rule. Hence, aggregation of damages allegedly owed to separate plaintiffs may be permitted only in the limited situation in which two or more plaintiffs unite to enforce a single title or right in which they have a common and undivided interest.[239]

Determination of whether the amount in controversy exceeds the jurisdictional minimum, exclusive of interests and costs, will involve a rather straightforward inquiry in a case in which the amount the plaintiff stands to gain is the same as the amount the defendant stands to lose. This will normally be the case in a suit for damages. However, some cases — notably those involving a request for injunctive or other equitable relief and most class actions — require more complex analysis. Whether these cases are found to have met the jurisdictional minimum may well turn on an initial decision concerning the viewpoint from which the matter in controversy is measured. For example, in an action seeking injunctive relief, a plaintiff may not stand to benefit by an amount in excess of the jurisdictional amount; however, the cost of compliance to the defendant might well be in excess of the jurisdictional amount.[240] In such a case, if the plaintiff files a state-court action praying for damages in an amount far below the federal minimum, should the defendant be deprived of access to the federal courts if the defendant desires to remove the case? Similarly, if the plaintiff in the same case prefers to file originally in federal district court, should that plaintiff be precluded from doing so because the value of the object of the litigation is not worth the jurisdictional amount from its point of view, although an excess of the jurisdictional amount is at stake in the suit from the defendant's point of view?

The various positions on viewpoint that have been considered by various courts may be summarized as follows:

---

[238] Only Congress should change rule. Snyder v. Harris, 394 U.S. 332, 341 (1969).

[239] Single title or right. Snyder v. Harris, 394 U.S. 332, 335 (1969); *see* Pinel v. Pinel, 240 U.S. 594, 596 (1916) (no aggregation of claims to shares of an estate arising from one will); Troy Bank v. G.A. Whitehead & Co., 222 U.S. 39, 39 (1911) (aggregation allowed for enforcement of state law vendor's lien because that claim was single and undivided); Clay v. Field, 138 U.S. 464, 479–480 (1891) (no aggregation for claim of dower and partnership profits arising from one tract of land); Allen v. R & H Oil & Gas Co., 63 F.3d 1326, 1330 & n.4 (5th Cir. 1995) (aggregation is allowed if plaintiffs unite to assert common, joint, integrated, or undivided right).

[240] Example of injunctive relief. *See, e.g.,* Bedell v. H.R.C. Ltd., 522 F. Supp. 732, 735 (E.D. Ky. 1981) (removing defendant could have lost $400,000 if permanent injunction halting project were to be granted; monetary value to plaintiffs not considered).

1. The plaintiff's viewpoint, which tests the sufficiency of the amount in controversy from the perspective of the plaintiff only, on the theory that this approach is likely to produce greater certainty of result and promote simplicity.
2. The viewpoint of either the plaintiff or the defendant, known as the "either viewpoint" rule.
3. The viewpoint of the party seeking to invoke federal jurisdiction. Under this standard, the court looks to the plaintiff's viewpoint in a case filed originally in federal court, and to the defendant's viewpoint in a case brought to the federal courts by removal from a state court.

The majority of federal courts have chosen to use the plaintiff viewpoint rule. In fact, a strong argument can be fashioned that the Supreme Court has adopted the plaintiff viewpoint rule, at least in most diversity class actions.[241] When this viewpoint is employed, it is used regardless of the nature of the action; it applies both to declaratory and equitable relief actions.[242]

One may reasonably question whether the plaintiff viewpoint rule legitimately fosters the purposes served by the jurisdictional minimum. As previously noted the jurisdictional-amount requirement reflects a congressional judgment that federal judicial resources should be devoted only to those diversity cases in which the financial stakes rise to a predetermined level. It is difficult to understand why those financial stakes are not implicated when *either* party stands to gain or lose the statutorily determined amount or its equivalent. Of course, the plaintiff-viewpoint rule has the obvious effect of reducing the number of cases qualifying for diversity jurisdiction. It is doubtful, however, that reliance on this fact as the sole justification for the plaintiff's viewpoint is legitimate.

Although the plaintiff-viewpoint rule has much to recommend it, it should not be applied if to do so destroys jurisdiction when a substantial claim clearly in excess of the minimum amount is involved. Because the jurisdictional amount was enacted primarily to measure substantiality of the suit, the question of whether the controversy is substantial should not be answered unqualifiedly by looking only to the value of that which the plaintiff stands to gain or lose. For example, if plaintiff seeks an injunction to have defendant remove an office building encroaching on one foot of plaintiff's land, the value of the matter in controversy to plaintiff may be trivial, while the expense in removal to the defendant if the injunction is granted would be clearly in excess of the jurisdictional amount. In such a case, the courts should recognize that a substantial controversy is involved and look to the effect of the suit on either party to the litigation.

Another approach taken by some courts is to view the amount in controversy from the point of view of the party seeking to invoke federal jurisdiction. Under this rule, the court would look to the plaintiff's viewpoint in a case brought originally in federal court and to the defendant's viewpoint in a case removed to federal court

[241] Rule in diversity class actions. Snyder v. Harris, 394 U.S. 332, 338, (1969).

[242] Nature of action. Myers v. Long Island Lighting Co., 623 F. Supp. 1076, 1079 (E.D.N.Y. 1985).

from a state court.[243] Although this rule has certain attractive features, such as tying the controlling viewpoint to the burden of proof as to jurisdiction, there are two problems with it. The first is the possibility of anomalous results. Under the rule, if a case originally brought in federal court were dismissed for failure to meet the jurisdictional amount from the plaintiff's viewpoint, it could yet end up in federal court if the plaintiff reinstituted the case in state court and the defendant, from whose point of view the required amount was present, then removed it.[244] This possibility introduces the second, more fundamental problem. Removal is allowed only of actions of which the district courts have original jurisdiction.[245] But the "burden of proving jurisdiction viewpoint" rule could lead to a situation in which the federal court would assume removal jurisdiction even though it could not assert original jurisdiction.

---

[243] Viewpoint of party invoking federal jurisdiction. McCarty v. Amoco Pipeline Co., 595 F.2d 389, 395 (7th Cir. 1979).

[244] Anomalous result. McCarty v. Amoco Pipeline Co., 595 F.2d 389, 395 (7th Cir. 1979).

[245] 28 U.S.C. § 1441.

# Chapter 4

# FEDERAL QUESTION JURISDICTION

## § 4.01 NATURE AND PURPOSES OF FEDERAL QUESTION JURISDICTION

A significant function performed by the federal courts today is the adjudication and protection of federal rights and interests. Before any case may be heard in federal court, two conditions must be met. First, Article III, Section 2 of the Constitution, which describes the kinds of cases to which the federal judicial power may extend, must authorize it; and second, Congress must have vested in the federal courts the power to hear those cases. If either of these factors is absent, the federal courts are not empowered to hear the case. In federal question litigation, both conditions have, in varying degrees, been met. Article III provides that the federal judicial power shall extend to all cases "arising under" the Constitution, laws or treaties of the United States.[1] And Congress has provided for federal court jurisdiction over federal questions in 28 U.S.C. § 1331. Despite significant differences in interpretation, the language of the current federal question statute[2] is strikingly similar to that of the constitutional provision: "The district courts shall have original jurisdiction of all civil actions *arising under the Constitution, laws or treaties of the United States*."[3]

The primary purpose of the 1875 grant of federal question jurisdiction is to ensure the availability of a forum designed to minimize the danger of hostility toward, and especially suited to the vindication of, federally created rights. Because the selection process for the appointment of federal judges generally ensures a minimum degree of competence, because federal judges are exposed day after day to issues of federal law, and because federal judges may often be more sympathetic to federal interests than are other judges,[4] it is generally assumed that adjudication of cases arising under federal law is an important — if not the central — element of the work of the federal courts.[5] The mere fact that federal question jurisdiction exists does not automatically mean that such jurisdiction is exclusive. In fact, the

---

[1] U.S. Const., art. III, § 2.

[2] The statute finds its origins in the Judiciary Act of 1875, 18 Stat. 470 (1875).

[3] 28 U.S.C. § 1331(a) (emphasis added).

[4] *See* Redish, *Reassessing the Allocation of Judicial Power Between State and Federal Courts: Federal Jurisdiction and "The Martian Chronicles,"* 78 Va. L. Rev. 1769, 1773–75 (1992); Mishkin, *The Federal "Question" in the District Courts*, 53 Colum. L. Rev. 137, 158 (1953).

[5] *See* American Law Institute, Study of the Division of Jurisdiction Between State and Federal Courts 164–168 (1969).

situations in which federal jurisdiction is exclusive are relatively few in number.[6] In most cases, then, federal question jurisdiction is designed to provide the litigants with the option to go to federal court for the adjudication and protection of federal rights — the plaintiff by means of a suit initiating the court's original jurisdiction under Section 1331, and the defendant by resort to removal.[7] It is therefore generally the case that absent exclusive federal jurisdiction, a federal question case will be heard in state court only if both parties decline to exercise their option to go to federal court; the plaintiff through filing in federal court originally, and the defendant through removal.

In addition to Section 1331, the general federal question statute, there are various other jurisdictional statutes that are derived from the "Arising Under" Clause contained in Article III. These include jurisdiction for suits arising under the patent laws[8] and for suits arising under any act of Congress regulating commerce,[9] among others. The test for suits "arising under" the patent laws is identical to that of Section 1331,[10] as is the test for suits "arising under" any act of Congress relating to commerce.[11]

Federal jurisdiction under Section 1338 for patent and copyright cases is vested exclusively in the federal courts, prompting some to suggest that there should be a difference in the scope of "arising under" jurisdiction in that statute.[12] The argument is that if the consequence of a finding of federal jurisdiction is the exclusion of state court jurisdiction, the courts should be more hesitant to find federal jurisdiction. Of course, the opposite argument could just as easily be fashioned: because Congress has expressed fear about state court adjudication of cases arising under the patent and copyright laws, the federal courts should be especially concerned about reaching a conclusion that will vest jurisdiction exclusively in state court. Whatever one thinks of these competing arguments, however, Supreme Court doctrine on the issue is clear; the definitions of "arising under" in the patent jurisdiction and general federal question jurisdiction statutes are identical.[13]

---

[6] Exclusive federal jurisdiction is rare. *See* Tafflin v. Levitt, 493 U.S. 455, 460 (1990) (exclusive federal jurisdiction over cases arising under federal law has been exception rather than rule); Redish & Muench, *Adjudication of Federal Causes of Action in State Court*, 75 Mich. L. Rev. 311 (1976).

[7] *See* 28 U.S.C. § 1441.

[8] 28 U.S.C. § 1338(a).

[9] 28 U.S.C. § 1337.

[10] "Arising under" test under § 1338. Gunn v. Minton, 133 S. Ct. 1059, 185 L. Ed. 2d 72, 79 (2013) ("arising under" interpreted identically under 28 U.S.C. § 1331 and § 1338(a)); Holmes Group, Inc. v. Vornado Air Circulation Sys., Inc., 535 U.S. 826, 829–830 (2002).

[11] "Arising under" test in suits under § 1337. Peyton v. Railway Express Agency, Inc., 316 U.S. 350, 352 (1942).

[12] Should exclusive jurisdiction make a difference? *See* T.B. Harms Co. v. Eliscu, 339 F.2d 823, 828 (2d Cir. 1964) (exclusive federal jurisdiction granted for issues arising under Copyright Act).

[13] "Arising under" test under § 1338. Holmes Group, Inc. v. Vornado Air Circulation Sys., Inc., 535 U.S. 826, 829–830 (2002) (same test applies in determining scope of "arising under" jurisdictional grants under general statute conferring federal question jurisdiction and 28 U.S.C. § 1338; expressly rejecting contrary argument based on need for patent law uniformity); Christianson v. Colt Indus. Operating Corp., 486 U.S. 800, 808 (1988) (cases interpreting language in § 1331 that is identical to that in § 1338

# § 4.02 THE CONSTITUTIONAL PROVISION

## [1] Constitutional Origins

Though the phrase "arising under" is hardly self-explanatory, the framers of the Constitution provided little clarification of its meaning in Article III, Section 2. The originator of the phrase appears to have been James Madison.[14] In defining the phrase, Madison stated that "[w]ith respect to the laws of the Union, it is . . . necessary and expedient that the judicial power should correspond with the legislative."[15] According to one authority, this interpretation seems to have been shared by those who favored the "Arising Under" Clause.[16]

It is doubtful, however, that Madison's statement provides complete illumination of the meaning of the constitutional phrase. Certainly, if Congress has the power to pass laws, it is reasonable to allow the federal judiciary the power to interpret and enforce those laws. However, the framers failed to indicate whether they intended the "Arising Under" Clause to allow federal courts to adjudicate cases in which issues of federal law were merely tangential or indirect. It has been suggested that perhaps Madison and his associates preferred ambiguity, since a precise definition might have led to opposition that might have limited the scope of the federal judicial power.[17] Thus, it was left to the Supreme Court to refine the meaning of the constitutional language.

## [2] The *Osborn* Decision

The Supreme Court's first major interpretation of the "Arising Under" Clause of Article III came in *Osborn v. Bank of the United States*.[18] The Bank sought to enjoin the auditor of Ohio from collecting taxes from it under an Ohio statute exacting "a tax from all banks, and individuals, and companies, and associations of individuals, that may transact banking business in this State, without being allowed to do so by the laws thereof."[19] After first holding that the federal statute creating the Bank allowed the suit,[20] Chief Justice Marshall considered whether Article III authorized Congress to provide this jurisdiction. In the Court's words, "the question is, whether [the suit] arises under a law of the United States."[21] Under the facts of *Osborn*, it was clear that the suit "arose" under federal law because the entire basis of the Bank's claim was that the Supremacy Clause of the

have applied same test); Pratt v. Paris Gas Light & Coke Co., 168 U.S. 255, 259 (1897) (exclusive jurisdiction vested in federal courts over cases arising under patent laws).

[14] *See* Forrester, *The Nature of a "Federal Question,"* 16 Tul. L. Rev. 362, 365 (1942).

[15] 16 Tul. L. Rev. at 366.

[16] 16 Tul. L. Rev. at 366.

[17] 16 Tul. L. Rev. at 367.

[18] First Supreme Court interpretation. Osborn v. Bank of the United States, 22 U.S. (9 Wheat.) 738, 746 (1824).

[19] Facts of case. 22 U.S. at 740.

[20] Suit allowed under statute that created Bank. 22 U.S. at 817, 818.

[21] Question is whether suit arises under federal law. 22 U.S. at 819.

Constitution[22] precluded a state from taxing the Bank, a federal instrumentality. But Marshall's decision went well beyond the limited facts. He stated, "We think, then, that when a question to which the judicial power of the Union is extended by the constitution, forms an ingredient of the original cause, it is in the power of Congress to give the Circuit Courts jurisdiction of that cause, although other questions of fact or law may be involved in it."[23] Previously in the opinion he had stated that, "if it be a sufficient foundation for jurisdiction, that the title or right set up by the party, may be defeated by one construction of the constitution or law of the United States, and sustained by the opposite construction, provided the facts necessary to support the action be made out, then all the other questions must be decided as incidental to this, which gives that jurisdiction."[24] But while this language was subsequently relied on to define the scope of the federal question statute, the remainder of Marshall's opinion makes it clear that he did not intend so narrow a construction of the "Arising Under" Clause of Article III.

To illustrate the potentially broad reach of his interpretation of the "arising under" phrase, Marshall posited a hypothetical case, which actually described a companion decision.[25] "Take the case of a contract," Marshall wrote. "When a Bank sues, the first question which presents itself, and which lies at the foundation of the cause, is, has this legal entity a right to sue? Has it a right to come, not into this Court particularly, but into any Court? This depends on a law of the United States."[26] In other words, even in a case as seemingly "unfederal" as a mundane breach of contract dispute, in which the entire litigation turns on questions of state law, the fact that the Bank is a party always raises the initial question of whether Congress has authorized the Bank to sue, and this issue will present a question solely of federal law. Once this initial question is recognized, according to Marshall, the federal court can proceed to decide the remainder of the case, though only matters of state law are involved.[27]

But what is to happen *after* the Bank's right to sue has been conclusively determined in the first case presenting the issue? If the issues does not arise in a future case because it has been recently and conclusively determined, where is the federal peg on which to hang the constitutional power of the federal courts to adjudicate what are now exclusively nonfederal issues? Marshall's response to this question must be described as disingenuous:[28]

> The right to sue, if decided once, is decided forever; but the power of Congress was exercised antecedently to the first decision on that right, and if it was constitutional then, it cannot cease to be so, because the particular

---

[22] U.S. Const., art. VI, cl. 2.

[23] Jurisdiction available when ingredient of cause is federal question. 22 U.S. at 823.

[24] Jurisdiction available when claim is determined by federal law. 22 U.S. at 822.

[25] Hypothetical case. *See* Bank of the United States v. Planters' Bank of Georgia, 22 U.S. (9 Wheat.) 904, 905 (1824).

[26] Bank's right to sue is federal question. Osborn v. Bank of the United States, 22 U.S. (9 Wheat.) 738, 823 (1824).

[27] Federal court with jurisdiction may resolve state law issues. 22 U.S. at 822.

[28] Subsequent suits concerning bank. 22 U.S. at 824.

> question is decided. It may be revived at the will of the party, and most probably would be renewed, were the tribunal to be changed. But the question respecting the right to make a particular contract, or to acquire a particular property, or to sue on account of a particular injury, belongs to every particular case, and may be renewed in every case. The question forms an original ingredient in every cause.

Marshall appears to be saying three things: (1) if a federal question "forms an ingredient of the original cause,"[29] the entire case can be heard in federal court, even though the remainder of the case is nonfederal; (2) though the issue raised by the "federal ingredient" may have been conclusively decided in a prior case, it *may* always be raised again and the fact that it actually is not raised is deemed irrelevant; (3) therefore, in any case in which a federal issue *could* be raised — apparently regardless of how clear the answer or how small the likelihood that it actually will be raised — Congress has the power under Article III to vest jurisdiction in the federal courts.

If Marshall is to be taken literally, he has created a classic tail-wagging-the-dog situation. The mere possibility of a federal issue is sufficient to authorize Congress to bring a case into federal court under the "Arising Under" Clause, even though in actuality the entire case will have absolutely nothing to do with federal law. Since it is a rare case indeed in which a creative attorney (or, for that matter, a creative court or Congress) could not devise a conceivable federal issue, a literal reading of Marshall's language in *Osborn* would give Congress virtually unlimited power to bring cases into federal court.[30]

In a separate opinion, Justice Johnson argued that "the principle of a possible occurrence of a question as a ground of jurisdiction . . . will admit of an enormous accession, if not an unlimited assumption, of jurisdiction."[31] Johnson concluded that the "Arising Under" Clause referred only to cases that *do* present a federal issue.[32] "From a purely etymological point of view," commentators have written:[33]

> Johnson, it seems clear, wins the argument. Literally a case "arising under" federal law connotes a case in which a federal issue is actually presented, and any other case is beyond the reach of this branch of federal judicial power. This is a plausible construction. It has the undeniable appeal of giving to the words construed their "natural import."

---

[29] Ingredient of original cause. 22 U.S. at 823.

[30] *See* Chadbourn & Levin, *Original Jurisdiction of Federal Questions*, 90 U. Pa. L. Rev. 639, 649 (1942) ("[I]n the *Osborn* case Marshall was construing for the future, and characteristically he construed broadly in order to allow future change and growth.") Once again, it should be emphasized that the mere fact that Congress possesses such broad power does not necessarily mean that Congress actually has exercised it. Indeed, it never has.

[31] Dissenting opinion. Osborn v. Bank of the United States, 22 U.S. (9 Wheat.) 738, 889 (1824). (Johnson, J., dissenting; emphasis omitted).

[32] Narrower interpretation argued. *See* 22 U.S. at 885; Chadbourn & Levin, *Original Jurisdiction of Federal Questions*, 90 Va. L. Rev. 639, 647 (1942).

[33] Chadbourn & Levin, *Original Jurisdiction of Federal Questions*, 90 Va. L. Rev. 639, 647–648 (1942).

But they further noted that Marshall's reason for rejecting this interpretation becomes apparent when the practical consequences of adopting it are considered.[34] It is true that Marshall's definition provided future Congresses with needed flexibility in determining the scope of federal court jurisdiction. It can be argued, however, that Marshall's opinion goes too far in defining the potential reach of federal court power by authorizing federal courts, under the federal question provision of Article III, to adjudicate virtually any case, regardless of how peripheral or remote the federal issue.

Not all commentators have agreed that Marshall intended so sweeping a power in his description of the constitutional scope of the "arising under" language. One commentator, for example, while recognizing that Marshall quite properly attributed broad scope to the constitutional language,[35] suggested limiting *Osborn* to situations in which federal instrumentalities or preexisting federal interests are involved.[36] Under this somewhat narrower reading of *Osborn*, Congress is empowered to authorize federal courts to hear cases in which no issue of substantive federal law will arise, but only if the consequences would affect a federal instrumentality or a preexisting federal statutory program.

Support for this reading of *Osborn* arguably derives from Chief Justice Marshall's distinction of suits by the Bank from suits by a naturalized alien or a federally chartered corporation. Under Marshall's view, if the act of Congress was a simple act of incorporation and contained nothing more, the issue might have been decided differently. Similarly, even though a naturalized citizen is indeed made a citizen under an act of Congress, this fact alone would not allow Congress to vest jurisdiction in the federal courts to adjudicate all cases involving that person. The difference, explained Marshall, is that the act creating the Bank "proceeds to bestow upon the being it has made, all the faculties and capacities which that being possesses. Every act of the Bank grows out of this law, and is tested by it."[37] If Marshall had intended that whenever a conceivable issue of federal law existed, Congress could vest jurisdiction in the federal courts, presumably the mere act of federal incorporation would be sufficient to bring a case involving that corporation under the "Arising Under" Clause, since a question might always be raised concerning the meaning of the act.

It may be that protecting the federal instrumentality against possible state court prejudice was a significant, if not the primary, motivation for Marshall's decision.[38]

---

[34] 90 U. PA. L. REV. at 647–648.

[35] Mishkin, *The Federal "Question" in the District Courts*, 53 COLUM. L. REV. 137, 160 (1953) (footnote omitted).

[36] 53 COLUM. L. REV. at 187 ("[T]he purpose of the *Osborn* decision was the protection of the Bank in all its legal relations, including those governed wholly by state law.").

[37] All bank's powers come from federal law. Osborn v. Bank of the United States, 22 U.S. (9 Wheat.) 738 (1824).

[38] Explanations of Marshall's position in later cases. *See* Textile Workers Union v. Lincoln Mills, 353 U.S. 448, 481 (1957) (Frankfurter, J., dissenting; "Marshall's holding was undoubtedly influenced by his fear that the bank might suffer hostile treatment in the state courts that could not be remedied by an appeal on an isolated federal question."); *but see* Mesa v. California, 489 U.S. 121, 136 (1989) (elimination of requirement that federal defense be present for removal of state action to federal court by federal

As has been argued, ultimate appellate review would be inefficient to prevent or rectify discrimination against the Bank in the application of state law or treatment of evidence. Only an initial federal forum would be adequate.[39] It is difficult to deny, however, that much of the language of *Osborn* is not so limited, and certain commentators[40] and courts[41] have acknowledged that Marshall intended *Osborn* to have a broader reach.

### [3] Post-*Osborn* Developments: *Textile Workers Union v. Lincoln Mills*

It is by no means clear that if the issue arose today, a broad reading of *Osborn* would be given strict adherence. The question rarely has arisen because the mere fact that Congress has constitutional power to extend federal question jurisdiction does not mean that Congress has exercised that power, as indeed it generally has not.

In one instance in which congressional action might have been thought to reach the outer limits of *Osborn*, the Supreme Court avoided the issue. Section 301(a) of the Labor Management Relations Act[42] provides federal jurisdiction for suits for violation of contracts between an employer and a labor organization representing employees in an industry affecting commerce. It was not clear whether by this section, Congress intended to vest in the federal courts power to develop a substantive federal common law of labor agreements, or merely to provide access to a federal forum, but with the federal court interpreting and applying state substantive law. If Congress had, in fact, intended the latter interpretation, serious questions would arise concerning the applicable scope of the "Arising Under" Clause of Article III because the federal court would be adjudicating a case presenting absolutely no issue of substantive federal law.

In *Textile Workers Union v. Lincoln Mills*, the Supreme Court avoided the need to interpret the "Arising Under" Clause of Article III by construing Section 301(a) to vest in the federal courts the power to develop their own principles of substantive law.[43] In dissent, Justice Frankfurter rejected the majority's interpretation of congressional intent. Because he assumed that Congress had intended, under the "Arising Under" Clause, to vest the federal courts with power to hear cases involving purely state law, Frankfurter felt compelled to reach the

---

officer under 28 U.S.C. § 1442(a) would raise serious doubt whether, in enacting § 1442(a), Congress would have expanded jurisdiction of federal courts beyond constitutional bounds). In light of *Mesa*, it appears that the Supreme Court does not accept such a version of *Osborn*.

[39] Mishkin, The *Federal "Question" in the District Courts*, 53 Colum. L. Rev. 137, 187 (1953).

[40] *See* Forrester, *The Nature of a "Federal Question,"* 16 Tul. L. Rev. 362, 370 (1942) ("[in *Osborn*] Marshall said, in effect, that if it is a 'federal question' once, it cannot cease to be so merely because the particular question is decided").

[41] *Osborn* broadly applied *See, e.g.*, T.B. Harms Co. v. Eliscu, 339 F.2d 823, 825 (2d Cir. 1964) (constitutional grant held under *Osborn* to extend "to every case in which federal law furnished a necessary ingredient of the claim even though this was antecedent and uncontested").

[42] 29 U.S.C. § 185(a).

[43] § 301 of LMRA construed to avoid constitutional issue. Textile Workers Union v. Lincoln Mills, 353 U.S. 448, 456 (1957) (substantive law to apply in suits under § 301(a) is federal common law).

constitutional issue.[44] The language of the statute appears to support Frankfurter's interpretation. The legislative history is, at best, inconclusive.

As Justice Frankfurter recognized, Marshall's language in *Osborn* could be thought to provide a basis to uphold the legislation under the "Arising Under" Clause. "The contribution of federal law [to interpretation of Section 301(a)]," Justice Frankfurter wrote, "might consist in postulating the right of a union, despite its amorphous status as an unincorporated association, to enter into binding collective-bargaining contracts with an employer."[45] Under this approach, the situation would be closely analogous to the one presented in *Osborn*.[46] Thus, under what Justice Frankfurter called the "traditional interpretation" of *Osborn*,[47] a strong argument could be made that Section 301(a), even were it to be interpreted to do no more than provide a federal forum, falls within the parameters of *Osborn*.

Justice Frankfurter was not willing to concede, however, that the traditional interpretation given *Osborn* was the proper one. He suggested that *Osborn* might possibly be limited on the ground that a federal instrumentality, the Bank of the United States, was involved.[48] And, while acknowledging the possible similarity of *Lincoln Mills* to *Osborn*, he noted that the historical setting was vastly different, and that the Bank was completely the creature of federal law, one engaged in carrying out essential governmental functions.[49] But Frankfurter argued that even if the broader view of *Osborn* represented the accepted interpretation, its foundation was subject to criticism.[50]

## [4] Current Status of Constitutional Scope of Federal Question Jurisdiction

The Supreme Court considered the constitutional scope of the "Arising Under" Clause in *Verlinden B.V. v. Central Bank of Nigeria*. The issue in the case was whether the Foreign Sovereign Immunities Act of 1976 (FSIA), by authorizing a foreign plaintiff to sue a foreign state in a United States District Court on a nonfederal cause of action, violated Article III. Section 2 of the Act extends federal

---

[44] Dissent addressed constitutional issue. 353 U.S. at 462 (Frankfurter, J., dissenting).

[45] Federal law concerning power of unions. 353 U.S. at 479 (Frankfurter, J., dissenting).

[46] Approach based on *Osborn*. 353 U.S. at 480 (Frankfurter, J., dissenting) ("Section 301 would, under this view, imply that a union is to be viewed as a juristic entity for purposes of acquiring contract rights under a collective-bargaining agreement, and that it has the right to enter into such a contract and to sue upon it. This was all that was immediately and expressly involved in the *Osborn* case.").

[47] Traditional interpretation. 353 U.S. at 471 (Frankfurter, J., dissenting) (footnote omitted) (federal jurisdiction under the "Arising Under" Clause, though limited to cases involving potential federal questions, has such flexibility that Congress may confer it whenever there is, in the background, some federal proposition that might be challenged, despite remoteness of likelihood of actual presentation of question).

[48] Involvement of federal instrumentality. 353 U.S. at 471 n.4 (Frankfurter, J., dissenting).

[49] Different historical setting. 353 U.S. at 480–481 (Frankfurter, J., dissenting).

[50] *Osborn* subject to criticism. 353 U.S. at 481–482 ("There is nothing in Article III that affirmatively supports the view that original jurisdiction over cases involving federal questions must extend to every case in which there is the potentiality of appellate jurisdiction.").

jurisdiction to civil actions against a foreign state as to any claim for relief in personam with respect to which the foreign state is not entitled to immunity either under Title 28 or under any applicable international agreement.[51]

The Court found that it did not need to decide the precise boundaries of Article III jurisdiction because the case did not involve a mere speculative possibility that a federal question may arise at some point in the proceeding. Rather, a suit against a foreign state under the FSIA necessarily raised questions of substantive federal law at the very outset, and hence clearly "arose under" federal law, as that term is used in Article III.[52]

This was because, in the court's words,[53]

> [t]he statute must be applied in the district Courts in every action against a foreign sovereign, since subject matter jurisdiction in any such action depends on the existence of one of the specified exceptions to foreign sovereign immunity. . . . At the threshold of every action in a District Court against a foreign state, therefore, the court must satisfy itself that one of the exceptions applies — and in doing so it must apply the detailed federal law standards set forth in the Act. Accordingly, an action against a foreign sovereign arises under federal law, for purposes of Article III jurisdiction.

*Verlinden* makes clear that the constitutional scope of the "arising under" jurisdiction remains broad, enabling Congress to use the federal courts as a means of protecting important federal interests.[54] However, because the Court in *Verlinden* found that substantive federal law was inescapably implicated in every application of the Act, no matter how preliminarily,[55] it expressly avoided deciding the question of *Osborn's* current validity. The Court also made clear, however, that a statute that merely confers federal jurisdiction cannot constitute the federal law under which an action arises.[56]

The Supreme Court debated the outer scope of Article III's "Arising Under" Clause in *Gutierrez de Martinez v. Lamagno.* There plaintiffs alleged that they had suffered physical injuries and property damage as a result of an accident in Colombia caused by the negligence of the respondent, a federal employee. The Attorney General, acting under the Westfall Act,[57] certified that respondent was acting within the scope of his employment at the time of the incident. Under the Act, on certification, the federal employee is ordinarily dismissed from the action, the

---

[51] 28 U.S.C. § 1330.

[52] Suit against foreign state arises under federal law. Verlinden B.V. v. Central Bank of Nigeria, 461 U.S. 480, 493 (1983).

[53] Application of statute. 461 U.S. at 493–494.

[54] Broad jurisdiction. 461 U.S. at 497.

[55] Involvement of substantive federal law. 461 U.S. at 493.

[56] Mere conferring of federal jurisdiction does not constitute "arising under." 461 U.S. at 496; *see* Osborn v. Bank of the United States, 22 U.S. (9 Wheat.) 738 (1824); *see also In re* TMI Litigation Cases Consolidated II, 940 F.2d 832, 850 (3d Cir. 1991) (central teaching of *Osborn* is that case cannot be said to arise under federal statute if statute is nothing more than jurisdictional grant).

[57] 28 U.S.C. § 2679(d)(1).

United States is substituted as defendant, and the case proceeds under the Federal Tort Claims Act (FTCA).[58] If the action was filed in state court, it must be removed to federal court because federal jurisdiction is exclusive under the FTCA, and the certification establishes scope of employment for purposes of removal.[59] Under the facts of this case, however, the substitution would result in the action's dismissal because it fell within an exception to the Federal Tort Claims Act's waiver of sovereign immunity.[60] Plaintiffs (whose suit was premised on diversity of citizenship) sought to obtain judicial review of the Attorney General's scope-of-employment certification so as to be able to proceed against the employee.[61]

The majority found the certification to be reviewable on nonjurisdictional grounds, finding that Congress did not intend to foreclose judicial review.[62] However, the jurisdictional problem is that if there is neither diversity nor a federal question, there will be federal jurisdiction only if the United States is a party under the FTCA,[63] and the case will proceed under the FTCA only if there is a certification. Hence, if the certification is reviewed and overturned, it is arguable that there is no basis for federal jurisdiction.[64]

Justice Souter, joined by three other justices in dissent, focused primarily on this point. He argued that the Court should not infer congressional intent to authorize judicial review because to do so might give rise to serious Article III problems if diversity is absent and the case has been removed from state court. He first noted that under the FTCA, once a state tort action has been removed to a federal court after a certification by the Attorney General, it may never be remanded to the state system because the statute makes the Attorney General's certification conclusive for purposes of removal.[65] Thus, if a federal court could review and possibly reverse the Attorney General's certification that the federal employee was acting within the scope of his employment, the result would be a nonremandable federal court adjudication of a claim that does not implicate federal law in any way. Such a reading, Justice Souter suggested, would cause the statute at the very least to approach the limit of Article III, if it does not cross the line. It was, therefore, just the case for adhering to the Court's practice of declining to construe a statute in such a way as to test the limits of Article III's if presented with a sound alternative.[66]

---

58 28 U.S.C. § 2680(k); *see* 28 U.S.C. § 2679(d)(4).

59 28 U.S.C. § 2679(d)(2); *see* 28 U.S.C. § 1346(b).

60 *See* 28 U.S.C. § 2680(k) (claims arising in foreign country excluded).

61 Judicial review sought for scope-of-employment certification. Gutierrez de Martinez v. Lamagno, 515 U.S. 417, 420 (1995).

62 Certification reviewable on nonjurisdictional grounds. Gutierrez de Martinez v. Lamagno, 515 U.S. 417, 423–426 (1995).

63 *See* 28 U.S.C. § 1346(b).

64 Arguably no basis for jurisdiction. *See* Gutierrez de Martinez v. Lamagno, 515 U. S. 417, 434–435 (1995).

65 Article III problems. 515 U.S. at 440–441 (Souter, J., dissenting); *see* 28 U.S.C. § 2679(d)(2).

66 Limit of Article III approached or crossed. 515 U.S. at 441 (Souter, J., dissenting).

Four of the five-justice majority were prepared to address the issue by finding no jurisdictional problem. Justice Ginsburg, in Part IV of the opinion in which only three justice joined, discussed the jurisdictional implications of their conclusion for the scope of Article III's "Arising Under" Clause. She did not believe the Article III problem to be a "grave" one. While in a case removed to federal court there may no longer be a federal question once the federal employee is resubstituted as defendant, there had been a nonfrivolous federal question, certified by the local U.S. Attorney, at the time when the case was removed to federal court; namely, whether the employee was acting within the scope of his federal employment. Because a case under the Westfall Act raises a question of substantive federal law at the very outset, it clearly "arises under" federal law as that term is defined in Article III.[67] As a result, under a theory of supplemental jurisdiction and in a manner reminiscent of the approach taken by Chief Justice Marshall in *Osborn*, she found that the federal court could also resolve all of the remaining state law issues.[68]

Justice Souter rejected this reasoning as unduly facile. He reasoned that the challenge to the certification is the equivalent of a challenge to the essential jurisdictional fact that the United States is a party, and that the federal court's jurisdiction to review scope of employment (on the Court's theory) is merely an example of any court's necessary authority to rule on a challenge to its own jurisdiction to try a particular action. The Court's reliance on the fact of the certification, then "simply obliterates the distinction between the authority to determine jurisdiction that is the subject of the challenge, and the party whose jurisdictional claim was challenged will never lose."[69]

Justice Souter is surely correct in his assertion that Justice Ginsburg's construction of Article III pushes the constitutional envelope. In the unlikely event that the Court would rigorously adhere to the broad construction of Chief Justice Marshall's opinion in *Osborn*, it is possible that Justice Ginsburg's analysis would be valid. Even this conclusion is far from clear, however. Chief Justice Marshall may not have required much to bring a case within the scope of Article III's "Arising Under" Clause, but he did require the existence of at least a potential question of federal law to be resolved by the federal court. Given that the statute seems to render the Attorney General's certification to be conclusive for purposes of removal, it is not exactly clear what federal "question" Justice Ginsburg believed existed that needed — even potentially — to be resolved by the federal court. Thus, while Chief Justice Marshall in *Osborn* might have been accused of allowing the tail to wag the dog, Justice Ginsburg is perhaps vulnerable to the criticism that she is wagging the dog without even a tail by which to do so. Justice Ginsburg's position simply ignores all of the constitutional questions and concerns that had previously been raised about overbroad interpretations of Article III.[70]

---

[67] No jurisdictional problem. 515 U.S. at 434–435 (quoting *Verlinden B.V. v. Central Bank of Nigeria*, 461 U.S. 480, 493 (1983)).

[68] Supplemental jurisdiction over remaining state law issues. 515 U.S. at 435–436.

[69] Justice Souter rejects reasoning. Gutierrez de Martinez v. Lamagno, 515 U.S. 417, 442–443 (1995) (Souter, J., dissenting).

[70] Broad interpretation of "arising under" had previously been subject to question. *See, e.g.*, Gully v. First Nat'l Bank, 299 U.S. 109, 113–114 (1936) (earlier cases were "less exacting" than more recent ones);

Any questions that might have remained about the propriety of the broadest possible interpretation of Article III seem to have been resolved by Justice Ginsburg in her majority opinion in *Osborn v. Haley*.[71] The facts of this case directly presented the question of whether an Attorney General certification that the defendant was a United States employee acting within the scope of his employment at the time of his alleged acts under the Westfall Act could, consistent with Article III, create federal jurisdiction even if no issue of federal law would ever arise in the case. The Court, without a great deal of analysis, rejected any possible Article III challenges to Attorney General certifications under the statute in such a case.[72]

In *Osborn v. Haley*, the plaintiff alleged that the defendant, a federal employee, tortiously interfered with the plaintiff's employment contract. The plaintiff filed suit in state court, asserting that the defendant's conduct was not within the scope of the defendant's federal employment. The local United States Attorney, acting on behalf of the Attorney General, issued a "conclusive" certification that the defendant was, in fact, acting within the scope of his federal employment at the time of the incident in question, and removed the case to federal court under 28 U.S.C. § 2679(d)(2).[73] The United States Attorney's certification automatically vested the federal district court with jurisdiction without any possibility of remand, even if the court subsequently found that the employee had not even engaged in the alleged behavior.[74] Thus, there would exist the possibility that resolution of the case would have nothing to do with defendant's duties as a federal officer, for the simple reason that he had not even engaged in the alleged acts in the first place. Nonetheless, under the statute, the federal court, because of the erroneous certification, would effectively have exclusive jurisdiction in the case.[75]

This situation was not a mere theoretical possibility in *Osborn v. Haley* because, after removing the case to the federal district court, the United States Attorney contradicted any possible factual basis for the certification by claiming that the

---

Puerto Rico v. Russell & Co., 288 U.S. 476, 485 (1933) (Osborn rule, dealing with actions brought by federally chartered corporations, has not been extended to other classes of cases, and has been restricted by successive statutes).

[71] *Osborn v. Haley* case. *See* Osborn v. Haley, 549 U.S. 225, 243–246 (2007) (question of propriety of Attorney General's Westfall Act certification will always present a sufficient federal question to satisfy Article III's "arising under" requirement).

[72] No Article III problems found. Osborn v. Haley, 549 U.S. 225, 243–246 (2007) ("the Westfall Act's command that a district court retain jurisdiction over a case removed pursuant to § 2679(d)(2) does not run afoul of Article III.").

[73] *Osborn v. Haley* facts. Osborn v. Haley, 549 U.S. 225, 231–235 (2007) (Attorney General issued "conclusive" certification that Haley was acting with scope of his employment at time of incident alleged in plaintiff's complaint, but, in fact, denied that incident alleged in plaintiff's complaint ever took place).

[74] Certification is conclusive for removal purposes. 28 U.S.C. § 2679(d)(2) ("The certification of the Attorney General shall conclusively establish scope of office or employment for purposes of removal."); Osborn v. Haley, 549 U.S. 225, 239–241 (2007) ("Congress gave district courts no authority to return cases to state courts on the grounds that the Attorney General's certification was unwarranted.").

[75] Westfall Act certification provides exclusive jurisdiction. Osborn v. Haley, 549 U.S. 225, 245–246 (2007) ("the Westfall Act's command that a district court retain jurisdiction over a case removed pursuant to § 2679(d)(2) does not run afoul of Article III. . . . We agree that Westfall Act certification is proper when a federal officer charged with misconduct asserts, and the Government determines, that the incident or episode in suit never occurred.").

defendant's actions alleged by the plaintiff had never occurred.[76] Given these facts, the district court could well conclude that the certification was factually erroneous,[77] but the certification would still provide the sole ground for assertion of federal jurisdiction in the case.

Because the United States Attorney was claiming that the alleged behavior never occurred at all, the district court rejected the United States Attorney's certification that the defendant had acted within the scope of his federal employment at the time of the alleged events. The district court, therefore, refused to substitute the United States as a party, and attempted to remand the action to state court, despite the provision in 28 U.S.C. § 2672(d)(2) that the certification was "conclusive . . . for the purposes of removal." The district court's orders were appealed to the Sixth Circuit, which reversed and instructed the district court to retain jurisdiction over the case.[78]

The Supreme Court affirmed the Sixth Circuit's ruling. Among other things, the Supreme Court ruled that a certification under the Westfall Act that the employee was acting within the course of his employment at the time of the alleged incident is proper and controlling, even if the government subsequently denies that the incident occurred at all.[79] According to the Supreme Court, the purpose of the certification under the Act is to protect individual employees from the burden of defending meritless suits. Thus certification serves that purpose even when the government's position is that the incident asserted in the suit never occurred.[80] Furthermore, the Supreme Court concluded that the district court's remand order was reviewable on appeal.[81]

On the Article III question, the Supreme Court found that the federal jurisdiction conferred by an Attorney General certification under the Act is conclusive, even if it is ultimately found to be erroneous. Justice Ginsburg held that this jurisdictional conclusion did not violate Article III. She reasoned that, whenever the Attorney General makes a certification under the Westfall Act, and thus confers federal jurisdiction in the case, there always exists a federal question sufficient to

---

[76] Osborn v. Haley, 549 U.S. 225, 235–236 (2007) (government denied allegations in its answer, and, on motion for reconsideration, submitted declarations asserting that there was no tortious interference because there was no communication between government employee and party that refused to hire plaintiff).

[77] Osborn v. Haley, 549 U.S. 225, 235–236 (2007) (district court did so conclude, arguing that government could certify Haley's actions, as alleged in complaint, were within scope of his federal employment only if it admitted that those actions occurred).

[78] Osborn v. Haley, 549 U.S. 225, 235–236 (2007).

[79] Westfall Act certification proper, even when government denies occurrence. Osborn v. Haley, 549 U.S. 225, 246–248 (2007) ("We agree that Westfall Act certification is proper when a federal officer charged with misconduct asserts, and the Government determines, that the incident or episode in suit never occurred.").

[80] Purpose of Westfall Act. Osborn v. Haley, 549 U.S. 225, 246–249 (2007) ("it would make scant sense to read the Act as leaving an employee charged with an intentional tort to fend for himself when he denies wrongdoing" [footnote omitted]).

[81] Improper attempt to remand after Westfall Act certification is reviewable. Osborn v. Haley, 549 U.S. 225, 238–243 (2007) ("of the two antishuttling commands, § 1447(d) and § 2679(d)(2), only one can prevail. We hold that § 2679(d)(2) controls.").

support federal jurisdiction. The federal question is whether the individual defendant does, in fact, have immunity under the Westfall Act. This is true, even though the district court lacks discretion to reject the Attorney General's certification and even if only state law claims and factual issues remained after the resolution of this federal question.[82]

The problem with Justice Ginsburg's Article III reasoning is that the federal question she finds to support federal jurisdiction comes ominously close to an impermissible jurisdictional bootstrap. According to her reasoning, the certification under the Westfall Act may vest a federal court with jurisdiction even when there is no other federal question or diversity of citizenship, because the question of whether the defendant is immune under the Westfall Act creates a federal question sufficient to satisfy Article III. Such a conclusion arguably stretches Article III's "arising under" language beyond its logical limit.

The only basis for finding federal question jurisdiction in *Haley* is the presence of the federal issue whether the defendant has Westfall Act immunity because he was acting within the scope of his duties as a federal officer at the time of his alleged actions. Yet according to the U.S. Attorney's argument following certification, the defendant had not even engaged in the behavior in the first place. The certification under the Westfall Act, then, seems to automatically create a federal question, even if none actually exists in the case. The Act thus appears to allow the Attorney General to create a federal question simply by invocation of its certification authority, even if the Attorney General immediately abandons the factual assumptions that necessarily underlie that certification. For jurisdictional purposes, then, the certification effectively becomes a self-fulfilling prophecy.

It is significant, however, that none of the other Justices writing in *Osborn v. Haley* challenged Justice Ginsburg on this point. Justice Souter, concurring and dissenting in part, was exclusively concerned with the conclusion that the remand order was appealable, asserting that the Court should have reviewed only the district's court's erroneous refusal to substitute the United States as a defendant.[83] Justice Breyer was concerned only with the question of whether a Westfall Act certification that an individual employee acted within the course of his or her federal employment could ever be proper when the government's position was that the incident asserted in the lawsuit never occurred.[84]

---

[82] Westfall Act certifications always present federal question that satisfies Article III. Osborn v. Haley, 549 U.S. 225, 243–245 (2007) ("In the case before us, the question [of whether Article III permits federal jurisdiction] would arise only if, after full consideration, the District Court determines that Haley in fact engaged in the tortious conduct outside the scope of his employment charged in Osborn's complaint. At that point, however, little would be left to adjudicate, at least as to Haley's liability. Because a significant federal question (whether Haley has Westfall Act immunity) would have been raised at the outset, the case would "arise under" federal law, as that term is used in Article III.").

[83] Limited scope of Souter's dissent. *See* Osborn v. Haley, 549 U.S. 225, 253–254 (2007) ("I would reaffirm the rule that a district court's remand order is unreviewable").

[84] Limited scope of Breyer's dissent. *See* Osborn v. Haley, 549 U.S. 225, 255–261 (2007) ("I continue to believe that the Westfall Act permits the Attorney General to certify only when accepting, at least conditionally, the existence of some kind of 'incident.' ").

## [5] Protective Jurisdiction

While the current status of the *Osborn* interpretation of Article III's "Arising Under" Clause is not entirely clear, scholars have developed another theory, generally referred to as "protective jurisdiction," to justify the vesting by Congress of power in the federal courts to adjudicate cases that do not directly present issues of substantive federal law.[85]

It should be emphasized that this doctrine, like *Osborn*, is not itself a means of obtaining federal jurisdiction, nor is it intended to serve as an interpretation of current federal question statutes. Rather, it is merely a method of determining the constitutionality under Article III of congressional attempts to vest jurisdiction in the federal courts over purely state law matters. Absent such a congressional assertion of federal question jurisdiction, the theory of protective jurisdiction is wholly irrelevant.

Though as previously noted, Congress has not often attempted to enact such a jurisdictional statute, the validity of protective jurisdiction is, at least as a theoretical matter, an important issue. There may be a number of occasions in which Congress deems it necessary to provide a federal forum, even though the substantive law to be applied is derived wholly from the states.[86]

Protective jurisdiction is in reality a label used to describe two completely different theories.[87] These theories are called the "greater includes the lesser" view and the "partial occupation" view.

The "greater includes the lesser" view of protective jurisdiction assumes that if Congress could, in the exercise of its enumerated or implied powers under Article I of the Constitution, pass substantive legislation on a particular matter, then this "greater" power logically includes within it the "lesser" power to provide the federal courts with jurisdiction over cases in the area, even though the substantive principles of decision are to be supplied by state law. One commentator provided this illustration:[88]

> Where, for example, Congress by the commerce power can declare as federal law that contracts of a given kind are valid and enforceable, it must be free to take the lesser step of drawing suits upon such contracts to the district courts without displacement of the states as sources of the operative, substantive law.

This theory has been summarized in the following manner: "A case is one 'arising under' federal law within the sense of Article III whenever it is comprehended in a valid grant of jurisdiction as well as when its disposition must be governed by the

[85] *See* Goldberg-Ambrose, *The Protective Jurisdiction of the Federal Courts*, 30 UCLA L. Rev. 542, 546–547 (1983) ("The concept of protective jurisdiction tends to arise in situations in which Congress has authorized a federal forum, the accepted minimum requirements for a case to arise under federal law are not met, and no other basis for federal jurisdiction can be found under article III of the Constitution.").

[86] *See* Mishkin, *The Federal "Question" in the District Courts*, 53 Colum. L. Rev. 137, 184–185 (1953).

[87] *See generally* Note, *The Theory of Protective Jurisdiction*, 57 N.Y.U. L. Rev. 933 (1982).

[88] Wechsler, *Federal Jurisdiction and the Revision of the Judicial Code*, 13 Law & Contemp. Prob. 216, 224 (1948) (footnote omitted).

national law."[89] Employing this approach then, Congress could assure litigants the protection of a federal forum any time it possessed the power to legislate substantively in a particular area.

Whether the "greater includes the lesser" approach adds to the broad constitutional power provided to Congress by *Osborn* is questionable.[90] Theoretically, at least, it is correct to think that this theory extends Congress's constitutional power beyond that established in *Osborn*. Under this interpretation, there need not be present even a potential federal question. As a practical matter, however, if Chief Justice Marshall's language in *Osborn* is to be taken literally, it will be a rare case indeed in which not even a conceivable federal issue can be found lurking in the background.

Others have questioned the logic of the "greater includes the lesser" theory. "Surely the truly technical restrictions of Article III are not met or respected," wrote Justice Frankfurter in his dissent *Textile Workers Union v. Lincoln Mills*, "by a beguiling phrase that the greater power here must necessarily include the lesser."[91]

The "partial occupation" version of protective jurisdiction, in contrast, is narrower than the "greater includes the lesser" theory in some ways, and broader in others.[92] The crux of the "partial occupation" theory is as follows:[93]

> [W]here there is an articulated and active federal policy regulating a field, the "arising under" clause of Article III apparently permits the conferring of jurisdiction on the national courts of all cases in the area — including those substantively governed by state law.

Like the "greater includes the lesser" theory, the "partial occupation" theory reads the "Arising Under" Clause of Article III to authorize Congress to vest in the federal courts the power to adjudicate certain cases in which all governing substantive principles will be derived from state law. This is the one significant link

---

[89] Wechsler, *Federal Jurisdiction and the Revision of the Judicial Code*, 13 LAW & CONTEMP. PROB. 216, 225 (1948).

[90] Professor Wechsler apparently thought that it does. "The power of the Congress to confer the federal judicial power must extend, as Marshall held, to every case that might involve an issue under federal law. It should extend, I think, beyond this to all cases in which Congress has authority to make the rule to govern disposition of the controversy but is content instead to let the states provide the rule so long as jurisdiction to enforce it has been vested in a federal court." Wechsler, *Federal Jurisdiction and the Revision of the Judicial Code*, 13 LAW & CONTEMP. PROB. 216, 224 (1948) (footnote omitted).

[91] "Greater includes the lesser" theory of protective jurisdiction rejected. *See* Textile Workers Union v. Lincoln Mills, 353 U.S. 448, 473–475 (1957) (Frankfurter, J., dissenting); *see also* Goldberg-Ambrose, *The Protective Jurisdiction of the Federal Courts*, 30 UCLA L. REV. 542, 590–591 (1983) (criticism of "greater includes the lesser" logic as rationale for protective jurisdiction); Mishkin, *The Federal "Question" in the District Courts*, 53 COLUM. L. REV. 137, 190 (1953) (author, proponent of his own variant of protective jurisdiction, criticizes "greater includes the lesser" theory on ground that theory would validate jurisdictional statute even though federal government had failed to evince any concern in outcome of cases brought under it).

[92] *See* Cross, *Congressional Power to Extend Jurisdiction to Disputes Outside Article III: A Critical Analysis From the Perspective of Bankruptcy*, 87 NW. U. L. REV. 1188, 1214 (1993); Goldberg-Ambrose, *The Protective Jurisdiction of the Federal Courts*, 30 UCLA L. REV. 542, 592–595 (1983).

[93] *See* Mishkin, *The Federal "Question" in the District Courts*, 53 COLUM. L. REV. 137, 192 (1953).

connecting the two versions of protective jurisdiction. It is there, however, that the similarity ends. Unlike the "greater includes the lesser" theory, the "partial occupation" theory, lets nothing turn on whether or not Congress could pass substantive legislation in the field of law in question. Ironically, while advocates of the "greater includes the lesser" theory believe that it extends *Osborn*, advocates of the "partial occupation" theory criticize the "greater includes the lesser" theory's prerequisite that Congress be able to pass substantive legislation before it can vest jurisdiction without actually passing such legislation precisely because this requirement narrows *Osborn*.[94]

In this sense, then, the "partial occupation" theory of protective jurisdiction seems to give Congress greater power than the "greater includes the lesser" theory. But the "partial occupation" theory imposes a precondition that advocates of the "greater includes the lesser" theory never consider relevant. Under the "partial occupation" theory, before Congress may vest jurisdiction in the federal courts to hear cases based solely on state law, it would have to be clear that there is an articulated and active federal policy regulating a field. The rationale is that Congress has the authority to protect its preexisting programs from being undermined by state court adjudication of related questions, even though those questions involve purely matters of state law.[95] Under the "partial occupation" theory then, cases of protective jurisdiction "arise under" the preexisting legislative program rather than under the jurisdictional statute itself.

Support for this theory is said to be found in various Supreme Court decisions. *Osborn* itself has been viewed as an illustration of this version of protective jurisdiction.[96] But it is not clear that, aside from the creation of the Bank and the establishment of limited regulation of its operation, Congress actually had evinced the "articulated and active federal policy" that is a prerequisite to the application of this form of protective jurisdiction.[97]

Stronger support for the "partial occupation" theory may be found in the so-called bankruptcy cases. These decisions upheld the constitutionality of the provisions in the bankruptcy law[98] that allow the trustee in bankruptcy under certain circumstances to bring a plenary suit in federal court to recover on causes of action originally belonging to the bankrupt, even though the substance of the suit concerned solely issues of state law.[99] Though the Court's reasons for upholding the constitutionality of these provisions were unclear, advocates of the "partial occupa-

---

94 53 Colum. L. Rev. at 189 (footnote omitted).

95 *See* 53 Colum. L. Rev. at 196 ("The use of the federal trial courts to protect a congressional program seems no less meet than their use to vindicate a specific federal right.").

96 53 Colum. L. Rev. at 187.

97 *See* 53 Colum. L. Rev. at 193 (acknowledging that *Osborn* case might be limited on ground that interest on whose behalf federal forum was invoked was government agency).

98 11 U.S.C. § 46(b).

99 Bankruptcy cases supporting partial-occupation theory of protective jurisdiction. Schumacher v. Beeler, 293 U.S. 367, 371 (1934); *see* Williams v. Austrian, 331 U.S. 642, 646 (1947); *see also* Cross, *Congressional Power to Extend Federal Jurisdiction to Disputes Outside Article III: A Critical Analysis From the Perspective of Bankruptcy*, 87 Nw. U. L. Rev. 1188 (1993) (analysis of intersection of Article III's "Arising Under" Clause and bankruptcy law).

tion" theory view the situation as one in which Congress had established and affirmatively enacted statutes expressing a national policy in the area concerned.[100] From this perspective, the bankruptcy cases seem to support the "partial occupation" theory of protective jurisdiction more than they do the "greater includes the lesser" theory, because it is by no means clear that Congress could, under its Article I power, substantively legislate over all causes of action of a bankrupt. On the other hand, because there could always be a question of federal law lurking in the background of these cases,[101] it is arguable that the bankruptcy cases simply represent a logical application of the *Osborn* interpretation of the "Arising Under" Clause of Article III.

In his dissent in *Lincoln Mills,* Justice Frankfurter expressed strong reservations about the "partial occupation" version of protective jurisdiction, much as he had about the "greater includes the lesser" version.[102] "Protective jurisdiction," said Frankfurter, "once the label is discarded, cannot be justified under any view of the allowable scope to be given to Article III."[103] In *Lincoln Mills*, however, Justices Burton and Harlan concluded that Section 301 was not intended to authorize the development by the federal courts of substantive principles of federal law, but nevertheless viewed the Act as constitutional under a theory of protective jurisdiction.[104] Until Congress attempts to employ the power that the commentators have suggested exists under protective jurisdiction, however, it remains to be seen whether the courts will give the doctrine significant credence.

In two more recent statements on federal question jurisdiction, the Supreme Court has expressly avoided the question of protective jurisdiction's validity. In a footnote in *Verlinden V.B. v. Central Bank of Nigeria*, the Court stated that "[i]n view of our conclusion that proper actions by foreign plaintiffs under the Foreign Sovereign Immunities Act are within Article III's 'arising under' jurisdiction, we need not consider petitioner's alternative argument that the Act is constitutional as

---

[100] Mishkin, *The Federal "Question" in the District Courts*, 53 COLUM. L. REV. 137, 195 (1953).

[101] Bankruptcy cases and "partial occupation" theory. *See* Textile Workers Union v. Lincoln Mills, 353 U.S. 448, 472 (1957) (Frankfurter, J., dissenting) ("[T]he trustee's right to sue might be challenged on obviously federal grounds — absence of bankruptcy or irregularity of the trustee's appointment or of the bankruptcy proceedings.").

[102] Reservations about "partial occupation" theory. 353 U.S. at 476 ("partial occupation" theory is as expansive as "greater includes the lesser" version, "save for dubious advantage of limiting incursions on state judicial power to situations in which State's feelings may have been tempered by early substantive federal invasions); *see also* Goldberg-Ambrose, *The Protective Jurisdiction of the Federal Courts*, 30 UCLA L. REV. 542, 548 (1983) (Partial occupation incorrectly draws line between cases arising under federal law in ordinary sense and those requiring exercise of protective jurisdiction because it underestimates significance of presence of some federal law in Bank's state contract claim in *Osborn*).

[103] Protective jurisdiction not justifiable. 353 U.S. at 474; *see* Note, *Over-Protective Jurisdiction: A State Sovereignty Theory of Federal Questions*, 102 HARV. L. REV. 1948 (1989) (critique of broad theory of protective jurisdiction and proposal for relatively narrow construction of Article III's "arising under" jurisdiction).

[104] Protective jurisdiction applied. 353 U.S. at 460 (Burton, J., concurring). *See also* the opinion of Judge Magruder in International Bhd. of Teamsters, Local 25 v. W.L. Mead, Inc., 230 F.2d 576, 580 (1st Cir. 1956) (§ 301 is constitutional because Congress has some power to confer "protective jurisdiction"). Justice Burton did not make clear, however, which form of protective jurisdiction he intended to adopt.

an aspect of so-called 'protective jurisdiction.' "[105]

More recently, in *Mesa v. California*, the Court was faced with the issue of whether a federal employee could remove a state criminal prosecution for traffic violations to federal court under the federal officer removal statute.[106] The Court construed the statute to require the presence of a federal defense and suggested that the opposite construction would give rise to serious "arising under" problems under Article III.[107] In so holding, the Court was more openly negative in its attitude towards protective jurisdiction. In rejecting the government's reliance on protective jurisdiction to provide constitutional support for removal without a federal defense, the Court reasoned:[108]

> We have, in the past, not found the need to adopt a theory of "protective jurisdiction" to support Art. III "arising under" jurisdiction . . . and we do not see any need for doing so here because we do not recognize any federal interests that are not protected by limiting removal to situations in which a federal defense is alleged. In these prosecutions, no state court hostility or interference has even been alleged by petitioners and we can discern no federal interest in potentially forcing local district attorneys to choose between prosecuting traffic violations hundreds of miles from the municipality in which the violations occurred or abandoning those prosecutions.

While the Court's assessment of the facts in *Mesa* may well have been accurate, its analysis was extremely narrow in a number of respects. The Court failed to deal fully with two conceivable factual variations: (1) a case in which local hostility to federal officers actually is alleged, and (2) the possibility of an express congressional judgment, contained in a newly-enacted statute, that fear of state court hostility is, as a general matter, a sufficient basis for a federal officer's invocation of federal jurisdiction on removal.

In a separate concurring opinion, Justice Brennan correctly pointed out that it is not at all inconceivable that Congress's concern about local hostility to federal authority could come into play in some circumstances in which the federal officer is unable to present any federal defense. In support, he noted that "[t]he days of widespread resistance by state and local governmental authorities to acts of Congress and to decisions of this court in the areas of school desegregation and voting rights are not so distant that we should be oblivious to the possibility of harassment of federal agents by local-law enforcement authorities. Such harassment could well take the form of unjustified prosecution for traffic or other offenses, to which the federal officer would have no immunity or other federal defense. The removal statute . . . might well have been intended to apply to such unfortunate

---

[105] Protective jurisdiction argument not addressed. Verlinden B.V. v. Central Bank of Nigeria, 461 U.S. 480, 491 n.17 (1983).

[106] 28 U.S.C. § 1442(a)(1) (federal officer may remove state criminal prosecution to federal court for or relating to any act under color of office or on account of any right, title, or authority claimed under any act of Congress for apprehension or punishment of criminals).

[107] Removal by federal officer requires federal defense. Mesa v. California, 489 U.S. 121, 136 (1989).

[108] 489 U.S. at 137–138.

and exceptional circumstances."[109] While Justice Brennan believed that the Court correctly refrained from deciding whether removal in such a situation is possible due to the fact that the issue was not presented, he joined in the Court's opinion because it had expressly left open the possibility that if a federal officer is prosecuted because of local hostility to his function, careful pleading, demonstrating the close connection between the state prosecution and the federal officer's performance of his duty might adequately replace the specific averment of a federal defense.[110] By this statement, the Court quite probably meant that the federal officer defendant's mere assertion that the state prosecution is motivated by hostility to him for the very reason that he is a federal officer might itself be deemed a "federal defense," thereby meeting the requirement of a substantive federal issue as a prerequisite to the invocation of Article III's "arising under" jurisdiction.

It is true, of course, that the Court could rightfully argue that its function is not to decide hypothetical cases. Yet the Court has often been willing to employ an individual case to expound on and provide clarity on a broader legal question. In the case of protective jurisdiction, it would not have been unreasonable for the Court to have taken the opportunity in *Mesa* to clarify the doctrine's reach, at least for the important and limited situation of potential state court hostility towards federal officers.

At first blush, one might think that *Osborn v. Haley* presents the question left open in *Mesa*: a suit against a federal officer under state law when the defense is not that the action was done in performance of the federal officer's duties, but rather a simple denial. The *Osborn v. Haley* Court believed, however, that the requirement of a federal issue was satisfied by the Westfall Act itself, which, when invoked, necessarily raises the question of whether the statute's requirements have been satisfied.[111] Despite the arguably circular nature of reliance on the act vesting jurisdiction in the federal courts, given the Court's assumption about the presence of an issue of federal law it need not have faced the protective jurisdiction question.

## § 4.03 28 U.S.C. § 1331: THE FEDERAL QUESTION STATUTE

### [1] Constitutional and Statutory Federal Question Provisions Compared

The general federal question statute, 28 U.S.C. § 1331, gives federal district courts original jurisdiction of "all civil actions arising under the Constitution, laws, or treaties of the United States."[112] Despite the striking similarity between this statutory language and that of Article III, Section 2, it is well established that the scope of the statute is considerably narrower than that of the constitutional

[109] 489 U.S. at 140 (Brennan, J., concurring).

[110] 489 U.S. at 140 (Brennan, J., concurring, quoting lead opinion, 489 U.S. at 132).

[111] Westfall Act certifications always present federal question that satisfies Article III. Osborn v. Haley, 549 U.S. 225, 243–245 (2007) ("Because a significant federal question (whether Haley has Westfall Act immunity) would have been raised at the outset, the case would "arise under" federal law, as that term is used in Article III.").

[112] 28 U.S.C. § 1331.

provision.[113] It is now universally understood that Congress did not intend to exercise the full potential of its power in enacting the general federal question statute.[114]

Given the similarity of the wording of the statute and the constitutional provision, it could be reasonably inferred that the two provisions were intended to be conterminous. One commentator argued that the primary drafter of the Senate bill for the original general federal question statute, which was enacted in 1875, did, in fact, intend to vest full constitutional power in the lower federal courts.[115] However, other scholars argued that a broad reading of the constitutional provision is justified because it is difficult to anticipate all of the problems that may confront future congresses, but a similarly broad reading of the statutory provision would flood the federal courts with countless cases totally unrelated to federal law. It is unlikely, they argued, that Congress would have intended to give such a broad interpretation to a general statutory grant of jurisdiction.[116]

### [2] Interpretation of the General Federal Question Jurisdiction Statute

Over the years, there has been substantial disagreement among both courts and scholars concerning the scope and meaning of the general federal question jurisdiction statute. That debate has focused largely on the meaning of the phrase "arising under."[117] But while the controversy may rage on an academic level, the disputes generally concern the outer fringes of the legal doctrines (as is true of many such controversies). As a practical matter, the overwhelming majority of actual cases fall either clearly within or without the federal question statute.[118] As one commentator has persuasively argued, "[t]he federal courts do not sit to give material for law review articles. Their business is the vindication of the rights

---

[113] Statute's narrower scope. Shoshone Mining Co. v. Rutter, 177 U.S. 505, 506 (1900) (in determining whether statute that authorized action to settle adverse mining claims "in a court of competent jurisdiction" conferred federal jurisdiction, issue was not extent of congressional power to confer jurisdiction, but intent to exercise that power).

[114] No congressional intent to exercise full potential. Verlinden B.V. v. Central Bank of Nigeria, 461 U.S. 480, 494–495 (1983); Romero v. International Terminal Operating Co., 358 U.S. 354, 379 n.51 (1959) (limits of general federal question statute are not limits on constitutional power of Congress to confer federal jurisdiction).

[115] Argument that Congress *did* intend to vest full constitutional power. Forrester, *The Nature of a "Federal Question,"* 16 Tul. L. Rev. 362, 374–375 (1942) (what little contemporary legal commentary that existed concurred in this interpretation).

[116] Different interpretations of statute and constitutional provision justified. *See* Mishkin, *The Federal "Question" in the District Courts*, 53 Colum. L. Rev. 137, 162–163 (1953); Cohen, *The Broken Compass: The Requirement That a Case Arise "Directly" Under Federal Law*, 115 U. Pa. L. Rev. 890, 891 (1967).

[117] *See* 28 U.S.C. § 1331.

[118] Cohen, *The Broken Compass: The Requirement That a Case Arise "Directly" Under Federal Law*, 111 U. Pa. L. Rev. 890, 906 (1967) ("It is the unusual, novel, atypical claim which presents the problem.").

conferred by federal law."[119]

A number of Supreme Court cases from the first half of the twentieth century addressed the parameters of statutory federal question jurisdiction. While these decisions were by no means fully internally consistent, it was not until the *Merrell Dow* decision in 1986[120] that the Court's doctrine degenerated into a significant state of uncertainty. Before one can understand the sources of that uncertainty, however, it is necessary to examine the conceptual and doctrinal evolution of the federal question statute.

The early historical focus of judicial interpretation of the federal question statute was on suits involving federal causes of action. This gave rise to the "creation test." Under this test, federal jurisdiction generally exists if the claims arise under either a federal statute or federal common law.[121]

Over the years, the Court began to expand the federal question statute's reach to include certain cases presenting state law causes of action that implicate issues of federal law. This gave rise to the "substantial federal question test." The question in these cases is whether the state law cause of action poses a substantial federal question, which has proven to be a more troublesome query.

### [a] Creation Test: Case Arises Under Law That Creates Cause of Action

The rule that a case arises under the law that creates the cause of action was set forth in the 1916 case of *American Well Works Co. v. Layne Bowler Co.* The case began in state court and was removed to federal court. It involved a claim of trade libel, under state law, premised on the plaintiff's contention that the defendants had falsely charged that parts of plaintiff's product infringed defendants' patents and had improperly sued or threatened to sue those who used plaintiff's product.[122] It appeared that the case would ultimately turn entirely on whether the product did, in fact, infringe defendants' patents, purely a question of federal law. If it did infringe the patents, defendants' conduct would likely have been proper under applicable state tort law.

Justice Holmes, writing for the Court, refused to find original federal jurisdiction. Rather, he found that a suit arises under the law that creates the cause of action. Because the cause of action in the case arose from state trade libel law rather than federal patent law, the case arose under state law, rather than federal law.[123]

---

[119] Wechsler, *Federal Jurisdiction and the Revision of the Judicial Code*, 13 LAW & CONTEMP. PROB. 216, 225 (1948).

[120] *Merrell Dow*. Merrell Dow Pharmaceuticals, Inc. v. Thompson, 478 U.S. 804 (1986).

[121] Federal statute or common law. Illinois v. City of Milwaukee, 406 U.S. 91, 100 (1972); *but see* Shoshone Mining Co. v. Rutter, 177 U.S. 505, 508 (1900).

[122] Issue in *American Well Works*. American Well Works Co. v. Layne & Bowler Co. 241 U.S. 257, 258–259 (1916).

[123] Suit arises under law that creates cause of action. American Well Works Co. v. Layne & Bowler Co. 241 U.S. 257 (1916).

Holmes's "creation test" seems consistent with his general legal philosophy, premised largely on principles of legal positivism.[124] Regardless of abstract legal philosophy, however, Holmes's reasoning has a certain practical appeal. "The State is master of the whole matter," he argued, "and if it saw fit to do away with actions of this type altogether, no one, we imagine, would suppose that they still could be maintained under the patent laws of the United States."[125] Yet there is also a serious practical drawback to his approach. In a sense, Holmes's test might be accused of putting form over substance. If many of the significant issues in the case are to turn on principles of federal law, is it advisable to deny federal jurisdiction merely because the vehicle for presenting those actions is state-created?

Holmes's creation test has in a certain sense half survived, which is to say that it really has not survived at all. The actual holding of *American Well Works*, that a cause of action created by state law cannot present a federal question, has been abandoned. However, the corollary remains; a cause of action created under federal law generally does present a federal question.[126]

One prestigious lower federal court judge many years ago noted that "Mr. Justice Holmes's formula [in *American Well Works*] is more useful for inclusion than for the exclusion for which it was intended."[127] In other words, federal question jurisdiction exists if the cause of action is created by federal law, but the mere fact that the cause of action does not derive from federal law will not automatically preclude a finding of federal question jurisdiction, as Holmes had intended. Under this approach, satisfying the *American Well Works* test would be a sufficient but not a necessary means of meeting the statutory "arising under" requirement.

On occasion, federal question jurisdiction has been rejected even though the cause of action derived solely from federal law. Cases that so hold have their origins in the Supreme Court case of *Shoshone Mining Co. v Rutter*, which predated *American Well Works* by 16 years. The case concerned application of a congressional plan for settling conflicting claims of miners. The federal law established a system that allowed miners to file patents on their claims. If an adverse claim was also filed, the adverse claimant could bring suit in a "court of competent jurisdiction" to ascertain true ownership. The statute provided that the right to possession was to be determined by local customs or rules of miners in the several mining

---

124 *See generally* Biddle, Justice Holmes, Natural Law, and the Supreme Court (1961).

125 American Well Works Co. v. Layne & Bowler Co. 241 U.S. 257, 260.

126 Federally created cause of action presents federal question. Mims v. Arrow Fin. Servs., LLC, 132 S. Ct. 740, 181 L. Ed. 2d 881, 893 (2012) ("there is no serious debate that a federally created claim for relief is generally a sufficient condition for federal-question jurisdiction" [citations omitted]; district court had federal question jurisdiction over private claim brought under federal Telephone Consumer Protection Act); *but see* Shoshone Mining Co. v. Rutter, 177 U.S. 505, 508 (1900). Congress may divest federal courts of this jurisdiction, expressly or by fair implication, but merely granting state courts jurisdiction over a statutory claim does not accomplish this. Mims v. Arrow Fin. Servs., LLC,132 S. Ct. 740, 181 L. Ed. 2d 881, 894–899 (2012) (Congress did not divest federal courts of federal question jurisdiction over private claims under Telephone Consumer Protection Act; state and federal courts have concurrent jurisdiction over such claims).

127 Holmes's formula more useful for inclusion. T.B. Harms Co. v. Eliscu, 339 F.2d 823, 827 (2d Cir. 1964) (Friendly, J.).

districts, so far as they were applicable and not inconsistent with federal law.[128]

The Supreme Court held that a suit brought by an adverse claimant to determine the true ownership of a mining claim did not "arise under" federal law for purposes of statutory federal question jurisdiction. In the Court's words:[129]

> Inasmuch . . . as the "adverse suit" to determine the right of possession may not involve any question as to the construction or effect of the Constitution or laws of the United States, but may present simply a question of fact as to the time of the discovery of mineral, the location of the claim on the ground, or a determination of the meaning and effect of certain local rules and customs prescribed by the miners of the district, or the effect of state statutes, it would seem to follow that it is not one which necessarily arises under the Constitution and laws of the United States.

While the Court in *Shoshone Mining* attempted to distinguish statutes that merely authorized an action to establish a right from those that created new rights,[130] it still appears that under Holmes's narrow test, there should have been federal question jurisdiction, and therefore, that *Shoshone Mining* should have been overruled in *American Well Works*. Federal law was solely responsible for the adverse claimant's right to sue, so the cause of action was clearly created under federal law.

Despite the fact that Holmes's opinion in *American Well Works* came 16 years after *Shoshone Mining*, *Shoshone Mining* is still followed on occasion.[131] Indeed, several modern commentators have spoken favorably of the decision.[132] One commentator, for example, while not questioning Congress's constitutional power to vest the federal courts with jurisdiction over cases like *Shoshone Mining*, reasoned that "[t]o bring all these suits into the federal courts would place upon them — and many of the litigants — an unnecessary burden."[133]

*Shoshone Mining*, therefore, is an exception to the general dictate of Holmes's creation test in *American Well Works*.

### [b] Substantial Federal Question Test for State Law Claims

Justice Holmes's narrow interpretation of federal question jurisdiction in *American Well Works* was essentially abandoned five years later in *Smith v. Kansas City Title & Trust Co.* In *Smith*, a shareholder sued a corporation in federal court,

---

128 Facts of *Shoshone Mining*. Shoshone Mining Co. v Rutter, 177 U.S. 505, 508 (1900).

129 177 U.S. at 509.

130 177 U.S. at 510.

131 *Shoshone Mining* followed. *See, e.g.*, Oneida Indian Nation v. County of Oneida, 414 U.S. 661, 683–684 (1974) (Rehnquist, J., concurring) (suit to enforce right that takes its origin in federal law is not necessarily one arising under Constitution or laws of United States, citing *Shoshone Mining*).

132 *See, e.g.*, Wechsler, *Federal Jurisdiction and the Revision of the Judicial Code*, 13 Law & Contemp. Prob. 216, 225 (1948); *but see* Currie, *Federal Jurisdiction in a Nutshell* 111 (2d ed. 1981) (referring to *Shoshone Mining* as "erroneous").

133 Mishkin, *The Federal "Question" in the District Courts*, 53 Colum. L. Rev. 157, 162 (1953).

seeking to enjoin the corporation from investing corporate funds in farm loan bonds issued under the authority of the Federal Farm Loan Act. Missouri law prohibited corporations from investing in illegal securities. Plaintiff claimed that the bonds were illegal because the federal act under which they were issued violated the United States Constitution. The suit clearly could not have been brought in federal court under Holmes's creation test. The cause of action itself — the actual vehicle for getting into court — was wholly state-created.[134]

The Supreme Court found that there was federal question jurisdiction in *Smith*, adopting a considerably broader test than the *American Well Works* test. The Court held that if it appears from the plaintiff's pleadings that the right to relief depends on the construction or application of the Constitution or federal law, and that the federal claim is not merely colorable but rests upon a reasonable foundation, there is federal question jurisdiction.[135] Because the controversy in *Smith* concerned the constitutional validity of an act of Congress that was directly at issue,[136] the Court concluded that federal question jurisdiction was present.

Not surprisingly, Justice Holmes vigorously dissented in *Smith*. He argued, as he had held in *American Well Works*, that it was evident that the cause of action arose not under any law of the United States but wholly under Missouri law, and that a suit cannot be said to arise under any other law than the one that creates the cause of action.[137] But the majority apparently recognized that regardless of the technical source of the suit, the entire case would turn on issues of federal constitutional law. Because a significant — if not primary — purpose for providing federal question jurisdiction is to take advantage of the federal courts' expertise on matters of federal law, the majority's interpretation appears preferable.

13 years after the Supreme Court's broadening decision in *Smith*, the Court appeared to narrow the inquiry once again. In *Moore v. Chesapeake & Ohio Railway*, the question was whether a suit authorized by the Employers' Liability Act of Kentucky could be thought to "arise under" the Federal Safety Appliance Act, which itself did not create a private cause of action. Under the terms of the state statute, an employee could not be found to have been contributorily negligent or to have assumed the risk in any case in which a common carrier's violation of any federal or state statute enacted for the safety of employees contributed to the injury or death of an employee. The Court concluded that the Federal Safety Appliance Act, which required the use of certain equipment for all cars employed on any railroad in interstate commerce, was a federal safety statute within the meaning of the state law. An important issue in the adjudication of the state cause of action, then, would be whether the standards required by the Act had been violated.[138] Under *Smith*, it would certainly seem that this issue would be a sufficient federal question because the result would turn on the construction of the Act.

---

[134] Issue in *Smith*. Smith v. Kansas City Title & Trust Co., 255 U.S. 180, 199 (1921).

[135] Cause "arises under" if right to relief depends on construction of federal law. 255 U.S. at 199.

[136] 255 U.S. at 201.

[137] 255 U.S. at 214 (Holmes, J., dissenting).

[138] Issue presented in Moore. Moore v. Chesapeake Ohio Railway, 291 U.S. 205, 213 (1934).

Surprisingly, the Court found that there was no federal question jurisdiction in *Moore*. The Court acknowledged that questions arising in state court actions to recover for injuries sustained by employees in intrastate commerce and relating to the scope or construction of the Federal Safety Appliance Act were federal questions, subject to Supreme Court review.[139] Nevertheless, the Court refused to find federal jurisdiction, holding that the mere incorporation of federal law into state law by reference does not create federal jurisdiction.[140]

It has been argued that *Smith* and *Moore* are in conflict,[141] and this position appears at least reasonable, if not compelling. In each, state law provided the cause of action, but each still presented a significant issue of federal law; yet the Court found jurisdiction in *Smith* and denied it in *Moore*.[142] A possible distinction between the two decisions, at least in their facts, is that the federal issue in *Smith* was raised on the face of plaintiff's well-pleaded complaint while the federal issue in *Moore* would properly arise only as a reply to a defense of contributory negligence or assumption of risk. Under the "well-pleaded complaint" rule (discussed below), federal question jurisdiction is not available under these circumstances. However, the Court in *Moore* did not explicitly rely on this fact.

To the extent *Smith* and *Moore* are in conflict, it appears that the principle enunciated in *Smith* was the one widely followed by lower federal courts for the next 50 years. However, in *Merrell Dow Pharmaceuticals, Inc. v. Thompson* (discussed below),[143] a majority of the Court found a basis on which to distinguish between *Smith* and *Moore*. In so doing, the Court added substantial confusion to the statutory "arising under" doctrine.

### [c] Supreme Court Retreats: *Merrell Dow Pharmaceuticals, Inc. v. Thompson*

For 50 years, the generally broad view of "arising under" jurisdiction prevailed without serious challenge. But in 1986, in *Merrell Dow Pharmaceuticals, Inc. v. Thompson*,[144] the Supreme Court, in an era of overcrowded federal dockets, revisited the issue and struck off in a quite different direction.

The question in *Merrell Dow*, according to Justice Stevens's opinion for the Court, was whether the incorporation of a federal standard into a state-law private action made the action one "arising under the Constitution, laws, or treaties of the United States" if Congress intended that there not be a federal private action for

---

[139] Federal questions subject to Court review. Moore v. Chesapeake & Ohio Railway, 291 U.S. 205, 213 (1934).

[140] Incorporation of federal standard does not confer federal jurisdiction. Moore v. Chesapeake & Ohio Railway, 291 U.S. 205, 214 (1934).

[141] *See* Currie, *Federal Jurisdiction in a Nutshell* 109 (2d ed. 1981); *see also* Greene, *Hybrid State Law in the Federal Courts*, 83 Harv. L. Rev. 289, 323 (1969).

[142] *See* Currie, *Federal Jurisdiction in a Nutshell* 109 (2d Ed. 1981) ("[i]n *Moore* as well as in *Smith* the result turned upon the construction of federal law, but in both cases the federal law provided no remedy").

[143] Merrell Dow Pharms., Inc. v. Thompson, 478 U.S. 804 (1986).

[144] Merrell Dow Pharms., Inc. v. Thompson, 478 U.S. 804 (1986).

violations of that federal standard.[145] Foreign plaintiffs had sued a pharmaceutical company in state court alleging that a child had been born with multiple deformities because the mother had ingested defendant's drug, Bendectin, during pregnancy. Damages were requested on various common law theories of liability as well as on an alleged violation of the Federal Food, Drug and Cosmetic Act[146] because Benedictin's labeling failed to provide adequate warning of its danger. The federal statute did not expressly provide for a private damage remedy. However, plaintiffs argued that violation of the federal statute gave rise to a rebuttable presumption of negligence and proximately caused the injuries at issue.[147] Defendant removed the case to federal court, claiming that plaintiffs' reference to the federal statute gave rise to federal question jurisdiction. The district court, relying on *Smith v. Kansas City Title*[148] discussed above, denied plaintiffs' motion to remand. The Sixth Circuit reversed, and the Supreme Court affirmed.

In many ways, the district court was correct to view *Smith* and *Merrell Dow* as analogous. In both, the substantive standard of decision was to be determined by reference to federal law, but federal law was relevant only because state law chose to make it so.[149] But the Supreme Court declined to find federal question jurisdiction in *Merrell Dow*, while nevertheless purporting to adhere to *Smith*. In *Merrell Dow*, the Court's jurisdictional analysis began with the assumption that no implied private remedy for damages could be inferred from the Food, Drug, and Cosmetic Act. On the basis of this assumption, the Court rejected federal question jurisdiction.[150] The Court reasoned that because Congress had not intended to create a private federal remedy in the statute, either explicitly or implicitly, it would "flout, or at least undermine, congressional intent to conclude that the federal courts might nevertheless exercise federal question jurisdiction and provide remedies for violations of that federal statute solely because the violation of the federal statute is said to be a 'rebuttable presumption' or a 'proximate cause' under state law, rather than a federal action under federal law."[151] In a footnote, the Court reasoned that "[w]hen we conclude that Congress had decided not to provide a particular federal remedy, we are not free to 'supplement' that decision in a way that makes it meaningless."[152]

Both the Court's reasoning and its conclusion in *Merrell Dow* are subject to serious question. Initially, the Court improperly confused the *substantive* issue of

---

[145] Issue in *Merrell Dow*. Merrell Dow Pharms., Inc. v. Thompson, 478 U.S. 804, 805 (1986).

[146] 21 U.S.C. § 301 *et seq.*

[147] Merrell Dow Pharms., Inc. v. Thompson, 478 U.S. 804, 806 (1986).

[148] Smith v. Kansas City Title & Trust Co., 255 U.S. 180 (1921).

[149] In *Smith*, the issue was whether federal law made the securities at issue in a state law shareholders' action illegal. In *Merrell Dow*, the issue was whether violation of the federal labeling standard was proof of negligence in a state law products liability action.

[150] No federal question jurisdiction because federal act did not create private cause of action. Merrell Dow Pharms., Inc. v. Thompson, 478 U.S. 804, 816 (1986).

[151] Exercising jurisdiction would undermine congressional intent. Merrell Dow Pharmaceuticals, Inc. v. Thompson, 478 U.S. 804, 812 (1986) (footnote omitted).

[152] Court cannot supplement congressional decision. Merrell Dow Pharmaceuticals, Inc. v. Thompson, 478 U.S. 804, 812 n.10 (1986).

the federal statute's reach with the *jurisdictional* question of whether a state cause of action incorporating a standard set forth in federal law gives rise to federal question jurisdiction. To provide federal *jurisdiction* for a state-created cause of action (assuming that the state cause of action is not preempted by Congress's failure to provide a private federal remedy) does not itself "supplement" the federal remedy; the *state* remedy itself has already done that. A congressional decision not to provide a federal remedy for a particular harm addressed by federal law does not necessarily imply congressional disapproval of the provision of a federal forum for adjudication of a state cause of action turning on the interpretation of that federal law.

It is, of course, possible that Congress's failure to provide a private remedy for violation of a federal statute should, as a matter of substantive law, act to preempt a state's provision of a private remedy. But unless this conclusion is reached under traditional preemption analysis — a matter of substantive constitutional law wholly unrelated to the issue of federal question jurisdiction — Congress's decision not to create a private damage remedy in no way automatically implies any congressional judgment about adjudication of the state cause of action. As Justice Brennan persuasively noted in dissent, "[c]learly, the decision not to provide a federal remedy should not affect federal jurisdiction unless the reasons why Congress withholds a federal remedy are also reasons for withholding federal jurisdiction."[153]

It could perhaps be argued that by failing to provide an enforceable cause of action, Congress indicated its determination that there was no discernible federal interest in adjudicating a state cause of action that enforces the federal statutory standard. Whether this is, in fact, to be deemed Congress's determination turns on an assessment of the level of federal interest in how the federal statutory standard is interpreted in a state cause of action. Viewed from this perspective, it is by no means clear that merely because Congress does not choose to provide its own remedy, it would not want a federal forum available to adjudicate a state remedy for violation of the federal standard. It is one thing to have no enforcement at all; it is quite another to have enforcement that is adjudicated only in state court. If one accepts the traditional values thought to be served by federal question jurisdiction, one might reasonably choose to make a federal forum available for adjudication even of a purely state-created cause of action enforcing the federal statutory standard. This is because once the state is allowed to enforce the federal statute, state court misinterpretation of the federal statute could give rise to several potentially harmful results. Initially, there is a danger of over-deterrence, caused by the state court's incorrect application of the statute to conduct not sought to be regulated.[154] Thus, though Congress's failure to provide a private remedy does not automatically invalidate state enforcement, Congress may have a legitimate interest in assuring that the federal act is properly interpreted if the state does choose to

[153] Dissent: Lack of federal remedy should not affect jurisdiction. Merrell Dow Pharmaceuticals, Inc. v. Thompson, 478 U.S. 804, 825 (1986) (Brennan, J., dissenting). Justice Brennan was joined in dissent by Justices White, Marshall, and Blackmun.

[154] Of course, if state law on its face overextends the federal statutory standard, the likelihood that the state cause of action will be found to be preempted substantially increases. The situation discussed in text, on the other hand, is one in which state law itself merely incorporates the federal standard by reference, but the state court, misinterpreting the federal law, overextends the federal standard.

enforce it. Moreover, Congress may have a legitimate interest in preventing precedential confusion caused by the dramatic increase in the number of courts that are called on to construe the statute.

It might be replied that these arguments, even if accepted, prove too much because they logically lead to the conclusion that federal jurisdiction should be exclusive, a result no one would rationally reach in such a situation. After all, if the concern is the fear of state court misinterpretation or lack of uniformity, more must be done than merely making federal courts available. Otherwise, parties would not be prevented from choosing the state forum, thereby giving rise to the very problems sought to be avoided by making federal courts available forums in the first place. But the same could be said of *all* federal question jurisdiction. Yet for the most part, the availability of the federal forum is not thought to automatically preclude concurrent state court jurisdiction. Though many of the same policy arguments employed to justify federal question jurisdiction could logically lead also to a finding of exclusive federal jurisdiction, the difference is generally one of degree. Hence, the traditional arguments used to justify federal question jurisdiction appear fully applicable to the suit in *Merrell Dow*, much as they were in *Smith*.

It might be thought that the Court's refusal to find federal question jurisdiction in *Merrell Dow* should logically lead to an overruling of *Smith* and a return to the narrow search for the source of the cause of action of *American Well Works*. Surprisingly, however, the Court purported not to overrule *Smith*. In a footnote, Justice Stevens's opinion saw a difference between *Smith* and *Moore v. Chesapeake & Ohio*[155] and found *Merrell Dow* to fall closer to *Moore*. He stated:[156]

> [T]he difference in results [in *Smith* and *Moore*] can be seen as manifestations of the differences in the nature of the federal issues at stake. [I]n *Smith* . . . the issue was the constitutionality of an important federal statute. . . . In *Moore*, in contrast, the Court emphasized that the violation of the federal standard as an element of state tort recovery did not fundamentally change the state tort nature of the action.

It is difficult to glean a coherent, workable standard for the decision of future cases from this analysis. Perhaps the Court intended to adopt a rule that a state cause of action will give rise to federal question jurisdiction only if that cause of action implicates a federal *constitutional* question. That test is met in *Smith* but not in either *Moore* or *Merrell Dow*. However, the Court in *Merrell Dow* did not explicitly adopt this constitutional-statutory dichotomy, though it would have been quite easy to do so had the Court intended such a rule. In any event, such a dichotomy would make little sense. Federal statutory questions have traditionally given rise to federal question jurisdiction as freely as have constitutional questions. And as long as the outcome of the case will have a direct impact on matters of only state concern, it is difficult to understand how the federal interest is somehow more substantial when the federal issue implicated by the state cause of action is constitutional than when it is statutory.

---

155 Moore v. Chesapeake & Ohio Railway, 291 U.S. 205 (1934).

156 Distinction between *Moore* and *Smith*. Merrell Dow Pharmaceuticals, Inc. v. Thompson, 478 U.S. 804, 814–815 n.12 (1986).

If the Court did not intend adoption of such an easily applied test, as seems likely, the only alternative is a vague and subjective "federal interest" standard that will translate into any federal issue implicated by a state cause of action that the judge happens to find sufficiently "important."

Surely, the values of consistency and predictability are not fostered by the *Merrell Dow* test. More significantly, the "importance" of the federal interest has never been used to distinguish among federal questions for jurisdictional purposes if the cause of action is itself federal. Because the effect on the federal issue incorporated in state law is likely to be the same, regardless of what that federal issue is, there are no more logical grounds on which to distinguish among federal issues when the federal question is incorporated by state law than when federal law provides the cause of action directly.

It should be emphasized that this criticism would not apply if the court had simply overruled *Smith* and returned to the *American Well Works* principle that there is federal question jurisdiction only if federal law creates the cause of action. Such a standard, of course, suffers from its own difficulties. The Court's reasoning in *Smith* indicates recognition that the federal judiciary's expertise may be needed to interpret federal law, even if the state is the technical source of the cause of action. However, by trying to draw a pragmatically unworkable and logically indefensible dichotomy among the many federal standards that have been incorporated by reference into state law, the Court left federal question jurisdiction in an unfortunate state of confusion.

In *Grable & Sons Metal Prods., Inc. v. Darue Engineering & Manufacturing*, the Supreme Court held that the national interest in providing a federal forum for federal tax litigation is sufficiently substantial to support federal question jurisdiction over a state law quiet title action related to land obtained at a federal tax sale.[157] The Court concluded that the lack of a federal cause of action to try claims of title to land obtained at a federal tax sale does not bar federal-question jurisdiction over a state-law quiet-title action that raises a disputed issue of federal tax law.[158]

In *Grable*, the Court expressly rejected the idea that *Merrell Dow* requires a federal cause of action to support federal question jurisdiction. Thus, the fact that federal law did not provide a quiet title action that could have been brought against the defendants did not preclude federal jurisdiction.[159] Read as a whole, the Court reasoned, *Merrell Dow* did not overturn decades of precedent to convert a federal cause of action from a sufficient condition into a necessary one. In fact, the Court noted, *Merrell Dow* expressly approved the exercise of jurisdiction in *Smith*, in

[157] National interest in federal forum for federal tax litigation supports federal question jurisdiction. Grable & Sons Metal Prods., Inc. v. Darue Eng'g & Mfg., 545 U.S. 308, 314–316 (2005) (Court unanimously holds that challenge to meaning of federal tax statute raises substantial questions of federal law sufficient for jurisdiction even though case did not present federal cause of action).

[158] Lack of federal quiet title action does not preclude federal question jurisdiction. Grable & Sons Metal Prods., Inc. v. Darue Eng'g & Mfg., 545 U.S. 308, 314–316 (2005).

[159] Federal cause of action not required. Grable & Sons Metal Prods., Inc. v. Darue Eng'g & Mfg., 545 U.S. 308, 312–320 (2005) (analyzing ) *Merrell Dow Pharmaceuticals, Inc. v. Thompson*, 478 U.S. 804 (1986).

which there was no federal cause of action available to the plaintiff. In a concurring opinion, in *Grable* Justice Thomas suggested that he might consider limiting federal question jurisdiction to suits in which federal law creates the cause of action.[160]

Even when a state-law claim presents a substantial federal question, the exercise of federal jurisdiction is appropriate only if it would be consistent with congressional judgment about the sound division of labor between state and federal courts, the Court noted in *Grable*. Thus, the federal question raised by the state-law claim must be not only substantial and actually disputed, but also one that a federal forum may entertain without disturbing any congressionally approved balance of federal and state judicial responsibilities. Because arising-under jurisdiction to hear a state-law claim always raises the possibility of upsetting the state-federal line drawn (or at least assumed) by Congress, the presence of a disputed federal issue and the ostensible importance of a federal forum are never necessarily dispositive. There must always be an assessment of any disruptive potential in exercising federal jurisdiction.[161] Unfortunately, such an interest-balancing approach is difficult to apply in specific cases, raising the danger of unpredictability and wasted judicial resources in resolving individual cases.

In *Grable,* the Supreme Court summarized the past-*Merrell Dow* test for determining whether federal question jurisdiction exists over state-law claims as follows: "[D]oes a state-law claim necessarily raise a stated federal issue, actually disputed and substantial, which a federal forum may entertain without disturbing any congressionally approved balance of federal and state judicial responsibilities?"[162] When all four of these requirements are met, jurisdiction in federal court is proper because there is a serious federal interest in claiming the advantages thought to be inherent in a federal forum, which can be vindicated without disrupting Congress's intended division of labor between state and federal courts.[163]

In *Empire Healthchoice Assurance, Inc. v. McVeigh,* the Supreme Court emphasized that federal jurisdiction over a state-law claim based on the fact that federal law is a necessary element of the claim is reserved for a "special and small category" of cases.[164] Specifically, the court held that a carrier's claim for reimbursement of benefits paid to a federal employee under a health plan governed

---

160 Concurring Justice willing to consider requiring federal cause of action. Grable & Sons Metal Prods., Inc. v. Darue Eng'g & Mfg., 545 U.S. 308, 320 (2005) (Thomas, J., concurring, suggests willingness to consider returning to *American Well Works* rule limiting federal question jurisdiction to cases in which federal law creates cause of action pleaded on face of complaint); *see* American Well Works Co. v. Layne & Bowler Co., 241 U.S. 257, 260 (1916).

161 Balancing test. Grable & Sons Metal Prods., Inc. v. Darue Eng'g & Mfg., 545 U.S. 308, 312–315 (2005); *see also* Franchise Tax Board of California v. Construction Laborers Vacation Trust, 463 U.S. 1, 8 (1983) ("arising under" masks welter of issues regarding interrelation of federal and state authority and proper management of federal judicial system).

162 Summary of test. Grable & Sons Metal Prods., Inc. v. Darue Eng'g & Mfg., 545 U.S. 308, 314 (2005).

163 Federal interest in claiming advantages inherent in federal forum. Gunn v. Minton, 133 S. Ct. 1059, 185 L. Ed. 2d 72, 79–80 (2013) (reiterating 4-part *Grable* test).

164 Special and small category of cases. Empire Healthchoice Assurance, Inc. v. McVeigh, 547 U.S. 677, 699 (2006).

by the Federal Employees Health Benefits Act (FEHBA) from the employee's third-party tort recovery does not "arise under" federal law for purposes of federal court jurisdiction under Section 1331. The Court pointed out that claims seeking recovery from the proceeds of state-court litigation are ordinarily resolved in state courts, and there is no clear signal from Congress that they should be treated as "arising under" federal law.[165]

In *Empire Healthchoice*, the Court distinguished *Grable* on the ground that the dispute in *Grable* centered on the action of a federal agency and its compatibility with a federal statute; the question qualified as "substantial"; and its resolution was not only dispositive of the case, but would be controlling in numerous other cases. Here, the reimbursement claim was triggered by the settlement of a state-court personal injury action rather than by the action of a federal department, agency, or service; the bottom-line practical issue was the share of that settlement properly payable to the carrier; and the reimbursement claim was fact-bound and situation-specific. There may have been an issue as to the extent to which the reimbursement should take into account attorney's fees expended to obtain the tort recovery, but that could be determined by the state court, which was competent to apply relevant federal law and was in the best position to determine the lawyer's part in obtaining, and his or her fair share in, the tort recovery. Finally, the United States' interest in attracting able workers to the federal workforce and in their health and welfare did not warrant turning the reimbursement claim into a federal case.[166]

Four justices dissented in *Empire Healthchoice*, arguing that the case arose under federal common law. The dissent reasoned that obligations to and rights of the United States under its contracts are governed exclusively by federal law. Because the plaintiff's claim was based on the interpretation of a federal contract, it should have been governed by federal common law. As such, the dissent concluded, the federal courts had jurisdiction over it pursuant to Section 1331.[167]

In *Gunn v. Minton*, the Court explained that to be "substantial" in the sense intended in *Grable*, the disputed question of federal law must be important to the federal system as a whole, not merely to the particular parties involved in the suit.[168] The Court held that there was no federal question jurisdiction over an action alleging legal malpractice in a patent infringement case, because the disputed federal question (whether the plaintiff would have prevailed in a patent infringement case if his lawyers had timely made an experimental-use argument) was insufficiently substantial. Because of the backward-looking nature of a legal malpractice claim, the federal question was presented in a merely hypothetical sense. Regardless of how the question was answered, the plaintiff's patent would

---

[165] No jurisdiction over insurer's reimbursement claim. Empire Healthchoice Assurance, Inc. v. McVeigh, 547 U.S. 677, 683 (2006).

[166] *Grable* distinguished. Healthchoice Assurance, Inc. v. McVeigh, 547 U.S. 677, 700–701 (2006).

[167] Dissent: Case arose under federal common law. Healthchoice Assurance, Inc. v. McVeigh, 547 U.S. 677, 706–707 (2006) (Breyer, J., dissenting).

[168] Question must be important to system as whole. Gunn v. Minton, 133 S. Ct. 1059, 185 L. Ed. 2d 72, 81 (2013) ("it is not enough that the federal issue be significant to the particular parties in the immediate suit; . . . The substantiality inquiry under *Grable* looks instead to the importance of the issue to the federal system as a whole.").

remain invalid.[169] Moreover, resolution of the question by a state court would not undermine the development of a uniform body of patent law.[170] Finally, even if a patent examiner could be bound by a Texas trial court's interpretation of the scope of the plaintiff's original patent, the result would be limited to the parties and patents that had been before the state court. Such fact-bound and situation-specific effects are insufficient to establish federal arising-under jurisdiction.

### [3] To Fall Within Federal Question Jurisdiction, the Federal Issue Must Be "Substantial"

Whatever test a court ultimately employs to determine whether a suit "arises under" federal law for purposes of the federal question statute, it is universally accepted that the issue of federal law must be "substantial." In the words of the Supreme Court, the claim of federal law must not be "so patently without merit" that the allegation could be called "insubstantial," "implausible," or "frivolous."[171] This should not be confused with "substantial" as used in the "substantial federal question test," in which it means important to the federal system as a whole.[172]

While this requirement has always been deemed a jurisdictional prerequisite, such an inquiry in reality goes to the merits of the allegations in the pleadings. Thus, a dismissal for lack of substantiality is, for all practical purposes, equivalent to a dismissal for failure to state a claim upon which relief may be granted.[173] The difference is that a case will be dismissed for lack of substantiality only in the most extreme cases.[174]

---

[169] Question was hypothetical. Gunn v. Minton, 133 S. Ct. 1059, 185 L. Ed. 2d 72, 81–82 (2013) ("No matter how the state courts resolve that hypothetical 'case within a case,' it will not change the real world result of the prior federal patent litigation.").

[170] Uniform body of patent law would not be undermined. Gunn v. Minton, 133 S. Ct. 1059, 185 L. Ed. 2d 72, 82 (2013) (allowing state court to resolve malpractice case would not undermine development of uniform body of patent law).

[171] Federal law issue must be substantial. *See, e.g.*, Franchise Tax Bd. v. Construction Laborers Vacation Trust, 463 U.S. 1, 8–9 (1983) (well-pleaded complaint requires resolution of substantial question of federal law); Hagans v. Lavine, 415 U.S. 528, 535, 542–543 (1974) ("we cannot say that the equal protection issue tendered by the complaint was either frivolous or so insubstantial as to be beyond the jurisdiction of the District Court"); Oneida Indian Nation v. County of Oneida, 414 U.S. 661, 666–667 (1974) (plaintiffs' claims could not be said to be so insubstantial, implausible, foreclosed by prior decisions, or otherwise completely devoid of merit as not to involve federal controversy within jurisdiction of district court, whatever may be ultimate resolution on merits); Bell v. Hood, 327 U.S. 678, 682–683 (1946) (suit may sometimes be dismissed for lack of jurisdiction if alleged federal claim clearly appears to be immaterial and made solely for purpose of obtaining jurisdiction, or if it is wholly insubstantial and frivolous); Smith v. Kansas City Title & Trust Co., 255 U.S. 180, 201–202 (1921).

[172] "Substantial" as used in "substantial federal question test." Gunn v. Minton, 133 S. Ct. 1059, 185 L. Ed. 2d 72, 81 (2013) (to satisfy substantial federal question test, "it is not enough that the federal issue be significant to the particular parties in the immediate suit; . . . The substantiality inquiry under *Grable* looks instead to the importance of the issue to the federal system as a whole.").

[173] Dismissal as jurisdictional is questionable. *See* Bell v. Hood, 327 U.S. 678, 683 (1946) (accuracy of calling these dismissals jurisdictional has been questioned).

[174] Substantiality lacking only in extreme cases. *See* Steel Co. v. Citizens for a Better Env't, 523 U.S. 83, 98 (1998) ("Dismissal for lack of subject-matter jurisdiction because of the inadequacy of the federal claim is proper only when the claim is so insubstantial, implausible, foreclosed by prior decisions of this

## § 4.04 THE WELL-PLEADED COMPLAINT RULE

### [1] Historical Origins

Application of the general federal question jurisdiction statute has been limited by an additional doctrine, usually referred to as the "well-pleaded complaint" rule. The doctrine received detailed articulation in the Supreme Court's decision in *Louisville & Nashville R.R. v. Mottley*. Plaintiffs had sued to enforce a contract of settlement between themselves and the railroad, under which the railroad granted them free lifetime passes on its trains. The complaint stated that defendant had refused to renew their passes and alleged that the refusal to comply with the contract was based solely on an intervening act of Congress that prohibited the giving of free passes or free transportation. The complaint also alleged that the act in question did not prohibit giving the Mottleys passes, and that, if not so construed, the act would violate due process.[175]

Though resolution of the case would probably turn entirely on issues of federal statutory and constitutional construction, the Supreme Court refused to find federal jurisdiction. The Court stated that a suit arises under the Constitution and laws of the United States only if the plaintiff's statement of the cause of action shows that it is based on those laws or that Constitution.[176] In so stating, the Court was interpreting only the language of the federal question statute, not that of Article III.

In *Mottley*, the plaintiffs' complaint showed clearly that the case would turn on issues of federal law. But in so doing, the complaint had anticipated a defense that it was assumed would be asserted by the defendant, and this was not a proper function of a complaint. Thus developed the "well-pleaded complaint" rule: a case will be said to "arise under" federal law only if the presence of the federal issue or issues can be ascertained from the plaintiff's well-pleaded complaint, that is, a complaint that does not anticipate possible federal defenses that the defendant might raise.[177]

### [2] Rationale for Rule

Under the well-pleaded complaint rule, federal jurisdiction generally exists only when a federal question is presented on the face of the *plaintiff's* properly pleaded complaint.[178] Under the rule, the presence of neither a federal defense[179] nor a

Court, or otherwise completely devoid of merit as not to involve a federal controversy" (citations and internal quotation marks omitted).

175 Issues in *Mottley*. Louisville & Nashville R.R. v. Mottley, 211 U.S. 149, 150–151 (1908).

176 211 U.S. at 152.

177 Well-pleaded complaint rule. *See* Oklahoma Tax Comm'n v. Graham, 489 U.S. 838, 840–841 (1989) (well-pleaded complaint contains what necessarily appears in plaintiff's statement of his or her own claim, unaided by anything alleged in anticipation of avoidance of defenses defendant may interpose).

178 Federal question on face of plaintiff's properly pleaded complaint. *See, e.g.*, Franchise Tax Bd. v. Construction Laborers Vacation Trust, 463 U.S. 1, 10–11, n.9 (1983).

179 Federal defense insufficient. *See* Franchise Tax Bd. v. Construction Laborers Vacation Trust, 463 U.S. 1, 10–11, n.9 (1983) (expressly declined to adopt rule that answer as well as complaint may be

federal counterclaim is sufficient to establish federal question jurisdiction.

Commentators have often been highly critical of the well-pleaded complaint rule and, it would seem, with good reason.[180] As the *Mottley* case so dramatically illustrates, application of the rule may result in excluding from federal court cases that will ultimately turn entirely on significant and unresolved issues of federal law.[181] Nevertheless, neither the Supreme Court nor Congress has expressed any inclination to alter it in any way.[182]

In defense of the rule, it could be argued that until a federal issue appears in a case, the federal court lacks authority even to demand a response from the defendant. Therefore, it would be unwise to allow federal jurisdiction to attach on plaintiff's mere speculation that the defendant will raise a federal defense, since in so doing, the court may be required to expend effort in a case in which it will ultimately lack jurisdiction.

The well-pleaded complaint rule has also been justified on the ground that without it, a defendant could upset a plaintiff's choice of forum. In the words of the Supreme Court:[183]

> [T]he presence of a federal question . . . in a defensive argument does not overcome the paramount policies embodied in the well-pleaded complaint rule — that the plaintiff is the master of the complaint, that a federal question must appear on the face of the complaint, and that the plaintiff may, by eschewing claims based on federal law, choose to have the cause heard in state court. . . . [A] defendant cannot, merely by injecting a federal question into an action that asserts what is plainly a state-law claim, transform the action into one arising under federal law, thereby selecting the forum in which the claim shall be litigated. If a defendant could do so, the plaintiff would be master of nothing.

This argument, however, makes no sense. The plaintiff may very well be master of the complaint, but he or she is not master of the defenses that defendant may choose to employ, and these defenses are as likely to implicate federal law as is the plaintiff's complaint. Nor has it ever been understood that the plaintiff is undisputed master of the choice of a federal forum. Indeed, the entire concept of removal

---

consulted before determination is made whether case arises under federal law); Board of Painesville v. City of Painesville, 200 F.3d 396, 399 (6th Cir. 1999) (federal defense insufficient).

[180] *See, e.g.*, Redish, *Reassessing the Allocation of Judicial Business Between State and Federal Courts: Federal Jurisdiction and "The Martian Chronicles,"* 78 Va. L. Rev. 1769, 1794–1797 (1992).

[181] The Mottleys subsequently brought suit in state court, and, as expected, defendant raised a defense under the federal statute. The Mottleys responded with their statutory and constitutional arguments. The case ultimately reached the Supreme Court, where the Court decided the federal issues in favor of the defendant railroad. *See* Louisville & Nashville R.R. v. Mottley, 219 U.S. 467, 472 (1911).

[182] No alteration of well-pleaded complaint rule. *See* Calstar v. State Comp. Ins. Fund, 636 F.3d 538, 542 (9th Cir. 2011) (*Grable & Sons Metal Prods., Inc. v. Darue Eng'g & Mfg.*, 545 U.S. 308 (2005), did not implicitly overturn well-pleaded complaint rule, which has long been basic principle marking boundaries of federal question jurisdiction, in favor of new "implicates significant federal issues" test).

[183] Plaintiff is master of complaint. Caterpillar, Inc. v. Williams, 482 U.S. 386, 398–399 (1987); *see also* Warner v. Ford Motor Co., 46 F.3d 531, 534 (6th Cir. 1995) (involving federal preemption exception to well-pleaded complaint rule).

authorizes a defendant, under certain circumstances, to overturn the plaintiff's initial choice of a state forum. Ultimately then, this argument amounts to a form of question-begging because it leaves unresolved the issue central to the viability of the well-pleaded complaint rule, namely, whether the federal interest in resolving a case that may turn on issues of federal law justifies the assertion of federal question jurisdiction, even if those issues arise solely as a defense.

Regardless of whether the arguments used to justify the well-pleaded complaint rule are accepted, there would seem to be absolutely no reason, other than the desire to reduce the federal courts' case load, to deny removal to federal court of state cases in which a federal issue is raised as a defense. Yet it is firmly established that there can be no removal under these circumstances. The removal statute provides that civil cases may be removed to federal court only if the district courts of the United States have original jurisdiction.[184] Because under the well-pleaded complaint rule the district courts do not have original jurisdiction unless the federal issue appears on the face of the well-pleaded complaint, it follows that there can be no removal jurisdiction in such a case.

Against the attacks on the well-pleaded complaint rule, one judicial commentator has suggested that the distinction drawn by the rule "is not quite so arbitrary as it sounds."[185] He reasons in the following manner:

> In many [such cases] the federal defense would have little merit — would, indeed, have been concocted purely to confer federal jurisdiction — yet this fact might be impossible to determine, with any confidence, without having a trial before the trial. Of course, frivolous federal claims are also a problem when only plaintiffs can use them to get into court, but a less serious problem. If the plaintiff gets thrown out of federal court because his claim is frivolous, and must start over in state court, he has lost time; and the loss may be fatal if meanwhile the statute of limitations has run. But the defendant may be delighted to see the plaintiff's case thrown out of federal court when the court discovers that the federal defense is frivolous.

It is doubtful, however, that a court would be required to hold "a trial before the trial" in order to determine whether a federal defense had been concocted solely for the purpose of creating federal jurisdiction. Indeed, under Rule 11 of the Federal Rules of Civil Procedure, such a pretrial inquiry into the factual accuracy of and motivation for pleadings is a relatively common occurrence.[186] There is no reason to believe — at least absent more empirical support than is provided — that vigorous enforcement of Rule 11's requirements will not adequately prevent the feared type of conduct.

In any event, it is by no means clear that the assumed danger of manufactured federal question jurisdiction is not just as great for plaintiffs as for defendants. Experience should teach us that a plaintiff who is intent on harassing a defendant or increasing the defendant's expenses in order to encourage settlement of a sham

---

[184] 28 U.S.C. § 1441(a).

[185] Posner, The Federal Courts: Crisis and Reform 190 (1985).

[186] Fed. R. Civ. P. 11.

claim (for example, a "strike suit" plaintiff) is just as likely to file a frivolous federal claim as a defendant is to raise a bogus federal defense. Moreover, it is not unreasonable to imagine that a plaintiff who possesses a legitimate state claim would consider adding a contrived federal issue to the complaint, in order to obtain the shorter dockets, more advanced discovery procedures, and possibly better judges in federal court. Hence, the discrimination caused by the well-pleaded complaint rule against defendants who raise a federal issue remains irrational. Even if the assessment that frivolous defense claims raise a greater concern is true, however, this concern fail to outweigh the value of having cases that will ultimately turn on a federal issue adjudicated in federal forum. Despite the controversy to which the well-pleaded complaint rule has given rise over the years, however, it is still well accepted and universally employed in the federal courts.

## [3] Application in Removal Actions

Generally, a defendant cannot remove a case from state court to federal court unless the federal court would have had concurrent original jurisdiction of the case.[187] Because the well-pleaded complaint rule requires that the federal question appear in plaintiff's complaint, a case may not be removed to federal court on the basis of a federal defense that the defendant might possibly raise to defeat plaintiff's claim.[188] Therefore, the well-pleaded complaint rule allows a plaintiff to foreclose federal jurisdiction by choosing to forgo a potential federal claim and to proceed solely under state law.

## [4] Application to Declaratory Judgment Actions

Despite its questionable rationale, the reach of the "well-pleaded complaint" rule was substantially expanded by the Supreme Court in *Skelly Oil Co. v. Phillips Petroleum Co.* In that case, Phillips had contracted to purchase gas from Skelly, among others, for resale to another party. Under the terms of the contract, the seller retained the right to terminate if the ultimate purchaser of the gas failed to obtain a required certificate issued by the Federal Power Commission before a specified date. There was a two-month grace period after the certificate date before the notice of termination could be delivered.

The Commission did issue a certificate one day before the grace period expired, but the certificate imposed certain conditions. Skelly, the seller, contending that a conditional certificate was not a certificate as specified in the contract, gave notice of termination immediately on expiration of the grace period. Phillips, the buyer, then sought a declaratory judgment in federal court to the effect that a proper certificate had, in fact, been obtained and that the contract was still in force.[189]

---

[187] 28 U.S.C. § 1441(a).

[188] Case not removable on basis of defense. Franchise Tax Bd. v. Construction Laborers Vacation Trust, 463 U.S. 1, 12 (1983) (action to collect taxes under state law; case not removable even if defense — that federal law preempts state law — was anticipated in plaintiff's complaint, and both parties agree it is the only issue in case); *see* The Fair v. Kohler Die & Specialty Co., 228 U.S. 22, 25 (1913) (party who brings suit is entitled to decide on what law he or she will rely).

[189] Facts of *Skelly*. Skelly Oil Co. v. Phillips Petroleum Co., 339 U.S. 667, 670 (1950).

Justice Frankfurter, speaking for the Court, refused to find federal question jurisdiction. The Court reasoned that Phillips was suing for breach of contract, and had simply anticipated and responded to Skelly's expected "federal" defense, that a proper certificate of convenience and necessity had not been issued. So viewed, the case fell directly within the well-pleaded complaint rule; it presented a complaint positing a state cause of action and anticipating a federal defense.[190]

The case might well have been decided on other grounds. Chief Justice Vinson, dissenting in part, stated that he had real doubts as to whether there was a federal question presented at all, even though interpretation of the contract between private parties would require an interpretation of a federal statute and the action of a federal regulatory body."[191] The asserted federal question in *Skelly* was whether the Federal Power Commission actually had issued the certificate in question. Though on first examination this appears to present an appropriate federal question, it should be recalled that the only reason the issue was relevant was that the private agreement among the parties made it so. Thus viewed, the case seems similar to the situation in which a federal standard has been gratuitously incorporated by reference in a state statute. Therefore, it is unclear whether, the *Mottley* issue aside, federal jurisdiction should have been found in *Skelly*. The majority declined to reach this "incorporation-by-reference" issue.

In *Skelly*, the Court established the rule that the well-pleaded complaint rule applies in actions brought under the Declaratory Judgment Act,[192] but that the inquiry must be inverted. In order to determine whether a declaratory judgment action "arises under" federal law, a court will ask whether, absent the availability of declaratory relief, the case could have brought in federal court. In answering this question, said the Court, the nature of the potential coercive action that the defendant might bring against the declaratory judgment plaintiff must be analyzed. The court will ask whether in this hypothetical suit, a federal question would be presented.

Justice Frankfurter's reasons in *Skelly* for this extension of *Mottley* were not especially compelling. First, he argued that allowing these cases to be brought into federal court would significantly increase the volume of federal litigation.[193] But if an important issue of federal law is involved, certainly it is no answer to assert that the district courts will be unduly burdened. Justice Frankfurter further argued that hearing these cases would "embarrass" the district courts (and the Supreme Court on potential review) in that matters of local law would often be involved, and the district courts would either have to decide doubtful questions of state law or hold cases pending disposition of state issues by state courts.[194] This argument is puzzling. Cases brought under the Declaratory Judgment Act that effectively

---

[190] No federal question jurisdiction to hear declaratory relief action that anticipates defense based on federal law. Skelly Oil Co. v. Phillips Petroleum Co., 339 U.S. 667, 673–674 (1950).

[191] 339 U.S. at 679 (Vinson, C.J., concurring in part and dissenting in part).

[192] 28 U.S.C. § 2201.

[193] Purpose to reduce volume of federal litigation. Skelly Oil Co. v. Phillips Petroleum Co., 339 U.S. 667, 673 (1950) (volume of litigation would swell if suit for declaration of rights could be brought in federal court merely because anticipated defense derived from federal law).

[194] 339 U.S. at 673.

anticipate a federal defense may ultimately turn solely on that federal issue. More importantly, even if these cases do implicate state law, they are certainly not the only ones in which a federal court may be required to determine issues of state law. Indeed, the doctrine of supplemental jurisdiction[195] contemplates that federal courts will be called on to decide related state-law issues. The dangers alluded to by Justice Frankfurter would seem to be no more nor less prevalent in cases in which a declaratory judgment is sought.

It might also be argued that allowing a declaratory judgment action to circumvent the well-pleaded complaint rule would violate the accepted principle that the Declaratory Judgment Act was not intended to expand the subject matter jurisdiction of the federal courts. Recently, however, commentators, after carefully examining the legislative history, have argued that that history requires recognition of the fact that Congress expanded federal courts' jurisdiction when it created the cause of action embodied in the Declaratory Judgment Act and that Congress could not have done so inadvertently.[196]

In any event, allowing declaratory judgment actions to be heard in federal court in cases in which the well-pleaded complaint rule would otherwise have barred the action does not actually expand federal jurisdiction. Under the established limits on federal jurisdiction imposed in *Mottley*, a federal court lacks federal question jurisdiction unless the federal issue appears in the plaintiff's well-pleaded complaint. Because of the Declaratory Judgment Act, the federal issue *does* properly appear in the complaint. Thus, while the Declaratory Judgment Act might expand the number of cases heard in federal court, it does not expand the rules of federal jurisdiction. Rather, it merely alters the application of those rules in specific cases.

It is true that the declaratory judgment action places the defendant's anticipated federal defense in the complaint, and if that defense is allowed to give rise to federal jurisdiction, the well-pleaded complaint rule would appear to be undermined. But there are essential differences between anticipation of the railroad's federal defense in *Mottley* on the one hand, and a similar anticipation in a declaratory judgment action on the other. In the former, the anticipation is not "well-pleaded" because it has no place in a properly drafted complaint; in the latter, the anticipation is at the very heart of the declaratory judgment action. While this distinction may appear overly technical, it ultimately explains why the purposes thought to be served by the well-pleaded complaint rule are inapplicable in a classic declaratory judgment action.

The declaratory judgment action was developed, according to one scholar, to remedy situations in which one of the parties to a dispute had no other way to take the initiative to get it judicially settled and would be seriously prejudiced by the other party's delay in initiating proceedings.[197] Thus, a classic declaratory

---

[195] *See* 28 U.S.C. § 1367.

[196] *See* Doernberg & Mushlin, *The Trojan Horse: How the Declaratory Judgment Act Created a Cause of Action and Expanded Federal Jurisdiction While the Supreme Court Wasn't Looking*, 36 U.C.L.A. L. Rev. 529, 588 (1989).

[197] James, Civil Procedure 26 (1965); *see also* Note, *Developments in the Law: Declaratory*

judgment action is, in many respects, a mirror image of an eventual suit. The plaintiff in the declaratory judgment action is the party whose conduct is likely to be ultimately challenged. In other words, the plaintiff would be, absent use of the declaratory judgment device, the eventual defendant. Instead, the plaintiff seeks a judicial declaration that the activity that has been performed or will be undertaken is proper. In this situation, the plaintiff's complaint *must* anticipate the eventual defense, or else it would effectively say nothing. More important, when the federal issue is raised in a complaint in a classic declaratory judgment action, the court is assured — unlike in *Mottley* — that a federal issue will be present in the case, for the defendant cannot refuse to deal with issues raised in the declaratory complaint. The court will therefore not need to expend effort in a case in which it will subsequently be determined that it lacks jurisdiction — one of the dangers the well-pleaded complaint rule is presumably attempting to avoid. Thus, there are clear distinctions between the *Mottley* situation and that of a classic declaratory judgment action.

The action in *Skelly,* however, was not a classic declaratory judgment action. In effect, the plaintiff in *Skelly* was suing for breach of contract, seeking specific performance of its terms. It was not a case in which plaintiff would be prejudiced by being required to await an affirmative action brought by the defendant. The plaintiff could simply have brought a suit directly for breach of contract. If the case had been brought in this manner, it is likely that the complaint could not have raised the question of the adequacy of the certificate without improperly anticipating a possible defense to the breach of contract action. In this context, the case would have been identical to *Mottley.* Plaintiff's attempt to characterize its case as a declaratory judgment, then, might well have been a conscious effort to circumvent the well-pleaded complaint rule. *Skelly* was therefore not an ideal case for testing *Mottley*'s applicability to a declaratory judgment action, and it is unfortunate that the Supreme Court saw fit to use the case as a vehicle for categorically expanding the well-pleaded complaint rule to encompass all declaratory judgment actions.[198]

A subsequent Supreme Court decision raising the *Skelly* doctrine underscores the doctrine's frailties. The case was *Duke Power Co. v. Carolina Environmental Study Group, Inc.* Plaintiffs challenged the constitutionality of the provision of the Price-Anderson Act[199] imposing a limitation of $560 million on private liability for nuclear accidents resulting from the operation of federally licensed private nuclear power plants.[200] Suit was brought against the United States Nuclear Regulatory Commission (the federal agency responsible for issuing licenses) and the Duke

---

*Judgments, 1941–1949*; 62 HARV. L. REV. 787, 788–790 (1949).

198 Rule applied in classic declaratory relief case. *See* Public Serv. Comm'n v. Wycoff Co., 344 U.S. 237, 248 (1952) (two years after *Skelly*, Supreme Court applied well-pleaded complaint rule in classic declaratory judgment action, though case involved numerous additional complications concerning appropriate scope of declaratory relief).

199 42 U.S.C. § 2210.

200 In 1975, the Act was amended to provide that in the event of a nuclear incident involving damages in excess of the amounts of aggregate liability, the Congress was to thoroughly review the particular incident and take whatever action it deemed necessary and appropriate to protect the public from the consequences of a disaster of this magnitude. 42 U.S.C. § 2210(e).

Power Company, a public utility that was constructing nuclear power plants. Plaintiffs sought a declaration that the Act was an unconstitutional violation of the Fifth Amendment's Due Process Clause.[201]

Though neither the parties nor the lower court had raised the issue of subject matter jurisdiction, both the majority and concurring opinions examined at great length whether the suit actually arose under federal law. Chief Justice Burger's opinion for the majority found jurisdiction under Section 1331, because the plaintiffs were making two basic challenges to the Act, both of which found their moorings in the Fifth Amendment.[202] But concurring Justice Rehnquist argued that whatever federal issues there were in the case arose in anticipation of a defense, and thus fell under the well-pleaded complaint rule. The fact that declaratory relief was sought was irrelevant, he said, because of *Skelly*.[203] Justice Rehnquist viewed the case as a suit against Duke Power under a state cause of action for a nuclear accident in which damages in excess of the statutory limit were sought. In this theoretical case, plaintiffs were anticipating the federal defense of the Price-Anderson Act, which plaintiffs alleged was unconstitutional.[204]

The majority responded that "the complaint was more fairly read as stating a claim against the NRC directly under the Due Process Clause of the Fifth Amendment" than as stating a state cause of action against Duke Power.[205] So viewed, the case arose under the Constitution. The fact that declaratory relief was sought did not automatically render *Skelly* applicable. It is only if the complaint in the hypothetical action mirrored by the declaratory judgment action would have contained no federal question that federal question jurisdiction will not be found.

While in the abstract, the majority's analysis is clearly correct, there were several difficulties in applying it to the facts of *Duke Power*. Most importantly, it is difficult to see how the NRC was a proper defendant of plaintiffs' constitutional claims. Although the NRC was the licensing agent, it had absolutely nothing to do with either imposition or enforcement of the limitation on liability.

This difficulty illustrates the awkwardness of the Court's finding of both standing and ripeness in the case. There simply had been no injury inflicted on the plaintiffs as a result of the Act's damage limitation. But if one were to assume a "pure" fact situation, Justice Rehnquist's analysis is all too persuasive. Assume that a nuclear power plant accident at Duke Power's plant has resulted in damages of catastrophic proportions, well beyond the $560 million limit. Assume further that the injured parties and their survivors have brought a class action against Duke Power to recover their actual damages. The suit would, of course, be an action under state tort law, either on negligence or strict liability grounds. Duke Power would undoubtedly raise the defense that its liability was limited by the terms of the Price-Anderson Act, and plaintiffs would respond that the Act is

---

[201] Issue in *Duke Power*. Duke Power Co. v. Carolina Envtl. Study Group, Inc., 438 U.S. 59 (1978).

[202] 438 U.S. at 69.

[203] 438 U.S. at 98 (Rehnquist, J., concurring).

[204] 438 U.S. at 97 (Rehnquist, J., concurring) (constitutionality of Act becomes relevant only if Duke Power Co. were to invoke Act as defense to suit for recovery under their state right of action).

[205] 438 U.S. at 69 n.13.

unconstitutional. So stated, the case presents an obvious *Mottley* problem. Nor could plaintiffs circumvent *Mottley* by seeking a declaration that the Price-Anderson Act was unconstitutional, because such an attempt would be barred by *Skelly*. Thus, in a case involving a vital matter of federal policy as well as important and difficult questions of federal law, suit could not be brought in federal court. Such a result demonstrates that Justice Frankfurter's specious logic in *Skelly* allows a distinct misallocation of federal judicial power. Thus, while the well-pleaded complaint rule of *Mottley* is itself questionable, its extension to actions brought under the Federal Declaratory Judgment Act in *Skelly* appears even more dubious.

*Skelly*'s holding that the well-pleaded complaint rule applies to declaratory judgment actions was extended in *Franchise Tax Board v. Construction Laborers Vacation Trust for Southern California* to actions brought in *state* court under *state* declaratory judgment actions and removed to federal court, even if the case presents the question of whether a federal statute preempts state law. The principal question in dispute in *Franchise Tax Board* was whether the Employment Retirement Income Security Act of 1974 (ERISA) permits state tax authorities to collect unpaid state income taxes by levying on funds held in trust for the taxpayer under an ERISA-covered vacation benefit plan.[206]

The Construction Laborers Vacation Trust was established as a mechanism for administering the provisions of a collective bargaining agreement that grants construction workers a yearly paid vacation. The trust agreement expressly prohibited any assignment, pledge, or encumbrance of funds held in trust by CLVT. The plan that CLVT administered was "unquestionably" considered an employee welfare benefit plan within the meaning of ERISA.[207]

The Franchise Tax Board (FTB) is a state agency in charge of enforcing California's personal income tax law. As such, it was authorized to require any person in possession of credits or personal property belonging to a taxpayer to withhold the amount of any tax, interest, or penalties due from the taxpayer and to transfer those funds to the FTB. The FTB filed a complaint in state court against the Trust, alleging that it had failed to comply with three tax levies. The complaint also stated:

> The Board contends that defendants are obligated and required by law to pay over to the Board all amounts held . . . in favor of the Board's delinquent taxpayers. On the other hand, defendants contend that section 514 of ERISA preempts state law and that the trustees lack the power to honor the levies made upon them by the State of California.[208]

The FTB sought a declaratory judgment of its rights to obtain the funds from the Trust, as well as damages for defendants' failure to honor the levies. The Trust removed the case to federal district court, purporting to base jurisdiction on the presence of a federal question.

---

206 Issue in *Franchise Tax Board*. Franchise Tax Bd. v. Construction Laborers Vacation Trust, 463 U.S. 1, 3–4 (1983).

207 463 U.S. at 4–5 (footnotes omitted).

208 *See* 463 U.S. at 6.

The preemption question was clearly an issue of federal law, ultimately implicating both congressional intent in ERISA and the Constitution's Supremacy Clause. And, by Justice Brennan's own admission, it was an important one that affects thousands of federally regulated trusts and all nonfederal tax collection systems, and must eventually receive a definitive, uniform resolution.[209] Yet, "for reasons involving more history than logic,"[210] the Court held that the well-pleaded complaint rule precluded federal jurisdiction.[211]

Justice Brennan viewed the issue before the Court to be whether the doctrine of *Skelly Oil* limits original federal court jurisdiction if a question of federal law appears on the face of a well-pleaded complaint for a state law declaratory judgment.[212] In answer to that question, the Court initially acknowledged that its interpretation of the federal Declaratory Judgment Act in *Skelly Oil* did not apply of its own force to an action brought under a *state* declaratory judgment statute.[213] Nevertheless, it concluded that "fidelity to [the] spirit [of *Skelly*] leads us to extend it to state declaratory judgment actions as well."[214]

This conclusion is harmful to the policies served by federal question jurisdiction, indefensible in logic, and not commanded by precedent. Initially, it is not difficult to see how the Court's conclusion in *Franchise Tax Board* is harmful to the policies underlying federal question jurisdiction. Few issues of federal law are more fundamental than the question of federal law's preemption of state law.[215] Yet the Court's holding dictates that the lower federal courts have no input into the decision-making process on a matter of such strong federal interest. Moreover, as the Court acknowledged, *Skelly* in no way dictated the Court's holding because that case was concerned solely with suits brought under the *federal* Declaratory Judgment Act. It should be recalled that one of the key justifications for extending the well-pleaded complaint rule to federal declaratory judgment actions was that, by its terms, the Act provides that it does not extend federal jurisdiction. But *state* declaratory judgment statutes, of course, contain no such limitations. Thus, *Skelly*'s logic is inapplicable to the situation in *Franchise Tax Board*. In support of its extension of *Skelly*, the Court argued:[216]

> If federal district courts could take jurisdiction, either originally or by removal, of state declaratory judgment claims raising questions of federal law, without regard to the doctrine of *Skelly Oil*, the federal Declaratory Judgment Act — with the limitations of *Skelly Oil* read into it — would

---

209 463 U.S. at 4.

210 463 U.S. at 4.

211 Well-pleaded complaint rule precludes federal jurisdiction over defense of federal preemption. Franchise Tax Bd. v. Construction Laborers Vacation Trust, 463 U.S. 1, 21–22 (1983).

212 463 U.S. at 17.

213 463 U.S. at 17 (emphasis in original).

214 463 U.S. at 18.

215 *See* Segreti, *Vesting the Whole "Arising Under" Power of the District Courts in Federal Preemption Cases*, 37 Okla. L. Rev. 539, 567 (1984) (federal preemption of state law displaces state regulatory authority, is based on Supremacy Clause of United States Constitution, and makes federal law source of governing rules of decision in disputes within regulatory borders).

216 463 U.S. at 18.

> become a dead letter. For any case in which a state declaratory judgment action was available, litigants could get into federal court for a declaratory judgment despite our interpretation of [the federal Act], simply by pleading an adequate state claim for a declaration of federal law. Having interpreted the Declaratory Judgment Act of 1934 to include certain limitations on the jurisdiction of federal district courts to entertain declaratory judgment suits, we should be extremely hesitant to interpret the Judiciary Act of 1875 and its 1887 amendment [that is, the general federal question jurisdiction statute] in a way that renders the limitations in the later statute nugatory.

The questionable nature of the Court's analysis can be seen by examination of the last quoted sentence. Contrary to the Court's assertion, *Skelly* did not hold that the Declaratory Judgment Act includes certain limitations on the jurisdiction of federal district courts. It simply held that the requirements of jurisdiction were not impliedly repealed or modified by passage of the Declaratory Judgment Act. In the Declaratory Judgment Act, Congress enlarged the range of remedies in the federal courts but did not extend their jurisdiction.[217] These two characterizations are by no means identical. If the Court were to interpret the general federal question statute to include suits brought under a state declaratory judgment statute that raise federal issues, the Federal Declaratory Judgment Act would not be rendered nugatory in any way. For as *Skelly* held, that Act does not itself *limit* federal jurisdiction, it merely *fails to extend* it, and therefore, is wholly neutral concerning the jurisdictional treatment to be given to state declaratory judgment actions.

The Court in *Franchise Tax Board* noted one additional policy in support of its refusal to extend federal question jurisdiction to state declaratory judgment actions:[218]

> There are good reasons why the federal courts should not entertain suits by the States to declare the validity of their regulations despite possibly conflicting federal law. States are not significantly prejudiced by an inability to come to federal court for a declaratory judgment in advance of a possible injunctive suit by a person subject to federal regulation. They have a variety of means by which they can enforce their own laws in their own courts, and they do not suffer if the preemption questions such enforcement may raise are tested there.

The ultimate irony of the Court's argument is that, in *Franchise Tax Board*, it was the private defendant, not the state agency, who had sought federal adjudication of the preemption question through removal.[219] Thus, even if the well-pleaded

---

[217] Declaratory Judgment Act enlarged remedies, but did not extend jurisdiction. Skelly Oil Co. v. Phillips Petroleum Co., 339 U.S. 667, 671 (1950) (operation of Declaratory Judgment Act is procedural only, and although enlarging range of available remedies, does not extend jurisdiction of federal courts).

[218] States have less need of federal forum to meet federal defenses. Franchise Tax Bd. v. Construction Laborers Vacation Trust, 463 U.S. 1, 21 (1983).

[219] *See* 463 U.S. at 20 n.20. 29 U.S.C. § 1132(a)(3) expressly provides:

> [A civil action may be brought] by a participant, beneficiary, or fiduciary (A) to enjoin any act or practice which violates any provision of this subchapter or the terms of the plan, or (B) to obtain other appropriate equitable relief (i) to redress such violations or (ii) to enforce any provision of this subchapter.

complaint rule were to preclude general federal question jurisdiction over a suit to enjoin enforcement of state law on preemption grounds, ERISA itself authorizes such a suit, at least under certain circumstances.[220] If a private litigant can obtain federal jurisdiction over an ERISA preemption claim, however, it is all the more puzzling why the Court would choose to deny federal jurisdiction when the very same litigant, as a state court defendant, seeks removal to federal court. In any event, if the other requirements of federal question jurisdiction have been met, there is no basis for the Court to refuse jurisdiction solely because of the nature of the litigant who is seeking access to federal court. Whichever litigant invokes the federal court's jurisdiction, there exists a systemic interest in employing federal judicial expertise to resolve so sensitive and important a federal issue as preemption. Moreover, one can fault the Court for denying federal jurisdiction on the grounds that a particular litigant has an adequate alternative forum in state court. In light of the long-established presumption in favor of concurrent state court jurisdiction over federal questions, the fact that a litigant's interests can be satisfied in state court cannot logically dictate a denial of federal question jurisdiction.[221]

### [5] Application of Well-Pleaded Complaint Rule to Defense of Federal Preemption

Four years after *Franchise Tax Board*, the Court in *Metropolitan Life Insurance Co. v. Taylor* noted an important, if somewhat confusing, "corollary" to its application of the well-pleaded complaint rule in preemption cases.

A former employee had sued his former employer and its insurer in state court, alleging breach of contract, retaliatory discharge, and wrongful termination of disability benefits. The defendants removed the case to federal court, claiming federal question jurisdiction over the disability benefits claim because of ERISA, and pendent jurisdiction over the remaining state claims. Though the district court allowed removal, the court of appeals reversed, concluding that the well-pleaded complaint rule applied because ERISA arose only as a defense to the state claims.[222]

The Supreme Court, in an opinion by Justice O'Connor, found federal question jurisdiction present and therefore allowed removal. While acknowledging that federal preemption is ordinarily a federal defense to the plaintiff's suit, and as such, it does not appear on the face of a well-pleaded complaint,[223] Justice O'Connor added that a corollary of the well-pleaded complaint rule is that

---

220 The Court left open whether a litigant could sue under ERISA to enjoin or to declare invalid a state tax levy, despite the Tax Injunction Act, 28 U.S.C. § 1341, which provides that district courts may not enjoin, suspend or restrain the assessment, levy or collection of any tax under State law if a plain, speedy and efficient remedy may be had in state court. *See* 463 U.S. at 20 n.21.

221 On the general subject of federal preemption and the well-pleaded complaint rule, *see* Collins, *The Unhappy History of Federal Question Removal*, 71 Iowa L. Rev. 717 (1986); Segreti, *Vesting the Whole "Arising Under" Power of the District Courts in Federal Preemption Cases*, 37 Okla. L. Rev. 439 (1984); Comment, *Federal Preemption, Removal Jurisdiction, and the Well-Pleaded Complaint Rule*, 51 U. Chi. L. Rev. 634 (1984).

222 Facts of *Metropolitan Life*. Metropolitan Life Ins. Co. v. Taylor, 481 U.S. 58, 60 (1987).

223 481 U.S. at 63.

Congress may so clearly preempt a particular area that any civil complaint raising this select group of claims is necessarily federal in character.[224] On the basis of this jurisdictional analysis, she concluded that although in *Franchise Tax Board*, the Court held that ERISA preemption, without more, does not convert a state claim into an action arising under federal law,[225] if, as in *Metropolitan Life*, a state cause of action is not only preempted by ERISA but also falls within ERISA's enforcement provisions regarding the bringing of a civil action to recover benefits or to resolve other specified disputes,[226] the "corollary" applied.[227]

Subsequent decisions have recognized the *Metropolitan Life* corollary, referring to it as the doctrine of "complete preemption."[228] However, the label is unfortunate because the doctrine is not one of preemption, but rather one of federal jurisdiction. Removal and preemption are two distinct concepts, and the fact that a claim may ultimately prove to be preempted does not establish that it is removable to federal court.[229] A better term is "jurisdictional" preemption because it is a doctrine that not only preempts the substantive state law, but also supports federal jurisdiction to address the issue regardless of in what stance the matter is brought before the federal court. It should be emphasized that *Metropolitan Life* did not alter the general rule that a claim of federal preemption ordinarily is a defense that fails to meet the well-pleaded complaint rule.[230]

To understand the jurisdictional distinction the Supreme Court has drawn between the situations in *Franchise Tax Board* and *Metropolitan Life*, it is necessary to understand the subtle but important distinctions in the nature of federal preemption. The concept of federal preemption means that Congress, by the enactment of substantive federal legislation, has, either explicitly or implicitly, superseded relevant state law that could undermine achievement of the goals of the federal statute.[231] But state law can interfere with federal law in a number of different ways, thus resulting in different types of preemption.

Though different commentators employ different labels, it makes sense to recognize roughly three forms of preemption: "field" preemption, "conflict" preemption," and "complete" preemption.[232] In the case of "field" preemption,

---

224 481 U.S. at 63–64.

225 481 U.S. at 64.

226 29 U.S.C. § 1132(a).

227 Some areas are preempted and outside of well-pleaded complaint rule. Metropolitan Life Ins. Co. v. Taylor, 481 U.S. 58, 64 (1987).

228 *Metropolitan Life* corollary recognized. *See* Caterpillar Inc. v. Williams, 482 U.S. 386, 393 (1987) (independent corollary to well-pleaded complaint rule known as complete preemption doctrine).

229 Claim may be preempted, but not necessarily within federal question jurisdiction. Caterpillar, Inc., v. Williams, 482 U.S. 386, 398 (1987) (fact that defendant ultimately prove that plaintiff's claims are preempted does not establish that they are removable to federal court).

230 Preemption is still defense that fails to meet rule. Metropolitan Life Ins. Co. v. Taylor, 481 U.S. 58, 63–64 (1987).

231 Concept of preemption. *See, e.g.*, Pacific Gas & Elec. Co. v. State Energy Res. Conservation & Dev. Comm'n, 461 U.S. 190, 203–204 (1983).

232 For an interesting exploration of the permutations of preemption, see S. Candice Hoke, *Preemption Pathologies and Civic Republican Values*, 71 B.U. L. Rev. 687 (1991).

state law is preempted because it provides remedies for the harm sought to be regulated by federal law. In the case of "conflict" preemption, the state cause of action is superseded because it directly clashes with — and therefore undermines — federal law. For example, a state tort suit against one protected by federal immunity is preempted because it "negatively" undermines the goal of the federal immunity.[233] In the case of "complete" preemption, which has been found to exist only on rare occasions, federal legislative regulation is so pervasive that it effectively transforms state causes of action into claims under the federal statute.

While these differences in the nature of preemption analysis do not directly implicate jurisdictional issues in general or the well-pleaded complaint rule in particular, jurisdictional considerations are implicated by the way defendants to the state cause of action may employ the different forms of preemption. A defendant to a state suit may raise preemption either for purposes of "avoidance" or for purposes of "characterization." "Avoidance" means that the defendant is relying on federal preemption to defeat — or "avoid" — the state claim. The goal is dismissal. "Characterization," on the other hand, means that the defendant relies on federal preemption merely to redescribe as federal what the plaintiff has labeled as a state cause of action. It in no way avoids or defeats plaintiff's suit; the goal is to establish federal jurisdiction.

A state court defendant may rely on either conflict or field preemption for avoidance purposes if a state cause of action aids plaintiffs in a manner not contemplated by federal law. However, if the argument is grounded in a theory of complete preemption, that is, that federal law is so pervasive in its reach that, even though the plaintiff has characterized the suit as state-based, it must be deemed federal in nature, the defendant is merely attempting to recharacterize plaintiff's claim as federal, rather than state. Put another way, in complete preemption cases, federal law so transforms the substantive area that any complaint alleging facts that come within the statute's scope necessarily "arises under" federal law, even if the plaintiff pleads a state law claim only. It is not just that a preemption defense is present, but that it is so pervasive that the claim must be deemed completely federal from its inception. On the other hand, if the claim of preemption is insufficiently complete to confer federal question jurisdiction, the state court will simply apply federal law in determining whether the claim is preempted.[234]

In *Avco Corp. v. Aero Lodge*, on which the Supreme Court later relied in *Metropolitan Life v. Taylor* to fashion the complete preemption exception to the well-pleaded complaint rule,[235] the Court allowed removal to federal court of a state court suit seeking an injunction against a strike on the basis of a no-strike clause in the contract. Though the plaintiff had characterized its suit solely in terms of breach of contract (a state cause of action), the Supreme Court held that because Section 301(a) of the Labor Management Relations Act[236] had effectively

---

[233] Conflict preemption. *Cf.* Howard v. Lyons, 360 U.S. 593, 597 (1959) (state libel suit against federal officer is controlled by federal law).

[234] State court may apply federal law to resolve preemption defense that is not complete.

[235] Metropolitan Life Ins. Co. v. Taylor, 481 U.S. 58, 64 (1987).

[236] LMRA § 301. 29 U.S.C. § 185.

preempted the entire field of labor contracts, the suit was in reality brought under this federal statute and could therefore be removed to federal court on the basis of federal question jurisdiction.[237] This rule does not apply to labor contracts if the employer is the United States, any of the 50 states, or a political subdivision of a state.[238]

If, however, either conflict or field preemption is invoked, the state cause of action is claimed to be in direct conflict with the federal law. In this situation, the state court defendant's reliance on preemption is not for the purpose of recharacterizing plaintiff's state cause of action as federal. Rather, the defendant is attempting to *defeat* the state suit, either because state law is in direct conflict with federal law or because it furthers the federal legislative interest in ways not contemplated by the federal statute. If a state court defendant (or a federal plaintiff in a declaratory judgment action anticipating a state suit) cites federal preemption for purposes of *avoidance* of the state claim, the federal issue appears solely as a defense and, therefore, does not authorize federal question jurisdiction because of the well-pleaded complaint rule. On the other hand, if a state court defendant, attempting to remove the case to federal court, correctly cites federal preemption solely to *recharacterize* plaintiff's claim as federal in nature, the federal issue is not a defense, but rather actually provides the basis of the plaintiff's cause of action. As such, it meets the requirements of even the strict *American Well Works* test[239] of federal question jurisdiction.

Viewed in the light of this analysis, the *Metropolitan Life* exception to *Franchise Tax Board* appears to make sense, at least if one begins analysis by accepting the premises of the well-pleaded complaint rule in the first place. If preemption dictates that plaintiff's suit be viewed as federal, the federal issue appears on the face of the complaint; if preemption is used to defeat a state cause of action, however, the federal issue is solely a defense, and therefore cannot provide the basis for federal question jurisdiction. The Court in *Metropolitan Life* was saying that the plaintiff's claim for benefits in state court, though characterized by him as a state law claim, should be recharacterized as a federal claim because ERISA's enforcement provisions have a preemptive impact in the area of suits for benefits. In *Franchise Tax Board*, however, the tax levy under state law was claimed to conflict directly with the federal right, and thus the preemption issue appeared solely as a defense. Hence, under the well-pleaded complaint rule, federal question jurisdiction was not present in *Franchise Tax Board* but was present in *Metropolitan Life*.

The lower federal courts have had difficulty understanding and applying the Supreme Court's distinction between complete preemption and other preemption defenses that do not provide for federal jurisdiction under the well-pleaded complaint rule. Beyond cases involving ERISA, the LMRA, the National Bank Act,

---

[237] LMRA § 301 completely preempts field of labor contracts. Avco Corp. v. Aero Lodge, I.A.M. & A.W., 390 U.S. 557, 560 (1968).

[238] No preemption if employer is U.S., state, or political subdivision of state. *See* 29 U.S.C. § 152(2) (defining "employer" to exclude "the United States . . . or any State or political subdivision thereof.").

[239] Strict requirements are met. American Well Works Co. v. Layne & Bowler Co., 241 U.S. 257, 260 (1916).

and certain tribal claims, substantial uncertainty exists about the applicability of the complete preemption corollary.

The Court in *Avco*[240] had given great weight to the presence of clear congressional intent to preempt state actions, clearly manifested in both language and legislative history, and this element was emphasized in *Metropolitan Life*.[241] The Court further emphasized in *Metropolitan Life* that the drafters of ERISA had purposely mirrored the language of the Labor Management Relations Act, and that in both statutes, Congress had also manifested its intent by creating federal private causes of action to enforce the statute.[242] A number of courts have focused on the presence or absence of a federal cause of action as essentially the determinative factor.

However, the Court in *Metropolitan Life* left unclear the question of whether, in the absence of manifest congressional intent, a federal statute's preemptive force should be treated as a close question or instead as a question in which a court should be reluctant to find that this extraordinary power had been exercised. Courts have adopted several significantly different standards. A number of circuits have taken a relatively liberal approach to finding complete preemption outside of ERISA and LMRA, but others have been considerably more restrictive in their analysis.

---

[240] Avco Corp. v. Aero Lodge, I.A.M. & A.W., 390 U.S. 557, 560 (1968).

[241] Complete preemption in extraordinary areas. Metropolitan Life Ins. Co. v. Taylor, 481 U.S. 58, 65 (1987) (noting that it had previously held in *Avco* that in some "extraordinary areas" Congress could completely preempt state claims).

[242] Both ERISA and LMRA create private causes of action. Metropolitan Life Ins. Co. v. Taylor, 481 U.S. 58, 65 (1987).

# Chapter 5

# SUPPLEMENTAL JURISDICTION

## § 5.01 THE BACKGROUND OF SUPPLEMENTAL JURISDICTION

Supplemental jurisdiction has proven to be an important component of federal jurisdiction because it allows federal courts to entertain claims over which they have no independent basis of subject matter jurisdiction. When those claims are sufficiently tied to suits properly in federal court, supplemental jurisdiction fosters the interests of efficient judicial administration. And if the initial basis for federal jurisdiction is the presence of a federal question, supplemental jurisdiction removes artificial deterrents to litigants in their desire to have their federal claims adjudicated in federal court.[1] However, because of concerns over the need both to obey constitutional dictates and to avoid undue encroachment on the scope of state judicial authority, both Congress and the Supreme Court have imposed limits on the concept's reach that have often given rise to substantial confusion.

Originally a judge-made doctrine, supplemental jurisdiction was codified by Congress in 28 U.S.C. § 1367, applicable to cases filed on or after December 1, 1990.[2] The statute has been subject to significant criticism from commentators, primarily because of both simple errors in drafting and a failure to resolve the numerous doctrinal problems and ambiguities that had evolved from judicial interpretation of the doctrine in its judge-made form. With certain major exceptions,[3] the statute was apparently intended simply to codify much of the preexisting judicial doctrine — ambiguities, inconsistencies, and all. The federal courts are now having to wrestle with the newly-created problems identified by critics of the statute, as well as with the many preexisting doctrinal ambiguities that Congress failed to resolve.

Before one explores those doctrinal ambiguities, however, one must first have a basic understanding of both the terminology employed in the use of supplemental jurisdiction and its historical development. The following two sections therefore focus on these preliminary issues.

---

[1] *See* Schenkier, *Ensuring Access to Federal Courts: A Revised Rationale for Pendent Jurisdiction*, 75 Nw. U. L. Rev. 245 (1980).

[2] Pub. L. 101-650, § 310(c), 104 Stat. 5089 (1990) 1990 U.S. Code Cong. & Admin. News 6802.

[3] Cases overruled by statute. The leading examples — indeed, the very impetus to its enactment — was the statute's overruling of the Supreme Court's holdings in Aldinger v. Howard, 427 U.S. 1 (1976) and Finley v. United States, 490 U.S. 545 (1989), refusing to recognize pendent party jurisdiction in federal question cases.

## § 5.02 NOMENCLATURE

### [1] Supplemental Jurisdiction

Supplemental jurisdiction is a statutory term[4] that is generally viewed by the courts and commentators as encompassing both what courts previously referred to as "pendent" jurisdiction and "ancillary" jurisdiction.[5] The term "supplemental jurisdiction" now encompasses three separate though historically and conceptually related concepts: pendent claim jurisdiction, pendent party jurisdiction, and ancillary jurisdiction. Supplemental jurisdiction under the statute thus addresses both the assertion of claims for which there is no independent basis for federal jurisdiction and disputes involving parties who are not otherwise before the court.[6] There is some suggestion in the courts, possibly including the Supreme Court, that statutory supplemental jurisdiction may not encompass all previous instances of ancillary jurisdiction.[7]

For supplemental jurisdiction to exist, there must be at least one claim over which the district court does have original jurisdiction. Original jurisdiction means independent federal subject matter jurisdiction. Without a claim over which the court has original jurisdiction, there is nothing for the claim in question to be supplemental to.[8]

### [2] Pendent Claim Jurisdiction

The term "pendent jurisdiction" traditionally described the basis for a court's exercise of jurisdiction to hear a claim for which there is no independent basis of federal jurisdiction, but that arises out of a "common nucleus of operative fact" with a properly asserted claim that does fall within the federal court's subject matter jurisdiction.[9] For example, an alleged incident of unlawful arrest might give rise simultaneously to claims against the same individual for violation of federally protected civil rights and under state tort law for battery and false imprisonment. Although there may have been no independent federal jurisdictional basis on which to adjudicate the state tort claims, those claims could be joined and heard with the § 1983 claim because they were within the pendent jurisdiction of the federal court. Such claims were sometimes referred to as "pendent state claims."

---

[4] *See* 28 U.S.C. § 1367.

[5] Supplemental jurisdiction encompasses ancillary and pendent jurisdiction. Perhaps the earliest uses of the term appeared in Matasar, *Rediscovering "One Constitutional Case": Procedural Rules and the Rejection of the Gibbs Test for Supplemental Jurisdiction,* 71 Cal. L. Rev. 1399, 1402 n.3 (1983), and Freer, *A Principled Statutory Approach to Supplemental Jurisdiction,* 1987 Duke L.J. 34.

[6] *See* 28 U.S.C. § 1367(a).

[7] Supplemental jurisdiction may not totally subsume ancillary jurisdiction. *See* Kokkonen v. Guardian Life Ins. Co., 511 U.S. 375, 378–379 (1994).

[8] Court must have original jurisdiction over at least one claim. Exxon Mobil Corp. v. Allapattah Servs., Inc., 545 U.S. 546, 551–555, 558–560 (2005) (supplemental jurisdiction requires original jurisdiction over at least one claim).

[9] Pendent jurisdiction. United Mine Workers of Am. v. Gibbs, 383 U.S. 715, 725 (1966).

The mere fact that a federal court had *power* to assert pendent claim jurisdiction, however, did not mean that it was required to exercise it. The Supreme Court recognized several factors that could justify a district court's exercise of its discretion not to assert pendent jurisdiction.[10]

## [3] Pendent Party Jurisdiction

Pendent claim jurisdiction presupposed one plaintiff and one defendant, with an independent jurisdictional basis existing for one of the claims but not for the other. Pendent party jurisdiction, on the other hand, constitutes the extension of pendent jurisdiction to include the assertion of jurisdiction over parties who are not named in any claim that is independently cognizable by the federal court.[11] For example, a plaintiff might assert a claim against one defendant for a federal civil rights violation and against a different defendant for a violation of state tort law arising from the same occurrence. While in this respect pendent party jurisdiction was strikingly similar to ancillary jurisdiction, the main difference was often thought to be that pendent claim jurisdiction extended pendent jurisdiction over a *plaintiff's* nonfederal claim against a new party not subject to jurisdiction under the principal federal claim. In contrast, the theory went, ancillary jurisdiction extended jurisdiction to parties or claims brought in by nonplaintiffs under the various procedural devices afforded by the Federal Rules of Civil Procedure. Yet in certain situations, ancillary jurisdiction had, in fact, been extended to add parties at plaintiff's request.[12] In any event, it is unclear why this fact should make a difference, at least in cases in which the original plaintiff's claim is based on the presence of a federal question.[13] The Supreme Court, in rejecting the concept of pendent party jurisdiction, failed adequately to distinguish the concept of ancillary jurisdiction, which extended jurisdiction over additional parties.[14] Whether the concept of pendent party jurisdiction is viable proved to be one of the most contentious elements of the historical development of supplemental jurisdiction.

## [4] Ancillary Jurisdiction

The term "ancillary jurisdiction" traditionally described the assertion of jurisdiction over claims or parties over whom the federal court lacked independent subject matter jurisdiction, but that arose out of the same conduct, transaction or occurrence as the plaintiff's original claim, to which federal subject matter jurisdiction extended. The Supreme Court has noted that ancillary jurisdiction has been asserted for two separate, though sometimes related, purposes: (1) to permit

---

[10] Discretion not to exercise pendent claim jurisdiction. *See* United Mine Workers of Am. v. Gibbs, 383 U.S. 715, 726–727 (1966).

[11] Pendent party jurisdiction defined. Finley v. United States, 490 U.S. 545, 549 (1989).

[12] Ancillary jurisdiction used to add parties at plaintiff's request. *See* Supreme Tribe of Ben-Hur v. Cauble, 255 U.S. 356, 366–367 (1921) (ancillary jurisdiction used in plaintiffs' diversity class action).

[13] In diversity cases, it could be argued that a plaintiff-defendant dichotomy is justified by a desire to deter resort to the diversity jurisdiction.

[14] Supreme Court's effort to distinguish ancillary from pendent party jurisdiction. *See* Aldinger v. Howard, 427 U.S. 1, 9–13 (1976) (declining to decide whether there are any "principled" differences between pendent and ancillary jurisdiction).

disposition, by a single court, of claims that are, in varying respects and degrees, factually interdependent; and (2) to enable a court to manage its proceedings, vindicate its authority, and effectuate its decrees.[15]

With regard to its first purpose, ancillary jurisdiction primarily involves the resolution of disputes involving nonparties to the primary action.[16] The Federal Rules of Civil Procedure do not, in and of themselves, create an independent basis for federal jurisdiction.[17] Though the Rules may provide for the introduction of new parties through impleader (Rule 14), joinder (Rules 19, 20), and intervention (Rule 24), those rules presuppose some basis for jurisdiction. Thus, in order to be heard in federal court, claims against parties joined under those rules must find some distinct basis for federal jurisdiction, such as diversity of citizenship or federal question jurisdiction. If no other jurisdictional basis existed, ancillary jurisdiction historically authorized adjudication of these claims if they arose out of the same transaction or occurrence as the main claim. Usually, though not always, ancillary jurisdiction applied if the joined claims were asserted by a party other than the plaintiff.[18]

The second purpose served by ancillary jurisdiction supported certain tangential proceedings, including proceedings for enforcement of the court's decrees;[19] proceedings connected with property in the custody and control of the court and under the court's jurisdiction;[20] proceedings for the distribution of settlement funds; independent actions in equity to obtain relief from judgment; and proceedings to resolve fee disputes and lien claims between litigants and their attorneys.

Enforcement of a settlement agreement in a federal case does not automatically fall within a district court's ancillary jurisdiction. Such an action is ordinarily one for breach of contract, which should be heard in state court unless the action has its own basis for jurisdiction.[21] The same rule has been applied to an action to

---

15 Functions of ancillary jurisdiction. Peacock v. Thomas, 516 U.S. 349, 355 (1996); Kokkonen v. Guardian Life Ins. Co., 511 U.S. 375, 378–379 (1994).

16 Ancillary jurisdiction extends to nonparties to primary action. Aldinger v. Howard, 427 U.S. 1, 9–13 (1976).

17 Federal Rules do not confer jurisdiction. Fed. R. Civ. P. 82; Owen Equip. & Erection Co. v. Kroger, 437 U.S. 365, 370 (1978) ("it is axiomatic that the Federal Rules of Civil Procedure do not create or withdraw federal jurisdiction").

18 Ancillary jurisdiction applied to claims asserted other than by plaintiff. Moore v. New York Cotton Exch., 270 U.S. 593, 610 (1926) (pre-Federal Rules landmark case holding that compulsory counterclaim is supported by ancillary jurisdiction after main claim has been dismissed on merits).

19 Ancillary jurisdiction over enforcement proceedings. *See* Dugas v. American Sur. Co., 300 U.S. 414, 428 (1937).

20 Ancillary jurisdiction over property. *See* Freeman v. Howe, 65 U.S. (24 How.) 450, 457 (1861), (in proceedings in rem, court has jurisdiction to determine all rights to property); *see also* Oklahoma v. Texas, 258 U.S. 574, 581 (1922) ("it long has been settled that claims to property or funds of which a court has taken possession and control through a receiver or like officer may be dealt with as ancillary to the suit wherein the possession is taken and the control exercised—and this although independent suits to enforce the claims could not be entertained in that court"); Devex Corp. v. General Motors Corp., 569 F. Supp. 1354, 1359–1360 (D. Del. 1983) (involving payment of prejudgment interest into court).

21 Ancillary jurisdiction rejected over enforcement of settlement agreement when not incorporated in

interpret a settlement agreement. However, the district court does have ancillary jurisdiction over the enforcement action if the order dismissing the action specifies that the district court retains jurisdiction over the settlement agreement or the agreement is incorporated into the order.[22] District courts also have ancillary jurisdiction over actions to enforce settlements during litigation, before the case is dismissed.[23]

## § 5.03 HISTORICAL BACKGROUND OF SUPPLEMENTAL JURISDICTION

Ancillary jurisdiction was first recognized by the Supreme Court in the 1860 case of *Freeman v. Howe,* although it was not so labeled. There the Court held that mortgagees of a piece of property that was the subject of litigation in federal court could intervene in the suit even though they were not diverse from the original parties to the action.[24]

The Supreme Court further expounded the doctrine 66 years later in *Moore v. New York Cotton Exchange,* in which the plaintiff had filed a federal antitrust claim against a defendant, who in turn filed a counterclaim against the plaintiff based on state law. The Court held that the district court could exercise jurisdiction over the counterclaim because it arose out of the same transaction as the original claim. In so holding, it defined "transaction" as "a word of flexible meaning. It may comprehend a series of many occurrences, depending not so much upon the immediateness of their connection as upon their logical relationship."[25]

Over the years, especially after the enactment of the liberal joinder devices of the Federal Rules in 1938, federal courts continued to expand the concept of ancillary jurisdiction to include not only compulsory counterclaims, but also crossclaims under Federal Rule of Civil Procedure 13(g),[26] third-party impleader claims under Rule 14(a),[27] and claims asserted by and against intervenors of right under Rule 24(a).[28]

---

order Kokkonen v. Guardian Life Ins. Co., 511 U.S. 375, 380–381 (1994).

22 Ancillary jurisdiction if order retains jurisdiction or incorporates agreement. *See* Kokkonen v. Guardian Life Ins. Co. of Am., 511 U.S. 375, 381 (1994).

23 Ancillary jurisdiction over settlements during litigation. T Street Development, LLC v. Dereje and Dereje, 586 F.3d 6, 10 (D.C. Cir. 2009) (district court had jurisdiction to decide whether parties had entered into binding settlement while specific performance suit was still pending before court; enforcement of settlement during litigation enables court to manage proceedings).

24 First recognition of ancillary jurisdiction. Freeman v. Howe, 65 U.S. (24 How.) 450, 460 (1860).

25 Ancillary jurisdiction extended to counterclaims. Moore v. New York Cotton Exch., 270 U.S. 593, 609–610 (1926).

26 Ancillary jurisdiction extended to crossclaims. Scott v. Fancher, 369 F.2d 842, 844 (5th Cir. 1966) (crossclaim between citizens of same state arising out of same transaction is ancillary to original suit); *see also* Perdue, *Finley v. United States: Unstringing Pendent Jurisdiction,* 76 Va. L. Rev. 539, 544 (1990).

27 Ancillary jurisdiction extended to impleader claims. Perdue, *Finley v. United States: Unstringing Pendent Jurisdiction,* 76 Va. L. Rev. 539 (1990).

28 Ancillary jurisdiction extended to claims in intervention. Smith Petroleum Serv. v. Monsanto Chem. Co., 420 F.2d 1103, 1113–1114 (5th Cir. 1970) (no independent ground of jurisdiction need be

## [1] Development of the Judge-Made Doctrine of Pendent Jurisdiction

The doctrine of pendent claim jurisdiction had its early roots in the Supreme Court's decision in *Osborn v. Bank of United States*. In defining the outer limits of Congress's power to vest the federal courts with federal question jurisdiction, Chief Justice Marshall there recognized that "there is scarcely any case, every part of which depends on the constitution, laws, or treaties of the United States." The Court therefore held that when a case involves a federal question, Congress has the power to confer jurisdiction on the district courts, even though other questions of fact or law may be involved.[29] Although this decision did not directly concern the exercise or creation of pendent claim jurisdiction, the Court in *Osborn* did recognize the possibility that Congress could at some point confer jurisdiction on the federal courts to hear state law claims when the case as a whole involved a federal question and those state law claims were part of the same "case" for purposes of Article III.

In 1909, the Supreme Court exercised the first form of pendent claim jurisdiction without any congressional authorization to do so. In *Siler v. Louisville & Nashville R.R.*, a railroad sued in federal court alleging that a state court order regulating rates violated both federal and state Constitutions. First, the Supreme Court held that it had jurisdiction over the state claim because of its connection to the federal question raised in the case. Then the Court proceeded to decide the case based on state law grounds rather than on federal constitutional issues. In doing so, the Court stated that if a case can be decided without reference to questions arising under the federal Constitution, that course is usually pursued and is not departed from without important reasons.[30] Thus, the Court in *Siler* established that federal trial courts may assert jurisdiction over state law issues even if the ultimate decision is not based on the federal question raised in the case.

The Supreme Court further expounded on pendent jurisdiction in *Hurn v. Oursler*, in which the plaintiffs filed suit for copyright infringement under federal law and two counts of unfair competition under state law. The district court had dismissed the copyright infringement action on the merits and then dismissed the state law causes of action for lack of jurisdiction. The Supreme Court reversed in part, holding that when state and federal claims are simply different grounds asserted in support of the same cause of action, the federal court has jurisdiction over both claims. In the case itself, the Court described the claims of infringement and unfair competition as "so precisely rest[ing] upon identical facts as to be little more than the equivalent of different epithets to characterize the same group of circumstances." Furthermore, the two claims were described as seeking to enjoin but one single wrong rather than to enjoin distinct wrongs. As such, the Court held

---

shown to support intervention as matter of right under Rule 24(a).

[29] First recognition of pendent jurisdiction. Osborn v. Bank of United States, 22 U.S. (9 Wheat.) 738, 823 (1824) ("[W]hen a question to which the judicial power of the Union is extended by the constitution forms an ingredient of the original cause, it is in the power of Congress to give the Circuit courts jurisdiction of that cause, although other questions of fact or of law may be involved in it.").

[30] Federal court may resolve state claims under state law. Siler v. Louisville & Nashville R.R., 213 U.S. 175, 193 (1909).

that they constituted but one single cause of action over which the federal court had jurisdiction.[31]

The Supreme Court modified both the structure and doctrine of pendent jurisdiction in *United Mine Workers of America v. Gibbs,* in which it laid the foundation for the modern concept of supplemental jurisdiction. In *Gibbs,* the plaintiff brought an action against a labor union for alleged violations of Section 303 of the Labor Management Relations Act, along with claims under state common law. Because the parties were nondiverse, the initial question was whether the state law claim was properly adjudicated in federal court in the absence of diversity. The Supreme Court held that it was.[32] Declaring the *Hurn* test for pendent jurisdiction to be "unnecessarily grudging," the Court expanded the concept of pendent claim jurisdiction, stating:[33]

> Pendent jurisdiction . . . exists whenever there is a claim "arising under [the] Constitution, the Laws of the United States, and Treaties made, or which shall be made, under their Authority . . ." and the relationship between that claim and the state claim permits the conclusion that the entire action before the court comprises but one constitutional "case." The federal claim must have substance sufficient to confer subject matter jurisdiction on the court . . . . The state and federal claims must derive from a common nucleus of operative fact. But if, considered without regard to their federal or state character, a plaintiff's claims are such that he would ordinarily be expected to try them all in one judicial proceeding, then, assuming substantiality of the federal issues, there is *power* in federal courts to hear the whole.

After *Gibbs,* the federal courts generally took an expansive view of the doctrines of pendent and ancillary jurisdiction, invoking them whenever it was expedient to resolve all claims arising from a common factual base in a single action. However, in the mid-1970s, the Supreme Court began to place certain limitations on the use of pendent or ancillary jurisdiction to support claims against additional parties, most of which were questionable in their logic.

In 1976, the Supreme Court, in *Aldinger v. Howard,* focused for the first time on the need for congressional authorization for jurisdiction, at least in cases in which additional parties were involved.[34] In *Aldinger,* the plaintiff, a county employee, filed a civil rights action under 42 U.S.C. § 1983 against her boss, and a state-law claim against the county itself under the theory of vicarious liability. The issue before the Court was whether pendent party jurisdiction could be exercised over the plaintiff's claim against the county.[35]

---

[31] Claims constituting single cause of action. Hurn v. Oursler, 289 U.S. 238, 246–247 (1933).

[32] Liberal test for pendent claim jurisdiction. United Mine Workers of Am. v. Gibbs, 383 U.S. 715, 725–728 (1966).

[33] United Mine Workers of Am. v. Gibbs, 383 U.S. 715, 725 (1966) (emphasis in original).

[34] *See* Perdue, *Finley v. United States: Unstringing Pendent Jurisdiction,* 76 VA. L. REV. 539, 547 (1990).

[35] Aldinger v. Howard, 427 U.S. 1, 4–5 (1976).

The Supreme Court held that pendent jurisdiction could not be exercised in this instance. But in so holding the Court, in an opinion by Justice Rehnquist, sent conflicting signals as to its rationale. From one perspective, the decision appeared to represent more of an interpretation of Section 1983 and its jurisdictional counterpart.[36] The status of the law at that time was that a local governmental entity was not a "person acting under color of state law" within the meaning of Section 1983, and was not amenable to suit under that statute.[37] The Court found that to extend pendent jurisdiction over a state law claim against the municipality would undermine Congress's decision to exclude municipalities from the scope of Section 1983.[38] To the extent that this substantive preemption theory is deemed to have provided the Court's rationale, however, its wisdom is subject to serious question. As dissenting Justice Brennan pointed out, there is a significant difference between the extension of federal *jurisdiction* to adjudicate a *state law claim* on the one hand and the creation of a *substantive federal right* on the other.[39] The fact that Congress chose not to create the latter does not necessarily imply that it automatically opposed the former.

On the other hand, much of the Court's analysis in *Aldinger* referred to the question of the proper scope of pendent jurisdiction. In so doing, the Court expressed concern that pendent party jurisdiction would extend federal court subject matter jurisdiction beyond that authorized by Congress. Such a result, the Court reasoned, would violate the principle that the federal courts are courts of limited jurisdiction, as dictated by congressional action.[40]

But, while the Court's recognition of the separation-of-powers problem was commendable as an abstract matter, its reliance on it in rejecting pendent party jurisdiction is questionable because it proves too much. First of all, it is difficult to understand why the exact same logic did not prove fatal for pendent claim jurisdiction. Both doctrines would extend federal jurisdiction to claims not statutorily authorized by Congress to be heard in federal court. Moreover, the doctrine of ancillary jurisdiction — much like the concept of pendent party jurisdiction — generally involved the judicially created assertion of jurisdiction over a party to whom Congress had not extended jurisdiction. It would therefore appear that ancillary jurisdiction should suffer from the same separation-of-powers defect as pendent party jurisdiction. In short, the Court's critique of pendent party jurisdiction could just as easily have been directed toward all of embodiments of supplemental jurisdiction as they existed at the time of that decision.

The Court in *Aldinger v. Howard* left open the possibility that pendent party jurisdiction would be viable if the federal court's jurisdiction over the plaintiff's main claim was exclusive; that is, if it could only be brought in federal court.[41]

---

36 *See* 28 U.S.C. § 1343.

37 *See* Monroe v. Pape, 365 U.S. 167, 191 (1961), *overruled in* Monell v. Dep't of Social Servs. 436 U.S. 658 (1978).

38 Pendent party jurisdiction rejected. Aldinger v. Howard, 427 U.S. 1, 16–17 (1976).

39 427 U.S. at 23 (Brennan, J., dissenting).

40 427 U.S. at 15.

41 Aldinger v. Howard, 427 U.S. 1, 18 (1976).

However, in 1989 in *Finley v. United States* the Court resolved the issue left open in *Aldinger* against the exercise of pendent-party jurisdiction.[42]

In *Finley*, the plaintiff filed a Federal Torts Claims Act claim against the FAA, seeking damages for the death of family members killed in a plane crash. She joined a state law claim against a local utility, which was a nondiverse defendant. Although there was no independent basis of federal jurisdiction over the latter claim, it clearly met the *Gibbs* standard in that it arose from a common nucleus of operative fact. The case fit within the unresolved area in *Aldinger* because the FAA may not be sued in state courts,[43] and thus, two parallel proceedings in state and federal court would be required unless there was federal jurisdiction over the state claim.

Nonetheless, the Court rejected federal jurisdiction over the claim because it determined that Congress had not expressly provided for it. The Court's narrow holding was that there was no pendent party jurisdiction over parties other than the United States under the Federal Tort Claims Act. However, the opinion's broad language indicated that except for a narrow range of proceedings covered by ancillary jurisdiction, there could be no supplemental jurisdiction over new parties in any situation in which Congress had not passed a statute expressly providing for it. The majority stated that neither the convenience of the litigants nor considerations of judicial economy could suffice to justify extension of the doctrine of ancillary jurisdiction beyond the bounds of Congressional authorization. In reaching its decision, the Court focused on the distinction between the assertion of jurisdiction over parties already before the federal court on the one hand and over parties who were never properly before the Court on the other hand.[44]

## [2] Enactment of the Supplemental Jurisdiction Statute

The Court in *Finley*, in the view of some, cast doubt on the viability of the concepts of pendent and ancillary jurisdiction.[45] Courts disagreed as to whether the decision was to be read broadly to terminate the use of ancillary jurisdiction over claims asserted through third-party practice under the Federal Rules if they lacked an independent jurisdictional basis. Some courts concluded that *Finley* left ancillary jurisdiction over these claims unchanged. However, other courts concluded that *Finley* had effectively ruled out ancillary jurisdiction over these claims. Such was the state of affairs when the supplemental jurisdiction statute was enacted in 1990.

What proved to be the most important part of *Finley* was the concluding statement in Justice Scalia's majority opinion:[46]

---

[42] Finley v. United States, 490 U.S. 545, 556 (1989).

[43] *See* 28 U.S.C. § 1346(b).

[44] Pendent party jurisdiction virtually eliminated. Finley v. United States, 490 U.S. 545, 552–556 (1989); *see* 28 U.S.C. § 1346(b).

[45] *See* Lee & Wikins, *An Analysis of Supplemental Jurisdiction and Abstention with Recommendations for Legislative Action*, 1990 B.Y.U. L. Rev. 321, 339.

[46] Finley v. United States, 490 U.S. 545, 556 (1989).

Whatever we say regarding the scope of jurisdiction conferred by a particular statute can of course be changed by Congress. What is of paramount importance is that Congress be able to legislate against a background of clear interpretive rules, so that it may know the effect of the language it adopts.

## § 5.04 SUPPLEMENTAL JURISDICTION STATUTE: AN OVERVIEW

### [1] Background

In 1988, as provided by the Judicial Improvements and Access to Justice Act,[47]Chief Justice Rehnquist created a 15-member Federal Courts Study Committee to analyze the federal court system and to recommend reforms. After the committee's review of the federal system had begun, the Supreme Court decided *Finley v. United States*. It was a subcommittee of the Federal Courts Study Committee that initially suggested the codification of the doctrines of ancillary and pendent jurisdiction under the name of supplemental jurisdiction. The Committee's Report recommended that Congress expressly authorize the federal courts to hear any claims arising out of the same transaction or occurrence as a claim within federal jurisdiction, including claims within federal question jurisdiction that require the joinder of additional parties.[48]

After consideration in committee of various alternative measures, Congress ultimately adopted the version largely proposed by three academics.[49] The statute was signed into law by President Bush on December 1, 1990.[50] As a result, the judge-made doctrines of pendent and ancillary jurisdiction were finally codified under the combined heading, "supplemental jurisdiction." In addition, the statute reversed the effect of the holdings in *Aldinger v. Howard* and *Finley*, by expressly authorizing pendent party jurisdiction in at least certain situations.

Problems and uncertainties in the interpretation of the supplemental jurisdiction statute have been numerous, and its drafting has been the subject of substantial criticism. Congress itself described the statute as "implementing noncontroversial reforms" that were "in keeping with the finest traditions of carefully considered federal court improvements legislation."[51] Ironically, however, it was Congress's and the academic drafters' apparent desire to avoid "controversial" reforms that gave rise to many of the enormous problems that developed in the judiciary's attempt to interpret the Act's provisions. The defect in

---

[47] Pub. L. 100-702, 102 Stat. 4642, 4645 (1988).

[48] Report of the Federal Courts Study Committee, 3 (April 2, 1990). Three members of the Committee opposed the creation of pendent party jurisdiction (at p. 48).

[49] Wolf, *Codification of Supplemental Jurisdiction: Anatomy of a Legislative Proposal*, 14 W. New Eng. L. Rev. 1, 18–19 (1992).

[50] Pub. L. 101-650, § 310, 104 Stat. 5089, 5113–5114 (codified at 28 U.S.C. § 1367). The provision concerning supplemental jurisdiction is often referred to simply as the supplemental jurisdiction statute.

[51] Federal Courts Study Committee Implementation Act of 1990, H.R. 734, 101st Cong. 2d Sess. (1990).

the drafters' strategy was the fact that they consciously sought to avoid dealing with many of the inconsistencies and anomalies that had evolved over the years in the development of the judge-made doctrines of pendent and ancillary jurisdiction, apparently in an attempt to assure passage. As one commentator noted,[52]

> In describing the supplemental jurisdiction provision as noncontroversial, Congress . . . viewed the statute only from one angle of a prism, as a response to the problems caused by the Supreme Court's decision in *Finley* . . . . Viewed in that light, perhaps the supplemental jurisdiction statute was noncontroversial . . . . When viewed from another angle of the prism, however, the controversy generated by the supplemental jurisdiction statute becomes more understandable.

The statute failed on other levels as well. The structural advantage of a statute over purely common law development is that its adoption presents a unique opportunity — one largely not available in the "patch quilt" evolutionary method employed by the common law process — to provide a substantial degree of coherence in both law and policy. By seeking uncritically to codify most of the preexisting judge-made doctrines regardless of their numerous ambiguities and inconsistencies, the statute failed the legislative obligation to clarify the law because the codified doctrines that are themselves are often inconsistent or confusing. In fact, the apparent attempt in the statute to codify inconsistent doctrine actually *increased* doctrinal confusion.

### [2] Subsection (a): Supplemental Jurisdiction over Claims That Are "Part of the Same Case or Controversy," and that Involve Joinder or Intervention of Additional Parties

Subsection (a) of the supplemental jurisdiction statute represents a broad grant of supplemental jurisdiction, extending to the full extent of Article III. Subject to the exceptions provided in subsections (b) and (c) or as expressly provided otherwise by federal statute, in any civil action in which the district court has original jurisdiction, it also has supplemental jurisdiction over "all other claims that are so related to claims in the action within original jurisdiction that they form part of the same case or controversy under Article III of the United States Constitution."[53] In *Daimlerchrysler Corp. v. Cuno*, the Supreme Court held that a federal court may not exercise supplemental jurisdiction over a claim that does not itself satisfy the Article III case or controversy requirements, including standing.[54] In *Daimlerchrysler*, plaintiffs who paid state and city taxes sued various state and city officials and a manufacturer in state court, alleging that state franchise tax credits and city property tax exemptions given to the manufacturer violated the Commerce Clause of the U.S. Constitution and injured the plaintiffs by diminishing the funds available to the city and the state, imposing a

---

[52] *See* Moore, *The Supplemental Jurisdiction Statute: An Important But Controversial Supplement to Federal Jurisdiction*, 41 Emory L.J. 31, 32–33 (1992).

[53] 28 U.S.C. § 1367(a).

[54] Article III must be satisfied. Daimlerchrysler Corp. v. Cuno, 547 U.S. 332, 351–353 (2006).

"disproportionate burden" on the plaintiffs. The Court held that the plaintiffs failed to satisfy the injury and redressability elements of Article III standing with respect to the state franchise tax credit.[55] The Court then held that the plaintiffs' standing to challenge the local property tax exemption did not give rise to supplemental jurisdiction over the state tax claim under *Gibbs*, which permits a federal court to exercise supplementary jurisdiction over state-law claims that "derive from a common nucleus of operative fact" with a claim over which the court has federal-question jurisdiction.[56] The Court saw no reason to read *Gibbs* to permit a federal court to exercise supplemental jurisdiction over a claim that does not itself satisfy the Article III requirements, particularly in light of Supreme Court precedent that a plaintiff must demonstrate standing for each claim he or she seeks to press.[57] In *Daimlerchrysler*, the plaintiffs' failure to establish an Article III injury with respect to their state taxes precluded federal jurisdiction over their claim concerning those taxes even if they did establish such an injury with respect to municipal taxes.[58]

Subsection (a) specifically provides that district courts do not have supplemental jurisdiction when it is "expressly provided otherwise by Federal statute."[59] A number of statutes have been held to "expressly provide otherwise," precluding the exercise of supplemental jurisdiction. Others have been held not to preclude the exercise of supplemental jurisdiction.

The last sentence of subsection (a) provides that supplemental jurisdiction includes claims that involve the joinder or intervention of additional parties.[60] This sentence clearly overrules both *Aldinger v. Howard* and *Finley v. United States* by permitting pendent-party jurisdiction in all federal question cases.[61] However, as described in the next subsection, this extension of supplemental jurisdiction is severely limited in certain diversity cases by subsection (b).

### [3] Subsection (b): Refusal to Extend Supplemental Jurisdiction to Diversity Claims Brought by Plaintiffs Under Specified Joinder Devices

Subsection (b) of the Supplemental Jurisdiction Statute provides that supplemental jurisdiction does not extend to claims in diversity actions under specified procedural joinder devices. In any civil action in which the court's original jurisdiction is founded solely on diversity, the court does not have supplemental jurisdiction over claims made under the joinder devices if exercising supplemental jurisdiction over the claim would be inconsistent with the jurisdictional

---

55 Injury and redressability not established. Daimlerchrysler Corp. v. Cuno, 547 U.S. 332, 342–350 (2006).

56 Common nucleus of operative fact. *See* United Mine Workers v. Gibbs, 383 U.S. 715, 725 (1966).

57 Standing for each claim. *See* Allen v. Wright, 468 U.S. 737, 752 (1984).

58 Federal jurisdiction precluded. Daimlerchrysler Corp. v. Cuno, 547 U.S. 332, 350–353 (2006).

59 28 U.S.C. § 1367(a).

60 28 U.S.C. § 1367(a).

61 *See* H.R. Rep. No. 734, 101st Cong., 2d Sess. (1990), reprinted at 1990 U.S. Code Cong. & Admin. News 6860, 6875.

requirements of the diversity statute.[62] The specified claims are the following:

1. Claims by plaintiffs against persons made parties under any of the following Federal Rules of Civil Procedure:
   a. Rule 14 (impleading third-parties by defendants and by plaintiffs against whom a counterclaim has been asserted)
   b. Rule 19 (compulsory joinder);
   c. Rule 20 (permissive joinder); and
   d. Rule 24 (intervention).
2. Claims by persons proposed to be joined under Rule 19 (concerning necessary and indispensable parties); and
3. Claims by persons seeking to intervene under Rule 24.

Subsection (b) applies to cases removed to federal court by defendants, as well as to cases originally brought in federal court.[63]

The legislative history expressly states that the net effect of subsection (b) is to implement the principal rationale of the Supreme Court's decision in *Owen Equip. & Erection Co. v. Kroger*.[64] The Court in *Owen Equipment* held that in a diversity case, ancillary jurisdiction did not extend to a plaintiff's claim against a third-party defendant impleaded by defendant. To hold otherwise, the Court reasoned, would enable a plaintiff to sue the diverse defendant solely for the purpose of creating federal jurisdiction, and then to wait for that defendant to implead the nondiverse tortfeasors before proceeding against them.[65] Subsection (b) reaffirms this result under Rule 14 and extends it to the other situations under other rules by which additional parties may be brought into the action.

An examination of the joinder devices to which the extension of supplemental jurisdiction is expressly denied reveals one common theme: they are all devices used by plaintiffs, who are often the parties seeking voluntarily to invoke the benefits of diversity jurisdiction. While commentators have debated whether Section 1367(b) reflects an anti-diversity bias,[66] it is difficult to understand how the statute could be read in any other manner than as a collateral statutory attack on diversity jurisdiction. Section 1367(b) quite obviously stands as a deterrent to

---

[62] 28 U.S.C. § 1367(b); *see* 28 U.S.C. § 1332.

[63] Section 1367(b) applies to removed cases. Griffin v. Lee, 621 F.3d 380, 385 (5th Cir. 2010) (Section 1367(b) precluded exercise of supplemental jurisdiction over claim of attorney who intervened under Rule 24 seeking imposition of lien on client/plaintiff's recovery).

[64] H.R. Rep. No. 734, 101st Cong., 2d Sess. (1990), reprinted at 1990 U.S. Code Cong. & Admin. News 6860, 6875 n.16.

[65] No ancillary jurisdiction over plaintiff's claim against impleaded third-party defendant. Owen Equip. & Erection Co. v. Kroger, 437 U.S. 365, 373–377 (1978).

[66] *Compare* Freer, *Compounding Confusion and Hampering Diversity: Life After Finley and the Supplemental Jurisdiction Statute,* 40 Emory L.J. 445 (1991) (arguing that § 1367(b) reflects anti-diversity bias) *with* Rowe Jr., Burbank, & Mengler, *Compounding or Creating Confusion About Supplemental Jurisdiction? A Reply to Professor Freer,* 40 Emory L.J. 943 (1991) (rejecting anti-diversity bias characterization); *see also* Arthur & Freer, *Grasping at Burnt Straws: The Disaster of the Supplemental Jurisdiction Statute,* 40 Emory L.J. 963 (1991).

plaintiffs who might be tempted to invoke diversity jurisdiction.[67] For plaintiffs seeking to invoke the diversity jurisdiction, Congress appears to have adopted the following statement of Justice Stewart in *Owen Equipment*: "[The] efficiency plaintiff seeks so avidly is available without question in the state courts."[68]

The existence of a bias against diversity jurisdiction is certainly not a new development. Both Congress and the Supreme Court have, on various occasions, expressed at best lukewarm enthusiasm for diversity and on occasion a clearly negative attitude towards this branch of subject matter jurisdiction. Congress most assuredly possesses the power to place hurdles in the path of those who wish to invoke diversity jurisdiction. Yet problems plague Congress's use of Section 1367(b) to accomplish this goal. Initially, the use of Section 1367(b) as a backdoor means of reflecting lack of enthusiasm for the entire diversity enterprise suffers from serious process defects. If it is thought today that Congress has struck an incorrect balance in shaping diversity jurisdiction, that issue should be openly confronted as part of the political process. Every time such a frontal assault on the scope of the diversity statute has been attempted, however, it has largely failed, with the exception of periodic raises in the jurisdictional minimum amount in controversy. Because its negative impact on diversity jurisdiction is indirect, and because it received so little public attention and debate at the time of the statute's enactment,[69] Section 1367(b) may accomplish many of the goals sought to be achieved by the very frontal assaults on diversity jurisdiction that have largely failed to date. Thus, even though the enactment of Section 1367(b) met all of the technical requirements of the legislative process, one may reasonably question whether the interests of representative democracy were served.

Following the enactment of the supplemental jurisdiction statute, circuit courts had debated whether each plaintiff must be considered individually for purposes of ascertaining the amount in controversy for diversity jurisdiction, or whether the supplemental jurisdiction statute altered this rule to permit the exercise of federal jurisdiction over claims that did not meet the jurisdictional minimum.[70] Section 1367(b) expressly excludes a number of joinder devices from the reach of supplemental jurisdiction when sought to be invoked by plaintiffs in diversity cases.[71] However, Rule 23 is omitted from the list.[72] Nevertheless, the legislative history reveals a Congressional desire to adhere to the holding of *Zahn v.*

---

[67] *See* Redish, *Reassessing the Allocation of Judicial Business Between State and Federal Courts: Federal Jurisdiction and "The Martian Chronicles,"* 78 Va. L. Rev. 1769, 1820 (1992) ("Because it denies diversity plaintiffs the substantial efficiency benefits of supplemental jurisdiction, § 1367 could be seen as a reflection of Congress's lukewarm support for diversity jurisdiction itself.").

[68] Owen Equip. & Erection Co. v. Kroger, 437 U.S. 365, 376 (1978) (quoting *Kenrose Mfg. Co. v. Fred Whitaker Co.*, 512 F.2d 890, 894 (4th Cir. 1972)).

[69] *See* Freer, *Compounding Confusion and Hampering Diversity: Life After Finley and the Supplemental Jurisdiction Statute,* 40 Emory L.J. 445, 470–474 (1991).

[70] Circuit split. *See* Exxon Mobil Corp. v. Allapattah Servs., Inc., 545 U.S. 546, 549–552 (2005) (addressing split of authority and citing cases).

[71] *See* 28 U.S.C. § 1367(b) (excluding claims by plaintiffs against persons made parties under Fed. R. Civ. Proc. 14, 19, 20, or 24).

[72] *See* 28 U.S.C. § 1367(b).

*International Paper Co.*[73] that supplemental jurisdiction could not be used by class action plaintiffs who independently failed to meet the amount-in-controversy requirement for diversity jurisdiction.[74] Because of Section 1367's poor drafting, then, it took many years — and countless lawyer hours — to resolve the issue of *Zahn*'s continuing validity under the Supplemental Jurisdiction Act.

Resolving the split of authority, the Supreme Court held in *Exxon Mobil Corp. v. Allapattah Servs., Inc.* that when at least one named plaintiff satisfies the amount-in-controversy requirement (and the other elements of jurisdiction are present), a district court may exercise supplemental jurisdiction over the claims of other plaintiffs in the same Article III case or controversy, even if those claims are for less than the jurisdictional minimum for diversity jurisdiction.[75] The Court held that Section 1367 legislatively overturned the Supreme Court's decision in *Zahn v. International Paper Co.*, which had held that each plaintiff, including all class members, must allege damages that meet the jurisdictional amount requirements of the diversity jurisdiction statute.[76] The Court explained that when one plaintiff's claim or claims meet the jurisdictional amount, there is a "civil action of which the district courts have original jurisdiction" within the meaning of the supplemental jurisdiction statute. The court then has supplemental jurisdiction over other diverse plaintiffs' claims that fail to meet the amount in controversy. In other words, as long as one claim in the plaintiff's well-pleaded complaint meets the test for original jurisdiction, the district court has supplemental jurisdiction, subject only to specified exceptions, over all other diverse plaintiffs' claims that form part of the same case and controversy.[77]

The Court made clear that this expansive interpretation of supplemental jurisdiction does not extend jurisdiction over additional parties whose presence defeats the requirement of complete diversity. The reason for the different treatment of the diversity requirement and the amount-in-controversy requirement according to the Court in *Allapattah* lies in their differing purposes. The amount-in-controversy requirement is fulfilled by a single claim of sufficient importance to warrant a federal forum and is not negated by additional, smaller claims. A failure of diversity, on the other hand, "contaminates" the action, removing any justification for providing a federal forum.[78] Such reasoning,

---

[73] *Zahn* case. Zahn v. International Paper Co., 414 U.S. 291, 301–302 (1973).

[74] H.R. Rep. No. 734, 101st Cong., 2d Sess. (1990), reprinted at 1990 U.S. Code Cong. & Admin. News 6860, 6874–6875 and set forth in § 106App.01 (citing *Zahn* and stating that 28 U.S.C. § 1367(b) was not intended to affect requirements of the diversity jurisdiction statute, 28 U.S.C. § 1332, in diversity-only class actions).

[75] Supplemental jurisdiction extends to members' claims below jurisdictional minimum. Exxon Mobil Corp. v. Allapattah Servs., Inc., 545 U.S. 546, 549 (2005) (5-4 opinion holds that as long as one plaintiff meets jurisdictional requisite, supplemental jurisdiction supports federal jurisdiction over claims of other diverse plaintiffs' claims).

[76] Supplemental jurisdiction statute overturns *Zahn*. Exxon Mobil Corp. v. Allapattah Servs., Inc., 545 U.S. 546, 557–566 (2005); *see* Zahn v. International Paper Co., 414 U.S. 291, 301 (1973).

[77] If one claim meets test for original jurisdiction, supplemental jurisdiction extends to claims from same case or controversy. Exxon Mobil Corp. v. Allapattah Servs., Inc., 545 U.S. 546, 559 (2005).

[78] Inapplicable to non-diverse parties. Exxon Mobil Corp. v. Allapattah Servs., Inc., 545 U.S. 546, 562–566 (2005).

however, appears both vague and illogical. Jurisdictional amount and complete diversity are *both* requirements of subject matter jurisdiction. Indeed, of the two, it is only the jurisdictional minimum which appears expressly on the face of the diversity statute. If the abandonment of the jurisdictional minimum to allow suit by plaintiffs who fail to meet that minimum somehow fails to "contaminate" the jurisdictional minimum, it is difficult to understand why one cannot view the abandonment of the complete diversity requirement as merely a selective departure from that jurisdictional requirement. In a sense, of course *all* forms of supplemental jurisdiction "contaminate" the suit by circumventing established statutory requirements of subject matter jurisdiction. It all seems to turn on how one is willing to conceptualize and characterize the supplemental jurisdiction dynamic in the first place.

### [4] Subsection (c): Discretionary Decline of Supplemental Jurisdiction

In *United Mine Workers v. Gibbs*, the Supreme Court indicated that under certain circumstances, a federal court may exercise its discretion not to assert pendent jurisdiction over state claims, even though the court has the power to do so.[79] Subsection (c) of Section 1367 codifies the discretionary factors that justify a refusal to exercise supplemental jurisdiction. The district court may decline to exercise supplemental jurisdiction over a claim under any of the following circumstances:[80]

1. The claim raises a novel or complex issue of state law;
2. The claim substantially predominates over the claim or claims over which the court has original jurisdiction;
3. The court has dismissed all claims over which it had original jurisdiction; or
4. In exceptional circumstances, there are other compelling reasons for declining jurisdiction.

The legislative history indicates that the first three factors codify considerations recognized as relevant under prior law, particularly in *United Mine Workers of America v. Gibbs*.[81] The fourth factor acknowledges that occasionally there may exist other compelling reasons for a district court to decline supplemental jurisdiction.[82] Nevertheless, there is not perfect congruence between the *Gibbs* factors and the statutory factors. The court's exercise of its discretion under Section 1367(c) is not a jurisdictional matter. Thus, the court's determination may

---

[79] Discretion to not exercise supplemental jurisdiction. United Mine Workers of Am. v. Gibbs, 383 U.S. 715, 726–727 (1966).

[80] 28 U.S.C. § 1367(c).

[81] *See* H.R. Rep. No. 734, 101st Cong., 2d Sess. (1990), reprinted at 1990 U.S. Code Cong. & Admin. News 6860, 6875 n.15; *see* United Mine Workers of Am. v. Gibbs, 383 U.S. 715, 726–727 (1966); Borough of W. Mifflin v. Lancaster, 45 F.3d 780, 788 (3d Cir. 1995).

[82] H.R. Rep. No. 734, 101st Cong., 2d Sess. (1990), reprinted at 1990 U.S. Code Cong. & Admin. News 6860, 6875.

be reviewed for abuse of discretion, but may not be raised at any time, as a jurisdictional defect may be.[83]

When the district court has the power to exercise supplemental jurisdiction under Section 1367(a), the court need not address whether it should decline jurisdiction under Section 1367(c) if neither party has raised the issue. Similarly, the court of appeals need not decide sua sponte whether the district court abused its discretion in applying or failing to apply Section 1367(c).

### [5] Subsection (d): Statute of Limitations

Subsection (d) of the supplemental jurisdiction statute enacts a salutary tolling provision to save supplemental claims that have been dismissed in federal court for assertion in state court. The period of limitations for any claim asserted under subsection (a), and for any other claim in the same action that is voluntarily dismissed at the same time as or after the dismissal of the claim under subsection (a), is tolled while the claim is pending and for a period of 30 days after it is dismissed, unless state law provides for a longer tolling period.[84] The legislative history indicates that the provision's purpose is to prevent the loss of claims to statutes of limitations if state law might fail to toll the running of the limitation period while a supplemental claim is pending in federal court. It also eliminates a possible disincentive from such a gap in tolling if a plaintiff might wish to seek voluntary dismissal of other claims in order to pursue the entire matter in state court, after a federal court dismisses a supplemental claim.[85]

## § 5.05 SAME CASE OR CONTROVERSY UNDER ARTICLE III

The supplemental jurisdiction statute authorizes supplemental jurisdiction over all other claims in the action so related to the claim falling within original jurisdiction that they form part of the same case or controversy under Article III of the United States Constitution.[86] Thus, Congress has chosen to equate the outer reaches of supplemental jurisdiction with the constitutional limits of subject matter jurisdiction under Article III.

The legislative history indicates that by use of the "same case or controversy" standard, Congress intended to codify the scope of supplemental jurisdiction first articulated by the Supreme Court in *United Mine Workers v. Gibbs*,[87] which

---

[83] Inquiry under § 1367(c) is not jurisdictional. Carlsbad Tech., Inc. v. HIF Bio., Inc., 556 U.S. 635, 640 (2009).

[84] 28 U.S.C. § 1367(d).

[85] *See* H.R. Rep. No. 734, 101st Cong., 2d Sess. (1990), reprinted at 1990 U.S. Code Cong. & Admin. News 6860, 6876; *see also* Wittner v. Banner Health, 720 F.3d 770, 781 (10th Cir. 2013) (as long as plaintiffs file state court action within 30 days of district court's dismissal, they should face no statute of limitation bar in state court).

[86] 28 U.S.C. § 1367(a).

[87] *See* H.R. Rep. No. 734, 101st Cong., 2d Sess. (1990), reprinted at 1990 U.S. Code Cong. & Admin. News 6860, 6875 n.15.

suggests that the test is to be the "common nucleus of operative facts."[88] However, the test traditionally employed in the judge-made doctrine of ancillary jurisdiction differed, at least linguistically, from the *Gibbs* standard. Ancillary jurisdiction could apply, said the Supreme Court in *Moore v. New York Cotton Exchange,* if the claims arise out of the "same transaction or occurrence."[89] The "same transaction or occurrence" standard continued to be employed in ancillary jurisdiction cases, even after *Gibbs'* adoption of the "common nucleus" standard for pendent claims.[90]

There exists some confusion in the legislative history of Section 1367 as to why Congress ultimately chose the "same case or controversy" language, rather than the "same transaction or occurrence" standard, which had been employed in earlier drafts of the statute. The "same case or controversy" language first appeared in the proposal submitted by the academic drafters.[91] Despite this seemingly unnecessary confusion, it is unlikely that use of different statutory language would have had any practical impact on the scope of supplemental jurisdiction.

In any event, an examination of Justice Brennan's opinion in *Gibbs,* however, reveals that his "common nucleus" test was itself designed to give effect to Article III's "case-or-controversy" directive. He stated, "Pendent jurisdiction . . . exists whenever there is a claim arising under [the] Constitution, the Laws of the United States, and Treaties made, or which shall be made, under their Authority . . .' and the relationship between that claim and the state claim permits the conclusion that the entire action before the court comprises but one constitutional 'case.' "[94] In so stating, he was no doubt drawing on Chief Justice Marshall's analysis in *Osborn v. Bank of the United States.*[95] Although courts employing a purely textual interpretive approach could no doubt choose to define the phrase, "same case or controversy" in Section 1367 in a manner untied to the prestatutory pendent jurisdiction doctrine, the federal courts generally seem to have deemed the phrase to incorporate the *Gibbs* "common nucleus of operative fact" standard.

The problem with the supplemental jurisdiction statute's attempt to codify the *Gibbs* test is that the *Gibbs* test itself suffered from serious ambiguities at the time of its creation, and over the years, it was subjected to a wide range of lower court interpretations. While, of course, generally phrased statutory language cannot avoid all uncertainties in its application to specific contexts, a statute that continues use of a vague and confused judicially-created standard can hardly be thought to represent an analytical advance. As one commentator has noted, "the Supreme Court [has treated] the case requirement as a receptacle, filling it with specific

---

88 Common nucleus of operative facts. *See* United Mine Workers of Am. v. Gibbs, 383 U.S. 715, 725 (1966).

89 Same transaction or occurrence. Moore v. New York Cotton Exch., 270 U.S. 593, 609–611 (1926).

90 "Same transaction or occurrence" standard applied in ancillary jurisdiction. *See, e.g.,* Wigglesworth v. Teamsters Local Union No. 592, 68 F.R.D. 609, 611 (E.D. Va. 1975) (same transaction or occurrence standard in determining whether counterclaim is compulsory or permissive under Rule 13).

91 *See* Federal Courts Study Committee Implementation Act and Civil Justice Reform Act: Hearing on H.R. 5381 and 3898 Before the Subcommittee on Courts, Intellectual Property and the Administration of Justice of the House Committee on the Judiciary, 101st Cong., 2d Sess., at 722 (1990).

94 United Mine Workers of Am. v. Gibbs, 383 U.S. 715, 725 (1966).

95 Osborn v. Bank of the United States, 22 U.S. (9 Wheat.) 738, 817–871 (1824).

doctrines [only] as the need arises. Working from the outside in, the Court [has sought] to reach the central definitional issue by solving, ad hoc, the problems it poses."[96] Thus, even if it were beyond dispute that — as Section 1367's legislative history indicates — the *Gibbs* "common nucleus" test controls interpretation of the statute's "same case or controversy" language, the interpretive problems would continue to exists.

## § 5.06 JOINDER OR INTERVENTION OF ADDITIONAL PARTIES

Subsection (b) of the supplemental jurisdiction statute expressly prohibits the extension of supplemental jurisdiction in diversity cases over claims by plaintiffs against persons made parties under Rule 14, 19, 20, or 24 of the Federal Rules of Civil Procedure, or over claims by persons proposed to be joined as plaintiffs under Rule 19, or seeking to intervene as plaintiffs under Rule 24.[97] Rule 14 deals with impleader or "third-party practice"; Rule 19 concerns compulsory joinder of necessary and indispensable parties; Rule 20 concerns permissive joinder of parties; and Rule 24 concerns intervention. As previously noted, by singling out the use of multi-party devices by *plaintiffs,* Section 1367(b) inescapably reveals its "anti-diversity bias." Those who seek to bring suit in federal court in diversity cases are expressly and unambiguously denied use of the very same strategic procedural devices that are available to both plaintiffs and defendants in federal question cases and to defendants in diversity cases.

In most instances, the statute mirrors prestatutory common law practice. In the prestatutory decision in *Owen Equipment & Erection Co. v. Kroger,* for example, the Supreme Court refused to extend ancillary jurisdiction to a claim by a plaintiff against a nondiverse third-party defendant who had been impleaded by the defendant under Rule 14, even though that rule authorizes such a procedural move.[98] The Court reached this conclusion, even though at the time it was well accepted that ancillary jurisdiction did apply to a Rule 14 third-party claim made by the defendant against a nondiverse impleaded party.[99]

One could, of course, debate whether, as a matter of policy, the diversity jurisdiction should in fact be deemed less worthy than federal question jurisdiction.[100] Even if one were to assume that an anti-diversity bias is justified as a matter of social policy, however, one may question whether the virtually nonexistent preenactment debate over Section 1367 justifies so unambiguous, albeit indirect, an attack on diversity. Moreover, if the drafters' goal were in fact to deter resort to the

---

[96] Bandes, *The Idea of a Case,* 42 Stan. L. Rev. 227, 227–228 (1990).

[97] 28 U.S.C. § 1367(b).

[98] *See* Fed. R. Civ. P. 14(a) (plaintiff may assert any claim against third-party defendant arising out of transaction or occurrence that is subject matter of plaintiff's claim against third-party plaintiff).

[99] Prestatutory rule that ancillary jurisdiction does not support plaintiff's claim against impleaded third party. Owen Equip. & Erection Co. v. Kroger, 437 U.S. 365, 376 (1978).

[100] The debate over the continued viability of the diversity jurisdiction has raged for many years. *See* Freer, *Compounding Confusion and Hampering Diversity: Life After,* Finley *and the Supplemental Jurisdiction Act,* 40 Emory L.J. 445 (1991).

diversity jurisdiction, their failure to extend the barriers of Section 1367(b) to defendants who remove cases to federal court is totally lacking in rationality. Finally, several serious problems of draftsmanship have rendered Section 1367(b) something of an interpretive nightmare.

Until the Supreme Court's 2005 opinion in *Exxon Mobil Corp. v. Allapattah Services, Inc.* clarified that supplemental jurisdiction can be applied to class plaintiffs' claims for less than the jurisdictional minimum so long as one named class member meets the jurisdictional amount in controversy,[101] courts and commentators disagreed regarding the application of supplemental jurisdiction in Rule 23 diversity class actions.[102] Much of the controversy stemmed from *Zahn v. International Paper Co.*, a Supreme Court case predating the 1990 enactment of the supplemental jurisdiction statute. In *Zahn*, the Supreme Court held that each member of a class action invoking diversity of citizenship jurisdiction must satisfy the jurisdictional minimum amount in controversy requirement, except in the relatively rare case in which the claims could be described as "joint."[103] After Congress enacted Section 1367, the supplemental jurisdiction statute,[104] the circuit courts split over the issue of whether the statute overruled *Zahn*. A number of courts, relying on the statute's legislative history, concluded that Section 1367 was not intended to overrule *Zahn* while other courts reached the opposite conclusion. In *Exxon Mobil Corp. v. Allapattah Services, Inc.*, the Court concluded that the supplemental jurisdiction statute *did* legislatively overturn *Zahn*.[105] The Court held that the supplemental jurisdiction statute permits the exercise of diversity jurisdiction over the claims of other plaintiffs in the same Article III case or controversy, even if those claims are for less than the jurisdictional minimum, provided that at least one named plaintiff satisfies the amount-in-controversy requirement and the other elements of jurisdiction are present.[106]

The Court's decision in *Allapattah* also resolved uncertainty about the application of Section 1367(b) to Rule 20 joinder. Under Rule 20 permissive joinder, all persons may join in one action as plaintiffs if they assert any right to relief jointly, severally, or in the alternative in respect of or arising out of the same transaction, occurrence, or series of transactions or occurrences and if any question of law or fact common to all these persons will arise in the action.[107] Section 1367(b) prohibits supplemental jurisdiction in a diversity case over claims by plaintiffs against

---

[101] *Exxon* case. Exxon Mobil Corp. v. Allapattah Servs., 545 U.S. 546, 549, 552–566 (2005).

[102] *See, e.g.*, Freer, *Compounding Confusion and Hampering Diversity: Life After Finley and the Supplemental Jurisdiction Statute*, 40 Emory L.J. 445, 485 (1991); Rowe, Burbank & Mengler, *Compounding or Creating Confusion About Supplemental Jurisdiction? A Reply to Professor Freer*, 40 Emory L.J. 943, 961 (1991).

[103] Each class member must meet jurisdictional amount in controversy requirement. Zahn v. International Paper Co., 414 U.S. 291, 301 (1973).

[104] 28 U.S.C. § 1367.

[105] Supplemental jurisdiction statute overturns *Zahn*. *See* Exxon Mobil Corp. v. Allapattah Servs., Inc., 545 U.S. 546, 567–568 (2005).

[106] Supplemental jurisdiction extends to members' claims below jurisdictional minimum. Exxon Mobil Corp. v. Allapattah Servs., Inc., 545 U.S. 546, 549–550 (2005).

[107] Fed. R. Civ. P. 20(a).

persons joined under Rule 20,[108] but does not prohibit use of supplemental jurisdiction over claims against joined parties if the basis for jurisdiction is a federal question.

The relevance to and use of supplemental jurisdiction in diversity cases involving joinder under Rule 20 is a good deal more complicated than joinder in federal question cases. By its terms, Section 1367(b) provides that in cases based on diversity, supplemental jurisdiction does not extend to claims by plaintiffs *against* persons made parties under Rule 20.[109] Even the statute's academic drafters have acknowledged the interpretive difficulty caused by the provision's silence about supplemental jurisdiction over nondiverse parties proposed to be added as *plaintiffs* under Rule 20 after initial filing, given that the explicit restriction extends only to supplemental jurisdiction over claims by existing plaintiffs *against* persons made parties under Rule 20.[110] They note that "[o]riginal filing of a diversity complaint by two plaintiffs, one of them not of diverse citizenship from a defendant, remains barred by the complete diversity interpretation of the requirements for original diversity jurisdiction. Literally, though, section 1367(b) does not bar an original complete-diversity filing and subsequent amendment to add a nondiverse coplaintiff under Rule 20, taking advantage of supplemental jurisdiction over the claim of the new plaintiff against the existing defendant."[111]

The problem, as the drafters acknowledge, is that the statute's prohibition refers only to claims "against" persons made parties under Rule 20, a restriction that, by its terms, fails to reach joinder of persons *aligned* with the plaintiff. "We can only hope," the drafters concluded, "that the federal courts will plug that potentially gaping hole in the complete diversity requirement — either by regarding it as an unacceptable circumvention of original diversity jurisdiction requirements, or by reference to the intent not to abandon the complete diversity rule that is clearly expressed in the legislative history of section 1367."[112]

The legislative history does indicate that Section 1367, in accordance with case law, is intended to prohibit the joinder or intervention of persons as plaintiffs if adding them is inconsistent with diversity requirements.[113] However, it is, of course, the unambiguous text, not the legislative history, that was subjected to the legislative process. It is therefore the text that legally controls.[114] And that text, as the drafters themselves have acknowledged, clearly provides that the bar against

---

[108] 28 U.S.C. § 1367(b).

[109] 28 U.S.C. § 1367(b).

[110] Rowe, Burbank, & Mengler, *Compounding or Creating Confusion About Supplemental Jurisdiction? A Reply to Professor Freer,* 40 Emory L.J. 943, 961 n.91 (1991).

[111] Rowe, Burbank, & Mengler, *Compounding or Creating Confusion About Supplemental Jurisdiction? A Reply to Professor Freer,* 40 Emory L.J. 943, 961 n.91 (1991).

[112] Rowe, Burbank, & Mengler, *Compounding or Creating Confusion About Supplemental Jurisdiction? A Reply to Professor Freer,* 40 Emory L.J. 943, 961 n.91 (1991).

[113] H.R. Rep. No. 734, 101st Cong., 2d Sess. (1990), reprinted at 1990 U.S. Code Cong. & Admin. News 6860, 6875

[114] Unambiguous statutory text precludes reliance on legislative history. Exxon Mobil Corp. v. Allapattah Servs., 545 U.S. 546, 567 (2005) (concluding that the text of Section 1367 was unambiguous, and that it was unnecessary to consult the legislative history when construing the statute).

supplemental jurisdiction in cases of Rule 20 joinder is limited to claims by plaintiffs *against* persons made parties under the rule.[115]

The Supreme Court, applying the statute as written, acknowledged this drafting anomaly in *Exxon Mobil Corp. v. Allapattah Servs.*, noting that it is not clear why Congress would have drafted Section 1367(b) to withhold supplemental jurisdiction over plaintiffs joined as parties "needed for just adjudication" under Rule 19, but would allow supplemental jurisdiction over plaintiffs permissively joined under Rule 20. The Court opined that one explanation for the different treatment of Rule 19 and Rule 20 is that Congress might have been concerned that extending supplemental jurisdiction to Rule 19 plaintiffs would allow circumvention of the complete diversity rule: a nondiverse plaintiff might be omitted intentionally from the original action but joined later under Rule 19 as a necessary party. More generally, Congress might have concluded that federal jurisdiction is appropriate only if the district court would have original jurisdiction over the claims of all those plaintiffs who are so essential to the action that they could be joined under Rule 19.[116]

The Court, however, did what the statutory drafters had urged years earlier by refusing to allow supplemental jurisdiction to remove the complete diversity requirement. There is language in *Exxon Mobil* that distinguishes between added plaintiffs whose claims do not satisfy the amount-in-controversy requirement on the one hand and those whose presence destroys complete diversity, on the other hand. The Court explained that under the "contamination theory," the inclusion of a claim or party falling outside the district court's original jurisdiction somehow "contaminates" every other claim in the complaint, depriving the court of original jurisdiction over any of the claims. The Court opined that this theory "can make some sense" in the context of the complete diversity requirement, because the presence of nondiverse parties on both sides of a suit eliminates the justification for providing a federal forum. In contrast, the theory "makes little sense" with respect to the amount-in-controversy requirement, which is meant to ensure that a dispute is sufficiently important to warrant attention in the federal courts.[117]

A variation of the diversity jurisdictional-amount issue involves the joinder of claims by a single plaintiff against two or more defendants, some of which allege a sufficient jurisdictional amount and others that do not. Rule 20(a) allows the joinder of defendants in a single action for claims against them arising out of the same transaction or occurrence.[118] The courts that have decided this issue have uniformly held that the supplemental jurisdiction statute does not provide supplemental jurisdiction for the insufficient claim, although they have on occasion employed different reasoning.

---

115 28 U.S.C. § 1367(b).

116 Drafting incongruities not absurd. Exxon Mobil Corp. v. Allapattah Servs., 545 U.S. 546, 565 (2005).

117 Contamination theory considered by Court. Exxon Mobil Corp. v. Allapattah Servs., 545 U.S. 546, 559–562 (2005) ("The presence of a single nondiverse party may eliminate the fear of bias with respect to all claims, but the presence of a claim that falls short of the minimum amount in controversy does nothing to reduce the importance of the claims that do meet this requirement.").

118 Fed. R. Civ. P. 20(a).

Before enactment of the Supplemental Jurisdiction Statute, claims *by or against* intervenors of right under Rule 24(a) were uniformly held to be supported by ancillary jurisdiction.[119]Under Section 1367(b), however, claims against nondiverse parties asserted by persons seeking to intervene *as plaintiffs* are not supported by supplemental jurisdiction in a diversity action, even if intervention is by right under Rule 24(a). One may question the wisdom of this result, in light of the very purposes that Section 1367(b) can properly be deemed to serve. In addition to changing the former practice, the rule punishes not the plaintiff who chose the federal forum in a diversity case, but rather an absentee who presumably had nothing to do with the choice of forum. This treatment, then, can be justified only by either a mindless prejudice against plaintiffs, laziness in statutory drafting, or an aimless "scatter gun" attempt to curb the federal courts' diversity jurisdiction. None of these can be deemed a legitimate rationale for legislative action.

Under judicial construction of Section 1367, a party may not intervene as a defendant solely for the purpose of asserting a claim against a nondiverse plaintiff. The intervenor must be potentially liable to the plaintiff on the primary claim in order to be treated as a defendant to whom supplemental jurisdiction may apply under Section 1367(b).

## § 5.07 DISCRETIONARY DECLINE OF SUPPLEMENTAL JURISDICTION

### [1] Scope of Statutory Factors

The supplemental jurisdiction statute sets forth four factors on which a court may exercise its discretion to decline supplemental jurisdiction.[120] These factors are similar, but not identical, to the factors identified in *United Mine Workers of America v. Gibbs*. In *Gibbs*, the Supreme Court emphasized that the existence of *power* in a district court to exercise pendent jurisdiction did not necessarily mean that the court should actually exercise such jurisdiction. Rather, the district court possesses a certain amount of discretion to decline to exercise such jurisdiction under certain circumstances.[121] The Court articulated the following circumstances under which pendent state claims could properly be dismissed:[122]

1. If the federal claims are dismissed before trial;
2. If it appears that the state issues substantially predominate, whether in terms of proof, of the scope of the issues raised, or of the comprehensiveness of the remedy sought; and
3. If separation of the state and federal claims is justified by reasons independent of jurisdictional considerations, such as the likelihood of jury

[119] Claims by or against intervenors. *See* Owen Equip. & Erection Co. v. Kroger, 437 U.S. 365, 375 n.18 (1978); Blake v. Pallan, 554 F.2d 947, 955 (9th Cir. 1977).

[120] 28 U.S.C. § 1367(c).

[121] Discretion to decline pendent claim jurisdiction. United Mine Workers of Am. v. Gibbs, 383 U.S. 715, 726 (1966).

[122] 383 U.S. at 726–727.

confusion.

The first and second factors set forth in *Gibbs* are carried forward in the statute as Section 1367(c)(2) and (3).[123] *Gibbs'* third factor is not specifically articulated in the statute. However, the statute includes two additional criteria: that the claim raises a novel or complex issue of state law,[124] and that in exceptional circumstances, there exist other compelling reasons for declining jurisdiction.[125]

Several circuits have taken the approach that Section 1367(c) merely incorporates the discretionary factors set forth in *Gibbs* and its progeny. Further, the legislative history indicates that Section 1367 was intended to codify the factors deemed relevant under prior law.[126] Other courts have found the lack of congruency between the factors enumerated in *Gibbs* and those set out in Section 1367(c) to be significant. They conclude that by listing the four factors, Congress intended to alter and restrict the previous common law analysis.[127]

Courts have construed use of the mandatory term "shall" in the supplemental jurisdiction statute to mean that a federal court must exercise supplemental jurisdiction if it is found to exist, unless one of the exceptions of subsection (c) applies. It is arguable that this position represents some change from pre-Section 1367 law. In *Gibbs,* the Supreme Court emphasized that pendent jurisdiction is a doctrine of discretion, not of plaintiff's right, and that it need not be exercised in every case in which it is found to be present. The Court found the justification for pendent claim jurisdiction to lie in considerations of judicial economy, convenience, and fairness to litigants. But, if these factors were not present, the Court indicated that a federal court should hesitate to exercise jurisdiction over state law claims. The Court stated that needless decisions of state law should be avoided, both as a matter of comity and to promote justice between parties by procuring for them a surer-footed reading of applicable law.[128] But, under the statute, the fact that one of the factors enumerated in Section 1367(c) is found to be present does not automatically imply that the district court should necessarily decline to exercise supplemental jurisdiction.

The lower courts generally construed the *Gibbs* factors not to represent an all-inclusive list, but as merely illustrative of the kinds of considerations that might cause a court to choose to exercise its discretion not to hear pendent claims. In contrast, Section 1367(c) has been construed to provide the exclusive means by which supplemental jurisdiction may be declined by a court. Unless a court properly invokes a Section 1367(c) category in exercising its discretion to decline to assert supplemental jurisdiction, that jurisdiction must be exercised. A district court no longer possesses discretion to refuse to exercise supplemental jurisdiction

---

[123] *See* 28 U.S.C. § 1367(c)(2), (3).

[124] 28 U.S.C. § 1367(c)(1).

[125] "Other compelling reasons" for declining jurisdiction. 28 U.S.C. § 1367(c)(4).

[126] H. R. Rep. No. 734, 101st Cong., 2d Sess. (1990), reprinted at 1990 U.S. Code Cong. & Admin. News 6802, 6875.

[127] Statute alters *Gibbs* factors. *See* 28 U.S.C. § 1367(c).

[128] Broader discretion to decline jurisdiction under *Gibbs*. United Mine Workers of Am. v. Gibbs, 383 U.S. 715, 726–727 (1966).

on grounds not enumerated categories, the court retains broad discretion to determine whether to exercise or decline jurisdiction on the indicated ground. Stated differently, supplemental jurisdiction *must* be exercised in the absence of any of the four Section 1367(c) factors; once a court determines the existence of one or more statutory factors, the additional *Gibbs* considerations may, by their presence or absence, influence the court in its decision concerning the exercise of that discretion.

### [2] Novel or Complex Issue of State Law

Section 1367(c)(1) gives the district court discretion to dismiss a claim supported only by supplemental jurisdiction if the claim raises a novel or complex issue of state law.[129] It is often used to decline jurisdiction in cases in which state law in the area is unsettled, or the issue is one of first impression. It also may be invoked to avoid construction of a state constitutional provision in federal court. Section 1367(c)(1) has also been cited to support discretionary declination of supplemental jurisdiction over claims that would raise novel and complex issues of foreign law.

### [3] When Supplemental Claim Substantially Predominates

Section 1367(c)(2) provides the district court with the discretion to dismiss a claim supported only by supplemental jurisdiction if that claim substantially predominates over the claim or claims over which the district court has original jurisdiction.[130] This rule represents a codification of one of the factors articulated in *United Mine Workers v. Gibbs*. In *Gibbs*, the Supreme Court stated that if it appears that the pendent state issues substantially predominate, whether in terms of proof, the scope of the issues raised, or the comprehensiveness of the remedy sought, the state claims may be dismissed without prejudice and left for resolution to state tribunals.[131] Because Section 1367(c)(2) codifies this element of *Gibbs*, the district court's analysis under Section 1367(c)(2) should track this standard. Decisions have indicated that in general, the question of whether state law predominates should be answered by looking to the nature of the claims as set forth in the pleading and by determining whether the state law claims are more complex or require more judicial resources to adjudicate, or are more salient in the case as a whole than the federal law claims.

Supplemental jurisdiction should be declined only if there is an overriding countervailing interest to be served by relegating state claims to state court. This will normally be true only if a state claim constitutes the real body of a case, to which the federal claim is only an appendage. Underlying Section 1367(c)(2) is the philosophy that the federal courts should not tolerate attempts to litigate an essentially state-law case in the federal forum. The fact that the federal claims have been resolved does not necessarily mean that the state law claims predominate over the federal claims.

---

129 Novel or complex state issue. 28 U.S.C. § 1367(c)(1).

130 28 U.S.C. § 1367(c)(2).

131 *Gibbs* standard regarding predominating state claim. United Mine Workers of Am. v. Gibbs, 383 U.S. 715, 726–727 (1966).

## [4] Dismissal of Jurisdiction-Conferring Claim

Section 1367(c)(3) provides the district court with discretion to dismiss a claim supported only by supplemental jurisdiction if it has dismissed all claims over which it had original jurisdiction.[132] This rule represents a codification of one of the factors articulated in *United Mine Workers v. Gibbs,*[133] and cases construing the former *Gibbs* standard may still be relevant in interpreting the statute.[134]

Dismissal of supplemental claims is not required on dismissal of all federal claims. The district court retains the power to hear a supplemental state claim after dismissal of all federal claims if, on balance, the underlying values indicate that it should be heard. When a federal court dismisses all claims supporting the exercise of original jurisdiction, the court must reassess its jurisdiction by engaging in a pragmatic and case-specific evaluation of a myriad of considerations that may bear on the determination of whether to exercise supplemental jurisdiction. There is no presumption in favor of dismissal unless all of the federal claims are dismissed before trial. However, if the federal claim was dismissed for lack of subject matter jurisdiction, the district court has no discretion to retain the supplemental claims for adjudication. The dismissal means that there never was a valid claim within the court's original jurisdiction to which the state claims may be supplemental. Therefore, the district court has no discretion to exceed the scope of its Article III power and must dismiss the state law claims without prejudice.

Subsection (c)(3) requires that *all* claims over which it has original jurisdiction must have been dismissed before a district court may rely on that provision as a basis for dismissing the supplemental claims. This refers to all claims in the case, not just those claims asserted against a particular defendant.

## [5] Reasons to Retain Jurisdiction

A federal court will often retain jurisdiction over a supplemental claim after dismissal of all jurisdiction-conferring claims if substantial judicial resources have already been committed in the federal court. Declining to exercise supplemental jurisdiction under those circumstances may result in a substantial duplication of effort if the matter is to be adjudicated in another court.[135] The district court is in the best position to judge the extent of resources invested in a case, and appellate deference to its decision to retain or decline supplemental jurisdiction is common.

In making the determination concerning the extent of resources that have been invested, the court should consider whether those resources may be used in the

---

[132] 28 U.S.C. § 1367(c)(3).

[133] *Compare* 28 U.S.C. § 1367(c)(3) *with* United Mine Workers of Am. v. Gibbs, 383 U.S. 715, 726–727 (1966).

[134] Cases construing *Gibbs* are still relevant. McCullough v. Branch Banking & Trust Co., Inc., 844 F. Supp. 258, 260 (E.D.N.C. 1993), *aff'd other grounds,* 35 F.3d 127 (4th Cir. 1994) (exercise of discretion under 1367(c)(3) may be guided by principles that guided exercise of judicial discretion under doctrine of pendent jurisdiction).

[135] Substantial duplication of effort. *See* Rosado v. Wyman, 397 U.S. 397, 404–405 (1970) (common sense policy of pendent jurisdiction involves conservation of judicial energy and avoidance of multiplicity of litigation).

state forum. If the district court has conducted significant proceedings so as to become familiar with the case, the parties, and the subject matter, then retention of jurisdiction is appropriate. However, other expended resources, such as discovery, may be largely reusable in state court. Similarly, the investigation of facts and research of state law is the same whether the case remains in federal court or is dismissed in favor of a state forum.

### [6] Compelling Reasons Under Exceptional Circumstances

Section 1367(c)(4) allows the district court to decline to exercise supplemental jurisdiction if, in exceptional circumstances, there are other compelling reasons to decline jurisdiction.[136] In the view of some circuits, by providing for this exercise of discretion only under "exceptional circumstances," Congress has sounded a note of caution that the bases for declining jurisdiction should be extended beyond those of subsections (c)(1) through (c)(3) only if the circumstances are truly unusual. Declining jurisdiction under (c)(4) should be the exception, rather than the rule. Moreover, if the court elects to decline jurisdiction under (c)(4), it must articulate exactly what exceptional circumstances are present.

---

136 28 U.S.C. § 1367(c)(4).

# Chapter 6

# REMOVAL JURISDICTION

## PART A
## NATURE AND PURPOSE OF REMOVAL JURISDICTION

### § 6.01 OVERVIEW OF REMOVAL JURISDICTION

Removal jurisdiction is peculiar in that it permits defendants to remove an action properly brought in one system of courts, our state courts, into another system of courts, our federal district courts. Our federal system of government, which created our dual system of federal and state courts, provides the predicate for the "judicial curiosity" that is removal.[1] Although there are other doctrines or procedures that may defeat the plaintiff's choice of a proper forum, only removal effects the actual assignment of a case from one judicial system to another. Thus, although it may be possible to transfer a case from one federal district court to another district court within the federal court system, and it may be possible to convince a court to dismiss a case on the ground that it was brought in a proper but inconvenient forum and there is no other convenient forum within that system,[2] only the removal statutes allow a case to be taken from a proper forum in one judicial system automatically to another.

Removal jurisdiction is not explicitly mentioned in Article III or elsewhere in the United States Constitution. Commentators have noted that although Article III sets out the scope of the federal judicial power by enumerating the kinds of cases that the federal courts may hear, the Constitution does not set forth the procedures for invoking federal court jurisdiction.[3] Removal is one of three ways of invoking federal jurisdiction. The other ways are to initiate an action by filing a complaint in federal court,[4] or by seeking federal court review of state court judgments.[5]

Removal, the third procedure for invoking federal jurisdiction, is the most peculiar and difficult of the three. Congress provided for removal jurisdiction in the

---

[1] Tinney v. McClain, 76 F. Supp. 694, 698 (N.D. Tex. 1948) ("The removal statute is a judicial curiosity incidental to our dual system of government"); *see generally* Ch. 11, *Dual Federal-State Judicial Systems.*

[2] *See* Ch. 10, *Change of Venue.*

[3] *See* Erwin Chemerinsky, Federal Jurisdiction 322 (2d Ed. 1994).

[4] *See* 1 Moore's Federal Practice Ch. 3, *Commencing an Action* (Matthew Bender 3d ed.).

[5] *See* 17A Moore's Federal Practice Ch. 120, *Dual State and Federal Judicial Structure* (Matthew Bender 3d ed.).

Judiciary Act of 1789,[6] the first legislation implementing Article III's judicial power. The history of removal jurisdiction is filled with confusion and incoherence. What was said in 1912 about removal is just as relevant today: "[t]hat there is no other phase of American jurisprudence with so many refinements and subtleties, as relate to removal proceedings, is known by all who have to deal with them."[7] Nonetheless, removal is an important aspect of federal jurisdiction. In 2013, approximately 11%, or over 32,000, of the cases pending in federal court were removed cases.[8] Moreover, it appears that removal significantly improves a defendant's chances of prevailing on the merits.[9]

This chapter covers the standards for removal under the general removal statute.[10] Under the general removal statute,[11] a defendant generally may invoke federal jurisdiction if the case originally could have been filed in federal court.[12] Usually, such removal jurisdiction is grounded in either diversity or federal question jurisdiction (*see* § 6.08[2] (discussion of diversity cases), § 6.08[3] (discussion of federal question cases)). In addition to the general removal provision, other statutes provide the right to remove in special situations, such as cases involving federal officers,[13] civil rights,[14] and bankruptcy.[15] For a discussion of the requirements under the special statutes, *see* 16 Moore's Federal Practice Ch. 107, *Removal* § 107.15 (Matthew Bender 3d ed.).

The removal statutes are designed to provide defendants with a federal forum to litigate federal claims and state claims with diverse parties. The original purpose of removal jurisdiction in federal question cases was to ensure that the tribunal better informed on questions of federal law would adjudicate the matter. In diversity cases, removal jurisdiction was designed to protect nonresident defendants from any perceived prejudice or preference of the state court regarding the resident plaintiffs.[16] Indeed, the Class Action Fairness Act of 2005 was enacted specifically to protect non-resident defendants, providing such defendants with an expanded

---

[6] Ch. 20, 1 Stat. 73, § 12 (Congress first provided for removal by alien defendants, by out-of-state citizens, and in certain land grant cases involving more than $500).

[7] Hagerla v. Mississippi River Power Co., 202 F. 771, 773 (S.D. Iowa 1912) (McPherson, J.).

[8] Admin. Off. U.S. Cts., Judicial Business of the United States Courts 2013, Table C-8 (2013), http://www.uscourts.gov/uscourts/Statistics/JudicialBusiness/2013/appendices/C08Sep13.pdf, last visited June 9, 2014.

[9] *See* Clermont & Eisenberg, *Do Case Outcomes Really Reveal Anything About the Legal System? Win Rates and Removal Jurisdiction*, 83 Cornell L. Rev. 581 (1998) (finding that successful removal significantly improves defendant's chances of prevailing on the merits).

[10] 28 U.S.C. § 1441.

[11] 28 U.S.C. § 1441(a).

[12] 28 U.S.C. § 1441(a); *see* Metcalf v. Watertown, 128 U.S. 586, 589 (1888).

[13] 28 U.S.C. § 1442.

[14] 28 U.S.C. § 1443.

[15] 28 U.S.C. § 1452.

[16] Stifel v. Hopkins, 477 F.2d 1116, 1125 (6th Cir. 1973) (citing Moore's Federal Practice); China Basin Props., Ltd. v. Allendale Mut. Ins. Co., 818 F. Supp. 1301, 1304 (N.D. Cal. 1992) (diversity jurisdiction provides neutral forum for citizens of another state or nation).

right of removal (*see* § 6.08[6] (discussion of The Class Action Fairness Act ("CAFA"))).

Although providing a federal forum is the goal of removal, the effect of removal is to deprive the state court of an action properly within its jurisdiction, which raises federalism concerns.[17] Moreover, if a state has consented to suit in its own courts, but not in federal courts, any action brought against the state must be litigated in the state court and may not be removed to federal court under the general removal statute.[18] However, in *Lapides v. Board of Regents*, the Supreme Court held that if the state itself removes the case, the state's Eleventh Amendment immunity is waived.[19]

In deciding whether to exercise the right to remove a case from state court to federal court, a defendant faces many considerations, some practical, some less so. Many times the decision whether to remove will depend on defendant's counsel's knowledge of local practice norms. Some of the practical considerations include whether the defendant's counsel is more familiar with the Federal Rules of Civil Procedure and Evidence than with the state rules, and whether there are procedures available or evidentiary rules in the federal court that are more advantageous to the client. Another consideration is the right to jury trial. In some cases, it is more likely that a matter could be tried to a jury in federal court than it would be in state court. The right to seek interlocutory appeals may differ in the federal and state courts. Defendant's counsel may consider the relative congestion in the state and federal court civil dockets, the physical convenience of the federal and state courthouses, the existence or lack of mandatory alternative dispute resolution procedures, and the relative propensity of state and federal juries to award large verdicts.

A factor that may favor removal would be the availability within the federal court system of a statute allowing the defendant to seek a transfer to a more convenient forum in a different state.[20] Further, although the *Erie* doctrine requires the federal court to apply the state law that the state court would apply,[21] in an area of unclear state law a federal judge's interpretation of state law may differ from that of a lower state court judge. Similarly, if the defendant's case raises particularly unpopular issues, it may be preferable to litigate in a federal court, where the judges handling the case will have the life tenure protections of Article III,[22] rather than in a state court, where the judges may be elected and therefore tend to be

---

[17] *See* Merrell Dow Pharmaceuticals, Inc. v. Thompson, 478 U.S. 804, 809 (1986); Carpenter v. Wichita Falls Indep. Sch. Dist., 44 F.3d 362, 365 (5th Cir. 1995).

[18] Gwinn Area Cmty. Sch. v. Michigan, 741 F.2d 840 (6th Cir. 1984) (action may not be removed unless state waives its Eleventh Amendment immunity and unequivocally expresses its consent to suit in federal court). *See generally* Ch. 14, *The Eleventh Amendment and State Sovereign Immunity.*

[19] Lapides v. Board of Regents of Univ. Sys. of Georgia, 535 U.S. 613, 618–624 (2002) (anomalous or inconsistent for state to invoke federal jurisdiction, contending that "[j]udicial power of the United States" extends to case at hand, and then to claim Eleventh Amendment immunity, denying that "[j]udicial power of the United States" extends to case at hand).

[20] *See* 28 U.S.C. § 1404(a); *see generally* Ch. 9, *Change of Venue.*

[21] *See* Ch. 15, *Applicable Law in Federal Court: The Erie Doctrine.*

[22] *See* U.S. Const., Art. III § 1; *see generally* Ch. 1, *The Structure of the Federal Judicial System.*

subject to political considerations. A complete analysis of removal jurisdiction is contained in 16 Moore's Federal Practice Ch. 107, *Removal* (Matthew Bender 3d ed. 1997).

## § 6.02 COMPARING REMOVAL JURISDICTION TO FEDERAL COURT ORIGINAL JURISDICTION

Removal jurisdiction of federal courts is entirely a creature of statute.[23] In contrast, the statutory basis for original federal jurisdiction (federal question and diversity) derives from Article III of the Constitution.[24] Original jurisdiction in the federal district courts is discussed in detail in Ch. 3, *Diversity Jurisdiction*, and Ch. 4, *Federal Question Jurisdiction*.

Because removal jurisdiction requires that the case originally could have been filed in federal court, removal jurisdiction is generally coextensive with diversity and federal question jurisdiction.[25]

However, some limitations apply to removal jurisdiction:

- The existence of a resident defendant generally precludes removal of a diversity case.[26]
- A one-year limit generally applies to removal of diversity cases.[27]
- The failure to comply with the statutory removal procedure may limit removal jurisdiction (*see* § 6.09).
- Some cases involving concurrent jurisdiction, such as cases arising under the Jones Act, are exempt from removal.[28]

In addition, special statutes authorize removal in certain specified situations (*see* § 6.01). In some of these cases, there is no statutory counterpart granting original jurisdiction to federal courts.

---

[23] Hurt v. Dow Chem. Co., 963 F.2d 1142, 1145 (8th Cir. 1992); *see* 28 U.S.C. § 1441 *et seq.*; *see also* Libhart v. Santa Monica Dairy Co., 592 F.2d 1062, 1064 (9th Cir. 1979) (statutory removal jurisdiction is constitutional exercise of congressional authority under necessary and proper clause of Constitution); U.S. Const., Art. I § 8.

[24] U.S. Const., Art. III § 2; *see* 28 U.S.C. §§ 1331, 1332; *see also* State Farm Fire & Casualty Co. v. Tashire, 386 U.S. 523, 530–531 (1967).

[25] *See* Northbrook Nat'l Ins. Co. v. Brewer, 493 U.S. 6, 12 (1989); Caterpillar, Inc. v. Williams, 482 U.S. 386, 392 (1987).

[26] 28 U.S.C. § 1441(b). *But see* 28 U.S.C. § 1453(b) (class actions removed under the Class Action Fairness Act of 2005 are not subject to the forum defendant rule); *see* § 6.08[6].

[27] 28 U.S.C. § 1446(b). *But see* 28 U.S.C. § 1453(b) (class actions removed under the Class Action Fairness Act of 2005 are not subject to the one year limit); *see* § 6.08[6].

[28] *See, e.g.*, 46 U.S.C. § 688 (Jones Act); Lackey v. Atlantic Richfield Co., 990 F.2d 202, 207 (5th Cir. 1993).

## § 6.03 REMOVAL STATUTES STRICTLY CONSTRUED

For over the last hundred years, the federal courts have construed the removal statutes to effectuate the congressional purpose generally to restrict removal jurisdiction.[29] Further, as a creature of statute, the removal right is strictly construed.[30] Because the effect of removal is to deprive the state court of jurisdiction over a case properly before the state court, removal raises federalism concerns that mandate strict construction.[31] Thus, a strong presumption exists against removal jurisdiction.[32] Because courts must rigorously enforce Congress's intent to restrict federal jurisdiction in controversies between citizens of different states,[33] all doubts are resolved in favor of remand.[34]

Recent developments have cast some doubt on the axioms that removal is strictly construed and that a presumption exists against removal (*see* 16 Moore's Federal Practice § 107.06). For example, the Supreme Court has held that the 30-day removal period is not triggered until the defendant is formally served (*see* § 6.09[2][a]).[35] Nevertheless, federal courts continue to recite these axioms. Perhaps these axioms are best understood in the context of the statutory nature of removal and the limited jurisdiction of federal courts.[36]

Apart from the question of congressional intent and other policy considerations, strict construction of the right of removal makes good sense. An order denying a motion to remand a case to state court is ordinarily not appealable until after a final

---

29 Shamrock Oil & Gas Corp. v. Sheets, 313 U.S. 100, 108 (1941) (denying plaintiffs right to remove: "[n]ot only does the language of the Act of 1887 evidence the Congressional purpose to restrict the jurisdiction of the federal courts on removal, but the policy of the successive acts of Congress regulating the jurisdiction of the federal courts is one calling for the strict construction of such legislation"); *see* American Fire & Cas. Co. v. Finn, 341 U.S. 6, 10–12 (1951) (articulating restrictive test for removal under 28 U.S.C. § 1441(c)); Long v. Bando Mfg. of Am., Inc., 201 F.3d 754, 757 (6th Cir. 2000) (because federalism concerns are implicated, removal statutes are narrowly construed); California v. United States, 215 F.3d 1005, 1010–1014 (9th Cir. 2000).

30 Burns v. Windsor Ins. Co., 31 F.3d 1092, 1095 (11th Cir. 1994); Hurt v. Dow Chem. Co., 963 F.2d 1142, 1144 (8th Cir. 1992); Salveson v. Western States BankcardAss'n, 731 F.2d 1423, 1426 (9th Cir. 1984).

31 Long v. Bando Mfg. of Am., Inc., 201 F.3d 754, 757 (6th Cir. 2000) (because federalism concerns are implicated, removal statutes are narrowly construed); Palkow v. CSX Transp., Inc., 431 F.3d 543, 555 (6th Cir. 2005) (no substantial federal question justified removal of state-law perjury claim based on testimony that occurred in federal court).

32 *See* Gaus v. Miles, Inc., 980 F.2d 564, 566 (9th Cir. 1992) (presumption against removal).

33 St. Paul Mercury Indem. Co. v. Red Cab Co., 303 U.S. 283, 288 (1938); Miera v. Dairyland Ins. Co., 143 F.3d 1337, 1339 (10th Cir. 1998) (citing *St. Paul* case).

34 *See* Libhart v. Santa Monica Dairy Co., 592 F.2d 1062, 1064 (9th Cir. 1979) (federal jurisdiction rejected when any doubt as to initial removal rights); Fajen v. Found. Reserve Ins. Co., 683 F.2d 331, 333 (10th Cir. 1982).

35 Murphy Bros., Inc. v. Michetti Pipe Stringing, Inc., 526 U.S. 344, 355 (1999) (interpreting "through service or otherwise" language of 28 U.S.C. § 1446(b) to require formal service).

36 *See* Manguno v. Prudential Prop. and Cas. Ins. Co., 276 F.3d 720, 723 (5th Cir. 2002) (ambiguities should be construed against removal because statute should be strictly construed in favor of remand); Bauer v. Transitional Sch. Dist., 255 F.3d 478, 482 (8th Cir. 2001); Russell Corp. v. American Home Assur. Co., 264 F.3d 1040, 1050 (11th Cir. 2001) (rejecting fairness approach in permitting later served defendants 30 days in which to remove because federal courts are of limited jurisdiction).

judgment or order is filed in the case (*see* § 6.13).[37] If the court of appeals determines that the case should have been remanded on the ground that there was no federal jurisdiction, the judgment on the merits must also be vacated because of the lack of jurisdiction. If the case was improperly remanded, at least the state court judgment will not be invalidated because of a lack of subject matter jurisdiction. Nonetheless, the district court must evaluate the removal question carefully, because the opportunity for review of remand decisions is quite limited (*see* § 6.13).

# PART B
# BASIS OF REMOVAL JURISDICTION

## § 6.04 FOUR BASIC ELEMENTS FOR REMOVAL

The general removal statute, Section 1441,[38] presents four essential elements for determining whether removal is proper:[39]

• First, only a "civil action brought in a State court" may be removed under Section 1441.

• Second, the civil action must be one "of which the district courts of the United States have original jurisdiction."

• Third, only "the defendant or the defendants" may remove.

• Fourth, the action must be removed to the district court for the district and division embracing the state court action.

## § 6.05 DEFENDANTS' OPTION TO REMOVE

### [1] Only Defendants May Remove

The general removal statute provides for removal by "the defendant or the defendants."[40] Similarly, the procedure for removal requires a "defendant or defendants" to file the notice of removal.[41] Accordingly, under the general removal statute, only defendants are permitted to remove a civil action from a state court to the district court for the district and division within which the action is pending. Plaintiffs are not permitted to remove an action under the general removal statute.[42] Thus, a plaintiff who elected state court jurisdiction when filing the

---

[37] *See also* 16 Moore's Federal Practice Ch. 107, *Removal* (Matthew Bender 3d ed.) (discussion of appellate review of orders denying remand).

[38] 28 U.S.C. § 1441. *See* 28 U.S.C. § 1455 with respect to removal of criminal prosecutions.

[39] 28 U.S.C. § 1441(a).

[40] 28 U.S.C. § 1441(a).

[41] 28 U.S.C. § 1446(a).

[42] *See* Shamrock Oil & Gas Corp. v. Sheets, 313 U.S. 100, 104–106 (1941) (rule depends on removal statute, not state statute that renders plaintiff a defendant in counterclaim); *see* American Home

complaint may not subsequently remove the action to federal court, even if a counterclaim would treat the plaintiff as a defendant under state law. In contrast, some of the special removal statutes set forth above may permit parties other than defendants to remove.[43] For example, any party may remove an action asserting federal claims arising out of federal patent or copyright law.

## [2] Determining Status as Defendant

### [a] Federal Law Governs Determination

Federal law applies to determine whether a party is a defendant, and it prevails over a state court's characterization or alignment of the parties.[44] As used in Section 1441(a),[45] the word *defendant* means the original plaintiff's defendant. Thus, generally, a party who was not a defendant in the plaintiff's original suit will not be re-characterized as a "defendant" by reason of the filing of later claims filed against that party in answers, third-party complaints, or claims in intervention. Similarly, a non-party, even one that claims to be a real party in interest, may not remove or participate in the removal of a case.[46]

In determining whether a party is a defendant, however, the federal courts apply a functional test. For example, if the plaintiff brings an action in state court, but the action has been brought for some ancillary purpose, such as to seek discovery, and the defendant files a counterclaim that is within federal jurisdiction, the plaintiff may remove the action on the theory that the counterclaim is the "mainspring" of the action.[47]

In other cases, however, where the original plaintiff is defending a counterclaim or cross-claim, the plaintiff does not become a "defendant" for removal purposes. Refusing to allow plaintiffs to remove based on claims against them is consistent with the strict construction of the removal statute and with the purpose of complete

---

Assurance Co. v. RJR Nabisco Holdings Corp., 70 F. Supp. 2d 296, 298 (S.D.N.Y. 1999) (unserved nonparty claiming to be real party in interest may not file notice of removal or participate in removal of case).

[43] *See, e.g.*, 28 U.S.C. § 1454(b) (civil action in which party asserts claim for relief arising under federal law relating to patents, plant variety protection, or copyright may be removed by any party).

[44] Chicago, Rock Island & Pac. R.R. Co. v. Stude, 346 U.S. 574, 580 (1954) (relevant issue is construction of federal removal statute, not state statute); Shamrock Oil & Gas Corp. v. Sheets, 313 U.S. 100, 107 (1941) (plaintiff characterized as defendant under state law may not remove based on counterclaim); *see* Progressive West Ins. Co. v. Preciado, 479 F.3d 1014, 1017–1018 (9th Cir. 2007) (applying *Shamrock* rule to case under Class Action Fairness Act) (*see* § 6.08[6] for discussion of the Class Action Fairness Act); Yakama Indian Nation v. Washington Dep't of Revenue, 176 F.3d 1241, 1248–1249 (9th Cir. 1999).

[45] 28 U.S.C. § 1441(a).

[46] American Home Assurance Co. v. RJR Nabisco Holdings Corp., 70 F. Supp. 2d 296, 298 (S.D.N.Y. 1999) (unserved party claiming to be real party in interest may not file notice of removal).

[47] *See, e.g.*, General Motors Corp. v. Gunn, 752 F. Supp. 729 (N.D. Miss. 1990) (manufacturer of car involved in accident sought discovery seeking to inspect owner's car; when owner of car counterclaimed for wrongful death, alleging design and manufacturing defects, plaintiff manufacturer was entitled to remove, based on diversity jurisdiction, and to have parties realigned).

diversity rule.[48] Again and again, the courts have reaffirmed the general rule that it would vitiate congressional intent to allow plaintiffs to engage in an end run around the complete diversity rule. However, one could argue that for removal purposes, there is no need to worry about such an "end-run," because the plaintiff has not invoked federal jurisdiction in the first place. On the other hand, to permit the state court plaintiff to sit back and await the filing of federal claims against it, and then assert federal jurisdiction through removal jurisdiction, seems to violate the same policy of preventing plaintiffs, as opposed to defendants, from using the liberal joinder rules together with liberal supplemental jurisdiction to invoke federal jurisdiction.[49]

### [b] Whether Additional Counterclaim Defendants, Cross-Claim Defendants, Third-Party Defendants, or Defendant Intervenors May Remove

#### [i] Additional Counterclaim Defendants and Cross-Claim Defendants Generally May Not Remove

The courts generally do not permit removal by additional counterclaim co-party defendants or cross-claim defendants. This is because of the general rule that *defendant* means the plaintiff's defendant. A counterclaim by a defendant against a plaintiff to which an additional co-party is added[50] is a claim asserted by a defendant. Accordingly, the co-party on the counterclaim is not a "defendant" for removal purposes. Similarly, when a cross-claim is asserted by a defendant,[51] and not the plaintiff, the cross-claim defendant may not remove on the basis of that there is federal jurisdiction over the cross-claim. Applying the general rule that *defendant* means plaintiff's defendant precludes removal because the cross-claim is asserted by the co-party defendant, not the plaintiff. This view comports with the firmly embedded principle to construe the right of removal narrowly.

However, an additional counterclaim defendant may remove a case under Section 1441(c), which permits removal when a cause of action within federal question jurisdiction is joined with one or more otherwise non-removable claims or causes of action.[52] The other counterclaim defendants may not have been able to remove because they were originally plaintiffs. But because the federal claims asserted against him would have been removable if he had been sued on them

---

[48] *See* Ch. 4, *Diversity Jurisdiction.*

[49] *See* Ch. 5, *Supplemental Jurisdiction.*

[50] *See* Palisades Collections LLC v. Shorts, 552 F.3d 327, 328–329 (4th Cir. 2008) (because additional counterclaim defendants were not defendants against whom the original plaintiff asserted claims, they were not "defendants" within the meaning of either removal statute; citing MOORE'S FEDERAL PRACTICE); Westwood Apex v. Contreras, 644 F.3d 799, 801 (9th Cir. 2011) (remanding case removed by additional counterclaim defendants).

[51] *In re* Crystal Power Co., Ltd., 641 F.3d 78, 80–81 (5th Cir. 2011) (crossclaim defendant may not remove because not "true defendant;" citing *Shamrock Oil & Gas Corp.*, 313 U.S. 100, 106, 61 S. Ct. 868, 85 L. Ed. 1214 (1941), in which Court held that counterclaim defendant may not remove).

[52] State of Texas v. Walker, 142 F.3d 813, 816 (5th Cir. 1998) (additional counterclaim defendant permitted to remove under § 1441(c)); *see* 28 U.S.C. § 1441(c).

alone, the counterclaim defendant may be permitted to remove under Section 1441(c).[53] For further discussion of removal under Section 1441(c), *see* § 6.08[5].

### [ii] Third-Party Defendants

There are myriad and diverging views on whether third-party defendants may remove an action. Some courts granting third-party defendants the right of removal hold that there should be no difference between defendants and third-party defendants.[54] Further, special removal statutes[55] may provide an independent basis for a third-party defendant seeking to remove certain types of cases.

Some courts hold that a third-party cause of action is not removable if the main claim could not have been originally filed in federal court and removal is based solely on the third-party claim.[56] Other courts prohibit third-party defendants from removing a case when the original defendants did not seek removal, under the theory that it would be unjust to permit a party not sued by the plaintiff to compel the plaintiff to try the case in a forum not of the plaintiff's choice.[57] Other courts consider the third-party cause of action to be merely incidental or ancillary to the main nonremovable claim and not a separate controversy.[58]

One court pointed out that some of the rationales for opposing third-party defendant removal may not apply to a third party defendant that has been impleaded by the plaintiff. In that case, the third-party defendant may be more like a traditional defendant, a party antagonistic to the plaintiff.[59] However, at least one other court held that a third-party defendant impleaded by a plaintiff/counterclaim-defendant cannot remove because the third-party defendant is not a

---

[53] State of Texas v. Walker, 142 F.3d 813, 816 (5th Cir. 1998) (university president was sued as additional counterclaim defendant by original defendant, who had been sued by university for alleged conversion and breach of contract; president was permitted to remove based on civil rights claims against him).

[54] *See* Motor Vehicle Cas. Co. v. Russian River County Sanitation Dist., 538 F. Supp. 488, 491–492 (N.D. Cal. 1981) (third-party defendant not deprived of removal rights based on accidental nature of being joined as third party rather than being initially named as defendant).

[55] *See* 16 Moore's Federal Practice Ch. 107, *Removal* (Matthew Bender 3d ed.).

[56] *See* Carl Heck Eng'rs, Inc. v. LaFourche Parish Police Jury, 622 F.2d 133, 135 (5th Cir. 1980) (such cases proceed on two theories: (1) treating impleaded third-party action as incidental to main action and not separable, and (2) holding it is unjust to permit party not sued by original plaintiff to compel plaintiff into forum not selected by plaintiff).

[57] *See* Thomas v. Shelton, 740 F.2d 478, 486–489 (7th Cir. 1984); Lewis v. Windsor Door Co., 926 F.2d 729, 732 (8th Cir. 1991).

[58] St. John's University v. Certain Underwriters at Lloyd's, 760 F. Supp. 2d 381, 383–384 (S.D.N.Y. 2011) (third-party defendants impleaded by insurer-defendant not permitted to remove action; because insurer-defendant's subrogee status would not accrue unless and until 18 plaintiffs in underlying suit recovered compensation from insured-plaintiff by settlement or judgment and insured-plaintiff recovered from insurer-defendant, "there is no pending case or controversy and no 'separate and independent' action on which to base a removal"); Hyde v. Carder, 310 F. Supp. 1340, 1342 (W.D. Ky. 1970) (impleaded third-party cause of action is incidental to main claim and not separable).

[59] Wiatt v. State Farm Ins. Co., 560 F. Supp. 2d 1068, 1077 (D.N.M. 2007) (citing Moore's Federal Practice; issue of whether third-party defendant may remove not decided, because third-party defendant did not establish diversity jurisdiction over claims against it).

defendant within the meaning of 28 U.S.C. § 1441.[60]

The better view, consistent with the principle that removal jurisdiction is to be strictly construed, is that third-party claims are not removable under the general removal statute because only a party defending against non-derivative claims asserted by the original plaintiff ought to be able to remove. If the original defendant had no right to remove, or chose not to, an impleaded defendant should not be permitted to remove, absent express statutory authority. As in the case of counterclaims and cross-claims, third-party defendants are not *defendants* within the meaning of the removal statute (subject to the caveats discussed in [a], *above*).[61]

#### [iii] Defendant Intervenors

Assuming that the original action would have been removable, and if the time for removing an action has not passed, and the original defendants join in the notice of removal or may be disregarded for removal purposes, the action may be removable by an intervening defendant.[62] On the other hand, consistent with the analysis above, if the sole basis for removing the action is the claim raised through the intervention of the intervening defendant, the intervener may not remove the action.[63]

### [c] Generally All Defendants Must Join in Removal

When a defendant removes under the general removal statute, all defendants must join in the notice of removal.[64] This joining requirement is satisfied if, for example, a defendant who did not join in the properly filed removal notice files a written consent to removal within the statutory time for filing the notice of

---

[60] Garnas v. American Farm Equip. Co., 502 F. Supp. 349, 351 n. 7 (D.N.D. 1980) (citing Moore's Federal Practice; based on pre-1990 and 2011 amendment to § 1441(c)).

[61] FirstBank P.R. v. Gittens, 466 F. Supp. 2d 614, 617–621 (D.V.I. 2006) (citing Moore's Federal Practice; 28 U.S.C. § 1441(a) unambiguously limits removal to defendant, which means initial defendant or defendant against whom plaintiff has asserted claim); First Nat'l Bank of Pulaski v. Curry, 301 F.3d 456, 462–467 (6th Cir. 2002) (citing Moore's Federal Practice; Sixth Circuit adopted majority view that third party defendants are not "defendants" for purposes of 28 U.S.C. § 1441(a)); Penn v. Pierce, 2008 U.S. Dist. LEXIS 73890, at *1–*2 (M.D. Ala. Sept. 25, 2008) (citing Moore's Federal Practice for "better view" that third-party claims are not removable).

[62] McKinney Econ. Dev. Corp. v. McKinney Shores Props., Inc., 2010 U.S. Dist. LEXIS 103680 (E.D. Tx. Aug. 27, 2010) (quoting Moore's Federal Practice); *see also* First Indep. Bank v. Trendventures, L.L.C., 2008 U.S. Dist. LEXIS 6577 (E.D. Mich. Jan. 30, 2008).

[63] McKinney Econ. Dev. Corp. v. McKinney Shores Props., Inc., 2010 U.S. Dist. LEXIS 103680 (E.D. Tx. Aug. 27, 2010) (quoting Moore's Federal Practice); Hopkins Erecting Co. v. Briarwood Apartments, 517 F. Supp. 243, 248 (E.D. Ky. 1981).

[64] 28 U.S.C. § 1446(b); *see* Chicago, Rock Island & Pac. Ry. v. Martin, 178 U.S. 245, 248 (1900); Esposito v. Home Depot U.S.A., Inc., 590 F.3d 72, 75 (1st Cir. 2009) (either unanimity requirement was satisfied by defendant's answer in federal court or lack of unanimity was cured by defendant's opposition to remand); Downey v. Ambassador Development, LLC, 568 F. Supp. 2d 28, 29–31 (D.D.C. 2008) (dissolved limited liability company named as defendant was required to join in removal because under applicable District of Columbia law, dissolved company may be subject to suit, and dissolved company had capacity to retain counsel and engage in winding up process; case remanded). See generally § 6.09.

removal.[65]

Although generally all defendants must join in the notice of removal, nominal or formal parties are not required to join in the notice.[66] "Nominal" has been defined in various ways. A party will be characterized as nominal if there is no possibility the plaintiff would be able to establish a cause of action against the party.[67] Similarly, other courts have stated that a defendant is nominal if there is no reasonable basis to impose,[68] or legal possibility of,[69] legal liability. Those against whom no real relief is sought have also been considered nominal.[70]

Additionally, any defendant that was not served with state court process need not join in the notice of removal.[71]

This unanimity requirement serves the interests of plaintiffs, defendants, and the courts. It benefits plaintiffs by preventing defendants from splitting the litigation, forcing the plaintiff to pursue the case in two separate forums. It benefits defendants by precluding one defendant from imposing its forum choice on codefendants. And it helps courts by preventing needless duplication of litigation.[72]

Although all courts agree generally on the requirement of unanimity, the circuits are split as to exactly what form a co-defendant's consent must take. The statute itself does not speak directly to this issue, stating only, "A defendant or defendants desiring to remove any civil action . . . from a State court shall file in the [appropriate] district court of the United States a notice of removal signed pursuant to Rule 11 of the Federal Rules of Civil Procedure . . . ."[73] It is clear from this language that a defendant may express its desire to remove by signing the notice of removal filed by co-defendants, but most circuits hold that something less explicit

---

[65] *See, e.g.*, Adams v. Lederle Lab., 569 F. Supp. 234, 243, 246 (W.D. Mo. 1983) (joinder rule does not include nondomiciliary defendants not served at time of removal; each defendant served before removal has 30 days after service of complaint on him or her to join in or consent to removal); Albonetti v. GAF Corp. Chem. Group, 520 F. Supp. 825, 828 (S.D. Tex. 1981) (joinder rule satisfied if all defendants served on or before removal notice thereafter timely file own removal notice, or written joinder in or consents to removal).

[66] *See, e.g.*, Northern Ill. Gas Co. v. Airco Indus. Gases, 676 F.2d 270, 272–273 (7th Cir. 1982); *see* Wilson v. Oswego Township, 151 U.S. 56, 64 (1894) (joinder or nonjoinder of formal parties does not defeat diversity).

[67] *See, e.g.*, Norman v. Cuomo, 796 F. Supp. 654, 658 (N.D.N.Y. 1992) (non-joining defendants were nominal in suit concerning state legislative district boundaries because declaration against them would provide no relief to plaintiffs).

[68] *See, e.g.*, Shaw v. Dow Brands, Inc., 994 F.2d 364, 369 (7th Cir. 1993) (parent corporation that had no connection with manufacture, sale, or distribution of product at issue probably nominal).

[69] *See, e.g.*, Creed v. Commonwealth of Virginia, 596 F. Supp. 2d 930, 935 (E.D. Va. 2009) (Commonwealth not necessarily nominal party in suit concerning death of prisoner).

[70] *See, e.g.*, Thorn v. Amalgamated Transit Union, 305 F.3d 826, 833 (9th Cir. 2002) (international union was nominal party in suit against local).

[71] *See* Murphy Bros., Inc. v. Michetti Pipe Stringing, Inc., 526 U.S. 344, 350 (1999) (". . . one becomes a party officially, and is required to take action in that capacity, only upon service of a summons or other authority-asserting measure stating the time within which the party served must appear and defend").

[72] *See* Esposito v. Home Depot U.S.A., Inc., 590 F.3d 72, 75 (1st Cir. 2009).

[73] 28 U.S.C. § 1446(a).

than actually signing the notice will suffice.[74]

The failure of all defendants to join in the removal notice constitutes a procedural defect.[75] If the defect is not objected to within 30 days, most courts properly hold that objection to the defect is deemed waived.[76] The district court may enable the removing defendants to cure the defect by allowing all served defendants to join in the removal notice prior to entry of judgment.[77] Under the *Grubbs* rule, the existence of subject matter jurisdiction at the time of judgment ordinarily cures any defect in removal procedure.[78] However, when the trial court's judgment must be reversed on the merits and the case remanded to the trial court for further proceedings, the rationale of efficiency, judicial economy, and the interest in finality of judgments that underlies the *Grubbs* rule does not apply and the case should be remanded to state court.[79]

If, on the other hand, removal is based on a federal question claim that is joined to a claim that is not within the original or supplemental jurisdiction of the district court or a claim that has been made nonremovable by statute, only the defendants to the federal question claim need join in or consent to the removal.[80] Similarly, if removal is based on a specific statutory authorization for removal, only those defendants who are defendants to the removable claim must join in the removal

---

[74] *See* Esposito v. Home Depot U.S.A., Inc., 590 F.3d 72, 76 (1st Cir. 2009) (gathering cases concerning satisfaction of unanimity requirement); Pietrangelo v. Alvas Corp., 686 F.3d 62, 66 (2d Cir. 2012) (defendants satisfied requirement of independently expressing consent to removal by submitting letters to court within 30-day removal period, despite letters' noncompliance with local format rules); Pritchett v. Cottrell, Inc., 512 F.3d 1057, 1062 (8th Cir. 2008) ("[E]ach defendant need not necessarily sign the notice of removal" (citation omitted)). *See* 16 Moore's Federal Practice Ch. 107, § 107.11[1][c].

[75] *See* Flagler v. Budget Rent a Car System, Inc., 538 F. Supp. 2d 557, 558 n. 1 (E.D.N.Y. 2008) (plaintiff waived objection based on failure of all defendants to join notice of removal); Page v. City of Southfield, 45 F.3d 128, 133 (6th Cir. 1995) (district court may not remand sua sponte based on violation of rule of unanimity); Loftis v. United Parcel Serv., Inc., 342 F.3d 509, 516–517 (6th Cir. 2003) (co-defendant's opposition to removal and timely motion to remand empowered district court to enforce unanimity requirement even though parties did not raise it); McMahon v. Bunn-O-Matic Corp., 150 F.3d 651, 653–654 (7th Cir. 1998) (failure of all defendants to join in removal is procedural defect).

[76] *See* McMahon v. Bunn-O-Matic Corp., 150 F.3d 651, 653–654 (7th Cir. 1998) (defect in removal procedure other than lack of subject matter jurisdiction is forfeited if not raised within 30 days of removal; failure of all defendants to join in removal was waived absent timely objection); Parrino v. FHP, Inc., 146 F.3d 699, 703 (9th Cir. 1998) (failure of one defendant to join in removal notice until almost two months after service of complaint is procedural defect that was cured by joinder; because procedural defect was cured before entry of judgment, reversal and remand were not warranted).

[77] Destfino v. Reiswig, 630 F.3d 952, 957 (9th Cir. 2011) (if not all properly served defendants join in removal petition, district court may enable removing defendants to cure defect by allowing all served defendants to join in removal notice prior to entry of judgment).

[78] *See* Grubbs v. General Elec. Credit Corp., 405 U.S. 699, 702 (1972).

[79] *See* Marshall v. Manville Sales Corp., 6 F.3d 229, 231–232 (4th Cir. 1993) (summary judgment reversed and case remanded to district court to remand to state court for wrongful removal); Prize Frize, Inc. v. Matrix (U.S.) Inc., 167 F.3d 1261, 1265–1267 (9th Cir. 1999) (citing Moore's Federal Practice; removal was procedurally defective when removal notice plainly admitted on its face that not all defendants had joined; district court ordered to remand to state court following reversal of judgment of dismissal).

[80] 28 U.S.C. § 1441(c)(2). *See* § 6.08[5].

notice.[81] Further, any single defendant, even a local defendant, may seek removal in multistate class actions covered by the Class Action Fairness Act of 2005.[82] Similarly, not all defendants need join in removal of a case pursuant to the Multiparty, Multiforum Trial Jurisdiction Act.[83] For more discussion on removal procedures, see § 6.09.

### [3] Removing Defendants Have Burden of Proving Removal Is Proper

The removing defendant bears the burden of establishing federal jurisdiction,[84] and ordinarily the existence of federal jurisdiction must be determined from the face of the plaintiff's complaint.[85] It is the party who urges jurisdiction that bears the burden of demonstrating that the case is one that is properly before the federal tribunal.[86] In addition, the removing defendant bears the burden of establishing that the defendant complied with the removal procedures.[87]

However, the courts are divided as to whether the Class Action Fairness Act of 2005 (CAFA)[88] shifted the burden of establishing federal jurisdiction in CAFA removal cases,[89] with most holding that the burden remains with the party

---

[81] *See, e.g.*, Dillon v. Mississippi Military Dep't, 23 F.3d 915, 919 (5th Cir. 1994) (federal officer removal); Davis v. FSLIC, 879 F.2d 1288, 1289 (5th Cir. 1989) (FSLIC removal); Ely Valley Mines, Inc. v. Hartford Accident & Indem. Co., 644 F.2d 1310, 1314–1315 (9th Cir. 1981) (federal officer removal); Akin v. Ashland Chem. Co., 156 F.3d 1030, 1034–1035 (10th Cir. 1998) (federal officer removal; result unaffected by fact that removal also was supported by federal question jurisdiction as action arose from incidents occurring on air force base).

[82] P.L. No. 109-2, 119 Stat. 4; 28 U.S.C. § 1453(b) (class actions removed under the Class Action Fairness Act of 2005 do not require the consent of all defendants); *see* § 6.08[6].

[83] Pettitt v. Boeing Co., 606 F.3d 340, 343 (7th Cir. 2010) (removal under MMTJA does not require joinder of all defendants); *see* 28 U.S.C. § 1441(e)(1) ("a defendant may . . . remove . . . if the action could have been brought . . . under section 1369" (emphasis added)).

[84] Wilson v. Republic Iron & Steel Co., 257 U.S. 92, 97 (1921); *See* Meritcare Inc. v. St. Paul Mercury Ins. Co., 166 F.3d 214, 222 (3d Cir. 1999); Long v. Bando Mfg. of Am., Inc., 201 F.3d 754, 757 (6th Cir. 2000) (party seeking removal bears burden of showing district court jurisdiction); Kanter v. Warner-Lambert Co., 265 F.3d 853, 857–858 (9th Cir. 2001) (citing MOORE'S FEDERAL PRACTICE; defendant's failure to specify plaintiff's citizenship, not stated in complaint or notice of removal, is fatal to assertion of diversity citizenship and removal); Prize Frize, Inc. v. Matrix (U.S.) Inc., 167 F.3d 1261, 1265 (9th Cir. 1999) (burden of establishing federal jurisdiction is on party seeking removal; removal statute strictly construed against removal).

[85] Westinghouse Elec. Corp. v. Newman & Holtzinger, P.C., 992 F.2d 932, 934 (9th Cir. 1993); *see* Ch. 4, *Diversity Jurisdiction*.

[86] *See* Meyerson v. Showboat Marina Casino P'ship, 312 F.3d 318, 321 (7th Cir. 2002) (defendants' repeated failures to establish diversity of citizenship warranted remand and order to show cause against imposition of sanctions); United Computer Sys., Inc. v. AT&T Info. Sys., Inc., 298 F.3d 756, 763 (9th Cir. 2002) (corporate defendants met burden of proof by submitting affidavits of knowledgeable company officials specifying state of incorporation and providing statistics showing number of corporate employees, income, sales, and location of top management).

[87] Parker v. Brown, 570 F. Supp. 640, 642 (S.D. Ohio 1983) (burden goes to issue of federal jurisdiction and to issues of compliance with statutes governing right of removal); Burns v. Windsor Ins. Co., 31 F.3d 1092, 1094–1095 (11th Cir. 1994).

[88] P.L. No. 109-2, § 4.

[89] *See* 28 U.S.C. §§ 1332(d)(10), 1453(b).

choosing federal court[90] and a few holding that the party opposing removal bears the initial burden of demonstrating that the action should be remanded.[91] For further discussion, *see* § 6.08[6].

## [4] Defendant's Waiver of Right to Remove

### [a] Forum Selection Clauses

A defendant may waive the right to remove a case from state to federal court by a contractual forum selection clause.[92] Forum selection clauses are prima facie valid and are enforceable absent a clear showing that enforcement would be unjust or unreasonable,[93] or that the clause is invalid because of fraud, undue influence, overreaching, undue bargaining power, or the like.[94] This principle of prima facie validity is equally applicable to international forum selection clauses and to domestic forum selection clauses.[95] In a diversity case, state law governs the enforceability of a contractual forum selection clause on a motion for remand.[96]

---

[90] *See* Blockbuster, Inc. v. Galeno, 472 F.3d 53, 57–58 (2d Cir. 2006); Morgan v. Gay, 471 F.3d 469, 472–473 (3d Cir. 2006); Strawn v. AT & T Mobility LLC, 530 F.3d 293, 297–298 (6th Cir. 2008); Werner v. KPMG LLP, 415 F. Supp. 2d 688, 694–695 (S.D. Tex. 2006); Brill v. Countrywide Home Loans, Inc., 427 F.3d 446, 447 (7th Cir. 2005); Abrego v. Dow Chem. Co., 443 F.3d 676, 683–686 (9th Cir. 2006).

[91] *See* Natale v. Pfizer, Inc., 379 F. Supp. 2d 161 (D.Mass. 2005), *aff'd on other grounds*, 424 F.3d 43 (1st Cir. 2005); Harvey v. Blockbuster, Inc., 384 F. Supp. 2d 749, 752 (D.N.J. 2005); *but see* Morgan v. Gay, 471 F.3d 469, 472–473 (3d Cir. 2006) ("It should take more than a few lines in a Senate Judiciary Committee Report and some vague language in a statute's 'Findings and Purposes' section to reverse the well-established proposition that the party seeking removal carries the jurisdiction-proving burden.").

[92] *See* National Equipment Rental, Ltd. v. Szukhent, 375 U.S. 311, 315–316 (1964) (contractual designation of agent for service of process constitutes consent to jurisdiction); Yakin v. Tyler Hill Corp., 566 F.3d 72, 76 (2d Cir. 2009) ("Parties are free to bind themselves to forum selection clauses that trump what would otherwise be a right to remove cases to federal courts"); New Jersey v. Merrill Lynch & Co., Inc., 640 F.3d 545, 547 (3d Cir. 2011) (forum selection clause providing "exclusive jurisdiction . . . shall lie in the appropriate courts of the State [of] New Jersey" waived defendant's right to remove case to federal court in New Jersey); Waters v. Browning-Ferris Indus., Inc., 252 F.3d 796, 797 (5th Cir. 2001); Ocwen Orlando Holdings Corp. v. Harvard Property Trust, LLC, 526 F.3d 1379, 1381 (11th Cir. 2008) (forum selection clauses interpreted according to ordinary contract principles and may constitute waivers of right to remove).

[93] Carnival Cruise Lines, Inc. v. Shute, 499 U.S. 585, 595 (1991); M/S Bremen v. Zapata Off-Shore Co., 407 U.S. 1, 5, 10, 15–19 (1972) (applicable standard for federal courts sitting in admiralty; defendant filing to limit liability not a waiver). *See* New Jersey v. Merrill Lynch & Co., Inc., 640 F.3d 545, 547 (3d Cir. 2011) (contractual waivers of right to remove usually upheld if reasonable and voluntary and enforcement is not inconsistent with public policy).

[94] Carnival Cruise Lines, Inc. v. Shute, 499 U.S. 585, 595 (1991); M/S Bremen v. Zapata Off-Shore Co., 407 U.S. 1, 12–15 (1972).

[95] Carnival Cruise Lines, Inc. v. Shute, 499 U.S. 585, 594–597 (1991).

[96] *See* Autoridad de Energia Electrica de P.R. v. Ericsson, Inc., 201 F.3d 15, 18 (1st Cir. 2000) (applying law of Puerto Rico to determine enforceability of forum selection clause); Roberts & Schaefer Co. v. Merit Contracting, Inc., 99 F.3d 248, 254 (7th Cir. 1996); *see* Ch. 9, *Change of Venue*. For extensive discussion of forum selection clauses, *see* 17 MOORE'S FEDERAL PRACTICE Ch. 111, *Change of Venue* (Matthew Bender 3d ed.).

The forum selection clause claimed to amount to a waiver of the right to remove must be clear and unequivocal[97] and must contain obligatory language that mandates a particular forum as the exclusive forum for the resolution of any dispute between the parties.[98]

A remand order based on the enforceability of a forum selection clause is not a statutory remand and therefore review is not barred under Section 1447(c) (*see* § 6.13).[99]

### [b] Other Methods of Waiving Right to Remove

A defendant may waive the right to remove a state court action to federal court by failing to file the removal notice within the statutory time limits (see § 6.09).[100] A defendant also may waive the right to remove a state court action to federal court by taking actions in state court, after it is apparent that the case is removable, that manifest the defendant's intent to (1) have the case adjudicated in state court and (2) abandon the right to a federal forum.[101] However, an intent to waive the right to remove to federal court and to submit to state court jurisdiction must be clear and unequivocal, and the defendant's actions must be inconsistent with the right to remove. For example, the following acts, when taken by a defendant, constitute a waiver of the defendant's right to remove to federal court: (1) participating in state court proceedings, such as seeking some form of affirmative relief, when the defendant is not compelled to take the action;[102] (2) moving in state court to compel arbitration;[103] (3) filing a motion to dismiss the state court complaint;[104] (4)

---

[97] Capital Bank & Trust Co. v. Associated Int'l Ins. Co., 576 F. Supp. 1522, 1524 (M.D. La. 1984) (waiver was clear and unequivocal when purpose of choice of forum clause was to compel defendant insurer to submit to insured's choice of forum).

[98] *See* Autoridad de Energia Electrica de P.R. v. Ericsson Inc., 201 F.3d 15, 18 (1st Cir. 2000) (no waiver in contract stating that parties agree to submit to jurisdiction of Puerto Rican courts); Dixon v. TSE Int'l Inc., 330 F.3d 396, 397 (5th Cir. 2003) (contract providing that "Courts *of* Texas" have jurisdiction waives right to remove to federal court); Waters v. Browning-Ferris Indus., Inc., 252 F.3d 796, 797–798 (5th Cir. 2001) (waiver when contract provision makes it unequivocally clear that other party has right to choose the forum in which any dispute will be heard).

[99] *See* 28 U.S.C. § 1447(c), (d); *see, e.g.*, Autoridad de Energia Electrica de P.R. v. Ericsson, Inc., 201 F.3d 15, 16–18 (1st Cir. 2000) (review of remand order based on forum selection clause is not barred by § 1447(c)); Yakin v. Tyler Hill Corp., 566 F.3d 72, 75 (2d Cir. 2009) (rationale behind § 1447(d)'s nonreviewability rule (prevention of delay) is not applicable when district court with subject-matter jurisdiction remands case on basis of its interpretation of forum-selection clause); New Jersey v. Merrill Lynch & Co., Inc., 640 F.3d 545, 547 (3d Cir. 2011) (remand based on contractual waiver of right to remove in forum selection clause is reviewable).

[100] *See* 28 U.S.C. 1446(b); *see generally* 16 Moore's Federal Practice Ch. 107, *Removal* (Matthew Bender 3d ed.).

[101] George v. Al-Saud, 478 F. Supp. 773, 774 (N.D. Cal. 1979).

[102] Virginia Beach Resort & Conference Ctr. Hotel Ass'n Condominium v. Certain Interested Underwriters at Lloyd's, 812 F. Supp. 2d 762, 764–767 (E.D. Va. 2011) (defendant waived right to remove by filing permissive counterclaim in state court after removability became clear and eight days before filing notice of removal; under facts of this case, filing of counterclaim demonstrated clear and unequivocal intention to remain in state court); Zbranek v. Hofheinz, 727 F. Supp. 324, 325 (E.D. Tex. 1989) (seeking injunction and moving for summary judgment); Isaacs v. Group Health, Inc., 668 F. Supp. 306, 308–309 (S.D.N.Y. 1987) (filing permissive cross-complaint).

[103] McKinnon v. Doctor's Assocs., Inc., 769 F. Supp. 216, 220 (E.D. Mi. 1991).

continuing with the state court trial when the case became removable early in the proceedings;[105] (5) seeking a continuance in state court, without notifying the plaintiff or the state court of the intention to remove the case in interim;[106] (6) arguing and losing an issue in state court — removal in this situation would operate as an appeal of an adverse state court decision;[107] or (7) participating in state court proceedings before formally entering an appearance in the case.[108]

Because an intent to waive the right to remove to federal court and to submit to state court jurisdiction must be clear, the following acts, when taken by a defendant, do not constitute a waiver of the defendant's right to remove to federal court: (1) filing a pleading, such as an answer or demurrer, or other pleading raising a defense that might be conclusive on the merits;[109] (2) opposing a motion for a temporary restraining order[110] or a motion for a preliminary injunction;[111] (3) opposing certification of a class in a class action suit on procedural grounds;[112] (4) failing to remove a previous action based on the same claim;[113] or (5) appointing an agent for service of process in the state where the action is pending.[114]

---

[104] Scholz v. RDV Sports, Inc., 821 F. Supp. 1469, 1470–1471 (M.D. Fla. 1993).

[105] Aynesworth v. Beech Aircraft Corp., 604 F. Supp. 630, 637 (W.D. Tex. 1985) (defendant removed after jury deliberations resulted in mistrial).

[106] Chicago Title & Trust Co. v. Whitney Stores, Inc., 583 F. Supp. 575, 577 (N.D. Ill. 1984) (if defendant disclosed intention to remove, plaintiff and court might have acted differently).

[107] Rosenthal v. Coates, 148 U.S. 142, 147 (1893) (defendant may not experiment in state court and appeal adverse decision in federal court); Hill v. Citicorp, 804 F. Supp. 514, 516–517 (S.D.N.Y. 1992) (filing and litigating motion to dismiss, arguing forum non conveniens); Estate of Krasnow v. Texaco, Inc., 773 F. Supp. 806, 808–809 (E.D. Va. 1991) (state court ruling on defendant's demurrer constitutes waiver; one defendant's waiver precluded removal by other defendants); Kiddie Rides USA, Inc. v. Elektro-Mobiltechnik GMBH, 579 F. Supp. 1476 (C.D. Ill. 1984) (defendant removed to appeal adverse ruling on motion to vacate attachment order).

[108] FDIC v. First Mortgage Investors, 459 F. Supp. 880, 882 (E.D. Wis. 1978) (removing defendant conducted state defense from behind the scenes; as a constructive party, defendant consented to state court jurisdiction).

[109] Cogdell v. Wyeth, 366 F.3d 1245, 1249 (11th Cir. 2004) (filing of motion to dismiss in state court does not waive removal rights if case is removed before state court can rule on motion and defendant takes no additional steps to have state court rule on motion before removal); Yusefzadeh v. Nelson, Mullins, Riley & Scarborough, LLP, 365 F.3d 1244, 1246–1247 (11th Cir. 2004) (motion to dismiss in state court does not waive defendant's removal rights if state procedural rules require filing of responsive pleadings before removal deadline).

[110] Rose v. Giamatti, 721 F. Supp. 906, 922 (S.D. Ohio 1989).

[111] Miami Herald Publ'g Co. v. Ferre, 606 F. Supp. 122, 124 (S.D. Fla. 1984).

[112] Adams v. Lederle Lab., 569 F. Supp. 234, 246–247 (W.D. Mo. 1983).

[113] Baker v. Firestone Tire & Rubber Co., 537 F. Supp. 244, 247 (S.D. Fla. 1982) (plaintiff voluntarily dismissed earlier personal injury action).

[114] Wright v. Continental Cas. Co., 456 F. Supp. 1075, 1079 (M.D. Fla. 1978).

## § 6.06 CASES ORIGINALLY FILED IN "STATE COURT" MAY BE REMOVED

Only cases originally filed and pending in state court may be removed.[115] The term *state court* includes the superior court of the District of Columbia, and the term *state* includes the District of Columbia.[116] In most circuits, whether a particular state tribunal is a *state court* for removal purposes depends on the tribunal's function, not on the name of the tribunal.[117] For example, if a tribunal is labeled as an administrative board, but the proceeding before it is judicial in nature, such as a contract action, the proceeding may be removable.[118] Even when the state agency's administrative findings are subject to deferential on-the-record review, the case may be removable.[119] Some circuits, on the other hand, have rejected the functional test in favor of a straightforward approach based on the clear, unambiguous language of Section 1441. In these circuits, removal is permitted only from an actual state court, not from an administrative agency or other entity that conducts court-like adjudications.[120] This comports with the principle that removal statutes should be strictly construed to limit, not expand, federal jurisdiction.[121]

Whether the court has limited or general jurisdiction is irrelevant to the question of whether a state judicial body is a *state court* for removal purposes. For example, a justice of the peace court is a state court.[122] However, the term *state court* does not include tribal courts.[123]

---

[115] 28 U.S.C. §§ 1441(a), 1446(a); Ristuccia v. Adams, 406 F.2d 1257, 1258 (9th Cir. 1969).

[116] 28 U.S.C. § 1451.

[117] Upshur County v. Rich, 135 U.S. 467 (1890); Volkswagen de Puerto Rico, Inc. v. Puerto Rico Labor Relations Bd., 454 F.2d 38 (1st Cir. 1972).

[118] Wirtz v. United Distillers & Vintners, N. Am., Inc., 224 F.3d 708, 710–714 (7th Cir. 2000) (applying functional analysis to determine that Illinois Liquor Control Commission, from which action had been removed to federal court, was not state court was not state court, because its powers were different from powers of courts and competing interests weighed against removal); Floeter v. C.W. Transp., Inc., 597 F.2d 1100, 1102 (7th Cir. 1979).

[119] City of Chicago v. International College of Surgeons, 522 U.S. 156 (1997) (The Supreme Court held that a case raising federal claims and state claims calling for review of deferential on-the-record administrative findings was removable.).

[120] *See, e.g.*, Or. Bureau of Labor & Indus. *ex rel.* Richardson v. U.S. West Communs., Inc., 288 F.3d 414, 417–420 (9th Cir. 2002) (functional test rejected, because plain language of § 1441 does not authorize removal of proceedings from administrative agency, regardless of how court-like proceedings may be); Porter Trust v. Rural Water Sewer & Solid Waste Mgmt. Dist. No. 1, 607 F.3d 1251, 1254–1255 (10th Cir. 2010) (applying plain language of § 1441(a) rather than functional test, court held that county board of county commissioners was not "state court" for purposes of § 1441(a), even though it exercised judicial function in de-annexation proceedings).

[121] Oregon Bureau of Labor & Indus. *ex rel.* Richardson v. U.S. West Communs., Inc., 288 F.3d 414, 417–420 (9th Cir. 2002) (functional test improperly expands federal removal jurisdiction).

[122] Katz v. Herschel Mfg. Co., 150 F. 684 (D. Neb. 1906).

[123] Becenti v. Vigil, 902 F.2d 777 (10th Cir. 1990) (tribal action against federal official may not be removed to federal court under 28 U.S.C. § 1442(a)(1), which permits removal of actions from "state courts," because tribal court is not state court).

Most of the statutes providing for removal apply to "civil actions."[124] Proceedings that occur before a civil action is filed have been held not to fall within the scope of removal jurisdiction. For example, courts have held that a proceeding to obtain a court order to take a pre-suit investigatory deposition under state law is not a "civil action" subject to removal.[125] It would be difficult for a federal court to determine with any certainty whether it had federal question or diversity jurisdiction over such a petition, because such petitions do not articulate a specific claim against a particular defendant and do not necessarily even lead to an actual suit.[126] However, the federal official removal statute was amended in 2011 to specify that a proceeding in which a judicial order, including a subpoena for testimony or documents, is sought or issued against the United States, a federal agency, or a federal officer is removable regardless of whether it is ancillary to another proceeding.[127]

Before the enactment of the Judicial Improvements Act of 1985,[128] the doctrine of *derivative jurisdiction* required that, for proper removal, the state court in which the action was initiated must have subject matter jurisdiction over the action. Under this doctrine, removal jurisdiction was derivative, and the federal court could not

---

[124] *See* 28 U.S.C. § 1441(a) (general removal statute; "any civil action . . . may be removed . . ."); 28 U.S.C. § 1442(a) (federal officer or agency removal; "A civil action or criminal prosecution . . . may be removed . . . "); 28 U.S.C. § 1443 (removal of civil rights cases; "Any of the following civil actions or criminal prosecutions . . . may be removed . . . "); 28 U.S.C. § 1452(a) (bankruptcy removal; "A party may remove any claim or cause of action in a civil action . . . "); 28 U.S.C. § 1453 ("A class action may be removed . . . "); *see also* 28 U.S.C. § 1442a ("civil or criminal prosecution" against member of armed forces removable); 28 U.S.C. § 1444 (removal of foreclosure "action" against United States); *but see* 9 U.S.C. § 205 (removal of "action or proceeding" relating to arbitration); 12 U.S.C. § 1819(b)(2)(B) (Federal Deposit Insurance Corporation "may . . . remove any action, suit or proceeding . . . "); *see also* 28 U.S.C. § 1442(c) ("civil action" and "criminal prosecution" include proceedings in which judicial order is sought or issued).

[125] Mayfield-George v. Texas Rehab. Comm'n, 197 F.R.D. 280, 283 (N.D. Tex. 2000) (petition seeking depositions to investigate whether petitioners had cause of action against Texas Rehabilitation Commission in connection with alleged assault by vocation counselor remanded to state court because it was "not a 'civil action' under § 1441(b)" because it asserted no claim or cause of action on which relief could be granted, and even if it was a "civil action," it was not action over which federal courts had original jurisdiction); McCrary v. Kan. City S. Ry. Co., 121 F. Supp. 2d 566, 569 (E.D. Tex. 2000) (because pre-suit petition for deposition under Texas Rules of Civil Procedure is not "civil action" subject to removal, petition does not start 30-day time limit for removal); *see* Price v. Johnson, 600 F.3d 460, 462 (5th Cir. 2010) (proceeding under Tex. R. Civ. P. 202.1, seeking order to take pre-suit investigatory deposition, remanded by district court because proceeding was not "civil action" within meaning of 28 U.S.C. § 1442 (federal officer removal); remand order unreviewable because it was based on subject matter jurisdiction).

[126] Davidson v. Southern Farm Bureau Cas. Ins. Co., 2006 U.S. Dist. LEXIS 40654, at *5–*10 (S.D. Tex. June 19, 2006) (proceeding involving petition to take pre-suit deposition remanded; "it would be difficult for a federal court to determine, with any certainty, that it has federal question or diversity jurisdiction over a Rule 202 petition, since the petition articulates no specific claims against any particular civil defendants."); *but see* Cornyn v. Real Parties in Interest, 110 F. Supp. 2d 514, 518–522 (E.D. Tex. 2000) (term "civil action" in removal statutes is intended to distinguish civil proceedings from criminal ones; Tex. R. Civ. P. 202 proceeding is "civil action" subject to removal because it possesses all elements of judicial proceeding, namely, (1) controversy between parties, (2) pleadings, (3) request for relief, and (4) requirement of judicial determination).

[127] 28 U.S.C. § 1442.

[128] Pub. L. No. 99-336, 100 Stat. 633 (1986).

acquire jurisdiction if none existed in state court.[129] The Judicial Improvements Act of 1985 added a new subsection to the general removal statute, removing this jurisdictional roadblock. Thus, a federal court is not precluded from hearing and determining any claim in a civil action because the state court from which the action was removed lacked jurisdiction over the claim.[130]

## § 6.07 CASES MUST BE REMOVED TO FEDERAL DISTRICT COURT FOR DISTRICT AND DIVISION EMBRACING STATE COURT ACTION

A defendant seeking to remove an action from state court must file a notice of removal in the federal district court for the district and division within which the state action is pending.[131] Venue principles applicable to actions originally filed in the federal courts have no applicability to removed actions. Accordingly, it is irrelevant that venue would not have been proper under the general venue statute[132] in the district to which a case is properly removed.[133] Removal of a case to the wrong district court is a procedural defect that does not deprive the district court of subject matter jurisdiction.[134] However, on removal, any party may seek a transfer under the change of venue statutes.[135]

## § 6.08 FEDERAL DISTRICT COURT MUST HAVE ORIGINAL JURISDICTION OVER REMOVED CASE

### [1] "Original Jurisdiction" Defined

An action filed in state court may not be removed unless the federal district courts have original jurisdiction of the action.[136] First, the federal court must be presented with a case or controversy within the meaning of Article III to establish original jurisdiction to allow removal (*see* Ch. 2 *Issues of Justiciability*).[137] It is important to note that state courts may have more liberal standing requirements for bringing state law claims than Article III would permit. If a plaintiff has standing under such state rules, but lacks Article III standing, the case is not

---

129 Lambert Run Coal Co. v. Baltimore & Ohio R.R. Co., 258 U.S. 377, 382 (1922); McClellan v. Kimball, 623 F.2d 83, 86 (9th Cir. 1980).

130 28 U.S.C. § 1441(f); *see* Sorosky v. Burroughs Corp., 826 F.2d 794, 801 (9th Cir. 1987).

131 28 U.S.C. § 1446(a).

132 28 U.S.C. § 1391. *See* Ch. 8, Venue.

133 Polizzi v. Cowles Magazines, Inc., 345 U.S. 663, 665–666 (1953).

134 Peterson v. BMI Refractories, 124 F.3d 1386, 1388, 1394 (11th Cir. 1997).

135 *See* Ch. 9, *Change of Venue*.

136 28 U.S.C. § 1441(a). *See, e.g.*, Hollis v. Florida State Univ., 259 F.3d 1295, 1299–1300 (11th Cir. 2001) (district court had jurisdiction over removed case notwithstanding defect in state court's jurisdiction over suit as originally filed).

137 Lee v. American Nat'l Ins Co., 260 F.3d 997, 1002–1005 (9th Cir. 2001) (case not removable if no case or controversy presented).

removable.[138] If the plaintiff does not have Article III standing, the case must be remanded, not dismissed.[139]

Second, a federal court only has *original jurisdiction* over any case for which Congress has provided for original federal subject matter jurisdiction. Most removed cases involve diversity of citizenship (*see* Ch. 4 and [2], *below*) or federal questions (*see* Ch. 3 and [3], *below*).[140] A complete analysis of the subject matter jurisdiction of the federal district courts is contained in MOORE'S FEDERAL PRACTICE Ch. 102, *Diversity Jurisdiction*; Ch. 103, *Federal Question Jurisdiction*; Ch. 104, *Specific Grants of Federal Question Jurisdiction*; Ch. 105, *Other Subject Matter Jurisdiction Statutes*; Ch. 106, *Supplemental Jurisdiction*; and Ch. 120, *Dual State and Federal Judicial Structure* (Matthew Bender 3d ed.).

## [2] Diversity of Citizenship Cases

### [a] "Diversity Jurisdiction" Defined

A district court has *diversity jurisdiction* over any civil action in which the amount in controversy exceeds the sum or value of $75,000, exclusive of interest and costs (*see* [g], *below*; *see* § 6.08[6] for a discussion of liberalized provisions for the removal of class actions),[141] and the action is between:[142]

- Citizens of different states;[143]
- Citizens of a state and citizens or subjects of a foreign state;[144]
- Citizens of different states, with foreign citizens or subjects as additional parties; [145]or
- A foreign state as plaintiff and citizens of a state or of different states as defendants.[146]

Federal courts' diversity jurisdiction is not exclusive; rather, generally, it is concurrent with that of state courts. A diversity case typically involves state-law claims, which necessarily are within the jurisdiction of state courts. The federal courts do not exercise diversity jurisdiction in domestic relations cases; therefore, suits seeking the issuance of a divorce, alimony, or child custody decree may not be removed based on diversity jurisdiction.[147] This exception is of long standing and is

---

[138] Lee v. American Nat'l Ins. Co., 260 F.3d 997, 1002–1005 (9th Cir. 2001).

[139] McGee v. Solicitor Gen. of Richmond County, 727 F.3d 1322, 1326 (11th Cir. 2013) (district court should have remanded case to state court because plaintiff did not have standing).

[140] *See* Caterpillar, Inc. v. Williams, 482 U.S. 386, 392 (1987); *see also* 28 U.S.C. §§ 1331, 1332.

[141] 28 U.S.C. § 1332(a).

[142] 28 U.S.C. § 1332(a).

[143] 28 U.S.C. § 1332(a)(1).

[144] 28 U.S.C. § 1332(a)(2).

[145] 28 U.S.C. § 1332(a)(3).

[146] 28 U.S.C. § 1332(a)(4); *see* 28 U.S.C. § 1603(a) (*foreign state* defined).

[147] Ankenbrandt v. Richards, 504 U.S. 689, 693–701 (1992) (diversity jurisdiction exception for domestic relations cases inapplicable to tort action for damages for sexual and physical abuse).

supported by sound policy considerations: the issuance of these decrees frequently involves the retention of jurisdiction by the issuing court and the deployment of social workers to monitor compliance. As a matter of judicial economy, state courts are more suited to work of this type than are federal courts, which lack the close association with state and local government organizations dedicated to handling issues that arise out of conflicts over divorce, alimony, and child custody decrees.[148]

However, the domestic relations exception is narrow and encompasses only cases involving the issuance of a divorce, alimony, or child custody decree. Therefore, the exception does not preclude diversity jurisdiction over an action alleging that a parent's tort against children resulted in damages,[149] or when an alleged violation of constitutional rights arises in a domestic relations context.[150]

Similarly, federal courts also lack diversity jurisdiction over probate cases and, therefore, may not probate a will or administer a decedent's estate.[151] However, a suit asserting a claim against a decedent's estate that is separate from probate administration may be removed on a diversity basis.[152]

### [b] Determining Citizenship

The rules for determining the citizenship of individuals, representative parties, permanent resident aliens, corporations, and partnerships for diversity purposes are the same for removal jurisdiction as for original federal diversity jurisdiction. The determination of citizenship for diversity purposes is covered in detail in Ch. 4, *Diversity Jurisdiction*.

### [c] Complete Diversity Generally Required

In general, diversity jurisdiction is conferred on a federal court only if there is complete diversity.[153] *Complete diversity* requires that none of the defendants be a citizen of the same state as any of the plaintiffs. If any plaintiff and any defendant share citizenship of the same state, diversity is incomplete and the federal court

---

148 504 U.S. at 693–701 (policy mandating state court jurisdiction of divorce, alimony, and child custody decrees not challenged by Congress); Fernos-Lopez v. Figarella Lopez, 929 F.2d 20, 22–23 (1st Cir. 1991) (strong state interest, relative expertise of state courts, state court duty and ability to provide ongoing services, and undesirability of potentially incompatible federal and state decrees as basis for exception); Thomas v. New York City, 814 F. Supp. 1139, 1146 (E.D.N.Y. 1993) (exception based on policy that states traditionally adjudicate marital and child custody disputes and have greater competence and expertise than federal courts).

149 Ankenbrandt v. Richards, 504 U.S. 689, 693–701 (1992).

150 Franks v. Smith, 717 F.2d 183, 185 (5th Cir. 1983).

151 Markham v. Allen, 326 U.S. 490, 494 (1946).

152 Marshall v. Marshall, 547 U.S. 293, 311–12 (2006) ("the probate exception reserves to state probate courts the probate or annulment of a will and the administration of a decedent's estate; it also precludes federal courts from endeavoring to dispose of property that is in the custody of a state probate court. But it does not bar federal courts from adjudicating matters outside those confines and otherwise within federal jurisdiction.").

153 28 U.S.C. § 1332(a); Carden v. Arkoma Assocs., 494 U.S. 185, 190–192 (1990); Strawbridge v. Curtiss, 7 U.S. (3 Cranch) 267, 267–268 (1806) (no diversity if plaintiff and defendant share citizenship of state, even if not state where action filed).

lacks jurisdiction.[154] However, some diversity based jurisdictional statutes do not require complete diversity. For example, the Class Action Fairness Act of 2005 requires only *minimal diversity* meaning that there is federal original or removal jurisdiction when any plaintiff or class member is diverse from any defendant.[155]

In determining the diversity of the parties, it is unclear whether the court must examine the citizenship of unserved defendants.[156] In any event, unserved defendants may be disregarded if the complaint fails to state a colorable cause of action against them, or if the plaintiff voluntarily abandons the suit against them.[157]

The citizenship of defendants sued under fictitious names, such as "Doe" defendants, is disregarded when named defendants attempt to remove the case to federal court.[158] Any attempt to replace Doe defendants with identified non-diverse defendants is subject to court approval.[159]

Although removal jurisdiction generally requires that all defendants join in the notice of removal, the joinder of nominal, unknown, sham, and fraudulently joined defendants cannot prevent removal, and their existence is disregarded for purposes of determining diversity.[160]

---

[154] Owen Equip. & Erection Co. v. Kroger, 437 U.S. 365, 373–374 (1978); Strawbridge v. Curtiss, 7 U.S. (3 Cranch) 267 (1806)).

[155] 28 U.S.C. § 1332(d)(2).

[156] McCall v. Scott, 239 F.3d 808, 813 n.2 (6th Cir. 2001), *modified*, 250 F.3d 997 (2001) (inclusion of unserved resident defendant in case in which complete diversity of citizenship exists does not defeat removal); Pecherski v. General Motors Corp., 636 F.2d 1156, 1160–1161 (8th Cir. 1981) (unserved local defendant does not preclude removal); Zaini v. Shell Oil Co., 853 F. Supp. 960, 963 (S.D. Tex. 1994) (service is irrelevant in determining jurisdiction; court examines citizenship of all named defendants); Windac Corp. v. Clarke, 530 F. Supp. 812, 813 (D. Neb. 1982) (voluntary appearance of unserved local defendant precludes removal).

[157] *See* Lopez v. General Motors Corp., 697 F.2d 1328, 1332 (9th Cir. 1983) (omission of local defendants from amended complaint filed before removal constitutes voluntary abandonment).

[158] 28 U.S.C. § 1441(b)(1); Doleac v. Michalson, 264 F.3d 470, 475–477 (5th Cir. 2001) (citizenship of defendants sued under fictitious names is disregarded for purposes of determining removal jurisdiction); Soliman v. Phillip Morris, Inc., 311 F.3d 966, 971 (9th Cir. 2002) (citizenship of Doe defendants is disregarded for removal purposes and only becomes relevant when plaintiff seeks leave to substitute new named defendant).

[159] *See* 28 U.S.C. § 1447(e) (after removal, court may deny joinder of additional defendants whose presence would destroy subject matter jurisdiction or permit joinder and remand to state court); *see, e.g.*, Newcombe v. Adolf Coors Co., 157 F.3d 686, 690–691 (9th Cir. 1998) (no prejudice in refusing to allow joinder).

[160] *See* Heritage Bank v. Redcom Labs., Inc., 250 F.3d 319, 323 (5th Cir. 2001) (if nondiverse party is fraudulently joined, removal is not precluded); Casias v. Wal-Mart Stores, Inc., 695 F.3d 428, 432 (6th Cir. 2012) (fraudulent joinder is "a judicially created doctrine that provides an exception to the requirement of complete diversity;" Bradley Timberland Res. v. Bradley Lumber Co., 712 F.3d 401, 404–405 (8th Cir. 2013) (denial of motion to remand affirmed; defendant who did not consent to removal had been fraudulently joined); Murphy v. Aurora Loan Servs., LLC, 699 F.3d 1027, 1031 (8th Cir. 2012) (district court properly retained jurisdiction over facially nondiverse case, determined that nondiverse defendant was fraudulently joined, dismissed that defendant, and refused to remand); Morris v. Princess Cruises, Inc., 236 F.3d 1061, 1067–1068 (9th Cir. 2001) (nondiverse defendant properly deemed fraudulently joined and disregarded when plaintiff's complaint failed to state claim for negligent representation against that defendant as matter of state law and plaintiff's admissions in remand motion made it abundantly obvious that she could not possibly prevail).

To establish that an in-state defendant has been fraudulently joined, the removing party must show either that (1) there is no possibility that the plaintiff would be able to establish a cause of action against the in-state defendant in state court, or (2) there has been outright fraud in the plaintiff's pleadings of jurisdictional facts.[161] The burden of persuasion placed on the party alleging fraudulent joinder is substantial.[162]

Under the procedural rules of some states, a plaintiff may join claims and parties that lack a relationship to other claims in a case. In an attempt to block any future removal attempts by the defendant, a plaintiff may strategically add nondiverse plaintiffs or defendants in a state-court action even though the plaintiffs' or defendants' claims do not arise out of the same transaction or occurrence or series of transactions or occurrences as would be required under Federal Rule of Civil Procedure 20. Some courts have adopted the "fraudulent misjoinder" (sometimes referred to as "procedural misjoinder") doctrine to address this tactic.

Fraudulent misjoinder is based on a lack of connection between the claims of diverse and nondiverse plaintiffs or the claims against diverse and nondiverse defendants. Under the doctrine, diversity jurisdiction survives if the nondiverse parties have been fraudulently misjoined. The Eleventh Circuit has adopted the doctrine,[163] and several other circuits have acknowledged the doctrine.[164]

---

[161] Boyer v. Snap-On Tools Corp., 913 F.2d 108, 111 (3d Cir. 1990) (joinder is fraudulent when no reasonable basis in fact or colorable ground supporting claim against joined defendant or no real, good faith intention to seek judgment against joined defendant or joint judgment); Parks v. New York Times Co., 308 F.2d 474, 478 (5th Cir. 1962); American Dredging Co. v. Atlantic Sea Con, Ltd., 637 F. Supp. 179, 183 (D.N.J. 1986) (if failure to state claim against local defendant is obvious, joinder is fraudulent; if real possibility exists that plaintiff stated claim, case should be remanded); *see* B., Inc. v. Miller Brewing Co., 663 F.2d 545, 550 (5th Cir. 1981).

[162] Cuevas v. BAC Home Loans Servicing, LP, 648 F.3d 242, 249–250 (5th Cir. 2011) (nondiverse defendant improperly joined because there was no reasonable basis to predict plaintiffs might be able to recover against that defendant); Heritage Bank v. Redcom Labs., Inc., 250 F.3d 319, 323 (5th Cir. 2001) (applicant was fraudulently joined in letter of credit issuer's declaratory judgment suit seeking to determine issuer's duty to honor presentment because claim was justiciable); *see* Travis v. Irby, 326 F.3d 644, 646–647 (5th Cir. 2003) (citing Moore's Federal Practice); Dutcher v. Matheson, 733 F.3d 980, 988 (10th Cir. 2013) (defendants failed to clear "high hurdle" to prove fraudulent joinder); Ross v. Citifinancial, Inc., 344 F.3d 458, 462–463 (5th Cir. 2003) (reasonable possibility of recovery, not merely theoretical one, defeats removal); Filla v. Norfolk Southern Ry. Co., 336 F.3d 806, 811 (8th Cir. 2003) (nondiverse defendant is fraudulently joined in state-court action and will not defeat removal jurisdiction when applicable state precedent precludes existence of cause of action against that defendant; if "colorable" cause of action, joinder is not fraudulent, and remand is mandatory); Dutcher v. Matheson, 733 F.3d 980, 988 (10th Cir. 2013) (two possibilities for demonstrating fraudulent joinder).

[163] Tapscott v. MS Dealer Service Corp., 77 F.3d 1353, 1360 (11th Cir. 1996), *abrogated on other grounds by Cohen v. Office Depot, Inc.*, 204 F.3d 1069 (11th Cir. 2000) (parties were fraudulently misjoined).

[164] *See* Crockett v. R.J. Reynolds Tobacco Co., 436 F.3d 529, 533 (5th Cir. 2006) (citing *Tapscott v. MS Dealer Serv. Corp.*, 77 F.3d 1353, 1360 (11th Cir. 1996) as support for proposition that joinder can be improper even if there is no fraud in pleadings and plaintiff has ability to recover against each defendant); *In re* Benjamin Moore & Co., 309 F.3d 296, 298 (5th Cir. 2002) (citing *Tapscott* as support for conclusion that district court erred in failing to consider whether diversity jurisdiction was defeated because among 17 plaintiffs who had nothing in common with each other, only four had asserted claims that related in any way to nondiverse defendants); *In re* Prempro Products Liability Litigation, 591 F.3d 613, 622 (8th Cir. 2010) (even if court adopted fraudulent misjoinder doctrine, any misjoinder of claims

When an original defendant seeks removal, a federal court is not bound by the plaintiff's alignment of the parties in the original state court pleading, and may realign the parties according to their substantive interests.[165] A federal court will determine the true interests of the parties to evaluate whether their positions as plaintiffs and defendants conform to their real interests, and the court will ascertain whether a bona fide controversy exists between citizens of different states. To ascertain that there is an actual, substantial controversy between citizens of different states, federal courts must look beyond the pleadings and arrange the parties according to their respective positions in the dispute.[166]

The Class Action Fairness Act of 2005 (CAFA)[167] greatly expanded the scope of diversity jurisdiction in large, multistate class actions. CAFA includes special jurisdictional and procedural provisions that permit district courts to exercise original and removal subject matter jurisdiction over multistate class actions based on minimal diversity.[168] Specifically, CAFA permits federal subject matter jurisdiction over multistate class actions in which the aggregated amount in controversy exceeds the sum or value of $5,000,000, exclusive of interest and costs, and either:[169]

• Any member of a class of plaintiffs is a citizen of a state different from any defendant;

• Any member of a class of plaintiffs is a foreign state or a citizen or subject of a foreign state and any defendant is a citizen of a state; or

• Any member of a class of plaintiffs is a citizen of a State and any defendant is a foreign state or a citizen or subject of a foreign state.

### [d] Time for Ascertaining Diversity of Citizenship

For removal purposes, diversity of citizenship generally is ascertained at the time that the lawsuit is commenced and again at the time of removal.[170] Further, diversity must be maintained throughout the proceeding, because the addition of a nondiverse party after removal may require remand.[171] The Supreme Court has crafted a narrow exception to this general rule. In *Caterpillar v. Lewis*, the Court

---

by women and survivors of women who were allegedly injured by taking hormone replacement therapy drugs manufactured by different companies was not so egregious that it would constitute fraudulent misjoinder); Lafalier v. State Farm Fire and Cas. Co., 2010 U.S. App. LEXIS 17588, at **18–**21 (10th Cir. Aug. 19 2010) (unpublished) ("There may be many good reasons to adopt procedural misjoinder, as the Insurers argue. But we need not decide that issue today, because the record before us does not show that adopting the doctrine would change the result in this case.").

165 *See* City of Indianapolis v. Chase Nat'l Bank, 314 U.S. 63, 69 (1941).

166 City of Indianapolis v. Chase Nat'l Bank, 314 U.S. 63, 69 (1941).

167 P.L. No. 109-2, 119 Stat. 4; *see* 28 U.S.C. § 1332(d).

168 Pub. L. 109-2, § 4, 119 Stat. 4, 9; see 28 U.S.C. §§ 1332(d), 1453.

169 28 U.S.C. § 1332(d)(2).

170 *See* Grupo Dataflux v. Atlas Global Group, L.P., 541 U.S. 567 (2004) (Court upheld dismissal for lack of subject-matter jurisdiction); Freeport-McMoRan, Inc. v. K N Energy, 498 U.S. 426, 428–429 (1991) (case originally filed in federal court); Pullman Co. v. Jenkins, 305 U.S. 534, 537 (1939); Koenigsberger v. Richmond Silver Mining Co., 158 U.S. 41 (1895).

171 28 U.S.C. § 1447(e); *see* Yniques v. Cabral, 985 F.2d 1031, 1035–1036 (9th Cir. 1993) (nondiverse party joined after removal requires remand, not dismissal).

held that a district court's failure to grant the plaintiff's motion to remand a case improperly removed on diversity grounds is not fatal to the adjudication of the case so long as federal jurisdictional requirements are satisfied by the time the judgment is entered.[172]

In *Grupo Dataflux v. Atlas Global Group, L.P.*, however, the Supreme Court held that the *Caterpillar* exception does not apply when parties who were not diverse at the time of filing become diverse before trial as a result of a party's change of citizenship, rather than because of a change in the identity of the parties.[173] The Supreme Court explained that the *Caterpillar* exception applies only to the cure of a *statutory* defect (the requirement that there be complete diversity at the time of removal), not to a *jurisdictional* defect. The defect in *Caterpillar* had been cured by the post-settlement dismissal of the non-diverse defendant, which has long been an acceptable way to cure a defect in diversity.[174]

With regard to cases initially filed in federal court, a well-established rule provides that if diversity jurisdiction is established, jurisdiction may not be divested by subsequent events.[175] Specifically, diversity jurisdiction, once established, is not divested by a subsequent change in the citizenship of the existing parties.[176] This rule applies to removed cases as well; a change in citizenship subsequent to removal does not divest the federal district court of jurisdiction.

### [e] Removal Precluded if Any Defendant Is Citizen of State in Which Action Is Filed

Removal is permissible only if none of the parties in interest properly joined and served as defendants is a citizen of the state in which the action is filed.[177] Thus, even if complete diversity exists, removal is precluded if a local defendant is served; after service on the forum defendant, even nonresident defendants may not seek removal.[178] This rule is often called the "forum defendant rule."[179]

The justification for this rule is simple. Given that the purpose of diversity jurisdiction is to provide litigants with an unbiased forum by protecting out-of-state litigants from local prejudices, it makes no sense to allow an in-state defendant to take advantage of removal. Similarly, the theory goes, out-of-state defendants will be cloaked with the "home court" advantage presented by being sued along with an

---

172 Caterpillar, Inc. v. Lewis, 519 U.S. 61 (1996) (after motion to remand, all claims involving nondiverse defendant were settled and that defendant was dismissed as party to action).

173 Grupo Dataflux v. Atlas Global Group, L.P., 541 U.S. 567, 574–575 (2004).

174 Grupo Dataflux v. Atlas Global Group, L.P., 541 U.S. 567, 573–574 (2004).

175 *See, e.g.*, Mollan v. Torrance, 22 U.S. (9 Wheat.) 537, 539 (1824); Wichita R.R. & Light Co. v. Public Util. Comm'n, 260 U.S. 48, 54 (1922).

176 Wichita R.R. & Light Co. v. Public Util. Comm'n, 260 U.S. 48, 54 (1922) (diverse when breach of contract action arose and when federal proceedings commenced).

177 28 U.S.C. § 1441(b)(2); Hurt v. Dow Chem. Co., 963 F.2d 1142, 1144–1145 (8th Cir. 1992).

178 GE Betz, Inc. v. Zee Co., 718 F.3d 615, 632 (7th Cir. 2013) (if forum defendant has been properly joined and served, *no* defendant may remove). *See* Windac Corp. v. Clarke, 530 F. Supp. 812, 814 (D. Neb. 1982) (general voluntary appearance of local defendant even without actual service precludes removal).

179 Ethington v. General Elec. Co., 575 F. Supp. 2d 855, 858 (N.D. Ohio 2008).

in-state defendant by an out-of-state plaintiff. Of course, this argument fails to take account of the possible finger-pointing that could occur among the defendants, which would put the out-of-state defendant very much at a disadvantage in terms of the local-bias perspective. Nonetheless, the general removal statute expressly precludes removal if any of the defendants is a citizen of the state in which the action was brought.[180]

Some recent cases have addressed whether to permit removal *by* a forum defendant who has not yet been *served*.[181] The language of the forum defendant rule would seem to permit such removal. It provides that cases in which federal jurisdiction is based only on complete diversity "may not be removed if any of the parties in interest *properly joined and served* as defendants is a citizen of the State in which such action is brought" (emphasis added).[182] However, a literal interpretation of the rule would provide an opportunity for gamesmanship by forum defendants who, by monitoring the state docket, could remove actions to federal court before the plaintiff has a chance to serve them, thereby avoiding the rule. Courts that refuse to follow this literal interpretation point out that the "joined and served" language in the rule was intended to prevent gamesmanship by plaintiffs, who might otherwise name an in-state defendant against whom there is no valid claim merely to prevent removal by the other defendants. Allowing local defendants to rush to remove newly filed state court cases before the plaintiff has a chance to serve them would turn Congressional intent to prevent litigant gamesmanship on its head.[183] Thus, some district courts have granted timely motions to remand after pre-service removals by forum defendants.[184] However, some courts have denied remand under those circumstances.[185]

---

[180] 28 U.S.C. § 1441(b)(2).

[181] *See* Ethington v. General Elec. Co., 575 F. Supp. 2d 855, 860–864 (N.D. Ohio 2008) (collecting cases and following trend prohibiting removal by unserved forum defendant).

[182] 28 U.S.C. § 1441(b)(2).

[183] DeAngelo-Shuayto v. Organon USA, Inc., 2007 U.S. Dist. LEXIS 92557, at *8–*15 (D.N.J. Dec. 12, 2007) (articulating reasoning and analysis adopted by later cases); Ethington v. General Elec. Co., 575 F. Supp. 2d 855, 860–864 (N.D. Ohio 2008) (collecting cases).

[184] *See, e.g.*, DeAngelo-Shuayto v. Organon USA, Inc., 2007 U.S. Dist. LEXIS 92557, at *15 (D.N.J. Dec. 12, 2007) (articulating reasoning and analysis adopted in later cases); Sullivan v. Novartis Pharmaceuticals Corp., 575 F. Supp. 2d 640, 643–647 (D.N.J. 2008) (literal reading of 28 U.S.C. § 1441(b) would conflict with congressional intent); *In re* Darvocet, Darvon & Propoxyphene Prods. Liab. Litig., 2012 U.S. Dist. LEXIS 99835, at *42–*45 (E.D. Ky. July 17, 2012) (in-state defendant cannot avoid statutory prohibition against removal by removing case before service); Vivas v. Boeing Co., 486 F. Supp. 2d 726, 734 (N.D. Ill. 2007) (allowing unserved forum defendant to remove diversity action would "frustrate the consistent efforts of both Congress and the courts to determine diversity jurisdiction based on the genuine interests of the parties to the controversy" and would "provide a vehicle for defendants to manipulate the operation of the removal statutes").

[185] *See, e.g.*, Flores v. Merck & Co. (*In re* Fosamax Prods. Liab. Litig.), 2008 U.S. Dist. LEXIS 57473, at *37–*38 (S.D.N.Y. July 28, 2008); Ripley v. Eon Labs Inc., 622 F. Supp. 2d 137, 140 (D.N.J. 2007); Thomson v. Novartis Pharms., 2007 U.S. Dist. LEXIS 37990, at *11–*15 (D.N.J. May 22, 2007); Frick v. Novartis Pharms. Corp., 2006 U.S. Dist. LEXIS 9178, at *3–*7 (D.N.J. Feb. 23, 2006) (all interpreting 28 U.S.C. § 1441(b) literally and permitting unserved New Jersey defendants to remove case from New Jersey state court); Terry v. J.D. Streett & Co., 2010 U.S. Dist. LEXIS 100251, at *6 (E.D. Mo. Sept. 23, 2010) (unserved forum defendant allowed to remove diversity action).

The courts are split on whether the ban on local defendants is procedural or jurisdictional. Most courts hold that the ban is procedural and, assuming complete diversity, that the defect is waived if the plaintiff fails to move to remand on this ground within 30 days of the notice of removal.[186] However, one court of appeals has held that the presence of a local defendant constitutes a jurisdictional defect that may be raised at any time.[187]

### [f] Procedures for Determining Diversity of Parties

A case is removable based on diversity jurisdiction if the initial pleading setting forth the claim for relief on which the action or proceeding is based alleges facts indicating diversity.[188] If the initial complaint does not disclose the citizenship of the parties, the case is not removable unless the defendant, in the notice of removal, can affirmatively plead, and later prove, the existence of diversity. If the complaint is indeterminate on its face, the defendant must scrutinize the complaint to determine removability unless the complaint provides "no clue" that the case is removable.[189]

### [g] Satisfaction of Amount in Controversy Requirement

#### [i] Amount Must Exceed $75,000 in Cases Outside Class Action Fairness Act of 2005

To support diversity jurisdiction, the amount in controversy must exceed $75,000, exclusive of interest and costs.[190] The test to determine the amount in controversy is not the sum that is ultimately awarded to the plaintiff, but the sum that is demanded by the plaintiff when the complaint is filed,[191] or, in the event of removal, on the day the suit was removed.[192]

---

186 *See, e.g.*, Samaan v. St. Joseph Hosp., 670 F.3d 21, 28 (1st Cir. 2012) (plaintiff waived objection to removal by forum defendant by failing to raise issue); Farm Constr. Serv. v. Fudge, 831 F.2d 18, 21–22 (1st Cir. 1987) (forum-defendant rule is nonjurisdictional); Assaf v. Trinity Med. Ctr., 696 F.3d 681, 685 (7th Cir. 2012) (plaintiff waived objection to removal by forum defendant by failing to object within 30 days); Hurley v. Motor Coach Indus., Inc., 222 F.3d 377, 379–380 (7th Cir. 2000) (forum-defendant rule limiting diversity jurisdiction is non-jurisdictional and subject to waiver); *In re* Shell Oil Co., 932 F.2d 1518, 1522–1523 (5th Cir. 1991); Ravens Metal Products, Inc. v. Wilson, 816 F. Supp. 427, 428–429 (S.D. W. Va. 1993).

187 Hurt v. Dow Chem. Co., 963 F.2d 1142, 1144–1145 (8th Cir. 1992); *see* Horton v. Conklin, 431 F.3d 602, 605 (8th Cir. 2005) (noting split in circuits and adhering to rule in *Hurt*).

188 *See* 28 U.S.C. § 1446(b).

189 *See* Adams v. Lederle Lab., 569 F. Supp. 234, 243, 244–245 (W.D. Mo. 1983) (service of process address not a clue); Keller v. Carr, 534 F. Supp. 100, 102 (W.D. Ark. 1981) (defendant expected to know own citizenship); Kaneshiro v. North American Co. for Life & Health Ins., 496 F. Supp. 452, 456–457, 460 (D. Haw. 1980) (averment of residence in complaint is clue regarding citizenship that defendant must act on in 30 days).

190 28 U.S.C. § 1332(a) (increased from $50,000, effective January 1997).

191 St. Paul Mercury Indem. Co. v. Red Cab. Co., 303 U.S. 283, 289–290 (1938) (recovery of less than jurisdictional amount does not divest federal court of jurisdiction).

192 Pullman Co. v. Jenkins, 305 U.S. 534, 537 (1939); *see* Smith v. American Gen. Life & Accident Ins. Co., Inc., 337 F.3d 888, 896–897 (7th Cir. 2003) (attorney's fees incurred by insured in pursuing statutory and common law fraud claims after removal notice was filed do not count toward satisfying requisite

Traditionally, in cases in which the amount in controversy in diversity cases is in doubt, the Supreme Court had drawn a sharp distinction between original jurisdiction and removal jurisdiction. For cases brought originally in federal court, it must appear to a legal certainty that the plaintiff cannot recover the jurisdictional amount to justify dismissal.[193] For cases instituted in state court and removed, a strong presumption arises that the plaintiff has not claimed an amount large enough to confer jurisdiction on a federal court and that the parties have not colluded to that end.[194] Every attorney is an officer of the court; in addition to the duty of diligently researching the client's case, the attorney has a duty of candor to the court. Therefore, the plaintiff's claim, if it is specific and drafted by an attorney, generally deserves deference and the presumption of truth.[195]

Uncertainty as to the amount in controversy may arise if the state court complaint does not allege the amount of damages sought. A defendant seeking removal can usually determine an appropriate range of damages through discovery. In addition, some state courts have jurisdictional limits that preclude a state court from awarding damages greater than specified amounts and that can serve as a basis for ascertaining the maximum amount in controversy for removal purposes.

The amount in controversy is determined based on the plaintiff's complaint at the time that the notice of removal is filed.[196] A plaintiff may not change the amount in controversy after removal in an attempt to defeat diversity jurisdiction. Most courts hold that a plaintiff's post-removal stipulation or amendment reducing the amount in controversy or limiting the types of relief sought has no bearing on the amount in controversy for diversity purposes.[197]

---

amount in controversy); BEM I, L.L.C. v. Anthropologie, Inc., 301 F.3d 548, 552–553 (7th Cir. 2002) (relevant date for determining amount in controversy in removed case is date of removal, not date original complaint was filed in state court); Freeport-McMoRan, Inc. v. K N Energy, 498 U.S. 426, 428 (1991) (amount in controversy in nonremoval diversity case is determined based on plaintiff's complaint when action is filed).

[193] 303 U.S. at 288–289; *see* Ch. 4, *Diversity Jurisdiction.*

[194] 303 U.S. at 288–290.

[195] 303 U.S. at 288–289 (plaintiff may evade federal court simply by asking for less than jurisdictional amount); Burns v. Windsor Ins. Co., 31 F.3d 1092, 1094–1095 (11th Cir. 1994) (presumption that plaintiff's counsel understands that choice and representations about damages have important legal consequences and raise significant ethical implications for court officer).

[196] Pullman Co. v. Jenkins, 305 U.S. 534, 537 (1939); *see* Freeport-McMoran, Inc. v. K N Energy, 498 U.S. 426, 428 (1991) (amount in controversy in nonremoval diversity case is determined based on the plaintiff's complaint at the time that the action is filed).

[197] Yong Qin Luo v. Mikel, 625 F.3d 772, 776 (2d Cir. 2010) (plaintiff could not deprive federal courts of jurisdiction by agreeing to limit damages to $75,000 on appeal, after she had refused such limitation at initial status conference and then submitted $600,000 settlement demand); Purple Passion, Inc. v. RCN Telecom Servs., Inc., 406 F. Supp. 2d 245, 246–247 (S.D.N.Y. 2005) (citing MOORE'S FEDERAL PRACTICE; post-removal amendment of complaint reducing damages to below jurisdictional minimum did not deprive district court of diversity jurisdiction); Werwinski v. Ford Motor Co., 286 F.3d 661, 666–668 (3d Cir. 2002) (amount in controversy not limited to costs of repairing or replacing defective transmissions when complaint's prayer for relief also clearly sought recovery for compensatory damages, all or part of sums paid to purchase or lease automobiles, and ill-gotten profits); *see also* Gebbia v. Wal-Mart Stores, Inc., 233 F.3d 880, 883 (5th Cir. 2000); Hunt v. Davita, Inc., 680 F.3d 775, 777–778 (7th

Pursuant to 2011 amendments to Section 1446, when a case that was commenced on or after January 6, 2012, is removed on the basis of diversity jurisdiction, the sum demanded in good faith in the initial pleading is deemed to be the amount in controversy, subject to the following two exceptions:[198]

(1) if the initial pleading seeks non-monetary relief; or

(2) the initial pleading seeks a money judgment, but state practice either does not permit demand for a specific sum or permits recovery of damages in excess of the amount demanded.

In either event, the notice of removal may assert the amount in controversy.[199] Removal will be proper on the basis of the amount asserted in the removal notice if the district court finds, by the preponderance of the evidence, that the amount in controversy exceeds the jurisdictional minimum for diversity jurisdiction.[200]

A suit for equitable relief, such as a suit solely for injunctive relief, is often difficult to evaluate monetarily. For example, an injunction-based action may have far less monetary value to a plaintiff than to a defendant, who may be required to spend in excess of $75,000 to comply with an injunction ultimately imposed by the court.[201] Although there are cases permitting an inquiry from the defendant's point of view, the general rule is that the value of the cause of action or the amount in controversy is determined from the plaintiff's point of view, that is, what the plaintiff will recover or avoid losing if the suit is successful.[202] This rule is consistent with the general principle of strict construction of the right of removal, and it protects the plaintiff's initial choice of forum.

---

Cir. 2012); *In re* Shell Oil Co., 970 F.2d 355, 356 (7th Cir. 1992); Hargis v. Access Capital Funding, LLC, 674 F.3d 783, 789–790 (8th Cir. 2012).

198 28 U.S.C. § 1446(c)(2).

199 28 U.S.C. § 1446(c)(2)(A).

200 28 U.S.C. § 1446(c)(2).

201 United Food and Commercial Workers Union, Local 919 v. Centermark Properties, 30 F.3d 298, 304–305 (2d Cir. 1994) (union seeking injunctive relief); Bedell v. H.R.C. Ltd., 522 F. Supp. 732, 735 (E.D. Ky. 1981) (determination of appropriate amount can be difficult in cases involving only injunctive relief, when benefit to plaintiff has different value than loss to defendant if relief is granted); Melkus v. Allstate Ins. Co., 503 F. Supp. 842, 846 (E.D. Mich. 1980).

202 Northup Properties v. Chesapeake Appalachia, 567 F.3d 767, 770–771 (6th Cir. 2009) (amount in controversy in declaratory judgment action measured by value of object of litigation; value of loss of mineral lease measured from plaintiff lessee's perspective, considering discounted future cash flow, leaseholds' minimum value, and cost to drill well); *but see* McCarty v. Amoco Pipeline Co., 595 F.2d 389, 395 (7th Cir. 1979) (in injunction action to remove encroaching building, court should recognize existence of substantial controversy and examine effect of suit on either party); Kheel v. Port of N.Y. Auth., 457 F.2d 46, 48–49 (2d Cir. 1972) (amount in controversy for jurisdictional purposes should be measured strictly from plaintiff's perspective); Myers v. Long Island Lighting Co., 623 F. Supp. 1076, 1078 (E.D.N.Y. 1985).

### [ii] Amount Must Exceed $5,000,000 in Class Action Fairness Act of 2005 Cases

The amount in controversy for class actions under the Class Action Fairness Act must exceed the sum or value of $5,000,000, exclusive of interest and costs.[203] The value of the plaintiffs' claims must be aggregated to determine the requisite amount in controversy.[204] It is not necessary that any individual plaintiff's claim exceed the jurisdictional minimum amount in controversy for non-CAFA diversity cases.[205]

Although the Class Action Fairness Act provides for aggregation of class members' claims, it requires that each plaintiff's claim in a *mass action* meet the same standard as under the general diversity statute.[206] Accordingly, federal jurisdiction exists only over the claims of mass action plaintiffs that exceed the $75,000 traditional diversity jurisdiction amount.[207]

There is a question whether the 2011 Jurisdiction and Venue Clarification Act ("JVCA") amendments to Section 1446, which adopts a preponderance of the evidence standard, applies to Class Action Fairness Act cases. The stronger argument is that they do not. Section 1446(c)(2) refers explicitly to cases removed under Section 1332(a), which concerns diversity jurisdiction generally, not Section 1332(d), the CAFA jurisdiction provision.[208] Based on this language, some district courts have held that the new rules do not apply to CAFA cases.[209] On the other hand, removal of CAFA cases is generally governed by Section 1446,[210] and some courts have suggested, therefore, that the new rules might apply to CAFA cases.[211]

---

[203] 28 U.S.C. § 1332(d)(2).

[204] 28 U.S.C. § 1332(d)(6).

[205] Cappuccitti v. DirectTV, Inc., 623 F.3d 1118, 1122 (11th Cir. 2010) (district court had subject matter jurisdiction over class action brought on behalf of over 100 persons whose claims, in aggregate, exceeded $5 million, even though no single plaintiff's claim exceeded $75,000).

[206] *See* 28 U.S.C. § 1332(d)(11)(B)(i).

[207] *See* 28 U.S.C. § 1332(a).

[208] 28 U.S.C. § 1446(c)(2) ("If removal of a civil action is sought on the basis of the jurisdiction conferred by *section 1332(a)*, the sum demanded in good faith in the initial pleading shall be deemed to be the amount in controversy, except that . . . " [emphasis added]).

[209] Bolton v. United States Nursing Corp., 2012 U.S. Dist. LEXIS 152387, at *11 (N.D. Cal. Oct. 23, 2012) (plaintiff's argument that JVCA amendments logically apply to CAFA cases "is insufficient to allow this court to rewrite the plain language of the statute, which creates exceptions to the legal certainty standard that are specifically limited to traditional diversity cases."); Sims v. AT&T Mobility Servs. LLC, 2013 U.S. Dist. LEXIS 27262, at *8 n.2 (E.D. Cal. Feb. 27, 2013) ("Defendant's argument that 28 U.S.C. § 1446(c)(2)(A) requires a preponderance standard is unpersuasive because that statute refers only to removals under 28 U.S.C. § 1332(a), not CAFA.").

[210] *See* 28 U.S.C. § 1453(b) ("[a] class action may be removed to a district court of the United States in accordance with section 1446.").

[211] *See* Smith v. Manhattan Club Timeshare Ass'n, 2013 U.S. Dist. LEXIS 38760, at *4–*5 (S.D.N.Y. Mar. 15, 2013) (conclusion that defendants must prove amount in controversy by preponderance of evidence "is reinforced, if not required, by the Federal Courts Jurisdiction and Venue Clarification Act of 2011; at the very least, the JVCA arguably supports the conclusion that the preponderance-of-the-evidence standard applies to a removing defendant invoking jurisdiction pursuant to CAFA.); Frederick v. Hartford Underwriters Ins. Co., 683 F.3d 1242, 1245–1247 & n.2 (10th Cir. 2012) ("We recognize that

Some courts cite to the Supreme Court's reasoning in *Standard Fire Ins. Co. v. Knowles*.[212] In *Knowles*, the Supreme Court ruled that because plaintiff cannot legally bind members of proposed class before a class is certified, prospective class representative's precertification stipulation that plaintiffs will not seek total aggregate damages of more than five million dollars will not prevent removal of class action under Class Action Fairness Act. Invoking *Knowles*, the Ninth Circuit held that the preponderance of the evidence standard applies.[213] The Eighth and Tenth Circuits also hold that a party seeking to remove under CAFA must establish the amount in controversy by a mere preponderance of the evidence regardless of whether the complaint alleges an amount below the CAFA jurisdictional minimum.[214] On the other hand, although Congress may well have intended the JVCA language to apply to all cases, its specific reference to § 1332(a) could trump the argument that the preponderance standard applies through the general language of CAFA that states that removal is governed by § 1446.

### [h] Removal May Be Possible When Later Developments Create Diversity

If a case is not removable based on the plaintiff's initial pleading, but the plaintiff takes some voluntary action that changes the nonremovable status of the case, such as by dismissing a nondiverse defendant, the case may become removable.[215] For example, if the plaintiff amends the state court complaint to increase the amount in controversy over the jurisdictional requisite, the action becomes removable unless the one-year limit (*see* § 6.09[2][a][iii]) on diversity removal has expired.[216] As another example, a suit becomes removable when the plaintiff voluntarily settles the claim against the nondiverse defendant and amends the complaint accordingly.[217] Similarly, if the plaintiff voluntarily moves to another state after the complaint was filed, and that move creates diversity, the defendant is entitled to remove within 30 days after notice of the change (*see* § 6.09[2]), provided that the defendant can satisfy the one-year rule.[218]

---

the Federal Courts Jurisdiction and Venue Clarification Act of 2011 ('JVCA') may modify this procedure).

[212] Standard Fire Ins. Co. v. Knowles, 133 S. Ct. 1345, 185 L. Ed. 2d 439 (2013) (because plaintiff cannot legally bind members of proposed class before class is certified, prospective class representative's precertification stipulation that plaintiffs will not seek total aggregate damages of more than five million dollars will not prevent removal of class action under Class Action Fairness Act).

[213] Rodriguez v. AT & T Mobility Servs., LLC, 728 F.3d 975, 977 (9th Cir. 2013) (*Lowdermilk* reasoning for imposing burden to prove amount in controversy to legal certainty is "clearly irreconcilable" with Supreme Court's reasoning in *Knowles; Lowdermilk* overruled, and proper burden of proof is preponderance of evidence).

[214] Bell v. Hershey Co., 557 F.3d 953, 958 (8th Cir. 2009); *see* Hartis v. Chicago Title Ins. Co., 656 F.3d 778, 781 (8th Cir. 2009) (under *Bell's* preponderance standard, jurisdictional fact is not whether damages are greater than requisite amount, but whether fact finder *might* legally conclude that they are).

[215] DeBry v. Transamerica Corp., 601 F.2d 480, 487–488 (10th Cir. 1979) (28 U.S.C. § 1446 permits filing of removal notice after case becomes removable on filing of new or amended paper).

[216] Tokarz v. Texaco Pipeline, Inc., 856 F. Supp. 403, 404 n.2, 404 (N.D. Ill. 1993).

[217] Kilpatrick v. Arrow Co., 425 F. Supp. 1378, 1379–1381 (W.D. La. 1977).

[218] *See* DeBry v. Transamerica Corp., 601 F.2d 480, 488 (10th Cir. 1979); *see also* 28 U.S.C. § 1446(b).

In contrast, involuntary changes in a case do not create removability if the plaintiff's complaint was not removable originally.[219] Thus, for example, the death of a nondiverse defendant does not create removability.[220] Moreover, defendants may not seek to manufacture diversity. For example, a defendant cannot create diversity by moving to another state after the plaintiff files the original complaint in state court.[221] In any event, if a case stated by the initial pleading is not removable, but subsequent events render the case removable, the defendant has 30 days to remove the action after receiving, through service or otherwise, a copy of an amended pleading, motion, order, or other paper from which it may first be ascertained that the case is removable.[222] However, a case generally may not be removed based on diversity jurisdiction more than a year after the commencement of the action in state court; therefore, if the defendant ascertains the existence of diversity after the one-year period, the defendant generally is precluded from removal.[223] This one-year limitation applies only to diversity cases.[224] These time limits are discussed in § 6.09[2].

## [3] Federal Question Cases

### [a] Federal Question Jurisdiction

The district courts have original *federal question jurisdiction* of civil actions arising under the Constitution, laws, or treaties of the United States.[225] If the case involves a federal question, the case is removable without regard to the citizenship of the parties.[226]

Federal question jurisdiction generally is not exclusive: state courts also have jurisdiction to hear most federal question cases.[227] A complete analysis of federal question subject matter jurisdiction is contained in MOORE'S FEDERAL PRACTICE Ch. 103, *Federal Question Jurisdiction*; Ch. 104, *Specific Grants of Federal Question Jurisdiction*; Ch. 106, *Supplemental Jurisdiction*; and Ch. 120, *Dual State and Federal Judicial Structure* (Matthew Bender 3d ed.).

---

219 Self v. General Motors Corp. 588 F.2d 655, 657–659 (9th Cir. 1978) (because plaintiff is master of complaint, involuntary changes cannot make case removable).

220 For further discussion of the effect of involuntary changes that show a basis for removal, *see* § 6.09[2].

221 Kilpatrick v. Arrow Co., 425 F. Supp. 1378, 1380 (W.D. La. 1977).

222 28 U.S.C. § 1446(b); *see* 28 U.S.C. § 1332 (diversity jurisdiction).

223 28 U.S.C. § 1446(b).

224 *See* 28 U.S.C. § 1446(b).

225 28 U.S.C. § 1331; *see* U.S. Const., Art. III § 2; *see* Ch. 4, *Federal Question Jurisdiction.*

226 28 U.S.C. § 1441(b).

227 *See* Lockerty v. Phillips, 319 U.S. 182, 187 (1943) (Congress could have decided against creating inferior federal courts and relied on state courts to adjudicate federal law).

### [b] "Federal Question" Defined

Article III of the Constitution provides that the federal judicial power extends to all cases arising under the Constitution, laws, or treaties of the United States.[228] For a case to be within the district court's federal question jurisdiction, there must be a statute conferring jurisdiction on the courts. The constitutional scope of jurisdiction is not self-executing.[229] Accordingly, for a case to be removable as a federal question, it must be a case that could have been brought in a district court as a federal question under Section 1331,[230] or another statute authorizing specific grant of jurisdiction.[231] Although the language of Section 1331 essentially mirrors that of Article III's "arising under" jurisdiction, the meaning of a federal question for statutory purposes is far more limited than that for Article III.[232] Federal question jurisdiction under Section 1331 generally includes claims that arise under a federal statute or federal common law.[233] It also includes certain state-law claims that raise actually disputed and substantial federal issues.[234] A thorough discussion of the parameters of federal question jurisdiction is beyond the scope of this chapter, but may be found in 15 Moore's Federal Practice, Ch. 103, *Federal Question Jurisdiction.*

The presence or absence of federal question jurisdiction is governed by the *well-pleaded complaint rule*, which provides that federal jurisdiction exists only if a federal question is affirmatively and distinctly presented on the face of the plaintiff's properly pleaded complaint. The rule makes the plaintiff the master of the complaint; thus, the plaintiff may avoid federal jurisdiction by forgoing a potential federal claim and relying exclusively on state law, unless the state claims are completely preempted.[235] The federal law under which a claim arises must be a direct and essential element of the plaintiff's cause of action to establish federal

---

[228] U.S. Const., Art. III § 2; *see* Sheldon v. Sill, 49 U.S. (How.) 441, 448–449 (1850) (inferior federal court has jurisdiction conferred by statute).

[229] *See* Ch. 1, *The Structure of the Federal Judicial System.*

[230] 28 U.S.C. § 1331.

[231] See generally, 15 Moore's Federal Practice, Ch. 104, *Specific Grants of Federal Question Jurisdiction.*

[232] *See* Ch. 4, *Federal Question Jurisdiction.*

[233] Illinois v. City of Milwaukee, 406 U.S. 91, 100 (1972); *but see* Shoshone Mining Co. v. Rutter, 177 U.S. 505, 508 (1900) (suit by adverse claimant to determine true ownership of mining claim did not "arise under" federal law for purposes of statutory federal question jurisdiction).

[234] Gunn v. Minton, 133 S. Ct. 1059 (2013) ("state legal malpractice claims based on underlying patent matters will rarely, if ever, arise under federal patent law for purposes of § 1338(a). Although such cases may necessarily raise disputed questions of patent law, those cases are by their nature unlikely to have the sort of significance for the federal system necessary to establish jurisdiction."); Grable & Sons Metal Prods., Inc. v. Darue Eng'g & Mfg., 545 U.S. 308, 314 (2005) ("[T]he question is, does a state-law claim necessarily raise a stated federal issue, actually disputed and substantial, which a federal forum may entertain without disturbing any congressionally approved balance of federal and state judicial responsibilities").

[235] Louisville & Nashville R.R. v. Mottley, 211 U.S. 149 (1908); Caterpillar, Inc. v. Williams, 482 U.S. 386, 392 (1987); Franchise Tax Bd. v. Construction Laborers Vacation Trust, 463 U.S. 1, 6, 9–10, 27–28 (1983). *See* Bracken v. Matgouranis, 296 F.3d 160 163–164 (3d Cir. 2002) (fact that plaintiffs anticipated state law defense of absolute privilege in their complaint by alleging that defense would violate their First Amendment rights is not sufficient basis for federal question jurisdiction as to support removal).

question jurisdiction. Therefore, if a plaintiff's well-pleaded complaint filed in state court does not allege any federal question, the defendant ordinarily may not remove the case to federal court, even if his or her defense or counterclaim is based on federal law.[236]

A case may not be removed to federal court on the basis of a federal defense, including the defense of preemption, even if the defense is anticipated in the plaintiff's complaint, and even if both parties concede that the federal defense is the only question truly at issue.[237] The complete preemption doctrine provides an exception to the well-pleaded complaint rule.[238] If a plaintiff alleges a cause of action based on state law, and the defendant asserts that federal law completely preempts the state cause of action and provides the exclusive cause of action and remedy, federal question jurisdiction may exist even though the complaint does not appear to allege a federal question. Whether federal jurisdiction exists depends on the nature and scope of the preemption of state law.[239]

In general, a defendant may not allege a federal question counterclaim and seek removal on that basis. The plaintiff generally is the master of the complaint (*see* [c], *below*).[240]

### [c] Plaintiff Generally Is Master of Complaint

The plaintiff is the master of the complaint and is not required to assert federal claims, even if they exist.[241] Ordinarily, the plaintiff's selection of a cause of action is controlling and ends the removal inquiry. However, in the area of complete preemption, when the true gravamen of the action is a federal claim (such as deprivation of pension plan benefits) the plaintiff cannot avoid preemption (and federal jurisdiction) by pleading a purported state claim.[242] If the plaintiff alleges only federal claims and dismisses them on removal, obviously there is nothing more for the federal court to do. There is no part of the case to consider remanding or dismissing. If the complaint alleges both state law and federal claims, the state law claims may fall within the federal district court's supplemental jurisdiction so long

---

236 Franchise Tax Bd. v. Construction Laborers Vacation Trust, 463 U.S. 1, 7–12 (1983) (action to collect taxes under state law; case not removable even if defense — that federal law preempts state law — was anticipated in plaintiff's complaint, and both parties agree it is only issue in case); *see* The Fair v. Kohler Die & Specialty Co., 228 U.S. 22, 25 (1913) (party who brings suit is entitled to decide what law he or she will rely on).

237 Caterpillar, Inc. v. Williams, 482 U.S. 386, 393 (1987); Franchise Tax Bd. v. Construction Laborers Vacation Trust, 463 U.S. 1, 10, 22 (1983).

238 Stikes v. Chevron USA, Inc., 914 F.2d 1265, 1267 (9th Cir. 1990) (Labor Management Relations Act completely preempts state law claims).

239 *See* 16 Moore's Federal Practice Ch. 107, *Removal* (Matthew Bender 3d ed.).

240 Caterpillar, Inc. v. Williams, 482 U.S. 386, 392 (1987) (plaintiff is master of complaint); Salveson v. Western States Bankcard Ass'n, 731 F.2d 1423, 1427 (9th Cir. 1984) (when case involves both federal and state grounds, plaintiff is free to ignore federal question and file in state court).

241 Caterpillar, Inc. v. Williams, 482 U.S. 386, 392 (1987) (plaintiff is master of complaint).

242 Ortiz-Bonilla v. Federación de Ajedrez de P.R., Inc., 734 F.3d 28, 38 (1st Cir. 2013) (federal court did not have removal jurisdiction over plaintiffs' second complaint, which did not include federal causes of action that had been asserted in first complaint); *see* Sorosky v. Burroughs Corp., 826 F.2d 794, 799–801 (9th Cir. 1987) (court will examine case to determine whether preempted by ERISA).

as the state and federal claims form part of the same case and controversy in a transactional sense.[243] Thus, the federal court has the power to hear and determine the state claims as well as the federal claims. Accordingly, if the plaintiff dismisses the federal claims, the district court has the power to retain jurisdiction over the state law claims.[244] As a practical matter, however, most district judges will exercise their discretion under the supplemental jurisdiction statute and dismiss the remaining state law claims (see Ch. 5).[245] The plaintiff's right to dismiss the federal claims is subject to Rule 41, which limits the opportunity for the plaintiffs to voluntarily dismiss an action or claims.[246]

Some defendants object to such practices as manipulative. The courts, however, are generally loath to impose sanctions when a party seeks to maintain the advantage in forum selection within the bounds of legal doctrine and the facts. For example, in one case the plaintiff filed an employment discrimination action in state court. After the action was removed to federal court, the plaintiff dismissed the federal claim and moved to remand. The district court imposed sanctions for "manipulative pleading practices." The Ninth Circuit reversed, finding no basis for sanctions against either party under Rule 11,[247] or under Section 1447(c),[248] which permits the discretionary award of attorney's fees for improvident removal. The Ninth Circuit noted that the plaintiff was entitled to file any claims with a legal and factual basis in state court, and that the defendants were entitled to remove if there was federal jurisdiction. It further noted, however, that the plaintiff was entitled to drop the federal claims, and that it would then be up to the district court to determine whether to remand or retain jurisdiction. "We are not convinced that such practices were anything to be discouraged."[249]

An important exception to the "plaintiff is the master of the complaint" rule. Under the "artful pleading" rule, an action may be removed to federal court even though the complaint purports to assert only state-law claims if the state-law claims are completely preempted by federal law.[250] The artful pleading rule does not apply to ordinary preemption, also known as partial or defensive preemption.

---

[243] *See* Ch. 5, *Supplemental Jurisdiction.*

[244] Albingia Versicherungs A.G. v. Schenker Int'l, Inc., 344 F.3d 931, 934–939 (9th Cir. 2003) (no abuse of discretion in exercising supplemental jurisdiction over related state law claims, particularly when plaintiff sought dismissal or remand only after adverse judgment).

[245] 28 U.S.C. § 1367(c)(3) (district court may decline to exercise supplemental jurisdiction when "district court has dismissed all claims over which it has original jurisdiction").

[246] Fed. R. Civ. P. 41; *see* 8 Moore's Federal Practice Ch. 41, *Dismissal of Actions* (Matthew Bender 3d ed.).

[247] Fed. R. Civ. P. 11; *see generally* 2 Moore's Federal Practice Ch. 11, *Signing Pleadings, Motions and Other Papers; Representations to the Court*; *Sanctions* (Matthew Bender 3d ed.).

[248] 28 U.S.C. § 1447(c).

[249] Baddie v. Berkeley Farms, Inc., 64 F.3d 487, 490 (9th Cir. 1995).

[250] *See* Metropolitan Life Ins. Co. v. Taylor, 481 U.S. 58, 64–65 (1987) ("One corollary of the well-pleaded complaint rule developed in the case law, however, is that Congress may so completely pre-empt a particular area that any civil complaint raising this select group of claims is necessarily federal in character"; removal upheld based on complete preemptive effect of Employee Retirement Income Security Act of 1974); *see* 29 U.S.C. § 1132(a)(1)(B).

Removal of a complaint that purports to assert only state-law claims may also be permitted if a federal statute expressly provides for removal. For example, the Price-Anderson Act[251] not only gives federal courts jurisdiction over tort actions arising out of nuclear accidents, but also expressly provides for removal of such actions brought in state court even when they assert only state-law claims.[252] Another example is the Securities Litigation Uniform Standards Act,[253] which expressly provides for the removal of covered class actions and permits the court to look beyond the face of the complaint to determine whether the case is removable.[254] Congress also has provided for removal in a case in which the plaintiff alleges only state law claims, but the defendant files a counterclaim alleging a federal patent or copyright violation.[255]

### [4] Removal of Claims Under Section 1441(a) and (b) That Are Supported by Other Grants of Federal Jurisdiction

When a defendant seeks removal under a special removal statute that does not require the federal court to have original jurisdiction of the case, the well-pleaded complaint rule does not apply.[256] For example, a federal officer may remove a civil or criminal action brought against him or her for any act performed under color of office, even if the federal court would not have had original jurisdiction of the case.[257] However, such an action is not removable unless the case presents a substantial federal question.[258] However, since the removal statute does not require that the federal court have original jurisdiction, the necessary federal question need not have been apparent on the face of the complaint; it may be raised in the defendant federal officer's answer to the complaint or notice of removal.[259]

---

[251] 42 U.S.C. § 2014(hh).

[252] *See* Beneficial Nat'l Bank v. Anderson, 539 U.S. 1, 6 (2003) (Price-Anderson Act cited as example of statute in which Congress created exception to rule that case will not be removable if complaint does not affirmatively allege federal claim).

[253] Securities Litigation Uniform Standards Act of 1998, 1998 Enacted S. 1260, 105 Enacted S. 1260, 112 Stat. 3227, 3228, codified at 15 U.S.C. 77p ("SLUSA").

[254] *See* Romano v. Kazacos, 609 F.3d 512, 519 (2d Cir. 2010) (district court's refusal to remand case to state court affirmed because, looking beyond face of complaint to substance of allegations, complaint fell within scope of SLUSA).

[255] See 28 U.S.C. § 1454 ("A civil action in which *any party* asserts a [patent or copyright] claim . . . may be removed.")

[256] Mesa v. California, 489 U.S. 121, 134–136 (1989).

[257] 28 U.S.C. § 1442(a)(1).

[258] Mesa v. California, 489 U.S. at 134–135.

[259] Mesa v. California, 489 U.S. at 136 (removal statute overcomes well-pleaded complaint rule, which would otherwise preclude removal even if federal defense were alleged); *see* 28 U.S.C. § 1442(a)(1).

## [5] Removal When Federal Question Claim Is Joined to Nonremovable Claim

### [a] Entire Case Removed; Nonremovable Claims Remanded

Whenever a removable claim or cause of action within federal question jurisdiction[260] is joined with otherwise nonremovable claims or causes of action (claims that are not within the original or supplemental jurisdiction of the district court or that have been made nonremovable by statute), the entire action may be removed.[261] However, the district court must then sever the claims that are not within its original or supplemental jurisdiction or that have been made nonremovable by statute and remand them to the state court from which the action was removed.[262] The district court must retain jurisdiction over the removable claims,[263] with the possible exception of claims over which it has supplemental jurisdiction, which it might decline to exercise under Section 1367(c) (*see* Ch. 5, *Supplemental Jurisdiction*). These provisions apply to cases commenced on or after January 6, 2012.[264]

From 1990 to 2012, Section 1441(c) provided for removal of the entire case when a "separate and independent" claim or cause of action within federal question jurisdiction was joined with one or more otherwise non-removable claims. Under that version of the statute, the district court had discretion either to determine all of the issues in the case or to remand all matters in which state law predominated.[265] This raised constitutional issues, because it appeared to provide district courts with discretion to exercise jurisdiction over claims that were not within its original or supplemental jurisdiction, arguably in violation of Article III.[266] This problem is avoided under the amended statute, because the district court is now required to remand the claims over which it does not have original or supplemental jurisdiction.[267]

### [b] Only Defendants to Federal Question Claim Must Consent to Removal

When a claim over which the district court has federal-question jurisdiction is joined to a claim over which the district court has neither original nor supplemental jurisdiction, or that has been made nonremovable by statute, only the defendants

---

260 28 U.S.C. § 1331.

261 28 U.S.C. § 1441(c)(1).

262 28 U.S.C. § 1441(c)(2).

263 Court must retain removable claims. Bivins v. Glanz, 2012 U.S. Dist. LEXIS 106871, at *4 (N.D. Okla. Aug. 1, 2012) ("The Court must sever and remand the nonremovable claim and retain all other removed claims that are within the Court's original or supplemental jurisdiction.").

264 Pub. L. No. 112–63, § 105, 125 Stat. 758 (2011).

265 *See* former 28 U.S.C. § 1441(c).

266 *See* U.S. Const., Art. III.

267 28 U.S.C. § 1446(c)(2).

against whom the federal-question claim is asserted are required to join in or consent to the removal.[268] Moreover, when a case is removed under Section 1441(c), only the defendants against whom the federal question claims are asserted must join or consent to removal.[269] This makes sense because parties who are defendants only with respect to the claims over which the district court has neither original nor supplemental jurisdiction or that have been made nonremovable by statute ought not be able to defeat the federal question defendant's right to remove.[270]

The case of parties who are defendants only with respect to claims over which the district court has supplemental jurisdiction is different. When a case including only claims over which a district court has either federal-question jurisdiction or supplemental jurisdiction is removed under Section 1441(a), all parties must consent to removal, including those who are defendants only as to the claims over which the district court has only supplemental jurisdiction.[271] In that situation, the supplemental-jurisdiction defendants can prevent removal by refusing to consent to removal. However, when a case includes federal-question claims, supplementary claims, and one or more claims over which the district court has neither original nor supplemental jurisdiction or that is nonremovable by statute, and the case is removed under Section 1441(c), the consent of parties who are defendants only on the supplemental-jurisdiction claims is not required.[272] This result preserves the right of the federal-question defendants to have the claims against them heard in federal court, but at the expense of the right of any non-consenting supplemental-jurisdiction claim defendants to keep the claims against them in state court. However, they can seek to have the district court decline to exercise its supplemental jurisdiction (see Ch. 5).

## [6] Removal of Class Actions

### [a] Class Actions Generally May Be Removed to Federal Court

The Class Action Fairness Act of 2005 (CAFA)[273] authorizes the removal of certain class actions involving multistate parties.[274] Under CAFA, removal is permissible based on minimal diversity. In addition, a class action involving multistate parties that is not initially removable may become removable as the case progresses. For example, state court plaintiffs may amend the complaint to increase the amount of damages in excess of the CAFA jurisdictional amount so as to permit

---

268 28 U.S.C. § 1441(c)(2); *see* § 107.11[1][d].

269 Thomson v. Oklahoma Employment Security Comm'n, 2012 U.S. Dist. LEXIS 95118, at *3–*4 (W.D. Okla. July 10, 2012) ("Even when a district court severs and remands nonremovable claims from an action under the recently amended § 1441(c)(2), defendants against whom a federal question claim has been asserted are required to join in or consent to removal.").

270 28 U.S.C. § 1441(c)(2).

271 28 U.S.C. § 1446(b)(2)(A).

272 28 U.S.C. § 1441(c)(2).

273 P.L. No. 109-2, 119 Stat. 4.

274 28 U.S.C. §§ 1332(d)(10), 1453(b).

removal to federal court.[275] Moreover, under CAFA, there is no overall one-year time limitation on removal as under the general removal statute.[276]

CAFA defines a "class action" as any civil action filed under Rule 23 of the Federal Rules of Civil Procedure or similar state statute or rule of judicial procedure authorizing an action to be brought by one or more representative persons as a class action, both before and after the entry of a class certification order by the court.[277]

CAFA specifically excludes certain types of class actions from its scope. Thus, CAFA's special removal provisions do not apply to any of the following types of class actions:

- *Certain securities actions excluded.* CAFA's removal procedures do not apply to any class action that solely involves a claim concerning a covered security as defined under § 16(f)(3) of the Securities Act of 1933 and § 28(f)(5)(E) of the Securities Exchange Act of 1934.[278]
- *Actions concerning fiduciary duties and related obligations concerning securities excluded.* CAFA's removal procedures do not apply to any class action that solely involves a claim that relates to the rights, duties (including fiduciary duties), and obligations relating to or created by or pursuant to any security as defined under § 2(a)(1) of the Securities Act of 1933 and the regulations issued under that section.[279]
- *Actions concerning intracorporate and business organization litigation excluded.* CAFA's removal procedures do not apply to any class action that solely involves a claim that relates to the internal affairs or governance of a corporation or other form of business enterprise and arises under or by virtue of the laws of the state in which the corporation or business enterprise is incorporated or organized.[280]

Several circuits have held that once the removing party has established the general requirements of CAFA, the party seeking remand bears the burden of proving one of these exceptions to CAFA jurisdiction.[281]

---

[275] *See, e.g.*, 28 U.S.C. § 1332(d)(4).

[276] *Cf.* 28 U.S.C. § 1446(b).

[277] 28 U.S.C. § 1332(d)(1)(B), (8); *see* College of Dental Surgeons of Puerto Rico v. Connecticut General Life Ins. Co., 585 F.3d 33, 39–40 (1st Cir. 2009) (complaint that alleged harm to dentists as group and sought class-wide relief fell within scope of CAFA); Erie Ins. Exch. v. Erie Indem. Co., 722 F.3d 154, 158 (3d Cir. 2013) (suit filed by insurance exchange members under state rules that contain none of Rule 23's class action requirements was not "class action" subject to CAFA jurisdiction).

[278] 28 U.S.C. § 1453(d)(1); *see* 15 U.S.C. § 78p(f)(3); 15 U.S.C. § 78bb(f)(5)(E); *see generally* 15 U.S.C. §§ 77p, 77z-1, 78bb, 78u-4 (excepted claims would still be subject to Private Securities Litigation Reform Act (PSLRA) and Securities Litigation Uniform Standard Act of 1998 (SLUSA), both addressed in Ch. 23, *Class Actions*, § 23.190).

[279] 28 U.S.C. § 1453(d)(3); *see* 15 U.S.C. § 77b(a)(1).

[280] 28 U.S.C. § 1453(d)(2).

[281] Greenwich Fin. Servs. Distressed Mortgage Fund 3 LLC v. Countrywide Fin. Corp., 603 F.3d 23, 26 (2d Cir. 2010) ("once the general requirements of CAFA jurisdiction are established, plaintiffs have the burden of demonstrating that remand is warranted on the basis of one of the enumerated

## [b] CAFA Makes Removal of Class Actions More Common

### [i] Only Minimal Diversity Required

Congress has vested the district courts with original jurisdiction of any civil action in which the matter in controversy exceeds the aggregated sum or value of $5,000,000, exclusive of interest and costs, that is a class action under the following circumstances:[282]

- Any member of a class of plaintiffs is a citizen of a state different from any defendant;
- Any member of a class of plaintiffs is a foreign state or a citizen or subject of a foreign state and any defendant is a citizen of a state; or
- Any member of a class of plaintiffs is a citizen of a state and any defendant is a foreign state or a citizen or subject of a foreign state.

The scope of expanded jurisdiction provided by CAFA becomes more apparent when these minimal diversity requirements are compared to the diversity of citizenship requirements applicable in other, non-CAFA actions. In those actions, the "complete diversity" rule applies. The "complete diversity" rule requires that each named class representative must be a citizen of a different state from each defendant (*see* § 6.08[2]).[283]

### [ii] Amount in Controversy Is to Be Aggregated

Federal district courts have original jurisdiction over any class action governed by CAFA in which the matter in controversy exceeds the sum or value of $5,000,000, exclusive of interest and costs,[284] provided that CAFA's minimal diversity requirements are met. Class members' claims may be aggregated to determine the requisite amount in controversy.[285] It is not necessary that any individual plaintiff's claim exceed the jurisdictional minimum amount in controversy for non-CAFA diversity cases.[286]

Most courts, including all of the circuits that have considered the issue, have held that a defendant seeking to remove a case under CAFA has the burden of establishing the amount in controversy.[287] This is in accord with the long-standing

---

exceptions"); Appert v. Morgan Stanley Dean Witter, Inc., 673 F.3d 609, 618–619 (7th Cir. 2012) (plaintiff had burden to show that securities exception applied).

282 28 U.S.C. § 1332(d)(2).

283 28 U.S.C. § 1332(a); *see* Strawbridge v. Curtiss, 7 U.S. (3 Cranch) 267, 267 (1806); *accord* Supreme Tribe of Ben-Hur v. Cauble, 255 U.S. 356, 365 (1921).

284 28 U.S.C. § 1332(d)(2).

285 28 U.S.C. § 1332(d)(6).

286 Cappuccitti v. DirectTV, Inc., 623 F.3d 1118, 1122 (11th Cir. 2010) (district court had subject matter jurisdiction over class action brought on behalf of over 100 persons whose claims, in aggregate, exceeded $5 million, even though no single plaintiff's claim exceeded $75,000). *See* 15 Moore's Federal Practice § 107.14[2][g] and 15 Moore's Federal Practice Ch. 102, *Diversity Jurisdiction*, for further discussion.

287 Amoche v. Guarantee Trust Life Ins. Co., 556 F.3d 41, 48 (1st Cir. 2009); Blockbuster, Inc. v.

rule in non-CAFA cases placing the burden of proving that subject matter jurisdiction exists on the removing defendant.

A precertification stipulation by a prospective class representative that the plaintiffs will not seek total aggregate damages of more than five million dollars does not defeat federal jurisdiction over the proposed class action under CAFA. This is because a plaintiff cannot legally bind members of a proposed class before the class is certified. Therefore, such a stipulation does not effectively reduce the value of the putative class members' claims.[288]

### [c] When CAFA Jurisdiction Will Not Be Exercised

Assuming CAFA's basic minimal diversity and amount in controversy provisions are met, CAFA provides plaintiff's the opportunity to persuade the district court to remand the action. First, as discussed below, under 28 U.S.C. § 1332(d)(3), federal district courts *may* decline jurisdiction under CAFA in the interests of justice.

Second, as discussed immediately below, there are two situations involving essentially local conflicts in which a district court *must* decline to exercise jurisdiction under CAFA. In these two situations, the district court may retain the case only if there is some other, non-CAFA basis for jurisdiction, such as a federal question or traditional diversity of citizenship. The two CAFA exceptions do not preclude federal courts from exercising subject matter jurisdiction over class actions on these other bases.[289]

The first situation in which the district court *must* decline to exercise jurisdiction under CAFA is known as the "local-controversy" exception. This applies when all of the following are true:[290]

- More than two-thirds of the members of all proposed plaintiff classes, in the aggregate, are citizens of the state in which the action was originally filed.
- At least one defendant who is a citizen of the state in which the action was originally filed is also a defendant "from whom significant relief is sought" by members of the plaintiff class or classes and "whose alleged conduct forms a significant basis for the claims asserted" by the proposed plaintiff class or classes.
- The members of the plaintiff class or classes incurred "principal injuries" resulting from the alleged conduct (or any related conduct) of each

---

Galeno, 472 F.3d 53, 57–58 (2d Cir. 2006) ("Every circuit court that has considered this issue has reached the same conclusion," that is, that burden remains on defendant); *see also* Morgan v. Gay, 471 F.3d 469, 472–473 (3d Cir. 2006); Brill v. Countrywide Home Loans, Inc., 427 F.3d 446, 447 (7th Cir. 2005); Bell v. Hershey Co., 557 F.3d 953, 956 (8th Cir. 2009); Abrego v. Dow Chem. Co., 443 F.3d 676, 685–686 (9th Cir. 2006); Thomas v. Bank of Am. Corp., 570 F.3d 1280, 1283 (11th Cir. 2009); Miedema v. Maytag Corp., 450 F.3d 1322, 1328–1330 (11th Cir. 2006).

[288] Standard Fire Ins. Co. v. Knowles, 133 S. Ct. 1345, 185 L. Ed. 2d 439, 444 (2013) ("Because his precertification stipulation does not bind anyone but himself, Knowles has not reduced the value of the putative class members' claims," and, therefore, stipulation did not prevent removal).

[289] *See* 28 U.S.C. § 1332(a).

[290] 28 U.S.C. § 1332(d)(4)(A).

defendant in the state in which the action was originally filed.

- During the three-year period preceding the filing of the class action, no other class action has been filed asserting the same or similar factual allegations against any of the defendants on behalf of the same or other persons.

The "local-controversy" exception is to be construed narrowly, with all doubts resolved in favor of the federal court's exercising CAFA jurisdiction.[291]

The second exception to CAFA jurisdiction is known as the "home state controversy" exception. It applies when "two-thirds or more of the members of all proposed plaintiff classes in the aggregate" and "the primary defendants" are all citizens of the state in which the action was originally filed.[292] The phrase "in the aggregate" has been interpreted as requiring the court to consider all of the proposed plaintiff classes in the action before the court, not all of the potential class members in *all* suits with similar allegations.[293] The use of the term "the primary defendants" rather than "a primary defendant" indicates that the exception applies only when all of the primary defendants are residents of the state in which the action was filed.[294]

Unlike the local-controversy exception, the home state exception is framed entirely in terms of the parties' citizenship. There is no reference to the existence of other class actions asserting similar allegations.[295] Therefore, the fact that a suit meeting the requirements of the home state exception may, in fact, be part of a larger national or international controversy is irrelevant for purposes of CAFA jurisdiction.[296]

Whether either the local-controversy or the home state exception applies is determined based on the class the plaintiff proposed when the suit was filed.

---

[291] *See* S. Rep. No. 109-14 at 39, 42 (2005), *as reprinted in* 2005 U.S.C.C.A.N. 38; Opelousas Gen. Hosp. v. Fairpay Solutions, Inc., 655 F.3d 358, 360 (5th Cir. 2011) (local controversy exception intended to be narrow, with all doubts resolved in favor of exercising jurisdiction); Evans v. Walter Indus., Inc., 449 F.3d 1159, 1163–1164 (11th Cir. 2006) (exception inapplicable; plaintiffs failed to prove that more than two-thirds of class were Alabama citizens or that relevant defendant was "significant").

[292] 28 U.S.C. § 1332(d)(4)(B).

[293] Hannaford Bros. Co. Customer Data Sec. Breach Litig., 564 F.3d 75, 78–79 (1st Cir. 2009) (plural "classes" used in statute because single complaint may contain multiple classes; court considered only citizenship of members of proposed classes in case before it, not citizenship of members of proposed classes in previously filed national class actions involving defendant); *In re* Sprint Nextel Corp., 593 F.3d 669, 672 (7th Cir. 2010) (same language in local controversy exception could not refer to members of proposed classes in other cases, and it would be "surprising" if language meant something different in home state exception; court considered only citizenship of members of proposed classes in case before it, not citizenship of members of proposed classes in all text messaging antitrust cases).

[294] Vodenichar v. Halcón Energy Props., 733 F.3d 497, 506 (3d Cir. 2013) (home state exception inapplicable because one of defendants was not from home state); Anthony v. Small Tube Mfg. Corp., 535 F. Supp. 2d 506, 515 (E.D. Pa. 2007) (plaintiff failed to establish that primary defendants were residents of state in which suit was filed).

[295] *Compare* 28 U.S.C. § 1332(d)(4)(B) *with* 28 U.S.C. § 1332(d)(4)(A).

[296] *In re* Sprint Nextel Corp., 593 F.3d 669, 673 (7th Cir. 2010) (fact that text messaging antitrust case filed in Kansas may be part of larger national controversy concerning text messaging is irrelevant in determining whether home state controversy exception applies).

Subsequent developments, such as a district court determination that class members from other states do not have standing, do not destroy federal jurisdiction by bringing the case within the scope of the exceptions. This follows from the principle that subject-matter jurisdiction depends on the state of things when the suit is filed, not on later developments.[297]

If the other requirements of the local-controversy or home state exception are met, the plaintiffs may ensure that the exception applies by defining the class in such a way that only citizens of the state in which the suit is filed are class members.[298]

Several circuit and district courts have held that although the removing defendant bears the burden of proving the basic aspects of CAFA jurisdiction, the party objecting to federal jurisdiction under the home state or local-controversy rule bears the burden of showing that the rule applies.[299] Placing the burden on the party asserting an exception to jurisdiction comports with longstanding Section 1441(a) doctrine concerning the burden of showing exceptions to jurisdiction and with congressional intent to do the same with CAFA.

Federal district courts *may* decline jurisdiction under CAFA in the interests of justice and looking at the totality of the circumstances if all of the following are true:[300]

- More than one-third of the members of all proposed plaintiff classes, in the aggregate, are citizens of the state in which the action was originally filed.
- Fewer than two-thirds of the members of all proposed plaintiff classes, in the aggregate, are citizens of the state in which the action was originally

---

[297] Morrison v. YTB Int'l, Inc., 649 F.3d 533, 535–536 (7th Cir. 2011) ("Subject-matter jurisdiction depends on the state of things when suit is filed; what happens later does not detract from jurisdiction already established"; district court's conclusion that out-of-state class members could not obtain relief under Illinois Consumer Fraud Act did not change fact that most members of only "proposed class" lived outside Illinois).

[298] *In re* Hannaford Bros. Co. Customer Data Sec., 564 F.3d 75, 78–81 (1st Cir. 2009) (class defined to include only Florida citizens); *See also* Johnson v. Advance America, 549 F.3d 932, 938 (4th Cir. 2008); *In re* Sprint Nextel Corp., 593 F.3d 669, 676 (7th Cir. 2010).

[299] *In re* Sprint Nextel Corp., 593 F.3d 669, 673–676 (7th Cir. 2010) (likelihood that most of members of class consisting of Kansas residents with Kansas cell phone numbers and billing addresses were Kansas citizens was insufficient to satisfy burden; plaintiffs should have submitted evidence that two-thirds of class members were Kansas domiciliaries or businesses or defined class to include only Kansas citizens); Westerfeld v. Independent Processing, LLC, 621 F.3d 819, 823 (8th Cir. 2010) (once CAFA's basic jurisdictional requirements are satisfied, burden shifts to party seeking to establish that local-controversy exception applies); Kaufman v. Allstate New Jersey Ins. Co., 561 F.3d 144, 153–154 (3d Cir. 2009) (plaintiff seeking remand had burden of establishing that local controversy exception applied); *see also* Preston v. Tenet Healthsystem Memorial Med. Center, 485 F.3d 804, 812 (5th Cir. 2007); Frazier v. Pioneer Ams. LLC, 455 F.3d 542, 546 (5th Cir. 2006); Hart v. Fedex Ground Package Sys. Inc., 457 F.3d 675, 680 (7th Cir. 2006); Serrano v. 180 Connect, Inc., 478 F.3d 1018, 1023–1024 (9th Cir. 2007); Evans v. Walter Indus., Inc., 449 F.3d 1159, 1164 (11th Cir. 2006); *see also* Mattera v. Clear Channel Communications, Inc., 239 F.R.D. 70, 78–79 (S.D.N.Y. 2006) (in case originally filed in federal court, burden on defendant objecting to federal jurisdiction to prove exception applies; placing burden on party seeking to avail itself of CAFA exception best furthers CAFA's stated purpose of allowing federal courts to hear more interstate class actions).

[300] 28 U.S.C. § 1332(d)(3).

filed.

- The "primary" defendants are citizens of the state in which the action was originally filed.[301]

In deciding whether to decline jurisdiction under this provision, the court is to look at the following factors:[302]

- Whether the claims involve matters of national or interstate interest.
- Whether the claims will be governed by laws of the state in which the action was originally filed or of other states.
- Whether the class action has been pleaded in a manner that seeks to avoid federal jurisdiction.
- Whether the action was brought in a forum with a distinct nexus with the class members, the alleged harm, or the defendants.
- Whether the number of citizens of the state in which the action was originally filed in all proposed plaintiff classes in the aggregate is substantially larger than the number of citizens from any other state, and the citizenship of the other members of the proposed class is dispersed among a substantial number of states.
- Whether, during the three-year period before the class action was filed, one or more other class actions asserting the same or similar claims on behalf of the same or other person have been filed.

However, if there is some basis for federal jurisdiction other than CAFA, such as federal question or complete diversity, the district court may not decline to exercise jurisdiction under this provision.[303]

### [d] "Mass Actions" May Also Be Removed

CAFA generally treats a "mass action" as a class action. Mass actions are removable in the same manner as class actions.[304] A "mass action," with certain exceptions, is any civil action other than a class action in which monetary relief claims of 100 or more persons are proposed by the plaintiff to be tried jointly on the ground that the claims involve common questions of law or fact.[305] Whether the claims actually proceed to a joint trial is irrelevant.[306]

---

301 *See* Caruso v. Allstate Ins. Company, 469 F. Supp. 2d 364, 368–370 (E.D. La. 2007) (comparing "significant" as used in local controversy exception with "primary" as used in home state controversy exception; referring to dictionary definition of "primary" as "first in importance; chief; principal; main"); *see also* Kearns v. Ford Motor Co., 2005 U.S. Dist. LEXIS 41614, at *26 (C.D. Cal. Nov. 21, 2005).

302 28 U.S.C. § 1332(d)(3). *See* Martin v. Lafon Nursing Facility of the Holy Family, Inc., 548 F. Supp. 2d 268, 278–279 (E.D. La. 2008) (based on statutory factors, claims against nursing home for its alleged failure to protect residents from Hurricane Katrina present "quintessential example" of type of "truly localized" controversy Congress intended to except from CAFA).

303 *See* 28 U.S.C. § 1332(a).

304 28 U.S.C. § 1332(d)(11)(A).

305 28 U.S.C. § 1332(d)(11)(B)(i), (ii); *see generally* Knight, *The CAFA Mass Action Numerosity Requirement: Three Problems With Counting to 100*, 78 Fordham L. Rev. 1875 (2010).

306 Visendi v. Bank of America, N.A., 733 F.3d 863, 868 (9th Cir. 2013) (district court's post-removal

All of the circuits to have decided the issue and some district courts have held that a district court may not aggregate individual related state court actions, each with fewer than 100 plaintiffs, to form a removable mass action. The plain language of the statute precludes such treatment, limiting "mass actions" to actions in which "claims of 100 or more persons are proposed to be tried jointly . . . ."[307] In addition, the statutory exclusion of actions in which claims are joined on a motion by the defendant or solely for pretrial proceedings[308] indicates congressional intent that such actions not be treated as mass actions. This result is consistent with the general rules that the plaintiffs may choose their forum, and that there is a presumption against federal removal jurisdiction.[309]

Some courts have held that a motion by the plaintiffs for consolidation may bring the case within the definition of mass action if it explicitly, or even implicitly, proposes a joint trial.[310] However, the Ninth Circuit held that a motion for coordination that did not explicitly propose a joint trial and that focused on pretrial proceedings did not render the cases a mass action subject to CAFA removal.[311] The Ninth Circuit, however, has vacated its opinion for rehearing en banc. These cases teach that when determining whether the plaintiffs have proposed a joint trial, it is important to look to the text of the state consolidation statute in question as well as the plaintiffs' contemporaneous statements regarding the purpose of their consolidation request.[312]

An important difference between class actions and mass actions under CAFA is the applicable amount in controversy. A class action is removable if the aggregated

---

conclusion that plaintiff's claims were improperly joined did not affect court's jurisdiction, because at time of removal, plaintiffs proposed joint trial).

307 28 U.S.C. § 1332(d)(11)(A).

308 28 U.S.C. § 1332(d)(11)(B)(ii)(II), (IV) (" 'mass action' shall not include any civil action in which . . . (II) the claims are joined upon motion of a defendant; . . . [or] (IV) the claims have been consolidated or coordinated solely for pretrial proceedings").

309 *See* 28 U.S.C.§ 1332(d)(11)(B)(i) (defining "mass action"); Anderson v. Bayer Corp., 610 F.3d 390, 393–394 (7th Cir. 2010) (four mostly identical state court personal injury complaints against manufacturer of prescription drug could not be removed as mass action because each had fewer than 100 plaintiffs and Congress explicitly stated defendant's request for consolidation is not basis for removal of mass action); *see also* Koral v. Boeing Co., 628 F.3d 945, 947 (7th Cir. 2011) (plaintiff's prediction that state court might decide to hold joint trial of separate suits involving airplane crash is not "proposal" for joint trial; state court's decision to conduct joint trial on its own initiative would not support removal as mass action); Tanoh v. Dow Chemical Co., 561 F.3d 945, 952–956 (9th Cir. 2009) (seven similar cases against single defendant, each involving fewer than 100 plaintiffs, could not be removed as "mass action" under CAFA); Scimone v. Carnival Corp., 720 F.3d 876, 880–887 (11th Cir. 2013) (separate actions, each with less than 100 plaintiffs, may not be removed as "mass action" merely because claims revolve around common questions of law or fact).

310 *In re* Abbott Labs., Inc., 698 F.3d 568, 572–573 (7th Cir. 2012) (motion to consolidate and transfer related state court cases to one circuit court "through trial" constituted proposal for joint trial, triggering CAFA's mass action jurisdiction); Atwell v. Boston Scientific Corp., 740 F.3d 1160, 1165–1166 (8th Cir. 2013) (inevitable result of joint assignment would be joint trial or exemplar trial with legal issues applied to remaining cases, either of which would render cases "mass action" subject to removal).

311 Romo v. Teva Pharms. USA, Inc., 731 F.3d 918, 922–923 (9th Cir. 2013) (motion for coordination that focused on pretrial proceedings did not amount to proposal for joint trial); vacated and rehearing, en banc by 742 F.3d 909 (2014).

312 *See* Koral v. Boeing Co., 628 F.3d 945, 947 (7th Cir. 2011).

claims of the class exceed $5,000,000.[313] With respect to mass actions, *each* plaintiff's claims must exceed $75,000.[314] Additionally, a removed mass action may not be transferred subsequently to another court for consolidated pretrial procedures under 28 U.S.C. § 1407, unless a majority of the *plaintiffs* in the action request transfer (*see* Ch. 10 (Multidistrict Litigation).[315] This anti-transfer provision applies only to mass actions, not to certified class actions or actions proposed for certification.[316]

### [e] Actions Brought by State Attorneys General

If a state attorney general files a suit as a class action and it meets the other requirements for removability under the Class Action Fairness Act, the court may permit removal.[317] However, most courts have refused to treat a suit filed by a state attorney general as a removable mass action if the suit was filed in the name of the attorney general alone rather than as a class action.[318] The Supreme Court has made clear that if the state attorney general files an action as a *parens patriae* action, it is not a removable mass action. In *Mississippi ex rel. Hood v. AU Optronics Corp.*, in a unanimous opinion, the Supreme Court held that only actual plaintiffs are to be considered in determining whether the 100 plaintiff numerosity requirement for a mass action is satisfied. Therefore, a suit filed by a state attorney general, with the state as the sole plaintiff, does not constitute a mass action. This is true even if relief is sought on behalf of 100 or more of the state's citizens.[319]

---

[313] 28 U.S.C. § 1332(d)(2).

[314] *See* 28 U.S.C. § 1332(a), (d)(11)(B)(i).

[315] 28 U.S.C. § 1332(d)(11)(C)(i); *see* 28 U.S.C. § 1407; *see generally* Ch. 112, *Multidistrict Litigation*.

[316] 28 U.S.C. § 1332(d)(11)(C)(ii).

[317] *See, e.g.*, *In re* Katrina Canal Litig. Breaches, 524 F.3d 700, 706 (5th Cir. 2008) ("With citizens of Louisiana joined as plaintiffs there is minimal diversity.").

[318] Purdue Pharma L.P. v. Kentucky, 704 F.3d 208, 212 (2d Cir. 2013) (parens patriae suits brought by state attorneys general are not removable as class actions under CAFA); West Virginia v. CVS Pharmacy, Inc., 646 F.3d 169, 172 (4th Cir. 2011) (state attorney general's parens patriae action was not class action within meaning of CAFA); State of Mississippi *ex rel.* Hood v. AU Optronics Corp., 701 F.3d 796, 799 (5th Cir. 2012), *rev'd on other grounds*, 134 S. Ct. 736, 187 L. Ed. 2d 654 (2014) (state attorney general's suit against manufacturers and distributors of liquid crystal display panels was not class action under CAFA jurisdiction); LG Display Co. v. Madigan, 665 F.3d 768, 772 (7th Cir. 2011) (state attorney general's parens patriae action was not class action under CAFA); Missouri *ex rel.* Koster v. Portfolio Recovery Assocs., 686 F. Supp. 2d 942, 944–947 (E.D. Mo. 2010) (state attorney general's suit was not class action under CAFA); Washington v. Chimei Innolux Corp., 659 F.3d 842, 847–850 (9th Cir. 2011) (parens patriae suits filed by state attorneys general in Washington and California were not class actions within meaning of CAFA).

[319] Mississippi *ex rel.* Hood v. AU Optronics Corp., 134 S. Ct. 736, 187 L. Ed. 2d 654, 663–668 (2014) (only actual plaintiffs are considered in determining whether suit is mass action under CAFA, so suit with State of Mississippi as only plaintiff is not mass action); *see* 28 U.S.C. § 1332(d)(11)(B)(i).

## [f] Special CAFA Removal Rules

### [i] Any Single Defendant May Remove

Removal procedures for class actions under the CAFA are generally the same as for other civil actions.[320] Chapter 6, Part C discusses these rules. However, CAFA expressly provides that covered class actions may be removed by any defendant without the consent of any other defendant.[321] For example, in a case that was originally filed before CAFA's effective date, the one defendant who had been added to the case after the effective date was able to remove the entire case to federal court.[322] In actions that fall outside of CAFA's scope, all the defendants must join in the notice of removal or the case is not removable.[323]

### [ii] Defendant's Local Citizenship Does Not Preclude Removal

CAFA expressly provides that covered class actions are removable without regard to whether any defendant is a citizen of the state in which the action was brought.[324] In actions that are outside CAFA's scope, the defendants may remove a civil action from state court to federal court on the basis of diversity of citizenship only if none of the defendants is a citizen of the state in which the action was originally brought.[325]

### [iii] One-Year Limitation on Removal Does Not Apply

The one-year absolute limitation on removal in diversity cases does not apply to multistate class actions under CAFA.[326] Under the general removal procedure statute, a notice of removal must ordinarily be filed within 30 days after receipt of the initial pleading or service of summons. If the case stated by the initial pleading is not removable, the notice of removal may be filed within 30 days after receipt of an amended pleading or other paper from which it may first be ascertained that the case is or has become removable. However, a case generally may not be removed based on diversity jurisdiction more than one year after commencement of the action.[327]

The 30-day requirement remains applicable to removal of class actions under CAFA (*see* § 6.09[a]). CAFA changes only the absolute one-year limitation on

---

[320] *See* 28 U.S.C. § 1453(b).

[321] 28 U.S.C. § 1453(b); United Steel v. Shell Oil, 549 F.3d 1204, 1208 (9th Cir. 2008) (statutory provision overrides judge-created requirement that each defendant consent to removal).

[322] Lowery v. Alabama Power Co., 483 F.3d 1184, 1195–1198 (11th Cir. 2007).

[323] *See* 28 U.S.C. § 1446(b). *See* § 6.05[2][c].

[324] 28 U.S.C. § 1453(b).

[325] 28 U.S.C. § 1441(b). *See* § 6.08[2][e].

[326] 28 U.S.C. § 1453(b).

[327] 28 U.S.C. § 1446(b). *See* § 6.09[2][a][iii].

removal[328] However, the elimination of the one-year limitation is significant. It means that if the removability of a class action becomes apparent at the later stages of an action, the action is still removable. Thus, under appropriate circumstances, a defendant may remove at any time, even several years after commencement of the action in state court, provided the notice of removal is filed within 30 days after receipt of a pleading or other paper from which the defendant first may ascertain that the action is or has become removable.[329]

### [g] Accelerated Appellate Review of Remand Order Is Possible

#### [i] Standard for Discretionary Review

CAFA expressly provides that a court of appeals may, in its discretion, accept an appeal from an order of a district court either granting or denying a motion to remand if a timely application is made to the appellate court.[330] The provision applies to both class actions and mass actions removed pursuant to CAFA.[331] It applies to sua sponte remand orders as well as to orders made in response to a party's motion.[332] It applies only to orders under CAFA;[333] in actions outside CAFA's special procedural provisions, an order granting or denying a motion to remand a case based on a lack of subject matter jurisdiction or procedural defect is not reviewable, on appeal or otherwise (*see* § 6.13).[334] The Supreme Court has jurisdiction to review a court of appeals' decision on appeal of a remand under CAFA.[335]

Several circuits have indicated that the presence of a CAFA-related question is

---

328 28 U.S.C. § 1453(b).

329 *See* 28 U.S.C. §§ 1446(b), 1453(b).

330 28 U.S.C. § 1453(c)(1); *see also* Fed. R. Civ. P. 6(a) (computation of time periods). BP America, Inc. v. Oklahoma *ex rel.* Edmondson, 613 F.3d 1029, 1032–1034 (10th Cir. 2010) (28 U.S.C. § 1447(c) does not deprive courts of appeals of jurisdiction to review remand order under 28 U.S.C. § 1453(c)(1)); Tmesys, Inc. v. Eufaula Drugs, Inc., 462 F.3d 1317, 1318–1319 (11th Cir. 2006) (court of appeals has jurisdiction to review district court's order to remand that is based on determination that CAFA does not apply, at least to extent of reexamining that jurisdictional issue).

331 Abraham v. St. Croix Renaissance Group, L.L.L.P., 719 F.3d 270, 275 (28 U.S.C. § 1453(c)(1) applies to mass actions); *see* 28 U.S.C. § 1332(d)(11)(A) (mass action deemed to be removable class action for purposes of 28 U.S.C. § 1453).

332 Watkins v. Vital Pharms., Inc., 720 F.3d 1179, 1181 (9th Cir. 2013) (insulation of sua sponte district court orders remanding class actions "would be inconsistent with CAFA's clearly expressed intention that the class actions are exempt from the general jurisdictional rule that district court remand orders are not reviewable on appeal").

333 Patterson v. Dean Morris, LLP, 448 F.3d 736, 742–743 (5th Cir. 2006) (CAFA's appellate provision not available to review otherwise non-reviewable decision to equitably remand; state court class action had commenced before effective date of CAFA, so CAFA was inapplicable); Saab v. Home Depot U.S.A., Inc., 469 F.3d 758, 759–760 (8th Cir. 2006).

334 28 U.S.C. § 1447(c), (d).

335 28 U.S.C. § 1254; Hertz Corp. v. Friend, 559 U.S. 77, 83–84 (2010) (60-day time limit for court of appeals decision (*see* 28 U.S.C. § 1453(c)) does not deprive Supreme Court of subsequent jurisdiction to review case).

an important factor in the decision whether to exercise discretion to review a CAFA remand order. The courts relied in part on a senate report stating that the courts were given discretion to review remand orders under CAFA in large part to "develop a body of appellate law interpreting [CAFA]," although the report was actually published after CAFA was enacted.[336]

The courts of appeals have identified a number of other factors as relevant to its decision whether to exercise its discretion to review a district court's remand of a case removed under CAFA. The First Circuit specified that this list of factors is merely a guide; the factors serve "as buoys to mark channels of inquiry." With that caveat, the court listed the following factors:[337]

- The presence of an important CAFA-related question.
- Whether the CAFA question presented (1) is unsettled, (2) appears to be wrongly decided or at least debatable, and (3) is consequential to the resolution of the particular case.
- Whether the question is likely to evade effective review if left for consideration only after final judgment.
- Whether the question is likely to recur.
- Whether the order being appealed is sufficiently final to position the case for intelligent review.
- The balance of relevant harms to both parties if an immediate appeal is entertained or refused.

Other courts have adopted the First Circuit's list of factors as a useful guide.[338]

Circuit courts also have held that once an appeal of a remand of a CAFA class action is accepted, the appellate court has discretion to consider any errors in the remand order, not just CAFA-related errors.[339]

### [ii] Time for Application for and Resolution of Discretionary Appeal

A party seeking to appeal a remand order under CAFA must apply to the court of appeals not more than 10 days after entry of the order.[340] If a court of appeals accepts an appeal, the court must complete all action on the appeal, including

---

336 *See* S. Rep. No. 109-14, at 49 (2005). *See, e.g.*, Coleman v. Estes Express Lines, Inc., 627 F.3d 1096, 1100 (9th Cir. 2010) (presence of important CAFA-related question identified as key factor); College of Dental Surgeons of Puerto Rico v. Connecticut General Life Ins. Co., 585 F.3d 33, 38 (1st Cir. 2009); Alvarez v. Midland Credit Management, Inc., 585 F.3d 890, 893–894 (5th Cir. 2009).

337 College of Dental Surgeons of Puerto Rico v. Connecticut General Life Ins. Co., 585 F.3d 33, 38–39 (1st Cir. 2009) (case was "good prototype" for review considering listed factors).

338 *See, e.g.*, Coleman v. Estes Express Lines, Inc., 627 F.3d 1096, 1100 (9th Cir. 2010); BP America, Inc. v. Oklahoma *ex rel.* Edmondson, 613 F.3d 1029, 1034–1035 (11th Cir. 2010).

339 Walker v. Trailer Transit, Inc., 727 F.3d 819, 823 (7th Cir. 2013) (review of order granting or denying remand is not limited to CAFA-specific issues; appeal concerned time limits specified in general removal statute); *see also* Brill v. Countrywide Home Loans, Inc., 427 F.3d 446, 451–452 (7th Cir. 2005); Coffey v. Freeport McMoran Copper & Gold, 581 F.3d 1240, 1247–1248 (10th Cir. 2009).

340 28 U.S.C. § 1453(c)(1) (effective December 1, 2009).

rendering judgment, not later than 60 days after the date on which the appeal was filed.[341] The 60-day period begins to run when the court of appeals grants the application to appeal, not when the appellants file their application to appeal.[342] If good cause is shown, and if it is in the interests of justice, an appellate court may extend the 60-day period for an additional period "not to exceed 10 days."[343] Otherwise, appellate courts may extend the 60-day period only if all the parties to the proceeding agree to the extension. In this situation, the court may extend the 60-day period "for any period of time."[344]

A court's failure to comply with the 60-day time limit for resolving a discretionary appeal under CAFA has a very serious consequence for the appellant. If the court fails to render a final judgment on the appeal before the end of the 60-day period (or any extended period), the appeal is denied automatically by operation of law.[345]

# PART C
# REMOVAL PROCEDURES AND EFFECT OF REMOVAL

## § 6.09 PROCEDURES FOR REMOVAL

### [1] Notice of Removal

The defendant seeking removal must file a "notice of removal" containing a short and plain statement of the grounds for removal.[346] For example, in a case removed on the basis of diversity jurisdiction, the removal notice must allege complete diversity of citizenship, at the time the case was filed in state court or at the time of removal,[347] and the notice must allege facts showing that the amount-in-controversy requirement is met (*see* § 6.08[2][g]).[348]

---

[341] 28 U.S.C. § 1453(c)(2) ("If the court of appeals accepts an appeal under paragraph (1), the court shall complete all action on such appeal, including rendering judgment, not later than 60 days after the date on which such appeal was filed, unless an extension is granted under paragraph (3).").

[342] College of Dental Surgeons of P.R. v. Connecticut Gen. Life Ins. Co., 585 F.3d 33, 37 (1st Cir. 2009) (entry of order granting application to appeal starts accrual of 60-day period); *see also* Ditolla v. Doral Dental IPA of N.Y., 469 F.3d 271, 274–275 (2d Cir. 2006); Morgan v. Gay, 471 F.3d 469, 472 (3d Cir. 2006); Patterson v. Dean Morris, L.L.P. 444 F.3d 365, 367–370 (5th Cir. 2006); *In re* Mortg. Elec. Registration Sys., 680 F.3d 849, 853 (6th Cir. 2012).

[343] 28 U.S.C. § 1452(c)(3)(B); *see, e.g.*, Abraham v. St. Croix Renaissance Group, L.L.L.P., 719 F.3d 270, 280–281 n.12 (3d Cir. 2013) (period extended because compliance with 60-day deadline would have resulted in abbreviated circulation period for precedential opinion).

[344] 28 U.S.C. § 1453(c)(3)(A).

[345] 28 U.S.C. § 1453(c)(4).

[346] 28 U.S.C. § 1446(a); *see* Fed. R. Civ. P. 8(a); Laughlin v. KMart Corp., 50 F.3d 871, 873 (10th Cir. 1995) (notice of removal must plainly indicate that federal jurisdictional requirements are met).

[347] *See* Washington-East Washington Joint Authority v. Roberts & Schaefer Co., 180 F. Supp. 15, 16–18 (D. Pa. 1960) (record must affirmatively show diversity at time of removal and commencement in state court to divest state court of jurisdiction).

[348] Laughlin v. KMart Corp., 50 F.3d 871, 873 (10th Cir. 1995) (if neither plaintiff's complaint nor

The notice of removal must be signed pursuant to Rule 11 of the Federal Rules of Civil Procedure.[349] Rule 11 authorizes the imposition of sanctions if papers are filed containing statements that are not well grounded in fact and warranted by law.[350]

In general, all defendants must "join in" the notice of removal, but not all are required to actually sign the notice.[351] However, a defendant with an independent right of removal, such as a federal agency or officer, may remove the entire case without the consent of other defendants.[352] Similarly, when a case is removed under the Class Action Fairness Act,[353] or under § 1441(c) (see § 6.08[5]), any defendant may remove without the consent of other defendants. *Join in* has been defined to mean support in writing. Therefore, defendants who do not sign the removal notice should submit a written statement to the court stating that they agree to the removal.[354] Promptly after filing a notice of removal, the defendant or defendants must give written notice of the filing to all adverse parties and must file a copy of the notice with the clerk of the state court where the case was filed.[355]

## [2] Time for Removal

### [a] When Notice of Removal Must Be Filed

#### [i] Within 30 Days After Defendant Receives Copy or Service of Initial Pleading Showing Basis for Removal

The notice of removal must be filed within 30 days after the earlier of the date that (1) the defendant receives, generally through service (*see* [c], *below*), a copy of the initial pleading setting forth the claim for relief (and showing the basis for removal) on which the action or proceeding is based; or (2) the summons is served on the defendant, if the initial pleading has been filed in state court and is not

---

defendant's notice of removal set forth amount in controversy, subject matter jurisdiction was lacking, even though search of record or permitting amendment of pleadings would have revealed that case clearly met jurisdictional amount); Gaus v. Miles, Inc., 980 F.2d 564, 566–567 (9th Cir. 1992) (simple allegation that amount in controversy exceeds jurisdictional amount neither overcomes strong presumption against removal nor satisfies defendant's burden of setting forth facts supporting claim amount in removal notice).

[349] 28 U.S.C. § 1446(a); *see* Fed. R. Civ. P. 11; *see also* Beard v. Lehman Bros. Holdings, Inc., 458 F. Supp. 2d 1314, 1318–1319 (M.D. Ala. 2006) (inauthentic signatures of lawyers were insufficient to affect their clients' joinder in removal petition, because Fed. R. Civ. P. 11 requires personal signatures).

[350] Fed. R. Civ. P. 11; *see generally* 2 Moore's Federal Practice Ch. 11, *Signing Pleadings, Motions and Other Papers; Representations to the Court; Sanctions* (Matthew Bender 3d ed.).

[351] *See* § 6.05[2][c].

[352] Dillon v. Mississippi Military Dep't, 23 F.3d 915, 918–919 (5th Cir. 1994) (federal officer removal); Davis v. FSLIC, 879 F.2d 1288, 1289 (5th Cir. 1989) (FSLIC removal); *see, e.g.*, 28 U.S.C. § 1442(a)(1) (federal agency and officer removal).

[353] *See* 28 U.S.C. § 1453((b).

[354] Roe v. O'Donohue, 38 F.3d 298, 301 (7th Cir. 1994).

[355] 28 U.S.C. § 1446(d).

required to be served on the defendant.[356] This 30-day period is strictly construed.[357] However, the triggering event for commencing the 30-day period in cases that are initially removable is also strictly construed. In *Murphy Brothers, Inc. v. Michetti Pipe Stringing, Inc.*, the Supreme Court held that the 30-day clock is triggered by formal service.[358]

A case is removable when the initial pleading enables the defendant to "intelligently ascertain" removability from the face of the pleading, such that the defendant can make a short and plain statement of the grounds for removal.[359] A pleading enables a defendant to intelligently ascertain removability when it provides the necessary facts to support a removal petition.[360] This standard requires defendants to apply a reasonable amount of intelligence in ascertaining removability, but it does not require defendants to look beyond the initial pleading.[361] For example, a defendant does not have a duty of inquiry if the initial pleading or other document is "indeterminate" with respect to removability. Thus, even if a defendant could have or actually has discovered grounds for removal through its own investigation, it does not lose the right to remove.[362]

### [ii] Within 30 Days After Defendant Receives Paper First Showing Basis for Removal

If the case stated by the initial pleading is not removable, the defendant may file a notice of removal within 30 days after receipt, through service or otherwise, of a copy of an amended pleading, motion, order, or other paper from which it first may be ascertained that the case has become removable.[363] For example, this situation

---

[356] 28 U.S.C. § 1446(b)(1); *In re* Willis, 228 F.3d 896, 897 (8th Cir. 2000) (30-day period begins running on receipt of complaint only when complaint explicitly discloses that plaintiff seeks damages in excess of jurisdictional minimum, rule promotes certainty and judicial efficiency by not requiring courts to query what particular defendant subjectively knows).

[357] *See* May v. Johnson Controls, Inc., 440 F. Supp. 2d 879, 882–884 (W.D. Tenn. 2006) (noting "very few exceptions" to rule that 30-day deadline is mandatory, court granted motion to remand because removal occurred one day after statutory deadline); Liebig v. DeJoy, 814 F. Supp. 1074, 1076 (M.D. Fla. 1993) (30-day time limit is mandatory and may not be extended by court).

[358] Murphy Bros., Inc. v. Michetti Pipe Stringing, Inc., 526 U.S. 344 (1999).

[359] Whitaker v. American Telecasting, Inc., 261 F.3d 196, 205–206 (2d Cir. 2001) (diversity cases require facts supporting amount in controversy and domicile of parties).

[360] Whitaker v. American Telecasting, Inc., 261 F.3d 196, 205–206 (2d Cir. 2001) (diversity cases require facts supporting amount in controversy and domicile of parties); Rowe v. Marder, 750 F. Supp. 718, 721 (W.D. Pa. 1990), *aff'd*, 935 F.2d 1282 (3d Cir. 1991); Sprague v. American Bar Ass'n, 166 F. Supp. 2d 206, 209 (E.D. Pa. 2001) (service of writ by summons and civil cover sheet did not inform defendants of facts showing case was removable).

[361] *See* Whitaker v. American Telecasting, Inc., 261 F.3d 196, 205–206 (2d Cir. 2001) (summons did not provide reasonable basis for diversity jurisdiction because it failed to identify defendants' addresses); *See* Foster v. Mutual Fire, Marine & Inland Ins. Co., 986 F.2d 48, 54 (3d Cir. 1993) (relevant test is what documents said, not what defendants purportedly knew).

[362] Roth v. CHA Hollywood Med. Ctr., L.P., 720 F.3d 1121, 1125 (9th Cir. 2013).

[363] 28 U.S.C. § 1446(b). *See, e.g.*, Proctor v. Vishay Intertechnology Inc., 584 F.3d 1208, 1223–1224 (9th Cir. 2009) (case timely removed within 30 days of amendment including allegations that met requirements for removal under Securities Litigation Uniform Standards Act (15 U.S.C. § 78bb(f))); Lovern v. General Motors Corp., 121 F.3d 160, 162 (4th Cir. 1997) (defendant timely filed notice of removal 28 days

might result if an original defendant who shared citizenship with a plaintiff, thereby precluding removal, is dropped as a party from the case pursuant to an agreement between the plaintiff and that defendant. A new 30-day period will commence from the date that the remaining defendant receives the paper manifesting that the claims against the non-diverse defendant have been dismissed.[364]

The rationale for permitting removal after a change by the plaintiff stems from the idea that the plaintiff is the master of the complaint. Subject to limitations such as the artful pleading rule (*see* § 6.08[3][c]), the plaintiff is entitled to bring an action alleging only state law claims against non-diverse defendants in order to defeat the possibility of removal. According to this rationale, if the plaintiff voluntarily decides to drop non-diverse defendants, or change domicile, for example, the plaintiff presumably is no longer insistent on keeping the action in the state courts and the action therefore becomes removable.[365]

#### [iii] No Later Than One Year After Commencement of Action in Diversity Case

A case that is not removable based on the initial pleading generally may not be removed on the basis of diversity jurisdiction more than one year after the action was commenced, unless the district court finds that the plaintiff acted in bad faith in order to prevent a defendant from removing the action.[366] A finding that the plaintiff deliberately failed to disclose the actual amount in controversy to prevent removal will be deemed a finding of bad faith.[367] This provision, adopted in 2011, applies to cases commenced on or after January 6, 2012.[368]

Before this 2011 amendment, it was unclear whether the one-year limit applied to cases that were removable on the basis of the initial pleadings as well as to cases that became removable later.[369] Some courts applied the one-year limit to all cases, regardless of whether there was a basis for removal at the time the action was

---

after receipt of police report and eight days after receipt of interrogatory answers revealing plaintiff's citizenship, even though notice was filed 88 days after service of complaint that did not reveal plaintiff's citizenship).

364 28 U.S.C. § 1446, Commentary on 1988 Revision of Section 1446; *see* H.R. Rep. No. 100-889, at 71 (1988).

365 Self v. General Motors Corp. 588 F.2d 655, 656–659 (9th Cir. 1978) (because plaintiff is master of complaint, only plaintiff's voluntary changes can make case removable); *see also* California v. Keating, 986 F.2d 346, 348 (9th Cir. 1993).

366 28 U.S.C. § 1446(c)(1).

367 28 U.S.C. § 1446(c)(3)(B).

368 Pub. L. No. 112-63, § 105, 125 Stat. 758 (2011).

369 *See* former 28 U.S.C. § 1446(b) ("If the case stated by the initial pleading is not removable, a notice of removal may be filed within thirty days after receipt by the defendant, through service or otherwise, of a copy of an amended pleading, motion, order or other paper from which it may first be ascertained that the case is one which is or has become removable, except that a case may not be removed on the basis of jurisdiction conferred by section 1332 of this title more than 1 year after commencement of the action.").

commenced.[370] Others held that the one-year limitation applied only to cases that were not initially removable.[371] Some courts applied an equitable estoppel exception to prevent plaintiffs from unfairly taking advantage of the one-year limitation,[372] but others declined to make any exceptions.[373]

The 2011 amendment to Section 1446 resolved these issues by restricting the one-year limit in two ways. First, it clarified that the limit applies only to cases that are not initially removable.[374] Second, it added an explicit exception for cases in which the district finds that the plaintiff acted in bad faith in order to prevent a defendant from removing the case.[375]

Additionally, the one-year rule does not apply to cases removed under the Class Action Fairness Act (see § 6.08[6][f][iii]).

#### [iv] When 30-Day Period for Removal Begins to Run

If the case is initially removable, the 30-day period during which the defendant must remove begins to run at the earlier of the following times: (1) when the defendant receives, generally through service, a copy of the initial pleading setting forth the claim for relief that underlies the proceeding; or (2) when the summons is served on the defendant, if the initial pleading has been filed in state court but is not required to be served on the defendant.[376]

If the case is not initially removable, the 30-day period during which the defendant must file a notice of removal begins to run when the defendant receives, through service or otherwise, a copy of an amended pleading, motion, order, or other paper from which it may first be ascertained that the case has become removable.[377] It is the earliest such pleading or paper, not the latest, that triggers the 30-day period.[378] For example, if the plaintiff amends the complaint and the

---

[370] *See, e.g., In re* Uniroyal Goodrich Tire Co., 104 F.3d 322, 324 (11th Cir. 1997).

[371] Johnson v. Heublein Inc., 227 F.3d 236, 241 (5th Cir. 2000) (citing MOORE'S FEDERAL PRACTICE; one-year limitation applies only when case was not initially removable); Brierly v. Alusuisse Flexible Packaging, Inc., 184 F.3d 527, 534 (6th Cir. 1999) (one-year limit imposed on removal based on diversity applies only to actions that become removable sometime after suit initially commenced, and not to actions that are removable when initially filed).

[372] *See, e.g.*, Tedford v. Warner-Lambert Co., 327 F.3d 423, 426–428 (5th Cir. 2003) (equitable tolling exception applied; plaintiff dismissed only nondiverse defendant after one-year removal period ended.

[373] *See* Lovern v. General Motors Corp., 121 F.3d 160, 163 (4th Cir. 1997) (removal statute safeguards against strategic delay by erecting "absolute bar to removal" of diversity cases more than one year after commencement of action).

[374] 28 U.S.C. § 1446(c)(1) ("A case may not be removed under subsection (b)(3) [concerning cases not removable as stated in initial pleading] on the basis of jurisdiction conferred by section 1332 more than 1 year after commencement of the action . . . ."

[375] 28 U.S.C. § 1446(c)(1).

[376] 28 U.S.C. § 1446(b); *see* Murphy Bros., Inc. v. Michetti Pipe Stringing, Inc., 526 U.S. 344, 347–349 (1999).

[377] 28 U.S.C. § 1446(b).

[378] Garrett v. Cook, 652 F.3d 1249, 1256 (10th Cir. 2011) ("It is the earliest pleading putting a defendant on notice of removability that counts, not the latest one."; argument that 30-day period had not

amended complaint makes the case removable, the 30-day period runs from the service of the amended complaint.[379] Similarly, if the plaintiff increases the amount in controversy through responses to interrogatories, the 30-day period begins when the defendant receives those responses.[380] Or, if the plaintiff raises a federal statutory claim in a memorandum in support of a motion for an injunction, the 30-day period begins when the memorandum is filed.[381]

Each defendant has 30 days to remove under Section 1441, beginning when that defendant receives or is served with the initial pleading or summons or paper.[382] Thus, if the defendants are served at different times, they will have different removal deadlines. If one of the later-served defendants files a notice of removal, any earlier-served defendant may consent to that removal, even if the earlier-served defendant did not initiate or consent to removal earlier.[383] These rules were added to Section 1446 in 2011, effective with respect to all cases commenced on or after January 6, 2012.[384]

Prior to the 2011 amendments, the circuits were split as to how to apply the 30-day deadline when multiple defendants were served at different times. Under the "first-served defendant" rule, if the case was removable when the first defendant was served, the 30-day removal period for all defendants, including those who had not yet been served, began to run at that time.[385] Under the "last-served defendant rule," which was followed by more courts, the 30-day period was calculated separately for each defendant.[386]

### [b] Initial Pleading Commencing Removal Time

Determining what constitutes an initial pleading may be difficult, particularly in states where plaintiffs are not required to file a complaint in order to commence an action. Given the pervasive anti-removal perspective, doubts as to what constitutes an initial pleading should be resolved in favor of an earlier filing of the notice of removal. Given the further pervasive anti-diversity perspective, it is entirely likely

---

begun to run because third amended complaint had not been served on defendant was red herring, because earlier complaints were undisputedly served on him).

379 *See* Hamilton v. Hertz Corp., 607 F. Supp. 1371, 1373–1374 (removal period runs from date of receipt of proposed order granting leave to amend complaint).

380 Miller v. Stauffer Chemical Co., 527 F. Supp. 775, 777–778 (D. Kan. 1981) (nonremovable case becomes removable on date of service of amended complaint; court record sole source to determine when nonremovable case becomes removable).

381 Hubbard v. Union Oil Co. of California, 601 F. Supp. 790, 793–794 (S.D. W. Va. 1985).

382 28 U.S.C. § 1446(b)(2)(B).

383 28 U.S.C. § 1446(b)(2)(C).

384 Pub. L. No. 112-63, § 105, 125 Stat. 758 (2011).

385 *See* Getty Oil v. Insurance Co. of N. Am., 841 F.2d 1254, 1262–1263 (5th Cir. 1988) (citing Moore's Federal Practice; "In cases involving multiple defendants, the thirty-day period begins to run as soon as the first defendant is served (provided the case is then removable.)").

386 *See, e.g.*, Marano Enters. v. Z-Teca Rests., 254 F.3d 753, 755–757 (8th Cir. 2001) (citing Moore's Federal Practice, holding that each defendant has 30 days after receiving service within which to file removal notice regardless of when or if previously served defendants filed removal notices); Delalla v. Hanover Ins., 660 F.3d 180, 185–189 (3d Cir. 2011) (joining majority of circuits in adopting later-served rule, which is better supported by text and is more equitable).

that what constitutes an initial pleading in a diversity case is different from, and perhaps less formal than, an initial pleading in a federal question case.[387]

In any event, the Supreme Court clarified in *Murphy Brothers, Inc. v. Michetti Pipe Stringing, Inc.* that in states where the service of the summons commences the action, but the local rules do not require that the complaint or initial pleading be filed or served at that time, the time for removal runs after service of formal process and when the complaint is made available through filing.[388]

If a pleading is served before the complaint, such as a motion for a temporary restraining order or other extraordinary relief, indicates removability, the 30-day removal period commences from receipt of that pleading.[389] Under the Supreme Court's *Murphy Brothers* rule, assuming formal service of the pleading or a summons with the pleading, the 30-day period should run from such service.[390]

### [c] Receipt May Be by Service or "Otherwise"

In general, notice of removal must be filed within 30 days after the defendant receives, through service or otherwise, a copy of the initial pleading.[391] In *Murphy Brothers, Inc. v. Michetti Pipe Stringing, Inc.*, the Supreme Court explained the purpose and meaning of the language "through service or otherwise," which previously had divided the lower courts. The touchstone is formal service.

States have varying commencement and complaint filing procedures. For example, in some states service of the summons commences the action without the necessity of filing a pleading until later. In these states, under the language of Section 1446(b), the period for removal could expire before the defendant obtained access to the complaint. The language "service or otherwise," as construed by the Supreme Court in *Murphy Brothers*, however, provides a uniform approach to the commencement of the removal period by extending the commencement of the 30-day period until a served defendant actually receives the complaint that forms the basis for the lawsuit. Under *Murphy Brothers*, the timeliness of removal turns on when, if at all, service was effected. The date of service is determined by state law. Thus, the 30-day federally mandated period for filing the notice of removal is measured from the service date according to state law.[392]

Traditionally, receipt by an agent designated by a defendant for service of process starts the 30-day removal period.[393] However, under *Murphy Brothers*, it is

---

387 *See* 28 U.S.C. § 1446.

388 Murphy Bros., Inc. v. Michetti Pipe Stringing, Inc., 526 U.S. 344, 354 (1999) (formal service required).

389 Williams v. Beyer, 455 F. Supp. 482, 484–485 (D.N.H. 1978) (petition for appointment of arbitrator).

390 Murphy Bros., Inc. v. Michetti Pipe Stringing, Inc., 526 U.S. 344, 347–348 (1999) (formal service required).

391 28 U.S.C. § 1446(b)(1).

392 City of Clarksdale v. Bellsouth Telecommunications, 428 F.3d 206, 210 (5th Cir. 2005).

393 Tech Hills II Assocs. v. Phoenix Life Mut. Ins. Co., 5 F.3d 963, 968 (6th Cir. 1993) (actual receipt by authorized agent sufficient); Getty Oil v. Insurance Co. of N. Am., 841 F.2d 1254, 1263 n.12 (5th Cir. 1988).

unlikely that receipt by persons unauthorized to accept service of process is sufficient.[394] Further, service on a statutory agent appointed as a matter of law may not commence the 30-day removal period.[395] Rather, the 30-day removal period commences only on the receipt of the initial pleading by the defendant.[396]

It is also questionable after *Murphy Brothers* whether *otherwise* includes attempted service by mail under a state counterpart of federal Rule 4[397] that is ineffective because the recipient refuses to sign and return the acknowledgment.[398]

### [d] Effect of Lack of Service on All Defendants

Most courts hold that if one or more defendants are not served, they do not need to join in the notice of removal (*see* § 6.05[2][c]).[399]

### [e] Other Paper

If the case stated by the initial pleading is not removable, the defendant may file a notice of removal within 30 days after receipt, through service or otherwise, of a copy of an amended pleading, motion, order, or other paper from which it may first be ascertained the case is one that has become removable.[400] *Other paper* is any other document that is part and parcel of the state court proceedings and that has its origin and existence by virtue of state court processes.[401] Section 1446 specifies that if the case stated by the initial pleading is not removable solely because the amount in controversy does not exceed the jurisdictional minimum, information relating to the amount of controversy in the record of the state proceeding or in responses to discovery must be treated as "other paper."[402] Other items have been held by courts to constitute "other paper." For example, correspondence between parties, such as a statement of damages letter identifying the damages and losses suffered by the plaintiff, constitutes "other paper" that may be considered in

---

394 *See* Schollenberger v. Sears, Roebuck & Co., 876 F. Supp. 153, 154–155 (E.D. Mich. 1995).

395 *See* Cox v. Sprung's Transport & Movers, Ltd., 407 F. Supp. 2d 754, 756 (D.S.C. 2006) (substituted service on state motor vehicles department did not commence 30-day removal period); Hibernia Cmty. Dev't Corp. v. U.S.E. Cmty. Servs. Group, Inc., 166 F. Supp. 2d 511, 513 (E.D. La. 2001) (30-day removal period begins only on receipt of initial pleading by defendant, not on receipt by statutory agent.

396 Hibernia Cmty. Dev't Corp. v. U.S.E. Cmty. Servs. Group, Inc., 166 F. Supp. 2d 511, 513 (E.D. La. 2001).

397 *See* Fed. R. Civ. P. 4.

398 *See* Robert E. Diehl, Inc. v. Morrison, 590 F. Supp. 1190, 1191 (M.D. Pa. 1984) (distinguishing refused mail, which triggers running of 30-day period, from unclaimed mail).

399 *See, e.g.*, Adams v. Lederle Lab., 569 F. Supp. 234, 243 (W.D. Mo. 1983).

400 28 U.S.C. § 1446(b).

401 *See, e.g.*, Chapman v. Powermatic, Inc., 969 F.2d 160, 163–164 (5th Cir. 1992) (receipt of sworn answers revealing removability required to start removal period, not previous correspondence); Phillips v. Allstate Ins. Co., 702 F. Supp. 1466, 1468–1469 (C.D. Cal. 1989) (only papers filed in case trigger removal period).

402 28 U.S.C. § 1446(c)(3)(A) ("If the case stated by the initial pleading is not removable solely because the amount in controversy does not exceed the amount specified in section 1332(a), information relating to the amount in controversy in the record of the State proceeding, or in responses to discovery, shall be treated as an 'other paper' under subsection (b)(3)").

determining the amount in controversy for purposes of removal.[403] Similarly, "other paper" includes discovery depositions,[404] answers to written interrogatories,[405] responses to requests for admission,[406] settlement agreements,[407] and offers of judgment specifying an amount in excess of the jurisdictional minimum.[408] A civil cover sheet filed with the complaint has also been held to constitute "other paper,"[409] but another judge from the same district disagreed with this result.[410] The Eighth Circuit has held that plaintiffs' attorneys statements at a court hearing on their motions for assignment of several cases to a single judge constituted "other paper" for purposes of triggering the 30-day removal period.[411] The court noted that the statements had been transcribed, "like deposition testimony," but did not specify whether the 30-day period began to run when the statements were made or

---

[403] Sunburst Bank v. Summit Acceptance Corp., 878 F. Supp. 77, 80–81 (S.D. Miss. 1995) (demand letter indicating amount in controversy); Rodgers v. Northwestern Mut. Life Ins. Co., 952 F. Supp. 325, 327–328 (W.D. Va. 1997) (settlement offer constituted other paper); Addo v. Globe Life & Accident Ins. Co., 230 F.3d 759, 761 (5th Cir. 2000) (post-complaint letter from insurance beneficiary's attorney to insurer offering to settle case for amount greater than federal jurisdictional minimum is "other paper"); Cohn v. Petsmart, Inc., 281 F.3d 837, 840 (9th Cir. 2002) (demand letter for $100,000); *but see* Chapman v. Powermatic, Inc., 969 F.2d 160, 163–164 (5th Cir. 1992) (receipt of sworn answers revealing removability required to start removal period, not previous correspondence indicating jurisdictional sum).

[404] Brooks v. Solomon Co., 542 F. Supp. 1229, 1230–1231 (N.D. Ala. 1982); S.W.S. Erectors, Inc. v. Infax, Inc., 72 F.3d 489, 494 (5th Cir. 1996) (deposition transcript is other paper); Peters v. Lincoln Elec. Co., 285 F.3d 456, 465–466 (6th Cir. 2002) (deposition testimony serves as "other paper" to trigger removal period); Huffman v. Saul Holdings Ltd. P'ship, 194 F.3d 1072, 1077–1079 (10th Cir. 1999) (30-day period commences with giving of state-court deposition not receipt of deposition transcript; court noted because Fed. R. Civ. P. 30 does not specify deadline for obtaining transcript, date of receipt may be subject to manipulation).

[405] Jackson v. Mississippi Farm Bureau Mut. Ins. Co., 947 F. Supp. 252, 254 (S.D. Miss. 1996) (plaintiffs' unsigned, unfiled interrogatory responses that were sent to defendants' counsel indicating that plaintiffs based claim on U.S. Constitution were "other paper," even though references to U.S. Constitution were removed from responses plaintiffs ultimately filed); Akin v. Ashland Chem. Co., 156 F.3d 1030, 1035–1036, 1035 n.2 (10th Cir. 1998) (answer to interrogatory gave first unequivocal notice of removal rights).

[406] Murchison v. Progressive Northern Ins. Co., 564 F. Supp. 2d 1311, 1314 (E.D. Ok. 2008).

[407] Garcia v. MVT Servs., 589 F. Supp. 2d 797, 803–804 (W.D. Tex. 2008) (on receipt of settlement agreement in which plaintiffs agreed to drop only nondiverse defendant from case, remaining defendant could have ascertained that case was removable).

[408] *In re* Willis, 228 F.3d 896, 897 (8th Cir. 2011) (30-day period began running on receipt of offer of judgment (following initial round of discovery) specifying amount in excess of jurisdictional minimum, not on receipt of initial complaint that did not explicitly disclose that plaintiff sought damages in excess of jurisdictional minimum).

[409] Henderson v. Target Stores, 431 F. Supp. 2d 1143, 1144 (D. Colo. 2006) (pursuant to state rules, complaint did not state dollar amount sought, but on civil cover sheet filed with complaint, plaintiff had checked box indicating she sought more than $100,000, from which defendant could have determined that diversity jurisdiction existed.

[410] Harding v. Sentinel Ins. Co., Ltd., 490 F. Supp. 2d 1134, 1134–1136 (D. Colo. 2007) (cover sheet opting out of Colorado's simplified pretrial procedures insufficient to establish amount in controversy).

[411] Atwell v. Boston Scientific Corp., 740 F.3d 1160, 1162 (8th Cir. 2013) ("Only when plaintiffs' attorneys made clear the extent of consolidation being sought at the state court motions hearing did Boston Scientific have a basis for removal.").

when they were transcribed.[412]

On the other hand, the Eighth Circuit also held that discovery responses submitted in a separate case were not "other paper" that triggered a new 30-day removal period.[413] The Ninth Circuit held that a document received before receipt of the initial pleading cannot constitute "other paper" for purposes of triggering the 30-day removal period. In that case, the paper in question was a demand letter sent several months before suit was filed. The court pointed out that if that letter constituted "other paper" for purposes of the 30-day removal period, the defendant would have been required to remove the case before it was filed, which is not possible.[414]

In general, to constitute "other paper," the paper must result from the voluntary act of a plaintiff and give the defendant notice of the changed circumstances that now support federal jurisdiction.[415] Thus, most courts do not consider a court decision in an unrelated case to be an "order or other paper" that will trigger an additional 30-day removal period.[416] However, the Third and Fifth Circuits have held that, in limited circumstances, an unrelated decision may constitute an "order or other paper" when the cases involve similar factual situations and legal issues and the other case, although not expressly authorizing removal, provides a basis for filing a second removal petition in the case.[417]

Some courts do not require that the defendant receive a *paper* indicating removability. Rather, if the defendant actually knows or is on notice that grounds exist for removal, the time for removal begins when the defendant acquires that

---

[412] Atwell v. Boston Scientific Corp., 740 F.3d 1160, 1162 (8th Cir. 2013) ("These oral statements, made at a court hearing and later transcribed, like deposition testimony, satisfy § 1446(b)(3)'s 'other paper' requirement.").

[413] Dalton v. Walgreen Co., 721 F.3d 492, 494 (8th Cir. 2013) (discovery responses filed in separate case involving one of same plaintiffs and similar claims, but different defendant, who happened to be represented by same counsel as defendant in this case, did not constitute "other paper" for purposes of 30-day removal period).

[414] Carvalho v. Equifax Info. Servs., LLC, 629 F.3d 876, 885–886 (9th Cir. 2010) (demand letter sent before complaint was filed could not trigger 30-day removal period); *see* 28 U.S.C. § 1446(b).

[415] Addo v. Globe Life & Accident Ins. Co., 230 F.3d 759, 761 (5th Cir. 2000) (post-complaint letter from insurance beneficiary's attorney to insurer offering to settle case for amount greater than federal jurisdictional minimum is "other paper" that begins running of 30-day removal period provided that letter is not plainly sham).

[416] *See* Gruner v. Blakeman, 517 F. Supp. 357, 360–361 (D. Conn. 1981) (subsequent decision in related case did not constitute "order or other paper"); Lozano v. GPE Controls, 859 F. Supp. 1036, 1038 (S.D. Texas 1994) (judicial opinion in unrelated case is not "other paper"); *but see* Davis v. Time Ins. Co., 698 F. Supp. 1317, 1321 (S.D. Miss. 1988) (suggesting that if new Supreme Court decision indicates case is subject to preemption, character of litigation is changed so as to make new suit that is removable).

[417] Doe v. American Red Cross, 14 F.3d 196, 198 (3d Cir. 1993) (successive removal permitted after intervening Supreme Court decision established original federal jurisdiction over Red Cross); Green v. R.J. Reynolds Tobacco Co., 274 F.3d 263, 266–268 (5th Cir. 2001) (second removal petition permitted after judgment in unrelated case involving same defendants and similar factual situation and legal conclusion; court noted that rule is applicable in very narrow circumstances); Landry v. Cross Country Bank, 431 F. Supp. 2d 682, 686 (S.D. Tex. 2003) (case became removable on date of Supreme Court's holding in *Beneficial Nat'l Bank v. Anderson*, 539 U.S. 1 (2003), that National Banking Act completely preempts state law usury claims against national banks).

knowledge.[418] However, courts are split on whether to impose a duty to investigate and determine removability when the initial pleading indicates that the right to remove *may* exist.[419] When it is apparent that removal may be justified, some courts impose a duty on potential movants to investigate potential reasons for removal.[420] Other courts require that the right to remove must be unequivocally apparent from the pleading. These courts impose no duty to investigate when the pleading merely indicates a possible right to remove.[421] In fact, the Ninth Circuit has held that even if a defendant actually has discovered grounds for removal through its own investigation, the 30-day clock does not begin to run until after some paper generated by the plaintiff is received.[422]

## [3] Whether Court Should Evaluate Subject Matter Jurisdiction Before Personal Jurisdiction

The Supreme Court has held that district courts have discretion to decide a personal jurisdiction issue before a subject matter jurisdiction issue in appropriate cases. For example, district courts may adjudicate relatively simple challenges to personal jurisdiction in removal cases before resolving the more difficult issue of subject matter jurisdiction.[423] This ruling validates the long-standing practice of many district courts who routinely decided relatively easy motions to dismiss for lack of personal jurisdiction before tackling the more difficult questions involving subject matter jurisdiction presented by the case.[424]

---

[418] Kanter & Eisenberg v. Madison Assocs., 602 F. Supp. 798, 801 (N.D. Ill. 1985) (if defendant learns that case removable after service of complaint, removal period runs from date knowledge acquired); *but see* Rivers v. International Matex Tank Terminal, 864 F. Supp. 556, 559 (E.D. La. 1994) (knowledge of removability acquired at deposition insufficient).

[419] Akin v. Ashland Chem. Co., 156 F.3d 1030, 1035–1036, 1035 n.2 (10th Cir. 1998) (collecting cases).

[420] *See* Scott v. Greiner, 858 F. Supp. 607, 610 & n.2 (S.D. W. Va. 1994) (motion for more definite statement required when federal question jurisdiction could not be ascertained from complaint).

[421] Whitaker v. American Telecasting, Inc., 261 F.3d 196, 205–206 (2d Cir. 2001) (reasonable basis for removal requires defendants to apply reasonable amount of intelligence, but does not require defendants to look beyond initial pleading); Mumfrey v. CVS Pharmacy, Inc., 719 F.3d 392, 399–400 (5th Cir. 2013) ("the thirty-day removal period under the first paragraph [of 28 U.S.C. § 1446(b)] is triggered only where the initial pleading '*affirmatively reveals on its face* that the plaintiff is seeking damages in excess of the minimum jurisdictional amount of the federal court"); Walker v. Trailer Transit, Inc., 727 F.3d 819, 824–826 (7th Cir. 2013) (30-day removal clock never started to run, because defendant never received pleading or paper that specifically disclosed amount of monetary damages sought; defendant removed based on confirmation that class sought percentage of disputed fees plus defendant's executive's estimate of damages based on that theory of recovery); Kuxhausen v. BMW Fin. Servs. NA LLC, 707 F.3d 1136, 1139 (9th Cir. 2013) (applying no-duty-to-investigate rule to removal under Class Action Fairness Act); Akin v. Ashland Chem. Co., 156 F.3d 1030, 1035–1036, 1035 n.2 (10th Cir. 1998) (rejecting argument that duty to investigate arises when removal may be proper; initial pleading was ambiguous and gave no unequivocal notice of removal rights, which was first given in answer to interrogatory).

[422] Roth v. CHA Hollywood Med. Ctr., L.P., 720 F.3d 1121, 1125 (9th Cir. 2013).

[423] Ruhrgas AG v. Marathon Oil Co., 526 U.S. 574 (1999).

[424] Ruhrgas AG v. Marathon Oil Co., 526 U.S. 574 (1999).

# § 6.10 EFFECT OF REMOVAL

## [1] Federal Court May Issue All Orders and Process Necessary

After removal, the federal court may issue all orders necessary for the proper advancement of the removed case.[425] Removal is automatically effected by the filing of a notice of removal with the district court, the state court, and the parties;[426] the federal court need not issue any specific order to effectuate removal.[427]

## [2] State Court Divested of Jurisdiction

Once a copy of the notice of removal is filed with the clerk of the state court in which the action is pending, the state court is divested of jurisdiction. The state court must stop all proceedings unless and until the case is remanded.[428] Any state court action after the filing of the removal notice is void ab initio,[429] even if the case is subsequently remanded because the initial removal was improper.[430] Further, the state court has no authority to act after a federal court dismisses rather than remands a case.[431] Despite this prohibition, courts have held that the "proceed no further" language does not bar state courts from performing ministerial acts that do not affect the merits of the dispute between the parties. Thus, state courts may permit actions such as the routine destruction of old files, allowing parties to remove documents for proper legal purposes, or any similar action that requires a court order.[432]

---

[425] *See* Granny Goose Foods, Inc. v. Brotherhood of Teamsters & Auto Truck Drivers, 415 U.S. 423, 437 (1974); *see* Fairbank v. Wunderman Cato Johnson, 212 F.3d 528, 531 (9th Cir. 2000) (federal court may grant summary judgment after removal even though state court denied motion).

[426] 28 U.S.C. § 1446(d).

[427] *See* Rollwitz v. Burlington N. R.R., 507 F. Supp. 582, 584 (D.C. Mass. 1981).

[428] 28 U.S.C. § 1446(d). *See* Brown v. Kerkhoff, 462 F. Supp. 2d 976, 980 (S.D. Iowa 2006) (district court refused to give effect to state court order filed after notice of removal despite waste of judicial resources).

[429] *See* Sweeney v. Resolution Trust Corp., 16 F.3d 1, 4 (1st Cir. 1994) (state court's entry of judgment after removal was void ab initio); Allman v. Hanley, 302 F.2d 559, 562 (5th Cir. 1962) (post-removal state court service of process was void ab initio); Ward v. Resolution Trust Corp., 972 F.2d 196, 198 (8th Cir. 1992) (quashing of state court, post-removal service of process affirmed because state court's action was void ab initio). *See* Ackerman v. Exxonmobil Corp., 734 F.3d 237, 249–250 (4th Cir. 2013) (state court had no jurisdiction over removed case, but that did not prevent state court from allowing amendment of complaint in second state court case that defendants argued was parallel to removed case).

[430] Ford Motor Credit Co. v. AA Plumbing, Inc., 2000 U.S. Dist. LEXIS 11388, at *11 (E.D. La. Aug. 2, 2000) (state court judgment issued one day after case was removed was void, despite district court's later remand).

[431] Murray v. Ford Motor Co., 770 F.2d 461, 463 (5th Cir. 1985) (state court cannot set aside default judgment after removal notice).

[432] *See, e.g.*, Master Equip., Inc. v. Home Ins. Co., 342 F. Supp. 549, 552 (E.D. Pa. 1972) (state court could correct its own records to remove default judgment that federal court would otherwise order stricken); Lawrence v. Chancery Court, 188 F.3d 687, 692–693 (6th Cir. 1999) (citing Moore's Federal Practice).

The power of a federal court to enjoin state court proceedings once a case has been removed is recognized as an "expressly authorized" exception to the Anti-Injunction Act, which generally prohibits federal courts from enjoining state court proceedings (*see* § 12.03[1][b][ii]).[433] The exception extends to a second, substantially identical suit filed in state court in order to subvert removal.[434]

## [3] Effect of Prior State Court Orders

In general, the federal court takes the case on removal exactly as the case stood in state court.[435] Thus, if a party takes advantage of a state's expedited summary judgment procedures by filing a summary judgment motion in state court, the federal court will evaluate the merits of the motion after removal as if the motion had originally been filed in federal court.[436] Interlocutory orders for preliminary relief entered by the state court, such as injunctions, attachments, and sequestrations, as well as associated security filed, such as bonds, remain in effect pursuant to federal law.[437] Additionally, state court rulings (including discovery orders and all other orders up to and including judgment) remain in effect until modified or supplanted by the federal court.[438] The district court is free to dissolve or modify the state court orders because state court orders are not considered to be the "law of the case."[439]

---

[433] Vendo Co. v. Lektro-Vend Corp., 433 U.S. 623, 640 (1977); *see* 28 U.S.C. § 2283 ("A court of the United States may not grant an injunction to stay proceedings in a State court except as expressly authorized by Act of Congress, or where necessary in aid of its jurisdiction, or to protect or effectuate its judgments.").

[434] *See* Davis Intern., LLC v. New Start Group, 488 F.3d 597, 605–606 (3d Cir. 2007) (noting unanimous view of courts that plaintiff's fraudulent attempt to subvert removal statute implicates "expressly authorized" exception to Anti-Injunction Act and may warrant granting of anti-suit injunction, but leaving question of merits of injunction for district court on remand). authorized by § 1446(e) in enjoining the proceedings in the state court").

[435] *See* Sun Forest Corp. v. Shvili, 152 F. Supp. 2d 367, 387 (S.D.N.Y. 2001) (after removal, district court takes removed action in posture in which it existed in state court at time of removal and must give effect to all actions and procedures accomplished in state court before removal).

[436] Sun Forest Corp. v. Shvili, 152 F. Supp. 2d 367, 387 (S.D.N.Y. 2001) (district court takes removed action in posture in which it existed in state court at time of removal and must give effect to all actions and procedures accomplished in state court before removal).

[437] 28 U.S.C. § 1450; *see* Rorick v. Devon Syndicate, Ltd., 307 U.S. 299, 309 & n.5 (1939); *see also* Sun Forest Corp. v. Shvili, 152 F. Supp. 2d 367, 387 (S.D.N.Y. 2001) (district court takes removed action in posture in which it existed in state court at time of removal and must give effect to all actions and procedures accomplished in state court before removal).

[438] *See* Granny Goose Foods, Inc. v. Brotherhood of Teamsters & Auto Truck Drivers, 415 U.S. 423, 437 (1974) (*ex parte* temporary restraining order).

[439] Louisiana v. Guidry, 489 F.3d 692, 698 (5th Cir. 2007) (district court was free to consider defendant's summary judgment motion even though motion encompassed many arguments rejected by state trial court in its judgment overruling defendant's peremptory exceptions); Quinn v. Aetna Life & Casualty Co., 616 F.2d 38, 40 (2d Cir. 1980); *see* 18 Moore's Federal Practice Ch. 134, *Stare Decisis, Law of the Case, and Judicial Estoppel* (Matthew Bender 3d ed.).

## [4] Law to Be Applied in Removed Case

A removed civil case is subject to the federal rules of civil procedure.[440] However, if removal is grounded in diversity, substantive legal issues are governed by state law.[441]

## [5] Venue Objections After Removal

The general federal venue provisions[442] do not apply to removed cases. Rather, removal venue is determined by the removal statute itself,[443] which provides that venue is automatically proper if the case is removed to the federal district and division embracing the place where the action is filed in state court.[444] Nevertheless, after proper removal, a case may be transferred to another district for the convenience of the parties and the witnesses.[445] Transfer of venue is discussed in Ch. 9, *Change of Venue*. A contractual designation of forum cannot override the venue dictated by the removal statute.[446] Once in federal court, however, a motion to transfer venue be made to enforce the forum selection clause (*see* § 9.04[5]).

---

[440] Fed. R. Civ. P. 81; Willy v. Coastal Corp., 503 U.S. 131, 134–135 (1992); Hollis v. Florida State Univ., 259 F.3d 1295, 1299 (11th Cir. 2001) (citing Moore's Federal Practice; properly removed actions subject to federal procedural rules).

[441] Erie R.R. v. Tompkins, 304 U.S. 64, 78 (1938); *see* Ch. 15, *Applicable Law in Federal Court: The Erie Doctrine.*

[442] *See* 28 U.S.C. § 1391; *see generally* Ch. 8, *Determination of Proper Venue*; Ch. 9, *Change of Venue*; Ch. 10, *Multi-District Litigation.*

[443] Polizzi v. Cowles Magazines, 345 U.S. 663, 665–666 (1953); Hartford Fire Ins. Co. v. Westinghouse Elec. Corp., 725 F. Supp. 317, 320 (S.D. Miss. 1989) (defendant's motion to remove confers venue over defendant).

[444] *See* 28 U.S.C. § 1441(a); Polizzi v. Cowles Magazines, Inc., 345 U.S. 663, 665–667 (1953).

[445] *See* 28 U.S.C. § 1404(a); Hartford Fire Ins. Co. v. Westinghouse Elec. Corp., 725 F. Supp. 317, 321–322 (S.D. Miss. 1989).

[446] Kerobo v. Southwestern Clean Fuels, Corp., 285 F.3d 531, 534–536 (6th Cir. 2002) (removal must be made to venue provided by removal statute regardless of what parties' forum selection clause provides).

# PART D
# POST-REMOVAL PROCEDURES

## § 6.11 PROCEDURES AFTER REMOVAL

### [1] Remand

#### [a] Who May Seek Remand

Whenever it appears, at any time before final judgment, that the federal district court lacks subject matter jurisdiction, the court must remand the case.[447] The lack of subject matter jurisdiction may not be waived, either by the court or by the parties.[448] The lack of subject matter jurisdiction mandates remand, even if the plaintiffs have engaged in vexatious litigation while pursuing their claim.[449] Procedural defects are treated differently. *Procedural defect* in the removal context generally refers to any defect that does not go to the question of whether the case could originally have been filed in federal district court, thus including all nonjurisdictional defects existing at the time of removal.[450] Most courts hold that a district court may not remand a removed case on its own motion based on defects in the removal procedure.[451]

The grounds for remand listed in Section 1447(c), lack of subject matter jurisdiction and procedural defects, are not the exclusive bases for remand.[452] For example, some cases hold that actions may be remanded based on abstention grounds.[453] However, a court may not remand a properly removed case solely

---

[447] 28 U.S.C. § 1447(c).

[448] *See* 28 U.S.C. § 1447(c).

[449] Mills v. Harmon Law Offices, P.C., 344 F.3d 42, 45–46 (1st Cir. 2003) (federal court must remand when subject matter jurisdiction appears to be lacking in removed case; court has no authority to dismiss).

[450] *In re* Allstate Ins. Co., 8 F.3d 219, 221 (5th Cir. 1993).

[451] *See, e.g.*, Page v. City of Southfield, 45 F.3d 128, 132–134 (6th Cir. 1995) (district courts lack discretion to remand sua sponte for procedural defects within or after 30-day period); Fax Telecommunicaciones Inc. v. AT&T, 138 F.3d 479, 485 (2d Cir. 1998); Ariel Land Owners, Inc. v. Dring, 351 F.3d 611, 614–615 (3d Cir. 2003); *In re* FMC Corp. Packaging Sys. Div., 208 F.3d 445, 450–451 (3d Cir. 2000); Ellenburg v. Spartan Motors Chassis, Inc., 519 F.3d 192, 198–199 (4th Cir. 2008); Pettitt v. Boeing Co., 606 F.3d 340, 342–343 (7th Cir. 2010); Kelton Arms Condo. Owners Ass'n, Inc. v. Homestead Ins. Co., 346 F.3d 1190, 1192–1193 (9th Cir. 2003); Corporate Management Advisors v. Artjen Complexus, Inc., 561 F.3d 1294, 1296 (11th Cir. 2009); Whole Health Chiropractic & Wellness, Inc. v. Humana Med. Plan, Inc., 254 F.3d 1317, 1319–1321 (11th Cir. 2001); *but see* Averdick v. Republic Fin. Servs. Inc., 803 F. Supp. 37, 41–42 (E.D. Ky. 1992) (district court may remand sua sponte at any time; statutory limitation on time for parties' motion does not restrict court's power to remand sua sponte).

[452] Carnegie-Mellon Univ. v. Cohill, 484 U.S. 343, 353–357 (1988); *see* 28 U.S.C. § 1447(c).

[453] *See, e.g.*, Bennett v. Liberty Nat'l Fire Ins. Co., 968 F.2d 969, 970–971 (9th Cir. 1992); Corcoran v. Ardra Ins. Co., Ltd., 842 F.2d 31, 36 (2d Cir. 1988).

because of a crowded court docket.[454]

Typically, it is the plaintiff who seeks remand to state court, electing to return to the forum previously selected by the plaintiff.[455] Whenever the federal court lacks subject matter jurisdiction, the court, the plaintiff, or the defendant may seek to remand the case.[456] Additionally, a defendant who was not served before removal and who did not join in the notice of removal may move to remand on any basis.[457]

### [b] Defects in Removal Procedure

What constitutes a defect in removal procedure is not entirely clear. In general, a *defect in removal procedure* refers to any defect that does not go to the question of whether the case could originally have been filed in federal district court, and the term includes all non-jurisdictional defects existing at the time of removal.[458] There are numerous examples of procedural defects. For example, when removal is prohibited by statute, such as the prohibition against removal of state workers' compensation claims,[459] improper removal is a procedural defect.[460] Most courts hold that filing a notice of removal after the 30-day time period is a procedural defect.[461] Similarly, as a general rule, the failure of all the defendants to join in the removal notice constitutes a procedural defect.[462] Some courts hold that the defendant's residence in the forum state in a diversity action constitutes a procedural defect that is waived if the plaintiff fails to object within 30 days of the notice of removal (*see* § 6.08[2][e]).[463] However, other courts hold that existence of

---

454 Thermtron Prods., Inc. v. Hermansdorfer, 423 U.S. 336, 344–346 (1976) (decided under pre-1988 version of statute).

455 *See* 28 U.S.C. § 1447(c).

456 American Fire & Cas. Co. v. Finn, 341 U.S. 6, 16–19 (1951).

457 *See, e.g.*, Getty Oil, Div. of Tex. v. Insurance Co. of N. Am., 841 F.2d 1254, 1263 (5th Cir. 1988).

458 *In re* Allstate Ins. Co., 8 F.3d 219, 221 (5th Cir. 1993).

459 *See* 28 U.S.C. § 1445(c).

460 *See, e.g.*, Pierpoint v. Barnes, 94 F.3d 813, 818–820 (2d Cir. 1996) (remand to state court of action under Death on High Seas Act, on ground that such actions are not removable, is based on defect in removal procedure and therefore is not reviewable).

461 May v. Johnson Controls, Inc., 440 F. Supp. 2d 879, 881 (W.D. Tenn. 2006) (time limit for removal is procedural requirement, not jurisdictional requirement); Barnes v. Westinghouse Elec. Corp., 962 F.2d 513, 516 (5th Cir. 1992) (time limit for removal can be waived); Wilson v. General Motors Corp., 888 F.2d 779, 781 (11th Cir. 1989); *but see* Rashid v. Schenck Const. Co., 843 F. Supp. 1081, 1087–1088 (S.D. W. Va. 1993) (One year limit for removing diversity cases is jurisdictional and cannot be waived).

462 McMahon v. Bunn-O-Matic Corp., 150 F.3d 651, 653–654 (7th Cir. 1998) (failure of all defendants to join in removal is procedural defect); Parrino v. FHP, Inc., 146 F.3d 699, 703 (9th Cir. 1998) (failure of one defendant to join in removal notice until almost two months after service is procedural defect cured by joinder; because defect was cured before entry of judgment, reversal and remand were not warranted); *but see* Prize Frize, Inc. v. Matrix (U.S.) Inc., 167 F.3d 1261, 1265–1267 (9th Cir. 1999) (citing Moore's Federal Practice; removal procedurally defective when notice plainly admitted that not all defendants had joined; district court ordered to remand to state court following reversal of its judgment of dismissal despite presence of subject matter jurisdiction at judgment).

463 Samaan v. St. Joseph Hosp., 670 F.3d 21, 28 (1st Cir. 2012) (plaintiff waived objection to removal by forum defendant by failing to raise issue); *In re* Shell Oil Co., 932 F.2d 1518, 1522–1523 (5th Cir. 1991); Ravens Metal Products, Inc. v. Wilson, 816 F. Supp. 427, 428 (S.D. W. Va. 1993).

a local defendant constitutes a jurisdictional defect that can be raised at any time.[464]

Similarly, there is a split of authority as to whether the failure to remove a case based on diversity jurisdiction within the one-year time limit[465] is a jurisdictional or procedural defect.[466] Some courts have held that the failure to meet the one-year limit is procedural. Therefore, if the plaintiff fails to file a timely motion to remand, the defect is waived and the case may remain in federal court.[467] Other courts, however, have held to the contrary, granting remand orders based on motions filed after the one-year period.[468] Moreover, holding the one-year limit to be procedural might encourage defendants to remove cases more than a year after they have been filed in the hope the plaintiff will not timely move to remand.

### [c] Time for Making Motion for Remand

A motion to remand a case based on a defect in the removal procedure must be filed within 30 days after the notice of removal is filed in federal court.[469] This 30-day limit has been strictly construed by the federal courts.[470] However, if the case was removed on a basis that later proves false, and a new basis for removal is asserted, to which the plaintiff did not have an opportunity to object, the plaintiff must be given an additional 30 days to challenge removal on the new basis.[471] In

---

[464] Hurt v. Dow Chem. Co., 963 F.2d 1142, 1144–1145 (8th Cir. 1992); *see* Horton v. Conklin, 431 F.3d 602, 605 (8th Cir. 2005) (noting split in circuits, adhering to rule in *Hurt*).

[465] *See* 28 U.S.C. § 1446(b).

[466] *Compare* Barnes v. Westinghouse Elec. Corp., 962 F.2d 513, 516 (5th Cir. 1992) (failure to meet one-year limit is procedural); Foiles by Foiles v. Merrell Nat'l Labs., 730 F. Supp. 108, 110 (N.D. Ill. 1989) (failure to meet one-year limit is procedural); Gray v. Moore Business Forms, Inc., 711 F. Supp. 543, 544–545 (N.D. Cal. 1989) (failure to meet one-year limit is procedural); *with* Brock by Brock v. Syntex Labs., Inc., 791 F. Supp. 721, 722–723 (E.D. Tenn. 1992), *aff'd without opinion*, 7 F.3d 232 (1993) (failure to meet one-year limit is jurisdictional); Smith v. MBL Life Assurance Corp., 727 F. Supp. 601, 602–603 (N.D. Ala. 1989); Perez v. General Packer, Inc., 790 F. Supp. 1464, 1470–1471 (C.D. Cal. 1992) (failure to meet one-year limit is jurisdictional).

[467] *See* Zerafa v. Montefiore Hosp. Hous. Co., Inc., 403 F. Supp. 2d 320, 327–328 (S.D.N.Y. 2005) (noting that other district courts in circuit have found time limitation to be procedural); Ariel Land Owners, Inc. v. Dring, 351 F.3d 611, 614–615 (3d Cir. 2003) (as matter of first impression, one year rule is procedural and not jurisdictional); Barnes v. Westinghouse Elec. Corp., 962 F.2d 513, 516 (5th Cir. 1992) (failure to meet one-year limit is procedural); Music v. Arrowood Indem. Co., 632 F.3d 284, 287–288 (6th Cir. 2011) (plaintiff forfeited one-year limit on removal by not timely moving for remand).

[468] *See* Lovern v. General Motors Corp., 121 F.3d 160, 163 (4th Cir. 1997) (dicta indicating that one-year limit is "absolute bar to removal" of diversity cases more than one year after commencement of action); Perez v. General Packer, Inc., 790 F. Supp. 1464, 1471 (C.D. Cal. 1992) (one-year rule is jurisdictional).

[469] 28 U.S.C. § 1447(c); *see* 28 U.S.C. § 1446(a).

[470] *In re* Shell Oil Co., 932 F.2d 1523, 1528–1529 (5th Cir. 1991); Ravens Metal Prods., Inc. v. Wilson, 816 F. Supp. 427, 428 (S.D. W. Va. 1993) (in diversity action, fact that defendant was resident in forum state was procedural defect that was waived by plaintiff's failure to object to removal in 30 days); Harmon v. OKI Sys., 115 F.3d 477, 479 (7th Cir. 1997) (defendant's failure to correctly allege grounds for removal jurisdiction was procedural in nature, not jurisdictional, because diversity jurisdiction existed at time of removal; accordingly, plaintiff waived right to seek remand because motion was not made within 30 days after removal); Brown v. Prudential Ins. Co., 954 F. Supp. 1582, 1584 (S.D. Ga. 1997) (30-day period for moving to remand commences on filing of removal notice in federal court, not state court).

[471] Caggiano v. Pfizer, Inc., 384 F. Supp. 2d 689, 691–692 (S.D.N.Y. 2005).

addition, some courts have held that the time period may be equitably tolled and that "quirks" in local rules will not render an otherwise timely filed motion untimely.[472]

The 30-day limit does not apply to motions to remand that are based on something other than a removal procedure defect.[473] If the motion to remand is based on some other type of defect that is not jurisdictional, the motion to remand must be made within a "reasonable" time.[474] If the motion is based on a jurisdictional defect, it can be made at any time. Thus, whenever it appears, at any time before final judgment, that the district court lacks subject matter jurisdiction, the case must be remanded.[475] The 30-day limit applies only to procedural objections and not to a lack of subject matter jurisdiction. Additionally, when a plaintiff moves to remand to state court after the applicable time limit, and the defendant does not raise the issue of untimeliness, the defect is waived and the district court may remand the case.[476]

### [d] Denial of Remand Based on Futility Exception

Some defendants have argued that a federal district court should dismiss the case rather than remand if a remand to state court would be futile, in the sense that the state court would inevitably dismiss the case as well.[477] However, it is unclear whether the futility doctrine is viable. In *International Primate Protection League v. Tulane Educational Fund*,[478] the Supreme Court discussed the futility doctrine but did not negate it, holding that in that case the barriers to the suit in state court were not "sufficiently certain" to render remand futile. Accordingly, the Court

---

472 Federal Ins. Co. v. Tyco Int'l, 422 F. Supp. 2d 357, 370–372 (S.D.N.Y. 2006) (discussion of cases in which time period was equitably tolled or failure to comply with local rule did not render motion untimely).

473 Graphic Communs. Local 1B v. CVS Caremark, 636 F.3d 971, 974–975 (8th Cir. 2011) (application of local controversy provision was not "defect" within meaning of 28 U.S.C. § 1447(c), so 30-day limit did not apply); Kamm v. ITEX Corp., 568 F.3d 752, 757 (9th Cir. 2009) (application of forum selection clause not "defect" within meaning of 28 U.S.C. § 1447(c), so 30-day limit did not apply); Snapper, Inc. v. Redan, 171 F.3d 1249, 1258 (11th Cir. 1999) ("defect" limited to removal defects).

474 Graphic Comm'ns Local 1B v. CVS Caremark, 636 F.3d 971, 976 (8th Cir. 2011) (case remanded for district court to determine whether time it took plaintiffs to move to remand was "reasonable"); Kamm v. ITEX Corp., 568 F.3d 752, 757 (9th Cir. 2009) (pre-statute "reasonable time frame" standard applies to remand motions not governed by statute); Snapper, Inc. v. Redan, 171 F.3d 1249, 1258 (11th Cir. 1999) (pre-statute "reasonable" time frame applies in cases not covered by statute).

475 28 U.S.C. § 1447(c); *see* Fed. R. Civ. P. 12(h)(3).

476 Student A v. Metcho, 710 F. Supp. 267, 269 (N.D. Cal. 1989); Roe v. O'Donohue, 38 F.3d 298, 301–302 (7th Cir. 1994) (questioning whether defendant causing untimely remand motion should be estopped from raising objection); Student A v. Metcho, 710 F. Supp. 267, 269 (N.D. Cal. 1989); *but see In re* Shell Oil Co., 932 F.2d 1523, 1528–1529 (5th Cir. 1991) (defendants may assert 30-day rule violation after 30 days when district court had opportunity to consider argument before deciding motion for reconsideration).

477 *See, e.g.*, International Primate Protection League v. Tulane Educ. Fund, 500 U.S. 72, 87–89 (1991); Maine Ass'n of Interdependent Neighborhoods v. Comm'r Maine, Dep't of Human Services, 876 F.2d 1051, 1054–1055 (1st Cir. 1989).

478 International Primate Protection League v. Tulane Educ. Fund, 500 U.S. 72 (1991).

remanded the case.[479]

The courts of appeals are split on whether to recognize the Futility Exception.[480]

### [e] Remand of Entire Case or Part of Case

When federal and state court claims are joined in an action removed to federal court, there is a question whether the federal court must retain or remand the entire case, or whether the court may retain the federal claims and remand the state law claims. [481] With respect to cases commenced on or after January 6, 2012, Section 1441(c) requires the district court to sever and remand claims that would have been nonremovable except that they were joined with a federal question claim (*see* § 6.08[5]).[482] This includes claims over which the district court has neither original nor supplemental jurisdiction and claims that have been made nonremovable by statute.[483] Prior to the enactment of the Federal Courts Jurisdiction and Venue Clarification Act of 2011, there was some controversy over whether the Section 1441(c) remand provision applied to cases removed under Section 1441(a) as well as those removed under Section 1441(c),[484] but as amended, the provision is clearly limited to cases removed under Section 1441(c).

If there is supplemental jurisdiction under Section 1367, the appropriate basis for declining to exercise jurisdiction is Section 1367(c) (*see* Ch. 5, *Supplemental Jurisdiction*).[485] In many of such cases, however, the court will decline to remand the state law claims when it is under a duty to exercise jurisdiction over the federal claim, because it would be inefficient to require the plaintiff to proceed in two forums.[486]

---

479 500 U.S. at 87–89.

480 *Compare* Asarco, Inc. v. Glenara, Ltd., 912 F.2d 784, 787 (5th Cir. 1990) (case dismissed because federal court's ruling that state court lacked jurisdiction bound state court); Deutsch v. Turner Corp., 324 F.3d 692, 718–719, & n.22 (9th Cir. 2003) (after determining that California statute was unconstitutional, Ninth Circuit declined to remand cases of uncertain federal jurisdiction based on futility exception as state court would simply dismiss claims with prejudice), *with* Hill v. Vanderbilt Capital Avisors, LLC, 702 F.3d 1220, 1226 (10th Cir. 2012) (plain language of § 1447(c) requires remand, rather than dismissal, of removed action over which federal court lacks jurisdiction, but regardless of propriety of futility exception, remand order was unreviewable because it was colorably based on lack of jurisdiction); *see* Bromwell v. Michigan Mut. Ins. Co., 115 F.3d 208, 213–214 (3d Cir. 1997); Roach v. West Virginia Reg'l Jail & Correctional Facility Auth., 74 F.3d 46, 49 (4th Cir. 1996); Coyne v. American Tobacco Co., 183 F.3d 488, 496–497 (6th Cir. 1999); Smith v. Wisconsin Dep't of Agriculture, 23 F.3d 1134, 1139 (7th Cir. 1994); University of S. Alabama v. American Tobacco Co., 168 F.3d 405, 410 (11th Cir. 1999).

481 Emrich v. Touche Ross & Co., 846 F.2d 1190, 1196 (9th Cir. 1988); *see* Carnegie-Mellon Univ. v. Cohill, 484 U.S. 343, 357 (1988).

482 28 U.S.C. § 1441(c)(2); *see* Pub. L. No. 112-63, § 105, 125 Stat. 758 (2011) (effective date).

483 28 U.S.C. § 1441(c)(1)(B).

484 Kabealo v. Davis, 829 F. Supp. 923, 926 (S.D. Ohio 1993), *aff'd without opinion*, 72 F.3d 129 (6th Cir. 1995) (some courts hold that Section 1441(c) could provide basis for remanding entire case, even if removal was based on Section 1441(a), but there is no authority for that proposition).

485 *See, e.g.*, Williams v. Huron Valley School Dist., 858 F. Supp. 97, 100 (E.D. Mich. 1994); Administaff, Inc. v. Kaster, 799 F. Supp. 685, 688 (W.D. Tex. 1992); Texas Hosp. Ass'n v. National Heritage Ins. Co., 802 F. Supp. 1507 (W.D. Tex. 1992); Padilla v. City of Saginaw, 867 F. Supp. 1309, 1315 (E.D. Mich. 1994); Williams v. Huron Valley School Dist., 858 F. Supp. 97, 100 (E.D. Mich. 1994).

486 *See, e.g.*, Roe v. Little Company of Mary Hosp., 800 F. Supp. 620 (N.D. Ill. 1992); *In re* City of

Another proper approach, appropriate when the court questions whether jurisdiction exists over the state law claims, is to sever the state law claims under Fed. R. Civ. P. 21, remand the state law claims, and retain jurisdiction over the federal question claims.[487]

## [2] Effect of Post-Removal Changes in Case

### [a] Federal Claims Dismissed; State Claims Remaining

If the federal claim that formed the basis of federal question jurisdiction is dismissed, the court has discretion to determine whether or not to retain, remand, or dismiss the supplemental state law claims.[488] If the federal question is eliminated relatively soon after removal, it is ordinarily preferable to remand the case rather than dismiss the case.[489] Remand is generally preferable to avoid potential procedural problems, such as the effect of the statute of limitations, and the delay and cost of filing new pleadings in state court.[490]

An order remanding state claims based on supplemental jurisdiction is subject to appellate review.[491] If the federal question is eliminated soon after removal, retaining the supplemental state law claims may constitute an abuse of discretion.[492]

---

Mobile, 75 F.3d 605, 607 (11th Cir. 1996) (federal court discretion to remand under Section 1367(c) does not include discretion to remand state court case that includes properly removed federal claim; Section 1441(c) remand provision is inapplicable if removal is made under Section 1441(a), and federal and state claims are not "separate and independent").

[487] Fielder v. Credit Acceptance Corp., 188 F.3d 1031, 1039 (8th Cir. 1999).

[488] *See* Carnegie-Mellon Univ. v. Cohill, 484 U.S. 343, 357 (1988); *see, e.g.*, Taylor v. First of Am. Bank-Wayne, 973 F.2d 1284, 1286–1288 (6th Cir. 1993) (federal court retains and rules on state law claims); Nishimoto v. Federman-Bachrach & Assocs., 903 F.2d 709, 715 (9th Cir. 1990); Lyster v. First Nationwide Bank Fin. Corp., 829 F. Supp. 1163, 1165–1166 (N.D. Cal. 1993) (post-removal elimination of federal claim does not require remand); Certilman v. Becker, 807 F. Supp. 307, 309 (S.D.N.Y. 1992) (court discretion to remand after dismissal of federal claims).

[489] Carnegie-Mellon Univ. v. Cohill, 484 U.S. 343, 357 (1988) (possible abuse of discretion to retain case when federal claims dropped in early stages of litigation).

[490] Carnegie-Mellon Univ. v. Cohill, 484 U.S. 343, 357 (1988) (court may evaluate whether plaintiff used manipulative tactics to control forum); Robertson v. Neuromedical Ctr., 161 F.3d 292, 296 (5th Cir. 1998) (after dismissing federal claims before trial, even though not jurisdictionally insubstantial, court abused discretion in not remanding state claims); Payne v. Churchich, 161 F.3d 1030, 1043 (7th Cir. 1998) (when district court dismisses all federal claims before trial, usual and preferred course is to remand state claims absent countervailing considerations); *See* Albingia Versicherungs A.G. v. Schenker Int'l, Inc., 344 F.3d 931, 939 (9th Cir. 2003) (federal courts may decline supplemental jurisdiction, and ordinarily should, after dismissal of jurisdiction-conferring claim, but dismissal is not mandatory); *but see* Acri v. Varian Assocs., 114 F.3d 999, 1000 (9th Cir. 1997) (pre-trial dismissal of all federal claims has never required dismissal of properly removed state law claims).

[491] Executive Software N. Am., Inc. v. United States Dist. Court, 24 F.3d 1545, 1548–1550 (9th Cir. 1994); Travelers Ins. Co. v. Keeling, 996 F.2d 1485, 1485–1489 (2d Cir. 1993) (collateral order subject to appeal when order decides whether dispute resolved in state court).

[492] Carnegie-Mellon Univ. v. Cohill, 484 U.S. 343, 357 (1988); Enochs v. Lampasas County, 641 F.3d 155, 161 (5th Cir. 2011) (district court abused discretion by retaining jurisdiction when federal claims were deleted at infancy of case and all statutory and common law factors weighed heavily in favor of remand); Harrell v. 20th Century Ins. Co., 934 F.2d 203, 205 (9th Cir. 1991).

### [b] Diversity Cases

If the main action on which diversity jurisdiction depends is settled, federal jurisdiction over a third-party claim that existed when the trial began survives that settlement.[493] The general rule in diversity cases is that if the jurisdictional requisites are present when the action begins, subsequent events do not ordinarily defeat the district court's jurisdiction.[494] Similarly, if the plaintiff settles the federal claim on which jurisdiction is based, the federal court retains supplemental jurisdiction over the surviving third-party complaint.[495]

Removability is ordinarily determined as of the date the notice of removal is filed.[496] If the amount in controversy exceeds the jurisdiction minimum at that time, the plaintiff's subsequent reduction of the amount in controversy does not deprive the federal court of jurisdiction.[497] Indeed, the Supreme Court has remarked that it has "consistently held that if jurisdiction exists at the time an action is commenced, such jurisdiction may not be divested by subsequent events."[498]

In contrast, if the state court complaint does not allege a specific amount of damages, a post-removal declaration by the plaintiff that the amount in controversy is less than the jurisdictional minimum may be sufficient to show a lack of removal jurisdiction unless the defendant rebuts the declaration.[499]

Because the amount in controversy is determined by the amount demanded in good faith when the complaint is filed, a final verdict that is less than the jurisdictional minimum does not deprive the federal court of jurisdiction.[500]

---

[493] Hill v. Rolleri, 615 F.2d 886, 888–889 (9th Cir. 1980) (plaintiffs settled case after removal; federal court retains jurisdiction over third-party claims).

[494] St. Paul Mercury Indem. Co. v. Red Cab Co., 303 U.S. 283, 290 (1938); Hardenbergh v. Ray, 151 U.S. 112, 118 (1894); Mollen v. Torrance, 22 U.S. 537, 539, 6 L. Ed. 154 (1824).

[495] Dery v. Wyer, 265 F.2d 804, 808 (2d Cir. 1959) (plaintiff settled FELA claim; federal court retains jurisdiction over third-party indemnity action); *see* 28 U.S.C. § 1367(c) (court may decline to exercise its jurisdiction over third-party claim if all claims over which court had original jurisdiction have been dismissed).

[496] Pullman Co. v. Jenkins, 305 U.S. 534, 537 (1939).

[497] St. Paul Mercury Indem. Co. v. Red Cab. Co., 303 U.S. 283, 290–294 (1938); *see* Carnegie-Mellon Univ. v. Cohill, 484 U.S. 343, 356–358 (1988) (court has discretion to exercise jurisdiction); Purple Passion, Inc. v. RCN Telecom Servs., Inc., 406 F. Supp. 2d 245, 246–247 (S.D.N.Y. 2005) (citing Moore's Federal Practice; post-removal amendment reducing claim below jurisdictional amount does not deprive district court of jurisdiction); Gebbia v. Wal-Mart Stores, Inc., 233 F.3d 880, 883 (5th Cir. 2000) (citing Moore's Federal Practice; post-removal affidavits may be considered in determining amount in controversy only if jurisdictional basis was ambiguous at time of removal); Rogers v. Wal-Mart Stores, Inc., 230 F.3d 868, 872–873 (6th Cir. 2000) (binding or non-binding post-removal stipulation reducing amount in controversy to below jurisdictional minimum does not deprive federal court of jurisdiction).

[498] Freeport-McMoRan, Inc. v. K N Energy, Inc., 498 U.S. 426, 428 (1991).

[499] Asociacion Nacional de Pescadores v. Dow Quimica de Colombia S.A., 988 F.2d 559, 565 (5th Cir. 1993).

[500] St. Paul Mercury Indem. Co. v. Red Cab. Co., 303 U.S. 283, 289–290, 296 (1938) (recovery of less than jurisdictional amount does not divest federal court of jurisdiction).

### [c] Addition of Nondiverse Parties

After removal, if a plaintiff seeks to join additional defendants, and the joinder of any additional defendants would destroy subject matter jurisdiction,[501] the court has discretion (1) to deny joinder of the nondiverse defendants and retain the action or (2) to permit joinder and remand the action to state court.[502] Before 1989, the general rule was that a district court that permitted the joinder of a nondiverse party to a removed case should remand the case to state court. The 1989 enactment of Subsection 1447(e) codified that rule.[503] If the court allows the plaintiff to join a nondiverse party, Section 1447(e) requires remand of the complaint to state court, because the district court no longer has subject matter jurisdiction.[504] This statute is designed to prevent a plaintiff from forum shopping by waiting until late in the case to join all nondiverse defendants, and then seeking remand.[505] However, if the district court was unaware that joinder would destroy diversity, it may reconsider its decision permitting joinder when the plaintiff moves to remand.[506]

When the district court allows the joinder of nondiverse parties, the court of appeals has the power to dismiss those parties to cure defects in diversity jurisdiction.

### [d] When Plaintiff Dismisses Nondiverse Party

In general, a plaintiff may avoid removal and obtain an order of remand by joining a nondiverse party. If the plaintiff then voluntarily dismisses the nondiverse party, however, either before or after removal, the remaining defendant may remove, provided that the one-year limit has not expired (*see* § 6.08[2][h],

---

[501] *See* Strawbridge v. Curtiss, 7 U.S. (3 Cranch.) 267 (1806) (federal court loses its diversity jurisdiction when nondiverse party is joined or intervenes).

[502] 28 U.S.C. § 1447(e); *see* H.R. Rep. No. 889, at 72–73 (1988) (option of permitting joinder and retaining case rejected); Casa Office Machines, Inc. v. Mita Copystar Am., Inc., 42 F.3d 668, 674 (1st Cir. 1994).

[503] *See* 28 U.S.C. § 1447(e); Yniques v. Cabral, 985 F.2d 1031, 1035 (9th Cir. 1993); Miller v. Grgurich, 763 F.2d 372, 373 (9th Cir. 1985); Takeda v. Northwestern Nat'l Life Ins. Co., 765 F.2d 815, 821 (9th Cir. 1985); Desert Empire Bank v. Insurance Co. of N. Am., 623 F.2d 1371, 1376, 1377 (9th Cir. 1980).

[504] Yniques v. Cabral, 985 F.2d 1031, 1035 (9th Cir. 1993); Doleac v. Michalson, 264 F.3d 470, 479–492 (5th Cir. 2001) (appellate court lacks jurisdiction to review district court order permitting joinder of party whose presence destroys diversity of citizenship and remanding case to state court); Cobb v. Delta Exps., Inc., 186 F.3d 675, 676–677 (5th Cir. 1999) (fraudulent joinder doctrine inapplicable when plaintiff seeks to join additional non-diverse defendants after case is properly removed; rather, court has discretion under 28 U.S.C. § 1447(e) to refuse to permit joinder, or to permit joinder but then remand the case to state court); Templeton v. Nedlloyd Lines, 901 F.2d 1273, 1275 (5th Cir. 1990) (28 U.S.C. § 1447(e) does not preclude voluntary dismissal under Fed. R. Civ. P. 41(a)(2)); *but see* Morris v. Princess Cruises, Inc., 236 F.3d 1061, 1068–1069 (9th Cir. 2001) (joinder of nondiverse defendants following removal destroyed diversity jurisdiction but did not divest district court of subject matter jurisdiction because court would have had original admiralty jurisdiction over suit if originally brought in federal court).

[505] *See, e.g.*, Le Duc v. Bujake, 777 F. Supp. 10, 12 (E.D. Mo. 1991) (joinder denied because made shortly before trial scheduled to commence).

[506] Schur v. L.A. Weight Loss Centers, Inc., 577 F.3d 752, 759 (7th Cir. 2009) (on motion to remand, district court judge allowed to review magistrate's order permitting joinder of nondiverse defendants).

§ 6.09[2][a][iii]).[507]

The question arises, however, whether judgment may be entered if the district court erroneously finds that subsequent events, such as settling claims against a non-diverse party, have rendered the case removable. If the jurisdictional defect is never cured, the judgment will be vacated on appeal. If however, the jurisdictional defect is cured by the time the matter is adjudicated and judgment is entered, the Supreme Court has held that the judgment may stand.[508]

### [3] Costs and Attorney's Fees

An order remanding a case to state court may require the losing defendant to pay the prevailing plaintiff's just costs and any actual expenses, including attorney's fees, incurred as a result of the removal.[509] Costs and fees "incurred as a result of removal" are limited to those incurred in federal court that would not have been incurred had the case remained in state court. Therefore, a party's costs of opposing removal, seeking remand, and other expenses incurred because of the improper removal may be awarded. By contrast, ordinary litigation expenses that would have been incurred had the action remained in state court are not recoverable.[510]

However, the statutory authority limiting an award of attorney's fees to actual fees incurred as a result of removal requires district courts to conduct some sort of reasonableness inquiry. In *Huffman v. Saul Holdings Ltd. P'ship*, the district court on remand awarded fees incurred in the district court, appellate fees, and fees for preparing the fee application itself per request without conducting an independent inquiry into the reasonableness of the amounts charged. The district court refused to consider any objections to the reasonableness of the fees. The appellate court reversed, holding that the phrase "incurred as a result of the removal" qualifies, informs, and narrows the meaning of "actual expenses, including attorney fees." The question then becomes whether some of the fees charged were incurred as a result of removal or, for example, as a result of unreasonable billing practices. The district court must make this determination, and must conduct an inquiry into the reasonableness of the time entries contained in the fee petition. Unreasonably high fees are not incurred as a result of removal; rather, excessive fee requests flow from and accumulate by means of improper billing practices and are not recoverable under Section 1447(c).[511]

---

[507] Rowe v. Johns-Manville Corp., 658 F. Supp. 122, 123–124 (E.D. Pa. 1987) (voluntary dismissal of all nondiverse defendants, through settlement or otherwise, makes case removable); Heniford V. American Motor Sales Corp., 471 F. Supp. 328, 336–337 (D.S.C. 1979) (dismissing nondiverse party during closing argument triggers removability).

[508] Caterpillar, Inc. v. Lewis, 519 U.S. 61 (1996) (after motion to remand, all claims involving nondiverse defendant were settled and that defendant was dismissed as party to action).

[509] 28 U.S.C. § 1447(c); *see* Garbie v. DaimlerChrysler Corp., 211 F.3d 407, 410–411 (7th Cir. 2000) (expenses incurred as result of removal include expenses in district court as well as those incurred on appeal in battling removal and defending award).

[510] *See, e.g.*, Avitts v. Amoco Prod. Co., 111 F.3d 30, 32 (5th Cir. 1997).

[511] Huffman v. Saul Holdings Ltd. P'ship, 262 F.3d 1128, 1131–1135 (10th Cir. 2001) (ruling reflects

The court's discretion to award attorney's fees under Section 1447(c) is triggered only if the court first finds that the defendant's decision to remove was legally improper; the propriety of the defendant's removal continues to be central in determining whether to impose fees.[512] In other words, the district court, in exercising its discretion to impose fees and costs, should distinguish removals that present a close question or are only technically defective from those that present no credible basis for federal jurisdiction.[513] As a practical matter, most courts refuse to award the plaintiff costs and fees when the defendant had a legitimate or colorable legal ground for removal or when the remand is based on procedural defects. This standard recognizes the purposes of the statute: to deter removals sought for the purpose of prolonging litigation and imposing costs on the opposing party, while not undermining Congress' decision to afford defendants a right to remove when the statutory criteria are satisfied.[514]

The standard for awarding attorney's fees under the removal statute[515] is something less than that required for an award of attorney's fees under Rule 11.[516] In addition to a statutory award, Rule 11 authorizes the imposition of sanctions when papers are filed containing statements that are not well grounded in fact and warranted by law.[517] A federal court is authorized to impose Rule 11 sanctions in the removal context, even if the court determines that removal was improper on the ground that the federal court lacks subject matter jurisdiction.[518] Under Rule 11, a federal court may (1) award attorney's fees as sanctions against a party who acts in bad faith or whose conduct is vexatious, and (2) sanction a party who makes a frivolous motion for remand.[519]

In addition to its power under Rule 11, a federal court has inherent power to award attorney's fees as sanctions against a party or an attorney who acts in bad faith or whose conduct is tantamount to bad faith,[520] or a losing party who has acted vexatiously, wantonly, or for oppressive reasons.[521]

---

general policy of district courts — that they are duty-bound to ensure that award of attorney's fees is reasonable).

512 Daleske v. Fairfield Communities, 17 F.3d 321, 324 (10th Cir. 1994); *see* 28 U.S.C. § 1447(c); Avitts v. Amoco Prod. Co., 111 F.3d 30, 32 (5th Cir. 1997).

513 Gray v. New York Life Ins. Co., 906 F. Supp. 628, 634 (N.D. Ala. 1995).

514 Martin v. Franklin Capital Corp., 546 U.S. 132, 140 (2005).

515 28 U.S.C. § 1447(c).

516 *See* Fed. R. Civ. P. 11; Gray v. New York Life Ins. Co., 906 F. Supp. 628, 635–637 (N.D. Ala. 1995); *see generally* 2 Moore's Federal Practice Ch. 11, *Signing Pleadings, Motions and Other Papers; Representations to the Court; Sanctions* (Matthew Bender 3d ed.).

517 Fed. R. Civ. P. 11(c); *see generally* Georgene Vairo, Rule 11 Sanctions: Case Law Perspectives and Preventive Measures (3d ed.).

518 *See* Fed. R. Civ. P. 11; Willy v. Coastal Corp., 503 U.S. 131 (1992).

519 *See* Fed. R. Civ. P. 11(b), (c); Chase v. Shop'N Save Warehouse Foods, Inc., 110 F.3d 424, 430–431 (7th Cir. 1997) (Rule 11 sanctions imposed on remand motion that was frivolous because court had previously denied plaintiff's identical motion in identical prior suit); *cf.* Roadway Express, Inc. v. Piper, 447 U.S. 752, 763–768 (1980) (sanctions under Fed. R. Civ. P. 37).

520 *See* Roadway Express, Inc. v. Piper, 447 U.S. 752, 763–768 (1980); Toledo Scale Co. v. Computing Scale Co., 261 U.S. 399, 426–428 (1923).

521 *See* 28 U.S.C. § 1927; Rich Co. v. United States *ex rel.* Industrial Lumber Co., 417 U.S. 116, 129

The district court retains jurisdiction, even after remand, to award attorney's fees. The award of attorney's fees is a collateral matter and the district court retains jurisdiction over an award even though the court has been divested of jurisdiction over the merits of the case.[522]

## § 6.12 STATE COURT JURISDICTION AFTER REMAND

Once a case is remanded, and the federal court mails a certified copy of the remand order to the state court, the remand is effected and the state court has jurisdiction to proceed with the case.[523] Typically, the state court "will give effect to all pleadings filed in federal court and to all rulings made by the federal court" while the case was in federal court.[524] Although the mailing of the copy of the remand order to the state court is automatic, counsel should order certified copies of the entire federal court file for the state court.

Once the remand is effected, the federal court lacks further jurisdiction over the case except that the court retains authority to adjudicate collateral matters, such as costs, fees, and sanctions.[525] For example, a remanding federal court cannot order that the plaintiff be estopped from recovering more than the requisite jurisdictional amount in state court.[526] Similarly, a remanding federal court cannot enjoin a party's efforts to obtain relief in bankruptcy court pertaining to that case.[527] The rule that the federal court lacks further jurisdiction once the case has been remanded has been applied to cases remanded under the Class Action Fairness Act.[528]

---

(1974); Vaughan v. Atkinson, 369 U.S. 527, 530–531 (1962).

522 Willy v. Coastal Corp., 503 U.S. 131, 132–133 (1992) (Rule 11 sanctions); Moore v. Permanente Medical Group, Inc., 981 F.2d 443, 445 (9th Cir. 1992); Buster v. Greisen, 104 F.3d 1186, 1188 (9th Cir. 1997).

523 28 U.S.C. § 1447(c); *see* Arnold v. Garlock, Inc., 278 F.3d 426, 437 (5th Cir. 2001) (order remanding case for lack of subject matter jurisdiction is not self-executing; certified copy of order must be mailed to clerk of state court).

524 *See, e.g.*, Wagh v. Metris Direct, Inc., 348 F.3d 1102, 1112–1113 (9th Cir. 2003), *as amended*, 352 F.3d 1187 (9th Cir. 2003).

525 Covanta Onondaga, Ltd. v. Onondaga County Res. Recovery Agency, 318 F.3d 392, 395 (2d Cir. 2003) (once district court relinquishes jurisdiction by remand, court has no jurisdiction to make any orders; court noted that case did not involve court acting under All Writs Act to aid or protect its jurisdiction and court did not retain authority to adjudicate collateral matters, such as costs, fees, and sanctions); *In re* C & M Props., L.L.C., 563 F.3d 1156, 1161–1162 (10th Cir. 2009) (any further litigation in federal court after remand is like playing "air guitar").

526 Christopher v. Stanley-Bostitch, Inc., 240 F.3d 95, 99–100 (1st Cir. 2001) (appellate court could review portion of remand order purporting to determine estoppel question in state court proceeding).

527 Covanta Onondaga, Ltd. v. Onondaga County Res. Recovery Agency, 318 F.3d 392, 400–401 (2d Cir. 2003) (after remand based on mandatory abstention, court improperly granted defendant's motion to enjoin plaintiff, debtor in pending bankruptcy case, from seeking bankruptcy court stay of remanded state-court action).

528 Conway v. Purdue Pharma, L.P. (*In re* Oxycontin Antitrust Litig.) 2011 U.S. Dist. LEXIS 117124, at *35 (S.D.N.Y. Oct. 6, 2011) ("once the Clerk of Court mailed a certified copy of the remand order to the state court, this Court was without authority to act on a motion in the case").

## § 6.13 APPELLATE REVIEW OF REMAND ORDER

### [1] Orders Denying Remand

In general, the existence of appellate jurisdiction in a specific federal court over a given type of case is dependent on authority expressly conferred by the constitution and statute.[529] The primary statutory grant of jurisdiction to the courts of appeals confers jurisdiction to review final decisions and orders of the district courts.[530] A refusal to remand, in and of itself, is not a final order and may not be reviewed until a final judgment is entered.[531] Unless the denial of the motion to remand is one of the few instances in which an interlocutory appeal is permissible, as discussed below, a court's decision to deny remand and to retain the case is not subject to review.[532]

After the case reaches final judgment, the issue of removal is reviewable on appeal from the final judgment.[533] The denial of a remand motion is a question of federal subject matter jurisdiction and statutory construction that is subject to review de novo.[534]

If a motion to remand is denied, the propriety of removal may be reviewable by interlocutory appeal if the order refusing to remand is certified.[535] Whenever a district judge in a civil action issues an order that is not otherwise appealable, and the judge believes that (1) the order involves a controlling question of law as to which substantial grounds exist for a difference of opinion, and (2) an immediate appeal from the order may materially advance the ultimate termination of the litigation, the judge must so certify in the order. The court of appeals, in its discretion, may permit an immediate appeal if the party seeking remand files an application within 10 days after the entry of the order denying remand.[536] Absent certification, an appeal of an order denying remand is only permitted when the appeal of the refusal to remand is joined with an appeal of a final order.[537]

---

[529] Carroll v. United States, 354 U.S. 394, 399 (1957); American Fire & Casualty Co. v. Finn, 341 U.S. 6, 17–18 (1951); *In re* Carter, 618 F.2d 1093, 1098 (5th Cir. 1980); *see* Maxwell v. First National Bank of Monroeville, 638 F.2d 32, 35 (5th Cir. 1981).

[530] 28 U.S.C. § 1291; *see* B., Inc. v. Miller Brewing Co., 663 F.2d 545, 547–550 (5th Cir. 1981).

[531] *See* New Jersey, Dep't of Treasury, Div. of Inv. v. Fuld, 604 F.3d 816, 819–824 (3d Cir. 2010) (appellate court did not have jurisdiction to review denial of remand under collateral order doctrine); Missouri *ex rel.* Nixon v. Prudential Health Care, 259 F.3d 949, 955 (8th Cir. 2001) (citing Moore's Federal Practice); Huffman v. Saul Holdings Ltd. P'ship, 194 F.3d 1072, 1076 (10th Cir. 1999); B., Inc. v. Miller Brewing Co., 663 F.2d 545, 547–550 (5th Cir. 1981).

[532] *See* Neal v. Brown, 980 F.2d 747, 748 (D.C. Cir. 1992).

[533] *See* City of Warren v. City of Detroit, 495 F.3d 282, 286 (6th Cir. 2007); O'Halloran v. University of Washington, 856 F.2d 1375, 1378–1379 (9th Cir. 1988).

[534] *See* Huffman v. Saul Holdings Ltd. P'ship, 194 F.3d 1072, 1076 (10th Cir. 1999) (because removal is issue of statutory construction, propriety of removal is reviewed de novo); Carpenter v. Wichita Falls Indep. Sch. Dist., 44 F.3d 362, 365 (5th Cir. 1995).

[535] *See* 28 U.S.C. § 1292(b); *see also* Sheeran v. General Elec. Co., 593 F.2d 93, 97 (9th Cir. 1979).

[536] 28 U.S.C. § 1292(b).

[537] *See, e.g.*, O'Halloran v. University of Washington, 856 F.2d 1375, 1381 (9th Cir. 1988).

In limited circumstances, immediate appellate review also may be sought by writ of mandamus.[538] However, mandamus is an extraordinary remedy available only in extreme situations if the party seeking the writ demonstrates a clear and indisputable right to the writ.[539] For example, a petition for a writ of mandamus must demonstrate that the district court committed a clear error of law in retaining the case, approaching the magnitude of an unauthorized exercise of judicial power (or a failure to exercise that power when under a duty to do so).[540] A writ of mandamus is appropriate when the denial of immediate review of an order denying remand would render any subsequent review impossible.[541]

## [2] Orders Granting Motion to Remand

In general, an order granting a motion to remand a case to the state court from which it was removed is not reviewable on appeal or otherwise.[542] A remand order based on a lack of subject matter jurisdiction is not subject to review,[543] even if the district court does not cite or refer to Section 1447(c).[544] Similarly, remand orders based on 28 U.S.C. Section 1447(e) are not reviewable. Section 1447(e) gives the court discretion to join additional defendants whose joinder would destroy subject matter jurisdiction and remand the case to state court (*see* § 6.11[2][c]).[545] Such orders fall within the general prohibition on review of remand orders provided by Section 1447(d).[546] However, an appellate court may evaluate the merits of an unreviewable remand order in the context of an immediate appeal of an order awarding of attorney fees and costs under Section 1447(c).[547] *See* § 6.11[3] for a discussion of awarding costs and attorney's fees to the prevailing party in a motion for remand.

The Supreme Court has not decided whether an appellate court may look beyond a district court's characterization of the basis for remand as lack of subject-

---

538 *See* 28 U.S.C. § 1651; *see* 19 MOORE'S FEDERAL PRACTICE Ch. 204, *Extraordinary Writs* (Matthew Bender 3d ed.).

539 *See* Trans. Penn Wax Corp. v. McCandless, 50 F.3d 217, 227 (3d Cir. 1995); Clorox Co. v. U.S. Dist. Ct. for N.D. of California, 779 F.2d 517, 519–520 (9th Cir. 1985) (extraordinary review by mandamus only when same review unobtainable by contemporary ordinary review); Rohrer, Hibler & Replogle, Inc. v. Perkins, 728 F.2d 860, 862–863 (7th Cir. 1984) (mere error insufficient to justify mandamus).

540 Trans. Penn Wax Corp. v. McCandless, 50 F.3d 217, 227 (3d Cir. 1995).

541 Rohrer, Hibler & Replogle, Inc. v. Perkins, 728 F.2d 860, 862–863 (7th Cir. 1984).

542 28 U.S.C. § 1447(d).

543 Things Remembered, Inc. v. Petrarca, 516 U.S. 124, 129 (1995). See, e.g., Calabro v. Aniqa Halal Live Poultry Corp., 650 F.3d 163, 165 (2d Cir. 2011) ("Because the district court's decision to remand this case rested on its determination that it was without subject-matter jurisdiction, we lack appellate jurisdiction to review it").

544 *See* 28 U.S.C. § 1447(c); *see, e.g., In re* WTC Disaster Site, 414 F.3d 352, 368 (2d Cir. 2005) (failure to mention 28 U.S.C. § 1447(c) irrelevant because lack of subject-matter jurisdiction was clearly ground for remand); Heaton v. Monogram Credit Card Bank of Ga., 231 F.3d 994, 997–999 (5th Cir. 2000) (remand order was based on lack of subject matter jurisdiction; order expressed doubt as to subject matter jurisdiction and stated that doubts should be resolved in favor of remand).

545 *See* 28 U.S.C. § 1447(e).

546 *In re* Florida Wire & Cable Co., 102 F.3d 866, 867–868 (7th Cir. 1996); *see* 28 U.S.C. § 1447(d).

547 Mints v. Educational Testing Service, 99 F.3d 1253, 1257, 1261 (3d Cir. 1996).

matter jurisdiction.[548] However, in *Powerex Corp. v. Reliant Energy Servs., Inc.*, the Court stated that if an appellate court *does* look behind the district court's characterization, once it confirms that the characterization was colorable, it may look no further. The Court reasoned that further scrutiny of the district court's reasons could result in lengthy appellate disputes about whether an arguably jurisdictional ground was properly jurisdictional, frustrating the purpose of the ban on appellate review of remand orders. Moreover, the Court pointed out, "the line between misclassifying a ground as subject-matter jurisdiction and misapplying a proper ground of subject-matter is sometimes elusively thin."[549]

Remand orders based on a timely raised defect in removal procedure are not subject to review,[550] regardless of whether the remand order is erroneous.[551] Thus, a remand order based on a defendant's failure to file the removal notice within the prescribed 30-day time limit is not subject to review.[552] Similarly, a remand order based on the fact that less than all of the defendants joined in the notice of removal within the 30-day limit is not reviewable because it is based on a procedural defect.[553]

However, an order for remand based on an *untimely* motion to remand for procedural defects is reviewable by mandamus.[554] Finally, even though an appellate court may not review the merits of a remand order, it may be able to review a sua sponte remand order based on procedural grounds, to determine

---

[548] Kircher v. Putnam Funds Trust, 547 U.S. 633, 641–642 (2006) ("even if it is permissible to look beyond the court's own label," district court's remand order was unmistakably premised on lack of subject matter jurisdiction, so Court declined to address issue of whether, and to what extent, appellate court may delve beyond district court's own statements of reasons for remand); *see* 547 U.S. at 650 (Scalia, J, concurring: "The Court should end this delay by holding that appellate courts cannot look beyond the stated basis for the district court's order.").

[549] Powerex Corp. v. Reliant Energy Servs., 551 U.S. 224, 233–234 (2007) ("Even assuming, however, that § 1447(d) permits appellate courts to look behind the district court's characterization, . . . we conclude that review of the District Court's characterization of its remand as resting upon lack of subject-matter jurisdiction, to the extent it is permissible at all, should be limited to confirming that that characterization was colorable. Lengthy appellate disputes about whether an arguable jurisdictional ground invoked by the district court was properly such would frustrate the purpose of § 1447(d)").

[550] Things Remembered, Inc. v. Petrarca, 516 U.S. 124, 129 (1995); Thermtron Prods., Inc. v. Hermansdorfer, 423 U.S. 336, 342 (1976); Price v. PSA, Inc., 829 F.2d 871, 874 (9th Cir. 1987) (nonstatutory remands not immune from review).

[551] *In re* Ocean Marine Mut., 3 F.3d 353, 355–356 (11th Cir. 1993); *see* Thermtron Prods., Inc. v. Hermansdorfer, 423 U.S. 336, 343 (1976).

[552] *In re* Uniroyal Goodrich Tire Co., 104 F.3d 322, 324, 325 (11th Cir. 1997) (court of appeals lacked jurisdiction to consider whether district court erred in remanding case to state court when remand order was based on plaintiff's claim that defendant failed to file removal notice within 30-day time limit).

[553] Phoenix Container, L.P. v. Sokoloff, 235 F.3d 352, 354–355 (7th Cir. 2000) (appellate court lacked jurisdiction to review remand order based on conclusion that removal was untimely; court rejected argument that district court's use of extra-statutory criteria to determine timeliness made order reviewable because judicial code statutes are interrelated rather than self-contained); *In re* Ocean Marine Mut., 3 F.3d 353, 355–356 (11th Cir. 1993); Wilson v. General Motors Corp., 888 F.2d 779, 781 n.1 (11th Cir. 1989) (failure to comply with 28 U.S.C. § 1446(a), (b) constitutes procedural defect).

[554] *In re* Shell Oil Co., 932 F.2d 1518, 1522 (5th Cir. 1991); Air-Shields, Inc. v. Fullam, 891 F.2d 63 (3d Cir. 1989).

whether the district court had authority to issue the order.[555]

Remand orders based on grounds other than a lack of subject matter jurisdiction or a procedural defect are subject to review.[556] Additionally, a remand order based on the abstention doctrine is subject to immediate appellate review.[557] An abstention-based remand order is appealable as a final decision, because it effectively puts the litigants out of court.[558]

Remands based on the following types of nonstatutory grounds have been held subject to appellate review: when a district court remands a case over which the court had subject matter jurisdiction because of a crowded court docket;[559] when the remand is based on a determination that a forum selection clause barred removal[560] or that a party waived its removal rights;[561] remand orders based on public policy considerations;[562] and remand orders based on post-removal changes in a properly removed case.[563]

---

555 Page v. City of Southfield, 45 F.3d 128, 131–132 (6th Cir. 1995); *In re* Allstate Ins. Co., 8 F.3d 219, 221–223 (5th Cir. 1993); *In re* First Nat'l Bank of Boston, 70 F.3d 1184, 1187–1190 (11th Cir. 1995).

556 Thermtron Prods., Inc. v. Hermansdorfer, 423 U.S. 336, 344–346 (1976) (review of remand order granted on the basis that district court had crowded docket); Gravitt v. Southwestern Bell Tel. Co., 430 U.S. 723, 724 (1977) (emphasizing narrow scope of permissible review).

557 Quackenbush v. Allstate Ins. Co., 517 U.S. 706, 712 (1996); Bennett v. Liberty Nat'l Fire Ins. Co., 968 F.2d 969, 970 (9th Cir. 1992) (reviewable because abstention is a matter of discretion); *see, e.g.*, Wallace v. Louisiana Citizens Prop. Ins. Corp., 444 F.3d 697, 700–701 (5th Cir. 2006) (remand of Hurricane Katrina-related case under 28 U.S.C. § 1369(b) is reviewable because based on abstention).

558 Moses H. Cone Memorial Hospital v. Mercury Constr. Corp., 460 U.S. 1, 9 (1983); Idlewild Bon Voyage Liquor Corp. v. Epstein, 370 U.S. 713, 715 (1962); *see* 28 U.S.C. § 1291.

559 Thermtron Prods., Inc. v. Hermansdorfer, 423 U.S. 336, 344 (1976) (remand based on crowded court docket impermissible).

560 Autoridad de Energia Electrica de P.R. v. Ericsson, 201 F.3d 15, 17–18 (1st Cir. 2000) (remand order based on forum selection clause is reviewable by interlocutory appeal under collateral order doctrine); New Jersey v. Merrill Lynch & Co., Inc., 640 F.3d 545, 547 (3d Cir. 2011) (remand based on defendant's waiver of right to remove in forum selection clause was reviewable); Suter v. Munich Reinsurance Co., 223 F.3d 150 (3d Cir. 2000); Findwhere Holdings, Inc. v. Systems Env't, 626 F.3d 752, 755 (4th Cir. 2010) (remand based on forum selection clause does not fall within general prohibition of appellate review for remand orders pursuant to 28 U.S.C. § 1447(c)); Waters v. Browning-Ferris Indus., Inc., 252 F.3d 796, 797 (5th Cir. 2001) (remand based on contractual forum selection clause is reviewable); Public Sch. Ret. Sys. v. State St. Bank, 640 F.3d 821, 825 (8th Cir. 2011) (remand based on contractual forum-selection clause is not based on procedural defect or lack of subject matter jurisdiction and, therefore, is reviewable); Snapper, Inc. v. Redan, 171 F.3d 1249, 1260 (11th Cir. 1999) (when forum selection clause clearly indicated state and federal forums in Georgia were proper, but plaintiff sought to exclude itself from contractual provision, clear and unequivocal standard for waiving right to remove was inapplicable; rather, ordinary contract principles applied).

561 Clorox Co. v. U.S. Dist. Ct. for N.D. of California, 779 F.2d 517, 520 (9th Cir. 1985) (employee handbook stated that suits could be filed in state or federal court).

562 Kolibash v. Committee on Legal Ethics, 872 F.2d 571, 576 (4th Cir. 1989) (remand of ethical action against U.S. attorney removed under 28 U.S.C. § 1442 improper; because key actions arose form official duties, removal proper even when federal defense not pleaded).

563 Executive Software N. Am., Inc. v. United States Dist. Court, 24 F.3d 1545, 1548–1550 (9th Cir. 1994) (dismissal of sole federal claim after removal); Matter of Shell Oil Co. 970 F.2d 355, 356 (7th Cir. 1992) (plaintiff waived damages exceeding amount in controversy after removal).

## [3] Standard of Review

On appeal, a district court's denial of a motion to remand is reviewed de novo.[564] Similarly, an appeal of a remand order based on the abstention doctrine is reviewed de novo.[565]

Further, a remand order based on a forum selection clause is reviewed de novo.[566] In contrast, a district court's decision to remand state-law claims after declining to exercise supplemental jurisdiction is reviewed for abuse of discretion.[567]

On a petition for mandamus (*see* [1][b][iii], *above*), the writ will issue only if there has been a usurpation of judicial power or a clear abuse of discretion.[568]

---

[564] Pietrangelo v. Alvas Corp., 686 F.3d 62, 64 (2d Cir. 2012) ("We review a district court's denial of a motion to remand de novo."); *see* Marcella v. Capital Dist. Physicians' Health Plan, Inc., 293 F.3d 42, 46–47 (2d Cir. 2002) (under its "special obligation" to ensure federal subject matter jurisdiction, appellate court considered issue de novo; decision was made notwithstanding fact that party had failed to timely object to magistrate judge's order denying remand based on ERISA preemption and even though district court had held that magistrate judge's ruling was law of case); Roland v. Green, 675 F.3d 503, 511 (5th Cir. 2012) (denial of motion to remand reviewed de novo).

[565] *See, e.g.*, Privitera v. California Bd. of Medical Quality Assurance, 926 F.2d 890, 895 (9th Cir. 1991).

[566] *See, e.g.*, Autoridad de Energia Electrica de P.R. v. Ericsson, 201 F.3d 15, 17–18 (1st Cir. 2000); Findwhere Holdings, Inc. v. Systems Env't, 626 F.3d 752, 755 (4th Cir. 2010) (district court decision on issue of contract interpretation, including interpretation of forum selection clause, reviewed de novo).

[567] *See, e.g.*, Esab Group, Inc. v. Zurich Ins. PLC, 685 F.3d 376, 393 (4th Cir. 2012) (district court did not abuse discretion in remanding nonarbitrable claims to state court).

[568] Schlagenhauf v. Holder, 379 U.S. 104, 110–111 (1964).

# Chapter 7

# PERSONAL JURISDICTION IN FEDERAL COURTS

## § 7.01 OVERVIEW OF PERSONAL JURISDICTION

### [1] Legislative and Judicial Jurisdiction Distinguished

Courts and scholars use the term "jurisdiction" in several different ways in the law. Jurisdiction, the power to say (*dictio*) what the law is (*juris*), can be exercised through legislation or through adjudication. Legislative jurisdiction refers to the state's authority to enact and to apply its laws (both decisional and statutory), and to conduct all business incidental to its law-making function. Legislation is effective with respect to all persons and property that have the adequate territorial connections with the state.[1] Judicial jurisdiction, on the other hand, refers to power of the courts to hear a dispute and to render a valid judgment, one that will be recognized by other courts.[2] Judicial jurisdiction is effective only with respect to certain persons or property. Before a person or property may be subjected to the court's jurisdiction, the person or property must have the adequate territorial connection with the state — *basis* — *and* certain prescribed steps — *process* — must be taken to subject that person or property to the court's authority.[3] The purpose of this chapter is simply to outline the elements of personal jurisdiction in federal courts. Thus, a broad overview of these *basis* and *process* requirements is provided in [2], *below*. For a complete discussion of the *basis* aspect of personal jurisdiction, *see* 16 Moore's Federal Practice, Ch. 108. For a complete discussion of the *process* aspect of personal jurisdiction in federal courts, see 1 Moore's Federal Practice, Ch. 4, *Summons*.

### [2] Basis and Process Requirements for Personal Jurisdiction

#### [a] Basis Establishes Required Connection with Sovereign

Two requirements must be satisfied before a court may exercise jurisdiction over a particular person or property.[4] First, there must be a proper connection between the person or property and the state's (or sovereign's) territory. The kind of connection or relationship that suffices for jurisdiction is referred to as the

[1] *See* Black's Law Dictionary 982 (9th ed. 2009).

[2] *See* Black's Law Dictionary 929 (9th ed. 2009).

[3] *See* Restatement (Second) of Judgments Ch. 2, § 1 (1982).

[4] Restatement (Second) of Judgments Ch. 2, § 1 (1982).

jurisdictional *basis*.[5] If a basis exists, the person or property is said to be *amenable* to jurisdiction.

### [b] Process Establishes Required Steps to Subject Person or Thing to Court's Power

A second requirement must be satisfied before a court may exercise jurisdiction over a particular person. A court may not exert power over a person unless certain prescribed steps are taken to connect the person to the court's power. This requirement is called the *process* of invoking jurisdiction. In other words, even if a person is *amenable* to jurisdiction, a court may not exert power over a person without the person's consent unless certain prescribed steps are taken.[6] This *process* requirement typically entails service of process in conformity with statutory and due process requirements.

Conversely, even if proper service was made, a court may not exercise jurisdiction over the defendant unless the defendant has the required contacts with the jurisdiction and is thus amenable to jurisdiction there.[7]

## [3] Categories of Jurisdiction

### [a] In Personam Jurisdiction Defined

The type of connection or relationship between a person, generally the defendant, or property and the state determines the type of jurisdiction a court may exercise and the type of judgment it may render. *In personam* jurisdiction is required when a personal money judgment or an injunction is sought against the defendant. If the defendant has an appropriate connection with the state, the court may exercise personal jurisdiction over the defendant and enter an *in personam* judgment.[8] A judgment *in personam* is a judgment that determines whether the

---

[5] *See, e.g.*, SEC v. Ross, 504 F.3d 1130, 1138 (9th Cir. 2007) (familiar minimum contacts test, coupled with statutory authorization, provides basis for exercise of jurisdiction, while service of process is mechanism by which court actually acquires jurisdiction).

[6] *See, e.g.*, Overton v. United States, 925 F.2d 1282, 1284 (10th Cir. 1991) (statute, 28 U.S.C. § 1391(e), providing that service on federal defendants be by certified mail beyond territorial limits of district court in which suit was instituted, is venue statute, "not a grant of nationwide *in personam* jurisdiction."); Greenspun v. Del E. Webb Corp., 634 F.2d 1204, 1207 (9th Cir. 1980) (two-step test to determine propriety of jurisdiction); *see also* Restatement (Second) of Judgments Ch. 2, § 1 (1982).

[7] *See, e.g.*, Overton v. United States, 925 F.2d 1282, 1284 (10th Cir. 1991) (statute, 28 U.S.C. § 1391(e), providing that service on federal defendants be by certified mail beyond territorial limits of district court in which suit was instituted, is venue statute, "not a grant of nationwide *in personam* jurisdiction."). For discussion of methods of service of process and constitutional limits on personal jurisdiction, beyond that included in this chapter, see Moore's Federal Practice Ch. 4, *Summons*, and Ch. 108, *Territorial Jurisdiction: Jurisdiction Over Persons and Property* (Matthew Bender 3d ed.).

[8] 16 Moore's Federal Practice, Ch. 108, *Territorial Jurisdiction: Jurisdiction Over Persons and Property* § 108.02[1] (Matthew Bender 3d ed.). *See, e.g.*, Walden v. Fiore, 134 S. Ct. 1115 (2014) ("For a State to exercise jurisdiction consistent with due process, the defendant's suit-related conduct must create a substantial connection with the forum State."); Daimler AG v. Bauman, 134 S. Ct. 746 (2014); Goodyear Dunlop Tires Operations, S.A. v. Brown, 131 S. Ct. 2846 (2011) ("A state court's assertion of jurisdiction exposes defendants to the State's coercive power, and is therefore subject to review for

defendant must do or refrain from doing some specific act, or pay the plaintiff a sum of money.[9]

There are two types of *in personam* jurisdiction. *Specific* jurisdiction exists when the lawsuit arises out of or is sufficiently related to a defendant's contacts with the forum state.[10] *General* jurisdiction, which is more difficult to obtain, exists when the defendant's contacts with the forum state are so pervasive that the defendant may be sued there on any cause of action whether or not the lawsuit is related to such contacts.[11] In addition, some traditional bases for jurisdiction continue to exist.[12] For a complete discussion of *in personam* jurisdiction, *see* 16 Moore's Federal Practice Ch. 108, *Territorial Jurisdiction: Jurisdiction Over Persons and Property* Part D (Modern Jurisdictional Theory: Minimum Contacts and Purposeful Availment & E (Modern Application of Traditional Bases: Personal Jurisdiction Based on Presence, Domicile, and Consent) (Matthew Bender 3d ed.).

### [b] Jurisdiction over Property Distinguished

A state may also assert its power over any property within its borders. Thus, jurisdiction over property enables a court to adjudicate an action *in rem* (or *quasi-in rem*). A judgment in an *in rem* action is effective to determine interests of persons in specific property. Unlike an in *personam judgment*, however, an *in rem* judgment does not impose any personal obligation on the defendant. The only type of judgment a court may render by virtue of its jurisdiction over property is one that affects that particular piece of the defendant's property.[13] Moreover, jurisdic-

---

compatibility with the Fourteenth Amendment's Due Process Clause. Assertion of jurisdiction over an out-of-state corporation must comply with "traditional notions of fair play and substantial justice."); J. McIntyre Mach., Ltd. V. Nicastro, 131 S. Ct. 2780 (2011) ("Due process protects the defendant's right not to be coerced except by lawful judicial power. As a general rule, the exercise of judicial power is not lawful unless the defendant "purposefully avails itself of the privilege of conducting activities within the forum State, thus invoking the benefits and protections of its laws."); World-Wide Volkswagen Corp. v. Woodson, 444 U.S. 286, 292 (1980) (one function of *International Shoe* approach to jurisdiction is to protect defendant against burdens of litigating in distant or inconvenient forum); Rush v. Savchuk, 444 U.S. 320, 332 (1980) (due process limitations on state court jurisdiction primarily serve to protect defendant).

[9] Hanson v. Denckla, 357 U.S. 235, 246, n.12 (1958) (citing Restatement (First) of Judgments §§ 5–9); *see* Restatement (Second) of Judgments Ch. 2, Introductory Note b, § 5 (1982).

[10] *See, e.g.*, Walden v. Fiore, 134 S. Ct. 1115 (2014) ("For a State to exercise jurisdiction consistent with due process, the defendant's suit-related conduct must create a substantial connection with the forum State."); J. McIntyre Mach., Ltd. V. Nicastro, 131 S. Ct. 2780 (2011) ("Due process protects the defendant's right not to be coerced except by lawful judicial power. As a general rule, the exercise of judicial power is not lawful unless the defendant "purposefully avails itself of the privilege of conducting activities within the forum State, thus invoking the benefits and protections of its laws."); World-Wide Volkswagen Corp. v. Woodson, 444 U.S. 286, 292 (1980) (one function of *International Shoe* approach to jurisdiction is to protect defendant against burdens of litigating in distant or inconvenient forum).

[11] *See, e.g.*, Daimler AG v. Bauman, 134 S. Ct. 746 (2014); Goodyear Dunlop Tires Operations, S.A. v. Brown, 131 S. Ct. 2846 (2011) ("A state court's assertion of jurisdiction exposes defendants to the State's coercive power, and is therefore subject to review for compatibility with the Fourteenth Amendment's Due Process Clause. Assertion of jurisdiction over an out-of-state corporation must comply with "traditional notions of fair play and substantial justice.").

[12] *See, e.g.*, Burnham v. Superior Court, 495 U.S. 604, 609 (1990) (service on defendant within forum state provides *in personam* jurisdiction).

[13] *See* Shaffer v. Heitner, 433 U.S. 186, 212 (1977) (jurisdiction over property requires adequate

tion over property is subject to the same constitutional restrictions that govern personal jurisdiction.[14] This topic is discussed further in § 7.04. For a complete discussion of *in rem* jurisdiction, *see* 16 MOORE'S FEDERAL PRACTICE Ch. 108, *Territorial Jurisdiction: Jurisdiction Over Persons and Property* G (Matthew Bender 3d ed.) (Jurisdiction over Property).

## [4] Consequences of Lack of Jurisdiction

### [a] Effect of Lack of Jurisdiction

Jurisdiction is required for a court to exert power over the particular person or property in a dispute. A court without jurisdiction over the defendant may not hear the dispute. If the court proceeds to hear the action, its judgment will be invalid and unenforceable.[15] Lack of jurisdiction is also a valid ground for one state court or federal court to refuse to enforce another state court's judgment.[16]

### [b] Jurisdictional Error Can Be Grounds for Collateral Attack on Judgment

A mistake in jurisdiction may be challenged either in the court in which the action is originally brought (*i.e.*, first forum or F-1) or, if no such challenge is made in F-1 and the mistake in jurisdiction is not waived, in a later proceeding in a different court (*i.e.*, F-2).[17] The former type of challenge is called a direct attack; the latter is called a collateral attack. The assertion of lack of jurisdiction of the F-1 court as a defense in a subsequent proceeding to enforce the judgment in F-2 is a typical example of a collateral attack.

### [c] Defect May Be Waived

Personal jurisdiction requirements serve to protect the defendant from being compelled to litigate in a forum with which the defendant has an insufficient connection.[18] Consequently, the defendant may waive personal jurisdiction, either

---

relation between defendant, forum, and litigation); *see also* Hanson v. Denckla, 357 U.S. 235, 246 n.12 (1958).

[14] *See*; *see also* 16 MOORE'S FEDERAL PRACTICE Ch. 108, *Territorial Jurisdiction: Jurisdiction Over Persons and Property* (Matthew Bender 3d ed.).

[15] *See* Burnham v. Superior Court, 495 U.S. 604, 609 (1990) (citing cases); *see also* RESTATEMENT (SECOND) OF JUDGMENTS Ch. 2, § 1 (1982) (court's judgment is invalid without jurisdiction).

[16] D'Arcy v. Ketchum, 52 U.S. (11 How.) 165, 176 (1851) (full faith and credit statute is not meant to enforce judgments in which rendering court lacked jurisdiction over defendant or defendant's property).

[17] *See* Restatement (Second) of Judgments Ch. 2, § 10 (1982).

[18] *See, e.g.*, Walden v. Fiore, 134 S. Ct. 1115 (2014) ("For a State to exercise jurisdiction consistent with due process, the defendant's suit-related conduct must create a substantial connection with the forum State."); Daimler AG v. Bauman, 134 S. Ct. 746 (2014); Goodyear Dunlop Tires Operations, S.A. v. Brown, 131 S. Ct. 2846 (2011) ("A state court's assertion of jurisdiction exposes defendants to the State's coercive power, and is therefore subject to review for compatibility with the Fourteenth Amendment's Due Process Clause. Assertion of jurisdiction over an out-of-state corporation must comply with "traditional notions of fair play and substantial justice."); J. McIntyre Mach., Ltd. V. Nicastro, 131 S. Ct. 2780 (2011) ("Due process protects the defendant's right not to be coerced except by lawful judicial

expressly, by consenting to jurisdiction, or impliedly, by failing to object in a timely manner using the proper procedure.[19] If the defendant is willing to waive the requirement, the court should not raise personal jurisdiction concerns on its own motion, because the defendant's consent is sufficient to give the court jurisdiction.[20] This rule is in contrast to that for subject matter jurisdiction problems. The parties may not consent to subject matter jurisdiction; rather, the court is obligated to raise the problem sua sponte, and must dismiss if subject matter jurisdiction is lacking (*see* [4][a], *below*).

### [5] Jurisdiction over Persons and Property Distinguished From Related Concepts

#### [a] Subject Matter Jurisdiction or "Competence"

Jurisdiction over subject matter or "competence" refers to the power of a particular court to hear a case of the type in question and to render a valid judgment.[21] Unlike personal jurisdiction, defects in subject matter jurisdiction may not be waived,[22] nor may the parties by consent or stipulation confer subject matter jurisdiction on a court of limited jurisdiction, such as a federal court.[23] Further, a federal court has the duty to examine its own subject matter jurisdiction at any stage in the proceedings.[24] Indeed, possible subject matter defects may be raised

---

power. As a general rule, the exercise of judicial power is not lawful unless the defendant "purposefully avails itself of the privilege of conducting activities within the forum State, thus invoking the benefits and protections of its laws."); World-Wide Volkswagen Corp. v. Woodson, 444 U.S. 286, 292 (1980) (one function of *International Shoe* approach to jurisdiction is to protect defendant against burdens of litigating in distant or inconvenient forum); Rush v. Savchuk, 444 U.S. 320, 332 (1980) (due process limitations on state court jurisdiction primarily serve to protect defendant).

[19] *See* Fed. R. Civ. P. 12(h)(1), (3); *see also* 16 Moore's Federal Practice Ch. 108, *Territorial Jurisdiction: Jurisdiction Over Persons and Property* (Matthew Bender 3d ed.).

[20] *See* Fed. R. Civ. P. 12(h)(1).

[21] *See* Ruhrgas Ag v. Marathon Oil Co., 526 U.S. 574, 583-84 (1999) (The requirement of subject-matter jurisdiction is nonwaivable and delimits federal-court power, while restrictions on a court's jurisdiction over the person are waivable and protect individual rights. "The character of the two jurisdictional bedrocks unquestionably differs. Subject-matter limitations on federal jurisdiction serve institutional interests. They keep the federal courts within the bounds the Constitution and Congress have prescribed. Accordingly, subject-matter delineations must be policed by the courts on their own initiative even at the highest level. . . . Personal jurisdiction, on the other hand, "represents a restriction on judicial power . . . as a matter of individual liberty." Therefore, a party may insist that the limitation be observed, or he may forgo that right, effectively consenting to the court's exercise of adjudicatory authority."). *See* Fed. R. Civ. P. 12(h)(2) & (3); Restatement (Second) of Judgments Ch. 2, Introductory Note, § 11 (1982).

[22] American Fire & Cas. Co. v. Finn, 341 U.S. 6, 17–18 (1951) ("The jurisdiction of the federal courts is carefully guarded against expansion by judicial interpretation or by prior action or consent of the parties."); *see* Fed. R. Civ. P. 12(h)(3).

[23] Industrial Addition Ass'n v. Commissioner, 323 U.S. 310, 313 (1945) ("Want of jurisdiction, unlike want of venue, may not be cured by consent of the parties; but when the court has jurisdiction, it has power to decide the case brought before it, even though the court having venue is one sitting in another circuit.").

[24] *See* Ruhrgas Ag v. Marathon Oil Co., 526 U.S. 574, 583–84 (1999).

for the first time on appeal, on the court's own motion or by the parties.[25]

For discussion of the sources of subject matter jurisdiction in the federal courts, see Ch. 4, *Diversity Jurisdiction*, Ch. 3, *Federal Question Jurisdiction*, and Ch. 5, *Supplemental Jurisdiction*.[26]

### [b] Subject Matter Jurisdiction of Federal and State Courts Distinguished

The federal courts are courts of limited subject matter jurisdiction. They may hear cases only when empowered to do so by the Constitution and by act of Congress.[27] Thus, before a federal court may hear a case, some ground for federal subject matter jurisdiction must be established and must affirmatively appear in the pleadings.[28] The two principal heads of federal subject matter jurisdiction are federal question jurisdiction[29] and diversity of citizenship jurisdiction.[30]

State courts, on the other hand, may be courts of general subject matter jurisdiction. Such courts have the power to exercise jurisdiction over all cases except those that are given by the legislature of that state exclusively to specialized courts in areas such as probate or domestic relations. Further, a case is usually presumed to be within the jurisdiction of a court of general jurisdiction until its jurisdiction is challenged.

Generally, if a federal court has subject matter jurisdiction over a particular type of case, the state courts will have concurrent jurisdiction over such cases. However, in some federal question cases, such as patents, copyrights, and plant variety protection,[31] certain admiralty cases,[32] and bankruptcy cases and proceedings, [33] federal courts have exclusive subject matter jurisdiction. In most areas of federal

---

[25] Mansfield & C.L.M. Ry. Co. v. Swan, 111 U.S. 379, 382–386 (1884) ( "[T]he first duty of this court is . . . to examine the sufficiency of [the] plea, and thus to take care that . . . this court shall [not] use the judicial power of the United States in a case to which the constitution and laws of the United States have not extended that power."); Fed. R. Civ. P. 12(h)(3) ("If the court determines at any time that it lacks subject-matter jurisdiction, the court must dismiss the action.").

[26] For more detailed discussion of subject matter jurisdiction in the federal courts, see MOORE'S FEDERAL PRACTICE Ch. 102, *Diversity Jurisdiction*, Ch. 103, *Federal Question Jurisdiction*, Ch. 104, *Specific Grants of Federal Question Jurisdiction*, Ch. 105, *Other Subject Matter Jurisdiction Statutes*, and Ch. 106, *Supplemental Jurisdiction* (Matthew Bender 3d ed.).

[27] Victory Carriers, Inc. v. Law, 404 U.S. 202, 212 (1971) ("Due regard for the rightful independence of state governments, which should actuate federal courts, requires that they scrupulously confine their own jurisdiction to the precise limits which [a federal] statute has defined," quoting *Healy v. Ratta*, 292 U.S. 263, 270 (1934)); *see* 28 U.S.C. § 1251 et seq.

[28] Norton v. Larney, 266 U.S. 511, 515–516 (1925) ("[T]he jurisdiction of a federal court must affirmatively and distinctly appear and cannot be helped by presumptions or by argumentative inferences drawn from the pleadings."); *see* Utah Fuel Co. v. Nat'l Bituminous Coal Comm'n, 306 U.S. 56, 59 (1939) (jurisdiction or facts on which it rests must be distinctly averred in pleadings); Fed. R. Civ. P. 8(a)(1) (party invoking jurisdiction must allege facts showing that case is within court's subject matter jurisdiction).

[29] *See* 28 U.S.C. § 1331; *see* Ch. 4, *Federal Question Jurisdiction*.

[30] *See* 28 U.S.C. § 1332; *see* Ch. 3, *Diversity Jurisdiction*.

[31] *See* 28 U.S.C. § 1338.

[32] *See* 28 U.S.C. § 1333.

subject matter jurisdiction, however, federal and state courts have concurrent jurisdiction. Either court system is authorized to entertain the case at the choice of the litigant.[34]

For further discussion of the relationship between state and federal courts and the history of the dual system, see Ch. 11, *Dual Federal-State Judicial Systems.*

### [c] Venue

If a defendant has the kind of connections with the territory of a sovereign entity to be subject to personal jurisdiction there, any court within that territory may be able to exercise personal jurisdiction over the defendant. Venue rules, however, may designate which of those courts is the proper court to hear the action. State court venue rules typically provide that the action be brought in the county or district where the defendant lives, or where the cause of action arose, or where the property is located. The general federal venue statute is similar. It requires that an action be brought in the federal district court in which any defendant resides if all the defendants reside in the same state, or in which a substantial part of the events or omissions giving rise to the claim occurred, or a substantial part of property that is the subject of the action is situated, or, if neither of these options are available, where any defendant is found or subject to personal jurisdiction.[35]

Although both venue and personal jurisdiction rules are concerned with the convenience of the parties and witnesses,[36] venue differs from both personal and subject matter jurisdiction. Rules of venue give the defendant a privilege not to be sued in a forum other than one designated as proper; they do not affect the court's power over the particular person or property in question or the court's competence to hear a particular type of case.[37]

Unlike subject matter jurisdiction,[38] and like personal jurisdiction, a defendant may consent to venue, or waive venue objections by failure to make a timely

---

[33] *See* 28 U.S.C. § 1334. For discussion of these special jurisdiction statutes, see Moore's Federal Practice Ch. 104, *Specific Grants of Federal Question Jurisdiction*, and Ch. 703, *Admiralty Jurisdiction* (Matthew Bender 3d ed.).

[34] *See* The Moses Taylor, 71 U.S. (4 Wall.) 411, 423–424 (1866) (state courts have "unquestioned concurrent cognizance of nearly all the cases mentioned in the third article of the second section of the Constitution"); *see also* Charles Dowd Box Co. v. Courtney, 368 U.S. 502, 508 (1962) (in favor of concurrent jurisdiction "where it is not excluded by express provision, or by incompatibility in its exercise arising from the nature of the particular case"); Testa v. Katt, 330 U.S. 386, 394 (1947) (state courts of general jurisdiction normally must entertain federal claims unless federal jurisdiction over them is exclusive).

[35] *See, e.g.*, 28 U.S.C. § 1391 (general federal venue statute); *see* Ch. 8, *venue*.

[36] *See* Olberding v. Illinois Cent. R. Co., 346 U.S. 338, 340 (1953) (venue is "a limitation designed for the convenience of litigants, and, as such, may be waived by them"); 28 U.S.C. § 1404(a) (transfers for convenience).

[37] Neirbo Co. v. Bethlehem Shipbuilding Corp., 308 U.S. 165, 167–168 (1939) (jurisdiction is court's power to adjudicate, whereas venue relates only to place where court should exercise judicial authority: "This basic difference between the court's power and the litigant's convenience is historic in the federal courts.").

[38] *See* Industrial Addition Ass'n v. Commissioner, 323 U.S. 310, 313 (1945) ("Want of jurisdiction, unlike want of venue, may not be cured by consent of the parties; but when the court has jurisdiction,

objection.[39] However, a defendant may challenge personal jurisdiction in a collateral attack (*see* § 7.09), but may not raise a venue objection in a separate proceeding.[40]

If personal jurisdiction is lacking or venue is improper, and a timely objection is made by the defendant, the case may be dismissed, or it may be transferred to a court of proper venue.[41] If subject matter jurisdiction is lacking, the case must be dismissed (*see* [a], *above*).

For a detailed discussion of venue and change of venue, see Ch. 8, *Venue*, and Ch. 9, *Change of Venue*.

### [d] Jurisdiction and Choice-of-Law

Choice-of-law rules guide the selection of the law to apply to a dispute involving parties or events connected with more than one state or nation. Although choice-of-law and jurisdictional determinations both require assessment of the relationship between the forum and the litigation, they are different inquiries.[42] Nevertheless, a choice-of-law clause in a contract may be a relevant contact for jurisdictional purposes.[43]

The fact that a state court will exercise judicial jurisdiction in an action does not automatically mean that the substantive law the court will apply will be the law of that state. Often the laws of a state or nation other than that of the forum will control the resolution of the problem.

Choice of law issues in the federal courts are discussed in Ch. 15, *Applicable Law in Federal Court: The Erie Doctrine*.

## § 7.02 PERSONAL JURISDICTION IN FEDERAL COURTS

### [1] Due Process Clause of Fifth Amendment Limits Federal Courts' Exercise of Jurisdiction

Like a state court, a federal court may assert jurisdiction in a particular case only if an adequate *basis* for the exercise of jurisdiction exists and the appropriate *process* is used. As in the state courts, the basis and process requirements for

---

it has power to decide the case brought before it, even though the court having venue is one sitting in another circuit.").

[39] Farmers Elevator Mut. Ins. Co. v. Carl J. Austad & Sons, Inc., 343 F.2d 7, 11 (8th Cir. 1965) (venue may be changed by consent of parties and objection to venue may be waived by failure to make timely objection); *see* Fed. R. Civ. P. 12(h)(1), (3).

[40] Farmers Elevator Mut. Ins. Co. v. Carl J. Austad & Sons, Inc., 343 F.2d 7, 11 (8th Cir. 1965) (objection to venue may not be raised in separate proceeding).

[41] 28 U.S.C. § 1406(a).

[42] Keeton v. Hustler Magazine, Inc., 465 U.S. 770, 778 (1984) ("choice of law concerns should [not] complicate or distort the jurisdictional inquiry"); *see* Hanson v. Denckla, 357 U.S. 235, 254 (1958) (choice of law considerations are generally irrelevant to jurisdictional analysis).

[43] Burger King Corp. v. Rudzewicz, 471 U.S. 462, 482 (1985) (agreement to be bound by local laws can help determine "whether a defendant has 'purposefully invoked the benefits and protections of a State's laws' for jurisdictional purposes").

jurisdiction in federal court actions are subject to constitutional and statutory limits. However, the source of constitutional due process limits on the exercise of federal court jurisdiction is the Due Process Clause of the Fifth Amendment, rather than the Due Process Clause of the 14th Amendment, which limits the exercise of jurisdiction in state court actions.

The constitutional requirements for invoking jurisdiction (the "process" requirements) under the Fifth and 14th amendments are the same: each requires notice and the opportunity to be heard. However, the basis requirements for the exercise of jurisdiction differ. While the due process requirements of the 14th Amendment essentially require that a defendant have minimum contacts with a particular state, the due process requirements of the Fifth Amendment look to the territory of the United States as a whole.[44] Under the modern *International Shoe* contacts-based approach, a state court will not have a basis for exercising personal jurisdiction unless the defendant has certain "minimum contacts" with a state, "such that the maintenance of the suit does not offend 'traditional notions of fair play and substantial justice.' "[45] Thus, as a constitutional matter, the "minimum contacts" due process limits of *International Shoe* and its progeny on federal courts generally relate to the defendant's contacts with the nation as a whole, rather than the defendant's contacts with a particular state.[46]

Although it has been questioned whether Congress may constitutionally extend the reach of a federal court's process beyond that of the state courts in the state in which the federal court sits in all cases,[47] Congress has expressly provided for nationwide service of process in special types of cases, such as statutory impleader.[48]

---

44 *See* 16 Moore's Federal Practice Ch. 108, *Territorial Jurisdiction: Jurisdiction Over Persons and Property* (Matthew Bender 3d ed.).

45 International Shoe Co. v. Washington, 326 U.S. 310, 316 (1945) (personal jurisdiction rules must focus on defendant's contacts with forum state).

46 *See* Mississippi Publ'g Corp. v. Murphree, 326 U.S. 438, 442 (1946) ("Congress could provide for service of process anywhere in the United States."); *In re* "Agent Orange" Prod. Liab. Litig., 818 F.2d 145, 163 (2d Cir. 1987) (Fifth Amendment Due Process Clause did not bar exercise of personal jurisdiction over class member in Agent Orange litigation who lacked contacts with forum state); Texas Trading & Milling Corp. v. Federal Republic of Nigeria, 647 F.2d 300, 315 (2d Cir. 1981) (assertion of personal jurisdiction using Fifth Amendment analysis "must be applied with caution in an international context," citing Arthur von Mehren & Donald Trautman, *Jurisdiction to Adjudicate: A Suggested Analysis*, 79 Harv. L. Rev. 1121, 1127 (1966)); Modern Mailers, Inc. v. Johnson & Quin, Inc., 844 F. Supp. 1048, 1051 (E.D. Pa. 1994) (Due Process Clause of Fifth Amendment applies to diversity action, limiting Pennsylvania's long-arm statute); Paulson Inv. Co. v. Norbay Sec., Inc., 603 F. Supp. 615, 618 (D. Or. 1984) ("When a federal statute authorizes worldwide service of process, a court must decide whether the party which has been served has had minimum contacts with the United States as a whole."); *see also* ALI, Study of the Division of Jurisdiction Between State and Federal Courts, 437–441 (A.L.I. 1969).

47 *See* Abraham, *Constitutional Limitations Upon the Territorial Reach of Federal Process*, 8 Vill. L. Rev. 520 (1963).

48 28 U.S.C. § 2361; *see also* Fed. R. Civ. P. 4(k) 1993 Advisory Committee Note; *see generally* 4 Moore's Federal Practice, Ch. 22, *Interpleader*.

## [2] Relation Between Jurisdiction and Rule 4 (Summons)

Apart from constitutional requirements, there are other limitations on the exercise of jurisdiction in federal court actions. Indeed, the most important limitation derives from the process aspect of personal jurisdiction in federal courts. It has long been "the unmalleable principle of law . . . that federal courts . . . must ground their personal jurisdiction on a federal statute or rule."[49] Rule 4 of the Federal Rules of Civil Procedure controls the question of service, and therefore by extension the question of personal jurisdiction.

Rule 4 has the effect in most cases of limiting federal district court jurisdiction to the same extent the 14th Amendment restricts state assertions of personal jurisdiction. Most states permit extraterritorial service; but of course, they are empowered to do so only when there would be a valid basis for exercising jurisdiction in the state, through a long-arm statute or by general jurisdictional theories. The *Omni* case presents a case in point.[50] There, the plaintiffs alleged violations of the Commodities Exchange Act against various defendants, including several foreign defendants who lacked "minimum contacts" with the state of Louisiana, the state in which the federal action was brought. The CEA did not provide for nationwide or worldwide service. In a 9-6 vote en banc, the Fifth Circuit held that there was no personal jurisdiction over the foreign defendants, even though they may have had minimum contacts with the United States, when they did not have minimum contacts with the forum state. According to the majority, the federal district court was limited by Rule 4, which at the time permitted federal service of process on out-of-state defendants only to the extent permitted by state long-arm statutes. Because the defendants lacked minimum contacts with the forum state, out-of-state service was not permitted. The dissent wrote that federal courts had the power to allow nationwide service, assuming Fifth Amendment nationwide "minimum contacts" existed, in federal question cases whether or not Congress had enacted a nationwide service of process statute.

The Supreme Court rejected the dissent's approach, finding no applicable federal service statute, no authorization for out-of-state service in Rule 4 itself, and no federal common-law power to permit service in federal question cases. It accordingly affirmed in an 8-0 opinion.[51] The Court, however, refused to consider the constitutional question of whether minimum contacts with the nation are sufficient, as opposed to minimum contacts with the forum, to allow the federal court to exercise personal jurisdiction. In reaction to the *Omni* case, amendments to Rule 4 were promulgated to permit nationwide jurisdiction in federal question cases when there was no state in which personal jurisdiction could otherwise be obtained, so long as the defendant has minimum contacts with the United States satisfying the Fifth Amendment due process test.[52]

---

[49] George v. Omni Capital International, Ltd., 795 F.2d 415, 423 (5th Cir. 1986) (en banc), *aff'd sub nom.* Omni Capital International, Ltd. v. Rudolf Wolff & Co., 484 U.S. 97 (1987).

[50] 795 F.2d at 423.

[51] Omni Capital International, Ltd. v. Rudolf Wolff & Co., 484 U.S. 97 (1987).

[52] *See* Fed. R. Civ. P. 4(k)(2).

Thus, although it is possible for federal courts to exercise essentially nationwide personal jurisdiction, in most cases, by operation of Rule 4, which governs service of a summons and complaint in federal courts,[53] federal court personal jurisdiction is generally coextensive with state court personal jurisdiction. To put it another way, there may be a constitutional *basis* for exercising personal jurisdiction because of a defendant's contacts with the United States as a whole, there may not be a statutory *process* for invoking jurisdiction.

Section [3], *below*, and § 7.03 discuss Rule 4 as it relates to the jurisdictional basis and process of invoking jurisdiction. For a complete discussion of service of process, including the nature of the summons, actions in forma pauperis, who may be served and who is immune from service, who may effect service, time limitations for service, and in what manner service must be effected as well as waiver of service, see 1 Moore's Federal Practice Ch. 4, *Summons* (Matthew Bender 3d ed.). For detailed discussion of service in federal courts, other than service of a summons, see 1 Moore's Federal Practice Ch. 4.1, *Serving Other Process*, and Ch. 5, *Service and Filing Pleadings and Other Papers* (Matthew Bender 3d ed.)

## [3] Procedures for Invoking Jurisdiction ("Process") Under Rule 4

### [a] Defendant May Waive Service of Process

The waiver of service provision in Federal Rule of Civil Procedure 4(d) replaces the mail service provision of former Rule 4(c)(2)(C)(ii).[54] Unlike the former rule, which effected actual service by a streamlined method,[55] the revised rule, Rule 4(d), specifies a procedure that does not purport to provide a method of service, only a request for waiver of service.[56] It does not secure jurisdiction of the defendant's person on the basis of the plaintiff's mailing.[57]

Soliciting a waiver is not mandatory. Rule 4 provides that, to avoid costs, the plaintiff "may," but is not required to, notify a defendant of the option to waive

---

[53] Fed. R. Civ. P. 4; *see* 1 Moore's Federal Practice Ch. 4, *Summons* (Matthew Bender 3d ed.).

[54] Fed. R. Civ. P. 4 Advisory Committee Notes to 1993 Amendments, 146 F.R.D. 401, 560–561 (1993); 28 U.S.C. App. R. 4(d) (1993).

[55] Former Fed. R. Civ. P. 4(c)(2)(C)(ii) provided that the mailing of a summons and complaint to the defendant would achieve valid service if the defendant signed an acknowledgment form and returned it in the enclosed postage-paid envelope.

[56] Fed. R. Civ. P. 4(d); *see* Fed. R. Civ. P. 4 Advisory Committee Notes to 1993 Amendments, 146 F.R.D. 401, 561 (1993); 28 U.S.C. App. R. 4(d) (1993).

[57] *See* Fed. R. Civ. P. 4 Advisory Committee Notes to 1993 Amendments, 146 F.R.D. 401, 565 (1993); 28 U.S.C. App. R. 4(d) (1993) ("The provisions of former subsection (c)(2)(C)(ii) of this rule may have been misleading to some parties [*see, e.g.*, Morse v. Elmira Country Club, 752 F.2d 35,39 (2d Cir. 1984) (receipt of mailed summons, if deliberately not acknowledged, is, nonetheless, sufficient to confer jurisdiction)] . . . Some plaintiffs, not reading the rule carefully, supposed that receipt by the defendant of the mailed complaint had the effect . . . of establishing jurisdiction of the court over the defendant's person. . . . The revised rule is clear that, if the waiver is not returned and filed, . . . the action will not otherwise proceed until formal service is effected.").

service.[58] If the plaintiff opts to use this procedure, the notice and request must meet the requirements set forth in Rule 4(d)(2).[59] If the defendant waives service, no other process is required to invoke the court's jurisdiction. However, the process element is completed only after the defendant executes the waiver and returns it to the plaintiff.[60]

Waiver of service does not constitute a submission to jurisdiction. The defendant who waives service may still object to the *basis* for personal jurisdiction.[61]

### [b] Service of Process May Be Effected by Several Methods

Service of process under the revised rules may be obviated by the waiver procedure of Federal Rule of Civil Procedure 4(d) (*see* [a], *above*).[62] When this consensual arrangement is not used, however, service of process on an individual may be accomplished within the United States by any of the following means:[63]

- Personal delivery of the summons and complaint to the individual defendant or to an authorized agent.
- Leaving the process at the dwelling house of an individual defendant with a person of suitable age and discretion who resides there.
- Service pursuant to the law of the state in which the district court sits.
- Service pursuant to the law of the state where service is effected.

Mail service, which was abolished by the 1993 amendments to Rule 4,[64] is available to a federal plaintiff only if the state in which the federal court sits, or the state where the defendant resides, provides for mail service.[65] Similarly, other state methods of service, such as posting and publication, are permitted if authorized in the appropriate state.[66]

A defendant in a foreign country who has not waived service of process may be served in the following ways:[67]

---

58 Fed. R. Civ. P. 4(d)(2).

59 *See* Fed. R. Civ. P. 4(d)(2).

60 Desormeaux v. Wackenhut Servs., 1994 U.S. Dist. Lexis 15384, at *2–*3 (E.D. La. Aug. 16, 1994) (return receipt obtained by postal company from defendant does not constitute acknowledgment for waiver of service).

61 Fed. R. Civ. P. 4(d)(1); Fed. R. Civ. P. 4 Advisory Committee Notes to 1993 Amendments, 146 F.R.D. 401, 563 (1993); 28 U.S.C. App. R. 4(d) (1993).

62 Fed. R. Civ. P. 4(d) (plaintiff mails request to defendant to waive formal service).

63 Fed. R. Civ. P. 4(e).

64 *See* Fed. R. Civ. P. 4.

65 Fed. R. Civ. P. 4(e)(1); *see, e.g.*, Cal. Civ. Proc. Code § 415.30 (authorizing service by mail).

66 Fed. R. Civ. P. 4(e)(1); *see, e.g.*, Fla. Stat. § 49.11 (authorizing service by posting in prominent locations), and Fla. Stat. § 49.021 (authorizing service by publication); *see also* §§ 108.90–108.91 (constitutional limitations).

67 Fed. R. Civ. P. 4(f).

- Service by an internationally agreed on means, such as the Hague Convention.[68]
- If no internationally agreed on method exists, by personal delivery or any form of mail requiring a signed receipt, unless those methods are prohibited by the foreign country's law.
- If personal delivery or mail is prohibited by the foreign country's law, by any manner prescribed by the foreign country's law or directed by the foreign authority in response to a letter of request.
- Service directed by the court by any means not prohibited by international agreement.

For a complete discussion of all aspects of methods of service, including service on infants and incompetents, corporations, government entities, and foreign countries, time limits, and required forms, see 1 MOORE'S FEDERAL PRACTICE Ch. 4, *Summons* (Matthew Bender 3d ed.).

## § 7.03 LIMITATIONS ON BASES FOR PERSONAL JURISDICTION UNDER RULE 4

### [1] Service of Process Generally Establishes Personal Jurisdiction Only Over Defendants Who Could Be Amenable to Jurisdiction in State in Which Federal Court Sits

Although process may be served on individuals and corporations anywhere in the United States[69] and outside the United States as authorized by Rule 4(f),[70] such service generally will support personal jurisdiction only over defendants "who could be subjected to the jurisdiction of a court of general jurisdiction in the state in which the district court is located."[71] Service alone does not confer jurisdiction.[72] There are some exceptions, however (*see* [3], *below*).

In addition to the constitutional limits on the jurisdiction of state courts, the exercise of jurisdiction in state courts must also meet any state statutory limits on the exercise of jurisdiction over nonresident defendants. These statutory limits are referred to as long-arm statutes. Long-arm statutes take two basic forms. The simpler type directs the court to exercise jurisdiction on any basis not inconsistent with the constitution of that state or the United States.[73] The other statutes,

---

[68] *See* 16 MOORE'S FEDERAL PRACTICE Ch. 108, *Territorial Jurisdiction: Jurisdiction Over Persons and Property* (Matthew Bender 3d ed.).

[69] Fed. R. Civ. P. 4(e), (g), (h).

[70] Fed. R. Civ. P. 4(f).

[71] Fed. R. Civ. P. 4(k)(1)(A).

[72] Indianapolis Colts, Inc. v. Metropolitan Baltimore Football Club Ltd. Partnership, 34 F.3d 410, 411–412 (7th Cir. 1994) (explaining applicability of Fed. R. Civ. P. 4(k)(1)(A), then turning to analysis of basis for jurisdiction).

[73] *See, e.g.*, Cal. Civ. Proc. Code § 410.10.

commonly called "enumerated act" statutes, direct the court to exercise jurisdiction over any defendant who commits one of several enumerated acts in the forum state. The Illinois, Wisconsin, and New York statutes were among the first enumerated act statutes.[74] These statutes, and the one adopted by the Commissioners on Uniform State Laws in the Uniform Interstate and International Procedure Act,[75] are the most influential formulations. In recent years, several states have amended their enumerated act statutes to combine enumerated act provisions with a general "any constitutional basis" provision. Finally, a few states have conferred long-arm jurisdiction on their courts by amending their "doing business" statutes to cover individuals and the types of activities not traditionally included in the term.[76]

### [2] Personal Jurisdiction in Federal District Courts Is Subject to State Long-Arm Statutes

Personal jurisdiction in federal courts is also subject to state long-arm statutes and constitutional limits on state courts' personal jurisdiction for these reasons: Although Federal Rule of Civil Procedure 4(e) allows service anywhere in the United States, Rule 4(k)(1)(A) states that such service will be effective to confer personal jurisdiction only if the defendant could be subjected to jurisdiction in the courts of the state in which the district court is located.[77] Although there are exceptions to this rule,[78] most cases, particularly cases based on state law, do not come under any of the exceptions. Consequently, although federal process can be, but is not required to be, served in accordance with state procedure, and can be served anywhere in the country,[79] federal courts must look to the state long-arm statutes to determine whether the defendant is subject to (amenable to) jurisdiction there (*see* [3], *below*). Federal courts generally must apply the relevant state statute even when the cause of action is purely federal.[80] Thus, federal courts must use state long-arm statutes to determine whether there is an appropriate

---

[74] *See, e.g.*, 735 Ill. Comp. Stat. 5/2-209.

[75] Uniform Interstate and International Procedure Act § 10.03, 13 U.L.A. 361.

[76] For complete discussion of "doing business" statutes, see 16 MOORE'S FEDERAL PRACTICE Ch. 108, *Territorial Jurisdiction: Jurisdiction Over Persons and Property* (Matthew Bender 3d ed.).

[77] Fed. R. Civ. P. 4(e), (k)(1)(A). The 1993 amendment to Rule 4 separated basis and process elements of personal jurisdiction for the first time. Before 1993, Rule 4's restrictions on the bases for personal jurisdiction were embodied in language that spoke only in terms of service of process.

[78] *See* Fed. R. Civ. P. 4(k)(1)(B) (100-mile bulge jurisdiction for parties joined under Fed. R. Civ. P. 14 or Fed. R. Civ. P. 19); Fed. R. Civ. P. 4(k)(1)(C) (federal statute may specifically confer jurisdiction over parties); Fed. R. Civ. P. 4(k)(2) (defendant in federal question cases in which defendant has sufficient minimum contact with the United States, but not with any one state); *see also* Ch. 4, *Summons*.

[79] Fed. R. Civ. P. 4(e)(1) (authorizing service according to state law in state where district court is located); Fed. R. Civ. P. 4(e)(2) (authorizing service by personally delivering copy of summons and complaint to defendant, by leaving such copies at residence or abode with person of suitable age and discretion, or by delivering such copies to agent authorized to receive service of process).

[80] *See, e.g.*, Graphic Controls Corp. v. Utah Medical Products, 149 F.3d 1382, 1385–1386 (Fed. Cir. 1998) (courts in Federal Circuit, when applying state long-arm statute in patent case, will defer to interpretation of relevant state and federal courts, but Federal Circuit does not defer to interpretations of other state and federal courts with respect to federal constitutional minimum contacts analysis); *but see* Fed. R. Civ. P. 4(k)(2) (exception to rule requiring application of state statutes for district court

*basis* for jurisdiction (but are not limited by those statutes for the *process* of invoking jurisdiction). Although federal courts are governed by the Due Process Clause of the Fifth Amendment, and not that of the Fourteenth Amendment, federal courts must look to the Fourteenth Amendment's limitations on state court jurisdiction because Federal Rule of Civil Procedure 4 so requires.[81] For a discussion of Fourteenth Amendment standards, *see* 16 Moore's Federal Practice Ch. 108.

### [a] Fourteenth Amendment Due Process Limits Stem From Territorial Scope of State Sovereignty

In *Pennoyer v. Neff*, the Supreme Court announced a general theory of due process limitations on state court jurisdiction that governed for almost seventy years,[82] until its holding in *International Shoe Co. v. Washington*.[83] Although *Pennoyer v. Neff* was a full faith and credit case,[84] and, as a result, the Court's comments about due process were dicta, the case has been accepted as equating the jurisdictional requirements of full faith and credit with those of due process.

### [b] Due Process Limits Exercise of State Court Jurisdiction

Although the analytical framework to determine whether the state has a jurisdictional basis sufficient to satisfy the Due Process Clause has been expanded by the Supreme Court's seminal decision in *International Shoe*, and its progeny,[85]

---

jurisdiction over defendant in suit based on federal law when no state would have jurisdiction over defendant).

81 *See* 16 Moore's Federal Practice Ch. 108, *Territorial Jurisdiction: Jurisdiction Over Persons and Property* § 108.123 (Matthew Bender 3d ed.).

82 Pennoyer v. Neff, 95 U.S. 714 (1877). Although the case's discussion of due process rather than its holding is significant, the facts are familiar to those who have studied the law: Mitchell sued Neff in state court in Oregon for $300 in attorney's fees. Neff did not reside in Oregon and was not personally served. Service was made by publication in a local newspaper, in accordance with the Oregon statute. Neff did not appear, and Mitchell obtained a default judgment. To satisfy the judgment, a piece of land belonging to Neff was sold at a sheriff's sale. Neff later sued Pennoyer, who had acquired the land, in federal court in Oregon to recover the property. Pennoyer's right to the land depended on the validity of the judgment in *Mitchell v. Neff* and, therefore, on whether service by publication was adequate to give the Oregon state court jurisdiction over Neff's person or over the property. Neff claimed that such service was inadequate for personal jurisdiction and that the federal court in Oregon was, therefore, not obliged to give full faith and credit to the state court's judgment. The Supreme Court held that the Oregon state court lacked jurisdiction over Neff because he was neither domiciled in Oregon nor served with process in Oregon. The Court also held that the Oregon state court lacked jurisdiction over the property because the property was not attached at the beginning of the action.

83 International Shoe Co. v. Washington, 326 U.S. 310, 316 (1945) (personal jurisdiction rules must focus on defendant's contacts with forum state); *see* §§ 108.30–108.31.

84 The 14th Amendment was not ratified until after the *Mitchell v. Neff* judgment had been rendered.

85 *See* International Shoe Co. v. Washington, 326 U.S. 310, 316 (1945) and its progeny, discussed in 16 Moore's Federal Practice Ch. 108, §§ 108.30–108.43. *See, e.g.*, Walden v. Fiore, 134 S. Ct. 1115 (2014) ("For a State to exercise jurisdiction consistent with due process, the defendant's suit-related conduct must create a substantial connection with the forum State."); Daimler AG v. Bauman, 134 S. Ct. 746 (2014); Goodyear Dunlop Tires Operations, S.A. v. Brown, 131 S. Ct. 2846 (2011) ("A state court's

beyond the three traditional bases enunciated in *Pennoyer v. Neff*,[86] the Due Process Clause continues to limit the states' exercise of judicial jurisdiction. A court that exercises jurisdiction over the defendant in the absence of a proper jurisdictional basis has violated the defendant's right not to be deprived of property without due process and, thus, its judgment is invalid.[87]

### [3] Statutory Exceptions Authorize Broader Personal Jurisdiction

#### [a] 100-Mile Bulge Service for Certain Parties

Federal Rule of Civil Procedure 4(k)(1)(B) preserves the traditional "100-mile bulge" exception, permitting service on persons impleaded under Federal Rule of Civil Procedure 14, or added under Federal Rule of Civil Procedure 19, anywhere in the United States that is within 100 miles of the federal courthouse where the action is pending.[88] Persons served under this exception are not required to have minimum contacts with the forum state, even in diversity actions. Rather, it is sufficient to obtain jurisdiction over such persons if they are subject to jurisdiction in the bulge state[89] or in either the bulge or the forum state.[90]

#### [b] Nationwide Service of Process for Certain Claims

Personal jurisdiction also may be obtained over persons who would not be subject to state court jurisdiction in statutory impleader actions,[91] and whenever authorized by federal statute. There are varieties of actions in which Congress has authorized nationwide, and in some cases, worldwide, service of process.[92] These

---

assertion of jurisdiction exposes defendants to the State's coercive power, and is therefore subject to review for compatibility with the Fourteenth Amendment's Due Process Clause. Assertion of jurisdiction over an out-of-state corporation must comply with "traditional notions of fair play and substantial justice."); J. McIntyre Mach., Ltd. V. Nicastro, 131 S. Ct. 2780 (2011) ("Due process protects the defendant's right not to be coerced except by lawful judicial power. As a general rule, the exercise of judicial power is not lawful unless the defendant "purposefully avails itself of the privilege of conducting activities within the forum State, thus invoking the benefits and protections of its laws."); World-Wide Volkswagen Corp. v. Woodson, 444 U.S. 286, 292 (1980) (one function of *International Shoe* approach to jurisdiction is to protect defendant against burdens of litigating in distant or inconvenient forum); Rush v. Savchuk, 444 U.S. 320, 332 (1980) (due process limitations on state court jurisdiction primarily serve to protect defendant).

[86] *See* Pennoyer v. Neff, 95 U.S. 714, 724–726 (1877) (three bases for jurisdiction: presence, consent, and domicile); *see also* §§ 108.20–108.22.

[87] *See* Burnham v. Superior Court, 495 U.S. 604, 609 (1990) (citing cases); *see also* Restatement (Second) of Judgments Ch. 2, § 1 (1982) (court's judgment is invalid without jurisdiction).

[88] Fed. R. Civ. P. 4(k)(1)(B).

[89] *See* Bellum v. PCE Constructors Inc., 407 F.3d 734 (5th Cir. 2005) (holding that 100-mile distance under former Fed. R. Civ. P. 4(f) is to be measured "as the crow flies"); Senzarin v. Abbott Severance Pay Plan for Employees, 361 Fed. Appx. 636 (6th Cir. 2010) (same).

[90] Sprow v. Hartford Ins. Co., 594 F.2d 412, 416 (5th Cir. 1979) (jurisdiction may be obtained over person with sufficient contact with bulge or forum state).

[91] 28 U.S.C. § 1335.

[92] Fed. R. Civ. P. 4(k)(1)(C), (D); *see* Fed. R. Civ. P. 4 Advisory Committee Notes to 1993

include, for example, cases arising under the 1934 Securities Exchange Act,[93] the Employee Retirement Income Security Act (ERISA),[94] the Racketeer Influenced and Corrupt Organizations Act (RICO),[95] and the Clayton Act (antitrust actions).[96]

Federal statutes allowing nationwide service of process are intended to permit jurisdiction to the full extent of due process.[97] Most courts therefore look to the defendant's contacts with the nation as a whole and do not require contacts with the forum state (although the statutes themselves usually require some sort of contact with the federal district where the suit is brought).[98]

However, a few courts insist that due process requires that the exercise of jurisdiction under federal nationwide service statutes be fair and reasonable. Under this view, the test is whether it is fair to require the defendant to defend in a particular federal court. Minimum contacts with the forum state are not required, and contact with the United States as a whole may, or may not, support jurisdiction, depending on whether the exercise of jurisdiction in a particular case is reasonable.[99]

---

Amendments, 146 F.R.D. 401, 571 (1993); 28 U.S.C. App. R. 4(d) (1993).

[93] 15 U.S.C. § 78aa (authorizing service in any district defendant inhabits or may be found).

[94] 29 U.S.C. § 1132(e) (authorizing nationwide service when venue is proper).

[95] 18 U.S.C. § 1965 (special venue statute authorizing nationwide service of process).

[96] 28 U.S.C. § 1391 (venue statute).

[97] *See* Leasco Data Processing Equip. Corp. v. Maxwell, 468 F.2d 1326, 1339 (2d Cir. 1972) (provision of Securities Exchange Act, 15 U.S.C. § 78aa, relating to jurisdiction and venue is intended to extend personal jurisdiction to full reach permitted by Due Process Clause).

[98] *See, e.g., In re* Automotive Refinishing Paint Antitrust Litig., 358 F.3d 288, 293, 297–299 (3d Cir. 2004) (personal jurisdiction in federal antitrust litigation is assessed on basis of defendant's aggregate contacts with U.S. as whole); Pinker v. Roche Holdings, Ltd., 292 F.3d 361, 369 (3d Cir. 2002) ("a federal court's personal jurisdiction may be assessed on the basis of the defendant's national contacts when the plaintiff's claim rests on a federal statute authorizing nationwide service of process"); Busch v. Buchman, Buchman, & O'Brien, Law Firm, 11 F.3d 1255, 1258 (5th Cir. 1994) (when federal court is attempting to exercise personal jurisdiction over defendant in action based on federal statute providing for nationwide service of process, relevant inquiry is whether defendant has had minimum contacts with United States, not with forum state); United Liberty Life Ins. Co. v. Ryan, 985 F.2d 1320, 1330 (6th Cir. 1993) (action under Securities Exchange Act, 15 U.S.C. § 78aa, requires national contacts approach); Go-Video, Inc. v. Akai Elec. Co., 885 F.2d 1406, 1413 (9th Cir. 1989) (explaining rationale behind requiring national, rather than state contacts, since causes litigated are matters of exclusive federal jurisdiction, thereby making concerns of state sovereignty inapplicable and rejecting argument that *Insurance Corp. of Ireland, Ltd. v. Compagnie des Bauxites de Guinee*, 456 U.S. 694 (1982), prohibits national contacts approach).

[99] *See, e.g.*, Filler v. Lernout (*In re* Lernout & Hauspie Sec. Litig.), 337 F. Supp. 2d 298, 311–319 (D. Mass. 2004) (to establish jurisdiction under nationwide service statute, plaintiff must show (1) that defendant had minimum contacts with U.S. and (2) that exercising jurisdiction over defendant would satisfy due process because it comports with "traditional notions of fair play and substantial justice"); Farr v. Designer Phosphate & Premix Int'l, Inc., 777 F. Supp. 890, 893–894 (D. Kan. 1991) (exercise of jurisdiction must not be unreasonable, considering burden on defendant to defend locally, foreseeability of local litigation, plaintiff's interest in obtaining complete and effective relief, interest in having matter heard there, and public interest in efficient resolution of matter); Oxford First Corp. v. PNC Liquidating Corp., 372 F. Supp. 191, 203–204 (E.D. Pa. 1974) (analyzing fairness to defendant to defend in particular federal court as determinant of due process context of nationwide service statutes, and concluding that fairness requires considerations of connection between action and locale of federal court, as well as contact between defendant and United States as whole).

### [c] Rule 4(k)(2) Confers Jurisdiction for Claims Arising Under Federal Law When No Federal Statute Authorizes Nationwide Service and No State Authorizes Jurisdiction

Even in the absence of a federal statute specifically authorizing nationwide service (*see* [b], *above*), defendants may be subject to nationwide process under Rule 4(k)(2), which was adopted after the Supreme Court's *Omni* decision (*see* § 7.02[2]).[100] This rule allows a court to exercise personal jurisdiction over foreign defendants who are not subject to personal jurisdiction in any particular state, but who do have minimum contacts with the nation as a whole. The rule applies if three elements are met: (1) the plaintiff's claim must be one arising under federal law; (2) the defendant must be beyond the jurisdictional reach of any state court of general jurisdiction; and (3) the federal court's exercise of jurisdiction must comply with constitutional minimum contacts requirements and other federal law.[101] The analysis to determine whether the exercise of jurisdiction complies with constitutional requirements is essentially the same as in traditional personal jurisdiction analysis, except that the court considers contacts with the nation as a whole, not just those with the forum state.[102]

Rule 4(k)(2) applies to "claims arising under federal law."[103] The Rule's "arising under" language is the same as that used in 28 U.S.C. § 1331, the statute conferring

---

[100] Fed. R. Civ. P. 4(k)(2); *see also* Central States, Se. & Sw. Areas Pension Fund v. Reimer Express World Corp., 230 F.3d 934, 940–942 (7th Cir. 2000) (Fed. R. Civ. P. 4(k)(2) permits jurisdiction to be exercised based on service in foreign country, provided other conditions of rule are satisfied and no other statute specifically prohibits worldwide service or indicates that worldwide service would be improper).

[101] Fed. R. Civ. P. 4(k)(2); *see also* Central States, Se. & Sw. Areas Pension Fund v. Reimer Express World Corp., 230 F.3d 934, 940–942 (7th Cir. 2000) (Fed. R. Civ. P. 4(k)(2) permits jurisdiction to be exercised by service of process in foreign country even if statute does not specifically state that such service is proper, provided other conditions of rule are satisfied and no other statute prohibits jurisdiction or indicates that jurisdiction would be improper); Pebble Beach Co. v. Caddy, 453 F.3d 1151, 1158–1160 (9th Cir. 2006) (Fed. R. Civ. P. 4(k)(2) requires plaintiff to prove three factors: (1) claim arises under federal law, (2) defendant is not subject to personal jurisdiction in any state, and (3) federal court's exercise of personal jurisdiction comports with due process; in this case, exercise of jurisdiction did not comport with due process because defendant's activities were not "purposefully directed" at United States); Synthes (U.S.A.) v. G.M. Dos Reis Jr. Ind. Com. de Equip. Medico, 563 F.3d 1285, 1293–1294 (Fed. Cir. 2009) (Fed. R. Civ. P. 4(k)(2) allows court to exercise personal jurisdiction over defendant if (1) plaintiff's claim arises under federal law, (2) defendant is not subject to jurisdiction in any state's courts of general jurisdiction, and (3) exercise of jurisdiction comports with due process).

[102] *See, e.g.*, Porina v. Marward Shipping Co., 521 F.3d 122, 127 (2d Cir. 2008) ("First, we ask whether the defendant has sufficient minimum contacts with the forum to justify the court's exercise of personal jurisdiction . . . . In the case before us, the question is whether [the defendant] has sufficient affiliating contacts with the United States in general, rather than with New York in particular, with which it has none."); Abelesz v. OTP Bank, 692 F.3d 638, 660 (7th Cir. 2012) ("The difference between litigating under state law in state court and under federal law in federal court is that the federal Constitution and federal law allow a plaintiff to aggregate a defendant's contacts with the entire nation rather than with the forum state. The underlying constitutional requirements for minimum contacts under either a general jurisdiction or specific jurisdiction analysis remain the same."); Holland America Line Inc. v. Wartsila North American, Inc., 485 F.3d 450, 462 (9th Cir. 2007) (contacts with U.S. were insufficient to support exercise of jurisdiction).

[103] Fed. R. Civ. P. 4(k)(2); *see, e.g.*, Porina v. Marward Shipping Co., 521 F.3d 122, 127 (2d Cir. 2008)

general federal question jurisdiction on federal district courts.[104] Presumably, use of that language in the Rule limits the application of Rule 4(k)(2) to cases that meet the tests for federal question jurisdiction,[105] and in most cases that means that the claim must assert a federally created cause of action.[106]

### [d] Supplemental Personal Jurisdiction: Service Based on Nationwide Contacts May Be Available to Reach Defendant Sued on Claim Giving Rise to Supplemental Jurisdiction

Although Rule 4(k)(2) applies only to cases arising under federal law and does not specifically address the question of supplemental personal jurisdiction, the Advisory Committee Notes suggest that service based on nationwide contacts is available to reach defendants sued on a claim that gives rise to supplemental jurisdiction (*see* Ch. 5).[107]

Supplemental (or pendent) personal jurisdiction refers to a situation in which the defendant is sued in federal court in a state where that defendant would not have been subject to jurisdiction but for the nationwide service statute. With regard to subject matter jurisdiction, the plaintiff may add a state law claim based on the same core of facts as in the federal action even though there is no diversity of citizenship with respect to those claims (see Ch. 5). However, with regard to personal jurisdiction, the courts are divided on whether the federal court may exercise personal jurisdiction over that state law claim when the personal jurisdiction depends on the nationwide service statute.

For example, almost all the courts that have considered the issue since 1970 have upheld supplemental or pendent personal jurisdiction in cases arising under the

---

(plaintiffs' claims relied on general maritime law and therefore arose under federal law for purposes of Fed. R. Civ. P. 4(k)(2)).

[104] *See* 28 U.S.C. § 1331; *see also* 16 Moore's Federal Practice Ch. 103, §§ 103.05 (numerous jurisdictional statutes use same "arising under" language, which derives from U.S. Const., Art. III); & 103.31 (extensive analysis of meaning of "arising under" language in general federal question jurisdiction statute).

[105] *See* 15 Moore's Federal Practice Ch. 103, §§ 103.31–103.33 (analysis of types of claims that satisfy "arising under" test of 28 U.S.C. § 1331).

[106] *See, e.g.*, Flag Co. v. Maynard, 376 F. Supp. 2d 849, 852–854 (N.D. Ill. 2005) (exercise of jurisdiction under Fed. R. Civ. P. 4(k)(2) was proper in RICO case); Holland America Line Inc. v. Wartsila North American, Inc., 485 F.3d 450, 461 (9th Cir. 2007) (admiralty claims "arose under federal law" for purposes of Fed. R. Civ. P. 4(k)(2)); *but see* Getz v. Boeing Co., 654 F.3d 852, 858–860 (9th Cir. 2011) (claims for product liability, negligence, wrongful death, and loss of consortium did not arise under federal law because they did not allege violation of federal right or seek enforcement of federal law; existence of federal defense did not transform claims into federal cause of action);

[107] Fed. R. Civ. P. 4, advisory committee note of 1993 (if Fed. R. Civ. P. 4(k)(2) permits jurisdiction over a federal claim, "then 28 U.S.C. 1367(a) provides supplemental jurisdiction over related claims against the defendant, subject to its discretion to decline exercise of jurisdiction under 28 U.S.C. § 1367(c)"); *see generally* Jon Heller, Note, *Pendent Personal Jurisdiction and Nationwide Service of Process*, 64 N.Y.U. L. Rev. 13 (1989); *see also* 28 U.S.C. § 1367, Commentary (statute codifies as "supplemental"jurisdiction doctrines previously known as "pendent" and "ancillary" jurisdiction, but does not address question of supplemental personal jurisdiction).

Securities Act and Securities Exchange Act.[108] Although cases involving the use of supplemental personal jurisdiction when the defendant is a corporation served under the Clayton Act[109] are rare, at least one court has upheld supplemental personal jurisdiction in an antitrust action.[110] On the other hand, at least one court has refused to take supplemental personal jurisdiction of related claims in a bankruptcy case.[111] Moreover, cases are divided on exercising supplemental personal jurisdiction over related claims when the defendant is served under the special service provisions of the Racketeer Influenced and Corrupt Organizations Act (RICO)[112] or the Employee Retirement Income Security Act (ERISA).[113]

---

[108] *See* 15 U.S.C. § 78aa (authorizing service in any district defendant inhabits or may be found); *see, e.g.*, COMSAT Corp. v. Finshipyards S.A.M., 900 F. Supp. 515, 525 (D.D.C. 1995) (if personal jurisdiction is established under Fed. R. Civ. P. 4, court could decide to exercise supplemental jurisdiction over plaintiff's non-federal claims against defendant; here, plaintiff failed to state federal claim); Newman v. Comprehensive Care Corp., 794 F. Supp. 1513, 1520 (D. Or. 1992) (if court has personal jurisdiction over federal securities fraud claim, it possesses personal jurisdiction over defendants with regard to state law claims; however, personal jurisdiction for federal securities litigation did not exist); Stuart-James Co., Inc. v. Rossini, 736 F. Supp. 800, 803–804 (N.D. Ill. 1990) ( "[T]he Illinois long-arm statute is . . . irrelevant to establishing personal jurisdiction over the defendants on the pendent state claims . . . . Instead the focus must be exclusively on 15 U.S.C. § 78aa.").

[109] 28 U.S.C. § 1391 (general venue statute).

[110] *See* Miller Pipeline Corp. v. British Gas plc, 901 F. Supp. 1416, 1423–1424 (S.D. Ind. 1995) (court noted that Seventh Circuit has held that "pendent personal jurisdiction applies in particular to cases like this one, 'in which personal jurisdiction of one claim was based on a federal statute authorizing nationwide service of process,' " asserting pendent personal jurisdiction over patent law claim in antitrust case).

[111] *See In re* New York Trap Rock Corp. v. Compania Naviera Perez Companc, S.A.C.F.I.M.F.A., 155 B.R. 871, 890 (Bankr. S.D.N.Y. 1993), *aff'd*, 160 B.R. 876 (S.D.N.Y.), *and aff'd in part, vacated in part*, 42 F.3d 747 (2d Cir. 1994) (there is no doctrine of pendent personal jurisdiction and "[e]ven if the doctrine . . . existed, the *Debreceni* case [*Debreceni v. Bru-Jell Leasing Corp.*, 710 F. Supp. 15, 19–20 (D. Mass 1989)] is in accord with Fed. Bankr. R. 7004(e), which this court has held earlier in this opinion requires application of a state's long-arm statute. Consequently, the court will not invoke the theory of pendent personal jurisdiction, if in fact it exists and is applicable in bankruptcy cases, to exercise personal jurisdiction over the Defendants.").

[112] *See* 18 U.S.C. § 1965 (special venue statute authorizing nationwide service of process); *see, e.g.*, Rolls-Royce Motors, Inc. v. Charles Schmitt & Co., 657 F. Supp. 1040, 1056 (S.D.N.Y. 1987) (Where a federal statute authorizes nationwide service of process, and the federal and state claims derive from a 'common nucleus of operative fact,' *Gibbs v. United Mine Workers*, 383 U.S. 715, 725 (1966), courts have been willing to assert [pendent personal] jurisdiction over the related state law claims in the interest of judicial economy.); First Fin. Leasing Corp. v. Hartge, 671 F. Supp. 538, 541 (N.D. Ill. 1987) (dictum that provision authorizing nationwide service of process that would confer pendent personal jurisdiction over defendant for RICO claims, if plaintiff could make requisite showing, "still would not provide jurisdiction as to the pendent state claims"); *see also* VMS/PCA Ltd. Partnership v. PCA Partners Ltd. Partnership, 727 F. Supp. 1167, 1173–1174 (N.D. Ill. 1989) (doctrine of pendent venue was applicable to state law claims that arose out of same nucleus of operative facts as RICO claims for which venue was proper).

[113] *See* 29 U.S.C. § 1132(e) (authorizing nationwide service when venue is proper); *see, e.g.*, Rice v. Nova Biomedical Corp., 38 F.3d 909, 913 (7th Cir. 1994) (asserting pendent personal jurisdiction over claim of intentional interference with business relationship when claim over which court exercised personal jurisdiction was based on federal statute authorizing national service); IUE AFL-CIO Pension Fund v. Herrmann, 9 F.3d 1049, 1056–1059 (2d Cir. 1993) (upholding pendent personal jurisdiction, rather than "supplemental" jurisdiction because case was begun before 28 U.S.C. § 1367 took effect); Debreceni v. Bru-Jell Leasing Corp., 710 F. Supp. 15, 19–20 (D. Mass. 1989) (dismissing pendent common law fraud claim for lack of personal jurisdiction and holding that state's long-arm statute was controlling

The better analysis may be to permit a court to assert supplemental personal jurisdiction over a defendant with respect to a claim for which there is no independent basis of personal jurisdiction, provided the state law claim arises out of a common nucleus of operative facts with the federal claim over which the court does have personal jurisdiction. In other words, if supplemental subject-matter jurisdiction exists, generally supplemental personal jurisdiction ought to as well. This position serves judicial economy, avoidance of piecemeal litigation, and overall convenience of the parties. Fairness concerns can still be addressed by the court, because the exercise of supplemental personal jurisdiction is never mandatory. The decision whether to exercise supplemental personal jurisdiction in a given case is committed to the discretion of the district court.[114]

## § 7.04 LIMITATIONS ON JURISDICTION OVER PROPERTY IN CIVIL ACTIONS

There is no specific provision in Federal Rule of Civil Procedure 4 for attaching property in quasi-in rem actions. If the defendant cannot be served with process by any method permitted under Rule 4, the court may obtain jurisdiction over the defendant's property located within the federal district if authorized by federal statute[115] or "under the circumstances and in the manner provided by state law in that district."[116]

The court's power under Rule 4(n)(2), however, is subject to certain limitations, including due process concerns. First, the property itself is not a sufficient basis for jurisdiction for claims unrelated to the property.[117] Thus, for claims that are unrelated to the property, due process requires that the defendant have contacts with the forum state sufficient to meet the minimum contacts requirement.[118] Second, due process also requires a showing of some exigent circumstance to permit *ex parte* attachment of a defendant's property.[119] Third, in order to seize property under Rule 4(n)(2), that property must be located within the court's jurisdiction.[120]

---

statute with regard to determining whether court could exercise personal jurisdiction over defendant in pendent common law claim).

[114] *See, e.g.*, Action Embroidery Corp. v. Atlantic Embroidery, Inc., 368 F.3d 1174, 1177–1180 (9th Cir. 2004) (district court had discretion whether to retain or dismiss pendent state-law claims); Action Embroidery Corp. v. Atlantic Embroidery, Inc., 368 F.3d 1174, 1177–1180 (9th Cir. 2004) (district court had discretion whether to retain or dismiss pendent state-law claims).

[115] Fed. R. Civ. P. 4(n)(1).

[116] Fed. R. Civ. P. 4(n)(2).

[117] Shaffer v. Heitner, 433 U.S. 186, 212 (1977) (property alone is not sufficient basis for jurisdiction, although its presence may tip balance in favor or exercising jurisdiction); *see* § 108.80.

[118] Shaffer v. Heitner, 433 U.S. 186, 207 (1977) ("The standard for determining whether an exercise of jurisdiction over the interests of persons is consistent with the Due Process Clause is the minimum-contacts standard elucidated in *International Shoe*."); *see* § 108.80[1].

[119] Connecticut v. Doehr, 501 U.S. 1, 18 (1991) (Connecticut statute that authorized prejudgment attachment of real estate that did not provide for preattachment hearing or require showing of some exigent circumstances violated due process requirements).

[120] Fed. R. Civ. P. 4(n)(2); *see* First Charter Land Corp. v. Fitzgerald, 643 F.2d 1011, 1014–1016 (4th

Finally, such seizure is permitted only if the defendant cannot be served with summons under Rule 4.[121]

For further discussion of Federal Rule of Civil Procedure 4(n), see 1 MOORE'S FEDERAL PRACTICE Ch. 4, *Summons*.

## § 7.05 RULE 45 (SUBPOENAS): JURISDICTION OVER WITNESS REQUIRES PROPER JURISDICTIONAL BASIS AND PROPER SERVICE OF PROCESS

A nonparty witness cannot be compelled to testify at a trial, hearing, or deposition unless the witness is subject to the personal jurisdiction of the court or other tribunal. Like jurisdiction over a defendant, jurisdiction over a nonparty witness requires a proper basis for jurisdiction and proper service of process (*see* MOORE'S FEDERAL PRACTICE § 108.01[2]).

In most states, however, the permissible bases for jurisdiction over a nonparty witness are limited to presence and consent.[122] Moreover, personal service of the subpoena on the witness generally is required.[123]

Although there is no general federal long-arm statute for service of subpoenas, Federal Rule of Civil Procedure 45(c) authorizes federal district courts to issue subpoenas to facilitate the taking of depositions in actions pending in other federal courts.[124] Rule 45(c) authorizes service of subpoenas within 100 miles of the place of trial, deposition, or hearing specified in the subpoena, or service at any other place, if authorized by federal statute.[125] Service of a subpoena directed at a witness (who is a United States national or resident) in a foreign country is governed by 28 U.S.C. § 1783 (the Walsh Act).[126] Federal Rule of Civil Procedure 28 authorizes federal courts to order the depositions of witnesses in foreign countries in connection with actions pending in United States federal courts.[127]

For further discussion of Rules 28 and 45, see Ch. 28, *Persons Before Whom Depositions May Be Taken*, and Ch. 45, *Subpoena*, respectively.

---

Cir. 1981) (court properly obtained jurisdiction over defendant's notes and bank account even though other court had possession of property).

121 Fed. R. Civ. P. 4(n)(2); *see* Citizens and S. Nat'l Bank v. Auer, 514 F. Supp. 631, 634 (E.D. Tenn. 1977) (plaintiffs failed to demonstrate personal service was impracticable because there was no showing of diligence in attempting to determine present whereabouts of defendants).

122 *See* Estate of Mirsky, 546 N.Y.S.2d 951, 953 (1989) (out-of-state service of subpoena is void).

123 *See In re* Smith, 126 F.R.D. 461, 462 (E.D.N.Y. 1989) ("Nowhere in Rule 45 is the Court given discretion to permit alternative service [other than personal service] in troublesome cases."); *see generally* Rhonda Wasserman, *The Subpoena Power:* Pennoyer's *Last Vestige*, 74 MINN. L. REV. 37 (1989) (discussion of subpoenas in state courts, including list of state statutes).

124 Fed. R. Civ. P. 45(a)(2).

125 Fed. R. Civ. P. 45(b)(2).

126 Fed. R. Civ. P. 45(b)(3).

127 Fed. R. Civ. P. 28(b).

## § 7.06 OBJECTIONS TO JURISDICTION MAY BE FORFEITED BY FAILURE TO COMPLY WITH DISCOVERY ORDERS

In *Insurance Corp. of Ireland, Ltd. v. Compagnie des Bauxites de Guinee*, the Supreme Court upheld the use of discovery sanctions under Federal Rule of Civil Procedure 37 to establish personal jurisdiction.[128] In this case, the defendants (foreign insurance companies) objected to the assertion of jurisdiction over them by the district court in Pennsylvania. The plaintiffs attempted to use discovery devices to show that the defendants' contacts with Pennsylvania satisfied the minimum requirement. The defendants, however, repeatedly failed to comply with discovery requests and orders.[129] The Supreme Court upheld the district court's ruling (as a discovery sanction under Rule 37(b)) that the court had jurisdiction over the defendants. The Court reasoned that the defendants initially had the option of default and collateral attack. Instead, having submitted to the jurisdiction of the court for the purpose of challenging jurisdiction, the defendants also submitted to the court's procedures for adjudicating that issue and sanctions, including discovery rules and sanctions.[130]

## § 7.07 COURT WILL NOT EXERCISE JURISDICTION OBTAINED BY FORCE OR FRAUD

A court will not exercise jurisdiction over a defendant if personal service was obtained by force or fraud.[131] Similarly, a court will not exercise jurisdiction in a quasi-in rem action if the presence of the defendant's property in the forum state is the result of fraud or force.[132]

The limits on jurisdiction based on fraud and force are less important today then they were when personal service of process within the forum state was the only

---

[128] Insurance Corp. of Ireland, Ltd. v. Compagnie des Bauxites de Guinee, 456 U.S. 694, 709 (1982) (jurisdictional objection may be forfeited by failure to comply with discovery orders).

[129] Insurance Corp. of Ireland, Ltd. v. Compagnie des Bauxites de Guinee, 456 U.S. 694, 696–700 (1982) (foreign corporation that failed to cooperate in discovery on questions of jurisdiction was sanctioned by court's finding that jurisdiction existed over corporation).

[130] 456 U.S. at 705 ("The expression of legal rights is often subject to certain procedural rules: The failure to follow those rules may well result in a curtailment of the rights.").

[131] *See* Restatement (Second) of Conflict of Laws § 82 (1971); *see, e.g.*, Wyman v. Newhouse, 93 F.2d 313, 315 (2d Cir. 1937) (fraud effecting jurisdiction is equivalent of lack of jurisdiction); E/M Lubricants, Inc. v. Microfral, S.A.R.L., 91 F.R.D. 235, 237–238 (N.D. Ill. 1981) (state will not exercise jurisdiction if defendant is tricked into entering state and then served with process).

[132] *See, e.g.*, Forbess v. George Morgan Pontiac Co., 135 So. 2d 594, 596 (2d Cir. 1961) (jurisdiction is not acquired over nonresident who has been fraudulently induced into entering forum state solely for purpose of securing jurisdiction); Commercial Air Charters, Inc. v. Sundorph Aeronautical Corp., 57 F.R.D. 84, 88–89 (D. Conn. 1972) (court will not exercise jurisdiction over defendant who has been tricked by plaintiff into entering jurisdiction in order to be served with process); *but see* Siro v. American Express Co., 99 Conn. 95, 121 A. 280, 282 (Conn. 1923) (plaintiff's act of creating debt due defendant company from its agent in order to obtain service by foreign attachment did not constitute fraud or deceit in procuring service).

adequate basis for personal jurisdiction over a nonresident defendant.[133] Modern long-arm statutes now permit state courts to exercise jurisdiction over nonresident defendants without such in-state service. However, the Supreme Court's decision in *Burnham v. Superior Court*, holding that jurisdiction based on personal service and physical presence generally is not contrary to due process,[134] has renewed the need for a doctrine that denies jurisdiction when the defendant's presence within the forum state has been obtained by force or fraud.

## § 7.08 SOME PARTIES MAY BE IMMUNE FROM JURISDICTION

For policy reasons, courts typically have held some defendants immune from service of process and have refused to exercise jurisdiction over them.[135] Diplomatic representatives from foreign nations, for example, generally have been granted immunity from service of process for reasons of comity. Other defendants have been held immune from service because exercising jurisdiction over them would hamper the state's administration of justice.[136] This type of immunity generally extends only to persons who voluntarily enter the territory for the sole purpose of participating in a trial or a deposition,[137] although, in some states, immunity also extends to persons participating in arbitration or settlement negotiations.[138]

---

[133] Burnham v. Superior Court, 495 U.S. 604, 613 (1990) ("Most States, moreover, had statutes or common-law rules that exempted from service of process individuals who were brought into the forum by force or fraud.").

[134] 495 U.S. at 622 ("For new procedures . . . the Due Process Clause requires analysis to determine whether 'traditional notions of fair play and substantial justice' have been offended.").

[135] *See* Restatement (Second) of Conflict of Laws § 83 (1971).

[136] *See, e.g.*, Viking Penguin, Inc. v. Janklow, 98 F.R.D. 763, 766–767 (S.D.N.Y. 1983) (defendant was immune from service while in New York solely to attend deposition proceeding pending in federal court in South Dakota because defendant's presence in New York benefitted both defendant and federal court in South Dakota); Higgins v. Garcia, 522 So. 2d 95, 96 (Fla. Dist. Ct. App. 1988) (upholding immunity of corporate officer served while in state to give deposition on corporation's behalf).

[137] *See* Sivnksty v. Duffield, 137 W. Va. 112, 71 S.E.2d 113, 114–115 (W. Va. 1952) (defendant had no immunity from civil service in tort action based on same accident for which he was incarcerated and awaiting trial).

[138] *See, e.g.*, E/M Lubricants, Inc. v. Microfral, S.A.R.L., 91 F.R.D. 235, 238 (N.D. Ill. 1981) (plaintiff's duty is "to forego service of process on a defendant who is in the jurisdiction for the exclusive purpose of discussing settlement"); Pavlo v. James, 437 F. Supp. 125, 126–127 (S.D.N.Y. 1977) (defendant was immune from service while attending arbitration in court outside territorial jurisdiction of defendant's residence); Lee v. Stevens of Fla., Inc., 578 So. 2d 867, 868 (Fla. Dist. Ct. App. 1991) (court found no reason to distinguish arbitration from judicial proceeding for purpose of immunity rule).

## § 7.09 PROCEDURES FOR CHALLENGING JURISDICTION

### [1] Defendant May Challenge Jurisdiction in State Court by Making Special Appearance or by Default and Collateral Attack

In state courts, defendants may make a special appearance for the purpose of litigating the court's jurisdiction over them without making a general appearance and, thus, consenting to the court's exercise of jurisdiction. The right to appear specially is not a constitutional right, but all states permit some form of special appearance. The technical requirements for making a special appearance vary from state to state, as do the types of acts by the defendant that turn an attempted special appearance into a general appearance.[139]

### [2] Defendant May Challenge Jurisdiction in Federal Court by Filing Rule 12 Motion to Dismiss or Raising Jurisdictional Defense in Answer or by Default and Collateral Attack

In federal courts, there is no longer a requirement for a special appearance. Instead, defendants may attack the court's jurisdiction over them by filing a motion to dismiss at the beginning of the litigation,[140] by including the jurisdictional objection in the answer,[141] or by not appearing in the action, allowing the plaintiff to obtain the judgment by default, and then collaterally attacking the default judgment for lack of jurisdiction (*see* § 7.01[3]). A defendant who appears must raise the objection to jurisdiction (either by proper pre-pleading motion or in the initial responsive pleading) in order not to waive the defect.[142]

If a defendant in a federal court makes a timely and successful objection to personal jurisdiction, it does not necessarily mean the action will be dismissed. In *Goldlawr, Inc. v. Heiman*, the Supreme Court recognized that a federal court in which both personal jurisdiction and venue were lacking could transfer the case, under 28 U.S.C. § 1406(a), to a federal court where venue and personal jurisdiction would be proper.[143] Such a transfer to cure a lack of personal jurisdiction can also be made when venue is proper, and transfer, accordingly, is made under 28 U.S.C. § 1404(a).[144] The power to transfer a case to cure a lack of jurisdiction is now

---

[139] *See* Richman & Reynolds, Understanding Conflicts of Laws, Second Edition, pp. 72–75 (Matthew Bender, 1993).

[140] Fed. R. Civ. P. 12(b).

[141] Fed. R. Civ. P. 12(b).

[142] *See* Fed. R. Civ. P. 12(b), (g), (h)(1) (defendant waives his or her jurisdiction objection if: (1) defendant makes a Rule 12 motion but does not include objection to personal jurisdiction, or (2) defendant does not make a Rule 12 motion, and does not include objection in answer).

[143] Goldlawr, Inc. v. Heiman, 369 U.S. 463, 466 (1962) (court has power to transfer case in which personal jurisdiction is lacking).

[144] *See* Corke v. Sameiet M.S. Song of Norway, 572 F.2d 77, 78–81 (2d Cir. 1978) (offering three different rationales to explain result).

codified in 28 U.S.C. § 1631. Although some courts have interpreted 28 U.S.C. § 1631 as applying only when it is subject matter jurisdiction that is lacking, the language of the statute is broad enough to permit its application in cases in which personal jurisdiction is lacking, and it has been so interpreted in several federal courts.[145] See generally, Chapter 9 (Change of Venue).

If a motion is made under Federal Rule of Civil Procedure 12, some practitioners recommend combining it with an alternative (less drastic) motion to transfer venue under 28 U.S.C. § 1404(a) or 28 U.S.C. § 1406(a), reasoning that if a court is given this choice, it increases the likelihood that at least one motion will be granted.[146]

---

[145] Western Smelting & Metals, Inc. v. Slater Steel, Inc., 621 F. Supp. 578, 582 (N.D. Ind. 1985) (when case is transferred because of lack of jurisdiction, law of transferee forum applies); *see also* Tellschow v. Aetna Cas. & Sur. Co., 585 F. Supp. 593, 594 (S.D. Fla. 1984) (cause of action was transferred because plaintiff did not allege sufficient contacts to establish personal jurisdiction); Nelson v. International Paint Co., 716 F.2d 640, 643 (9th Cir. 1983) (statute would have authorized transfer, except for fact that it could not be applied retroactively).

[146] *See* Ch. 9, *Change of Venue*. For a complete discussion of the procedural aspects of Rule 12, see 2 Moore's Federal Practice Ch. 12, *Defenses and Objections: When and How Presented; Motion for Judgment on the Pleadings; Consolidating Motions; Waiving Defenses; Pretrial Hearing* (Matthew Bender 3d ed.).

# DIVISION II

# VENUE

# Chapter 8

# VENUE

## § 8.01 OVERVIEW OF VENUE

### [1] *Venue* Defined as Proper District Court in Which to File Action

*Venue* concerns the appropriate district court in which an action may be filed.[1] Venue statutes generally are concerned with convenience. They seek to channel lawsuits to an appropriately convenient court, given the matters raised and the parties involved in an action.[2] Thus, venue principles must be contrasted with personal jurisdiction principles[3] and subject matter jurisdiction principles[4] in at least two important respects. First, and perhaps most important, venue rules do not implicate the court's power either to bind the litigants before it, as personal jurisdiction rules do; or to decide a particular type of case, as subject matter jurisdiction rules do. Thus, no constitutional rights are implicated by the venue statutes, and accordingly, any rights conferred by the federal venue statutes are waivable.[5]

Second, because the object of venue rules is to determine a convenient locality for the litigation, venue is determined according to judicial district, rather than by state.[6] Many states are composed of more than one federal judicial district. So, for example, in a multidistrict state, any judicial district within the state may have personal jurisdiction over the defendants, but venue may be proper in only one of the districts.

If an action is filed in an improper judicial district, the district court may dismiss the action on a timely and proper objection or, in the interest of justice, may transfer the case to a district in which the action could have been brought.[7]

---

[1] *See* Nat'l Labor Relations Bd. v. Line, 50 F.3d 311, 314 (5th Cir. 1995) ( "[v]enue is necessarily defined as the appropriate district court to file an action"); Whiting v. Hogan, 855 F. Supp. 2d 1266, 1282 (D.N.M 2012); City of Waco v. Schouten, 385 F. Supp. 2d 595, 599 (W.D. Tex 2005).

[2] Leroy v. Great Western United Corp., 443 U.S. 173, 185 (1979).

[3] *See generally* Ch. 7, *Personal Jurisdiction in Federal Courts.*

[4] *See generally* Ch. 3, *Diversity Jurisdiction*, Ch. 4, *Federal Question Jurisdiction*, and Ch. 5, *Supplemental Jurisdiction.*

[5] Leroy v. Great Western United Corp., 443 U.S. 173, 183–187 (1979).

[6] *See, e.g.*, 28 U.S.C. § 1391(a), (b) (general venue statute); *cf.* 28 U.S.C. § 1332 (diversity jurisdiction depends on state citizenship).

[7] 28 U.S.C. § 1406(a).

Transferring the action is the favored disposition.[8] Transfer of venue is discussed in Ch. 9, *Change of Venue.*

Because venue rules do not raise any constitutional issues and because they are concerned with convenience, interpretation and application of the venue statutes should be relatively simple. Moreover, modern jet travel and the reality of corporate existence, as well as technological advances in communications, which facilitate the discovery process, should reduce the instances in which venue is an issue. Thus, the courts generally should construe venue statutes liberally. Although Congress is not required to provide a federal forum for all claims, the Supreme Court has said that Congress, in general, does not intend to create venue gaps. Thus, in construing venue statutes, it is reasonable to prefer the construction that avoids leaving such a gap.[9] Nonetheless, venue limitations remain important, particularly in the context of some specialized venue statutes where policy concerns may justify a relatively strict application. Venue statutes designate the proper court or courts for a civil litigation that is within federal subject matter jurisdiction.[10]

Congress has amended the venue statutes repeatedly over the last several decades. Important amendments to the venue statutes made in 1966, 1988, 1990, and 2011 completed a four-stage/four-decade-long process of eliminating venue as a significant constraint on choice of federal forum. Indeed, the 1990 Act,[11] provides the basis for expansive forum-shopping. And, the 2011 amendments simplify and clarify important venue rules.

## [2] Federal Statutes Control Venue of All Civil Actions in Federal Courts

Federal venue statutes govern the venue of all civil actions brought in the federal district courts.[12] The proper venue for an action is determined without regard to whether the action is considered to be "local" or "transitory" in nature.[13] Venue is a procedural matter that may be regulated by Congress. Thus, the federal venue statutes control even in diversity cases in which substantive matters are generally governed by state law under the *Erie* Doctrine.[14]

---

[8] *See, e.g.*, Szulik v. Tag V.I., 858 F. Supp. 2d 532, 547 (E.D.N.C. 2012) (rather than dismissing for improper venue, courts favor finding that it is in the interests of justice to transfer venue).

[9] Atl. Marine Constr. Co. v. United States Dist. Court, 134 S. Ct. 568, 578 (2013) ("Congress does not in general intend to create venue gaps, which take away with one hand what Congress has given by way of jurisdictional grant with the other." Smith v. United States, 507 U.S. 197, 203 (1993) (internal quotation marks omitted)); Brunette Mach. Works, Ltd., v. Kockum Indus., Inc., 406 U.S. 706, 710–711 & ns. 8, 9 (1972) (Congress generally does not intend to leave venue gaps, "which take away with one hand what Congress has given by way of jurisdictional grant with the other").

[10] *See* 28 U.S.C. § 1390(a).

[11] The Judicial Improvements Act of 1990, Pub. L. No. 101-650, 104 Stat. 5089 (codified as amended at 28 U.S.C. § 1391).

[12] *See* 28 U.S.C. § 1390.

[13] *See* 28 U.S.C. § 1391(a)(1) (as amended Dec. 7, 2011, effective Jan. 6, 2012).

[14] *See* Stewart Org., Inc. v. Ricoh Corp., 487 U.S. 22, 32 (1988) (28 U.S.C. § 1404(a), regarding transfer of venue, was procedural rule within Congress's power, and governed decision whether to give effect to

The Federal Rules of Civil Procedure do not control venue, and may not be construed to extend or limit venue of actions in the federal courts, except with respect to admiralty or maritime claims.[15] Admiralty or maritime claims, however, are not governed by the general venue statute, but instead are controlled by special rules contained in a supplement to the Federal Rules of Civil Procedure.[16]

### [3] Venue Is Determined by General Venue Statute Unless Special Statute Exists

The general venue statute, Section 1391(b), governs venue of civil actions "[e]xcept as otherwise provided by law."[17] The venue choices available under the general statute are discussed in § 8.02. This provision must be read together with Section 1391(c), which defines where a party resides for venue purposes.[18] This topic is discussed in § 8.03[4].

Special venue statutes apply in a number of areas, including those statutes contained in Chapter 87 of Title 28 and many others (*see generally* 17 Moore's Federal Practice Chapter 110, § 110.60, table of venue provisions).[19] For each special statute, the question arises whether the statute is exclusive or is supplemented by the general venue provisions. The resolution of this question depends on analysis of the precise language of the special statute, together with other evidence of congressional intent in appropriate cases.[20]

Generally, special venue statutes have been considered to be non-exclusive if the statute is read as originally intended to expand rather than contract venue. In the Jones Act and antitrust areas, for example, the courts have read the general venue provisions as supplementing the special statutes applicable to those areas.[21] Similarly, the general venue statute supplements the special statutory venue provisions in the Federal Arbitration Act that govern proceedings to confirm, vacate, or modify arbitration awards. The Federal Arbitration Act provisions were intended only to expand existing venue choices.[22]

---

parties' forum-selection clause pursuant to motion to transfer); *see generally* Ch. 15, *Applicable Law in Federal Court: The Erie Doctrine.*

[15] Fed. R. Civ. P. 82.

[16] *See* Fed. R. Civ. P. 9(h), 82, Supplemental Rule F(9); *see generally* 17 Moore's Federal Practice Ch. 110, *Determination of Proper Venue* (venue in admiralty cases), Division XI, *Admiralty Practice* (Matthew Bender 3d ed.).

[17] *See* 28 U.S.C. § 1391(a), (b).

[18] *See* 28 U.S.C. § 1391(c).

[19] The special venue statutes are discussed in detail in 17 Moore's Federal Practice, Ch. 110, *Determination of Venue* (Matthew Bender 3d ed.).

[20] *See* VE Holding Corp. v. Johnson Gas Appliance Co., 917 F.2d 1574, 1577 (Fed. Cir. 1990) ("Facially, there is little consistency from area to area").

[21] *See* Pure Oil Co. v. Suarez, 384 U.S. 202, 205–207 (1966) (Section 1391(c) applied in Jones Act case); Go-Video, Inc. v. Akai Elec. Co., 885 F.2d 1406, 1409–1413 (9th Cir. 1989) (antitrust cases may be brought under special antitrust statutes or under general venue statute: "[A]s a general matter, courts have interpreted special venue provisions to supplement, rather than preempt, general venue statutes").

[22] Cortez Byrd Chips, Inc. v. Bill Harbert Constr. Co., 529 U.S. 193, 199 (2000) ("We hold the FAA provisions permissive . . . . The enactment of the special venue provisions in the FAA . . . had an

The special venue provision applicable in patent infringement actions, on the other hand, was long considered to be the exclusive provision governing these actions. The Supreme Court interpreted this statute to have restricted venue of infringement actions under the law in effect when it was first enacted.[23] Other special venue statutes have been held to be exclusive based on Congressional intent. For example, the special venue statute contained in the Civil Rights Act of 1964 (Title VII) controls venue for actions under the Act to the exclusion of the general venue statute. The Act shows a congressional intent that venue be limited to district courts with a connection to the alleged discrimination, as provided by the special statute.[24] Other courts have ruled that certain statutes are exclusive citing the maxim that specific provisions control over more general ones.[25]

## [4] Plaintiff Generally May Choose Among Proper Venues

Normally, the plaintiff will invoke one of the venue options provided for in the general venue statute or an applicable special venue statute. In some cases, however, a contract will contain a forum selection clause. Two questions arise when a case involves a forum selection clause.

The first question is whether the district court will enforce a forum selection clause when an action is filed in a district permitted by the clause, but that district is not a proper venue under the applicable venue statute. Courts generally will enforce the agreement. In the first place, defendants may waive objection to venue.[26] Second, the Supreme Court has made clear that it generally will enforce such agreements.[27] Thus, when a defendant moves to dismiss a case when a plaintiff has invoked a forum selection clause, courts generally will deny the motion.[28]

The second question is whether the district court will enforce the forum selection clause at the insistence of the defendant when the plaintiff chooses a different, but otherwise proper, forum under the applicable venue provisions. The answer depends in part on whether the clause in question requires the case to be brought *only* in a specified state (or foreign) court, or if it allows the case to be

---

obviously liberalizing effect"); *see* 9 U.S.C. §§ 9–11 (proceedings to confirm, vacate, or modify arbitration awards "may" be brought in district court for district where arbitration award made).

[23] Stonite Products Co. v. Melvin Lloyd Co., 315 U.S. 561, 564–567 (1942) (predecessor to 28 U.S.C. § 1392(a) did not supplement patent infringement venue statute); Fourco Glass Co. v. Transmirra Prods. Corp., 353 U.S. 222, 224–225 (1957) (general statute governing corporations, former 28 U.S.C. § 1391(c), did not supplement patent infringement venue statute, 28 U.S.C. § 1400(b)); Joslyn Mfg. Co. v. Amerace Corp., 729 F. Supp. 1219, 1222 (N.D. Ill. 1990).

[24] *See* 42 U.S.C. § 2000e — 5(f)(3); Bolar v. Frank, 938 F.2d 377, 379 (2d Cir. 1991) (interpreting Rehabilitation Act of 1973, 29 U.S.C. § 701 et seq., which incorporates Title VII venue provision).

[25] *See* Fourco Glass Co. v. Transmirra Prods. Corp., 353 U.S. 222, 228–229 (1957); *see also* Stonite Products Co. v. Melvin Lloyd Co., 315 U.S. 561, 564–567 (1942) (special statute governing patent infringement actions was exclusive).

[26] *See* Neirbo Co. v. Bethlehem Shipbuilding Corp., 308 U.S. 165, 167–168 (1939).

[27] Carnival Cruise Lines v. Shute, 499 U.S. 585, 590–594 (1991); M/S Bremen v. Zapata Off-Shore Co., 407 U.S. 1, 8–20 (1972).

[28] *See* Medicine Shoppe Int'l, Inc. v. Browne, 683 F. Supp. 731, 732–733 (E.D. Mo. 1988) (motion to transfer denied when plaintiff brought suit in court specified by forum selection clause).

brought in either federal or state court. If an action is brought in a forum that is proper under the venue states, but a valid forum selection clause requires that the action be maintained in another forum, then a party may seek to enforce the clause through a motion for convenience transfer under 28 U.S.C. § 1404(a). When a party files such a motion, the district court should transfer the case unless extraordinary circumstances unrelated to the convenience of the parties clearly disfavor a transfer.[29] If the forum selection clause requires that the action be maintained only in a state court, or in the courts of a foreign country, so that transfer is not possible, then the action may be dismissed under forum non conveniens principles.[30] These matters are discussed in detail in Ch. 9, *Transfer of Venue*.

Before the Supreme Court's decision in *Atlantic Marine Construction Co. v. United States District Court*, some circuits considered that a forum selection clause could be enforced through a motion to transfer or dismiss based on improper venue under 28 U.S.C. § 1406(a), or a motion to dismiss for improper venue under Rule 12(b)(3). These circuits reasoned that venue was wrong or improper because of the effect of the forum selection clause. However, in *Atlantic Marine* the Court observed that the propriety of venue depends exclusively on whether the court in which the case was brought satisfies the requirements of federal venue laws. The general venue statute, 28 U.S.C. § 1391, "makes clear that venue in 'all civil actions' must be determined in accordance with the criteria outlined in that section. That language cannot reasonably be read to allow judicial consideration of other, extrastatutory limitations on the forum in which a case may be brought."[31]

## [5] Pleading and Burden of Proof as to Venue

Venue requirements pose a restraint on the filing of actions that is separate from and in addition to subject matter jurisdiction and personal jurisdiction. Venue provisions come into play only after subject matter jurisdiction, the court's power to decide the action, has been established. If venue requirements are not satisfied, the district court is not deprived of subject matter jurisdiction, although dismissal of the case may be appropriate if a timely objection to the venue is interposed.[32] Conversely, venue statutes cannot confer jurisdiction.[33] Because venue provisions do not restrict the court's power to adjudicate, the litigants may waive venue objections (*see generally* Ch. 9, *Change of Venue* (discussion of waiver)).[34]

---

[29] Atlantic Marine Constr. Co. v. United States Dist. Court, 134 S. Ct. 568, 187 L. Ed. 2d 487, 494 (2013).

[30] Atlantic Marine Constr. Co. v. United States Dist. Court, 134 S. Ct. 568, 187 L. Ed. 2d 487, 499–500 (2013).

[31] Atlantic Marine Constr. Co. v. United States Dist. Court, 134 S. Ct. 568, 187 L. Ed. 2d 487, 496 (2013).

[32] Polizzi v. Cowles Magazines, Inc., 345 U.S. 663, 665 (1953); *see* 28 U.S.C. §§ 1404, 1406(a).

[33] Andrus v. Charlestone Stone Prods. Co., 436 U.S. 604, 608 n.6 (1978); Powell v. Offshore Navigation, Inc., 644 F.2d 1063, 1064 n.1 (5th Cir. 1981).

[34] 28 U.S.C. § 1406(b) ("Nothing in this chapter shall impair the jurisdiction of a district court of any matter involving a party who does not interpose timely and sufficient objection to the venue"); Olberding v. Illinois C. R. Co., 346 U.S. 338, 340 (1953).

This distinction is recognized in the definition of venue contained in the venue statutes:[35]

> As used in this chapter, the term "venue" refers to the geographic specification of the proper court or courts for the litigation of a civil action that is within the subject-matter jurisdiction of the district courts in general, and does not refer to any grant or restriction of subject-matter jurisdiction providing for a civil action to be adjudicated only by the district court for a particular district or districts.

Venue must also be distinguished from personal jurisdiction, which is the court's power over the person or property of the defendant and is acquired by service of process on the defendant (*see* Ch. 7; *see generally* MOORE'S FEDERAL PRACTICE, Ch. 4, *Summons*; Ch. 108, *Territorial Jurisdiction: Jurisdiction over Persons and Property*). The venue statutes do not affect the necessity of acquiring personal jurisdiction over the defendants by proper service of process.[36]

Venue simply concerns the place where this judicial authority may be exercised. In other words, venue provisions do not limit the power of the court but instead relate to the convenience of the litigants and witnesses and the proper allocation of judicial business.[37] Venue serves the purpose of protecting a defendant from the inconvenience of having to defend an action in a trial court that is either remote from the defendant's residence or from the place where the acts underlying the controversy occurred.[38]

Another distinction between venue on the one hand and subject matter jurisdiction on the other relates to pleading and burdens of proof. The party invoking federal jurisdiction must plead and prove that federal subject matter jurisdiction exists (*see* 2 MOORE'S FEDERAL PRACTICE, Ch. 8, *General Rules of Pleading*, and Ch. 12, *Defenses and Objections: When and How Presented; Motion for Judgment on the Pleadings; Consolidating Motions; Waiving Defenses; Pretrial Hearing*).[39] Thus, for example, a plaintiff must plead the basis for subject matter jurisdiction in the first paragraph of the complaint; failure to do so may result in dismissal at any time during the litigation for lack of subject matter jurisdiction.[40]

---

[35] 28 U.S.C. § 1390(a).

[36] KM Enters., Inc. v. Global Traffic. Techs., Inc., 725 F.3d 718, 723–724 (7th Cir. 2013) ("While personal jurisdiction governs a court's power over a defendant, federal venue rules determine in which judicial district (among those that have the power to hear a given suit) a suit should be heard. Unlike personal jurisdiction, which has a constitutional dimension, civil venue is a creature of statute, intended to limit the potential districts where one may be called upon to defend oneself in any given matter to those that are fair and reasonably convenient.").

[37] Lindahl v. Office of Personnel Mgmt., 470 U.S. 768, 793 n.30 (1985) (citing *Neirbo Co. v. Bethlehem Shipbuilding Corp.*, 308 U.S. 165, 168 (1939)); *see also* Leroy v. Great Western United Corp., 443 U.S. 173, 183–184 (1979) ("in most instances, the purpose of statutorily specified venue is to protect the defendant against the risk that a plaintiff will select an unfair or inconvenient place of trial").

[38] *See* VE Holding Corp. v. Johnson Gas Appliance Co., 917 F.2d 1574, 1576 (Fed. Cir. 1990) (citing MOORE'S FEDERAL PRACTICE).

[39] Capron v. Van Noorden, 6 U.S. (2 Cranch) 126 (1804); McNutt v. General Motors Acceptance Corp., 298 U.S. 178, 182 (1936).

[40] Fed. R. Civ. P. 8(a)(1), 12(b)(1), (h)(3).

In contrast, a plaintiff need not allege the basis for filing in a particular district court although it may be good practice to do so to forestall challenges to venue (*see* 2 Moore's Federal Practice, Ch. 8, *General Rules of Pleading*). Unlike subject matter jurisdiction, venue is not a matter that must be raised by the proponent of the forum. Rather, venue, like personal jurisdiction, involves a privilege personal to the defendant because the purpose of venue statutes is to prevent litigation from being conducted in a forum that is inconvenient or unfair to the defendant because the forum lacks a sufficient connection with the events giving rise to the claim. Accordingly, any defendant that fails to timely object waives venue objections.[41]

When the defendant timely objects to venue, courts should treat the venue question as an affirmative defense. Therefore, the defendant has the burden of establishing that venue is improper.[42] Nevertheless, it should be noted that a number of courts, apparently relying on an analogy to subject matter jurisdiction, have stated that the plaintiff has the burden of proving venue.[43]

If the district court finds that venue is improper, it may dismiss the action. However, the preferred disposition is to transfer the action to a district in which it might have been brought in the first place (*see* Ch. 9, Change of Venue).[44] Challenges to venue and the procedures for transfer are discussed in detail in 17 Moore's Federal Practice Ch. 111, *Change of Venue*, and in 2 Moore's Federal Practice Ch. 12, *Defenses and Objections: When and How Presented; Motion for Judgment on the Pleadings; Consolidating Motions; Waiving Defenses; Pretrial Hearing*.

Because courts view venue problems as relatively unimportant, especially after Congress's efforts to liberalize the general venue provisions, they are not inclined to grant motions to dismiss. They are far more likely to transfer the action. Accordingly, defendants making motions to dismiss for improper venue ought to consider requesting the court in the alternative to transfer the action pursuant to Section 1406 (*see* Ch. 9, *Change of Venue* (discussion of differences between Sections 1404 and 1406)).[45] Although the court has the authority to transfer on its own motion, it is wise to raise the matter in the motion to dismiss so that the full range

---

[41] Fed. R. Civ. P. 8(a), 12(b)(3) (motion to dismiss for proper venue); Fed. R. Civ. P. 12(h)(1) (venue objection waived if not made in first responsive pleading).

[42] Myers v. American Dental Ass'n, 695 F.2d 716, 724 (3d Cir. 1982) (citing Moore's Federal Practice, venue is affirmative, dilatory defense, so that defendant has burden of proof); Simon v. Ward, 80 F. Supp. 2d 464, 466–468 (E.D. Pa. 2000) (defendant is required to make evidentiary showing that venue is improper in order to gain dismissal or transfer); *In re* Peachtree Lane Assocs., Ltd., 150 F.3d 788, 794 (7th Cir. 1998) (venue is presumed to be proper in district in which case is filed, and party challenging venue bears burden of establishing by preponderance of evidence that district chosen by plaintiff was improper venue).

[43] *See* Johnson v. Washington Gas Light Co., 89 F. Supp. 2d 45, 47 (D.D.C. 2000) (plaintiff met burden of showing that venue was proper in district); Gulf Ins. Co. v. Glasbrenner, 417 F.3d 353, 355 (2d Cir. 2005) (if district court holds evidentiary hearing, plaintiff must demonstrate venue by preponderance of evidence); Lieb v. American Pac. Int'l, Inc., 489 F. Supp. 690, 696 (E.D. Pa. 1980) (plaintiff bears burden of proving that venue is proper); *See* Bartholomew v. Virginia Chiropractors Ass'n, 612 F.2d 812, 816 (4th Cir. 1979) (plaintiff bears burden of proving that venue is proper).

[44] *See, e.g.*, Scott v. Monsanto Co., 868 F.2d 786, 788–789 (5th Cir. 1989).

[45] 28 U.S.C. § 1406.

of remedies for the filing in an allegedly improper district will be considered.

## § 8.02 GENERAL VENUE STATUTE GOVERNS MOST CIVIL ACTIONS

### [1] Overview of Venue Possibilities

The general venue statute, 28 U.S.C. § 1391(b), sets out three venue possibilities, one based on the defendants' residence, one based on the location of the operative events, and a fallback provision. Specifically, a civil action may be brought in:[46]

1. A district in which any defendant resides, if all defendants are residents of the state in which the district is located (*see* [2], *below*).
2. A district in which a substantial part of the events or omissions giving rise to the claim occurred, or a substantial part of property that is the subject of the action is situated (*see* [3], *below*).
3. If there is no district in which an action may otherwise be brought, any judicial district in which any defendant is subject to the court's personal jurisdiction with respect to the action (*see* [4], *below*).

As amended in 2011, this statute applies to all civil actions.[47] Formerly, the statute contained separate provisions governing diversity actions and federal question actions. These provisions were identical as to the first two venue choices listed above, but differed in language as to the third (*see* [d], *below*).

### [2] District Where Any Defendant Resides, If All Defendants Reside in Same State

Under Section 1391(b)(1), a civil action governed by the general venue statute may be brought in a judicial district in which any defendant resides, if all defendants are residents of the state in which the district is located.[48] The plaintiff's residence, on the other hand, is no longer relevant to venue under this statute, although this was an alternative in diversity cases until eliminated by the 1990 amendments to the general venue statute. For discussion of the determination of place of residence for purposes of the statute, *see* § 8.03.

Before being amended in 2011, the statute provided that venue was proper in "a judicial district where any defendant resides, if all defendants reside in the same State," rather than "if all defendants are residents of the state in which the district is located." The former statute, like the present version, was intended to provide for venue in cases with multiple defendants in the same state. However, as explained in the Committee Report to the 2011 amendment, it was thought that the

---

[46] 28 U.S.C. § 1391(b).

[47] *See* 28 U.S.C. § 1391(a), (b).

[48] 28 U.S.C. § 1391(b)(1).

former language might have unintended consequences, and therefore the present language was substituted:[49]

> For example, consider a suit brought against both a resident (natural person) in Illinois and a corporation that does substantial business in every state, including Illinois, and the litigation arose from events that occurred in Illinois. Under current subsection 1391(c), the corporation could be considered a resident of Illinois and every other state, by virtue of its being subject to personal jurisdiction in all those states. A plaintiff might sue both defendants in any other district where the corporation happens to reside, such as the Southern District of New York, on the theory that, because all defendants reside in the same state (Illinois) as provided in 28 U.S.C. § 1391(a) and (b), venue is proper in any other district where "any defendant resides." Proposed paragraph 1391(b)(1) would alter the statutory language to preclude such a result, while achieving the intended goal of the original statute.

In other words, in the hypothetical presented, venue would, and should, be proper only in a district in Illinois. Both defendants reside in Illinois, so venue is properly restricted to a district in that state.

### [3] District Where Substantial Part of Events or Omissions Occurred or Where Property Is Situated

Under Section 1391(b)(2), a civil action governed by the general venue statute may be brought in a judicial district in which a substantial part of the events or omissions giving rise to the claim occurred, or a substantial part of the property that is the subject of the action is situated.[50] Venue is not limited to a single district "where the claim arose,"[51] but may be proper in several districts. For a discussion of the determination of where a substantial part of the events or omissions occurred, *see* § 8.04.

This provision addresses the "litigation breeding problem" that existed before Congress's 1988 and 1990 amendments. Prior to the amendments, venue was proper only in the one district "in which the claim arose," giving rise to disputes over which of several districts connected with the lawsuit was the single district in which the claim arose. Now, instead of venue being proper only in the one district "where the claim arose," venue is proper in any district "in which a substantial part of the events or omissions giving rise to the claim occurred." The intent is to provide more options to those bringing suit. Several districts may serve as the locus of "substantial events or omissions."

---

[49] H.R. Rep. No. 112-10, at 19 (2011).

[50] 28 U.S.C. § 1391(b)(2).

[51] *See* LeRoy v. Great W. United Corp., 443 U.S. 173, 185 (1979). *See generally* 17 Moore's Federal Practice, § 110 App.106.

### [4] If No Other Option Applies, Where Any Defendant Is Subject to Personal Jurisdiction

Under Section 1391(b)(3), if there is no district in which an action may otherwise be brought under Section 1391(b)(1) or (2), the action may be brought in *any* judicial district in which *any* defendant is subject to the court's personal jurisdiction with respect to the action.[52] This is a fall-back provision, designed to deal with the problem of where venue should lie when the significant events giving rise to the claim arise outside the United States. In such cases, it may be impossible to find a district in which a substantial part of the events or omissions giving rise to the claim occurred. Accordingly, Section 1391(b)(2) venue will be unavailable.[53] Similarly, given the transnational flavor of the case, all the defendants may not reside in the same state; thus, venue will be unavailable under Section 1391(b)(1).[54] Under these circumstances, the fallback provision applies. In general, Congress does not intend to create venue gaps which would prevent the federal courts from exercising their jurisdiction. The fallback provision ensures that, so long as the court has personal jurisdiction over a defendant, venue will always lie somewhere.[55]

Section 1391(b)(3) applies only when there is no district in which the action could otherwise be brought under Section 1391(b)(1) or (2). The policy for this limitation on the use of subsection (3) is clear. In a multi-defendant case, at least one of the defendants may reside in a different state from the other defendants, or may have relatively little connection with the district. Thus, the out-of-state defendant would be burdened by having to litigate in the district in which the other defendants reside. Of course, out-of-state defendants may have a good argument that the court has no personal jurisdiction over them in that district. But, out-of-state defendants will be unsuccessful with motions to dismiss under statutes that allow for nationwide or other extraterritorial service in certain federal question cases such as antitrust, securities fraud, and RICO cases. Moreover Rule 4(k)(2) now permits extraterritorial service on defendants in federal question cases when the defendants are not otherwise subject to jurisdiction in any state's courts and the exercise of jurisdiction is consistent with due process.[56]

The language requiring that the defendant be subject to personal jurisdiction "with respect to such action" was added by the 2011 amendment. The change was intended to avoid the possibility of a reading of the statute that would allow an overly broad assertion of venue.[57]

When determining personal jurisdiction for venue purposes, the court must determine whether the defendant is subject to personal jurisdiction with respect to

---

[52] 28 U.S.C. § 1391(b)(3).

[53] *See* 28 U.S.C. § 1391(b)(2).

[54] *See* 28 U.S.C. § 1391(b)(1).

[55] *See* Atlantic Marine Constr. Co. v. United States Dist. Court, 134 S. Ct. 568, 187 L. Ed. 2d 487, 497 (2013).

[56] *See* Fed. R. Civ. P. 4(k)(2). *See* Ch. 7, Personal Jurisdiction.

[57] *See* H.R. Rep. No. 101-734, at 20 (1990).

the district in which the plaintiff has filed suit (in multidistrict states), not with respect to the state as a whole. The court must focus on contacts with the particular district; it is not sufficient that the defendant would be subject to personal jurisdiction by virtue of contacts with another district in that state.[58] For an extensive discussion of personal jurisdiction, *see* 16 MOORE'S FEDERAL PRACTICE Ch. 108, *Territorial Jurisdiction: Jurisdiction over Persons and Property.*

However, the venue statute does not create an additional basis for personal jurisdiction. Thus, even though venue may be proper in a district in which any defendant is subject to personal jurisdiction, if all the defendants are not subject to jurisdiction in the same district, it will be necessary to bring separate actions in different districts in order to obtain relief against all the defendants.[59]

Before the 2011 amendment to Section 1391, the statute contained separate subsections governing federal question and diversity cases, and the language of the two subsections differed slightly. Former Section 1391(b)(3), which applied to all cases in which jurisdiction was not founded solely on diversity of citizenship grounds, provided that venue was proper in a "judicial district in which any defendant may be found." Former Section 1391(a)(3), applicable to cases in which jurisdiction was founded solely on diversity, provided that venue was proper "in a district in which any defendant is subject to personal jurisdiction at the time the action is commenced." This difference in language probably did not create any practical difference because the word "found," as used in venue statutes,[60] generally has been interpreted to mean where a defendant was subject to personal jurisdiction.[61] But the 2011 amendments put diversity and other cases on par, and thus eliminated any possibility of litigation over the different terminology.

## § 8.03 WHERE PARTY "RESIDES" DEPENDS ON NATURE OF PARTY

### [1] Individual Resides in District of Domicile

The district of an individual defendant's residence is a proper venue under the general venue statute, and the district of residence of either the defendant or plaintiff may be a proper venue under a number of special venue statutes (*see generally* 17 MOORE'S FEDERAL PRACTICE § 110.60 (table of venue statutes)).[62] Thus,

---

[58] *See* 28 U.S.C. § 1391(c); Milwaukee Concrete Studios, Ltd. v. Fjeld Mfg. Co., 8 F.3d 441, 445–446 (7th Cir. 1993) (citing MOORE'S FEDERAL PRACTICE); *cf.* Fed. R. Civ. P. 4(k) (proper service confers personal jurisdiction if party could be subjected to jurisdiction of court of general jurisdiction in state in which district court is located).

[59] *See* H.R. Rep. No. 101-734, at 23 (1990).

[60] *See, e.g.*, 28 U.S.C. § 1400(a) (copyright venue statute, discussed in 17 MOORE'S FEDERAL PRACTICE § 110.39[2]); 15 U.S.C. §§ 15, 22 (antitrust venue statute, discussed in 17 MOORE'S FEDERAL PRACTICE § 110.45); 29 U.S.C. § 1132(e)(2) (ERISA venue statute, discussed in § 110.49).

[61] "Found" means where party is subject to personal jurisdiction. *See* Freeman v. Bee Machine Co., 319 U.S. 448, 452 (1943) ("found" in venue sense does not necessarily mean physical presence).

[62] *See* 28 U.S.C. § 1391(b) (general venue statute, discussed in 17 MOORE'S FEDERAL PRACTICE § 110.02);

a determination of an individual's residence is critical for determining proper venue.

Under the 2011 amendments to the general venue statute, and for purposes of all venue statutes, a natural person, including an alien lawfully admitted for permanent residence in the United States, is deemed to reside in the judicial district in which that person is domiciled.[63] A person's domicile is that place where the person has his or her true, fixed, and permanent home, and to which he or she has the intention of returning in the future although he or she may presently be absent from there. Domicile thus often turns on the subjective factor of intent.[64] Determination of residence or domicile is a question for the trier of fact.[65]

Citizenship for diversity purposes is defined as equivalent to domicile. Thus, diversity cases discussing citizenship will be instructive on domicile for venue purposes.[66] This topic is discussed in Ch. 3, *Diversity Jurisdiction*.

---

28 U.S.C. § 1391(e) (venue in suits against federal officials, discussed in 17 MOORE'S FEDERAL PRACTICE § 110.31).

[63] 28 U.S.C. § 1391(c)(1); *see also* Shaw v. Quincy Mining Co., 145 U.S. 444, 449, 12 S. Ct. 935, 36 L. Ed. 768 (1892). *See* Manley v. Engram, 755 F.2d 1463, 1466 n.3 (11th Cir. 1985) ("It is well settled that an individual's mere residence in a state is not enough for purposes of establishing the propriety of venue there. Rather, it is the individual's 'permanent' residence — i.e., his domicile — that is the benchmark for determining proper venue."); MacNeil v. Whittemore, 254 F.2d 820, 821 (2d Cir. 1958) (defendant with only summer home in Vermont was not resident of Vermont for venue purposes); Ellingburg v. Connett, 457 F.2d 240, 241 (5th Cir. 1972) (interpreting 28 U.S.C. § 1391(e); plaintiff's place of incarceration was not equivalent to "residence" for venue purposes); Holmes v. United States Bd. of Parole, 541 F.2d 1243, 1248–1249 (7th Cir. 1976) (venue was proper in suit by prisoner in district of domicile, not place of incarceration as argued by government).

[64] *See* Flanagan v. Shively, 783 F. Supp. 922, 935 (M.D. Pa. 1992), *aff'd*, 980 F.2d 722 (3d Cir. 1992) (prisoner does not become "resident" of state for venue purposes by virtue of incarceration there if prisoner was resident of another state before incarceration and there is no indication that prisoner intends to relocate on release); Manley v. Engram, 755 F.2d 1463, 1466 n.3 (11th Cir. 1985) (member of military stationed in Georgia was domiciled in Florida, which he considered his permanent residence; although venue was thus improper in Georgia district court, transfer was appropriate on *plaintiff's* motion because defendant withheld information about his actual domicile so that plaintiff could not in exercise of due diligence have discovered defendant's true residence prior to filing suit).

[65] *See* Hill v. Gregory, 241 F.2d 612, 613–614 (7th Cir. 1957) (although individual lived in Illinois, court did not abuse discretion in finding that he resided in Mississippi for venue purposes, considering among other factors: Mississippi was where he was registered to vote and where he voted, he made frequent trips to Mississippi and kept property there, and he intended to return to Mississippi).

[66] *See, e.g.*, Mas v. Perry, 489 F.2d 1396, 1399–1400 (5th Cir. 1974) ("For diversity purposes, citizenship means domicile; mere residence in the State is not sufficient. . . . . . . . A person's domicile is the place of 'his true, fixed, and permanent home and principal establishment, and to which he has the intention of returning whenever he is absent therefrom.' "); Townsend v. Bucyrus-Erie Co., 144 F.2d 106, 108–109 (10th Cir. 1944) (although citizenship for diversity purposes and residence for venue purposes are not necessarily synonymous terms, they are related and existence of one is cogent evidence of other; both embody concept of domicile or place called home as distinguished from transitory or temporary place of abode).

## [2] Residence of Aliens

An alien who has been lawfully admitted for permanent residence in the United States is deemed to reside in the judicial district in which that person is domiciled.[67] Thus, for venue purposes a resident alien is treated the same as a resident citizen (*see* [1], *above*). A nonresident alien, on the other hand, may be sued in any district (and this is also true for nonresident citizens).[68] For further discussion of treatment of nonresidents, *see* 17 Moore's Federal Practice § 110.30.

This treatment of resident aliens was added to the venue statute by the 2011 Jurisdiction and Venue Clarification Act.[69] Before that, resident aliens were treated the same as nonresident aliens and could be sued in any district. Aliens were treated differently from domestic parties because of a conception of residence for venue purposes that depended on state citizenship. Accordingly, an alien was not considered to be a resident of a state, or district in a state, because an alien is not a citizen of the state.[70]

Under this former law, the residence of alien defendants was not relevant, but residence of alien plaintiffs could be significant for purposes of certain statutes that name the residence of the plaintiff as a proper venue.[71] Courts considering actions by permanent resident aliens under these statutes showed a willingness to allow venue in the district of the alien's actual residence or domicile, notwithstanding the lack of citizenship.[72] This approach harmonizes the current venue statute with the diversity jurisdiction statute, which treats aliens who are admitted as permanent residents and are domiciled in a state in the same manner, for purposes of determining diversity jurisdiction, as citizens of that state.[73]

One problem that may arise under the statute after the 2011 amendments to the general venue statutes, however, is how to deal with an illegal alien who is

---

[67] 28 U.S.C. § 1391(c)(1).

[68] 28 U.S.C. § 1391(c)(3).

[69] *See* Pub. L. No. 112-63, § 205, 125 Stat. 758 (2011) (amendment effective Jan. 6, 2012 and applies to any action commenced in federal district court on or after that date, and to any action removed from state court to federal district court and that had been commenced, within meaning of state law, in state court on or after that date).

[70] *See* Brunette Mach. Works, Ltd., v. Kockum Indus., Inc., 406 U.S. 706, 709–710 (1972) (alien defendant is by definition citizen of no district); Galveston, H. & S. A. R. Co. v. Gonzales, 151 U.S. 496, 506–507 (1894) (alien plaintiff, for venue purposes, is assumed not to reside in any judicial district regardless of where alien actually lives); Alegria v. United States, 945 F.2d 1523, 1526 (11th Cir. 1991) ("It is generally accepted that an alien, for purposes of establishing venue, is presumed by law not to reside in any judicial district of the United States regardless of where he or she actually lives").

[71] *See, e.g.*, 28 U.S.C. § 1402 (suits against United States); *see also* 17 Moore's Federal Practice § 110.41.

[72] *See* Arevalo-Franco v. United States Immigration and Naturalization Serv., 889 F.2d 589, 591 (5th Cir. 1989) (Freedom of Information Act Complaint may be filed in district where complainant, whether a citizen or an alien, in fact resides: "There is nothing in the FOIA to indicate that Congress intended to distinguish between citizens and aliens when it enacted 5 U.S.C. § 552(a)(4)(B) and used the word 'person' therein."); Williams v. United States, 704 F.2d 1222, 1227 (11th Cir. 1983) ("a resident alien taxpayer may establish venue under 28 U.S.C.A. § 1402(a)(1) for purposes of contesting a jeopardy assessment").

[73] *See* 28 U.S.C. § 1332(a)(2).

domiciled in a state. The residence of a natural person under Section 1391(c)(1) is that person's domicile. The provision for natural persons includes lawful permanent resident aliens but does not expressly exclude illegal aliens. And, Section 1391(c)(3) refers only to non-residents. The best approach here would be to ignore the U.S. domicile of the illegal alien and treat that person as a non-resident. This approach allows the plaintiff to ignore the illegal alien's residence for venue purposes. That surely is Congress's intent, but the lack of clarity creates an issue.

Nonresident aliens, on the other hand, clearly do not reside in any district. Possibly, a venue statute that designates only the county of residence of the plaintiff as a proper venue is unconstitutional as applied to nonresident aliens to the extent it denies nonresident aliens a right granted to residents.[74]

## [3] Public Official Sued in Official Capacity Resides Where Official Performs Official Duties

A public official, when sued in an official capacity rather than as an individual, resides for venue purposes in the district of his or her official residence; that is, where he or she performs his or her official duties.[75] This rule applies to state as well as federal officials. An official may have more than one residence under this principle.[76] Formerly, this rule acted to restrict mandamus actions against federal officials to the District of Columbia. Now, however, actions in the nature of mandamus are subject to the liberal venue requirements of Section 1391(e), and need not be brought in the district of the defendant's residence.

## [4] Residence of Corporation or Other Legal Entity

### [a] Defendant That Is Corporation or Other Entity Resides Where It Is Subject to Personal Jurisdiction

Any entity with the capacity to sue and be sued in its common name under applicable law, whether or not incorporated, is deemed to reside, if a defendant, in any judicial district in which it is subject to the court's personal jurisdiction with respect to the civil action in question.[77] If the entity is a plaintiff, it is deemed to reside only in the judicial district in which it maintains its principal place of

---

[74] *See* Alegria v. United States, 945 F.2d 1523, 1528 (11th Cir. 1991) (court reversed dismissal for lack of venue under 28 U.S.C. § 1402(a) because it found no rational basis for treating aliens and citizens differently for venue purposes in internal revenue jeopardy assessment case); *Contra* Malajalian v. United States, 504 F.2d 842, 844–845 (1st Cir. 1974) (plaintiff was not denied forum because suit could be brought in Court of Claims).

[75] Official sued in official capacity resides where he or she performs official duties. *See* Butterworth v. Hill, 114 U.S. 128, 132 (1885). *5th Circuit. See* Florida Nursing Home Ass'n v. Page, 616 F.2d 1355, 1360 (5th Cir. 1980), *rev'd on other grounds*, 450 U.S. 147 (1981) (citing Moore's Federal Practice). *6th Circuit. See* O'Neill v. Battisti, 472 F.2d 789, 791 (6th Cir. 1972) (citing Moore's Federal Practice). *9th Circuit. See* Earnst v. Secretary of Interior, 244 F.2d 344, 345 (9th Cir. 1957) (official residence was Washington, D.C.).

[76] Rule applies to state officials.

[77] 28 U.S.C. § 1391(c)(2).

business.[78]

When determining personal jurisdiction for venue purposes, the court must make a separate inquiry into personal jurisdiction as it existed when the complaint was filed, irrespective of subsequent consent or waiver.[79] This definition of residence for defendants essentially equates venue and personal jurisdiction (*see generally* 16 Moore's Federal Practice Ch. 108, *Territorial Jurisdiction: Jurisdiction over Persons and Property*), except with respect to multidistrict states as discussed in [b], *below*. This broad definition of venue was intended to eliminate many of the problems of interpretation that arose under an older version of the statute, which provided that a corporation's residence for venue purposes was where it was incorporated, licensed to do business, or doing business.[80]

Before being amended in 2011, Section 1391(c) governed corporations only. However, partnerships and other unincorporated associations were usually treated the same as corporations. As amended, the statute applies equally to all types of entitles able to sue or be sued in its common name (*see* [c], *below*).

Section 1391(c) was amended in 1988 to provide that it applied to all venue statutes in Ch. 87 of the United States Code, and amended again in 2011 to provide that it applied "for all venue purposes." Therefore, the definition of residence contained in Section 1391(c) applies "for all venue purposes," and therefore applies to all venue statutes.[81]

### [b] Personal Jurisdiction Determined With Respect to Each District in Multidistrict States

In states with more than one judicial district, venue is determined by considering personal jurisdiction with respect to each district rather than to the state as a whole. A corporate defendant resides in any district in a multidistrict state in which, at the time the action is commenced, it would be subject to personal jurisdiction if that district were a separate state.[82] There is a question whether the minimum contacts due process analysis developed under *International Shoe* and its progeny (*see generally* 16 Moore's Federal Practice Ch. 108, *Territorial Jurisdiction:*

---

[78] 28 U.S.C. § 1391(c)(2).

[79] DSMC, Inc. v. Convera Corp., 273 F. Supp. 2d 14, 19 (D.D.C. 2002) (to determine residence of corporation for purposes of general venue statute, court is required to make independent inquiry into whether jurisdiction existed at time action was commenced); Wine Mkts. Int'l v. Bass, 939 F. Supp. 178, 180 (E.D.N.Y. 1996) (court should assess situation as it existed when complaint was filed, irrespective of subsequent consent or waiver).

[80] *See generally* 17 Moore's Federal Practice § 110App.105; § 110App.07[2] (committee notes to 1988 amendment).

[81] 28 U.S.C. § 1391(c) (as amended Dec. 7, 2011); *see* Pub. L. No. 112-63, § 205, 125 Stat. 758 (2011) (amendment effective Jan. 6, 2012 and applies to any action commenced in federal district court on or after that date, and to any action removed from state court to federal district court and that had been commenced, within meaning of state law, in state court on or after that date).

[82] 28 U.S.C. § 1391(d); *see, e.g.*, Bicicletas Windsor, S.A. v. Bicycle Corp. of America, 783 F. Supp. 781, 785–786 (S.D.N.Y. 1992) (in addition to determination of personal jurisdiction, in multidistrict states statute requires "a hypothetical analysis of personal jurisdiction confined to" the district of suit).

*Jurisdiction over Persons and Property*),[83] controls the question of whether the corporation is subject to personal jurisdiction, rather than an analysis that also considers the applicable state long-arm statute, which may be more restrictive than the constitutional test in some states. Some courts have held that only the constitutional minimum contacts test must be complied with.[84] For example, in a breach of contract action, a district court for the Southern District of New York used only a federal "minimum contacts" analysis, rather than turning to New York's jurisdictional statute, which is more restrictive. The court found personal jurisdiction over the defendant in the Southern District to satisfy the venue requirement of Section 1391(c) because the corporation solicited business in district. However, more than mere solicitation would have been required under the New York long-arm statute.[85]

Other states require that both the minimum contacts test and the state long arm statute be satisfied. For example, a district court in North Carolina applied the state long arm statute as part of its corporate residence venue analysis. The plaintiff, a North Carolina corporation, sued defendants (a New York corporation, a South Carolina corporation, and a Pennsylvania corporation) alleging breach of contract. Under Section 1391(c), the district court found personal jurisdiction by using the state's long-arm statute both in the state of North Carolina and within the Western District. Thus, venue was properly laid in the Western District of North Carolina.[86]

In light of the purpose of venue statutes, as well as Congress's intent to liberalize venue rules, the first result makes more sense. When applying Section 1391(c), the courts ought to consider only the federal constitutional test. This approach is further supported by the additional point that federal law governs the question of venue (*see* 17 MOORE'S FEDERAL PRACTICE § 110.01[2]).

If the corporation is subject to personal jurisdiction in the state at large, but there is no one district with sufficient contacts to support personal jurisdiction, the corporation resides in the district in which it has the most significant contacts.[87] The "most significant contacts" language is not explained in the statute or in the legislative history.[88] Personal jurisdiction is concerned with "minimum contacts" linking the defendant, the litigation, and the forum (*see* 16 MOORE'S FEDERAL PRACTICE Ch. 108, *Territorial Jurisdiction: Jurisdiction over Persons and Property*), and does not ordinarily require a comparison of contacts between forums to determine which one is best. Nonetheless, the purpose of the new language is clearly to avoid the possibility that the venue statute may once again become a technical barrier to filing suit in a particular district when all the jurisdictional requirements are met.

---

[83] International Shoe Co. v. State of Washington, 326 U.S. 310 (1945).

[84] *See* Bicicletas Windsor, S.A. v. Bicycle Corp. of America, 783 F. Supp. 781, 786 (S.D.N.Y. 1992).

[85] Bicicletas v. Bicycle Corp. of America, 783 F. Supp. 781, 786 (S.D.N.Y. 1992).

[86] DP Riggins and Assoc's, Inc. v. American Bd. Co., 796 F. Supp. 205, 211 (W.D.N.C. 1992).

[87] 28 U.S.C. § 1391(c).

[88] *See* Oakley, *Recent Statutory Changes in the Law of Federal Jurisdiction and Venue: The Judicial Improvements Acts of 1988 and 1990*, 24 U.C. DAVIS. L. REV. 735, 773–774 (1991) (suggesting that "most significant contacts" language "presumably locates venue in that district within a multidistrict state in which suit was most foreseeable").

### [c] Unincorporated Associations Are Treated as Corporations

As amended in 2011, Section 1391(c) applies equally to corporations and unincorporated associations. Any entity with the capacity to sue and be sued in its common name under applicable law, whether or not incorporated, is deemed to reside, if a defendant, in any judicial district in which it is subject to the court's personal jurisdiction with respect to the civil action in question.[89] If the entity is a plaintiff, it is deemed to reside only in the judicial district in which it maintains its principal place of business.[90]

Before this amendment, federal statutes had not explicitly defined the residence of labor unions, partnerships, and other unincorporated associations for general venue purposes. This question arises in those cases in which an unincorporated association has the capacity to sue or be sued as an entity, so that it is necessary to determine the residence of the entity for purposes of the general venue statute or other venue statutes using residence as a criterion. Generally, capacity to sue or be sued is determined by the laws of the state in which the district court is located. Additionally, notwithstanding the state law, a partnership or other unincorporated association may sue or be sued as an entity for the purpose of enforcing for or against it a substantive right under the U.S. Constitution or federal laws.[91]

In the absence of an explicit statutory directive, the courts often treated unincorporated associations as analogous to corporations for the purposes of venue, and allowed suit if venue would be proper under the applicable jurisdictional statute pertaining to residence of corporations.[92] This treatment has been afforded various types of unincorporated associations, including labor unions, partnerships, limited partnerships, joint ventures, and trusts.[93]

---

[89] 28 U.S.C. § 1391(c)(2).

[90] 28 U.S.C. § 1391(c)(2).

[91] Fed. R. Civ. P. 17(b); *see generally* 4 MOORE'S FEDERAL PRACTICE Ch. 17; *Plaintiff and Defendant; Capacity; Public Officers*; *see also* Ch. 23.2, *Actions Relating to Unincorporated Associations*.

[92] *See* Denver & Rio Grande W. R.R. v. Brotherhood of R.R. Trainmen, 387 U.S. 556, 562 (1967) ("[w]e think it most nearly approximates the intent of Congress to recognize the reality of the multi-state, unincorporated association such as a labor union and to permit suit against that entity, like the analogous corporate entity, wherever it is 'doing business' "); *cf.* Carden v. Arkoma Assocs., 494 U.S. 185, 195 (1990) (for purposes of diversity jurisdiction, citizenship of unincorporated association depends on citizenship of all its members).

[93] *See* Denver & Rio Grande W. R.R. v. Brotherhood of R.R. Trainmen, 387 U.S. 556, 562 (1967) (labor union); MacCallum v. New York Yankees P'ship, 392 F. Supp. 2d 259, 262–264 (D. Conn. 2005) (limited partnership was treated as "corporation" for purposes of 28 U.S.C. § 1391(c), and considered to be resident of forum district because it could be served there); Kingsepp v. Wesleyan Univ., 763 F. Supp. 22, 28 (S.D.N.Y. 1991) (Dartmouth College, created as charitable trust, was treated as corporation and its residence was determined under § 1391(c)); Penrod Drilling Co. v. Johnson, 414 F.2d 1217, 1222–1224 (5th Cir. 1969) (Jones Act case extending Brotherhood of R.R. Trainmen rule to partnerships, and suggesting that other unincorporated associations, such as agricultural societies, co-ops, banking associations, charitable associations, news associations, and religious societies, should be treated this way); Decker Coal Co. v. Commonwealth Edison Co., 805 F.2d 834, 841–842 (9th Cir. 1986) (residence of joint venture between two corporations was joint venture's principal place of business).

When Congress amended Section 1391(c) in 2011 to clarify residency rules, it may have inadvertently omitted one clarification. Section 1391(c) deals with the residence of any entity. Section 1391(d) discusses residency of corporations in multidistrict states. It would have been preferable for Congress to provide the same residence rule for corporations and other entities in Section 1391(d) as well as in Section 1391(c). Perhaps Congress intends for the rules discussed above as well as Section 1391(c)'s approach to apply when determining the residence of unincorporated entities for purposes of venue in multidistrict states.

### [5] Personal Jurisdiction for Residence Purposes Must Be Determined With Respect to the Civil Action in Question

Under Section 1391(c) as amended in 2011, an entity that is a defendant resides where it is subject to personal jurisdiction "with respect to the civil action in question."[94]

Before it was amended in 2011, Section 1391(c) provided that a corporation was deemed to reside in any judicial district in which the corporation was subject to personal jurisdiction "at the time the action is commenced." This language was omitted in the 2011 revision. This omission probably was not intended to work a significant change.

## § 8.04 DISTRICT WHERE SUBSTANTIAL PART OF EVENTS OR OMISSIONS OCCURRED IS DETERMINED BY FACTS OF CASE

Under the general venue statute as amended in 1990, venue is proper in any district in which "a substantial part of the events or omissions giving rise to the claim occurred."[95] Before the amendment, this statute allowed venue in "the judicial district . . . in which the claim arose." The 1990 amendment, which had long been recommended by the American Law Institute, avoids the phrase "in which the claim arose," which was thought to be litigation breeding, and clarifies that it is not necessary to identify a single location in cases in which substantial parts of the underlying events occurred in more than one district.[96]

---

[94] 28 U.S.C. § 1391(c)(2).

[95] 28 U.S.C. § 1391(b)(2).

[96] H.R. Rep. No. 101-734, at 23 (1990). *See* Gulf Ins. Co. v. Glasbrenner, 417 F.3d 353, 355–358 (2d Cir. 2005) (statute permits venue in multiple judicial districts as long as "a substantial part" of underlying events took place in those districts); Mitrano v. Hawes, 377 F.3d 402, 405–406 (4th Cir. 2004) (court rejected "weight of the contacts" test because 1990 venue amendment permits venue in more than one judicial district); First of Mich. Corp. v. Bramlet, 141 F.3d 260 (6th Cir. 1998) (Sixth Circuit reversed dismissal on improper venue grounds after de novo review, because district court used incorrect venue standard. Under the 1990 amendments to statute, which were designed to broaden the number of places where venue might be proper, it is no longer necessary to find "the" district where the most activity occurred, but rather any district in which any substantial part of case arose); Woodke v. Dahm, 70 F.3d 983, 985 (8th Cir. 1995) ("The statute does not posit a single appropriate district for venue; venue may be proper in any of a number of districts, provided only that a substantial part of the events giving rise to the claim occurred there"); Jenkins Brick Co. v. Bremer, 321 F.3d 1366, 1371 (11th Cir. 2003) ("The new language thus contemplates some cases in which venue will be proper in two or more districts.").

Before the 1990 amendment, in *LeRoy v. Great Western United Corp.*, the Supreme Court had indicated that a claim might arise in more than one district only in unusual cases. The court identified various factors to be considered in determining the locus of a claim, including availability of witnesses and evidence and the convenience of the defendant.[97] Because it is no longer necessary to determine the best venue, these factors that compare venues will have less significance.[98]

Instead, the statutory language requires the court to determine the locus of any substantial part of the events or omissions on which the claim is based.[99] "Substantiality," for this purpose, is more a qualitative than a quantitative inquiry. Courts measure it by assessing the overall nature of the plaintiff's claims and the nature of the specific events or omissions in the forum, and not by simply adding up the number of contacts.[100] In making its determination, the court ought not focus solely on the matters that gave rise to the filing of the action, but rather should look at the entire progression of the underlying claim.[101] For example, in contract cases, courts must consider not only the place of performance but all relevant events such

---

[97] LeRoy v. Great W. United Corp., 443 U.S. 173, 185 (1979) ("[T]he broadest interpretation of the language of § 1391(b) that is even arguably acceptable is that in the unusual case in which it is not clear that the claim arose in only one specific district, a plaintiff may choose between those two (or conceivably even more) districts that with approximately equal plausibility — in terms of the availability of witnesses, the accessibility of other relevant evidence, and the convenience of the defendant (but not of the plaintiff) — may be assigned as the locus of the claim").

[98] Estate of Himoud Saed Abtan v. Blackwater Lodge & Training Ctr., 611 F. Supp. 2d 1, 8 (D.D.C. 2009) (no longer appropriate to ask which district is "best" venue or which has most significant connection to claim; rather, proper question is whether forum has substantial connection to claim, whether or not other forums had greater contacts); Bates v. C & S. Adjusters, Inc., 980 F.2d 865, 867 (2d Cir. 1992) ("Since the new statute does not, as a general matter, require the District Court to determine the best venue, these [*LeRoy*] factors will be of less significance"); Employers Mut. Cas. Co. v. Bartile Roofs, Inc., 618 F.3d 1153, 1165–1166 (10th Cir. 2010) (venue is not limited to district with the *most* substantial events or omissions; statute contemplates that venue may be appropriate in more than one district provided substantial part of underlying events took place in each of those districts; citing MOORE'S FEDERAL PRACTICE); Uffner v. La Reunion Francaise, S.A., 244 F.3d 38, 41–43 (1st Cir. 2001) (in determining whether location is "substantial," court must look to entire sequence of events underlying claim, rather than try to identify single triggering event).

[99] First of Mich. Corp. v. Bramlet, 141 F.3d 260, 263 (6th Cir. 1998) (general venue statute permits plaintiff to file case in any forum with substantial connection to plaintiff's claim); Gulf Ins. Co. v. Glasbrenner, 417 F.3d 353, 355–358 (2d Cir. 2005) (district courts must take adjective "substantial" seriously; significant events or omissions material to plaintiff's claim must have occurred in district in question, even if other material events occurred elsewhere); Uffner v. La Reunion Francaise, S.A., 244 F.3d 38, 41–43 (1st Cir. 2001) (in suit alleging bad faith insurance claim resulting from loss of vessel, jurisdiction where loss occurred was "substantial" for venue purposes); Estate of Himoud Saed Abtan v. Blackwater Lodge & Training Ctr., 611 F. Supp. 2d 1, 8 (D.D.C. 2009) (in case involving claims by Iraqis under Alien Tort Claims Act against government contractor security firm operating in Iraq, firm's federal contracts did not create "substantial connection" with District of Columbia as they were only tangentially connected to claims; nor did existence of congressional and criminal investigations, in District of Columbia, into firm's activities in Iraq create any connection between claims and forum).

[100] *See* Daniel v. American Bd. of Emergency Med., 428 F.3d 408, 431–435 (2d Cir. 2005) (whether events or omissions constitute "substantial part" of events or omissions giving rise to claim is not quantitative but is to be decided by considering nexus between events or omissions and nature of claims).

[101] Uffner v. La Reunion Francaise, S.A., 244 F.3d 38, 41–43 (1st Cir. 2001) (court must look to entire sequence of events underlying claim, rather than try to identify single triggering event); Mitrano v. Hawes, 377 F.3d 402, 405–406 (4th Cir. 2004) (court should no longer focus only on those matters that are in dispute or that directly led to action, but should review entire sequence of events underlying claim to

as where the contract was negotiated or executed, where the alleged breach occurred, and where the alleged harm occurred, in order to determine whether some substantial part of these events occurred in the forum state.[102]

## § 8.05 VENUE MUST BE PROPER FOR EACH JOINED CAUSE OF ACTION

Generally, when multiple causes of action are joined, venue must be established for each separate cause of action.[103] This rule would appear to create a problem for much modern multi-claim and multi-party litigation. There is no real problem, however, because since early in the twentieth century, the courts have interpreted the meaning of a cause of action broadly. The Federal Rules of Civil Procedure provide for the pleading of claims.[104] Since *Hurn v. Oursler* was decided in 1933, factually interrelated claims have been considered to be one cause of action with two or more grounds of relief. If venue is proper for one ground, this will support adjudication of the related ground.[105]

As an additional or alternative rationale for allowing venue over joined causes of actions, courts have relied on a theory of "pendent" venue analogous to the pendent jurisdiction doctrine (now called supplemental jurisdiction, *see* Ch. 5).[106]

---

determine if venue is proper); Employers Mut. Cas. Co. v. Bartile Roofs, Inc., 618 F.3d 1153, 1166 (10th Cir. 2010) (court should look to entire progression of events underlying claim; quoting Moore's Federal Practice); Estate of Himoud Saed Abtan v. Blackwater Lodge & Training Ctr., 611 F. Supp. 2d 1, 8 (D.D.C. 2009) (court should not focus only on those matters that are in dispute or that directly lead to filing of action, but should review entire sequence of events underlying claim).

[102] *See, e.g.*, Kirkpatrick v. Rays Group, 71 F. Supp. 2d 204, 212 (W.D.N.Y. 1999) (when complaint is based on contract dispute, courts consider variety of factors in determining whether venue is proper, including (1) where contract was negotiated or executed; (2) where contract was to be performed; (3) where alleged breach occurred; and (4) where alleged harm occurred); Mitrano v. Hawes, 377 F.3d 402, 405–406 (4th Cir. 2004) (work performed under contract constituted "substantial part" of events giving rise to claim for breach of contract); *see also* Gulf Ins. Co. v. Glasbrenner, 417 F.3d 353, 355–358 (2d Cir. 2005) (Second Circuit explicitly declined to decide whether negotiation and issuance of contract in given judicial district, standing alone, would be sufficient to lay venue in that district).

[103] *See* Beattie v. United States, 756 F.2d 91, 100 (D.C. Cir. 1984).

[104] Fed. R. Civ. P. 8(a).

[105] *See* Hurn v. Oursler, 289 U.S. 238, 245–246 (1933) (factually interrelated copyright and unfair competition claims were same cause of action); General Foods Corp v. Carnation Co., 411 F.2d 528, 531–532 (7th Cir. 1969) (multiple claims on single patent all relating to same subject matter were one cause of action: "To hold as Carnation would have us do would create an intolerable situation. It would mean that an action for patent infringement in a situation such as we have here would be tried piecemeal, some claims in one jurisdiction and others in another. Confusion would be engendered and a multiplicity of suits invited"); Beattie v. United States, 756 F.2d 91, 101 (D.C. Cir. 1984) (negligence claims against federal officials in Washington and against Navy air traffic controllers in Antarctica constituted one cause of action).

[106] *See* 18 U.S.C. § 1367; *see* Travis v. Anthes Imperial Ltd., 473 F.2d 515, 528–529 (8th Cir. 1973) (When venue is proper on federal claims, it is also proper on pendent state claims); Solow Bldg. Co. v. ATC Assocs. Inc., 175 F. Supp. 2d 465, 469–470 (S.D.N.Y. 2001) (court could exercise pendent venue over one claim when that claim was factually related to second claim for which venue was proper, and second claim was primary claim); Hsin Ten Enter. USA, Inc. v. Clark Enters., 138 F. Supp. 2d 449, 462 (S.D.N.Y. 2000) (pendent venue permitted over patent claims when related trademark claim was properly venued and was substantial or primary claim, and exercise of pendent venue would result in judicial efficiency

## § 8.06 COUNTERCLAIMS, CROSS-CLAIMS, AND THIRD-PARTY CLAIMS NOT AFFECTED BY VENUE RULES

The venue statutes govern where an action may be instituted initially. They have no application to new claims against existing parties, including counterclaims, cross-claims, or claims in intervention. This can be seen from a literal reading of the venue statutes, which typically speak in terms of where an action "may be brought."[107] In the same manner, third-party claims joining new parties need not meet venue requirements because they are regarded as ancillary to the existing suit.[108] Of course, if the plaintiff files an amended complaint adding additional parties or claims, venue rules must be satisfied for that complaint and satisfied with respect to each named defendant.

## § 8.07 CLASS ACTIONS: VENUE DETERMINED AS TO NAMED PARTIES

Venue in class actions is determined by the same statutes that would apply if the action were not a class action. Venue is proper if the statutory requirements are met with respect to the named parties. Members of the class other than the representative party or parties need not be considered. Class actions are discussed in detail in 5 Moore's Federal Practice Ch. 23, *Class Actions* (Matthew Bender 3d ed.).

## § 8.08 ACTION IS REMOVED TO DISTRICT IN WHICH STATE COURT ACTION PENDING

Under the general removal statute, a civil action brought in state court may, if original jurisdiction over the action exists in the federal district courts, be removed by the defendant or defendants to the U.S. district court for the district and division embracing the place where the state action is pending.[109] This provision controls venue for removed actions; the venue statutes that would have applied had the action been brought originally in federal court are not applicable.[110] After removal, however, the action may be transferred to another district under the venue transfer

---

and convenience to parties and would avoid piecemeal litigation); High River Ltd. Partnership v. Mylan Labs., Inc., 353 F. Supp. 2d 487, 493–494 (M.D. Pa. 2005) (citing Moore's Federal Practice; under pendent venue doctrine, which borrows largely from principles of supplemental jurisdiction, venue exists when pendent claims arise out of same operative facts as main claims for which venue is already established); SEC v. Bilzerian, 378 F.3d 1100, 1107 (D.C. Cir. 2004) (when ancillary jurisdiction exists over claim, venue is proper); *see also* Ch. 5, *Supplemental Jurisdiction.*

[107] *See* Beattie v. United States, 756 F.2d 91, 100 (D.C. Cir. 1984).

[108] Lone Star Package Car Co. v. Baltimore & O. R. Co., 212 F.2d 147, 152 (5th Cir. 1954) (third-party claim is ancillary to main suit and therefore venue is not required); United States v. Acord, 209 F.2d 709, 713–714 (10th Cir. 1954) (third-party defendant may be brought in without regard to venue, because venue in ancillary proceeding rests on venue in main proceeding).

[109] 28 U.S.C. § 1441(a); *see generally* Ch. 6, *Removal.*

[110] Polizzi v. Cowles Magazines, Inc., 345 U.S. 663, 665–666 (1953) (whether corporation was "doing business" in district for purposes of former version of 28 U.S.C. § 1391(c) was irrelevant, since action was removed to proper district as specified by 28 U.S.C. § 1441(a)); *see, e.g.*, Hartford Fire Ins. Co. v. Westinghouse Elec. Corp., 725 F. Supp. 317, 320 (S.D. Miss. 1989).

statutes.[111] Also, if the plaintiff files an amended complaint in federal court adding new claims or new defendants after removal, venue must be proper with respect to the new claims or new defendants under the applicable general or special venue provision.[112] The reason for this is that the amended complaint will be treated as a new action, and a determination must be made as to whether venue would have been proper there in the first place.

---

[111] *See* 28 U.S.C. §§ 1404, 1406; Bentz v. Recile, 778 F.2d 1026, 1028 (5th Cir. 1985) (transfer to district where personal jurisdiction was available was proper under 28 U.S.C. § 1404 allowing transfer to more convenient forum); Mortensen v. Wheel Horse Products, Inc., 772 F. Supp. 85, 89–91 (N.D.N.Y. 1991) (transfer was proper under 28 U.S.C. § 1406 when action was removed to wrong district); *see generally* Ch. 9, *Change of Venue*.

[112] *See* Freeman v. Bee Machine Co., 319 U.S. 448, 457 (1943).

# Chapter 9

# CHANGE OF VENUE

## PART A
## SIGNIFICANCE OF DIFFERENCES IN TRANSFER OR DISMISSAL DEVICES

### § 9.01 OVERVIEW OF STATUTORY TRANSFER AND COMMON LAW DISMISSAL DEVICES

Over the last several decades, Congress has amended the general venue statute several times (*see* § 8.01[1]).[1] The thrust of these amendments has been to expand significantly the options available to plaintiffs seeking the best federal forum for bringing suit. Congress and the courts have provided several devices that may be used to have an action transferred or dismissed when the plaintiff chooses a relatively inconvenient forum:

- *Section 1404(a) convenience transfer.* The court may transfer an action based on the convenience transfer statute, Section 1404(a) (*see* §§ 9.02–9.06).[2] In many cases, a plaintiff will choose to file a civil action in a federal district court in which venue is proper, but which is inconvenient to some or all of the parties and witnesses involved. For example, the plaintiff may choose to file an action in a proper but inconvenient federal district court because he or she believes that the result that would be obtained there would be better, because of choice of law or other considerations. The liberalized provisions in the general venue statute, together with the Supreme Court's approach to personal jurisdiction matters (pursuant to which the Court focuses primarily on the defendant's purposeful contacts with the forum state, and rarely focuses on convenience factors),[3] make it relatively easy for a plaintiff to engage in forum

---

[1] *See* 28 U.S.C. § 1391; *see generally* 17 Moore's Federal Practice Ch. 110, *Determination of Proper Venue* (Matthew Bender 3d ed.).

[2] 28 U.S.C. § 1404(a).

[3] *Compare* Burger King Corp. v. Rudzewicz, 471 U.S. 462, 472–476 (1985) (focusing on defendants' purposeful contacts with forum and looking to convenience transfer statute as basis for curing inconvenience) *with* Asahi v. Superior Court, 480 U.S. 102, 113–116 (1987) (only case in which Supreme Court found forum state lacked jurisdiction because of the fairness factors, as opposed to a defendant's lack of purposeful contacts with the forum state); *see also* Daimler AG v. Bauman, 134 S. Ct. 746, 187 L. Ed. 2d 624 (2014) (rejecting assertion of general jurisdiction over German corporation based on contacts of its subsidiary); Walden v. Fiore, 134 S. Ct. 1115, 188 L. Ed. 2d 12 (2014) (the inquiry into the "minimum

shopping. Thus, the need for a convenience-based transfer mechanism is apparent.

- *Section 1406(a) improper venue transfer.* When an action is brought in a district court in which venue is improper, the court may either dismiss the action or it may transfer the action to a federal district or division in which it could have been brought.[4] For example, if the plaintiff files in a district court in which venue is improper, Section 1406(a) provides for the cure of the defect in the court's discretion (*see* §§ 9.07–9.13).[5]
- *Section 1631 transfer.* If a plaintiff files in a federal district court that lacks jurisdiction typically because a federal statute vests exclusive subject matter jurisdiction over a particular category of cases or appeals in another federal court, Section 1631 provides for transfer to that federal court (*see* §§ 9.14–9.15).[6]
- *Transfer of multidistrict litigation.* The Judicial Panel on Multidistrict Litigation may transfer related civil actions pending in a number of federal district courts for coordinated or consolidated pretrial proceedings.[7] This topic is discussed in Ch. 10, *Multidistrict Litigation.*
- *Forum non conveniens dismissal.* Even if the plaintiff files in an appropriate federal court, if there is no federal district to which the action can or should be transferred, as, for example, when the facts suggest that the better forum is a court in a foreign country, then, and only then, may the common law doctrine of *forum non conveniens* be invoked, and in appropriate cases the action will be dismissed (*see* §§ 9.18–9.26).

Important consequences flow from the use of the transfer or dismissal devices. Thus, it is important for a party to determine which statute or doctrine the court is likely to invoke so that he or she can better evaluate whether the motion is likely to succeed, and whether those consequences are desirable for that party.

---

contacts" necessary to create specific jurisdiction focuses "on the relationship among the defendant, the forum, and the litigation.", quoting Keeton v. Hustler Magazine, Inc., 465 U. S. 770 (1984)); Hanson v. Denckla, 357 U.S. 235, 253–54 (1958), World Wide Volkswagen Corp. v. Woodson, 444 U.S. 286, 298 (1980); *see generally* 16 MOORE'S FEDERAL PRACTICE Ch. 108, *Territorial Jurisdiction: Jurisdiction over Persons and Property* (Matthew Bender 3d ed.).

[4] 28 U.S.C. § 1406(a).

[5] 28 U.S.C. § 1406(a).

[6] 28 U.S.C. § 1631.

[7] 28 U.S.C. § 1407.

# PART B
# TRANSFER WHEN VENUE IS PROPER BUT INCONVENIENT

## § 9.02 PURPOSE OF SECTION 1404(a) CONVENIENCE TRANSFER

Recognizing that the "broad venue provisions in federal Acts often resulted in inconvenient forums," Congress intended Section 1404(a) to remedy this situation by authorizing easy transfer of actions to a more convenient federal forum.[8] This transfer statute has a broad remedial purpose: "to prevent the waste 'of time, energy and money' and 'to protect litigants, witnesses and the public against unnecessary inconvenience and expense.' "[9] To the extent there is an alternative federal forum, the district court lacks the power to dismiss.[10]

Thus, under Section 1404(a), even though venue is proper in the court in which the plaintiff brought the action, in general the court is empowered to transfer the action to another federal forum if two requirements are met:

- The court must determine that transfer of the action will enhance the convenience of the parties and witnesses, and is in the interest of justice (*see* § 9.04).[11]
- The proposed transferee district must be one in which the action "might have been brought" originally (*see* § 9.03),[12] or to which all parties have consented (*see* § 9.03[1][a]).[13]

---

[8] Ferens v. John Deere Co., 494 U.S. 516, 522 (1990); Piper Aircraft Co. v. Reyno, 454 U.S. 235, 254 (1981) (Section 1404(a) enacted to allow "easy change of venue"); Van Dusen v. Barrack, 376 U.S. 612, 616 (1964) (Section 1404(a) "reflects an increased desire to have federal civil suits tried in the federal system at the place called for in the particular case by considerations of convenience and justice").

[9] 376 U.S. at 616, *quoting* Continental Grain Co. v. Barge FBL-585, 364 U.S. 19, 26 (1960).

[10] Bacon v. Liberty Mut. Ins. Co., 575 F.3d 781, 783 (8th Cir. 2009) (district court erred when it dismissed suit believing either state or federal courts in Nebraska to be more appropriate forum).

[11] 376 U.S. at 615; *In re* Joint Eastern & Southern Dists. Asbestos Litigation, 22 F.3d 755, 762 (7th Cir. 1994).

[12] Van Dusen v. Barrack, 376 U.S. 612, 634 (1964) ("This transfer power is, however, expressly limited by the final clause of Section 1404(a) restricting transfer to those federal districts in which the action 'might have been brought' ").

[13] 28 U.S.C. § 1404(a) (civil action may be transferred "to any district or division to which all parties have consented").

## § 9.03 TRANSFEREE COURT MUST BE ONE IN WHICH ACTION "MIGHT HAVE BEEN BROUGHT" OR TO WHICH ALL PARTIES CONSENT

### [1] Requirements for Transferee Court

#### [a] Transferee Court Must Have Proper Venue, Subject Matter, and Personal Jurisdiction

Under Section 1404(a), assuming the other requirements for convenience transfer are met, a district court may transfer an action "to any other district or division where it might have been brought."[14] The Supreme Court in *Hoffman v. Blaski* interpreted the quoted language to mean that the proposed transferee district must be one in which the plaintiff properly could have filed the action initially.[15] Accordingly, the transferor court may not transfer an action unless it first determines that, at the time the action was originally filed, (1) venue would have been proper in the proposed transferee district;[16] (2) the transferee court would have had subject-matter jurisdiction;[17] and (3) the transferee court could have exercised personal jurisdiction over the defendants.[18] Alternatively, a district court may transfer an action to any district or division if all the parties consent (*see* § 9.03[1][b]).

#### [b] Transfer to Any District Possible Based on Consent of All Parties

A court may transfer a civil action under Section 1404(a) to any other district or division to which all parties have consented.[19] This authority exists whether or not the other district or division is one where the action "might have been brought." Consent transfer is possible only when all parties agree and only if the court finds that transfer would be for the convenience of the parties and witnesses and in the interest of justice.[20] The language allowing transfer to be based on consent was added by amendment in 2011.[21] At the same time, Section 1404(d) was amended to provide that transfers to the District Court of Guam, the District Court for the

---

[14] 28 U.S.C. § 1404(a).

[15] Hoffman v. Blaski, 363 U.S. 335, 343–344 (1960).

[16] 363 U.S. at 343 (denying transfer when venue not proper in transferee court).

[17] Bacik v. Peek, 888 F. Supp. 1405, 1413 (N.D. Ohio 1993) (Section 1404(a) permits transfer to court with proper venue, personal, and subject matter jurisdiction); Packer v. Kaiser Foundation Health Plan, 728 F. Supp. 8, 11 (D.D.C. 1989) (transferee court must have subject matter jurisdiction, proper venue, and personal jurisdiction over defendant).

[18] Hoffman v. Blaski, 363 U.S. 335, 343–344 (1960).

[19] 28 U.S.C. § 1404(a).

[20] 28 U.S.C. § 1404(a); *see* H.R. Rep. No. 112-10, at 24, 112th Cong. 1st Sess. (2011).

[21] *See* Pub. L. No. 112-63, §§ 204, 205, 125 Stat. 758 (2011) (change effective Jan. 6, 2012, and applicable to any action commenced in federal district court on or after that date, and to any action removed from state court that had been commenced, within meaning of state law, in state court on or after that date).

Northern Mariana Islands, or the District Court of the Virgin Islands are not permitted under Section 1404(a).[22] This change was thought necessary to clarify that the amendment allowing consent transfer was not intended to allow transfer of an action from an Article III district court to a territorial district court lacking Article III status.[23]

Before the statutory change, courts could not consider the defendant's consent to the transferee venue because transfer was authorized only to a court where the action "might have been brought." In *Hoffman v. Blaski*, the Supreme Court ruled that a lack of proper venue in the proposed transferee district precluded transfer. The court went on to state that transfer was unauthorized on the additional ground that the transferee court could not have asserted personal jurisdiction over the defendant at the time the action was initially filed. The rationale for this decision was to prevent giving the defendant the power to unilaterally defeat the plaintiff's privilege of selecting venue.[24] Critics of the decision, however, pointed out that it overstated the defendant's ability to defeat the plaintiff's privilege of selecting the forum, noting that the determination whether to transfer ultimately is resolved by the court based on considerations of convenience and fairness, and is not within the defendant's control.[25] Nevertheless, lower courts were required to follow *Hoffman v. Blaski's* rule that the transferee court must have personal jurisdiction independent of the defendant's consent, until this rule was partially abrogated by the 2011 amendment.[26] Yet, *Hoffman's* rational of avoiding giving defendants the ability to unilaterally deprive plaintiffs of their chosen forum is preserved by requiring that all parties consent to transfer.

### [2] Options When Venue in Proposed Transferee Court Is Proper as to Some Defendants and Not as to Others

When one or more defendants as to whom venue would not have been proper in the transferee district are "alleged to be only indirectly connected" to the events that form the main subject matter of the action, the court in which the action was

---

22 *See* 28 U.S.C. § 1404(d).

23 *See* H.R. Rep. No. 112-10, at 24, 112th Cong. 1st Sess. (2011).

24 Transfer was not allowed if transferee court lacked personal jurisdiction over defendant at time of filing. Hoffman v. Blaski, 363 U.S. 335, 342–344 (1960).

25 Convenience and fairness factors control transfer. *See* Hoffman v. Blaski, 363 U.S. 335, 363 (1960) (Frankfurter, J., dissenting); Schertenleib v. Traum, 589 F.2d 1156, 1163 (2d Cir. 1978) (noting criticism and refusing to extend *Hoffman v. Blaski* to context of motion to dismiss on forum non conveniens ground).

26 Defendant's consent to personal jurisdiction was not enough. *2d Circuit. See, e.g.*, Morales v. Navieras de Puerto Rico, 713 F. Supp. 711, 712 (S.D.N.Y. 1989); Alexander & Alexander v. Donald F. Muldoon & Co., 685 F. Supp. 346, 349–350 (S.D.N.Y. 1988). *3d Circuit. See, e.g.*, Sunbelt Corp. v. Noble, Denton & Associates, Inc., 5 F.3d 28, 32–33 (3d Cir. 1993). *5th Circuit. But see* Liaw Su Teng v. Skaarup Shipping Corp., 743 F.2d 1140, 1148–1149 (5th Cir. 1984) (transfer permitted when objecting defendant earlier had "effectively consented to venue and personal jurisdiction" in transferee court). *9th Circuit. See, e.g.*, Commercial Lighting Prods., Inc. v. United States Dist. Court, 537 F.2d 1078, 1079 (9th Cir. 1976). *10th Circuit. See, e.g.*, Chrysler Credit Corp. v. Country Chrysler, Inc., 928 F.2d 1509, 1515 (10th Cir. 1991) ("Section 1404(a) does not allow a court to transfer a suit to a district which lacks personal jurisdiction over the defendants, even if they consent to suit [there]").

originally brought has discretion to sever the claims against these defendants and transfer the action against the remaining defendants to the more convenient forum.[27] In such an instance, if "the administration of justice would be materially advanced by severance and transfer," the court in which the action originally was brought may sever under Rule 21 even properly joined claims, thus creating two separate actions, to permit transfer of the one while retaining jurisdiction of the other.[28] "Otherwise, a plaintiff could preclude the court from considering whether transfer would serve the interest of justice by including a defendant, not subject to suit in the more convenient district, who was in some manner peripherally involved in the alleged wrongdoing."[29]

However, the court should deny severance of the claims against one or more defendants as to whom venue would not have been proper in the proposed transferee court when these defendants are so involved in the transactions at issue in the action that the transfer of the claims against the other defendants "would require the same issues to be litigated in two places."[30]

### [3] Party Moving for Transfer Has Burden of Proving Transferee Court Proper

The party seeking transfer (usually the moving party is a defendant) has the burden of establishing the requisites for convenience transfers, including the burden of clearly establishing that the action properly could have been brought in the first instance in the transferee district unless all parties have consented to transfer.[31]

---

[27] Wyndham Associates v. Bintliff, 398 F.2d 614, 618 (2d Cir. 1968); *see* Carver v. Knox County, Tenn., 887 F.2d 1287, 1293 (6th Cir. 1989) (citing *Wyndham Associates*, severing claims against certain defendants and transferring them to another district).

[28] Wyndham Associates v. Bintliff, 398 F.2d 614, 618 (2d Cir. 1968); *see* Fed. R. Civ. P. 21; *see generally* 4 MOORE'S FEDERAL PRACTICE Chapter 21, *Misjoinder and Nonjoinder of Parties* (Matthew Bender 3d ed.).

[29] *See* 398 F.2d at 619.

[30] Sunbelt Corp. v. Noble, Denton & Associates, Inc., 5 F.3d 28, 33–34 (3d Cir. 1993) (severance and transfer denied when co-defendants attributed cause of plaintiff's injury to each other's negligence).

[31] Shutte v. Armco Steel Corporation, 431 F.2d 22, 24–25 (3d Cir. 1970) (transfer was abuse of discretion when substantial doubt existed as to whether transferee court would have had personal jurisdiction); Volkswagen de Mexico, S.A. v. Germanischer Lloyd, 768 F. Supp. 1023, 1029 (S.D.N.Y. 1991) ("party seeking transfer bears the burden of establishing personal jurisdiction over the defendants in the transferee forum").

# § 9.04 TRANSFER MUST BE BASED ON "CONVENIENCE OF PARTIES AND WITNESSES, IN THE INTEREST OF JUSTICE"

## [1] Courts Apply Flexible and Discretionary Analysis

The decision as to whether transfer is warranted under Section 1404(a), assuming the threshold requirements relating to the proposed transferee forum are met, lies within the broad discretion of the district court.[32] Resolution of the transfer motion thus requires the court to make a "flexible and individualized analysis," and to "weigh in the balance a number of case-specific factors" to determine whether the proposed transferee district would be a more convenient forum for the litigation.[33]

## [2] List of Factors to Be Considered

When considering a Section 1404(a) convenience transfer motion, the court must determine that transfer of the action will accomplish the following statutory requirements:[34]

1. Enhance the convenience of the parties;
2. Enhance the convenience of the witnesses; and
3. Be in the interest of justice.

In addition to these three statutory elements, the courts consider a variety of other factors thought to have a bearing on the determination.[35] While there is no definitive list of factors that must be considered, courts typically look to some or all of the following "public" and "private" interest factors to determine whether the proposed alternative forum would better serve the convenience and interest of justice requirements:

- The plaintiff's original choice of forum;

---

[32] Reese v. CNH America LLC, 574 F.3d 315, 320 (6th Cir. 2009) (district courts have broad discretion to determine when convenience or interest of justice make transfer appropriate), Reversed by, remanded by: Reese v. CNH Am. LLC, 694 F.3d 681, 2012 U.S. App. LEXIS 19207, 2012 FED App. 331P (6th Cir.), 2012 FED App. 0331P (6th Cir.), 54 Employee Benefits Cas. (BNA) 1077, 194 L.R.R.M. (BNA) 2006 (6th Cir. Mich. 2012); Ventress v. Japan Airlines, 486 F.3d 1111, 1118 (9th Cir. 2007); Filmline (Cross-Country) Productions, Inc. v. United Artists Corp., 865 F.2d 513, 520 (2d Cir. 1989); *see* 28 U.S.C. § 1404(a); Jarvis Christian College v. Exxon Corp., 845 F.2d 523, 528 (5th Cir. 1988); Cote v. Wadel, 796 F.2d 981, 984 (7th Cir. 1986).

[33] Stewart Org., Inc. v. Ricoh Corp., 487 U.S. 22, 29 (1988); Ventress v. Japan Airlines, 486 F.3d 1111, 1118 (9th Cir. 2007) ("Weighing of the factors for and against transfer involves subtle considerations and is best left to the discretion of the trial judge.").

[34] 28 U.S.C. § 1404(a); Van Dusen v. Barrack, 376 U.S. 612, 616 (1964).

[35] Jumara v. State Farm Ins. Co., 55 F.3d 873, 879 (3d Cir. 1995) ("courts have not limited their consideration to the three enumerated factors [in Section 1404(a)]"); Coffey v. Van Dorn Iron Works, 796 F.2d 217, 220 (7th Cir. 1986) (three statutory factors "are best viewed as placeholders for a broader set of considerations"). *See* 17 Moore's Federal Practice Ch. 111, § 111.13 for a complete discussion of all factors.

- Where the events at issue in the lawsuit ("the operative events") took place;
- The convenience of the parties;
- The convenience of the witnesses;
- The comparative availability of compulsory process to compel the attendance of unwilling witnesses;
- The location of the physical evidence;
- The enforceability of the judgment;
- In which forum the case can be tried more inexpensively and expeditiously;
- The relative court congestion in the two forums;
- The public interest in local adjudication of local controversies;
- The relative familiarity of the courts with the applicable law;
- Whether transfer is in the "interest of justice";
- Which forum would better serve judicial economy; and
- Whether a contractual clause specifies a specific forum to resolve contractual disputes.

These factors are generally the same as those to be considered on a motion to dismiss under the common law doctrine of forum non conveniens, which are laid out in *Gulf Oil Co. v. Gilbert* and *Piper Aircraft Co. v. Reyno* (*see* § 9.21[2][b]).[36]

## [3] Convenience Factors

When considering these factors, it is axiomatic that the plaintiff's choice of forum is given significant weight and will not be disturbed unless the other factors weigh substantially in favor of transfer.[37] It is clear, however, that Section 1404(a) motions to transfer venue, although derived from the common-law doctrine of dismissal for forum non conveniens require that less weight be given to the plaintiff's choice of forum than was received under the common law doctrine.[38] The weight accorded to plaintiff's choice of forum may depend on various

[36] *See* Gulf Oil Co. v. Gilbert, 330 U.S. 501, 508 (1947); Piper Aircraft Co. v. Reyno, 454 U.S. 235, 250 (1981).

[37] *See, e.g.*, *In re* Volkswagen of Am., Inc., 545 F.3d 304, 314–315 (5th Cir. 2008) (mandamus granted directing district court to transfer case when district court erroneously applied stricter forum non conveniens standard); Employers Mut. Cas. Co. v. Bartile Roofs, Inc., 618 F.3d 1153, 1167 (10th Cir. 2010) (plaintiff's choice of forum should rarely be disturbed unless balance of factors is "strongly in favor of the movant"); *In re* Warrick, 70 F.3d 736, 740 (2d Cir. 1995) (plaintiff's choice of forum "entitled to substantial consideration"); Jumara v. State Farm Ins. Co., 55 F.3d 873, 879 (3d Cir. 1995) ("courts normally defer to a plaintiff's choice of forum"); Schexnider v. McDermott Int'l, Inc., 817 F.2d 1159,1162 (5th Cir. 1987) ("plaintiff's choice of forum should rarely be disturbed").

[38] *See, e.g.*, Employers Mut. Cas. Co. v. Bartile Roofs, Inc., 618 F.3d 1153, 1167–1168 n.13 (10th Cir. 2010) (noting that § 1404 was intended to revise common law and that courts therefore enjoy greater discretion to transfer case pursuant to § 1404 than to dismiss action based on forum non conveniens); *In re* Volkswagen of Am., Inc., 545 F.3d 304, 314–315 (5th Cir. 2008); Norwood v. Kirkpatrick, 349 U.S. 29, 32 (1955) (although plaintiff's choice of forum is still a factor to be considered, Section 1404(a) transfers

circumstances. For example, the weight given to the plaintiff's choice may be lessened in declaratory judgment actions in which the plaintiff has filed a preemptive action in order to deprive the "natural plaintiff" of its choice of forum.[39] Moreover, connections made in anticipation of litigation or with the intent of manipulating venue should not be considered in the transfer analysis. Thus, if a company establishes an office in a particular forum, or takes the step of incorporating there, and these acts are in anticipation of litigation, they do not weigh in favor of the forum.[40]

The plaintiff's choice generally is given added weight if the plaintiff resides in the chosen forum.[41] However, even if the plaintiff resides in the chosen forum, if the operative events did not take place in that district, many courts assign the plaintiff's choice of forum less weight.[42] The place where the operative events occurred often will be the place where the majority of significant witnesses and physical evidence is located, additional factors that favor transfer.

A similar significant factor is the relative convenience of the parties. The "logical starting point" for analyzing the convenience of the parties is a consideration of their residences in relation to the district chosen by the plaintiff and the proposed transferee district.[43] It is generally presumed that the most convenient district for a party to litigate in is the district of or near his or her residence.[44] Thus, when the plaintiff resides in the chosen forum and the defendant resides in the proposed

---

should be granted on " 'a lesser showing of inconvenience' than is required for dismissal under the doctrine of forum non conveniens").

39 Piedmont Hawthorne Aviation, Inc. v. TriTech Envtl. Health & Safety, Inc., 402 F. Supp. 2d 609, 616 (M.D.N.C. 2005) (strong presumption in favor of plaintiff's choice of forum is lessened in declaratory judgment action filed to deprive other party of its choice of forum).

40 *In re* Microsoft Corp., 630 F.3d 1361, 1364–1365 (Fed. Cir. 2011) (Federal Circuit granted mandamus to order Eastern District of Texas to transfer patent case to more convenient forum); *In re* Zimmer Holdings, Inc., 609 F.3d 1378, 1381 (Fed. Cir. 2010) ("Our assessment of the realities of this case makes it clear that the Eastern District of Texas is convenient only for MedIdea's litigation counsel. . . . This is a classic case where the plaintiff is attempting to game the system by artificially seeking to establish venue by sharing office space with another of the trial counsel's clients.").

41 Dwyer v. General Motors Corp., 853 F. Supp. 690, 694 (S.D.N.Y. 1994) (other factors not sufficient to justify transfer when plaintiff resided in chosen district); Apache Products Co. v. Employer Ins. of Wausau, 154 F.R.D. 650, 653 (S.D. Miss. 1994) (plaintiff's choice of forum entitled to more weight if plaintiff resides in that district).

42 *See, e.g., In re* Volkswagen of Am., Inc., 545 F.3d 304, 314–315 (5th Cir. 2008) (mandamus granted directing district court to transfer case when district court erroneously applied stricter forum non conveniens standard); IBM Credit Corp. v. Definitive Computer Services, Inc., 1996 U.S. Dist. LEXIS 2385 (N.D. Cal. Feb. 29, 1996) ("ordinarily, where the forum lacks any significant contact with the activities alleged in the complaint, plaintiff's choice of forum is given considerably less weight, even if the plaintiff is a resident of the forum"). *But see* Dwyer v. General Motors Corp., 853 F. Supp. 690, 694 (S.D.N.Y. 1994) (denying transfer from district of plaintiff's residence despite fact that operative events occurred elsewhere; denial of transfer was appropriate because even though operative events did not take place in plaintiff's chosen forum, as they also did not take place in district to which defendant sought transfer).

43 *See* U.S. Fidelity & Guar. Co. v. Republic Drug Co., Inc., 800 F. Supp. 1076, 1080 (E.D.N.Y. 1992).

44 Morales v. Navieras de Puerto Rico, 713 F. Supp. 711, 713 (S.D.N.Y. 1989) ("Because plaintiff is a resident of Puerto Rico, he does not, nor can he, seriously argue that New York is a more convenient forum [for him] than Puerto Rico").

transferee district, one or the other unavoidably will be inconvenienced whether transfer is granted or not. In such a case, generally the weight given to the plaintiff's choice of forum will tip the balance against transfer, unless the other relevant factors, such as the convenience of witnesses or the interest of justice, weigh strongly in favor of transfer.[45]

Because the convenience of the parties often cancel each other out, the convenience of witnesses has been called "the most powerful factor governing the decision to transfer a case."[46] The convenience of the witnesses also is determined by reference to their residence in relation to the district in which the action is pending and to the proposed transferee district.[47] Thus, when the majority of both parties' material witnesses are located in the district to which transfer is sought, transfer is likely to be granted even though the transfer may cause the plaintiff some inconvenience by having to litigate in a forum outside his or her home district.[48]

The convenience of expert witnesses, as opposed to fact witnesses, "is of little or no significance on a motion to transfer,"[49] although the relative cost of transporting them to the respective districts may be considered in connection with the determination as to where the action can be tried more inexpensively and expeditiously.

The materiality of the prospective witnesses' testimony, and not merely the number of prospective witnesses, will determine the extent to which their convenience will be weighed.[50] Given the importance of the convenience of

---

[45] *See In re* National Presto Indus., Inc., 347 F.3d 662, 663–665 (7th Cir. 2003) (when plaintiff and defendant are in different states, there is no choice of forum that will avoid imposing inconvenience on one or the other, but "the tie is awarded to the plaintiff"); Icon Indus. Controls Corp. v. Cimetrix, Inc., 921 F. Supp. 375, 384 (W.D. La. 1996) (denying transfer from plaintiff's residence to defendant's residence because other factors did not strongly favor transferee forum).

[46] Gundle Lining Const. Corp. v. Fireman's Fund Ins. Co., 844 F. Supp. 1163, 1166 (S.D. Tex. 1994) (relative convenience of witnesses "the most important factor"); Hernandez v. Graebel Van Lines, 761 F. Supp. 983, 990 (E.D.N.Y. 1991) (convenience of witnesses is "probably the single-most important factor in the analysis").

[47] Burstein v. Applied Extrusion Technologies, Inc. 829 F. Supp. 106, 109–112 (D. Del. 1992) (convenience of witnesses analyzed in terms of where they "work and/or reside" relative to both districts).

[48] *In re* Volkswagen of Am., Inc., 545 F.3d 304, 315–319 (5th Cir. 2008) (district court abused its discretion by not considering difference in convenience to witnesses between existing venue and proposed venue, including additional travel time, additional meal and lodging expenses, and time witnesses must be away from regular employment; mandamus granted to order district court to transfer); Burstein v. Applied Extrusion Technologies, Inc., 829 F. Supp. 106, 109–112 (D. Del. 1992) (transfer granted when majority of witnesses located in proposed transferee district); Hernandez v. Graebel Van Lines, 761 F. Supp. 983, 989 (E.D.N.Y. 1991) (when all witnesses except for plaintiff and his two treating physicians resided in district to which transfer sought, that fact weighed strongly in favor of transfer).

[49] Dwyer v. General Motors Corp., 853 F. Supp. 690, 693 (S.D.N.Y. 1994); Hernandez v. Graebel Van Lines, 761 F. Supp. 983, 989–990 (E.D.N.Y. 1991).

[50] Employers Mut. Cas. Co. v. Bartile Roofs, Inc., 618 F.3d 1153, 1169 (10th Cir. 2010) (materiality of testimony rather than number of prospective witnesses will determine weight to be given this factor; quoting Moore's Federal Practice); Scheidt v. Klein, 956 F.2d 963, 966 (10th Cir. 1992) (district court

witnesses, it is obvious that another important factor is the amenability of significant nonparty witnesses to subpoena at the respective forums.[51] Under Rule 45, a subpoena requiring the attendance of a witness at a hearing or trial may be served at any place within the district in which the hearing or trial is being held, or within 100 miles of where the witness resides, is employed, or regularly transacts business in person.[52] Thus, that the majority of material non-party witnesses may not be subject to the compulsory process of one of the courts, but are within the subpoena power of the other, militates heavily in favor of the latter district.[53]

The location of the documents and other physical evidence relevant to the dispute is a factor to be considered in the transfer convenience analysis.[54] Although this factor is usually considered in the context of securing the documents for trial, it is also relevant in terms of the ease of conducting merits-related discovery in a location that is near the pertinent documents.[55] The location of documents is a relatively less important consideration in the transfer convenience analysis, given "the comparatively low cost of transporting documents."[56] If, however, the documents at issue are voluminous,[57] or in the possession of non-party witnesses beyond the reach of the transferor court's subpoena power,[58] a transfer to the district in which the documents are located may be appropriate.[59] If a viewing of immovable physical evidence by the fact-finder is necessary, this will weigh in favor of the forum in which the evidence is located.[60] On the other hand, photographs or videotapes of the property may suffice, especially when a visual inspection is not of

must receive "some factual information relative to the materiality of witness testimony and [other relevant] considerations").

[51] *See In re* Volkswagen of Am., Inc., 545 F.3d 304, 316–317 (5th Cir. 2008) (when proper venue existed that enjoyed subpoena power for both depositions and trial, this factor weighed in favor of transfer; mandamus granted to order district court to transfer).

[52] *See* Fed. R. Civ. P. 45(c)(1)(A).

[53] *In re* Volkswagen of Am., Inc., 545 F.3d 304, 316–317 (5th Cir. 2008) (when proper venue existed that enjoyed subpoena power for both depositions and trial, this factor weighed in favor of transfer; mandamus granted to order district court to transfer); Hernandez v. Graebel Van Lines, 761 F. Supp. 983, 990 (E.D.N.Y. 1991) (when majority of witnesses were beyond subpoena power of transferor court, transfer was favored to district where these witnesses resided).

[54] *See In re* Warrick, 70 F.3d 736, 741 (2d Cir. 1995); Mobil Oil Corp. v. S.E.C., 550 F. Supp. 67, 70–71 (S.D.N.Y. 1982) (transferring case when over 7,000 documents expected to be produced); Scheidt v. Klein, 956 F.2d 963, 965 (10th Cir. 1992).

[55] Enplanar, Inc. v. Marsh, 11 F.3d 1284, 1291 (5th Cir. 1994).

[56] *See* Pennwalt Corp. v. Purex Industries, Inc., 659 F. Supp. 287, 290 (D. Del. 1986).

[57] McEvily v. Sunbeam-Oster Co., Inc., 878 F. Supp. 337, 348 (D.R.I. 1994).

[58] Falconwood Financial Corp., v. Griffin, 838 F. Supp. 836, 841 (S.D.N.Y. 1993) (recognizing that although discovery rules permit defendants to compel document production in certain instances by non-parties outside of transferor court's subpoena power, transfer was still necessary because without transfer, defendants could not compel testimony of author of documents, and under discovery rules, non-party could avoid document production if significant expense involved).

[59] Enplanar, Inc. v. Marsh, 11 F.3d 1284, 1291 (5th Cir. 1994) (ease of conducting merits-related discovery).

[60] *See, e.g.*, Dicken v. United States, 862 F. Supp. 91, 94 (D. Md. 1994) (when "core issue" in tort claim was condition of staircase, actual inspection was preferable to photographs).

utmost importance.[61]

Many courts have noted that the location of documents has become less significant as technological advances make the copying, storage, and transfer of documents easier. Nevertheless, "less significant" does not mean "not significant." A court may not merely disregard this factor and should still consider it to the extent it bears on the convenience calculus.[62] The ease with which documents may be transferred also, to an extent, puts the location of documents within the power of the parties. However, courts should not allow parties to manipulate venue in anticipation of a transfer motion through their own deliberate acts.

Another factor militating in favor of transfer is whether the court in which the action originally is brought is more congested than the district to which transfer is sought.[63] Similarly, because, in general, federal courts favor adjudication of diversity actions by the court that sits in the state whose substantive laws will govern the case,[64] if the choice of law rules of the transferor state dictate that another state's laws apply to the action (*see* § 9.06), then this will favor transfer to the federal courts of that state.[65]

### [4] Interest of Justice Factors

The courts deal with the "interest of justice" factor in a variety of ways. For the most part, although the interest of justice is treated as a separate component in the transfer analysis,[66] most courts consider it to be made up of an amalgam of the

---

[61] *See, e.g.*, S-Fer Int'l, Inc. v. Paladion Partners, Ltd., 906 F. Supp. 211, 215 (S.D.N.Y. 1995) (when lease, rather than property itself, was main focus of dispute, jury could view property by photographs or videotapes and transfer to site of property was not warranted); *see also* Dwyer v. General Motors Corp., 853 F. Supp. 690, 693 (S.D.N.Y. 1994) (no transfer when jury visit to site was not imperative).

[62] *In re* Volkswagen of Am., Inc., 545 F.3d 304, 316 (5th Cir. 2008) ("That access to some sources of proof presents a lesser inconvenience now than it might have absent recent developments does not render this factor superfluous . . . . [T]he district court erred [by not considering] this factor because it does weigh in favor of transfer."); *In re* Apple, Inc., 602 F.3d 909, 914 (8th Cir. 2010) ("While electronic filing may lessen the inconvenience of document handling, if the need arises to refer to original documents or evidence in the litigation, Northern California would prove more convenient."); *In re* Link_A_Media Devices Corp., 662 F.3d 1221, 1224 (Fed. Cir. 2011) ("The district court also refused to consider two of the private interest factors in a Third Circuit venue inquiry: the convenience of the witnesses and the location of the books and records. Rather than analyze the merits of the parties' arguments relating to these factors, the district court stated that these issues are 'outdated, irrelevant, and should be given little weight, if any, except for those rare exceptions where truly regional defendants are litigating.' While advances in technology may alter the weight given to these factors, it is improper to ignore them entirely." (citations omitted)).

[63] Coady v. Ashcraft & Gerel, 223 F.3d 1, 11 (1st Cir. 2000) (district court erred when it denied transfer on grounds that two judicial vacancies existed in transferee court; court should not have considered this factor, which is materially different from docket congestion); Parsons v. Chesapeake & O. Ry. Co., 375 U.S. 71, 73 (1963) (condition of transferor court's docket is legitimate consideration in transfer analysis).

[64] Laumann Mfg. Corp. v. Castings USA, Inc., 913 F. Supp. 712, 721–722 (E.D.N.Y. 1996); *In re* Eastern Dist. Repetitive Stress Injury Lit., 850 F. Supp. 188, 194, 196 (E.D.N.Y. 1994).

[65] Van Dusen v. Barrack, 376 U.S. 612, 645 (1964) (trial in state in which federal judges are more familiar with the governing laws a factor to be considered in motions for transfer).

[66] Coffey v. Van Dorn Iron Works, 796 F.2d 217, 220 (7th Cir. 1986) ("interest of justice" is "a separate

public interest factors relating to the efficient administration of the court system, such as the interests of conserving judicial resources, avoiding court congestion, and the avoiding the difficulties of applying another state's law.[67] Thus, if transfer of an action would obviate having two actions involving the same or similar issues proceeding in different districts, the "interest of justice" will be served by transfer.[68]

Similarly, if the issue of whether the transferor court has personal jurisdiction over the defendant is a difficult one, transfer to a district where jurisdiction is certain may be in the interest of justice because it may conserve judicial resources by allowing the transferor court to avoid addressing the personal jurisdiction issue — at least in those circuits that permit transfer even if the transferor court lacks personal jurisdiction over the defendant.[69] Other courts do not treat the interest of justice component as a separate factor, but rather simply conclude that, given the aggregate of the other relevant factors, the transfer either is or is not in the interest of justice.[70]

The "judicial economy" factor in the convenience transfer analysis comes into play whenever two separate actions involving the same or similar issues and parties are proceeding in different districts. The fact that a related action is pending in the proposed transferee district is an important consideration that can override plaintiff's choice of forum because transfer of the second action will promote judicial economy and avoid the possibility of inconsistent results.[71] Judicial economy is served by having the two actions in the same district even though

---

component" in the transfer analysis, and "may be determinative in a particular case, even if the convenience of the parties and the witnesses might call for a different result").

[67] *See* Stewart Org., Inc. v. Ricoh Corp., 487 U.S. 22, 30 (1988) (interest of justice factor encompasses the "public interest factors of systemic integrity and fairness").

[68] *See* Ferens v. John Deere Co., 494 U.S. 516, 531 (1990) ("To permit a situation in which two cases involving precisely the same issues are simultaneously pending in different District Courts leads to the wastefulness of time, energy and money that Section 1404(a) was designed to prevent"). *See* Banjo Buddies Inc. v. Renosky, 156 F. Supp. 2d 22, 25 (D. Me. 2001) (conservation of judicial resources may justify transfer of venue; quoting Moore's Federal Practice); *but see* Eagle Auto Mall Corp. v. Chrysler Group, LLC, 760 F. Supp. 2d 421, 425–426 (E.D.N.Y. 2011) (balance of factors did not favor transfer even though three cases raising similar issues were consolidated in another district).

[69] *See* Cherry Communications, Inc. v. Coastal Telephone Co., 906 F. Supp. 452, 455 n.4 (N.D. Ill. 1995) (interest of justice served by transferring case to district where personal jurisdiction was not difficult issue); Datasouth Computer Corp. v. Three Dimensional Technologies, Inc., 719 F. Supp. 446, 452, (W.D.N.C. 1989) (interest of justice served by transferring case to district where personal jurisdiction was not difficult issue).

[70] Pilates, Inc. v. Pilates Institute, Inc., 891 F. Supp. 175, 183 (S.D.N.Y. 1995) (interest of justice factor "based on the totality of circumstances"); Constitution Reinsurance Corp. v. Stonewall Ins. Co., 872 F. Supp. 1247, 1250–1251 (S.D.N.Y. 1995) (interest of justice determined by totality of circumstances); Hernandez v. Graebel Van Lines, 761 F. Supp. 983, 991–992 (E.D.N.Y. 1991) (balance of all relevant factors made transfer in the interest of justice).

[71] Ferens v. John Deere Co., 494 U.S. 516, 531 (1990), *quoting* Continental Grain Co. v. Barge FBL-585, 364 U.S. 19, 26 (1960) ("To permit a situation in which two cases involving precisely the same issues are simultaneously pending in different District Courts leads to the wastefulness of time, energy and money that Section 1404(a) was designed to prevent"). *See* Research Automation, Inc. v. Schrader-Bridgeport Int'l, Inc., 626 F.3d 973, 979 (7th Cir. 2010) (ordinary rule that plaintiff's choice of forum must be afforded deference loses its significance when identical suits are filed in distinct venues, since each case has a plaintiff and the choice of one of them must necessarily be disturbed).

actual consolidation of the actions may not be possible.[72] The litigation of related claims before the same judge may conserve judicial resources and avoid inconsistent rulings, and having related litigation in the same district may allow pretrial discovery to be conducted more efficiently.[73] Transfer also may foster judicial economy by avoiding multiple litigation when the defendant needs to implead a third party defendant who may only be joined in the transferee district because he or she is not subject to the jurisdiction of the transferor court.[74] On the other hand, "judicial economy" does not mean that the court may transfer for the sole reason that transferring the action will give the court the means to dispose of a burdensome or inconvenient action without addressing the merits.[75]

If two actions involving the same parties and identical issues ("mirror image" actions) are pending in different districts, whether filed in those courts originally or removed there, competing motions to dismiss or transfer to the other district frequently are made in both actions.[76] In general, under the "first-filed rule," the first-filed action will be given priority and be allowed to proceed in favor of the later action,[77] unless convenience or other special circumstances dictate departure from the rule.[78] The first-filed rule advances "the inherently fair concept that the party

---

[72] FUL Inc. v. Unified School Dist. No. 204, 839 F. Supp. 1307, 1313 (N.D. Ill. 1993) (consolidation need not be certain); Fairfax Dental Ltd. v. S.J. Filhol Ltd., 645 F. Supp. 89, 92 n.2 (E.D.N.Y. 1986) ("[t]here is no requirement that consolidation be certain before this court can consider the fact that a related action is pending in the proposed transferee court").

[73] Bally Mfg. Co. v. Kane, 698 F. Supp. 734, 739 (N.D. Ill. 1988) (discovery could be streamlined if related actions in same district); Fairfax Dental (Ireland) Ltd. v. S.J. Filhol Ltd., 645 F. Supp. 89, 91–92 (E.D.N.Y. 1986) (even without consolidation, in actions involving same patent before same judge, ruling on patent validity could be used in both actions).

[74] Falconwood Financial Corp. v. Griffin, 838 F. Supp. 836, 841–842 (S.D.N.Y. 1993) (transfer would allow defendant to join necessary third party and would avoid necessity of two separate actions); Biggers v. Borden, Inc., 475 F. Supp. 333, 336–337 (E.D. Pa. 1979) (transfer to allow impleader of third-party defendant).

[75] *In re* Warrick, 70 F.3d 736, 740 (2d Cir. 1995) (district court abused discretion when it transferred action to district in which previous action presenting same issue recently had been dismissed for sole purpose of having transferee court dispose of second action on same grounds); *In re* Scott, 709 F.2d 717, 721 (D.C. Cir. 1983) ("inconvenience to the court is a relevant factor [in transfer analysis] but, standing alone, it should not carry the day").

[76] *See, e.g.*, Stroock & Stroock & Lavan v. Valley Systems, Inc., 1996 U.S. Dist. LEXIS 182 (S.D.N.Y. Jan. 10, 1996).

[77] Banjo Buddies Inc. v. Renosky, 156 F. Supp. 2d 22, 25 (D. Me. 2001) (first-filed rule applies when actions involve same parties and identical issues; transfer will be denied if there is no overlap of issues; quoting MOORE'S FEDERAL PRACTICE); Fire Eagle L.L.C. v. Bischoff (*In re* Spillman Dev. Group), 710 F.3d 299, 306 (5th Cir. 2013) (under first-to-file rule, when related cases are pending before two federal courts and issues substantially overlap, court in which case was last filed may refuse to hear it; transfer that accorded with this rule was not abuse of discretion); Northwest Airlines, Inc. v. American Airlines, Inc., 989 F.2d 1002, 1006 (8th Cir. 1993) ("To conserve judicial resources and avoid conflicting rulings, the first-filed rule gives priority, for purposes of choosing among possible venues when parallel litigation has been instituted in separate courts, to the party who first establishes jurisdiction"); First City Nat. Bank & Trust Co. v. Simmons, 878 F.2d 76, 80 (2d Cir. 1989) ("The first to file rule embodies considerations of judicial administration and conservation of resources"). *See also* Feinstein v. Brown, 304 F. Supp. 2d 279, 282–283 (D.R.I. 2004) (when action was removed to federal court, date of filing in state court rather than date of removal was considered for purposes of deciding which of two actions was first filed).

[78] Coady v. Ashcraft & Gerel, 223 F.3d 1, 11 (1st Cir. 2000) (when identical actions are proceeding

who commenced the first suit should generally be the party to attain its choice of venue."[79]

The courts do not apply the first-filed rule mechanically, and various policies and circumstances may lead the courts to depart from the rule.[80] For example, if the convenience factors under section 1404(a) weigh in favor of the second-filed action, the courts may disregard the first-filed rule.[81] Moreover, the courts generally give less weight to the first-filed rule when the competing actions were filed within a short time of each other.[82]

In addition, another circumstance justifying departure from the first-filed rule is that the first action was an anticipatory filing, i.e., the action, usually a declaratory judgment action, was filed after the other party gave notice of its intention to sue.[83]

## [5] Forum Selection Clauses Enforced Under § 1404(a)

In *Atlantic Marine Construction Co. v. United States District Court*, the Supreme Court clearly ruled that the appropriate motion to enforce a forum selection clause that points to a federal forum is a motion for convenience transfer under § 1404(a). Moreover, the court ruled that when a defendant files such a motion, a district court should transfer the case "unless extraordinary

---

concurrently in two federal courts, first-filed action is generally preferred; district court erred by denying transfer to first-filed district on grounds that judicial emergency existed because of two judicial vacancies in transferee district); Midwest Motor Express, Inc. v. Central States S.E. & S.W., 70 F.3d 1014, 1017 (8th Cir. 1995) ("compelling circumstances" may require disregard of first-filed rule); Merrill Lynch, Pierce, Fenner & Smith, Inc. v. Haydu, 675 F.2d 1169, 1174 (11th Cir. 1982) ("in the absence of compelling circumstances" the first-filed rule should be applied).

[79] *See* Ontel Prods., Inc. v. Project Strategies Corp., 899 F. Supp. 1144, 1150, 1153 n.13 (S.D.N.Y. 1995) (not applying first-filed rule because there was "negligible time difference" in filing of actions).

[80] *See* TransCanada Power Mktg., Ltd. v. Narragansett Elec. Co., 402 F. Supp. 2d 343, 347–354 (D. Mass. 2005) (courts may depart from first-filed rule if balance of convenience substantially favors second-filed action, or if special circumstances justify transfer, such as when party bringing first-filed suit engaged in misleading conduct in order to prevail in race to courthouse); Research Automation, Inc. v. Schrader-Bridgeport Int'l, Inc., 626 F.3d 973, 980–981 (7th Cir. 2010) (while strict application of first-filed rule would have certainty and ease of application, the cost, i.e., an "unseemly race to the courthouse," would be too high).

[81] New York Marine and Gen. Ins. Co. v. LaFarge North America, Inc., 599 F.3d 102, 112–113 (2d Cir. 2010) (transfer to first-filed jurisdiction is inappropriate when balance of convenience favors second-filed action; in absence of special circumstances, first-filed rule is not dispositive but is only presumption that may be rebutted by proof of desirability of proceeding in forum of second-filed action).

[82] Ontel Products., Inc. v. Project Strategies Corp., 899 F. Supp. 1144, 1153 (S.D.N.Y. 1995) ("the [first-filed] rule is usually disregarded where the competing suits were filed merely days apart" and holding that rule was inapplicable there because actions were filed on same day).

[83] Research Automation, Inc. v. Schrader-Bridgeport Int'l, Inc., 626 F.3d 973, 980 (7th Cir. 2010) (Seventh Circuit does not adhere to first-filed rule when one part files its lawsuit in anticipation of impending suit; similarly, when parallel cases involve declaratory judgment action and action seeking coercive relief, Seventh Circuit ordinarily gives priority to coercive action regardless of which was filed first); Boatmen's First Nat. Bank of Kansas City v. KPERS, 57 F.3d 638, 641 (8th Cir. 1995) (two "red flags" indicating that first-filed rule should be disregarded: "first, that the 'first' suit was filed after the other party gave notice of intention to sue . . . and second, that the action was for declaratory judgment rather than for damages or equitable relief").

circumstances unrelated to the convenience of the parties clearly disfavor a transfer."[84]

In the typical case not involving a forum-selection clause (*see* § 9.04[1]–[4]), a district court considering a § 1404(a) motion, must evaluate both the convenience of the parties and various public-interest factors. When a forum selection clause is involved, however, the clause represents the parties' agreement as to the proper forum. This fact requires three changes to the § 1404(a) calculus:[85]

1. The plaintiff's choice of forum merits no weight. Rather, as the party defying the forum-selection clause, the plaintiff bears the burden of establishing that transfer to the forum for which the parties bargained is unwarranted.
2. A court evaluating a defendant's § 1404(a) motion to transfer based on a forum-selection clause should not consider arguments about the parties' private interests. When parties agree to a forum-selection clause, they waive the right to challenge the preselected forum as inconvenient or less convenient for themselves or their witnesses, or for their pursuit of the litigation. A court may consider arguments about the public interest factors only, and these factors will rarely defeat a transfer motion.
3. When a party bound by a forum-selection clause has filed suit in a different forum, a § 1404(a) transfer of venue will not carry with it the original venue's choice-of-law rules (*see* § 9.06).

The Supreme Court also discussed the effect of forum selection clauses in its earlier decision, *Stewart Organization Inc. v. Ricoh Corp.* In *Stewart*, the Court held that the weight to be given a forum selection clause in a diversity case should be determined by federal law, specifically the standards contained in Section 1404(a) itself, and not state law pertaining to forum selection clauses or *The Bremen* standards.[86] The Court stated that, by its terms, Section 1404(a) requires the district court to resolve a transfer motion by using a "flexible and individualized" analysis, "weigh[ing] in the balance a number of case-specific factors."[87] Accordingly, *Stewart* was understood as requiring that a forum selection clause be treated as only one of a number of factors to be weighed in deciding whether transfer was warranted by considerations of fairness and convenience.

---

[84] Atlantic Marine Constr. Co. v. United States Dist. Court, 134 S. Ct. 568, 187 L. Ed. 2d 487, 494, 500 (2013).

[85] Atlantic Marine Constr. Co. v. United States Dist. Court, 134 S. Ct. 568, 187 L. Ed. 2d 487, 494, 500–502 (2013) ("Although the Court of Appeals correctly identified § 1404(a) as the appropriate provision to enforce the forum-selection clause in this case, the Court of Appeals erred in failing to make the adjustments required in a § 1404(a) analysis when the transfer motion is premised on a forum-selection clause. When the parties have agreed to a valid forum-selection clause, a district court should ordinarily transfer the case to the forum specified in that clause. Only under extraordinary circumstances unrelated to the convenience of the parties should a § 1404(a) motion be denied. And no such exceptional factors appear to be present in this case.").

[86] Stewart Org., Inc. v. Ricoh Corp., 487 U.S. 22, 29–30 (1988); *see* 28 U.S.C. 1404(a); *see also* M/S Bremen v. Zapata Off-Shore Co., 407 U.S. 1, 12–13 (1972).

[87] Stewart Org., Inc. v. Ricoh Corp., 487 U.S. 22, 29 (1988).

Now, however, under the *Atlantic Marine* formulation, the clause will nearly always have dispositive weight.

The *Atlantic Marine* approach applies only when the forum selection clause is mandatory. Forum selection clauses may be either "permissive" or "mandatory." Some courts have held that in deciding whether to transfer under Section 1404(a), a permissive clause is entitled to less weight than a mandatory clause,[88] while other courts hold that the permissive nature of the clause should not affect its weight.[89] The better view is for the courts to consider the permissive nature of the forum selection clause. The plaintiff ought to come forward with some explanation as to why the clause should not be enforced, but given the permissive nature of the clause, the explanation by the plaintiff need not be as substantial as it should be to defeat a mandatory clause.

In addition, if the forum selection clause is a "limited" one, the dispute may not fall within the scope of the clause and the clause in that case will not be given any weight in a Section 1404(a) motion to transfer.[90] Interpreting the language of the forum selection clause is, therefore, an integral part of the transfer analysis when the parties dispute the meaning of the language.[91] When interpretation is required, the court of appeals general applies a de novo standard of review to the district court's interpretation of the language, and an abuse of discretion standard to the district court's balancing of the transfer factors.[92]

## § 9.05 STANDING TO BRING MOTION TO TRANSFER ON CONVENIENCE GROUNDS

### [1] Plaintiff or Defendant May Bring Motion

A plaintiff, as well as a defendant, may move to transfer venue on convenience grounds under Section 1404(a).[93] Of course, since the plaintiff chose the venue in the first place, in most cases it will be the defendant who is seeking to change it.

---

88 *See, e.g.*, Orix Credit Alliance, Inc. v. Mid-South Materials Corp., 816 F. Supp. 230, 234 (S.D.N.Y. 1993); *see* 28 U.S.C. § 1404(a).

89 Haagen-Dazs Shoppe Co., Inc. v. Born, 897 F. Supp. 122, 125 (S.D.N.Y. 1995); Stateline Power Corp. v. Kremer, 404 F. Supp. 2d 1373, 1380–1381 (S.D. Fla. 2005) (court considered permissive forum selection clause as having great weight in venue transfer analysis, as existence of clause indicated that, at time contract was signed, defendant did not consider possibility of litigating in Florida to be inconvenient).

90 *See, e.g.*, S-Fer Int'l, Inc. v. Paladion Partners, Ltd., 906 F. Supp. 211, 213–214 (S.D.N.Y. 1995) (forum selection clause providing that action "for enforcement of any obligation" in lease agreement had to be brought in specified forum did not cover claims for tort and rescission of lease for fraudulent inducement).

91 Terra Int'l, Inc. v. Mississippi Chem. Corp., 119 F.3d 688, 692 (8th Cir. 1997) ("Before a district court can even consider a forum selection clause in its transfer analysis, it [must first] decide whether the clause applies to the type[s] of claims asserted in the lawsuit").

92 Terra Int'l, Inc. v. Mississippi Chem. Corp., 119 F.3d 688, 692 (8th Cir. 1997) (de novo review is appropriate standard for district court's interpretation of forum selection clause language); Northern Cal. Dist. Council of Laborers v. Pittsburg-Des Moines Steel Co., 69 F.3d 1034, 1036 n.3 (9th Cir. 1995).

93 Ferens v. John Deere Co., 494 U.S. 516, 524 (1990); *see* 28 U.S.C. § 1404(a).

However, there may be circumstances that would lead the plaintiff to want to seek a transfer.

Before granting a plaintiff's motion to change venue on convenience grounds, some courts require the plaintiff to show that circumstances have changed since the action was filed.[94] However, several more recent cases reach a contrary conclusion, allowing transfer on the plaintiff's motion without a showing of changed circumstances.[95] Given Section 1404(a)'s broad remedial purpose of allowing "easy" change of venue so that the litigation can proceed in a convenient forum, the latter decisions refusing to impose this additional requirement on the plaintiff seem the better reasoned, even though they seem to permit unfettered forum shopping. For example, the plaintiff may choose a proper but inconvenient forum to take advantage of a favorable rule of law that would be applied by that court. Under the Supreme Court's *Ferens* decision, the plaintiff could move to transfer under Section 1404(a), and, if successful, take the favorable rule of law along (*see* § 111.20[1][a][ii]).[96]

Certainly, such forum shopping is permissible. Nonetheless, to avoid harassment of defendants and to ensure the judicious use of Section 1404(a) transfers, it is appropriate that the plaintiff be put to a higher burden of persuasion in seeking the transfer over the objection of the defendant.

### [2] Courts Split on Whether Third-Party Defendant Has Standing to Bring Motion

The courts are split on whether a third-party defendant has standing to move for a convenience transfer under Section 1404(a).[97] The decisions granting third-party defendants standing to move for a convenience transfer represent the better view. The courts denying standing have relied on authority prohibiting third parties from raising objections to venue. Allowing such objections would frustrate

---

[94] *See* Anadigics, Inc. v. Raytheon Co., 903 F. Supp. 615, 617 (S.D.N.Y. 1995) (requisite changed circumstances present because plaintiff's transfer motion was in response to defendant's transfer motion); James v. Daley & Lewis, 406 F. Supp. 645, 648 (D. Del. 1976) (transfer denied because no change of circumstances); Moore v. McKibbon Bros., Inc., 41 F. Supp. 2d 1350, 1356 (N.D. Ga. 1998) (motion to transfer by plaintiffs was granted when, at time of filing, plaintiffs did not know they had choice of forum and only learned through discovery of alternative forum where personal jurisdiction and venue were proper).

[95] *See, e.g.*, Central Hudson Gas & Elec. Corp. v. Empresa Naviera Santa S.A., 769 F. Supp. 208, 209 (E.D. La. 1991) (no change of circumstances required); American Home Assur. Co. v. Glovegold, Ltd., 153 F.R.D. 695, 700 (M.D. Fla. 1994) (plaintiff need not show changed circumstances to obtain convenience transfer); Cordis Corp. v. Siemens-Pacesetter, Inc., 682 F. Supp. 1200, 1203 (S.D. Fla. 1987) (plaintiff does not need to show changed circumstances to obtain convenience transfer); *see also* Anglo American Ins. Group, PLC v. Calfed, Inc., 916 F. Supp. 1324, 1329 (S.D.N.Y. 1996) (plaintiff moving for transfer must show change of circumstances *or* that transfer in interest of justice);

[96] *See* Ferens v. John Deere Co., 494 U.S. 516 (1990).

[97] *See* Stringfellow v. S.D. Warren Co., 1991 U.S. Dist. LEXIS 16479 (W.D. Mich. Oct. 15, 1991) (in dictum, court discusses split of authority and concludes that allowing standing is more in keeping with language and purpose of Section 1404(a)).

the purpose underlying Rule 14[98] by making it more likely that related claims would be tried in different forums. However, this concern does not apply in a Section 1404(a) motion, which seeks transfer of the entire case to another forum.[99] Moreover, in light of the language and policy considerations of Section 1404(a), which authorizes the court to transfer an action if it determines that another federal forum is more convenient for the parties and witnesses, there is no valid reason for precluding third-party defendants from moving for a convenience transfer.[100]

### [3] Court May, on Its Own Motion, Transfer on Convenience Grounds

The district court may transfer an action under Section 1404(a) on its own motion.[101] One Court has said that sua sponte transfers on convenience grounds "should be reserved for exceptional circumstances," such as a pending related action in another district with which the transferred action could be consolidated.[102] Most courts, however, simply follow the traditional analysis of whether the "convenience" and "interest of justice" factors warrant transfer of the case to a district other than that originally selected by the plaintiff.[103] Of course, before transferring venue on its own motion, the court should give the parties notice and an opportunity to be heard.[104]

## § 9.06 CHOICE OF LAW FOLLOWING SECTION 1404(A) CONVENIENCE TRANSFER

### [1] Choice of Law in Diversity Cases

#### [a] Generally, Transferor State's Law and Choice of Law Rules Apply

##### [i] Rule Originated with *Van Dusen* Case

In *Van Dusen v. Barrack*, the Supreme Court held that in diversity cases, following a transfer for convenience pursuant to Section 1404(a), the court to which the action has been transferred generally must apply the same state law, including

---

98 *See* Fed. R. Civ. P. 14; *see generally* 3 Moore's Federal Practice Ch. 14, *Third-Party Practice* (Matthew Bender 3d ed.).

99 Stringfellow v. S.D. Warren Co., 1991 U.S. Dist. LEXIS 16479, at *2 (W.D. Mich. Oct. 15, 1991).

100 Krupp Intern., Inc. v. Yarn Industries, Inc., 615 F. Supp. 1103, 1107 (D. Del. 1985).

101 Ferens v. John Deere Co., 494 U.S. 516, 530 (1990) (dicta); *see also* 28 U.S.C. § 1404(a).

102 *In re* Scott, 709 F.2d 717, 721 (D.C. Cir. 1983) (sua sponte transfer not justified merely because large number of prisoners' Freedom of Information Act cases represent burden on District of Columbia Court).

103 Haskel v. FPR Registry, Inc., 862 F. Supp. 909, 916 (E.D.N.Y. 1994); Robinson v. Town of Madison, 752 F. Supp. 842, 847 (N. D. Ill. 1990).

104 Starnes v. McGuire, 512 F.2d 918, 934 (D.C. Cir. 1974).

any applicable choice of law rules, that the transferor court would have applied had the action remained there.[105] Pursuant to the *Erie* doctrine,[106] the transferor court, as a court sitting in diversity, generally would have applied the law, including the choice of law rules, of the state in which it sits.[107] The Supreme Court's holding in *Van Dusen* was intended to ensure that the plaintiff is not deprived of the law he or she expected to be applied by filing the action in the transferor court.[108] The Court views Section 1404(a) as merely a "housekeeping measure" that does not carry with it a change in the applicable law.[109] The statute deals with the "placement of litigation in the federal courts," and merely authorizes "a change of courtrooms,"[110] not a change in applicable law. The Court stated in *Van Dusen* that, since a Section 1404(a) convenience transfer presupposes that the plaintiff has chosen a proper venue, plaintiffs should therefore be allowed to retain "whatever advantages may flow from the state laws of the forum they have initially selected," following transfer to a more convenient forum.[111] Although the Court noted that it might seem "undesirable to let the plaintiff reap a choice-of-law benefit from the deliberate selection of an inconvenient forum," such a result was necessary because under our federal system, when a plaintiff has a choice of two proper forums that have different laws, the plaintiff is entitled to exercise his or her venue privilege by selecting the forum with the most favorable law or choice of law rules.[112]

Moreover, if a Section 1404(a) convenience transfer were accompanied by a change in the applicable law, it would create an opportunity for defendants to forum shop for more favorable law. That is, defendants could use Section 1404(a) as a forum shopping device to obtain a "change of law as a bonus for a change of venue."[113] Since no such opportunity is available to defendants in state court, unless they were successful in persuading the state court to dismiss on forum non conveniens grounds, it likewise must be unattainable in diversity cases. Finally, if the choice of law rule were otherwise, the remedial purpose of Section 1404(a), which is to grant transfer on the basis of convenience and fairness, might be frustrated. Courts might be reluctant to grant transfer under Section 1404(a), even

---

[105] Van Dusen v. Barrack, 376 U.S. 612, 627 (1964); Ferens v. John Deere Co., 494 U.S. 516, 524–527 (1990). *See* Liberty Synergistics Inc. v. Microflo Ltd., 718 F.3d 138, 153–154 (2d Cir. 2013) (governing law does not change following transfer of venue for convenience under § 1404(a); court is required to apply state law that would have been applied had there been no change of venue, regardless of which party initiated transfer); Yelton v. PHI, Inc., 669 F.3d 577, 580 (5th Cir. 2012) (after transfer under 28 U.S.C. § 1404, choice of law rules of transferor court are applied).

[106] *See generally* Ch. 15, *Applicable Law in Federal Court: The Erie Doctrine*.

[107] *See* Erie R. Co. v. Tompkins, 304 U.S. 64, 78–80 (1938); *see also* Klaxon Co. v. Stentor Elec. Mfg. Co., 313 U.S. 487, 496 (1941) (forum state's choice of law rules govern).

[108] *See* Ferens v. John Deere Co., 494 U.S. 516, 524–527 (1990) (following a convenience transfer, "the transferee court must follow the choice of law rules that prevailed in the transferor court").

[109] Van Dusen v. Barrack, 376 U.S. 612, 636–637 (1964).

[110] 376 U.S. at 636.

[111] 376 U.S. at 633.

[112] 376 U.S. at 634; *see also* Ferens v. John Deere Co., 494 U.S. 516, 527–528 (1990) (under our federal system, plaintiffs have opportunity to forum shop for favorable law when there is a choice between two proper forums that have different substantive laws).

[113] Ferens v. John Deere Co., 494 U.S. 516, 527–528 (1990), *quoting* Van Dusen v. Barrack, 376 U.S. 612, 638 (1964).

though another forum was clearly more convenient, if application of the transferee state's laws could result in dismissal of the plaintiff's claim, such as in the case where the transferee forum has a shorter statute of limitations than the transferor forum or does not recognize a claim that is actionable in the transferor forum.[114]

There is an exception to this general rule in cases in which a § 1404(a) transfer is ordered due to a forum selection clause (*see* § 9.04[5]).[115]

### [ii] *Ferens* Extended *Van Dusen* Rule to Cases in Which Plaintiff or Court Moves for Convenience Transfer

The *Van Dusen* rule that the transferee court must apply the same substantive law that the transferor court would have applied has been extended to diversity actions in which the plaintiff moves for a convenience transfer,[116] and when the court sua sponte orders transfer under Section 1404(a).[117]

In *Ferens v. John Deere Co.*, the Supreme Court acknowledged that applying the transferor state's law would seem to reward plaintiffs for conduct that "seems manipulative." Nonetheless, it held that the policies underlying the *Van Dusen* rule required that result.[118] In so holding, the court noted that since venue was proper in the transferor court, the plaintiff was entitled to select that forum and have its laws apply. In *Ferens*, the plaintiffs, with the help of the convenience transfer statute, were able to have their cake and eat it too: application of another state's more favorable law *and* a convenient forum. The plaintiffs brought their diversity action in a district whose state law was favorable to them (a longer statute of limitations), and in which venue was proper but highly inconvenient for both them and the defendant. By then moving to transfer to a more convenient forum (the district of plaintiffs' residence) the plaintiffs were able to carry the favorable state law to the convenient forum, under whose state law the claim would have been time-barred.[119]

Nonetheless, plaintiffs seeking a transfer should be required to articulate more persuasive reasons to justify a transfer than in the usual case. Only when the balance of all the factors in a Section 1404(a) analysis tip heavily in favor of transfer

---

114 Van Dusen, 376 U.S. 612, 638 (1964); Ferens v. John Deere Co., 494 U.S. 516, 527–528 (1990).

115 Atlantic Marine Constr. Co. v. United States Dist. Court, 134 S. Ct. 568, 187 L. Ed. 2d 487, 494, 500–502 (2013) (§ 1404(a) is the appropriate provision to enforce forum-selection clause, and the Court of Appeals erred in failing to make the adjustments required in a § 1404(a) analysis when the transfer motion is premised on a forum-selection clause; when the parties have agreed to a valid forum-selection clause, a district court should ordinarily transfer the case to the forum specified in that clause; when transfer is ordered, the plaintiff's presumed choice of law advantage protected by the *Van Dusen* rule does not apply).

116 Ferens v. John Deere Co., 494 U.S. 516, 527–528 (1990); *see* Van Dusen v. Barrack, 376 U.S. 612, 627 (1964).

117 Muldoon v. Tropitone Furniture Co., 1 F.3d 964, 965–966 (9th Cir. 1993); *see also* Ferens v. John Deere Co., 494 U.S. 516, 523, 530–531 (1990).

118 Ferens v. John Deere Co., 494 U.S. 516, 531 (1990).

119 494 U.S. at 531.

should the court grant the motion at the plaintiff's behest. In relatively rare cases, the courts may find the test for transfer to be met. But in most cases, the balance will not tip so clearly and the courts may properly find that it is not in the interest of justice to permit the transfer. In either case, the lower courts will be keeping in mind the systemic costs of litigating in one venue or the other. As the *Ferens* majority pointed out, there is no guarantee that the district court will grant the plaintiffs' motion. Indeed, the Court remanded the case for just such a determination to be made.[120]

### [b] Transferor State's Choice of Law Rules May Dictate Application of Another State's Law

It is important to note that the *Van Dusen* rule does not necessarily result in application of the law of the state in which the transferor court sits. Instead, when a case is transferred under Section 1404(a), *Van Dusen* requires the same choice of law analysis that would have been applied in the transferor court to be conducted by the transferee court, which may require the transferee court to apply its own law, the law of the transferor court, or some other state's law. Under *Erie* and its progeny, the whole law of the state must be applied, including its choice of law rules (*see* Ch. 15, Applicable Law in Federal Court: The *Erie* Doctrine).[121] The choice of law rules of the states generally require the courts to engage in an issue by issue analysis to determine which state's law should apply to the various issues in the case.[122]

### [2] Choice of Law in Federal Question Cases: Generally, Transferee Court Follows Its Own Circuit's Interpretation of Law

Following a Section 1404(a) convenience transfer in a federal question case, in contrast to diversity cases, the transferee court ordinarily should apply the law as interpreted by its own circuit, and should not be required to apply the precedent of the transferor circuit. Thus, the *Van Dusen* rule (*see* [1], *above*) generally does not apply in federal question cases.[123] An important justification for the transferee

[120] Ferens v. John Deere Co., 494 U.S. 516 (1990).

[121] Ferens v. John Deere Co., 494 U.S. at 517, 527; Klaxon Co. v. Stentor Elec. Mfg. Co., 313 U.S. 487, 496 (1941); Erie R. Co. v. Tompkins, 304 U.S. 64, 78–80 (1938).

[122] *See generally* Ch. 15, *Applicable Law in Federal Court: The Erie Doctrine*; 17A Moore's Federal Practice Ch. 124, *The Erie Doctrine and Applicable Law* (Matthew Bender 3d ed.).

[123] *See, e.g.*, E.E.O.C. v. Northwest Airlines, Inc., 188 F.3d 695, 700–701 (6th Cir. 1999) (court of appeals should apply law of its own circuit in federal question cases, since federal law is presumed to be uniform, whether or not it is in fact); Murphy v. FDIC, 208 F.3d 959, 964–966 (11th Cir. 2000) (transferee court should follow its own interpretation of federal law, not that of transferor court); Olcott v. Delaware Flood Co., 76 F.3d 1538, 1546 (10th Cir. 1996) (ordinarily, transferee court should apply its own circuit's precedent to transferred federal claims); Wilborn v. Dep't of Health and Human Services, 49 F.3d 597, 600 (9th Cir. 1995) ("following a transfer under 28 U.S.C. § 1404(a), when reviewing federal claims, a transferee court in this circuit is bound only by our circuit's precedent"); Eckstein v. Balcor Film Investors, 8 F.3d 1121, 1126 (7th Cir. 1993) (following a 28 U.S.C. § 1404(a) transfer, "a transferee court normally should use its own best judgment about the meaning of federal law when evaluating a federal claim").

court applying its own circuit's interpretation to federal claims is that, "until the Supreme Court speaks, the federal circuit courts are under duties to arrive at their own determinations of the merits of federal questions presented to them."[124]

# PART C
# TRANSFER OR DISMISSAL IF VENUE IS IMPROPER

## § 9.07 PURPOSE OF SECTION 1406(a) IMPROPER VENUE TRANSFER STATUTE

Section 1406(a) allows a district court to cure the defect of "a case laying venue in the wrong division or district."[125] Section 1406(a) was enacted to authorize the court to transfer, instead of dismiss, an action when venue is improper, and to "avoid . . . the injustice which had often resulted to plaintiffs from dismissal of their actions merely because they had made an erroneous guess with regard to the existence of some elusive fact of the kind upon which venue provisions often turn."[126] Thus, the enactment of Section 1406(a) was in keeping with the general trend in legislative changes affecting federal court procedure "of removing whatever obstacles may impede an expeditious and orderly adjudication of cases and controversies on their merits."[127] Prior to the enactment of Section 1406(a), if the plaintiff lay venue in the wrong district, the district court's sole option was to dismiss the action. Although the dismissal was without prejudice, it nevertheless often had the harsh result of divesting the plaintiff of his or her cause of action, if, for example, the statute of limitations had expired in the meantime.[128]

Some courts have given a broad reading to the concept of when venue is "wrong," and effect transfer under Section 1406(a) to remove other procedural obstacles in the original district which make it a "wrong" venue for the action, i.e., a lack of personal jurisdiction over the defendant or the bar of the statute of limitations.

---

[124] Menowitz v. Brown, 991 F.2d 36, 40 (2d Cir. 1993); *In re* Korean Airlines, 829 F.2d 1171, 1176 (D.C. Cir. 1987), *aff'd on other grounds sub nom.* Chan v. Korean Airlines, Ltd., 490 U.S. 122 (1989) ("if . . . more than one interpretation of federal law exists, the Supreme Court of the United States can finally determine the issue and restore uniformity in the federal system").

[125] 28 U.S.C. § 1406(a).

[126] Goldlawr, Inc. v. Heiman, 369 U.S. 463, 466 (1962).

[127] 369 U.S. at 466.

[128] *See* Burnett v. New York Central Railroad Co., 380 U.S. 424, 430 (1965) (Section 1406(a) prevents "the unfairness of barring a plaintiff's action solely because a prior timely action is dismissed for improper venue after the applicable statute of limitations has run"); Goldlawr, Inc. v. Heiman, 369 U.S. 463, 466 (1962) (purpose of Section 1406(a) was to avoid injustices such as plaintiff "losing a substantial part of its cause of action under the statute of limitations" because it made a mistake in venue).

## § 9.08 TRANSFEROR COURT'S PREREQUISITES FOR TRANSFER FOR IMPROPER VENUE

### [1] Transferor Court Needs Subject Matter Jurisdiction

A district court has no power to transfer an action under Section 1406(a) unless it has subject matter jurisdiction — that is, diversity, federal question, or some other basis for subject matter jurisdiction over the action — and must dismiss the action if subject matter jurisdiction is lacking.[129] If, however, the court lacks jurisdiction because a special jurisdictional statute applies to confer exclusive jurisdiction in another court, transfer under § 1404 is not available,[130] but transfer to the court with exclusive jurisdiction may be available under 28 U.S.C. § 1631 (*see* §§ 9.14, 9.15).[131]

### [2] Transferor Court Need Not Have Personal Jurisdiction

When venue is wrong in the district in which the plaintiff has originally brought the action, a district court may transfer the action to another district under Section 1406(a) whether or not the transferor court has personal jurisdiction over the defendant.[132] If, however, the transferor court concludes that the lack of personal jurisdiction over the defendant should have been obvious to the plaintiff, the court may deny transfer as not "in the interest of justice," and instead may dismiss the action.

### [3] Venue Must Be "Wrong"

The majority of the courts agree that Section 1406(a) is the appropriate vehicle to transfer or dismiss the action when venue is "wrong."[133] Venue is "wrong," and a Section 1406(a) motion to dismiss or transfer is appropriate, when venue is improper in the district in which the action originally was brought because it fails to comply with the applicable venue statute.[134]

---

[129] Standing Stone Media v. indiancountrytoday.com, 193 F. Supp. 2d 528, 536 (S.D.N.Y. 2002) (court had authority to transfer case when it had subject matter jurisdiction because case arose under federal law, the Anticybersquatting Consumer Protection Act, 15 U.S.C. § 1125(d)).

[130] Lloyd v. FDIC, 22 F.3d 335, 338 (1st Cir. 1994) (because transferee court lacked subject-matter jurisdiction under special jurisdictional provision relating to FDIC, transfer to it under 28 U.S.C. § 1404(a) was improper and appellate court ordered it to retransfer action to transferor court); Landmark Land Co., Inc. v. Office of Thrift Supervision, 948 F.2d 910, 913 (5th Cir. 1991) (transfer erroneous because transferee court did not have jurisdiction under bankruptcy jurisdiction statute); United States v. Copley, 25 F.3d 660, 662 (8th Cir. 1994) (transfer unauthorized because transferee court lacked jurisdiction under special jurisdictional statute relating to revocation proceedings).

[131] *See* 28 U.S.C. § 1631.

[132] Goldlawr, Inc. v. Heiman, 369 U.S. 463, 466 (1962) ("The language of 28 U.S.C. § 1406(a) is amply broad enough to authorize the transfer of cases, however wrong the plaintiff may have been in filing his case as to venue, whether the court in which it was filed had personal jurisdiction over the defendants or not").

[133] *See* 28 U.S.C. § 1406(a); Van Dusen v. Barrack, 376 U.S. 612, 634 (1964) ("Section 1406(a) provides for transfer from forums in which venue is wrongly or improperly laid").

[134] *See* 28 U.S.C. § 1406(a); *see* Atlantic Marine Constr. Co. v. United States Dist. Court, 134 S. Ct.

Some courts define venue as "wrong" only if it is technically wrong because it fails to satisfy the applicable venue statute, while others define venue as "wrong" in an additional circumstance, i.e., when even though venue is technically correct, some other obstacle in the transferor court, such as a lack of personal jurisdiction over the defendant, would prevent the action from proceeding further there.[135]

## § 9.09 PREREQUISITES FOR PROPOSED TRANSFEREE COURT WHEN VENUE IS IMPROPER IN TRANSFEROR COURT: TRANSFEREE COURT MUST BE ONE IN WHICH ACTION "COULD HAVE BEEN BROUGHT"

When an action is filed laying venue in the wrong district, if the district court decides transfer is "in the interest of justice," it may transfer it to "any district or division in which it could have been brought."[136] The phrase "in which it could have been brought" has been construed to mean that the proposed transferee forum must have been one in which it would have been proper to file the action initially, that is, it would have had proper venue, subject matter jurisdiction, and personal jurisdiction over the defendant.[137] This meaning is the same as the meaning attributed to the phrase "might have been brought" in the convenience transfer statute, Section 1404(a) (*see* § 9.03, *above*).[138]

## § 9.10 COURT MAY TRANSFER IN INTEREST OF JUSTICE OR DISMISS WITHOUT PREJUDICE WHEN VENUE IS WRONG

### [1] Transfer Should Be Usual Remedy for Improper Venue

When venue is wrong in the district court in which the plaintiff has filed the action, the court must either transfer it, if the court determines that it is in the interest of justice to do so, or must dismiss the action without prejudice.[139] Even if the defendant has moved only for dismissal for improper venue under Section

568, 187 L. Ed. 2d 487, 494, 500–502 (2013) (the question whether venue is "wrong" is governed by the general venue statute, 28 U.S.C. § 1391); *see generally* Ch. 8, *Venue*.

[135] Goldlawr, Inc. v. Heiman, 369 U.S. 463, 466 (1962) ("The language of 28 U.S.C. § 1406(a) is amply broad enough to authorize the transfer of cases, however wrong the plaintiff may have been in filing his case as to venue, whether the court in which it was filed had personal jurisdiction over the defendants or not").

[136] 28 U.S.C. § 1406(a).

[137] Minnette v. Time Warner, 997 F.2d 1023, 1026 (2d Cir. 1993) (district court properly denied motion to transfer action to district in which venue would not have been proper).

[138] *See* 28 U.S.C. § 1404(a).

[139] Minnette v. Time Warner, 997 F.2d 1023, 1026 (2d Cir. 1993); *see* 28 U.S.C. § 1406(a); Johnson v. Payless Drug Stores Northwest, Inc., 950 F.2d 586, 588 (9th Cir. 1991); Hapaniewski v. City of Chicago Heights, 883 F.2d 576, 579 (7th Cir. 1989) ("A district court must dismiss such a suit if it denies the transfer [under Section 1406(a)]").

1406(a), the court may order the action transferred, if transfer is otherwise appropriate.[140]

Although some courts have stated that transfer should be the usual remedy, not dismissal,[141] in practice some courts dismiss rather than transfer, even when the statute of limitations has since run and will bar a new action filed in the proper district. The better approach, especially in this instance, is for the court to transfer. Such an approach comports with the purpose of Section 1406(a) (*see* § 9.07).[142]

The court may dismiss without prejudice, rather than transfer, if the plaintiff so requests. A plaintiff may wish to do this for strategic reasons. However, the dismissal will then be considered voluntary (even though contingent on the court's decision that venue is improper or inconvenient) and the plaintiff will not be able to appeal the dismissal or the court's decision on venue.[143]

### [2] Court May Transfer If in Interest of Justice

When venue is wrong in the court in which a case was brought, the court may transfer to another court with proper venue if (1) the proposed transferee court is one in which the action "could have been brought"; and (2) transfer is "in the interest of justice."[144] If the district court dismisses without first considering whether transfer is in the interest of justice, the dismissal order will be vacated as an abuse of discretion.[145]

The "interest of justice" is an amorphous standard, left largely undefined by the courts. Ordinarily, "transfer will be in the interest of justice because normally dismissal of an action that could be brought elsewhere is 'time consuming and justice-defeating.' "[146] The purpose of the improper venue transfer statute is to avoid the harsh result of dismissal of the action "merely because [plaintiffs] had

---

[140] Concession Consultants, Inc. v. Mirisch, 355 F.2d 369, 371 n.3 (2d Cir. 1966) ("And where the motion asks only that the suit be dismissed, the court may properly, *sua sponte*, order it transferred").

[141] *See, e.g.*, Szulik v. Tag V.I., 858 F. Supp. 2d 532, 547 (E.D.N.C. 2012) (rather than dismissing for improper venue, courts favor finding that it is in the interests of justice to transfer venue); Estate of Bank v. Swiss Valley Farms Co., 286 F. Supp. 2d 514, 521–522 (D. Md. 2003) (transfer is favored for any reason that constitutes impediment to decision on merits in transferor district but would not be impediment in transferee district); Davis V. American Soc'y of Civil Eng'rs, 290 F. Supp. 2d 116, 120 (D.D.C. 2003) (while court has discretion whether to dismiss or transfer, interest of justice generally requires transfer).

[142] *See* Goldlawr, Inc. v. Heiman, 369 U.S. 463, 466 (1962) (transfer will ordinarily be in interest of justice).

[143] *See* Dearth v. Mukasey, 516 F.3d 413, 414–416 (6th Cir. 2008) ("By dismissing their case without prejudice, the district court put the plaintiffs in the same legal position as if the case had never been brought. It would be unfair to allow them the ability both to start anew in any district and to appeal the underlying basis of a ruling that likely would not have been appealable until the end of the now-dismissed case.").

[144] 28 U.S.C. § 1406(a); Minnette v. Time Warner, 997 F.2d 1023, 1026 (2d Cir. 1993); Costlow v. Weeks, 790 F.2d 1486, 1488 (9th Cir. 1986) (transfer required only when it is in the interest of justice); Wood v. Santa Barbara Chamber of Commerce, 705 F.2d 1515, 1523 (9th Cir. 1983).

[145] *See, e.g.*, Clayton v. Morioka, 1995 U.S. App. LEXIS 37504 (4th Cir. Nov. 14, 1995) (unpublished) (district court did not properly exercise its discretion when it dismissed without considering transfer).

[146] Goldlawr, Inc. v. Heiman, 369 U.S. 463, 466 (1962); *cf.* Miller v. Hambrick, 905 F.2d 259, 262 (9th

made an erroneous guess with regard to the existence of some elusive fact upon which venue provisions often turn."[147] Thus, for example, many lower courts have transferred rather than dismissed when the statute of limitations has expired after the plaintiff filed the action originally.[148] If the court dismisses, the case would be barred; but if the court transfers a case that was timely filed in the improper forum within the limitations period, the case can continue in the new forum.[149]

The court may dismiss an action pursuant to a Section 1406(a) motion if venue is wrong and transfer is not in the interest of justice.[150] For example, transfer will not be in the interest of justice and courts will dismiss if the plaintiff brought the action in the wrong district (1) for some improper purpose, e.g., the action was brought in the wrong district in bad faith in an attempt to circumvent an adverse ruling in a related action pending elsewhere,[151] (2) to harass the defendant with litigation in a remote forum,[152] or (3) if "blatant forum shopping" led the plaintiff not to bring the action in the proper district in the first instance.[153]

Moreover, the fact that the statute of limitations will bar the refiling of the action in the proper district does not require the conclusion that transfer is in the interest of justice.[154] Some courts have seized on the Supreme Court's description of a mistake on plaintiff's part as an "elusive" fact,[155] and have refused to transfer when the plaintiff's mistake was "obvious" or "foreseeable."[156]

---

Cir. 1990), (quoting *Goldlawr*, discussing transfer under Section 1631, which has same interest of justice requirement).

[147] Goldlawr, Inc. v. Heiman, 369 U.S. 463, 466 (1962).

[148] Gonzalez v. Hasty, 651 F.3d 318, 324–325 (2d Cir. 2011) (while courts enjoy considerable discretion in deciding whether to transfer in interests of justice, compelling reason for transfer is generally acknowledged when plaintiff's case, if dismissed, would be time-barred on refiling in proper forum); Lafferty v. St. Riel, 495 F.3d 72, 81 (3d Cir. 2007) ("When a judge elects to transfer rather than dismiss a case filed in an improper forum, he elects to allow parties to preserve their claim 'in the interest of justice' ").

[149] *See* Lafferty v. St. Riel, 495 F.3d 72, 82 (83 (3d Cir. 2007) (date of filing for limitations purposes is initial filing date in transferor forum, even if case is not docketed in transferee forum until after limitations period has run).

[150] *See* 28 U.S.C. § 1406(a).

[151] *Cf. In re* Hall, Bayoutree Associates, Ltd., 939 F.2d 802, 805–806 (9th Cir. 1991) (citing Moore's Federal Practice, court held that, under bankruptcy transfer statute modeled after Section 1406(a), district court properly dismissed rather than transferred when filing in forum lacking proper venue was done for bad faith reasons).

[152] King v. Russell, 963 F.2d 1301, 1304 (9th Cir. 1992).

[153] Wood v. Santa Barbara Chamber of Commerce, Inc., 705 F.2d 1515, 1523 (9th Cir. 1983).

[154] Hapaniewski v. City of Chicago Heights, 883 F.2d 576, 580 (7th Cir. 1989).

[155] *See* Goldlawr, Inc. v. Heiman, 369 U.S. 463 (1962).

[156] *See, e.g.*, Continental Ins. Co. v. M/V Orsula, 354 F.3d 603, 607–608 (7th Cir. 2003) (district court did not abuse its discretion in dismissing for improper venue after statute of limitations had run, rather than transferring, when proper forum required by forum selection clause was clear to plaintiff); Nichols v. G.D. Searle & Co., 991 F.2d 1195, 1201–1202 (4th Cir. 1993) (because plaintiff's attorney should have realized action was filed in wrong district as precedent was clear that defendant's activities in state were insufficient to subject them to general jurisdiction, court did not abuse its discretion in dismissing rather than transferring action even though action could not be refiled in proper district because statute of limitations apparently had since run); Spar, Inc. v. Information Resources, Inc., 956 F.2d 392, 394 (2d Cir.

## § 9.11 STANDING TO OBJECT TO IMPROPER VENUE

Because venue ordinarily must be proper as to each defendant,[157] any defendant may object that venue is improper as to him or her (but may not object as to another defendant), and the court must either dismiss the action against that defendant or transfer it to a district with proper venue. If there are other defendants as to whom venue is proper, the court may retain the action as to these defendants unless the dismissed defendant was an indispensable party (*see* 4 MOORE'S FEDERAL PRACTICE Ch. 19, *Required Joinder of Parties*).

At any time before the defendant has waived the objection to improper venue, a district court properly may raise on its own motion the issue of lack of proper venue, and may dismiss or transfer the action on that ground, as long as the court first has given the parties adequate notice and an opportunity to be heard on the issue.[158] Notice is necessary because the defendant may wish to waive any objection to the plaintiff's chosen forum.[159]

In general, the plaintiff, by bringing an action in a district lacking proper venue, automatically waives the right to object to improper venue in that district.[160] If, however, the plaintiff, through no fault of his or her own, was mistaken as to the residence of the defendant and as a consequence filed the action in the wrong district, the plaintiff's right to object to improper venue in the original district is not waived and the plaintiff may move to transfer the action under Section 1406(a) when he or she discovers the defendant's true residence.[161]

## § 9.12 WAIVER OF OBJECTION TO IMPROPER VENUE

A defendant loses the right to obtain a transfer or dismissal of the action for improper venue under Section 1406(a) unless he or she preserves this defense by making a timely and sufficient objection to improper venue and by avoiding conduct

---

1992) (transfer was not in interest of justice as "reasonably diligent" plaintiff should have known venue was wrong because action was time-barred by transferor court's statute of limitations).

[157] *See* Ch. 8, *Venue*; *see generally* 17 MOORE'S FEDERAL PRACTICE Chapter 110, *Determination of Proper Venue* (Matthew Bender 3d ed.).

[158] Stjernholm v. Peterson, 83 F.3d 347, 348 (10th Cir. 1996) (at any time before the defendants waive the objection to improper venue, "a district court may raise on its own motion an issue of defective venue or lack of personal jurisdiction, but the court may not dismiss without first giving the parties an opportunity to be present their views on the issue"); Costlow v. Weeks, 790 F.2d 1486, 1488 (9th Cir. 1986) ("in the absence of waiver, we can find no reason to hold that the district court erred by raising the issue of defective venue on its own motion").

[159] Lipofsky v. New York State Workers' Compensation Board, 861 F.2d 1257, 1258 (11th Cir. 1988) (reversing sua sponte dismissal when parties were not given chance to respond, noting that "defendants in some cases may wish to waive the defense [of improper venue] and the plaintiffs ought to have an opportunity to respond to the defenses before their cases are dismissed").

[160] Olberding v. Illinois Central Railway Co., 346 U.S. 338, 340 (1953).

[161] Manley v. Engram, 755 F.2d 1463, 1467–1471 (11th Cir. 1985) ("we hold that where a diligent plaintiff files suit in good faith in the district of the individual defendant's apparent residence, but later discovers that the defendant subjectively considers another state his permanent residence, the plaintiff will not be deemed to have automatically waived his right to object to venue in the original forum or to seek a transfer under Section 1406(a)").

that might be considered an implicit waiver.[162] The defense of improper venue is easily waived and waiver can occur in several ways,[163] including failure to comply with Rule 12 (*see* 2 Moore's Federal Practice Ch. 12, *Defenses and Objections: When and How Presented; Motion for Judgment on the Pleadings; Consolidating Motions; Waiving Defenses; Pretrial Hearing*) or by conduct through which the defendant is deemed to have implicitly abandoned the objection. Note, however, that waiver of improper venue does not preclude a Section 1404(a) motion to transfer on the basis of convenience of the parties or the witnesses (*see* § 9.02).[164]

The defense of improper venue is waived unless it is included in the defendant's first response to the complaint, whether that response is (1) a pre-answer motion to dismiss, (2) an answer to the complaint.[165]

Even if the defendant complies with Rule 12 by including the objection to improper venue in his or her first response to the complaint, the objection may still be waived by other conduct that may be viewed as an implicit submission to the court's jurisdiction.[166] For example, the defendant's participation in the action before making his or her first response to the complaint may result in a finding of waiver of the defense of improper venue. In one case, for example, the defendant waived its objection to improper venue when, prior to its answer in which it objected to lack of venue, defendant (1) moved for a hearing on the plaintiff's motion for an ex parte temporary restraining order, (2) moved for permission for its counsel to appear pro hac vice, (3) moved for an extension of time to file its answer, and (4) entered into a stipulation pursuant to which the parties agreed to try to resolve their dispute by, among other things, agreeing to limited expedited discovery and agreeing to a later hearing on the preliminary injunction if the parties could not resolve their dispute pursuant to a stipulation.[167]

---

[162] *See* 28 U.S.C. § 1406(b) ("Nothing in this chapter shall impair the jurisdiction of a district court of any matter involving a party who does not interpose timely and sufficient objection to venue"); *see also* King v. Russell, 963 F.2d 1301, 1303, 1305 (9th Cir. 1992) (action could not be dismissed under either 28 U.S.C. § 1406(a) or Fed. R. Civ. P. 12(b)(3) when defendants waived improper venue defense by not raising it in first pre-answer motion); Broadcasting Co. v. Flair Broadcasting, 892 F.2d 372, 377 (4th Cir. 1989) (defendant loses right to dismiss or transfer for improper venue under Section 1406(a) if objection has been waived).

[163] Leroy v. Great Western United Corp., 443 U.S. 173, 180 (1979) (venue is personal privilege that may be waived); Neirbo Co. v. Bethlehem Shipbuilding Corp., 308 U.S. 165, 168 (1939) (venue objection "may be lost by failure to assert it seasonably, by formal submission in a cause, or by submission through conduct").

[164] *See* 28 U.S.C. § 1404(a).

[165] *See* Fed. R. Civ. P. 12(h)(1) ("[a] defense of . . . improper venue . . . is waived . . . (A) if omitted from a motion in the circumstances describe in subdivision (g), or (B) if it is neither made by motion under this rule nor included in a responsive pleading or an amendment thereof permitted by Rule 15(a) to be made as a matter of course"); Fed. R. Civ. P. 12(g) ("If a party makes a motion under this rule but omits therefrom any defense or objection then available to the party which this rule permits to be raised by motion, the party shall not thereafter make a motion based on the defense or objection so omitted"); *See generally* 2 Moore's Federal Practice Ch. 12, *Defenses and Objections: When and How Presented; Motion for Judgment on the Pleadings; Consolidating Motions; Waiving Defenses; Pretrial Hearing* (Matthew Bender 3d ed.).

[166] *See* Neirbo Co. v. Bethlehem Shipbuilding Corp., 308 U.S. 165, 168 (1939) (objection to venue also may be waived "by submission [in a cause] through conduct").

[167] Manchester Knitted Fashions v. Amalgamated, 967 F.2d 688, 691 (1st Cir. 1992).

The majority of the courts hold that, in general, the defendant's act of removing the action from state court waives or cures any objection that venue would have been improper under the federal general venue statute[168] had the action been commenced in the district court originally.[169] This is so because the venue of removed actions is governed by the removal statute itself, which provides that the proper venue of a removed action is "the district of the United States for the district and division embracing the place where such action is pending,"[170] and the general venue provisions of Section 1391 have "no application" to removed actions.[171] In contrast, the act of removal does not waive the right to object in federal court to *state* court venue if objections have been properly preserved.[172]

## § 9.13 CHOICE OF LAW FOLLOWING TRANSFER FOR IMPROPER VENUE

Following a transfer under Section 1406(a), "the transferee court should apply whatever law it would have applied had the action been properly commenced there,"[173] including the choice of law rules of the state in which the transferee court sits.[174]

The rationale for this rule is to prevent impermissible forum-shopping. If the plaintiff were allowed to benefit by "capturing" the law of the forum by filing an action there despite improper venue and then moving to transfer to a proper venue, it would allow plaintiffs to forum shop by filing actions wherever state law was most advantageous, regardless of whether venue was proper in that district or not.[175] Indeed, the fact that the transferee court is not constrained to apply the law that the transferor court would have applied in diversity cases is one of the key consequential differences between Section 1404(a) transfers and Section 1406 transfers.

---

[168] 28 U.S.C. § 1391; *see generally* Ch. 8, *Venue*.

[169] Polizzi v. Cowles Magazines, Inc., 345 U.S. 663, 665 (1953); Seaboard Rice Milling Co. v. Chicago, Rock Island & Pacific R.R. Co., 270 U.S. 363, 366 (1926).

[170] 28 U.S.C. § 1441(a).

[171] Polizzi v. Cowles Magazines, Inc., 345 U.S. 663, 665 (1953) ("The venue of removed action is governed by 28 U.S.C. § 1441(a)" and the general venue provision "has no application"); *see generally* Ch. 6, *Removal*.

[172] *See* Lambert v. Kysar, 983 F.2d 1110, 1113 n.3 (1st Cir. 1993) ("the filing of a removal petition in a diversity action, without more, does not waive the right to object in federal court to the state court venue").

[173] *See, e.g.*, Schaeffer v. Village of Ossining, 58 F.3d 48, 49 (2d Cir. 1995).

[174] *See, e.g.*, Lafferty v. St. Riel, 495 F.3d 72, 81 (3d Cir. 2007) (ordinarily rule is that, following transfers, transferee forum's substantive laws apply); Jackson v. West Telemarketing Corp. Outbound, 245 F.3d 518, 523 (5th Cir. 2001) (after transfer under 28 U.S.C. § 1406(a), transferee district court should apply its own state law, including choice of law rules).

[175] *See, e.g.*, Eggleton v. Plasser & Theurer Export Von Bahnbaumaschinen Gesellschaft, 495 F.3d 582, 588–589 (8th Cir. 2007) (applying law of transferor forum would be unfair to defendant, who would be made to suffer choice-of-law consequences of plaintiff's mistake, and encourages procedural gamesmanship by creating an incentive for plaintiffs to engage in undue forum shopping); *see also* LaVay Corp. v. Dominion Federal Sav. & Loan Ass'n, 830 F.2d 522, 526 (4th Cir. 1987).

# PART D
# TRANSFER TO COURT WITH EXCLUSIVE SUBJECT MATTER JURISDICTION

## § 9.14 SECTION 1631 IS BROADLY PHRASED TO ALLOW TRANSFER BETWEEN FEDERAL COURTS

Ordinarily, a district court must dismiss an action if it lacks subject matter jurisdiction, i.e., diversity, federal question, or some other basis for jurisdiction.[176] If, however, the district court lacks subject matter jurisdiction over particular categories of actions or appeals because a federal statute vests exclusive subject matter jurisdiction in a specified federal court, the district court may transfer the action to that court under Section 1631.[177] Section 1631 was enacted as part of the Federal Courts Improvement Act of 1982,[178] and is a broadly phrased provision authorizing a federal court, if it determines that "there is a want of jurisdiction" as to a civil action or appeal filed with it, to transfer the action or appeal "to any other court in which the action or appeal could have been brought at the time it was filed or noticed" in the original court.[179]

Although all courts agree that the statute was intended to allow transfer of an action or appeal under these circumstances, some courts have concluded that this is the sole purpose of the statute,[180] while others have interpreted it as authorizing transfer to cure additional defects in the transferor court, such as a lack of personal jurisdiction or improper venue.[181]

---

[176] *See generally* Ch. 3, *Diversity Jurisdiction*; Ch. 4, *Federal Question Jurisdiction.*

[177] *See* 28 U.S.C. § 1631.

[178] Pub. L. No. 97-164, § 301.

[179] 28 U.S.C. § 1631; *see* Ross v. Colorado Outward Bound School, Inc., 822 F.2d 1524, 1526 (10th Cir. 1987) ("Congress gave broad authority to permit the transfer of an action between any two federal courts. [Section 1631] controls the action of a federal court when it finds that it lacks jurisdiction but that another federal court has jurisdiction"); McLaughlin v. Arco Polymers, Inc., 721 F.2d 426, 429 (3d Cir. 1983) (Section 1631 "is broadly drafted to allow transfer between any two Federal courts"); *see also* S. Rep. No. 275, at 30, *reprinted in* 1982 U.S. Code Cong. & Admin. News 11, 40.

[180] McTyre v. Broward Gen. Med. Ctr., 749 F. Supp. 102, 105 (D.N.J. 1990) (28 U.S.C. § 1631 applies only when subject matter jurisdiction is lacking in transferor court); Levy v. Pyramid Co. of Ithaca, 687 F. Supp. 48, 51 (N.D.N.Y. 1988), *aff'd on other grounds*, 871 F.2d 9 (2d Cir. 1989) (Section 1631 "was only intended to apply to cases in which the transferor court lacks SUBJECT matter jurisdiction") (emphasis in original).

[181] Ross v. Colorado Outward Bound School, Inc., 822 F.2d 1524, 1527 (10th Cir. 1987) (when transferor court lacks personal jurisdiction, transfer to proper court should be made pursuant to 28 U.S.C. § 1631).

## § 9.15 PREREQUISITES FOR TRANSFEREE COURT

Before transferring under Section 1631, the district court in which the action or appeal originally was filed must ascertain that the proposed transferee court is one in which the action "could have been brought at the time it was filed or noticed."[182] Although this phrase has not been interpreted as frequently as the similar phrases in the other transfer statutes, it has been interpreted in a similar fashion, requiring that at the time the action or appeal was filed in the original court, the transferee court would have had (1) subject matter jurisdiction,[183] (2) proper venue,[184] and (3) personal jurisdiction over the defendant.[185]

# PART E
# APPELLATE REVIEW OF TRANSFER ORDERS

## § 9.16 TRANSFER ORDERS USUALLY NOT IMMEDIATELY APPEALABLE

As a general rule, orders granting or denying transfer under any of the transfer statutes, Section 1404 (transfer of case from one proper venue to another for convenience), Section 1406 (transfer of case in which venue was improper), or Section 1631 (transfer when subject matter jurisdiction, or in some courts, personal jurisdiction, is lacking), are not immediately appealable because ordinarily these orders do not end the litigation. Thus, they are not "final decisions" for the purpose of appellate jurisdiction.[186] There is one exception to this rule, however. An order granting or denying a motion to transfer an action to the United States Court of Federal Claims under Section 1631 is immediately appealable.[187] In contrast, if the

---

[182] 28 U.S.C. § 1631.

[183] United States Marine, Inc. v. United States, 722 F.3d 1360, 1365 (Fed. Cir. 2013) (for the transfer order to be correct district court must lack jurisdiction over plaintiff's action, and the Claims Court must have jurisdiction over its action); Kolek v. Engen, 869 F.2d 1281, 1284 (9th Cir. 1989) (transfer to appellate court was proper because at time appeal was filed in wrong court, appellate court would have had exclusive jurisdiction over appeal).

[184] *See, e.g.*, Ross v. Colorado Outward Bound School, Inc., 822 F.2d 1524, 1527 (10th Cir. 1987) (transferor court correctly determined that venue would be proper in transferee court); Grimsley v. United Engineers & Constructors, Inc., 818 F. Supp. 147, 148–149 (D.S.C. 1993) (transferee court must have subject matter jurisdiction, proper venue, and personal jurisdiction).

[185] *See, e.g.*, Grynberg v. Ivanhoe Energy, Inc., 2012 U.S. App. LEXIS 14254, at *53–*54 (10th Cir. July 18, 2012) (unpublished opinion) (district court properly declined to transfer action when plaintiffs failed to show that transferee court would have had personal jurisdiction over defendants; citing Moore's Federal Practice); Grimsley v. United Engineers & Constructors, Inc., 818 F. Supp. 147, 148–149 (D.S.C. 1993) (transferee court must be able to exercise personal jurisdiction over defendant).

[186] *See* 28 U.S.C. § 1291 (providing for appeals only from "final decisions of the district courts of the United States"); Subsalve USA Corp. v. Watson Mfg., Inc., 462 F.3d 41, 47 (1st Cir. 2006) (transfer order under 28 U.S.C. § 1631 was not final order and was not immediately appealable, so that court of appeals lacked jurisdiction to review it); SongByrd, Inc. v. Estate of Grossman, 206 F.3d 172, 176 (2d Cir. 2000) (citing Moore's Federal Practice, "A transfer order is an interlocutory order that is not immediately reviewable by appeal").

[187] Section 1292 authorizes interlocutory review of transfer orders to Court of Claims under Section

court dismisses the action rather than transfers it, the order is immediately appealable as a final judgment.[188] Section 1406(a) expressly authorizes the court to dismiss the action for improper venue unless it finds that transfer is in the interest of justice (*see* § 9.10).

Orders granting or denying transfer fall outside the collateral order exception to the final judgment rule,[189] which permits immediate review if the interlocutory order would be "effectively unreviewable" after a final judgment is entered in the case.[190] On the other hand, courts have noted that there are several possible, though limited, avenues to secure immediate review of the transfer order, i.e., by a writ of mandamus, by certification of the transfer order, or by indirect review by way of a motion for retransfer in the transferee court. Thus, these courts have noted that transfer orders are not "effectively unreviewable" after final judgment.[191]

The losing party to a motion to transfer venue may request that the district court certify the transfer order as one qualifying for immediate appeal.[192] Although certification has been granted to allow immediate review of transfer orders,[193] it is somewhat rare.[194]

An appellate court always has the power to grant mandamus relief to review transfer orders.[195] Generally, however, mandamus is only available when the losing party has no other adequate means of obtaining relief from the adverse order.[196] In an appropriate case, mandamus review is available because most courts recognize that it is almost impossible to correct an erroneous transfer order by appellate

---

1631. 28 U.S.C. § 1292(d)(4)(A) (Federal Circuit has exclusive jurisdiction to review interlocutory orders of district court granting or denying motions to transfer to United States Court of Federal Claims under 28 U.S.C. § 1631); *see* United States v. D.L. Kaufman, 175 F.3d 970, 972 (Fed. Cir. 1999) (28 U.S.C. § 1292(d)(4)(A) permits interlocutory review of orders granting or denying transfer to Court of Federal Claims).

[188] Cook v. Fox, 537 F.2d 370, 371 (9th Cir. 1976).

[189] *See, e.g.*, F.D.I.C. v. McGlamery, 74 F.3d 218, 221 (10th Cir. 1996) (in dicta, court stated that "[t]he courts have almost universally agreed that transfer orders fall outside the scope of the collateral order exception").

[190] Cohen v. Beneficial Indus. Loan Corp., 337 U.S. 541, 546 (1949) (generally speaking, the collateral order doctrine is an exception to the rule limiting immediate appeals to final orders, and allows review of interlocutory orders if, among other requirements, they would be "effectively unreviewable" after a final judgment is entered in the case).

[191] *See, e.g.*, Roofing & Sheet Metal Serv. v. La Quinta Motor Inns, Inc., 689 F.2d 982, 987 (11th Cir. 1982) (availability of mandamus means transfer order not effectively unreviewable).

[192] *See* 28 U.S.C. § 1292(b) (district court is permitted to certify that interlocutory order should be immediately appealable because it involves controlling question of law as to which there is substantial ground for difference of opinion, and that immediate appeal may materially advance ultimate termination of litigation; court of appeals may then, in its discretion, grant immediate appeal); *see* 19 Moore's Federal Practice Ch. 203, *Interlocutory Orders* (Matthew Bender 3d ed.).

[193] *See* Red Bull Associates v. Best Western Intern., Inc., 862 F.2d 963 (2d Cir. 1988); *see also* Contraves Inc. v. McDonnell Douglas, Corp., 889 F. Supp. 470, 474 (M.D. Fla. 1995) (certifying order granting transfer under 28 U.S.C. § 1404(a) based on forum selection clause to appellate court).

[194] *See* Garner v. Wolfinbarger, 433 F.2d 117, 120 (5th Cir. 1970) (orders granting or denying transfer generally should not be certified).

[195] Van Dusen v. Barrack, 376 U.S. 612, 615 n.3 (1964).

[196] Sunbelt Corp. v. Noble, Denton & Associates, Inc., 5 F.3d 28, 30 (3d Cir. 1993).

review after a trial, and even if the order ultimately is reversed, the expense and inconvenience of retrying the case would be extremely burdensome.[197] Mandamus may be warranted even when the party did not seek reconsideration of the transfer order or ask the district court to certify the case for interlocutory appeal under 28 U.S.C. § 1292(b).[198]

Because mandamus is considered an extraordinary remedy, however,[199] the petitioner generally must show an error on the part of the district court of a higher magnitude than "mere error." For example, the order must be a "gross" abuse of discretion,[200] or, at the very least, "clearly erroneous" or a "clear-cut abuse of discretion."[201]

However, some courts of appeals have become more expansive in allowing mandamus review of the denial of motions to transfer. For example, sitting en banc, a divided Fifth Circuit held that the defendant was entitled to mandamus in a product liability case in which the district court had denied a motion to transfer under § 1404(a).[202] While the opinion purports to adhere to a relatively stringent test for granting mandamus to correct erroneous transfer orders, the Fifth Circuit actually applied the test quite expansively to enable the defendant to avoid litigation in a particular division of the Eastern District of Texas, which had become known as a plaintiff-friendly forum.[203] Similarly, the Federal Circuit has followed the same expansive approach to allowing mandamus and ordered the district court to transfer

---

[197] Sunbelt Corp. v. Noble, Denton & Associates, Inc., 5 F.3d at 30 ("the possibility of an appeal in the transferee forum following a final judgment . . . is not an adequate alternative").

[198] *In re* Apple, Inc., 602 F.3d 909, 912 (8th Cir. 2010) ("even if we assume that interlocutory review would be available . . . we may proceed to consider the petition for writ of mandamus").

[199] Allied Chemical Corp. v. Daiflon, Inc. 449 U.S. 33, 34 (1980) ("the remedy of mandamus is a drastic one, to be invoked only in extraordinary situations"); *see also* Roofing & Sheet Metal Serv. v. La Quinta Motor Inns, Inc., 689 F.2d 982, 987 (11th Cir. 1982) (court indicated that although "a majority of circuits have at least suggested that the writ [of mandamus] might issue to correct an abuse of discretion [in the grant or denial of a transfer order] in some circumstances," mandamus has "rarely issued" in such a context).

[200] *In re* Tripati, 836 F.2d 1406, 1407 (D.C. Cir. 1988).

[201] *In re* Federal-Mogul Global, Inc., 300 F.3d 368, 378–384 (3d Cir. 2002) (court of appeals refused to issue writ of mandamus overruling order denying transfer when district court's decision did not amount to clear error of law approaching magnitude of unauthorized exercise of judicial power); *In re* Volkswagen of Am., Inc., 545 F.3d 304, 309 (5th Cir. 2008) (en banc) ("mandamus will be granted [on] a determination that there has been a clear abuse of discretion"); *In re* Horseshoe Entm't, 337 F.3d 429, 431–432 (5th Cir. 2003) (writ of mandamus granted when court found that district court clearly abused its discretion by considering improper factors and ignoring relevant factors with respect to decision to transfer venue); *In re* LimitNone, LLC, 551 F.3d 572, 575–576 (7th Cir. 2008) (party seeking mandamus must show that order so far exceeds proper bounds of judicial discretion as to be legitimately considered usurpative in character, or in violation of clear and indisputable legal right, or at very least patently erroneous); *In re* Genentech, Inc., 566 F.3d 1338, 1341 (Fed. Cir. 2009) (writ of mandamus is available only in extraordinary situations to correct "clear abuse of discretion"); *see generally* 19 Moore's Federal Practice Ch. 204, *Extraordinary Writs* (Matthew Bender 3d ed.).

[202] *See In re* Volkswagen of Am., Inc., 545 F.3d 304, 310 (5th Cir. 2008) (en banc) (district court "clearly" abuses its discretion when court's errors result in "patently erroneous result").

[203] *In re* Volkswagen of Am., Inc., 545 F.3d 304, 309–310, 318 (5th Cir. 2008) (en banc) (district court clearly abused its discretion in denying transfer motion when no factors favored chosen venue and only connection between case and forum was plaintiff's choice to file there).

the cases.[204] For example, the Federal Circuit granted mandamus in a patent case filed in a district court within the Third Circuit. Applying the Third Circuit's "exacting standard" for mandamus, the Federal Circuit nevertheless directed the district court to transfer the case, finding that the district court had failed to balance the public and private interest factors fairly and instead had elevated two of the factors to overriding importance.[205] Although mandamus is not available in every case,[206] these cases indicate a greater willingness on the part of the courts of appeals to order mandamus to correct transfer decisions, and a corresponding lessening of the broad discretion traditionally accorded district courts in these matters.

If the district court grants transfer of venue, the losing party may obtain "indirect review" of the transfer order by making a motion in the transferee court to retransfer the case.[207] The "law of the case" doctrine,[208] however, generally discourages transferee courts from revisiting the prior rulings of the transferor court, especially the transfer order itself.[209]

## § 9.17 DETERMINATION OF PROPER CIRCUIT IN WHICH TO SEEK APPELLATE REVIEW

### [1] Appellate Review If Motion to Transfer Denied

If the motion to transfer is denied, the losing party may seek immediate appellate review via certification or mandamus in the Court of Appeals embracing the district court in which the action is pending. Of course, this is the same circuit

---

[204] *See In re* Microsoft Corp., 630 F.3d 1361, 1363–1365 (Fed. Cir. 2011) (Federal Circuit granted mandamus to order Eastern District of Texas to transfer patent case to more convenient forum when denial of transfer was patently erroneous); *In re* TS Tech United States Corp., 551 F.3d 1315, 1321–1322 (Fed. Cir. 2008) (defendant met its "difficult burden" of demonstrating clear abuse of discretion when district court denied transfer from venue with no meaningful ties to case).

[205] *In re* Link_A_Media Devices Corp., 662 F.3d 1221, 1222–1223 (Fed. Cir. 2011) (mandamus may be used to correct an improper transfer order if the petitioner can establish a "clear and indisputable" right to the writ; standard is an exacting one, requiring the petitioner to establish that the district court's decision amounted to a failure to meaningfully consider the merits of the transfer motion).

[206] *In re* Vistaprint Ltd., 628 F.3d 1342, 1344–1347 (Fed. Cir. 2010) (district court for Eastern District of Texas did not clearly abuse its discretion in denying transfer of patent case, even though factors relating to convenience favored transfer, when judicial economy favored retaining action; judicial economy favored retaining action because court had substantial experience in construing patent that was at issue, and another case involving same patent was pending there).

[207] F.D.I.C. v. McGlamery, 74 F.3d 218, 221 (10th Cir. 1996) ("Indirect review of [transfer orders] can be obtained by bringing a motion to retransfer in the transferee court").

[208] *See* 18 Moore's Federal Practice Ch. 134, *Stare Decisis, Law of the Case, and Judicial Estoppel* (Matthew Bender 3d ed.).

[209] Christianson v. Colt Indus. Operating Corp., 486 U.S. 800, 816 (1988) (law of case doctrine applies even more to transfer decisions than it does to other issues); *See also* McGuire v. United States, 707 F.3d 1351, 1359 (Fed. Cir. 2013) (*Christianson* applies when transferor court has made merits rulings while it had jurisdiction over case; law of case doctrine did not prevent transferee court from revisiting merits decisions of transferor court that were made without jurisdiction).

in which any appeal from a final judgment would be filed.[210]

### [2] Appellate Review If Motion to Transfer Granted

If the motion to transfer is granted, and the transfer is to a district court within another circuit, certain steps must be taken to preserve the ability to obtain appellate review. The losing party may file a mandamus petition or seek certification in the transferor circuit, but only in the time period before which the record is physically transferred to the transferee court. This is so because generally the transferor court, including the circuit court, loses jurisdiction as soon as the files in the case are transferred and docketed in the transferee court.[211]

# PART F
# COMMON LAW DOCTRINE OF FORUM NON CONVENIENS DISMISSAL

## § 9.18 PURPOSE OF FORUM NON CONVENIENS DOCTRINE

Under the common-law doctrine of forum non conveniens, the district court "may decline to exercise its jurisdiction, even though the court has jurisdiction and venue, when it appears that the convenience of the parties and the court and the interests of justice indicate that the action should be tried in another forum."[212] Dismissal on forum non conveniens grounds "has the practical effect of requiring the plaintiff to refile [the] complaint in a more convenient forum elsewhere."[213]

## § 9.19 DOCTRINE APPLIES IN FEDERAL COURTS ONLY WHEN ALTERNATIVE FORUM IS ABROAD

Since the convenience transfer statute, Section 1404(a), was enacted in 1948, the federal doctrine of forum non conveniens has continuing application only in cases in which the alternative forum is abroad.[214] Before Section 1404(a) was enacted,

---

[210] *See, e.g.*, Cottman Transmission Sys., Inc. v. Martino Distrib., Inc., 36 F.3d 291, 296 (3d Cir. 1994) (transferor circuit would hear appeal from denial of transfer).

[211] Midwest Motor Express, Inc. v. Central States S.E. & S.W., 70 F.3d 1014, 1016 (8th Cir. 1995) ("the rule that jurisdiction follows the file avoids the procedural and jurisdictional snarl that would likely ensue if two courts were simultaneously working on the same case"); *see also* Hudson United Bank v. Chase Manhattan Bank of Connecticut, N.A., 43 F.3d 843, 845 n.4 (3d Cir. 1994); Chrysler Credit Corp. v. Country Chrysler, Inc., 928 F.2d 1509, 1516–1517 (10th Cir. 1991); *see* Lou v. Belzberg, 834 F.2d 730, 733 (9th Cir. 1987) (transferor court loses jurisdiction when case files docketed in transferee court); Robbins v. Pocket Beverage Co., Inc., 779 F.2d 351, 355 (7th Cir. 1985) (transferor court loses jurisdiction when case files docketed in transferee court).

[212] Piper Aircraft Co. v. Reyno, 454 U.S. 235, 250 (1981).

[213] Howe v. Goldcorp. Investments, Ltd., 946 F.2d 944, 947 (1st Cir. 1991).

[214] American Dredging Co. v. Miller, 510 U.S. 443, 448–450 n.2 (1994); *see* 28 U.S.C. § 1404(a); *see also* Sinochem Int'l Co. v. Malaysia Int'l Shipping Corp., 549 U.S. 422, 428–430 (2007) (common-law doctrine

federal courts dismissed actions on forum non conveniens grounds when the alternative forum was a foreign country, a state court, or another federal forum.[215] Section 1404(a) was enacted to avoid the harsh remedy of dismissal by authorizing the district courts to transfer an action in which venue was proper to another federal district court also having proper venue that was a more convenient forum for the litigation (*see* § 9.02).[216]

## § 9.20 COURT MUST APPLY FEDERAL LAW OF FORUM NON CONVENIENS

A federal court in a diversity action must apply the federal law of forum non conveniens in resolving a motion to dismiss when the alternative forum is a foreign tribunal, not the state forum non conveniens law of the district in which the court is sitting.[217] Federal law applies because "[t]he forum non conveniens doctrine is a rule of venue, not a rule of decision and, therefore, the *Erie* doctrine does not require the application of state forum non conveniens rules."[218] In addition, the "strong federal interests" of the federal forum's ability to manage the cases before it and the doctrine's "foreign policy implications" militate in favor of applying federal law to the issue of forum non conveniens.[219]

## § 9.21 COURT WEIGHS MULTIPLE FACTORS IN DECIDING FORUM NON CONVENIENS MOTION

### [1] Doctrine Is Flexible

The doctrine of forum non conveniens is a "flexible" one, with the court weighing multiple factors relating to fairness and convenience based on the particular facts of the case in deciding the motion.[220] Indeed, the Supreme Court has cautioned that "[i]f central emphasis [is] placed on any one factor, the forum non conveniens

---

of forum non conveniens has continuing application in federal courts only when alternative forum is abroad "and perhaps in rare instances where a state or territorial court serves litigational convenience best").

[215] *See* Gulf Oil Corp. v. Gilbert, 330 U.S. 501 (1947) (upholding dismissal of action in New York district court when Virginia was more convenient forum).

[216] Norwood v. Kirkpatrick, 349 U.S. 29, 32 (1955).

[217] *See* Ravelo Monegro v. Rosa, 211 F.3d 509, 511–512 (9th Cir. 2000) (federal law governed forum non conveniens motion in federal court, since interests of federal forum in self-regulation, in administrative independence, and in self-management are more important than any interest in uniformity between federal and state forums in single state).

[218] Rivendell Forest Products, Ltd. v. Canadian Pacific Ltd., 2 F.3d 990, 992 (10th Cir. 1993); *see generally* Ch. 15, *Erie Doctrine*; 17 MOORE'S FEDERAL PRACTICE Ch. 124, *The Erie Doctrine and Applicable Law* (Matthew Bender 3d ed.).

[219] Blanco v. Banco Industrial de Venezuela, S.A., 997 F.2d 974, 981 (2d Cir. 1993) (it is not the business of the federal courts to assume the responsibility for supervising the integrity of the judicial system of another sovereign nation).

[220] Piper Aircraft Co. v. Reyno, 454 U.S. 235, 249 (1981) ("each case turns on its facts"); *see* Windt v. Qwest Communs. Int'l, Inc., 529 F.3d 183, 188 (3d Cir. 2008) (district court is afforded substantial flexibility in evaluating forum non conveniens motion, and each case turns on its facts).

doctrine would lose much of the very flexibility that makes it so valuable."[221] The downside of the doctrine's flexible nature is that it makes "uniformity and predictability of outcome almost impossible."[222]

## [2] Two Elements Required for Dismissal

The party moving for forum non conveniens dismissal must demonstrate (1) the existence of an adequate alternative forum, and (2) that the balance of relevant private and public interest factors favor dismissal.[223]

### [a] First Element: Alternative Forum Must Be Adequate

In resolving a forum non conveniens motion, the threshold inquiry is whether there is an "adequate" alternative forum available for adjudication of the dispute.[224] If there is no adequate alternative forum available, the court has no discretion to dismiss and must retain the action.[225]

Although adequacy is a threshold consideration, only in "rare" circumstances will the alternative forum be held inadequate despite the defendant's amenability to process there.[226] For example, the alternative forum will be considered inadequate if it "does not permit litigation of the subject matter of the dispute" at all or if the plaintiff demonstrates "significant legal or political obstacles to conducting litigation

---

[221] Piper Aircraft Co. v. Reyno, 454 U.S. at 249.

[222] American Dredging Co. v. Miller, 510 U.S. 443, 454–456 (1994). *See* Simona Grossi, *Forum Non Conveniens as a Jurisdictional Doctrine*, 75 *U. Pitt. L. Rev.* __ , __ (2014) (forthcoming) (describing history of forum non conveniens doctrine and how federal court decisions have become increasingly unpredictable).

[223] Piper Aircraft Co. v. Reyno, 454 U.S. 235, 254 n.22 (1981); Agudas Chasidei Chabad v. Russian Federation, 528 F.3d 934, 950 (D.C. Cir. 2008) (court must decide (1) whether adequate alternative forum is available and (2) whether balancing of private and public interest factors strongly favors dismissal); Creative Technology, Ltd. v. Aztech Sys. PTE, Ltd., 61 F.3d 696, 699 (9th Cir. 1995).

[224] Piper Aircraft Co. v. Reyno, 454 U.S. 235, 254 n.22 (1981); *see* Stroitelstvo Bulgaria Ltd. v. Bulgarian-American Enter. Fund, 589 F.3d 417, 421 (7th Cir. 2009) (threshold requirement for any forum non conveniens dismissal is existence of alternative forum that is both available and adequate).

[225] *See* DRFP L.L.C. v. Republica Bolivariana de Venezuela, 622 F.3d 513, 518 (6th Cir. 2010) (decision that foreign forum does not provide adequate alternative forum is matter of law reviewed de novo rather than for abuse of discretion); Fireman's Fund Ins. Co. v. Thyssen Mining Constr. of Can., Ltd., 703 F.3d 488, 495 (10th Cir. 2012) (even though New Mexico was inconvenient forum under private and public interest factors, court could not dismiss when action in Canadian forum would be barred by statute of limitations: "Sometimes an inconvenient forum is the *only* available forum").

[226] Piper Aircraft Co. v. Reyno, 454 U.S. 235, 254 n.22 (1981) ("In rare circumstances, however, where the remedy offered by the other forum is clearly unsatisfactory, the other forum may not be an adequate alternative, and the initial requirement may not be satisfied"); DiRienzo v. Philip Servs. Corp., 232 F.3d 49, 57 (2d Cir. 2000), *adopted in part, vacated in part on other grounds en banc*, 294 F.3d 21, 29 (2d Cir. 2002) (only on rare occasions is remedy in alternative forum so unsatisfactory that forum is inadequate; Canadian forum was adequate forum for litigation of securities fraud claims, despite differences between U.S. and Canadian securities laws and class action procedures); Bhatnagar v. Surrendra Overseas Ltd., 52 F.3d 1220, 1225 n.3 (3d Cir. 1995) (referring to conclusion in Note, *Review and Appeal of Forum Non Conveniens and Venue Transfer Orders*, 59 Geo. Wash. L. Rev. 715, 727–728 (1991), that as of March 1991, out of "hundreds" of reported forum non conveniens decisions, "only six reported decisions involved pretrial decisions *not* to dismiss") (emphasis in original).

in the alternative forum."[227]

Although the courts are reluctant to hold an alternative forum inadequate, some courts have created special rules for allocating the burden of proof with respect to adequacy of the foreign forum. The defendant has the ultimate burden of persuasion on whether the foreign forum will provide a remedy, but only when the plaintiff has substantiated allegations of serious corruption or delay in the foreign court system. When the allegations are insubstantially supported, the district court may reject them without considering any evidence from the defendant. When the plaintiff produces significant evidence documenting partiality or delay typically associated with the adjudication of similar claims, and these conditions are so severe as to call the adequacy of the forum into doubt, then the defendant has the burden to persuade the district court that the facts are otherwise. This approach correctly forbids dismissal to alternative forums that realistically are not capable of producing any remedy for the plaintiff's injuries, without crediting cursory attacks on foreign legal systems simply because they are somewhat slower or less elaborate than those in the United States.[228]

Thus, when a district court decides to dismiss a case on *forum non conveniens* grounds, it may not rely on a mere "justifiable belief" in the adequacy of the foreign forum.[229] Rather, the district court, keeping in mind that the party seeking dismissal bears the burden of proving the adequacy of the foreign forum, must engage in a full analysis of the question and carefully examine all submissions to support a determination that it has a justifiable belief that the foreign forum is adequate.[230]

Moreover, the possibility that less favorable substantive law will be applied in the foreign forum is only relevant in the forum non conveniens inquiry when "the remedy provided by the alternative forum is so clearly inadequate or unsatisfactory that it is no remedy at all," because, for example, the alternative forum "does not permit litigation of the subject matter of the dispute."[231] Thus, as long as the alternative forum provides some potential avenue for redress, that forum generally will be considered adequate. In the Supreme Court's seminal *Piper* decision, for example, the possibility that the alternative forum would not recognize a strict liability theory did not make the forum inadequate because the plaintiff would still

---

[227] *See* Mercier v. Sheraton Intern., Inc., 981 F.2d 1345, 1350 (1st Cir. 1992) (citing as example Castro's Cuba unavailable to Cuban political refugees as alternative forum).

[228] Leon v. Millon Air, Inc., 251 F.3d 1305, 1312–1314 (11th Cir. 2001) (defendant was not required to offer proof on adequacy issue when plaintiffs did not meet their burden of producing significant evidence documenting partiality or delay in foreign court system). *See also* Abdullahi v. Pfizer, Inc., 562 F.3d 163, 189 (2d Cir. 2009) ("while the plaintiff bears the initial burden of producing evidence of corruption, delay or lack of due process in the foreign forum, the defendant bears the ultimate burden of persuasion as to the adequacy of the forum").

[229] Bank of Credit & Commerce Int'l Ltd. v. State Bank of Pakistan, 273 F.3d 241, 247–248 (2d Cir. 2001) (district court is not excused from engaging in full analysis of adequacy of forum by concluding that it has justifiable belief in adequacy of forum).

[230] 273 F.3d at 247–248 (district court must engage in full analysis of question of adequacy and carefully review parties' submissions to support justifiable belief in adequacy of forum determination).

[231] Piper Aircraft Co. v. Reyno, 454 U.S. 235, 254 (1981).

be able to pursue negligence claims in that forum.[232] Some courts, however, have interpreted *Piper* to mean that less favorable law in the foreign forum, even if it does not rise to the level of depriving the plaintiff of all remedies, still carries some weight in favor of retaining the action.[233]

A district court need not start from scratch in making this analysis, but should be guided by precedent. If previous appellate decisions have found a particular foreign forum to be available and adequate, the district court should not reach a contrary conclusion unless plaintiffs can show evidence distinguishing the case from the precedent, an order from the foreign court dismissing the precise case for lack of jurisdiction, or reliable evidence of some change in the law of the foreign forum.[234]

Finally, if there is doubt as to whether the alternative foreign forum will entertain the action, the district court should condition the dismissal on the foreign court's acceptance of the case.[235] The district court may impose other conditions to ensure the adequacy of the foreign forum. In one case, for example, dismissal was conditioned on an American defendant's agreement to make available in the alternative forum witnesses and evidence to the same extent as it would have in district court.[236] In some cases the defendant has been required to waive a statute of limitations defense that might otherwise bar litigation in the foreign forum.[237] However, while it is appropriate to make dismissal subject to conditions placed on the parties, courts should avoid conditions that may be viewed as having the effect of undermining the considered policies of the foreign forum.[238]

---

[232] 454 U.S. at 247, 254–255 ("The possibility of a change in substantive law should ordinarily not be given conclusive or even substantial weight in the forum non conveniens inquiry"); *see* Gonzalez v. Chrysler Corp., 301 F.3d 377, 380–383 (5th Cir. 2002) (inappropriate to denounce legitimate policy choice of foreign country and replace it with court's own view); DRFP L.L.C. v. Republica Bolivariana de Venezuela, 622 F.3d 513, 520 (6th Cir. 2010) ("fact that the law in Venezuela *may* not be favorable to [plaintiff] . . . does not render . . . Venezuela [an] unavailable and inadequate [forum] as a matter of law.").

[233] *See, e.g.*, Wilson v. Humphreys (Cayman) Ltd., 916 F.2d 1239, 1246 (7th Cir. 1990) (district court did not abuse discretion in retaining action and giving some weight to fact that law in foreign forum was disadvantageous to plaintiff); Lehman v. Humphrey Cayman, Ltd., 713 F.2d 339, 343 (8th Cir. 1983).

[234] *In re* Ford Motor Co., 591 F.3d 406, 412–413 (5th Cir. 2009) (earlier decision by Fifth Circuit Court of Appeals created "a nearly airtight presumption" that Mexico was available forum, so that district court clearly erred in denying dismissal in favor of Mexican court).

[235] Bank of Credit and Commerce Int'l (Overseas) Ltd. v. State Bank of Pakistan, 273 F.3d 241, 247 (2d Cir. 2001); Blanco v. Banco Industrial de Venezuela, 997 F.2d 974, 983–984 (2d Cir. 1993); Vasquez v. Bridgestone/Firestone, Inc., 325 F.3d 665, 671–672, 675 (5th Cir. 2003).

[236] *See, e.g.*, Mercier v. Sheraton Int'l, Inc., 981 F.2d 1345, 1353 (1st Cir. 1992).

[237] *See* Carijano v. Occidental Petroleum Corp., 643 F.3d 1216, 1234–1235 (9th Cir. 2011) (district courts are not required to impose conditions on forum non conveniens dismissals, but it is an abuse of discretion to fail to do so when there is a justifiable reason to doubt that a party will cooperate with foreign forum).

[238] *See* Gross v. BBC, 386 F.3d 224, 234–235 (2d Cir. 2004) (Second Circuit urged district court to be "cognizant of the prudential choices made by foreign nations and not to impose conditions on parties that may be viewed as having the effect of undermining the considered policies of the transferee forum").

### [b] Second Element: Convenience of Parties and Ends of Justice Must Be Best Served by Dismissing Action

The formulation of the degree of inconvenience that the defendant must show to justify a dismissal of the action on forum non conveniens grounds varies. The Supreme Court has said that trial in the plaintiff's chosen forum is inappropriate when it would cause " 'oppressiveness and vexation to a defendant . . . out of all proportion to plaintiff's convenience,' or when . . . 'considerations affecting the court's own administrative and legal problems' " make the forum inappropriate.[239] Some lower courts emphasize the need for a showing of a likelihood of "serious unfairness" if the district court retains the action,[240] while others speak more in terms of simple convenience.[241]

Once the court has decided that the proposed alternative forum is adequate, "it must proceed to balance public and private interests to determine whether the convenience of the parties and the ends of justice would best be served by dismissing the action."[242]

The private interest factors include the following (*see* 17 Moore's Federal Practice Ch. 111, § 111.74[3][c]):[243]

- The relative ease of access to sources of proof.
- The relative availability of compulsory process to secure the attendance of unwilling witnesses.
- The cost of obtaining attendance of willing witnesses.
- Whether a view of the premises at issue in the action is necessary.
- The enforceability of judgments.
- The defendant's inability to implead a necessary third party.
- The cost of obtaining or translating evidence.
- The plaintiff's financial hardship that would be incurred if the action is brought in the alternative forum.

---

239 American Dredging Co. v. Miller, 510 U.S. 443 (1994), *quoting* Piper Aircraft Co. v. Reyno, 454 U.S. 235, 241 (1981).

240 *See* Iragorri v. International Elevator, Inc., 203 F.3d 8, 15 (1st Cir. 2000) (court properly applied standard that forum non conveniens dismissal is proper when balance of factors "strongly favors" alternative forum, and this standard is not independent standard from "oppressiveness and vexation" formulation but is distillation of that language); Zions First Nat'l Bank v. Moto Diesel Mexicana, S.A. de C.V., 629 F.3d 520, 525–526 (6th Cir. 2010) (when U.S. plaintiff selects U.S. forum, forum non conveniens determination must indicate that district court considered whether any oppression and vexation to defendant was out of all proportion to plaintiff's convenience); Ravelo Monegro v. Rosa, 211 F.3d 509, 513–514 (9th Cir. 2000) (court should dismiss only when facts establish such oppression and vexation of defendant as to be out of proportion to plaintiff's convenience).

241 *See, e.g.*, Great Prize, S.A. v. Mariner Shipping Pty., Ltd., 967 F.2d 157, 160 (5th Cir. 1992) ("Convenience is the cornerstone of the [forum non conveniens] inquiry").

242 *See* Murray v. British Broadcasting Corp., 81 F.3d 287, 293 (2d Cir. 1996).

243 Piper Aircraft Co. v. Reyno, 454 U.S. 235 (1981); Gulf Oil Co. v. Gilbert, 330 U.S. 501 (1947).

Frequently, most of these private interest factors favor the forum in which the events at issue in the lawsuit took place, because often the bulk of the witnesses, the physical evidence, and necessary third parties are located in the same place.[244]

The public interest factors include the following (*see* MOORE'S FEDERAL PRACTICE Ch. 111, § 111.74[3][d]):[245]

- The administrative difficulties flowing from court congestion.
- The local interest in having localized controversies decided in their home forum.
- The imposition of jury duty on the citizens of a forum that is unrelated to the subject of the litigation.
- The interest in having a case tried in a forum familiar with the law that governs the action.
- The avoidance of unnecessary problems in conflicts of law or in the application of foreign law.

## § 9.22 DEFERENCE TO PLAINTIFF'S CHOICE OF FORUM

### [1] Courts Give Deference to American Plaintiff's Choice of Forum

When the plaintiff is an American citizen or resident, the plaintiff's choice of forum is accorded significant deference and "should rarely be disturbed" by dismissal of the action on forum non conveniens grounds.[246] A plaintiff should not be deprived of the advantages of his or her home jurisdiction except on a clear showing of facts that either (1) establish such oppressiveness and vexation to a defendant as to be out of all proportion to the plaintiff's convenience, or (2) make trial in the chosen forum inappropriate because of considerations affecting the court's own administrative and legal problems.[247] Also, when foreign as well as

---

[244] Allstate Life Ins. Co. v. Linter Group, Ltd., 994 F.2d 996, 1002 (2d Cir. 1993) ("since all of the Bank's allegedly fraudulent activity occurred in Australia, most relevant documents . . . and [m]ost witnesses and other sources of proof are also located in Australia").

[245] Piper Aircraft Co. v. Reyno, 454 U.S. 235 (1981); Gulf Oil Co. v. Gilbert, 330 U.S. 501 (1947).

[246] Piper Aircraft Co. v. Reyno, 454 U.S. 235, 257 (1981); Gulf Oil Co. v. Gilbert, 330 U.S. 501 (1947); *see, e.g.*, Adelson v. Hananel, 510 F.3d 43, 53–54 (1st Cir. 2007) (defendant must overcome strong presumption in favor of U.S. forum selected by U.S. plaintiff by showing that private and public interest factors strongly favor dismissal); Iragorri v. United Techs. Corp., 274 F.3d 65, 70–73 (2d Cir. 2001) (en banc) (deference afforded plaintiff's choice is greater to extent it was motivated by legitimate reasons, including convenience and ability to obtain jurisdiction over defendant, and diminishes to extent it was motivated by tactical advantage); DiFederico v. Marriott Int'l, Inc., 714 F.3d 796, 802–803 (4th Cir. 2013) (defendant seeking dismissal against non-citizen plaintiff must show that factors "strongly favor" another forum; citizen plaintiff's choice of forum is entitled to even greater deference, and should be overridden only when defendant establishes such oppressiveness and vexation as to be out of all proportion to plaintiff's convenience); *see also* Duha v. Agrium, Inc., 448 F.3d 867, 873–875 (6th Cir. 2006); Gullone v. Bayer Corp. (*In re* Factor VIII or IX Concentrate Blood Prods. Litig.), 484 F.3d 951, 955 (7th Cir. 2007); Carey v. Bayerische Hypo-Und Vereinsbank AG, 370 F.3d 234, 237–239 (2d Cir. 2004).

[247] Koster v. Lumbermens Mut. Cas. Co., 330 U.S. 518, 524 (1947) ("In any balancing of conveniences,

domestic plaintiffs are present in the suit, the choice of a U.S. forum is nevertheless entitled to a strong presumption of convenience because of the U.S. plaintiff or plaintiffs.[248]

Nonetheless, an American plaintiff's choice of a United States forum is not immunized against forum non conveniens dismissal.[249] For example, less deference is indicated if it appears that the plaintiff's choice was motivated by forum-shopping reasons, such as (1) attempts to win a tactical advantage resulting from local laws, (2) the habitual generosity of juries in the forum, (3) the plaintiff's popularity or the defendant's unpopularity in the region, or (4) the inconvenience and expense to the defendant resulting from litigation in the forum. The degree of deference is not dispositive, but is only the first level of inquiry, and the court must continue to analyze the remaining private and public interest factors to determine whether dismissal is warranted.[250]

## [2] Foreign Plaintiff's Choice of Forum Generally Given Less Deference

When the plaintiff is a foreign citizen, his or her choice of forum generally is entitled to less deference than that of an American plaintiff.[251] This rule "is not based on a desire to disadvantage foreign plaintiffs" but rather on the assumption that a United States forum is not the most convenient forum when a foreign plaintiff files in a federal court.[252] Instead, the court may suspect that the foreign plaintiff's choice of forum springs from disfavored motives, such as a desire to obtain the benefit of more favorable United States law,[253] or to harass the defendant.[254]

---

a real showing of convenience by a plaintiff who has sued in his home forum will normally outweigh the inconvenience the defendant may have shown").

248 Carijano v. Occidental Petroleum Corp., 643 F.3d 1216, 1228–1229 (9th Cir. 2011) (in suit based on environmental contamination in Peruvian rainforest, U.S. environmental organization was named as plaintiff as well as 25 Peruvians; U.S. plaintiff was entitled to strong presumption that its choice of forum was convenient).

249 *See* Piper Aircraft Co. v. Reyno, 454 U.S. 235, 253 n.23 (1981) (citizen's choice of forum not given dispositive weight); *see, e.g.*, Interface Partners Int'l Ltd. v. Hananel, 575 F.3d 97, 102 (1st Cir. 2009) (there is no automatic right to presumption of deference, and court should deny presumption to plaintiffs acting with vexatious and oppressive motive).

250 *Compare* Iragorri v. United Techs. Corp., 274 F.3d 65, 70–73 (2d Cir. 2001) (en banc) (district court did not accord appropriate deference to plaintiff's choice of forum when there was no indication of forum shopping); *with* Interface Partners Int'l Ltd. v. Hananel, 575 F.3d 97, 102–103 & n.7 (1st Cir. 2009) (plaintiff's choice was not entitled to any heightened deference when plaintiff had originally filed suit in Israel and had litigated and conducted discovery there for nearly four years before seeking dismissal and refiling in U.S. court; plaintiff's conduct was sufficient to show that he acted with oppressive or vexatious motive or, at least, acted solely for reasons of litigation strategy).

251 Piper Aircraft Co. v. Reyno, 454 U.S. 235, 256 (1981).

252 454 U.S. at 255–256 ("Because the central purpose of any forum is to ensure that the trial is convenient, a foreign plaintiff's choice deserves less deference").

253 Empresa Lineas Maritimas Argentinas, S.A. v. Schichua-Unterweser, 955 F.2d 368, 373 (5th Cir. 1992).

254 Gulf Oil Co. v. Gilbert, 330 U.S. 501, 508 (1947).

Although the degree of deference is reduced, it has not been articulated with greater precision than simply to say that "some weight must still be given to a foreign plaintiff's choice of forum."[255] Therefore, the defendant still must overcome the presumption in favor of the foreign plaintiff's choice of forum by showing that the balance of convenience favors trial in the foreign forum.[256]

## § 9.23 COURT HAS NO POWER TO DISMISS ACTIONS ARISING UNDER CERTAIN FEDERAL STATUTES

The doctrine of forum non conveniens has been held inapplicable to cases arising under a few federal statutes that contain special venue provisions providing for venue in the district courts of the United States. Forum non conveniens dismissal will be held unavailable if the language and legislative purpose of the statute reveal a Congressional intent to vest in the plaintiff an absolute power to choose a United States forum, and thus implicitly to deprive the court of its discretionary power to defeat the plaintiff's venue choice by application of the doctrine of forum non conveniens. For example, such an intent has been discerned in actions pursuant to the Federal Employers' Liability Act (FELA).[257]

Finding no such Congressional intent, courts have held that a court may grant a forum non conveniens dismissal of (1) claims arising under the United States Copyright Act,[258] (2) a bankruptcy provision providing for venue of bankruptcy related wrongful death, tort, and personal injury actions,[259] (3) securities fraud,[260] (4) the Lanham Act,[261] (5) RICO,[262] (6) the Warsaw Convention,[263] (7) the Montreal

---

[255] Bhatnagar v. Surrendra Overseas Ltd., 52 F.3d 1220, 1226 n.4 (3d Cir. 1995) (court indicated that "it does not mean that his or her decision is entitled to *no* deference," and acknowledged that "the deference evaluation cannot be done with mathematical precision") (emphasis in original); R. Maganlal & Co. v. M.G. Chemical Co. Inc., 942 F.2d 164, 168 (2d Cir. 1991) (dismissal for forum non conveniens should be exception not rule even when plaintiff is foreign).

[256] Iragorri v. United Techs. Corp., 274 F.3d 65, 70–73 (2d Cir. 2001) (en banc) (district court did not accord appropriate deference to plaintiff's choice of forum when there was no indication of forum shopping); Ravelo Monegro v. Rosa, 211 F.3d 509, 513–514 (9th Cir. 2000) (although foreign plaintiff's choice of forum receives less deference, "less deference is not the same thing as no deference," and under circumstances it was abuse of discretion to deny foreign plaintiffs' their choice of forum).

[257] 45 U.S.C. § 51; *see* Baltimore & Ohio R.R. Co. v. Kepner, 314 U.S. 44 (1941); Creative Technology, Ltd. v. Aztech Sys. PTE, Ltd., 61 F.3d 696, 699–700 (9th Cir. 1995) (in dicta, court stated "[t]he forum non conveniens doctrine is inapplicable to certain federal statutes, such as . . . the Federal Employer's Liability Act (FELA) which contain special provisions mandating venue in the United States").

[258] 17 U.S.C. § 101 *et seq.*; *see, e.g.*, Creative Technology, Ltd. v. Aztech Sys. PTE, Ltd., 61 F.3d 696, 699–700 (9th Cir. 1995).

[259] 28 U.S.C. § 157(b)(5); *see, e.g.*, Baumgart v. Fairchild Aircraft Corp., 981 F.2d 824, 829–831 (5th Cir. 1993).

[260] 15 U.S.C. §§ 77q(a), 78j(b); *see, e.g.*, Allstate Life Ins. Co. v. Linter Group, Ltd., 994 F.2d 996, 1002 (2d Cir. 1993); Howe v. Goldcorp Inv., Ltd., 946 F.2d 944, 947–950 (1st Cir. 1991).

[261] 15 U.S.C. §§ 1051–1127; *see, e.g.*, Wells Fargo & Co. v. Wells Fargo Express Co., 556 F.2d 406, 431 (9th Cir. 1977).

[262] 18 U.S.C. § 1961 *et seq.*; *see, e.g.*, Transunion Corp. v. Pepsico, Inc., 811 F.2d 127, 130 (2d Cir. 1987); Alfadda v. Fenn, 966 F. Supp. 1317, 1332 (S.D.N.Y. 1997) (federal courts may apply forum non conveniens doctrine in securities fraud actions under RICO).

Convention governing damages for death or personal injury by international air travel passengers,[264] and (8) the Death on the High Seas Act.[265]

Additionally, there is a split of authority in the circuits as to whether a district court may dismiss an action on forum non conveniens grounds if American law governs the action. Some circuits hold that, in the context of Jones Act and maritime cases, if the court determines that American law applies to the action, then the action may not be dismissed on forum non conveniens grounds.[266] In contrast, other circuits have held that a choice of law determination has no bearing on the forum non conveniens analysis, even for Jones Act or maritime cases.[267] *Piper Aircraft Co. v. Reyno* held that ordinarily the district court should avoid conducting a choice of law analysis because it is incompatible with the purpose of the forum non conveniens doctrine and also poses substantial practical problems.[268]

## § 9.24 FORUM SELECTION CLAUSE MAY AFFECT ANALYSIS OF MOTION

### [1] Mandatory Forum Selection Clause Enforced Through Motion to Dismiss Under Forum Non Conveniens Principles

When a party seeks to enforce a forum selection clause that requires an action to be brought only in state court, or the courts of a foreign country, transfer is not possible — the transfer statutes, § 1404(a), § 1406, and § 1631, allow transfer only to other federal courts. The Supreme Court, in *Atlantic Marine Construction Co. v. United States District Court*, has indicated that in this situation, a motion to dismiss based on forum non conveniens grounds, as opposed to a motion to transfer under § 1406 or Fed. R. Civ. P 12(b)(6), is the appropriate means of seeking to

---

263 U.S.C. § 1502; *In re* Air Crash Disaster Near New Orleans, 821 F.2d 1147, 1162 (5th Cir. 1987), *vacated on other grounds*, 490 U.S. 1032 (1989).

264 Pierre-Louis v. Newvac Corp., 584 F.3d 1052, 1056–1058 (11th Cir. 2009) (while Montreal Convention includes provision specifying fora in which plaintiff may bring suit, it also provides that questions of procedure shall be governed by law of forum court, and for U.S. fora this includes law of forum non conveniens).

265 Loya v. Starwood Hotels & Resorts Worldwide, Inc., 583 F.3d 656, 660–663 (9th Cir. 2009) (Death on the High Seas Act, 46 U.S.C. § 30301 *et seq.*, which created remedy in admiralty for wrongful deaths more than a marine league from shore, neither explicitly nor implicitly rejects application of forum non conveniens doctrine).

266 46 U.S.C. § 688(a); *see* Membreno v. Costa Crociere S.P.A., 425 F.3d 932, 936 (11th Cir. 2005) (first step in determining whether action should be dismissed for forum non conveniens is to determine whether U.S. law should be applied to case).

267 *In re* Air Crash Disaster Near New Orleans, 821 F.2d 1147, 1163 (5th Cir. 1987), *vacated on other grounds sub nom.*, Pan American World Airways, Inc. v. Lopez, 490 U.S. 1032 (1989) (fact that American law applies does not prevent dismissal of Jones Act and maritime cases on forum non conveniens grounds); Cruz v. Maritime Co. of Philippines, 702 F.2d 47, 48 (2d Cir. 1983) (choice of law determination is not involved in forum non conveniens analysis for Jones Act or any other cases).

268 Piper Aircraft Co. v. Reyno, 454 U.S. 235, 251 (1981).

enforce a clause that requires litigation in a state or foreign forum.[269]

### [2] Normal Forum Non Conveniens Analysis Applies to Permissive Forum Selection Clause

When the forum selection clause is permissive, the normal forum non conveniens analysis applies.[270]

## § 9.25 PROCEDURES ON FORUM NON CONVENIENS DISMISSAL MOTION

### [1] Timing of Motion

A motion for forum non conveniens dismissal is timely if it is made within a reasonable time after the defendant has become aware of the facts that form the basis for the motion.[271] Even if the defendant has moved in a timely fashion, however, if extensive discovery on the merits has taken place or if the court has expended significant resources on the case, considerations of judicial economy weigh in favor of retaining the action.[272]

A defendant's removal of the action from state court does not bar the defendant from subsequently moving to dismiss on forum non conveniens grounds.[273]

---

[269] Atlantic Marine Constr. Co. v. United States Dist. Court, 134 S. Ct. 568, 187 L. Ed. 2d 487, 499–500 (2013) (quoting Sinochem Int'l Co. v. Malaysia Int'l Shipping Corp., 549 U. S. 422, 430 (2007)).

[270] *See* AAR Int'l, Inc. v. Nimelias Enters. S.A., 250 F.3d 510, 523–527 (7th Cir. 2001) (court noted that it would be reasonable to apply traditional forum non conveniens analysis rather than *Bremen* standards to permissive forum selection clauses, although *Bremen* standards applied in this case when there was also unambiguous language providing that defendant would not object to venue in Illinois); Blanco v. Banco Industrial de Venezuela, 997 F.2d 974, 979–980 (2d Cir. 1993); Neo Sack, Ltd. v. Vinmar Impex, Inc., 810 F. Supp. 829, 833 (S.D. Tex. 1993).

[271] *See* Lony v. E.I. Du Pont de Nemours & Co., 935 F.2d 604, 607 (3d Cir. 1991) (motion must be made within reasonable time "after the facts or circumstances . . . have developed and become known"); *but see* Aldana v. Del Monte Fresh Produce N.A., Inc., 578 F.3d 1283, 1291 (11th Cir. 2009) (there is generally no time limit on when motion to dismiss for forum non conveniens must be made).

[272] *See* Genpharm Inc. v. Pliva-Lachema a.s., 361 F. Supp. 2d 49, 59 (E.D.N.Y. 2005) (while there is no specified time limit on when motion to dismiss on forum non conveniens can be made, delay in bringing motion is factor to be considered in court's evaluation of whether forum is convenient); *but see* Mercier v. Sheraton Int'l, Inc., 981 F.2d 1345, 1355 (1st Cir. 1992) (upholding district court's determination that progress of litigation in that case was not so significant as to merit retention of the action).

[273] Davis Int'l, LLC v. New Start Group Corp., 488 F.3d 597, 603 (3d Cir. 2007) (neither doctrine of unclean hands nor doctrine of estoppel precluded defendants in removed case from moving for dismissal on forum non conveniens grounds); PT United Can Co. v. Crown Cork & Seal Co., 138 F.3d 65, 73–75 (2d Cir. 1998) (district court did not abuse its discretion in dismissing on forum non conveniens after removal).

## [2] Court May Dismiss on Forum Non Conveniens Grounds Without First Deciding Jurisdictional Issues

A district court has discretion to consider a defendant's forum non conveniens motion before taking up any other threshold objection. The court need not first resolve whether it has subject-matter jurisdiction or personal jurisdiction over the defendant if it determines that, in any event, a foreign tribunal is plainly the more suitable arbiter of the merits of the case. The Supreme Court so ruled in *Sinochem Int'l Co. v. Malaysia Int'l Shipping Corp.*[274] While a court must determine jurisdictional issues before it proceeds to the merits, forum non conveniens is a non-merits ground for dismissal that does not entail an assumption of law-making power. Accordingly, the court may dispose of an action by a forum non conveniens dismissal, bypassing questions of subject-matter and personal jurisdiction, when considerations of convenience, fairness, and judicial economy warrant doing so.

Nevertheless, if a court can readily determine that it lacks jurisdiction over the cause or the defendant, the proper course would be to dismiss on that ground.[275] In most cases, jurisdiction does not involve a difficult inquiry, and both judicial economy and the consideration ordinarily accorded the plaintiff's choice of forum should impel the federal court to consider jurisdictional issues first. When subject-matter or personal jurisdiction is difficult to determine, and forum non conveniens considerations weigh heavily in favor of dismissal, the court properly may take the less burdensome course.[276]

## [3] Defendant Has Burden of Proving All Elements

It is the defendant's burden to show that a forum non conveniens dismissal is warranted.[277] Thus, to prevail on a motion to dismiss based on forum non conveniens, the defendant must show that there is an adequate alternative forum

---

[274] Sinochem Int'l Co. v. Malaysia Int'l Shipping Corp., 549 U.S. 422, 425 (2007) ("We hold that a district court has discretion to respond at once to a defendant's forum non conveniens plea, and need not take up first any other threshold objection. In particular, a court need not resolve whether it has authority to adjudicate the cause (subject-matter jurisdiction) or personal jurisdiction over the defendant if it determines that, in any event, a foreign tribunal is plainly the more suitable arbiter of the merits of the case."); *see, e.g.*, Figueiredo v. Republic of Peru, 665 F.3d 384, 389 (2d Cir. 2011) ("Although courts are normally obliged to consider issues of subject matter jurisdiction prior to other issues, the Supreme Court has approved the practice of this Court . . . of exercising discretion to consider an FNC dismissal without first adjudicating issues of subject matter jurisdiction . . . . We have concluded that it is appropriate to do so in this case.").

[275] Sinochem Int'l Co. v. Malaysia Int'l Shipping Corp., 549 U.S. 422, 436 (2007) ("If, however, a court can readily determine that it lacks jurisdiction over the cause or the defendant, the proper course would be to dismiss on that ground."); *see also* Ruhrgas AG v. Marathon Oil Co., 526 U.S. 574, 578 (1999) (while there is no unyielding jurisdictional hierarchy, and court may consider personal jurisdiction before subject matter jurisdiction in interest of judicial economy, ordinarily subject matter jurisdiction will not involve difficult inquiry and should be decided first).

[276] Sinochem Int'l Co. v. Malaysia Int'l Shipping Corp., 549 U.S. 422, 435–436 (2007) ("where subject-matter or personal jurisdiction is difficult to determine, and forum non conveniens considerations weigh heavily in favor of dismissal, the court properly takes the less burdensome course.").

[277] *See, e.g.*, Jiali Tang v. Synutra Int'l, Inc. 656 F.3d 242, 248–250 (4th Cir. 2011) (moving party bears burden of showing that adequate alternative forum exists); Leon v. Millon Air, Inc., 251 F.3d 1305,

and that in light of the relevant public and private interest factors, the balance of convenience tilts strongly in favor of the foreign forum.[278]

## § 9.26 APPELLATE REVIEW

### [1] Grant of Forum Non Conveniens Motion Is Appealable as Final Order

An order granting a motion to dismiss on forum non conveniens grounds is appealable as a final judgment.[279] The dismissal is still considered final even if the district court makes the dismissal conditional upon the fulfillment by the defendant of certain terms, and thus retains jurisdiction which could be reasserted in the event that the defendant fails to comply with such conditions.[280]

### [2] Denial of Forum Non Conveniens Motion Subject to Limited Review

The district court's denial of a forum non conveniens motion does not fall within the collateral order doctrine, and is not immediately appealable under 28 U.S.C. § 1291.[281] For an interlocutory order to come within the collateral order exception, among other things, it must decide an issue that is completely separate from the merits of the action.[282] In balancing the various factors necessary to determine whether a particular forum is so inconvenient as to warrant dismissal, "the district court generally becomes entangled in the merits of the underlying dispute."[283] For example, in evaluating the availability of witnesses and the relative access to sources of proof, the court must examine the substance of the dispute to determine whether the evidence cited by the parties is relevant to the plaintiff's claim or to any potential defenses. Accordingly, allowing automatic interlocutory review of the denial of such a motion would waste judicial resources by "requiring repetitive appellate review of substantive questions in the case."[284]

---

1312–1314 (11th Cir. 2001) (defendant ordinarily has burden of persuasion on all elements of forum non conveniens question); Bhatnagar v. Surrendra Overseas Ltd., 52 F.3d 1220, 1226, 1230 (3d Cir. 1995) (defendant failed to meet burden when it did not rebut plaintiff's evidence that it would take Indian courts up to 25 years to resolve ordinary personal injury action).

[278] Peregrine Myanmar Ltd. v. Segal, 89 F.3d 41, 46 (2d Cir. 1996) (when adequacy of alternative forum was not disputed, defendant had burden of showing that *Gilbert* factors "tilt strongly in favor of" alternative forum).

[279] *See* Abad v. Bayer Corp., 563 F.3d 663, 665 (7th Cir. 2009) (dismissal of case on grounds of forum non conveniens is deemed final judgment and appealable even though it does not end litigation).

[280] *See* Koke v. Phillips Petroleum Co., 730 F.2d 211, 216 (5th Cir. 1984).

[281] 28 U.S.C. § 1291; *see also* King v. Cessna Aircraft Co., 562 F.3d 1374, 1378–1379 (11th Cir. 2009) (court of appeals did not have jurisdiction to review denial of motion to dismiss, nor was this matter sufficiently connected to appealable dismissal of other parties on forum non conveniens grounds to allow review under pendent appellate jurisdiction); *see* 19 Moore's Federal Practice Ch. 203, *Interlocutory Orders* (Matthew Bender 3d ed.).

[282] *See* Cohen v. Beneficial Indus. Loan Corp., 337 U.S. 541, 546–547 (1949).

[283] Van Cauwenberghe v. Biard, 486 U.S. 517, 528 (1988).

[284] 486 U.S. at 528.

The district court, on the other hand, retains jurisdiction over the interlocutory order and has the power to reconsider and reverse its decision for any reason it deems sufficient.[285]

Because the district court has considerable flexibility in deciding a forum non conveniens motion, in certain cases the court may be able to decide that dismissal is appropriate without extensive inquiry into the merits of the underlying dispute.[286] In such a case, immediate review might save both the court and the parties substantial time and expense, and the district court therefore may certify the order for interlocutory review under 28 U.S.C. § 1292(b).[287] The court of appeals, in its discretion, may then accept the order for immediate appeal.[288] Both the district court and the court of appeals must agree that the case is a proper candidate for immediate review before the normal rule requiring a final judgment will be overridden.[289]

Mandamus is available to review the denial of a motion to dismiss on forum non conveniens grounds, although at least one circuit has suggested that it is only available if certification has been denied.[290] In addition, although mandamus relief theoretically is available, it is difficult to show entitlement to the remedy. The movant must show a clear cut abuse of discretion.[291]

## [3] Court's Grant or Denial of Motion Subject to Abuse of Discretion Standard

A district court's grant or denial of a motion to dismiss on the grounds of forum non conveniens may be reversed only if there has been a clear abuse of discretion.[292] When the district court "has considered all relevant public and private interest factors, and when its balancing of these factors is reasonable, its

---

[285] *See* Saqui v. Pride Central America, LLC, 595 F.3d 206, 210 (5th Cir. 2010) (district court was free to reconsider its denial even in absence of new evidence or intervening change in or clarification of substantive law).

[286] Van Cauwenberghe v. Biard, 486 U.S. at 529.

[287] 28 U.S.C. 1292(b) (certification is appropriate when order "involves a controlling question of law as to which there is substantial ground for difference of opinion and . . . an immediate appeal from the order may materially advance the ultimate termination of the litigation").

[288] Van Cauwenberghe v. Biard, 486 U.S. at 529–530.

[289] *See In re* Ford Motor Co., 344 F.3d 648, 653–655 (7th Cir. 2002) (mandamus was not available remedy to compel district court to certify issue for immediate appeal under 28 U.S.C. § 1292(b)).

[290] *In re* Air Crash Disaster Near New Orleans, 821 F.2d 1147, 1167 (5th Cir. 1987) ("an unsuccessful defendant may seek certification . . . or if this is denied, the defendant can petition this court for a writ of mandamus").

[291] *See In re* Ford Motor Co., 344 F.3d 648, 651–653 (7th Cir. 2002) (mandamus relief was not granted when district court did not abuse its authority, regardless of whether its decision on forum non conveniens would have been upheld on appeal from final decision, when its decision was based on careful consideration of relevant factors); Carlenstolpe v. Merck & Co., Inc., 819 F.2d 33, 35 (2d Cir. 1987) (when district court has considered *Gilbert* factors, mandamus relief is available on demonstration "not of mere error, but of a clear-cut abuse of discretion").

[292] *See* Jiali Tang v. Synutra Int'l, Inc. 656 F.3d 242, 248 (4th Cir. 2011) (forum non conveniens dismissal reviewed for abuse of discretion, and district court's decision deserves substantial deference); Saqui v. Pride Central America, LLC, 595 F.3d 206, 213 (5th Cir. 2010) ("clear abuse of discretion"

decision deserves substantial deference."[293] Even though the district court's decision is accorded substantial deference, however, the appellate court must still conduct a "meaningful" review of the decision.[294] However, when the decision is made on a purely legal basis, as when a court denies a motion to dismiss because it has determined that there is no available alternative forum, the decision is reviewed de novo.[295]

---

standard applies; party opposing dismissal must "plainly demonstrate" that party is highly unlikely to obtain justice in alternative forum).

[293] Piper Aircraft Co. v. Reyno, 454 U.S. 235, 257 (1981) (upholding district court's dismissal of product liability action based on determination that Scotland was more convenient site for trial).

[294] Delta Air Lines, Inc. v. Chimet S.p.A., 619 F.3d 288, 295 (3d Cir. 2010) (although decision to grant or deny forum non conveniens motion lies within district court's sound discretion, decision should be exercised in structured discretion founded on procedural framework guiding district court's decision making process); R. Maganlal & Co., Inc. v. M.G. Chemical Co., Inc., 942 F.2d 164, 169 (2d Cir. 1991) (district court's discretion not so broad as to preclude meaningful review into whether district court "reached an erroneous conclusion on either the facts or the law").

[295] DRFP L.L.C. v. Republica Bolivariana de Venezuela, 622 F.3d 513, 518 (6th Cir. 2010) (decision that Venezuela did not provide an adequate alternative forum because Venezuelan law would not permit litigation of the subject matter of the suit, was purely matter of law and reviewed de novo).

# Chapter 10

# MULTIDISTRICT LITIGATION

## § 10.01 CONDUCT OF MULTIDISTRICT LITIGATION

### [1] Overview of Multidistrict Litigation Statute

#### [a] Purpose of Multidistrict Litigation Statutory Scheme

Since the 1960s, complex litigation increasingly has occupied the attention of the federal district courts. Many types of disputes, ranging from antitrust and securities cases to mass disaster and mass tort cases, result in the filing of related cases in different district courts throughout the United States. There may also be parallel related cases filed in state courts around the country. Although at present there are no mechanisms for authorizing the formal consolidation of state court cases filed in different states, or for coordinating related state and federal litigation, Congress has enacted a statutory scheme for consolidating and coordinating related cases filed in different federal district courts.[1]

When civil actions involving one or more common questions of fact are pending in different judicial districts, the multidistrict litigation statute authorizes the Judicial Panel on Multidistrict Litigation to consolidate and transfer them to a single district for coordinated or consolidated pretrial proceedings.[2] The purpose of this transfer procedure is to conserve judicial resources and to avoid the delays that would inevitably result if all aspects of each action, such as discovery, were conducted separately. However, this procedure applies only to *pretrial* proceedings. The statute permits the transferee court to deal with the pretrial proceedings that are common to all the actions in a single unified setting, but then requires that the actions be remanded to the districts from which they were transferred for trial, if necessary.[3]

In addition to providing for greater efficiencies in the pretrial process, multidistrict consolidation and transfer have proven to be a useful complement, and at times, alternative to class actions that could not otherwise proceed.[4] For example,

---

[1] 28 U.S.C. § 1407.

[2] 28 U.S.C. § 1407. In 1968, Congress enacted legislation creating the Judicial Panel on Multidistrict Litigation as a result of the successful efforts of the Coordinating Committee for Multiple Litigation of the United States District Courts, which supervised nationwide discovery proceedings during a wave of electrical equipment antitrust cases that threatened to inundate the federal courts.

[3] 28 U.S.C. § 1407(a).

[4] *See, e.g., In re* Zyprexa Prods. Liab. Litig., 467 F. Supp. 2d 256 , 269–270 (E.D.N.Y. 2006) (MDL

in 1991, the Multidistrict Litigation Panel transferred 26,639 federal asbestos cases pending at that time to the Eastern District of Pennsylvania.[5] In many cases, especially in mass tort cases, the federal district courts and parties try to use the class action device to achieve efficiencies and a quicker and cheaper resolution of the litigation (*see* 5 Moore's Federal Practice, Ch. 23, *Class Actions*). Use of class actions, however, remains highly controversial, and the courts are not shy about reversing what they perceive to be improper class certifications.[6] After the reversal of the asbestos class action settlement in 1997,[7] the cases in the asbestos MDL remained to be resolved. During 2006 to 2014 alone, another 186,591 federal cases were transferred to the MDL. However, as of April 2014, only 2,845 remained unresolved.[8] Thus, the asbestos example serves to show the rather substantial benefits that may be achieved through the use of the statutory scheme provided by Congress, and the result is certainly consistent with Congress's purpose to provide the courts with a transfer and consolidation tool that facilitates the just and efficient conduct of such actions. Indeed, since its enactment almost 50 years ago, the Panel has transferred almost 400,000 lawsuits, ranging from securities, and consumer actions, to mass tort cases, for pretrial purposes.[9]

### [b] Operation of Judicial Panel on Multidistrict Litigation

The Judicial Panel on Multidistrict Litigation consists of seven circuit and district court judges chosen by the Chief Justice of the United States.[10] The Panel may transfer civil actions involving one or more common questions of fact that are pending in different judicial districts to any federal district court for coordinated or consolidated pretrial proceedings if it determines that the transfer will be for the convenience of the parties and witnesses and will promote the just and efficient conduct of the actions. The Panel has prescribed its own rules of procedure that detail the mechanics of such a transfer (*see* § 10.02).[11] At the conclusion of the

---

litigation administered as a "quasi-class action"); Sperberg v. Firestone Tire & Rubber Co., 61 F.R.D. 70, 78 (N.D. Ohio 1973); *In re* 7-Eleven Franchise Antitrust Litig., 358 F. Supp. 286, 287 (J.P.M.L. 1973); *see also In re* Plywood Anti-Trust Litig., 76 F.R.D. 570, 587 (E.D. La. 1976) ("conflicting class allegations in the complaints was a basic reason for centralizing all actions in this district").

[5] *In re* Asbestos Prod. Liab. Litig., 771 F. Supp. 415 (J.P.M.L. 1991).

[6] *See* Wal-Mart Stores, Inc. v. Dukes, 131 S. Ct. 2541, 180 L. Ed. 2d 374 (2011) (reversing class action certification in nationwide employment discrimination lawsuit), Reversed by, remanded by: Odle v. Wal-Mart Stores, Inc., 747 F.3d 315, 2014 U.S. App. LEXIS 5958, 97 Empl. Prac. Dec. (CCH) P45047, 122 Fair Empl. Prac. Cas. (BNA) 532 (5th Cir. Tex. 2014).

[7] Amchem Prods., Inc. v. Windsor, 521 U.S. 591, 620, 629 (1997) ("The safeguards provided by the Rule 23(a) and (b) class-qualifying criteria . . . are not impractical impediments . . . " and "Rule 23, which must be interpreted with fidelity to the Rules Enabling Act and applied with the interests of absent class members in close view, cannot carry the large load . . . " often required in mass tort cases).

[8] MDL-875, Asbestos Products Liability Litigation Caseload Statistics, Office of the Clerk of the Court (E.D.PA. May 2014), https://www.paed.uscourts.gov/documents/MDL/MDL875/MDL%20875%20Stats%20as%20of%20end%20of%20April.pdf (last visited June 4, 2014).

[9] Margaret S. Williams and Tracey E. George, *Who Will Manage Complex Civil Litigation? The Decision to Transfer and Consolidate Multidistrict Litigation*, 10 J. Empir. Stud. 424, 427–28 (2013).

[10] 28 U.S.C. § 1407(d).

[11] 28 U.S.C. § 1407(f); *see* Rules of Procedure, Judicial Panel on Multidistrict Litigation. The Rules have been amended several times and their numbering in case citations is therefore not consistent.

pretrial proceedings, each transferred action is to be remanded to the district from which it was transferred, for trial or further proceedings, unless the action has been terminated in the course of the consolidated pretrial proceedings (*see* § 10.05[3]).

A transfer proceeding may be initiated by motion filed with the Panel or by the Panel itself.[12] All parties in the actions for which coordinated or consolidated pretrial proceedings are contemplated are given notice of a hearing to determine whether a transfer should be ordered.[13] If a subsequent civil action is filed in a district court that involves common questions of fact with actions that have already been transferred (a "tag-along action"), it may also be transferred and consolidated with the previously transferred actions (*see* § 10.02[3]). A transfer order issued by the Panel is reviewable only by extraordinary writ issued by a court of appeals. An order denying a motion to transfer an action for consolidated pretrial proceedings, however, may not be reviewed at all.[14]

### [c] Jurisdiction of Judicial Panel on Multidistrict Litigation

A case may be transferred under the multidistrict litigation statute only if the prospective transferor court has subject matter jurisdiction over the action. In most cases, if the federal court lacks subject matter jurisdiction, the action must be dismissed. However, in the rare case in which one federal court lacks subject matter jurisdiction, but another federal court does have jurisdiction, the case may be transferred to the latter federal court.[15] It would then be proper for the action to be transferred under the multidistrict litigation statute.[16]

Once the threshold requirement that the transferor court have subject matter jurisdiction is met, the Panel may transfer an action to *any* district; personal jurisdiction and venue objections will not prevent the Panel from transferring a case (*see* § 10.03[2]). Similarly, a lack of personal jurisdiction in the transferor court is not a ground for opposing a transfer, because any party contesting personal jurisdiction may make the appropriate motion before the transferee court.[17] Thus, it can be said that the Multidistrict Panel has a wider range of options in terms of where actions may be transferred than is possible under the convenience transfer statute, 28 U.S.C. § 1404(a).[18]

In another respect, however, the jurisdiction of the Multidistrict Panel is quite limited. The Panel may make determinations, *sua sponte* or on motion, on whether

---

12 28 U.S.C. § 1407(c)(i), (ii).

13 28 U.S.C. § 1407(c).

14 28 U.S.C. § 1407(e); *see* 28 U.S.C. § 1651.

15 *See* 28 U.S.C. § 1631 (federal court may, after determining that "there is a want of jurisdiction," may transfer "to any other court in which the action or appeal could have been brought at the time it was filed or noticed"); *see generally* Ch. 9, *Change of Venue*.

16 *See* 28 U.S.C. § 1407.

17 *See In re* Ivy, 901 F.2d 7, 9 (2d Cir. 1990) (Judicial Panel on Multidistrict Litigation had jurisdiction to transfer Agent Orange case in which jurisdictional objection was pending).

18 *See* Ch. 9, *Change of Venue*.

related actions ought to be transferred for pretrial purposes.[19] The Panel also has the power to remand to the transferor court actions that have not been terminated in the transferee court.[20] Finally, the Panel is empowered to prescribe rules for the conduct of its business.[21] However, the Multidistrict Litigation Panel may not rule on substantive or procedural matters other than these transfer and remand questions. These determinations are made by the transferor court prior to transfer and after remand, and by the transferee court after transfer until an action is remanded.

### [2] Multidistrict Litigation Defined

*Multidistrict litigation* simply means related actions pending in more than one district court.[22] There is no quantifiable definition of multidistrict litigation. The only statutory requirements are that the cases be civil actions involving one or more common questions of fact pending in different districts, and that the Panel determine that grouping them together for coordinated or consolidated pretrial proceedings will be for the convenience of the parties and promote the just and efficient conduct of the actions (*see* § 10.03[1]).[23] Although there must be more than one action by definition, there are no numerical requirements specifying either the minimum number of actions or the minimum number of districts that must be involved before a transfer may be considered by the Panel. As few as two cases may warrant multidistrict litigation transfer,[24] while at the other extreme 26,639 asbestos cases filed in districts all over the United States unquestionably qualify as multidistrict litigation.[25]

---

19 28 U.S.C. § 1407(a).

20 28 U.S.C. § 1407(a).

21 28 U.S.C. § 1407(f).

22 28 U.S.C. § 1407. *See* Patricia D. Howard, *A Guide to Multidistrict Litigation*, 124 F.R.D. 479, 481 (1989).

23 28 U.S.C. § 1407(a).

24 *See In re* Clark Oil & Ref. Corp. Antitrust Litig., 364 F. Supp. 458, 458 (J.P.M.L. 1973).

25 *See In re* Asbestos Prod. Liab. Litig. (No. VI), 771 F. Supp. 415, 416 (J.P.M.L. 1991); *see also In re* Agent Orange Prod. Liab. Litig., 597 F. Supp. 740, 749–750 (E.D.N.Y. 1984), *aff'd in part and rev'd in part on other grounds*, 818 F.2d 145 (2d Cir. 1987) ("[s]ome 600 separate cases have been sent to this district from all over the country with an estimated fifteen thousand named plaintiffs"); *In re* Temporomandibular Joint (TMJ) Implants Prods. Liab. Litig., 844 F. Supp. 1553 (J.P.M.L., Feb 25, 1994) (173 actions); *In re* San Juan Dupont Plaza Hotel Fire Litig., 1988 U.S. Dist. LEXIS 17332 (D.P.R. Dec. 2, 1988) (275 actions).

# § 10.02 PRACTICE AND PROCEDURE BEFORE JUDICIAL PANEL ON MULTIDISTRICT LITIGATION

## [1] Practice Before Panel and Representation in Transferred Actions

The Judicial Panel on Multidistrict Litigation has prescribed its own rules of procedure.[26] These rules provide that every member in good standing of the Bar of any federal district court is entitled to practice law before the Judicial Panel on Multidistrict Litigation without condition. No special admission procedures exist. More importantly, the rules specify that any attorney of record in any action transferred to another district court under the multidistrict litigation statute may continue to represent his or her client in any district court to which the action is transferred, and that the parties to such an action are not required to engage local counsel in the district to which the action is transferred.[27]

All attorneys filing pleadings with the Judicial Panel on Multidistrict Litigation must do so using the Panel's electronic case filing system (ECF).[28] "Pleadings" as used in the Panel Rules refers to all papers, motions, responses, or replies of any kind.[29] Pro se individuals may file in paper form.

## [2] Who May Seek Transfer and Consolidation

A proceeding to transfer an action under the multidistrict litigation statute may be initiated by the Judicial Panel on Multidistrict Litigation itself or by a party in any action in which coordinated or consolidated pretrial proceedings may be appropriate.[30] If the proceedings are initiated by a party, the process is begun by filing a motion for transfer and a brief in support of the motion with the Clerk of the Panel.[31] A copy of the motion must also be filed in the district court in which the moving party's action is pending,[32] and in each district court in which an action is pending that will be affected by the motion.[33]

In some cases, the Multidistrict Litigation Panel learns of the pendency of related or similar cases filed in different district courts and the Panel itself initiates the transfer proceedings. In such cases,[34] the Clerk of the Panel serves a show-cause order on all the parties involved, directing them to show cause why the actions should not be transferred for coordinated or consolidated pretrial

---

[26] 28 U.S.C. § 1407(f) (statutory authority for Panel to prescribe rules). 28 U.S.C. § 1407(f); Rules of Procedure, Judicial Panel on Multidistrict Litigation, Rule 1 *et seq.* (effective October 4, 2010).

[27] Rules of Procedure, Judicial Panel on Multidistrict Litigation, Rule 2.1(c).

[28] Rules of Procedure, Judicial Panel on Multidistrict Litigation, Rules 1.1(d), 3.2(b) (effective October 4, 2010.

[29] Rules of Procedure, Judicial Panel on Multidistrict Litigation, Rules 1.1(g).

[30] 28 U.S.C. § 1407(c)(i), (ii).

[31] Rules of Procedure, Judicial Panel on Multidistrict Litigation, Rule 6.2(a).

[32] 28 U.S.C. § 1407(c)(ii).

[33] Rules of Procedure, Judicial Panel on Multidistrict Litigation, Rule 6.2(a).

[34] *See* 28 U.S.C. § 1407(c)(i).

proceedings. Any party or counsel served with a show-cause order is also obliged to notify the Clerk of the Panel of any other federal district court actions related to the litigation encompassed by the show-cause order so that they may be considered by the Panel as well. This duty to notify includes not only additional actions that are pending at the time the show-cause order is issued, but also related federal actions that are filed subsequently.[35] Although not required by statute, the Panel generally sends copies of show-cause orders to the districts in which actions appearing on the show-cause order are pending.[36]

## [3] Conditional Transfer Orders for Tag-Along Actions

A *tag-along action* is a civil action pending in a district court that involves common questions of fact with either (1) actions on a pending motion to transfer to create a multidistrict litigation, or (2) actions previously transferred to an existing multidistrict litigation, and which the Panel would consider transferring under Section 1407.[37] Any party or counsel in actions previously transferred under Section 1407 must promptly notify the Clerk of the Panel of any potential tag-along actions in which that party is also named or in which that counsel appears.[38] When faced with a potential tag-along action, the Panel has several options: filing a conditional transfer order, filing a show-cause order, or declining to act.[39]

If the Clerk of the Judicial Panel on Multidistrict Litigation learns of a potential tag-along action pending in a district court other than the transferee district court, the Clerk may enter a conditional transfer order. Such an order will provide for the transfer of the tag-along action to the previously designated transferee district court.[40] The Clerk must then serve the conditional transfer order on each party to the litigation and allow them to object.[41]

Whether the Panel will transfer a tag-along action depends on whether the requirements for transfer under the multidistrict litigation statute are met.[42] Because the Panel has already made a determination that the standards for transfer have been met, it is unlikely that the Panel will decline to transfer the tag-along action.[43] However, to defeat transfer, litigants in the tag-along action may argue that their action is not suitable for transfer because the case is far along in

---

[35] Rules of Procedure, Judicial Panel on Multidistrict Litigation, Rule 8.1(a).

[36] Patricia D. Howard, *A Guide to Multidistrict Litigation*, 124 F.R.D. 479, 482 (1989).

[37] Rules of Procedure, Judicial Panel on Multidistrict Litigation, Rule 1.1(h).

[38] Rules of Procedure, Judicial Panel on Multidistrict Litigation, Rule 7.1(a); *see In re* Bank of Am. Wage & Hour Empl. Litig., 740 F. Supp. 2d 1207, 1211 n.3 (D. Kan. 2010) (court enjoined party from proceeding with class action settlement in case pending in another federal district court until party had notified Panel of other case, as required by Rule 7.1(a), and allowed Panel to determine whether other case should be transferred and consolidated with multidistrict litigation).

[39] Rules of Procedure, Judicial Panel on Multidistrict Litigation, Rule 7.1(a).

[40] Rules of Procedure, Judicial Panel on Multidistrict Litigation, Rule 7.1(b).

[41] Rules of Procedure, Judicial Panel on Multidistrict Litigation, Rule 7.1(b).

[42] *See* 28 U.S.C. § 1407(multidistrict litigation statute).

[43] *See In re* General Motors Class E Buyout Sec. Litig., 696 F. Supp. 1546, 1546–1547 (J.P.M.L. 1988).

discovery or that their case raises questions that are sufficiently distinct from those in the transferred actions.[44]

## [4] Termination and Remand

In many cases, an action that had been transferred for consolidated or coordinated pretrial proceedings under the multidistrict litigation statute is disposed of completely in the transferee court.[45] A case that has been completely disposed of need not be remanded to the transferor district by the Judicial Panel on Multidistrict Litigation, but rather is terminated and dismissed by the transferee district court. Although the essential purpose of the multidistrict litigation statute is to achieve pretrial efficiency — for example, by supervising discovery — the transferee judge also has the authority to decide all pretrial motions, including motions that may be dispositive,[46] such as motions for judgment approving a settlement, for dismissal, for judgment on the pleadings, for summary judgment, for involuntary dismissal under Rule 41(b), for an order striking an affirmative defense, for voluntary dismissal under Rule 41(a), and for an order to quash service of process.[47] The vast majority of cases are terminated in the transferee court. When an action is terminated in the transferee court, the clerk of the transferee district court must send a copy of the order terminating the action to the Clerk of the Panel.[48]

When pre-trial proceedings have concluded and an action has not yet been terminated, the action must be remanded back to the transferor court for trial.[49] If a transferred action has not been terminated in the transferee district court, the Panel must remand it to the transferor district at the conclusion of the coordinated or consolidated pretrial proceedings.[50] Proceedings for remand may be initiated by a party, at the suggestion of the transferee district court, or by the Panel itself. Although remand proceedings may be initiated by any of the parties involved, actions transferred under the multidistrict litigation statute may be actually remanded only by order of the Panel.[51]

Most transferred actions are remanded on the suggestion of the transferee district court judge, indicating that the coordinated or consolidated pretrial

---

[44] *See* 17 Moore's Federal Practice § 112.05.

[45] *See* 17 Moore's Federal Practice § 112.07[1].

[46] *In re* Temporomandibular Joint (TMJ) Implants Prod. Liab. Litig., 97 F.3d 1050, 1055 (8th Cir. 1996); *see also* 28 U.S.C. § 1407(b); *In re* Agent Orange Prod. Liab. Litig., 597 F. Supp. 740, 751–752 (E.D.N.Y. 1984), *aff'd in part and rev'd in part on other grounds*, 818 F.2d 145 (2d Cir. 1987) (transferee court assumes complete jurisdiction for pretrial purposes and has authority to settle all pretrial motions including dispositive motions such as those for summary judgment or approval of a settlement).

[47] Stanley A. Weigel, *The Judicial Panel on Multidistrict Litigation, Transferor Courts and Transferee Courts*, 78 F.R.D. 575, 582–583 (1978); *see* Fed. R. Civ. P. 41(a), (b).

[48] Rules of Procedure, Judicial Panel on Multidistrict Litigation, Rule 10.1(a); *see* Patricia D. Howard, *A Guide to Multidistrict Litigation*, 124 F.R.D. 479, 486 (1989).

[49] 28 U.S.C. § 1407(a); Rules of Procedure, Judicial Panel on Multidistrict Litigation, Rule 10.1(b).

[50] 28 U.S.C. § 1407(a); Rules of Procedure, Judicial Panel on Multidistrict Litigation, Rule 10.1(b).

[51] 28 U.S.C. § 1407(a). *See In re* Wilson, 451 F.3d 161, 165 (3d Cir. 2006) (transferee court has no authority to remand case on its own; rather, Panel must order remand; citing Moore's Federal Practice).

proceedings assigned to the judge by the Panel have been successfully completed. A judge should make such a suggestion when he or she perceives that his or her role in the case has ended.[52] The Panel defers to the views of the transferee judge and is reluctant to order a remand absent a suggestion to do so from the transferee judge.[53]

## § 10.03 BASES FOR ORDERING TRANSFER OF AN ACTION

### [1] Prerequisites for Transfer

#### [a] Balancing Statutory Prerequisites

There are three requirements for obtaining transfer under the multidistrict litigation statute. The "civil actions" pending in different districts must involve (1) "one or more common questions of fact," and transfer must be (2) "for the convenience of parties and witnesses," and must (3) "promote the just and efficient conduct of such actions."[54] The party moving for transfer has the burden of showing that the statutory requirements for transfer are met.[55]

When balancing the three requirements for transfer, the Panel keeps in mind the overall purpose of the multidistrict litigation statute to achieve efficiencies in the pretrial process. Thus, a review of the many decisions of the Panel shows that the Panel does not give equal weight to the three factors. Given the statutory purpose, the most important factor is whether the transfer will result in the just and efficient conduct of the action.[56]

---

[52] *See*, e.g., *In re* Patenaude, 210 F.3d 135, 142–146 (3d Cir. 1999) (court refused to issue writ of mandamus to compel remand of asbestos cases when individual settlement negotiations and conferences were ongoing and transferee court was conducting discovery on overlapping issues that affected many asbestos cases, even if not the plaintiffs' cases); *In re* Wilson, 451 F.3d 161, 165 (3d Cir. 2006) (suggestion to remand from transferee court indicates that coordinated or consolidated pretrial proceedings assigned to it have been successfully completed; citing Moore's Federal Practice); *In re* Activated Carbon-Based Hunting Clothing Mktg. & Sales Practices Litig., 840 F. Supp. 2d 1193, 1201 (D. Minn. 2012) ("Although 'the Court is leaving some pretrial work undone' by suggesting remand, it believes that 'the central purpose of the JPML referral has been achieved' now that discovery is over, class certification has been denied, and what remain are a handful of cases requiring individualized proof on many state-specific issues.").

[53] Rules of Procedure, Judicial Panel on Multidistrict Litigation, Rule 10.3(a); *In re* Asbestos Prods. Liab. Litig. (No. VI), 771 F. Supp. 415, 422 n.8 (J.P.M.L. 1991) ("Those parties who may seek early remand of their actions or claims are reminded of (i) Panel Rule 14(d)'s expression of the Panel's reluctance to order remand absent a suggestion of remand from the transferee judge, and (ii) the special affidavit requirement of that Rule."); *In re* Air Crash Disaster Near Chicago, 476 F. Supp. 445, 450 n.6 (J.P.M.L. 1979) (Panel places great weight on transferee judge's suggestion that remand has become appropriate).

[54] 28 U.S.C. § 1407(a).

[55] *See In re* Chiropractic Antitrust Litig., 483 F. Supp. 811, 813 (J.P.M.L. 1980).

[56] *See* generally Margaret S. Williams and Tracey E. George, *Who Will Manage Complex Civil Litigation? The Decision to Transfer and Consolidate Multidistrict Litigation*, 10 J. Empir. Stud. 424,

### [b] Actions Involving Common Questions of Fact

The fundamental statutory requirement for transferring related civil actions pending in different judicial districts to a centralized forum for coordinated or consolidated pretrial proceedings is that they involve one or more common questions of fact.[57] The multidistrict litigation statute was enacted as a means of conserving judicial resources by avoiding duplicative parallel discovery and other pretrial proceedings in related actions, and if this fundamental requirement is not met consolidation serves no purpose.[58]

A common question of fact among related cases generally is not difficult to identify, and if common questions of fact are present, and the other statutory requirements are met, the Panel will order transfer.[59] However, if the degree of commonality does not rise to the level that a transfer under the multidistrict litigation statute would serve the overall convenience of the parties and witnesses and promote the just and efficient conduct of the entire litigation, the transfer will be denied, because the separate actions can be conducted separately just as efficiently. For example, if the only common fact among a group of personal injury claims is a claim of "such generality that it covers a number of different ailments for each of which there are numerous possible causes other than the tortious conduct of one of the defendants," a transfer for coordinated or consolidated pretrial proceedings would be inappropriate.[60]

The Panel has interpreted the common-questions requirement quite broadly to achieve the efficiency purposes of the multidistrict litigation statute. For instance, even though the statute refers to common questions of "fact," the Panel in complex cases has justified transfer on the basis of important or dispositive questions of law, as well as the existence of some common questions of fact.[61] The complexity of the

---

427–28 (2013); John F. Cooney, Comment, *The Experience of Transferee Courts Under the Multidistrict Litigation Act*, 39 U. Chi. L. Rev. 588, 594 (1972).

[57] 28 U.S.C. § 1407(a); *In re* "Factor VIII or IX Concentrate Blood Prods." Prods. Liab. Litig., 853 F. Supp. 454, 455 (J.P.M.L. 1993).

[58] Ranger Ins. Ltd. v. BP PLC (*In re* Oil Spill by the Oil Rig Deepwater Horizon), 764 F. Supp. 2d 1352, 1353 (J.P.M.L. 2011), Reversed by, remanded by: Lake Eugenie Land & Dev., Inc. v. BP Exploration & Prod. (*In re* Deepwater Horizon), 732 F.3d 326, 2013 U.S. App. LEXIS 20188, 2014 A.M.C. 80 (5th Cir. La. 2013) (Panel will generally decline to transfer declaratory judgment insurance actions when they appear to present strictly legal questions, requiring little or no discovery, while transfer may be warranted if actions require and rely on same factual discovery as already-centralized actions); *see In re* Food Lion, Inc., 73 F.3d 528, 532 (4th Cir. 1996).

[59] *In re* Toyota Motor Corp. Unintended Acceleration Mktg. Sales Practices & Prods. Liab. Litig., 704 F. Supp. 2d 1379, 1381 (J.P.M.L. 2010) (cases involved common questions of fact when each action before the Panel asserted economic damages on behalf of certain classes and/or individuals stemming from an alleged defect in certain Toyota vehicles that causes sudden, unintended acceleration), vacated by Alfen v. Toyota Motor Sales, U.S.A., Inc. (*In re* Toyota Motor Corp. Unintended Acceleration Mktg.), 287 F.R.D. 614, 2013 U.S. Dist. LEXIS 60119 (C.D. Cal. 2013); *In re* Temporomandibular Joint (TMJ) Implants Prods. Liab. Litig., 844 F. Supp. 1553, 1554 (J.P.M.L. 1994); *In re* Gross Common Carrier, Inc., Freight Undercharge Claims Litig., 843 F. Supp. 1506, 1507–1508 (J.P.M.L. 1994); Fung v. Abex Corp., 816 F. Supp. 569, 573 (N.D. Cal. 1992) (centralization is proper if common questions of fact exist relating to wrongful death and injury claims allegedly resulting from asbestos exposure).

[60] *In re* Repetitive Stress Injury Litig., 11 F.3d 368, 373 (2d Cir. 1993); *see* 28 U.S.C. § 1407.

[61] *See In re* Mutual Fund Sales Antitrust Litig., 361 F. Supp. 638, 640 (J.P.M.L. 1973).

common questions will have an impact on the Panel's decision whether to transfer if there are relatively few cases. Similarly, the Panel will balance the complexity of the common questions against the number of common questions in determining whether a transfer is appropriate. If there are few common questions, and the questions are not complex or individual factual issues predominate, the Panel generally will not order a transfer.[62] On the other hand, there need not be a predominance of common questions to justify transfer if the Panel believes that the transfer is otherwise appropriate to achieve the just and efficient conduct of the actions.[63] Nor is there any bar to combining different types of actions based on different legal theories provided there is a significant factual overlap.[64] Rather, the cases will be transferred and it will be left to the transferee judge to work with the parties to develop a discovery plan that takes into account the common and the individual factual questions.[65]

### [c] Convenience of Parties and Witnesses

The second fundamental requirement of the multidistrict litigation statute is that the convenience of the parties and the witnesses be weighed as a factor in determining whether a transfer should be ordered.[66] However, in view of the fact that the Panel has the authority to consolidate and transfer cases even over the objections of all of the parties,[67] some commentators have suggested that this requirement is basically ignored in practice.[68]

The decisions and orders of the Judicial Panel on Multidistrict Litigation as well as the reported cases that have touched on this issue indicate that the Panel views the question of convenience from the group perspective rather than from the point of view of any one party or witness. As several decisions have expressed it, the Panel must look to the overall convenience of *all* the parties and witnesses rather than looking to the individual convenience of *each* party and *each* witness.[69]

---

[62] *See In re* Asbestos School Prods. Liab. Litig., 606 F. Supp. 713, 714 (J.P.M.L. 1985); *In re* Westinghouse Elec. Corp. Employment Discrimination Litig., 438 F. Supp. 937, 939 (J.P.M.L. 1977).

[63] *See In re* Microsoft Corp. Windows Operating Sys. Litig., 2000 U.S. Dist. LEXIS 5559, at *6–*7 (J.P.M.L. Apr. 25, 2000) (common questions sufficient to permit § 1407 transfer despite presence of additional or differing legal theories because all underlying actions arise from common factual core); *In re* Multidistrict Civil Antitrust Actions Involving Antibiotic Drugs, 299 F. Supp. 1403 (J.P.M.L. 1969).

[64] *In re* BP Sec., 734 F. Supp. 2d 1380, 1382–1383 (J.P.M.L. 2010) (Panel frequently includes securities fraud and ERISA actions in same MDL docket; "Our experience so far has taught us that combining these kinds of cases in one MDL has produced good results and efficiencies.").

[65] *See In re* Multi-Piece Rim Prods. Liab. Litig., 464 F. Supp. 969, 974 (J.P.M.L. 1979); *In re* Upjohn Co. Antibiotic "Cleocin" Prod. Liab. Litig., 450 F. Supp. 1168, 1170 (J.P.M.L. 1978).

[66] 28 U.S.C. § 1407(a); S. Rep. No. 454, 90th Cong., 1st Sess. 2 (1967).

[67] *See In re* Air Crash Disaster at Florida Everglades on December 29, 1972, 549 F.2d 1006, 1013 (5th Cir. 1977) ("courts may order consolidation of cases without consent and over the objections of parties").

[68] Blake M. Rhodes, *The Judicial Panel on Multidistrict Litigation: Time for Rethinking*, 140 U. Penn. L. Rev. 711, 720 (1991).

[69] *In re* Dow Co. "Sarabond" Prods. Liab. Litig., 664 F. Supp. 1403, 1404 (D. Colo. 1987); *In re* Vernitron Sec. Litig., 462 F. Supp. 391, 393–394 (J.P.M.L. 1978) (claims of extreme inconvenience and prohibitive cost for party to obtain local counsel rejected because of total savings, possibility of prudent, efficient apportionment of work, and no necessity of hiring local counsel); *In re* Swine Flu Immunization

In cases in which parties complain that a transfer under the multidistrict litigation statute will be inconvenient or expensive, the Panel generally rejects such complaints and suggests instead that the transferee court employ the various techniques discussed in the Manual for Complex Litigation,[70] such as developing case management plans, appointment of lead and liaison counsel, aggressive supervision of discovery, shared discovery, and appropriate motion practice and the like, to minimize the inconvenience and expenses for peripheral parties, or those involved in only one or two cases.[71] For example, there is no need for all counsel to participate in pretrial conferences in the transferee court; at least some depositions may be taken in the district in which they reside, and, with respect to depositions taken in inconvenient districts, the transferee court can enter orders providing for delayed examinations.[72] Moreover, parties to tag-along cases generally achieve the automatic benefit of having access to discovery that has already been had in the multidistrict litigation.[73]

### [d] Just and Efficient Conduct of Actions

The third and most important requirement for transfer under the multidistrict litigation statute is that the Panel must determine whether consolidating and transferring the related civil actions will promote the just and efficient conduct of the actions.[74] This requirement essentially implements the purpose of the Multi-district Litigation Act.[75]

The term "efficiency" in this context usually refers to saving judicial resources.[76] Efficient judicial administration can be achieved by conducting the pretrial proceedings in the related cases in one forum, where the duplication of discovery that would result from trying the actions separately can be avoided. One judge may also issue a single ruling on pretrial matters, thus avoiding repeated rulings on the same issue and the possibility of conflicting rulings issued by several judges.[77] As the

---

Prods. Liab. Litig., 453 F. Supp. 648, 649–650 (J.P.M.L. 1978) (that parties would be financially unable to participate if action was transferred from Oregon to Washington, D.C., was not deemed valid objection in light of overall economy to be gained and available safeguards).

[70] Federal Judicial Center, Manual for Complex Litigation (Fourth).

[71] *See In re* Commodity Credit Corp. Litig. Involving Grain Shipments, 364 F. Supp. 462, 463 (J.P.M.L. 1973); *see also In re* Sugar Indus. Antitrust Litig. (East Coast), 471 F. Supp. 1089, 1094 (J.P.M.L. 1979); *In re* Multidistrict Litig. Involving Butterfield Patent Infringement, 328 F. Supp. 513, 514 (J.P.M.L. 1970).

[72] *In re* Sugar Indus. Antitrust Litig. (East Coast), 471 F. Supp. 1089, 1094 (J.P.M.L. 1979); *In re* Commodity Credit Corp. Litig. Involving Grain Shipments, 364 F. Supp. 462, 463 (J.P.M.L. 1973).

[73] *In re* Swine Flu Immunization Prods. Liab. Litig., 446 F. Supp. 244, 247 (J.P.M.L. 1978).

[74] 28 U.S.C. § 1407(a).

[75] S. Rep. No. 454, 90th Cong., 1st Sess. 2 (1967) ("the main purpose of transfer for consolidation or coordination of pretrial proceedings is to promote the ends of efficient justice"); H.R. Rep. No. 90-1130, at 1 (1968), *reprinted in* 1968 U.S. Code Cong. & Admin. News pp. 1898, 1900 ("it is expected that such transfer is to be ordered only where significant economy and efficiency in judicial administration may be obtained").

[76] *In re* Food Lion, Inc., 73 F.3d 528, 532 (4th Cir. 1996).

[77] *See In re* Bridgestone/Firestone Inc., ATX, ATX II, and Wilderness Tires Products Liability Litig., 2000 U.S. Dist. LEXIS 15926 (J.P.M.L. Oct. 24, 2000); *In re* Managed Care Litig., 2000 U.S. Dist. LEXIS

Panel has put it, a transfer under the multidistrict litigation statute will always result in some inconvenience to the parties, so the main question becomes "whether the objectives of the statute [judicial efficiency] are sufficiently served to justify the necessary inconveniences of transfer and remand."[78]

Given this fundamental goal of the multidistrict litigation statute, the Panel will refuse to transfer cases if the actions are nearing trial in the transferor forum or if discovery is already well along. Consolidating the actions in these circumstances will not conserve any judicial resources, and "[u]nder these circumstances, transfer will not further the purposes of section 1407."[79]

### [e] Mass Actions May Not Be Transferred

There is a statutory limitation on the power of the Panel to transfer (under the multi-district litigation statute) a "mass action" (as that term is defined by Class Action Fairness Act of 2005) (*see* § 6.08[6][d]).[80] In this context, the term "mass action" means any civil action (other than a class action) in which the plaintiffs propose a joint trial for monetary relief claims of 100 or more persons. [81] The MDL court may not transfer a mass action to another court for consolidated pretrial procedures under Section 1407, unless a majority of the plaintiffs in the action request transfer.[82]

The statutory limitation on transfer applies to only those mass actions removed to federal court on the basis of the limited or minimal diversity of citizenship subject matter jurisdiction created by the Class Action Fairness Act of 2005.[83] The Class Action Fairness Act creates a special form of limited or minimal diversity jurisdiction for large, multi-state class actions in which sufficient diversity of citizenship exists when one plaintiff and one defendant are citizens of different

---

15927 (J.P.M.L. Oct. 23, 2000); *In re* Air Crash Disaster Near Chicago, 476 F. Supp. 445, 447 (J.P.M.L. 1979) (listing benefits of consolidated pretrial proceedings).

[78] *In re* "East of the Rockies" Concrete Pipe Antitrust Litig., 302 F. Supp. 244, 255–256 (J.P.M.L. 1969) (listing factors relevant to that decision).

[79] *In re* "Lite Beer" Trademark Litig., 437 F. Supp. 754, 755 (J.P.M.L. 1977); *see also In re* Engle Progeny Tobacco Prods. Liab. Litig., 2007 U.S. Dist. LEXIS 93627 (J.P.M.L. Dec. 12, 2007) (coordinated proceedings were not warranted when discovery on common fact issues had already occurred in underlying state action, and any remaining common questions were not sufficiently complex or numerous to justify transfer); *In re* Asbestos Prods. Liab. Litig. (No. VI), 771 F. Supp. 415, 418 (J.P.M.L. 1991) (many of actions were well advanced, with some of actions pending for up to four years, and trial dates or discovery cutoff dates had been set in several actions; accordingly, transfer would not further purposes of statute); *In re* Cable Tie Patent Litig., 487 F. Supp. 1351, 1354 (J.P.M.L. 1980) (transfer denied when movant did not meet burden of demonstrating that transfer will further purposes of statute); *see generally* 17 Moore's Federal Practice Ch. 112, *Multidistrict Litigation* (Matthew Bender 3d ed.).

[80] *See* 28 U.S.C. § 1332(d)(11)(C)(i).

[81] 28 U.S.C. § 1332(d)(11)(B)(i).

[82] 28 U.S.C. § 1332(d)(11)(C)(i). The transfer ban transfer does not apply when: 1) The case is no longer being treated as a mass action in that, at the time of the transfer, it has been formally certified as a class action under Rule 23 (28 U.S.C. § 1332(d)(11)(C)(ii)(I)); or 2) A majority of the plaintiffs in the action request the transfer. 28 U.S.C. § 1332(d)(11)(C)(ii)(II).

[83] *See* 28 U.S.C. § 1332(d)(11)(C)(i).

states.[84] With a few changes with respect to the calculation of the required minimum amount in dispute, this type of limited or minimal diversity of citizenship subject matter jurisdiction is available as the basis for federal court subject matter jurisdiction in a mass action case as well in a class action.[85] The availability of this type of subject matter jurisdiction will support the removal of a mass action from state court to federal court.[86]

### [2] Selection of Transferee Forum

In many cases, the more difficult question before the Panel is not whether the related actions should be grouped together and transferred for coordinated or consolidated pretrial proceedings, but to which district they should be transferred.[87] The statutory framework for dealing with multidistrict litigation requires the Panel to determine that a transfer will be for the convenience of the parties and witnesses and that it will promote the just and efficient conduct of the actions, but otherwise provides no guidance for deciding where to transfer the actions.[88]

The Panel has developed its own general guidelines for selecting the transferee district, taking into account the specific facts of the cases and sometimes the wishes of the parties. The Panel is not restricted by venue and personal jurisdiction considerations when determining to which district court the cases ought to be transferred.[89] Rather, so long as the convenience of the parties and witnesses is served, and most importantly, a just and efficient conduct of the actions can be achieved, the Panel may transfer the actions to any district. One might argue that it violates the due process "minimum contacts" test to permit an action to be transferred to a district court that may not have been able to exercise jurisdiction in the first place.[90] Such an argument, however, fails. First, the only restriction on

---

84 *See* 28 U.S.C. § 1332(d)(2).

85 *See* 28 U.S.C. § 1332(d)(11)(B)(i). *See generally* Margaret S. Williams and Tracey E. George, *Who Will Manage Complex Civil Litigation? The Decision to Transfer and Consolidate Multidistrict Litigation*, 10 J. Empir. Stud. 424 (2013).

86 28 U.S.C. § 1332(d)(11)(A). For further discussion of removal of mass actions based on limited or minimal diversity jurisdiction, see Moore's Federal Practice Ch. 23, *Class Actions* and Ch. 107, *Removal*.

87 *See, e.g., In re* Regents of the University of California, 964 F.2d 1128, 1136 (Fed. Cir. 1992); *In re* Air Fare Litig., 322 F. Supp. 1013, 1015 (J.P.M.L. 1971) ("[a]s is so often the case, the real issue among the parties is not whether these actions should be transferred under Section 1407 but rather to which district they should be transferred"); *see also* Richards, *An Analysis of the Judicial Panel on Multidistrict Litigation's Selection of Transferee District and Judge*, 78 Fordham L. Rev. 311 (2009) (overview of factors used by MDL panel when selecting transferee district).

88 28 U.S.C. § 1407(a).

89 *See* Pinney v. Nokia, Inc., 402 F.3d 430, 451–452 (4th Cir. 2005) (28 U.S.C. § 1407 is itself venue statute that allows Panel to override plaintiff's choice of forum when requirements of statute are met); *In re* Ivy, 901 F.2d 7, 9 (2d Cir. 1990) (Judicial Panel on Multidistrict Litigation had jurisdiction to transfer Agent Orange case in which jurisdictional objection was pending); *In re* New York City Mun. Sec. Litig., 572 F.2d 49, 51 (2d Cir. 1978) ("We begin by noting that § 1407, unlike §§ 1404 and 1406, authorizes transfer of an action to 'any district' and not simply to a district where the action could have been brought").

90 *See generally* Ch. 7, *Personal Jurisdiction in Federal Courts*.

the *federal* court's exercise of personal jurisdiction is the Fifth Amendment, rather than the Fourteenth Amendment (*see* § 7.02[1]). Thus, the question is whether the parties had "minimum contacts" or sufficient affiliating contacts with *the United States as a whole* to justify the exercise of personal jurisdiction.[91]

The Panel will consider a number of factors when deciding the appropriate transferee forum. One group of factors concerns the convenience of the parties and witnesses. Thus, the Panel will look to the parties' principal places of business,[92] the location of documents and witnesses necessary to the actions,[93] and the centrality of the location for the convenience of the parties and witnesses, or where the most cases have already been filed.[94] Another helpful barometer as to the most convenient place to transfer the actions is the prior transfer of a case or cases under the convenience transfer statute.[95] The Panel will therefore look at the decisions rendered by district courts under the convenience transfer statute in the cases involved.[96]

Similarly, the Panel will look to the district in which the broader-based of the actions, as well as the earliest to be filed, was originally brought,[97] which district has the most cases pending,[98] and the district in which a bankruptcy action involving the defendant is pending.[99] Generally, transferring actions pursuant to these factors results in greater convenience to most of the parties and witnesses.

The Panel will also look at a number of factors that concern the just and efficient conduct of the actions. Thus, for example, the Panel will look at the condition of the

---

[91] *See* Omni Capital Int'l v. Rudolf Wolff & Co., 484 U.S. 97, 111 (1987) (suggesting, without deciding, that Congress could constitutionally permit service of process on defendants who in the aggregate have sufficient affiliating contacts with the United States); Wells Fargo & Co. v. Wells Fargo Express Co., 556 F.2d 406, 418 (9th Cir. 1977) (reviewing cases permitting aggregation of contacts to meet Fifth Amendment minimum contacts with the United States test, and surveying federal statutes permitting service in such cases). *See generally* Moore's Federal Practice Ch. 4, *Summons*; Ch. 108, *Territorial Jurisdiction: Jurisdiction Over Persons and Property*).

[92] *In re* "Factor VIII or IX Concentrate Blood Prods." Prods. Liab. Litig., 853 F. Supp. 454, 455 (J.P.M.L. 1993).

[93] *In re* Air Crash Disaster Near Coolidge, Arizona on May 6, 1971, 362 F. Supp. 572, 573 (J.P.M.L. 1973).

[94] *In re* Pet Food Prods. Liab. Litig., 499 F. Supp. 2d 1346, 1347 (J.P.M.L. 2007) (transfer to District of New Jersey was appropriate when about one-third of pending actions were already there and pretrial proceedings were advancing well); *In re* Wheat Farmers Antitrust Class Action Litig., 366 F. Supp. 1087, 1088 (J.P.M.L. 1973).

[95] *See* 28 U.S.C. § 1404(a); Ch. 9, *Change of Venue*.

[96] *In re* Warehouse Constr., Contract Litig., 387 F. Supp. 734, 735–736 (J.P.M.L. 1975); *see* 28 U.S.C. § 1404(a) (convenience transfer statute).

[97] *In re* Regents of the University of California, 964 F.2d 1128, 1136 (Fed. Cir. 1992).

[98] *In re* BP p.l.c. Sec. Litig., 734 F. Supp. 2d 1376, 1379 (J.P.M.L. 2010) (Southern District of Texas was appropriate court when plaintiffs' securities fraud claims would require significant discovery into defendant's Gulf Coast operations, which were based primarily in Houston, Texas); *In re* Republic National-Realty Equities Sec. Litig., 382 F. Supp. 1403, 1407 (J.P.M.L. 1974).

[99] *In re* American Continental Corp./Lincoln Sav. & Loan Sec. Litig., 130 F.R.D. 475, 476 (J.P.M.L. 1990).

potential transferee forum's docket.[100] If that district has a crowded docket, it may not be efficient to transfer the cases there. On the other hand, if that district appears to be the best forum from a convenience standpoint, the Panel may order the cases transferred there and then appoint a district court judge from another district to handle the cases there.[101] Even if no actions are pending in a particular district, the Panel may consider transferring the cases there if overall administrative efficiencies would result.[102]

Mass tort litigation presents the Panel with another consideration. If a large number of cases have been brought in the courts of a particular state, the Panel may decide to transfer federal actions to a district in that state, so that the federal and state courts can cooperate in the conduct of discovery and other matters. The Panel also considers the geographic dispersion of the cases. If the cases are widely dispersed, it may look to a district that has a judge experienced in multidistrict litigation and that has the capacity to handle complex litigation.[103]

Another consideration is the type of case. The differences in type of proof, and in the nature of the litigation or the litigants involved, may determine where the actions should be transferred. For example, domestic air crash cases are generally transferred to the district in which the crash took place. Typically, it will be that district in which much of the key physical evidence will be located. As noted above, cases related to a bankruptcy proceeding are generally transferred to the district in which the bankruptcy proceeding is pending, which, in turn, is generally located in the district in which the debtor resides. Given the importance of documents relating to the debtor's financial condition in most actions related to a bankruptcy, that would be a singularly important factor. When the federal government is involved in a multidistrict litigation, the Panel will often transfer cases to the district in which the government's action is pending. For example, in the antitrust context, the place where a grand jury investigation is taking place will often then be the district in which much key evidence will be collected.[104]

Although the Panel will not hesitate to transfer cases under the multidistrict litigation statute when it thinks it is appropriate to do so, it often will transfer a case to the district that a majority of litigants think is the best, if the other convenience factors seem equally balanced.[105] On the other hand, if there is substantial disagreement among the parties, the Panel may transfer the action to a

---

[100] *In re* Peruvian Rd. Litig., 380 F. Supp. 796, 798 (J.P.M.L. 1974).

[101] *In re* San Juan, Puerto Rico Air Crash Disaster, 316 F. Supp. 981, 982 n.3 (J.P.M.L. 1970).

[102] *In re* BP p.l.c. Sec. Litig., 734 F. Supp. 2d 1376, 1379 (J.P.M.L. 2010) (fact that no constituent action was currently pending in Southern District of Texas was not impediment to its selection as transferee district); *In re* Swine Flu Immunization Prods. Liab. Litig., 446 F. Supp. 244, 247 (J.P.M.L. 1978); *In re* Cement & Concrete Antitrust Litig., 437 F. Supp. 750, 753 (J.P.M.L. 1977) ("In appropriate circumstances we would order a group of actions to a district in which none of the actions is pending").

[103] Judge experienced in complex litigation. *See In re* Vioxx Prods. Liab. Litig., 360 F. Supp. 2d 1352, 1353 (J.P.M.L. 2005).

[104] *In re* Cement & Concrete Antitrust Litig., 437 F. Supp. 750, 753 (J.P.M.L. 1977); *see generally* Levy, *Complex Multidistrict Litigation and the Federal Courts*, 40 Fordham L. Rev. 41, 58 (1971).

[105] *In re* Cutter Labs., Inc. "Braunwald-Cutter" Aortic Heart Valve Prods. Liab. Litig., 465 F. Supp. 1295, 1297–1298 (J.P.M.L. 1979).

"neutral" forum. For instance, in the breast-implant litigation, one group of attorneys strongly favored a transfer to a district in California, to judges who were familiar with and had tried cases. Another group of attorneys favored transfer to an experienced judge in Ohio. The Panel declined to take sides in what was a hotly contested matter, and instead transferred the actions to a judge highly experienced in complex litigation in Alabama.[106]

## [3] Selection of Transferee Judge

The multidistrict litigation statute requires the Panel to assign the transferred cases to a particular judge or judges to conduct the actions in the transferee district.[107] Even though the Panel generally assigns the actions to a judge who is a member of the transferee district court, and the presence of a judge in that district may well have been a factor in selecting that district as the transferee forum,[108] the judge or judges need not be members of the transferee district court.[109]

In choosing a judge, the Panel generally will look for a judge who is most familiar with the particular facts and legal issues raised by the cases.[110] Clearly, the efficiency purposes of the statute are well served by such a consideration.[111] Especially in the case of particularly complex multidistrict litigation, the Panel will be likely to assign the cases to a judge who has already demonstrated an ability to handle such litigation. For example, the Panel transferred the "mega-mass tort" breast-implant litigation to the Northern District of Alabama and assigned the litigation to Judge Sam Pointer, a former member of the Panel, Chair of the Board of Editors of the Manual for Complex Litigation, Chair of the Judicial Conference's Advisory Committee on Civil Rules, and an experienced multidistrict transferee judge.[112]

In making this selection, however, one of the things the Panel does *not* consider is the litigants' dissatisfaction with past or anticipated rulings of a prospective transferee judge.[113]

---

[106] *In re* Silicone Gel Breast Implants Prod. Liab. Litig., 793 F. Supp. 1098, 1101 (J.P.M.L. 1992).

[107] 28 U.S.C. § 1407(b); *see also* Richards, *An Analysis of the Judicial Panel on Multidistrict Litigation's Selection of Transferee District and Judge*, 78 Fordham L. Rev. 311 (2009) (overview of factors used by MDL panel when selecting transferee judge).

[108] *In re* Data Gen. Corp. Antitrust Litig., 470 F. Supp. 855, 859 (J.P.M.L. 1979) (that district court judge was familiar with legal and factual issues was factor in transferring actions to that district).

[109] 28 U.S.C. § 1407(b).

[110] *See generally* Margaret S. Williams and Tracey E. George, *Who Will Manage Complex Civil Litigation? The Decision to Transfer and Consolidate Multidistrict Litigation*, 10 J. Empir. Stud. 424 (2013).

[111] *In re* Multidistrict Private Civil Treble Damage Antitrust Litigation Involving IBM, 302 F. Supp. 796, 800 (J.P.M.L. 1969).

[112] *In re* Silicone Gel Breast Implants Prods. Liab. Litig., 793 F. Supp. 1098, 1101 (J.P.M.L. 1992).

[113] *See, e.g., In re* Holiday Magic Sec. and Antitrust Litig., 433 F. Supp. 1125, 1126 (J.P.M.L. 1977); *In re* Molinaro/Catanzaro Patent Litig., 402 F. Supp. 1404, 1406 (J.P.M.L. 1975); *In re* Glenn W. Turner Enters. Litig., 368 F. Supp. 805, 806 (J.P.M.L. 1973).

## § 10.04 JURISDICTION AND AUTHORITY OF TRANSFEROR COURTS

### [1] Orders Issued Prior to Transfer and During Pendency of Action Before Judicial Panel

A transfer under the multidistrict litigation statute becomes effective when the Panel's order of transfer is filed with the clerk of the transferee court.[114] Thereafter it is generally accepted that the jurisdiction of the transferor court ceases, and the transferee court assumes complete pretrial jurisdiction.[115]

However, the mere pendency of a motion to transfer, of an order to show cause, or of a conditional transfer order before the Judicial Panel on Multidistrict Litigation in no way limits the jurisdiction of the court in which the action is pending,[116] and all discovery in progress and all orders of the transferor court remain in effect after transfer unless and until they are modified by the transferee judge.[117] Although a pending motion to transfer does not automatically stay proceedings, the transferor court has the authority to do so if appropriate. The court should consider, among other matters, whether (1) the issues in question are easily capable of arising in multiple cases, (2) the issues involve common questions of law and fact that relate to the cases already transferred, and (3) it would serve judicial economy to have the questions resolved by the transferor court.[118]

On the other hand, the pendency of settlement negotiations or motions, including dispositive motions such as motions to dismiss, does not limit the authority of the Panel to order transfer. The theory is that any such matters may be handled by the transferee court if and when transfer is ordered.[119]

---

[114] 28 U.S.C. § 1407(c); Rules of Procedure, Judicial Panel on Multidistrict Litigation, Rule 2.1(d).

[115] *See In re* Plumbing Fixture Cases, 298 F. Supp. 484, 495–496 (J.P.M.L. 1968).

[116] Rules of Procedure, Judicial Panel on Multidistrict Litigation, Rule 2.1(d); Illinois Mun. Ret. Fund v. Citigroup, 391 F.3d 844, 850 (7th Cir. 2004) (pendency of conditional order of transfer did not divest transferor court of jurisdiction to determine whether to remand removed case to state court); General Elec. Co. v. Byrne, 611 F.2d 670, 673 (7th Cir. 1979).

[117] *See In re* Penn Central Sec. Litig., 62 F.R.D. 181, 187 (E.D. Pa. 1974); *In re* Plumbing Fixture Cases, 298 F. Supp. 484, 496 (J.P.M.L. 1968).

[118] Rutherford v. Merck & Co., Inc., 428 F. Supp. 2d 842, 845–846 (S.D. Ill. 2006) (court should be reluctant to grant stay when subject matter jurisdiction is in question; court should conduct at least limited review of remand motion before granting stay and, if it appears removal was improper, should promptly complete its consideration and remand case to state court); Kohl v. American Home Prods. Corp., 78 F. Supp. 2d 885, 888 (W.D. Ark. 1999) (transferor court decided to hear motion to remand to state court, denied remand, and stayed all other proceedings pending transfer); Conroy v. Fresh Del Monte Produce, Inc., 325 F. Supp. 2d 1049, 1053–1054 (N.D. Cal. 2004) (transferor court decided to hear motion to remand to state court when motion could be readily resolved and granting stay would lead to judicial inefficiency and delay resolution of jurisdictional issue); Conroy v. Fresh Del Monte Produce, Inc., 325 F. Supp. 2d 1049, 1053–1054 (N.D. Cal. 2004) (transferor court decided to hear motion to remand to state court when motion could be readily resolved and granting stay would lead to judicial inefficiency and delay resolution of jurisdictional issue).

[119] *See, e.g., In re* Oil Spill by "Amoco Cadiz" off Coast of France on March 16, 1978, 471 F. Supp. 473, 478 (J.P.M.L. 1979); *In re* Investors Funding Corp. of New York Sec. Litig., 461 F. Supp. 673, 675 (J.P.M.L. 1978).

### [2] Motions and Orders Before Court at Time of Transfer

The transferor court retains jurisdiction until the Panel's order transferring an action is entered. Thus, the transferor court has the power to decide any pending motions or take any other proper action. Once an action or group of actions is transferred, however, the transferor court or courts are divested of jurisdiction to decide the pending matters. Thus, the general rule regarding a pending motion before the transferor court at the time an action is officially transferred is that a subsequent decision on the motion by the transferor court is a nullity.[120]

Although the governing statute is silent on the precise fate of matters *sub judice* at the time a case is officially transferred,[121] Rule 2.1(d) states in pertinent part:[122]

> The pendency of a . . . conditional transfer order . . . before the Panel pursuant to 28 U.S.C. § 1407 does not affect or suspend orders and pretrial proceedings in any pending federal district court action and does not limit the pretrial jurisdiction of that court. An order to transfer . . . pursuant to 28 U.S.C. § 1407 shall be effective only upon its filing with the clerk of the transferee district court.

This provision and its earlier analogs has been consistently interpreted by the Panel and the courts as divesting the transferor court of jurisdiction at the moment of transfer.[123]

> On change of venue the overwhelming authority holds that the jurisdiction and powers of the transferee court are coextensive with that of the transferor court; that the transferee court may make any order to render any judgment that might have been rendered by the transferor court in the absence of transfer; that after an order changing venue the jurisdiction of the transferor court ceases; and that thereafter the transferor court can issue no further orders, and any steps taken by it are of no effect. These principles are applicable to a transfer under Section 1407 from the time of entry of the orders of transfer until the time of entry of an order to remand.[124]

Because the transferor court may not exercise jurisdiction over an action once a Panel order transferring the action is entered, the Panel will consider whether

---

120 Cooper v. Family Dollar Stores, Inc., 2009 U.S. Dist. LEXIS 59801, at *4 (D.N.J. July 14, 2009); Glasstech, Inc. v. AB Kyro OY, 769 F.2d 1574, 1576–1577 (Fed. Cir. 1985).

121 *See* 28 U.S.C. § 1407.

122 Rules of Procedure, Judicial Panel on Multidistrict Litigation, Rule 2.1(d).

123 Allen v. Bayer Corp., 460 F.3d 1217, 1230–31 (9th Cir. 2006) (When the transfer becomes effective, the jurisdiction of the transferor court ceases and the transferee court has exclusive jurisdiction.); *see* Manual for Complex Litigation (Fourth), § 20.131 ("[a] transfer under § 1407 becomes effective when the order granting the transfer is filed in the office of the clerk of the transferee court. At that point, the jurisdiction of the transferor court ceases and the transferee court has exclusive jurisdiction."). *See In re* UpJohn Co. Antibiotic Cleocin Prods. Liab. Litig., 664 F.2d 114, 118 (6th Cir. 1981) ("power of the Panel on Multidistrict Litigation under 28 U.S.C. § 1407 to transfer district court proceedings from one court to another should divest the transferor court of any further authority").

124 *In re* Plumbing Fixture Cases, 298 F. Supp. 484, 495 (J.P.M.L. 1968).

motions are pending when deciding whether and when to transfer a case.[125] In one instance, for example, the Panel stated that "[o]n principles of comity, where appropriate, the Panel has in the past timed its actions and constructed its orders in a manner which will permit the transferor courts (and Courts of Appeals if they are involved) to reach timely decisions on particular issues without abrupt, disconcerting, untimely or inappropriate orders of transfer by the Panel."[126] In another decision the Panel stated that it was "reluctant to transfer any action that has an important motion under submission with a court,"[127] and in yet another, the Panel denied a transfer when the plaintiff's motions for a preliminary injunction were pending before the court.[128]

## [3] Upon Remand of Action

When, at the conclusion of the coordinated or consolidated pretrial proceedings, an action is remanded to the district court from which it was transferred, it is transferred to the transferor judge's regular docket for further proceedings and trial.[129] Generally, the transferor district court judge has complete control of the action from that point onward.

One of the features of multidistrict litigation, however, is that following remand, transferor judges should not modify orders issued by the transferee judges. The rationale for this position is that allowing the transferor courts (and possibly their courts of appeal) to reconsider the transferee court's orders would frustrate the very purposes of the multidistrict litigation statute by leading to piecemeal litigation. The Panel and the courts properly hold the view that if a party wishes to appeal a decision of the transferee court, the better practice is to allow that appeal prior to remand.[130] Similarly, if the case is remanded back to the original transferor court, that court should use the law of the case doctrine to determine whether to revisit a decision of the transferee court.[131]

---

[125] *In re* L.E. Lay & Co. Antitrust Litig., 391 F. Supp. 1054, 1056 (J.P.M.L. 1975) (on principles of comity, Panel will be reluctant to transfer any action that has important motion under submission with transferor court); *see* Manual for Complex Litigation, § 31.131 at 252 (3d ed. 1995).

[126] *In re* Plumbing Fixture Cases, 298 F. Supp. 484, 496 (J.P.M.L. 1968).

[127] *In re* L.E. Lay & Co. Antitrust Litig., 391 F. Supp. 1054, 1056 (J.P.M.L. 1975).

[128] *In re* Professional Hockey Antitrust Litig., 352 F. Supp. 1405, 1407 (J.P.M.L. 1973); *see also* Stanley A. Weigel, *The Judicial Panel on Multidistrict Litigation, Transferor Courts and Transferee Courts*, 78 F.R.D. 575, 577 (1978).

[129] Manual for Complex Litigation (Fourth), § 20.133.

[130] *In re* Food Lion, Inc., 73 F.3d 528, 532–533 (4th Cir. 1996); *see* 28 U.S.C. § 1407.

[131] *In re* Ford Motor Co., 580 F.3d 308, 312 (5th Cir. 2009) (under law of case doctrine, district court should have granted rehearing on forum non conveniens motion when transferee court's decision not to dismiss on forum non conveniens grounds was clearly erroneous and would work manifest injustice; error was serious enough to require mandamus relief ordering district court to dismiss in favor of Mexican forum).

## § 10.05 JURISDICTION AND AUTHORITY OF TRANSFEREE COURT

### [1] Scope of Authority

#### [a] Judicial Authority

Coordinated or consolidated pretrial proceedings ordered under the multidistrict litigation statute are conducted by a judge, or on rare occasions by two judges, to whom the actions are assigned by the Judicial Panel on Multidistrict Litigation. The litigation is usually transferred to a judge in the transferee court, but occasionally the Panel has selected a judge designated to sit specially in the transferee district on an intracircuit or intercircuit assignment.[132]

A judge who has been assigned multidistrict litigation has two distinct grants of judicial authority. The first is to preside over the transferred actions by exercising his or her authority as a member of the district court to which the actions have been transferred.[133] Thus, when a judge is temporarily assigned to the transferee district to conduct pretrial proceedings in multidistrict litigation, he or she sits as a judge of the court to which he or she is temporarily assigned.[134] The second grant of authority permits a judge who has been assigned multidistrict litigation to exercise the powers of a district judge in *any* judicial district in order to supervise depositions being conducted in those other districts.[135] The judge to whom the actions are assigned exercises not only the judicial power of a judge of the transferee district but also "the powers of a district judge in any district for purposes of conducting pretrial depositions in such coordinated or consolidated pretrial proceedings."[136] This supervisory power over depositions in other districts may be exercised in person or by telephone.[137]

#### [b] Conduct of Pretrial Proceedings

The transferee judge has complete control of the coordinated or consolidated pretrial proceedings and has all the pretrial powers over the transferred actions that could be exercised by a district court under the Federal Rules of Civil Procedure.[138] Thus, the transferee judge has the power to supervise all pretrial matters and to rule on all pretrial motions.[139]

---

[132] 28 U.S.C. § 1407(b); *see* 28 U.S.C. § 291 *et seq.*; Manual for Complex Litigation (Fourth), § 20.131.

[133] 28 U.S.C. § 1407(b).

[134] *In re* Corrugated Container Antitrust Litig., 662 F.2d 875, 881 (D.C. Cir. 1981).

[135] 28 U.S.C. § 1407(b).

[136] 28 U.S.C. § 1407(b).

[137] *In re* Corrugated Container Antitrust Litig., 662 F.2d 875, 881 (D.C. Cir. 1981) (power of judge handling depositions conducted in another judicial district by telephone to hold witness in contempt and impose jail sentence and monetary fine); *see* 28 U.S.C. § 1407(b).

[138] *In re* Agent Orange Prod. Liab. Litig., 996 F.2d 1425, 1435 (2d Cir. 1993) (transferee judge has all pretrial jurisdiction transferor judge would have had if transfer had not occurred).

[139] *In re* Plumbing Fixture Cases, 298 F. Supp. 484, 493–496 (J.P.M.L. 1968).

The transferee judge may modify, expand, or vacate prior orders issued by the transferor courts.[140] A transferee judge may, for example, exclude issues by pretrial order,[141] set aside pretrial orders issued by the transferor court,[142] and vacate and modify protective orders entered by the transferor courts.[143] In appropriate cases, the transferee judge may sanction the parties for conduct engaged in before the transferor court.[144]

The transferee court's power to expand or vacate prior orders is congruent with that of the transferor court. Accordingly, this power is appropriately limited by the law of the case doctrine: the transferee court should modify or vacate a prior order only in extraordinary circumstances, such as when the initial decision was clearly erroneous or would work a manifest injustice.[145]

The transferee judge has the authority to decide all pretrial motions, including dispositive motions.[146] Although the transferee judge has the power to grant summary judgment motions, it may not compromise the Seventh Amendment rights of the litigants in a multidistrict litigation to a jury trial.[147] For example, it is proper for a transferee court to hold a mini-trial to determine whether 10 test-case plaintiffs' expert evidence was sufficient to raise a triable issue of fact, and to grant summary judgment if the court found that it did not.[148] However, the transferee court may not then extrapolate from a grant of summary judgment in the test cases and dismiss the claims of the remaining 2000 plaintiffs alleging personal injuries.[149]

Clearly, the transferee court has the power to manage discovery. The key purpose of the multidistrict litigation statute is to provide the transferee judge with the discretion to develop an effective and efficient pretrial program. Thus, transferee courts have determined a wide range of discovery issues, including motions to

---

140 *See, e.g., In re* Plumbing Fixture Cases, 298 F. Supp. 484, 489 (J.P.M.L. 1968).

141 *In re* Multi-Piece Rim Prods. Liab. Litig., 464 F. Supp. 969, 975 (J.P.M.L. 1979).

142 Firestone Tire & Rubber Co., 653 F.2d 671, 676–677 (D.C. Cir. 1981).

143 *In re* Upjohn Co. Antibiotic Cleocin Prods. Liab. Litig., 664 F.2d 114, 118 (6th Cir. 1981).

144 *See In re* S.E. Banking Corp., 204 F.3d 1322, 1331–1332 (11th Cir. 2000).

145 *In re* Pharmacy Benefit Managers Antitrust Litig., 582 F.3d 432, 438–443 (3d Cir. 2009) (after transfer, transferee court's discretion to modify or vacate orders of transferor court is limited by law of the case doctrine, so that transferee court erred by vacating order to compel arbitration). *See* Moore's Federal Practice Ch. 134, *Stare Decisis, Law of the Case, and Judicial Estoppel.*

146 Lexecon Inc. v. Milberg Weiss Bershad Hynes & Lerach, 523 U.S. 26, 37 (1998) (Panel is not required to issue "ceremonial" remand orders in cases concluded by summary judgment or dismissal); *In re* African-American Slave Descendants Litig., 471 F.3d 754, 756 (7th Cir. 2006) (transferee court may decide motion to dismiss even if plaintiff has not agreed to let court decide merits); *In re* Korean Air Lines Co., Ltd., 642 F.3d 685, 699–701 (9th Cir. 2011) (transferee court's authority is broad and encompasses power to decide dispositive pretrial motions, although court must articulate and apply traditional legal standards governing such motions); *In re* Temporomandibular Joint (TMJ) Implants Prod. Liab. Litig., 872 F. Supp. 1019, 1024 (D. Minn. 1995); *see also* 28 U.S.C. § 1407(b).

147 *In re* TMI Litig., 193 F.3d 613, 725 (3d Cir. 1999), *amended*, 199 F.3d 158 (3d Cir. 2000).

148 *In re* TMI Litig., 193 F.3d 613, 724–725 (3d Cir. 1999), *amended*, 199 F.3d 158 (3d Cir. 2000).

149 *In re* TMI Litig., 193 F.3d 613, 727 (3d Cir. 1999), *amended*, 199 F.3d 158 (3d Cir. 2000).

compel discovery, attorney-client privilege issues, and the like.[150] Additionally, the transferee court has the power in cases subject to the automatic discovery stay provisions of the Private Securities Litigation Reform Act to stay discovery in any related state court actions.[151] The transferee court may designate a United States Magistrate Judge to resolve nondispositive matters.[152] Transferee courts also have the power to determine class certification issues[153] and other preliminary matters in cases filed as class actions.[154] Indeed, the problems raised by the very existence of class actions have been cited by the Panel as a reason for transfer.[155]

In terms of dispositive motions, the transferee court's authority extends to motions for judgments approving consent decrees[156] or settlements,[157] for dismissal,[158] for judgment on the pleadings,[159] for summary judgment,[160] for involuntary dismissal under Federal Rule of Civil Procedure 41(b),[161] to strike an

---

[150] *In re* Data Gen. Corp. Antitrust Litig., 470 F. Supp. 855, 858–859 (J.P.M.L. 1979); *see In re* Zyprexa Prods. Liab. Litig., 375 F. Supp. 2d 190, 192 (E.D.N.Y. 2005) (court suggested use of special master to act on behalf of all plaintiffs and conduct general discovery).

[151] *See* Newby v. Enron Corp., 338 F.3d 467, 472–473 (5th Cir. 2003) (affirming transferee court order enjoining discovery in related state court action).

[152] *In re* San Juan Dupont Plaza Hotel Fire Litig., 117 F.R.D. 30, 32 (D.P.R. 1987) (as ordinary consequence of transferee judge's additional duties in multidistrict litigation proceedings, judge may designate magistrate to resolve nondispositive motions).

[153] *In re* New England Mut. Life Ins. Co., 183 F.R.D. 33, 44–45 (D. Mass. 1998) (certifying class at this stage had significant advantages in terms of judicial efficiency, without any significant risk of increasing complexity under present circumstances); *In re* Ski Train Fire in Kaprun, Austria on Nov. 11, 220 F.R.D. 195, 200–201 (S.D.N.Y. 2003) (grant of jurisdiction under 28 U.S.C. § 1407 empowers court to rule on wide range of preliminary legal and factual questions, including class certification); *In re* Phar-Mor, Inc. Sec. Litig., 875 F. Supp. 277, 281 (W.D. Pa. 1994) (court certified defendant class); *In re* Copley Pharm., Inc. "Albuterol" Prods. Liab. Litig, 161 F.R.D. 456, 470 (D. Wyo. 1995) (court denied motion to decertify class).

[154] Preliminary matters in class actions. *See, e.g.*, *In re* Hannaford Bros. Co., 252 F.R.D. 66, 67–69 (D. Me. 2008) (court appointed interim counsel to represent putative class pending certification decision, pursuant to Rule 23(g)(3)).

[155] *In re* New York City Mun. Sec. Litig., 439 F. Supp. 267, 270 (J.P.M.L. 1977).

[156] *In re* Temporomandibular Joint (TMJ) Implants Prod. Liab. Litig., 872 F. Supp. 1019, 1024 (D. Minn. 1995); *see also* 28 U.S.C. § 1407(b).

[157] *See In re* Zyprexa Prods. Liab. Litig., 233 F.R.D. 122, 122–123 (E.D.N.Y. 2006) (court approved global settlement and also used its general equitable powers to ensure that attorney's fees were reasonable); Dier v. Merck & Co. (*In re* Vioxx Prods. Liab. Litig.), 2010 U.S. App. LEXIS 16998, at **8–**9 (5th Cir. July 16, 2010) (unpublished) (district court approved master settlement agreement to which plaintiffs could opt in; those plaintiffs who did not choose to opt in did not have standing to challenge master settlement agreement on appeal); *In re* Corrugated Container Antitrust Litig., 659 F.2d 1332, 1335 (5th Cir. 1981).

[158] *See* Pinney v. Nokia, Inc., 402 F.3d 430, 452–453 (4th Cir. 2005) (transferee court properly considered and granted motion to dismiss five consolidated class actions on federal preemption grounds, even though motion to dismiss on same grounds had been denied by one transferor court); *In re* African-American Slave Descendants Litig., 471 F.3d 754, 756–757 (7th Cir. 2006) (district court properly considered and granted motion to dismiss for lack of subject matter jurisdiction); *In re* King Resources Co. Sec. Litig., 385 F. Supp. 588, 590 (J.P.M.L. 1974).

[159] Kaiser Indus. Corp. v. Wheeling-Pittsburgh Steel Corp., 328 F. Supp. 365, 371 (D. Del. 1971).

[160] Humphreys v. Tann, 487 F.2d 666, 668 (6th Cir. 1973).

[161] *See In re* Asbestos Prods. Liab. Litig., 718 F.3d 236, 248 (3d Cir. 2013) (under Fed. R. Civ. P. 41(b),

affirmative defense,[162] for voluntary dismissal under Federal Rule of Civil Procedure 41(a),[163] to quash service of process,[164] and to remand removed cases to state court.[165]

A transferee court also has the power under the All Writs Act and the Anti-Injunction Act[166] to enjoin parties in related state court actions from seeking preliminary relief in the state court without leave of the transferee court.[167] The use of injunctions in this context raises difficult federalism concerns. Accordingly, such power may be invoked only in exceptional circumstances (*see* Ch. 12, *The Anti-Injunction Acts*).

There are a number of matters and issues that the transferee court may not address. For example, the transferee court may not initially consolidate actions for trial purposes under Federal Rule of Civil Procedure 42.[168] Also, a transferee court may not assert jurisdiction over parties who have not yet been served with process. For example, a transferee court lacks the power to order an unserved defendant to

---

court properly dismissed claims of 12 plaintiffs with prejudice for failure to comply with court order requiring medical report showing, inter alia, complete asbestos exposure history; "Rule 41(b) is intended to allow judges to enforce orders pertaining to the progress of their cases. Nowhere is this more important, in terms of the degree of difficulty and the impact, than in multidistrict litigation cases, where the very purpose of the centralization before the transferee judge is the efficient progress of the cases in preparation for trial."); *In re* Four Seasons Sec. Laws Litig., 63 F.R.D. 115, 120 (W.D. Okla. 1974); *see also* Fed. R. of Civ. P. 41(b).

[162] *In re* REA Express, Inc., Private Treble Damage Antitrust Litig., 386 F. Supp. 1406, 1407 (J.P.M.L. 1975).

[163] Humphreys v. Tann, 487 F.2d 666, 668 (6th Cir. 1973); *see also* Fed. R. Civ. P. 41(a).

[164] *In re* King Resources Co. Sec. Litig., 385 F. Supp. 588, 590 (J.P.M.L. 1974); *see* Stanley A. Weigel, *The Judicial Panel on Multidistrict Litigation, Transferor Courts and Transferee Courts*, 78 F.R.D. 575, 582–583 (1978).

[165] *In re* Vioxx Prods. Liab. Litig., 360 F. Supp. 2d 1352, 1354 (J.P.M.L. 2005) (pendency of motion to remand removed action to state court was not sufficient basis to avoid inclusion in consolidated proceedings, since motion could be presented to and decided by transferee court); *In re* New England Mut. Life Ins. Co. Sales Practices Litig., 324 F. Supp. 2d 288, 291–292 (D. Mass. 2004) (while only Judicial Panel on Multidistrict Litigation is empowered to remand cases to transferor courts, this was irrelevant when question was whether court could decide motion to remand removed action to state court).

[166] *See* 28 U.S.C. §§ 1651, 2283.

[167] Newby v. Enron Corp., 338 F.3d 467, 473–476 (5th Cir. 2003) (order enjoining state court actions affirmed when (1) preliminary relief sought in state courts threatened to interfere with transferee court determinations, (2) there was danger of inconsistent and duplicative relief, and (3) state court actions appeared to be deliberate attempt to flaunt federal court's jurisdiction); Newby v. Enron Corp., 302 F.3d 295, 302 (5th Cir. 2002) (district court had power to issue narrowly tailored injunction under All Writs Act to enjoin repeatedly vexatious litigants from filing future state court actions without leave of court); *see also* Newby v. Enron Corp., 542 F.3d 463, 474 (5th Cir. 2008) (when attorneys sought leave of court to file state court actions, court properly denied leave as to actions that were clearly barred by limitations as filing would be futile, but court should have granted leave to file suit in which actions were arguably not barred so that state court could decide question under applicable state law). *See also In re* Checking Account Overdraft Litig., 859 F. Supp. 2d 1313, 1322 (S.D. Fla. 2012) (All Writs Act authorizes district court judges to enjoin proceedings in another federal court; "[T]he All Writs Acts was designed for situations where the proposed settlement and release of claims in another judicial district would interfere with the MDL Court's disposition of those same claims.").

[168] *In re* Penn Central Commercial Paper Litig., 62 F.R.D. 341, 344 (S.D.N.Y. 1974), *aff'd without opinion*, 515 F.2d 505 (2d Cir. 1975); *see* Fed. R. Civ. P. 42.

reimburse the plaintiffs' steering committee for expenses in connection with multidistrict litigation discovery.[169]

## [2] Governing Substantive Law

### [a] Choice of Law Principles

In general, the choice of law rules that must be applied by the transferee court that receive cases under the multidistrict litigation statute[170] are consistent with the rules to be applied by transferee courts that receive cases under the convenience-transfer statute.[171] Thus, in diversity cases, the general rule is that the transferee court must apply the law that the transferor court would have applied (*see* [b], *below*); but in federal-question cases, the transferee court may apply the law of its own circuit (*see* [c], *below*).

### [b] State Law

In diversity jurisdiction based multidistrict litigation that has been transferred to a central forum for coordinated or consolidated pretrial proceedings, the transferee federal district court must apply the substantive state law of the transferor district,[172] including its choice of law rules.[173] This means that the *Van Dusen*[174] and *Ferens*[175] rules applicable when a case is transferred under the convenience transfer statute[176] require the transferee court to apply the same law that the transferor court would have applied. Just as in *Van Dusen* and *Ferens*, when a diversity case is transferred under the multidistrict litigation statute,[177] the state law that would have applied in the transferor court continues to apply in the transferee court, because the transfer accomplished "but a change of court-

---

169 *In re* Showa Denko K.K. L-Tryptophan Prods. Liab. Litig., 953 F.2d 162, 165–166 (4th Cir. 1992).

170 28 U.S.C. § 1407.

171 28 U.S.C. § 1404(a); *see* Ch. 9, *Change of Venue.*

172 *See In re* Norplant Contraceptive Prods. Liab. Litig., 215 F. Supp. 2d 795, 804 (E.D. Tex. 2002) (court looked to state law of transferor courts to determine applicability of "learned intermediary" doctrine in products liability litigation involving prescription device); *In re* Gen. Am. Life Ins. Co. Sales Practices Litig., 391 F.3d 907, 911–912 (8th Cir. 2004) (transferee court was required to apply Pennsylvania statute of limitations, which the transferor court would have applied); *In re* Guidant Corp. Implantable Defibrillators Prods. Liab. Litig., 489 F. Supp. 2d 932, 935–936 (D. Minn. 2007) (choice of law rules of state of transferor court continue to apply even if complaint is amended in transferee court); *In re* Silicone Gel Breast Implants Prod. Liab. Litig., 887 F. Supp. 1463, 1465 (N.D. Ala. 1995); *In re* United States Office Prods. Co. Sec. Litig., 251 F. Supp. 2d 77, 90 (D.D.C. 2003) (in diversity actions, transferee court applies choice-of-law rules of state where transferor court sits); *In re* Lou Levy & Sons Fashions, 988 F.2d 311, 313 (2d Cir. 1993).

173 *In re* Norplant Contraceptive Prods. Liab. Litig., 215 F. Supp. 2d 795, 804 (E.D. Tex. 2002) (court looks to law of transferor district's state to determine which jurisdiction's law governs each case); *In re* Nucorp Energy Sec. Litig., 772 F.2d 1486, 1492 (9th Cir. 1985).

174 Van Dusen v. Barrack, 376 U.S. 612 (1964).

175 Ferens v. John Deere Co., 494 U.S. 516 (1990).

176 28 U.S.C. § 1404(a); *see* Ch. 9, *Change of Venue.*

177 28 U.S.C. § 1407.

rooms."[178]

## [c] Federal Law

When a claim or defense arises under federal law, the transferee court must consider whether to apply the law of its circuit or that of the transferor court. When examining the *Van Dusen*[179] and *Ferens* rules[180] in the context of the multidistrict litigation statute, however, the courts have generally concluded that these rules rest on principles advanced by the *Erie* doctrine,[181] and that those principles do not "figure in the calculus when the law to be applied is federal, not state."[182] Accordingly, most courts have held that a transferee court should be free to decide a federal claim in the manner it views as correct, without deferring to the interpretation of that federal law made by a transferor circuit.[183]

The position of some courts is that an interpretation of federal law made by a transferee court may bind the transferor courts as the "law of the case" if several cases are remanded to transferor courts outside the transferee circuit, even though their interpretation of the applicable federal law might be different from that of the transferee court. The courts properly have reasoned that if this were not the case, transfers under the multidistrict litigation statute would be counterproductive because they would generate, rather than reduce, the duplicated and protracted litigation that Congress sought to check in enacting the Multidistrict Litigation Act.[184]

There is some conflict among the circuits regarding whether the *Van Dusen* and *Ferens* rules apply to statute of limitations issues arising under the courts' federal-question jurisdiction. Some courts have held that although *Van Dusen* arose in a diversity jurisdiction cases, it found it to be equally applicable "whenever

---

[178] *See* Van Dusen v. Barrack, 376 U.S. 612, 639 (1964).

[179] Van Dusen v. Barrack, 376 U.S. 612 (1964).

[180] Ferens v. John Deere Co., 494 U.S. 516 (1990).

[181] Erie Railroad v. Tompkins, 304 U.S. 64 (1938).

[182] *In re* Korean Air Lines Disaster of Sept. 1, 1983, 829 F.2d 1171, 1174 n.5 (D.C. Cir. 1987), *aff'd on other grounds sub nom.* Chan v. Korean Air Lines, 490 U.S. 122 (1989); *but see In re* UMWA Employee Benefit Plans Litig., 854 F. Supp. 914, 919 (D. D.C. 1994) (*Van Dusen* not limited to state law).

[183] *In re* Korean Air Lines Disaster, 829 F.2d 1171, 1176 (D.C. Cir. 1987), *aff'd on other grounds sub nom.* Chan v. Korean Air Lines, Ltd., 490 U.S. 122 (1989); *see generally* Richard L. Marcus, *Conflicts Among Circuits and Transfers Within the Federal Judicial System*, 93 Yale L.J. 677 (1984); *but see* Robert A. Ragazzo, *Transfer and Choice of Law: The Appellate Model*, 93 Mich. L. Rev. 704 (1995) (arguing that when case is transferred for pretrial purposes only, law of transferor court should be applied). *See* Desiano v. Warner-Lambert & Co., 467 F.3d 85, 90–91 (2d Cir. 2006) (while court must defer to other circuit's interpretation of questions of state law from state within that circuit, as to issues of federal law each circuit must reach its own conclusions, and this obligation does not change in context of transferred cases).

[184] *In re* Korean Air Lines Disaster, 829 F.2d 1171, 1176 (D.C. Cir. 1987), *aff'd on other grounds sub nom.* Chan v. Korean Air Lines, Ltd., 490 U.S. 122 (1989) (court of appeals noted that, should cases eventually be returned to transferor courts, transferee court's interpretation of Warsaw Convention, which had been affirmed by court of appeals, would be law of case); *see also* United States ex rel. Staley v. Columbia/HCA Healthcare Corp., 587 F. Supp. 2d 757, 761–763 (W.D. Va. 2008) (reconsideration of transferor court's decision striking two paragraphs of complaint would be contrary to principles of both multidistrict litigation system and law of case doctrine, citing Moore's Federal Practice).

different federal courts . . . use different [federal] rules."[185] Other courts have concluded that the *Van Dusen* rule applies only in diversity actions and that it does not apply in a case transferred under the multidistrict litigation statute to a federal court that construes the relevant federal law differently than the federal court in which the action was filed.[186]

## [3] Power to Remand, Retain, or Transfer Actions

### [a] Authority over Remands

The multidistrict litigation statute permits the transfer of a group or groups of related civil actions to a central forum for the conduct of coordinated or consolidated pretrial proceedings. Once pretrial proceedings have been concluded, any transferred action that has not been terminated is then to be remanded to the district from which it was transferred.[187] The transferee court may suggest to the Panel that it issue a remand order for an action or group of actions, but it may not order a remand itself. A suggestion to remand from the transferee district court provides the indication that the coordinated or consolidated pretrial proceedings assigned to it by the Panel have been successfully completed.[188] The Panel is reluctant to order a remand absent a suggestion to do so from the transferee court,[189] and a party seeking a remand without a suggestion to do so from the transferee judge bears a very heavy burden of persuasion.[190]

### [b] No Power to Retain or Transfer Actions

Statistically, few multidistrict litigation actions transferred to a central forum for the conduct of coordinated or consolidated pretrial proceedings are ever remanded for trial or further proceedings in the district from which they were transferred.[191]

---

185 *See, e.g.*, Eckstein v. Balcor Film Investors, 8 F.3d 1121, 1127 (7th Cir. 1993).

186 *See, e.g.*, Menowitz v. Brown, 991 F.2d 36, 40–41 (2d Cir. 1993); *see* 28 U.S.C. § 1407.

187 28 U.S.C. § 1407(a); Rules of Procedure, Judicial Panel on Multidistrict Litigation, Rule 14(b).

188 Rules of Procedure, Judicial Panel on Multidistrict Litigation, Rule 7.6.

189 Rules of Procedure, Judicial Panel on Multidistrict Litigation, Rule 7.6; *see In re* Richardson-Merrell, Inc. "Bendectin" Prods. Liab. Litig., 606 F. Supp. 715, 716 (J.P.M.L. 1985) (remanding cases with support of transferee judge and notice that Panel is "greatly influenced by the transferee judge's suggestion that remand is appropriate").

190 Rules of Procedure, Judicial Panel on Multidistrict Litigation, Rule 7.6; *see In re* Data Gen. Corp. Antitrust Litig., 510 F. Supp. 1220, 1226 (J.P.M.L. 1979) ("Absent a notice of suggestion of remand from the transferee judge to the Panel, any party advocating remand before the Panel bears a strong burden of persuasion"); *see* Stanley A. Weigel, *The Judicial Panel on Multidistrict Litigation, Transferor Courts and Transferee Courts*, 78 F.R.D. 575, 584 (1978).

191 Margaret S. Williams and Tracey E. George, *Who Will Manage Complex Civil Litigation? The Decision to Transfer and Consolidate Multidistrict Litigation*, 10 J. Empir. Stud. 424, 426 & n.9 (2013), *citing* Emery G. Lee, Margaret S. Williams, Richard A. Nagareda, Joe S. Cecil, Thomas E. Willging & Kevin M. Scott, *The Expanding Role of Multidistrict Consolidation in Federal Civil Litigation: An Empirical Investigation*, working paper (detailing how, when, and where MDL cases are resolved); *see also* Marc Galanter, *The Vanishing Trial: An Examination of Trials and Related Matters in Federal and State Courts*, 1 J. Empirical Legal Stud. 459 (2004) (demonstrating that trial is rare in litigation generally). As Richard Nagareda has explained, "consolidated pretrial proceedings at the behest of the

Most are terminated in the transferee court by some form of pretrial disposition. But if a case is not terminated in the transferee court by pretrial disposition, it must be remanded to the original district from which it was transferred (*see* [a], *above*).[192] The transferee court has no authority to retain a case for trial, *sua sponte*, once it has completed pretrial proceedings.[193]

Prior to the Supreme Court's 1998 decision in *Lexecon, Inc. v. Milberg, Weiss Bershad Hynes & Lerach*, some transferee courts had invoked the convenience transfer statute to transfer cases to themselves for trial purposes.[194] The *Lexecon* decision reversed the practice of self-assignment by transferee courts, as well as a growing body of case law that sought to justify the trend, generally on grounds of efficiency.[195]

The *Lexecon* court did not expressly address the potential power of a transferee court to use the venue statutes to transfer a case to another district (not the transferor district) after pretrial proceedings.[196] Presumably this procedure also would be invalid in light of *Lexecon's* clear mandate to honor the multidistrict litigation statute's language requiring a case to be remanded to the transferor district on completion of pretrial proceedings.[197]

Nor did *Lexecon* consider whether it would be appropriate for the transferee court to retain the case if all parties consented and the transferee court is a court where the action might have been filed in the first place.[198] At the time of the

---

MDL Panel already form a setting ripe for plaintiffs' lawyers and defendants to begin discussions about a comprehensive peace." Richard A. Nagareda, Mass Torts in a World of Settlement 260 (2007). Ninth Circuit Judge Alex Kozinski has taken a different view, concluding that the small numbers of cases returned to the transferor court "tell the story of a remarkable power grab by federal judges who have parlayed a narrow grant of authority to conduct consolidated discovery into a mechanism for systematically denying plaintiffs the right to trial in their forum of choice." *In re* Am. Cont'l Corp./Lincoln Sav. & Loan Sec. Litig., 102 F.3d 1524 (9th Cir. 1996) (Kozinski, J., dissenting), *rev'd sub. nom.*, Lexecon Inc. v. Milberg Weiss Bershad Hynes & Lerach, 523 U.S. 26 (1998).

[192] 28 U.S.C. § 1407(a).

[193] Lexecon, Inc. v. Milberg, Weiss Bershad Hynes & Lerach, 523 U.S. 26, 40–41 (1998) (there is no "self-assignment power in a transferee court"); Armstrong v. LaSalle Bank Nat'l Ass'n, 552 F.3d 613, 615–616 (7th Cir. 2009) (plaintiffs need not assert right to remand; presumption is that case will be remanded at close of pre-trial proceedings); *In re* Cessna 208 Series Aircraft Prods. Liab. Litig., 2009 U.S. Dist. LEXIS 12852, at *12–*14 (D. Kan. Feb. 19, 2009) (*Lexecon* rule meant that court had no authority to grant plaintiff's motion seeking separate trial of airworthiness issue under Fed. R. Civ. P. 42; court indicated it was willing to consider other alternatives to remand consistent with *Lexecon*, such as bellwether trial or intercircuit assignment).

[194] *See* 28 U.S.C. §§ 1404, 1406 (venue statutes); *see also* Administrative Office of the United States, L. Mecham, *Judicial Business of the United States Courts: 1995 Report of the Director*, 32, *cited in* Lexecon, Inc. v. Milberg, Weiss Bershad Hynes & Lerach, 523 U.S. 26, 31–33 (1998) (out of 39,228 cases transferred for consolidated pretrial proceedings and terminated by 9/30/95, 3,787 ultimately required trial, and 279 of those were retained by transferee courts).

[195] *See, e.g.*, *In re* Fine Paper Antitrust Litig., 685 F.2d 810, 820 (3d Cir. 1982) (transferee judge has power to order transfer under venue statutes).

[196] *See* 28 U.S.C. §§ 1404, 1406 (venue statutes).

[197] Lexecon, Inc. v. Milberg, Weiss Bershad Hynes & Lerach, 523 U.S. 26, 40–41 (1998) ("[N]one of the arguments raised can unsettle the straightforward language imposing the Panel's responsibility to remand."); *see* 28 U.S.C. § 1407(a) (multidistrict litigation statute).

[198] *See* 28 U.S.C. § 1404(a); Hoffman v. Blaski, 363 U.S. 335, 343–344 (1960).

*Lexecon* decision, the convenience transfer statute allowed a court to transfer a case to a district where venue would be proper if the case had been filed there in the first place. A 2011 amendment to this statute liberalized transfer possibilities still further; a court may now also transfer a case, with the consent of all parties, to any district whether or not the case might have been brought there originally.[199]

### [c] Power to Retain Actions for Settlement Purposes

Although the *Lexecon* opinion makes clear that the transferee court lacks the power to retain actions for trial purposes without the consent of all parties, it has the power to retain actions while it continues efforts to settle the actions. A case need not be remanded to the original court as long as "coordinated or consolidated pretrial proceedings" are continuing, and this term is interpreted broadly.[200] Even though no further discovery is being conducted in the proceeding, continuing to allow the transferee judge to engage in the centralized management of individual settlement negotiations is consistent with the goals of the MDL statute. The transferee judge's knowledge of the recurring issues in the litigation and the major players facilitates that court's ability to assist in settling cases with particular defendants.

## [4] Appeal of Decisions of Transferee Court

The multidistrict litigation statute sets forth the ground rules for when and how an order of the Judicial Panel on Multidistrict Litigation may be reviewed.[201] There is no mechanism for reviewing an order of the Panel denying transfer. All other orders of the Panel are reviewable only by extraordinary writ issued by a court of appeals.[202] A petition to review an order setting a transfer hearing, or any other order rendered prior to transfer (other than an order denying transfer) must be filed in the court of appeals having jurisdiction over the district in which the hearing is held.

Petitions to review orders of transfer and orders issued following a transfer must be filed in the court of appeals having jurisdiction over the transferee

---

[199] 28 U.S.C. § 1404(a). *See* H.R. Rep. No. 112-10, at 24, 112th Cong. 1st Sess. (2011)) ("Such mutually agreed upon and judicially approved transfers would be proper in any action, including actions that have been centralized for pre-trial proceedings by the Judicial Panel on Multidistrict Litigation under 28 U.S.C. § 1407."); *see generally* Ch. 111, *Change of Venue*.

[200] *See In re* Patenaude, 210 F.3d 135, 145 (3d Cir. 1999) (remand may be refused when "the possibility exists that even individual settlement negotiations will be more efficient if facilitated by a judge who is intimately familiar with the general issues and many of the parties."); *see also In re* Wilson, 451 F.3d 161, 169–172 (3d Cir. 2006) ("[O]ur determination in *Patenaude* that § 1407(a) was satisfied did not hinge on the MDL judge having engaged in centralized management of the negotiations. Rather, we held that the phrase 'coordinated and consolidated' was broad enough to include the conduct of individual, non-global settlement negotiations, which in *Patenaude* happened to be conducted under the close supervision of the MDL judge.").

[201] 28 U.S.C. § 1407(e).

[202] 28 U.S.C. § 1407(e); *see* 28 U.S.C. § 1651. *See, e.g.*, *In re* Patenaude, 210 F.3d 135, 142–146 (3d Cir. 2000) (writ of mandamus was available to review district court order refusing to remand cases, although here court found that writ should be denied).

district.[203] Thus, for example, the court of appeals for the transferee court will have jurisdiction to determine the propriety of the Panel's order of transfer, as well as the underlying questions of lack of subject-matter jurisdiction, if a litigant seeks review of transfer orders, even if there is a question whether an action was properly removed that was pending at the time the Panel transferred the action.[204]

Although the multidistrict litigation statute does not explicitly say which court of appeals has jurisdiction over appeals from orders issued by the district court to which a case is transferred, most cases hold that it is the court of appeals covering the transferee court rather than the one covering the transferor court.[205] Such a rule makes more sense than permitting review by the court of appeals for the transferor court. If there are to be any efficiency gains by ordering the transfer, it hardly makes sense to permit multiple appeals to different courts of appeals, which may not rule consistently. The one exception to this general rule applies to cases in which Congress has allocated appellate jurisdiction to a court of appeals for a circuit other than the one in which the transferee court is located. For example, the Federal Circuit has exclusive appellate jurisdiction in patent cases.[206]

Aside from the judicial authority a transferee judge holds in his or her own district, a judge who has been assigned multidistrict litigation also has the powers of a district judge in *any* district in order to supervise depositions being conducted in those other districts (*see* [1][a], *above*).[207] Any appeal from a judge's orders issued in this capacity must be filed in the court of appeals having jurisdiction over the deposition district. For example, a transferee judge might issue an order of contempt over the telephone from his or her home district to a witness being deposed in another judicial district. Any appeal of that contempt order must be taken to the court of appeals having jurisdiction over the deposition district, because the contempt order was issued pursuant to the transferee judge's exercise of powers as a district judge in the deposition district rather than as a sitting judge in the district court to which the multidistrict litigation has been assigned.[208] The Sixth Circuit has applied this same principle not only to deposition-related orders but to other types of discovery orders against non-parties.[209]

Once an action is remanded to the transferor district, it will be the court of appeals for the transferor district that will have appellate jurisdiction over any unreviewed matters.[210] That court of appeals will have appellate jurisdiction over any unreviewed rulings made by the transferee court prior to transfer as well as

---

203 28 U.S.C. § 1407(e); *see* 28 U.S.C. § 1651.

204 *In re* Ivy, 901 F.2d 7, 9 (2d Cir. 1990).

205 *In re* Plumbing Fixture Cases, 298 F. Supp. 484, 496 (J.P.M.L. 1968).

206 *See* 28 U.S.C. § 1295.

207 28 U.S.C. § 1407(b).

208 *In re* Corrugated Container Antitrust Litig., 662 F.2d 875, 876 (D.C. Cir. 1981).

209 Appeal of discovery orders against non-parties located in another district must be taken to court of appeals for that district. United States ex rel. Pogue v. Diabetes Treatment Ctrs. of Am., Inc., 444 F.3d 462, 467–469 (6th Cir. 2006) (order compelling non-party to turn over certain documents and finding that non-party had waived any privilege was properly appealed to court of appeals for circuit where non-party was located).

210 Allegheny Airlines, Inc. v. LeMay, 448 F.2d 1341, 1344–1345 (7th Cir. 1971).

rulings[211] made by the transferor court subsequent to remand.

[211] 448 F.2d at 1344–1345 (dismissal of third-party complaints by transferee court would be reviewed by court of appeals for transferor court after final judgment is entered in remanded case).

# DIVISION III

# INTERRELATIONSHIP OF STATE AND FEDERAL COURTS

# Chapter 11

# DUAL FEDERAL-STATE JUDICIAL SYSTEMS

## § 11.01 HISTORICAL BASIS FOR THE ESTABLISHMENT OF STATE AND FEDERAL SYSTEMS

### [1] Colonial Courts

In the American judicial experience, colonial courts were the predecessors of state courts, which existed before the establishment of federal courts. Colonial courts antedated the Constitution by many years.[1] Initially, in some colonies, the judicial function was merged with the legislative function.[2] However, after the English Revolution in 1688, the American colonies moved to create independent judicial bodies similar to the independent judiciary being developed in England.[3] Until the American Revolution, the English Privy Council had the authority to review and invalidate decisions of the highest colonial tribunal and to veto colonial legislation. Thus, even before the Constitution established a Supreme Court, there existed an American tradition of judicial review of colonial court decisions.

### [2] Admiralty Courts

The origins of the federal court system emerged from the development of American admiralty courts. Prior to the Revolution, colonial governors were usually commissioned vice-admirals and they or a specially appointed judge held vice-admiralty courts, with jurisdiction over cases of prize and capture.[4] When the American Revolution began, the vice-admiralty courts ceased, and Congress filled the void by asking the states to set up admiralty courts for the trial of rights of capture, with final appeal to Congress.[5] Appeals were heard in Congress at first by ad hoc committees and later by a standing committee.[6] While originally the states readily allowed appeals to Congress, the states subsequently attempted to restrict this right.[7] Finally, the system proved unworkable when one state refused to follow

---

1 *See* Pound, Organization of Courts (1940) 26–90.

2 Pound, Organization of Courts (1940) 26–57.

3 Pound, Organization of Courts (1940) 58.

4 Jameson, The Predecessor of the Supreme Court, in Essays in the Constitutional History of the United States (1889) 5.

5 1 Carson, The Supreme Court of the United States (1902) 44.

6 1 Carson, The Supreme Court of the United States (1902) 50, 51.

7 Jameson, The Predecessor of the Supreme Court, in Essays in the Constitutional History of the United States (1889) 11; 1 Carson, The Supreme Court of the United States (1902) 46.

the mandate of the committee, and the committee stopped hearing appeals, pending clarification of its powers. The reason for this failure was that the congressional committee could not compel a state court to follow its mandate. Thus, in 1780 Congress established a "Court of Appeals in Prize Cases."[8] This Court was set up as an independent judicial body, but after debate Congress again denied it necessary enforcement powers and the Court had to look to state courts for enforcement of its decrees.[9]

## [3] Federal Courts Under the Articles of Confederation

The Articles of Confederation created the first independent federal courts of limited jurisdiction.[10] Article IX provided Congress with the power of "appointing courts for the trial of piracies and felonies committed on the high seas and establishing courts for receiving and determining finally appeals in all cases of captures." Under this Article, Congress was the last resort on appeal in boundary disputes between states. The federal Court of Appeals in Prize Cases continued after the ratification of the Articles of Confederation.[11] But jurisdiction that had been granted under Article IX in cases of piracies and felonies on the high seas was delegated to special courts composed of state admiralty or superior court judges.[12] Congress rarely exercised its appellate powers in cases affecting the boundaries between states.

Under the Articles of Confederation Congress lacked, or refused to assert, many powers necessary to the operation of a sovereign nation, even asking the states for tribunals or statutes to punish offenses against the law of nations. While the states apparently did not respond, Pennsylvania held, in one case, that the law of nations was part of its internal law.[13] Moreover, Congress asked the states to provide laws and a forum to punish treason, and turned to state courts for the enforcement of penalties for official misdemeanors under the postal laws.[14] Finally, Congress requested that the states provide laws for settling military accounts and to provide for the recovery of debts due the United States.[15]

The central failure of the appellate system under the Articles of Confederation was that the system depended for its enforcement on the very courts and officers whose judgments were reversed. And, in areas where there was no federal

---

8 Jameson, The Predecessor of the Supreme Court, in Essays in the Constitutional History of the United States (1889) 29, 32.

9 Jameson, The Predecessor of the Supreme Court, in Essays in the Constitutional History of the United States (1889) 28; 1 Carson, The Supreme Court of the United States (1902) 56.

10 Jameson, The Predecessor of the Supreme Court, in Essays in the Constitutional History of the United States (1889) (dealing solely with the history of the Court of Appeals in Case of Capture); 1 Carson, The Supreme Court of the United States (1902) 31–86.

11 Jameson, The Predecessor of the Supreme Court, in Essays in the Constitutional History of the United States (1889) 32.

12 1 Carson, The Supreme Court of the United States (1902) 65.

13 Respublica v. DeLongchamp, 1 U.S. (Dall.) 111 (1784) (conviction for violating the law of nations by insulting and assaulting the Secretary of the French legation).

14 1 Carson, The Supreme Court of the United States (1902) 84.

15 1 Carson, The Supreme Court of the United States (1902) 85.

appellate jurisdiction, Congress looked futilely to state courts for enforcement of what essentially were national interests, and which often were antagonistic to the interests of the states.

### [4] Constitutional Creation of a Federal Judiciary

Article III of the United States Constitution, establishing federal judicial power, reflects the lessons and failures under the Articles of Confederation. The drafters agreed that there should be a Supreme Court of the United States and plans submitted to the Constitutional Convention included a Supreme Court.[16] Further, the drafters envisioned Supreme Court judicial review of state laws claimed to violate the federal Constitution.[17] Also, the drafters concurred that if the Nation were to survive, certain matters could not be left solely to state courts. Thus, to protect the country from adverse foreign reactions to state decisions in regard to foreign representatives, Article III vested original jurisdiction in the Supreme Court of "cases affecting Ambassadors, other public ministers and consuls." And the further grant of original jurisdiction, to the Supreme Court, of controversies between two or more states may be traced to the recognition under the Articles that if civil war was to be avoided, the federal government must arbitrate conflicts between states, especially as to territorial claims.[18]

Although the drafters agreed that the federal system should include one Supreme Court, opinion was divided concerning the necessity for lower federal courts. Some felt that they would be too expensive, and duplicative of existing state facilities, and that there should be none. But Madison and others stated that the weight of appeals to the Supreme Court would be too great without lower federal courts, and that it would be impossible to correct a biased state court's findings of facts on appeal.[19] The compromise was that the Constitution did not itself create any inferior federal courts but gave Congress the power to do so, and to vest those courts with such jurisdiction as it saw fit to confer.[20]

Article III gave Congress the power to create inferior federal courts and to vest them with jurisdiction over cases arising under the Constitution, laws and treaties; cases of admiralty and maritime jurisdiction; controversies to which the United States shall be a party; and controversies between citizens of the same state claiming lands under grants of different states, a sensitive matter of considerable importance at that time. Also Congress was given power to vest federal courts with jurisdiction over suits between citizens of different states or between citizens of a state and foreign states, citizens or subjects.[21] Thus, the Constitution laid a basis

---

[16] 1 Carson, The Supreme Court of the United (1902) 90 *et seq.*

[17] Warren, The Making of the Constitution (1928) 320, 323.

[18] Warren, The Making of the Constitution (1928) 544; *see also* 17 Moore's Federal Practice Ch. 120, *Dual State and Federal Judicial Structure* (Matthew Bender 3d ed.).

[19] 1 Carson, The Supreme Court of the United States (1902) 89–93; Warren, The Making of the Constitution (1928) 326.

[20] *See* Ch. 1, *The Structure of the Federal Judicial System.*

[21] *See* Ch. 1, *The Structure of the Federal Judicial System*; Ch. 3, *Diversity Jurisdiction*; Ch. 4, *Federal Question Jurisdiction.*

for federal jurisdiction paralleling that of state courts over private law suits.

### [5] State Courts at the Ratification of the Constitution

At the time of the Constitutional convention, a well-developed system of state courts existed, which were modeled after the English system. State court jurisdiction was not disturbed by the adoption of the Constitution, and state courts were to continue to protect federally-created as well as state-created rights. State courts would also have jurisdiction over matters within federal judicial power, unless Congress exclusively committed a particular matter to the federal courts.

Thus a dual system of courts antedated both the American Revolution and the Constitution. The colonial experience laid the groundwork for the dual federal-state judicial system that evolved after the ratification of the Constitution. This experience demonstrated the need for a strong, independent, central court system with certain matters assigned exclusively to federal jurisdiction, concurrent with a state court system with independent jurisdiction.

At the time of ratification, most state court institutions and jurisprudence were chiefly derived from the English legal system. Those few states with French and Spanish colonial heritage retained legal institutions and jurisprudence derived from those countries. The English development of separate law and equity courts was replicated, to varying degrees, among state court systems. However, because there was hostility toward equity among many colonists, when the colonies became states there was great variance in maintaining this separation of law and equity courts. Today a few states still have separate law and equity courts; others have a unified court system with divergent law and equity procedures; while most states have merged law and equity in a unified legal system.

## § 11.02 THE DUAL COURT SYSTEM AND THE JUDICIARY ACTS OF 1789 AND 1875

Following the adoption of the Constitution, Congress enacted the legislation creating the federal judiciary and prescribing its jurisdiction under the power granted by Article III.[22] The first Judiciary Act of 1789 provided for the Court's organization and dealt with both the Court's original jurisdiction and its appellate jurisdiction over federal and state courts.[23] The Act created inferior federal courts and prescribed their respective jurisdiction. The Judiciary Act of 1789 thus created the dual court system that has continued to the present. Although Congress has created and abolished federal courts, and has expanded or modified federal jurisdiction, the essence of the dual judicial system has changed little.

The first Judiciary Act contemplated concurrent jurisdiction between state and federal courts over several types of cases; and, since it did not vest either the district or circuit courts with jurisdiction of suits arising under the Constitution,

---

[22] Warren, *New Light on the History of the Federal Judiciary Act of 1789*, 37 HARV. L. REV. 49 (1923).

[23] Act of Sept. 24, 1789, ch. 20, 1 Stat. 73; *see also* 17 MOORE'S FEDERAL PRACTICE Ch. 120, *Dual State and Federal Judicial Structure* (Matthew Bender 3d ed.).

laws or treaties of the United States,[24] jurisdiction over these matters was impliedly committed to the state courts. The dual system was capped by § 25 of the Act, which conferred appellate jurisdiction on the Supreme Court to review a final judgment of the highest court of a state that invalidated a treaty or federal statute, sustained the validity of a state statute against a federal claim of invalidity, or construed the Constitution, a treaty, or a statute against the claim.

There was no doubt in the minds of a majority of members of the first Congress that power existed in Congress to vest exclusive jurisdiction over certain matters in the federal courts, and to leave certain matters (as general federal question jurisdiction) to the state courts for initial resolution. The Congress also endorsed this scheme by providing concurrent jurisdiction over certain matters in both federal and state courts. The pattern envisioned by Hamilton[25] was accepted by Congress. Yet it was not without much controversy that this scheme was finally established. Even though the concept of federal review of state court decisions had been partially accepted prior to the Constitution, the right of the Supreme Court to review a state court decision was not easily admitted by the states. However, this power was the keystone of the whole structure of concurrent jurisdiction. Aside from the abortive "Midnight Judges" Act of 1801 (repealed the following year), it was not until 1875 that the lower federal courts were given general original or removal jurisdiction over federal question cases.[26] Under the first Judiciary Act, federal judicial power over such matters was confined to the Supreme Court's appellate power to review state court judgments turning on federal issues. And even after the federal courts had been given federal question jurisdiction in 1875, because the federal issue had to appear in plaintiff's well-pleaded complaint,[27] many cases that involved federal issues still had to be litigated in the state courts, with final appellate review by the Supreme Court.

## § 11.03 VARIATIONS AMONG CONTEMPORARY STATE COURT SYSTEMS

A typical state judicial system has courts of general original jurisdiction (that is, trial courts) and courts of appellate review, including a state high court of final appeal. Arizona, for example, has a general jurisdiction trial court system that handles all cases at law and in equity when the amount in controversy is $1,000 or more.[28] Arizona has intermediate courts of appeals[29] and a state Supreme Court.[30]

---

[24] *See* 15 Moore's Federal Practice Ch. 100, *The Structure of the Federal Judicial System* (Matthew Bender 3d ed.).

[25] Federalist No. 82.

[26] *See* 15 Moore's Federal Practice Ch. 100, *The Structure of the Federal Judicial System*, Ch. 103, *Federal Question Jurisdiction* (Matthew Bender 3d ed.).

[27] *See* Ch. 4, *Federal Question Jurisdiction*.

[28] *See* Ariz. Const., Art. VI, §§ 14–18 (inferior trial courts of more limited jurisdiction include justice courts, small claims courts, and municipal courts); *see also* Ariz. Rev. Stat. §§ 22-201, 22-402, 22-503.

[29] *See* Ariz. Rev. Stat. §§ 12-120, 12-120.04, 12-120.21.

[30] *See* Ariz. Const., Art. VI.

Not all states have a three-tier judicial system. Some states with small populations, such as North Dakota, have general jurisdiction trial courts,[31] but a single state Supreme Court[32] to handle appeals directly from trial courts. There are no intermediate appellate courts. Texas has intermediate appellate courts that handle both civil and criminal appeals from the trial courts,[33] but a separate Supreme Court to handle final civil appeals and a separate Court of Criminal Appeals to handle final criminal appeals and death-penalty appeals.[34] Delaware still has separate trial courts for matters at law[35] and for matters in equity.[36]

The sole federal constitutional limit on state court systems is that a state may provide for courts of limited jurisdiction, but only so long as the limitation on jurisdiction does not discriminate against out-of-state litigants or against the enforcement of federal rights.[37]

## § 11.04 THE CONTEMPORARY FEDERAL COURT SYSTEM

### [1] Courts of Limited Jurisdiction

By and large, federal courts, in contrast to state courts, are *not* courts of general jurisdiction. Article III of the Constitution as well as federal statutes limit the jurisdiction of each federal court.[38] For example, a federal court may not adjudicate a matter that does not qualify as a "case or controversy" under Article III of the Constitution.[39]

### [2] Article III Courts

Article III of the Constitution provides for a single Supreme Court and authorizes, but does not require, Congress to create inferior federal courts. Congress has exercised the constitutional authority given under Article III by creating a structure of trial courts known as federal district courts, and intermediate courts of appeals known as United States Courts of Appeals. These courts are called Article III courts.[40]

---

31 *See* N.D. Cent. Code §§ 27-05-06, 27-07.1-17 (called District and County Courts).

32 *See* N.D. Cent. Code § 27-02-04.

33 *See* Tex. Code Crim. P. Art. 4.03; Tex. Gov. C. § 22.201 *et seq.*

34 *See* Tex. Const. Art. 5 §§ 1, 3, 5.

35 *See* Delaware Const. Art. IV § 7.

36 *See* Del. Code tit. 10, §§ 341, 342.

37 *See* McKnett v. St. Louis & San Francisco Ry. Co., 292 U.S. 230, 233–234 (1934) (action under Federal Employers' Liability Act); Chambers v. Baltimore & Ohio R.R. Co., 207 U.S. 142, 148–149 (1907); *see also* U.S. Const., Art. IV § 2, cl. 1 (citizens of each state entitled to privileges and immunities of citizens in other states).

38 Aldinger v. Howard, 427 U.S. 1, 14–15 (1976) (federal courts' jurisdiction marked out by Congress).

39 *See* Flast v. Cohen, 392 U.S. 83, 94–95 (1968); *see generally* Ch. 2, *Issues of Justiciability.*

40 *See* Ch. 1, *The Structure of the Federal Judicial System.*

The primary Article III trial courts are the federal district courts. Periodically, Congress determines whether to create new federal district courts, and at the end of the twentieth century, the United States is divided into more than ninety federal districts.[41] Some more populous states have more than one federal district court,[42] while other states may have only one federal judicial district.[43] Federal district courts typically are denominated by geographical location, such as the Southern, Eastern, Western, and Northern Districts of New York.[44] In addition, some federal courts may have divisions within the district.[45]

At the intermediate appellate level, the United States is divided into thirteen judicial circuits.[46] The United States Supreme Court is the highest court of appeal for the entire federal judicial system, and the only constitutionally mandated federal court.[47] The Supreme Court entertains appeals from both the lower federal courts as well as the highest available state courts. It is a court of limited jurisdiction.

### [3] Article I Courts

Congress, in carrying out its powers under Article I of the Constitution,[48] has "wide discretion to assign the task of adjudication in cases arising under federal law to [special] legislative tribunals."[49] These special, legislative tribunals are often referred to as Article I courts. The Tax Court is an example of such a legislative or Article I tribunal.[50]

Although Congress has the power to create tribunals for the limited purpose of enforcing the laws it creates, it may not use these tribunals to undermine the separation of powers built into the Constitution. The full range of ordinary court cases may not be shunted off from Article III courts to these special tribunals in which the judges may serve at the pleasure of the Congress or the President instead of for "good behavior" as in Article III courts.[51] The Supreme Court has consistently ruled that the Constitution restricts the jurisdiction of legislative

---

41 *See generally* 28 U.S.C. § 81 *et seq.*

42 *See, e.g.*, 28 U.S.C. §§ 84, 89, 90, 124 (California and Texas each have four districts, while Florida and Georgia have three districts each).

43 *See, e.g.*, 28 U.S.C. §§ 86–88 (Connecticut, Delaware, and District of Columbia each have single federal judicial district).

44 *See, e.g.*, 28 U.S.C. § 112.

45 *See, e.g.*, 28 U.S.C. § 84(c) (Central District of California has three divisions).

46 28 U.S.C. § 41.

47 *See* U.S. Const., Art. III § 1.

48 *See* U.S. Const., Art. I § 8, cl. 18 (Congress has power to create laws that are necessary and proper to carry out powers Constitution vests in legislative branch of government).

49 *See* Freytag v. Commissioner, 501 U.S. 868, 889 (1991) (legislative tribunals, such as Tax Court, could appoint "special trial judge" under statutory authority without violating "appointments clause" of constitution).

50 *See* Ch. 1, *The Structure of the Federal Judicial System* (discussion of Article 1 courts).

51 *See* Ch. 1, *The Structure of the Federal Judicial System.*

courts. In general, legislative or Article I courts may not adjudicate matters that are "inherently judicial."[52]

## § 11.05 CONSEQUENCES OF A DUAL COURT SYSTEM

### [1] Parallel State and Federal Proceedings: Repetitive Lawsuits

The existence of a dual court system with concurrent jurisdiction gives rise to the possibility of repetitive suits in federal and state courts. Repetitive suits occur when a plaintiff files multiple actions based on similar or identical causes of action against the same defendant in different forums.[53] Multiple class actions brought against the same defendant on the same claim by different lead plaintiffs in different forums also are an example of repetitive lawsuits.[54]

A plaintiff may file repetitive actions for a variety of reasons, and such multiple filings are not prohibited by law. Thus, a plaintiff might file repetitive actions in order to obtain a speedier adjudication of the plaintiff's claim, if there is docket congestion and a backlog of cases in a particular forum. Second, a plaintiff might file repetitive actions to avoid an anticipated adverse judgment after one court issues an adverse interlocutory ruling on a preliminary matter.[55]

Third, a plaintiff might file repetitive actions in order to ensure that the plaintiff will obtain personal jurisdiction over the defendant, somewhere.[56] Fourth, a plaintiff might file repetitive actions to gain a tactical advantage based on different procedural rules in the two courts. For example, a plaintiff might file in both state court and federal court in order to use more liberal federal discovery procedures to prepare for trial in the state court.[57]

---

[52] *See, e.g.*, Northern Pipeline Constr. Co. v. Marathon Pipe Line Co., 458 U.S. 50, 76–87 (1982) (Article I bankruptcy courts created under Bankruptcy Act of 1978 were given jurisdiction that was unconstitutionally broad); *see also* Commodity Futures Trading Comm'n v. Schor, 478 U.S. 833, 856 (1986) (Commission could decide inherently judicial matters as adjunct to Article III court, since its orders could be enforced only by action of Article III court).

[53] *See* Allan D. Vestal, *Repetitive Litigation*, 45 Iowa L. Rev. 525 (1960); *see, e.g.*, Tovar v. Billmeyer, 609 F.2d 1291, 1292–1293 (9th Cir. 1980) (plaintiff sued in state court to compel city to issue permit for adult bookstore and while state court action was pending, plaintiff filed action in federal court for declaratory and injunctive relief).

[54] *See, e.g.*, Smith v. Bayer Corp., 131 S. Ct. 2368, 180 L. Ed. 2d 341, 346 (2011) (similar class actions in state and federal court).

[55] *See, e.g.*, Graziano v. Pennell, 371 F.2d 761, 764 (2d Cir. 1967) (preclusion order); Beaver v. Borough of Johnsonburg, 375 F. Supp. 326, 328 (W.D. Pa. 1974) (dismissal based on laches).

[56] *See, e.g.*, O'Hare Int'l Bank v. Lambert, 459 F.2d 328, 330 (10th Cir. 1972) (during pendency of its appeal from dismissal entered by federal court in Illinois based on lack of personal jurisdiction over defendants, plaintiff commenced identical actions in federal district courts in Illinois, Oklahoma, Arkansas, and Texas).

[57] *See, e.g.*, Mottolese v. Kaufman, 176 F.2d 301, 303–304 (2d Cir. 1949).

Fifth, a classic reason for filing repetitive law suits is simple forum-shopping.[58] Forum-shopping may include considerations of possible applicable law, jury pools and jury selection methods, prior disposition of similar litigation (including remedies and damage awards), and knowledge about the presiding judicial officers. Sixth, a plaintiff might file multiple class complaints in order to become the lead plaintiff, or to control the proceedings, or to become eligible to collect attorney fees for representing the class. Finally, a plaintiff might file repetitive actions simply to harass the defendant.[59]

## [2] Parallel State and Federal Proceedings: Reactive Lawsuits

The existence of a dual court system with concurrent jurisdiction also gives rise to the possibility of a defendant's attempting to respond to one lawsuit by filing a separate reactive lawsuit against the plaintiff. A reactive suit occurs when the defendant in one suit responds by filing a second lawsuit in another court system, seeking relief against the plaintiff based on the same transaction or occurrence that is the subject matter of the first suit.[60]

The most common form of reactive lawsuit is the federal declaratory judgment action, which state court defendants typically institute in federal court. After being sued in state court a defendant may file a federal declaratory judgment action for a declaration of rights and duties under applicable law. If the federal court issues a favorable declaratory judgment prior to the state court's resolution of the issue, the federal declaratory judgment may preclude relitigation of the issue in state court. A reactive suit might also seek affirmative relief that a defendant might otherwise have to assert in an answer and counterclaim in the first suit.[61]

Similar to the plaintiff's reasons for filing repetitive lawsuits, defendants have many reasons for filing reactive lawsuits. A defendant might file a reactive suit in order to gain a tactical advantage by becoming the plaintiff in the second action. Second, a defendant might file a reactive lawsuit to harass the plaintiff in the original action, by burdening the plaintiff with the expense and inconvenience of litigating in two forums. Third, a defendant might file a reactive action to take advantage of the second court's familiarity with the applicable law, or to obtain the application of favorable substantive law by taking advantage of the second forum's choice-of-law rules.[62] Similarly a defendant might file a reactive lawsuit to gain a tactical advantage based on different procedural rules in the two courts. For example, a party sued in state court might file reactive suit in federal court to take

---

[58] *See, e.g.*, Mars, Inc., v. Standard Brands, Inc., 386 F. Supp. 1201, 1204–1205 (S.D.N.Y. 1974).

[59] For discussion of sanctions for filing frivolous pleadings and pursuing vexatious litigation, *see* 2 Moore's Federal Practice Ch. 11, *Sanctions: Signing Pleadings, Motions, and Other Papers: Representations to the Court* (Matthew Bender 3d ed.).

[60] *See* Allan D. Vestal, *Reactive Litigation*, 47 Iowa L. Rev. 11 (1961).

[61] *See, e.g.*, Microsoftware Computer Sys., Inc. v. Ontel Corp., 686 F.2d 531, 533 (7th Cir. 1982).

[62] *See, e.g.*, PPG Industries, Inc. v. Continental Oil Co., 478 F.2d 674, 676 (5th Cir. 1973) (Louisiana corporation, sued in Texas state court for declaration of rights under contract, brought action based on same issues in Louisiana federal court, based on belief that Louisiana choice-of-law rules and substantive contract law were more favorable than Texas law).

advantage of more liberal federal discovery procedures.[63]

Fourth, a defendant might file a reactive lawsuit in order to obtain a speedier adjudication of the dispute,[64] or to gain preclusive effect of another court's favorable judgment (*see* [3], *below*). Fifth, a defendant might file a reactive lawsuit in order to have a federal court adjudicate a defense or counterclaim based on federal law. This is particularly important when the case does not involve diversity of citizenship. If a federal question is raised only in a defense or counterclaim, the defendant usually is unable to secure a hearing on that federal question in a federal forum by way of removal.[65] Therefore, if the defendant wishes to have the federal question adjudicated by a federal court, he or she must file a reactive suit.[66]

Sixth, a defendant might file a reactive lawsuit in order to have a federal court adjudicate a case that involves diversity of citizenship and that has been filed in a state court in the defendant's home state. Because the case was filed in the defendant's home state, the defendant is not entitled to remove the case to federal court, despite diversity of citizenship.[67] If the defendant wishes to have the case adjudicated by a federal court, he or she must file a reactive suit.

## [3] Duplicative Litigation and Preclusion Doctrine

A final judgment in one suit generally has the effect of precluding relitigation of the identical claim in a duplicative suit.[68] More complex questions of preclusion arise when, for example, a plaintiff litigates to judgment a state-law claim in state court and then seeks to litigate a federal claim in federal court, based on the same facts as the state-law claim.[69]

In this context, preclusive effects include both claim preclusion and issue preclusion. Claim preclusion refers to res judicata in a narrow sense, that is, the effect of a judgment in foreclosing litigation of matters that could have and should have been raised in an earlier suit. Issue preclusion refers to collateral estoppel, that is, the effect of a judgment in foreclosing relitigation of an issue that has been actually litigated and decided.[70]

Neither federal nor state courts have the power to simply ignore the preclusive effects of judgments that have been rendered. In federal court, the Full Faith and

---

[63] *See, e.g.*, Aetna State Bank v. Altheimer, 430 F.2d 750, 758 (7th Cir. 1970) (federal rules permitted more liberal discovery than state rules, so plaintiff filed repetitive suits).

[64] *See, e.g.*, Applegate v. Devitt, 509 F.2d 106, 107–109 (8th Cir. 1975) (actions in state court normally delayed three years in coming to trial).

[65] *See* Ch. 4, *Federal Question Jurisdiction.*

[66] *See, e.g.*, Oliver v. Fort Wayne Educ. Ass'n, Inc., 820 F.2d 913, 914–915 (7th Cir. 1987) (defense based on First and Fourteenth Amendments could not be removed to federal court because plaintiff's complaint did not raise federal question).

[67] *See* Ch. 3, *Diversity Jurisdiction.*

[68] Angel v. Bullington, 330 U.S. 183, 186–187 (1947).

[69] *See, e.g.*, Migra v. Warren City Sch. Dist. Bd. of Educ., 465 U.S. 75, 79–80 (1984) (tort claim in state court followed by civil rights claim in federal court).

[70] *See* Marrese v. American Academy of Orthopaedic Surgeons, 470 U.S. 373, 376 n.1 (1985).

Credit Act[71] requires federal courts to give state court judgments the same force and effect that the state courts would give.[72] The preclusion law of the state in which a state court judgment is rendered determines whether the state judgment precludes subsequent litigation of a claim or issue in federal court, unless Congress has enacted an express exception to the Full Faith and Credit Act.[73] Congress may enact exceptions to the Full Faith and Credit Act's requirement that state court judgments be given preclusive effect. However, federal courts may not imply such an exception; it must be explicit, or the intent to create an exception must be clear and manifest from a statute or its legislative history or operation.[74]

A state court judgment must also be given full faith and credit by the courts of other states.[75] Litigants thus may initiate a race to judgment in filing repetitive and reactive lawsuits in state and federal court, because of the preclusive effect of the first judgment rendered. A final judgment of one court in an in personam case ordinarily will preclude further duplicative proceedings in the other court.[76]

## [4] Mechanisms for Coping with Duplicative Litigation

If duplicative lawsuits are filed solely within the federal court system, various statutes and procedural rules are available to coordinate the efficient resolution of such duplicative litigation. Thus, if repetitive or reactive suits are pending in different federal district courts, the suits may be transferred to one particular federal district court and consolidated for pre-trial proceedings, or for a consolidated trial.[77]

There are no similar provisions for dealing with simultaneous duplicative state court and federal court litigation. Thus, if federal and state courts have concurrent jurisdiction, both courts ordinarily may go forward with their proceedings until one court renders a final judgment. The pendency of a suit in the federal or state court does not bar the other court's jurisdiction of the same cause of action.[78] In all *in*

---

[71] *See* 28 U.S.C. § 1738.

[72] Matsushita Elec. Indus. Co. v. Epstein, 516 U.S. 367 (1996) (federal courts must give Delaware settlement judgment full faith and credit, even though it purports to dispose of securities claims within exclusive federal court jurisdiction); Migra v. Warren City Sch. Dist. Bd. of Educ., 465 U.S. 75, 79–80 (1984).

[73] Matsushita Elec. Indus. Co. v. Epstein, 516 U.S.367, 369 (1996); Marrese v. American Academy of Orthopaedic Surgeons, 470 U.S. 373, 380 (1985).

[74] *See* Migra v. Warren City Sch. Dist. Bd. of Educ., 465 U.S. 75, 81–83 (1984) (no exception created by civil rights statute, 42 U.S.C. § 1983); Kremer v. Chemical Constr. Corp., 456 U.S. 461, 468 (1982) (no exception created by employment discrimination provisions of Title VII of 1964 Civil Rights Act).

[75] U.S. Const., Art. IV § 1; 28 U.S.C. § 1738; *see* Riley v. New York Trust Co., 315 U.S. 343, 348–349 (1942) (preclusive effect of state judgment on proceedings in another state).

[76] *See* Donovan v. City of Dallas, 377 U.S. 408, 412 (1964) (state court and federal court, having concurrent jurisdiction of in personam suits, may proceed at least until one court renders judgment, which will then be res judicata).

[77] *See* 28 U.S.C. §§ 1404, 1406, 1407; *see also* Fed. R. Civ. P. 42 (consolidation of different actions in single district that involve common questions of fact); *see generally* 8 Moore's Federal Practice Ch. 42, *Consolidation; Separate Trials* (Matthew Bender 3d ed.).

[78] Stanton v. Embrey, 93 U.S. 548, 554 (1876).

*personam* cases, the two courts simply proceed to judgment. When the first court renders a judgment, the successful party may attempt to assert its favorable judgment as preclusive of further proceedings in the other forum. The only real exception to this rule is if the case is based on *in rem* jurisdiction. In cases based on *in rem* jurisdiction, the court that first acquires jurisdiction over the res generally has exclusive jurisdiction to proceed.[79]

In the interest of federal-state comity and the conservation of judicial resources, Congress and the Supreme Court have developed statutory and doctrinal means to allow federal courts to minimize duplicative litigation without abdicating their obligation to adjudicate matters within their jurisdiction.[80] As the following chapters discuss, these mechanisms consist primarily of: (1) the Anti-Injunction Act,[81] which delineates when federal courts may and may not issue injunctions staying state court proceedings; (2) federal abstention doctrines, which permit federal courts to stay or dismiss their own proceedings under certain circumstances; and (3) state court abstention doctrines, which permit the same effect.

[79] Penn Gen. Casualty Co. v. Pennsylvania *ex rel.* Schnader, 294 U.S. 189, 195 (1935) (receivership proceedings); *see also* Ch. 7, *Personal Jurisdiction in Federal Courts* (discussion of in rem jurisdiction, or jurisdiction over property).

[80] Colorado River Water Conservation Dist. v. United States, 424 U.S. 800, 817 (1976) (federal courts have "virtually unflagging obligation . . . to exercise the jurisdiction given them").

[81] *See* 28 U.S.C. § 2283.

# Chapter 12

# THE ANTI-INJUNCTION ACTS

## § 12.01 HISTORY OF THE ANTI-INJUNCTION ACTS

### [1] Early Anti-Injunction Legislation

Federal courts, since 1793, have been specifically limited by statute in their ability to enjoin state court proceedings. The first anti-injunction legislation was no more than one sentence in a small section of a two-page statute. The provision merely stated that no "writ of injunction [shall] be granted to stay proceedings in any court of a state."[1] It is unclear why the anti-injunction provision was inserted into the general statute and, until the 1874 codification of federal laws into the Revised Statutes, federal courts almost completely ignored the anti-injunction provision. In fact, the Supreme Court mentioned the provision only once, in *Watson v. Jones* in 1871.[2]

In 1874 Congress inserted the anti-injunction provision in its own section and substantially changed the statutory language to specifically limit federal court power to enjoin state court proceedings. The new section provided: "The writ of injunction shall not be granted by any court of the United States to stay proceedings in any court of a State, except in cases where such injunction may be authorized by any law relating to proceedings in bankruptcy."[3] This provision was included, unchanged, in the Judicial Code of 1911,[4] where it remained until the 1948 revision that created the modern Anti-Injunction Act.

### [2] Theory of the Anti-Injunction Statutes

The Anti-Injunction Act is founded on the principles of federalism, which ensure states those powers not surrendered to the national government and not otherwise restrained by the "supreme Law of the Land" set forth in the Constitution, laws, or treaties of the United States.[5]

---

1 Act of Mar. 2, 1793, ch. 22, § 5, 1 Stat. 335.

2 Watson v. Jones, 80 U.S. (13 Wall.) 679 (1872).

3 Rev. Stat. of 1874, ch. 12, § 720, 18 Stat. 134.

4 § 265, Judicial Code of 1911, 28 U.S.C. § 379 (1940).

5 *See* Toucey v. New York Life Ins. Co., 314 U.S. 118, 130–132 (1941); Atlantic Coast Line R.R. Co. v. Brotherhood of Locomotive Eng'rs, 398 U.S. 281, 285 (1970).

In creating a dual court system,[6] the framers of the constitution sought to reconcile two competing principles: state sovereignty versus a cohesive federal union. State sovereignty proponents argued that separate federal courts were unnecessary because state courts were competent to protect state and federal rights. Strong federalist proponents claimed that a federal court system was necessary to resolve federal issues. The constitutional compromise established two essentially separate legal systems. The constitution created the Supreme Court, and Congress created federal trial and appellate courts with limited jurisdiction. Each state was left to create its own court system with broad jurisdiction.

The courts soon recognized that this dual system could not function if state and federal courts conflicted over control of litigation. So, to "prevent needless friction between state and federal courts" the respective governments addressed this potential tension through anti-injunction legislation.[7]

### [3] Judicial Interpretation of Federal Injunctive Power Before 1948

Although the Supreme Court recognized early in constitutional history that the Anti-Injunction Act was based on principles of comity, for many years the federal courts did not treat the prohibition against injunctions as an absolute bar.[8] Instead, federal courts recognized numerous situations in which federal courts could stay or enjoin state court proceedings. Thus, under early practice, federal courts issued injunctions against state proceedings in cases involving bankruptcy proceedings,[9] removal actions,[10] limitation of shipowners' liability,[11] interpleader,[12] real property,[13] and res judicata determinations.[14] Through 1941, the Anti-Injunction Act was observed more in its exceptions than in its prohibition.[15]

### [4] The *Toucey* Decision

In 1941 the Supreme Court decided *Toucey v. New York Life Ins. Co.*, in which the Court directly addressed the question, "[d]oes a federal court have power to stay a proceeding in a state court simply because the claim in controversy has previously been adjudicated in the federal court?"[16] The Court's majority opinion interpreted the Anti-Injunction Act literally and narrowly, indicating that federal courts had no such power. The Court noted the important congressional policy of

---

6 *See generally* Ch. 11, *Dual Federal-State Judicial Systems.*

7 Oklahoma Packing Co. v. Gas Co., 309 U.S. 4, 9 (1940).

8 Toucey v. New York Life Ins. Co., 314 U.S. 118, 135–136 (1941).

9 314 U.S. at 132.

10 Dietzsch v. Huidekoper, 103 U.S. 494, 498 (1881).

11 Providence & N.Y.Steamship Co. v. Hill Mfg. Co., 109 U.S. 578, 599 (1883).

12 Dugas v. American Surety Co., 300 U.S. 414, 428 (1937).

13 Toucey v. New York Life Ins. Co., 314 U.S. 118, 135–136 (1941).

14 314 U.S. at 133–135.

15 314 U.S. at 141–142.

16 Toucey v. New York Life Ins. Co., 314 U.S. 118 (1941).

preventing needless friction between state and federal courts. Citing a litany of prior precedents applying the relitigation doctrine, the Court nonetheless held that "[l]oose language and a sporadic, ill-considered decision cannot be held to have imbedded in our law a doctrine which so patently violates the expressed prohibition of Congress."[17]

The Court recognized that an exception to the Act could stem from express congressional authorizations, and accepted the established rule that a court first acquiring jurisdiction over a *res* could enjoin all others from also exercising jurisdiction over the same *res*.[18] It rejected all other exceptions.

A vigorous dissent argued that federal courts must have the power to protect their decrees against relitigation of the same claims in state court. The dissent cited numerous precedents for the principle that a court has the right to execute its decrees to avoid relitigation and forced reliance on res judicata, and noted that for more than a half century courts had widely accepted the rule that, despite the prohibition of the Anti-Injunction Act, federal courts retained the power to prevent relitigation of previously determined issues.[19]

### [5] Legislative Reaction to *Toucey* Decision

In direct response to the *Toucey* decision, Congress in 1948 enacted the relitigation exception as part of the revised modern Anti-Injunction Act. The Reviser's Note indicates:

> The exceptions specifically include the words "to protect or effectuate its judgments," for lack of which the Supreme Court held that the Federal courts are without power to enjoin relitigation of cases and controversies fully adjudicated by such courts (*See Toucey v. New York Life Insurance Co.*, . . . A vigorous dissenting opinion . . . notes that at the time of the 1911 revision of the Judicial Code, the power of the courts of the United States to protect their judgments was unquestioned and that the revisers of that code noted no change and Congress intended no change).

Therefore, the revised statute restored the basic relitigation exception as federal courts generally understood and interpreted it prior to the *Toucey* decision.

## § 12.02 THE MODERN ANTI-INJUNCTION ACT

### [1] The Anti-Injunction Acts

The general Anti-Injunction Act provides, simply: "A court of the United States may not grant an injunction to stay proceedings in a State court except as expressly authorized by Act of Congress, or where necessary in aid of its

[17] 314 U.S. at 139.

[18] 314 U.S. at 139.

[19] 314 U.S. at 146–153.

jurisdiction, or to protect or effectuate its judgments."[20] A separate Tax Anti-Injunction Act provides: "The district courts shall not enjoin, suspend or restrain the assessment, levy or collection of any tax under State law where a plain, speedy and efficient remedy may be had in the courts of such State."[21]

### [2] Purpose of Anti-Injunction Acts

The modern Anti-Injunction Acts prohibit federal courts from enjoining state court proceedings in most circumstances. Generally, the Anti-Injunction Act contains a clear and sweeping prohibition against federal court power to enjoin or stay state court proceedings. The Act is an affirmative proscription against federal court interference in state court proceedings unless one of three enumerated exceptions listed in the Act applies. However, in certain very limited circumstances, federal courts may restrain state court proceedings.

The Anti-Injunction Act creates a presumption in favor of permitting parallel litigation in state and federal courts. Doubts as to a federal injunction's propriety should be resolved in favor of allowing the state court action to proceed in an orderly fashion to finally determine the controversy.[22]

The Anti-Injunction Act is deeply rooted in federalist principles of government and has a well-established history. The Act is based on notions of comity and a need to prevent needless friction between state and federal courts.[23]

### [3] Broad Prohibition on Federal Injunctive Power

A federal court may not enjoin state court proceedings except "as expressly authorized by Act of Congress, or where necessary in aid of its jurisdiction, or to protect or effectuate its judgments."[24] These are the only three exceptions to the prohibition. They are narrow, and are "not to be enlarged by loose statutory construction."[25] The Anti-Injunction Act therefore applies as a broad prohibition on the power of federal courts to enjoin state court proceedings.[26]

---

[20] 28 U.S.C. § 2283.

[21] 28 U.S.C. § 1341.

[22] *See* Atlantic Coast Line R.R. v. Brotherhood of Locomotive Eng'rs, 398 U.S. 281, 295 (1970).

[23] *See* Amalgamated Clothing Workers of Am. v. Richman Bros., 348 U.S. 511, 514–516 (1955).

[24] 28 U.S.C. § 2283.

[25] Atlantic Coast Line R.R. Co. v. Brotherhood of Locomotive Eng'rs, 398 U.S. 281, 287 (1970); *see also* Chick Kam Choo v. Exxon Corp., 486 U.S. 140, 146 (1988).

[26] *See* Chick Kam Choo v. Exxon Corp., 486 U.S. 140, 146 (1988); Atlantic Coast Line R.R. Co. v. Brotherhood of Locomotive Eng'rs, 398 U.S. 281, 287 (1970) (language in Act is admittedly broad); Amalgamated Clothing Workers of Am. v. Richman Bros., 348 U.S. 511, 515–516 (1955) (Act is clear-cut prohibition qualified only by specifically defined exceptions).

## [4] Application of Anti-Injunction Act

### [a] What Constitutes a Court

The Anti-Injunction Act limits the power of a "court of the United States" to enjoin state proceedings. For purposes of the Anti-Injunction Act, a "court of the United States" is defined to include the United States Supreme Court, the courts of appeals, and the federal district courts (the Act applies to the District Court for Puerto Rico, but does not apply to the district courts for the Canal Zone, Guam, the Northern Mariana Islands, or the Virgin Islands). The Act also applies to the Court of International Trade and any court created by Congress whose judges hold office during good behavior.

The Anti-Injunction Act prohibits the federal courts from restraining parallel state court proceedings. The Anti-Injunction Act also prohibits restraining state agencies that perform activities that are judicial in nature. However, the Anti-Injunction Act does not protect legislative or administrative functions performed by a state agency.[27] A federal court determines the nature of a state agency by evaluating the character of the agency's proceedings, rather than the body or entity in which they occur. A judicial body is not a "court" for purposes of the Anti-Injunction Act when it performs legislative or administrative functions.[28] Further, the Act does not bar an injunction against future state court proceedings.[29] Judicial activities that come within the definition of "court" activities include state Supreme Court review of estate tax assessments;[30] activities of a state Industrial Accident Commission;[31] post-judgment garnishment proceedings;[32] and heirship proceedings within federal court jurisdiction.[33]

However, certain non-judicial state activities fall outside the Act's protection. For example, such activities include an election recount by a statutory, court-ordered, court-appointed recount committee;[34] the administrative enforcement of a state statute;[35] the administrative adjudication of an Agricultural Labor Relations Board;[36] state disbarment proceedings, prior to court adjudication;[37] legislative proceedings;[38] state public service commission proceedings concerning a utility's

---

27 Prentis v. Atlantic Coast Line Co., 211 U.S. 210, 224 (1908).

28 Prentis v. Atlantic Coast Line Co., 211 U.S. 210, 224–226 (1908).

29 *See* Pathways, Inc. v. Dunne, 329 F.3d 108, 114 (2d Cir. 2003).

30 Hill v. Martin, 296 U.S. 393, 402 (1935).

31 North Pacific S.S. v. Industrial Accident Comm'n, 23 F.2d 109, 110 (9th Cir. 1918).

32 Garrett v. Hoffman, 441 F. Supp. 1151, 1157–1158 (D.C. Pa. 1977).

33 Miami County Nat'l Bank v. Bancroft, 121 F.2d 921, 923 (10th Cir. 1941) (federal courts have equity jurisdiction to determine whether litigants are heirs of deceased and their share in estate).

34 Roudebush v. Hartke, 405 U.S. 15, 21–22 (1972).

35 American Motor Sales Corp. v. Runke, 708 F.2d 202, 204–205 (6th Cir. 1983).

36 Bud Antle, Inc. v. Barbosa, 45 F.3d 1261, 1271–1272 (9th Cir. 1994)

37 Taylor v. Kentucky State Bar Ass'n, 424 F.2d 478, 482 (6th Cir. 1970).

38 Virginia Nat'l Bank v. Virginia ex rel. State Corp. Comm'n, 320 F. Supp. 260, 265 (D.C. Va. 1970).

certification;[39] the activities of a "condemnation court" board of appraisers selected by the state Supreme Court, in connection with municipal acquisition of utility property;[40] a county court approval of Indian land conveyance under a federal statute;[41] and proceedings before a state liquor authority.[42]

### [b] What Constitutes an "Injunction"

The Anti-Injunction Act extends to declaratory judgments and other orders that have essentially the same effect as an injunction. Thus, the Anti-Injunction Act prohibits any federal court order that, though not specifically enjoining a state proceeding, would decide or preempt a pending state proceeding.[43] Federal declaratory judgments may have injunctive effects and therefore come within the Anti-Injunction prohibition. However, a federal court is not prohibited from issuing a declaratory judgment if a claim turns on a question of federal law more familiar to the federal court, and the state court would not normally determine the issue.[44]

A temporary restraining order or a preliminary injunction may constitute and injunction. For example, a temporary restraining order barring an employer from seeking to enforce non-compete agreements in any court except the federal district court in San Diego was held to violate the Anti-Injunction Act.[45] The order violated the Act because ordering the employer not to proceed in other courts was tantamount to enjoining pending state proceedings, even though the parties and issues were similar but not identical.

The issue of what constitutes an injunction is a legal one, subject to de novo appellate review.[46]

### [c] What Constitutes a "Proceeding"

For Anti-Injunction purposes, the term *proceeding* comprehensively includes:[47]

> All steps taken or which may be taken in the state court or by its officers from the institution to the close of the final process. It applies to appellate as well as to original proceedings; and is independent of the doctrine of res judicata. It applies alike to actions by the court and by its ministerial

---

[39] Delaware Coach Co. v. Public Serv. Comm'n of State of Del., 265 F. Supp. 648, 653 (D.C. Del. 1967).

[40] Central Elec. & Gas Co. v. City of Stromsburg, 192 F. Supp. 280, 295 (D.C. Neb. 1960).

[41] Armstrong v. Maple Leaf Apartments, 508 F.2d 518, 523 (10th Cir. 1974).

[42] Engelman v. Cahn, 425 F.2d 954, 958 (2d Cir. 1969).

[43] Texas Employers' Ins. Ass'n v. Jackson, 862 F.2d 491, 504–508 (5th Cir. 1988) (declaratory judgment precluded when it would have same effect as injunction).

[44] Thiokol Chemical Corp. v. Burlington Industries, Inc., 448 F.2d 1328, 1332 (3d Cir. 1971) (declaratory judgment permitted on federal question); *see* Steffel v. Thompson, 415 U.S. 452, 460–461 (1974) (declaratory judgment on constitutional question permitted in extraordinary circumstances). For general discussion of declaratory judgments, see 12 Moore's Federal Practice Ch. 57, *Declaratory Judgment* (Matthew Bender 3d ed.).

[45] *See* Bennett v. Medtronic, Inc., 285 F.3d 801, 804–05 (9th Cir. 2002).

[46] *Id.*, 285 F.3d at 805.

[47] Hill v. Martin, 296 U.S. 393, 403 (1935).

officers; applies not only to an execution issued on a judgment, but to any proceeding supplemental or ancillary taken with a view to making the suit or judgment effective. The prohibition is applicable whether such supplementary or ancillary proceeding is taken in the court which rendered the judgment or in some other. And it governs a privy to the state court proceeding . . . as well as the parties of record. Thus, the prohibition applies whatever the nature of the proceedings, unless the case presents facts which bring it within one of the recognized exceptions.

Thus, for example, the Anti-Injunction Act extends to discovery and permits district courts to enjoin state discovery to protect the integrity of a federal court order. Private dispute resolution mechanisms instituted pursuant to an agreement between the parties, such as arbitration, are not judicial proceedings. Therefore, a federal court may enjoin arbitration proceedings that threaten to interfere with a pending federal litigation.[48] Arbitration pursuant to a private agreement is not a judicial proceeding, even if the state courts could eventually become involved because the state courts have the power to confirm, modify, vacate, or enforce the arbitration award. However, an arbitration proceeding that is ordered by a state court is a proceeding that is protected by the Anti-Injunction Act.

The Anti-Injunction Act does not apply to state administrative proceedings. The plain language of the Anti-Injunction Act refers only to federal court injunctions to stay proceedings in state court. An injunction related to an administrative proceeding does not impact state courts.[49] Similarly, the proceedings of a federal agency are exempt from the terms of the Anti-Injunction Act, which applies only to proceedings in a "court of the United States."[50]

An injunction restrains parties to a lawsuit, rather than the court. However, it is immaterial, for the purposes of the Anti-Injunction Act, that an injunction is directed to the parties and not the state court.[51]

Although the Act prevents injunctions against any proceedings after the suit is instituted, it does not prohibit a federal court from issuing an injunction restraining a party from instituting state proceedings (*see* [5][d], *below*).[52]

---

[48] Pridential real estate Affiliates, Inc. v. PPR Realty, Inc., 204 F.3d 867 (9th Cir. 2000); Six Clinics Holding Corp., II v. Cafcomp Sys., Inc., 119 F.3d 393, 398 (6th Cir. 1997).

[49] United States Fidelity & Guar. Co. v. Lee Inv. LLC, 641 F.3d 1126, 1136 (9th Cir. 2011); Entergy, Arkansas, Inc. v. State of Nebraska, 210 F.3d 887, 900–01 (8th Cir. 2000).

[50] American Airlines, Inc. v. Dep't of Transp., 202 F3d 788, 802 (5th Cir. 2000).

[51] Oklahoma Packing Co. v. Oklahoma Gas & Elec. Co., 309 U.S. 4, 9 (1940) (immaterial that injunction directed to parties rather than proceedings); Gloucester Marine Rys. Corp. v. Charles Parisi, Inc., 848 F.2d 12, 15 (1st Cir. 1988) (injunction applied to parties).

[52] Dombrowski v. Pfister, 380 U.S. 479, 484 n.2 (1965); *see* B & A Pipeline Co. v. Dorney, 904 F.2d 996, 1002 (5th Cir. 1990) (injunction prohibited party from commencing proceedings); Phillips v. Chas. Schreiner Bank, 894 F.2d 127, 131 (5th Cir. 1990) (injunction prohibited party from commencing proceedings).

## [5] Parties and Proceedings Beyond Scope of Act

### [a] United States Government

The Anti-Injunction Act does not prohibit the United States from obtaining an injunction of state proceedings to prevent threatened irreparable injury to a national interest. In such circumstances, the United States government may use injunctive power to stay state court proceedings, free from the Act's severe restriction.[53] However, a federal court will not automatically grant an injunction simply on the government's application,[54] and principles of comity and equitable entitlement apply. Absent some express superseding power, the United States may not maintain a federal suit that interferes with valid state *in rem* or *quasi in rem* jurisdiction.[55]

### [b] Federal Agencies

In general, the Anti-Injunction Act prohibits federal boards, agencies, and corporations from obtaining an injunction of state proceedings. However, the Anti-Injunction Act does not apply to a federal entity if the agency properly can be equated to the United States as sovereign, and the agency asserts a superior federal interest.[56] This exception to the Anti-Injunction Act for federal agencies does not apply automatically.

### [c] Strangers to Earlier Litigation

Under the "strangers to the state court proceedings" exclusion, the Anti-Injunction Act does not bar an injunction when the party requesting injunctive relief in the federal court was neither a party, nor in privity with a party, to an earlier state court proceeding sought to be enjoined.[57] A third party is a stranger to the litigation if a prior judgment would not collaterally estop the party in successor litigation.[58]

---

[53] Leiter Minerals, Inc. v. United States, 352 U.S. 220, 225–226 (1957).

[54] United States v. Sid-Mars Rest. & Lounge, Inc., 644 F.3d 270, 272–73 (5th Cir. 2011) (injunction is not automatically proper merely because the U.S. seeks it); U.S. v. Certified Indus., Inc. 361 F.2d 857, 859 (2d Cir. 1966).

[55] *See* U.S. v. Augspurger, 452 F. Supp. 659, 668 (D.C.N.Y. 1978). *In rem* jurisdiction is discussed in Ch. 7, *Personal Jurisdiction in Federal Courts*.

[56] NLRB v. Nash-Finch Co., 404 U.S. 138, 147 (1971).

[57] *See* County of Imperial v. Munoz, 449 U.S. 54, 59–60 (1980) (Act does not apply to "strangers to the state court proceeding"); Commodities export v. Detroit Int'l Bridge Co., 695 F.3d 518, 527 (6th Cir. 2012) (Anti-Injunction Act did not apply because plaintiff in federal suit was not party to state court litigation).

[58] Iantosca v. Step Plan Services, Inc., 604 F.3d 24, 32 (1st Cir. 2010); Prudential Real Estate Affiliates, Inc., 204 F.3d at 877–80.

### [d] Commencement of Proceedings

The Anti-Injunction Act does not prohibit injunctions restraining the commencement of state court proceedings. This was the well-settled rule under the former Anti-Injunction Act,[59] and it remains the rule today.[60] Federal courts, however, are divided as to whether a federal injunction can issue when there is no state court proceeding when the injunction is sought, but a state action is commenced before the federal court acts on the application. Some courts have ruled that an injunction may issue in this situation,[61] while others have held that the Act bars an injunction in these circumstances, unless an exception applies.[62] The Supreme Court granted *certiorari* to answer this question in *Roth v. Bank of the Commonwealth*, but dismissed the petition when the parties settled,[63] so the Court has yet to resolve the conflict.

### [e] Arbitration Proceedings

The Anti-Injunction Act does not prohibit federal courts from enjoining arbitration proceedings when state court proceedings are not involved.[64] More precisely, when an arbitration proceeding is private and voluntary, and the state courts have not become involved (and may never become involved) in the proceeding, the Anti-Injunction Act does not apply.[65] In *Kelly v. Merrill, Lynch, Pierce, Fenner & Smith* plaintiffs sued their securities broker in federal court, alleging violations of SEC Rules. After the defendant prevailed on summary judgment, the plaintiffs commenced arbitration proceedings over four state claims that involved the same conduct in the earlier action. The district court issued an injunction, holding that the arbitration was barred by res judicata. The court of appeals affirmed, holding that the Anti-Injunction Act did not apply because state court proceedings were not involved.

Arbitration that involves a judicial inquiry, such as an adjudication to decide and enforce parties' rights and liabilities, is considered a state court proceeding that the Act protects. Stated differently, arbitration is a "state proceeding" for the purposes

---

59 *See* 28 U.S.C. § 379; Jewel Tea Co. v. Lee's Summit, 198 F. 532, 539 (W.D. Mo. 1912) (federal court may enjoin party from commencing state court proceedings); Pathways, Inc. v. Dunne, 329 F.3d 108, 114 (2d Cir. 2003).

60 Dombrowski v. Pfister, 380 U.S. 479, 484 n.2 (1965) (Anti-Injunction Act does not apply to proceedings not yet commenced).

61 Hyde Park Partners, L.P. v. Connolly, 839 F.2d 837, 842 n.6 (1st Cir. 1988).

62 *See* Denny's Inc. v. Cake, 364 F.3d 521, 531 (4th Cir. 2004); Martingale LLC v. City of Louisville, 361 F.3d 297, 302–04 (6th Cir. 2004); Roth v. Bank of the Commonwealth, 583 F.2d 527, 531–535 (6th Cir. 1978), *cert. dismissed*, 442 U.S. 925 (1979).

63 *See* 442 U.S. 925.

64 Prudential Real estate Affiliates, Inc., 204 F.3d at 879; Six clinics Holding Corp., II, 119 F.3d at 398–99; Kelly v. Merrill Lynch, Pierce, Fenner & Smith, 985 F.2d 1067, 1069 (11th Cir. 1993) (federal court has authority to enjoin arbitration); *cf.* McDonald v. City of West Branch, 466 U.S. 284, 287–288(1984) (arbitration is not "judicial proceeding" for purposes of full faith and credit statute, 28 U.S.C. § 1738.

65 *See* McDonald v. City of West branch, 466 U.S. 284, 287–288 (1984); Prudential Real Estate Affiliates, Inc., 204 F.3d at 879–80.

of the Anti-Injunction Act if the arbitration has been ordered or its award enforced by a state court in judicial (as opposed to merely ministerial) proceedings.[66] Thus, when a state court orders and oversees an arbitration, and the parties have recourse to the court over the results, a federal court may not enjoin the state arbitration (unless it falls within an exception to the Anti-Injunction Act).[67]

### [f] Suits in Foreign Countries

The Anti-Injunction Act does not apply to suits in foreign countries.[68] Determining the appropriateness of an international antisuit injunction is a highly nuanced exercise. Courts must accommodate the presumption in favor of concurrent jurisdiction as well as conflicting, and often mutually exclusive, national policies without unduly interfering with the judicial processes of a foreign sovereign.[69] Generally, principles of international comity require restraint regarding extraterritorial interference with international litigation. Federal courts ordinarily will not issue an injunction against a foreign proceeding if the foreign litigation poses no threat to federal court jurisdiction or to any important national public policy.[70]

### [g] Temporary Restraining Orders

The Anti-Injunction Act does not prohibit a federal court from issuing a temporary restraining order to preserve existing conditions while it determines whether it has jurisdiction. Thus, a federal court may stay state proceedings temporarily while it considers whether the Act applies.[71] However, other temporary restraining orders may violate the Anti-Injunction Act.[72]

---

66 Prudential Real Estate Affiliates, Inc., *id.*

67 Prudential Real Estate Affiliates, Inc., *id.*; Empire Blue Cross & Blue Shield v. Janet Greeson's A Place For Us, Inc., 985 F.2d 459, 461–462 (9th Cir. 1993) (court-ordered arbitration, award to be submitted to court for approval).

68 *See* Quaak v. Klynveld Peat Marwick Goerdeler Bedrijfsrevisoren, 361 F.3d 11, 16–19 (1st Cir. 2004).

69 *Id.*, 361 F.3d at 16–17 (formidable task to determine propriety of international antisuit given paucity of guidance from Supreme Court and circuit precedent).

70 *Id.*, 361 F.3d at 17–19 (rejecting a liberal approach to assigns low priority to interest of international comity and undermines presumption in favor of concurrent parallel proceedings); Stonington Partners, Inc. v. Lernout & Hauspie Speech Prods., N.V., 310 F.3d 118, 126 (3d Cir. 2002); China Trade & Dev. Corp. v. M/V Choong Yong, 837 F.2d 33, 35–36 (2d Cir. 1987) (federal courts have power to enjoin foreign suits).

71 United States v. United Mine Workers of Am., 330 U.S. 258, 292–293 (1947).

72 Bennett v. Medtronic, Inc., 285 F.3d 801, 805–07 (9th Cir. 2002).

## § 12.03 EXCEPTIONS TO THE ANTI-INJUNCTION ACT

### [1] First Exception: "Expressly Authorized" by Act of Congress

#### [a] Function of Exception

Federal courts may enjoin state court proceedings "as expressly authorized by Act of Congress."[73] The congressional act need not specifically refer to the Anti-Injunction Act, nor is there any prescribed formula for authorization.[74] However, the congressional act must create an enforceable, specific, and uniquely federal right or remedy that a state proceeding could frustrate if not enjoined.[75] Beyond these general strictures, however, the Court has provided little guidance concerning what federal statutes are within the exception. A statutory precursor of the Anti-Injunction Act gave federal courts the power to issue injunctions against state court proceedings only under laws relating to bankruptcy proceedings.[76] Over time, the Supreme Court recognized that to give intended effect to other federal statutes, courts needed to construe those statutes to permit injunction of state court proceedings.[77] Thus, despite the lack of express authorization, the Supreme Court recognized the federal courts' ability to enjoin state proceedings under statutes regarding removal,[78] limitation of shipowners' liability,[79] farm mortgages,[80] and interpleader.[81]

The 1948 revision of the Judicial Code removed the express exception for bankruptcy from the Anti-Injunction Act and added the current language, "except as expressly authorized by Act of Congress."[82] Supreme Court opinions are divided concerning which statutes fall within this exception,[83] and lower federal courts similarly disagree.

#### [b] Recognized Express Exceptions

##### [i] Bankruptcy Proceedings

The current Anti-Injunction Act does not specifically include an exception for bankruptcy proceedings. However, the "expressly authorized" exception to the broad prohibition of the Anti-Injunction Act permits a federal court to enjoin state

---

[73] 28 U.S.C. § 2283.

[74] Amalgamated Clothing Workers of Am. v. Richman Bros., 348 U.S. 511, 516 (1955).

[75] Mitchum v. Foster, 407 U.S. 225, 237–238 (1972).

[76] Rev. Stat. of 1874, ch. 12, § 720.

[77] *See* Toucey v. New York Life Ins. Co., 314 U.S. 118, 132 (1941).

[78] Kern v. Huidekoper, 103 U.S. 494, 498 (1881).

[79] Providence & N.Y.S.S. Co. v. Hill Mfg. Co., 109 U.S. 578, 599–601 (1883).

[80] Kalb v. Feuerstein, 308 U.S. 433, 439–440 (1940).

[81] Dugas v. American Surety Co. of N.Y., 300 U.S. 414, 428–429 (1937).

[82] 28 U.S.C. § 2283.

[83] *See* Vendo Co. v. Lektro-Vend Corp., 433 U.S. 623 (1977) (three separate opinions).

court proceedings in bankruptcy.[84] Courts recognized and applied this exception before the 1948 revision of the Anti-Injunction statute;[85] the prior Anti-Injunction Act provided that "[t]he writ of injunction shall not be granted by any court of the United States to stay proceedings in any court of a State, except in cases where such injunction may be authorized by any law relating to proceedings in bankruptcy."[86]

Although the current Anti-Injunction Act does not specifically include an exception for bankruptcy proceedings, Section 362 of the Bankruptcy Code provides express authorization by allowing for a broad stay of litigation, lien enforcement, and other actions that would affect or interfere with a debtor's property or estate.[87] A federal court's ability to stay state court proceedings becomes effective on filing of the debtor's bankruptcy petition.

### [ii] Removal Actions

Federal courts have long recognized removal actions as an "expressly authorized" exception to the Anti-Injunction Act.[88] The removal statute provides that when a state court defendant files a removal petition in federal court (with a copy to the state court clerk), posts bond, and gives written notice to all adverse parties, "the State court shall proceed no further unless and until the case is remanded."[89] This language expressly authorizes a federal court to enjoin state court proceedings regarding a case removed to federal court.[90] If the removal is proper, a federal court may issue an injunction against state proceedings even if the defendant sought removal solely to avoid the Act's prohibition.[91] And, the federal court may issue an injunction if the state plaintiff files a second substantially identical state court suit in order to subvert removal.[92] The Anti-Injunction exception for removal cases applies only so long as the federal court maintains jurisdiction. The power to enjoin the state court proceeding ends if the federal court remands the case or dismisses it without prejudice.[93]

---

[84] Vendo Co. v. Lektro-Vend Corp., 433 U.S. 623, 640 (1977).

[85] Toucey v. New York Life Ins. Co., 314 U.S. 118, 132 (1941).

[86] Judicial Code of 1911 § 265.

[87] 11 U.S.C. § 362.

[88] French v. Hay, 89 U.S. (22 Wall.) 250, 252 (1875). Removal in general is discussed in Ch. 6, *Removal*.

[89] 28 U.S.C. § 1446(d).

[90] Vendo Co. v. Lektro-Vend Corp., 433 U.S. 623, 640 (1977).

[91] Hyde Park Partners, L.P. v. Connolly, 839 F.2d 837, 841–842 (1st Cir. 1988).

[92] Lou v. Belzberg, 834 F.2d 730, 740–741 (9th Cir. 1987) (plaintiff's second suit, although similar to first, contained none of the federal claims and was thus properly instituted in state court).

[93] *See* Hickey v. Duffy, 827 F.2d 234, 243 (7th Cir. 1987).

### [iii] Civil Rights Actions

The Supreme Court has construed the Civil Rights Act[94] as providing another "expressly authorized" exception to the Anti-Injunction Act.[95] The Civil Rights Act authorizes an aggrieved party to bring a "suit in equity" to redress civil rights deprivations under color of state law.[96] For several years lower federal courts equivocated on whether the Civil Rights Act also supplied an express exception to the Anti-Injunction Act.[97] The Supreme Court laid the theoretical groundwork in 1965 for identifying situations in which a federal court injunction might issue to prevent state violations of constitutional rights. In *Dombrowski v. Pfister*, the Court held that a federal court could issue an injunction against state enforcement of criminal statutes, if "extraordinary circumstances" presented a great, immediate danger of irreparable loss or injury.[98] The Court carefully noted, however, that in the case before it extreme circumstances had threatened the plaintiffs, and that no state proceedings were pending at the time the plaintiffs sought federal injunctive relief. The Court therefore specifically declined to decide whether civil rights actions generally were within the Anti-Injunction Act's "expressly authorized" exception.[99]

By the early 1970s, the Court again suggested that certain circumstances might justify a federal court's issuing an injunction to prevent state violation of constitutional rights in criminal proceedings. Thus in *Younger v. Harris* the Court held that "the possible unconstitutionality of a statute 'on its face' does not in itself justify an injunction against good-faith attempts to enforce it." The availability of injunctive relief under the Anti-Injunction Act, at least in criminal proceedings, requires a showing of "bad faith, harassment, or other unusual circumstances."[100] The Court's *Younger* holding rested on equitable principles, and the Court again did not explicitly decide whether the Anti-Injunction Act barred or permitted issuance of an injunction.[101]

Finally, in 1972, the Court in *Mitchum v. Foster* squarely held that the Civil Rights Act embodies a legislative exception to the Anti-Injunction Act.[102] The Court relied heavily on the Civil Rights Act's legislative history in reaching its conclusion. The Court suggested that Congress intended the Civil Rights Act to open federal courts to private citizens to enforce the Fourteenth Amendment

---

94 42 U.S.C. § 1983.

95 Mitchum v. Foster, 407 U.S. 225, 243 (1972).

96 42 U.S.C. § 1983.

97 *See, e.g.*, Baines v. City of Danville, 337 F.2d 579, 590 (4th Cir. 1964) (Civil Rights Act does not create exception to Anti-Injunction Act); Machesky v. Bizzell, 414 F.2d 283, 291 (5th Cir. 1969) (principles of comity imbedded in the Anti-Injunction Act must yield to First Amendment rights); Sheridan v. Garrison, 415 F.2d 699, 702–706 (5th Cir. 1969) (Anti-Injunction Act is no bar to injunction of state criminal proceedings involving free speech).

98 Dombrowski v. Pfister, 380 U.S. 479, 483–485 (1965) (state repeatedly threatened continued criminal prosecution for violation of statute).

99 380 U.S. at 484.

100 Younger v. Harris, 401 U.S. 37, 49 (1971).

101 *See* 401 U.S. at 49, 54.

102 Mitchum v. Foster, 407 U.S. 225, 243 (1972).

against state action, and to use the federal courts as guardians of the people's federal rights from unconstitutional action under color of state law.[103] In so holding, the Court more broadly articulated three elements necessary for a statutory provision to qualify as an "expressly authorized" exception to the Anti-Injunction Act: (1) the legislation must create a "uniquely federal right or remedy"; (2) the right or remedy must be enforceable in a federal court of equity; and (3) the right or remedy could be frustrated if the federal court was not permitted to enjoin a state court proceeding. The Court also required a finding that the statute could be given its intended scope only if the federal court had the ability to stay state court proceedings.[104]

### [iv] Antitrust Actions

The Clayton Act[105] does not fall within the "expressly authorized" exception to the Anti-Injunction Act.[106] In *Vendo Co. v. Lektro-Vend Corp.*, the Supreme Court reviewed the various criteria in *Dombrowski v. Pfister*,[107] *Younger v. Harris*,[108] and *Mitchum v. Foster*.[109] Focusing on the test enunciated in *Mitchum*, the Court concluded that the Clayton Act was not congressional legislation "[which] could be given its intended scope only by the stay of a state court proceeding."[110]

In reviewing the Clayton Act's legislative history, the Court found that Congress did not focus on any necessary interaction between federal and state judicial proceedings in enforcing federal antitrust policy. The *Vendo* Court was extremely concerned that the Clayton Act appeared to lack the type of legislative intent that had supported the *Mitchum* ruling. Reviewing its holdings in *Dombrowski*, *Younger*, and *Mitchum*, the Court suggested that "[b]y limiting the statutory exceptions of § 2283 and its predecessors to these few instances, we have clearly recognized that the Act countenancing the federal injunction must *necessarily interact with, or focus upon, a state judicial proceeding*."[111]

The Clayton Act, which authorizes a private action for injunctive relief against individuals and private entities, does not "by its very essence contemplate or envision the necessary interaction with state judicial proceedings." The Civil Rights Act, on the other hand, authorizes private actions for injunctive relief against violations of constitutional rights under color of state law, that is, through state action. Unlike federal civil rights legislation, nothing in the Clayton Act's legislative history supported a congressional intent that the Clayton Act include an "expressly authorized" exception to the Anti-Injunction Act.[112] The Court noted that "[t]he

---

[103] 407 U.S. at 237–238.

[104] 407 U.S at 237–238.

[105] 15 U.S.C. § 26.

[106] Vendo Co. v. Lektro-Vend Corp., 433 U.S. 623, 641 (1977).

[107] Dombrowski, 380 U.S. 479 (1965) (great and immediate danger of irreparable loss).

[108] Younger v. Harris, 401 U.S. 37 (1971) (bad faith, harassment, or other unusual circumstances).

[109] Mitchum v. Foster, 407 U.S. 225 (1972) (unique federal rights requiring special federal protection).

[110] Vendo Co. v. Lektro-Vend Corp., 433 U.S. 623, 632 (1977).

[111] 433 U.S. at 640–641 (emphasis added).

[112] 433 U.S. at 640–641.

critical aspects of the legislative history recounted in *Mitchum* which led [it] to conclude that § 1983 was within the 'expressly authorized' exception to § 2283 are wholly absent from the relevant history of § 16 of the Clayton Act."[113]

The *Vendo* Court was sharply divided, however, and unable to obtain a majority opinion; three opinions expressed widely divergent views.[114] Justice Blackmun concurred, emphasizing that the Clayton Act should be considered an expressly authorized exception to the Anti-Injunction Act when state court proceedings are "themselves part of a series of 'baseless, repetitive claims' that are being used as an anticompetitive device." If a party seeking a federal injunction could show this, the party satisfies traditional prerequisites for equitable relief and the federal court should issue an injunction.[115] Justice Blackmun's requirement alludes to the necessary state involvement before a federal statute will be found to expressly authorize federal injunction of state judicial proceedings. In *Vendo*, there were no allegations of state governmental involvement of any kind, nor any indication that the Clayton Act, as applied, violated a constitutional right or a public interest.

The dissenting Justices argued that the Clayton Act falls squarely within the "expressly authorized" exception in all cases.[116] They concluded that Section 16 of the Clayton act satisfies the *Mitchum* test because it creates a federal remedy that can only be given its intended scope if it includes the power to stay state-court proceedings in appropriate cases. Without that power, the dissent argued, a private litigant's business might be ruined before the litigant has a remedy against state-court litigation seeking, for example, enforcement of an invalid patent, a covenant not to compete, or an executory merger agreement.[117]

### [c] Inconsistent Application of "Expressly Authorized" Exception

Lower courts have struggled to reconcile the Court's decision in *Vendo Co. v. Lektro-Vend Corp.*[118] with *Mitchum v. Foster*,[119] often with inconsistent and conflicting results.[120] However, the *Vendo* opinion clarifies the second part of the

---

[113] 433 U.S. at 635.

[114] 433 U.S. at 626–666.

[115] 433 U.S. at 643–645 (Blackmun, J. concurring).

[116] 433 U.S. at 650–651 (Stevens, J. dissenting).

[117] 433 U.S. at 656–657 (Stevens, J. dissenting).

[118] Vendo Co. v. Lektro-Vend Corp., 433 U.S. 623 (1977).

[119] Mitchum v. Foster, 407 U.S. 225, 225 (1972).

[120] *See, e.g.*, 1975 Salaried Retirement Plan v. Nobers, 968 F.2d 401, 405 (3d Cir. 1992) (no express authorization in ERISA and therefore state court claims preempted by ERISA fall within Act's prohibitions); United States Steel Corp. Plan for Employee Ins. Benefits v. Musisko, 885 F.2d 1170, 1175 (3d Cir. 1989) (ERISA did not expressly authorize injunction of state court proceedings); Texas Employer's Ins. Ass'n v. Jackson, 862 F.2d 491, 502–504 (5th Cir. 1988) (no "expressly authorized" exception for Longshore and Harbor Workers' Compensation Act); Sycuan Band of Mission Indians v. Roache, 788 F. Supp. 1498, 1509–1511 (S.D. Cal. 1992), *aff'd*, 54 F.3d 535 (9th Cir. 1994) (Indian Gaming Regulatory Act, a unique and comprehensive scheme to regulate Indian gambling, expressly authorizes federal court injunction of state proceedings); Oxford House-Evergreen v. City of Plainfield, 769 F. Supp. 1329, 1341 (D.N.J. 1991) (Fair Housing Act matter fell within "expressly authorized" exception).

*Mitchum* test, which may help to identify appropriate circumstances for application of the exception.

Several federal courts have determined that certain statutes "expressly authorize" federal injunction of state proceedings and are within the Anti-Injunction Act exception. These statutes include the Anti-Drug Abuse Act of 1988,[121] and the Agricultural Credit Act.[122]

Other federal courts have determined that various federal statutes and rules do not expressly authorize federal courts to enjoin state court proceedings. These statutes and rules include the Longshore and Harbor Workers' Compensation Act;[123] the Federal Rules of Civil Procedure;[124] the antitrust laws;[125] the Equal Credit Opportunity Act;[126] and the Americans with Disabilities Act.[127]

The federal circuits disagree whether certain provisions under the Employee Retirement Income Security Act (ERISA) expressly authorize the injunction of state court proceedings, or do not so permit restrain of such proceedings.[128]

## [2] Second Exception: "When Necessary in Aid of" Federal Court Jurisdiction

### [a] Function of Exception

The Anti-Injunction Act permits federal courts to enjoin state court proceedings when "necessary in aid of" the federal court's jurisdiction.[129] Despite this seemingly permissive language, this exception applies only in strictly limited situations. Federal courts may issue injunctions to restrain state proceedings in removed

---

[121] 21 U.S.C. § 848(q)(4)(B); McFarland v. Scott, 512 U.S. 849 (1994) (right to qualified counsel in post-conviction proceedings to vacate or set aside death sentence, read in conjunction with federal habeas corpus statute, 28 U.S.C. § 2251, provides federal courts with express discretionary authorization to enter stay of execution, not barred by Anti-Injunction Act, at time party requests counsel).

[122] 7 U.S.C. § 24 *et seq.*; Zajac v. Fed. Land Bank of St. Paul, 887 F.2d 844, 855–856 (8th Cir. 1989) (Agricultural Credit Act expressly authorizes federal court injunction to prevent state foreclosure proceedings in violation of Act; squarely within Anti-Injunction Act exception).

[123] 33 U.S.C. § 921(d); Tex. Employers' Ins. Ass'n v. Jackson, 862 F.2d 491, 503–504 (5th Cir. 1988) (no "expressly authorized" exception for Longshore and Harbor Workers' Compensation Act).

[124] *In re* Temple, 851 F.2d 1269, 1272 n.3 (11th Cir. 1988) (Federal Rules are not congressionally enacted legislation and therefore not "expressly authorized" exceptions to Anti-Injunction Act).

[125] 15 U.S.C. § 26; Village of Bolingbrook v. Citizens Utils. Co. of Ill., 864 F.2d 481, 483–485 (7th Cir. 1988) (aims of antitrust laws may be secured without federal injunction against state case).

[126] Bledsoe v. Fulton Bank, 940 F. Supp. 804, 807–809 (E.D. Pa. 1996).

[127] Lussier v. Dep't. of Hwy. Safety & Motor Vehicles, 972 F. Supp. 1412, 1418–22 (M.D. Fla. 1997).

[128] Cf. Gilbert v. Burlington Indus., Inc., 765 F.2d 320, 329 (2d Cir. 1985) (state suits over ERISA benefits may be enjoined) with trustees of Carpenters' Health & Welfare v. Darr, 694 F.3d 803, 807–11 (7th Cir. 2012) (ERISA's injunction authorization is limited); United States Steel Corp. Plan for Employee Ins. Benefits v. Musisko, 885 F.2d 1170, 1176–78 (3d Cir. 1989) (neither language nor legislative history of ERISA injunction provision demonstrate congressional intent to authorize injunctions against state court action).

[129] Atlantic Coast Line R.R. Co. v. Brotherhood of Locomotive Eng'rs, 398 U.S. 281, 288 (1970).

cases[130] and when the federal court first acquires jurisdiction in parallel *in rem* actions.[131] However, federal courts are also authorized to enjoin state proceedings in removed cases under the "expressly authorized" exception (*see* [1], *above*).

The Reviser's Note to the Anti-Injunction Act provides little guidance in interpreting the "necessary in aid of jurisdiction" exception:[132]

> The phrase "in aid of its jurisdiction" was added to conform to [the All Writs Statute] and to make clear the recognized power of the Federal courts to stay proceedings in State cases removed to the district courts.

The Supreme Court's interpretation of this exception has not greatly elucidated the concept of "in aid of its jurisdiction:"[133]

> First, a federal court does not have inherent power to ignore the limitations of § 2283 and to enjoin state court proceedings merely because those proceedings interfere with a protected federal right or invade an area preempted by federal law, even when the interference is unmistakably clear . . . . Second, if the district court does have jurisdiction, it is not enough that the requested injunction is related to that jurisdiction, but it must be necessary to prevent a state court from so interfering with a federal court's consideration or disposition of a case as to seriously impair the federal court's flexibility and authority to decide that case.

Indeed, it is difficult to say exactly when and in what situations the "necessary in aid of jurisdiction" exception will apply. It does not apply simply because the federal court has exclusive jurisdiction,[134] nor in the case of simultaneous duplicative litigation in both federal and state courts (unless the proceedings are *in rem*).[135] There is some suggestion that it applies to certain duplicative mass tort litigation.[136] The Supreme Court has not yet considered the applicability of the "in

---

[130] Mitchum v. Foster, 407 U.S. 225, 234 (1972); *see generally* Ch. 6, *Removal.*

[131] Atlantic Coast Line R.R. Co. v. Brotherhood of Locomotive Eng'rs, 398 U.S. 281, 295 (1970).

[132] *See* June 25, 1948, ch. 646, 62 Stat. 968, reprinted at 17 Moore's Federal Practice § 121App.05 (Matthew Bender 3d ed.); based on *former* § 265 of the Judicial Code of 1911 (Mar. 3, 1911, c. 231, § 265, 36 Stat. 1162), reprinted at 17 Moore's Federal Practice § 121App.03 (Matthew Bender 3d ed.).

[133] Atlantic Coast Line R.R. Co. v. Brotherhood of Locomotive Eng'rs, 398 U.S. 281, 294–295 (1970).

[134] 398 U.S. at 294–295.

[135] 398 U.S. at 295.

[136] Battle v. Liberty Nat'l Life Ins. Co., 877 F.2d 877, 882 (11th Cir. 1989) (lengthy, complex class action suit is much like res to be administered); *In re* Agent Orange Product Liability Litigation, 996 F.2d 1425, 1432 (2d Cir. 1993) (district court's intervention was in aid of its continuing jurisdiction over Agent Orange federal class action, not only to administer settlement fund, but also to ensure that settlement agreement as whole was enforced according to its terms); Carlough v. Amchem Prods., Inc., 10 F.3d 189, 204 (3d Cir. 1993) ("At this mature phase of settlement proceedings and after years of pre-trial negotiations, mass opting-out of . . . plaintiffs clearly would be disruptive to the district court'scourt's ongoing settlement management and would jeopardize the settlement's fruition"); Wesch v. Folsom, 6 F.3d 1465, 1472–1473 (11th Cir. 1993) (district court invested time and other resources in arduous task of reapportioning state's congressional districts, and state court claims were "substantially similar" to those before federal court); *In re* Baldwin United Corp., 770 F.2d 328, 336–338 (2d Cir. 1985) (in consolidated multidistrict securities litigation consisting of over 100 lawsuits against several defendants, after settlement but prior to entry of final judgment, officials from several different states made known

aid of jurisdiction" exception as it applies to parallel duplicative complex litigation.

### [b] Application of the Exception

#### [i] Removal Actions

As early as 1874, federal courts recognized removal as an expressly authorized congressional exception, and most courts continue to treat removal as falling within the "expressly authorized" exception to the Anti-Injunction Act.[137] There is some rationale, however, for treating removal cases as falling within the "necessary in aid of jurisdiction" exception. The Reviser's Note states that "[t]he phrase 'in aid of jurisdiction' was added . . . to make clear the recognized power of the federal courts to stay proceedings in State cases removed to the district courts."[138] Nonetheless, federal courts rarely have applied this exception to removed cases.[139]

#### [ii] Exclusive Federal Jurisdiction

Exclusive federal jurisdiction over a matter is not in itself sufficient to bring a case within the "necessary in aid of jurisdiction" exception to the Anti-Injunction Act's prohibition. Even when a state court invades a field Congress has preempted and the state court is wholly without jurisdiction, the district court may not invoke this exception.[140] State court proceedings normally should continue unimpaired by federal court intervention. Litigants may seek relief from state court errors in the state appellate courts and, if there is federal jurisdiction over an issue in the case, in the United States Supreme Court.[141] However, when Congress specifically vests exclusive jurisdiction in a federal agency with express authorization to enforce its orders in federal court, an injunction properly may issue in aid of jurisdiction to enforce an agency order.[142] In *Capital Service v. N.L.R.B.*, the NLRB brought suit in federal court to enjoin an employer from enforcing a state court injunction against union picketing in a labor controversy. The federal district court found that the union's conduct was subject to the Board's exclusive jurisdiction under Section 10(b) of the National Labor Relations Act, and that the state court action in granting the injunction invaded the Board's and the district court'scourt's exclusive jurisdiction.[143]

The Supreme Court, however, limited it's *Capital Service* holding the following

---

their intention to commence proceedings against some of defendants based on same claims).

[137] Vendo Co. v. Lektro-Vend Corp., 433 U.S. 623, 640–641 (1977); Mitchum v. Foster, 407 U.S. 225, 234–237 (1972); French v. Hay, 89 U.S. (22 Wall.) 250 (1875).

[138] 28 U.S.C. § 2283 (Reviser's Note, 1948).

[139] *See* Hyde Park Partners L.P. v. Connolly, 839 F.2d 837, 842 (1st Cir. 1988) (state court issued orders on case that was subsequently removed and district court invalidated or enjoined enforcement of those orders).

[140] Amalgamated Clothing Workers of Am. v. Richman Bros., 348 U.S. 511, 515 (1955).

[141] Atlantic Coast Line R.R. Co. v. Brotherhood of Locomotive Eng'rs, 398 U.S. 281, 296 (1970).

[142] Capital Serv., Inc. v. NLRB, 347 U.S. 501, 504–505 (1954); Amalgamated Clothing Workers of Am. v. Richman Bros., 348 U.S. 511, 519–520 (1955).

[143] Capital Serv., Inc. v. NLRB, 347 U.S. 501, 505 (1954).

year in *Amalgamated Clothing Workers of Am. v. Richman Brothers* by indicating that *Capital Service* was decided under the "expressly authorized" exception, rather than the "necessary in aid of jurisdiction" exception.[144] In *Amalgamated Clothing Workers*, the Court held that a private cause of action seeking injunction of state proceedings regarding union conduct under § 10(b) did not come within the Anti-Injunction Act's "expressly authorized exception" because Congress explicitly gave jurisdiction to the district courts only on behalf of the NLRB on a petition by it.[145] Moreover, the case did not come within the "necessary in aid of jurisdiction" exception because the district court has no jurisdiction to enforce rights and duties that call for recognition by the NLRB.[146]

When Congress provides exclusive federal jurisdiction over Indian reservation gambling operations, a federal court may enjoin state court proceedings in aid of that jurisdiction. Because federal statutes mandate exclusive federal jurisdiction over criminal enforcement of state gaming laws in Indian country, state court proceedings are in derogation of federal jurisdiction. In such circumstances, state proceedings would violate federal-state comity, which the Anti-Injunction Act seeks to preserve. Therefore, a federal court may enjoin the state proceedings in order to preserve and aid federal jurisdiction.[147]

However, in a case brought by a member of an Indian tribe who was arrested on the reservation for allegedly violating New York cigarette tax laws, a federal district court declined to follow the Ninth Circuit precedent holding that Indian tribes may sue in federal court to enjoin state court proceedings. The district court distinguished those cases on the ground that they involved Indian tribes, rather than an individual member of a tribe.[148]

### [iii] Simultaneous Duplicative Litigation

The Supreme Court addressed the matter of simultaneous duplicative litigation in *Atlantic Coast Line R.R. Co. v. Brotherhood of Locomotive Engineers*.[149] The Court, relying on historical background and principles of federalism, found that state and federal courts were meant to have concurrent jurisdiction and neither system might prevent parties from simultaneously pursuing identical claims in different courts.

The "necessary in aid of jurisdiction" exception does not permit federal courts to enjoin state court proceedings merely because the state proceedings simultaneously duplicate the federal action.[150] The mere existence of a parallel action in state court does not constitute the level of interference necessary to

---

144 Amalgamated Clothing Workers of Am. v. Richman Bros., 348 U.S. 511, 515 (1955).

145 348 U.S. at 516–519.

146 348 U.S. at 519–521.

147 Sycuan Band of Mission Indians v. Roache, 54 F. 3d 535, 540–541 (9th Cir. 1994).

148 Bess v. Spitzer, 459 F. Supp. 2d 191, 202 (E.D.N.Y. 2006).

149 Atlantic Coast Line R.R. Co. v. Brotherhood of Locomotive Eng'rs, 398 U.S. 281, 295 (1970).

150 398 U.S. at 295; Standard Microsystems, Corp. v. Tex. Instruments, Inc., 916 F.2d 58, 60–61 (2d Cir. 1990) (identical actions brought in successive days in two different courts disputing interpretation of contract may proceed concurrently).

permit injunctive relief under the "necessary in aid of jurisdiction" exception to the Anti-Injunction Act.[151] Despite the general rule permitting simultaneous duplicative litigation, the federal courts traditionally have made an exception for concurrent *in rem* actions.[152] Concurrent *in personam* actions have been afforded much greater freedom to proceed independently, without federal interference in the state court proceedings.[153]

The "necessary in aid of jurisdiction" exception applies only when the federal court's flexibility and authority to decide a case are seriously impaired by the parallel state court proceeding. Thus, if a state court action is not filed until after a federal action has concluded, the state court action cannot be enjoined based on this exception. Under those circumstances, there can be no interference with the federal court's exercise of its jurisdiction, even if the state court action results in a judgment that conflicts with the settlement or judgment in the federal action.[154]

### [iv] The *In Rem* Exception

A federal court may issue an injunction in aid of its jurisdiction if that injunction is "necessary to prevent a state court from so interfering with a federal court's consideration or disposition of a case as to seriously impair the federal court's flexibility and authority to decide that case."[155] Federal courts have interpreted this standard to permit an injunction when federal and state proceedings involve the same *res*, or when parallel proceedings both are *in rem* or *quasi in rem*.[156] The *in rem* exception is well-settled. Even in *Toucey v. New York Life Insurance Co.*, the Supreme Court's narrowest interpretation of the Anti-Injunction Act exceptions, the Court recognized the *res* exception.[157] Federal courts continue to find the narrow *res* exception included within the Anti-Injunction Act's "in aid of jurisdiction" exception.[158] *In rem* actions that also seek to establish personal liability are governed by the rules governing parallel in *in rem* actions, when results depend on the property being delivered.[159]

When a conflict arises between federal and state *in rem* jurisdiction and the same *res* is the subject of both actions (which each court must control to provide relief), the court first assuming jurisdiction over the property may maintain and

---

151 Lou v. Belzberg, 834 F.2d 730, 740 (9th Cir. 1987).

152 Toucey v. New York Life Ins. Co., 314 U.S. 118, 135 (1941).

153 Moses H. Cone Memorial Hosp. v. Mercury Constr. Corp., 460 U.S. 1, 21–22 (1983).

154 Sandpiper Village v. Louisiana-Pacific, 428 F.3d 831, 848–47 (9th Cir. 2005) (injunction of state court proceedings on ground they would interfere with federal class action settlement did not fall within first exception because class action was resolved years before state action was filed).

155 Atlantic Coast Line R.R. Co. v. Brotherhood of Locomotive Eng'rs, 398 U.S. 281, 295 (1970).

156 Garcia v. Bauza-Salas, 862 F.2d 905, 909 (1st Cir. 1988). Actions in rem are discussed in Ch. 7, *Personal Jurisdiction in Federal Courts*.

157 Toucey v. New York Life Ins. Co., 314 U.S. 118, 135–136 (1941).

158 Hyde Constr. Co. v. Koehring, 388 F.2d 501, 508 (10th Cir.) (res exception falls within umbrella of "in aid of jurisdiction" provision of Anti-Injunction Act).

159 United States v. Bank of N. Y. & Trust Co., 296 U.S. 463, 463 (1936); Bennett v. Medtronic, Inc., 285 F.3d 801, 805–07 (9th Cir. 2002).

exercise that jurisdiction to the exclusion of the other.[160] Therefore, a federal court may issue an injunction against state proceedings to protect its *in rem* jurisdiction when the federal court acquires jurisdiction before the state court and the state proceedings interfere with the control and disposition of the *res*.[161] This exception to the Anti-Injunction Act applies only when the federal court acquires jurisdiction before the state court.[162]

When state court jurisdiction attaches first, the federal court is precluded from exercising jurisdiction over the same *res*.[163] This is true even if the United States is the plaintiff in the second federal action, and the United States ordinarily is entitled to have its claims determined in federal court.[164]

Pursuant to principles of intersystem comity and federalism, state and federal courts must respect each system's prior *in rem* jurisdiction. Thus, a federal court must respect and not interfere with a state court's prior *in rem* jurisdiction. A federal court must obey a state court injunction forbidding further federal proceedings with reference to the *res*.[165] After finding that a state court has prior *in rem* jurisdiction, a federal court should ordinarily abstain.[166] The superior *in rem* jurisdiction is exclusive only so far as necessary for the appropriate control and disposition of the property, and to avoid unseemly conflict. Moreover, exclusive *in rem* jurisdiction does not deprive the excluded court of power to make orders, including orders relating to the property, that do not violate the other court's exclusive right of control.[167]

In *Princess Lida v. Thompson*, the Supreme Court held that the *in rem* exception is not restricted to cases in which property is actually seized before commencement of a second suit. The exception applies as well in litigation to marshal assets, administer trusts, or liquidate estates, and in similar suits in which

---

[160] Donovan v. City of Dallas, 377 U.S. 408, 412 (1964) ("in cases where a court has custody of property, that is, proceedings in rem or quasi in rem . . . the state or federal court having custody of such property has exclusive jurisdiction to proceed"); James v. Bellotti, 733 F.2d 989, 993 (1st Cir. 1984) (relying on precedents of Penn Gen. Casualty Co. v. Pennsylvania ex rel. Schnader, 294 U.S. 189, 195 (1935) and Kline v. Burke Const. Co., 260 U.S. 226, 235 (1922)).

[161] Hyde Constr. Co., 388 F.2d at 508 (res exception falls within the umbrella of "in aid of jurisdiction" provision of Anti-Injunction Act).

[162] Trustees of Carpenters' Health & Welfare v. Darr, 694 F.3d 803, 811 (7th Cir. 2012) ("[N]ecessary in aid of . . . jurisdiction" exception inapplicable because state suit preceded federal suit).

[163] Kline v. Burke Const. Co., 260 U.S. 226, 229 (1922).

[164] United States v. Bank of New York & Trust Co., 296 U.S. 463, 463 (1935).

[165] *See* Princess Lida v. Thompson, 305 U.S. 456, 466 (1939) (court may not exercise jurisdiction over action if another court in previously filed action is exercising control over property at issue, and second court must exercise control over same property); Dailey v. National Hockey League, 987 F.2d 172, 176 (3d Cir. 1993) (*Princess Lida* doctrine is mechanical rule that requires federal court to yield its jurisdiction).

[166] *See* Moses H. Cone Memorial Hosp. v. Mercury Constr. Corp., 460 U.S. 1, 21–22 (1983); Colorado River Water Conservation Dist. v. United States, 424 U.S. 800, 819 (1976); *see generally* Ch. 13, *The Abstention Doctrine*.

[167] First Charter Land Corp. v. Fitzgerald, 643 F.2d 1011, 1015 (4th Cir. 1981) (order appointing property receiver or custodian is not invalid and non-controlling court may make further orders directing appointee to make certain dispositions of property when controlling court relinquishes it).

a court must control the property.[168] Actual possession of the *res* is not necessary to confer exclusive jurisdiction. Thus, if a prior suit is explicitly directed to a certain *res* and a court cannot proceed effectively without control of it, the action's pendency gives exclusive jurisdiction even against a later court that obtains actual possession.[169] Priority may depend on actual possession of the *res*, however, if the two actions are different, the courts are not asserting concurrent jurisdiction, or the prior complaint does not create constructive possession.[170]

### [v] Exception Does Not Apply to *In Personam* Proceedings

Federal courts carefully distinguish cases *in rem*, in which federal courts may issue an injunction, and cases *in personam*, in which a federal court may not issue an injunction (unless another exception applies). In *Kline v. Burke Construction Co.*, an early case interpreting the *in rem* exception, the Supreme Court stated:[171]

> [A] Controversy is not a thing, and a controversy over a mere question of personal liability does not involve the possession or control of a thing, and an action brought to enforce such a liability does not tend to impair or defeat the jurisdiction of the court in which a prior action for the same cause is pending. Each court is free to proceed in its own way and in its own time, without reference to the proceedings in the other court.

The *Kline* rule remains valid law. With certain narrow exceptions, the *res* exception applies only when both the state and federal actions are *in rem*, and both jurisdictions acquire control and disposition of the same *res*. If one action is *in personam*, the conflict does not exist.[172] Similarly, concurrent *in personam* actions between the same parties and involving the same subject matter may proceed simultaneously in the courts of the same forum or two or more forums. Concurrent *in personam* jurisdiction does not satisfy the "necessary in aid of jurisdiction" exception to the Anti-Injunction Act.[173]

Federal courts may not enjoin further prosecution of a pending *in personam* state action absent a showing that the case falls within one of the Anti-Injunction Act's three stated exceptions.[174] However, despite the restriction on enjoining state *in personam* proceedings under the "in aid of jurisdiction" exception, federal courts sometimes use the exception to enjoin parallel state class action proceedings that

---

[168] Princess Lida v. Thompson, 305 U.S. 456, 466–467 (1939).

[169] Bryan v. Speakman, 53 F.2d 463, 466 (5th Cir. 1932).

[170] Penn Gen. Casualty Co., 294 U.S. at 195; SEC v. Wencke, 622 F.2d 1363, 1371–1372 (9th Cir. 1980).

[171] Kline v. Burke Const. Co., 260 U.S. 226, 229–230 (1922).

[172] *See* Estate of Brennan v. Church of Scientology Flag, 645 F.3d 1267, 1274 (11th Cir. 2011); *In re* Prudential Ins. Co. of Am., 261 F.3d 355, 365 (3d Cir. 2001) ("aid of jurisdiction" exception usually applied only to parallel state *in rem* rather than *in personam* actions); Winkler v. Eli Lilly & Co., 101 F.3d 1196, 1202 (7th Cir. 1996).

[173] *See* Moses H. Cone Memorial Hosp. v. Mercury Constr. Corp., 460 U.S. 1, 21–22 (1983).

[174] *See* Atlantic Coast Line R.R. Co. v. Brotherhood of Locomotive Eng'rs, 398 U.S. 281, 286–287 (1970).

might jeopardize a complex federal settlement,[175] and state *in personam* proceedings that threaten to make complex multidistrict litigation unmanageable.[176] Moreover, a state court may never enjoin a federal court *in personam* action, even if the state court was the first to acquire jurisdiction.[177]

### [vi] Mischaracterization of Nature of Jurisdiction

In general, litigants may not invoke the *in rem* exception by cleverly characterizing the nature or jurisdiction of their claims. Most federal courts reject such attempts to mischaracterize *in personam* proceedings as *in rem* proceedings.[178] However, recently, some federal courts have been willing to apply the *in rem* exception more broadly.[179] Federal courts, especially in class actions and mass tort litigation, have suggested that the action itself is a kind of *res*, requiring federal injunctive power over state proceedings in aid of the federal court's jurisdiction.

### [vii] Class Actions and Complex Multidistrict Litigation

Although ordinarily the "necessary in aid of jurisdiction" exception does not apply to *in personam* proceedings, federal courts have applied the exception to enjoin parallel state court actions that threaten the management of complex federal litigation. For example, the First Circuit has applied the "in aid of jurisdiction" exception to school desegregation cases when conflicting orders threatened ongoing federal oversight.[180] Similarly, federal courts have applied the "in aid of jurisdiction" exception to consolidated multidistrict litigation when a parallel state proceeding threatens the court's ability to manage the litigation effectively.[181]

In addition, federal courts are increasingly willing to use the "necessary in aid of jurisdiction" exception to enjoin duplicative state class action proceedings, especially when the parallel state proceedings might jeopardize complex federal settlements. Federal courts also rely on the All Writs Statute, either alone or in conjunction with the Anti-Injunction Act's "in aid of jurisdiction" exception, to

---

[175] *See* Battle v. Liberty Nat'l Life Ins. Co., 877 F.2d 877, 882 (11th Cir. 1989).

[176] *See* Winkler v. Eli Lilly & Co., 101 F.3d 1196, 1201–1203 (7th Cir. 1996).

[177] Donovan v. City of Dallas, 377 U.S. 408, 411–414 (1964).

[178] *See, e.g.*, Phillips v. Chas. Schreiner Bank, 894 F.2d 127, 132 (5th Cir. 1990) (petitioner's "inventive argument" that claims against lender with debt secured by property constituted in rem exception rejected because lawsuit was ordinary in personam action); Mass. Casualty Ins. Co. v. Renstrom, 831 F. Supp. 1088, 1089–1090 (D.C.N.Y. 1993) (disability insurance policy, for purposes of suit seeking to recover under policy was not res to be administered by court).

[179] *See, e.g.*, *In re* Agent Orange Prod. Liab. Litig., 996 F.2d 1425, 1432 (2d Cir. 1993) (district court's intervention necessary to administer settlement fund and ensure that settlement agreement is adequately enforced).

[180] *See* Garcia v. Bauza-Salas, 862 F.2d 905, 909 (1st Cir. 1988).

[181] *See, e.g.*, Winkler v. Eli Lilly & Co., 101 F.3d 1196, 1201–1203 (7th Cir. 1996); Carlough v. Amchem Prods., Inc., 10 F.3d 189, 197 (3d Cir. 1993); *In re* Baldwin United Corp., 770 F.2d 328, 336 (2d Cir. 1985); *In re* Corrugated Container Antitrust Litig., 659 F.2d 1332, 1334–1335 (5th Cir. 1981).

justify enjoining duplicative state class action proceedings.[182]

Although some federal courts directly invoke the "in aid of" language, other federal courts have invoked the exception by analogizing the class action itself to a *res*, bringing the litigation within the *res* exception to the Act's prohibition.[183] In *Battle v. Liberty Nat. Life Ins. Co.*,[184] class members in a federal antitrust class action brought substantially similar claims in state court after final judgment was entered in the federal case. The Eleventh Circuit upheld an injunction as "necessary in aid of jurisdiction," reasoning that a lengthy, complex class action suit is much like a *res* to be administered. The court determined that the "necessary in aid of jurisdiction" exception is, in such a case, applicable to actions that are not technically *in rem*, and that the exception continues to apply after entry of final judgment.[185]

The Eleventh Circuit applied the same reasoning in *Juris v. Inamed Corp.*, which involved a federal class action against the manufacturer of silicone breast implants. The district court enjoined all members of the class from pursuing any state court claim covered by the federal settlement. The Eleventh Circuit held that this injunction fell within the "necessary in aid of [its] jurisdiction" exception to the Anti-Injunction Act because, as in *Battle*, the lengthy, complicated litigation over breast implants was the "virtual equivalent of a res."[186]

Federal courts have invoked the *in rem* exception to restrain parallel duplicative state asbestos litigation. In *Carlough v. Amchem Products*, a federal asbestos class action, a federal district court enjoined several dissident class plaintiffs from prosecuting a duplicative state class action. Relying on both the Anti-Injunction Act and the All Writs Statute, the Third Circuit upheld an injunction of the state proceedings, concluding that the federal class settlement was imminent after years of negotiations, the plaintiff class members had been afforded a reasonable opportunity to opt-out of the class, and the plaintiffs were trying to use the state suit to challenge the federal settlement. The court found that "at this mature phase of the settlement proceedings and after years of pre-trial negotiations, a mass opting-out of . . . plaintiffs would be disruptive to the district court's ongoing

---

182 *See, e.g.*, *In re* Agent Orange Product Liability Litigation, 996 F.2d 1425, 1432 (2d Cir. 1993) (removal of state case authorized by All Writs Statute); Carlough v. Amchem Prods., Inc., 10 F.3d 189, 204 (3d Cir. 1993) (injunction proper under All Writs Statute and Anti-Injunction Statute); *In re* Baldwin United Corp., 770 F.2d 328, 336–338 (2d Cir. 1985) (All Writs Statute and Anti-Injunction Act permitted injunction of suits by state officials in aid of federal court's jurisdiction over consolidated multidistrict securities litigation of over 100 lawsuits against several defendants).

183 *In re* Agent Orange Product Liability Litigation, 996 F.2d 1425, 1432 (2d Cir. 1993) (district court's removal of state case did not violate Anti-Injunction Act because removal was in aid of court's continuing jurisdiction over Agent Orange federal class action, not only to administer settlement fund, but also to ensure that settlement agreement as whole was enforced according to its terms); Battle v. Liberty Nat'l Life Ins. Co., 877 F.2d 877, 882 (11th Cir. 1989) (lengthy, complex class action suit is much like a res to be administered); *In re* Baldwin United Corp., 770 F.2d 328, 336–338 (2d Cir. 1985) ("the district court had before it a class action proceeding so far advanced that it was the virtual equivalent of a res over which the district judge required full control").

184 Battle v. Liberty Nat'l Life Ins. Co., 877 F.2d 877, 882 (11th Cir. 1989).

185 877 F.2d at 881–882.

186 Juris v. Inamed Corp., 685 F.3d 1294, 1339 (11th Cir. 2012).

settlement management and would jeopardize the settlement's fruition."[187]

The Third Circuit also has upheld an injunction to protect its jurisdiction, enjoining commencement or prosecution of a parallel state court action in another complex multidistrict class action. The action was against a diet drug manufacturer and involved a substantial number of claimants from multiple districts. The challenged injunction enjoined only an attempted mass opt-out that unquestionably interfered with the federal suit. However, individual plaintiffs were still permitted to opt-out.[188]

In *Wesch v. Folsom*, a federal court enjoined a simultaneous state proceeding in which the plaintiff class asserted claims regarding congressional redistricting substantially similar to those previously decided in a federal action. The court applied the "in aid of jurisdiction" exception even though all elements of *res judicata* were present, so that the relitigation exception would apply. The Third Circuit upheld the injunction, finding that the lengthy and complicated prior class action was the equivalent of a *res*, and the district court was merely exercising its continuing jurisdiction over that *res* in enjoining a state court suit filed after entry of judgment.[189]

## [3] Third Exception: "To Protect or Effectuate Federal Court Judgments" — The Relitigation Exception

### [a] Function of Exception

A federal court may issue an injunction to stay state court proceedings to protect or effectuate a federal court's judgment.[190] This exception, known as the relitigation exception, allows a party with a favorable federal judgment to protect that judgment by enjoining repetitive state court proceedings rather than relying on a plea of *res judicata*. The purpose of the exception is to prevent relitigation of matters that a federal court has fully adjudicated, and to prevent the harassment of successful federal litigants through repetitious state litigation. *Fully adjudicated* means actually decided.[191]

A federal court may enjoin any further state proceedings that attempt to relitigate previously adjudged matters, or that may impair the prior judgment's effect.[192] The injunction, however, may not exceed the bounds of matters that the federal court determined in the prior proceeding.[193]

---

187 *See* Carlough v. Amchem Prods., Inc., 10 F.3d 189, 204 (3d Cir. 1993).

188 *In re* Diet Drugs, 282 F.3d 220, 233–239 (3d Cir. 2002).

189 *See* Wesch v. Folsom, 6 F.3d 1465, 1472–1473 (11th Cir. 1993).

190 28 U.S.C. § 2283.

191 *See* Atlantic Coast Line R.R. Co. v. Brotherhood of Locomotive Eng'rs, 398 U.S. 281, 293.

192 *See* G.C. and K.B. Investments, Inc. v. Wilson, 326 F.3d 1096, 1106–07 (9th Cir. 2003); Rutledge v. Scott Chotin, Inc., 972 F.2d 820, 825 (7th Cir. 1992).

193 Next Level Communs. L.P. v. DSC Communs. Corp., 179 F.3d 244, 249–50 (5th Cir. 1999); Rath v. Gallup, Inc. 51 F.3d 791, 793 (8th Cir. 1994) (federal court determination that plaintiff was not

### [b] Scope of the Exception

Federal courts generally have applied the relitigation exception strictly and narrowly, with every benefit of the doubt going to the state court, and congruent with principles of *res judicata* and collateral estoppel.[194] The Supreme Court in *Smith v. Bayer Corp.* determined that the preclusive effect of a court's judgment is usually the prerogative of the second court, not the court that issued the judgment. Issuing an injunction pursuant to the relitigation exception amounts to "resorting to heavy artillery."[195]

The relitigation exception applies only when the issue decided by the federal court is the same as the issue to be decided by the state court.[196] The requirement of identical issues is illustrated in *Smith v. Bayer Corp.* Smith involved two proposed class actions against a single defendant, one proceeding in a West Virginia state court and the other proceeding in federal district court. The substantive claims in the two cases broadly overlapped, and the plaintiffs sought certification of the same class in each case. The federal district court denied class certification. Based on that denial, the defendant obtained an order from the same district court enjoining the West Virginia court from considering a class certification motion. The Eighth Circuit affirmed, holding that the injunction fell within the relitigation exception.[197] The Supreme Court reversed the Eighth Circuit's judgment, holding that the district court had exceeded its authority under that exception.[198]

The *Smith* Court reasoned that the class certification issue the state court was enjoined from deciding was not the same as the class certification issue that had been decided by the federal district court. In the federal case, the judge declined to certify the class under Federal Rule of Civil Procedure 23 because individual issues of fact concerning the harm to each plaintiff predominated over issues common to all members of the proposed class. The plaintiff in *Smith* sought certification of the same class, but because *Smith* was in state court, the propriety of certification was to be decided under West Virginia Rule 23 rather than Federal Rule 23. Although the two rules were worded virtually identically, the legal standards applied by West Virginia courts under its class action rule were different than those applied in federal courts, particularly with respect to the predominance requirement. Therefore, the Court concluded, the West Virginia court in *Smith* was not faced with the same legal question that had been resolved by the federal district court, and the district court's denial of class certification did not preclude the state's consideration

terminated for bringing ERISA claim did not permit injunction of state action seeking damages for wrongful termination in general).

194 Atlantic Coast Line R.R. Co. v. Brotherhood of Locomotive Eng'rs, 398 U.S. 281, 287 (1970).

195 Smith v. Bayer Corp., 131 S. Ct. 2368, 180 L. Ed. 2d 341 (2011); Atlantic Coast Line R.R. Co. v. Brotherhood of Locomotive Eng'rs, 398 U.S. 281, 287 (1970).

196 Smith v. Bayer Corp., *id.* (injunction inappropriate because issues were not the same); Wyly v. Weiss, 697 F.3d 131, 141–42 (2d Cir. 2012) (district court's order enjoining state court legal malpractice action permissible where malpractice rule identical to New York's).

197 *In re* Baycol Prods. Litig, 593 F.3d 716, 724 (2010), vacated by, remanded by, McCollins v. Bayer Corp. (*In re* Baycol Prods. Litig.), 2011 U.S. App. LEXIS 26708 (8th Cir. Minn. Aug. 4, 2011).

198 Smith v. Bayer, 131 S. Ct. 2368, 180 L. Ed. 2d 341 (2011).

of the class certification motion in *Smith*.[199]

The relitigation exception applies only when the parties to the state proceedings were parties to the federal proceeding or fall within one of the few exceptions to the general rule against binding nonparties.[200] In *Smith*, the Court held that the relitigation exception did not apply because the plaintiff in the state court case did not have the requisite connection to the federal case. The Court explained that subject to a few discrete, limited exceptions, as a fundamental general rule, only parties can be bound by prior judgments.[201]

### [c] Relationship to Res Judicata and Collateral Estoppel

The Supreme Court's 1988 majority opinion in *Chick Kam Choo v. Exxon Corp.* indicated that before a federal court may enjoin subsequent state proceedings, the parties in the federal suit must have actually disputed the issue, and the federal trier of fact must actually have resolved it.[202] In determining whether the relitigation exception applies, federal courts often have looked to the principles underlying *res judicata*. Indeed, the Supreme Court in *Chick Kam Choo* expressly noted that the relitigation exception is "founded in the well-recognized concepts of *res judicata* and collateral estoppel."[203]

Nonetheless, most federal courts have interpreted the exception far more narrowly than the doctrine of *res judicata* (which prohibits relitigation of all claims that were or could have been litigated in the earlier proceeding),[204] and more akin to collateral estoppel (which applies only to issues actually litigated).[205] The relitigation exception permits a federal court to enjoin state proceedings only as to those issues that federal courts have fully and finally decided.[206] This is consistent with the purposes of the Anti-Injunction Act, to respect comity and ensure the effectiveness and supremacy of federal law. As the Tenth Circuit explained, when a federal court affirmatively decides an issue, that decision is entitled to respect and finality. In contrast, when a federal court has not passed on a specific claim, the main concern raised by subsequent state litigation is harassment of the opposing party. This, then, is the province of *res judicata*, which a party is free to raise in a

---

199 *Id.*

200 *Id.*

201 *Id.*; Sandpiper Village v. Louisiana-Pacific, 428 F.3d 831, 848–49 (9th Cir. 2005) (state court action could not be enjoined under relitigation exception because party to state court action was not named party in federal class action and was not member of nationwide class, nor were his interests sufficiently parallel to class members' interests that privity could be implied).

202 Chick Kam Choo v. Exxon Corp., 486 U.S. 140, 148 (1988).

203 486 U.S. at 147.

204 *See* Restatement (Second) of Judgments § 24(1) (1982); *see generally* 18 Moore's Federal Practice Ch. 131, *Claim Preclusion and Res Judicata* (Matthew Bender 3d ed.).

205 *See* Jones v. The St. Paul Cos., Inc., 495 F.3d 888,892–94 (8th Cir. 2007) (joining majority of circuits, limiting relitigation exception to claims actually litigated in federal court); Vasquez v. Bridgestone/Firestone, Inc., 325 F.3d 665, 675–680 (5th Cir. 2003); Restatement (Second) of Judgments § 27 (1982); *see generally* 18 Moore's Federal Practice Ch. 132, *Issue Preclusion and Collateral Estoppel* (Matthew Bender 3d ed.).

206 486 U.S. at 148.

subsequent state proceeding and which state courts are presumed competent to resolve.[207]

The *Chick Kam Choo* decision, however, failed to distinguish between principles of *res judicata* and collateral estoppel — a lack of clarity that has engendered disparate lower court interpretations of *Chick Kam Choo*. Thus, although the Court did not directly hold that a claim must be actually litigated before the relitigation exception applies, several circuits have interpreted *Chick Kam Choo* to require actual litigation.[208]

Other federal courts, particularly the Ninth Circuit, have held that the relitigation exception applies both to issues actually litigated, and to matters that could have been litigated and are barred from relitigation by *res judicata*.[209] The Ninth Circuit concluded that any issue that has been "actually litigated" as contemplated by *Chick Kam Choo* would anyway be barred by collateral estoppel, thereby eliminating any need to rely on the principles of *res judicata*. This result, the court decided, would be contrary to the purposes of the Anti-Injunction Act as well as the Supreme Court's finding that the relitigation exception is based on the principles of both *res judicata* and collateral estoppel.[210] Therefore, if the prior federal decision "necessarily precludes" a certain result, an issue could thus be "decided" without having been actually litigated. Although the Ninth Circuit noted that five circuits apply the more limited "issues actually litigated" standard, the court interpreted *Chick Kam Choo* as holding that if "a prior federal decision 'necessarily precludes' a certain result, even if that result was not itself actually litigated, then an injunction is permissible under the relitigation exception."[211] The court therefore specifically disagreed with those circuits requiring issues to be actually litigated in a prior proceeding.

The Eleventh Circuit also applies the exception in the *res judicata* context. According to that court, the relitigation exception empowers a federal court to be the arbiter of the *res judicata* effects of its own judgment, permitting the litigant to seek an injunction from a federal court rather than having to argue the res judicata defense in state court.[212] The Fifth Circuit applies a four-part test to determine the

---

[207] Weyerhaeuser Co. v. Wyatt, 505 F.3d 1104, 1110 (10th Cir. 2007).

[208] *See, e.g.*, Kidder, Peabody & Co. v. Maxus Energy Corp., 925 F.2d 556, 565 (2d Cir. 1991) (federal court had not determined state damages issue that was covered under terms of injunction); Santopadre v. Pelican Homestead & Sav. Ass'n, 937 F.2d 268, 273 (5th Cir. 1991) (court may go beyond judgment and look to pleadings to determine issues actually litigated); Farias v. Bexar County Bd. of Trustees, 925 F.2d 866, 879–880 (5th Cir. 1991) ("what looks like the same rodeo in a different arena is really a different rodeo" for purposes of relitigation exception); Am. Town Ctr. v. Hall 83 Assoc., 912 F.2d 104, 112 (6th Cir. 1990) (court enjoined only those claims that were actually litigated); Staffer v. Bouchard Transp. Co., 878 F.2d 638, 642–644 (2d Cir. 1989) (injunction will issue as to only those claims that were actually litigated); Roth v. Bank of the Commonwealth, 583 F.2d 527, 536 (6th Cir. 1978) (injunction otherwise permissible is impermissible as to those issues earlier court did not actually decide).

[209] Western Sys., Inc. v. Ulloa, 958 F.2d 864, 869–870 (9th Cir. 1992) (*Chick Kam Choo* decision does not show that distinction between res judicata and collateral estoppel was really intended).

[210] 958 F.2d at 869–870.

[211] 958 F.2d at 870.

[212] Juris v. Inamed Corp., 685 F.3d 1294, 1340 (11th Cir. 2012) (application of relitigation exception is appropriate when consideration of state law claims would be precluded by doctrine of *res judicata*).

applicability of the relitigation exception, asking whether: (1) the parties in the subsequent suit are identical to (or at least in privity with) the parties in the earlier suit, (2) the judgment in the prior suit was rendered by a court of competent jurisdiction, (3) the prior suit was concluded with a judgment on the merits, and (4) the same claim or cause of action was involved in both suits.[213]

Finally, federal law determines the preclusive effect of a federal judgment.[214]

### [d] Need for Final Judgment

A case need not be fully and finally determined on its merits before the relitigation exception will permit federal injunction of state proceedings. Indeed, nothing in the relitigation exception "limits its scope to final judgments" and Congress, in enacting the modern Anti-Injunction Act, intended it to apply to interlocutory as well as to final decrees.[215] Nevertheless, the Fifth Circuit requires that the prior federal court suit have concluded with a final judgment on the merits.[216]

Although there is no decisive test for determining what constitutes a judgment, many courts follow the rule that a judgment is "a decree and any order from which an appeal lies," as defined in the Federal Rules of Civil Procedure.[217] This flexible approach permits protection of federal determinations that have been "fully adjudicated," including some interlocutory orders.[218]

A federal injunction may enjoin state court litigation of issues actually decided on their merits, but may not enjoin aspects of the state proceedings the federal court did not address.[219] At least one court has held that "the legislative policy that permits a federal court to enjoin state court action when a federal court has decided a suit on its substantive merits has equal force when a critical underlying issue unrelated to the substantive merits of the action has been litigated to finality."[220] Thus, a preliminary injunction may be a judgment for purposes of the relitigation exception if the federal court decided the issues sought to be enjoined in the state proceedings.[221]

---

[213] Moore v. State Farm Fire & Cas. Co., 556 F.3d 264, 273 (5th Cir. 2009).

[214] Semtek Int'l, Inc. v. Lockheed Martin Corp., 531 U.S. 497 (2001); *In re* Bridgestone/Firestone, Inc. Prod. Liab. Litig., 333 F.3d 763, 767–68 (7th Cir. 2003).

[215] Sperry Rand Corp. v. Rothlein, 288 F.2d 245, 248–249 (2d Cir. 1961).

[216] New York Life Ins. Co. v. Gillispie, 203 F.3d 384, 387 (5th Cir. 2000).

[217] Fed. R. Civ. P. 54(a).

[218] *See, e.g.*, Rutledge v. Scott Chotin, Inc., 972 F.2d 820, 824–825 (7th Cir. 1992) (exception applies to partial summary judgment that has been made final and appealable by Fed. R. Civ. P. 54(b) procedure); Henry v. First Nat'l Bank of Clarksdale, 595 F.2d 291, 306 (5th Cir. 1979) (exception applies to interlocutory rulings, such as preliminary injunctions, that are appealable as of right); Baker v. Gotz, 415 F. Supp. 1243, 1250–1251 (D.C. Del. 1976) (injunction permissible under relitigation exception when critical underlying issue unrelated to substantive merits of action has been litigated to finality).

[219] Vasquez v. Bridgestone/Firestone, Inc., 325 F.3d 665, 675–680 (5th Cir. 2003); Roth v. Bank of the Commonwealth, 583 F.2d 527, 536 (6th Cir. 1978), *cert. dismissed*, 442 U.S. 925 (1979).

[220] Baker v. Gotz, 415 F. Supp. 1243, 1250 (D.C. Del. 1976).

[221] NBA v. Minn. Professional Basketball, Ltd. Partnership, 56 F. 3d 866, 871–872 (8th Cir. 1995).

A federal court's dismissal of an action with prejudice is a complete adjudication of the pleaded issues and bars further action between the parties as to those issues.[222] This rule does not apply to dismissals on *forum non conveniens* grounds, because such dismissals are on procedural grounds only.[223] The relitigation exception generally does not encompass procedural rulings.[224] The Seventh Circuit has held that a federal court decision finding a nationwide class inappropriate precludes any putative class member from obtaining certification of a nationwide class in state court.[225] Because the preclusive effect of a judgment rendered by the federal court depends on federal rather than state law, the Seventh Circuit rejected the argument that unnamed class members should not be bound by the prior decision barring a nationwide class. The court explained that so long as absent class members are adequately represented by the named litigants and class counsel, they are bound by a decision made on an issue that was actually litigated and resolved.[226]

### [e] Relationship to Full Faith and Credit Act

A federal court may enjoin state proceedings to protect or effectuate its judgments only prior to a state court's determination of the *res judicata* effects of the federal judgment.[227] If litigants raise an issue in state court, and the state court determines that *res judicata* does not apply to the federal judgment, the federal court must give full faith and credit to the state court's decision. The Full Faith and Credit Act[228] requires federal courts to give state judicial proceedings "the same full faith and credit . . . as they have by law or usage in the courts of such State . . . from which they are taken."[229] Even if the state court's rejection of a *res judicata* defense is erroneous, the federal court may not enjoin the state proceedings under the relitigation exception.[230]

In *Parsons Steel, Inc. v. First Alabama Bank*, plaintiffs instituted a state court action alleging fraud and a federal court action alleging violations of the Bank Holding Company Act. Both actions alleged the same conduct by the same defendants, and the parties conducted joint discovery. The federal action proceeded to trial on the liability issue, before the state trial. The federal jury returned a favorable plaintiff's verdict, but the district court granted the defendant a judgment notwithstanding the verdict. After the court entered its judgment, the defendants pleaded that judgment as *res judicata* and collateral estoppel in the state action. The state court ruled that *res judicata* did not bar the state action. In the state case, the jury awarded the plaintiffs a substantial judgment and the defendants returned

---

222 Daewoo Elec. Corp. of Am. v. Western Auto Supply Co., 975 F.2d 474, 478 (8th Cir. 1992).

223 Vasquez v. Bridgestone/Firestone, Inc., 325 F.3d 665, 675–680 (5th Cir. 2003).

224 *See* Chick Kam Choo v. Exxon Corp., 486 U.S. 140, 148 (1988).

225 *In re* Bridgestone/Firestone, Inc. Prods. Liab. Litig., 333 F.3d 763, 769 (7th Cir. 2003).

226 *Id.*

227 Parsons Steel, Inc. v. First Ala. Bank, 474 U.S. 518, 519 (1986).

228 28 U.S.C. § 1738.

229 28 U.S.C. § 1738.

230 *See* Parsons Steel, Inc. v. First Ala. Bank, 474 U.S. 518, 519 (1986).

to federal court and obtained an injunction barring plaintiffs from further prosecuting the state action.

The Supreme Court reversed the federal court's issuance of the injunction. The Court held that "[i]t has long been established that [the Full Faith and Credit Act] does not allow federal courts to employ their own rules of *res judicata* in determining the effect of state judgments."[231] States are permitted to determine the preclusive effect of judgments in their own courts, and after the state court has done so, federal courts must accept the state's determination that there is no preclusion.[232]

A federal court may issue an injunction of state court proceedings despite a state court's ruling that *res judicata* does not apply to the federal judgment if the state court's ruling would not be given preclusive effect by other courts in the state. In that case, the federal court may determine the propriety of an injunction under the general principles of equity, comity, and federalism.[233] However, in exercising its discretion, a federal court should keep in mind that the purpose of the Anti-Injunction Act is to prevent friction between federal and state courts by barring federal intervention in all but the narrowest of circumstances. The federal court must apply state law in determining the preclusive effect of the state court's ruling.[234]

### [f] Timing Considerations

The relitigation exception permits federal injunction of state proceedings only when the state court has not yet ruled on the merits of the *res judicata* defense. Once a litigant raises and the state court determines the *res judicata* effect of a federal judgment, that determination binds the federal courts.[235] Thus, timing considerations are particularly important when seeking injunctive relief against state judicial proceedings under the Anti-Injunction Act's relitigation exception. Although a litigant might obtain an injunction of repetitive state court proceedings while those proceedings are pending, once the state court determines not to give preclusive effect to a federal judgment the federal court is bound by the state court's determination. The party denied preclusive effect must appeal the preclusion decision in state court.[236]

Thus, the full faith and credit doctrine creates a strong incentive for successful federal litigants to seek a federal injunction of repetitive state actions immediately, and to avoid litigation of the preclusion issue in state court. However, a party who participates in a state court action and delays requesting a federal stay is not precluded from obtaining this relief, unless the party intended to relinquish the right to an injunction (which would constitute a waiver), or the opposing party

---

[231] 474 U.S. at 523 (citing Kremer v. Chemical Constr. Corp. 456 U.S. 461, 481–482 (1982)).

[232] 474 U.S. at 523.

[233] Brother Records, Inc. v. Jardine, 432 F.3d 939, 944–45 (9th Cir. 2005).

[234] Bryan v. Bellsouth Communications, Inc., 492 F.3d 231, 240 (4th Cir. 2007); Brother Records, Inc., *id.*

[235] 474 U.S. at 524–525.

[236] 474 U.S. at 524–525.

reasonably and detrimentally relied on the delay (which could constitute an estoppel against the federal litigant).[237]

## § 12.04 EQUITABLE ENTITLEMENT FOR RELIEF

A party seeking a federal injunction of state proceedings must satisfy both the requirements of the Anti-Injunction Act and those for obtaining equitable relief — namely, irreparable injury and lack of an adequate remedy at law.[238] Moreover, even if a federal court may enjoin state proceedings under the Anti-Injunction Act, it is not required to do so.[239] A federal court's power to issue an injunction against state proceedings is discretionary and, in considering whether to exercise the power, federal courts must consider principles of "equity, comity and federalism."[240] Thus, courts may decline to issue an injunction on equitable grounds when parties seek an injunction in bad faith or to harass an opponent,[241] but in other cases the equitable limitations on federal injunctive power are not so clear.

The Supreme Court has advised federal courts to exercise caution in issuing injunctions, and to err in favor of permitting state courts proceedings.[242] Hence, before a federal court will issue an injunction, litigants generally must make a strong showing that the federal case fits within an exception and that adequate state court proceedings are unavailable.[243]

Generally, federal injunctions against state court proceedings are disfavored, especially in dual litigation involving the relitigation exception.[244] A complainant must make a strong and unequivocal showing of relitigation of the same issue in order to overcome the federal court's proper disinclination to intermeddle in state court proceedings. Some federal courts, however, do not require a showing of equitable entitlement if the case is within the relitigation exception.[245] As a discretionary ruling, a district judge's decision regarding an injunction against state proceedings is subject to an abuse of discretion standard of review. Appellate courts will not disturb a district court's decision regarding a federal litigant's equitable

---

[237] Samuel C. Ennis & Co. v. Woodmar Realty Co., 542 F.2d 45, 48 (7th Cir. 1976).

[238] Mitchum v. Foster, 407 U.S. 225, 245 (1972); *see* Amwest Mortgage Corp. v. Grady, 925 F.2d 1162, 1164 (9th Cir. 1991).

[239] Chick Kam Choo v. Exxon Corp., 486 U.S. 140, 151 (1988).

[240] Mitchum v. Foster, 407 U.S. 225, 229–230 (1972).

[241] *See* Royal Ins. Co. of Am. v. Quinn-L Capital Corp., 960 F.2d 1286, 1300–1301 (5th Cir. 1992) (injunction denied on grounds of bad faith).

[242] Vendo Co. v. Lektro-Vend Corp., 433 U.S. 623, 630 (1977).

[243] Merle Norman Cosmetics, Inc. v. Victa, 936 F.2d 466, 468 (9th Cir. 1991) (nothing prevented employer from raising defenses of res judicata and collateral estoppel in state court); Bechtel Petroleum, Inc. v. Webster, 796 F.2d, 252, 253 (9th Cir. 1986) (doubts should be resolved in favor of permitting state courts to proceed in orderly fashion to judgment); Int'l Ass'n of Machinists & Aerospace Workers v. Nix, 512 F.2d 125, 131 n.9 (5th Cir. 1975) (party could rely on defenses of res judicata and collateral estoppel); S. Cal. Petroleum Corp. v. Harper, 273 F.2d 715, 718–719 (5th Cir. 1960) (discretion should be exercised in light of historical reluctance of federal courts to interfere with state judicial proceedings).

[244] *See* Bechtel Petroleum, Inc. v. Webster, 796 F.2d, 252, 253 (9th Cir. 1986).

[245] *In re* Nat'l Student Marketing Litig., 655 F. Supp. 659, 663 (D.D.C. 1987) (injunction issued on showing that case fit within exception; no additional showing necessary).

entitlement to injunctive relief in absence of abuse of discretion.[246]

When a state has a strong protectable interest, a litigant who seeks an injunction must make a stronger showing of equitable entitlement before the federal court may issue an injunction under any of the Anti-Injunction Act exceptions.[247] Federal courts have required this stronger showing especially for litigants invoking the "expressly authorized by Act of Congress" exception. When a state is significantly involved in a litigation, a litigant seeking to enjoin the proceedings must show the possibility of great and immediate irreparable injury that cannot be eliminated by a defense to the state proceeding.[248]

## § 12.05 THE ANTI-INJUNCTION ACT AND DECLARATORY JUDGMENTS

### [1] Declaratory Judgments Under Declaratory Judgment Act

The availability of the federal declaratory judgment action presents an opportunity for litigants to engage in duplicative parallel state and federal court litigation. Defendants in state court proceedings often seek a federal declaratory judgment in a reactive federal lawsuit. As several courts have noted, a purpose of the Federal Declaratory Judgment Act[249] is to provide litigants a means of judicial relief when a dispute is not sufficiently developed to authorize traditional coercive relief.[250] Because a prior federal declaratory judgment may have preclusive effects on a parallel state proceeding, federal declaratory judgment actions may be similar in effect to federal injunctive actions. Alternatively, a successful federal litigant who obtains a favorable declaratory judgment may use that judgment as the basis to seek an injunction of parallel state proceedings.

Federal declaratory judgment jurisdiction is discretionary and partially based in equitable principles. Thus, while the Declaratory Judgment Act grants federal courts the power to declare the rights and legal relations of parties, federal courts may withhold such relief on equitable grounds.[251] In considering whether to grant such jurisdiction and relief, federal courts assess whether the parties are involved in pending state court proceedings that may resolve the controversy, and whether there are possible inequities in one action having precedence.[252]

---

[246] *In re* Prudential Ins. Co. of Am., 261 F.3d 355, 363 (3d Cir. 2001) (decision to issue injunction reviewed for abuse of discretion).

[247] Daewoo Elec. Corp. of Am. v. Western Auto Supply Co., 975 F.2d 474, 478–479 (8th Cir. 1992).

[248] Goodrich v. Supreme Court of S.D., 511 F.2d 316, 317 (8th Cir. 1975).

[249] 28 U.S.C. § 2201(a). For general discussion of declaratory judgments, see 12 Moore's Federal Practice Ch. 57, *Declaratory Judgment* (Matthew Bender 3d ed.).

[250] Tex. Employers' Ins. Ass'n v. Jackson, 862 F.2d 491, 505 (5th Cir. 1988).

[251] *See* Franchise Tax Bd. v. Constr. Laborers Vacation Trust, 463 U.S. 1, 19–22 (1983).

[252] Rowan Companies, Inc. v. Griffin, 876 F.2d 26, 29 (5th Cir. 1989).

## [2] Declaratory Relief as an Injunctive Surrogate

Litigants may not use a federal declaratory judgment action to circumvent Anti-Injunction Act restrictions. Federal plaintiffs may not use the declaratory judgment action for the specific purpose of defeating an underlying state suit, or evading a state court determination of *res judicata*.[253] The Supreme Court has recognized the possible intrusive nature of federal declaratory judgment actions in relation to independent state court proceedings:[254]

> [O]rdinarily a declaratory judgment will result in precisely the same interference with and disruption of state proceedings that the long-standing policy limiting injunctions was designed to avoid. This is true for at least two reasons. In the first place, the Declaratory Judgment Act provides that after a declaratory judgment is issued the district court may enforce it by granting '[f]urther necessary or proper relief,' 28 U.S.C. § 2202, and therefore a declaratory judgment issued while state proceedings are pending might serve as the basis for a subsequent injunction against those proceedings to 'protect or effectuate' the declaratory judgment, . . . and thus result in a clearly improper interference with the state proceedings. Secondly, even if the declaratory judgment is not used as a basis for actually issuing an injunction, the declaratory relief alone has virtually the same practical impact as a formal injunction would.

Lower federal courts consistently agree that a federal court may not grant declaratory relief when there is a possibility that the declaratory judgment will have the same effect as enjoining pending state court proceedings, in violation of the Anti-Injunction Act.[255] Some federal courts emphatically have rejected use of the declaratory judgment action as a means to avoid the constraints of the Anti-Injunction Act:[256]

> To allow declaratory relief in these circumstances would be to transform section 2283 from a pillar of federalism reflecting the fundamental constitutional independence of the states and their courts, to an anachronistic, minor technicality, easily avoided by mere nomenclature or procedural sleight of hand.[257] Although the Anti-Injunction Act does not by its terms prohibit federal courts from issuing declaratory judgments that affect state court proceedings,[258] the Act does prohibit "the perversion of the purpose of declaratory judgment legislation which occurs when it is used to anticipate the result of litigation pending in another forum."[259]

---

[253] Tex. Employer's Ins. Ass'n v. Jackson, 862 F.2d 491, 505 (5th Cir. 1988).

[254] Samuels v. Mackell, 401 U.S. 66, 72 (1971).

[255] *See* Sun Ref. & Mktg. Co. v. Brennan, 921 F.2d 635, 639–640 (6th Cir. 1990).

[256] *See* Tex. Employer's Ins. Ass'n v. Jackson, 862 F.2d 491, 506–508 (5th Cir. 1988); *see also* Sun Ref. & Mktg. Co. v. Brennan, 921 F.2d 635, 638–639 (6th Cir. 1990); Golden Challenger Marinera v. Spalieris, 795 F. Supp. 802, 804–805 (E.D. La. 1992).

[257] Tex. Employer's Ins. Ass'n v. Jackson, 862 F.2d 491, 502–505 (5th Cir. 1988).

[258] Gloucester Marine Rys. Corp. v. Charles Parisi Inc., 848 F.2d 12, 15 (1st Cir. 1988).

[259] H.J. Heinz Co. v. Owens, 189 F.2d 505, 508 (9th. Cir. 1951).

There are, however, certain limited circumstances in which a federal court will grant declaratory relief even if the Anti-Injunction Act would bar an injunction.[260]

## § 12.06 THE ANTI-INJUNCTION ACT AND THE ALL WRITS STATUTE

The All Writs Statute gives federal courts the power to issue "all writs necessary or appropriate in aid of their respective jurisdictions and agreeable to the usages and principles of law."[261] The Anti-Injunction Act embodies limitations on the broad equitable powers of federal courts to issue writs, as authorized in the All Writs Statute.[262] The two statutes are compatible, however, as both require a showing of equitable entitlement. The Anti-Injunction Act simply imposes additional limitations on federal court power to enjoin state court proceedings.[263] In accordance with a long-standing rule,[264] the All Writs Statute must be construed in conjunction with the Anti-Injunction Act.[265] However, the Anti-Injunction Act does not create an independent jurisdictional basis.[266]

Federal courts have relied on the All Writs Statute, either alone or in conjunction with the Anti-Injunction Act's "in aid of jurisdiction" exception, to justify enjoining duplicative state class action proceedings. In the context of complex class action litigation, a federal district court may remove and enjoin prosecution of subsequent state court claims under the All Writs Act to enforce its ongoing orders against relitigation and to guard the integrity of its prior rulings over which it expressly retained jurisdiction.[267] However, like the Anti-Injunction Act, the All Writs Act does not confer jurisdiction on federal courts, and cannot therefore confer the

---

260 Steffel v. Thompson, 415 U.S. 452, 460–462 (1974) (plaintiff was repeatedly threatened with criminal prosecution for engaging in conduct prohibited by state law and declaratory relief was measurably less coercive and intrusive on state action than injunction).

261 28 U.S.C. § 1651.

262 *In re* Diet Drugs, 282 F.3d 220, 233 (3d Cir. 2002); *In re* Prudential Ins. Co. of Am., 261 F.3d 355, 364–67 (3d Cir. 2001); Kelly v. Merrill Lynch, Pierce, Fenner & Smith, Inc., 985 F.2d 1067, 1069 (11th Cir. 1993) (Anti-Injunction Act carves out exception to All Writs Statute).

263 *See* Mitchum v. Foster, 407 U.S. 225, 242–243 (1972).

264 *See* Kline v. Burke Const. Co., 260 U.S. 226, 229–230 (1922).

265 *See* Hayes Indus., Inc. v. Caribbean Sales Assoc., Inc., 387 F.2d 498, 500 (1st Cir. 1968); Kelly v. Merrill Lynch, Pierce, Fenner & Smith, 985 F.2d 1067, 1069 (11th Cir. 1993).

266 Newby v. Enron Corp., 302 F.3d 295, 300–03 (5th Cir. 2002); Sprint Spectrum L.P. v. Mills, 283 F.3d 404, 413 (2d Cir. 2002).

267 Matter of VMS Secur. Litig., 103 F.3d 1317, 1323–1326 (7th Cir. 1996) (under All Writs Act, district court properly removed to federal court and enjoined class action suit brought in state court by investors alleging that Prudential Securities fraudulently induced them to participate in two class action settlements in federal district court; federal district court had expressly retained jurisdiction over implementation and enforcement of settlements); *In re* Agent Orange Product Liability Litigation, 996 F.2d 1425, 1432 (2d Cir. 1993) (removal of state case authorized by All Writs Statute); Carlough v. Amchem Prods., Inc., 10 F.3d 189, 204 (3d Cir. 1993) (injunction proper under All Writs Statute and Anti-Injunction Statute); *In re* Baldwin United Corp., 770 F.2d 328, 336–338 (2d Cir. 1985) (All Writs Statute and Anti-Injunction Act permitted injunction of suits by state officials in aid of federal court's jurisdiction over consolidated multidistrict securities litigation of over 100 lawsuits against several defendants).

original jurisdiction required to support removal.[268]

## § 12.07 THE TAX ANTI-INJUNCTION ACT

### [1] Function of Tax Anti-Injunction Act

The Tax Anti-Injunction Act provides that "The district courts shall not enjoin, suspend or restrain the assessment, levy or collection of any tax under State law where a plain, speedy and efficient remedy may be had in the courts of such State."[269] The Tax Anti-Injunction Act is rooted in equity, federalism, comity, and the need of states to administer their own fiscal operations.[270] The primary purpose of the Tax Anti-Injunction Act is to limit federal interference with the important local concern of tax collection.[271] Federal courts broadly construe the prohibition against issuing federal injunctions against state tax collection. The prohibition barring tax injunctions applies only to federal district courts; it does not apply to suits between states in the Supreme Court's original jurisdiction.[272]

### [2] Application of the Tax Anti-Injunction Act

#### [a] Definition of What Constitutes a Tax

Federal courts liberally define and broadly apply the term "tax" under the Act. The Act's prohibition against federal injunctions extends to any state or local taxes imposed by state law.[273] Federal courts have not developed a generally recognized test for determining whether a particular fee or assessment is characterized as a tax. The characterization of an assessment as a tax usually depends on whether it primarily raises revenue or regulates activity; an assessment is a tax if it primarily raises revenue.[274] The Act's prohibitions do not apply to regulations, even though they also may raise revenue.[275] In examining the revenue's ultimate use, courts generally ask whether the revenue provides a general benefit to the public, or provides more narrow benefits to regulated companies or defrays an agency's regulatory costs.[276]

---

[268] Syngenta Crop Prot., Inc. v. Henson, 537 U.S. 28 (2002); Newby v. Enron Corp., 302 F.3d 295, 300–03 (5th Cir. 2002).

[269] 28 U.S.C. § 1341 (last amended 1948 ch. 646, June 25, 1948).

[270] *See* Tully v. Griffin, 429 U.S. 68, 73 (1976).

[271] California Grace Brethren Church, 457 U.S. 393, 408–409 (1982).

[272] Maryland v. Louisiana, 451 U.S. 725, 745 n.21 (1981).

[273] *See* Alnoa G. Corp. v. City of Houston, 563 F.2d 769, 771 (5th Cir. 1977); Non-Resident Taxpayers Ass'n v. Municipality of Phila., 478 F.2d 456, 458 (3d Cir. 1973).

[274] Retail Industry Leaders Ass'n v. Fielder, 475 F.3d 180, 189 (4th Cir. 2007).

[275] Genon Mid-Atlantic, LLC v. Montgomery County, MD, 650 F.3d 1021, 1023 (4th Cir. 2011); Chamber of Commerce of the United States v. Edmondson, 594 F.3d 742, 763–64 (10th Cir. 2010).

[276] Empress Casino Joliet v. Balmoral Racing Club, 651 F.3d 722, 728 (7th Cir. 2011); Neinast v. Texas, 217 F.3d 275, 278 (5th Cir. 2000).

Thus, a charge is likely to be classified as a tax if (1) the revenues go into the general fund, (2) the charge is enacted by the legislature (as opposed to an administrative agency, (3) the charge is called a "tax" in the statute, and (4) the statute is administered by the tax assessor. The Seventh Circuit has disdained the use of open-ended, multifactor tests for determining whether an exaction is a tax. The court has concluded that the only material distinction is between exactions designed to generate revenue (taxes) and exactions designed to punish (fines) or to compensate for a service that the state provides to the persons or firms on which the exaction falls (fees). All other factors are irrelevant.[277]

Most circuits employ a three-factor test to determine whether an assessment is a tax or a regulatory fee: (1) the entity that imposes the assessment, (2) the parties on whom the assessment is imposed, and (3) whether the assessment is expended for general public purposes or used for the regulation or benefit of the parties on whom the assessment is imposed.[278]

In addition, courts generally look to the revenue's ultimate use, asking whether the revenue provides a general benefit to the public, or provides more narrow benefits to regulated companies or defrays an agency's regulatory costs.[279] The label a state legislature gives an assessment is not dispositive.[280] Many forms of state revenue-raising fall within the Act's protection, including: (1) unemployment compensation and disability benefits contributions;[281] (2) truck registration fees;[282] (3) bail bond license fees;[283] (4) special assessment for street improvement;[284] (5) state-imposed hospital surcharges;[285] (6) payments by parolees to supervision and victim compensation funds;[286] (7) franchise fees, if charged in measurable amount and paid into city's general revenue account;[287] and (8) sewer connection and use charges.[288]

---

[277] Empress Casino, 651 F.3d at 727–30.

[278] Genon Mid-Atlantic, LLC, 650 F.3d 1021, 1023–26; Qwest Corp. v. City of Surprise, 434 F.3d 1176, 1183 (9th Cir. 2006).

[279] San Juan Cellular Tel. Co. v. Pub. Serv. Comm'n, 967 F.2d 683, 685 (1st Cir. 1992).

[280] Wright v. McClain, 835 F.2d 143, 144–145 (6th Cir. 1987) (revenues earmarked for specific purposes are generally not considered taxes, although parolee payments to specially designated funds, even though earmarked, are taxes, and are therefore subject to Tax Anti-Injunction Act).

[281] Sipe v. Amerada Hess Corp., 689 F.2d 396, 402 (3d Cir. 1982).

[282] Schneider Transp., Inc. v. Cattanach, 657 F.2d 128, 132 (7th Cir. 1981).

[283] A Bonding Co. v. Sunnuck, 629 F.2d 1127, 1130 (5th Cir. 1980).

[284] Alnoa, 563 F.2d at 771.

[285] Travelers Ins. Co. v. Cuomo, 14 F.3d 708, 713 (2d Cir. 1993).

[286] Wright v. McClain, 835 F.2d 143, 144 (6th Cir. 1987).

[287] Diginet, Inc. v. Western Union ATS, Inc., 845 F. Supp. 1237, 1239 (D.C. Ill. 1994).

[288] Kerns v. Dukes, 944 F. Supp. 1214, 1219–1222 (D. Del. 1996).

### [b] Plain, Speedy, and Efficient State Remedy

The Tax Anti-Injunction Act permits a federal court to enjoin a state's assessment or tax collection when there is no "plain, speedy and efficient remedy available in the courts of such State."[289] The question of what constitutes a "plain, speedy and efficient remedy" is the most frequently litigated issue under this Act. Historically, the Supreme Court applied this exception liberally, frequently finding state remedies inadequate. Thus, in contrast to its Anti-Injunction Act holdings, the Court found that even uncertainty about the effectiveness of state remedies was sufficient to permit federal review.[290]

More recently, however, the Court has narrowed its interpretation of the Tax Anti-Injunction Act and left state courts with broad powers in this area.[291] For example, the Court in *Rosewell v. LaSalle National Bank* significantly narrowed the exception for inadequate state proceedings and held that a substantive defect could not be the basis for such a finding. The Court noted that the substantive inadequacy of state remedies was irrelevant; it was concerned only with the procedural adequacy of state law.[292] The Court has expanded its *Rosewell* approach, holding that the Tax Anti-Injunction Act bars federal courts from deciding constitutional challenges to state and local taxes.[293] The Court also has held that "mere speculation" that the state courts would not entertain claims is insufficient to prevent application of the Tax Injunction Act.[294]

### [c] Relationship to Full Faith and Credit Act

The same full faith and credit principles that apply to the Anti-Injunction Act apply to the Tax Anti-Injunction Act as well. Thus, full faith and credit principles preclude a federal court from interfering with state court proceedings if the state court previously ruled on the issues involved.[295] In *Swanson v. Faulkner*, a federal district court held that a state tax refund statute did not provide a plain, speedy, and efficient remedy. In a dispute over whether the state's refund remedy satisfied due process, the state court later determined that the federal ruling had no preclusive effect because the district court's order was not final. A federal appellate court upheld the state court ruling, stating that: "If plaintiffs believed that the state court preclusion ruling was erroneous, their remedy was an appeal to the U.S. Supreme Court, not action in lower federal courts."[296]

---

[289] 28 U.S.C. § 1341.

[290] *See* Spector Motor Serv., Inc. v. McLaughlin, 323 U.S. 101, 105–106 (1944).

[291] Tully v. Griffin, 429 U.S. 68, 73 (1976) (state's remedy is not inadequate merely because it is unfair or imposes some hardship on those who wish to challenge it).

[292] Rosewell v. LaSalle Nat'l Bank, 450 U.S. 503, 514–515 (1981) (state remedy was "speedy" despite average delays in adjudication of two years because "docket congestion of this sort is not unusual").

[293] *See* California v. Grace Brethren Church, 457 U.S. 393, 408 (1982).

[294] Franchise Tax Bd. of Cal. v. Alcan Aluminum Unlimited, 493 U.S. 331, 340 (1990).

[295] Swanson v. Faulkner, 55 F. 3d 956, 964–965 (4th Cir. 1995).

[296] 55 F.3d at 965.

### [d] Declaratory Judgments Similar to Injunction

The Tax Anti-Injunction Act precludes federal declaratory judgment relief to the same extent and in the same circumstances as the Anti-Injunction Act prohibits declaratory judgment relief.[297] Since the purpose of the Tax Anti-Injunction Act is to prevent federal interference with state and local tax collection, a federal declaratory judgment invalidating and suspending state tax assessment and collection would violate the Act.

### [e] Exceptions to Tax Anti-Injunction Act

#### [i] United States Government

The Tax Anti-Injunction Act does not apply if the United States, as plaintiff, challenges a state tax.[298] The Supreme Court has held that permitting the United States to sue for injunctions is consistent with the presumption against consigning the federal government to state courts in general, and that the United States must have the means to protect itself from unconstitutional state exactions.[299]

The Supreme Court has held that instrumentalities of the United States, by virtue of that designation alone, do not have the same right as the United States to avoid the Tax Anti-Injunction Act. Specifically, the Court ruled that the Tax Anti-Injunction Act barred Production Credit Associations (PCAs) from seeking a federal injunction prohibiting the state from imposing sales taxes on them when they sued without the United States as a co-plaintiff. The Court noted that PCAs, which are corporations chartered by the Farm Credit Administration to make loans to farmers, are not granted the right to exercise government regulatory authority, but rather serve a specific commercial and economic purpose. The Court left open the question of whether a federal agency with broad regulatory power is exempt from the Tax Anti-Injunction Act when it sues in its own name.[300]

#### [ii] Original Supreme Court Jurisdiction

The Tax Anti-Injunction Act does not apply to suits within the Supreme Court's original jurisdiction.[301] Thus, the Supreme Court, which has original jurisdiction over disputes between states, has found it logical that the Court should hear such cases rather than either state court.

---

[297] California Grace Brethren Church, 457 U.S. 393, 408–410 (1982).

[298] Dep't of Employment v. United States, 385 U.S. 355, 357–358 (1966).

[299] Leiter Minerals, Inc. v. United States, 352 U.S. 220, 225–226 (1957) (federal government should be able to obtain injunction to prevent threatened irreparable injury to national interest free of severe restrictions imposed by Act); Dep't of Employment v. United States, 385 U.S. 355, 357–358 (1966); United States v. Broward County, Fla., 901 F.2d 1005, 1008 (11th Cir. 1990).

[300] Arkansas v. Farm Credit Services, 520 U.S. 821, 823–827 (1997).

[301] Maryland v. Louisiana, 451 U.S. 725, 741 (1981).

### [iii] Statutory Exceptions to Tax Anti-Injunction Act

Unlike the Anti-Injunction Act,[302] the Tax Anti-Injunction Act does not contain an exception for suits expressly authorized by Act of Congress. Nonetheless, the Supreme Court has recognized that some statutes authorize federal district courts to enjoin the assessment or collection of state taxes.[303] The Court is hesitant, however, to construe federal statutes as authorizing an exception to the Tax Anti-Injunction Act, and if possible the Court will decide a case on other grounds.[304]

302 28 U.S.C. § 2283.

303 Burlington N. R.R. v. Okla. Tax Comm'n, 481 U.S. 454, 457–458, 464 (1987) (section 306 of Railroad Revitalization and Regulatory Reform Act of 1976 prohibits state discrimination against railroad property and authorizes injunctions of violative taxes); Moe v. Confederated Salish and Kootenai Tribes of Flathead Reservation, 425 U.S. 463, 471–472 (1976) (28 U.S.C. § 1362 exempts Indian tribes from Act).

304 *See* Franchise Tax Bd. v. Constr. Laborers Vacation Trust, 463 U.S. 1, 19–20 (1983) (Court did not decide whether ERISA constitutes statutory exception to Tax Anti-Injunction Act, but hinted strongly that it does).

# Chapter 13

# THE ABSTENTION DOCTRINE

## § 13.01 ABSTENTION IN FEDERAL COURT PROCEEDINGS: INTRODUCTION

### [1] Declining the Jurisdiction of Federal Courts

Federal court access is limited by the requirements of subject matter jurisdiction and various justiciability doctrines. In addition, the Eleventh Amendment further circumscribes federal court access, preventing federal courts from hearing suits brought against state governments by citizens of other states.[1] Apart from these doctrines, abstention doctrines are judicially created and self-imposed limitations on courts' adjudication of cases that are properly within their jurisdiction. As such, abstention doctrines represent a kind of voluntary abdication of a court's rightful jurisdiction and are in tension with a right to federal court access that Congress has conferred through various jurisdictional statutes. The Supreme Court has suggested that federal courts have an "unflagging obligation" to exercise their validly conferred jurisdiction. Abstention doctrines, then, conflict with this general principle. However, the Supreme Court also has recognized that in some situations it may be highly appropriate or necessary for a federal court to yield its rightly conferred jurisdiction in deference to a parallel state court proceeding.

### [2] Rationales Underlying the Abstention Doctrines: General Approaches

The Supreme Court has identified a number of circumstances in which the federal courts should abstain from adjudicating a controversy, even though the case satisfies all jurisdictional requirements and presents a justiciable controversy. The abstention doctrines basically operate to yield proper federal court jurisdiction to a state tribunal, on the theory that the state tribunal is the more appropriate forum to hear and decide the suit. All abstention doctrines effectively operate to yield federal court jurisdiction to a state tribunal. At its most basic, the theory behind each abstention doctrine is that the state tribunal is the more appropriate forum to adjudicate the case. Considerations of intersystem comity undergird virtually all of absention's many doctrinal permutations.

The Supreme Court has articulated three possible abstention doctrines for federal litigation involving issues of unclear state law. These abstention doctrines

---

[1] U.S. Const., Amend. XI.

counsel the federal courts to abstain and refer the case to state court, rather than have the federal court construe the unsettled question of state law. The *Pullman* doctrine requires federal abstention if a state court determination of an unsettled state law question would avoid resolution of a federal constitutional issue.[2] *Thibodaux* abstention requires the federal court to yield jurisdiction in diversity cases involving certain kinds of important issues of unclear state law.[3] *Burford* abstention requires a federal court to defer to state tribunals when a litigation involves a complex and comprehensive state administrative statutory scheme.[4]

The Supreme Court has suggested that federal abstention is desirable in these circumstances because abstention avoids friction between the federal and state courts,[5] reduces the likelihood that a federal court will make an erroneous interpretation of state law,[6] and may avoid unnecessary constitutional rulings.[7] Considerations of federalism and intersystem comity, then, chiefly support federal abstention in litigation involving issues of unclear state law. Commentators have criticized these rationales, but the Supreme Court continues to rely on these theories.

The Supreme Court articulated a fourth type of abstention doctrine in *Younger v. Harris*.[8] As originally formulated by the Court, *Younger* abstention prohibited federal courts from enjoining state criminal proceedings without a showing of "extraordinary circumstances" to warrant federal intervention.[9] The Court rested *Younger* abstention on considerations of equity: "that courts of equity should not act . . . when the moving party has an adequate remedy at law [in state court] and will not suffer irreparable injury if denied equitable relief."[10] Additionally, the Court justified *Younger* abstention based on the notion of "Our Federalism," or the belief that "the National Government will fare best if the States and their institutions are left free to perform their separate functions in their separate ways."[11] Although the Supreme Court announced *Younger* abstention in the context of parallel state criminal proceedings, federal courts have expanded *Younger* principles to (1) declaratory and monetary relief, when there are pending state criminal proceedings; (2) declaratory and injunctive relief, when there are no pending state proceedings; (3) litigation where the state government is a party, or involves important state interests; (4) pending state administrative proceedings; and (5) state and local executive branch proceedings.

---

[2] Railroad Comm'n of Texas v. Pullman Co., 312 U.S. 496 (1941).

[3] Louisiana Power & Light Co. v. City of Thibodaux, 360 U.S. 25 (1959).

[4] Burford v. Sun Oil Co., 319 U.S. 315 (1943).

[5] Railroad Comm'n of Texas v. Pullman Co., 312 U.S. 496, 500 (1941); Louisiana Power & Light Co. v. City of Thibodaux, 360 U.S. 25, 28 (1959); Burford v. Sun Oil Co., 319 U.S. 315, 318, 332 (1943).

[6] Railroad Comm'n of Texas v. Pullman Co., 312 U.S. 496, 499–500 (1941); Louisiana Power & Light Co. v. City of Thibodaux, 360 U.S. 25, 29–30 (1959); Burford v. Sun Oil Co., 319 U.S. 315, 327–331 (1943).

[7] Railroad Comm'n of Texas v. Pullman Co., 312 U.S. 496, 499–501 (1941).

[8] Younger v. Harris, 401 U.S. 37 (1971).

[9] 401 U.S. at 53–54.

[10] 401 U.S. at 43–44.

[11] 401 U.S. at 44.

The Supreme Court announced a fifth abstention doctrine, known as *Colorado River* abstention, under which a federal court may abstain in the "interests of wise judicial administration." *Colorado River* abstention typically is invoked in situations involving parallel, duplicative federal-state litigation.[12] Federal courts generally may not abstain from deciding a case because of concurrent state litigation, unless there are truly "exceptional circumstances" that convince the federal court that abstention is warranted.[13] This rule derives from "the virtually unflagging obligation of the federal courts to exercise the jurisdiction given them," even though parallel federal-state litigation is wasteful.[14]

Abstention doctrines are not intended to alter policy choices that Congress itself considered and addressed. If a statute specifies the conditions under which a suit can proceed and the conditions are satisfied, the court should not rely on one of the abstention doctrines to avoid adjudicating the suit. Such a use of abstention may amount to an end-run around congressional will.[15]

Federal courts may raise the issue of abstention *sua sponte*, and this may be done at any point in the appellate process.[16] Although federal courts may raise the issue of abstention *sua sponte*, they are not required to do so because abstention does not implicate subject matter jurisdiction.[17] In addition, some federal courts have held that abstention is not available if the litigation arises under a statute that confers exclusive federal court jurisdiction.[18] The Supreme Court has yet to issue a definitive ruling on this issue.

## § 13.02 ABSTENTION TO AVOID FEDERAL CONSTITUTIONAL RULINGS: *PULLMAN* ABSTENTION

### [1] Origin of *Pullman* Doctrine

The Supreme Court, in *Railroad Comm'n of Texas v. Pullman Co.*,[19] established an abstention doctrine designed to further the Court's traditional policy of avoiding unnecessary constitutional decisions.[20] The *Pullman* doctrine holds that federal

---

12 Colorado River Water Conservation Dist. v. United States, 424 U.S. 800 (1976).

13 424 U.S. at 818–819.

14 424 U.S. at 817.

15 Chico Serv. Station, Inc. v. Sol Puerto Rico Ltd., 633 F.3d 20, 31 (1st Cir. 2011); Adkins v. Vim Recycling, Inc., 644 F.3d 483, 497 (7th Cir. 2011).

16 D.A. Osguthorpe Family P'ship v. Utah, Inc., 705 F.3d 1223, 1231 (10th Cir. 2013); Lamex Foods, Inc. v. Audeliz Lebron Corp., 646 F.3d 100, 112 n.15 (1st Cir. 2011).

17 Lamex Foods, Inc., 646 F.3d at 112 n.15.

18 Retirement Trust Fund of Plumbing v. Franchise Tax Bd., 909 F.2d 1266, 1274 (9th Cir. 1990) (abstention inappropriate with respect to ERISA claims, over which ERISA grants federal courts exclusive jurisdiction).

19 Railroad Comm'n of Texas v. Pullman Co., 312 U.S. 496 (1941).

20 Cincinnati v. Vester, 281 U.S. 439, 448–449 (1930).

abstention is appropriate if two interrelated elements are present in a case.[21] First, there must be an uncertain question of state law, and second, that question of state law must be susceptible of a construction that will either eliminate the need to decide the federal constitutional question altogether, or materially alter the way in which the federal court will view that issue.[22] When litigants challenge state actions on federal constitutional grounds, the *Pullman* decision directs federal district courts to avoid erroneously forecasting how the state courts would decide an unsettled state law question. Rather, *Pullman* counsels federal abstention to allow the state court to resolve questions of state law that might dispose of the entire litigation.[23]

The *Pullman* case involved an equal protection and due process challenge under the Fourteenth Amendment to an allegedly discriminatory Texas Railroad Commission regulation that required every sleeping car operated in Texas to have a conductor as well as a porter. In 1941, all the conductors were white and all the porters were African-American. The Pullman company and the railroads brought an action in federal district court to enjoin the Railroad Commission's regulation, alleging that the Commission lacked the authority to issue the regulation. The Pullman porters intervened, alleging that the regulation violated the Fourteenth Amendment's prohibition of racial discrimination. The federal district court enjoined enforcement of the regulation on the ground that Texas law did not give the Commission the authority to issue it.[24] No Texas court, however, had yet construed the statute nor decided whether the Commission had the authority to issue such a regulation under state law. The injunction was appealed directly to the Supreme Court.

The Supreme Court held that the federal district court should not have decided the challenge based on its interpretation of Texas law. Rather, the district court should have abstained by staying its proceedings, and retained jurisdiction pending a state court interpretation of state law.[25] The Court reasoned that if the state courts ruled that the Commission did not have the power to issue the regulation, the matter would end and the constitutional issues would not arise. If the state court upheld the regulation, however, the litigation could return to federal court to determine the constitutional issues.[26] Thus, in order to avoid both the wastefulness of a tentative decision on the state law question and the friction of a premature constitutional adjudication, the federal district court should have abstained.

---

[21] Railroad Comm'n of Texas v. Pullman Co., 312 U.S. 496, 499–501 (1941).

[22] Harris County Comm'rs Court v. Moore, 420 U.S. 77, 84 (1975); Kusper v. Pontikes, 414 U.S. 51, 54–55 (1973).

[23] Railroad Comm'n of Texas v. Pullman Co., 312 U.S. 496, 499–500 (1941).

[24] 312 U.S. at 497–499.

[25] 312 U.S. at 499–502.

[26] 312 U.S. at 500–501.

## [2] Prerequisites for *Pullman* Abstention

### [a] Required Elements

Federal courts may apply *Pullman* abstention if a litigation presents two interrelated elements: (1) an unsettled question of state law; and (2) the possibility that the state court's construction of the unsettled question will avoid the need to reach the federal constitutional issue, or at least materially change the nature of the problem.[27] These elements are interrelated and *both* must be present for the federal court to abstain. In recent years, however, several federal circuit courts have applied variations on a three-factor test that substantially incorporates the elements and concerns of the primary *Pullman* test.[28]

The Court has specifically held that abstention is inappropriate in cases involving only unsettled or difficult questions of state law and no federal constitutional question,[29] and has repeatedly stated that *Pullman* abstention is limited to situations in which both of these "special circumstances" are present.[30] Although the Supreme Court has clearly established that these circumstances must be present for *Pullman* abstention, the Court has offered limited guidance concerning when they exist.

### [b] Uncertain Question of State Law

*Pullman* abstention requires that there be an unsettled, uncertain, or unresolved state law question that only a state tribunal can construe.[31] Federal courts should not abstain if state law is certain and unambiguous, and there is nothing for a state court to construe. Moreover, the Court repeatedly has stated that if state law is certain and unambiguous, federal courts should not abstain from deciding consti-

---

[27] Bellotti v. Baird, 428 U.S. 132, 147 (1976) (*quoting* Harrison v. NAACP, 360 U.S. 167, 177 (1959)); Casiano-Montañez v. State Ins. Fund Corp., 707 F.3d 124, 128 (1st Cir. 2013) (two-factor test for *Pullman* abstention satisfied); Wisconsin Right to Life State PAC v. Barland, 664 F.3d 139, 150 (7th Cir. 2012); Hunter v. Hamilton County Bd. of Elections, 635 F.3d 219, 233 (6th Cir. 2011); Moore v. Hosemann, 591 F.3d 741, 745 (5th Cir. 2009); Siegel v. Le Pore, 234 F.3d 1163, 1174 (11th Cir. 2000).

[28] *See e.g.*, Hartford Courant Co. v. Pellegrino, 380 F.3d 83, 100 (2d Cir. 2004) (three-part test for court to abstain, including: (1) unclear state statute or state law question at issue, (2) resolution of a federal constitutional issue must depend on interpretation of the state law, (3) state law must be susceptible to an interpretation by a state court that would avoid or modify the federal constitutional issue). *See also* Planned Parenthood v. Farmer, 220 F.3d 127, 149–50 (3d Cir. 2000) (three-part test for court to abstain, including: (1) uncertain issue of state law underlying federal constitutional claims, (2) state law must be amenable to an interpretation that would narrow or obviate the need for adjudication of the federal constitutional claims, and (3) an erroneous federal construction of the state law would disrupt important state policies); Potrero Hills Landfill, Inc. v. County of Solano, 657 F.3d 876, 888 (9th Cir. 2011) (9th Circuit three-part test); Kansas Judicial review v. Stout, 519 F.3d 1107, 1118–19 (10th Cir. 2008) (three-part test).

[29] Meredith v. Winter Haven, 320 U.S. 228, 234–235 (1943).

[30] Kusper v. Pontikes, 414 U.S. 51, 54 (1973); Baggett v. Bullitt, 377 U.S. 360, 375 (1964); Zwickler v. Koota, 389 U.S. 241, 248 (1967).

[31] City of Meridian v. Southern Bell Tel. & Tel. Co., 358 U.S. 639, 640–641 (1959); Harman v. Forssenius, 380 U.S. 528, 534 (1965).

tutional claims.[32] If state courts have never interpreted a state law, it is unresolved and unsettled — the situation the *Pullman* case presented.[33] However, the fact that a state tribunal has never interpreted a statute is not enough to warrant abstention. Additionally, the state interpretation of the statute must have the potential for rendering a decision on the federal constitutional question unnecessary, or substantially modifying the constitutional question.[34] Not only state supreme court decisions will eliminate uncertainty concerning state law for purposes of abstention. Decisions from lower state courts, including even municipal courts, may also serve that function.[35] In contrast, administrative agency interpretations of an ambiguous statute will not necessarily resolve uncertainty for abstention purposes.[36]

### [c] State Construction Limiting Need for Federal Constitutional Ruling

#### [i] Statute Must Be Susceptible of Construction

Federal courts may invoke *Pullman* abstention only if the state judiciary's resolution of the unsettled question of law "might avoid, in whole or in part, the necessity for federal constitutional adjudication, or at least materially change the nature of the problem."[37] If state court interpretation of an unsettled state-law question will not result in a limiting construction that eliminates or materially changes the federal constitutional question, then federal court abstention may be inappropriate.[38] However, if a state court's construction of state law may avoid or limit a federal constitutional issue, abstention is appropriate.[39]

---

32 Hawaii Hous. Auth. v. Midkiff, 467 U.S. 229, 237 (1984); Wisconsin v. Constantineau, 400 U.S. 433, 439 (1971); Zwickler v. Koota, 389 U.S. 241, 250–251 (1967); Harman v. Forssenius, 380 U.S. 528, 535 (1965).

33 Railroad Comm'n of Texas v. Pullman Co., 312 U.S. 496, 496 (1941).

34 Harman v. Forssenius, 380 U.S. 528, 535 (1965).

35 Houston v. Hill, 482 U.S. 451 (1987).

36 United Servs. Auto Ass'n v. Muir, 792 F.2d 356, 362 (3d Cir. 1986).

37 Bellotti v. Baird, 428 U.S. 132, 147 (1976) (quoting Harrison v. NAACP, 360 U.S. 167, 177 (1959)); *see also* Colorado River Water Conservation Dist. v. United States, 424 U.S. 800, 813–814 (1976); Carey v. Sugar, 425 U.S. 73, 78–79 (1976); Kusper v. Pontikes, 414 U.S. 51, 54–55 (1973); Zwickler v. Koota, 389 U.S. 241, 249 (1967).

38 Houston v. Hill, 482 U.S. 451, 468–469 (1987) (ordinance not susceptible of limiting construction because its language is plain and its meaning unambiguous); Procunier v. Martinez, 416 U.S. 396, 404 (1974) (no reasonable interpretation of state statute would avoid or modify federal constitutional question); Harman v. Forssenius, 380 U.S. 528, 535 (1965) (uninterpreted state statute not fairly subject to any limiting interpretation); Baggett v. Bullitt, 377 U.S. 360, 375 (1964) (uncertain issue of state law could not be resolved by state court because statute was susceptible of an indefinite number of alternative meanings).

39 Fornaris v. Ridge Tool Co., 400 U.S. 41, 44 (1970) (retroactive application of Puerto Rican law not yet construed by Commonwealth's courts might be judicially narrowed and avoid all constitutional questions); Reetz v. Bozanich, 397 U.S. 82, 84 (1970) (conflict between Alaska Constitution and state law might be confined so as not to have any federal constitutional infirmity); Railroad Comm'n of Texas v. Pullman Co., 312 U.S. 496, 499–502 (1941).

### [ii] Standards for Construction

The Supreme Court has not established a definite standard for determining when state law is susceptible of a limiting construction. For example, the Court has alternatively required that the state statute be "obviously susceptible" of a limiting construction,[40] "fairly subject" to an interpretation that will render the federal constitutional question unnecessary or substantially modify that question,[41] or that it merely be "conceivable" that such a construction could be made.[42] However, the Court has also stated that a bare possibility that state courts might render adjudication of the federal question unnecessary is insufficient.[43]

The Court uses the various formulations interchangeably, reiterating more than one standard in a single case. In both *Hawaii* and *Houston v. Hill*, for example, the Court cited both the "fairly subject" and the "obviously susceptible" standards to conclude that federal court abstention was inappropriate.[44]

### [iii] Interpretive Approaches

In considering whether a state court could interpret a challenged statute in such a way to avoid or modify a federal constitutional issue, the federal courts allow for various approaches. A state court need not construe a challenged statute in its entirety, but it may give the statute a limiting construction by severing discrete unconstitutional subsections from the rest.[45] A court's construction of a state statute involves analysis of the statute and its legislative history. If that history is such that it permits no reasonable interpretation of the statute that would eliminate or modify the federal constitutional question, then abstention is inappropriate.[46]

State appellate courts do not necessarily have to review lower state court rulings. For example, if municipal courts have regularly applied an unambiguous statute, a federal court need not abstain until the state appellate courts have construed the statute.[47] Similarly, the Supreme Court has held that trial court interpretations of state law, such as those given in jury instructions, constitute "a ruling on a question of state law that is as binding on us as though the precise words had been written into the ordinance."[48] Administrative agency interpretation

---

[40] Zwickler v. Koota, 389 U.S. 241, 251 n.14 (1967).

[41] Houston v. Hill, 482 U.S. 451, 468 (1987); Hawaii Hous. Auth. v. Midkiff, 467 U.S. 229, 236–237 (1984); Harman v. Forssenius, 380 U.S. 528, 535 (1965).

[42] Fornaris v. Ridge Tool Co., 400 U.S. 41, 44 (1970).

[43] Hawaii Hous. Auth. v. Midkiff, 467 U.S. 229, 237 (1984) ("a bare, though unlikely, possibility that state courts might render adjudication of the federal question unnecessary" is insufficient).

[44] *See, e.g.*, Hawaii Hous. Auth. v. Midkiff, 467 U.S. 229, 238 (1984); Houston v. Hill, 482 U.S. 451, 468 (1987).

[45] Houston v. Hill, 482 U.S. 451, 468 (1987).

[46] *See* Procunier v. Martinez, 416 U.S. 396, 404 (1974).

[47] Houston v. Hill, 482 U.S. 451, 470 (1987).

[48] Terminiello v. Chicago, 337 U.S. 1, 4 (1949).

of an ambiguous statute, however, will not remove inherent ambiguity for abstention purposes.[49]

Several appellate courts have held that *Pullman* abstention is not appropriate when the federal constitutional question is whether, under the Supremacy Clause, federal law preempts state law. For the purposes of *Pullman* abstention, federal preemption is not considered a substantial constitutional issue. This is because although preemption has its doctrinal basis in the Constitution, the question in a Supremacy Clause preemption case is not one of constitutional interpretation, but rather one of comparing the federal and state statutes.[50]

The Supreme Court has not unambiguously decided whether abstention is discretionary or mandatory if a litigant establishes the requirements for *Pullman* abstention. In several cases, the Court has indicated that even if the requirements are met, a federal court may exercise its discretion to hear the case if there are substantial reasons for doing so.[51] However, in some cases the Supreme Court has suggested that abstention may be mandatory if *Pullman* requirements are satisfied.[52] All appellate courts have adopted the view that *Pullman* abstention involves an exercise of discretion.

## [3] Balancing Costs of Abstention

### [a] Considerations of Federalism Outweigh Concerns over Cost and Delay

*Pullman* abstention, then, typically involves a discretionary exercise of the federal court's equitable powers.[53] Many courts have concluded that abstention is not mandatory, even if the "special circumstances" exist.[54] If the federal court abstains, however, the state court must resolve the state law claims. Unless the litigants submit all issues to the state court, the case may return to federal court to resolve federal claims.[55] *Pullman* abstention, then, may require piecemeal adjudication, increasing costs and delay.

The Supreme Court has held that considerations of federalism — requiring deference to state courts for unsettled questions of state law — necessarily outweigh concerns over the transaction costs of *Pullman* abstention.[56] On the other hand, the Court has also indicated that the delay inherent in *Pullman* abstention

---

[49] United Servs. Auto. Ass'n v. Muir, 792 F.2d 356, 362 (3d Cir. 1986).

[50] Swift v. Wickham, 382 U.S. 111 (1965); United States v. Morros, 268 F.3d 695, 703–04 (9th Cir. 2002).

[51] Harman v. Forssenius, 380 U.S. 528, 535–37 (1965); Baggett v. Bullitt, 377 U.S. 360, 379 (1964).

[52] Babbitt v. UFW Nat'l Union, 442 U.S. 289 (1979); City of Meridian v. Southern Bell Tel. & Tel. Co., 358 U.S. 639 (1959).

[53] Baggett v. Bullitt, 377 U.S. 360, 375 (1964); Railroad Comm'n of Texas v. Pullman Co., 312 U.S. 496, 500 (1941).

[54] Baggett v. Bullitt, 377 U.S. 360, 375 (1964).

[55] England v. Louisiana State Bd. of Med. Exam'rs, 375 U.S. 411, 417 (1964).

[56] Chicago v. Fieldcrest Dairies, Inc., 316 U.S. 168, 172–173 (1942).

and its economic consequences are legitimate factors for a court to consider in deciding whether to abstain.[57] Several circuits have followed this approach, considering the economic and other costs of delay as factors weighing against abstention. In some cases, courts will opt for certification of the state law question rather than abstention as a faster and more convenient alternative.[58] A court may also take notice of other harms that would result from abstention.[59]

### [b] Litigation Involving Fundamental Rights

In litigation involving First Amendment claims, the Supreme Court has recognized that the delay associated with *Pullman* abstention may be of particular concern,[60] although this concern may not be sufficient to avoid abstention. Such concerns "[H]ave particular significance when, as in this case, the attack upon the statute on its face is for repugnancy to the First Amendment. In these cases, to force the plaintiff who has commenced a federal action to suffer the delay of state court proceedings might itself effect the impermissible chilling of the very constitutional right he seeks to protect."[61] However, the heightened concern in First Amendment cases does not preclude abstention in every First Amendment case.[62]

Other federal litigation involving basic civil liberties may also raise concerns about the delays inherent in *Pullman* abstention. In *Harman v. Forssenius*, for example, the Court refused to abstain in a case involving an alleged impairment of the right to vote.[63] Consistent with *Pullman* standards, the Court refused to abstain on the ground that the state statute was unambiguous. The Court further indicated, however, that because the statute allegedly impaired the "fundamental civil rights of a broad class of citizens," abstention would involve delays that would prejudice the plaintiffs' attempts to vindicate those rights.[64]

In litigation involving fundamental rights, then, the Supreme Court has encouraged federal courts to assess the nature of the alleged constitutional deprivation weighed against the probable consequences of abstention.[65]

---

57 Pike v. Bruce Church, Inc., 397 U.S. 137, 140 & n.3 (1970).

58 Arizonans for Official English v. Arizona, 520 U.S. 43, 75–76 (1997).

59 Aroostook Band of Micmacs v. Ryan, 404 F.3d 48, 72 (1st Cir. 2005) ("Since the Band has asserted a dignitary harm in being forced to defend itself before the Commission, let alone Maine courts, abstention would be tantamount to a decision on the merits against the Band.").

60 Baggett v. Bullitt, 377 U.S. 360, 379 (1964).

61 Zwickler v. Koota, 389 U.S. 241, 252 (1967) (challenge to state statute prohibiting distribution of anonymous handbills); Wolfson v. Brammer, 616 F.3d 1045, 1066 (9th Cir. 2010); Kansas Judicial review v. Stout, 519 F.3d 1107, 1118–19 (10th Cir. 2008).

62 Babbitt v. United Farm Workers Nat'l Union, 442 U.S. 289, 308–09 (1979) (abstention proper because state construction of ambiguous statute could avoid or substantially affect the constitutional question presented).

63 Harman v. Forssenius, 380 U.S. 528, 529 (1965).

64 380 U.S. at 535–537; *but see* Harrison v. NAACP, 360 U.S. 167, 168–173 (1959) (Supreme Court abstained from deciding Fourteenth Amendment challenge to state statutes allegedly designed to curtail activities of groups such as NAACP).

65 *See* Procunier v. Martinez, 416 U.S. 396, 404 (1974) (abstention inappropriate when First Amendment challenge involved); *cf.* Younger v. Harris, 401 U.S. 37, 51 (1971) (mere incidence of chilling

### [c] Adequate State Procedure

Another factor courts consider in deciding whether to abstain on the basis of *Pullman* is the adequacy of state procedures for resolving uncertain state law issues. In *Pullman*, the Court did not explicitly state that adequate state court procedures are a prerequisite for *Pullman* abstention. However, the Court noted that state law appeared to furnish easy and ample means for resolving the state law issue which involved the authority of the Texas Railroad Commission. Since that decision, courts have held or at least suggested that abstention is not appropriate if state procedures are inadequate to the task.[66]

## [4] Criticism of *Pullman* Abstention

The Supreme Court offered three rationales for its *Pullman* holdings, and commentators have criticized each. First, the Court stated that a major ground for abstention was to avoid friction between federal and state courts. Professor Field, however, has questioned whether this rationale justifies abstention,[67] suggesting two possible outcomes when a federal court decides a state law issue. First, the federal court could come to the same conclusion as the state court, in which case friction is nonexistent because the results are identical. Alternatively, the federal court could reach a conclusion different from the state court. In *Pullman*, this would have occurred if the state court upheld the regulation on state law grounds, but the federal court subsequently invalidated it on constitutional grounds. This result would exacerbate tension between the judicial systems, despite the federal court's abstention, because the federal decision would overrule (and render superfluous) the state decision.

The Supreme Court's second justification for the *Pullman* doctrine is that abstention reduces the likelihood of erroneous interpretations of state law. Commentators have criticized this rationale on the ground that federal courts often are asked to construe uncertain questions of state law. Under the *Erie* doctrine,[68] for example, federal courts apply state law in all diversity cases, and must interpret the state law when it is unclear or uncertain.[69] Moreover, federal judges are unlikely to err in their construction of state law, because they sit in the same state as the state judiciary and often practiced law there. It is questionable, therefore, whether federal judges are less capable of correctly interpreting state law than

---

effect on First Amendment rights insufficient to justify enjoining state action); *but see* Babbitt v. United Farm Workers Nat'l Union, 442 U.S. 289, 308–309 (1979) (Supreme Court abstained from deciding First Amendment challenge to ambiguous state law limiting deceptive union publicity).

[66] Biegenwald v. Fauver, 882 F.2d 748, 753 (3d Cir. 1989).

[67] Field, *Abstention in Constitutional Cases: The Scope of the* Pullman *Abstention Doctrine*, 122 U. Pa. L. Rev. 1071, 1090 (1974).

[68] Erie R.R. v. Tompkins, 304 U.S. 64 (1938); *see generally* Ch. 15, *Applicable Law in Federal Court: The Erie Doctrine*.

[69] *See* England v. Louisiana State Bd. of Med. Exam'rs, 375 U.S. 411, 426 (1964) (Douglas, J., concurring, criticizes *Pullman* abstention because under *Erie*, federal courts decide state law questions and the fact that those questions are complex or difficult is no excuse for a district court to refuse to hear the suit).

state court judges.[70]

Finally, the Supreme Court justified its *Pullman* decision as a means of avoiding unnecessary constitutional rulings. Thus, if a state court first invalidates state law, there then is no need for the federal court to reach the federal constitutional question. This accords with the principle that federal courts ought to avoid constitutional rulings whenever possible.[71] Federal courts, however, can achieve this goal by deciding state law issues first, and reaching constitutional questions only if necessary. In fact, the Supreme Court advocated this approach prior to *Pullman*.[72]

Commentators also have pointed to the significant transaction costs associated with *Pullman* abstention, as cases are shifted from federal to state court and then, often, back to federal court. These increased costs would seem undesirable unless there is some compelling justification.[73] Excessive transaction costs can be mitigated, however, by sending the entire case, including the federal constitutional claim, to the state court. Alternatively, federal courts may lessen delay by certifying specific issues to the state court.[74]

Commentators have proposed limiting abstention when federal court adjudication would disrupt important state policies, particularly when states have created tribunals for uniform review of state regulatory agency decisions. The American Law Institute has proposed procedures for state courts to resolve all issues, including federal constitutional questions, when a federal court abstains. The ALI proposals, however, would prohibit abstention in actions involving civil rights, voting rights, and equal protection challenges.[75] Congress has not enacted these proposals, however, and *Pullman* abstention remains a discretionary doctrine.

---

70 Field, *Abstention in Constitutional Cases: The Scope of the* Pullman *Abstention Doctrine*, 122 U. Pa. L. Rev. 1071, 1092–1093 & n.4 (1974).

71 *See* Ashwander v. TVA, 297 U.S. 288, 346–347 (1936) (Brandeis, J., concurring).

72 Siler v. Louisville & Nashville R.R., 213 U.S. 175 (1909).

73 Field, *Abstention in Constitutional Cases: The Scope of the* Pullman *Abstention Doctrine*, 122 U. Pa. L. Rev. 1071, 1086–1088 (1974).

74 Buchanan, Notes, *Pullman Abstention: Reconsidering the Boundaries*, 59 Temple L.Q. 1243, 1261–1262 (1986).

75 Field, *Abstention in Constitutional Cases: The Scope of the* Pullman *Abstention Doctrine*, 122 U. Pa. L. Rev. 1071, 1126–1129 (1974).

## § 13.03 ABSTENTION BECAUSE OF UNCLEAR STATE LAW IN DIVERSITY CASES: *THIBODAUX* ABSTENTION

### [1] Diversity Jurisdiction and the Propriety of Federal Abstention

In *Erie Railroad v. Tompkins*,[76] the Supreme Court ruled that federal courts must apply state law in diversity cases. *Erie* doctrine, then, requires federal courts to interpret and apply unclear or unsettled state law.[77] In *Meredith v. Winter Haven*, the Supreme Court further indicated that federal courts should not abstain just because state law is unclear, uncertain, or difficult to determine.[78] This rule is consistent with the rationale supporting diversity jurisdiction, which is intended to mitigate possible bias against out-of-state litigants. Thus, the basis of diversity jurisdiction is "the supposition that, possibly, the state tribunal[s] might not be impartial between their own citizens and foreigners."[79] Federal abstention, then, defeats this purpose by returning litigants to state court.[80]

### [2] *Thibodaux* Case

Although abstention generally contravenes the purpose of diversity jurisdiction, the Supreme Court in *Louisiana Power & Light Co. v. City of Thibodaux* indicated that some diversity litigation may warrant federal abstention.[81] In *Thibodaux*, the City of Thibodaux, Louisiana, initiated an eminent domain proceeding in state court to expropriate the property of a Florida power company. The power company removed the case to federal court, based on the parties' diversity of citizenship. The federal district court, on its own motion, stayed the action to allow the Louisiana Supreme Court to determine whether the city had the authority to exercise eminent domain power under state law.[82] At the time, Louisiana's eminent domain law was unclear: a state attorney general's opinion had concluded in a similar case that a Louisiana city did not have eminent domain power, while a Louisiana statute seemed to grant the power. The Louisiana courts had never interpreted the statute, and the federal district judge abstained to seek clarification from the Louisiana Supreme Court.[83] The Fifth Circuit Court of Appeals reversed the federal judge's stay of proceedings, holding that the case presented no special circumstances warranting abstention.

---

[76] Erie R.R. v. Tompkins, 304 U.S. 64 (1938); *see generally* Ch. 15, *Applicable Law in Federal Court: The Erie Doctrine*.

[77] *See* Propper v. Clark, 337 U.S. 472 (1949) (Frankfurter, J., dissenting).

[78] Meredith v. Winter Haven, 320 U.S. 228, 236 (1943).

[79] Pease v. Peck, 59 U.S. (18 How.) 595, 599 (1856).

[80] *See* Note, *Abstention and Certification in Diversity Suits: "Perfection of Means and Confusion of Goals,"* 73 YALE L.J. 850, 858 (1964).

[81] Louisiana Power & Light Co. v. City of Thibodaux, 360 U.S. 25 (1959).

[82] 360 U.S. at 25–26.

[83] 360 U.S. at 30.

The Supreme Court reversed, upholding abstention, reaffirming the doctrine that federal courts may stay proceedings pending a state court determination of a decisive state law. In arriving at its conclusion, the Court acknowledged the general *Meredith* principle that "the mere difficulty of state law does not justify a federal court's relinquishment of jurisdiction in favor of state court action."[84] The Court noted, however, that it required district courts to stay proceedings when litigation involved city-state relationships, or an uninterpreted state statute of questionable constitutionality.[85] The Court concluded that abstention was appropriate because the litigation involved an unresolved state law question. More importantly, the federal court had been asked to determine an intricate question of state sovereignty; namely, the nature and extent of a governmental delegation of power between the city and state. The underlying eminent domain proceeding, then, was "intimately involved with [the government's] sovereign prerogative."[86] Thus, the Court concluded that abstention was appropriate because the federal litigation implicated both an unresolved question of state law as well as inter-state governmental relations.

In *Thibodaux*, the district court did not dismiss the case, but merely stayed further proceedings in federal court until the Louisiana Supreme Court had been afforded the opportunity to interpret the state statute. The Supreme Court noted that this was not the abnegation of a judicial duty, but merely the "postponement of decision for its best fruition."[87] Eventually, the Court stated, the district court would award compensation if the taking were sustained.

## [3] The *Mashuda* Case

The Supreme Court has made it clear that abstention is not required in all diversity eminent domain litigation, in another case decided the same day as *Thibodaux*. In *Allegheny County v. Frank Mashuda Co.*, an individual challenged Pittsburgh's authority to take land subsequently leased to private corporations. State law was unambiguous, holding that the government did not have eminent domain power to take property for private use. The Court held that there was nothing inherent in eminent domain requiring abstention. In fact, the Court said that eminent domain "is no more mystically involved with sovereign prerogative" than numerous other interests federal courts frequently adjudicate.[88] The Supreme Court held that the district court should have exercised jurisdiction because this would not have entailed a premature or perhaps unnecessary decision of a constitutional question, created the hazard of unsettling some delicate balance in the federal-state relationship, or required the district court to guess at the resolution of uncertain and difficult issues of state law.

---

[84] 360 U.S. at 27 (relying on holding in Meredith v. Winter Haven, 320 U.S. 228, 236 (1943)).

[85] 360 U.S. at 28 (citing Chicago v. Fieldcrest Dairies, Inc., 316 U.S. 168, 171 (1942) and Leiter Minerals, Inc. v. United States, 352 U.S. 220, 229 (1957)).

[86] 360 U.S. at 28.

[87] 360 U.S. at 29.

[88] Allegheny County v. Frank Mashuda Co., 360 U.S. 185, 192 (1959).

## [4] Reconciling the *Thibodaux* and *Mashuda* Decisions

Although *Thibodaux* and *Mashuda* both involved eminent domain, the decisions are reconcilable. *Thibodaux* involved both eminent domain and an unclear state statute concerning the apportionment of power between a city and the state, while *Mashuda* involved only the power of eminent domain. The state statute in *Mashuda* was perfectly clear. Only two Justices in the majority in both cases (Justices Stewart and Whittaker), however, were persuaded by this distinction.[89] Also, the district court in *Mashuda* had dismissed the case,[90] while the district court in *Thibodaux* stayed the federal proceeding.[91] Thus, in *Thibodaux* the Court indicated that abstention is not the "abnegation of judicial duty," but only its postponement. The district court judge retained complete control over the litigation, and if the parties failed to promptly seek a state declaratory judgment, the district court judge could have proceeded to decide the question.[92] The Supreme Court has reaffirmed that the controlling distinction between *Thibodaux* and *Mashuda* is grounded in whether the federal court, in abstaining, orders a dismissal or a stay of proceedings.[93]

Justice Brennan also attempted to reconcile *Thibodaux* and *Mashuda* with reference to the fundamental reasons for diversity jurisdiction. The broad state law question in *Thibodaux* had substantial ramifications because it involved the power of a city (as opposed to the state) to condemn property. An adverse, possibly biased, state decision against the Florida power company additionally might have had significant adverse effects on Louisiana citizens. In *Mashuda*, on the contrary, a state court's decision would have had little effect beyond the parties.[94]

## [5] Prerequisites for *Thibodaux* Abstention

Viewed together, the *Thibodaux* and *Mashuda* decisions establish that the federal courts should abstain in diversity cases if there is uncertain state law *and* an important state interest that is "intimately involved" with the government's "sovereign prerogative." Rather than spelling out exactly what these "important state interests" are, the Supreme Court subsequently rephrased this doctrine in *Colorado River* by stating that *Thibodaux* abstention is appropriate when a diversity case presents difficult questions of state law bearing on policy problems of substantial public import whose importance transcends the result in the case.[95] In that case, the Court indicated that *Thibodaux* abstention is appropriate when a diversity case presents difficult questions of state law bearing on "policy problems

---

89 *See* Louisiana Power & Light Co. v. City of Thibodaux, 360 U.S. 25, 31 (1959) (Stewart, J., concurring).

90 Allegheny County v. Frank Mashuda Co., 360 U.S. 185, 188 (1959).

91 Louisiana Power & Light Co. v. City of Thibodaux, 360 U.S. 25, 26 (1959).

92 360 U.S. at 29.

93 Quackenbush v. Allstate Insurance Co., 517 U.S. 706 (1996).

94 *See* McGautha v. California, 402 U.S. 183, 261 & n.11 (1971) (Brennan, J., dissenting).

95 Colorado River Water Conservation Dist. v. United States, 424 U.S. 800, 814 (1976).

of substantial public import whose importance transcends the result in the case."[96] Thus, although a federal court is not permitted to decline jurisdiction merely because a dispute involves difficult and unresolved state law questions,[97] sometimes the subject may be of such intensely local concern that federal courts decline jurisdiction, even though *Erie* doctrine compels federal courts to apply state law.[98] The reasons for abstaining must be particularly compelling when a defendant who removed the case to federal court is the one urging abstention.[99]

### [6] Application of *Thibodaux* Abstention

The Supreme Court, in a *per curiam* opinion in *Kaiser Steel Corp. v. W. S. Ranch Co.*,[100] briefly addressed what substantial public policy problems may warrant abstention. The Court held that the Tenth Circuit should have stayed an action rather than decide whether condemnation of private land to secure water for a private business violated the New Mexico Constitution, which permitted the taking of private property only for "public use." The Court did not cite *Thibodaux* in its short *per curiam* opinion; however, its reasoning accorded with the rationales underlying *Thibodaux* abstention.

In this litigation, Kaiser Steel Corporation claimed authority under a state statute to enter a ranch company's land to use water rights New Mexico granted Kaiser. The ranch contended that if the state statute were construed to authorize private land condemnation, the law violated the state's constitution, which permitted private takings only for "public use." The central issue, then, was interpretation of "public use" in the New Mexico Constitution. The Court indicated that the federal district court should have abstained, rather than deciding this interpretive issue. The Court explained that "[t]he state law issue which is crucial in this case is one of vital concern in the arid State of New Mexico, where water is one of the most valuable natural resources."[101] Because the issue "is a truly novel one . . . [s]ound judicial administration requires" abstention so "that the parties in this case be given the benefit of the same rule of law which will apply to all other businesses and landowners concerned with the use of this vital state resource."[102] The Court remanded the case with directions that the action be stayed and that the district court retain federal jurisdiction to ensure a just disposition of the litigation should anything prevent a prompt state court determination. Justices Brennan, Douglas, and Marshall concurred, emphasizing the "special circumstances" of the state's vital concern with allocation of its water rights.[103]

Appellate courts have invoked *Thibodaux* abstention in diversity cases when there is an unclear issue of state law involving an important state interest that is

---

[96] 424 U.S. at 814.

[97] Meredith v. Winter Haven, 320 U.S. 228 (1943).

[98] Construction Aggregates Corp. v. Rivera DeVicenty, 573 F.2d 86, 91–92 (1st Cir. 1978).

[99] Hawthorne Sav. F.S.B. v. Reliance Ins. Co., 421 F.3d 835, 844 (9th Cir. 2005).

[100] Kaiser Steel Corp. v. W. S. Ranch Co., 391 U.S. 593 (1968).

[101] 391 U.S. at 594.

[102] 391 U.S. at 594.

[103] 391 U.S. at 595 (Brennan, J., concurring).

intimately involved with the government's sovereign prerogative.[104] When invoking *Thibodaux* abstention, courts often emphasize that resolution of the state law question could have consequences for the state's citizenry beyond its effect on the parties before the court. Conversely, when a court declines to abstain pursuant to *Thibodaux*, courts often cite a lack of broader consequences.[105] The lack of a difficult or uncertain question of state law will also preclude *Thibodaux* abstention.[106]

## [7] *Pullman* Abstention Distinguished

*Thibodaux* and *Pullman* abstention both entail federal litigation involving an unsettled or unclear state law question. Both doctrines permit abstention to allow state courts to address an unsettled issue before the federal court adjudicates the matter. Although the doctrines are very similar, there are some differences. *Pullman* and *Thibodaux* abstention may arise from different procedural postures. Thus, in *Pullman*, the litigation was originally brought in federal district court, while in *Thibodaux* the suit was initially filed in state court. Only then did the defendant remove the litigation to federal court.

*Pullman* abstention typically involves litigation in which a party raises a federal constitutional challenge to state action, based on an uncertain state law. The state law must be susceptible of a construction that will eliminate the need to decide the federal constitutional question, or that will materially alter the way the federal court views that issue.[107] *Thibodaux* abstention, however, involves suits that do not allege federal constitutional issues, but only state claims involving public policy problems of substantial import or local concern. *Thibodaux* abstention is warranted, then, so that the parties will "be given the benefit of the same rule of law which will apply to all other" litigants concerned with the issue.[108]

Moreover, as discussed above, *Pullman* abstention recognizes exceptions, while *Thibodaux* does not. Thus, the Supreme Court has held that in some instances a federal district court should not abstain but rather decide a federal constitutional challenge, even though the litigation presents valid *Pullman* abstention grounds. Such situations involve important constitutional interests such as voting rights. *Pullman* abstention should be declined in cases that involve the exercise of important constitutional rights that might suffer because of delay. In contrast, *Thibodaux* abstention recognizes no formal exceptions.

---

[104] *See e.g.* Keleher v. New England Tel. & Tel. Co., 947 F.2d 547, 551 (2d Cir. 1991) (abstention in case concerning state and local taxation).

[105] *See e.g.*, Superior Beverage Co. v. Schieffelin & Co., 448 F.3d 910, 915–17 (6th Cir. 2006) (*Thibodaux* abstention not warranted in case involving dispute over termination of alcohol distributorships, in part because case was ordinary commercial dispute, importance of which did not transcend results in case at bar).

[106] Id.; City of Tucson v. United States W. Commc'n, 284 F.3d 1128, 1134 (9th Cir. 2002).

[107] Harris County Comm'rs Court v. Moore, 420 U.S. 77, 84 (1975); Kusper v. Pontikes, 414 U.S. 51, 54–55 (1973).

[108] *See* Colorado River Water Conservation Dist. v. United States, 424 U.S. 800, 814 (1976); Kaiser Steel Corp. v. W. S. Ranch Co., 391 U.S. 593, 594 (1968); Construction Aggregates Corp. v. Rivera DeVicenty, 573 F.2d 86, 91–92 (1st Cir. 1978).

# § 13.04 ABSTENTION IN DEFERENCE TO COMPREHENSIVE STATE ADMINISTRATIVE PROCEDURES: *BURFORD* ABSTENTION

## [1] *Burford* Case

The Supreme Court recognized, in *Burford v. Sun Oil Co.*, that federal abstention also is appropriate to defer to comprehensive state administrative procedures.[109] In *Burford*, the Sun Oil Company initiated a federal lawsuit challenging the validity of a Texas Railroad Commission order granting Burford a permit to drill oil wells in east Texas. Sun Oil sought to enjoin the Commission's order as a denial of due process and a violation of state law.[110] The Supreme Court held that the federal district court should have dismissed the case in deference to an existing comprehensive state regulatory system, devised for the conservation of oil and gas in Texas. The Court emphasized the existence of the complex state administrative procedures regulating the oil and gas industry and the need for centralized decision-making in allocating oil drilling rights. The Court explained that since an oil and gas field is a single pool, one operator can conceivably draw the oil not only from under that operator's own surface area, but also from the most distant parts of the reservoir. A single agency, therefore, was best equipped to regulate an oil and gas field as a unit for conservation purposes.

The Court noted that one agency was best able to deal with the complicated and interlocking issues that arose in the industry because "the physical facts are such that an additional permit may affect . . . a well miles away." Therefore, the "standards applied by the Commission in a given case necessarily affect the entire state conservation system" for oil and gas, one of the state's "most important natural resources." The Court felt that the state needed an overall regulatory plan for this vital industry, rather than a system that responded to individual speculative interests.[111]

The Court also noted that Texas had created a comprehensive state-court system of administrative and judicial review of the Commission's actions, "which alone have the power to give definite answers to the question of state law posed [in the Commission's] proceedings." The Court described the Texas courts and the Railroad Commission as "working partners" regulating the oil industry. Texas law conferred jurisdiction to hear appeals from Commission orders on only one state district court (which thereby acquired specialized knowledge in the area) as a means of avoiding the "intolerable confusion" that would result if all state district courts had jurisdiction. The statutory scheme also provided for appellate review within the state judicial system.[112] The Court concluded that Texas had provided a unified method for the Railroad Commission to formulate policy and for the state courts to adequately and expeditiously determine cases. Moreover, the

---

[109] Burford v. Sun Oil Co., 319 U.S. 315 (1943).

[110] 319 U.S. at 314–317.

[111] 319 U.S. at 319–320.

[112] 319 U.S. at 325–327.

comprehensive statutory scheme preserved litigants' rights to an ultimate review in federal court.[113]

*Burford* abstention, then, is appropriate when a case involves an unclear state law question of vital local concern,[114] which must be addressed through a centralized, unified state administrative system.[115] Under these circumstances it is appropriate "that a federal equity court should step aside and leave a specialized system of state administration to function."[116]

## [2] Development of Doctrine Since *Burford*

### [a] *Alabama Public Service Commission* Case

The Supreme Court frequently has cited the *Burford* decision without expanding, modifying, or further explaining its scope. For example, the Court has cited *Burford* for the proposition that "the state question itself need not be determinative of state policy. It is enough that exercise of federal review of the question in a case and in similar cases would be disruptive of state efforts to establish a coherent policy with respect to a matter of substantial public concern."[117] The Court has reaffirmed that *Burford* abstention requires a matter of vital local concern[118] subject to a centralized state administration system.[119]

The Supreme Court upheld *Burford* abstention principles in *Alabama Public Service Commission v. Southern Railway Co.*[120] In that litigation, the Southern Railway Company applied to the state Public Service Commission to discontinue local train service that was operating at a loss. The Commission denied the request. Although procedures existed for the railway to seek state judicial review, the Railway instead filed suit in federal court. The Railway's federal claim alleged that the Commission's decision, forcing the Railway to operate at a loss, was an unconstitutional taking of property without due process.[121] The Supreme Court found that federal abstention was appropriate, distinguishing these facts from *Pullman* abstention. The Court indicated that this was not a situation in which a state court's clarification of state law might avoid or alter a federal court ruling on

---

113 319 U.S. at 333–334.

114 *See* Kaiser Steel Corp. v. W. S. Ranch Co., 391 U.S. 593, 595–596 (1968) (Brennan, J., concurring).

115 *See* Tafflin v. Levitt, 493 U.S. 455, 458 (1990).

116 *See* Great Northern Life Ins. Co. v. Read, 322 U.S. 47, 60 (1944) (Frankfurter, J., dissenting).

117 Colorado River Water Conservation Dist. v. United States, 424 U.S. 800, 814 (1976); *see also* Zwickler v. Koota, 389 U.S. 241, 257 (1967) (exercise of jurisdiction by federal court would disrupt state administrative process).

118 *See* Kaiser Steel Corp. v. W. S. Ranch Co., 391 U.S. 593, 595–596 (1968) (Brennan, J., concurring: "[T]he state law issue which is crucial in this case is one of vital concern in the arid State of New Mexico").

119 Tafflin v. Levitt, 493 U.S. 455, 458 (1990) ("Maryland's 'comprehensive scheme . . .' provided a proper basis for the district court to abstain under the authority of *Burford v. Sun Oil Co*").

120 Alabama Pub. Serv. Comm'n v. Southern Ry. Co., 341 U.S. 341 (1951).

121 341 U.S. at 343.

a constitutional question.[122] Rather, the Court justified abstention because of the important local interest in intrastate transportation services, and a state regulatory structure with adequate state procedures to ensure judicial review. The Court noted:[123]

> Not only has Alabama established its Public Service Commission to pass upon a proposed discontinuance of intrastate transportation service, but it has also provided for appeal from any final order of the Commission to the circuit court of Montgomery County as a matter of right. That court, after a hearing on the record certified by the Commission, is empowered to set aside any Commission order found to be contrary to the substantial weight of the evidence or erroneous as a matter of law, and its decision may be appealed to the Alabama Supreme Court. Further, the Supreme Court ultimately could review any federal questions arising out of Public Service Commission orders.

### [b] Criticism of *Alabama Public Service Commission*

The *Alabama Public Service Commission* has been criticized as a substantial expansion of *Burford* abstention.[124] In *Burford*, the Court stressed the need for a unified decision-making process in allocating drilling rights, subject to a comprehensive state administrative system. In the *Alabama Public Service Commission* decision, the Court did not similarly require — as a predicate to abstention — a unified state decision-making process or a detailed state regulatory structure. Conceivably, then, the *Alabama Public Service Commission* decision could justify abstention when litigants raise a federal constitutional challenge to a state administrative decision reviewable in state court.

The Supreme Court, however, has indicated it did not intend that *Alabama Public Service Commission* be read that broadly. In *McNeese v. Board of Education*, for example, the Court specifically rejected a request to apply *Burford* abstention. Instead, the Court held that African-American students could bring a federal suit challenging a segregated school system, without first exhausting the state's administrative procedures. In these circumstances the federal court should not abstain under *Burford* principles, even though schools are of vital local interest and are governed by a state administrative structure.[125]

Similarly, in *Zablocki v. Redhail*, the Court refused to require a federal court to abstain so that a state court could first review a state administrative decision.[126] In *Zablocki*, a Wisconsin statute prevented individuals from obtaining a marriage license unless their child support payments were current. The Court explicitly distinguished *Burford*, stating that "[u]nlike *Burford*, however, this case does not involve complex issues of state law, resolution of which would be 'disruptive of state

---

[122] 341 U.S. at 344.

[123] 341 U.S. at 348–349.

[124] *See* Field, *Abstention in Constitutional Cases: The Scope of the* Pullman *Abstention Doctrine*, 122 U. Pa. L. Rev. 1071, 1158–1159 (1974).

[125] McNeese v. Board of Educ., 373 U.S. 668, 670 (1963).

[126] Zablocki v. Redhail, 434 U.S. 374, 379 & n.5 (1978).

efforts to establish a coherent policy with respect to a matter of substantial public concern.' " The Court rejected abstention, stating that "there is, of course, no doctrine requiring abstention merely because resolution of a federal question may result in the overturning of a state policy."[127]

### [c] The *NOPSI* Decision

In *New Orleans Public Service, Inc. v. Council of New Orleans* (*NOPSI*), the Court emphasized that *Burford* abstention is appropriate only where there is a danger that federal court review would "disrupt the State's attempt to ensure uniformity in the treatment of an essentially local problem."[128]

In *NOPSI*, the Federal Energy Regulatory Commission (FERC) allocated the cost of the Grand Gulf 1 nuclear reactor among several jointly owned companies, including NOPSI, that had agreed to finance the reactor's construction and operation. NOPSI, which provides retail electrical service to New Orleans, then sought a rate increase from the New Orleans City Council, the local ratemaking body, to cover the increase in its wholesale rates resulting from the FERC's allocation of the Grand Gulf costs. The Council determined that the costs incurred should not be completely reimbursed through a rate increase, because NOPSI's management had been negligent in failing to diversify its supply portfolio by selling a portion of its Grand Gulf power after the risks of nuclear power became apparent.[129] NOPSI sought review of the Council's order in federal court, and the district court abstained on both *Burford* and *Younger* abstention grounds. The Supreme Court reversed as to both.

The Court described the *Burford* doctrine as requiring federal courts to decline to interfere with complex state regulatory schemes in cases involving (1) difficult state-law questions bearing on important policy problems, or (2) efforts to establish a coherent state policy for matters of substantial public concern. However, the Court noted that the mere existence of a complex state administrative procedure did not require abstention. The Court explained that "[w]hile *Burford* is concerned with protecting complex state administrative processes from undue federal interference, it does not require abstention whenever there exists such a process, or even in all cases where there is a 'potential for conflict' with state regulatory law or policy."[130] The rationales for *Burford* abstention were not implicated, moreover, because wholesale electricity was not chiefly bought and sold locally. Thus, federal review of the Council's decision "will not disrupt state resolution of distinctively local regulatory facts or policies."[131]

The *NOPSI* decision makes clear that the mere existence of state administrative procedures does not necessarily warrant abstention. *Burford* abstention requires that the primary purpose of a state's administrative system be to achieve a uniform and coherent policy regarding a matter of substantial public concern. *Burford*

---

127 434 U.S. at 379 & n.5.

128 New Orleans Pub. Serv., Inc. v. Council of New Orleans, 491 U.S. 350, 362–364 (1989).

129 491 U.S. at 352–353.

130 491 U.S. at 360–364.

131 491 U.S. at 364.

abstention is warranted, then, if federal review would "be disruptive of state efforts to establish a coherent policy."[132]

### [d] Post-*NOPSI* Applications of *Burford* Abstention

All circuits, with the possible exception of the Tenth, generally follow the *NOPSI* requirements for *Burford* abstention. In other words, they require either (1) a difficult question of state law bearing on a policy of substantial public import whose importance transcends the result in the case, or (2) a situation in which the exercise of federal review of the question in a case and in similar cases would be disruptive of state efforts to establish a coherent policy of substantial public concern.[133]

Beyond these guidelines, some circuit courts have specified additional factors that must be considered. For example, the Second Circuit looks at: (1) the degree of specificity of the state regulatory scheme, (2) the need to give one or another debatable construction to a state statute, and (3) whether the subject matter is traditionally one of state concern.[134] The Fifth Circuit considers five factors in deciding whether to abstain pursuant to *Burford*: (1) whether the cause of action arises under federal or state law, (2) whether the case requires inquiry into unsettled issues of state law or into local facts, (3) the importance of the state issue involved, (4) the state's need for a coherent policy in that area, and (5) the presence of a special state forum for judicial review.[135] The Ninth Circuit has articulated its own three-factor test,[136] and the Tenth Circuit has announced a four-factor test.[137]

The fundamental concern in *Burford* abstention is to prevent federal courts from bypassing a state administrative scheme and resolving issues of state law and policy that are committed to expert administrative resolution.[138] Thus, *Burford* abstention may be considered when an order from the federal court would interfere with the proceedings or orders of a state administrative agency.[139] When a federal court decision would not interfere with state administrative proceedings, *Burford* abstention may be inappropriate.[140] However, *Burford* abstention is not limited to suits that challenge the actions of state administrative agencies.[141]

---

[132] Colorado River Water Conservation Dist. v. United States, 424 U.S. 800, 814 (1976).

[133] *See e.g.*, Washington Gas Light Co. v. Prince George's City Council, 711 F.3d 412, 418 (4th Cir. 2013); Chico Serv. Station, Inc. v. Sol Puerto Rico, Ltd., 633 F.3d 20, 21 (1st Cir. 2011); National City Mortgage Co. v. Stephen, 647 F.3d 78, 83 (3d Cir. 2011); Adkins v. Vim Recycling, Inc., 644 F.3d 483, 504 (7th Cir. 2011).

[134] Liberty Mut. Ins. Co. v. Hurlbut, 585 F.3d 639, 650 (2d Cir. 2009); Planned Parenthood of Dutchess-Ulster, Inc. v. Steinhaus, 60 F.3d 122, 127 (2d Cir. 1995).

[135] Romano v. Greenstein, 721 F.3d 373, 380 (5th Cir. 2013); Sierra Club, Inc. v. Sandy Creek Energy Assocs., 627 F.3d 134, 144–45 (5th Cir. 2010).

[136] Poulos v. Caesars World, Inc., 379 F.3d 654, 671 (9th Circ. 2004).

[137] Grimes v. Crown Life Ins. Co., 857 F.2d 699, 704–05 (10th Cir. 1988).

[138] Adrian Energy Assocs. V. Michigan Pub. Serv. Comm'n, 481 F.3d 414, 423 (6th Cir. 2007).

[139] Chico Serv. Station, Inc. v. Sol Puerto Rico, Inc., 633 F.3d 20, 34 (1st Cir. 2011).

[140] Sevigny v. Employers Ins. of Wausau, 411 F.3d 24, 27–29 (1st Cir. 2005).

[141] Johnson v. Collins Entm't Co., 204 F.3d 573, 576 (4th Cir. 2000).

*Burford* abstention is not available unless there is an opportunity for timely and adequate state court review of the issues in the case. On the contrary, *Burford* abstention may be appropriate where plaintiffs are unable to obtain adequate and timely review of their claims.[142] Some circuits require or at least consider the existence of a specialized court to review the claim.[143] If *Burford* abstention is based on a question of difficult state law, the importance of the state law question must transcend the case at bar. Thus, a dispute concerning a private settlement agreement was not transcendent and did not merit *Burford* abstention.[144] In addition, a public policy in danger of disruption must be a state policy, and not a national policy.[145] A constitutional attack on an entire state regulatory system generally does not disrupt state efforts to establish a coherent policy so as to warrant *Burford* abstention.[146]

### [e] The *Quackenbush* Decision: Application to Legal Claims

The *Burford* Court framed the abstention issue in terms of a district court's discretion, sitting "in equity," to decline jurisdiction.[147] The circuits disagreed over whether *Burford* abstention was appropriate only when litigants sought equitable relief, or whether it was also available when litigants sought only legal relief (i.e., damages).[148]

In *Quackenbush v. Allstate Insurance Co.*, the Supreme Court resolved this split among the circuits. The Court held that a federal court's decision to dismiss and remand a damage suit, based on *Burford* principles, was improper. The Court concluded that abstention doctrines apply to actions "at law" only to defer or put off possible federal court adjudication, not to eliminate it forever by dismissal or remand.[149] In *Quackenbush*, the California Insurance Commissioner sought, in state court, to recover funds from Allstate Insurance Company due an insolvent insurance company under reinsurance agreements. Allstate removed the proceed-

---

[142] Raritan Baykeeper v. NL Indus., 660 F.3d 686, 689–90 (3d Cir. 2011); Chico Serv. Station, Inc., 633 F.3d at 32.

[143] Illinois Cent. R.R. Co. v. Guy, 682 F.3d 381, 392 (5th Cir. 2012); Adkins v. Vim Recycling, Inc., 644 F.3d 483, 504–05 (7th Cir. 2011).

[144] Gray v. Bush, 628 F.3d 779, 786 (6th Cir. 2012).

[145] Chico Serv. Station Inc., 633 F.3d at 33; Illinois Bel Tel. Co. v. Global Naps Ill., Inc., 551 F.3d 587, 595 (7th Cir. 2008).

[146] Vaqueria Tres Monjitas, Inc. v. Irizarry, 587 F.3d 464, 474–477 (1st Cir. 2009); Martin v. Stewart, 499 F.3d 360, 367–69 (4th Cir. 2007).

[147] Burford v. Sun Oil Co., 319 U.S. 315, 317–318 (1943).

[148] *Compare* Lac D'Amiante du Quebec, Ltee v. American Home Assurance Co., 864 F.2d 1033, 1045 (3d Cir. 1988) (*Burford* abstention appropriate in case seeking declaratory relief); Brandenburg v. Seidel, 859 F.2d 1179, 1192 & n.17 (4th Cir. 1988) (*Burford* abstention appropriate in action for damages); *and* Wolfson v. Mutual Benefit Life Ins. Co., 51 F.3d 141, 147 (8th Cir. 1995) (*Burford* abstention appropriate in action for damages); *with* Fragoso v. Lopez, 991 F.2d 878, 882 (1st Cir. 1993) (federal court can abstain under *Burford* only if it is "sitting in equity"); University of Maryland v. Peat Marwick Main & Co., 923 F.2d 265, 272 (3d Cir. 1991) (same); *and* Baltimore Bank for Coops. v. Farmer's Cheese Co-op., 583 F.2d 104, 111 (3d Cir. 1978) (same).

[149] Quackenbush v. Allstate Insurance Co., 517 U.S. 706, 718–720 (1996).

ings to federal court on diversity grounds and filed a motion to compel arbitration under the Federal Arbitration Act. The Commissioner moved to remand the proceedings to state court on *Burford* grounds, citing the important state interest in regulating insurance insolvencies and liquidations, and the undesirability of having inconsistent federal and state rulings. The district court agreed and dismissed the proceedings, remanding the entire case to state court. On appeal the Ninth Circuit reversed, holding that federal courts can abstain under *Burford* only when the relief being sought is equitable, and that in this instance the Commissioner sought only legal relief.[150]

The Supreme Court reviewed the historical development of the abstention doctrines and the discretionary power to abstain as courts "sitting in equity." The Court further noted, though, that abstention has never been treated as a technical equity rule. Instead, "we have recognized that the authority of a federal court to abstain from exercising its jurisdiction extends to all cases in which the court has discretion to grant or deny relief." The Court concluded that it had applied "abstention principles to actions 'at law' only to permit a federal court to enter a stay order that *postpones* adjudication of the dispute, not to dismiss the federal suit altogether."[151]

The Court further pointed out that the distinction between remand or dismissal orders and stays was the basis for its different holdings in *Thibodaux* and *Mashuda*, which cases otherwise were nearly identical. The Court concluded that when litigants seek equitable or discretionary relief, federal courts have the power to abstain by stays, dismissals, or remands. But in an action for damages, a federal court may only stay the action, not dismiss or remand it.[152] The Court repudiated as too broad the Ninth Circuit's pronouncement that "[T]he power of federal courts to abstain from exercising their jurisdiction, at least in *Burford* abstention cases, is founded upon a discretion they possess only in equitable cases."[153] Abstention, the Court concluded, is not limited to "equitable cases" but extends to all cases in which a federal court is asked to provide discretionary relief, and to damage actions as well.[154]

The *Quackenbush* decision, then, suggests that in cases seeking equitable or discretionary relief, federal courts not only may stay the action based on abstention principles, but also may decline to exercise jurisdiction altogether by dismissing or remanding the litigation. The decision also suggests that, in damage actions, federal courts may abstain and stay proceedings, but they may not dismiss such actions altogether.[155]

---

150 Garamendi v. Allstate Ins. Co., 47 F.3d 350, 355–356 (9th Cir. 1995).

151 Quackenbush v. Allstate Insurance Co., 517 U.S. 706, 718–720 (1996) (emphasis in original).

152 517 U.S. at 718–720.

153 Garamendi v. Allstate Ins. Co., 47 F.3d 350, 355–356 (9th Cir. 1995).

154 Quackenbush v. Allstate Insurance Co., 517 U.S. 706, 718–720 (1996).

155 For discussion of the procedural options in abstention proceedings, see § 13.07.

### [3] *Pullman* Abstention Distinguished

In *Pullman* abstention, as in *Burford* abstention, there must be an uncertain state law question. In *Pullman* abstention, however, that state law question must be susceptible of a construction that will eliminate the need to decide the federal constitutional question, or materially alter the way the federal court will view that issue.[156] In *Burford* abstention, however, state law issues predominate and federal constitutional issues are secondary. When a federal court invokes *Pullman* abstention, the federal court remands the case to state court for a clarification of the state law. A federal court invoking *Burford* abstention, however, defers to a state administrative agency or state procedures for judicial review of agency action.[157]

The most important distinction between *Pullman* and *Burford* abstention, however, is that in *Burford* abstention the federal district court should completely dismiss the action.[158] In contrast, federal courts applying *Pullman* or *Thibodaux* abstention remand the case but retain jurisdiction, allowing the case to return to federal court if necessary to hear any federal constitutional issues. Thus, *Burford* abstention does not merely postpone federal court jurisdiction, it eliminates it.[159]

## § 13.05 ABSTENTION TO AVOID INTERFERENCE WITH PENDING STATE PROCEEDINGS: "OUR FEDERALISM" — *YOUNGER v. HARRIS*

### [1] Pre-*Younger* Doctrine

Another consequence of dual system litigation concerns the ability of federal courts to enjoin parallel criminal proceedings. Through the early twentieth century, federal courts narrowly permitted such restraint only if a person about to be prosecuted in state court could show irreparable damage in absence of a federal injunction.[160] This policy was based on the equitable principle that a court should not restrain a criminal prosecution if a party seeking an injunction has an adequate legal remedy and will not suffer irreparable harm if denied the relief.

The policy disfavoring federal interference with state criminal proceedings also is based in comity considerations. The Supreme Court describes *comity* as "a proper respect for state functions, a recognition of the fact that the entire country is made up of a Union of separate state governments, and a continuance of the belief that the National Government will fare best if the States and their institutions are left free to perform their separate functions in their separate

---

[156] Harris County Comm'rs Court v. Moore, 420 U.S. 77, 84 (1975); Kusper v. Pontikes, 414 U.S. 51, 54–55 (1973).

[157] *See* Burford v. Sun Oil Co., 319 U.S. 315, 333–334 (1943).

[158] 319 U.S. at 334.

[159] *See* Louisiana Power & Light Co. v. City of Thibodaux, 360 U.S. 25, 29 (1959).

[160] *Ex parte* Young, 209 U.S. 123, 165 (1908).

ways."[161] This is the concept referred to as "Our Federalism."

Prior to its decision in *Younger v. Harris*, the Supreme Court repeatedly held that federal courts should not enjoin state officials from instituting criminal actions, unless absolutely necessary to protect constitutional rights. To justify a federal injunction, the danger of irreparable loss had to be great and immediate. If not, the person seeking the federal injunction had to present constitutional objections in state court. A state criminal prosecution brought in good faith, in which the defendant could present a constitutional defense, did not warrant federal interference with the state proceeding.[162]

The Supreme Court found an injunction warranted in *Dombrowski v. Pfister*.[163] In *Dombrowski*, the plaintiffs alleged that the Louisiana Subversive Activities and Communist Control Law were being used unconstitutionally to harass and threaten their civil rights work. They alleged that the statute was overbroad, violating the First Amendment. Their offices had been raided and files seized, and they were arrested for violating the statute. Although a judge dismissed the charges, a grand jury subsequently indicted the plaintiffs for the same offenses, and prosecutors continued to threaten them with the same law.[164] In the Court's view, these circumstances justified a federal injunction to prevent the immediate, irreparable loss of the plaintiff's federal constitutional rights. The Court also was satisfied that the repeated prosecutorial harassment demonstrated that the plaintiffs could not effectively assert their constitutional rights as a defense in a state action.[165]

## [2] *Younger* Decision and Rationale

The Supreme Court refined and elaborated the contours of federal power to enjoin state criminal proceedings in *Younger v. Harris*.[166] The plaintiff in *Younger* was indicted in state court under the California Criminal Syndicalism Act for distributing leaflets.[167] The plaintiff sought a federal injunction against the state criminal prosecution on the grounds that the Act (and prosecution) violated the First and Fourteenth Amendments. Relying on *Dombrowski*, the federal district court ordered injunctive relief, holding the California Act was unconstitutionally vague and overbroad. The Supreme Court, on appeal, concluded that the injunction "must be reversed as a violation of the national policy forbidding federal courts to stay or enjoin pending state court proceedings except under special circumstances."[168] The Court concluded that the district court had misread

---

161 Younger v. Harris, 401 U.S. 37, 44 (1971).

162 *See, e.g.*, Douglas v. City of Jeannette, 319 U.S. 157, 162 (1943); Watson v. Buck, 313 U.S. 387, 400–401 (1941); Beal v. Missouri Pac. R. Co., 312 U.S. 45, 50 (1941); Spielman Motor Sales Co. v. Dodge, 295 U.S. 89, 95 (1935); Fenner v. Boykin, 271 U.S. 240, 243–244 (1926).

163 Dombrowski v. Pfister, 380 U.S. 479 (1965).

164 380 U.S. at 482.

165 380 U.S. at 485–486.

166 Younger v. Harris, 401 U.S. 37 (1971).

167 *See former* Cal. Penal Code §§ 11400–11402 (repealed Stats. 1991, ch. 186 § 10).

168 Younger v. Harris, 401 U.S. 37, 41 (1971).

*Dombrowski* as having expanded the availability of injunctive relief against state criminal prosecutions. The lower court incorrectly interpreted *Dombrowski* as permitting an injunction whenever a state statute was found unconstitutionally vague or overbroad, absent a showing of bad faith or harassment.

The Court stated that the result in *Dombrowski* was instead based on long-established standards for equitable relief and principles of comity: "the basic doctrine of equity jurisprudence [is] that courts of equity should not act, and particularly should not act to restrain a criminal prosecution, when the moving party has an adequate remedy at law and will not suffer irreparable injury if denied equitable relief."[169] The Court concluded that the plaintiff could have raised the constitutional claim as a defense in the state court proceeding, and therefore the federal injunction was unnecessary. The Court also based its decision on the notion of "comity," stating:[170]

> The underlying reason for restraining courts of equity from interfering with criminal prosecutions is reinforced by an even more vital consideration, the notion of "comity," that is, a proper respect for state functions. This is the idea expressed by the phrase "Our Federalism"—the belief that "the National Government will fare best if the States and their institutions are left free to perform their separate functions in their separate ways."

The Supreme Court also held that the district court misread *Dombrowski* as permitting injunctive relief whenever a state statute is found unconstitutionally vague or overbroad in violation of the First Amendment. The Court expressly rejected the contention that First Amendment issues are sufficient to modify the rule against federal intervention in state court proceedings, stating that "[i]t is undoubtedly true . . . that [a] criminal prosecution under a statute regulating expression . . . may inhibit the full exercise of First Amendment freedoms. But this sort of 'chilling effect' should not by itself justify federal intervention."[171]

The *Younger* decision thus announced a firm bar against federal courts enjoining pending state court criminal prosecutions, and a strong policy of federal abstention in favor of those proceedings.[172] All circuit courts follow the *Younger* rule.[173]

---

[169] 401 U.S. at 43–44.

[170] 401 U.S. at 44.

[171] 401 U.S. at 50.

[172] *See* Ankenbrandt v. Richards, 504 U.S. 689, 716 n.9 (1992) (Blackmun, J., concurring: "*Younger* abstention is inappropriate on the facts before us, because of the absence of any pending state proceeding").

[173] *See, e.g.*, Nivens v. Gilchrist, 319 F.3d 151, 154–55 (4th Cir. 2003) (abstention proper because (1) federal suit was instituted to stop pending state criminal proceedings, (2) state had a very important substantial interest in preventing violations of its criminal laws, and (3) party had adequate opportunity to raise double jeopardy claim in state prosecution); Cedar Rapids Cellular Tel., L.P. v. Miller, 280 F.3d 874, 878–882 (8th Cir. 2002); For Your Eyes Alone, Inc. v. City of Columbus Georgia, 281 F.3d 1209, 1217–1220 (11th Cir. 2002).

## [3] Relationship of *Younger* Doctrine to Anti-Injunction Act

The *Younger* opinion explicitly states that the Court's decision was based on considerations of equity jurisprudence and comity, and not on the Anti-Injunction Act.[174] The Anti-Injunction Act provides that a federal court may not grant an injunction to stay proceedings in a state court except (1) as expressly authorized by federal law, (2) when necessary in aid of its jurisdiction, or (3) to protect or carry out its judgments.[175] A year after the Supreme Court decided *Younger*, the Court held that 42 U.S.C. § 1983, which authorizes civil actions for state deprivations of civil rights, provided an express statutory authorization for federal injunctions. Hence, in Section 1983 civil rights actions, federal courts could enjoin state court proceedings. In *Mitchum v. Foster*, the Court stated that "[t]he very purpose of § 1983 was to interpose the federal courts between the States and the people, as guardians of the people's federal rights — to protect the people from unconstitutional action under color of state law."[176]

The *Mitchum* decision is somewhat difficult to reconcile with *Younger*, which also was a civil rights action under Section 1983, but one in which the Supreme Court denied injunctive relief. The two decisions may be reconciled by viewing *Younger* abstention as a separate, distinct bar to federal injunctions. Thus, a litigant seeking an injunction must satisfy exceptions to both the Anti-Injunction Act and the *Younger* doctrine. Although suits under Section 1983 constitute an exception to the Anti-Injunction Act, they are not automatically an exception to *Younger* abstention.[177]

Even if the two cases can be reconciled technically, they are difficult to reconcile as a policy matter. The Court in *Mitchum* expressly based its decision on the federal courts' role in protecting people from state and local violations of constitutional rights. Congress distrusted state courts and enacted Section 1983 to allow federal courts to enjoin unconstitutional state court proceedings, "to protect the people from unconstitutional action under color of state law."[178] In *Younger*, the Court premised its decision on the notion that federal courts should not interfere with state courts, because state proceedings can sufficiently protect constitutional rights. *Younger* therefore rests on the contrary assumption that state courts can be trusted to uphold civil rights — an assumption expressly rejected in *Mitchum*.[179]

---

[174] Younger v. Harris, 401 U.S. 37, 54 (1971).

[175] 28 U.S.C. § 2283; *see generally* Ch. 12, *The Anti-Injunction Acts*.

[176] Mitchum v. Foster, 407 U.S. 225, 242–243 (1972).

[177] *See, e.g.*, First Alabama Bank v. Parsons Steel, Inc., 825 F.2d 1475, 1483 (11th Cir. 1987) ("the Supreme Court's mandate merely states, as did the opinion in *Mitchum*, that the fact an injunction may be permissible under an exception to the Anti-Injunction Act does not mean that the district court should not also consider whether such an injunction is appropriate under the principles reflected in the *Younger* doctrine").

[178] Mitchum v. Foster, 407 U.S. 225, 242 (1972).

[179] *See* Younger v. Harris, 401 U.S. 37, 51–52 (1971).

## [4] Criticism of *Younger* Doctrine

Commentators have criticized the *Younger* decision, questioning whether considerations of equity or comity justify the Court's conclusions. Traditional equity principles posit that a court should not issue an injunction if the party seeking the injunction has an adequate legal remedy. This usually refers to whether money damages will make the party whole. In *Younger*, however, the Court cited equity jurisprudence for the proposition that a federal court should not issue an injunction if the claims asserted in federal court could be raised in state court proceedings.[180] This is an unusual basis for refusing an injunction, and highly questionable. In fact, earlier Supreme Court opinions recognized the flaw in this reasoning when stating "[a]n adequate remedy at law as a bar to equitable relief in the federal courts refers to a remedy on the law side of federal courts. It was never a doctrine of equity that a federal court should exercise its judicial discretion to dismiss a suit merely because a state court could entertain it."[181]

*Younger* critics also question whether state court remedies may be adequate, challenging the parity assumption between state and federal courts.[182] In addition, one commentator has argued that state courts may not provide an adequate substitute for federal review, because state courts often may not be able to provide the same relief as federal courts, such as interlocutory, class-wide, or prospective remedies.[183]

Defenders of the *Younger* doctrine suggest that it is simply another decision among many that are consistent with the long-standing principle that equity courts should not enjoin pending state criminal prosecutions. The defenders of *Younger* doctrine stress the importance of the underlying concept of "Our Federalism" — of federal non-interference with state courts. In this view, *Younger* doctrine promotes harmony between state and federal courts, and it avoids insulting state judges with the presumption that state courts are incompetent to adjudicate constitutional questions.[184]

---

180 *See* 401 U.S. at 43–45 ("[o]ne . . . basic doctrine of equity jurisprudence [is] that courts of equity should not act, and particularly should not act to restrain a criminal prosecution, when the moving party has an adequate remedy at law").

181 *See, e.g.*, Alabama Pub. Serv. Comm'n v. Southern Ry. Co., 341 U.S. 341, 346 (1951) (Frankfurter, J., concurring).

182 Zeigler, *Federal Court Reform of State Criminal Justice Systems: A Reassessment of the* Younger *Doctrine from a Modern Perspective*, 19 U.C. Davis L. Rev. 31 (1985).

183 Laycock, *Federal Interference with State Prosecutions: The Need for Prospective Relief*, 1977 Sup. Ct. Rev. 193.

184 Redish, Federal Jurisdiction: Tension in the Allocation of Judicial Power, 344–345 (2d ed. 1990).

## [5] Expansion of *Younger* Doctrine

### [a] Pending State Proceedings: Availability of Declaratory and Monetary Relief

#### [i] Availability of Declaratory Relief

The Supreme Court has extended *Younger* principles to apply to requests for a federal declaratory judgment while there is a pending state criminal proceeding.[185] In *Samuels v. Mackell*,[186] a companion case to *Younger*, the Supreme Court held that the federal courts should not issue declaratory judgments regarding the constitutionality of state statutes when the person seeking declaratory relief also is subject to a pending state criminal prosecution. The Court based its decision on the same reasoning as in *Younger*. The Court declared that "ordinarily a declaratory judgment will result in precisely the same interference with and disruption of state proceedings that the long-standing policy limiting injunctions was designed to avoid."[187]

Federal declaratory judgments generally are less intrusive than injunctions against proceedings. A declaratory judgment is a statement of rights, not a binding order with enforceable sanctions. Thus, state authorities may choose to be guided by the federal court's declaratory judgment, but they are not ordinarily compelled to follow the decision.[188] In *Steffel v. Thompson*, however, the Court noted that the Declaratory Judgment Act provides that a district court may enforce a declaratory judgment by granting "further necessary or proper relief."[189] This statutory delegation, then, might serve as the basis for a federal injunction against state proceedings to "protect or effectuate" the declaratory judgment under the Anti-Injunction Act's third exception.[190] This would result in the same improper interference with the state proceedings as issuing an injunction initially.

The Court further stated that "even if a declaratory judgment is not used as a basis for actually issuing an injunction, declaratory relief alone has virtually the same practical impact as a formal injunction would." The Court therefore concluded that the same equitable principles that govern the propriety of issuing an injunction against a pending state criminal proceeding, also must govern the propriety of issuing a declaratory judgment. The Court stated that "where an injunction would be impermissible under these principles, declaratory relief should ordinarily be denied as well."[191] The circuit courts follow this rule.[192]

---

[185] For general discussion of declaratory judgments, *see* 12 Moore's Federal Practice Ch. 57, *Declaratory Judgment* (Matthew Bender 3d ed.).

[186] Samuels v. Mackell, 401 U.S. 66 (1971).

[187] 401 U.S. at 72.

[188] *See* Steffel v. Thompson, 415, U.S. 452, 482 (1974).

[189] 28 U.S.C. § 2202.

[190] 28 U.S.C. § 2283.

[191] Samuels v. Mackell, 401 U.S. 66, 73 (1971).

[192] *See, e.g.*, Hansel v. Town Court, 56 F.3d 391, 393 (2d Cir. 1995) (*Younger* abstention principles

### [ii] Availability of Monetary Relief

An unresolved *Younger* question is whether a federal court may award monetary damages to a state criminal defendant if a damage claim arises out of the same issues pending in state court. For example, if at the time a state is prosecuting a defendant under an allegedly unconstitutional statute, may a federal court award monetary damages to the defendant for injuries suffered in enforcing the statute? The Supreme Court has noted that this is an unresolved issue and has not directly confronted it. The Court upheld a federal stay in a money damages suit, pending a state criminal prosecution concerning the same issues.[193] However, the Court has made it clear that if the *Younger* doctrine applies, and if the damage claims are not redressable in state court, the most the district court may do is to stay the federal proceedings; dismissal is inappropriate in that circumstance.[194] But the Court has not affirmatively resolved the question whether *Younger* precludes a federal damage suit if the same matter is the subject of a pending state criminal proceeding.[195]

The circuit courts also have acknowledged that this remains an open question.[196] While some circuits have held that *Younger* doctrine bars a claim for monetary damages,[197] others have only *suggested* that a federal district court can adjudicate a claim for monetary damages when the *Younger* doctrine otherwise applies, noting that a damage award may be as disruptive of state proceedings as an injunction or declaratory relief.[198] Most federal decisions, however, have concluded that the federal courts should abstain on monetary damages claims when *Younger* abstention applies, because a stay does not foreclose the federal court from deciding the claim.[199] If damage claims can be brought in state court, outright dismissal might be appropriate.[200] On the other hand, some courts have suggested that *Younger* abstention does not apply to damage claims at all.[201]

---

extend to declaratory relief); Bongiorno v. Lalomia, 851 F. Supp. 606, 611 (D.N.J. 1994) (same); Traveler Ins. Co. v. Louisiana Farm Bureau Fed'n, Inc., 996 F.2d 774, 778 (5th Cir. 1993) (same); *accord* Nobby Lobby, Inc. v. City of Dallas, 970 F.2d 82, 86 (5th Cir. 1992).

193 Deakins v. Monaghan, 798 F.2d 632 (3d Cir. 1986), *aff'd*, 484 U.S. 193, 202 (1988).

194 American Consumer Publ'g Ass'n v. Margosian, 349 F.3d 1122, 1126–29 (9th Cir. 2003).

195 *See* Tower v. Glover, 467 U.S. 914, 922 (1984); Juidice v. Vail, 430 U.S. 327, 339 & n.16 (1977).

196 *See, e.g.*, American Consumer Publ'g Ass'n, 349 F.3d at 1126–29; Carroll v. City of Mount Clemens, 139 F.3d 1072, 1077 (6th Cir. 1998) (collecting cases on circuit split over whether *Younger* abstention applies to claims for monetary damages).

197 *See* Guerro v. Mulhearn, 498 F.2d 1249, 1252 (1st Cir. 1974).

198 *See* Rossi v. Gemma, 489 F.3d 26, 37 (1st Cir. 2007); Gilbertson v. Albright, 381 F.3d 965, 968 (9th Cir. 2004); D.L. v. Unified Sch. Dist., 392 F.3d 1223, 1228 (10th Cir. 2004).

199 Rossi v. Gemma, 489 F.3d 26, 37–38 (1st Cir. 2007); Kay v. City of Rancho Palos Verdes, 504 F.3d 803, 808 (9th Cir. 2007); Nivens v. Gilchrist, 444 F.3d 237, 248 (4th Cir. 2006).

200 Green v. Benden, 281 F.3d 661, 667 (7th Cir. 2002).

201 Morkel v. Davis, 2013 U.S. App. LEXIS 5202, at *12 (10th Cir. Mar. 15, 2103) (unpublished opinion) (monetary damages do not fall within the purview of Younger abstention); Marran v. Marran, 376 F.3d 143, 154 (3d Cir. 2004) (Supreme Court has never explicitly decided whether *Younger* abstention covers actions for damages, but *Deakins v. Monaghan*, 484 U.S. 193 (188) and *Quackenbush v. Allstate* Ins. Co., 517 U.S. 706 (1996) seem to indicate that abstention under *Younger* principles is not proper when damages are sought).

## [b] Absence of Pending State Proceedings: Availability of Declaratory and Injunctive Relief

### [i] Availability of Declaratory Relief

Neither the *Younger* decision nor the *Samuels* decision expressed a view on the propriety of federal injunctive or declaratory relief in the absence of pending state criminal proceedings. The Supreme Court partially answered this question in *Steffel v. Thompson*,[202] in which it held that a federal court could provide declaratory relief when there is no ongoing state prosecution. The plaintiff in *Steffel* was threatened with prosecution under a state trespass statute for distributing handbills at a shopping center protesting the Vietnam War. A companion had been arrested under the statute. The plaintiff filed a federal court suit seeking declaratory and injunctive relief against the threatened enforcement of the state statute, rather than risk arrest. The district court dismissed the suit based on *Younger* principles. The Supreme Court reversed, noting that the propriety of granting federal declaratory relief may be considered independent of a request for injunctive relief. The Court also stressed the appropriateness of declaratory relief in the absence of an ongoing state prosecution. The Court held that the *Younger* rationales simply were not applicable if there were no pending state proceedings, stating:[203]

> When no state criminal proceeding is pending at the time the federal complaint is filed, federal intervention does not result in duplicative legal proceedings or disruption of the state criminal justice system; nor can federal intervention, in that circumstance, be interpreted as reflecting negatively upon the state court's ability to enforce constitutional principles.

In addition, the Court noted that although a pending state prosecution provides a federal plaintiff with an opportunity to vindicate his or her constitutional rights, a federal refusal to intervene when there is no pending state proceeding may place "the hapless plaintiff between the Scylla of intentionally flouting state law and the Charybdis of forgoing what he believes to be constitutionally protected activity in order to avoid becoming enmeshed in a criminal proceeding."[204]

### [ii] Nature and Timing of State Proceedings

*Steffel* permits declaratory relief if there is no pending state proceeding and principles of equity, comity, and federalism are not of concern. The *Steffel* Court, however, did not define what constitutes a pending state proceeding. The facts in *Younger* and *Samuels* indicate that a state indictment or information constitutes a pending prosecution for *Younger* purposes. In contrast, pre-indictment proceedings before a grand jury do not constitute state proceedings in which a federal plaintiff's claims could ever be adjudicated. Abstention is not appropriate

---

[202] Steffel v. Thompson, 415 U.S. 452 (1974).

[203] 415 U.S. at 462.

[204] 415 U.S. at 462; *see also* Ankenbrandt v. Richards, 504 U.S. 689, 716 & n.9 (1992) (Blackmun, J., concurring, *Younger* is not applicable in absence of pending state proceeding).

because there is no pending state proceeding with adjudicatory powers unless the grand jury, at some future time, decides to return an indictment.[205] Some lower courts have held, however, that an arrest commences state court proceedings for *Younger* purposes.[206]

A related question concerns when a state court proceeding may be considered pending. In *Hicks v. Miranda*, the Supreme Court applied *Younger* principles and declined to interfere with a state criminal prosecution, despite a first-filed federal action.[207] In *Hicks*, the state prosecuted a theater owner the day after he filed a federal declaratory relief action. The police had seized copies of an allegedly obscene film and began proceedings to have the film declared obscene. The theater owner, not a party to the state proceedings, then filed a federal suit to have the state's obscenity law declared unconstitutional. The state amended its pleadings to include the owner, but the federal district court found that there were no state proceedings pending against the owner when he filed the federal lawsuit. Therefore the district court exercised jurisdiction, holding the state law unconstitutional. The Supreme Court reversed. The Court noted that the theater owner's interests already were being litigated in the state proceeding, but more importantly, those state proceedings provided him a forum to adjudicate his constitutional claims. The Court reasoned that because the federal suit was in its initial stages (the complaint was filed but no proceedings had occurred), the federal court should appropriately defer to the state court proceedings. The Court stated that "[n]either *Steffel v. Thompson*, nor any other case in this Court has held that for *Younger v. Harris* to apply, the state criminal proceeding must be pending on the day the federal case is filed." On the contrary, the Court held that "where state criminal proceedings are begun against the federal plaintiffs after the federal complaint is filed but before any proceedings of substance on the merits have taken place in the federal court, the principles of *Younger v. Harris* should apply in full force."[208]

Hicks therefore holds that federal courts must dismiss suits if there have been no "proceedings of substance on the merits" prior to the beginning of the state criminal prosecution. There are no firm guidelines, however, concerning what actions must occur in a federal lawsuit for this rule to apply. In *Hicks*, for example, a federal court's denial of a temporary restraining order was insufficient to refuse abstention.[209] However, a federal court's grant of a preliminary injunction was enough to allow a federal court to exercise jurisdiction, even when a state

---

205 Deakins v. Monaghan, 798 F.2d 632, 636–637 (3d Cir. 1986), *aff'd*, 484 U.S. 193, 202 (1988) (Third Circuit had ruled that *Younger* abstention was never appropriate for money-damages claim, but that ruling was affirmed by Supreme Court only on ground that stay rather than dismissal was appropriate remedy even if abstention were proper, and Third Circuit's ruling that denied abstention for equitable claims on grounds of ongoing grand jury proceedings was mooted by plaintiffs' subsequently-stated desire to proceed with its equitable claims solely in state court now that indictment had been returned against plaintiffs).

206 Rialto Theater Co. v. City of Wilmington, 440 F.2d 1326, 1326 (3d Cir. 1971); Eve Prods., Inc. v. Shannon, 439 F.2d 1073, 1073 (8th Cir. 1971).

207 Hicks v. Miranda, 422 U.S. 332 (1975).

208 422 U.S. at 349.

209 422 U.S. at 332.

subsequently instituted criminal charges.[210]

The Court also has held that *Hicks* applies when the only federal litigation that has occurred is the court's consideration of the abstention question,[211] and suggested that *Younger* abstention *might* apply if state court proceedings are *about* to begin.[212] Circuit court decisions vary in their understanding of what constitutes a pending proceeding for *Younger* abstention purposes. All circuits, however, generally follow the *Hicks* rule and defer to state proceedings if the federal litigation has conducted no proceedings of substance on the merits.[213]

### [iii] Availability of Injunctive Relief

The Court in *Steffel* focused on whether a federal court could provide declaratory relief in the absence of any pending state prosecution. It explicitly left open the question whether federal courts could enjoin state prosecutions *before* they are begun.[214] Because the Court in *Samuels* concluded that declaratory and injunctive relief basically are indistinguishable, injunctive relief ought to permissible if a federal court could issue a declaratory judgment. Thus, in *Doran v. Salem Inn, Inc.*, the Supreme Court upheld a preliminary injunction against threatened prosecution.[215]

In *Doran*, three bar owners brought a federal action seeking declaratory relief and a preliminary injunction preventing enforcement of a topless dancing ordinance. After the federal suit was filed and the court denied a temporary restraining order, one of the bar owners resumed offering topless dancing. The state court then instituted criminal proceedings. Subsequently, the federal district court granted preliminary injunctive relief to the bar owners. The Supreme Court affirmed the preliminary injunction granted to the two owners who complied with the ordinance pending a federal court decision. The Court reversed, however, with regard to the noncomplying owner being prosecuted in state court. The Court found that *Younger*, *Samuels*, and *Hicks* abstention principles applied to this owner, and that he was required to present all his claims in the state court

---

[210] Hawaii Hous. Auth. v. Midkiff, 467 U.S. 229, 238 (1984) ("A federal court action in which a preliminary injunction is granted has proceeded well beyond the embryonic stage . . . and considerations of economy, equity, and federalism counsel against *Younger* abstention at that point").

[211] Middlesex County Ethics Comm. v. Garden State Bar Ass'n, 457 U.S. 423, 436–437 (1982).

[212] Morales v. Trans World Airlines, 504 U.S. 374, 381 & n.1 (1992) (*Younger* imposes heightened requirements for injunction to restrain already-pending or about-to-be-pending state criminal action, or civil action involving important state interests).

[213] *See, e.g.*, Employers Resource Management Co. v. Shannon, 65 F.3d 1126, 1135 (4th Cir. 1995); Agriesti v. MGM Grand Hotels, Inc., 53 F.3d 1000, 1002 (9th Cir. 1995) (*Younger* abstention does not require imminent, but rather ongoing, state judicial proceedings; neither arrest nor issuance of misdemeanor citation by police officer is judicial in nature — these are executive acts that do not mark commencement of judicial proceedings); Fragoso v. Lopez, 991 F.2d 878, 885 (1st Cir. 1993) (the more embryonic a case, the more significant interference with state framework if federal tribunal does not yield); Royal Ins. Co. v. Quinn-L Capital Corp., 3 F.3d 877, 886 (5th Cir. 1993) (if substantial proceedings have occurred in federal court, that court need not abstain; federal court is allowed to proceed to prevent state from employing abstention as means of delay).

[214] Steffel v. Thompson, 415 U.S. 452, 463 (1974).

[215] Doran v. Salem Inn, Inc., 422 U.S. 922, 932 (1975).

proceedings. As to the other owners, the Court held that if there is no pending state court proceeding, individuals may receive a preliminary injunction because it does not disrupt any state court proceedings and there is no other forum available in which they may raise their constitutional claims.[216]

The Supreme Court reaffirmed these holdings in *Wooley v. Maynard*, extending these principles to permanent injunctions.[217] In *Wooley*, a Jehovah's Witness obscured the New Hampshire state motto "Live Free or Die" on his automobile license plates because it offended his religious beliefs. A New Hampshire statute made defacing the state motto a misdemeanor, and the state prosecuted the plaintiff three times in five weeks for this offense. Before he could be prosecuted again, the plaintiff brought a federal action challenging the statute on First Amendment grounds, seeking declaratory and injunctive relief. The Supreme Court declared the state statute unconstitutional and upheld the lower court's injunction. Although the Court acknowledged that there is a general policy against enjoining enforcement of state criminal statutes, it held that injunctions are appropriate in "exceptional circumstances" upon "a clear showing that an injunction is necessary in order to afford adequate protection of constitutional rights."[218]

### [c] Pending State Civil Proceedings

#### [i] Civil Enforcement Proceedings

The *Younger* abstention doctrine developed in the context of pending state criminal proceedings. Subsequently, the Court has applied *Younger* abstention when the state government is a party in state civil litigation. The Court first extended *Younger* abstention to civil cases in *Huffman v. Pursue, Ltd.*[219] In *Huffman*, state officials instituted and won a civil nuisance proceeding against an adult movie theater for violating an Ohio obscenity statute. Rather than pursue an Ohio appeal, the theater owner sought federal injunctive and declaratory relief under 42 U.S.C. § 1983. The federal district court ruled that the Ohio statute and proceedings violated the First Amendment. The Supreme Court reversed, holding that the district court should have abstained on *Younger* principles. The Court acknowledged that the lawsuit was a civil proceeding, but analogized it to a criminal case, in which *Younger* would clearly apply. The Court emphasized that the state's nuisance proceeding was "more akin to a criminal prosecution than are most civil cases." The Court noted that the state was a party to a proceeding, which was "both in aid of and closely related to criminal statutes which prohibit the dissemination of obscene materials," and concluded that federal intervention would be just as inappropriate "as it would be were this a criminal proceeding."[220]

In *Trainor v. Hernandez*, the Supreme Court clarified that *Younger* abstention

---

216 422 U.S. at 929–930.

217 Wooley v. Maynard, 430 U.S. 705 (1977).

218 430 U.S. at 712.

219 Huffman v. Pursue, Ltd., 420 U.S. 592 (1975).

220 420 U.S. at 604.

applies to all civil proceedings in which the state is a party.[221] In *Trainor*, the Illinois Department of Public Aid brought a state civil fraud proceeding to recover welfare benefits allegedly obtained by fraudulent means. The state obtained a writ of attachment against the defendant's savings. The defendant then brought a federal action challenging the statute's constitutionality and seeking declaratory and injunctive relief. The Court concluded that *Younger* abstention should apply even though the proceeding was wholly civil. The Court emphasized that the state was a party to the proceeding, acting to vindicate important state policies. Further, as in *Huffman*, the state might have initiated a criminal enforcement action. Rather than rely on analogies to criminal proceedings, however, the Court concluded that "the principles of *Younger* and *Huffman* are broad enough to apply to interference by a federal court with an ongoing civil enforcement action such as this, brought by the State in its sovereign capacity."[222]

### [ii] Proceedings Involving Important State Interests

In *Juidice v. Vail*, the Supreme Court extended *Younger* abstention to civil proceedings in which the state government is not a party.[223] In *Juidice*, a state court held several individuals in contempt for refusing to comply with subpoenas. They filed suit in federal court seeking injunctive and declaratory relief against the state's contempt proceedings. The Supreme Court held that *Younger* applied to restrain the federal court, even though the parties were private litigants. The Court based its conclusion on the importance of the state's interest in state contempt proceedings, which lie "at the core of the administration of a State's judicial system."[224] The *Juidice* decision therefore stands for the proposition that the *Younger* abstention doctrine applies to private civil litigation when there are important governmental interests at stake.

The Supreme Court's decision in the *Pennzoil* litigation further emphasized this proposition.[225] The *Pennzoil* case involved a Texas breach of contract action between Pennzoil and Texaco over the purchase of the Getty Oil Company, which resulted in a $10 billion jury verdict. Texaco was required to post a bond of over $13 billion in order to appeal in the state system. Instead, Texaco sued in federal court seeking to enjoin enforcement of the Texas bond requirement. The federal district court ruled in Texaco's favor and enjoined enforcement of the bond requirement. The Supreme Court reversed, holding that the court "should have abstained under the principles of federalism enunciated in *Younger v. Harris*."[226] The Court noted that the *Younger* equity and comity rationales were equally applicable in civil cases, and that a federal forum was unnecessary if state proceedings were available to raise constitutional issues. The Court analogized *Pennzoil* to *Juidice v. Vail*, noting that both involved deference to state courts. The Court concluded that the

---

221 Trainor v. Hernandez, 431 U.S. 434 (1977).

222 431 U.S. at 444.

223 Juidice v. Vail, 430 U.S. 327 (1977).

224 430 U.S. at 335.

225 Pennzoil Co. v. Texaco, Inc., 481 U.S. 1 (1987).

226 481 U.S. at 10.

"reasoning of *Juidice* controls" and federal abstention was warranted for the following reasons:[227]

> That case rests on the importance to the States of enforcing the orders and judgments of their courts. There is little difference between the State's interest in forcing persons to transfer property in response to a court's judgment and in forcing persons to respond to the court's process on pain of contempt. Both *Juidice* and this case involve challenges to the processes by which the State compels compliance with the judgments of its courts.

Pennzoil reaffirms the principle that federal abstention is appropriate in private state civil proceedings that involve an important state interest. In both *Pennzoil* and *Juidice*, that interest was the process "by which the State compels compliance with the judgments of its courts."[228] *Younger* abstention, however, is not warranted in all instances involving parallel state civil proceedings. The Supreme Court repudiated this broad application of *Younger* doctrine in *New Orleans Pub. Serv., Inc. v. Council of New Orleans (NOPSI)*.[229] Thus, the Court has indicated that federal abstention is not appropriate when the state judicial proceedings involve legislative or executive actions.

In *NOPSI*, the Court indicated that federal abstention is not appropriate when the state judicial proceedings involve legislative or executive actions rather than judicial functions.[230] The Federal Energy Regulatory Commission (FERC) allocated the cost of the Grand Gulf 1 nuclear reactor among several companies that agreed to finance the reactor's construction and operation. NOPSI, which provides retail electrical service to New Orleans, sought a rate increase from the New Orleans City Council to cover the increase in its wholesale rates resulting from FERC's allocation of the reactor's costs. The Council determined that NOPSI's costs should not be completely reimbursed through a rate increase because of management negligence in failing to diversify its supply portfolio.[231] NOPSI challenged the Council's order in federal court on federal preemption grounds, but the district court abstained based on both *Burford* and *Younger* principles. The Fifth Circuit affirmed. The Supreme Court reversed the district court's decision to abstain on *Younger* grounds, declaring that federal court abstention is not warranted in all instances where there are pending state court proceedings. The Court stated:[232]

> Although our concern for comity and federalism has led us to expand the protection of *Younger* beyond state criminal prosecutions, to civil enforcement proceedings [citing *Huffman*, *Trainor*, and *Moore*], and even to civil

---

227 481 U.S. at 13–14; *see also* Moore v. Sims, 442 U.S. 415, 423 (1979) (*Younger* "fully applicable to civil proceedings in which important state interests are involved").

228 481 U.S. at 13–14.

229 New Orleans Pub. Serv., Inc. v. Council of New Orleans, 491 U.S. 350 (1989).

230 *Id.*; Green v. Jefferson County Comm'n, 563 F.3d 1243, 1251 (11th Cir. 2009) (*Younger* inapplicable to review county commission's action affecting employee benefits, but dismissal required on grounds of *res judicata*).

231 491 U.S. at 353.

232 491 U.S. at 367–368.

> proceedings involving certain orders that are uniquely in furtherance of the state courts' ability to perform their judicial functions [citing *Juidice* (civil contempt order) and *Pennzoil* (requirement for the posting of a bond pending appeal)], it has never been suggested that *Younger* requires abstention in deference to a state judicial proceeding reviewing legislative or executive action. Such a broad abstention requirement would make a mockery of the rule that only exceptional circumstances justify a federal court's refusal to decide a case in deference to the States.

The Court concluded that rate-setting by the New Orleans City Council essentially was a legislative task, and courts had never applied *Younger* to prevent review of matters other than judicial proceedings.[233]

The *NOPSI* decision therefore suggests that federal court abstention is not required in all instances when there is pending state civil proceeding.[234] *Younger* abstention is appropriate for state civil enforcement proceedings with parallel criminal statutes, if there are important state interests. The circuit courts consistently have ruled that *Younger* abstention applies only in civil cases presenting an important state interest.[235]

### [d] Application to Pending State Administrative Proceedings

The *Younger* abstention doctrine developed in the context of federal power to enjoin pending state criminal proceedings. Subsequently, the Court considered the application of *Younger* principles to various pending state civil proceedings. In *Middlesex County Ethics Committee v. Garden State Bar Association*,[236] the Court applied *Younger* abstention to a state administrative proceeding. In *Middlesex*, state administrative bar disciplinary charges were brought against a New Jersey attorney for acting in a manner "prejudicial to the administration of justice." The attorney filed suit in federal court, alleging that the state bar regulations and investigation were unconstitutional. The Supreme Court upheld the federal court's decision to dismiss the federal suit in deference to the pending state administrative proceeding. The Court noted that "[t]he policies underlying *Younger* are fully applicable to noncriminal judicial proceedings when important state interests are involved."[237]

The Court considered the state bar disciplinary proceedings as judicial because the state supreme court ultimately reviewed the results. In addition, state bar

---

[233] 491 U.S. at 370.

[234] *See* Sprint Communications, Inc. v. Jacobs, 134 S. Ct. 584, 187 L. Ed. 2d 505 (2013) (*Younger* abstention not appropriate in case involving action before Iowa Utilities Board proceedings where state authority was invoked to settle civil dispute between two private parties).

[235] *See, e.g.*, Chaulk Servs. v. Massachusetts Comm'n Against Discrimination, 70 F.3d 1361, 1378–1379 (1st Cir. 1995) (sex discrimination); Williams v. Lambert, 46 F.3d 1275, 1278 (2d Cir. 1995) (state interest in welfare of illegitimate children); Schilling v. White, 58 F.3d 1081, 1084 & n.3 (6th Cir. 1995) (state interest in state judicial proceedings).

[236] Middlesex County Ethics Comm. v. Garden State Bar Ass'n, 457 U.S. 423 (1982).

[237] 457 U.S. at 432.

discipline was closely related to the functioning of the state's judicial system.[238] *Middlesex*, therefore, represents an extension of *Juidice* and *Pennzoil*, applying *Younger* principles to pending state civil proceedings that involve important state interests in the performance of judicial functions.

The Supreme Court has further extended *Younger* doctrine in relation to state administrative proceedings.[239] In *Ohio Civil Rights Commission*, a school fired a pregnant teacher who objected to a school's religious doctrine that mothers stay at home with preschool children.[240] The teacher filed a complaint with the Ohio Civil Rights Commission alleging unlawful sex discrimination in violation of Ohio law. She also alleged that her firing was impermissible retaliation for attempting to exercise her rights. The Commission concluded that probable cause existed to initiate an administrative proceeding. The school raised the First Amendment as a defense to the state proceedings and filed a federal suit to enjoin the administrative proceedings. The Supreme Court held that the federal court "should have abstained from adjudicating this case under *Younger v. Harris*."[241]

The Court stated that *Younger* principles apply to state administrative proceedings that are judicial in nature and when important state interests are at stake, provided the federal plaintiff has a fair opportunity to litigate any constitutional claims. The elimination of sex discrimination was a sufficiently important state interest to bring the case within the *Younger* doctrine. Moreover, the federal plaintiff had adequate opportunity to raise its First Amendment claim in the state proceedings. Even if the Ohio Civil Rights Commission could not consider the statute's constitutionality, the school still could raise the constitutional claim in state appellate review of the administrative proceedings.[242] The Court stressed it was not altering existing doctrine that a litigant need not exhaust state administrative procedures before filing a federal civil rights action.[243] If no state administrative proceedings are pending, a party may file a federal suit without recourse to available state administrative remedies. But once state administrative proceedings have begun, federal court abstention is required if important state interests are at stake.[244] The circuit courts all follow this rule.[245]

---

238 457 U.S. at 433–434.

239 Ohio Civil Rights Comm'n v. Dayton Christian Sch., 477 U.S. 619 (1986).

240 477 U.S. at 623.

241 477 U.S. at 625.

242 477 U.S. at 625–629.

243 *See* Patsy v. Board of Regents, 457 U.S. 496 (1982).

244 Ohio Civil Rights Comm'n v. Dayton Christian Sch., 477 U.S. 627 (1986).

245 *See, e.g.,* Doe v. Connecticut Dep't of Health Servs., 75 F.3d 81, 85 (2d Cir. 1996) (discipline proceeding of physician; abstention is appropriate with ongoing state judicial proceeding); Fieger v. Thomas, 74 F.3d 740, 744 (6th Cir. 1996) (attorney discipline proceeding is within state supreme court jurisdiction, and abstention is appropriate with ongoing state judicial proceeding); Chaulk Servs. v. Massachusetts Comm'n Against Discrimination, 70 F.3d 1361, 1378–1379 (1st Cir. 1995) (*Younger* prevents interference with pending state administrative proceedings if they are judicial in nature); Employers Resource Management Co. v. Shannon, 65 F.3d 1126, 1134 (4th Cir. 1995) (*Younger* expanded into state administrative proceedings that are judicial in nature).

The circuit courts have all applied *Younger* abstention in the context of ongoing administrative proceedings when the other requirements for *Younger* abstention have been present.[246]

Some courts have distinguished between the commencement of formal enforcement proceedings, which may trigger *Younger* abstention, and preliminary investigations during which enforcement is only threatened, which do not. Abstaining before formal enforcement proceedings are commenced would allow a state agency to keep a party's constitutional rights in limbo while the agency contemplated enforcement but refrained from undertaking it. Therefore, the period between the threat of enforcement and the onset of formal enforcement proceedings may be an appropriate time for a litigant to bring its constitutional challenges in federal court.[247]

For *Younger* abstention to apply, the state administrative proceedings must be judicial in nature.[248] Among the factors courts consider in determining whether the proceedings are judicial in nature are whether they are (1) initiated by a complaint, (2) adjudicative in nature, (3) governed by court rules or rules of procedure, and (4) employ legal burdens of proof.[249]

In determining whether *Younger* abstention applies to state administrative proceedings, courts may distinguish between cases in which the state is coercively enforcing its laws and those in which the federal plaintiff is seeking a remedy for a past wrong. Some courts hold that *Younger* abstention may be appropriate with respect to coercive proceedings, but not with respect to remedial proceedings.[250] Courts consider the following factors relevant to the distinction between coercive and remedial proceedings: (1) whether the federal plaintiff's participation in the state administrative proceeding was mandatory (coercive) or an option was available to the federal plaintiff to redress a wrong inflicted by the state (remedial), (2) whether the state proceeding is itself the wrong the federal plaintiff seeks to correct, and (3) whether the state administrative proceeding was initiated to punish the federal plaintiff for an alleged bad act (coercive).[251]

---

[246] Geier v. Missouri Ethics Comm'n, 715 F.3d 674, 678–80 (8th Cir. 2013); Laurel Sand & Gravel, Inc. v. Wilson, 519 F.3d 156, 165–67 (4th Cir. 2008); Maymo-Melendez v. Alvarez-Ramirez, 364 F.3d 27, 34–38 (1st Cir. 2004).

[247] Guillemard-Ginorio v. Contreras-Gomez, 585 F.3d 508, 518–20 (1st Cir. 2009) (no *Younger* abstention in suit filed while agency was investigating plaintiff, but before agency had instituted formal enforcement proceedings against plaintiff).

[248] Kendall v. Russell, 572 F.3d 126, 131 (3d Cir. 2009) (*Younger* doctrine only permits abstention when there are ongoing state proceedings that are judicial in nature).

[249] *Id.*, 572 F.3d at 131–32.

[250] Casiano-Montañez v. State Ins. Fund Corp., 707 F.3d 124, 128 (1st Cir. 2013); Guillemard-Ginorio, 585 F.3d at 522–23; Brown ex rel. Brown v. Day, 555 F.3d 882, 884 (10th Cir. 2009) (collecting and analyzing cases).

[251] *Id.*

### [e] Application to Executive Branches of State and Local Governments

Federal courts have not applied *Younger* abstention to limit federal review of state and local executive action. The Supreme Court, however, almost extended *Younger* doctrine in this context in *Rizzo v. Goode*.[252] In *Rizzo*, the federal district court issued an injunction against the Philadelphia Police Department after finding substantial evidence of racially motivated police brutality. The court also directed correction of the department's internal procedures. The Supreme Court reversed, concluding that the district court had exercised its jurisdiction improperly. The federal suit was nonjusticiable because it did not present a "real and immediate injury."[253] In reaching this conclusion, the Court further noted:[254]

> [T]he principles of federalism which play such an important part in governing the relationship between federal courts and state governments, though initially expounded and perhaps entitled to their greatest weight in cases where it was sought to enjoin a criminal prosecution in progress, have not been limited either to that situation or indeed to a criminal proceeding itself. We think these principles likewise have applicability where injunctive relief is sought, not against the judicial branch of the state government, but against those in charge of an executive branch of an agency of state or local governments such as petitioners here.

Thus, the Supreme Court in *Rizzo* suggested that abstention might be appropriate to limit federal review of state executive action, but the Court did not indicate when. Subsequent Court decisions have not elaborated this view.[255] Some circuit courts have cited the *Rizzo* decision as possibly extending *Younger* principles to state and local executive branches, but none has directly applied it.[256]

## [6] Exceptions to *Younger* Doctrine

### [a] Bad Faith Prosecutions

The Supreme Court in *Younger v. Harris* stated that in "extraordinary circumstances" federal courts may enjoin pending state criminal prosecutions. The Court identified three such exceptions to the *Younger* doctrine. Other exceptions are possible in extraordinary circumstances in which the danger of irreparable loss is

---

[252] Rizzo v. Goode, 423 U.S. 362 (1976).

[253] 423 U.S. at 372.

[254] 423 U.S. at 380.

[255] *See* City of Canton v. Harris, 489 U.S. 378, 392 (1989); City of Los Angeles v. Lyons, 461 U.S. 95, 132 (1983) (citing *Rizzo* with approval, but no further discussion of abstention principle).

[256] *See, e.g.*, Palmer v. City of Chicago, 755 F.2d 560, 581 (7th Cir. 1985) (Cudahy, Cir. J., dissenting in part and concurring in part) (even if *Younger* is to be extended, as in *Rizzo*, to include nonjudicial state action, it applies only where "the federal plaintiff can secure a full and fair hearing" on constitutional claims by raising them as defense in state enforcement proceeding); United States v. City of Yonkers, 856 F.2d 444, 454 (2d Cir. 1988), *rev'd on other grounds*, 493 U.S. 265, 269 (1990) (district court must exercise restraint in determining what actions ought to be required of state and local governmental official).

great and immediate.[257]

The first exception to the *Younger* doctrine is when a state initiates a bad faith prosecution.[258] The *Younger* court described this exception by reference to the *Dombrowski* case. *Dombrowski* involved repeated state prosecutions to harass rather than convict civil rights activists. The *Dombrowski* plaintiffs alleged that state officials seized their property and repeatedly threatened and arrested them, even though the state had no intention of prosecuting them. Instead, the plaintiffs alleged that the officials were using the state's criminal justice system to harass and dissuade them from their civil rights work.[259] The *Younger* court viewed *Dombrowski* as presenting an exception to the general prohibition on enjoining pending state criminal prosecutions. Litigants should be able to challenge state action in federal court, because bad faith state actions deny defendants the opportunity to assert constitutional claims, once the state court dismisses the bad faith action.[260]

The Supreme Court has defined a *bad faith prosecution* as a prosecution that "has been brought without reasonable expectation of obtaining a valid conviction."[261] The Court has not applied this exception since its *Younger* decision, but has rejected claims of bad faith prosecution in several cases, including allegations of repeated police brutality against farm workers;[262] unreasonable use of the state's contempt procedures to harass;[263] repeated seizures of an allegedly obscene movie;[264] and impermissible bias by the state judiciary.[265] The bad faith prosecution exception, then, may be limited to the *Dombrowski* facts: repeated state prosecutions solely to harass rather than to convict; coupled with the inability to assert constitutional claims in the state proceedings because of lack of prosecution.

The circuit courts have also applied the bad faith exception narrowly, imposing a heavy burden on the plaintiff seeking to invoke the exception, requiring more than mere allegations of bad faith or harassment.[266]

---

[257] Walck v. Edmondson, 472 F.3d 1227, 1232–34 (10th Cir. 2007); Hi Tech Trans, LLC v. New Jersey, 382 F.3d 295, 305 (3d Cir. 2004).

[258] Younger v. Harris, 401 U.S. 37, 53 (1971).

[259] Dombrowski v. Pfister, 380 U.S. 479 (1965).

[260] Younger v. Harris, 401 U.S. 37, 49–50 (1971) (quoting Dombrowski v. Pfister, 380 U.S. 479, 485–486 (1965)).

[261] Kugler v. Helfant, 421 U.S. 117, 126 & n.6 (1975).

[262] Allee v. Medrano, 416 U.S. 802, 804 (1974).

[263] Juidice v. Vail, 430 U.S. 327, 332 (1977).

[264] Hicks v. Miranda, 422 U.S. 332, 340 (1975).

[265] Moore v. Sims, 442 U.S. 415, 432 (1979).

[266] RTM Media, L.L.C. v. City of Houston, 584 F.3d 220, 229 (5th Cir. 2009); Diamond "D" Const. Corp. v. McGowan, 282 F.3d 191, 198–201 (2d Cir. 2002); Tindall v. Wayne County Friend of the Court, 269 F.3d 533, 539–40 (6th Cir. 2001).

### [b] Patently Unconstitutional Laws

The second exception to the *Younger* doctrine involves patently unconstitutional state laws. A federal court may enjoin a state proceeding in such circumstances.[267] As with the bad faith exception, the Supreme Court has not applied this exception to justify a federal injunction in any case since the *Younger* decision, and the exception has been characterized as "very narrow."[268]

Litigants raised this exception, however, in *Trainor v. Hernandez*.[269] In this litigation, the Illinois Department of Public Aid used a state attachment statute to recover welfare benefits allegedly obtained by fraudulent means. The plaintiffs challenged the statute's constitutionality in federal court. The district court found the statute to patently violate due process. The Supreme Court reversed, holding that the district court was wrong in applying the exception and refusing to abstain.[270] Dissenting Justices argued that the majority's opinion effectively "eliminates one of the exceptions from the doctrine."[271] Although the Court continues to cite the exception,[272] the Court has not further elaborated or applied it to any fact situation.

### [c] Unavailability of Adequate State Forum

The third exception to the *Younger* doctrine is the unavailability of an adequate state forum in which the federal plaintiff can raise a constitutional claim. The Court did not explicitly name this as one of the "extraordinary circumstances" warranting federal intervention, but rather mentioned it in discussing factors favoring abstention. Thus, the Court stated that if there are pending state proceedings, constitutional issues should be raised there "unless it plainly appears that this course would not afford adequate protection."[273]

The Court considered the adequacy of a state forum in *Gibson v. Berryhill*.[274] In *Gibson*, licensed optometrists who were corporate employees brought a federal action to enjoin proceedings before the Alabama Board of Optometry. The optometry board, composed entirely of private practitioners, was seeking to revoke the licenses of state optometrists who worked as employees rather than as private practitioners. The district court issued the injunction because it concluded that the board was biased in light of the economic benefit to its members of the revocation action. Without explicitly stating that *Younger* applied to this administrative proceeding, the Court stated:[275]

---

[267] Younger v. Harris, 401 U.S. 37, 53–54 (1971).

[268] Rossi v. Gemma, 489 F.3d 26 n.16 (1st Cir. 2007).

[269] Trainor v. Hernandez, 431 U.S. 434 (1977).

[270] 431 U.S. at 447.

[271] 431 U.S. at 463 (Stevens, J., dissenting).

[272] *See* Moore v. Sims, 442 U.S. 415, 424 (1979); New Orleans Pub. Serv., Inc. v. Council of New Orleans, 491 U.S. 350, 366–367 (1989).

[273] Younger v. Harris, 401 U.S. 37, 45 (1971) (quoting *Ex parte* Young, 209 U.S. 123 (1908)).

[274] Gibson v. Berryhill, 411 U.S. 564 (1973).

[275] 411 U.S. at 577–578.

> *Younger v. Harris* contemplates the outright dismissal of the federal suit, and the presentation of all claims, both state and federal, to the state courts. Such a course naturally presupposes the opportunity to raise and have timely decided by a competent state tribunal the federal issues involved. Here the predicate for a *Younger v. Harris* dismissal was lacking, for the appellees alleged, and the district court concluded, that the State Board of Optometry was incompetent by reason of bias to adjudicate the issues pending before it. If the District Court's conclusion was correct in this regard, it was also correct that it need not defer to the Board. Nor, in these circumstances, would a different result be required simply because judicial review, *de novo* or otherwise, would be forthcoming at the conclusion of the administrative proceedings.

Federal courts may intervene in pending state proceedings, then, if a state tribunal involved is biased and cannot constitutionally conduct appropriate hearings.

The Supreme Court rejected application of the exception, however, in *Kugler v. Helfant*.[276] In *Kugler*, a state municipal judge was indicted for alleged collusive behavior with a state deputy attorney general and New Jersey Supreme Court members. The plaintiff alleged that the state supreme court was so involved he could not receive an unbiased hearing. The United States Supreme Court disagreed, concluding that there was insufficient evidence that the state courts could not provide a fair hearing. The Court suggested that it was impossible to conclude that the state courts could not adequately resolve the plaintiff's constitutional claims, in light of state judicial disqualification procedures, as well as changes in the state supreme court personnel.[277]

Thus, state proceedings may be deemed inadequate if the federal litigant can demonstrate impermissible state bias, or that the state tribunal cannot afford adequate protection for the federal plaintiff's constitutional claims. The court may also decline to abstain under the *Younger* doctrine when the plaintiff has no state forum in which to raise a constitutional claim because the state court has ruled that the plaintiff's claim is not justiciable.[278]

## [d] Waiver

A final exception to the *Younger* doctrine is waiver. Parties seeking to invoke *Younger* abstention must raise it; federal courts will not raise it on their own (*sua sponte*).[279] In addition, a state government can waive its *Younger* abstention argument, thereby permitting a federal court to hear a suit. If a state "voluntarily chooses to submit to a federal forum, principles of comity do not demand that the federal court force the case back into the State's own system."[280]

---

[276] Kugler v. Helfant, 421 U.S. 117 (1975).

[277] 421 U.S. at 127–129.

[278] *See* Mockaitis v. Harcleroad, 104 F.3d 1522, 1528 (9th Cir. 1997) (priest seeking destruction of audio tape of him administering penance to jail inmate charged with murder had no remedy at law because state court had refused to hear his petition holding it did not present justiciable controversy).

[279] Swisher v. Brady, 438 U.S. 204, 213 & n.11 (1978).

[280] Ohio Bureau of Employment Servs. v. Hodory, 431 U.S. 471, 480 (1977).

## § 13.06 ABSTENTION FOR REASONS OF SOUND JUDICIAL ADMINISTRATION: *COLORADO RIVER* ABSTENTION

### [1] Parallel, Duplicative Litigation, and Judicial Efficiency

The problem of parallel, duplicative litigation involves what a federal court should do when a federal action essentially duplicates a simultaneous state lawsuit. When state and federal courts have concurrent jurisdiction of virtually identical lawsuits — litigation involving the same parties and the same claims — the Anti-Injunction Act prohibits the federal court from enjoining the state proceedings.[281] Generally, however, parallel, duplicative litigation wastes judicial time and resources and increases transaction costs.

Problems of duplicative litigation arise in several ways, but a common form of duplicative litigation is the reactive lawsuit. *Reactive* litigation occurs when a state defendant reciprocally files a federal suit concerning the same subject. The state defendant may file a reactive federal suit for several reasons, including perceptions of bias or sympathy, strategic or tactical advantages, or docket congestion. Additionally, a state defendant may reactively file a federal declaratory judgment action in order to take advantage of a federal court's declaration of rights and duties in the state action.[282]

Duplicative litigation also can also involve *repetitive* suits. In a repetitive suit, a state court plaintiff may file essentially the same suit in federal court. There are many possible reasons for such duplicative filing, including harassment, delay, or adverse rulings in the state forum.[283] As long as the state and federal courts have concurrent subject matter jurisdiction, no jurisdictional rules prohibit such parallel repetitive litigation.

Federal courts generally must exercise their validly conferred jurisdiction.[284] Moreover, federal courts need not dismiss or stay an action because of pending parallel state litigation.[285] Federal courts generally may not enjoin state proceedings, because the Anti-Injunction Act[286] and the *Younger* abstention doctrine generally prohibit this. Further, a state court cannot enjoin a federal court

---

[281] 28 U.S.C. § 2283.

[282] *See* Wilson, Comment, *Federal Court Stays and Dismissals in Deference to Parallel State Court Proceedings: The Impact of* Colorado River, 44 U. Chi. L. Rev. 641, 644 (1977); *see, e.g.,* Microsoftware Complex Sys., Inc. v. Ontel Corp., 686 F.2d 531 (7th Cir. 1982).

[283] *See* Wilson, Comment, *Federal Court Stays and Dismissals in Deference to Parallel State Court Proceedings: The Impact of* Colorado River, 44 U. Chi. L. Rev. 641, 643 (1977); *see, e.g.,* Tovar v. Billmeyer, 609 F.2d 1291 (9th Cir. 1980).

[284] Colorado River Water Conservation Dist. v. United States, 424 U.S. 800, 817 (1976) (duty stems from "the virtually unflagging obligation of the federal courts to exercise the jurisdiction given them").

[285] *See, e.g.,* Stanton v. Embrey, 93 U.S. 548, 554 (1877) (pendency of prior suit in another jurisdiction is not bar to subsequent suit in circuit court or in court below, even though two suits are for same cause of action).

[286] *See* 28 U.S.C. § 2283; *see generally* Ch. 12, *The Anti-Injunction Acts.*

proceeding,[287] nor are state courts obliged to abstain and defer to the federal courts. Federal courts may abstain from hearing a case, but only in very narrowly defined circumstances.

### [2] Inroads on the Problem of Duplicative Litigation

The Supreme Court found, in *Brillhart v. Excess Ins. Co.*, that federal court deference to a state proceeding might be appropriate in some circumstances apart from the traditional abstention doctrines.[288] In *Brillhart*, a federal court dismissed a diversity declaratory judgment action because there was similar pending state litigation. The Court held that federal refusal to exercise jurisdiction was appropriate if the state proceedings would adequately settle the controversy. The Court noted that the federal diversity suit involved state law issues, and that declaratory judgment actions are discretionary.[289] The Court concluded:[290]

> Ordinarily it would be uneconomical as well as vexatious for a federal court to proceed in a declaratory judgment suit where another suit is pending in a state court presenting the same issues, not governed by federal law, between the same parties. Gratuitous interference with the orderly and comprehensive disposition of a state court litigation should be avoided.

Lower courts subsequently used the *Brillhart* decision to expand the opportunities for federal courts to refuse to exercise their jurisdiction because of simultaneous state litigation. In most instances, the federal court stayed its proceedings, based on a broad discretionary power to control the court's docket.[291] The Supreme Court, however, implicitly disapproved of abstention as a docket-control mechanism.[292] Instead, the Supreme Court consistently has emphasized the federal courts' unflagging obligation to exercise its jurisdiction, and clearly indicated that abstention because of duplicative litigation is appropriate in only very limited, exceptional circumstances.

### [3] The *Colorado River* Decision: Exceptional Circumstances Defined

The Supreme Court has held that federal courts may abstain from exercising their validly conferred jurisdiction in certain exceptional circumstances of parallel, duplicative litigation. The federal courts may do so in the interests of sound judicial administration and economy.[293]

---

[287] General Atomic Co. v. Felter, 434 U.S. 12, 17 (1977); Donovan v. Dallas, 377 U.S. 408, 413 (1964).

[288] Brillhart v. Excess Ins. Co., 316 U.S. 491 (1942).

[289] *See* 28 U.S.C. § 2201.

[290] Brillhart v. Excess Ins. Co., 316 U.S.491, 495 (1942).

[291] *See, e.g.*, Weiner v. Shearson, Hammill & Co., 521 F.2d 817, 820 (9th Cir. 1975); Aetna State Bank v. Altheimer, 430 F.2d 750, 756 (7th Cir. 1970); Amdur v. Lizars, 372 F.2d 103, 106 (4th Cir. 1967); Mottolese v. Kaufman, 176 F.2d 301, 303 (2d Cir. 1949).

[292] Colorado River Water Conservation Dist. v. United States, 424 U.S. 800 (1976); *see* Moses H. Cone Memorial Hosp. v. Mercury Constr. Corp., 460 U.S. 1 (1983).

[293] Colorado River Water Conservation Dist. v. United States, 424 U.S. 800, 817 (1976).

In *Colorado River*, the United States, as trustee for Indian tribes, brought suit in federal court seeking a declaration of water rights on federal lands. The complaint named over one thousand defendants. A federal defendant filed a state motion to join the United States as a party to a state court proceeding concerning the same rights. Although the United States generally may not be sued in state court without its consent, the McCarran Amendment[294] provides such consent in state water rights actions. At the same time, several other federal defendants filed a motion seeking to dismiss the federal action for lack of subject matter jurisdiction. They alleged that the McCarran Amendment precluded the federal court from assuming jurisdiction over the question. Instead of dismissing the federal suit, the district court stayed its proceeding because of the parallel state proceedings. The Tenth Circuit reversed, finding that none of the recognized abstention doctrines applied.

The Supreme Court reversed and reinstated the district court's stay. The Court agreed that the case did not fit any recognized abstention doctrines. The Court also emphasized that the federal courts have a "virtually unflagging obligation . . . to exercise the jurisdiction given them." Accordingly, a federal court usually may not abstain from hearing a suit just because there is a pending parallel state litigation. Moreover, a pending state action does not bar a federal suit concerning the same subject matter, if the federal court has jurisdiction.[295] The Supreme Court nevertheless found that federal courts may abstain out of deference to pending state court proceedings under truly exceptional circumstances. The Court circumscribed this kind of abstention, however, suggesting that the "circumstances permitting the dismissal of a federal suit due to the presence of a concurrent state proceeding for reasons of wise judicial administration are considerably more limited than the circumstances appropriate for abstention."[296]

The Court identified four factors a federal court should consider when determining whether the interests of wise judicial administration outweigh a court's duty to exercise its jurisdiction. These factors include consideration of: (1) which court first assumed jurisdiction over the res involved in the actions, (2) the relative inconvenience of the federal forum, (3) the desirability of avoiding piecemeal litigation, and (4) the order of filing for the state and federal actions. The Court emphasized that no single factor was determinative, and that only the clearest justifications warrant dismissal of a federal proceeding.[297]

In *Colorado River*, the Court found that the federal court's abstention was appropriate because the McCarran Amendment reflected a congressional policy to avoid piecemeal litigation in adjudicating water rights. This policy was akin to the rule that jurisdiction should remain with the court that first assumes jurisdiction over a *res*. Thus, the adjudication of water rights, like questions over property, should be conducted in "unified proceedings" such as those available under the

---

[294] *See* 43 U.S.C. § 666.

[295] Colorado River Water Conservation Dist. v. United States, 424 U.S. 800, 817 (1976).

[296] 424 U.S. at 818.

[297] 424 U.S. at 818–819.

state system.[298] In finding abstention appropriate, the Court noted other persuasive factors, such as the apparent absence of federal proceedings beyond the complaint, the extensive involvement of state water rights, the close proximity of the state court, and the United States participation in other state water rights proceedings. Taken together, these factors constituted exceptional circumstances warranting federal abstention.[299]

### [4] The *Will* Decision: Exceptional Circumstances Revisited

The Supreme Court further elaborated circumstances justifying *Colorado River* abstention in *Will v. Calvert Fire Ins. Co.*[300] In *Will*, the Calvert Fire Insurance Company rescinded its membership in a reinsurance pool operated by American Mutual Reinsurance Company. American sued Calvert in state court for a declaratory judgment that the pool agreement remained in effect. Calvert's answer in state court alleged that the pool agreement was unenforceable, because it violated the 1933 Securities Act, Rule 10b-5 of the Securities Exchange Act of 1934, and the Illinois Securities Act. Calvert also counterclaimed for damages, except for the Rule 10b-5 violation, which was exclusively enforceable in the federal courts. Simultaneously with filing its state answer, Calvert filed a federal damage action for American's alleged violation of Rule 10b-5. American moved to dismiss or abate the federal action, arguing that the reinsurance agreement was not a security and the federal court should defer to the pending state proceedings. The district court agreed to stay the federal litigation; Calvert then obtained a writ of mandamus from the Seventh Circuit compelling District Judge Will to proceed with the federal suit.

The Supreme Court reversed, in a divided four-one-four decision, ruling that the district court had appropriately abstained. The plurality reasoned that district courts have discretion to abstain when there is an identical pending state litigation. Although the opinion recognized that the Court's prior *Colorado River* decision had stressed that federal courts must hear cases within their jurisdiction, the plurality instead relied on *Brillhart v. Excess Insurance Co.* for the proposition that "[i]t is equally well settled that a district court is under no compulsion to exercise that jurisdiction where the controversy may be settled more expeditiously in state court."[301] The plurality did not discuss the "extraordinary circumstances" required by *Colorado River*, but instead emphasized that federal abstention is discretionary when there is a parallel state court proceeding.

Justice Blackmun concurred in the judgment, but not the plurality's reasoning. He argued that *Colorado River* established that abstention due to parallel state proceedings was appropriate only in "extraordinary circumstances," and that *Brillhart* was no longer valid precedent. He suggested that the Seventh Circuit should have required reconsideration in light of *Colorado River*.[302]

---

[298] 424 U.S. at 819.

[299] 424 U.S. at 820.

[300] Will v. Calvert Fire Ins. Co., 437 U.S. 655 (1978).

[301] 437 U.S. at 662–663.

[302] 437 U.S. at 667–668 (Blackmun, J., concurring).

Four justices — Justices Brennan, Marshall, and Powell, and Chief Justice Burger — dissented. They argued that the plurality opinion was guilty of "[i]gnoring wholesale the analytical framework set forth in *Colorado River*."[303] They further argued that abstention must be rare and limited to "exceptional circumstances." The dissenters also argued that *Brillhart* had no application because it was a diversity suit, state law would govern the outcome, and most significantly, the federal action in *Brillhart* had sought a declaratory judgment. The Federal Declaratory Judgment Act vests federal courts with discretionary jurisdiction.[304] The dissenters pointed out that "[i]t was primarily because federal jurisdiction over declaratory judgment suits is discretionary that *Brillhart* found the District Court's deference to state-court proceedings permissible."[305] Thus, the dissenters considered the plurality opinion's reliance on *Brillhart* to be totally wrong, as was the failure to follow *Colorado River* abstention criteria.

### [5] The *Moses Cone* Decision: Exceptional Circumstances Expanded

The lack of a majority opinion in *Will*, and the plurality's reliance on *Brillhart* rather than the *Colorado River* "exceptional circumstances" language, engendered a good deal of doctrinal confusion in the federal courts.[306] The Supreme Court subsequently attempted to resolve this confusion and clearly rejected the plurality's suggestion in *Will* that *Brillhart* might have application beyond the context of declaratory judgments.[307]

In *Moses H. Cone*, the plaintiff brought a state action seeking a determination that its contract with the defendant construction company was not subject to arbitration. The construction company then brought a federal diversity action for a declaratory judgment compelling arbitration under the Federal Arbitration Act. The district court stayed its proceedings in deference to the pending state court proceedings, but the Court of Appeals reversed, finding abstention inappropriate.

The Supreme Court upheld the appellate decision that abstention was inappropriate and reaffirmed its *Colorado River* holding. The Court repeated that federal courts may abstain from exercising their jurisdiction only in exceptional circumstances, and the mere presence of a duplicative, parallel state proceeding was not enough to justify abstention. The Court warned that federal courts were not to use the four *Colorado River* factors as a mere checklist. Instead, federal courts should carefully balance all considerations involved. The *Colorado River* factors were "to be applied in a pragmatic, flexible manner with a view to the

---

303 437 U.S. at 674 (Brennan, J., dissenting).

304 28 U.S.C. § 2201 ("In a case of actual controversy within its jurisdiction . . . any court of the United States, upon the filing of an appropriate pleading, *may* declare the rights and other legal relations of any interested party seeking such declaration") (emphasis added).

305 437 U.S. at 671–672 (Brennan, J., dissenting).

306 *See* Platt, Note, *Abstention and Mandamus after Will v. Calvert Fire Ins. Co.*, 64 CORNELL L. REV. 566, 585 (1979).

307 Moses H. Cone Memorial Hosp. v. Mercury Constr. Corp., 460 U.S. 1 (1983).

realities of the case at hand."[308] In addition, the Court added a new factor: whether the litigation involved a federal question. Abstention in *Colorado River* was justified partially because the McCarran Amendment specifically made the adjudication of water rights *not* a federal question. Thus, the presence of a federal question should weigh against a federal court's abstention.[309]

The Court again stressed that federal courts generally must decide cases within their jurisdiction, stating:[310]

> We emphasize that our task in cases such as this is not to find some substantial reason for the *exercise* of federal jurisdiction by the district court; rather, the task is to ascertain whether there exist "exceptional" circumstances, the "clearest of justifications," that can suffice under *Colorado River* to justify the *surrender* of that jurisdiction. The Supreme Court therefore reaffirmed its *Colorado River* decision and restated that federal courts may not abstain when there is identical, concurrent state litigation, except in truly exceptional cases.

The Court reaffirmed the basic principles of *Colorado River* abstention in *Arizona v. San Carlos Apache Tribe*,[311] a case that duplicated the *Colorado River* litigation except for the plaintiff's identity. The Court found the same exceptional circumstances justifying federal court abstention.[312]

### [a] Six Factors Considered

In *Moses H. Cone*, the Court identified six factors as relevant to the determination of whether exceptional circumstances justify abstention: (1) which court first assumed jurisdiction over the res in the actions, (2) the relative convenience of the federal forum, (3) the desirability of avoiding piecemeal litigation, (4) the order in which state and federal court obtained jurisdiction, (5) the presence of federal law issues, and (6) whether the state forum would adequately protect the parties' interests. The Court had identified the first four factors in *Colorado River*. The Court added the latter two in *Moses H. Cone*.

None of the *Colorado River* factors weighed in favor of abstention in *Moses*. Consideration of the first three factors was straightforward. There was no assumption by either court of jurisdiction over any res or property, no contention that the federal forum was less convenient than the state forum, and no danger of piecemeal litigation as a result of litigating in federal court.

The Court explained that the fourth factor, the order in which the courts obtained jurisdiction, is not to be measured exclusively by which complaint was filed first. Rather, the court is to consider how much progress had been made in the two actions. The Court concluded that this factor weighed against the district court's stay, noting that no substantial proceedings had taken place in state court except an

---

308 460 U.S. at 21.

309 460 U.S. at 23–24.

310 460 U.S. at 25–26.

311 Arizona v. San Carlos Apache Tribe, 463 U.S. 545 (1983).

312 463 U.S. at 566.

abortive temporary injunction, while in the federal suit, the parties had taken most of the steps necessary to resolve the arbitrability issue.

The *Moses* Court then considered the fifth factor: the presence of federal law issues. The Court stated that in some rare circumstances, the presence of state law issues may weigh in favor of abstention. In contrast, the presence of federal law issues must always be a major consideration weighing against abstention. This factor weighed against abstention in *Moses*, because the Arbitration Act governed the case.

Finally, the Court considered whether the state forum would adequately protect the parties' interests. The Court acknowledged that state courts are as obligated as federal courts to grant stays of litigation under the Arbitration Act. However, the same was not necessarily true of orders to compel arbitration. Because there was substantial room for doubt that the construction company could obtain a state court order compelling arbitration, the Court concluded that this factor weighed against abstention.

Although the Court in *Moses H. Cone* identified six factors for courts to consider in determining whether to abstain in the face of a duplicative, parallel state proceeding, the Court also emphasized that court should not treat the factors as a checklist to be applied mechanically. Rather, the courts must carefully balance all of the important factors in a pragmatic, flexible manner, with the balance heavily weighted in favor of the exercise of jurisdiction, and against abstention. The weight to be given to any one factor will vary greatly from case to case, depending on the particular setting of the case.

## [6] Prerequisites for Colorado River Abstention

### [a] Parallel State Proceedings

The existence of a parallel, ongoing state court proceeding is a threshold requirement for *Colorado River* abstention.[313] Generally, suits are parallel when they have the same parties and the same issue.[314] However, the suits need not be identical to be considered parallel.[315] The presence of additional parties or claims in one case does not necessarily preclude a finding that the suits are parallel.[316] On the other hand, if the actions involve different issues, remedies, and proof requirements, they generally will not be considered parallel.[317] The mere fact that the issues in each proceeding may depend on some of the same facts does not make the proceedings parallel.[318] The critical consideration in determining whether federal

---

[313] American Family Life Assurance Co. v. Biles, 714 F.3d 887, 892 (5th Cir. 2013); Huon v. Johnson & Bell Ltd., 657 F.3d 641, 646 (7th Cir. 2011).

[314] American Family Life, 714 F.3d at 892.

[315] D.A. Osguthorpe Family P'ship v. ASC Utah, Inc., 705 F.3d 1223, 1233 (10th Cir. 2013); Beck v. Dobrowski, 559 F.3d 680, 686(7th Cir. 2009).

[316] Beck, 559 F.3d at 686.

[317] Huon, 657 F.3d at 646; Gannett Co., Inc. v. Clark Constr. Group, Inc., 286 F.3d 737, 741–43 (4th Cir. 2002).

[318] Scottsdale Ins. Co. v. Detco Indus., 426 F.3d 994, 997 (8th Cir. 2005).

and state suits are parallel is whether the state litigation will dispose of all claims raised in the federal action.[319] Any substantial doubt that the non-federal litigation will completely and promptly resolve the issues between the parties in the federal action precludes abstention on the basis of parallel litigation.[320] This is true even if the plaintiff in the federal action could have raised the issues in the state court proceeding and chose not to do so.[321]

### [b] Exceptional Circumstances

The second requirement for *Colorado* abstention is the presence of exceptional circumstances that justify deference to the state court proceedings. In determining whether abstention is appropriate, appellate courts generally apply the exceptional circumstances balancing test developed in *Moses H. Cone*, considering at least the four *Colorado River* factors and the two additional factors in *Moses H. Cone*.[322] However, courts have recognized that other factors may be considered and that the list is not meant to be exhaustive or rigid.[323]

Among other factors that courts consider are the vexatious or reactive nature of the state or federal filings, and the relative progress of the litigation in state and federal courts, which the Supreme Court considered under the fourth factor in *Moses H. Cone*. Courts also may consider the desire to avoid forum shopping, whether the state court proceedings will resolve all issues before the federal court, the presence of absence of concurrent jurisdiction, the availability of removal, and whether the concurrent cases involve a federal statute that evinces a policy favoring abstention. Because of the presumption against abstention, absent or neutral factors weigh against abstention and in favor of exercising federal jurisdiction.

## [7] Appropriateness in Declaratory Judgment Suits

### [a] *Wilton* Decision: District Court Has Discretion

In *Wilton v. Seven Falls Co.*, the Supreme Court resolved a split among the circuits and settled whether the *Brillhart* decision survived the Court's abstention decisions in *Colorado River* and *Moses H. Cone*. The Court held that *Brillhart* governs a district court's discretionary decision to stay a declaratory judgment action during pending parallel state proceedings.[324]

---

319 Beck, 559 F.3d at 686; AAR Int'l, Inc. v. Nimelias Enters. S.A., 250 F.3d 510, 517–20 (7th Cir. 2001).

320 Huon, 657 F.3d at 646; United States v. Rice, 605 F.3d 473, 476 (8th Cir. 2010).

321 Truserv. Corp. v. Flegles, 419 F.3d 584, 591–93 (7th Cir. 2005).

322 American Family Life, 714 F.3d at 892; D.A. Osguthorpe Family P'ship, 705 F.3d at 1234–35; Niagara Mohawk Power Corp. v. Hudson River-Black, 673 F.3d 84, 101–04 (2d Cir. 2012); R.R. Street & Co., Inc. v. Transport Ins. Co., 656 F.3d 966, 978–79 (9th Cir. 2011).

323 Tyrer v. City of S. Beloit, 456 F.3d 744, 751, 754 (7th Cir. 2006); Currie v. Group Ins. Comm'n, 290 F.3d 1, 10 (1st Cir. 2002).

324 Wilton v. Seven Falls Co., 515 U.S. 277, 287–289 (1995). For general discussion of declaratory judgment actions, see 12 Moore's Federal Practice Ch. 57, *Declaratory Judgment* (Matthew Bender 3d ed.).

This question had been unresolved for many years. The Supreme Court first addressed the issue in *Brillhart*, when it held that a federal court was "under no compulsion to exercise [its declaratory judgment] jurisdiction" if the controversy might be settled more expeditiously in state court.[325] The Court stated that abstention was discretionary, and the federal court should examine the scope of the pending state proceeding, the nature of available defenses, and whether the parties' claims could be adjudicated satisfactorily.[326]

The Court subsequently based its plurality decision in *Will* on the *Brillhart* decision. Some Justices, however, questioned whether the *Brillhart* holding survived the Supreme Court's *Colorado River* decision, which limited abstention to truly extraordinary circumstances.[327] The Court then reaffirmed this narrower standard in *Moses H. Cone*.[328] As a result, lower federal courts were divided over whether they had discretion to abstain in declaratory judgment actions involving parallel state proceedings. Some courts held that abstention was justified to avoid the risk of conflicting determinations of applicable law, while others held that they could not abstain because a declaratory judgment was not a sufficiently exceptional circumstance to justify abstention.[329]

In *Wilton v. Seven Falls Co.*, a case almost identical to *Brillhart*, the Supreme Court held that *Brillhart's* discretionary standard, rather than the *Colorado River* exceptional circumstances test, governs a district court's decision to stay a declaratory judgment action.[330] The *Wilton* case involved litigation over the ownership and operation of Texas oil and gas properties. In a state action, some underwriters refused to defend or indemnify the defendants under several commercial liability insurance policies. After the defendants lost, they notified the underwriters that they intended to file a state court action on the policies. The underwriters immediately filed a federal declaratory judgment action for a declaration that their policies did not cover the defendants' liability. The defendants filed their state court suit and moved to dismiss or, in the alternative, to stay the underwriters' federal action. The district court entered a stay because the state suit encompassed the same coverage issues in the federal action, and the Fifth Circuit affirmed.

---

[325] Brillhart v. Excess Ins. Co., 316 U.S. 491, 494 (1942).

[326] 316 U.S. at 495.

[327] Will v. Calvert Fire Ins. Co., 437 U.S. 655, 667–668 (1978) (Blackmun. J., concurring).

[328] Moses H. Cone Memorial Hosp. v. Mercury Constr. Corp., 460 U.S. 1, 25–26 (1983).

[329] *Compare, e.g.*, Employers Ins. of Wausau v. Missouri Elec. Works, 23 F.3d 1372, 1374 & n.3 (8th Cir. 1994) (pursuant to *Colorado River* and *Moses H. Cone*, district court may not stay or dismiss declaratory judgment action absent "exceptional circumstances") *and* Lumbermens Mut. Casualty Co. v. Connecticut Bank & Trust, 806 F.2d 411, 413–414 (2d Cir. 1986) (district court may not stay or dismiss declaratory judgment action absent "exceptional circumstances") *with* Travelers Ins. Co. v. Louisiana Farm Bureau Fed'n, Inc., 996 F.2d 774, 778 & n.12 (5th Cir. 1993) ("exceptional circumstances" test of *Colorado River* and *Moses H. Cone* is inapplicable in declaratory judgment actions) *and* Mitcheson v. Harris, 955 F.2d 235, 237–238 (4th Cir. 1992) ("exceptional circumstances" test is inapplicable in declaratory judgment actions).

[330] Wilton v. Seven Falls Co., 515 U.S. 277, 287 (1995).

The Supreme Court traced the history of the *Colorado River* abstention doctrine and concluded that subsequent decisions had "in no way undermine[d] the conclusion of *Brillhart* that the decision whether to defer to the concurrent jurisdiction of a state court is, in the last analysis, a matter committed to the district court's discretion."[331] The Court stressed the fact that the Declaratory Judgment Act is discretionary,[332] and concluded that "[d]istinct features of the Declaratory Judgment Act, we believe, justify a standard vesting district courts with greater discretion in declaratory judgment actions than that permitted under the 'exceptional circumstances' test of *Colorado River* and *Moses H. Cone.*"[333]

Thus, a discretionary standard governs a district court's decision to stay a declaratory judgment action during the pendency of parallel state court proceedings, while the more rigorous *Colorado River* exceptional circumstances test applies to all other abstention requests that implicate parallel duplicative litigation.[334]

The *Wilton* Court did not resolve the issue of whether the district court must still weigh considerations of comity, sound judicial administration, and policy against forum shopping before ruling on the merits of a claim for declaratory relief when a parallel state court action is anticipated, but never filed, because the dispute is settled.[335] The Ninth Circuit has held that a district court must consider whether existing state court remedies, such as indemnification or the right to seek a declaration under state law, will provide an adequate remedy for a party who files a claim under the Declaratory Judgment Act. Even when no related state court proceeding is ever filed because the underlying dispute is settled after the federal action for declaratory relief is filed, the district court still has a duty to weigh all relevant factors before exercising its discretion under the Declaratory Judgment Act.[336]

Several circuits have adopted an intermediate standard for determining whether abstention is appropriate in a declaratory judgment action when the state court proceedings are not parallel. These courts strike a balance between the broad discretion and exceptional circumstances standards.[337] The more lenient *Brillhart* (or *Wilton*) abstention analysis governs a district court's discretion to stay or dismiss when the federal suit seeks only a declaration of rights. If other relief is

---

331 Will v. Calvert Fire Ins. Co., 437 U.S. 655, 664 (1978).

332 28 U.S.C. § 2201 ("In a case of actual controversy within its jurisdiction . . . any court of the United States, upon the filing of an appropriate pleading, *may* declare the rights and other legal relations of any interested party seeking such declaration" [emphasis added]).

333 Wilton v. Seven Falls Co., 515 U.S. 277, 287 (1995).

334 *See* National Union Fire Ins. Co. v. Karp, 108 F.3d 17, 21–22 (2d Cir. 1997) (district court had discretion under *Wilton* rule to determine whether to abstain from deciding request for declaratory judgment regarding insurance coverage that was raised in interpleader action; *Wilton* applied even though insurer's claim was not brought exclusively under the Declaratory Judgments Act).

335 Wilton v. Seven Falls Co., 515 U.S. 277, 290 (1995) ("We do not attempt at this time to delineate the outer boundaries of [the district court's] discretion in . . . cases in which there are no parallel state proceedings").

336 Budget Rent-A-Car v. Crawford, 108 F.3d 1075, 1081 (9th Cir. 1997).

337 Scottsdale Ins. Co. v. Detco Indus., 426 F.3d 994, 998 (8th Cir. 2005); United States v. City of Las Cruces, 289 F.3d 1170, 1187 (10th Cir. 2002).

requested, the situation is less clear. The question of whether to apply Brillhart or the more stringent *Colorado River* standard has been approached in at least four different ways by the appellate courts.[338]

### [b] Appellate Review for Abuse of Discretion

The court of appeals reviews the district court's decision to grant or refrain from granting declaratory relief under an abuse of discretion standard.[339] In a series of decisions, the Ninth Circuit has addressed district court rulings on declaratory judgment cases involving state law issues. When the district court offers no indication that it considered the issue, and the district court's exercise of jurisdiction is not clearly improper, the court of appeals usually should remand the matter to the district court with directions to consider whether the exercise of jurisdiction is proper.[340] Therefore, the Ninth Circuit will vacate a district court's decision filed under the Declaratory Judgment Act, and remand with instructions to consider whether the facts demonstrate that the exercise of its discretionary jurisdiction is appropriate.

When the record contains no facts or circumstances that would permit the district court to exercise its discretionary jurisdiction, the appellate court will not remand an action filed under the Declaratory Judgment Act. Rather, the court will vacate the district court's decision on the merits and direct the district court to dismiss the action.[341] The appellate court also will not remand the case if the district court erred in exercising jurisdiction, but the error was harmless. In that instance, the appellate court will affirm the district court's decision.[342]

## [8] Unresolved Questions in *Colorado River* Abstention Stay of Proceedings — Retention of Federal Court Jurisdiction

### [a] Defining and Balancing Exceptional Circumstances

Federal courts should not abstain from deciding a case in deference to parallel, duplicative state litigation absent truly exceptional circumstances. Although the Supreme Court has indicated factors the district courts should weigh in determining whether to abstain,[343] the Court has not established a definitive list and many uncertainties remain. For example, the Court has ruled that *Colorado River*

---

338 *See* New England Ins. Co. v. Barnett, 561 F.3d 392, 395–96 (5th Cir. 2009) (describing four approaches and collecting cases).

339 Wilton v. Seven Falls Co., 515 U.S. 277, 288–289 (1995).

340 Government Employees Ins. Co. v. Dizol, 108 F.3d 999, 1008 (9th Cir. 1997), *vacated on other grounds*, 133 F.3d 1220 (9th Cir. 1998) (case remanded in view of genuine dispute regarding whether state court action was still pending because parties settled before federal action was filed).

341 Employers Reinsurance Corp. v. Karussos, 65 F.3d 796, 799–801 (9th Cir. 1995).

342 Golden Eagle Ins. Co. v. Travelers Cos., 95 F.3d 807, 810–812 (9th Cir. 1996) (case not remanded; district court's error in exercising jurisdiction was harmless because court applied relevant state law to undisputed material facts and came up with right answer).

343 *See* Colorado River Water Conservation Dist. v. United States, 424 U.S. 800, 820 (1976).

abstention is not "invariably" justified simply because a state defendant chooses to initiate new federal proceedings, rather than removing the existing suit to federal court.[344]

Lower courts have variously construed what facts constitute exceptional circumstances to warrant abstention. Typically the courts formally examine the *Colorado River* and *Moses H. Cone* standards (*see* [3], [5], *above*),[345] but no factor is controlling. Some lower courts also have acknowledged other considerations, in addition to the *Colorado River* and *Moses H. Cone* factors.[346]

### [b] Claims Within Exclusive Federal Jurisdiction

Federal courts have not resolved whether they may abstain when a claim is within exclusive federal jurisdiction. The Supreme Court did not decide this issue in *Will*, where the plaintiff alleged a Rule 10b-5 violation exclusively enforceable in federal court.[347] State courts may decide federal claims. The full faith and credit statute governs the preclusive effect of state judgments, and provides that state judicial proceedings "shall have the same full faith and credit in every court within the United States . . . as they have by law or usage in the courts of such State . . . from which they are taken."[348] This statute therefore requires federal courts to refer to state preclusion doctrine. The Supreme Court has stated:[349]

> It has long been established that § 1738 [the full faith and credit statute] does not allow federal courts to employ their own rules of *res judicata* in determining the effect of state judgments. Rather, it goes beyond the common law and commands a federal court to accept the rules chosen by the State from which the judgment is taken.

If a state preclusion law would bar subsequent federal adjudication of an exclusively federal issue, this would frustrate congressional intent in placing a matter within exclusive federal jurisdiction. In such circumstances, federal absten-

---

[344] Gulfstream Aerospace Corp. v. Mayacamas Corp., 485 U.S. 271, 290 (1988); *see generally* Ch. 6, *Removal*.

[345] *See* Colorado River Water Conservation Dist. v. United States, 424 U.S. 800, 820 (1976); Moses H. Cone Memorial Hosp. v. Mercury Constr. Corp., 460 U.S. 1, 25–26 (1983).

[346] *See, e.g.*, Elmendorf Grafica, Inc. v. D.S. America (East), Inc., 48 F.3d 46, 50 (1st Cir. 1995) ("exceptional circumstances" include (1) whether either court has assumed jurisdiction over res; (2) inconvenience of federal forum; (3) desirability of avoiding piecemeal litigation; (4) order in which forums obtained jurisdiction; (5) whether state or federal law controls; and (6) adequacy of state forum to protect parties' rights; another factor, mentioned but not applied in *Moses H. Cone*, is vexatious or reactive nature of federal lawsuit); Planned Parenthood of Dutchess-Ulster, Inc. v. Steinhaus, 60 F.3d 122, 126 (2d Cir. 1995) ("the presence of a federal basis for jurisdiction may raise the level of justification needed for abstention"); Williams v. Lambert, 46 F.3d 1275, 1283 (2d Cir. 1995) (*Colorado River* abstention turns on balancing six factors: (1) whether either state or federal court has assumed jurisdiction over res; (2) relative inconvenience of federal forum; (3) desirability of avoiding piecemeal litigation; (4) order in which actions were filed; (5) whether state or federal law provides rule of decision; and (6) whether state action will protect federal plaintiffs' rights).

[347] *See* Will v. Calvert Fire Ins. Co., 437 U.S. 655, 667 (1978).

[348] 28 U.S.C. § 1738.

[349] Marrese v. American Academy of Orthopedic Surgeons, 470 U.S. 373, 379 (1985); *see* Matsushita v. Epstein, 516 U.S. 367, 381–382 (1996).

tion in deference to pending concurrent state proceedings is not appropriate.[350] However, if a state decision will not bind the federal court, the federal court ultimately will decide the issue and abstention would serve no purpose. Either way, federal courts should not abstain in litigation involving issues within exclusive federal jurisdiction.

## § 13.07 PROCEDURAL OPTIONS IN ABSTENTION PROCEEDINGS

### [1] Stay of Proceedings, Retention of Federal Court Jurisdiction, or Dismissal

#### [a] *Pullman* Abstention

In *Pullman* abstention,[351] the case is sent to state court for a clarification of state law. However, the case may return to federal court to resolve remaining constitutional issues, if the state court does not resolve the entire litigation. The federal court retains jurisdiction but stays its proceedings pending a determination of state law. The Supreme Court, in *England v. Louisiana State Board of Medical Examiners*,[352] explained the procedures federal courts should follow in *Pullman* abstention cases. A party can choose to litigate all issues, including federal constitutional claims, in state court. A litigant who chooses this option, however, relinquishes the right to return to federal court. In the alternative, a party can choose to litigate state law questions in state court and reserve the right to return to federal court to determine federal law issues. This reservation does not have to be explicit. The Court held:[353]

> Such an explicit reservation is not indispensable; the litigant is in no event to be denied his right to return to the District Court unless it clearly appears that he voluntarily . . . [and] fully litigated his federal claims in the state courts. When the reservation has been made, however, his right to return will in all events be preserved.

Federal court abstention pursuant to *Pullman* principles, therefore, does not preclude subsequent federal litigation of federal claims. The traditional *res judicata* rule against claim-splitting does not apply. It is not clear, however whether collateral estoppel would bind a federal court to a state court's findings of fact. The *England* decision stressed the importance of federal fact-finding on constitutional issues,[354] but some courts have applied collateral estoppel in constitutional cases (but not involving abstention) and prevented fact relitigation.[355]

---

[350] *See* Will v. Calvert Fire Ins. Co., 437 U.S. 655, 670 (1978) (Brennan, J., dissenting. state court decisions should not have preclusive effect over matters within exclusive federal court jurisdiction).

[351] Railroad Comm'n of Texas v. Pullman Co., 312 U.S. 496, 500–501 (1941).

[352] England v. Louisiana State Bd. of Med. Exam'rs, 375 U.S. 411 (1964).

[353] 375 U.S. at 421–422.

[354] 375 U.S. at 416–417.

[355] *See* Allen v. McCurry, 449 U.S. 90, 105 (1980) (federal courts must accord collateral estoppel to

### [b] *Thibodaux* Abstention

*Thibodaux* abstention is treated similarly to *Pullman* abstention, but often with different results.[356] Thus, in *Thibodaux* abstention the case is sent to state court for a clarification of state law, and the case theoretically may return to federal court to resolve remaining federal constitutional issues. As in a *Pullman* abstention, the federal court retains jurisdiction, but stays its proceedings pending resolution of the state adjudication. In *Thibodaux* abstention, however, there rarely are remaining federal issues, because *Thibodaux* is invoked in federal diversity cases, which involve only state law questions. Sending a case to state court under *Thibodaux* abstention, therefore, is likely to terminate the federal proceeding, even though it technically remains on the federal docket until completion of the state proceedings.

### [c] *Burford* Abstention

Unlike *Pullman* and *Thibodaux* abstention, in which a case is sent to state court for clarification of the state law, but may return to federal court if necessary, under *Burford* abstention a federal court may completely dismiss the case. *Burford* abstention involves complex administrative procedures. Such abstention because of complex state administrative procedures does not merely postpone federal court adjudication, it completely displaces it. Although long-standing *Burford* abstention doctrine mandated dismissal of the federal action, the Supreme Court's decision in *Quackenbush* called this principle into question. *Quackenbush* suggests that when *Burford* abstention is involved, federal courts are not limited to a dismissal of the federal action, but "*Burford* might support a federal court's decision to postpone adjudication of a damage[] action pending the resolution by the state courts of a disputed question of state law."[357] Thus, *Burford* abstention may no longer direct a dismissal of the federal proceedings in every case, and *Burford* abstention may more appropriately be treated in the same manner as *Colorado River* abstention.

Following *Quackenbush*, several circuit courts have held that federal courts may not remand or dismiss a case based on *Burford* abstention when the plaintiff seeks monetary damages. In that event, the court may only stay the proceedings. The court may remand or dismiss if the plaintiff seeks only equitable or discretionary damages, i.e., claims for injunctive or declaratory relief.[358]

### [d] *Younger* Abstention

*Younger* abstention forbids federal courts from interfering in pending state proceedings under certain circumstances. *Younger* abstention contemplates the outright dismissal of the federal suit and the presentation of all federal and state claims to the state court. However, the Supreme Court has held that a district court may stay an action for damages based on *Younger* principles.

---

state court fact-finding in § 1983 cases); *accord* Astoria Fed. Sav. and Loan Ass'n v. Solimino, 501 U.S. 104, 110 (1991).

[356] *See* Louisiana Power & Light Co. v. City of Thibodaux, 360 U.S. 25, 28 (1959).

[357] Quackenbush v. Allstate Ins. Co., 517 U.S. 706, 730–31 (1996).

[358] Gray v. Bush, 628 F.3d 779, 785 (6th Cir. 2010); Dunn v. Cometa, 238 F.3d 38, 43 (1st Cir. 2001).

The circuit courts have split on whether *Younger* abstention supports the dismissal of a federal claim seeking money damages. A plurality now applies *Younger* abstention principles in some fashion to claims for damages.

### [e] *Colorado River* Abstention

*Colorado River* abstention, which applies because of duplicative concurrent state litigation, may result either in a stay or outright dismissal of the federal proceeding. In *Colorado River*, the Supreme Court dismissed the parallel federal proceeding,[359] but in *Moses H. Cone*, the Court left open the question whether a federal court should dismiss or stay its jurisdiction when ordering abstention because of duplicative state proceedings.[360] This distinction makes very little difference in *Colorado River* abstention, however, because the state court decision will have preclusive effect in any subsequent federal proceeding. As the Court stated in *Wilton v. Seven Falls*, "the action [a stay rather than a dismissal of the federal proceedings] is of little moment in this regard, because the state court's decision will bind the parties under principles of res judicata."[361]

There may be some situations, however, when the preclusive effect of the state proceedings will not completely resolve the entire litigation. In these situations a stay is preferable. As the Court noted, a stay avoids statute of limitations problems: "[W]here the basis for declining to proceed is the pendency of a state proceeding, a stay will often be the preferable course, [insofar as] it assures that the federal action can proceed without risk of a time bar if the state case, for any reason, fails to resolve the matter in controversy."[362] In fact, most circuits have held that a stay is generally preferable to dismissal because it may likely produce the same practical result, while leaving the docket open in case loose ends remain at the conclusion of the state proceedings.[363]

Remand is not an option when a district court abstains under Colorado River, because it would serve no purpose to send the federal case back to state court once it has been determined that the state court case is an adequate vehicle for the complete and prompt resolution of the issues.[364]

## [2] Dismissal Without Prejudice

A separate problem arises when a state court refuses to decide an unsettled question of state law because state constitutional law prevents advisory opinions. When a federal court abstains but does not dismiss the federal action, the case remains on its docket and the matter is stayed while pending in state court. The federal court retains jurisdiction and the case can return to federal court for

---

[359] Colorado River Water Conservation Dist. v. United States, 424 U.S. 800, 821 (1976).

[360] Moses H. Cone Memorial Hosp. v. Mercury Constr. Corp., 460 U.S. 1, 13–16 (1983).

[361] Wilton v. Seven Falls Co., 515 U.S. 277, 283–284 (1995).

[362] 515 U.S. at 287–289 & n.2.

[363] Jimenez v. Rodriguez-Pagan, 597 F.3d 18, 31–32 (1st Cir. 2010); Moorer v. Demopolis Waterworks & Sewer Bd., 374 F.3d 994, 998 (11th Cir. 2004).

[364] Saucier v. Aviva & Annuity Co., 701 F.3d 458, 465–66 (5th Cir. 2012).

resolution of remaining federal constitutional issues. Some state courts view federal abstention as a request for an advisory opinion, because the state judgment will not necessarily be final. The Texas Supreme Court, for example, has ruled that it cannot grant declaratory relief under state law if a federal court retains jurisdiction over the federal claim.[365]

The Supreme Court has held that, under these circumstances, a federal court should dismiss the case without prejudice: "In order to remove any possible obstacles to state-court jurisdiction, we direct the District Court to dismiss the complaint. The dismissal should be without prejudice so that any remaining federal claim may be raised in a federal forum after the Texas courts have been given the opportunity to address the state-law questions in this case."[366] Whether dismissal without prejudice addresses state courts' concerns regarding advisory opinions remains an open question.

## [3] Certification of Questions to State Court

Most states have statutes permitting federal courts to "certify" questions to the state courts for a decision on particular questions of state law. In states that have adopted this procedure, the United States Supreme Court, federal appellate courts,[367] and, in most but not all states, federal district courts,[368] can certify state law questions to the state court system.

Certification greatly simplifies abstention procedure and reduces delays and costs associated with abstention. Certification is more efficient and saves "time, energy, and resources."[369] The Supreme Court considers certification to be a factor a court must consider in deciding whether to abstain,[370] but the availability of a certification procedure is not an independent ground justifying an abstention decision.[371] Moreover, abstention may be required when the legal uncertainties of a case cannot be reduced to a few simply formulated abstract legal question so as to permit the alternative of certification.[372]

Circuit courts frequently certify questions rather than abstain.[373] Some courts, however, have refused to certify a question when the same issue is already being

---

365 United Servs. Life Ins. Co. v. Delaney, 396 S.W.2d 855 (1965); *see* Romero v. Coldwell, 455 F.2d 1163, 1167 (5th Cir. 1972); Barrett v. Atlantic Richfield Co., 444 F.2d 38, 45–46 (5th Cir. 1971).

366 Harris County Comm'rs Court v. Moore, 420 U.S. 77, 88–89 & n.14 (1975).

367 *See* Fla. App. R. 4.61; Haw. Sup. Ct. R. 20; Ind. App. R. 15(0); La. Sup. Ct. R. 12.

368 *See* Ala. Con. art. VI, § 140 (b) (3); Colo. App. R. 21.1; Okla. St. Ann. §§ 1601–1613; Md. Cts. & Jud. Proc. C. Ann. §§ 12-601–12-609; Mass. Sup. Ct. R. 3-21; Me. R. Civ. Pro. AR 76B; Minn. Stat § 480.061; Mont. Sup. Ct. R. 1; RI. Sup. Ct. R. 6; Wash. Rev. C. Ann. §§ 2.60.010–2.60.030.

369 Lehman Bros. v. Schein, 416 U.S. 386, 391 (1974).

370 Bellotti v. Baird, 428 U.S. 132, 151 (1976) ("the availability of certification greatly simplifies the analysis").

371 Houston v. Hill, 482 U.S. 451, 471 (1987) (availability of certification "is not in itself sufficient to render abstention appropriate").

372 Dunn v. Cometa, 238 F.3d 38, 43 (1st Cir. 2001).

373 Doyle v. City of Medford, 565 F.3d 536, 543–44 (9thCir. 2009); Kansas Judicial Review v. Stout, 519 F.3d 1107, 1119 (10th Cir. 2008).

litigated in the state court.[374]

## [4] Appeal of Abstention Orders

The Supreme Court has reviewed a number of abstention decisions but has directly addressed their appealability only in a few instances. In *Idlewild Bon Voyage Liquor Corp. v. Epstein*, for example, the Court held that a district court's decision to abstain and stay a proceeding under *Pullman* abstention was a final decision for purposes of appellate review.[375] The abstention order therefore was reviewable because it put the litigants "effectively out of court."[376] Similarly, the Court held that a district court's order staying a federal proceeding under *Colorado River* was a final decision that was immediately appealable,[377] because the order put the litigants effectively out of court and surrendered federal jurisdiction to a state court.[378] On the other hand, the Court has indicated that an order *denying* a *Colorado River* motion is "inherently tentative" and not a "conclusive determination within the meaning of the collateral-order doctrine and therefore not appealable under § 1291."[379]

In *Quackenbush v. Allstate Insurance Co.*, the Supreme Court also has held that a remand order issued under *Burford* abstention was immediately appealable under the statute conferring appellate jurisdiction[380] as well as the *Cohen* collateral-order doctrine.[381] Such *Burford* abstention effectively puts the litigants out of court and surrenders federal jurisdiction. More specifically, the remand order was appealable under the collateral-order doctrine because (1) it conclusively determined a disputed question completely separate from the merits, (2) the asserted rights were sufficiently important to warrant an immediate appeal, and (3) the remand order would not be subsumed in any other appealable district court order.[382] Although the *Quackenbush* decision specifically involved a *Burford* remand order, its holding should be equally applicable to *Pullman* remand orders.

Several circuits have held that an order denying *Younger* abstention is not immediately reviewable.[383] It does not qualify as a final decision subject to review.[384] Nor does it fit within the collateral order exception to the final decision

---

[374] Currie v. Group Ins. Comm'n, 290 F.3d 1, 13 (1st Cir. 2002); Nationwide Mut. Is. Co. v. Unauthorized Practice of Law Comm., 283 F.3d 650, 656–57 (5th Cir. 2002).

[375] *See* 28 U.S.C. § 1291. For general discussion of what orders are appealable final decisions, see 19 Moore's Federal Practice Ch. 202, *Final Judgments*, and Ch. 203, *Interlocutory Orders* (Matthew Bender 3d ed.).

[376] Idlewild Bon Voyage Liquor Corp. v. Epstein, 370 U.S. 713, 715 & n.2 (1962).

[377] *See* 28 U.S.C. § 1291.

[378] Moses H. Cone Memorial Hosp. v. Mercury Constr. Corp., 460 U.S. 1, 11 & n.11 (1983).

[379] Gulfstream Aerospace Corp. v. Mayacamas Corp., 485 U.S. 271, 278 (1988).

[380] *See* 28 U.S.C. § 1291.

[381] *See* Cohen v. Beneficial Indus. Loan Corp., 337 U.S. 541 (1949).

[382] Quackenbush v. Allstate Insurance Co., 517 U.S. 706, 712 (1996).

[383] Tarrant Regional Water Dist. v. Sevenoaks, 545 F.3d 906, 914 (10th Cir. 2008); Summers v. Leis, 368 F.3d 881, 889 (6th Cir. 2004).

[384] Summers, 368 F.3d at 889.

requirement, because it can effectively be reviewed on appeal from the final judgment.[385]

## [5] Standard of Review

The Supreme Court also has not articulated a clear standard for appellate review of abstention orders. In *Wilton*, the Court ruled that the appropriate standard of review for *Colorado River* abstention orders is an abuse-of-discretion standard.[386] The abuse of discretion standard has been applied to review *Colorado River* abstention in some circuits, but that discretion must be exercised within the narrow constraints of Colorado River's exceptional circumstances doctrine.[387] An appellate court reviews the district court's discretion to grant or refrain from granting declaratory relief under an abuse of discretion standard.[388] Most, but not all, lower courts apply the abuse-of-discretion standard to decisions whether to abstain under *Burford* or *Pullman*.[389]

In determining the standard of review for abstention cases, courts often distinguish between a district court's determination that the requirements of the particular abstention doctrine have been met and the actual decision to abstain. These courts specify that application of the abuse of discretion standard of review applies only to the decision whether to abstain. Whether the requirements of the particular abstention doctrine are satisfied generally is a question of law, which is review *de novo*.[390]

---

[385] Tarrant Regional Water Dist., 545 F.3d at 914; Summers, 368 F.3d at 889.

[386] Wilton v. Seven Falls Co., 515 U.S. 277, 289–290 (1995).

[387] National City Mortgage Co. v. Stephen, 647 F.3d 78, 82 (3d Cir. 2011); Adkins v. Vim recycling, Inc., 644 F.3d 483, 497 (7th Cir. 2011).

[388] Niagara Mohawk Power Corp. v. Hudson River-Black, 673 F.3d 84, 104 (2d Cir. 2012); United States v. City of Las Cruces, 289 F.3d 1170, 1179 (10th Cir. 2002).

[389] *See, e.g.*, Washington Gas Light Co. v. The Prince George's County Council Sitting as the Dist. Council, 711 F.3d 412, 417 (4th Cir. 2013); Wisconsin Right to Life State PAC v. Barland, 664 F.3d 139, 149–51 (7th Cir. 2011); Nat'l City Mortgage, 647 F.3d at 82; Adkins, 644 F.3d at 497.

[390] American Family Life Assurance Co. v. Biles, 714 F.3d 887, 891 (5th Cir. 2013); Saucier v. Aviva Life & Annuity Co., 701 F.3d 458, 462 (5th Cir. 2012); Chico Serv. Station, Inc. v. Sol Puerto Rico, 633 F.3d 20, 30 (1st Cir. 2011).

# Chapter 14

# THE ELEVENTH AMENDMENT AND STATE SOVEREIGN IMMUNITY

## § 14.01 HISTORICAL BACKGROUND: SOVEREIGN IMMUNITY IN ENGLAND

The doctrine of sovereign immunity goes back to ancient times.[1] Rooted in the theory of the divine rights of kings,[2] the doctrine finds its simplest expression in the maxim "the King can do no wrong." In that vein, Blackstone, a staunch supporter of the monarchy, eloquently stated the Crown's immunity: "Besides the attribute of sovereignty the law also ascribes to the king, in his political capacity, absolute perfection. The king can do no wrong."[3] But history teaches that the kings and queens of England did wrong, and were not above the rule of law. Indeed, "[t]he premise of Magna Carta, reissued by successive kings and reinforced by repeated baronial struggles, was that the king was not only capable of but disposed toward doing wrong; this premise and the actions taken upon it are the very foundation of the concept of government under law."[4]

Some scholars have commented, however, that another explanation for the evolution of the doctrine of sovereign immunity was the feudal structure, and not the alleged infallibility of the Crown. In feudal times, a petty lord could not be sued in his own courts by his vassals without his consent. But the feudal hierarchy subjected him to suit in the courts of his lord, irrespective of his consent. Thus, the realities of enforceability and not notions of infallibility immunized the petty lord from suits in his own courts. Because the king stood at the "apex of the feudal pyramid,"[5] there was no court above him to correct his misdeeds. So described, the

---

[1] For a discussion of sovereign immunity under Roman and medieval law and English common law, see Borchard, *Government Responsibility in Tort*, 36 Yale L.J. 1, 3–17 (1926).

[2] *See* James, *Tort Liability of Governmental Units and Their Officers*, 22 U. Chi. L. Rev. 610, 611 (1955).

[3] Erlich, Erlich's Blackstone 67 (1959).

[4] Engdahl, *Immunity and Accountability for Positive Government Wrongs*, 44 U. Colo. L. Rev. 1, 3 (1972); Borchard, *Government Responsibility in Tort*, 36 Yale L.J. 1, 18 (1926) (The concept "that the king was above the law did not prevail in thirteenth century England."); 1 F. Pollack & F. Maitland, The History of English Law 500 (1895) ("In the middle of the fourteenth century the common belief was that down to the time of Edward I the king could be sued like a private person and a judge said that he had seen a writ beginning with *Praecipe Henrico Regi Angliae*.").

[5] Engdahl, *Immunity and Accountability for Positive Government Wrongs*, 44 U. Colo. L. Rev. 1, 3 (1972).

Crown's immunity was "an accident."[6] As Justice Stevens noted in *Nevada v. Hall*, "[t]he King's immunity rested primarily on the structure of the feudal system and secondarily on a fiction that the King could do no wrong."[7]

With the breakdown of feudalism, and the rise of the nation state, the King was clothed in the garb of sovereignty:[8]

> Here, in the days of the later Tudors and Stuarts in England . . . "we are plunged into talk about kings who do not die, who are never under age, who are ubiquitous, who do no wrong and (says Blackstone) think no wrong; and such talk has not been innocuous." The ancient maxim that "the King can do no wrong" took on new meaning and came to stand for a notion that the sovereign was incapable of doing wrong. This was a substantive ground of immunity in addition to the mere lack of a court with power to enforce remedies against the king.

Nonetheless, the Crown never enjoyed absolute immunity from suit.[9] For example, an aggrieved subject could pursue a contract claim through a petition of right addressed to the King's Chancellor. As Chief Justice Cockburn stated in the famous case of *Feather v. The Queen*:[10]

> [T]he petition of right is open to the subject . . . where the land or goods or money of a subject have found their way into the possession of the Crown, and the purpose of the petition is to obtain restitution, or if restitution cannot be given, compensation in money, or where the claim arises out of a contract, as for goods supplied to the Crown or to the public service.

But petitions of right were not available for claims sounding in tort.[11]

---

[6] 1 F. POLLACK & F. MAITLAND, THE HISTORY OF ENGLISH LAW 502 (1895) ("He cannot be compelled to answer in his own court, but this is true of every petty lord of every petty manor; that there happens to be in this world no court above his court is, we may say, an accident."). *See also* Erlich, ERLICH'S BLACKSTONE 66 (1959) ("[N]o suit or action can be brought against the king, even in civil matters, because no court can have jurisdiction over him. For all jurisdiction implies superiority of power . . . but who, shall command the king? It is likewise, that by law the person of the king is sacred, even though the measures pursued in his reign be completely tyrannical and arbitrary: For no jurisdiction upon earth has power to try him in a criminal way; much less to condemn him to punishment.").

[7] Nevada v. Hall, 440 U.S. 410, 415 (1979).

[8] James, *Tort Liability of Governmental Units and Their Officers*, 22 U. CHI. L. REV. 610, 611–612 (1955) (quoting Maitland).

[9] *See* Jaffe, *Suits Against Governments and Officers: Sovereign Immunity (Part 1)*, 77 HARV. L. REV. 1, 2–19 (1963), for a history of sovereign immunity in England.

[10] Feather v. The Queen, (Q.B. 1865) 6 B & S 257, 122 Eng. Rep. 1191, 1204; *See also* Thomas v. The Queen (1874) L.R. 10 Q.B. 31.

[11] "Not only is there no precedent for a petition of right being entertained *in re*spect of a wrong in the legal sense of the term, but, if the matter is considered with reference to principle, it becomes apparent that the proceeding by petition of right cannot be resorted to by the subject in the case of a tort. For it must be borne in mind that the petition of right, unlike a petition addressed to the grace and favour of the Sovereign, is founded on the violation of some right *in re*spect of which, but for the immunity from all process with which the law surrounds the person of the Sovereign, a suit at law or equity could be maintained." *See* Feather v. The Queen (Q.B. 1865) 6 B & S 257, 122 Eng. Rep. 1191, 1205.

An individual who believed that his property was in the wrongful possession of the King could also resort to the remedy of *monstrans de droit*;[12] and sometimes this remedy was available without the King's consent.[13] In addition, the King could be sued in the Court of Exchequer to recover property wrongfully claimed by the Crown or to enforce a monetary obligation on which the Crown had defaulted. As early as 1668, the Court of Exchequer, in *Pawlett v. The Attorney General*, allowed a mortgagor to recover property that had escheated to the Crown by virtue of the mortgagee's attainder of treason.[14]

While the King could not be sued for the misdeeds of his officers, his officers were not similarly protected. The thirteenth century saw the King's Court of Exchequer entertain suits against the Exchequer's sheriffs and bailiffs. Mandamus and other prerogative writs were available to discipline the King's officers.[15] And Blackstone commented that "the prerogative of the crown" was "created for the benefit of the people" and could not "be exerted to their prejudice." Thus, "evil counselors" and "wicked ministers" could be punished "by means of indictments, and parliamentary impeachments."[16] Reasoning from the ancient doctrine that the King could do no wrong, "any wrong that was done in his name was, in the eyes of the law, not done by the king at all."[17] Thus, the King's servants and officers could be sued personally for trespasses committed by them in the name of the Crown.[18]

In sum, the Crown never enjoyed absolute immunity against judicial accountability for its misdeeds. While vital, the doctrine was well-tempered by the time it was imported to Plymouth Rock and Jamestown.[19]

---

[12] Jacobs, The Eleventh Amendment and Sovereign Immunity 5 n.6 (1972).

[13] Jaffe, *Suits Against Governments and Officers: Sovereign Immunity (Part 1)*, 77 Harv. L. Rev. 1, 6 n.10 (1963).

[14] Pawlett v. The Attorney General, (Ex 1668) Hadres 465, 145 Eng. Rep. 550.

[15] *See* Jacobs, The Eleventh Amendment and Sovereign Immunity 5 (1972); Jaffe, *Suits Against Governments and Officers: Sovereign Immunity (Part 1)*, 77 Harv. L. Rev. 1, 15–18 (1963).

[16] Erlich, Erlich's Blackstone 67 (1959).

[17] Engdahl, *Immunity and Accountability for Positive Government Wrongs*, 44 U. Colo. L. Rev. 1, 4 (1972).

[18] *See* Feather v. The Queen (Q.B. 1865) 6 B & S 257, 122 Eng. Rep. 1191, 1205 (where the court held that although a petition of right was not available to redress tort claims, "[a]s the Sovereign cannot authorize wrong to be done, the authority of the Crown would afford no defence to an action brought for an illegal act committed by an officer of the Crown."); Ashby v. White, 6 Mod. 45, 87 Eng. Rep. 808 (Q.B. 1702), *rev'd*, 1 Brown P.C. 45, 1 Eng. Rep. 417 (H.L. 1703) (discussed in Jaffe, *Suits Against Governments and Officers: Sovereign Immunity (Part 1)*, 77 Harv. L. Rev. 1, 15 (1963)).

[19] For additional discussion on the history of sovereign immunity in England, see Justice Iredell's dissent in *Chisholm v. Georgia*, 2 U.S. (2 Dall.) 419, 437–446 (1793), Justice Wilson's review in the *Chisolm* case at 459–461, and *Mayle v. Pennsylvania Dep't of Highways*, 479 Pa. 384, 388 A.2d 709 (1978).

## § 14.02 THE EARLY AMERICAN EXPERIENCE

### [1] Nineteenth Century Views on Sovereign Immunity

Blind adherence to the doctrine of sovereign immunity would have rendered the King unaccountable to his subjects. An exception to the doctrine, however, developed at common law that permitted individuals to sue the King's officers and officials. This exception was based on a fiction: because the King could do no wrong, only his officials could be the source of a citizen's grievance with his government. Thus, the King's officials were stripped of the immunity that shielded the King from suits by his subjects.

This fiction was transported to colonial America. Chief Justice Marshall, in *Osborn v. Bank of the United States*,[20] held that the Eleventh Amendment did not prohibit a federal court from imposing an injunction against the auditor and the treasurer of Ohio, requiring them to return money that they had seized from the Bank of the United States under an unconstitutional state statute: "It was proper, then, to make a decree against the defendants in the Circuit Court, if the law of the state of Ohio be repugnant to the constitution, or to a law of the United States made in pursuance thereof, so as to furnish no authority to those who took, or to those who received, the money for which this suit was instituted."[21]

In 1887, the Supreme Court reaffirmed the doctrine of *Osborn* in *In re Ayres*, stating:[22]

> Nothing can be interposed between the individual and the obligation he owes to the Constitution and laws of the United States, which can shield or defend him from their just authority, and the extent and limits of that authority the government of the United States, by means of its judicial power, interprets and applies for itself. If, therefore, an individual, acting under the assumed authority of a State, as one of its officers, and under color of its laws, comes into conflict with the superior authority of a valid law of the United States, he is stripped of his representative character, and subjected in his person to the consequences of his individual conduct. The State has no power to impart to him any immunity from responsibility to the supreme authority of the United States.

And in *Reagan v. Farmers' Loan & Trust Co.*, the Court applied its earlier reasoning in a suit seeking injunctive relief in which it was alleged that although a state official acted under a constitutional statute, the officer did so in a manner not authorized by the statute. The Court stated:[23]

> A valid law may be wrongfully administered by officers of the State, and so as to make such administration an illegal burden and exaction upon the individual . . . . They may go beyond the powers thereby conferred, and

---

[20] Osborn v. Bank of the United States, 22 U.S. (9 Wheat) 738 (1824).

[21] 22 U.S. (9 Wheat) at 859; *see also* Poindexter v. Greenhow, 114 U.S. 270, 291 (1885).

[22] *In re* Ayers, 123 U.S. 443, 507 (1887).

[23] Reagan v. Farmers' Loan & Trust Co., 154 U.S. 362, 390–391 (1894).

> when they do the fact that they are assuming to act under a valid law will not oust the courts of jurisdiction to restrain their excessive and illegal acts.

### [2] The Doctrine of *Ex Parte Young*

Fourteen years later, in 1908, the Court decided *Ex parte Young*. While *Young* is regarded as a landmark case, basically the Court forged no new ground relating to sovereign immunity. Rather, the Court acted in the tradition of *Osborn, Poindexter, Ayres*, and *Reagan*. Thus, the Court held that a suit in which it was alleged that a state official threatened to enforce an unconstitutional state statute was not a suit against the state. More specifically, the Court held that the Attorney General of Minnesota could be sued to enjoin him from enforcing railroad rates that were alleged to be unconstitutional. The Court refused to equate the suit with an action brought against the State of Minnesota:[24]

> The act to be enforced is alleged to be unconstitutional, and if it be so, the use of the name of the State to enforce an unconstitutional act to the injury of complainants is a proceeding without the authority of and one which does not affect the State in its sovereign or governmental capacity. It is simply an illegal act upon the part of the state official in attempting by the use of the name of the State to enforce a legislative enactment which is void because unconstitutional.

Hence, the rule of *Ex parte Young* treated a state official, whether acting under an allegedly unconstitutional statute or under a valid statute but in an unauthorized manner, as an ordinary tortfeasor — irrespective of his or her good intentions. And, that official could be sued as any other tortfeasor for prospective relief. *The Ex Parte Young* decision raised a great concern over the power of a single federal judge. Congress immediately recognized the problem, and, in 1910, Congress provided that a suit to enjoin a state official from enforcing a state statute alleged to be unconstitutional must be heard by a three-judge federal court with direct appeal to the Supreme Court.[25] In 1976, Congress eliminated the requirement that such an action be heard before a three-judge court, thereby eliminating direct appeal to the Supreme Court. By then, Congress decided that the need to protect state legislation against precipitate federal judicial action was outweighed by the drain on federal judicial manpower.[26]

## § 14.03 MODERN STATE SOVEREIGN IMMUNITY: THE IMPORTANCE OF THE ELEVENTH AMENDMENT FOR FEDERAL-STATE RELATIONS

The Eleventh Amendment and the doctrine of state sovereign immunity play an important role in the federal judicial system. Before the formation of the Union, each state was a sovereign entity and enjoyed the benefit of the common-law doctrine of sovereign immunity. That doctrine essentially held that a sovereign

---

[24] *Ex parte* Young, 209 U.S. 123, 159 (1908).

[25] Act of June 18, 1910, ch. 309, § 17, 36 Stat. 539, 557.

[26] Act of August 12, 1976, Pub. L. 94-381, 90 Stat. 1119.

cannot be sued without its consent.[27] Under the doctrine, a private litigant could not hale the state itself into its own courts. Further, since no state was subject to any other state's territorial jurisdiction, a state generally could not be sued in another state's courts. Consequently, the sovereign states did not have to worry about the indignity or financial effects of being sued.

The states surrendered some of their sovereignty to the federal union, indicated by the Constitution's Supremacy Clause.[28] However, each state retained sovereignty within its borders, including the rights, powers, and immunities they did not constitutionally surrender to the federal government.[29] Thus, for the first time since the states gained independence from England, each state existed within two jurisdictions, its own and the federal government. The Eleventh Amendment represents an attempt to define the limits of federal judicial power over the states. The Amendment and the Supreme Court's interpretation of the Amendment has been important in shaping federal-state relations.

The Eleventh Amendment provides: "The Judicial power of the United States shall not be construed to extend to any suit in law or equity, commenced or prosecuted against one of the United States by Citizens of another State, or by Citizens or Subjects of any Foreign State."[30] On its face, the Eleventh Amendment precludes only suits against states brought by out-of-state citizens in federal court. The Supreme Court, in construing the Amendment, however, has treated the Amendment as the embodiment of the doctrine of sovereign immunity. The Court therefore has applied the Amendment to circumstances outside its express terms.[31]

In interpreting and applying the Eleventh Amendment and the principle of state sovereign immunity, the Supreme Court endeavors to balance two competing policies:[32] (1) The states' interest in maintaining traditional concerns protected by sovereign immunity, such as the dignity and autonomy of state government, and the solvency of state treasuries; balanced against (2) the federal government's interest in ensuring compliance with the federal Constitution and laws, which are the supreme law of the land.[33]

The inquiry into the role of the Eleventh Amendment and its interplay with issues of federalism, separation of powers, limited federal government, and states' rights has been intense in recent years. The Supreme Court has issued a series of cases interpreting the scope of the Eleventh Amendment and its concomitant

---

[27] *See* Hans v. Louisiana, 134 U.S. 1, 15–18 (1890) (sovereign immunity was established fundamental legal principle at time of adoption of Constitution).

[28] U.S. Const., Art. VI, cl. 2 (Constitution and laws made pursuant to it are supreme law of land).

[29] Principality of Monaco v. Mississippi, 292 U.S. 313, 322–323 (1934) (states are immune from suit without their consent, except where there has been surrender of immunity in "the plan of the [constitutional] convention").

[30] U.S. Const., Amend. XI.

[31] *See, e.g.*, Hans v. Louisiana, 134 U.S. 1, 15 (1890) (state immune from suits by own citizens).

[32] *See* Pennhurst State Sch. and Hosp. v. Halderman, 465 U.S. 89, 105 (1984) (Court exerts efforts to harmonize principles of state sovereignty reflected in Eleventh Amendment with supremacy of federal Constitution and laws).

[33] *See* U.S. Const., Art. VI, cl. 2.

limitations on the authority of Congress to abrogate state immunity. These decisions collectively counsel that courts should not lightly conclude that Congress has the authority to abrogate state sovereign immunity under the Fourteenth Amendment or that Congress may use its spending power in a manner that ultimately effects a waiver of a state's Eleventh Amendment immunity. Courts must respect the Supreme Court's admonitions that the Eleventh Amendment restricts judicial power under Article III, and that Article I cannot be used to circumvent the limitations placed on federal jurisdiction. Therefore, Congress cannot use its power to exact waivers of the Eleventh Amendment through the exercise of its Article I spending powers to circumvent the anti-abrogation rule of *Seminole Tribe*.

The Supreme Court has cast some doubt on the continued validity of its earlier statements concerning the use of Article I powers to exact waivers of *Eleventh Amendment* immunity, at least with respect to bankruptcy laws. Without purporting to overrule these precedents, but noting that it is not required to follow dicta from a case in which a point was not fully debated, a closely divided Supreme Court held that the Bankruptcy Clause in Article I waives states' sovereign immunity with respect to a bankruptcy trustee's proceeding to set aside the debtor's preferential transfers to state agencies. The majority reasoned that in ratifying the Bankruptcy Clause, states agreed to subordinate whatever sovereign immunity they might otherwise have asserted in proceedings necessary to effectuate the *in rem* jurisdiction of the bankruptcy courts. Thus, Congress' power to subject the states to bankruptcy laws arises directly from the Constitution's Bankruptcy Clause in Article I, not from the section of the Bankruptcy Act indicating that state sovereign immunity is abrogated with respect to certain sections of the Act.[34]

In so holding, the Court noted that the sovereign immunity implications of the Bankruptcy Clause are not necessarily the same as those of other clauses in Article I, notably the Commerce Clause.[35] The Court emphasized that the Bankruptcy Clause's unique history and the singular nature of bankruptcy courts' jurisdiction persuaded the court that the clause represents a surrender of state sovereign immunity in certain federal proceedings.[36] Unconvinced, four Justices dissented, arguing that the majority ignored "settled doctrine" that nothing in Article I constitutes consent by the states to a waiver of their sovereign immunity.[37] The Supreme Court's attempts to achieve a satisfactory balance between these federal and state interests have been difficult. Jurists and commentators have criticized the Court's attempts to articulate a theory of the Eleventh Amendment that protects both state and federal interests.[38]

---

[34] Cent. Va. Cmty. College v. Katz, 546 U.S. 356, 373–378 (2006); *see* 11 U.S.C. § 106(a).

[35] U.S. Const., Art. I § 8 cl. 3.

[36] Central Va. Cmty. College v. Katz, 546 U.S. 356, 369 n.9 (2006).

[37] *Id.*

[38] *See, e.g.*, Atascadero State Hosp. v. Scanlon, 473 U.S. 234, 248 (1985) (Brennan, J., dissenting, joined by Marshall, Blackmun, and Stevens, JJ.) (Supreme Court's Eleventh Amendment doctrine "rests on flawed premises, misguided history, and an untenable vision of the needs of the federal system it purports to protect"); John J. Gibbons, *The Eleventh Amendment and State Sovereign Immunity: A Reinterpretation*, 83 Colum. L. Rev. 1889, 1891 (1983) ("hodgepodge of confusing and intellectually indefensible judge-made law").

## § 14.04 BASIS AND RATIFICATION OF ELEVENTH AMENDMENT

### [1] *Chisholm v. Georgia*

Article III of the Constitution provides that the federal judicial power extends to controversies "between a State and Citizens of another State" and "between a State . . . and foreign . . . Citizens or Subjects."[39] When the Constitution was drafted and offered for ratification, there was much debate whether this language represented an abrogation of the existing general rule of sovereign immunity — that a state may not be sued without its consent.[40] Neither the constitutional drafters nor ratifiers were unanimous in their interpretation of this Article III language.[41] Some read the language as an express nullification of state sovereign immunity.[42] Others argued that the language left the doctrine of sovereign immunity undisturbed, and merely extended federal judicial power to actions not barred by the doctrine (i.e., actions in which a state is the plaintiff or has consented to be sued).[43]

Not long after the states ratified the Constitution, the Supreme Court faced the issue of Article III's jurisdictional grant of cases involving states. In *Chisholm v. Georgia*,[44] a South Carolina citizen brought an original action in the Supreme Court to recover a debt that Georgia owed for the purchase of Revolutionary War supplies. The plaintiff contended that Article III and the Judiciary Act of 1789, which vested the Supreme Court with original jurisdiction of cases in which states were parties, abrogated state sovereign immunity. Georgia did not enter an appearance in the case, based on the belief that sovereign immunity protected the state from being sued without its consent.

The Supreme Court ruled for the plaintiff.[45] Four of five justices read Article III as authorizing suits against a state by citizens of other states.[46] Justice Iredell wrote a dissenting opinion. He reasoned that since sovereign immunity was a fundamental principle and Article III and the Judiciary Act did not specifically authorize suits against states, the Court should interpret these provisions as

---

[39] U.S. Const., Art. III § 2, cl. 1.

[40] *See* Hans v. Louisiana, 134 U.S. 1, 12–14 (1890); *see also* William A. Fletcher, *A Historical Interpretation of the Eleventh Amendment: A Narrow Construction of an Affirmative Grant of Jurisdiction Rather than a Prohibition Against Jurisdiction*, 35 Stan. L. Rev. 1033, 1045–1054 (1983) (reviewing debates over Article III and congressional deliberations on Judiciary Act of 1789); John J. Gibbons, *The Eleventh Amendment and State Sovereign Immunity: A Reinterpretation*, 83 Colum. L. Rev. 1889, 1902–1914 (1983) (summarizing ratification debates in Pennsylvania, Virginia, New York, and North Carolina).

[41] *See* Welch v. Texas Dep't of Highways and Pub. Transp., 483 U.S. 468, 482–484 (1987) (historical materials show that to extent this question was debated, intentions of framers and ratifiers were ambiguous).

[42] *See* 483 U.S. at 482–483 (Patrick Henry, George Mason, and Richard Henry Lee).

[43] 483 U.S. at 483 (Madison, Hamilton, and Marshall).

[44] Chisholm v. Georgia, 2 U.S. (2 Dall.) 419 (1793).

[45] 2 U.S. (2 Dall.) at 480.

[46] 2 U.S. (2 Dall.) at 450–479 (opinions of Blair, J.; Wilson, J.; Cushing, J.; and Jay, C.J.).

extending federal judicial power only to actions where states were plaintiffs.[47] The Supreme Court subsequently endorsed Justice Iredell's reasoning.[48] However, the Court never overruled *Chisholm*. Instead, soon after the Court rendered the *Chisholm* decision, Congress overruled it by enacting the Eleventh Amendment.

### [2] Reaction to *Chisholm;* Ratification of Eleventh Amendment

The *Chisholm* decision caused an uproar among state legislators and governors, because they feared more lawsuits against states to collect Revolutionary War debts.[49] At Congress's next meeting, legislators almost unanimously proposed the Eleventh Amendment, which the necessary state legislatures ratified soon thereafter.[50]

The swiftness with which the Eleventh Amendment was ratified is some evidence of the original intent behind Article III's grant of federal jurisdiction over cases in which states are parties.[51] Thus, although the Supreme Court's decision in *Chisholm* may have been based on an incorrect assessment of the framers' and ratifiers' intent, the Court subsequently referred to the response to *Chisholm* in interpreting the intended scope of Article III federal judicial power.[52]

## § 14.05 SCOPE OF CONSTITUTIONAL IMMUNITY: INTERPRETIVE THEORIES OF ELEVENTH AMENDMENT

### [1] Significance of Interpretive Theories

On its face, the Eleventh Amendment precludes only suits against states by out-of-state citizens, in federal court. However, the Supreme Court has construed the Eleventh Amendment more broadly than the literal text.[53] For example, the

---

[47] 2 U.S. (2 Dall.) at 429–450 (Iredell, J., dissenting).

[48] *See, e.g.*, Hans v. Louisiana, 134 U.S. 1, 18–19 (1890).

[49] 134 U.S. at 11 (*Chisholm* decision created "a shock of surprise throughout the country"); *see* 2 Charles Warren, The Supreme Court in United States History 99 (rev. ed. 1926) (reaction to *Chisholm* and adoption of Eleventh Amendment arose from fear of suits to collect war debts); *but see* Clyde E. Jacobs, The Eleventh Amendment and Sovereign Immunity 4, 69–70 (1972) (finding "practically" no evidence that Eleventh Amendment was intended to allow states to escape payment of obligations; citing strong support for Eleventh Amendment from creditor-oriented federalist majorities in Congress and state legislatures).

[50] Hans v. Louisiana, 134 U.S. 1, 11 (1890); *see* John V. Orth, The Judicial Power of the United States: The Eleventh Amendment in American History 12–29 (1987) (history of proposal and ratification of Eleventh Amendment).

[51] U.S. Const., Art. III § 2.

[52] *See, e.g.*, Hans v. Louisiana, 134 U.S. 1, 11–12 (1890) (citing reaction to *Chisholm* decision and adoption of Eleventh Amendment as evidence that Article III had not been intended to abrogate states' sovereign immunity against suits by their own citizens).

[53] *See* Principality of Monaco v. Mississippi, 292 U.S. 313, 322–323 (1934) (behind words of Amendment are postulates that limit and control, including postulate that states retain sovereign

Supreme Court has applied the Amendment, or the principle of sovereign immunity, to bar suits by in-state citizens.[54] Also, the Court has construed the Amendment to preclude damage suits against state officers for official conduct, but to allow injunctive actions against the same conduct.[55] The Court has held that Congress has a limited power to abrogate the states' Eleventh Amendment immunity.[56]

Decisions construing the Eleventh Amendment have generated much controversy. There has been no enduring consensus about the meaning and effect of the Eleventh Amendment, even among Supreme Court Justices.[57] However, various commentators have articulated several interpretive theories to explain and reconcile the Supreme Court's decisions. These theories are based on historical interpretations of the ratification of the Constitution and subsequent adoption of the Eleventh Amendment. The Court's resolution of many important Eleventh Amendment cases has centered on the particular interpretive theory the Court endorsed. Various Justices have espoused different theories, and as a result the Court has decided many important Eleventh Amendment cases by narrow majorities, accompanied by strong dissents.[58]

On occasion, the Court has overruled its own landmark Eleventh Amendment decisions.[59]

### [2] Constitutional Limitation on Subject Matter Jurisdiction

One Eleventh Amendment theory posits that sovereign immunity is a constitutional principle limiting federal court subject-matter jurisdiction.[60] Under this theory, Article III implicitly incorporated the full scope of state sovereign immunity, because sovereign immunity was a well-established principle predating

---

immunity to extent not surrendered in formation of Union).

[54] Hans v. Louisiana, 134 U.S. 1, 15 (1890).

[55] *Ex parte* Young, 209 U.S. 123, 159–160 (1908) (officer who violates federal law is stripped of state authority and therefore subject to injunctive relief action in individual capacity); Edelman v. Jordan, 415 U.S. 651, 662–665 (1974) (if damages would be payable from state treasury, state is real party in interest even though officials are nominal parties).

[56] Seminole' Tribe v. Florida, 517 U.S. 44, 57 (1996).

[57] *See, e.g.*, 517 U.S. at 72–73 (5-4 decision, holding that Congress has no Article I power to abrogate Eleventh Amendment; overruling *Pennsylvania v. Union Gas Co.*, 491 U.S. 1, 14–15 (1989), holding Article I Commerce Clause power enables abrogation of Eleventh Amendment).

[58] *See, e.g.*, Atascadero State Hosp. v. Scanlon, 473 U.S. 234, 248 (1985) (5-4 decision, with 3 dissenting opinions totaling 57 pages); Pennhurst State Sch. and Hosp. v. Halderman, 465 U.S. 89, 125–167 (1984) (5-4 decision, with 2 dissenting opinions).

[59] *See, e.g.*, Seminole Tribe v. Florida, 517 U.S. 44, 72–73 (1996) (5-4 decision overruling *Pennsylvania v. Union Gas Co.*, 491 U.S. 1 (1989), holding that Article I Commerce Clause power enables Congress to abrogate Eleventh Amendment); Welch v. Texas Dep't of Highways and Pub. Transp., 483 U.S. 468, 476–478 (1987) (5-4 decision overruling *Parden v. Terminal Ry.*, 377 U.S. 184, 192 (1964), holding that state's choice to operate railroad was constructive consent to suit under Federal Employers' Liability Act).

[60] Pennhurst State Sch. and Hosp. v. Halderman, 465 U.S. 89, 97–98 (1984) (fundamental principle of sovereign immunity limits grant of judicial authority in Article III).

the Constitution.[61] Thus, even though the Eleventh Amendment only partially states the principle of sovereign immunity (immunity against suits by citizens of other states and countries), sovereign immunity as a bar to federal suits against states by their own citizens is not precluded.[62]

The Supreme Court has endorsed this "constitutional limitation of subject-matter jurisdiction" theory. Thus, the Court has suggested that sovereign immunity is a broad constitutional principle,[63] and the Eleventh Amendment is merely an example.[64] These subsequent Court pronouncements recognize that the first Supreme Court should have decided *Chisholm* differently, making the Eleventh Amendment an unnecessary clarification of the sovereign immunity implicit in Article III.[65]

The Eleventh Amendment's specific wording, that "[t]he Judicial power of the United States shall not be construed to extend" to suits by non-resident citizens, also may be interpreted to support the theory that the Amendment limits federal courts' subject-matter jurisdiction.[66] A narrow Supreme Court majority currently favors this "constitutional limitation of subject-matter jurisdiction" theory.[67] The Court has noted that the Eleventh Amendment is sufficiently in the nature of a jurisdictional bar that a state may raise the defense for the first time on appeal.[68] However, the Court has not yet held that the Eleventh Amendment is jurisdictional in the sense that a court may raise and decide the defense on its own motion. This is because of the importance of state law in analyzing Eleventh Amendment questions, and the fact that a state may waive its immunity.[69]

## [3] Restoration of Common-Law Immunity From Suits

A second Eleventh Amendment theory is that the Amendment restored common-law state sovereign immunity that Article III and the *Chisholm* decision denied. This theory does not treat state sovereign immunity as a constitutional principle implicit in Article III. Rather, sovereign immunity is viewed as a common-law doctrine that became partially unavailable when the states adopted the Constitution. Under Article III (as interpreted in *Chisholm*), sovereign immunity

---

[61] *See* Employees of Dep't of Pub. Health and Welfare v. Department of Pub. Health and Welfare, 411 U.S. 279, 288–292 (1973) (Marshall, J., concurring); Hans v. Louisiana, 134 U.S. 1, 13 (1890) (suits against unconsenting states were not contemplated by Constitution in establishing federal judicial power).

[62] 134 U.S. at 15.

[63] Seminole Tribe v. Florida, 517 U.S. 44, 72–73 (1996).

[64] *Ex parte* New York, 256 U.S. 490, 497 (1921) (no federal jurisdiction to entertain suit against state brought by its own citizens, because of fundamental rule of sovereign immunity, of which Eleventh Amendment is "but an exemplification").

[65] *See* Hans v. Louisiana, 134 U.S. 1, 18–19 (1890) (endorsing dissenting opinion in *Chisholm*).

[66] U.S. Const., Amend. XI; *see* Missouri v. Fiske, 290 U.S. 18, 25–26 (1933) (Eleventh Amendment explicitly limits federal judicial power).

[67] Seminole Tribe v. Florida, 517 U.S. 44, 72–73 (1996) (5-4 decision holding that Congress cannot abrogate states' sovereign immunity under its Article I power, because sovereign immunity is constitutional principle).

[68] Edelman v. Jordan, 415 U.S. 651, 678 (1974).

[69] Patsy v. Board of Regents, 457 U.S. 496, 516 n.19 (1982).

was no longer applicable when non-residents brought suit against a state. However, Article III and *Chisholm* never affected state common-law immunity against suits by their own citizens.[70] When the states ratified the Eleventh Amendment, the Amendment restored state immunity against non-resident suits. According to this "restoration of common-law immunity" theory, sovereign immunity is not a constitutional doctrine and does not limit federal court subject-matter jurisdiction. Therefore, a state may waive sovereign immunity and Congress may abrogate it through validly enacted statutes.[71]

Moreover, although the Eleventh Amendment embodies immunity against non-resident suits, one commentator has suggested that Congress also may abrogate this immunity, arguing that Congress intended the Eleventh Amendment only to correct judicial misinterpretation of Article III jurisdiction. The Eleventh Amendment merely restored the common-law immunity that pre-existed the Constitution. Thus, neither Article III nor the Eleventh Amendment elevated state sovereign immunity to constitutional status. Since state sovereign immunity is merely a common-law doctrine without constitutional status, Congress could enact legislation to abrogate state sovereign immunity against suit.[72]

A difficulty with this theory, however, is that the Eleventh Amendment's language does not support the inference that the Amendment does not restrict congressional action to abrogate the immunity. Rather, the Amendment directly limits the permissible scope of federal judicial power. Under well-established principles of constitutional law, therefore, Congress generally cannot override such a provision, nor can a litigant waive it.[73]

The Supreme Court has endorsed the "restoration of common-law sovereign immunity" theory in its recognition that states voluntarily may waive sovereign immunity by consent.[74] Thus, the Court has recognized that immunity is merely a common-law defense available to a sovereign, rather than a constitutional limit on

---

[70] *See* U.S. Const., Art. III § 2, cl. 1, Amend. XI.

[71] Pennsylvania v. Union Gas Co., 491 U.S. 1, 13–20 (1989) (by ratifying Constitution, states impliedly consented to empower Congress to abrogate sovereign immunity by legislation enacted under Article I), *overruled by* Seminole Tribe v. Florida, 517 U.S. 44, 72–73 (1996).

[72] Field, *The Eleventh Amendment and Other Sovereign Immunity Doctrines: Part I*, 126 U. Pa. L. Rev. 515, 538–549 (1978) (arguing that neither Article III nor Eleventh Amendment constitutionalized common-law doctrine of sovereign immunity); Field, *The Eleventh Amendment and Other Sovereign Immunity Doctrines: Congressional Imposition of Suit Upon the States*, 126 U. Pa. L. Rev. 1203, 1261–1278 (1978); *see* Fletcher, *A Historical Interpretation of the Eleventh Amendment; A Narrow Construction of an Affirmative Grant of Jurisdiction Rather Than a Prohibition Against Jurisdiction*, 35 Stan. L. Rev. 1033, 1036–1037, 1063 (1983) (agreeing in part with Professor Field's theory); *see also Tribe, Intergovernmental Immunities in Litigation, Taxation, and Regulation: Separation of Powers Issues in Controversies About Federalism*, 89 Harv. L. Rev. 682, 693–699 (1976) (arguing that because Eleventh Amendment was adopted *in* reaction to judicial decision in *Chisholm v. Georgia*, its purpose is to restrict only *judicial* action; therefore, Amendment does not prevent Congress from enacting laws that abrogate state sovereign immunity); Nowak, *The Scope of Congressional Power to Create Causes of Action Against State Governments and the History of the Eleventh and Fourteenth Amendments*, 75 Colum. L. Rev. 1413, 1441–1445 (1975).

[73] *See* Pennsylvania v. Union Gas Co., 491 U.S. 1, 24 (1989) (Stevens, J., concurring) ("A statute cannot amend the Constitution"), *overruled by* Seminole Tribe v. Florida, 517 U.S. 44, 72–73 (1996).

[74] *See, e.g.*, Petty v. Tennessee-Missouri Bridge Comm'n, 359 U.S. 275, 276 (1959).

federal court subject-matter jurisdiction. Some Justices also have recognized this theory in concluding that a state's immunity from citizen suits arises not from the Eleventh Amendment, but rather from the common-law principle of sovereign immunity.[75]

A majority of Justices, however, has never accepted this theory.[76]

### [4] Restriction of Federal Diversity Jurisdiction

Another Eleventh Amendment theory is that the Amendment provides immunity only against federal diversity suits.[77] Proponents of this theory point out that the Eleventh Amendment's language carefully tracks the Article III language granting federal diversity jurisdiction. Since *Chisholm* involved diversity jurisdiction, proponents argue that the Eleventh Amendment was intended only to overrule the *Chisholm* Court's interpretation of the extent of Article III diversity jurisdiction. Under this theory, therefore, the Eleventh Amendment has no effect on Article III's other grants of jurisdiction, such as federal question jurisdiction.[78]

Proponents of this theory contend, then, that Article III abrogates state sovereign immunity in federal question cases. Therefore states, in ratifying the Constitution, effectively surrendered their sovereign immunity from such suits.[79]

---

[75] *See, e.g.*, Atascadero State Hosp. v. Scanlon, 473 U.S. 234, 259 (1985) (Brennan, J., dissenting, joined by Marshall, Blackmun, and Stevens, JJ.) ("There simply is no constitutional principle of state sovereign immunity, and no constitutionally mandated policy of excluding suits against States from federal court. . . . The original Constitution did not embody a principle of sovereign immunity as a limit on the federal judicial power. There is simply no reason to believe that the Eleventh Amendment established such a broad principle for the first time"); Employees of Dep't of Pub. Health and Welfare v. Department of Pub. Health and Welfare, 411 U.S. 279, 309–314 (1973) (Brennan, J., dissenting) ("Any intimation . . . that we may infer from the Eleventh Amendment a 'constitutional immunity,' . . . protecting States from . . . suits brought in federal court by its own citizens, must be rejected . . . . Thus, even if the Eleventh Amendment is a constitutional restraint upon suits against States by citizens of another State, *Hans* accords to nonconsenting States only a nonconstitutional immunity from suit by its own citizens."); *see also* Hans v. Louisiana, 134 U.S. 1 (1890).

[76] *See, e.g.*, Atascadero State Hosp. v. Scanlon, 473 U.S. 234 (1985) (four dissenters treated sovereign immunity as matter of common law, arguing that state's general consent to be sued was sufficient to waive immunity in federal court; majority treated sovereign immunity as fundamental constitutional principle embodied in Article III and Eleventh Amendment, holding that only specific consent to be sued in federal court would suffice to waive immunity in federal court); *see also* Pennsylvania v. Union Gas Co., 491 U.S. 1, 13–24 (1989) (5-4 decision; four members of majority treated sovereign immunity as matter of common law; fifth member of majority agreed with conclusion but not with reasoning; decision was later overruled by Seminole Tribe v. Florida, 517 U.S. 44, 72–73 (1996)).

[77] *See, e.g.*, Atascadero State Hosp. v. Scanlon, 473 U.S. 234, 260–290 (1985) (Brennan, J., dissenting) (detailed review of history of adoption of Eleventh Amendment, concluding that nothing in Amendment or Article III prevents federal courts from exercising federal-question jurisdiction over suits against states).

[78] Pennsylvania v. Union Gas Co., 491 U.S. 1, 23–29 (1989) (Stevens, J., concurring) (Eleventh Amendment carefully mirrors language of diversity clauses of Article III and provides only that federal judicial power shall not be construed to extend to these cases; nothing in text of Amendment in any way affects other grants of judicial power contained in Article III).

[79] *See* Employees of Dep't of Pub. Health and Welfare v. Department of Pub. Health and Welfare, 411 U.S. 279, 300–301 (1973) (Brennan, J., dissenting); Parden v. Terminal Ry., 377 U.S. 184, 192 (1964) ("[b]y empowering Congress to regulate commerce, then, the States necessarily surrendered any portion of

Proponents of this theory consequently question the Supreme Court's decision in *Hans v. Louisiana*,[80] to the extent that decision rests on a constitutional principle of state immunity from federal question suits.[81]

A difficulty with this "restriction of federal diversity jurisdiction" theory is that it ignores the Eleventh Amendment's plain language. The Amendment does not distinguish between suits according to different federal jurisdictional bases. Rather, the Amendment flatly states that the federal judicial power "shall not be construed to extend to *any* suit" against a state by non-residents (emphasis added). By its terms, therefore, the Amendment appears to apply to federal-question litigation brought against a state. Thus, the Supreme Court has rejected this "restriction of federal diversity jurisdiction" theory.[82]

## [5] Literal Reading of Eleventh Amendment

A fourth Eleventh Amendment theory is based on a straightforward application of the Amendment's literal language. Under this "textualist" theory, federal courts have no power to adjudicate any suit brought by a non-resident against a state, whether premised on diversity or federal question grounds. At the same time, a state would be subject to federal-question suits by its own citizens.[83] This textualist theory has a perceived shortcoming: the Amendment's textual distinction between suits by an out-of-state plaintiff and an in-state plaintiff does not appear rationally related to any commonly understood goal of the Amendment.[84] For example, if a purpose of the Eleventh Amendment was to protect states against Revolutionary War debt suits, it makes no sense for the Amendment to apply only to suits by out-of-state plaintiffs.

One commentator has suggested that the Eleventh Amendment's distinction may be rationalized on the basis of the "social contract" between a state and its own citizens, as opposed to out-of-state residents; or as a pragmatic compromise resulting from the political realities of the constitutional amendment process.[85] In

---

their sovereignty that would stand in the way of such regulation"), *overruled*, Welch v. Texas Dep't of Highways and Pub. Transp., 483 U.S. 468 (1987).

[80] Hans v. Louisiana, 134 U.S. 1, 1–3 (1890) (involving claimed violation of Contracts Clause by state's failure to pay debt).

[81] Atascadero State Hosp. v. Scanlon, 473 U.S. 234, 301–302 n.55 (1985) (Brennan, J., dissenting, joined by Marshall, Blackmun, and Stevens, JJ.) (if based on constitutional principle of sovereign immunity, *Hans* "rested on misconceived history and misguided logic"; however, *Hans* could be upheld if based on holding that underlying cause of action on debt did not exist under state law).

[82] Pennhurst State Sch. and Hosp. v. Halderman, 465 U.S. 89, 119–120 (1984) ("[t]he Amendment thus is a specific constitutional bar against hearing even federal claims that otherwise would be within the jurisdiction of the federal courts").

[83] *See* Marshall, *Fighting the Words of the Eleventh Amendment*, 102 Harv. L. Rev. 1342 (1989); Shreve, *Letting Go of the Eleventh Amendment*, 64 Ind. L.J. 601, 615 (1989).

[84] *See* Marshall, *Fighting the Words of the Eleventh Amendment*, 102 Harv. L. Rev. 1342, 1351–1352 (1989).

[85] *See* Martin H. Redish, Federal Jurisdiction: Tensions in the Allocation of Judicial Power 192–193 (2d ed. 1990); *see also* Marshall, *Fighting the Words of the Eleventh Amendment*, 102 Harv. L. Rev. 1342, 1352–1371 (1989).

any event, no Supreme Court Justice has accepted this textualist theory.[86]

### [6] *Alden v. Maine*

In *Alden v. Maine*, the Supreme Court in a 5 to 4 vote, held that Congress lacks authority under its Article I powers to subject nonconsenting states to private suits in their own courts. Resolving a case of first impression, the Supreme Court invalidated the provisions of the Fair Labor Standards Act (FLSA) enacted under Article I, that authorize private suits against states in their own courts without their consent.[87] The import of this case goes well beyond its specific holding.

The Supreme Court majority took a broad analytical approach in analyzing the historical basis of the states' sovereign immunity and its relationship to the Eleventh Amendment. By its terms, the Eleventh Amendment bars federal jurisdiction over suits brought against one state by citizens of another state or of a foreign state. As a result, the Court has sometimes referred to the states' immunity from suit as "Eleventh Amendment immunity." However, the Court explained that this phrase is something of a misnomer, for the sovereign immunity of the states neither derives from nor is limited by the terms of the Eleventh Amendment. Rather, the Constitution's structure and history and Court interpretations make clear that the states' immunity from suit is a fundamental aspect of sovereignty that states enjoyed before the ratification of the Constitution. The states retain this immunity today except as altered by certain constitutional Amendments.

The Supreme Court looked beyond the text of the Eleventh Amendment, examining British law, the Federalist Papers, debates over the ratification of the Constitution and the Eleventh Amendment, the legislative history and text of the Eleventh Amendment, and decisional law. The Court noted the lack of congressional attempts to abrogate sovereign immunity in state courts. The Court also noted that the generation that designed and adopted the federal system considered immunity from private suits central to sovereign dignity.

Views expressed in the ratification debates underscored the importance of state sovereign immunity. Article III, which extended the federal judicial power to controversies between states, raised grave concerns. Hence, proponents of the Constitution assured the people that the Constitution would not strip the states of their sovereign immunity. By the time of ratification, English law was well-established that the Crown could not be sued without consent in its own courts. These additional sources reflect a settled doctrinal understanding that the sovereign immunity of states derives not from the Eleventh Amendment but from the structure of the original Constitution. The Supreme Court has consistently interpreted the adoption of the Eleventh Amendment as conclusive evidence "that the decision in *Chisholm* was contrary to the well-understood meaning of the Constitution."[88]

---

[86] *See* Martin H. Redish, Federal Jurisdiction: Tensions in the Allocation of Judicial Power 193 (2d ed. 1990).

[87] Alden v. Maine, 527 U.S. 706, 712 (1999).

[88] Seminole Tribe v. Florida, 517 U.S. 44, 69 (1996).

Because the Eleventh Amendment confirmed rather than established state sovereign immunity, the scope of that immunity is demarcated not by the text of the Eleventh Amendment alone but by fundamental concepts implicit in the overall design of the Constitution.[89] Following this approach, the Court has upheld states' assertions of sovereign immunity in various contexts falling outside the literal text of the Eleventh Amendment and rejected requests to conform the principle of sovereign immunity to the strict language of the Eleventh Amendment. However, this "residual" sovereign immunity is limited to states and arms of states.[90]

The dissent in *Alden v. Maine* strongly rejected the notion that some inherent sovereign immunity was historically understood to apply to states. Further, sovereign immunity was not generally understood to be indefeasible or to be accorded much status, given its lack of coverage in the original Constitution. The dissent concluded that if the issue had been raised, state sovereign immunity would not have shielded a state from suit on a subject committed to national jurisdiction by Article I.[91]

## § 14.06 APPLICATION OF THE ELEVENTH AMENDMENT: ACTIONS BARRED

### [1] Suits Against State by Citizens of Another State

The Eleventh Amendment expressly prevents federal courts from exercising original jurisdiction of any suit against a state by citizens of another state.[92]

### [2] Suits Against State by Citizens of Foreign Country

The Eleventh Amendment expressly prevents federal courts from exercising original jurisdiction of any suit against a state by citizens of a foreign country.[93]

### [3] Suits Against State by Its Own Citizens

The Eleventh Amendment does not expressly prevent federal courts from exercising original jurisdiction over a suit against a state by its own citizens.[94] However, the Supreme Court has held that the Eleventh Amendment, or the principle of sovereign immunity exemplified by the Eleventh Amendment, prevents

---

[89] Alden, 527 U.S. at 713–35.

[90] Northern Ins. Co. v. Chatham County, 547 U.S. 189, 194–195 (2006) (quoting *Alden* and refusing to extend residual sovereign immunity to local governments not acting as arms of state).

[91] Alden v. Maine, 527 U.S. 706, 762–765 (1999).

[92] U.S. Const., Amend. XI; *see Ex parte* New York, 256 U.S. 490, 497 (1921) (federal courts lack jurisdiction to entertain suit against state by citizens of another state, because of Eleventh Amendment).

[93] U.S. Const., Amend. XI; *see Ex parte* New York, 256 U.S. 490, 497 (1921) (federal courts lack jurisdiction to entertain suits against state by citizens or subjects of foreign State, because of Eleventh Amendment).

[94] *See* U.S. Const., Amend. XI.

federal courts from exercising original jurisdiction over such suits.[95]

The general rule of sovereign immunity — that a state may not be sued without its consent — is a fundamental jurisprudential rule well-established when the states ratified and adopted the Constitution.[96] The history of the Eleventh Amendment demonstrates that federal judicial power granted in the Constitution was not intended to impair the fundamental rule of state sovereign immunity.[97] The Eleventh Amendment is an example of the application of sovereign immunity, but the Amendment's terms do not fully define the scope of the rule.[98] Accordingly, the Supreme Court consistently has applied sovereign immunity to bar suits against states by their citizens in federal court.[99]

### [4] Suits Against States in Admiralty

The Eleventh Amendment applies to suits "in law or equity."[100] The Supreme Court has held that the Amendment and sovereign immunity apply to actions not embraced by the language "any suit in law or equity." For example, a non-consenting state is immune from an admiralty or maritime suit in federal court by a private citizen, provided that the state is in possession of the *res*.[101] In contrast, the Eleventh Amendment does not bar federal court jurisdiction over *in rem* admiralty actions where the *res* is not within the state's possession.[102] For the Eleventh Amendment immunity to apply, the state's possession of the *res* must be actual, and not constructive.[103]

Because Congress enacted the Eleventh Amendment in reaction to the Supreme Court's *Chisholm* decision, its language was particularly directed toward the facts of the *Chisholm* case. *Chisholm* was a suit at law, and the Court held that Article III, Section 2, of the Constitution abrogated the states' traditional immunity to such suits. Consequently, since the Eleventh Amendment was phrased to reverse

---

[95] Hans v. Louisiana, 134 U.S. 1, 15–18 (1890) (it would be anomalous and unheard of to allow state to be sued by own citizens but not by citizens of other states or countries); Maysonet-Robles v. Cabrero, 323 F.3d 43, 53 (1st Cir. 2003); Lawson v. Shelby County, Tenn., 211 F.3d 331, 334 (6th Cir. 2000).

[96] 134 U.S. at 15 (cognizance of suits unknown to and forbidden by law was not contemplated by Constitution when establishing federal judicial power); *see Ex parte* New York, 256 U.S. 490, 497 (1921) (rule of sovereign immunity has important bearing on construction of Constitution).

[97] Hans v. Louisiana, 134 U.S. 1, 12–15 (1890) (it is absurd to suppose that language of Eleventh Amendment was intended to abrogate states' sovereign immunity against suits by their own citizens, in light of history of adoption of Amendment); *see* Welch v. Texas Dep't of Highways and Pub. Transp., 483 U.S. 468, 486 (1987) (Eleventh Amendment embodies broad constitutional principle of sovereign immunity).

[98] *Ex parte* New York, 256 U.S. 490, 497 (1921).

[99] Edelman v. Jordan, 415 U.S. 651, 662–663 (1974).

[100] U.S. Const., Amend. XI.

[101] *Ex parte* New York, 256 U.S. 490, 497–498 (1921) (admiralty *in rem* proceeding).

[102] California v. Deep Sea Research, 523 U.S. 491, 507–08 (1998).

[103] *Id.*; Aqua Log, Inc. v. Georgia, 594 F.3d 1330, 1335–37 (11th Cir. 2010); Great Lakes Exploration Group, L.L.C. v. Unidentified Wrecked and (For Salvage-Right Purposes), Abandoned Sailing Vessel, 522 F.3d 682, 689 (6th Cir. 2008).

that holding, it deals expressly with suits "in law or equity."[104] *Chisholm* did not purport to decide whether Article III abrogated states' sovereign immunity from other suits; thus, there was no need for the Eleventh Amendment to restore sovereign immunity for such other suits.[105] The states' swift ratification of the Eleventh Amendment, however, clearly demonstrated that Article III was not to be construed as inherently surrendering any portion of state sovereign immunity.[106] Therefore, to the extent that sovereign immunity applies to suits other than "in law or equity," states retain such immunity even though the Eleventh Amendment does not expressly encompass such other suits.[107]

## [5] Suits Against States by Foreign Countries

Although the Eleventh Amendment refers specifically to suits by *citizens* and *subjects* of foreign states, the Supreme Court has held that sovereign immunity also applies to suits by foreign countries.[108] A suit by a foreign country is subject to the fundamental constitutional principle that a sovereign state cannot be sued unless it consents or impliedly waives its immunity.[109] This sovereign immunity principle is implicit in the Article III grant of federal jurisdiction. Thus, for example, Article III's grant of federal judicial power over suits "between a State . . . and foreign States" does not abrogate sovereign immunity, but applies only when a state is the plaintiff or a state consents to suit.[110] Sovereign immunity is not limited merely because the Eleventh Amendment does not comprehensively set forth its full scope.[111] Nothing in the text or history of the Constitution indicates that a state's adoption inherently involved any waiver of sovereign immunity against suits by foreign countries. Therefore, a foreign country may not sue a non-consenting state in federal court, even though the Eleventh Amendment does not expressly bar such suits.[112]

## [6] Suits Against States by Native American Tribes

Although the Eleventh Amendment does not expressly apply to suits against states by Native American tribes, the Supreme Court has held that sovereign immunity applies to such suits.[113] Native American tribes are sovereigns.[114]

---

[104] 256 U.S. at 497–498.

[105] 256 U.S. at 497–498.

[106] *See* Hans v. Louisiana, 134 U.S. 1, 18–19 (1890).

[107] *Ex parte* New York, 256 U.S. 490, 497–498 (1921) (federal preemption of state laws affecting admiralty and maritime matters is not inconsistent with states' immunity from suit by private citizens in federal courts of admiralty and maritime jurisdiction).

[108] Principality of Monaco v. Mississippi, 292 U.S. 313, 330 (1934) (suit on bonds issued by state).

[109] 292 U.S. at 330.

[110] 292 U.S. at 321–322; *see* U.S. Const., Art. III § 2, cl. 1.

[111] 292 U.S. at 321–323.

[112] 292 U.S. at 330.

[113] Blatchford v. Native Village of Noatak, 501 U.S. 775, 776–780 (1991); Ysleta del Sur Pueblo v. Raney, 199 F.3d 281, 285 (5th Cir. 2000).

[114] Oklahoma Tax Comm'n v. Citizen Band Potawatomi Indian Tribe, 498 U.S. 505, 509 (1991) (tribes

Although the Eleventh Amendment does not expressly mention suits by other sovereigns, such litigation is subject to state sovereign immunity.[115] Therefore, a suit by a Native American tribe (another sovereign) against a state is not cognizable in federal court, unless the state consents or has impliedly waived its immunity.[116]

There is no indication in the Constitution's text that states intended to waive their sovereign immunity against suits by Native American tribes. Moreover, there is no compelling evidence that the drafters intended such a waiver.[117] Although in adopting the Constitution the states mutually waived their sovereign immunity against suits by each other, no Native American tribe was a party to the constitutional convention. Therefore, no such mutual waiver of immunity occurred between states and tribes.[118] For example, the Supreme Court has held that Native American tribes have immunity against suits by the states.[119] In this respect, Native Indian tribes are similar to foreign sovereigns.[120] Congress does not have the power to generally abrogate state sovereign immunity from suits by Native American tribes.[121] Congress has enacted a statute giving federal district courts original jurisdiction of civil actions arising under federal law, by any Indian tribe recognized by the Secretary of the Interior.[122] A purpose of this statute is to provide Native American tribes with federal court access that is at least as broad as the United States when it sues as a tribe's trustee.[123] The Court has held that this statute exempts Native American tribes from the Tax Injunction Act, which prevents citizens from suing in federal court to enjoin state tax collection.[124] However, the statutory grant of jurisdiction to Native American tribes does not generally abrogate state sovereign immunity under the Eleventh Amendment.[125]

---

are "domestic dependent nations" that exercise inherent sovereign authority over their members and territories).

[115] Principality of Monaco v. Mississippi, 292 U.S. 313, 322–323 (1934) (sovereign immunity bars suit by foreign country).

[116] Blatchford v. Native Village of Noatak, 501 U.S. 775, 776–780 (1991).

[117] 501 U.S. at 776–780.

[118] 501 U.S. at 776–780.

[119] Oklahoma Tax Comm'n v. Citizen Band Potawatomi Indian Tribe, 498 U.S. 505, 509 (1991).

[120] Blatchford v. Native Village of Noatak, 501 U.S. 775, 776–780 (1991).

[121] 501 U.S. at 786–788.

[122] 28 U.S.C. § 1362.

[123] 501 U.S. at 784.

[124] Moe v. Confederated Salish and Kootenai Tribes, 425 U.S. 463, 470–475 (1976) (Tax Injunction Act does not prevent United States from suing as tribe's trustee in federal court to enjoin collection of state tax; therefore, tribe may maintain such action in its own right); *see* 28 U.S.C. § 1341 (Tax Injunction Act).

[125] Blatchford v. Native Village of Noatak, 501 U.S. 775, 784–785 (1991) (state is immune from tribe's suit seeking payment of money allegedly owed under state revenue-sharing statute; federal jurisdictional statute's increase of tribal access to federal courts applies only "in certa*in re*spects").

## [7] Suits Against Persons and Entities Other Than State Governments

### [a] Suit Against State Officer in Official or Representative Capacity

An action against a state officer in the officer's official or representative capacity is considered an action against the state because the state is the real party in interest. The Eleventh Amendment bars such actions, even if the state is not a party of record.[126] Litigation against a state officer in some instances may effectively make the state a real party in interest, because a judgment will operate against the state. Thus, the Supreme Court has deemed a damage suit against a state officer, as a representative of the state, an action against the state. As such, the Eleventh Amendment bars the action.[127]

Even though Eleventh Amendment immunity belongs to the state, some agencies exercising state power may invoke that immunity to protect the state treasury from liability that would have the same practical consequences as a judgment against the state itself. If the agency or board acts as an arm of the state, it enjoys immunity from federal suit to the same extent as the state based on its performance of governmental functions.[128]

A suit against a state treasurer for a refund of illegally collected taxes is an action against the state. Although the state is not a nominal defendant, the suit is against one of its officers, the relief is a judgment against the officer in his or her official capacity and would compel payment from the public treasury. Thus, the judgment would have the same effect as if rendered against the state directly. Therefore, the Eleventh Amendment bars this type of suit.[129]

Federal courts treat litigation to enjoin the future violation of federal law as an individual-capacity suit, even if the suit purports to be an official-capacity suit and the litigants complain of conduct implementing state policy. In such a suit, since the state cannot confer authority to violate federal law, the officer is stripped of state authority. Thus, the suit effectively is against the officer in an individual capacity, rather than as a state representative. Therefore, state sovereign immunity does not protect against such suits for prospective injunctive relief.[130]

---

[126] Regents of Univ. of Cal. v. Doe, 519 U.S. 425, 431 (1997); Carter v. City of Philadelphia, 181 F.3d 339, 347 (3d Cir. 1999).

[127] *Ex parte* New York, 256 U.S. 490, 500–501 (1921) (action against state superintendent of public works for damages that would be paid out of state funds); *see* Will v. Michigan Dep't of State Police, 491 U.S. 58, 71 (1989) (suit against official in his or her official capacity is no different from suit against state).

[128] Hess v. Port Auth. Trans-Hudson Corp., 513 U.S. 30 (1994); Jones v. Washington Metro. Area Transit Auth., 205 F.3d 428, 432 (D.C. Cir. 2000).

[129] Smith v. Reeves, 178 U.S. 436, 438–439 (1900) (state statute authorizing such actions in state court did not waive state's Eleventh Amendment immunity from suit in federal court).

[130] *Ex parte* Young, 209 U.S. 123, 159 (1908).

### [b] Supplemental (Pendent) State-Law Claim Against State Officer

Federal courts have jurisdiction of suits against state officers to enjoin violations of federal law.[131] In such a suit, the plaintiff may seek to assert a supplemental claim that the defendant officer's conduct also violates state law. Generally, the federal court has supplemental jurisdiction over such an additional claim, if it arose from a common nucleus of operative facts as the federal-law claim. Such addition claims are sometimes called "pendent" claims. Under the codified supplemental jurisdiction statute, a federal court has supplemental jurisdiction of state claims if they "form part of the same case or controversy under Article III."[132] However, if the state claim is against an officer in an official capacity, the Eleventh Amendment overrides supplemental jurisdiction and prevents the federal court from hearing the claim.[133]

Supplemental jurisdiction is based on policies favoring efficient judicial administration, and convenience in deciding multiple claims in a single proceeding. However, state sovereignty embodied in the Eleventh Amendment's explicit limitation of federal judicial power outweighs these policies of convenience and economy.[134] Thus, a federal court cannot exercise supplemental jurisdiction of an official-capacity claim based on state law, even if the claim is solely for prospective injunctive relief.[135]

Moreover, the doctrine of *Ex parte Young* does not apply to an official-capacity suit alleging that the officer violated *state* law.[136] In *Ex parte Young*, the Supreme Court held the Eleventh Amendment does not bar a suit for prospective injunctive relief when a litigant alleges a state officer violated *federal* law. This is so even if the officer was implementing state policy. The Court adopted the legal fiction that in violating federal law, the officer is stripped of state authority and therefore is being sued in an individual capacity.[137] The fiction the Court adopted in *Ex parte Young* was necessary to permit the federal courts to vindicate federal rights and hold state officials responsible to the supreme authority of federal law.[138] However, in a claim based on state law violations, vindication of federal rights is not a concern, and state constitutional immunity takes precedence. Therefore, the *Ex parte Young* fiction is inapplicable to official-capacity claims based on state law violations, and the

---

131 209 U.S. at 159–160.

132 28 U.S.C. § 1367(a) (codifying substance of judicial doctrine of pendent jurisdiction); *see* United Mine Workers v. Gibbs, 383 U.S. 715, 725 (1966) (court may exercise pendent jurisdiction of additional claim based on common nucleus of operative fact with claim that gives court jurisdiction). For discussion of supplemental jurisdiction, see Ch. 5, *Supplemental Jurisdiction*.

133 *See* Pennhurst State Sch. and Hosp. v. Halderman, 465 U.S. 89, 119–123 (1984).

134 *See* 465 U.S. at 119–123 ("neither pendent jurisdiction nor any other basis of jurisdiction may override the Eleventh Amendment"; recognizing that denial of pendent jurisdiction might impair judicial economy and parties' convenience by encouraging plaintiffs to split causes of action).

135 465 U.S. at 106 (Eleventh Amendment bars any official-capacity suit based on violation of state law, whether for damages or injunctive relief, if relief sought would have direct impact on state itself).

136 465 U.S.at 106; Equity Athletics, Inc. v. Dept. of Educ., 639 F.3d 91, 107 (4th Cir. 2004).

137 *Ex parte* Young, 209 U.S. 123, 159–160 (1908).

138 Pennhurst State Sch. and Hosp. v. Halderman, 465 U.S. 89, 105–106 (1984).

Eleventh Amendment bars such claims.[139]

### [c] Suit Against Political Subdivision That Acts as Arm of State

The Eleventh Amendment does not ordinarily protect a political subdivision, such as a municipality or county, from suit in federal court.[140] However, a municipality or other political subdivision that effectively is acting as an agency or arm of the state government may have Eleventh Amendment protection.[141]

Whether a county official acts for the state or a local entity is not an all-or-nothing determination. An official or entity may be an arm of the state for some of its purposes, but not others.[142] The question is whether, when the official acts in a particular area or on a particular issue, the official acts for the state or the county.[143] Further, because the determination of whether a county official is acting as a local or state official depends on how the state treats the official, no inconsistency results from decisions that declare an officer to be a state official in one state and not in another.[144] For example, some courts have held that county sheriffs act as state officials when acting in a general law enforcement capacity,[145] while others do not.[146] Similarly, state universities may or may not be protected by Eleventh Amendment immunity.[147]

A political subdivision ordinarily will not be treated as a state arm entitled to Eleventh Amendment protection merely because the subdivision exercises a "slice of state power."[148] For a political subdivision to qualify as a state arm for Eleventh

---

[139] 465 U.S. at 105–106 ("it is difficult to think of a greater intrusion on state sovereignty than when a federal court instructs state officials on how to conform their conduct to state law").; Saahir v. Estelle, 47 F.3d 758, 760–61 (5th Cir. 1995); Ripley v. University of Tex. Health Sci. Ctr., 400 F. Supp. 2d 933, 936–38 (W.D. Tex. 2005).

[140] *See, e.g.*, Mt. Healthy City Sch. Dist. Bd. of Educ. v. Doyle, 429 U.S. 274, 279–281 (1977) (under state's law, school district was not considered part of state); Centro Familiar Cristiano v. City of Yuma, 651 F.3d 1163, 1168 (9th Cir. 2011).

[141] Pennhurst State Sch. and Hosp. v. Halderman, 465 U.S. 89, 123–124 (1984).

[142] *See* Regents of Univ. of Cal. v. Doe, 519 U.S. 425, 427 n.2 (1997) (finding it unnecessary to decide whether some state instrumentalities may qualify as arms of state for some but not all purposes); *see also* Scott v. O'Grady, 975 F.2d 366, 370 (7th Cir. 1992) (sheriff is local official when serving as "chief law enforcement officer" of county, but arm of state when enforcing state court order).

[143] McMillian v. Monroe County, Ala., 520 U.S. 781, 785–786 (1997) (examining whether sheriff was entitled to immunity when acting in law enforcement capacity); Marsh v. Butler County, Ala., 212 F.3d 1318, 1321–1326 (11th Cir. 2000).

[144] McMillian, 520 U.S. at 793–795.

[145] McMillian, 520 U.S.at 793 (Court reviewed state constitution and statutes, and how Eleventh Circuit and state supreme court construed those sources).

[146] Franklin v. Zaruba, 150 F.3d 682, 686 (7th Cir. 1998) (state constitution states that sheriff is county officer and state supreme court so holds).

[147] Richardson v. Southern Univ., 118 F.3d 450, 453–456 (5th Cir. 1997) (university and its Board of Supervisors were state agency); Durham v. Parks, 564 F. Supp. 244, 245–249 (D. Minn. 1983) (not state agency); *but see* Hoeffner v. University of Minn., 948 F. Supp. 1380, 1385–1390 (D. Minn. 1996) (state agency).

[148] Lake Country Estates, Inc. v. Tahoe Regional Planning Agency, 440 U.S. 391, 401 (1979).

Amendment purposes, a judgment against the subdivision essentially has to have the same practical consequences as a judgment against the state.[149] For example, the Court held that a county was a state arm entitled to Eleventh Amendment protection against a suit arising out of the county's operation of a program for mentally challenged patients. The county officials cooperated with state officials in operating the program, which the state almost entirely funded.[150]

### [d] Suits Against State Agencies and Boards Acting as Arm of State

#### [i] General Rule

The Eleventh Amendment protects against suits brought directly against a state in federal court. The state's Eleventh Amendment immunity also extends to any state agency that is an arm of the state government, such as a state health department, because the agency is considered part of the state.[151] This jurisdictional bar applies regardless of the nature of the relief sought. The jurisdictional bar applies to employees of a state agency or board sued in their official capacities with respect to claims for damages,[152] but not with respect to claims for injunctive relief.

To invoke the Eleventh Amendment, the entity must establish that (1) the suit is against the entity and (2) the entity is an arm of the state. Thus, the suit must be against the entity itself, involving a determination of the rights and liabilities of the entity. The Eleventh Amendment does not apply when the entity invoking immunity is sued only in its representative capacity.

A state's Eleventh Amendment protection ordinarily does not extend to a local municipality or other political subdivision, because these entities are not ordinarily part of state government. However, Eleventh Amendment immunity does extend to a political subdivision acting as an arm of the state.

---

[149] *See* 440 U.S. at 400–401 (action involving regional agency created by two states with congressional approval; Eleventh Amendment inapplicable because states did not intend to confer immunity on agency).

[150] Pennhurst State Sch. and Hosp. v. Halderman, 465 U.S. 89, 125–167 (1984); *see also* Mumford v. Basinski, 105 F.3d 264, 273–274 (6th Cir. 1997) (plaintiff's Section 1983 action against successor to domestic relations court judge who fired plaintiff for political activity was barred by Eleventh Amendment because domestic relations court was arm of state, rather than segment of county government; court was created and regulated by state law); *but see* Sonnenfeld v. City and County of Denver, 100 F.3d 744, 749 (10th Cir. 1996) (city and county of Denver were not arm of state entitled to Eleventh Amendment immunity when carrying out state policy in building airport absent showing of degree of state funding or that judgment would be paid out of state treasury).

[151] Hess. v. Port Auth. Trans-Hudson Corp., 513 U.S. 30, 44–51 (1994); McCormick v. Miami Univ., 693 F.3d 654, 661 (6th Cir. 2012).

[152] Coggeshall v. Mass. Bd. of Reg. of Psychologists, 604 F.3d 658, 662 (1st Cir. 2010).

### [ii] Tests for Determining Whether Agency or Board is Acting as Arm of State

The Supreme Court has not stated a precise rule to determine whether a state board or public entity is a state arm entitled to Eleventh Amendment protection. Instead, the Court has indicated that the determination is to be made on a case-by-case basis, balancing various factors:[153]

- Whether state funds would be used to pay a judgment against the entity. Thus, the entity's funding sources are relevant. If the state substantially funds the entity, those funds would be a probable source to satisfy any judgment against the entity. On the contrary, if the entity has taxing powers and can issue bonds, state funds might not be at risk in litigation against the entity. An indemnification agreement between a state instrumentality and a third party, such as the federal government or an insurance company, does not nullify the instrumentality's Eleventh Amendment immunity. The relevant test is whether the state would be liable for the judgment.
- The nature of the entity as created by state law. For example, if a state statute defines the "state" to exclude "political subdivisions," and "political subdivisions" include local school districts, then local school districts probably are not entitled to Eleventh Amendment protection. If Congress creates a multistate entity pursuant to the Compact Clause, the multistate entity presumptively does not qualify for Eleventh Amendment immunity unless there is reason to believe the states structured the entity to provide immunity, and Congress concurred.
- Whether the state intended to confer Eleventh Amendment immunity on the entity.
- Whether the entity exercises the state power and is under state control. For example, if the state government appoints the entity's executives, that tends to show that the entity exercises state power. If state government directs, guides, or vetoes the entity's activities, that also tends to show that the entity is acting for the government. However, a public entity ordinarily will not be treated as a state agency merely because the entity exercises a "slice of state power".
- Whether the entity performs functions typically performed by a state government. If the entity performs what usually are local functions, that tends to indicate that the entity is not a state arm.
- Whether the entity has the right to sue in its own name.
- Whether the entity has the power to hold property in its own name.

Federal courts, in assessing these different factors, may be unable to conclude definitively whether an entity is a state arm entitled to Eleventh Amendment immunity. In these circumstances, courts additionally may consider the two reasons for the Eleventh Amendment's existence: state dignity and the protection

[153] Lake Country Estates, Inc. v. Tahoe Regional Planning Agency, 440 U.S. 391 (1979).

of state treasuries. Thus, if a public entity is sufficiently distinct from the state and financially independent, a suit is not a threat to the state's dignity and the entity should not be deemed a state arm entitled to Eleventh Amendment protection.

#### [iii] Source of Payment and Legal Liability Are Critical Factors

The source of payment for the judgment has historically been considered the most critical factor in determining whether or not an agency or board is operating as an arm of the state. However, it is the entity's potential for legal liability that is determinative,[154] rather than the likelihood that the entity will be reimbursed by the state or the state's ability or inability to require a third party to reimburse it or to discharge the liability in the first instance.[155] Moreover, at least one circuit has concluded that it can no longer give primacy to the source-of-payment factor after the Supreme Court's statement that, although shielding state treasuries is an important function of sovereign immunity, "the doctrine's central purpose is to accord the States the respect owed them as joint sovereigns."[156] In any case, the fact that the federal government has agreed to indemnify a state instrumentality against litigation costs, including an adverse judgment, does not divest the state agency of Eleventh Amendment immunity.[157]

#### [iv] Federal Law Controls

In determining whether an entity is an arm of the state for Eleventh Amendment purposes, federal courts will consider how the entity is treated under state law. This determination is fact specific and to a great extent based on an examination of state law.[158] However, federal law governs the scope of Eleventh Amendment immunity and the determination whether an entity is an arm of the state.[159]

### [e] Administrative Actions

The Supreme Court has held that the Eleventh Amendment bars the Federal Maritime Commission from adjudicating a private party's complaint against a state agency.[160] In *Federal Maritime Commission v. South Carolina State Ports Authority*, a private cruise-ship operator brought suit against a state agency that had repeatedly denied the ship operator's requests to berth its cruise ship at the agency's facilities. The complaint, alleging violations of the Shipping Act of 1984, was filed with the Federal Maritime Commission (FMC), which is authorized to

---

154 Lowe v. Hamilton County Dept. of Job & Family Servs, 610 F.3d 321, 325 (6th Cir. 2010).

155 Shands Teaching Hosp. & Clinics, Inc. v. Beech St. Corp., 208 F.3d 1308, 1311–1313 (11th Cir. 2000).

156 Benn v. First Judicial Dist. of Pa., 426 F.3d 233, 239–40 (3d Cir. 2005).

157 Regents of Univ. of Cal. v. Doe, 519 U.S. 425, 431 (1997).

158 McMillian v. Monroe County, 520 U.S. 781, 786 (1997); Versiglio v. Bd. of dental Exam'rs, 686 F.3d 1290 (11th Cir. 2012); Kitchen v. Upshaw, 286 F.3d 179, 184–85 (4th Cir. 2002).

159 Versiglio, 686 F.3d at 1290.

160 Federal Mar. Comm'n v. South Carolina State Ports Auth., 535 U.S. 743, 752–761 (2002).

adjudicate claims under the Shipping Act. The complaint requested that the FMC (1) seek injunctive relief in federal district court, (2) direct the state agency to pay the complainant reparations, as well as interest and reasonable attorney's fees, and (3) issue an order commanding the state agency to cease and desist from violating the Shipping Act.

The complaint was referred to an administrative law judge. The state agency moved to dismiss, asserting that the state agency, as an arm of the state, was entitled to Eleventh Amendment immunity. Specifically, the state agency argued that the Eleventh Amendment prohibits Congress from enacting a statute authorizing a ship operator to file a complaint before the FMC, effectively suing the state for damages and injunctive relief. The administrative law judge agreed and dismissed the complaint. The FMC reversed, holding that state sovereign immunity is meant to cover proceedings before federal or state judicial tribunals, not Executive Branch administrative agencies like the FMC. The Fourth Circuit reversed the FMC's decision, reasoning that any proceeding in which a federal officer adjudicates disputes between private parties and unconsenting states is barred by the Eleventh Amendment, even if the forum is a federal administrative agency.

In a 5-4 decision, the Supreme Court affirmed the Fourth Circuit's holding. The majority held that state sovereign immunity, as exemplified by the Eleventh Amendment, covers not only proceedings before judicial tribunals, but also adjudicative proceedings conducted by agencies of the federal executive branch.[161] In examining whether state sovereign immunity applies to adjudications by the FMC, the Court assumed *arguendo* that the FMC does not exercise the judicial power of the United States in adjudicating complaints filed by private parties under the Shipping Act. This assumption did not end the inquiry, even though by its terms the Eleventh Amendment limits the exercise of "the judicial [p]ower" of the United States, since the sovereign immunity enjoyed by the states extends beyond the literal text of the Eleventh Amendment.

In determining whether the states' sovereign immunity extends to administrative adjudications, the Court first observed that the historical record of the original understanding of the Constitution was not helpful. Formalized administrative adjudications were all but unheard of in the late eighteenth and early nineteenth centuries, so the Court found it unsurprising that there was no specific evidence indicating whether the Framers believed that the states' sovereign immunity would apply in such proceedings. However, the Court applied a presumption that the Constitution was not intended to raise any proceedings against the states that were "anomalous and unheard of when the Constitution was adopted." The Court therefore attributed great significance to the fact that states were not subject to private suits in administrative adjudications at the time of the founding or at any time before the twentieth century. FMC adjudications are the type of proceedings from which the Framers would have thought the states possessed immunity when they agreed to enter the Union, and the Court stated that the similarities between FMC proceedings and civil litigation are "overwhelming."

[161] Federal Mar. Comm'n v. South Carolina State Ports Auth., 535 U.S. 743, 752–761 (2002).

For example, the FMC's Rules of Practice and Procedure show that FMC administrative proceedings bear a remarkably strong resemblance to civil litigation in federal courts, in terms of pleading requirements and discovery. Given the strong similarities between FMC proceedings and civil litigation, and given that the preeminent purpose of sovereign immunity is to accord the states the dignity that is consistent with their sovereign status, the Supreme Court held that sovereign immunity bars the FMC from adjudicating complaints filed by private parties against nonconsenting states.[162]

The Court's holding is consistent with *Seminole Tribe v. Florida*,[163] in which the Court ruled that Congress lacks the power under Article I of the Constitution to enact legislation abrogating the states' sovereign immunity. It would be quite strange to bar Congress from exercising its Article I powers to abrogate state sovereign immunity in Article III judicial proceedings, but to permit the use of those same Article I powers to create court-like administrative tribunals where sovereign immunity does not apply. The Supreme Court also rejected the argument that the FMC should not be barred from considering a private party's request for nonmonetary relief. The nature of the relief sought is irrelevant to the issue of whether the suit is barred by the Eleventh Amendment, and the Court found no reason why a different rule ought to apply in the realm of administrative adjudications.

In dissent, Justice Breyer wrote that the case involved a typical executive branch agency exercising typical executive branch powers to determine whether a particular person violated federal law. The majority opinion lacked any firm anchor in the Constitution. Because the outcome of an administrative adjudication is a commission order, which the commission cannot itself enforce under the Shipping Act without first obtaining a court order, the administrative adjudication should not constitute the "judicial power of the United States" as to invoke the Eleventh Amendment.[164]

The First Circuit has held that the Eleventh Amendment protects a state employer from being subjected to federal administrative proceedings to enforce the whistle blower provision of the Solid Waste Disposal Act (SWDA).[165] The First Circuit concluded that the Supreme Court's opinion in *Federal Maritime Comm'n v. South Carolina State Ports Authority* disposed of any argument that, as a general proposition, a state's traditional immunity from suit does not extend to administrative proceedings initiated and prosecuted by private parties. The court found no basis for distinguishing the Supreme Court's holding even though the Supreme Court case involved a different administrative agency, a different federal statute, and a different adjudication scheme. Proceedings under the Solid Waste Disposal

---

[162] Federal Mar. Comm'n v. South Carolina State Ports Auth., 535 U.S. 743, 755–764 (2002) (if framers thought it impermissible affront to state's dignity to be required to answer complaints of private parties in federal courts, it is inconceivable that framers would have found it acceptable to compel state to do same thing before administrative tribunal of agency; affront to state's dignity is not lessened when adjudication is before administrative tribunal).

[163] Seminole Tribe v. Florida 517 U.S. 44, 72 (1996).

[164] Federal Mar. Comm'n v. South Carolina State Ports Auth., 535 U.S. 743, 776–787 (2002).

[165] Rhode Island Dep't of Envt'l Mgmt. v. United States, 304 F.3d 31, 45–46 (1st Cir. 2002).

Act's whistleblower provisions share the same salient characteristics as the Shipping Act, and are of the type that the framers would have thought states immune when the states entered the union. Both proceedings are (1) adjudicated before an ALJ, whose role is similar to that of a trial judge, (2) conducted in a manner roughly conforming to the procedural rules that govern the course of a traditional civil lawsuit, and (3) culminate in a final decision that includes the types of relief typically available in civil litigation. Therefore, the First Circuit concluded that a state may invoke sovereign immunity in proceedings initiated by a private party under 29 C.F.R.

The First Circuit also concluded that a state does not waive its immunity by filing a nonstatutory review action in federal court to resolve the immunity issue. The state did not waive its immunity during the administrative proceeding, and the court discerned no attempt by the state to reverse its waiver decision by a change in forum.

## § 14.07 ACTIONS PERMITTED CONSISTENT WITH ELEVENTH AMENDMENT SOVEREIGN IMMUNITY

### [1] Suits by United States Government Against State

The Eleventh Amendment does not bar suits against a state in federal court by the federal government.[166] For example, the Eleventh Amendment did not bar a suit brought by the United States on behalf of the Cheyenne River Sioux Tribe and its members seeking a declaration that the state lacked jurisdiction to impose motor vehicle excise taxes and registration fees on tribe members living on the reservation, although the suit would have been barred had it been brought by the tribe.[167]

The First Circuit rejected an argument that state sovereign immunity is inapplicable when an order issuing from administrative proceedings can be enforced by the federal government. Although sovereign immunity is no barrier to a suit originated by the United States, the First Circuit found it significant that the Solid Waste Disposal Act also allows an individual complainant to enforce the administrative order by initiating a suit in federal court. Therefore, the federal government's role as a potential enforcer did not alter the state's entitlement to sovereign immunity.[168] Nevertheless, the federal government may intervene in the proceedings and remove the sovereign immunity bar.[169] Thus, if the United States

---

[166] *See, e.g.*, United States v. Mississippi, 380 U.S. 128, 140–141 (1965) (civil rights action by United States).

[167] United States v. South Dakota, 105 F.3d 1552, 1560 (8th Cir. 1997).

[168] Rhode Island Dep't of Envt'l Mgmt. v. United States, 304 F.3d 31, 52–55 (1st Cir. 2002) (ordinary role of federal government as enforcer of Secretary of Labor's orders does not alter state's entitlement to immunity; Secretary exercises no discretion in initiation of administrative proceedings).

[169] Rhode Island Dep't of Envt'l Mgmt. v. United States, 304 F.3d 31, 52–55 (1st Cir. 2002) (Secretary of Labor may intervene in the proceedings and remove the sovereign immunity bar); Ohio Envt'l Protection Agency v. United Sates Dep't of Labor. 121 F. Supp. 2d 1155, 1167 (S.D. Ohio 2000).

joins a suit after it has been initiated by otherwise-barred private parties and seeks the same relief as the private parties, the government's intervention generally cures any Eleventh Amendment immunity defect and the private parties may continue to participate in the suit.[170]

The Eleventh Amendment does not bar a suit by the federal government to enforce a federal statute or constitutional provision against a state merely because the suit seeks victim-specific relief on behalf of a private individual.[171] States have argued that in such cases, the federal government is merely standing in the place of the private individual, whose own suit would be barred by the Eleventh Amendment. The courts have disagreed, holding that such suits are permitted as long as the United States controls prosecution of the case and has an independent interest in enforcing the statute.[172]

### [2] Suits by One State Against Another

The Eleventh Amendment generally does not bar suits in federal court by one state against another.[173] However, the Eleventh Amendment will apply to bar a state's suit against another state if the suit actually attempts to obtain recovery for specific citizens.[174] For example, the Eleventh Amendment barred a state's suit seeking damages for designated citizens whose farms were damaged and crops lost when the state diverted a river.[175] The mere fact that a judgment may disproportionately benefit some of a state's citizens does not automatically involve the Eleventh Amendment, if the state is suing to vindicate its own substantial interests.[176] Thus, the Eleventh Amendment did not bar a state's suit to obtain an equitable apportionment of water rights, even though the suit would benefit a particular state citizen. The state sued in its own name and had a substantial interest in the suit's outcome by virtue of its ownership of the affected water rights,

---

170 Rhode Island Dep't of Envt'l Mgmt. v. United States, 304 F.3d 31, 52–55 (1st Cir. 2002).

171 *See* Alden v. Maine, 527 U.S. 706, 759–760 (1999) ("The difference between a suit by the United States on behalf of the employees and a suit by the employees implicates a rule that the National Government must itself deem the case of sufficient importance to take action against the State; and history, precedent, and the structure of the Constitution make clear that . . . States have consented to suits of the first kind but not of the second.").

172 United States v. Alabama Dep't of Mental Health, 673 F.3d 1320, 1327 (11th Cir. 2012) (suit by United States against Alabama Dep't of Mental Health seeking damages for particular individual for violation of Uniformed Services Employment and Reemployment Rights Act was not barred by *Eleventh Amendment*, because suit was "firmly under the control of the executive branch" and United States had significant interest in prosecuting case to achieve law's goal of encouraging service in armed forces); United States v. Mississippi Dep't of Pub. Safety, 321 F.3d 495, 499 (5th Cir. 2003) (*Eleventh Amendment* did not bar federal government's suit against state seeking injunctive relief and monetary damages and other compensatory relief under Americans With Disabilities Act for losses of individual allegedly fired in violation of Act, because federal government had interest in ensuring states' compliance with federal law and had control over case).

173 *See, e.g.*, Colorado v. New Mexico, 459 U.S. 176, 182 n.9 (1982) (suit for equitable apportionment of water rights); Maryland v. Louisiana, 451 U.S. 725, 745 n.21 (1981) (suit challenging constitutionality of state taxes).

174 Maryland v. Louisiana, 451 U.S. 725, 745 n.21.

175 North Dakota v. Minnesota, 263 U.S. 365, 375–376 (1923).

176 Colorado v. New Mexico, 459 U.S. 176, 182 n.9 (1982).

as trustee for its citizens. Even though one citizen would be the primary beneficiary of those rights in the short term, other citizens jointly could use the water or purchase water rights in the future. Accordingly, the state had not brought the suit to benefit one specific citizen, and the Eleventh Amendment did not bar it.[177]

## [3] Suits Against States in State Courts

### [a] Suits in Courts of Defendant State

The Eleventh Amendment does not affect state court jurisdiction to adjudicate suits against a state. Nevertheless, sovereign immunity, derived apart from the literal text of the Eleventh Amendment, bars a citizen from suing the citizen's own state.[178] However, a state may waive its sovereign immunity and consent to suit in its own courts.[179] A state's consent to suit in its own courts does not automatically operate as an Eleventh Amendment waiver.[180]

### [b] Suits in Other States' Courts

A state has no sovereign immunity against suits filed in other states' courts.[181] As a matter of comity, the forum state may grant another state immunity from suit, but the Constitution does not require that a forum state recognize any other state's sovereign immunity.[182]

### [c] Supreme Court Review

The Supreme Court has appellate jurisdiction to review state court decisions in actions against states.[183] The Eleventh Amendment by its terms applies to cases "commenced or prosecuted" in federal court. The Supreme Court has construed this language to refer only to suits invoking original federal court jurisdiction.[184] Thus, the Eleventh Amendment does not constrain the Supreme Court's appellate jurisdiction of cases from state courts.[185]

---

[177] 459 U.S. at 182 n.9.

[178] Alden v. Maine, 527 U.S. 706, 734–35 (1999) (Congress lacks authority under its Article I powers to subject non-consenting states to private suits in own courts).

[179] *See* Nevada v. Hall, 440 U.S. 410, 414 (1979) (only consent to be sued can modify state's absolute immunity from suit in its own courts).

[180] *See, e.g.*, Florida Dept. of Health and Rehabilitative Servs. v. Florida Nursing Home Ass'n, 450 U.S. 147, 149–150 (1981).

[181] Nevada v. Hall, 440 U.S. 410, 416–427 (1979).

[182] 440 U.S. at 416–427.

[183] *See* 28 U.S.C. § 1257(a) (appellate jurisdiction to review state court decisions involving federal questions).

[184] McKesson Corp. v. Division of Alcoholic Beverages and Tobacco, 496 U.S. 18, 29 (1990).

[185] 496 U.S. at 26–31.

### [4] Suits Against Political Subdivisions Such as Municipalities and Counties

The Eleventh Amendment generally bars only suits that name a state or one of its agencies as a defendant.[186] A political subdivision, such as a county or municipality, usually is not considered a part of the state. Therefore, the Eleventh Amendment ordinarily does not protect a political subdivision from suit in federal court.[187] However, the Eleventh Amendment may protect a municipality or political subdivision that effectively acts as a state agency or arm of state government.[188]

## § 14.08 EXCEPTIONS TO THE ELEVENTH AMENDMENT

### [1] Suits Against State Officers in Individual Capacity

#### [a] Distinction Between Official and Individual Capacity

In the early nineteenth century, the Supreme Court construed the Eleventh Amendment to preclude only suits naming a state as a defendant. Accordingly, the Eleventh Amendment did not bar suits against individual state officers.[189] Later, the Court modified this rule to extend the Eleventh Amendment's bar to suits in which a state, although not a named defendant, is the real party in interest. For example, the Eleventh Amendment may bar a suit against a state agency that exercises state power.[190] Similarly, a damage suit against a state officer may be treated as a suit against the state, if the officer is sued in an official capacity for acts carried out under state law authority. In effect, the suit is not against the official but against the official's office; therefore it is no different from a suit against the state.[191] Thus, if an individual sued in official capacity dies or leaves office while

---

[186] *See* Osborn v. Bank of the United States, 22 U.S. (9 Wheat) 738, 857–858 (1824); Florida Dept. of Health and Rehabilitative Servs. v. Florida Nursing Home Ass'n, 450 U.S. 147, 149–150 (1981) (state agency).

[187] *See, e.g.*, Will v. Michigan Dep't of State Police, 491 U.S. 58, 71 (1989) (explicitly reaffirming Monell's holding that local governments are not entitled to sovereign immunity under Section 1983); Central Familiar Cristiano v. City of Yuma, 651 F.3d 1163, 1168 (9th Cir. 2011) (Eleventh Amendment immunity does not apply to municipalities); United Disaster Response, LLC v. Omni Pinnacle, LLC, 511 F.3d 476, 479 (5th Cir. 2007) (parish not entitled to Eleventh Amendment immunity in absence of convincing evidence it is distinguishable from parishes or counties generally);

[188] Pennhurst State Sch. and Hosp. v. Halderman, 465 U.S. 89, 123–124 (1984) (county effectively acted as agency of state in administering particular state program).

[189] *See* Osborn v. Bank of the United States, 22 U.S. (9 Wheat) 738, 857–858 (1824) (whether suit is against state is determined by whether state is party of record).

[190] Florida Dept. of Health and Rehabilitative Servs. v. Florida Nursing Home Ass'n, 450 U.S. 147, 149–150 (1981) (Eleventh Amendment protection extends to state agency as well as to state itself); *but see* Mt. Healthy City Sch. Dist. Bd. of Educ. v. Doyle, 429 U.S. 274, 279–281 (1977) (suit against political subdivision of state may be brought in federal court, unless political subdivision is effectively acting as arm of state).

[191] Hafer v. Melo, 502 U.S. 21, 25 (1991); VIBO Corp., Inc. v. Conway, 669 F.3d 675, 691 (6th Cir. 2012).

litigation is pending, the successor automatically is substituted as defendant.[192] In an official-capacity suit, the state is the real party in interest, since the state treasury will pay any money judgment.[193]

These rules, however, do not bar a damage suit against a state officer in an individual capacity. Such a suit seeks to impose personal liability on the officer for actions under color of state law. Since the officer's personal assets will be used to satisfy any money judgment, the state is not the real party in interest. Accordingly, the Eleventh Amendment does not bar such a suit.[194] Moreover, a suit against an officer that does not seek damages from state funds is treated as an individual-capacity suit, even if it purports to name the officer in an official capacity. For example, in a suit to enjoin the future enforcement of an unconstitutional state statute, the statute is void and confers no state authority on the official. Thus, the suit effectively is against the official in an individual capacity, rather than as a state representative.[195]

Similarly, courts deem a suit to recover specific property held by a state officer (but not state-owned), as an individual-capacity suit. In such a suit, a plaintiff's favorable judgment will impose no burden on the state treasury, since the property does not belong to the state.[196]

### [b] Determining Whether Officer Is Being Sued in Individual Capacity

The characterization of a damage suit depends on the capacity in which the officer is sued, rather than the capacity in which the officer allegedly inflicted injury.[197] Thus, even if the officer was performing official functions when the alleged harm occurred, the suit is an individual-capacity suit if the plaintiff seeks a damage award against the officer personally.[198]

An individual-capacity suit is not transformed into an official-capacity suit because state funds may be available to reimburse an officer for personal liability in the performance of duties. Thus, a state's decision to indemnify its public servants does not confer Eleventh Amendment immunity on state officials sued in their

---

[192] 502 U.S. at 25; *see* Fed. R. Civ. P. 25(d)(1); Fed. R. App. P. 43(c) (1); S. Ct. R. 35.3.

[193] *See* Kentucky v. Graham, 473 U.S. 159, 165–166 (1985) (if damages would be payable from state treasury, state is real party in interest even though officials are nominal parties).

[194] *See* 473 U.S. at 165–166.

[195] *Ex parte* Young, 209 U.S. 123, 159–160 (1908).

[196] Florida Dep't of State v. Treasure Salvors, Inc., 458 U.S. 670, 697–699 (1982) (admiralty *in rem* proceeding; state had no colorable claim of ownership of property); *see* Tindal v. Wesley, 167 U.S. 204, 221–223 (1897) (judgment in such individual-capacity suit against officer case would not preclude state from bringing subsequent action to establish whatever claim it has to property).

[197] Hafer v. Melo, 502 U.S. 21, 27–29 (1991).

[198] 502 U.S. at 23–24 (suit for damages based on wrongful termination of employment); Scheuer v. Rhodes, 416 U.S. 232, 237–238 (1974) (damages recoverable from individual defendants notwithstanding that they hold public office).

personal capacity.[199]The Supreme Court has indicated that "it is obviously preferable for the plaintiff to be specific in the [complaint] to avoid any ambiguity" about the capacity in which the defendant officer is being sued.[200] Consequently, some lower courts have looked solely to a complaint's wording to determine whether a suit is against a state official in an individual or official capacity.[201] However, the Supreme Court also has noted that if a complaint does not clearly specify the capacity in which an official is sued, the proceedings typically indicate the nature of the liability.[202] For example, the trial record may provide evidence of an official's capacity, including the plaintiff's response to a summary judgment motion, opening statements, evidentiary rulings, and liability findings.[203] Thus, several lower courts have considered matters extrinsic to the complaint, such as the defenses, to determine the capacity in which a plaintiff has sued a defendant.[204]

## [2] Suits Against State Officers in Official Capacity

### [a] Suits for Monetary Relief Barred

Suits for monetary damages against state officials in their official capacities operate as suits against the state. As such, official capacity suits seeking monetary damages are barred.[205]

### [b] Suits for Injunctive Relief Permitted

Official capacity suits for injunctive relief are permitted under the Eleventh Amendment. Officials who violate federal law are stripped of state authority and do not act for the state because the state cannot confer authority to violate federal law.[206]

---

[199] *See e.g.*, Farid v. Smith, 850 F.2d 917, 923 (2d Cir. 1988); Blaylock v. Schwinden, 862 F.2d 1352, 1354 (9th Cir. 1988).

[200] Hafer v. Melo, 502 U.S. 21, 27 (1991).

[201] *See e.g.*, Wells v. Brown, 891 F.2d 591, 592 (6th Cir. 1989) (in action alleging deprivation of civil rights under 42 U.S.C. § 1983, plaintiff must specifically plead that damage suit is against state official in individual capacity); Nix v. Norman, 879 F.2d 429, 431 (8th Cir. 1989) (same); *see also* Fed. R. Civ. P. 9(a) (not necessary to aver party capacity except to extent required to show court's jurisdiction).

[202] Kentucky v. Graham, 473 U.S. 159, 167 n.14 (1985).

[203] Brandon v. Holt, 469 U.S. 464, 469–470 (1985) (allowing plaintiff to amend pleadings to conform to name municipality as defendant; record demonstrated that original defendant officer had been sued in official capacity).

[204] *See e.g.*, Houston v. Reich, 932 F.2d 883, 885 (10th Cir. 1991); Shabazz v. Coughlin, 852 F.2d 697, 700 (2d Cir. 1988) (complaint was ambiguous; court looked to record of defendant's summary judgment motion to determine that parties believed suit was against defendant in individual capacity).

[205] Will v. Michigan Dep't of State Police, 491 U.S. 58, 64 (1989); McCormick v. Miami Univ., 693 F.3d 654, 662 (6th Cir. 2012) (claims for monetary damages against faculty members of public university in their official capacities were barred by Eleventh Amendment).

[206] Miranda B. v. Kitzhaber, 328 F.3d 1181, 1187–88 (9th Cir. 2003) (official capacity suits seeking monetary damages for past breaches are barred).

### [c] Enforcement of Federal Consent Decree Permitted

The Eleventh Amendment allows the enforcement of a federal consent decree entered into by state officials if the decree springs from a federal dispute and furthers the objectives of federal law, even if the claimed violation does not constitute a violation of that federal law.[207]

The plaintiffs in *Frew v. Hawkins* filed a Section 1983 class action in federal district court seeking injunctive relief against various officials charged with operating the Texas Medicaid program. The individuals were sued in their official capacities and were represented by the state attorney general. The resulting consent decree required the state officials to follow a comprehensive plan for implementing the statutory requirements, in contrast with the brief and general provisions of the federal Medicaid statute. When the plaintiffs moved to enforce the consent decree, the state officials claimed that the Eleventh Amendment barred enforcement. The Fifth Circuit held that the Eleventh Amendment prevented enforcement unless a violation of the consent decree was also a statutory violation of a provision of the Medicaid Act that imposed a clear and binding obligation on the State.

The Supreme Court reversed, expressly rejecting the officials' argument that a federal court should not enforce a consent decree arising from an *Ex parte Young* suit unless the court first identifies violation of federal law at the enforcement stage. The Court emphasized that the state officials did not contend that the terms of the decree were impermissible under *Ex parte Young*. Rather, the officials challenged only the enforcement of the decree, not its entry, contending that enforcement would permit state officials to bind the state government to significantly more commitments than what federal law requires. Federal courts would have jurisdiction over not just federal law, but also everything else that officials agreed to when they entered into the decree. Thus, a state that is in full compliance with federal law could remain subject to federal court oversight through judicial proceedings brought to enforce the consent decree.[208]

The Supreme Court observed that a proper consent decree is a federal court order that springs from a federal dispute and furthers the objectives of federal law. Because the state had asserted its Eleventh Amendment immunity, the officials could not agree to a decree including remedies beyond the scope of *Ex parte Young*. Therefore, the plaintiffs' motion sought to enforce a remedy consistent with *Ex parte Young*, a remedy the state officials themselves had accepted when they asked the district court to approve the decree. Accordingly, the Supreme Court concluded that enforcing the agreement would not violate the Eleventh Amendment. The Court distinguished *Pennhurst State School and Hospital v. Halderman*, which held the *Ex parte Young* inapplicable to suits brought against state officials alleging violations of *state* law. In the present case, the consent decree was entered to implement a federal statute. Although the decree implemented the Medicaid statute

---

[207] Frew v. Hawkins, 540 U.S. 431, 436–440 (2004) (consent decree was enforceable under the principles of *Ex parte Younger*; court did not reach alternative theory that state waived its immunity by participating in litigation).

[208] *Id.*, 540 U.S. at 437–440.

in a highly detailed way, requiring some steps not specifically required by statute, that would be true of any effort to implement a general statute in a particular way. The decree reflected a choice among ways that a state could implement the Medicaid Act.

The Supreme Court acknowledged that the enforcement of consent decrees can undermine the sovereign interests and accountability of state governments. The remedies outlined in consent decrees might improperly deprive future officials of their legislative and executive powers, if those remedies were not limited to reasonable and necessary implementations of federal law. Remedies outlined in consent decrees involving state officers might improperly deprive future officials of their designated legislative and executive powers if not limited to reasonable and necessary implementations of federal law. Such remedies could also lead to federal court oversight of state programs for long periods of time, even absent ongoing violations of federal law.

However, the primary response to these state sovereignty concerns is based on the district court's equitable powers and the Federal Rules of Civil Procedure, not on the Eleventh Amendment. For example, Rule 60(b)(5) authorizes courts to modify decrees in light of changed circumstances. The Court emphasized that when a suit under *Ex parte Young* requires a detailed order to ensure compliance for prospective relief, and the decree requires state officials to administer a significant federal program, then federalism requires that state officials be given latitude and substantial discretion. Further, federal courts must exercise their equitable powers to ensure that state control be returned when the state satisfies the decree's objectives.

The Supreme Court's decision in *Frew* resolved a circuit split whether the Eleventh Amendment bars enforcement of a consent decree that imposes more detailed requirements than generally applicable federal law.

## [3] Suits Against Individual State Officers for Injunctive and Declaratory Relief

### [a] *Ex Parte Young* Doctrine

#### [i] Suits Permitted for Prospective Relief

The Eleventh Amendment does not bar a suit to enjoin a state officer from conduct that would violate federal law,[209] even if the conduct the plaintiff seeks to enjoin is the implementation of official state policy.[210] Suits against state officials to enjoining them from enforcing state laws that allegedly violate the federal constitution are not deemed against the state. By violating the federal

[209] Idaho v. Coeur D'Alene Tribe of Idaho, 521 U.S. 261, 269 (1997); McCormick v. Miami Univ., 693 F.3d 654, 662 (6th Cir. 2012); Indiana Prot., and Advocacy Servs. V. Indiana Family and Soc. Servs. Admin., 603 F.3d 365, 371 (7th Cir. 2010); Concilio de Salud Integral v. Perez-Perdomo, 551 F.3d 10, 18 (1st Cir. 2008); Nelson v. University of Texas at Dallas, 535 F.3d 318, 322 (5th Cir. 2008).

[210] *Ex parte* Young, 209 U.S. 123, 159–160 (1908) (suit to enjoin enforcement of unconstitutional state statute).

constitutional rights of citizens, state officials are stripped of any official or representative capacity. As such, they may be sued personally for the consequences of their unconstitutional conduct. This legal fiction is necessary to permit federal courts to vindicate federal rights and hold state officials responsible to the supreme authority of federal law. Such suits are not permitted against state agencies or the state itself.[211]

This rule is referred to as the doctrine of *Ex parte Young,*[212] after the case in which the Court articulated the rule. The legal fiction on which the *Ex parte Young* doctrine is based is called a fiction because the suit against the official or representative actually binds the state, just as would a suit against the state itself. The state stands behind the individual defendant as the real party in interest. Therefore, there is no need to join the state as a required party under Rule 19. The *Ex parte Young* doctrine operates as an exception to the general rule of sovereign immunity that states may be sued only with their consent. The doctrine and its underlying rationale do not extend to claims for retrospective relief.[213] The Supreme Court has affirmed the vitality of the *Ex parte Young* doctrine, even while strongly reaffirming states' immunity rights against suits. Examples of prospective injunctive relief include job reinstatement and injunctions against future violations of federal law. The application of the *Ex parte Young* doctrine turns on two considerations: (1) whether the plaintiff seeks prospective or retrospective relief, and (2) whether the alleged violation of federal law is ongoing and continuous.[214] Further, if Congress provides a detailed remedial scheme for the enforcement of a statutory right, the *Ex parte Young* doctrine does not apply and a plaintiff must pursue the prescribed statutory remedy.[215]

Prior to the Supreme Court's decision in *Verizon Maryland Inc. v. Public Service Commission,*[216] courts deciding the availability of suit under the *Ex parte Young* doctrine also considered whether "special sovereignty interests" would be implicated by a grant of equitable relief. In some exceptional cases, suit was not permitted because the relief sought would implicate such interests. That consideration has been called into question by the Court's decision in *Verizon.*

For the *Ex parte Young* exception to apply, the state official defendant must have "some connection with the enforcement" of the challenged act. Absent this nexus, a suit against a state official would be just an indirect means of suing the state and subject to sovereign immunity. In addition, the requirement that the defendant have a measure of proximity to and responsibility for the challenged state action ensures that a federal injunction will be effective with respect to the

---

211 Consejo de Salud v. Gonzalez-Feliciáno, 695 F.3d 83, 103 (1st Cir. 2012); Lewis v. University of Tex. Med. Branch, 665 F.3d 625, 630 (5th Cir. 2011).

212 *Ex parte* Young, 209 U.S. 123 (1908).

213 Council 31 of the Am. Fed'n of State, County, and Mun. Employees v. Quinn, 680 F.3d 875, 882–884 (7th Cir. 2012); Muscogee (Creek) Nation v. Oklahoma Tax Comm'n, 611 F.3d 1222, 1232–34 (10th Cir. 2010).

214 Council 31, 680 F.3d at 882–84; Lewis v. New Mexico dep't of Health, 261 F.3d 970, 975–78 (10th Cir. 2001) (Tenth Circuit applies four-part test to determine applicability of the *Ex parte Young* doctrine).

215 Seminole Tribe v. Florida, 517 U.S. 44, 73–76 (1996).

216 Verizon Md. Inc. v. PSC, 535 U.S. 635 (2002).

underlying claim.[217] Thus, any probe into the application of the *Ex parte Young* exception should determine the ability of the official to enforce the challenged statute under his or her statutory or constitutional powers and the demonstrated willingness of the official to enforce the statute.

If the challenged statute does not itself establish an actual enforcement connection, there must be sufficient indicia establishing the defendant's enforcement powers elsewhere in the state's laws.[218] It is not enough that the defendant merely possesses general authority to enforce the laws of the state.[219] However, the defendant need not be specifically empowered to enforce compliance with the statute at issue; it is enough that the defendant exercises duties that assist in giving effect to the law.[220]

When a public officer who is sued in the officer's official capacity dies, resigns, or otherwise ceases to hold office, the action does not abate; the successor is automatically substituted as defendant. Proceedings following the substitution will be in the name of the substituted party.

### [ii] *Ex parte Young* Case

In *Ex parte Young*, a Minnesota statute prescribed railway rates. Railway stockholders sued the company and the state's attorney general in federal court, seeking to enjoin the statute's enforcement, which allegedly violated the constitution. The federal court issued a preliminary injunction prohibiting the state's attorney general from enforcing the statute. When the attorney general violated the injunction, the federal court took the attorney general into federal custody. The attorney general then filed a petition for habeas corpus, asserting that the Eleventh Amendment barred the stockholders' suit. The attorney general argued that, since any action by him to enforce the statute was state action in carrying out its policy, the stockholders' suit effectively was a suit against the state.[221]

The Supreme Court held that because of the Constitution's superior authority, a state and its officers have no authority to enforce an unconstitutional state statute. Any proceeding to enforce an unconstitutional statute does not affect the state in its sovereign or governmental capacity. Accordingly, an attempt by a state officer to enforce such a statute simply is an illegal act, and the officer is stripped of official or representative character and is personally liable for the consequences of their individual conduct.[222] Under these circumstances, the state has no power to impart sovereign immunity for individual actions. The Court concluded that the Eleventh Amendment did not bar the stockholders' suit against the state attorney general,

---

[217] South Carolina Wildlife Federation v. Limehouse, 549 F.3d 324, 333 (4th Cir. 2008).

[218] K.P. LeBlanc, 627 F.3d 115, 124–25 (5th Cir. 2010); Chamber of Commerce of the United States v. Edmondson, 594 F.3d 742, 760 (10th Cir. 2010).

[219] McBurney v. Cuccinelli, 616 F.3d 393, 399 (4th Cir. 2010).

[220] Coalition to Defend Affirmative Action v. brown, 674 F.3d 1128, 1133–35 (9th Cir. 2012); Missouri Protection and Advocacy v. Carnahan, 499 F.3d 803, 807 (8th Cir. 2007).

[221] 209 U.S. at 159.

[222] 209 U.S. at 159–160.

either to have the statute declared unconstitutional, or to enjoin its enforcement.[223]

### [iii] Ongoing Violation of Federal Law Required

Ordinarily, *Ex parte Young* exception to Eleventh Amendment immunity applies only when an ongoing violation of federal law is alleged. This clearly encompasses violations of the United States Constitution or federal statutes.[224] Whether state officials are actually violating federal law is a merits question, not a question of Eleventh Amendment immunity. For the *Ex parte Young* exception to apply, the claim that federal law is being violated need not be meritorious, so long as it is not frivolous.[225]

The Supreme Court in *Verizon Maryland* held that a local exchange carrier's suit alleging that the 1996 Telecommunications Act preempts a state public utilities commission order requiring payment of reciprocal compensation to new participants in the local market may proceed under the *Ex parte Young* doctrine.[226] The case involved a dispute over whether an interconnection agreement required reciprocal compensation for calls made by one of LEC's customers to local access numbers of Internet Service Providers. After the commission issued an order requiring reciprocal compensation for the calls, one of the LECs filed suit in federal district court, seeking declaratory and injunctive relief, alleging that the commission's order violated the Telecommunications Act and a related FCC ruling. The named defendants included the state commission, its individual members in their official capacities, and the other competing LECs. The complaint asserted subject-matter jurisdiction under the general federal question statute and under the Telecommunications Act. The Supreme Court held that the plaintiff LEC could properly seek prospective injunctive relief — the essence of the complaint — against the individual commissioners under the doctrine of *Ex parte Young*. The Court found it unnecessary to decide whether the state public utilities commission had waived its Eleventh Amendment immunity by voluntarily participating in the regulatory regime set up by the Telecommunications Act.

The *Ex parte Young* exception does not apply to a claim that a state official is violating a state law or state constitution, because such claims do not implicate federal rights or federal supremacy concerns.[227] In addition, the Supreme Court has placed some limitations on the *Young* doctrine. If Congress provides a detailed remedial scheme for the enforcement of a statutory right, *Ex parte Young* does not apply and a plaintiff must pursue the statutory remedy.[228] Moreover, in *Idaho v. Coeur d'Alene Tribe of Idaho*, the Supreme Court indicated that *Ex parte Young* may not be applicable when the relief sought implicates important issues of state

---

223 209 U.S. at 159–160.

224 Verizon Md., Inc. v. Public Serv. Comm'n, 535 U.S. 635, 645–48 (2002).

225 *Id.*, 535 U.S.at 646.

226 *Id.*, 535 U.S. at 648.

227 McKinley v. Abbott, 643 F.3d 403, 406 (5th Cir. 2011); Spoklie v. Montana, 411 F.3d 1051, 1060 (9th Cir. 2005).

228 Seminole Tribe v. Florida, 517 U.S. 44, 75–76 (1996) (statutory remedy was much less severe than injunctive relief — including possibility of contempt sanctions — would have been).

sovereignty such as control over submerged lands.[229] Lower courts have also evaluated other state and federal interests under the reasoning of *Coeur d'Alene*, holding that "special sovereign interests" of the type present in *Coeur d'Alene* were not implicated, and often emphasizing the exceptional effect of the relief sought in that case and the narrow scope of the *Coeur d'Alene* exception.[230] Two circuits have opined that the Supreme Court, in *Verizon, Maryland Inc.* rejected "special sovereign interests" as a consideration in determining whether suit is available under the *Ex parte Young* doctrine.[231]

### [b] Consequences of *Ex parte Young*

Under the *Ex parte Young* doctrine, courts treat a suit against a state officer to enjoin a violation of federal law as an individual-capacity suit, even if the officer acts solely to enforce state law and the plaintiff seeks to prevent implementation of state policy.[232] Some Justices and commentators have criticized this application of *Ex parte Young*, because it seems to conflict with other Supreme Court decisions holding that the Eleventh Amendment bars damage actions against state officers when the state is the real party in interest.[233] However, commentators also have pointed out that the Supreme Court's "fictitious" distinction between a state and an officer is analogous to the common-law rule that imposes personal liability on an agent who acts in excess of the authority that a principal legally could confer.[234]

Another apparent inconsistency arises from the Supreme Court's definition of state action for Fourteenth Amendment purposes. The Fourteenth Amendment prohibits states from denying due process and equal protection, but it does not affect private conduct.[235] In a suit against a state officer to enjoin a Fourteenth

---

[229] Idaho v. Coeur d'Alene Tribe, 521 U.S. 261, 280–285 (1997) (Native American Tribe claimed ownership of submerged lands under lake and sought injunction against state to prohibit it from regulating or using lands; Supreme Court held suit was barred by Eleventh Amendment and did not fall within *Ex Parte Young* exception because Idaho's sovereign interest in its lands and waters would be significantly affected were the Tribe to prevail).

[230] *In re* Dairy Mart Convenience Stores, Inc., 411 F.3d 367, 371–72 (2d Cir. 2005); Carten v. Kent State Univ., 282 F.3d 391, 398 (6th Cir. 2002).

[231] Hill v. Kemp, 478 F.3d 1236, 1258–60 (10th Cir. 20007); Ameritech Corp. v. McCann, 297 F.3d 582, 587–88 (7th Cir. 2002).

[232] *Ex parte* Young, 209 U.S. 123, 159–160 (1908) (officer is "stripped of his official or representative character and is subjected in his person to the consequences of his individual conduct").

[233] *See* 209 U.S. at 174 (Harlan, J., dissenting) (injunctive relief in federal court prevents state from testing validity of its own law in its own courts); Tribe, *Intergovernmental Immunities in Litigation, Taxation, and Regulation: Separation of Powers Issues in Controversies About Federalism*, 89 Harv. L. Rev. 682, 687 (1976) (*Ex parte Young*'s distinction between suit against officer and suit against state is "unsatisfactory and conceptually unruly"); Martin H. Redish, Federal Jurisdiction: Tensions in the Allocation of Judicial Power 194 (2d ed. 1990) ("Court's analysis in *Young* has a distinct air of unreality about it"); *see also* Kentucky v. Graham, 473 U.S. 159, 165–166 (1985) (Eleventh Amendment bars damages suit against state officer when state is real party in interest); Edelman v. Jordan, 415 U.S. 651, 662–665 (1974) (if damages would be payable from state treasury, state is real party in interest even though officials are nominal parties).

[234] *See* Erwin Chemerinsky, Federal Jurisdiction 392 (2d ed. 1994); John V. Orth, The Judicial Power of the United States: The Eleventh Amendment in American History 133 (1987).

[235] U.S. Const., Amend. XIV § 1.

Amendment violation, therefore, the complaint must allege that the threatened violation would constitute state action, rather than the defendant's individual, unofficial act. However, because a complaint alleges that a defendant officer's threatened act would violate the Constitution, *Ex parte Young* treats the act as the defendant's individual conduct rather than a state act.[236] As a result, the officer's unconstitutional conduct constitutes state action under the Fourteenth Amendment but private conduct under the Eleventh Amendment.[237]

Despite these logical inconsistencies, the Supreme Court and commentators have accepted the *Ex parte Young* doctrine as necessary to permit the federal courts to vindicate federal rights. The doctrine is the result of the Court's efforts to harmonize state sovereignty reflected in the Eleventh Amendment with federal supremacy reflected in the Constitution and federal laws.[238] Thus, when a plaintiff alleges a continuing or future violation of federal law, the federal government's interest in ensuring compliance with federal law predominates, and a federal court has jurisdiction to enjoin the violation.[239] On the contrary, if a plaintiff alleges a past violation, the state's interest in maintaining its autonomy predominates and a federal court will not have jurisdiction to award damages.[240]

## [4] Suits Against State Officers in Individual Capacity for Monetary Relief

### [a] Prospective vs. Retroactive Relief

The doctrine of *Ex parte Young* applies only to suits against state officers for *injunctive* relief. Thus, the Eleventh Amendment still confers immunity on state officers against monetary damage suits paid by the state. If an action essentially seeks to recover money from the state, the state is the real, substantial party in interest, even though an individual state officer is the nominal defendant.[241] In such a case, the state's Eleventh Amendment immunity protects the officer, even though the alleged conduct violated federal law and would have stripped the officer of state authority in an injunctive relief suit.[242]

---

[236] *Ex parte* Young, 209 U.S. 123, 159–160 (1908) (officer is "stripped of his official or representative character and is subjected in his person to the consequences of his individual conduct").

[237] Pennhurst State Sch. and Hosp. v. Halderman, 465 U.S. 89, 104–105 (1984) (acknowledging "well-recognized irony" created by fiction used in *Ex parte Young*).

[238] *See* 465 U.S. at 105.

[239] Green v. Mansour, 474 U.S. 64, 68 (1985) (remedies designed to end continuing violation of federal law are necessary to vindicate federal interest in assuring supremacy of that law).

[240] 474 U.S. at 68–72 (federal "compensatory or deterrence interests" are insufficient to overcome dictates of Eleventh Amendment).

[241] Ford Motor Co. v. Department of Treasury, 323 U.S. 459, 464 (1945) (suit against state officers for refund of state taxes alleged to have been illegally collected; under state law, any judgment would have to be satisfied out of state treasury).

[242] Edelman v. Jordan, 415 U.S. 651, 664–666 (1974) (injunction was properly issued to require defendant officer to conform future conduct to law, but award of monetary damages for defendant officer's past conduct was improper, because damages would be paid from state funds).

The differing treatment of suits against state officers — depending on whether the remedy is injunctive relief or damages payable by the state — is grounded in the policy aim of protecting state treasuries.[243] However, even injunctive relief may have a significant direct effect on a state treasury. For example, an injunction ordering a state officer to comply with federal guidelines for processing welfare applications does not directly require the state to pay damages, but the state may incur substantial expenses in bringing state procedures into compliance with federal law.[244] The Supreme Court, in articulating a rationale for the different treatment of injunctive relief and damage suits, has focused on the nature of the relief rather than the effect of a potential judgment on the state treasury. Generally, an injunction is *prospective* in nature, because it addresses the defendant's *future* conduct. In contrast, a damage award is *retroactive* in nature, because it compensates the plaintiff for the defendant's *past* violations. The Supreme Court has relied on this distinction between prospective and retroactive relief to determine whether Eleventh Amendment immunity applies to suits brought against state officers.

Thus, the Eleventh Amendment protects a state officer against a suit in federal court for retroactive relief that would be paid out of the state treasury.[245] In contrast, the Eleventh Amendment ordinarily does not preclude a suit against an officer for prospective relief, even if the requested relief would require the expenditure of substantial state funds.[246]

A federal suit seeking damages against a state officer in an individual capacity, rather than an official capacity, is not considered a suit against the state. Therefore, the Eleventh Amendment does not protect the officer against such a suit.[247] If an official-capacity suit against a state officer is based on a violation of state rather than federal law, the Eleventh Amendment bars the suit from federal court, whether the relief is prospective or retroactive.[248]

---

[243] *See* 415 U.S. at 664–666 (Eleventh Amendment bars action for monetary relief payable from state treasury, notwithstanding that relief is labeled "equitable restitution").

[244] *See* 415 U.S. at 668.

[245] 415 U.S. at 668–669.

[246] 415 U.S. at 667–668 (expenditure of state funds as necessary result of compliance with prospective decree is permissible and often inevitable consequence of doctrine of *Ex parte Young*); *see also* Kostok v. Thomas, 105 F.3d 65, 68 (2d Cir. 1997) (Eleventh Amendment did not bar Medicaid patient's suit against Commissioner of State Social Services Department requesting declaration that state policy prohibiting Medicaid payment for customized wheelchair violated federal law and injunction against state's refusal to authorize payment).

[247] *See* Kentucky v. Graham, 473 U.S. 159, 165–166 (1985).

[248] Pennhurst State Sch. and Hosp. v. Halderman, 465 U.S. 89, 106 (1984) (federal court's grant of relief against state officer based on state law, whether prospective or retroactive, would not serve purpose of vindicating federal law and would conflict directly with federalism principles underlying Eleventh Amendment).

### [b] Determining Whether Relief Sought Is Prospective or Retroactive

It is not always easy for courts to determine whether the relief a plaintiff seeks is prospective or retroactive.[249] Although a direct court order to pay money from the state treasury to remedy past conduct ordinarily fits the definition of *retroactive* relief, under some circumstances a court may deem such an order *prospective* in nature.

For example, in *Milliken v. Bradley*,[250] the Supreme Court held that in ordering officials to end unconstitutional school segregation, a federal court may supplement this prospective remedy by ordering that the state bear some of the cost of remedial programs to eliminate future, ongoing vestiges of state-imposed segregation.[251] Although the order to provide special educational programs served as "compensation" to victims for harm caused by prior school segregation, the Supreme Court characterized the relief as prospective in nature. Thus, without the special programs, discrimination victims would continue to experience segregations' harmful effects until remedial programs helped dissipate the continuing effects of past misconduct.[252] The Court distinguished the order to pay for remedial programs from a retroactive damage award. The *Milliken* order was unlike a damage award, which usually is paid directly to the victim and is sufficient to compensate for wrongful conduct. The one-time money damage award in *Milliken* would not make the victims of school segregation whole, because they would continue to experience the effects of inferior education. Moreover, the order was unlike a damage award, because the state funds in *Milliken* were not paid directly to the victims.[253]

One commentator has criticized the *Milliken* decision as an unwarranted extension of the concept of prospective relief.[254] Another commentator has suggested that the real distinction between prospective relief and retroactive relief may be based on the manner in which funds are taken from the state treasury. Thus, a federal court order may be characterized as *prospective* relief if it appears simply to order a state officer to comply with the law, and the expenditure of state funds is incidental to compliance. However, a court order may be characterized as *retroactive* relief if it appears that a federal court is directing expenditure from the state treasury to a plaintiff.[255] Indeed, in characterizing the *Milliken* order for the payment of state funds as prospective relief, the Supreme Court found it important that the case did not involve " 'individual citizens' conducting a raid on the state

---

[249] *See, e.g.*, Sandoval v. Hagan, 197 F.3d 484, 500 (11th Cir. 2001); Florida Ass'n of Rehab. Facilities, Inc., v. Florida Dep't of Health and rehab. Servs., 225 F.3d 1208, 1220–22 (11th Cir. 2000).

[250] Milliken v. Bradley, 433 U.S. 267 (1977).

[251] 433 U.S. at 288–290.

[252] 433 U.S. at 288–290.

[253] 433 U.S. at 290 nn.21, 22.

[254] *See* David P. Currie, *Sovereign Immunity and Suits Against Government Officers*, 1984 Sup. Ct. Rev. 149, 162 (arguing that "prospective" expenditure of state funds in *Milliken* is no different in principle from payment of retroactive welfare benefits disapproved by Court in *Edelman*).

[255] *See* Erwin Chemerinsky, Federal Jurisdiction 397 (2d ed. 1994) (Eleventh Amendment seems to be concerned with preventing appearance of court taking money directly from state).

treasury for an accrued monetary liability."[256]

Courts have applied the prospective-retroactive distinction to bar certain official-capacity suits for declaratory relief. For example, if a plaintiff does not claim a continuing violation of federal law or a threat of a future violation, a federal declaratory judgment is inappropriate. The purpose of such a judgment could only be to provide a federal declaration on liability, with the hope that it would be *res judicata* in state-court proceedings. This would be an inappropriate exercise of federal judicial power because it would have the same effect as a damage award or restitution against the state.[257] However, even if the potential preclusive effect of the equitable apportionment of fault will apply in state court, the Eleventh Amendment does not bar a third-party claim by the United States when the primary purpose of the remedy is to reduce the federal government's potential liability.[258]

## [5] Ancillary Relief

The Eleventh Amendment's preclusion of official-capacity suits against state officers for retroactive monetary relief does not relieve a state of the obligation to spend the money necessary to comply with prospective relief against a state officer.[259] The expenditure of state funds by a state officer in complying with a federal court injunction is a permissible *ancillary* effect of the relief.[260]

Aside from the ancillary effect of prospective relief, a federal court has the power to make an ancillary order to pay money when it grants prospective relief. For example, a court may award attorneys' fees against a state agency that fails to comply with an injunction. In such a case, attorneys' fees or a contempt fine is properly treated as ancillary to the federal court's power to impose injunctive relief.[261] Moreover, such an award of attorneys' fees is distinguishable from a retroactive award of damages, because it constitutes reimbursement of expenses incurred in litigation seeking prospective relief, rather than retroactive liability for prelitigation conduct.[262] Similarly, the federal court has the power to order an enhancement of attorneys' fees as a sanction for a delay in payment of the awarded

[256] 433 U.S. at 290 n.22.

[257] Green v. Mansour, 474 U.S. 64, 72–73 (1985).

[258] Bethel Native Corp. v. Dep't of Interior, 208 F.3d 1171, 1175–77 (9th Cir. 2000).

[259] Hutto v. Finney, 437 U.S. 678, 690 (1978) (states not immune from obligation to obey costly federal-court orders of prospective relief; cost of compliance is ancillary to prospective order).

[260] Edelman v. Jordan, 415 U.S. 651, 667–668 (1974) ("ancillary" effect on state treasury is permissible consequence of federal court's grant of prospective decree requiring state officials to conform their conduct to federal law); Council 31 of the Am. Fed'n of State, County, and Mun. Employees v. Quinn, 680 F.3d 875, 882–83 (7th Cir. 2002).

[261] *See* Hutto v. Finney, 437 U.S. 678, 690–693 (1978) (instead of assessing award against individual defendant officers in their official capacities, trial court directed that fees be paid out of state department of correction funds; although it might have been better form to omit reference to department of correction, use of that language is not reversible error); Lawson v. Shelby County, 211 F.3d 331, 335 (6th Cir. 2000) (relief ancillary to injunctive relief, such as declaratory relief and attorneys' fees permitted).

[262] 437 U.S. at 695 n.24 (award of attorneys' fees not retroactive relief because it does not compensate plaintiff for injury that brought him or her into court).

fees. Such an enhancement is an exercise of the court's power to compute the fee award and does not represent compensation for the plaintiff's injury; therefore, it is not classified as retroactive relief so long as it is ancillary to other prospective relief.[263]

To avoid classification as impermissible retroactive relief, a court order that necessitates the payment of state funds must be ancillary to some other prospective relief the court awards. For example, if a court makes an appropriate prospective order requiring a state officer to conform the state's welfare program to federal guidelines, the court may then issue an ancillary order requiring notice be sent regarding state administrative procedures to claim past benefits wrongfully denied. Although state funds would be paid for the notice order, it is proper because it is ancillary to the court's prospective relief.[264] On the other hand, a court order to provide similar notice is impermissible retroactive relief if not ancillary to an order of prospective relief. Thus, after a suit is filed, the state officers might voluntarily bring the state welfare program into compliance with federal law. These actions would eliminate the need for the federal court to issue an injunction requiring compliance. Therefore, an order to give notice of procedures for claiming past benefits would stand alone and, under these circumstances, would amount to an impermissible grant of retroactive relief. Such an order would not be designed to prevent any ongoing federal law violation, nor would it be ancillary to any prospective relief.[265]

## § 14.09 WAIVER AND CONSENT

### [1] Explicit Waivers

A state may waive its Eleventh Amendment sovereign immunity by consent to suit in federal court,[266] or by actively participating in litigation and not asserting Eleventh Amendment immunity.[267] A state may consent to suit by making a general appearance in particular litigation[268] or by declaring in its constitution or a statute that it is willing to be sued.[269] However, a state constitutional provision or statute constitutes a consent to suit in federal court only if the consent is stated by

---

263 Missouri v. Jenkins, 491 U.S. 274, 278–279 (1989) (ancillary award of attorneys' fees is treated as part of costs of litigation, which have traditionally been awarded without regard for states' Eleventh Amendment immunity).

264 Quern v. Jordan, 440 U.S. 332, 349 (1979) (state would make actual determination and award of any retroactive benefits).

265 Green v. Mansour, 474 U.S. 64, 68–72 (1985) ("notice relief" would be appropriate only as case-management device in conjunction with prospective relief).

266 Port Auth. Trans-Hudson Corp. v. Feeney, 495 U.S. 299, 304–309 (1990) (assuming for argument that regional transportation authority created by two states is state agency with standing to claim immunity under Eleventh Amendment).

267 Johnson v. Rancho Santiago Cmty. Coll. Dist., 623 F.3d 1011, 1021–22 (9th Cir. 2010); New Hampshire v. Ramsey, 366 F.3d 1, 15–21 (1st Cir. 2004).

268 Ramsey, 366 F.3d at 15–21; Skelton v. Henry, 390 F.3d 614, 618 (8th Cir. 2004).

269 *See* Petty v. Tennessee-Missouri Bridge Comm'n, 359 U.S. 275, 276 (1959); Clark v. Barnard, 108 U.S. 436, 447–448 (1883) (general appearance waived Eleventh Amendment immunity).

(1) the most express language or (2) such overwhelming implications from the text that there is no room for any other reasonable construction.[270] Courts will indulge every reasonable presumption against a state's waiver of its sovereign immunity.[271] Thus, a constitutional or statutory provision specifically indicating the state's willingness to be sued in federal court is sufficient to waive the state's Eleventh Amendment immunity.[272]

A waiver of state sovereign immunity is ordinarily accomplished by legislation.[273] A state's waiver of Eleventh Amendment immunity will not be expanded beyond the scope of the waiver as expressly stated.[274] The scope of a state's waiver of its Eleventh Amendment immunity is determined by state law.[275]

On the other hand, a provision consenting to suit in a state's own courts does not constitute a waiver of the state's Eleventh Amendment immunity against suit in federal court.[276] Similarly, a general waiver of sovereign immunity, such as a statute allowing tax refund suits in "any court of competent jurisdiction," is not sufficient to waive the state's Eleventh Amendment immunity against suit in federal court.[277] Such a general waiver provision is ambiguous: it reasonably could be interpreted to apply only to suits in state court. Because of the importance of state sovereign immunity in the fundamental constitutional balance between the federal government and the states, the Supreme Court has construed such ambiguous and general consent-to-suit provisions, standing alone, as insufficient to waive Eleventh Amendment immunity.[278]

However, courts may construe a general consent-to-suit statute as waiving Eleventh Amendment immunity if it is accompanied by another provision clarifying

---

[270] Atascadero State Hosp. v. Scanlon, 473 U.S. 234, 241 (1985); VIBO Corp., Inc. v. Conway, 669 F.3d 675, 691 (6th Cir. 2012); AES Sparrow Point LNG v. Wilson, 589 F.3d 721, 727 (4th Cir. 2009).

[271] College Savings Bank v. Florida Prepaid Postsecondary Educ. Expense Bd., 527 U.S. 666, 682 (1999); MCI Telecomms. Corp. v. Ill. Bell Tel. Co., 222 F.3d 323, 338 (7th Cir. 2000).

[272] *See* Atascadero State Hosp. v. Scanlon, 473 U.S. 234, 241 (1985) (Eleventh Amendment immunity not waived by constitutional provision that did not specify intent to subject state to suits in *federal* court).

[273] *Id.*, 473 U.S. at 241.

[274] VIBO Corp., Inc. v. Conway, 669 F.3d 675, 692 (6th Cir. 2012) (state did not waive Eleventh Amendment immunity to private parties' suits on state law claims in federal court; any waiver of immunity in settlement agreement did not extend to suits involving private parties, and consent to federal arbitration was not consent to be sued in federal court for state law claims).

[275] Craven v. University of Col. Hosp. Auth., 260 F.3d 1218, 1231–32 (10th Cir. 2001).

[276] *See, e.g.*, Florida Dept. of Health and Rehabilitative Servs. v. Florida Nursing Home Ass'n, 450 U.S. 147, 149–150 (1981) (under state law, department of health was "body corporate" with capacity to "sue and be sued"); *see also* Hoeffner v. University of Minnesota, 948 F. Supp. 1380, 1391–1393 (D. Minn. 1996) (state did not waive Eleventh Amendment immunity by enacting Tort Claims Act, which waived state's sovereign immunity in state court suits, but did not expressly permit state to be sued in federal court).

[277] Kennecott Copper Corp. v. State Tax Comm'n, 327 U.S. 573, 577–579 (1946); Raper v. Iowa, 940 F. Supp. 1421, 1424–1426 (S.D. Iowa 1996) (state did not waive its Eleventh Amendment immunity for claims for overtime pay brought under Fair Labor Standards Act by enacting statute permitting employees to sue employers (including state employers) for wages in "any court of competent jurisdiction").

[278] Port Auth. Trans-Hudson Corp. v. Feeney, 495 U.S. 299, 306 (1990).

the ambiguity. For example, if a general consent provision is combined with another provision conditioning consent on venue in a certain judicial district, these provisions are sufficiently specific to be construed as a waiver of the state's Eleventh Amendment immunity.[279]

The fact that the state enters into a settlement agreement does not act as a waiver of immunity when the agreement or record does not reflect an unequivocal waiver.[280] In addition, a state does not waive its immunity by appearing in federal court to protest federal jurisdiction.[281]

### [2] Waiver by Removal

In *Lapides v. Board of Regents of University System of Georgia*, the Supreme Court held that a state waives its Eleventh Amendment immunity by affirmative litigation conduct when it removes a case to federal court, at least in the context of state law claims to which the state has explicitly waived sovereign immunity from state court proceedings.[282] In that case, a professor had sued the Board of Regents of the University System of Georgia in Georgia state court, claiming violations of both state and federal law. Georgia joined with the other defendants in removing the case to federal court, where the state then claimed Eleventh Amendment immunity. The Supreme Court concluded that by voluntarily joining in the removal, Georgia had voluntarily invoked the federal court's jurisdiction, thus waiving immunity under the long-standing principle that a state waives Eleventh Amendment immunity by voluntarily appearing in federal court.[283]

The effect of the Supreme Court's decision in *Lapides* in contexts other than state law claims to which the state has explicitly waived sovereign immunity from state court proceedings is unclear. In *Lapides*, the Supreme Court explicitly limited its holding to that context. However, in denying that its holding would cause confusion as to what conduct would constitute a waiver of Eleventh Amendment immunity, the Court did not mention this limitation, describing the rule broadly as a "clear [rule], easily applied" that "says that removal is a form of voluntary invocation of a federal court's jurisdiction sufficient to waive the State's otherwise valid objection to litigation of a matter (here of state law) in a federal forum."[284] This has led to differing interpretations by appellate courts.

Some courts have interpreted *Lapides* broadly, holding that by removing a case to federal court, a state waives immunity to all of the claims in the case.[285] In

---

[279] 495 U.S. at 307–308 (assuming for argument that regional transportation authority created by two states is state agency with standing to claim immunity under Eleventh Amendment; both states had enacted identical consent-to-suit statutes); *see* Great Northern Life Ins. Co. v. Read, 322 U.S. 47, 54–55 (1944) (procedural provisions contained in statute authorizing suits served to clarify that consent applied only to suits in state court).

[280] VIBO Corp., Inc., 669 F.3d at 692; Saahir v. Estelle, 47 F.3d 758, 761 (5th Cir. 1995).

[281] Union Elec. Co. v. Missouri Dep't of Conservation, 366 F.3d 655, 659–60 (8th Cir. 2004).

[282] Lapides v. Board of Regents of the Univ. Sys. of Ga., 535 U.S. 613, 616–20 (2002).

[283] *Id.*, 535 U.S. at 620.

[284] *Id.*, 535 U.S. at 623–24.

[285] Bd. of Regents of Univ. of Wis. Sys. v. Phoenix Int'l Software, Inc., 653 F.3d 448, 461 (7th Cir.

contrast, some courts have limited the *Lapides* holding to claims for which the state has waived immunity in state court. In other words, removal does not waive the state's sovereign immunity unless the claim could have been heard in state court under state-law immunity rules.[286] The First Circuit has held that a state's removal of a case to federal court waives the state's sovereign immunity only if the removal confers an unfair advantage on the removing state.[287]

The Supreme Court's holding in *Lapides* is in line with Supreme Court precedent holding that a state's voluntary appearance in federal court amounts to a waiver of its Eleventh Amendment immunity.

### [3] Participating in Federal Program Expressly Conditioned on Waiver

Congress may exercise its Spending Clause authority to condition the receipt of federal funds on a state waiver of sovereign immunity. Thus, states may waive their sovereign immunity by participating in a federal spending program that is expressly conditioned on a waiver of sovereign immunity.[288] In general, a federal spending program operates in the nature of a contract: in return for federal funds, states agree to comply with federally imposed conditions. Nothing in the Supreme Court's Eleventh Amendment decisions noting limitations on Congress's authority to abrogate state sovereign immunity bars Congress from conditioning federal grants on a state's consent to suit in federal court.

A state's continued participation in a federal program after the passage of legislation that makes participation contingent on a waiver of Eleventh Amendment immunity may constitute a waiver with respect to actions taken before the immunity-waiving legislation became part of the program.[289]

To effect a Spending Clause waiver, it must be clear in the legislation that acceptance of federal funds results in waiver of state immunity. The mere receipt of federal funds is insufficient to establish that a state consented to suit in federal court, and courts may not find waiver absent an "unequivocal indication" that the state intends to consent to federal jurisdiction.[290] In other words, conditions attached to the exercise of Congress's spending authority must be stated

---

2011); Lombardo v. Pennsylvania Dep't of Pub. Welfare, 540 F.3d 190, 196–98 (3d Cir. 2008).

[286] Bergemann v. Rhode Island Dep't of Env't Mgmt., 665 F.3d 336, 338, 342 (1st Cir. 2011); Watters v. Wash. Metro Area Transit Auth., 295 F.3d 36, 42 n.13 (D.C. Cir. 2002).

[287] Bergemann, 665 F.3d at 342.

[288] Alexander v. Sandoval, 532 U.S. 275 (2001) (Rehabilitation Act Amendments of 1986 expressly abrogates states' sovereign immunity against suits brought in federal court to enforce Title VI); College Sav. Bank v. Florida Prepaid Postsecondary Educ. Expense Bd., 527 U.S. 666, 679–87 (1999) (reaffirming constitutionality of conditioning federal funds on state sovereign immunity waiver); Pace v. Bogalusa City Sch. Bd., 403 F.3d 272, 283–85 (5th Cir. 2005) (acceptance of funds under Individuals with Disabilities in Education Act (IDEA) was waiver of immunity); *but see* San Lazaro Ass'n, Inc. v. Connell, 286 F.3d 1088, 1095 n.5 (9th Cir. 2002) (states do not consent to suits by accepting Medicaid funds; Medicaid statutory provision requiring waiver of sovereign immunity as condition of participation repealed in 1976).

[289] Islander East Pipeline v. Conn. Dep't of Environ., 467 F.3d 295, 304–07 (2d Cir. 2006).

[290] Sossamon v. Texas, 131 S. Ct. 1651, 179 L. Ed. 2d 700 (2011) ("A [s]tate's consent . . . must be

"unambiguously." Waiver determinations are subject to stringent, exacting standards because of the vital role of the Eleventh Amendment in preserving the federal balance.

Further, courts may not lightly conclude that principles of federalism and state sovereign immunity permit Congress to use its spending power in a manner that ultimately effects a waiver of Eleventh Amendment immunity. Courts rely on traditional canons of statutory construction to determine whether a statute and its accompanying administrative regulations provide states with the notice for imposing funding conditions. However, courts do not require the use of "consent" or "waiver" in the statute. In determining whether the statute clearly waives Eleventh Amendment immunity, the courts must view the statute from the perspective of a state official who is deciding whether the state should accept the funds.[291]

In order for an individual to sue a state or state agency in federal court under this waiver exception to Eleventh Amendment immunity, Congress must have intended to create a private right of action and a private remedy.[292] In *Alexander v. Sandoval*, the plaintiff challenged the Alabama Department of Public Safety's policy of administering driver's license examinations only in English as discriminatorily impacting non-English speakers based on national origin. The plaintiff further argued that the policy violated federal regulations prohibiting funding recipients from conduct that had the effect of subjecting individuals to discrimination. The United States Supreme Court held that, assuming that the regulations were statutorily authorized and resulted in discriminatory impact, no private right of action existed to enforce the regulations.[293]

The following laws have been held to meet the clear statement test and validly condition a waiver of state sovereign immunity on the receipt of federal funds under a federal Spending Clause program: Title VI of the Civil Rights Act, except that no private right of action exists under Title VI disparate-impact regulations that do not address intentional discrimination;[294] Title IX of the Education Amendments of 1972; The Individuals With Disabilities Education Act (IDEA); Section 504 of the Rehabilitation Act; The Randolph-Sheppard program, which provides work opportunities for blind; The 1996 Telecommunications Act, which preempts state regulatory authority over many aspects of local telephone service; The Energy Policy Act of 2005, which provides an expedited direct cause of action in the federal appellate courts to challenge a state administrative agency's order, action, or failure to act with respect to a permit application required under federal law in order to proceed with a natural gas facility project subject to Section 5 or 7 of the Natural Gas Act; The Religious Land Use and Institutionalized Persons Act (RLUIPA), which prohibits states from imposing substantial and unjustified burdens on the religious liberty of state prisoners.

---

unequivocally expressed in the text of the relevant statute . . ."); Bragg v. West Virginia Coal Ass'n, 248 F.3d 275, 298 (4th Cir. 2001).

[291] Hurst v. Texas dep't of Assistive & Rehab. Servs., 482 F.3d 809, 811 (5th Cir. 2007).

[292] Alexander v. Sandoval, 532 U.S. 275, 284–87 (2001).

[293] *Id.*

[294] Alexander v. Sandoval, 532 U.S. 275 (2001).

However, the RLUIPA waiver is limited to equitable relief; there is no waiver with respect to monetary damages.[295] The Act provides that a person may obtain "appropriate relief" in a private cause of action against a government for a RLUIPA violation. The Supreme Court concluded that this does not constitute a clear and unambiguous waiver of sovereign immunity with respect to monetary damages.

## [4] Implicit or Constructive Waivers Barred

In *College Sav. Bank v. Florida Prepaid Postsecondary Educ. Expense Bd.*, the Supreme Court rejected the concept of constructive waivers of state sovereign immunity[296] and expressly overruled any remaining portion of *Parden v. Terminal R. Co. of Alabama*.[297] The Court held that *Parden*'s doctrine of constructive waiver cannot be reconciled with the requirement that a state's waiver of sovereign immunity be unequivocal. Further, recognizing Congress's authority to exact constructive waivers of sovereign immunity through the exercise of its Article I powers would circumvent the holding of *Seminole Tribe of Florida v. Florida*.[298] In *College Sav. Bank* the Court held that the Trademark Remedy Clarification Act (TRCA), which subjects states to suits brought under Section 43 of the Lanham Act for false and misleading advertising, does not validly abrogate state sovereign immunity. The Court rejected the theory that Florida's commercial activities constituted a constructive waiver of its sovereign immunity.

The Court distinguished cases in which the Court had permitted Congress to extract waivers of sovereign immunity as a condition to congressional approval of an interstate compact, or as a condition to a grant of federal funds. For example, if Congressional approval of an interstate compact is conditioned on the proviso that federal courts will have jurisdiction of any matter the compact affects, the states will be deemed to have waived their Eleventh Amendment immunity by participation in the compact. Similarly, states may waive their sovereign immunity by participating in a federal program with dispute arbitration and enforcement of arbitration awards. States cannot form an interstate compact without first obtaining express congressional consent, so the granting of that consent is a "gratuity." Similarly, Congress is not obligated to exercise its Spending Clause power to disburse funds to the states, so such funds are "gifts." Accordingly, Congress has the power to condition such gratuities and gifts on states voluntarily taking certain actions.

The TRCA, however, clearly indicated that a state waives its immunity from Lanham Act suits by engaging in the interstate marketing and administration program. The Court held that rather than granting a gift or gratuity, Congress threatened a sanction: the exclusion of the state from otherwise permissible activity. Dissenting, Justices Breyer, Ginsburg, Souter, and Stevens argued that

---

[295] Sossamon v. Texas, 131 S. Ct. 1651, 179 L. Ed. 2d 700 (2011).

[296] College Sav. Bank v. Florida Prepaid Postsecondary Educ. Expense Bd., 527 U.S. 666, 675–81 (1999).

[297] Parden v. Terminal R. Co. of Ala. Docks Dep't, 377 U.S. 184, 186 (1964).

[298] College Sav. Bank, 527 U.S. at 685–87; *see* Seminole Tribe v. Florida, 517 U.S. 44, 47 (1996).

the *Parden* holding allowing constructive waivers should not be rejected, and strongly disagreed with the majority's assertion that *Parden*'s holding was a constitutional "anomaly" that "broke sharply with prior cases," was "fundamentally incompatible with later ones," and had been "narrowed . . . in every subsequent opinion."[299]

Even before the *College Savings* decision, courts disfavored constructive waivers of Eleventh Amendment immunity.[300] Thus, a court would not find a constructive waiver unless Congress expressly stated that particular state conduct would operate as a consent to suit in federal court.[301] A state did not constructively waive its Eleventh Amendment immunity merely by participating in a federal program and agreeing to receive and administer federal funds in compliance with federal law.[302] Even state acceptance of funds was not a constructive waiver of state immunity if the statute did not manifest a clear intent that a state's participation be conditioned on a waiver.

## § 14.10 SUITS PURSUANT TO FEDERAL STATUTES

### [1] Statutes Adopted Pursuant to Section 5 of Fourteenth Amendment

#### [a] Congressional Power to Abrogate State Sovereign Immunity

Congress may abrogate a state's Eleventh Amendment sovereign immunity in a particular federal statute for suits under that statute only if the statute (1) unequivocally expresses Congress's intent to abrogate immunity and (2) Congress enacted the statute pursuant to a constitutional provision that takes precedence over Article III and the Eleventh Amendment. The Supreme Court has expressly identified only one constitutional provision that empowers Congress to abrogate the states' sovereign immunity — Section 5 of the Fourteenth Amendment.[303] In addition, Congress's proper exercise of its Fourteenth Amendment enforcement powers requires a congruence and a proportionality between the injury to be prevented or remedied, and the means adopted to that end.[304]

The Fourteenth Amendment expressly regulates state conduct, prohibiting states from (1) enacting laws that abridge the privileges and immunities of citizens, (2) depriving any person of life, liberty, or property without due process of law, or (3) denying any person the equal protection of the laws.[305] Section 5 of the

[299] College Sav. Bank, 527 U.S. 666, 688–91 (1999).

[300] Atascadero State Hosp. v. Scanlon, 473 U.S. 234, 238 n.1 (1985).

[301] Welch v. Texas Dep't of Highways and Pub. Transp., 483 U.S. 468, 476–78 (1987).

[302] Florida Dep't Health and Rehabilitative Servs. V. Florida Nursing Home Ass'n, 450 U.S. 147, 150 (1981).

[303] *See* Seminole Tribe v. Florida, 517 U.S. 44, 59, 72–73 (1996).

[304] City of Boerne v. Flores, 521 U.S. 507, 519–20 (1997).

[305] U.S. Const., Amend. XIV § 1.

Fourteenth Amendment gives Congress the power to enact appropriate legislation to enforce the Amendment's provisions.[306] Congress adopted the Fourteenth Amendment in 1868, seventy years after the Eleventh Amendment. Because it was adopted subsequent to the Eleventh Amendment, and its substantive provisions expressly regulate state action, the Fourteenth Amendment supersedes or limits the Eleventh Amendment to the extent they are inconsistent.[307]

Therefore, Congress has the power to abrogate the states' Eleventh Amendment immunity by enacting appropriate legislation to enforce the Fourteenth Amendment.[308] For example, in the 1972 amendments to the Civil Rights Act of 1964, Congress expressly authorized federal courts to award money damages in favor of a private individual against a state government found to have subjected that individual to employment discrimination on the basis of race, color, religion, sex, or national origin.[309] The Eleventh Amendment does not bar such an individual's suit for money damages brought directly against a state in federal court, because Congress created the cause of action pursuant to Congress's enforcement power under Section 5 of the Fourteenth Amendment.[310]

### [b] Determining Congressional Intent to Abrogate Eleventh Amendment Immunity

Although Section 5 of the Fourteenth Amendment gives Congress the power to abrogate the states' Eleventh Amendment immunity, Congress has not done so in every enactment under the Fourteenth Amendment. In enacting legislation to enforce the Fourteenth Amendment,[311] Congress has discretion to decide whether to abrogate the states' immunity.[312] The Supreme Court has adopted a particularly strict standard for determining whether Congress actually intended, in a particular statute, to abrogate the states' Eleventh Amendment immunity. The Court has applied a strict standard because federal abrogation of sovereign immunity upsets the constitutional balance between the federal government and the states, and states cannot directly remedy a judicial misconstruction of their immunity.[313]

Thus, the Court has held that federal legislation abrogates state sovereign immunity only if Congress makes that intention unmistakably clear in the statutory

---

[306] U.S. Const., Amend. XIV § 5.

[307] *See* Fitzpatrick v. Bitzer, 427 U.S. 445, 453–456 (1976) (Fourteenth Amendment was intended to be enlargement of congressional power, with corresponding diminution of state sovereignty).

[308] 427 U.S. at 456 (in enforcing provisions of Fourteenth Amendment, Congress may provide for private suits against states that would be constitutionally impermissible in other contexts).

[309] 42 U.S.C. §§ 2000e(a), (f), 2000e — 2(a), 2000e — 5(a)–(g).

[310] Fitzpatrick v. Bitzer, 427 U.S. 445, 452 (1976) (congressional intent to subject states to suit was clearly present in legislation, which was not disputed to be exercise of Congress's Fourteenth Amendment power).

[311] U.S. Const., Amend. XIV § 5.

[312] *See* Fitzpatrick v. Bitzer, 427 U.S. 445, 456 (1976).

[313] Atascadero State Hosp. v. Scanlon, 473 U.S. 234, 242–243 (1985); *see* Port Auth. Trans-Hudson Corp. v. Feeney, 495 U.S. 299, 305 (1990).

language.[314] For example, language stating that "states are not immune" and similar language are sufficiently clear statements of Congressional intent to abrograte Eleventh Amendment immunity.[315] Further, language expressly authorizing a federal court suit against a state for violations of federal law is generally sufficient.[316] In contrast, language permitting citizen civil suits to enforce a statute's substantive provisions to the extent permitted by the Eleventh Amendment indicates that Congress had no intention to disturb the states' traditional immunity from suit.[317]

When a statute permits suits against "persons," a longstanding interpretive presumption held that the term "persons" does not include sovereigns.[318] Thus, statutory language providing a federal remedy against any "person" who receives funds under a federal program does not abrogate states' immunity against federal suit, even though states are recipients of funds under the program. Because the states occupy a special position in our constitutional system, they are not like any other class of recipients of federal aid, and a general authorization for suit in federal court is not the kind of unequivocal statutory language sufficient to abrogate the Eleventh Amendment.[319]

Similarly, the basic civil rights statute, 42 U.S.C. § 1983, creates a cause of action in federal court against "person" who, under color of state law, deprives another of civil rights under the Constitution or federal law.[320] The statute contains no definition or clarification of the word "person." Accordingly, the Supreme Court has held that although Section 1983 was enacted pursuant to Congress's Fourteenth Amendment power, it does not contain the clear, explicit language necessary to establish that Congress intended it to abrogate the states' Eleventh Amendment immunity.[321] If statutory language raises an inference that Congress intended that the states be subject to damage actions for violations, that is insufficient to abrogate the Eleventh Amendment. The statutory language indicating Congress's intent to subject the states to suit must be unequivocal.[322]

---

314 Kimel v. Florida Bd. of regents, 528 U.S. 62, 73 (2000) (ADEA satisfies simple yet stringent test to determine whether federal statute properly subjects states to suit by individuals; congressional intent is unmistakably clear); Dellmuth v. Muth, 491 U.S. 223, 228–32 (1989); Atascadero State Hosp. v. Scanlon, 473 U.S. 234, 242–243 (1985) (pre-and post-enactment legislative history and inferences from general statutory language are insufficient to establish abrogation if statute does not unequivocally express Congress's intention to abrogate).

315 Kimel v. Florida Bd. of regents, 528 U.S. 62, 73–74 (2000).

316 Seminole Tribe, 517 U.S. at 57.

317 Rhode Island Dep't of Envt'l Mgmt. v. United States, 304 F.3d 31, 51–52 (1st Cir. 2002).

318 Vermont Agency of Natural resources v. United States, 529 U.S. 765, 780–81 (2000).

319 473 U.S. at 242–246 (Rehabilitation Act of 1973).

320 42 U.S.C. § 1983.

321 Quern v. Jordan, 440 U.S. 332, 345 (1979); *see* Pennhurst State Sch. and Hosp. v. Halderman, 465 U.S. 89, 99 (1984); *see also* Will v. Michigan Dep't of State Police, 491 U.S. 58, 71 (1989) (state may not be sued in state court for violation of Section 1983).

322 Dellmuth v. Muth, 491 U.S. 223, 232 (1989) (Education of the Handicapped Act, 20 U.S.C. § 1400 *et seq.*).

On at least one occasion, the Supreme Court has looked to legislative history to find sufficient congressional intent that particular legislation abrogates the Eleventh Amendment. In *Hutto v. Finney*,[323] the Court considered whether 42 U.S.C. § 1988 permits a federal court to award attorneys' fees as costs against a state. Section 1988 provides that such fees may be awarded as costs to the prevailing party in a suit brought under certain civil rights statutes. Section 1988 does not specifically include or exclude states among the parties against whom attorneys' fees may be taxed as costs. The Senate and House Reports on Section 1988 both contained express statements that the legislation contemplated attorneys' fee awards against states.[324]

In light of the clear congressional intent in the legislative history, and because Section 1988 applies to suits based on civil rights statutes that regulate state conduct, the Court construed Section 1988's language as applicable to all litigants, including states.[325] The Supreme Court's reliance on legislative history in *Hutto* conflicts with other decisions that have required the statute to contain a clear, explicit expression of intent to abrogate states' immunity.[326] Congressional abrogation of the Eleventh Amendment, however, was not an indispensable rationale for the *Hutto* decision: the Court also stated that it has never viewed the Eleventh Amendment as barring awards of litigation costs, even in suits between states and individual litigants. Unlike a retroactive damage award that would bring the Eleventh Amendment into play, an award of costs (including applicable attorneys' fees) constitutes reimbursement of litigation expenses seeking prospective relief, rather than retroactive liability for prelitigation conduct. Accordingly, an award of costs is a form of ancillary relief that is not affected by the Eleventh Amendment.[327]

### [c] Enactment Must Fall Within Congress's Section 5 Enforcement Powers Under Fourteenth Amendment

#### [i] Abrogation Only Pursuant to Section 5

Congress may abrogate state sovereign immunity only when acting to enforce the constitutional rights of the Fourteenth Amendment pursuant to Section 5.[328] Establishing that a Congressional enactment falls within Congress's Section 5 authority does not require that Congress explicitly state the basis of its power to legislate. In other words, the constitutionality of congressional acts does not depend on recitals of the power under which it undertakes to exercise authority. Therefore, Congress need not expressly refer to Section 5 of the Fourteenth

---

323 Hutto v. Finney, 437 U.S. 678 (1978).

324 437 U.S. at 694 (quoting from Senate Report and House Report).

325 437 U.S. at 693–698 (attorneys' fees awarded as costs in suit brought under 42 U.S.C. § 1983).

326 *See, e.g.*, Dellmuth v. Muth, 491 U.S. 223, 230 (1989) (legislative history generally will be irrelevant to judicial inquiry into whether Congress intended to abrogate Eleventh Amendment); Atascadero State Hosp. v. Scanlon, 473 U.S. 234, 242–246 (1985); Pennhurst State Sch. and Hosp. v. Halderman, 465 U.S. 89, 99 (1984); *but see* Quern v. Jordan, 440 U.S. 332, 345 (1979) (citing legislative history as evidence that Congress had not intended Section 1983 to abrogate Eleventh Amendment).

327 437 U.S. at 695 n.24.

328 Seminole Tribe of Florida, 517 U.S. at 59.

Amendment. However, even though Congress is not required to recite the words "Section 5," "Fourteenth Amendment," or "equal protection," courts must be able to discern "some legislative purpose or factual predicate" that supports the exercise of Fourteenth Amendment power.

Nonetheless, sovereign immunity claims are problematic if the congressional source of power is ambiguous or possibly impermissible. For example, Congress relied solely on the copyright clause of Article I when it extended the application of the Copyright Act to states. Because Congress may not abrogate state sovereign immunity under Article I authority, a question arises as to whether courts may consider another ground of constitutionality. In *Chavez v. Arte Publico Press*, the Fifth Circuit noted that Supreme Court precedent supports the view that courts may not consider a ground for constitutionality that Congress has not invoked in the legislation.[329]

The valid abrogation of state sovereign immunity requires that the challenged legislation must have been, or could have been, enacted pursuant to Section 5. In determining whether Congress "could have" enacted the statute pursuant to Section 5, courts typically rely on the legislative record for guidance. However, the Supreme Court has never established a procedural requirement that Congress must document in detail its reasons for adopting a statute, and courts are free to consider evidence beyond the legislative record.[330]

### [ii] Legislation Must Enforce Not Expand Rights

In recent terms, the Supreme Court has addressed the extent of legislative authority under Section 5. In each case, the Court has stressed that the language of Section 5 that gives Congress the power to "enforce" the Fourteenth Amendment must be taken seriously. Statutes that create new rights or that expand old rights do not "enforce" the amendment. Thus, legislation must meet a "proportionality and congruence" test.

In *City of Boerne v. Flores*, the Supreme Court announced a new standard for assessing whether Congress properly exercised its Fourteenth Amendment enforcement powers. In order for Congress to validly abrogate state sovereign immunity, the legislation must be remedial in nature, rather than creating or amending any substantive rights. To qualify as remedial legislation, "there must be a congruence and proportionality between the injury to be prevented or remedied and the means adopted to that end." The *City of Boerne* test is similar to the factor in *Katzenbach* that requires that the means chosen be "plainly adapted to that end."[331]

The proportionality inquiry has two facets: an evolution of the extent of the threatened constitutional violation and the legislative steps to remedy or prevent the violations. To determine the extent of the threatened violations, courts examine Congress's findings regarding the evils that the legislation addresses. Additionally,

---

[329] 204 F.3d 601, 604–05 (5th Cir. 2000).

[330] Florida Prepaid Postsecondary Educ. Expense Bd., 527 U.S. at 645–46.

[331] City of Boerne v. Flores, 521 U.S. 507 (1997).

courts must determine whether the legislative scope is so sweeping that the statute is not proportional to the evil addressed. In *City of Boerne*, the Court noted that remedial legislation may be within Congress's enforcement power, even if the legislation bars constitutional conduct and intrudes into "legislative spheres of autonomy previously reserved to states."[332]

In *Florida Prepaid Postsecondary Educ. Expense Bd. v. College Sav. Bank*, the Supreme Court provided an analytical framework that requires an examination of three aspects of the challenged legislation: (1) the nature of the injury to be remedied; (2) Congress's consideration of the adequacy of state remedies to redress the injury; and (3) the coverage of the legislation.[333] The first consideration involves the nature of the injury to be remedied and whether the state's conduct evinced a pattern of constitutional violations. The second consideration involves determining whether Congress studied the existence and adequacy of existing state remedies for the alleged violation. The third consideration involves determining whether Congress sought to limit the coverage of the challenged legislation to arguably constitutional violations. The judiciary, rather than the legislature, must determine what conduct violates the Fourteenth Amendment, and federal jurisprudence indicates that a deprivation must be intentional to fit within the meaning of the due process clause. Thus, Congress's failure to confine the scope of the legislation to intentional acts, such as by limiting remedies to certain types of infringement, cannot be reconciled with the principle that legislation pursuant to the Fourteenth Amendment must be proportionate to legitimate Section 5 ends.

In a concurring opinion in *Coleman v. Court of Appeals of Md.*, Justice Scalia described the "congruence and proportionality" test as a "flabby test" and "a standing invitation to judicial arbitrariness and policy-driven decisionmaking."[334] Moreover, he complained, to apply it, the Court must scour the legislative record in search of evidence that supports the congressional action, a task the Court is "ill suited to perform and ill advised to undertake." He argued that the Court should adopt an approach "that is properly tied to the text of § 5, which grants Congress the power 'to enforce, by appropriate legislation,' the other provisions of the Fourteenth Amendment." Outside of the context of racial discrimination, he would limit Congress's section 5 power to the regulation of conduct that itself violates the Fourteenth Amendment.

The "congruence and proportionality" test is applied on a claim-by-claim basis, considering the specific governmental services at issue. Congruence and proportionality are more likely to be found when the statute at issue is a response to a clearly discernible pattern of state encroachment on fundamental or other important constitutional rights that require a heightened level of scrutiny. Congruence and proportionality are less likely to be found if the rights at issue are not subject to heightened judicial scrutiny.[335]

---

332 *Id.*, 521 U.S. at 518.

333 Florida Prepaid Postsecondary Educ. Expense Bd., 527 U.S. at 639–647.

334 Coleman v. Court of Appeals of Md., 132 S. Ct. 1327, 182 L. Ed. 2d 296 (2012).

335 Tennessee v. Lane, 541 U.S. 509, 529 (2004); Nevada Dep't of Human Res. v. Hibbs, 538 U.S. 721, 735–36 (2003).

### [a] Statutes Abrograting State Sovereign Immunity

Concluding that Congress had exceeded the scope of its enforcement power under Section 5, the Supreme Court held that the congruence and proportionality test was not satisfied with respect to the Age Discrimination in Employment Act (ADEA),[336] the Patent and Plant Variety Protection Remedy Clarification Act,[337] the Religious Freedom Restoration Act (RFRA),[338] and the self-care provisions of the Family and Medical Leave Act.[339] In each case, the Supreme Court held that the legislative record failed to identify widespread and persisting deprivation of constitutional rights of the sort that Congress faced in enacting proper prophylactic Section 5 legislation. Additionally, the Court held that each Act was so out of proportion to a supposed remedial or preventive objective that it could not be understood as responsive to, or designed to prevent, unconstitutional behavior. Therefore, the means used by Congress were not congruent and proportional to the injuries that Congress attempted to remedy.

Lower federal courts have held that the following federal statutes abrogate state sovereign immunity under the Eleventh Amendment because these statutes contain a clear expression of Congress's intent to abrogate and the statutes were properly enacted pursuant to Section 5 of the Fourteenth Amendment: the Equal Pay Act (EPA); Title VII of the Civil Rights Act of 1964; the Railroad Revitalization and Regulatory Reform Act (4-R Act); and the Government Employee Rights Act (GERA).

In *City of Boerne*, the Court struck down the Religious Freedom and Restoration Act (RFRA) insofar as it applies to states and state entities as an unconstitutional exercise of Congress's Section 5 enforcement power. The Court held that the RFRA's provisions were "so out of proportion" to the pattern or practice of unconstitutional conduct burdening the exercise of religion that the RFRA could not be regarded as enforcing the provisions of the Fourteenth Amendment.[340]

At the end of the 1998–1999 term, the Supreme Court handed down two major decisions defining the scope of the states' sovereign immunity from suit and limiting Congress's ability to make federal law binding on the states in the trademark and patent infringement context. The Court concluded that states are immune from suit by individuals alleging unfair competition by states in the market and by patent owners for infringement by state universities and agencies[341] Following these two cases, the Fifth Circuit determined that the Copyright

---

[336] Kimel v. Florida Bd. of Regents, 528 U.S. 62, 67 (2000).

[337] Florida Prepaid Postsecondary Educ. Expense Bd., 527 U.S. at 646–47.

[338] City of Boerne, 521 U.S. at 533–34.

[339] Coleman v. Court of Appeals of Md., 132 S. Ct. 1327, 182 L. Ed. 2d 296 (2012).

[340] City of Boerne, 521 U.S. at 519–33.

[341] College Sav. Bank v. Florida Prepaid Postsecondary Educ. Expense Bd., 527 U.S. 666, 686–88 (1999); Florida Prepaid Postsecondary Educ. Expense Bd. v. College Sav, Bank, 527 U.S. 627, 646–48 (1999).

Remedy Clarification Act's extension to cover states does not validly abrogate state sovereign immunity.[342]

The Age Discrimination in Employment Act of 1967 (ADEA) does not validly abrogate state sovereign immunity. In *Kimel v. Florida Bd. of Regents*, the Supreme Court addressed and resolved a split among the circuit courts. First, the Court held that the ADEA satisfies the simple yet stringent test to determine whether a federal statute properly subjects states to suits by individuals: Congress made its intention to abrogate the states' immunity unmistakably clear in the language of the statute. This clear intent is manifested in statutory language authorizing employees to maintain actions for backpay against employers in any competent federal or state court of competent jurisdiction, and defining employers to include public agencies (state governments, political subdivisions, and state agencies).[343]

Nevertheless, the Court determined that the ADEA is not appropriate legislation under § 5 of the Fourteenth Amendment because it is out of proportion to any supposed remedial or preventive object. The ADEA imposes substantive requirements on state and local governments that are disproportionate to any unconstitutional conduct that conceivably could be targeted by the ADEA. Therefore, the ADEA's purported abrogation of state sovereign immunity is invalid.

Further, a review of the ADEA's legislative record reveals that Congress had virtually no reason to believe that state and local governments were unconstitutionally discriminating against their employees on the basis of age. Congress never identified any pattern of age discrimination by states, much less any discrimination whatsoever that rose to the level of constitutional violation. That failure confirms that Congress had no reason to believe that broad prophylactic legislation was needed.

### [*b*] Statutes Not Abrogating State Sovereign Immunity

In other cases, the Court held that the congruence and proportionality test was satisfied. For example, in *Tennessee v. Lane*, the Supreme Court held that Title II of the Americans with Disabilities Act (ADA) satisfies the congruence and proportionality test insofar as it applies to the class of cases implicating the fundamental right of access to the courts.[344] In *Nevada Dep't of Human Res. v. Hibbs*, the Court held that the family-care provisions of the Family and Medical Leave Act (FMLA) satisfied the congruence and proportionality test.[345]

Consequently, the Supreme Court and lower federal courts have held that various statutes do not abrograte sovereign immunity. For example, resolving a case of first impression, the Supreme Court in *Alden v. Maine* invalidated the

---

342 Chavez v. Arte Publico Press, 204 F.3d 601, 604–08 (5th Cir. 2000).

343 Kimel v. Florida Bd. of regents, 528 U.S. 62 (2000).

344 Tennessee v. Lane, 541 U.S. 509, 530–33 (2004).

345 Nevada Dep't of Human Res. v. Hibbs, 538 U.S. 721 (2003).

provisions of the Fair Labor Standards Act (FLSA), enacted under Article I, that authorize private suits against states in their own courts without their consent.[346] The Court held that Congress lacks authority under its Article I powers to subject nonconsenting states to private suits in their own courts. This holding was not particularly surprising, because the Court (by the same five-four vote) had already held in *Seminole Tribe v. Florida* that Congress may not constitutionally abrogate state sovereign immunity in federal courts relying on its Article I powers.

The Court also has held that the following statutes do not abrogate state sovereign immunity: the Individuals with Disabilities Education Act; the Jones Act; the Indian Gaming Regulatory Act; the Violence Against Women Act; and the Uniformed Services Employment and Reemployment Rights Act.

### [2] Statutes Adopted Under Other Congressional Powers

State sovereign immunity exemplified in the Eleventh Amendment is treated as a constitutional limitation of Article III federal judicial power.[347] Federal statutes cannot abrogate state sovereign immunity unless Congress enacts the statute pursuant to a constitutional provision that takes precedence over Article III and the Eleventh Amendment.[348] For example, a statute enacted by Congress pursuant to the Fourteenth Amendment may abrogate state sovereign immunity, because the Fourteenth Amendment was adopted well after the Constitution's ratification and adoption of the Eleventh Amendment, and the Fourteenth Amendment altered the pre-existing balance between federal and state power.[349]

Congress, therefore, has no power to abrogate state sovereign immunity against suits in federal court under any constitutional provision that existed when the states ratified the Eleventh Amendment. For example, Congress cannot exercise its power under the Interstate Commerce Clause, the Indian Commerce Clause, or any other Article I clause to abrogate state sovereign immunity.[350] Even in areas where federal jurisdiction is exclusive (such as Native American commerce, bankruptcy, copyright, and antitrust law), Congress cannot use its Article I power

---

346 Alden v. Maine, 527 U.S. 706, 712 (1999).

347 Seminole Tribe v. Florida, 517 U.S. 44, 72–73 (1996).

348 517 U.S. at 59, 72–73 (constitutional provision that predates Eleventh Amendment cannot serve as basis for statute limiting Eleventh Amendment).

349 517 U.S. at 59; Fitzpatrick v. Bitzer, 427 U.S. 445, 456 (1976) (in enforcing provisions of Fourteenth Amendment, Congress may provide for private suits against states that would be constitutionally impermissible in other contexts).

350 517 U.S. at 72–73 (overruling Pennsylvania v. Union Gas Co., 491 U.S. 1 (1989), which had held that Article I Commerce Clause power enables abrogation of Eleventh Amendment); *see* U.S. Const., Art. I § 8; *see also* Hoeffner v. University of Minnesota, 948 F. Supp. 1380, 1395–1396 (D. Minn. 1996) (Congress did not abrogate states' Eleventh Amendment immunity in Federal Drug and Cosmetic Act and Public Health Services Act; neither statute contains unequivocal expression of congressional intent to abrogate and both statutes were enacted under Interstate Commerce Clause, which does not empower Congress to abrogate Eleventh Amendment immunity); Union Pacific R.R. Co. v. Burton, 949 F. Supp. 1546, 1552–1554 (D. Wyo. 1996) (Congress did not have to power to abrogate states' Eleventh Amendment immunity in Railroad Revitalization and Regulatory Reform Act because Congress enacted Act pursuant to its power to regulate interstate commerce).

to abrogate state sovereign immunity.[351]

A few Supreme Court decisions seemed to suggest that Congress could exercise Article I powers as a basis for abrogating the Eleventh Amendment, but the Court either has overruled these decisions,[352] or the decisions actually involved statutes enacted under the Fourteenth Amendment,[353] In other cases, the Court never reached the constitutional issue because the statute did not clearly express a congressional intent to accomplish abrogation.[354]

The Supreme Court has expressly identified only one constitutional provision that empowers Congress to abrogate the states' sovereign immunity — Section 5 of the Fourteenth Amendment.[355] Conceivably, another constitutional amendment may confer such power on Congress if it was adopted after the Eleventh Amendment and altered the balance between federal and state power that existed at the time of its adoption.[356] For example, the Fifteenth, Nineteenth, Twenty-Fourth, and Twenty-Sixth Amendments are similar to the Fourteenth Amendment in that they expressly and directly regulate state conduct, and each Amendment authorizes Congress to enforce its provisions by appropriate legislation.[357] Thus, in a case that did not directly involve a claim of Eleventh Amendment immunity, the Supreme Court indicated that the Fifteenth Amendment authorizes a congressional "intrusion on state sovereignty" to protect against racial discrimination in state voting. The Court reasoned that the Fifteenth Amendment, like the Fourteenth, was specifically designed to expand federal power and permit a corresponding intrusion on state sovereignty. Accordingly, congressional power to enforce these "Civil War Amendments" by appropriate legislation may override

---

351 Seminole Tribe v. Florida, 517 U.S. 44, 72 n.16 (1996) (lower court decisions holding otherwise were decided under now-overruled decision in *Pennsylvania v. Union Gas Co.*, 491 U.S. 1 (1989)).

352 Pennsylvania v. Union Gas Co., 491 U.S. 1 (1989) (holding that Article I Commerce Clause power enables abrogation), *overruled by* Seminole Tribe v. Florida, 517 U.S. 44 (1996).

353 *See, e.g.*, Dellmuth v. Muth, 491 U.S. 223, 227 n.1 (1989) (Education of the Handicapped Act).

354 Seminole Tribe v. Florida, 517 U.S. 44, 54–56 (1996) (in most cases, Court first determines whether statute represents actual attempt to abrogate immunity, often making it unnecessary to determine constitutional question of existence of power to abrogate); *see, e.g.*, Hoffman v. Connecticut Dep't of Income Maintenance, 492 U.S. 96, 102 (1989) (language of Bankruptcy Code not sufficiently clear to establish intent to abrogate states' sovereign immunity); Atascadero State Hosp. v. Scanlon, 473 U.S. 234, 244–248 nn.4, 5 (1985) (unclear whether Rehabilitation Act of 1973 was enacted under Fourteenth Amendment or under Spending Clause of Article I, but Court never reached constitutional issue because statute did not establish congressional intent to abrogate states' immunity).

355 Seminole Tribe v. Florida, 517 U.S. 44, 59 (1996) (Fourteenth Amendment; rejecting Article I powers as basis for abrogation); *but see* City of Rome v. United States, 446 U.S. 156, 178–180 (1980) (indicating that Fifteenth Amendment is similar to Fourteenth in authorizing Congress to intrude on state sovereignty; case did not involve direct issue of state's Eleventh Amendment immunity from suit).

356 517 U.S. at 59 (rationale for holding that Fourteenth Amendment empowers Congress to abrogate Eleventh Amendment).

357 U.S. Const., Amend. XV (states may not deny or abridge voting rights on account of race); U.S. Const., Amend. XIX (states may not deny or abridge voting rights on account of sex); U.S. Const., Amend. XXIV (states may not deny or abridge voting rights in presidential or congressional elections on account of failure to pay tax); U.S. Const., Amend. XXVI (states may not deny or abridge, on account of age, voting rights of persons age 18 or over).

the principles of federalism that ordinarily limit congressional authority.[358] The Supreme Court has yet to consider whether the Nineteenth, Twenty-Fourth, or Twenty-Sixth Amendments may serve as the basis for a congressional abrogation of state sovereign immunity.

[358] *See* City of Rome v. United States, 446 U.S. 156, 178–180 (1980) (declaratory judgment action to test constitutionality of Voting Rights Act as applied to municipality; no direct Eleventh Amendment issue was raised, since state sovereign immunity cannot be asserted by municipalities).

# Chapter 15

# APPLICABLE LAW IN FEDERAL COURT: THE *ERIE* DOCTRINE

## PART A
## DEVELOPMENT OF THE *ERIE* DOCTRINE

## § 15.01 HISTORICAL BACKGROUND TO THE APPLICABLE LAW PROBLEM

### [1] Section 34 of Judiciary Act of 1789 and Doctrine of *Swift v. Tyson*

Section 34 of the original Judiciary Act of 1789, commonly known as the Rules of Decision Act, provided:

> *Laws of States as rules of decision.* The laws of the several states, except where the constitution, treaties or statutes of the United States shall otherwise require or provide, shall be regarded as rules of decision in trials at common law in the courts of the United States in cases where they apply.

Section 34 was first added to the Draft Bill of the Judiciary Act by a Senate amendment; this amendment as originally drafted read:

> And be it further enacted, That the Statute law of the several States in force for the time being and their unwritten or common law now in use, whether by adoption from the common law of England, the ancient statutes of the same or otherwise, except where the Constitution, Treaties or Statutes of the United States shall otherwise require or provide, shall be regarded as rules of decision in the trials at common law in the courts of the United States in cases where they apply.

However, before the amendment was submitted the words "Statute law" were stricken and the word "laws" was inserted and the words "in force for the time being and their unwritten or common law now in use, whether by adoption from the common law of England, the ancient statutes of the same or otherwise" also were stricken.[1] Whatever the original draftsman may have meant, the use of the

---

[1] *See* Warren, *New Light on the History of the Judiciary Act of 1789*, 37 Harv. L. Rev. 49, 86 (1923). Warren argued that the word "laws" was intended to include both statutory and case-made law because of these legislative language changes. He also stated that § 34 was prompted to quiet fears of many people that a different law would be applied in federal courts than was applied in state courts.

ambiguous words "the laws of the several states" gave rise to much controversy.

The United States Supreme Court first interpreted the meaning of the term "state law" as used in the Rules of Decision Act in 1842 in *Swift v. Tyson*.[2] This was an action in the circuit court of New York by a non-resident holder of a negotiable bill of exchange. The acceptor of the bill defended on the ground that he had been induced to accept the bill by fraud and that this defense was a bar against the plaintiff, because under New York decisions, which he contended were binding on the federal court, the plaintiff was not a holder for value because he had taken the bill in satisfaction of a pre-existing debt. The Supreme Court, in an opinion by Justice Story, declined to follow the New York decisions.

The Court held that federal courts must apply state statutes and constitutions and state court decisions construing them as the rule of decision in diversity cases. However, the *Swift* Court held that federal courts need only apply state common-law decisions on local or immovable matters, such as real property. Thus, "state law" did not include state court decisions on matters of commercial and contract law or general jurisprudence, such as torts, conflicts of law, and damages.[3] In those areas, the federal courts were free to evolve their own common law, which they did until the Supreme Court overruled *Swift* in its landmark 1938 decision in *Erie v. Tompkins*.[4] The *Erie* decision eliminated the general federal common law, although the federal courts retain the power to make common law in certain limited cases.

The Supreme Court decided to overrule *Swift* because the *Swift* doctrine had not achieved its expected result. *Swift* was supposed to create a uniform body of national substantive law because state courts were expected to adopt the general federal common law. However, a national common law failed to emerge because state courts continued to follow their own common law and because state and federal courts had difficulty distinguishing between cases involving general jurisprudence and those involving purely local matters.

The *Erie* Court also was concerned with the forum-shopping opportunities that diversity of citizenship jurisdiction afforded nonresident litigants under the *Swift* doctrine. When state and federal common law differed, nonresidents could choose the forum, state or federal, that offered the most favorable law, resulting in unfair discrimination against state citizens in which the federal court was located.[5]

---

[2] Swift v. Tyson, 41 U.S. (16 Pet.) 1 (1842).

[3] 41 U.S. (16 Pet.) at 18–19 ("state law" included only common-law decisions on "rights and titles to things having a permanent locality, such as the rights and titles to real estate and other matters immovable and intraterritorial in their national character").

[4] Erie R.R. Co. v. Tompkins, 304 U.S. 64 (1938).

[5] 304 U.S. at 74; *see, e.g.*, Black & White Taxi & Transfer Co. v. Brown & Yellow Taxi & Transfer Co., 276 U.S. 518, 522–525 (1928) (Kentucky corporation reincorporated in Tennessee solely to establish diversity of citizenship so that it could sue rival in federal court and take advantage of federal common law that was more favorable than Kentucky law).

## [2] The *Erie* Decision

### [a] Facts and Holdings

*Erie v. Tompkins* was a simple tort case. An Erie train injured Tompkins, a Pennsylvania citizen, while he was walking along the tracks in Pennsylvania. Since the Erie Railroad was a New York corporation, Tompkins sued in federal district court for the Southern District of New York, basing jurisdiction on diversity of citizenship. The railroad contended that Pennsylvania law applied and that, under Pennsylvania tort law, it was not liable for trespassers. The district court ruled for Tompkins, and the Court of Appeals for the Second Circuit affirmed on the theory that the federal courts were not bound to follow state law and could exercise their independent judgment whether the railroad was negligent.

The Supreme Court reversed, in an opinion authored by Justice Brandeis. In concluding that the federal court was required to apply state law, the Court reinterpreted the reference to "state law" in the Rules of Decision Act. According to the Court, the purpose of the Rules of Decisions Act is to make certain that, in all matters except those in which some federal law is controlling, the federal courts exercising jurisdiction in diversity cases will apply state law, as set forth in state constitutions, statutes, and judicial opinions. Judicial opinions include opinions enunciating state common law. The Court further declared that there was no general federal common law.[6]

### [b] Is *Erie* A Constitutionally Based Decision?

The Court further intimated that by making common law under the *Swift* doctrine, the federal courts invaded rights the Constitution reserved to the states. The Court did not point to a particular Constitutional provision the *Swift* doctrine violated, and many commentators have argued that the Court's constitutional analysis was dictum since the decision can rest on its reinterpretation of the Rules of Decision Act.[7] Thus, whether *Erie* establishes a rule of constitutional limitation is uncertain and much debated.[8] To begin, the issue concerning what Congress could constitutionally do was not before the Court. Second, it was highly unclear what constitutional provision *Swift v. Tyson* violated, especially since Justice Brandeis failed to cite any particular provision.

The most often suggested provision is the Tenth Amendment, which preserves to the states those powers that are not expressly delegated to the federal government. Justice Brandeis concluded that by failing to include state judicial decisions as "rules of decision" under Section 34, "in applying the *Swift* doctrine this Court and the lower courts have invaded rights which in our opinion are reserved by the

---

[6] Erie R.R. Co. v. Tompkins, 304 U.S. 64, 71–77 (1938).

[7] *See, e.g.*, Clark, *State Law in the Federal Courts: The Brooding Omnipresence of Erie v. Tompkins*, 55 Yale L.J. 267, 273 n.27 (1946).

[8] *See* Ely, *The Irrepressible Myth of Erie*, 87 Harv. L. Rev. 693 (1974); Friendly, *In Praise of Erie — And of the New Federal Common Law*, 39 N.Y.U. L. Rev. 383 (1964); Keefe, *In Praise of Joseph Story, Swift v. Tyson and "The" True National Common Law*, 18 Am. U. L. Rev. 316 (1969).

Constitution to the several states."[9] The broadest reading of this statement implies an unconstitutional invasion of Tenth Amendment rights; a narrower reading suggests an unconstitutional application of Section 34. Nonetheless, the Court did not hold Section 34 itself unconstitutional. The debate whether *Erie* established a rule of constitutional limitation was further fueled by Justice Reed's concurring opinion in which he contended that Article III, section 2 of the Constitution, coupled with the Necessary and Proper Clause of Article I, section 8 gave Congress the power to promulgate substantive rules for federal courts.[10]

### [c] Purposes of *Erie* Doctrine: The "Twin Aims" of *Erie*

Under the *Erie* doctrine, federal courts in diversity cases perform the role of another state trial court applying state statutes and common law. The *Erie* doctrine is rooted in a realization that it would be unfair for the result of litigation to depend on whether the suit is brought in state or federal court. Thus, the *Erie* doctrine has two purposes: (1) to assure uniform results in state and federal courts and discourage forum shopping between the state and federal system; and (2) to avoid inequitable administration of the laws.[11]

### [d] Promulgation of the Federal Rules of Civil Procedure

Congress enacted the Federal Rules of Civil Procedure in 1938, the same year the Court decided the *Erie* case. Before then, the Conformity Act of 1872 required the federal courts to follow state procedural law. In 1938 the federal courts transformed their approach to determining applicable law in federal cases, moving from vertical uniformity with state courts on procedure and horizontal uniformity in substance, to horizontal uniformity in procedure and vertical uniformity with state courts on substance. The *Erie* decision itself did not specifically address the substance/procedure dichotomy except for a statement in the concurring opinion that "[t]he line between procedural and substantive law is hazy, but no one doubts federal power over procedure."[12] The lower federal courts interpreted the *Erie* decision to mean that they were free to apply federal procedural law in diversity cases.[13]

---

[9] Erie R.R. Co. v. Tompkins, 304 U.S. 64, 79–80 (1938); *see* U.S. Const., Amendment X.

[10] Erie R.R. Co. v. Tompkins, 304 U.S. 64, 91–92 (1938); *see* U.S. Const., Article I § 8, Article III § 2.

[11] Guaranty Trust Co. v. York, 326 U.S. 99 (1945) ("[t]he nub of the policy that underlies *Erie R. Co. v. Tompkins* is that for the same transaction the accident of a suit by a non-resident litigant in a federal court instead of in a State court a block away should not lead to a substantially different result"); *see* Hanna v. Plumer, 380 U.S. 460, 464–472 (1965).

[12] Erie R.R. Co. v. Tompkins, 304 U.S. 64, 92 (1938) (Reed, J., concurring).

[13] *See, e.g.*, Connecticut Indem. Co. v. Lee, 168 F.2d 420, 423 (1st Cir. 1948); Brown v. Cranston, 132 F.2d 631, 633–634 (2d Cir. 1942).

# § 15.02 EARLY EFFORTS TO DISTINGUISH SUBSTANCE FROM PROCEDURE; OUTCOME-DETERMINATION ANALYSIS

## [1] The Outcome-Determination Test: The *Guaranty Trust* Decision

In developing the *Erie* doctrine, the Supreme Court has focused on creating an analytical framework for distinguishing between substance and procedure. Many legal rules are clearly substantive, such as the elements of a claim, and their application in diversity cases causes little difficulty.[14] However, some legal rules have both procedural and substantive characteristics, such as statutes of limitation, burdens of proof, and standards for setting aside a verdict. In addition, the Federal Rules of Civil Procedure themselves sometimes fall into the gray area between substance and procedure.

The Supreme Court initially suggested an analytical basis to distinguish substance and procedure in *Guaranty Trust Co. v. York*.[15] *Guaranty Trust* involved a class action in equity by noteholders against Guaranty Trust for an alleged breach of trust. Jurisdiction was based on diversity. The issue before the Supreme Court was whether the *Erie* doctrine required the federal court to apply the New York statute of limitations, which would have barred the suit. The court of appeals held that in an equity suit, a federal district court was not required to apply a state statute of limitations.[16] The Supreme Court acknowledged that the difference between substance and procedure depends on the context in which the question arises. A rule of law may be procedural for one purpose and substantive for another. The Court concluded that, for *Erie* purposes, a law that would apply if the suit were brought in state court is substantive if it would "significantly affect the result of a litigation for a federal court to disregard [the law]." Applying this outcome-determination analysis, the Court concluded that the federal court was obligated to apply the New York statute of limitations.[17]

The major weakness of the *Guaranty Trust* outcome-determination test is that it has no clearly defined limits. Virtually any state rule can affect a litigation's outcome, even those that are essentially judicial housekeeping rules. The broad outcome-determination test threatened the viability of the Federal Rules of Civil Procedure in diversity cases whenever a federal rule conflicted with a state rule. Nevertheless, the Court continued to apply the outcome-determination analysis[18]

---

[14] *See, e.g.*, McKethan v. Texas Farm Bureau, 996 F.2d 734, 741–742 (5th Cir. 1993) (state law determined elements of cause of action for intentional infliction of emotional distress and measure of damages).

[15] Guaranty Trust Co. v. York, 326 U.S. 99 (1945).

[16] 326 U.S. at 108–112.

[17] 326 U.S. at 108–112.

[18] *See, e.g.* Ragan v. Merchants Transfer and Warehouse Co., 337 U.S. 530, 531–534 (1949) (action barred under state law that required service by certain date for tolling statute of limitations even though Fed. R. Civ. P. 3 provides that action is commenced on date complaint is filed); Woods v. Interstate Realty Co., 337 U.S. 535, 537 (1949) (state statute closed doors to foreign corporations who failed to register to

for 13 years before articulating other standards, first in *Byrd v. Blue Ridge Electrical Cooperative, Inc.*[19] and *Hanna v. Plumer.*[20]

## [2] Refinement of the Outcome-Determination Test

The Supreme Court refined the *Guaranty Trust* pure outcome-determination test in considered dicta in *Hanna v. Plumer*. The *Hanna* Court explained that federal courts must not mechanically apply the *Guaranty Trust* outcome-determination test. Instead, the twin aims of the *Erie* rule must guide its application: (1) to assure uniform results in state and federal courts so that forum shopping between the state and federal system is discouraged; and (2) to prevent the party who chooses the forum from obtaining an advantage over the other party, avoiding an inequitable administration of the laws.[21] The forum-shopping that concerned the Court is the unfairness of providing plaintiffs who can sue in federal court an advantage unavailable to non-diverse plaintiffs who must proceed in state court, or unavailable to defendants who have no choice.[22]

Thus, in federal diversity suits the court is obliged to apply a state rule even if it decreases the plaintiff's chance of success on the merits, or results in smaller verdicts than in federal court. For example, in *Gasperini v. Center for Humanities, Inc.*, the Supreme Court concluded that a federal district court must apply a state standard for reviewing excessive jury verdicts. The federal court's failure to apply the more stringent state standard could lead to federal verdicts substantially higher than state verdicts in similar cases. This possible discrepancy might encourage plaintiffs to file in federal court, resulting in unfair discrimination against state citizens.[23]

The *Erie-Hanna* forum-shopping concern looks to state rules that decrease a plaintiff's likelihood of success in state court, thereby encouraging federal filing. However, federal courts have held that state rules that potentially increase a plaintiff's recovery, such as prejudgment interest rules, are outcome-determinative and federal courts must apply them. The courts also point to the forum-shopping opportunities for nonresident defendants who can remove a case to federal court, and the unfairness to resident defendants who lack that opportunity.[24]

---

do business in state); Cohen v. Beneficial Indus. Loan Corp. 337 U.S. 541, 543–545 (1949) (shareholder's derivative action dismissed for failure to comply with state requirements for security even though Fed. R. Civ. P. 23 contained no such requirements).

[19] Byrd v. Blue Ridge Rural Elec. Coop., 356 U.S. 525, 533–540 (1958).

[20] Hanna v. Plumer, 380 U.S. 460, 464–472 (1965).

[21] 380 U.S. at 468 ("The outcome-determination test therefore cannot be read without reference to the twin aims of the Erie rule: discouragement of forum-shopping and avoidance of inequitable administration of the laws").

[22] *See In re* Air Crash Disaster Near New Orleans, Louisiana on July 9, 1982, 821 F.2d 1147, 1157 (5th Cir. 1987).

[23] Gasperini v. Center for Humanities, Inc., 518 U.S. 415, 429–430 (1996) ("Erie precludes a recovery in federal court significantly larger than the recovery that would have been tolerated in state court").

[24] *See, e.g.*, S.A. Healy Co. v. Milwaukee Metro. Sewerage Dist., 60 F.3d 305, 310–312 (7th Cir. 1995) (state law imposing penalties on defendant for rejecting plaintiff's settlement demand applied);

Generally, however, when no federal statute or federal rule governs, a federal court sitting in diversity must apply forum state law if failure to apply state law would (1) significantly affect the outcome of the litigation and (2) encourage forum shopping or result in inequitable administration of the laws. The court must ask whether application of state law would have so important an effect on the fortunes of the litigants that the court's failure to apply state law would unfairly discriminate against forum state citizens, or likely cause a plaintiff to choose the federal court.[25]

## § 15.03 BALANCING OF COMPETING STATE AND FEDERAL INTERESTS: THE *BYRD* TEST

Seven years before *Hanna v. Plumer*, the Supreme Court announced a balancing test to determine when a federal court must apply state law in a diversity action. The Supreme Court's 1958 decision in *Byrd v. Blue Ridge Rural Electric Cooperative Inc.* was a departure from the Court's pure outcome-determination test. In *Byrd*, the Court acknowledged that "outcome" was only one factor a federal court should consider in choosing between state and federal law, but that other elements also were relevant.[26] The status of the *Byrd* test, in the wake of *Hanna v. Plumer* (*see* § 15.04) is uncertain.

*Byrd* was a federal diversity personal injury suit. Byrd, an injured employee, sued a utility company claiming its negligence caused his injuries. The utility argued that it was immune from suit because Byrd was a statutory employee and his exclusive remedy was under the state worker's compensation statute. South Carolina state practice permitted judges to decide whether a plaintiff was a statutory employee within the worker's compensation statute. The central *Erie* question was whether the federal judge had to follow this state practice and decide this question or should allow a jury to decide.[27]

The Supreme Court held that a jury should decide the issue in conformity with federal practice. In reaching this result, the Court reviewed the state rule and concluded that it was "merely a form and mode of enforcement of the immunity" and "not a rule intended to be bound up with the definition of the rights and obligations of the parties" in such a way that *Erie* required its application. The Court acknowledged that the litigation's outcome would be substantially affected by whether the judge or a jury decided the immunity issue. Therefore, if "outcome" were the only consideration, a strong case existed for the federal court to follow state practice. However, the Court concluded that affirmative countervailing considerations were present. The Court balanced the strong federal interest in maintaining the Seventh Amendment jury trial right against South Carolina's less

---

Commercial Union Ins. Co. v. Walbrook Ins. Co., Ltd., 41 F.3d 764, 772 (1st Cir. 1994) (state prejudgment interest rule applied).

[25] *See* Gasperini v. Center for Humanities, Inc., 518 U.S. 415, 428–429 (1996); Hanna v. Plumer, 380 U.S. 460, 468 n.9 (1965).

[26] Byrd v. Blue Ridge Rural Elec. Coop., 356 U.S. 525, 533–540 (1958).

[27] 356 U.S. at 525–528.

compelling policy of permitting judges to make the determination.[28]

Commentators have suggested that the *Byrd* test recognizes three interests: (1) the state's interest in having federal courts recognize and uphold its substantive rules and policies, (2) the federal court's interests in adhering to significant federal principles in the administration of justice, and (3) the litigants' interests in having a uniform outcome regardless of where the plaintiff sues.[29] However, commentators and courts continue to debate the correct formulation of the *Byrd* test. One approach evaluates whether a state rule is "bound up" with the accomplishment of state substantive policy. If so, the federal court must follow the state rule and should not balance it against other possible competing federal policies. Another approach requires federal courts to balance the three *Byrd* interests. In this formulation, whether a state rule is bound up with state substantive policy is a factor to consider in determining the strength of the state's interests.[30]

The *Byrd* analysis has proved difficult to apply since the opinion does not clarify how a federal court is to determine whether a state rule is bound up with the definition of the parties' rights and obligations. The *Byrd* opinion also provides no guidance for determining when a federal interest outweighs a state interest. Moreover, the relationship between the *Byrd* test and other *Erie* analytical models is not clear. The *Hanna* Court cited *Byrd* only for the proposition that the "[o]utcome-determination analysis was never intended to serve as a talisman."[31] It appears that the Court intended the Rules Enabling Act analysis (*see* § 15.04) to supplant *Byrd* for cases involving a conflict between federal rules and state law. Neither the *Hanna* opinion, nor the Court's later opinion in *Burlington Northern R.R. Co. v. Woods* (dealing with the application of Federal Rule of Appellate Procedure 38) suggest that balancing state and federal interests has any role in the Rules Enabling Act analysis.[32]

However, the *Byrd* test still appears applicable in cases that do not involve federal rules. In its 1996 decision in *Gasperini v. Center for Humanities* (*see* § 15.05), the Supreme Court stated that the outcome-determination test is an insufficient guide in cases presenting "countervailing federal interests." The Court suggested that the *Byrd* test might be appropriate when the outcome-determination test would require application of state law, but state law conflicts with federal interests.[33] The Court did not clarify what kind of countervailing federal interests are sufficient to invoke *Byrd*. Since both *Byrd* and *Gasperini* involved Seventh Amendment issues, presumably a constitutionally protected federal inter-

---

[28] 356 U.S. at 533–540.

[29] REDISH, FEDERAL JURISDICTION: TENSIONS IN THE ALLOCATION OF JUDICIAL POWER 216 (2d ed. 1990).

[30] CHEMERINSKY, FEDERAL JURISDICTION § 5.3 at 272 (1989).

[31] Hanna v. Plumer, 380 U.S. 460, 466–467 (1965).

[32] *See* 380 U.S. at 471 ("[w]hen a situation is covered by one of the Federal Rules . . . the court has been instructed to apply the Federal Rule, and can refuse to do so only if the Advisory Committee, this Court, and Congress erred in their prima facie judgment that the Rule in question transgresses neither the terms of the Enabling Act nor constitutional restrictions"); Burlington N. R.R. v. Woods, 480 U.S. 1, 3–8 (1987); *see also* John Hart Ely, *The Irrepressible Myth of Erie*, 87 HARVARD L. REV. 693, 718–738 (1974).

[33] Gasperini v. Center for Humanities, Inc., 518 U.S. 415, 436–437 (1996).

est qualifies. As a practical matter, many federal courts continue to apply the *Byrd* balancing test or hybrids of the *Byrd* test and the outcome-determination test.[34]

## § 15.04 *HANNA v. PLUMER:* DETERMINING WHETHER TO APPLY STATE LAW OR FEDERAL RULE OF CIVIL PROCEDURE

### [1] General *Hanna* Analytical Approach: Federal Rule Applies if Pertinent and Valid Under Rules Enabling Act

The Supreme Court's decision in *Hanna v. Plumer* provides federal courts with guidance, under a construction of the Rules Enabling Act, to determine whether to apply a state rule or a conflicting federal procedural rule.[35] Under a Rules Enabling Act[36] analysis, the federal court must apply the federal rule if (1) the scope of the rule is "sufficiently broad to cover the situation"; and (2) the rule is constitutional and a valid exercise of the Supreme Court's rulemaking power under the federal Rules Enabling Act. The federal rule controls when both conditions are satisfied, even if a state court applying state law would reach a different result.[37]

If the court determines that the scope of the federal rule is not sufficiently broad to cover the situation, the Rules Enabling Act analysis does not apply, and the court must look to other standards that the Supreme Court has developed to determine whether the *Erie* doctrine calls for the application of state law, such as the refined outcome-determination analysis (*see* § 15.02[2]).

### [2] Rules Enabling Act, Not Outcome-Determination, Is Test for Federal Rules

In *Hanna v. Plumer*, the Supreme Court held that Rule 4(d)(1) of the Federal Rules of Civil Procedure, rather than state law, governs the manner of service of process in federal diversity suits. The plaintiff, an Ohio resident, sued the executor of a deceased Massachusetts citizen in Massachusetts district court for injuries from an automobile accident allegedly caused by the decedent's negligence. State law required service by in-hand delivery to the executor within one year of the injury. Instead, the plaintiff served the executor by leaving copies of the summons and complaint with the executor's wife at his residence, in compliance with former Federal Rule 4(d)(1), shortly before the limitations period ran. Applying the

---

[34] *See, e.g.*, Hottle v. Beech Aircraft Corp., 47 F.3d 106, 109–110 (4th Cir. 1995) (state evidence rule excluding party's internal rules and regulations to show negligence was sufficiently bound up with state substantive policies to be applied in diversity case).

[35] Hanna v. Plumer, 380 U.S. 460, 463–465 (1965) (Federal Rules of Civil Procedure); *see also* Burlington N. R.R. v. Woods, 480 U.S. 1, 4–5 (1987) (Federal Rules of Appellate Procedure).

[36] 28 U.S.C. § 2072.

[37] Hanna v. Plumer, 380 U.S. 460, 471 (1965) ("[W]hen a situation is covered by one of the Federal Rules . . . the court has been instructed to apply the Federal Rule, and can refuse to do so only if the Advisory Committee, this Court, and Congress erred in their prima facie judgment that the Rule in question transgresses neither the terms of the Enabling Act nor constitutional restrictions").

*Guaranty Trust* outcome-determination test, the district court granted summary judgment against the plaintiff and the court of appeals affirmed.

The Supreme Court concluded that the scope of Rule 4(d)(1), which was designed to control service of process in diversity actions, was coextensive with state law regarding the method for serving process on an executor. The clash between Rule 4(d)(1) and the state service requirements was unavoidable because "Rule 4(d)(1) says — implicitly, but with unmistakable clarity — that in-hand service is not required in federal courts." The Court held that Rule 4(d)(1) was valid under the Rules Enabling Act and it therefore displaced the state service requirements.[38]

The *Hanna* opinion is significant because it distinguished situations involving conflicts between state law and a Federal Rule of Civil Procedure from those that did not, such as *Erie* itself. *Hanna*, therefore, provided a separate analytical framework for federal rules cases. Before *Hanna*, all *Erie* questions were subject to the "outcome-determination" analysis that required federal courts to apply state law if application of state law would have a significant effect on the litigation's outcome. In *Hanna*, the Supreme Court made clear that the Federal Rules of Civil Procedure typically will supplant conflicting state rules in diversity cases, even if the result is outcome-determinative, because the *Erie* doctrine is not the appropriate test of the validity and applicability of a Federal Rule of Civil Procedure.[39] The *Hanna* Court recognized that "the constitutional provision for the federal court system . . . carries with it congressional power to make rules governing the practice and pleading in those courts, which in turn includes a power to regulate matters which, though falling within the uncertain area between substance and procedure, are rationally capable of classification as either."[40]

### [3] Determining Scope (Pertinence) of Federal Rule Under Rules Enabling Act

#### [a] Federal Rule Must Be Sufficiently Broad to Control Situation

Under the *Hanna* Rules Enabling Act analysis, a Federal Rule of Civil Procedure or Appellate Procedure will displace a state rule in a diversity case only if the federal rule is sufficiently coextensive in scope with the state rule.[41] The determination of the federal rule's scope is critical. As a practical matter, once the federal court determines that the federal and state rules have the same scope, the federal rule usually will supplant the state rule because all federal rules presumptively satisfy the constitutional validity requirement of Rules Enabling Act analy-

---

[38] 380 U.S. at 463–464; *see* Fed. R. Civ. P. 4(d)(1); *see also* 28 U.S.C. § 2072 (Rules Enabling Act). For general discussion of service of process under the Federal Rules of Civil Procedure, *see* 1 Moore's Federal Practice Ch. 4, *Summons* (Matthew Bender 3d ed.).

[39] 380 U.S. at 472.

[40] 380 U.S. at 472.

[41] 380 U.S. at 470; *see* 28 U.S.C. § 2072 (Rules Enabling Act).

sis.[42] The *Hanna* Court itself retroactively validated several earlier Supreme Court decisions applying state rules because the scope of the federal rule was simply not broad enough to cover the point.[43]

Several Supreme Court decisions seem to indicate a need for a "direct collision" or conflict between the federal rule and state law.[44] However, more recent decisions affirm that the relevant *Hanna* inquiry is whether the federal law is "sufficiently broad to control the issue before the Court." Federal law and state law need not be perfectly coextensive and equally applicable for the federal rule to "cover the point in dispute."[45] Moreover, courts should not narrowly construe the federal rules to avoid a direct collision with state law, but should give federal rules their plain meaning.[46]

Typically, courts deem a federal rule sufficiently broad to control the issue when the court cannot give effect to both the federal and state rules. The court must apply Enabling Act analysis to choose between a federal rule and a state rule unless both "can exist side by side . . . each controlling its own intended sphere of coverage without conflict."[47] On the other hand, in *Shady Grove Orthopedic Assocs. v. Allstate Ins. Co.*,[48] five Justices, including the concurring and dissenting Justices, indicated that when determining whether a federal rule and a state law conflict, courts must be aware of and sensitive to important state and regulatory policies.

In several cases, courts have held that federal rules are not broad enough to displace state law. For example, the Court determined that Federal Rule of Civil Procedure 3 does not displace state law governing the tolling of statutes of limitation.[49] Federal Rule of Civil Procedure 4, which governs service of process in federal court, does not displace state law governing personal jurisdiction.[50] In addition, Federal Rule of Civil Procedure 23.1 does not displace state security requirements in shareholder derivative suits;[51] nor does Federal Rule of Civil Procedure 68 displace late law on attorney fees or penalties on losing defendants.[52]

---

[42] *See* Burlington N. R.R. v. Woods, 480 U.S. 1, 5 (1987).

[43] Hanna v. Plumer, 380 U.S. 460, 470 (1965); *see, e.g.*, Ragan v. Merchants Transfer and Warehouse Co., 337 U.S. 530, 531–534 (1949) (action barred under state law that required service by certain date for tolling statute of limitations even though Fed. R. Civ. P. 3 provides that action is commenced on date complaint is filed); Cohen v. Beneficial Indus. Loan Corp. 337 U.S. 541, 543–545 (1949) (shareholder's derivative action dismissed for failure to comply with state requirements for security even though Fed. R. Civ. P. 23 contained no such requirements).

[44] *See, e.g.*, Walker v. Armco Steel Corp., 446 U.S. 740, 749–753 (1980); Burlington N. R.R. v. Woods, 480 U.S. 1, 4 (1987).

[45] *See* Stewart Org., Inc. v. Ricoh Corp., 487 U.S. 22, 29–31 (1988) (case involved federal procedural statute).

[46] Walker v. Armco Steel Corp., 446 U.S. 740, 750 n.9 (1980).

[47] 446 U.S. at 752.

[48] Shady Grove Orthopedic Assocs. v. Allstate Ins. Co., 559 U.S. 393 (2010).

[49] Walker v. Armco Steel Corp., 446 U.S. 740 (1980); Guaranty Trust Co. v. York, 326 U.S. 99 (1945).

[50] Arrowsmith v. United Press Int'l., 320 F.2d 219, 225–26 (2d Cir. 1963).

[51] Cohen v. Beneficial Indus. Loan Corp., 337 U.S. 541 (1949).

[52] Tanker Mgmt., Inc. v. Brunson, 918 F.3d 1524, 1528 (11th Cir. 1990).

In other cases, federal courts have held that discretionary federal rules are sufficiently broad to conflict with similar mandatory state rules. For example, the Supreme Court held that Federal Rule of Civil Procedure 23 is broad enough to displace state law concerning criteria for pursuing a claim as a class action.[53] Federal Rule 66, which governs the appointment of a receiver in a diversity action, is sufficiently broad to displace state law.[54] In addition, the Court has determined that the scope of Federal Rule of Appellate Procedure 38, which gives appellate courts discretion to assess penalties for frivolous appeals, is sufficiently broad to conflict with an Alabama statute requiring the appellate court to impose a 10 percent penalty on an unsuccessful appellant. In addition to the conflict between Rule 38's discretionary operation and the state's mandatory provision, the purposes underlying the rule are sufficiently coextensive with the state statute to indicate that the rule occupies the entire field and precludes application of state law in federal diversity actions.[55] Similarly, the Ninth Circuit Court of Appeals held that Federal Rule of Civil Procedure 41(b), which permits a federal court to dismiss a suit for failure to prosecute, is sufficiently broad to conflict with Nevada Rule 41(e), which requires dismissal for failure to prosecute after five years.[56]

### [b] Rule Must Regulate Procedure

Congress has the power to make rules governing federal court practice under Article III of the United States Constitution and the Necessary and Proper Clause.[57] Congress enacted the Rules Enabling Act pursuant to this grant. The Federal Rules of Civil Procedure are presumed valid under both the Constitution and the Rules Enabling Act. The Advisory Committee on Civil Rules, the Judicial Conference, and the Supreme Court study and approve every rule amendment, which Congress then formally enacts. This rulemaking process imbues the federal rules and rule amendments with a presumption of validity.[58]

The Rules Enabling Act provides that the Supreme Court has the power to prescribe, by general rules, the forms of process, writs, pleadings, and motions, and the practice and procedure of the United States district courts in civil actions. However, these rules may not abridge, enlarge, or modify any substantive right, and must preserve the jury trial right.[59] In *Hanna*, the Supreme Court stated that a rule is valid under the Rules Enabling Act if the rule really regulates procedure — that is, regulates the judicial process for enforcing substantive rights and duties,

---

[53] Shady Grove Orthopedic Assocs., 559 U.S. 393 (2010).

[54] Canada Life Assur. Co. v. Lapeter, 563 F.3d 837, 842 (9th Cir. 2009).

[55] Burlington N. R.R. v. Woods, 480 U.S. 1, 4–8 (1987); *see generally* 20A Moore's Federal Practice Ch. 338, *Frivolous Appeal — Damages and Costs* (Matthew Bender 3d ed.).

[56] Harvey's Wagon Wheel, Inc. v. Van Blitter, 959 F.2d 153, 155 (9th Cir. 1992); see Fed. R. Civ. P. 41(b); *see generally* 8 Moore's Federal Practice Ch. 41, *Dismissal of Actions* (Matthew Bender 3d ed.).

[57] Hanna v. Plumer, 380 U.S. 460, 472–473 (1965) ("*Erie* and its offspring cast no doubt on the long-recognized power of Congress to prescribe housekeeping rules for federal courts"); *see* U.S. Const., Art. III (Judicial Department); U.S. Const., Art. I § 8, cl. 18 (Necessary and Proper Clause).

[58] Burlington N. R.R. v. Woods, 480 U.S. 1, 5 (1987).

[59] 28 U.S.C. § 2072 (Rules Enabling Act).

and for justly administering relief.[60] Thus, a Federal Rule of Civil Procedure is valid if it regulates matters commonly understood as procedural and matters that, though falling within the uncertain area between substance and procedure, are rationally capable of classification as either.[61] The *Hanna* Court attributed no significance to the substantive rights language in the Rules Enabling Act and did not consider the possibility that application of a federal rule in a diversity case could abridge or enlarge substantive rights of litigants under state law.

### [c] Rule May Not Abridge or Enlarge Substantive Rights

State procedural rules sometimes also further state substantive policies. Arguably, application of a federal rule in a diversity case could abridge or enlarge a litigant's state substantive rights in violation of the Rules Enabling Act. However, although the Court has considered the possibility in several cases, the Court has never found a federal rule to violate this provision. In *Burlington Northern R.R. v. Woods*, the Court stated that "[r]ules which incidentally affect litigants' substantive rights do not violate [the substantive rights] provision if reasonably necessary to maintain the integrity of that system of rules."[62] In *Sibbach v. Wilson & Co.*, the first case to consider the validity of a federal rule under the Enabling Act, the Court held that Rule 35, which permits a federal court to order a party to submit to a physical or mental exam when the party's condition is in controversy, did not violate the substantive rights language. However, if the Court had held Rule 35 invalid, applicable state law would have permitted the exam.[63]

Similarly, in *Business Guides v. Chromatic Communications Enterprises*, the Court rejected an argument that Rule 11 sanctions, for failing to conduct a reasonable inquiry before filing a pleading, violated the Rules Enabling Act. The sanctioned party argued that Rule 11 sanctions enlarged substantive rights in (1) authorizing fee shifting in absence of a federal statute and (2) effectively creating a federal tort of malicious prosecution. The Court concluded that Rule 11 does not shift fees because Rule 11 sanctions are not tied to the litigation's outcome. Furthermore, Rule 11 does not create a federal common-law action for malicious prosecution because the Rule's objective is to deter baseless findings, not compensate victimized parties.[64]

In *Shady Grove Orthopedic Assocs. v. Allstate Ins. Co.*, a plurality of four Justices argued that the test for validity of a federal rule under the Rules Enabling Act is not whether the rule affects a litigant's substantive rights, as most procedural rights do. What matters, according to these Justices, is what the rule itself *regulates*. If it really regulates procedure, governing only the manner and the means by which the litigants' rights are enforced, it is valid; if it alters the rules of

---

[60] Hanna v. Plumer, 380 U.S. 460, 464 (1965); *see* Sibbach v. Wilson & Co., 312 U.S. 1, 14 (1941).

[61] Hanna v. Plumer, 380 U.S. 460, 472 (1965).

[62] Burlington N. R.R. v. Woods, 480 U.S. 1, 5 (1987).

[63] Sibbach v. Wilson & Co., 312 U.S. 1, 14 (1941); *see* Fed. R. Civ. P. 35; *see generally* 7 Moore's Federal Practice Ch. 35, *Physical and Mental Examinations* (Matthew Bender 3d ed.).

[64] Business Guides, Inc. v. Chromatic Comm. Enterprises, 498 U.S. 533, 551–554 (1991); *see* Fed. R. Civ. P. 11; *see generally* 2 Moore's Federal Practice Ch. 11, *Signing Pleadings, Motions, and Other Papers; Representations to the Court; Sanctions* (Matthew Bender 3d ed.).

decision by which the court will adjudicate those rights, it is not.[65] These Justices concluded that rules allowing multiple claims by or against multiple parties to be litigated together, including rules about joinder, consolidation, and class actions are procedural, neither changing plaintiffs' separate entitlements to relief nor abridging defendants' rights, but merely altering how the claims are processed. The Court emphasized that for purposes of this analysis, it is not the substantive or procedural nature or purpose of the affected state law that matters, but rather the substantive or procedural nature of the federal rule.

Concurring in *Shady Grove*, Justice Stevens rejected the idea that the only criterion for determining validity is whether the federal law really regulates procedure. He emphasized the Enabling Act's prohibition on federal rules that "abridge, enlarge or modify any substantive right,"[66] concluding that there are some state procedural rules that federal courts must apply in diversity cases because they function as a part of the state's definition of substantive rights and remedies. However, Justice Stevens concurred in the Court's judgment, concluding that the New York law at issue in that case, which precluded class action suits in which the plaintiffs sought statutory penalties, was not such a rule.

The Ninth Circuit held that a state law precluding waiver of appealability of punitive damage awards does not override Federal Rule of Civil Procedure 50. Rule 50 prevents a party from raising an argument in a post-trial motion for judgment as a matter of law, unless the argument was raised in a pre-verdict motion.[67] The court reasoned that the state's no-waiver rule did not create any substantive right, and it did not add, subtract, or define any of the elements necessary to justify punitive damages. Rather, it merely established when and how those pre-existing substantive rules can be reviewed. Thus, in overriding the state's no-waiver rule, Rule 50 does not run afoul of the Rules Enabling Act because its application affects only the process of enforcing litigants' rights and not the rights themselves. The mere fact that the state's no-waiver rule is rooted in public policy did not render it substantive for *Erie* purposes.

There are a few cases in which federal courts have held that application of a federal rule would violate the Rules Enabling Act's substantive rights provision because the federal rule abridged, enlarged, or modified litigants' rights under state law. For example, the Fifth Circuit applied a state rule on compulsory counter-claims, rather than Federal Rule 13(a), in a diversity case involving a lender's remedy for default on promissory notes. The makers of the overdue notes contended that the holder was barred from collecting because the holder's predecessor, in prior litigation, had failed to file a compulsory counterclaim under Rule 13(a). Under the state compulsory counterclaim rule, the lender would not have been compelled to file the counterclaim because the lender was entitled to elect

---

[65] Shady Grove Orthopedic Assocs., 559 U.S. 393, — (2010) (Scalia, J., joined by Robert C.J., Thomas, J., and Sotomayor, J.; quoting Sibbach v. Wilson & Co., 312 U.S.1 (1941).

[66] Shady Grove, *id.* (Stevens J., concurring: "A federal rule, therefore, cannot govern a particular case in which the rule would displace a state law that is procedural in the ordinary use of the term but it is so intertwined with a state right or remedy that it functions to define the scope of the state-created right.").

[67] Freund v. Nycomed Amersham, 347 F.3d 752, 760–62 (9th Cir. 2003).

judicial or nonjudicial foreclosure, and the debtors had no right to force the lender to pursue a judicial foreclosure remedy. The court ruled that the debtors could not raise Federal Rule 13(a) to prevent the note holder from collecting because to do so would abridge the holder's substantive rights and enlarge the debtor's substantive rights.[68] In *Garman v. Campbell County Sch. Dist. No. I*, the Tenth Circuit applied the pleading requirements of the Wyoming Governmental Claims Act (WGCA) rather than Fed. R. Civ. P. 8(a)(1).[69] Rule 8(a)(1) requires only "a short and plain statement of the grounds for the court's jurisdiction." In contrast, the WGCA requires plaintiffs in suits against local governments to allege compliance with statutory filing requirements and compliance with constitutional signature and certification requirements. If those requirements are not met, a state court must dismiss the case for lack of jurisdiction. The Tenth Circuit concluded that the requirements are part of the substantive law of Wyoming. Permitting Rule 8(a)(1) to trump this substantive Wyoming law would "abridge, enlarge, or modify" the litigants' rights, in violation of the Rules Enabling Act. Therefore, the district court properly dismissed the complaint, which did not comply with the WGCA requirements, for lack of jurisdiction.

## § 15.05 ACCOMMODATION OF COMPETING STATE AND FEDERAL INTERESTS; *GASPERINI v. CENTER FOR HUMANITIES*

When outcome-determination analysis requires a federal court to apply state law, but state law conflicts with significant federal interests, the Supreme Court has attempted to accommodate both interests. In *Gasperini v. Center for Humanities*, the Supreme Court faced the question whether the federal courts could apply a New York law, prescribing the appellate review standard for excessive jury verdicts, without violating the Seventh Amendment. In a five to four decision, the Court held that the federal court could give effect to the state standard if the federal district court, rather than the court of appeals, applied it.[70]

Gasperini, an aspiring photojournalist, sued the Center for Humanities because the Center lost 300 slide transparencies he had lent it. The jury awarded Gasperini $450,000 in damages. The Center moved for a new trial under Rule 59, attacking the verdict on various grounds, including excessiveness. The district court denied the motion without comment. Under a New York statute, state appellate courts were required to rule that a jury award is excessive or inadequate if it "deviates materially from what would be reasonable compensation." The less rigorous federal standard required the district court to set the verdict aside only if it "shocked the conscience." The federal court of appeals would then review the district court's decision for abuse of discretion.

---

[68] Douglas v. NCNB Texas Nat'l Bank, 979 F.2d 1128, 1129–1131 (5th Cir. 1992); *see* Fed. R. Civ. P. 13(a); *see generally* 3 Moore's Federal Practice Ch. 13, *Counterclaim and Cross-Claim* (Matthew Bender 3d ed.).

[69] 630 F.3d 977, 984–85 (10th Cir. 2010) ("[p]ermitting the federal rules to trump substantive Wyoming law would 'abridge, enlarge, or modify' the litigants' rights in violation of the Rules Enabling Act.").

[70] Gasperini v. Center for Humanities, Inc., 518 U.S. 415, 438–439 (1996).

The Court of Appeals for the Second Circuit applied the New York standard of appellate review and ordered a new trial unless Gasperini would agree to a remittitur reducing the verdict to $100,000. The issues before the Supreme Court were (1) whether the *Erie* doctrine requires the state standard of review to be applied in federal court and (2) whether the Seventh Amendment's re-examination clause permits the state standard to be applied in federal court.[71] The reexamination clause provides that "no fact tried by a jury, shall be otherwise re-examined in any Court of the United States, than according to the rules of the common law."[72]

The Court concluded that *Erie* required that the New York state standard be applied in federal court because litigants could expect substantial variations between federal and state judgments if the federal court applied a "shocks the conscience" test to New York state damage awards. These substantial variations could encourage plaintiffs to file in federal rather than state court, leading to unfair discrimination against New York citizens.[73]

Turning to the Seventh Amendment question, the Court's majority opinion approved a line of appellate decisions holding that the Seventh Amendment permits appellate review of a district court's denial of a motion to set aside a jury verdict as excessive, under an abuse of discretion standard. The Court stated that "appellate review for abuse of discretion is reconcilable with the Seventh Amendment as a control necessary and proper to the fair administration of justice." Review by a federal appellate court under the "materially deviates" standard, however, would fail to attend to an essential characteristic of the federal court system.

The Court then resolved its conflicting conclusions on the *Erie* and Seventh Amendment issues by ruling that the federal court could respect New York's dominant interest without disrupting the federal system if the federal district court applied the state's "materially deviates" standard. The appellate court would then review the district court's decision only for abuse of discretion. The Court decided that it did not need to apply the *Byrd* balancing test, because in *Byrd*, the Court was faced with an either/or decision: either resolution of the issue by the judge as in state court, or trial by jury as in federal court.[74] Instead, in *Gasperini* the Court fashioned a compromise it believed would minimize the likelihood of discrepancies in state and federal verdicts, but not transgress the reexamination clause.[75] Thus, *Gasperini* and *Byrd* suggest that the outcome-determination test is inadequate when the state law impinges on a constitutionally protected federal interest. In such cases, the court should attempt to accommodate both interests if possible or apply the *Byrd* balancing test to determine whether the federal or state interest should prevail.

Three Justices, in a dissent by Justice Scalia, would have resolved the case under the Rules Enabling Act analysis rather than the outcome-determination test. They

---

71 Gasperini v. Center for Humanities, Inc., 518 U.S. 415, 426 (1996).

72 U.S. Const., Amend. VII.

73 Gasperini v. Center for Humanities, Inc., 518 U.S. 415, 429–430 (1996) ("*Erie* precludes a recovery in federal court significantly larger than the recovery that would have been tolerated in state court").

74 *See* Byrd v. Blue Ridge Rural Elec. Coop., 356 U.S. 525, 533–540 (1958).

75 Gasperini v. Center for Humanities, Inc., 518 U.S. 415, 436–437 (1996).

characterized the case as involving a conflict between state law and Federal Rule of Civil Procedure 59. Rule 59, in the dissenter's view, prescribes a federal standard that the district courts must apply to motions for new trials. The Scalia minority also would have ruled that the Seventh Amendment prohibits any appellate review of the district court's denial of a motion for a new trial for factual error.[76] Justice Stevens, in a separate dissent, agreed with the Court's *Erie* analysis, but would have ruled that the Seventh Amendment permits appellate courts to apply the state standard of review.[77]

# PART B
# SPECIFIC APPLICATIONS OF ERIE DOCTRINE

## § 15.06 RULE 3 DOES NOT DISPLACE STATE LAW GOVERNING TOLLING OF STATUTE OF LIMITATIONS

State statutes of limitations are substantive rules of law for *Erie* purposes. When jurisdiction is based on diversity of citizenship, a federal court is obliged to apply a state statute of limitations. In addition to the statute of limitations itself, state rules that are an integral part of the statute of limitations, such as tolling rules, apply to state claims brought in federal court.

Federal Rule of Civil Procedure 3, which states that "[a] civil action is commenced by filing a complaint with the court" does not determine when an action is commenced for the purpose of tolling the state statute of limitations.[78] In *Walker v. Armco Steel Corp.*, the Supreme Court held that the federal district court had to apply an Oklahoma statute that required service of process within 60 days after filing a complaint.[79] Since the action would have been barred for failure to meet the service requirement had it been brought in a Oklahoma state court, the action also was barred in federal court. In reaching this conclusion, the Court first determined that the scope of Rule 3 was not sufficiently broad to cover the situation. In the Court's view, Rule 3 was not intended to toll a state statute of limitations, or to displace state tolling rules. In diversity actions, Rule 3 governs the date from which various timing requirements of the federal rules begin to run, but does not affect state statutes of limitations. Since there was no conflict between the federal rule and state law, the *Hanna* Rules Enabling Act analysis was irrelevant.[80]

---

[76] *See* 518 U.S. at 449 (Scalia J. dissenting); *see* Fed. R. Civ. P. 59; *see generally* 12 Moore's Federal Practice Ch. 59, *New Trial; Altering or Amending a Judgment* (Matthew Bender 3d ed.).

[77] *See* Gasperini v. Center for Humanities, Inc., 518 U.S. 415, 439–440 (1996) (Stevens J. dissenting).

[78] Walker v. Armco Steel Corp. 446 U.S. 740, 748–751 (1980), *aff'g* Ragan v. Merchants Transfer & Warehouse Co., 337 U.S. 530, 533, 534 (1949); *see* Fed. R. Civ. P. 3.

[79] 446 U.S. at 752–753.

[80] 446 U.S. at 752–753; *see generally* 1 Moore's Federal Practice Ch. 3, *Commencing an Action* (Matthew Bender 3d ed.).

Applying the refined outcome-determination test, the Court noted that failure to apply the state service law might not create any problem of forum shopping, but would result in an "inequitable administration" of the law because a suit that could not be brought in state court could be maintained in federal court solely because of the fortuity of diversity citizenship.[81] Thus, in the absence of a federal rule directly on point, state service requirements that are "an integral part of the state statute of limitations" control in a state law action filed in federal diversity jurisdiction.[82]

State service requirements that are integral to the state statute of limitations may be found in statutes, court rules, or case law.[83] One federal appellate court has held that time computation provisions, like the commencement of action provisions, are an integral part of the statute of limitations. Thus, the federal court was required to use the state computation rules, rather than Federal Rule of Civil Procedure 6(a).[84]

The federal court's application of state limitations to state claims should be distinguished from a federal court's borrowing a state limitation to apply to a federal claim. In the former situation, the court must apply the state statute and all other provisions, such as tolling rules, that are "integral" to the state statute. In federal claim cases (litigation based on the federal court's federal question jurisdiction), it is less clear what the federal court may borrow that is integral to the state limitations provisions.[85]

Although service of process must be timely when a state limitations statute specifies that service is necessary to toll a limitations period, federal law determines the adequacy of the method of service.[86]

## § 15.07 RULE 4 DOES NOT DISPLACE STATE LAW GOVERNING PERSONAL JURISDICTION

Federal Rule of Civil Procedure 4, which governs service of process in federal court, does not implicitly mandate federal standards for determining when a nonresident is amenable to process. Rule 4(d)(3) describes the method for service

---

81 446 U.S. at 752–753.

82 446 U.S. at 751–753; *see also* Ragan v. Merchants Transfer & Warehouse Co., 337 U.S. 530, 533–534 (1949) (provisions integral to state statute of limitations must be applied in diversity cases).

83 Converse v. General Motors Corp., 893 F.2d 513, 515–516 (2d Cir. 1990) (state supreme court decision requiring service of process within limitations period applied in diversity action).

84 Alonzo v. ACF Prop. Mgmt., Inc., 643 F.2d 578, 580–581 (9th Cir. 1981) (case remanded to district court to determine whether day on which federal courts were closed constituted a holiday under state law); *see* Fed. R. Civ. P. 6(a); *see generally* 1 Moore's Federal Practice Ch. 6, *Computing and Extending Time; Time for Motion Papers* (Matthew Bender 3d ed.).

85 *Compare* West v. Conrail, 481 U.S. 35, 38–40 (1987) *with* Hardin v. Straub, 490 U.S. 536, 538–544 (1989).

86 Hanna v. Plumer, 380 U.S. 460, 463–464 (1965) (service was properly completed under Fed. R. Civ. P. 4 when plaintiff left summons with executor's wife, and state rule requiring in-hand service on executors was inapplicable); *but see* Witherow v. Firestone Tire & Rubber Co., 530 F.2d 160, 163–169 (3d Cir. 1976) (Fed. R. Civ. P. 4(h) granting judge discretion to amend or perfect service of process after expiration of limitations period did not supplant state service-of-process rules because they were integral part of state statute of limitations).

on a defendant. It does not address the validity of subjecting a nonresident corporation to service when a state long-arm statute does not reach the full extent of federal due process.[87] All appellate courts hold that state jurisdictional principles govern in federal diversity actions. Thus, state long-arm statutes govern a nonresident defendant's amenability to service in federal court.[88]

## § 15.08 RULE 15(c) INCORPORATES STATE RELATION-BACK RULES

Federal Rule of Civil Procedure 15(c) governs when an amended pleading relates back to the date of the original filing. Rule 15(c) permits an amendment that changes a party (usually to correct a misnomer or mistaken identity) to relate back to the original filing if the pleader satisfies certain conditions. The relation-back doctrine may permit a litigant to maintain a claim against the new party that the statute of limitations otherwise might bar. An amendment naming a new party relates back if the claim or defense the pleader asserts arose out of the occurrence in the original pleading and, within the period provided by Rule 4(m) for service (120 days after filing), the new party (1) receives notice of the action so as not be prejudiced in maintaining a defense on the merits, and (2) knew or should have known that, but for mistaken identity, the action would have been brought against the new party. Similarly, Rule 15(c) permits an amended claim or defense to relate back if the claim or defense arose out of the occurrence in the original pleading.[89]

Before 1991, federal courts divided on whether the state or federal relation-back rule applied when the state rule would permit the suit and the federal rule required dismissal. Decisions applying state law were based on the ground that application of Rule 15(c) would abridge substantive state rights in violation of the Rule Enabling Act, or that Rule 15(c) did not conflict with state law, because the state rule was not expressly a relation-back rule but rather was an integral part of the state statute of limitations.[90]

---

[87] *See* Fed. R. Civ. P. 4(d)(3); Arrowsmith v. United Press Int'l., 320 F.2d 219, 225–226 (2d Cir. 1963) (Congress has power to establish federal standard for personal jurisdiction in diversity cases but "[n]o federal statute or Rule of Civil Procedure speaks to the issue either expressly or by fair implication"); *see also* Fed. R. Civ. P. 4(e)–(k) (additional methods for service and territorial limits of effective service); Perkins v. Benguet Consolidated Mining Co., 342 U.S. 437, 440–441 (1952) (states not required to assert jurisdiction to limits of Due Process Clause); *see generally* Ch. 7, *Personal Jurisdiction in Federal Courts*; 1 Moore's Federal Practice Ch. 4, *Summons* (Matthew Bender 3d ed.).

[88] *See, e.g.*, Robinson v. Overseas Military Sales Corp., 21 F.3d 502, 510 (2d Cir. 1994) (personal jurisdiction over nonresident is governed by law of state in which federal court sits, subject to constitutional due process limitations); Pizarro v. Hoteles Concorde Int'l, 907 F. 2d 1256, 1258 (1st Cir. 1990) ("It is well established that in diversity cases, the district court's personal jurisdiction over a non-resident defendant is governed by the forum's long-arm statute").

[89] Fed. R. Civ. P. 15(c); *see* Fed. R. Civ. P. 4(j); *see generally* 3 Moore's Federal Practice Ch. 15, *Amended and Supplemental Pleadings* (Matthew Bender 3d ed.).

[90] *See, e.g.*, Diffley v. Allied-Signal, Inc. 921 F.2d 421, 423–424 (2d Cir. 1990) (statute that permitted plaintiffs to refile suit within six months after dismissal even though court lacked subject matter over original suit applied because it was part of state statute of limitations and did not conflict with Fed. R. Civ. P. 15(c)); Marshall v. Mulrenin, 508 F.2d 39, 44–45 (1st Cir. 1974) (state statute that would permit relation back even when new defendant did not have notice of suit applied over Fed. R. Civ. P. 15(c)).

The 1991 amendment to Rule 15(c) eliminated this potential conflict between Rule 15(c) and state law. The amendment provides that a change of party relates back to the original pleading if either Rule 15(c) is satisfied or relation back would be permitted by the law that provides the statute of limitations.[91] In other words, when state law provides the rule of decision in an action in federal court, the state relation-back rule applies if it is more liberal than the federal rule.

## § 15.09 RULE 23.1 AND STATE SECURITY REQUIREMENTS IN SHAREHOLDER DERIVATIVE SUITS

Federal Rule of Civil Procedure 23.1, which governs shareholder derivative suits,[92] does not displace state statutes that require plaintiff shareholders to post bond covering the corporation's expenses if the corporation prevails on the merits. In the pre-*Hanna* case of *Cohen v. Beneficial Industrial Loan Corporation*, the Supreme Court held that the plaintiffs had to satisfy a bond requirement to bring a federal diversity action.[93] The *Cohen* Court applied *Guaranty Trust* outcome-determination analysis. However, the *Hanna* Court implicitly reaffirmed *Cohen* by suggesting that the federal rule did not supplant state law, because the scope of Rule 23.1 was not sufficiently broad to cover the situation.[94] In fact, Rule 23.1 does not apply to security bonds (nor did its predecessor, which the Court considered in *Cohen*). Thus, courts may apply both Rule 23.1 and state bond requirements simultaneously.

## § 15.10 RULE 68 AND STATE LAW ON ATTORNEYS' FEES OR PENALTIES ON LOSING DEFENDANTS

Several federal courts have held that the scope of Federal Rule of Civil Procedure 68, which governs settlement offers,[95] is not broad enough to conflict with state law. The Seventh Circuit Court of Appeals held that Rule 68 did not conflict with a state penalty statute for an unsuccessful defendant who rejected a plaintiff's settlement demand, because Rule 68 only addresses penalties for unsuccessful plaintiffs who reject a defendant's settlement offer. Using the refined outcome-determination analysis, the court concluded that the court should apply the state rule governing penalties for unsuccessful plaintiffs.[96] The Eleventh Circuit Court of Appeals held that Rule 68 did not conflict with a state statute permitting a defendant to recover attorney's fees if the plaintiff unreasonably rejected a settlement offer or offer of judgment because Rule 68 does not provide for

---

[91] Fed. R. Civ. P. 15(c).

[92] *See generally* 5 Moore's Federal Practice Ch. 23.1, *Derivative Actions* (Matthew Bender 3d ed.).

[93] Cohen v. Beneficial Indus. Loan Corp, 337 U.S. 541, 543–545 (1949).

[94] Hanna v. Plumer, 380 U.S. 460, 470 (1965).

[95] *See* Fed. R. Civ. P. 68; *see generally* 13 Moore's Federal Practice Ch. 68, *Offer of Judgment* (Matthew Bender 3d ed.).

[96] S.A. Healy Co., v. Milwaukee Metro. Sewerage Dist., 60 F.3d 305, 310 (7th Cir. 1995).

attorneys' fees.[97]

## § 15.11 STATE LAWS AFFECTING ACCESS TO STATE COURTS: STATE DOOR-CLOSING STATUTES

State "door-closing" statutes make state court unavailable to certain types of litigants or cases. For example, a door-closing statute may prohibit a foreign corporation from suing in state court unless the corporation registers to do business in the state. Litigants barred from state courts by such statutes have attempted to bring suit in federal court when diversity exits. In a pair of pre-*Hanna* cases, *Angel v. Bullington* and *Woods v. Interstate Realty Co.*, the Supreme Court held that a federal court may not entertain a case that the state court would bar.[98] Arguably, the *Woods* and *Angel* holdings continue to apply after *Hanna* because state door-closing statutes are outcome-determinative, or because they do not involve the federal rules. Failure to apply the state statute significantly affects the litigation's outcome and encourages the plaintiff to choose the federal forum.

In a post-*Hanna* case, the Ninth Circuit applied a combination of the *Byrd* test and outcome-determination analysis to conclude that the plaintiffs' personal injury suit must be dismissed because under state law, their only remedy was an administrative claim for worker's compensation. The court reasoned that failure to apply state law would encourage forum-shopping and result in inequitable administration of the laws. Moreover, the state rule was intended to be bound up with the definitions of the parties' rights and obligations. Finally, the court could discern no countervailing federal considerations.[99]

However, in an earlier post-*Hanna* case, the Fourth Circuit also employed a combination of outcome-determination analysis and the *Byrd* test to conclude that a federal court need not apply a state door-closing statute when it does not evidence a clear state substantive policy, and failure to apply it would not lead to inequitable administration of the laws. The court did not apply a state statute that barred a nonresident from suing a foreign corporation on a cause of action arising outside the state. The court noted that the main purpose of the *Erie* doctrine is to prevent different legal treatment of parties merely because of a variation in their opponent's residence. Application of the state door-closing statute would result in just such a variation because the relief available in the federal court to the foreign residents would then turn on the state of the defendant's incorporation. Moreover, the non-resident plaintiffs had not chosen their forum frivolously. The suit involved

---

97 Tanker Mgmt., Inc. v. Brunson, 918 F.2d 1524, 1528 (11th Cir. 1990).

98 Angel v. Bullington, 330 U.S. 183, 191–192 (1947) (state statute precluding deficiency judgments in favor of mortgagees who foreclose prevented suit for deficiency judgment from being entertained in federal court); Woods v. Interstate Realty Co., 337 U.S. 535, 537 (1949) (state statute closed doors to foreign corporations that failed to register to do business in state).

99 Begay v. Kerr-McGee Corp., 682 F.2d 1311, 1317–1319 (9th Cir. 1982); *but see* Grand Bahama Petroleum Co. Ltd. v. Asiatic Petroleum Corp., 550 F.2d 1320 (2d Cir. 1977) (state statute did not bar foreign corporation from bringing diversity action under federal Arbitration Act because foreign corporation was seeking to vindicate federal rights).

multiple defendants, one of which could be served with process only in the state.[100] The court distinguished *Angel* and *Woods* on the grounds that the statutes in those cases both evidenced significant state substantive policies. The court was unable to ascertain a clear substantive state policy in this instance and concluded that the statute might be either a codification of the doctrine of forum non conveniens or a measure to relieve docket congestion.[101]

State door-closing statutes barring foreign corporations from suing in state court may conflict with Federal Rule of Civil Procedure 17(b), which provides that corporate capacity to sue is determined by the law of the state of incorporation. The Supreme Court did not address this potential conflict in *Woods*. However, at least one lower court has done so. A district court held that, instead of Rule 17(b), it had to apply a state statute that prevented a corporation from suing in the state unless it was qualified to do business there. Rule 17(b) would have permitted the suit, and therefore it abridged an existing state substantive right in violation of the Rules Enabling Act.[102]

## § 15.12 SANCTIONS UNDER FEDERAL COURT'S INHERENT POWER

Federal courts have inherent power to impose sanctions on a litigant for bad-faith conduct outside the scope of Federal Rule of Civil Procedure 11 and federal statutes. A federal court may invoke this power to assess attorneys' fees and related expenses against a party who has defrauded or attempted to defraud the court, filed false and frivolous pleadings, or engaged in delay tactics, oppression, and harassment.[103] The federal court may impose these sanctions notwithstanding state statutes or rules that prescribe the circumstances under which a prevailing party is entitled to an award. The *Hanna* outcome-determination test does not require the federal court to apply state law, because bad conduct sanctions do not implicate the twin aims of *Erie*. Imposition of sanctions under the court's inherent power depends on how the parties conduct themselves during the litigation and not on which party wins the lawsuit. Consequently, imposition of sanctions will not lead to forum-shopping. Similarly, imposition of sanctions will not result in inequitable administration of the law, because the court may impose sanctions on both citizens and non-citizens. Each party, by controlling their litigation conduct, has the power to determine whether sanctions are assessed.[104]

---

[100] Szantay v. Beech Aircraft Corp., 349 F.2d 60, 63–66 (4th Cir. 1965); *see also* Miller v. Davis, 507 F.2d 308, 312–318 (6th Cir. 1974) (following *Szantay* analysis, court applied state law depriving state courts of jurisdiction of suits involving foreign trusts).

[101] 349 F.2d at 63–66.

[102] McCollum Aviation, Inc. v. CIM Associates, Inc., 438 F. Supp. 245, 247 (S.D. Fla. 1977); *see* Fed. R. Civ. P. 17(b); *see generally* 4 MOORE'S FEDERAL PRACTICE Ch. 17, *Plaintiff and Defendant; Capacity; Public Officers* (Matthew Bender 3d ed.).

[103] *See generally* 2 MOORE'S FEDERAL PRACTICE Ch. 11, *Signing Pleadings, Motions, and Other Papers; Representations to the Court; Sanctions* (Matthew Bender 3d ed.).

[104] Chambers v. NASCO, Inc., 501 U.S. 32, 53–55 (1991) (Court upheld assessment of attorney's fees and costs against defendant who attempted to defraud court in breach of contract action, even though

## § 15.13 JURISDICTION AND VENUE ISSUES: CONTRACT CLAUSES PURPORTING TO CONFER PERSONAL JURISDICTION

The Eleventh Circuit has held that state law determines whether a forum selection clause containing the parties' consent to personal jurisdiction confers personal jurisdiction. On a motion to dismiss for lack of personal jurisdiction, the federal court had to determine whether to apply state or federal law to determine the effect of a contractual provision conferring personal jurisdiction. Determining that no federal rule or statute controlled, the court used outcome-determination analysis to resolve the *Erie* question. Federal law favors the enforcement of forum selection clauses. State law would enforce such clauses only if an independent ground for personal jurisdiction existed under the state long-arm statute. The court concluded that state law must be applied because application of federal law would violate the twin aims of *Erie*. Application of federal law would lead to forum shopping because plaintiffs would be encouraged to file in federal court to avoid dismissal for lack of jurisdiction under state law. Application of federal law would inequitably discriminate against forum state citizens because an action that the state court would bar could proceed in federal court "solely because of the fortuity that there is diversity of citizenship between the litigants."[105]

## § 15.14 FORUM NON CONVENIENS

The doctrine of forum non conveniens[106] has limited application in federal court. Since liberal transfer provisions permit litigants to transfer a case to a more convenient forum within the federal system,[107] the doctrine applies only when the alternative forum is abroad.[108] The Supreme Court has never answered the question whether the *Erie* doctrine requires a federal court sitting in diversity to apply state law on forum non conveniens.

Before adoption of the federal transfer provisions in 1948, earlier federal court decisions conflicted.[109] More recent authority characterizes forum non conveniens as an aspect of venue, and therefore a procedural matter for *Erie* purposes, even though differences between state and federal law of forum non conveniens can be

---

state law prohibited (1) punitive damage awards in breach of contract actions and (2) attorney's fee awards unless authorized by statute or contract).

[105] Alexander Proudfoot Co. World Headquarters v. Thayer, 877 F.2d 912, 916–919 (11th Cir. 1989); *but see* Northwestern Nat'l Ins. Co. v. Donovan, 916 F.2d 372, 374 (7th Cir. 1990) (parties agreed that federal law governed whether contractual consent to personal jurisdiction conferred personal jurisdiction over non-resident defendants and court concluded, but did not decide, that they were probably correct).

[106] *See generally* Ch. 9, *Change of Venue*.

[107] 28 U.S.C. § 1404(a).

[108] American Dredging Co. v. Miller, 510 U.S. 443, 449 n.2 (1994).

[109] *See* Gilbert v. Gulf Oil Corp., 153 F.2d 883, 885 (2d Cir. 1946), *rev'd on other grounds*, 330 U.S. 501 (1947) (federal courts need not apply state forum non conveniens doctrine); Weiss v. Routh, 149 F.2d 193, 194–195 (2d Cir. 1945) (state law controls forum non conveniens question in diversity case).

outcome determinative.[110] Thus, in those rare instances when the more convenient forum is in a foreign country and state and federal forum non conveniens doctrines differ, it appears that federal law applies.[111]

## § 15.15 FUNCTIONS OF JUDGE AND JURY

### [1] Federal Policy Favoring Jury Trial Applies

Under the *Byrd* decision, federal policy favoring a jury trial on disputed fact issues applies in diversity cases, even if under state law a judge would decide a disputed issue.[112] Applying the *Byrd* balancing test, federal courts have also concluded that federal law governs the number of jurors.[113]

### [2] Federal Law Generally Governs Review of Jury Verdicts

In general, federal law governs the role of the federal trial and appellate courts in reviewing the size of jury verdicts.[114] In reviewing a damage award, the district court must determine whether the jury's verdict is within state law standards, or whether the court should order a new trial or remittitur under Rule 59. The appellate court should then review the district court's determination under an abuse-of-discretion standard.[115] Review under an abuse of discretion standard is permitted by the Seventh Amendment's reexamination clause. "[A]ppellate review for abuse of discretion is reconcilable with the Seventh Amendment as a control necessary and proper to the fair administration of justice."[116]

When the state standard of review of a jury verdict is stricter than the federal standard, the outcome-determination test requires that federal courts apply the state standard. Failure to apply the state standard would lead to discrepancies in

---

110 Sibaja v. Dow Chemical Co., 757 F.2d 1215, 1219 (11th Cir. 1985) (federal law of forum non conveniens applies in diversity cases because doctrine is procedural); *see also* American Dredging Co. v. Miller, 510 U.S. 443, 453 (1994) (characterizing forum non conveniens as a venue matter that goes to process rather than substantive rights in context of admiralty case); Stewart Org., Inc. v. Ricoh Corp., 487 U.S. 22, 25–27 (1988).

111 *In re* Air Crash Disaster Near New Orleans, Louisiana on July 9, 1982, 821 F.2d 1147, 1157 (5th Cir. 1987), *vacated on other grounds*, 490 U.S. 1032 (1989) (federal doctrine applied to permit dismissal to foreign jurisdiction even though state law did not recognize forum non conveniens).

112 Byrd v. Blue Ridge Rural Elec. Coop., 356 U.S. 525, 533–540 (1958); Simler v. Conner, 372 U.S. 221, 222 (1963); Gallagher v. Wilton Enterprises, 962 F.2d 120, 122 (1st Cir. 1992) (federal court looks first to state law to determine elements of cause of action and remedies, then to federal law to characterize action and remedies as equitable or legal); *but see* Justice v Pennzoil Co., 598 F.2d 1339, 1343 (4th Cir. 1979) (state law applied, requiring ultimate question to be judicially decided based on jury findings).

113 Rideau v. Parkem Indus. Servs., Inc., 917 F.2d 892, 895 (5th Cir 1990) (number of jurors is not integral part of state-created right).

114 Donovan v. Penn Shipping Co., 429 U.S. 648, 649 (1977) (per curiam).

115 Browning-Ferris v. Kelco Disposal Inc., 492 U.S. 257, 279 (1989); *see* Fed. R. Civ. P. 59; *see generally* 12 MOORE'S FEDERAL PRACTICE Ch. 59, *New Trial; Altering or Amending a Judgment* (Matthew Bender 3d ed.).

116 Gasperini v. Center for Humanities, Inc., 518 U.S. 415, 435 (1996); *see* U.S. Const., Amend. VII; *see also* Consorti v. Armstrong World Indus., Inc., 103 F.3d 2, 4–5 (2d Cir. 1996).

verdicts, thus encouraging forum-shopping. However, the Seventh Amendment does not permit an appellate court to apply a stricter state standard. In such cases, the competing interests of the *Erie* doctrine and the Seventh Amendment can be accommodated if the federal district court, but not the appellate court, applies the stricter state standard (*see* § 15.05).[117]

## § 15.16 FEDERAL RULES OF EVIDENCE AND STATE EVIDENTIARY PROVISIONS

### [1] Federal Rules Generally Apply in Federal Court

*Erie* outcome-determination analysis is largely inapplicable to the Federal Rules of Evidence. Congress directly enacted the Federal Rules of Evidence in 1975,[118] and therefore the federal evidence rules do not come within the purview of the Rules Enabling Act.[119] Under the Rules of Decision Act[120] and the Supremacy Clause,[121] federal evidence rules apply in federal court, unless in enacting the rules Congress exceeded its powers to regulate federal courts.[122]

Presumably, the analytical approach to determine when a Federal Rule of Evidence is applicable is the same as for federal procedural statutes. That is, the Federal Rule of Evidence applies when it covers the disputed point and represents a valid congressional exercise of authority under the Constitution.[123] Under this approach, courts have held that the Federal Rules of Evidence ordinarily govern the admissibility of evidence in diversity cases.[124]

---

[117] Gasperini v. Center for Humanities, Inc., 518 U.S. 415, 430 (1996) ("Erie precludes a recovery in federal court significantly larger than the recovery that would have been tolerated in state court"); Steinke v. Beach Bungee, Inc., 105 F.3d 192, 197–198 (4th Cir. 1997) ($12 million verdict remanded to district court to apply South Carolina remittitur standard because record did not indicate on what basis district court denied defendant's motion for remittitur); Consorti v. Armstrong World Indus., Inc., 103 F.3d 2, 4–5 (2d Cir. 1996) (case remanded to district court so it could consider issue of remittitur under New York "deviates materially" standard, rather than federal "shocks conscience" standard).

[118] Pub. L. No. 93-595, 88 Stat. 1959 (1975).

[119] Flaminio v. Honda Motor Co., 733 F.2d 463, 470–471 (7th Cir. 1984) ("[h]aving been enacted by Congress rather than promulgated by the Supreme Court pursuant to the Rules Enabling Act, . . . the Federal Rules of Evidence are not subject to the Act's proviso that rules promulgated under it 'shall not abridge, enlarge or modify any substantive right' ").

[120] 28 U.S.C. § 1652.

[121] U.S. Const., Art. VI cl. 2.

[122] Flaminio v. Honda Motor Co., 733 F.2d 463, 470–472 (7th Cir. 1984) (Fed. R. Evid. 407 prohibiting admission of evidence of subsequent remedial measures in personal injury cases applies in diversity action even though state law would permit introduction of such evidence).

[123] *See* Stewart Org., Inc. v. Ricoh, 487 U.S. 22, 25–27 (1988); *but see* Stutzman v. CRST, Inc., 997 F.2d 291, 295 (7th Cir. 1993) (Federal Rule of Evidence is applicable if it "really regulates procedure — the judicial process for enforcing rights and duties recognized by substantive law and for justly administering remedy and redress for disregard or infraction of them").

[124] *See, e.g.*, 997 F.2d at 295 (Federal Rules of Evidence govern admissibility of expert testimony in federal diversity cases); Barron v. Ford Motor Co., 965 F.2d 195, 198 (7th Cir. 1992) ("Even in diversity cases the rules of evidence applied in federal courts are the Federal Rules of Evidence rather than state rules"); Kelly v. Crown Equip. Co., 970 F.2d 1273, 1275–1278 (3d Cir. 1992) (Fed. R. Evid. 407 applied in

### [2] Some State Evidentiary Rules Are Substantive and Are Applied in Federal Court

Although the federal rules of evidence ordinarily govern the admissibility of evidence in diversity cases, the federal courts have concluded that some state evidentiary rules are really rules of substantive law and must be applied whenever state law provides the rule of decision.[125]

# PART C
# DETERMINING THE CONTENT OF STATE LAW

## § 15.17 BINDING EFFECT OF STATE COURT DECISIONS

### [1] Decisions of State's Highest Court Are Binding on Federal Courts

The highest court of a state is the final arbiter of state law. When state law provides the rule of decision under the *Erie* doctrine, federal courts must generally accept a decision of the state's highest court as a definitive statement of state law.[126] The federal court is bound by a decision of the state's highest court, even if it believes the decision is unwise or incorrect.[127] However, the federal court may refuse to follow a decision of the state's highest court if clear and persuasive data indicate that the state's highest court would modify, limit, or overrule the decision.[128] Persuasive indications that a state's highest court would modify, limit, or overrule an earlier decision include a state's subsequent enactment or amendment of a statute that apparently changes the law as stated in the decision;[129] later decisions of the state's highest court that implicitly overrule the decision;[130] or dicta from the state's highest court criticizing or casting doubt on

---

diversity action because it is "arguably procedural" notwithstanding state law to the contrary).

[125] Hottle v. Beech Aircraft Corp., 47 F.3d 106, 109–110 (4th Cir. 1995) (state evidence rule excluding party's internal rules and regulations to show negligence was sufficiently bound-up with state substantive policies to apply in diversity case); Milam v. State Farm Mut. Auto Ins. Co., 972 F.2d 166, 170 (7th Cir. 1992) (federal court sitting in diversity will apply state substantive policy making it more difficult to prove state-law claim, even if state policy is nominally declared to be rule of evidence).

[126] West v. American Tel. & Tel. Co., 311 U.S. 223, 237–238 (1940); Doe v. Otte, 248 F.3d 832,839 (9th Cir. 2001); Retail Assocs., Inc. v. Macy's East, Inc., 245 F.3d 694, 698 (8th Cir. 2001).

[127] 311 U.S. at 237–238 (federal court must "ascertain from all the available data what the state law is and apply it rather than to prescribe a different rule, however superior it may appear").

[128] 311 U.S. at 237–238.

[129] Dawkins v. White Prods. Corp., 443 F.2d 589, 593–594 (5th Cir. 1971) (when long-arm statute was amended to provide for personal jurisdiction on basis of tort committed in state, federal court declined to follow state supreme court decision interpreting earlier version of statute as not permitting such jurisdiction).

[130] *See* Pauley v. Combustion Eng'g, Inc., 528 F. Supp. 759, 761–763 (D.C. W. Va. 1981) (district court concluded state supreme court would adopt particular interpretation of discovery rule in asbestos exposure cases because it had done so in other related types of cases).

the decision.[131]

A federal court may not refuse to follow a decision of a state's highest court merely because it is many years old. However, the Supreme Court has suggested that a federal court may decline to follow an old decision if a developing line of authorities, dicta, or legislative developments indicate that the state's highest court would no longer follow the decision.[132] Several appellate courts have followed this approach.[133] [134]

Further, a federal court may not refuse to follow a decision of the state's highest court that has not been overruled, despite the fact that the state supreme court had expressed clear misgivings about the decision and apparently limited the case to its facts. Only if the federal court could reasonably assume that the state court would overrule the decision if directly faced with the issue may a court disregard the precedent.

In some circumstances, a defendant may remove a case to federal court after the state's highest court has remanded the case to a lower state court.[135] The federal court must follow the state's highest court decision even if the highest court itself would not be bound on a second appeal. In *Moore v. Illinois Central Railway Co.*, for example, an employee brought suit in Mississippi state court for wrongful discharge. The trial court rendered judgment for the defendant. The Mississippi Supreme Court reversed and remanded. The plaintiff amended the complaint to confer diversity jurisdiction and the defendant removed the case. The district court followed the Mississippi Supreme Court's earlier decision. The appellate court reversed, declining to follow the state supreme court because the Mississippi Supreme Court does not regard itself bound by a former decision on a second appeal. The United States Supreme Court reversed, holding that federal appellate courts do not have the same power to reconsider state law interpretations as do the highest state courts which render a decision.[136]

Although a federal court must defer to and is bound by a state's highest court's construction of a statute, federal courts are not bound to adopt that court's legal conclusion regarding whether a legislature's purpose is to punish in order to determine whether the statute is subject to the requirements of the ex post facto clause. Federal courts must independently determine whether the state court's

---

131 Mason v. American Emery Wheel Works, 241 F.2d 906, 908–909 (1st Cir. 1957) (court declined to follow state supreme court decision in light of pervasive trend in other jurisdictions toward modern approach, and recent dictum from state supreme court indicating approval of trend).

132 Bernhardt v. Polygraphic Co., 350 U.S. 198, 204–205 (1956) (Supreme Court affirmed appellate conclusion that 1910 Vermont Supreme Court decision, holding arbitration agreements unenforceable, was current Vermont law).

133 *See, e.g.*, Miller v. Premier Corp., 608 F.2d 973, 984–987 (4th Cir. 1979) (court declined to apply 80 year-old state choice of law rule for usury cases with multi-state connections because of major intervening developments in choice of law theory and personal jurisdiction).

134 Invest Almaz v. Temple-Inland Forest Prods. Corp., 243 F3d. 57, 74–75 (1st. Cir. 2001).

135 *See generally* Ch. 6, *Removal.*

136 Moore v. Illinois Cent. R.R., 312 U.S. 630, 633–634 (1941).

statutory interpretation renders the statute punitive and thus potentially violative of the ex post facto clause.[137]

### [2] Decisions of Intermediate State Appellate Courts Usually Must Be Followed

When the state's highest court has not ruled on an issue, federal courts must decide the way the highest state court would rule if presented with the issue. Thus, federal courts should follow decisions of intermediate state appellate courts unless persuasive data indicate that the highest state court would decide the issue differently.[138] Although not binding on federal courts, decisions by a state's intermediate appellate court provides evidence of how the state's highest court would rule on the issue, and federal courts are entitled to consider those decisions.[139] It is immaterial whether the appellate court decision is published or unpublished.[140]

A federal court may refuse to follow an intermediate state appellate court decision if subsequent statutory enactments or amendments change state law;[141] if decisions of the state's highest court in analogous or related areas suggest that the highest court would decide the issue differently;[142] if the decision conflicts with a statute or statutory scheme;[143] if considered dicta of the state's highest court contradicts lower court decisions;[144] or if there are differences between state circuit and district courts.[145] However, a federal court may not ignore an intermediate court decision because it believes the decision wrong, bad policy, contrary to the majority rule in other jurisdictions, lacking common sense, or not

---

137 Doe v. Otte, 248 F.3d 832, 839 (9th Cir. 2001).

138 Hicks v. Feiock, 485 U.S. 624, 630 n.3 (1988), *quoting* West v. American Tel. & Tel. Co., 311 U.S. 223, 237–238 (1940); General refractories Co. v. Fireman's Fund Ins. Co., 337 F.3d 297, 303–04 (3d Cir. 2003); Stanek v. Greco, 323 F.3d 476, 478 (6th Cir. 2003).

139 Clark v. State Farm Mut. Auto Ins. Co., 319 F.3d 1234, 1240–41 (10th Cir. 2003); General refractories Co., 337 F.3d at 303–04 n.1.

140 Ziegler v. IBP Hog Market, 249 F.3d 509, 517–18 (6th Cir. 2001).

141 *See* Dawkins v. White Prods. Corp., 443 F.2d 589, 593–594 (5th Cir. 1971) (when long-arm statute was amended to provide personal jurisdiction for torts committed in state, federal court declined to follow state supreme court decision interpreting earlier statute not permitting such jurisdiction).

142 *See* Green v. Walker, 910 F.2d 291, 295–296 (5th Cir. 1990) (relying on Louisiana Supreme Court decision that doctor owed duty of due care to unborn child whose parents were patients, court held doctor had duty to use due care when performing employee physical even though Louisiana appellate court held to contrary).

143 *See* Ground Air Transfer, Inc. v. Westates Airlines, Inc., 899 F.2d 1269, 1275 (1st Cir. 1990) (court declined to follow intermediate court decision granting injunction in commercial case because state U.C.C. did not appear to allow such injunctions; court was convinced that state supreme court would not follow intermediate decision).

144 Nolan v. Transocean Air Lines, 365 U.S. 293, 293–296 (1961) (Supreme Court vacated and remanded appellate judgment to consider California Supreme Court decision containing considered dictum on point).

145 Bravo v. United States, 577 F.3d 1324, 1325–26 (11th Cir. 2009) (despite trend in state court decisions, "cross-currents" in those decisions required examination of all available data); Matheny v. Glen Falls Ins. Co., 152 F.3d 348, 354 (5th Cir. 1998).

"what it ought to be."[146]

For example, the Fifth Circuit declined to follow a Louisiana intermediate court decision that a property owner could be liable for a repair person's injuries under the Louisiana Civil Code. The Fifth Circuit concluded that the Louisiana Supreme Court would decide otherwise, based on (1) a subsequent Louisiana Supreme Court opinion holding that a property owner cannot be liable for injuries sustained on the property unless the owner exposed the injured person to an unreasonable risk, and (2) dicta from other Louisiana appellate cases that property owners could not be held liable for injuries to repair persons.[147] Similarly, the Seventh Circuit declined to follow an Illinois appellate decision that an employer unilaterally could modify an employment contract by inserting a disclaimer in the employee manual. The Seventh Circuit concluded that the Illinois Supreme Court would rule otherwise on general contract principles, requiring consideration to support a contract modification. The federal court also looked to an Illinois Supreme Court decision holding that parties may not unilaterally modify contracts.[148]

An intermediate court decision is binding on the federal court regardless of whether the state's highest court has refused to review it. However, the highest state court's refusal to review the intermediate court decision does strengthen the decision's binding effect.[149] When intermediate state appellate court decisions conflict, the federal court must determine which approach the state's highest court would likely adopt.[150] When state decisions set forth different doctrine, federal courts typically follow the majority position.[151] Finally, federal courts are not bound by state intermediate appellate dicta.[152]

## [3] Trial Court Decisions Usually Are Not Binding

When neither the state's highest court nor its intermediate appellate courts have ruled on an issue, federal courts should give some weight to state trial court decisions. Unpublished trial court decisions that are not binding on any other state courts also do not bind federal courts.[153]

---

146 Maska U.S., Inc. v. Kansa Gen. Ins. Co., 198 F.3d 74, 80 (2d Cir. 1999).

147 Ladue v. Chevron, 920 F.2d 272, 274–277 (5th Cir. 1991).

148 Robinson v. Ada S. McKinley Community Servs., Inc., 19 F.3d 359, 363–364 (7th Cir. 1994).

149 West v. American Tel. & Tel. Co., 311 U.S. 223, 237 (1940); *cf.* Exxon Co. v. Banque de Paris, 889 F.2d 674, 675–677 (5th Cir. 1989) (court followed Texas appellate opinion even though Texas Supreme Court had denied, rather than refused, writ of error).

150 Stifle v. Marathon Petroleum Co., 876 F.2d 552, 557–559 (7th Cir. 1989).

151 *See* FDIC v. McSweeney, 976 F.2d 532, 536 n.3 (9th Cir. 1992) (California Supreme Court would be unlikely to follow intermediate court decision that conflicted with "well-settled California law" and decision was therefore not binding).

152 *In re* Pladson, 35 F.3d 462, 466 (9th Cir. 1994) (court distinguished facts of one intermediate decision and declined to follow pure dicta in another, reversing denial of debtor's claimed homestead exemption).

153 King v. Order of United Commercial Travelers of Am., 333 U.S. 153, 153–162 (1948) (decision of South Carolina common pleas court not binding on federal district court); *see* Commissioner of Internal Revenue v. Bosch's Estate, 387 U.S. 456, 462–466 (1967) (state trial court decisions are not controlling when state law is rule of decision in federal question case).

Published state trial decisions or those with precedential value, however, may be controlling. In a widely criticized opinion, the Supreme Court held a federal district court was bound by two New Jersey chancery decisions. The Court concluded that (1) the decisions were printed with the state's highest court opinions in the New Jersey equity reports, (2) the chancery court had statewide jurisdiction, (3) only the Court of Errors and Appeals could review the decisions, and (4) the Court of Errors and Appeals would not set aside a uniform ruling except for compelling reasons.[154]

## § 15.18 APPELLATE COURTS MUST APPLY CHANGE IN STATE LAW THAT OCCURS WHILE APPEAL IS PENDING

In *Vandenbark v. Owen-Illinois Glass Co.*, the Supreme Court held that an appellate court must apply current state law when state law changes while an appeal is pending.[155] Similarly, a district court must recognize a change in state law that occurs while trial is pending.[156]

The purpose of the *Vandenbark* holding was to eliminate inconsistent federal and state law interpretations. However, inconsistency is eliminated only in states in which appellate courts apply subsequent changes to prior lower court decisions. In states that deny retroactive effect, the *Vandenbark* decision encourages different rather than similar results. In those states, a state appellate court would not consider any change that occurs while an appeal is pending; but in the same situation, federal appellate courts would be obliged to apply the subsequent state decision and reverse a lower federal court if necessary. Consistency can be achieved only if the federal appellate courts determine what effect the state appellate courts would give to the change. If the state courts would deny the subsequent change retroactive effect and leave the trial court's decision undisturbed, federal courts should act similarly. When state courts would apply the intervening change, federal courts should be required to do so. This approach is arguably more in keeping with the *Erie* doctrine.

The *Vandenbark* decision does not require federal appellate courts to make an independent determination whether a state will apply a change retroactively. Several appellate courts have acknowledged that applying state retroactivity rules

---

[154] Fidelity Union Trust Co. v. Field, 311 U.S. 169, 178 (1940); *see* King v. Order of United Commercial Travelers of Am., 333 U.S. 153, 153–162 (1948) ("Nor is our decision to be taken as promulgating a general rule that federal courts need never abide by determinations of state law by state trial courts. As indicated by the *Fidelity Union Trust Co.* case, other situations in other states may well call for a different result.").

[155] Vandenbark v. Owens-Illinois Glass Co., 311 U.S. 538, 541 (1941) (appellate court was required to consider statutory amendment and two overruled cases occurring after district court dismissed suit for failure to state cause of action); *see also* Mills v. Rogers, 457 U.S., 291, 302–303 (1982) (case remanded to appellate court in light of intervening state supreme court decision that, while not directly on point, could affect case); Huddleston v. Dwyer, 322 U.S. 232, 237–238 (1944) (case remanded to appellate court in light of intervening state supreme court decision).

[156] *See* Industrial Consultants, Inc. v. H.S. Equities, Inc., 646 F.2d 746, 747–749 (2d Cir. 1981) (district court properly followed state supreme court decision decided one year after action began).

would more closely achieve the uniformity sought in *Erie*. In these cases, the courts determined that the state courts would have applied change retroactively. Federal courts either have applied the "hard and fast approach" seemingly mandated by *Vandenbark*[157] or expressly declined to endorse this or a more flexible *Erie* approach, since both yield the same result.[158]

## § 15.19 DETERMINING STATE LAW WHEN IT IS UNSETTLED

### [1] Difficulty in Determining State Law Does Not Justify Dismissal

Difficulty in determining applicable state law does not warrant a district court to dismiss or stay its proceedings until a state court can do so. Absent special circumstances, federal district courts must decide questions involving the application of state law even if they are extremely difficult to resolve.[159] Under appropriate circumstances, federal courts may invoke the abstention doctrine to decline to decide a case even though the court has jurisdiction of a justiciable controversy.[160] Abstention due to unclear state law is "an extraordinary and narrow exception to the duty of a district court to adjudicate a controversy properly before it," and is permitted only under "exceptional circumstances."[161] The leading Supreme Court decision sanctioning abstention in diversity cases, *Louisiana Power and Light Co. v. Thibodaux*, indicates that a federal court may abstain only when (1) state law is unclear, and (2) the case intimately involves the state government's sovereign prerogative.[162]

The sovereign prerogative at issue in *Thibodaux* was whether a city had the power to take property under state eminent domain. Since the *Thibodaux* decision, the Supreme Court has done little to explain what other government interests might justify abstention in a diversity case. In the one subsequent case ordering abstention for unclear state law, the issue was the validity of a water use statute under the New Mexico constitution. The Supreme Court held that abstention was justified because of the state's vital interest in regulating water rights in such an arid state.[163]

Many states have adopted a certification procedure that permits the federal courts to certify an unsettled question of state law to the state's highest court for

---

[157] Nelson v. Brunswick Corp., 503 F.2d 376, 381 (9th Cir. 1974).

[158] *See* FBW Enterprises v. Victorio Co., 821 F.2d 1393, 1394–1396 (9th Cir. 1987) (court applied state supreme court decision interpreting state deficiency judgment legislation retroactively after concluding that state courts would also do so).

[159] Colorado River Water Conservation Dist. v. United States, 424 U.S. 800, 813–818 (1976); Meredith v. Winter Haven, 320 U.S. 228, 234 (1943).

[160] Abstention is discussed in detail in Ch. 13, *The Abstention Doctrine*.

[161] Allegheny County v. Frank Mashuda Co., 360 U.S. 185, 188–189 (1959).

[162] Louisiana Power & Light Co. v. City of Thibodaux, 360 U.S. 25, 25–31 (1959).

[163] Kaiser Steel Corp. v. W. S. Ranch Co., 391 U.S. 593, 593–594 (1968).

resolution. The Supreme Court has endorsed the certification process.[164] Certification is a voluntary procedure that rests in the federal court's sound discretion.[165] Certification is appropriate when either (1) the question is of first impression or likely to recur, (2) the question involves a question of state constitutional law, (3) state precedents clearly conflict or are unclear, (4) the applicable law is not the law of the state in which the federal court is located, (5) the unsettled law is outcome determinative, or (6) the issue is important to the state. The federal court is bound to follow state law declared by its highest court in response to a certified question.[166]

### [2] Federal Court Must Predict How State's Highest Court Would Rule

When state law is unsettled, the federal court must attempt to predict how the state's highest court would rule if confronted with the issue.[167]

In the absence of direct authority, the federal court may look to state high court decisions in related or analogous cases for an indication of how the state's highest court is likely to rule.[168] Similarly, considered dicta of the state's highest court is persuasive evidence of how the state court might rule. In absence of other authority, federal courts may follow the considered dicta of the state's highest court. Next, federal courts look at the relevant decisions of the state's intermediate courts. Some courts hold that decisions of intermediate state courts provide guidance but are not controlling, while other conclude that a federal court is bound by intermediate state precedent unless the court is convinced by other persuasive data that the highest court of the state would have decided otherwise. Federal courts also look to the policy underlying a statute or other pertinent public policy considerations.[169]

Additionally, federal courts may consider scholarly treatises, law review articles, and Restatements of the law.[170] Opinions of a state attorney general are

---

[164] Lehman Bros. v. Schein, 416 U.S. 386, 391 (1974) (certification saves "time, energy, and resources and helps build a cooperative judicial federalism").

[165] 416 U.S. at 391.

[166] Grover by Grover v. Eli Lilly & Co., 33 F.3d 716, 719 (6th Cir. 1994) ("A federal court that certifies a question of state law should not be free to treat the answer as merely advisory unless the state court specifically contemplates that result").

[167] *See* Commissioner of Internal Revenue v. Estate of Bosch, 387 U.S. 456, 465 (1967); Bernhardt v. Polygraphic Co., 350 U.S. 198 (1956); Avemco Ins. Co. v. Auburn Flying Serv., Inc., 242 F.3d 819, 822 (8th Cir. 2001); Stauth v. Nat'l Union Fire Ins. Co. of Pittsburgh, 236 F.3d 1260, 1267 (10th Cir. 2001); Sprint PCS L.P. v. Connecticut Siting Council, 222 F.3d 113, 115 (2d Cir. 2000).

[168] Maska U.S., Inc. v. Kansa Gen. Ins. Co., 198 F.3d at 78; Farris v. J.C. Penney Co., 176 F.3d 706, 713 (3d Cir. 1999).

[169] F.D.I.C. v. Ogden Copr., 202 F.3d 454, 460–61 (1st Cir. 2000); Jurrens v. Hartford Life Ins. Co., 190 F.3d 919, 922 (8th Cir. 1999).

[170] McKenna v. Ortho Pharm. Corp., 622 F.2d 657, 662–663 (3d Cir. 1980); Cox v. Nasche, 70 F.3d 1030, 1031 (9th Cir. 1995) (court relied on Restatement because it noted that Alaska state courts frequently did so).

persuasive, but not binding, authority.[171] A federal court may examine cases from other jurisdictions to determine what law the controlling state will adopt, particularly in the complete absence of any state decisions.[172]

If a higher federal court has ruled on a particular point of state law, a lower court will follow that decision in absence of an authoritative state decision. A prior federal appellate decision is persuasive,[173] and in some circuits controlling, in a subsequent case before an appellate court of the same circuit, absent supervening state court decisions.[174] Similarly, a federal court may be guided by another circuit's decisions.[175] However, when a federal court predicts how a state supreme court would rule, that holding establishes no precedent in state law.[176]

Circuit panels are for the most part bound by prior panel decisions closely on point,[177] subject to two exceptions. First, an existing panel decision may be undermined by subsequently announced controlling authority, such as a Supreme Court opinion, an en banc opinion of the circuit court, or a statutory overruling. The second exception covers those relatively rare instances when authority that postdates the original decision, although not directly controlling, nevertheless offers a sound reason for believing that the former panel would change its mind in light of fresh developments.[178] Further, if two decisions of previous federal panels within the same circuit conflict, the first decision constitutes binding precedent.[179]

In *F.D.I.C. v. Abraham*, the Fifth Circuit carefully analyzed the effects of a prior decision of a different panel of that circuit and an intervening state appellate court case in light of the continued silence of the state's highest court.[180] Preliminarily, the court reasoned that as a strict stare decisis court, one panel of the Fifth Circuit may not disregard, much less overrule, the decision of a prior panel. Thus, when considering a governing question of state law on which a prior panel has ruled, the subsequent panel's obligation to follow that ruling is not alleviated by intervening

---

[171] Florida *ex rel.* Shevin v. Exxon Corp., 526 F.2d 266, 275 (5th Cir. 1976).

[172] Cox v. Nasche, 70 F.3d 1030, 1031–1032 (9th Cir. 1995) (court concluded Alaska Supreme Court would follow majority of states in holding that signed release of information regarding employment created absolute privilege against defamation); Leon's Bakery Inc. v. Grinnell Corp., 990 F.2d 44, 48 (2d Cir. 1993) (federal court may consider all sources used by state's highest court, including decisions of other jurisdictions); Ross v. Creighton Univ., 957 F.2d 410, 414–415 (7th Cir. 1992) (Illinois Supreme Court would not recognize claim for educational malpractice because overwhelming majority of states had rejected it).

[173] *See* State Farm Mut. Auto. Ins. Co. v. Travelers Indem. Co., 433 F.2d 311, 312 (10th Cir. 1970) (court followed its prior decision in interpreting two insurance policies rather than unreported trial court decision).

[174] Roboserve, Ltd. v. Tom's Foods, Inc., 940 F.2d 1441, 1451 (11th Cir. 1991) (court declined to follow prior Eleventh Circuit decision because state intermediate appellate decision explicitly contradicted it).

[175] *See* Warren Bros. Co. v. Cardi Corp., 471 F.2d 1304, 1307–1308 (1st Cir. 1973) (court relied on analogous federal decisions interpreting Miller Act to interpret comparable state statute).

[176] Pacheco v. United States, 220 F.3d 1126, 1131 (9th Cir. 2000).

[177] Maine General Med. Ctr. v. Shalala, 205 F.3d 493, 497 (1st Cir. 2000).

[178] *Id.*

[179] Cohen v. Office Depot, Inc., 204 F.3d 1069, 1073–77 (11th Cir. 2000); United States v. Texas Tech. Univ., 171 F.3d 279, 285 (5th Cir. 1999).

[180] FDIC v. Abraham, 137 F.3d 264 (5th Cir. 1998).

decisions of intermediate state appellate courts unless the subsequent decisions are "clearly contrary" to a previous decision of the relevant circuit. Stated differently, the Fifth Circuit should not disregard its own precedent on the basis of a subsequent intermediate state appellate court decision unless that decision comprises unanimous or near-unanimous holdings from several — preferably a majority — of the intermediate appellate courts of the state in question. Of course, a different result may be required by a clearly contrary subsequent holding of the highest state court or a subsequent statutory authority, squarely on point. Further, a federal court may be guided by another circuit's decisions.

### [3] Policy Against Expanding State Law

Most federal courts conservatively predict how a state's highest court will rule on an unsettled state law issue. In general they hold that a federal court's role in applying state law is to rule on state law as it exists, and not to surmise or suggest its expansion.[181] The First and Seventh Circuits, in particular, have articulated a policy against expanding state law in diversity cases that the plaintiff elected to bring in federal court, as opposed to those the defendant removed to federal court.[182] However, the Seventh Circuit has suggested that it would be willing to take a less conservative approach in diversity cases a defendant removed to federal court.[183]

### [4] Interpreting Statutes Never Construed by State Court

When a state court has never construed a state statute, the federal court must exercise its independent judgment as to what the statute means, guided by any analogous decisions and the court's own interpretation of the statute's intended public policy. The federal court must carefully review available resources to predict how the state's highest court would interpret the statute. These resources include the statutory language, legislative history, the statutory scheme set in historical context, how the statute can be woven into the state law with the least distortion of the total statutory fabric, state decisional law, any federal cases that construe the

---

181 Karas v. American Family Ins. Co., 33 F.3d 995, 999–1001 (8th Cir. 1994) (court declined to permit plaintiff to recover damages for mental suffering in breach of contract action when state's highest court had not ruled on issue); Burris Chemical, Inc. v. USX Corp., 10 F.3d 243, 247 (4th Cir. 1993) (court declined to extend discovery rule, which can be applied to toll statute of limitations, to notice provision in contract); *but see* Saloomey v. Jeppesen & Co., 707 F.2d 671, 674–676 (2d. Cir. 1983) (court expanded state law by ruling that Connecticut would adopt most significant relationship test as its choice of law theory in aviation accident cases, even though state supreme court had specifically declined to adopt most significant relationship test for automobile accident cases).

182 *See, e.g.*, Martel v. Stafford, 992 F.2d 1244, 1247 (1st Cir. 1993) ("[w]e have repeatedly warned that a plaintiff who . . . selects a federal forum in preference to an available state forum may not expect the federal court to steer state law into unprecedented configurations"); Shaw v. Republic Drill Corp., 810 F.2d 149, 150 (7th Cir. 1987) ("our policy will continue to be one that requires plaintiffs desirous of succeeding on novel state law claims to present those claims initially in state court."

183 Haynes v. Alfred A. Knopf, Inc., 8 F.3d 1222, 1234 (7th Cir. 1993) ("If the plaintiffs had filed this case in an Illinois state court and it had been removed to the federal district court, they would have had no choice, and then we would have been duty-bound to be as innovative as we thought it plausible to suppose the Illinois courts would be"); Anderson v. Marathon Petroleum Co., 801 F.2d 936, 942 (7th Cir. 1986).

state statute, and scholarly works.[184] The rulings of a state administrative agency charged with enforcement and construction of a state statute or rule are entitled to respectful consideration.[185] And, in interpreting a state statute that state courts have not interpreted, the court may consider decisions interpreting an analogous federal statute.[186]

## § 15.20 COURT OF APPEALS *DE NOVO* REVIEW OF STATE LAW DETERMINATION

The court of appeals must review *de novo* a district court's determination of state law.[187] Before the Supreme Court's 1991 decision in *Salve Regina College v. Russell*, many appellate courts reviewed a district court's determination of state law under a deferential abuse of discretion standard. Under this standard, the appellate court would reverse the district court's determination only if it were clearly erroneous.[188]

In *Salve Regina*, the Court concluded that appellate deference to a district court's determination of state law is inconsistent with the twin aims of the *Erie* doctrine — discouraging forum-shopping and avoiding inequitable administration of the laws. According to the Court, deferential appellate review invites divergent development of state law among the federal trial courts even within a single state. Moreover, by denying a litigant access to meaningful review of state-law claims, deferential review creates a dual enforcement system for state-created rights, in which the substantive rule applied to a dispute may depend on the choice of forum.[189]

*De novo* review requires the appellate court to substitute its determination of an unsettled state law issue for the district court's when the appellate court would resolve the issue differently, but the appellate court cannot conclude that the

---

[184] Bensmiller v. E.I. DuPont De Nemours & Co., 47 F.3d 79, 82 (2d Cir. 1995) (court construed state long-arm jurisdiction statute); Travelers Ins. Co. v. 633 Third Assocs., 14 F.3d 114, 119–124 (2d Cir. 1994) (construing state waste statute, court concluded that equitable action would lie for failure to pay property taxes).

[185] *See* University of Tenn. v. Elliott, 478 U.S. 788, 797–799 (1986) (federal courts must accord state agency's fact-finding same preclusive effect it would be entitled in state courts where agency acted in judicial capacity and parties had adequate opportunity to litigate); Law Students Civil Rights Research Council, Inc. v. Wadmond, 401 U.S. 154, 167 (1971); Dionne v. Mayor and City Council of Baltimore, 40 F.3d 677, 679 (4th Cir. 1994) (federal court not required to consider preclusive effect under state law of state administrative decisions that state courts have not reviewed).

[186] Lenhardt v. Basic Institute of Technology, 55 F.3d 377, 380–381 (8th Cir. 1995) (court examined decisions under Title VII and Age Discrimination in Employment Act to interpret Missouri Human Rights Act).

[187] Salve Regina College v. Russell, 499 U.S. 225, 231–240 (1991) (appellate court erred by deferring to district court's interpretation of state law); Feldman v. Allstate Ins. Co., 322 F.3d 660,665 (9th Cir. 2003); Horsehead Indus., Inc. v. Paramount Communications, Inc., 258 F.3d 132, 140 (3d Cir. 2001).

[188] *See, e.g.*, Anderson v. Marathon Petroleum Co., 801 F.2d 936, 938 (7th Cir. 1986); Hylton v. John Deere, Co., 802 F.2d 1011, 1014–1015 (8th Cir. 1986) (deference to district court's interpretation of state law on unreasonably dangerous product liability).

[189] Salve Regina College v. Russell, 499 U.S. 225, 233–235 (1991).

district court's determination constitutes clear error.[190] The Ninth Circuit will not reverse a district court's construction of state law unless that construction is clearly wrong.[191]

# PART D
# CHOICE OF STATE SUBSTANTIVE LAW

## § 15.21 DETERMINING WHICH STATE LAW APPLIES IN DIVERSITY CASES

### [1] The *Klaxon* Rule: Court Generally Must Apply Choice of Law Rules of State in Which It Sits

Choice of state law questions may arise in applying the *Erie* doctrine in cases involving multistate contacts. Diversity cases often involve choice of law questions because the parties reside in different states. In addition, the cause of action may have arisen in a state other than the residence of either party. In such cases, a federal court must apply the choice of law rules of the state in which it sits to determine which state's substantive law applies (the *Klaxon* rule),[192] unless the claims implicate a significant federal policy.[193] Because federal choice of law rules are a species of federal common law and federal courts have severely limited authority to displace state law, a federal court must specifically find a significant conflict between some federal policy or interest and use state law before creating federal common law, displacing state choice of law rules.[194]

Absent a timely objection, the appellate court will follow the law the district court applied.[195] A federal court may not exercise independent judgment or follow general principles in selecting the law of the case, unless the forum state's rule would violate the constitution or the forum state has no ascertainable rule.[196] The

---

[190] *See, e.g., In re* McLinn, 739 F.2d 1395, 1397 (9th Cir. 1984) ("[t]he panel indicated that if the question of law were reviewed under the deferential standard that we have applied in the past, which permits reversal only for clear error, then they would affirm; but if they were to review the determination under an independent de novo standard, they would reverse").

[191] Farmers Ins. Exch. V. Law Offices of Conrado Sayas, 250 F.3d 1234, 1236 (9th Cir. 2001).

[192] Klaxon Co. v. Stentor Elec. Mfg. Co., 313 U.S. 487, 496 (1941) (federal court in Delaware was required to apply Delaware choice of law rule to determine which state's law governed addition of interest to judgment for damages for breach of contract executed and to be performed in New York); Griffin v. McCoach, 313 U.S. 498, 503 (1941) ("federal courts in diversity of citizenship cases are governed by the conflict of laws rules of the courts of the states in which they sit"); *In re* Volkswagen & Audi Warranty Extension, 692 F.3d 4, 17 (1st Cir. 2012); West American Ins. Co. v. RLI Ins. Co., 698 F.3d 1069, 1073 (8th Cir. 2012); Jorgensen v. Cassiday, 320 F.3d 906, 913 (9th Cir. 2003).

[193] *In re* Gaston & Snow, 243 F.3d 599, 605–07 (2d Cir. 2001).

[194] *Id.*

[195] *See* International Adm'rs v. Life Ins. Co., 753 F.2d 1373, 1376 (7th Cir. 1985) (appellate court approved district court's choice of state law since neither party objected and no compelling reason required disapproval of district court's choice).

[196] Klaxon Co. v. Stentor Elec. Mfg. Co., 313 U.S. 487, 496 (1941).

forum state's choice of law rules must be applied exactly as a state court would apply them. A federal court may not engraft exceptions or modifications on state conflict rules that "may commend themselves to the federal court, but which have not commended themselves to the State in which the federal court sits."[197]

For example, a plaintiff filed a diversity action in Texas federal court to recover damages for death and personal injuries resulting from the premature explosion of ammunition in Cambodia. Texas law permitted recovery under a theory of strict liability. Cambodian law required a showing of negligence. Texas conflict rules apparently would have required application of Cambodian law. The Fifth Circuit declined to apply the Texas conflict rules because (1) Cambodia had no interest in the case, (2) Cambodia had no right under international law to determine liabilities between foreign subjects arising out of a foreign power's military activities, and (3) the federal courts had no power to frustrate American policies by applying policies of a foreign government.[198] The Supreme Court reversed, holding that regardless of the Fifth Circuit's persuasive reasons, the district court had to follow Texas's conflict rules.[199]

The federal courts are divided concerning whether federal choice of law rules or forum choice of law rules apply in bankruptcy courts. Some circuits apply the choice of law rules of the forum state; others apply federal choice of law; while others have declined to resolve the issue.[200] After extensive analysis of federal common law and precedent, the Second Circuit concluded that the forum state's choice of law rules govern in bankruptcy courts hearing claims based on state law, in the absence of any conflicting and significant federal policy.[201]

The *Klaxon* rule can be criticized for undermining the *Erie* goal of eliminating forum shopping. While *Erie* helps to eliminate vertical forum shopping between state and federal courts, the *Klaxon* rule may encourage litigants to forum shop horizontally among federal courts for the most advantageous choice of law rule. Federal legislation to override the *Klaxon* rule has been proposed, but never enacted, for use in multiparty, multiforum mass tort litigation.[202]

## [2] After Transfer of Venue for Convenience, Transferor State's Choice of Law Rules Apply: The *Van Dusen* and *Ferens* Rules

When litigants transfer a case within the federal system from one venue to another under the convenience transfer statute, Section 1404(a) of Title 28,[203] the transferee court must apply the choice of law rules of the state in which the

---

197 Day and Zimmermann, Inc. v. Challoner, 423 U.S. 3, 3–5 (1975).

198 Day and Zimmerman, Inc. v. Challoner, 512 F.2d 77, 80 (5th Cir. 1975), *rev'd*, 423 U.S. 3 (1975).

199 423 U.S. at 3–5.

200 *In re* Mirant Corp., 675 F.3d 530, 536 (5th Cir. 2012).

201 *In re* Gaston & Snow, 243 F.3d at 605–07.

202 *See* H.R. 3406 § 6 (Multiparty, Multiforum Jurisdiction Act of 1990), 101st Cong. 2d Sess. (1990); American Law Institute, *Complex Litigation Project, Preliminary Draft* No. 3 § 6.01 (1990).

203 U.S.C. § 1404(a) ("[f]or the convenience of parties and witnesses, in the interest of justice, a

transferor court sits.[204] This rule applies regardless of which party initiates the transfer, either the defendant, (the *Van Dusen* rule) or the plaintiff (the *Ferens* rule). Thus, Section 1404(a) entitles the litigants only to a change of courtrooms, not a change of law.

There are three reasons for the *Van Dusen* and *Ferens* rules. First, Section 1404(a) should not deprive parties of state-law advantages that exist absent diversity jurisdiction. A Section 1404(a) convenience transfer assumes that the plaintiffs have chosen a proper venue so they should be allowed to retain "whatever advantages may flow from the state laws of the forum they have initially selected," following transfer to a more convenient forum.[205] Although the *Van Dusen* Court noted that it might seem "undesirable to let the plaintiff reap a choice-of-law benefit from the deliberate selection of an inconvenient forum," such a result was necessary because, under the federal system, when a plaintiff has a choice of two proper forums that have different laws, the plaintiff is entitled to exercise a venue privilege by selecting a forum with favorable choice of law rules.[206] Thus, Section 1404(a) should not deprive the plaintiff of the venue privilege and state law advantages that the plaintiff would have had if the plaintiff filed the action in state court (or remained in federal court) in the transferor district.[207]

Second, Section 1404(a) should not create or multiply opportunities for forum shopping. If a transfer for convenience were accompanied by a change in applicable law, defendants could use Section 1404(a) to obtain a "change of law as a bonus for a change of venue."[208] Since defendants do not have that opportunity in state court, they may not have it in federal diversity cases. Third, the decision to transfer venue under Section 1404(a) should turn on considerations of convenience and the interest of justice, rather than on the possible prejudice resulting from a change of law. If a change in law accompanied a change in venue, the remedial purpose of Section 1404(a) would be frustrated. Courts would be reluctant to grant a convenience transfer if application of the transferee state's laws could result in dismissal of the plaintiff's claim, such as when the transferee forum has a shorter statute of limitations or does not recognize a claim actionable in the transferor forum.[209]

The *Ferens* rule on plaintiff-initiated transfers has been criticized because it enables a plaintiff to engage in a file-and-transfer procedure that takes advantage of both a favored forum and favored law. This possibility thus encourages precisely the kind of forum shopping *Erie* was designed to eliminate.[210] The plaintiff in

---

district court may transfer any civil action to any other district or division where it might have been brought"); *see generally* Ch. 9, *Change of Venue.*

[204] Ferens v. John Deere Co., 494 U.S. 516, 521–532 (1990); Van Dusen v. Barrack, 376 U.S. 612, 626–640 (1964).

[205] 376 U.S. at 635–637.

[206] Ferens v. John Deere Co., 494 U.S. 516, 527–528 (1990); Van Dusen v. Barrack, 376 U.S. 612, 635–637 (1964).

[207] 494 U.S. at 527–528; 376 U.S. at 638.

[208] 494 U.S. at 527–528.

[209] 494 U.S. at 527–528; 376 U.S. at 638.

[210] 494 U.S. at 535–539 (Scalia, J. dissenting).

*Ferens* was unable to bring a personal injury action in his home forum because the limitations period had run. By filing suit in an inconvenient forum with a longer limitations statute, and then transferring to his home forum, the plaintiff was able to obtain both favored law (the longer statute of limitations) and a favored forum.[211] Although the *Ferens* Court acknowledged that applying the transferor state's law would reward plaintiffs for conduct that "seems manipulative," it held that the policies underlying the *Van Dusen* rule required that result.[212] The Court noted that since venue was proper in the transferor court, the plaintiff was entitled to select that forum and have its laws apply. A rule that would not allow the transferor state's laws to apply in a plaintiff-initiated transfer would merely "discourag[e] the occasional motions by plaintiffs to transfer inconvenient cases."[213] The undesirable consequence of such a rule would be that the suit would go forward in an inconvenient forum to the potential detriment of witnesses and the courts. This result would be inconsistent with the purpose of the convenience transfer statute.[214]

The Second Circuit extended the rules of *Van Dusen* and *Ferens* to bankruptcy court claims, holding that the bankruptcy court should look to the choice of law rules of the state where the underlying pre-petition complaint was filed when (1) the claim before the bankruptcy court is wholly derived from another claim already pending in a parallel, out-of-state, non-bankruptcy proceeding; and (2) the pending original, or "source," claim was filed prior to the commencement of the bankruptcy case. The court reasoned that in those circumstances, the commencement of the bankruptcy case approximates a defendant-initiated venue transfer; the claimant's participation in the bankruptcy is an extension of the state-court action. In fact, the bankruptcy claim and the state-law proceedings are functionally one and the same. Therefore, it would be unfair to allow the bankruptcy to deprive the claimant of the state-law advantages adhering to the exercise of the claimant's venue privilege.[215]

### [3] After Transfer Because of Improper Venue, Transferee Court Applies Choice of Law Rules of State in Which it Sits

When a case is transferred for improper venue,[216] the transferee court must apply the choice of law rules of the state in which it sits. In absence of such a rule, plaintiffs could benefit from bringing an action in an impermissible forum, which would encourage plaintiffs to file in states with plaintiff-favoring substantive rules.[217]

---

[211] 494 U.S. at 521–532.

[212] 494 U.S. at 531.

[213] 494 U.S. at 526.

[214] 494 U.S. at 529–530.

[215] *In re* Coudert Bros. LLP, 673 F.3d 180, 188–91 (2d Cir. 2012).

[216] *See generally* Ch. 9, *Change of Venue*.

[217] *See, e.g.*, LaVay Corp. v. Dominion Federal Sav. & Loan Ass'n, 830 F.2d 522, 526 (4th Cir. 1987); Manley v. Engram, 755 F.2d 1463, 1467 n.10 (11th Cir. 1985).

### [4] Applicable Law When Transferor Court Lacks Personal Jurisdiction

Appellate courts differ on whether Section 1404(a) or Section 1406(a) is the appropriate vehicle to transfer an action in which venue is technically proper, but the transferor court lacks personal jurisdiction over the defendant.[218] Many courts to which a case is transferred under Section 1404(a) do not apply the *Van Dusen* rule when the transferor court did not have personal jurisdiction over the defendant. Applying the *Van Dusen* rule in such a case would permit a plaintiff to benefit by bringing an action in an impermissible forum. The plaintiff could unfairly capture the law of the transferor forum by filing a federal action, when the state court would have dismissed it for want of jurisdiction. The plaintiff's only recourse would be to file the action in another state that has personal jurisdiction over the defendant and that state would apply its own laws. Therefore, applying the *Van Dusen* rule to cases in which the transferor court lacked personal jurisdiction would be contrary to the *Erie* doctrine because this would lead to different results in federal and state court. Moreover, application of the transferor state's law to a defendant over whom the transferor court could not exercise personal jurisdiction may violate constitutional due process guarantees.[219] Courts refusing to apply the *Van Dusen* rule to such cases instead hold that the substantive law of the transferee state, including its choice of law rules, govern.[220]

Other courts reach the same result through another analysis. When personal jurisdiction is absent, these courts refuse to treat a transfer motion as a motion under Section 1404(a), and instead require transfer to be effected under Section 1406(a) (the improper venue transfer statute). These courts reason that although venue technically is proper, it nonetheless is in the "wrong" district because the lack of personal jurisdiction would prevent the action from proceeding in that district.[221]

---

218 *See generally* Ch. 9, *Change of Venue.*

219 *See, e.g.,* Roofing & Sheet Metal Serv. v. La Quinta Motor Inns, Inc., 689 F.2d 982, 992 (11th Cir. 1982) ("application of a state's choice of law rules to a party over whom its courts cannot obtain personal jurisdiction might present problems of a constitutional dimension").

220 *See* Levy v. Pyramid Co. of Ithaca, 871 F.2d 9, 10 (2d Cir. 1989) (when transfer is "to cure a defect of personal jurisdiction over the defendant, the state law of the transferee forum governs the actions"); Caribbean Wholesales & Service Corp. v. US JVC Corp., 855 F. Supp. 627, 631 (S.D.N.Y. 1994) (in dicta, court indicated that when personal jurisdiction is lacking in transferor court, exception to *Van Dusen* rule is consistent with *Erie* doctrine); *but see* Myelle v. American Cyanamid Co., 57 F.3d 411, 412–413 (4th Cir. 1995) (transferor forums' choice of law rules applied despite place of personal jurisdiction in transferor court).

221 *See, e.g.,* Brower v. Flint Ink Corp., 865 F. Supp. 564, 568 (W.D. Iowa 1994) (only 28 U.S.C. § 1406(a) can effect transfer when transferor court lacks personal jurisdiction); Pittock v. Otis Elevator Co., 8 F.3d 325, 329 (6th Cir. 1993) (same).

# PART E
# FEDERAL COMMON LAW

## § 15.22 AUTHORITY OF FEDERAL COURTS TO CREATE FEDERAL COMMON LAW

### [1] General Principles

Unlike state courts, federal courts are not general common-law courts and do not possess a broad power to develop and apply their own rules of decision. According to the Federal Rules of Decision Act as interpreted by *Erie v. Tompkins*, state law, including state common law, provides the rule of decision in federal court except on matters governed by the Constitution or federal statutes.[222] The *Erie* decision made clear that federal courts may not create a general common law covering such areas as torts, contracts, and commercial transactions.[223]

The language of the Rules of Decision Act seems to preclude federal common law.[224] Moreover, the vesting of jurisdiction in the federal courts does not create authority to formulate federal common law.[225] However, Supreme Court decisions affirm that federal courts may create and apply federal common law in certain limited areas to effectuate congressional intent[226] or protect uniquely federal interests.[227] In addition to showing that the dispute implicates a uniquely federal interest, the proponent of the application of federal law must specifically indicate that state law conflicts with a significant policy or interest.[228] Federal courts may apply appropriate federal rules in areas in which Congress has manifested a desire to avoid significant conflict.[229]

Federal courts generally are hesitant to create federal common law, recognizing that Congress should make the decision to displace state law.[230] Thus, federal common law has been characterized as a "necessary expedient."[231] Federal

---

222 Erie R.R. Co. v. Tompkins, 304 U.S. 64, 78 (1938) ("[e]xcept in matters governed by the Federal Constitution or by Acts of Congress, the law to be applied in any case is the law of the State").

223 304 U.S. at 78 ("There is no general federal common law").

224 *See* 28 U.S.C. § 1652.

225 Texas Indus., Inc. v. Radcliff Materials, Inc., 451 U.S. 630, 640–641 (1981).

226 Textile Workers Union v. Lincoln Mills, 353 U.S. 448, 450 (1957).

227 Texas Indus., Inc. v. Radcliff Materials, Inc., 451 U.S. 630, 640 (1981); Oregon *ex rel.* State Land Bd. v. Corvallis Sand & Gravel Co., 429 U.S. 363, 371 (1977).

228 Certain Underwriters at Lloyd's London v. Argonaut Ins. Co., 500 F.3d 571, 577–81 (7th Cir. 2007); Woodward Governor Co. v. Curtiss-Wright Flight Sys., Inc., 164 F.3d 123, 128–29 (2d Cir. 1999).

229 Moriarty v. Svec., 164 F.3d 323, 327–28 (7th Cir. 1998).

230 *See* Wallis v. Pan American Petroleum Corp., 384 U.S. 63, 68 (1966).

231 Committee for Consideration of Jones Falls Sewage System v. Train, 539 F.2d 1006, 1008 (4th Cir. 1976) (en banc).

common law is created "[in] absence of an applicable Act of Congress,"[232] when the court must consider federal questions that "cannot be answered from federal statutes alone."[233] The Supremacy Clause makes federal common law binding on both state and federal courts.[234]

Federal common law is "subject to the paramount authority of Congress."[235] Federal common law is preempted when federal statutes or regulations address a question.[236]

In general, cases applying federal common law can be grouped into six areas:[237] (1) suits based on a federal statute containing a gap in applicable law requiring creation of interstitial federal common law; (2) suits by or against the United States or between private parties involving federal proprietary interests; (3) suits involving a controversy between states; (4) suits invoking principles of international relations or international law; (5) suits based on admiralty jurisdiction; and (6) suits involving Native American relations. A case may fall into more than one category.[238]

## [2] Areas in Which Federal Courts Create Common Law

### [a] Interstitial Federal Common Law

Federal courts may create "interstitial federal common law" when Congress has enacted a general regulatory scheme and indicated explicitly or implicitly that the federal courts are to fashion the substantive rules to effectuate the scheme.[239] In enacting federal statutory law, Congress often expressly delegates federal lawmaking authority to the courts, or implicitly does so by creating a general regulatory

---

[232] Clearfield Trust Co. v. United States, 318 U.S. 363, 367 (1943).

[233] D'Oench, Duhme & Co. v. FDIC, 315 U.S. 447, 469 (1942) (Jackson, J., concurring).

[234] U.S. Const., Art. VI, cl.2.

[235] New Jersey v. New York, 283 U.S. 336, 348 (1931).

[236] *See, e.g.,* American Elec. Power Co. v. Connecticut, 131 S. Ct. 2527, 180 L. Ed. 2d 435 (2011) (Clean Air Act and Environmental Protection Agency action authorized by Act displaced any federal common law public nuisance claims previously held by states against carbon dioxide emitters); City of Milwaukee v. Illinois, 451 U.S. 304, 315–332 (1981) (enactment of Federal Water Pollution Control Act Amendments of 1972 preempted federal common-law claim for abatement of nuisance caused by interstate water pollution); *see* Illinois v. City of Milwaukee, 406 U.S. 91 (1972) (""new federal laws and new federal regulations may in time pre-empt the field of federal common law of nuisance""); Arizona v. California, 373 U.S. 546 565–566 (1963) (Court declined to apply federal common-law doctrine of equitable apportionment it developed for interstate water disputes because majority concluded Congress had addressed question).

[237] *See* Texas Indus., Inc. v. Radcliff Materials, Inc., 451 U.S. 630 (1981) ("absent some congressional authorization to formulate substantive rules of decision, federal common law exists only in such narrow areas as those concerned with the rights and obligations of the United States, interstate and international disputes implicating the conflicting rights of states or our relations with foreign nations, and admiralty cases").

[238] *See, e.g.,* O'Melveny & Myers v. FDIC, 512 U.S. 79 (1994) (interstitial and proprietary interests); United States v. Little Lake Misere Land Co., 412 U.S. 580, 592–594 (1973) (interstitial and proprietary interests).

[239] Textile Workers Union v. Lincoln Mills, 353 U.S. 448, 450–451 (1957).

scheme with gaps or general language. In both instances, federal courts have created and applied *interstitial federal common law* to fill in the gaps in federal statutory provisions. Courts have created and applied interstitial federal common law under both federal statutes and the federal constitution.

The seminal case supporting the creation of interstitial federal common law is *Textile Workers Union v. Lincoln Mills*. In *Lincoln Mills*, a union sued an employer under Section 301 of the Labor Management Relations Act of 1947 to compel arbitration required by the parties' collective bargaining agreement. On its face, Section 301(a) does nothing more than grant federal subject matter jurisdiction over suits for contract violations between an employer and a union. The Supreme Court held that Section 301(a) "is more than jurisdictional — that it authorizes federal courts to fashion a body of federal law for the enforcement of these collective bargaining agreements and includes within that federal law specific performance of promises to arbitrate grievances under collective bargaining agreements."[240]

Federal courts have used the *Lincoln Mills* principle to create federal common-law rules under many federal statutory schemes, including the Employee Retirement and Income Security Act (ERISA),[241] and the Sherman Antitrust Act.[242] Further, federal common law governs the enforcement and interpretation of settlement agreements in Title VII cases because the settlements are inextricably linked to the underlying law of Title VII.[243]

The existence of gaps in a federal statutory structure is not sufficient to require creation of federal common law. State law will be used to fill gaps unless there is a significant conflict between some federal policy or interest and state law.[244] For example, for cases arising under federal statutes enacted before December 1, 1990, state law supplies the statute of limitations for actions based on a federal statute when the statute lacks a limitations provision.[245]

---

240 Textile Workers Union v. Lincoln Mills, 353 U.S. 448, 450–451 (1957); *see* 28 U.S.C. § 185(a) (§ 301 of Labor Management Relations Act of 1947).

241 *See* Firestone Tire & Rubber Co. v. Bruch, 489 U.S. 101, 110 (1989) ("courts are to develop a federal common law of rights and obligations under ERISA-regulated plans"); Guardian Life Ins. Co. v. Finch, 395 F.3d 238, 243 (5th Cir. 2004); *see also* 29 U.S.C. § 1001 *et seq.*; *but see* Weiner v. Klais & Co., 108 F.3d 86, 92 (6th Cir. 1997) (podiatrist did not have common-law claim for unjust enrichment against ERISA plan administrator as assignee of plan beneficiaries for services provided to them because creation of federal common law of unjust enrichment for plan beneficiaries would be inconsistent with ERISA).

242 *See* National Soc'y of Professional Eng'rs v. United States, 435 U.S. 679, 688 (1978) ("Congress, however, did not intend the text of the Sherman Act to delineate the full meaning of the statute or its application in concrete situations. The legislative history makes it perfectly clear that it expected the courts to give shape to the statute's broad mandate by drawing on common-law tradition"); *see also* 15 U.S.C. § 1.

243 Chavez v. New Mexico, 397 F.3d 826, 837–38 (10th Cir. 2005).

244 Wallis v. Pan American Petroleum Corp., 384 U.S. 63, 68 (1966).

245 *See, e.g.,* Wilson v. Garcia, 471 U.S. 261, 266–279 (1985) (civil rights claims under 42 U.S.C. § 1983 governed by state statutes of limitations for personal injury actions); *but see* 28 U.S.C. § 1658 (claims arising under federal statutes enacted after December 1, 1990, which do not provide limitations period, are subject to four-year statute of limitation).

### [b] Suits Involving Proprietary Interests of United States

#### [i] Federal Common Law Is Not Applied to Private Litigation Not Affecting Rights and Duties of United States

Federal law, including federal common law, applies in a suit that involves a proprietary interest of the United States. Proprietary interests are "uniquely federal interests" so committed by the Constitution and federal law that federal law preempts and replaces state law where necessary.[246] Federal proprietary interests requiring the application of federal common law include matters such as the rights and duties of the United States regarding commercial paper that it issues or holds;[247] the liability of United States property to local taxes;[248] the right of the United States to bring a tort action;[249] the rights and obligations of the United States under its contracts, particularly when the contracts bear heavily on a federal regulatory program;[250] and the civil liability of the United States for actions taken by a separate entity, i.e., whether the separate entity is so intimately involved with the federal government that it qualifies as a federal instrumentality.[251]

Federal common law may preempt and replace state law only when "necessary" to protect federal proprietary interests. Federal common law is necessary when (1) a uniform federal rule is needed to prevent the rights and duties of the United States from varying from state law when important federal policies are involved,[252] or (2) there is a significant conflict between some federal policy and state law.[253]

For example, in *United States v. Little Lake Misere Land Co.*, the Supreme Court held that federal law governed United States agreements to acquire land from private parties pursuant to the Migratory Bird Conservation Act. State law,

---

[246] *See* Boyle v. United Techs. Corp. 487 U.S. 500, 504–506 (1988).

[247] Clearfield Trust Co. v. United States, 318 U.S. 363, 366–367 (1943) (suit by U.S. to recover on government check cashed over forged endorsement); *see also* D'Oench, Duhme & Co. v. FDIC, 315 U.S. 447, 457–458 (1942) (right of FDIC to recover on note held as collateral was governed by federal common law).

[248] United States v. Allegheny County, 322 U.S. 174, 183 (1946).

[249] United States v. Standard Oil Co., 332 U.S. 301 (1947) (suit by U.S. against private party to recover expenses of injured soldier's hospitalization was governed by federal law; absent specific federal legislation, U.S. could not recover).

[250] United States v. Texas, 507 U.S. 529 (1993) (Debt Collection Act of 1982 did not abrogate United States' common-law right to collect prejudgment interest on debts owed to it by States); West Virginia v. United States, 479 U.S. 305 (1987) (federal standard applied to determine West Virginia's liability for prejudgment interest on debt arising from contractual obligation to reimburse U.S. for services rendered by Army Corp of Engineers).

[251] Commodities Export v. Detroit Int'l Bridge Co., 695 F.3d 518, 526–27 (6th Cir. 2012).

[252] Textile Workers Union v. Lincoln Mills, 353 U.S. 448, 366 (1957) (nationwide rule needed to govern rights and liabilities of U.S. on commercial paper it issues); West Virginia v. United States, 479 U.S. 305, 308–313 (1987) (single nationwide rule desirable to determine state liability for prejudgment interest on debt arising from contractual obligation to reimburse U.S.).

[253] Wallis v. Pan American Petroleum Corp., 384 U.S. 63, 68 (1966).

which indefinitely reserved underlying mineral rights to the landowners, did not apply because it conflicted with the federal program for protecting migratory birds.[254] However, in *United States v. Yazell*, the Supreme Court applied the (since-repealed) state law of coverture to prevent the United States from recovering from a woman on a loan that the small Business Administration made to her and her husband. The Court refused to create a federal common-law rule because it found no federal interest that justified overriding state law in the peculiarly local areas of family law and property. The Court emphasized that the SBA voluntarily negotiated a contract with knowledge of the woman's legal disabilities.[255]

### [ii] Federal Common Law Is Not Applied to Private Litigation Not Affecting Rights and Duties of United States

When "litigation is purely between private parties and does not touch the rights and duties of the United States," federal courts will not apply federal common law, even if the litigation tangentially involves federal proprietary interests.[256] In such cases, state law is used as the rule of decision unless it significantly conflicts with some federal policy or interest.[257] The Supreme Court has refused to apply federal common law in litigation between private parties incidentally involving federal proprietary interests. In *Bank of America v. Parnell*, the Supreme Court held that the ability of private parties to recover for conversion of United States bonds is governed by state law. Bank of America sued to recover funds Parnell obtained by cashing bonds issued by the United States Home Owner's Loan Corporation. The Supreme Court concluded that the presence of federal commercial interests in a suit between private parties did not justify the creation of federal common law because the federal interests would not be harmed by application of state law.[258] And in *Wallis v. Pan American Petroleum Corp.*, the Supreme Court concluded that state law regarding contract interpretation and the statute of frauds governed the assignment of an oil and gas lease under the Mineral Leasing Act of 1920. The application of state law presented no significant threat to any identifiable federal policy or interest.[259]

Similarly, in *Miree v. DeKalb County*, the survivors of plane crash victims attempted to sue a municipality as third-party beneficiaries of contracts between a municipality and the Federal Aviation Administration (FAA). The Supreme Court held that state law was not displaced because (1) the operations of the United States in connection with such FAA contracts would not be burdened by allowing state law to determine whether third-party beneficiaries could sue, and (2) any federal interest in the litigation outcome was far too speculative to justify the

---

[254] United States v. Little Lake Misere Land Co., 412 U.S. 580, 592–594 (1973).

[255] United States v. Yazell, 382 U.S. 341, 345–358 (1966).

[256] Bank of Am. v. Parnell, 352 U.S. 29, 33 (1956).

[257] Wallis v. Pan American Petroleum Corp., 384 U.S. 63, 68 (1966).

[258] Bank of Am. v. Parnell, 352 U.S. 29, 33 (1956).

[259] Wallis v. Pan American Petroleum Corp. 384 U.S. 63, 68–71 (1966).

application of federal law to transactions essentially of local concern.[260]

Finally, in *O'Melveny & Myers v. Federal Deposit Insurance Corporation*, the Court applied a state common-law rule that the knowledge of corporate officers acting against a corporation's interest (in this case a bank) would be imputed to the FDIC when it sued the bank's officers for breach of fiduciary duty as the corporation's receiver. The Court concluded that the case did not involve United States rights under nationwide programs, because the FDIC was suing to enforce the bank's rights, not its own. Moreover, the FDIC failed to identify a significant conflict between state law and an identifiable federal policy or interest.[261]

The Supreme Court also has applied state law in suits between family members to determine their rights under federal programs. In *Rose v. Rose*, the Supreme Court held that a state court had the right to order a veteran to pay child support from V.A. benefits because such benefits are intended to support the veteran's family.[262] But the Court has applied federal law when state and federal law conflict.[263]

The government's proprietary interests in litigation between private parties may be sufficiently strong to justify creation of federal common law in certain circumstances. In *Boyle v. United Technologies Corp.*, the Supreme Court held that federal common law should determine the tort liability of a contractor for design defects in equipment provided to the military, because significant federal interests were at stake. The application of state tort law could impair the government's ability to procure military equipment meeting its specifications. The Court created a federal common-law rule that a contractor is not liable for design defects when the federal government approves specifications for the equipment, the equipment meets the specifications, and the contractor warns the government about known design dangers.[264]

### [iii] Adopting State Law as Federal Common Law in Interstitial and Proprietary Interest Cases

In some cases involving federal proprietary interests or gaps in federal statutory schemes, the federal court borrows state law to provide the rule of decision rather than creating a new federal common-law rule. The presumption that state law should be incorporated into federal common law is particularly strong in areas in which private parties have entered legal relationships with the

---

260 Miree v. DeKalb County, 433 U.S. 25, 30 (1977).

261 O'Melveny & Myers v. FDIC, 512 U.S. 79 (1994).

262 Rose v. Rose, 481 U.S. 619, 625–636 (1987); *see also* Yiatchos v. Yiatchos, 376 U.S. 306, 309–313 (1964) (right of widow to federal bonds purchased by husband with community funds but payable on death to husband's brother was determined under state community property law).

263 *See* Ridgway v. Ridgway, 454 U.S. 46, 53–63 (1981) (insured serviceman's beneficiary designation under life policy issued pursuant to federal statute prevailed over constructive trust imposed on policy proceeds pursuant to state divorce decree); Wissner v. Wissner, 338 U.S. 655, 656–660 (1950) (state community property law did not determine estranged wife's entitlement to husband's federal life insurance benefits because federal law gave insured right to designate beneficiary).

264 Boyle v. United Techs. Corp., 487 U.S. 500, 504–506 (1988).

expectation that state law would govern their rights and obligations, such as commercial, property, and family law,[265] and corporation law.[266] Specifically, federal courts must balance three factors when deciding to create a common-law rule or incorporate state law as the federal rule of decision: (1) the need for a nationally uniform body of law; (2) whether application of state law would frustrate the specific objectives of federal programs; and (3) the extent to which application of a federal rule would disrupt commercial relationships based on state law.[267]

For example, the Supreme Court concluded that federal law should govern Small Business Administration and Farmers Home Administration loan programs, because those agencies performed federal functions. However, state law could establish the appropriate rule for establishing lien priority, because a national rule was unnecessary to protect federal interests underlying the loan programs.[268] Similarly, the Court concluded that in shareholder derivative actions under the Investment Company Act of 1940, state law should govern the demand futility exception and be adopted as the federal common-law rule. The Court declined to create a federal common-law rule obliging the representative shareholder to make a demand on the board of directors when state law would excuse the demand as futile. The Court concluded that "where a gap in the federal securities laws must be bridged by a rule that bears on the allocation of governing powers within the corporation, federal courts should incorporate state law into federal common law unless the particular state law in question is inconsistent with the policies underlying the federal statute."[269]

### [iv] Borrowing State Statutes of Limitations

All claims arising under federal statutes enacted after December 1, 1990 that do not provide a limitations period are subject to a four-year statute of limitations.[270] Analogous state limitations periods are not borrowed for such claims.

The Supreme Court, in *Jones v. R. R. Donnelley & Sons Co.*, held that this four-year statute of limitation applies to a claim that was made possible by a post-1990 amendment to a preexisting statute.[271] In *Jones*, plaintiffs' hostile work environment, wrongful discharge, and refusal to transfer claims did not state violations of the original version of 42 U.S.C. § 1981 per Supreme Court precedent. However, Congress amended Section 1981 in the Civil Rights Act of 1991 by adding a new subsection to define the term "make and enforce contracts" as including the "termination of contracts, and the enjoyment of all benefits, privileges, terms, and

---

[265] *See* De Sylva v. Ballentine, 351 U.S. 570, 580–81 (1956) (state law borrowed to determine whether illegitimate children should be allowed to renew copyrights of deceased parents).

[266] In Kamen v. Kemper Financial Services, Inc., 500 U.S. 90, 98 (1991).

[267] United States v. Kimbell Foods, Inc., 440 U.S. 715, 728 (1979).

[268] 440 U.S. at 728.

[269] In Kamen v. Kemper Financial Services, Inc., 500 U.S. 90, 108 (1991); *see also* Burks v. Lasker, 441 U.S. 471, 477–486 (1979) (state law governed whether disinterested directors of registered investment company have power to terminate nonfrivolous derivative action founded on Investment Company Act of 1940 and Investment Advisers Act of 1940).

[270] 28 U.S.C. § 1658.

[271] Jones v. R.R. Donnelley & Sons Co., 541 U.S. 369 (2004).

conditions of the contractual relationship."

It was undisputed that the plaintiffs' claims alleged violations of Section 1981 as amended. The critical question before the Court was whether plaintiffs' claims should be characterized as "arising under" the Civil Rights Act of 1991 or under Section 1981 as originally enacted. After addressing the lack of clarity in the four-year statute's "arising under" language, the Court reviewed the statute's legislative history, determining that the statute's central purpose was to minimize the need to borrow state statutes of limitations. This legislative history called for a broad interpretation of the four-year statute. The Court remarked that nothing in the text or history of the statute supported an interpretation that would limit its reach to entirely new sections of the United States Code. In deciding *Jones*, the Court resolved a circuit split.

When Congress has not expressly provided a statute of limitations governing actions based on a federal statute, federal courts must apply the most closely analogous state statute, unless application of the state statute would be inconsistent with underlying federal policies.[272] The determination of which state statute is most analogous is a question of federal law.[273] The federal district court must follow federal precedent even if the state court would apply a different statute of limitations. Moreover, the district court must follow federal precedent even in a case removed to federal court in which the state court would have applied a longer statute of limitations. Application of the shorter statute in federal court is not unfair to defendants because any defendant sued on a civil rights claim in state court can remove the case to federal court.[274]

When the analogous state limitations period would "frustrate or interfere with the implementation of national policies," or be "at odds with the purpose or operation of federal substantive law,"[275] the federal courts have looked to analogous federal law for a limitations statute more in harmony with the objectives of the action.[276] The adoption of an analogous federal limitations period is the exception. The court should decline to follow a state limitations period "only 'when a rule from elsewhere in federal law clearly provides a closer analogy than available state statutes, and when the federal policies at stake and the practicalities of litigation

---

[272] *See, e.g.*, Jones, 541 U.S. 369 (federal four year "catch-all" statute applied to plaintiffs' § 1981 claims that depended in part on language added to § 1981 after December 1, 1990); North Star Steel Co. v. Thomas, 515 U.S. 29 (1995) (state statute applies to actions under Worker Adjustment and Retraining Notification Act (WARN); Reed v. United Transportation Union, 488 U.S. 319, 323–334 (1989) (claims under § 101(a)(2) of the Labor-Management Reporting and Disclosure Act of 1959, 29 U.S.C. § 411(a)(2), governed by state personal injury statutes); Wilson v. Garcia, 471 U.S. 261, 266 (1985) (civil rights claims under 42 U.S.C. § 1983 governed by state statutes of limitations for personal injury actions).

[273] Agency Holding Corp. v. Malley-Duff & Assoc., 483 U.S. 143, 147 (1987).

[274] Kuhnle Bros. v. County of Geauga, 103 F.3d 516, 519–520 (6th Cir. 1997) (district court properly applied two-year statute to § 1983 claim in accordance with Sixth Circuit precedent, rather than four-year statute that would have applied had case not been removed).

[275] DelCostello v. Teamsters, 462 U.S. 151, 161 (1983).

[276] *See, e.g.*, Lampf, Pleva, Lipkind, Prupis & Petigrow v. Gilbertson, 501 U.S. 350, 362 (1991); Agency Holding Corp. v. Malley-Duff & Assoc., 483 U.S. 143, 146–156 (1987); DelCostello v. Teamsters, 462 U.S. 151, 171–72 (1983).

make that rule a significantly more appropriate vehicle for interstitial lawmaking.'"[277]

For example, in *DelCostello v. Teamsters*, the Supreme Court held that Section 10(b) of the National Labor Relations Act, which establishes a six month period for making charges of unfair labor practices to the NLRB, applied to an employee suit against an employer and a union. The suit alleged that the employer had breached a collective-bargaining agreement provision and the union had breached its duty of fair representation in a grievance-and-arbitration proceeding. The Court declined to borrow the state limitations period because the state law provided very short times for suit (generally 90 days) and thus failed to provide an aggrieved employee with a satisfactory opportunity to vindicate his or her rights.[278]

In applying a state limitations statute to an action arising under a federal statute, the federal court should give effect to the state's tolling provisions if they do not conflict with the federal statute's goals. In *Hardin v. Straub*, the Supreme Court concluded that a state provision tolling the statute of limitations during an inmate's disability should be applied to the inmate's Section 1983 suit because the tolling provision furthers Section 1983's remedial purposes by enhancing the inmate's ability to bring suit and recover damages.[279] On the contrary, federal law may preempt a state statute of limitations requiring the plaintiff to notify the defendant before filing suit. In *Felder v. Casey*, the Supreme Court held that state provisions that required the plaintiff to notify a governmental defendant before filing suit did not apply to a Section 1983 action because they were inconsistent with federal law.[280]

### [c] Application of Federal Common Law in Suits Between States

The *Erie* doctrine does not apply in suits between states.[281] In the absence of a relevant federal statute, the Supreme Court, which has original, exclusive jurisdiction over suits between states,[282] applies federal common law because neither state's laws can be fairly applied to resolve the dispute. When two states are in conflict, the Supreme Court "is called upon to settle that dispute in such a way as will recognize the equal rights of both and at the same time establish justice between them."[283]

---

277 Reed v. United Transportation Union, 488 U.S. 319 (1989).

278 DelCostello v. Teamsters, 462 U.S. 151, 169–172 (1983); *see also* Agency Holding Corp. v. Malley-Duff & Assoc., 483 U.S. 143, 146–156 (1987) (Clayton Act statute of limitations applied to civil enforcement actions under Racketeer Influenced and Corrupt Organizations Act (RICO).

279 Hardin v. Straub, 490 U.S. 536, 538–544 (1989); *see* 42 U.S.C. § 1983.

280 Felder v. Casey, 487 U.S. 131, 138–153 (1988) (Section 1983 action brought in state court).

281 *See* Hinderlider v. La Plata River & Cherry Creek Ditch Co., 304 U.S. 92, 110 (1938) (decided on same day as *Erie* and applying federal common law to determine apportionment of interstate stream).

282 28 U.S.C. § 1251(a).

283 Kansas v. Colorado, 206 U.S. 46, 97–98 (1907).

The Supreme Court has applied federal common law to resolve disputes between states concerning state boundaries[284] and, in many decisions, to resolve rights to interstate waters.[285] If Congress enacts a comprehensive statute governing apportionment of the interstate waters in question, however, the statute supplants federal common law.[286]

The Supreme Court applied federal common law in an Illinois suit against four Wisconsin cities to enjoin pollution of Lake Michigan.[287] Subsequently, however, the Court held that the 1972 amendments to the Water Pollution Control Act prevented a federal common-law action for nuisance as a result of pollution of interstate waters. The Court concluded that application of federal common law was unnecessary because the comprehensive regulatory statute established liability for water pollution.[288]

Federal common law also applies to suits between private litigants when the parties' rights and titles depend on state boundaries or interstate compacts. It is immaterial whether the states are or can be made parties to the suit.[289] Interstate compact agreements are federal law under the Compact Clause, and their interpretation presents a federal question.[290]

In general, however, state law applies to resolve title disputes between a single state and a private party. For example, state law determines title questions between riparian claimants and the state, when a river shifts its course by accretion or avulsion. But federal common law governs title suits between a state and a private party when a federal land patent or boundary demarcation is at issue.[291] Moreover, federal common law governs title disputes between the United States and a state or private party when the United States has never parted with its interest in the property.[292]

---

284 *See* Arkansas v. Tennessee, 246 U.S. 158 (1918) (when navigable stream forms interstate boundary, federal common law determines effect of change in stream bed on boundary).

285 *See, e.g.*, Nebraska v. Wyoming, 325 U.S. 589, 591 (1945) (doctrine of equitable apportionment applied to apportion interstate river waters among Nebraska, Wyoming, and Colorado); Hinderlider v. La Plata River & Cherry Creek Ditch Co., 304 U.S. 92, 110 (1938) ("[w]hether the water of an interstate stream must be apportioned between two states is a question of 'federal common law' upon which neither the statutes nor the decisions of either state can be conclusive"); New Jersey v. New York, 283 U.S. 336, 342 (1931); Connecticut v. Massachusetts, 282 U.S. 660, 670–671 (1931).

286 Arizona v. California, 373 U.S. 546, 575–586 (1963) (Boulder Canyon Project Act controlled apportionment of Colorado River waters among California, Arizona, and Nevada, rather than equitable apportionment doctrine).

287 Illinois v. City of Milwaukee, 406 U.S. 91, 98–108 (1971).

288 City of Milwaukee v. Illinois, 451 U.S. 304, 317–332 (1981).

289 *See* Hinderlider v. La Plata River & Cherry Creek Ditch Co., 304 U.S. 92, 110 (1938) (federal common law applied in suit between private party and state to determine validity of interstate compact).

290 *See* Cuyler v. Adams, 449 U.S. 433, 438–442 (1981) (interstate Agreement on Detainers was congressionally approved interstate compact and therefore subject to federal rather than state construction); *see* Nebraska v. Iowa, 406 U.S. 117, 117–127 (1972).

291 *See* Oregon *ex rel.* State Land Bd. v. Corvallis Sand & Gravel Co., 429 U.S. 363 (1977), *overruling* Bonelli Cattle Co. v. Arizona, 414 U.S. 313 (1973).

292 California *ex rel.* State Lands Comm'n v. United States, 457 U.S. 273, 278–283 (1982) (federal law determines dispute over accretions to oceanfront land where title rests with or was derived from federal

Although disputes between states predominately have involved land title and water rights, courts have applied federal common law to other areas, such as conflicting escheat claims among states.[293]

### [d] Federal Common Law and International Relations

Federal law governs suits affecting international relations. In *Banco Nacional de Cuba v. Sabbatino*, the Supreme Court held that federal law is the interpretive source for international law issues, even for diversity cases.[294] In *Sabbatino*, a financial agent of the Cuban government sought to recover the proceeds of a sugar shipment it claimed the Cuban government had nationalized. The district court held that the Cuban expropriation violated international law and granted summary judgment against Banco Nacional. The Supreme Court reversed, holding that it was inappropriate for the district court to have made any determination concerning the validity of the Cuban nationalization, since as a matter of federal common law, the act of state doctrine prohibited the United States courts from ruling on the internal acts of other sovereign governments. The Court deemed a uniform rule necessary to prevent the possibility that state courts could undermine the purposes behind the act-of-state doctrine.[295]

Congress and subsequent cases narrowed the act-of-state doctrine and affirmed that the executive and legislative branches are entrusted with foreign policymaking power.[296] The Supreme Court indicated that federal courts should not apply the act-of-state doctrine when the executive branch indicates its application would not advance American foreign policy interests.[297] Similarly, the Court has refused to apply the act-of-state doctrine "to acts committed by foreign sovereigns in the course of their purely commercial operations."[298]

Finally, the Court has held that the act-of-state doctrine does not bar a United States court from entertaining an action that may embarrass a foreign sovereign because it will impute an unlawful motivation in performing an official act. The act-of-state doctrine merely requires that courts deem valid foreign sovereign acts within their own jurisdictions.[299] Nonetheless, the basic *Sabbatino* rule that

---

government); Wilson v. Omaha Indian Tribe, 442 U.S. 653, 670 (1979) (federal law determines effect of accretive or avulsive changes in navigable stream when federal government is riparian owner).

[293] *See* Pennsylvania v. New York, 407 U.S. 206, 208–216 (1972); Texas v. New Jersey, 379 U.S. 674, 680–683 (1965) (court adopted as matter of federal law rule that state of creditor's last known address shown by debtor's records is entitled to escheat property owed to that creditor).

[294] Banco Nacional de Cuba v. Sabbatino, 376 U.S. 398, 421–427 (1964).

[295] 376 U.S. at 421–427 ("an issue concerned with a basic choice regarding the competence and function of the Judiciary and the National Executive in ordering our relationships with other members of the international community must be treated exclusively as an aspect of federal law").

[296] *See* 22 U.S.C. § 2370(e).

[297] First National City Bank v. Banco Nacional De Cuba, 406 U.S. 759, 762–776 (1972).

[298] Alfred Dunhill of London v. Cuba, 425 U.S. 682, 706 (1976) (Cuba's refusal to return funds Dunhill mistakenly paid for cigars purchased from expropriated businesses was not "act of state").

[299] W. S. Kirkpatrick & Co. v. Environmental Tectonics Corp., 493 U.S. 400, 404–410 (1990) (act-of-state doctrine did not prevent unsuccessful bidder for construction contract with Nigeria from suing successful bidder alleging it had bribed Nigerian officials).

empowers federal courts to create federal common law in actions relating to foreign affairs is still valid.[300]

## [e] Federal Common Law in Maritime and Admiralty Cases

The Constitution grants federal courts jurisdiction over admiralty and maritime cases, regardless of the amount in controversy, diversity of citizenship, or whether the controversy arises under a federal statute.[301] The Supreme Court has interpreted the Constitution's admiralty and maritime jurisdiction clause to contain three grants of federal power:[302] (1) Congress may confer admiralty and maritime jurisdiction on lower federal courts; (2) federal courts may develop and apply admiralty and maritime common law;[303] and (3) Congress may enact statutes revising and supplementing admiralty and maritime common law.

Congress has enacted legislation in many areas of maritime law, including worker's compensation for non-seamen maritime workers,[304] tort remedies for seamen killed or injured in the course of employment,[305] remedies for survivors of persons killed on the high seas,[306] carriage of goods under bills of lading,[307] and maritime liens.[308] Under the "savings to suitors" clause,[309] state courts have concurrent subject matter jurisdiction over most maritime matters. In exercising this jurisdiction, a state court may adopt whatever remedies it sees fit as long as it does not attempt to make changes in substantive maritime law. The state remedy may not work a material prejudice to the characteristic features of the general federal maritime law or interfere with the harmony and uniformity of that law in its international and interstate relations.[310]

Congress's power to enact maritime legislation, federal and state court concurrent jurisdiction, and the broad scope of maritime jurisdiction (extending to inland navigable waters),[311] has led to questions regarding the relationship between state

---

300 *See* First Natl. City Bank v. Banco Para El Comercio Ex., 462 U.S. 611, 621–623 (1983) (international law and federal common law determine whether courts should recognize separate juridical status of foreign instrumentality).

301 U.S. Const., Art. III § 2, cl. 3.

302 Romero v. Int'l Terminal Operating Co., 358 U.S. 354, 360–361 (1959).

303 *See* Chelentis v. Luckenbach S.S. Co., 247 U.S. 372, 382 (1918); Southern Pacific Company v. Jensen, 244 U.S. 205, 215–216 (1917).

304 33 U.S.C. §§ 901–950 (Longshore and Harbor Workers' Compensation Act).

305 46 U.S.C. § 688 (Jones Act).

306 46 U.S.C. §§ 761–766 (Death on the High Seas Act).

307 46 U.S.C. § 1300 *et seq.* (Carriage of Goods by Sea Act).

308 46 U.S.C. §§ 31321–31330.

309 *See* 28 U.S.C. § 1333 ("the district courts shall have original jurisdiction, exclusive of the courts of the States, of: (1) Any civil case of admiralty or maritime jurisdiction, saving to suitors in all cases all other remedies to which they are otherwise entitled").

310 *See* American Dredging Co. v. Miller, 510 U.S. 443 (1994) (state courts may not provide remedy in rem for any cause of action within admiralty jurisdiction).

311 *See* 46 U.S.C. § 740 ("The admiralty and maritime jurisdiction of the United States shall extend

and federal law. Thus, federal courts have developed a hierarchy of statutory and common law.

Federal statutes and United States treaties govern all proceedings within maritime jurisdiction, notwithstanding contrary prior federal common and state law.[312] Further, uniform substantive principles governing admiralty cases developed by the Supreme Court are federal common law under the Supremacy Clause, and all courts must apply them, unless preempted by federal statute.[313]

Courts may apply state law under the "maritime but local" doctrine if the law does not conflict with federal statutes, treaties, or the general federal maritime common law, and there is no need to create a uniform federal common-law rule.[314]

### [f] Federal Common Law and Native American Relations and Land Rights

Since the adoption of the Constitution, Native American relations have been the exclusive province of federal law. Numerous nineteenth-century Supreme Court decisions recognized that Native Americans have a federal common-law right to sue to enforce their aboriginal land rights.[315] The Court reaffirmed this principle in *County of Oneida v. Oneida Indian Nation*, holding that the Oneida Indians had a common-law right of action to sue for damages for land that New York purchased in 1795 in violation of federal law.[316] Moreover, the Court concluded that federal common-law actions by Native Americans to enforce aboriginal property rights are

---

to and include all cases of damage or injury, to person or property, caused by a vessel on navigable water, notwithstanding that such damage or injury be done or consummated on land"); *see also* Foremost Ins. Co. v. Richardson, 457 U.S. 668, 672–677 (1982) (collision between two pleasure boats on navigable waters falls within federal court admiralty jurisdiction); *but see* Executive Jet Aviation, Inc. v. Cleveland, 409 U.S. 249, 253–274 (1972) (no federal admiralty jurisdiction over aviation tort claims arising from flights by land-based aircraft between points within continental United States even if plane crashes in navigable waters; wrong must bear significant relationship to traditional maritime activity).

312 *See, e.g.,* Zicherman v. Korean Air Lines Co. 516 U.S. 217 (1996) (neither state nor general maritime law can provide basis for recovery of loss-of-society damages under Death on the High Seas Act (DOHSA); Miles v. Apex Marine Corp., 498 U.S. 19, 30–36 (1990) (Jones Act, rather than general maritime law, determines damages recoverable in action for wrongful death of seamen).

313 *See, e.g.,* Miles v. Apex Marine Corp., 498 U.S. 19, 23–26 (1990) (general maritime cause of action for wrongful death extended to seamen); Moragne v. States Marine Lines, Inc., 398 U.S. 375, 379–409 (1970) (creation of general maritime cause of action for wrongful death).

314 *See, e.g.,* Yamaha Motor Corp. v. Calhoun, 516 U.S. 199 (1996) (state wrongful death remedies not displaced by general maritime wrongful death action in cases when no federal statute specifies appropriate relief and decedent was not seaman, longshore worker, or person otherwise engaged in maritime trade); American Dredging Co. v. Miller, 510 U.S. 443 (1994) (federal admiralty law does not preempt state law of forum non conveniens because state doctrine does not interfere with harmony and uniformity of maritime law); Sun Ship, Inc. v. Pennsylvania, 447 U.S. 715, 717–726 (1980) (state may apply its workers' compensation scheme to land-based injuries that fall within compass of Longshore and Harbor Workers' Compensation Act); Askew v. American Waterways Operators, Inc., 411 U.S. 325, 329–344 (1973) (federal statute making maritime torts of shore damage caused by vessels on navigable water did not preempt state statute imposing strict liability on vessel owners for oil spills on navigable waters).

315 *See, e.g.,* Holden v. Joy, 84 U.S. (17 Wall.) 211 (1872); Mitchel v. United States, 34 U.S. (9 Pet.) 711, 746 (1835); Cherokee Nation v. Georgia, 30 U.S. (5 Pet.) 1, 17 (1831).

316 County of Oneida v. Oneida Indian Nation, 470 U.S. 226, 233–236 (1985).

not governed by any statute of limitations, and application of a state statute would be inconsistent with federal policies.[317]

# PART F
# APPLICATION OF FEDERAL LAW IN STATE COURTS

## § 15.23 STATE COURTS MUST HEAR FEDERAL CLAIMS IF THEY HAVE APPROPRIATE JURISDICTION UNDER STATE LAW

State courts have concurrent jurisdiction over claims arising under federal law unless the Constitution, federal statutes, or case law vests exclusive jurisdiction in the federal courts. State courts must hear federal law claims over which they have concurrent jurisdiction when state courts have jurisdiction to hear similar state law claims.[318] Federal law is enforceable in state courts because the Supremacy Clause makes federal law "the supreme law of the land" and charges state courts with a coordinate responsibility to enforce it.[319]

A state violates the Supremacy Clause if it refuses to entertain a category of federal claims, when the court entertains similar state law actions against state defendants. For example, in *Testa v. Katt* the Supreme Court held that the Rhode Island courts could not decline jurisdiction over treble damages claims under the federal Emergency Price Control Act when their jurisdiction was otherwise "adequate and appropriate under established local law." The Rhode Island court had declined to exercise jurisdiction because the federal act was a penal statute. If another state had enacted such a statute, the state court would not have been required to enforce it under the Full Faith and Credit Clause. Rejecting that argument, the Supreme Court observed that the Rhode Island court enforced the same type of claim arising under state law and claims for double damages under federal law. The Court concluded that the state court had adequate and appropriate jurisdiction under local law to adjudicate the suit and could not decline to exercise this jurisdiction by labeling the federal law as penal.[320]

States have the power to establish the structure and jurisdiction of their courts. Federal courts may not compel a state court to entertain a claim over which the state court has no jurisdiction under state law. Moreover, states are not required to create a court of competent jurisdiction to hear a case in which the federal claim is presented. However, a state rule may deprive a state court of jurisdiction to entertain a federal claim only if the rule really is a jurisdictional rule. A state court may not justify its refusal to entertain a federal claim simply by characterizing a

---

[317] 470 U.S. at 240–244.

[318] Testa v. Katt, 330 U.S. 386, 394 (1947).

[319] *See* Miles v. Illinois Central R.R., 315 U.S. 698, 703–704 (1942); Mondou v. New York, New Haven & Hartford R.R., 223 U.S. 1, 58 (1912) ("The existence of concurrent jurisdiction implies a duty to exercise it"); *see also* U.S. Const., Art. VI, cl. 2.

[320] Testa v. Katt, 330 U.S. 386, 394 (1947).

rule as jurisdictional. A rule is jurisdictional only if it deals with the court's power over the litigants and its competence over the subject matter.[321]

A state jurisdictional rule may not discriminate against federal actions. In *McKnett v. St. Louis and San Francisco Railway Co.*, a state court interpreted a state statute to permit suits against foreign corporations for injuries in another state, but to prohibit suits on federal actions under the same circumstances. Thus, the state court refused to exercise jurisdiction over a Federal Employer's Liability Act (FELA) action against a foreign corporation for an injury suffered in another state. The Supreme Court held that the Constitution prohibits state courts of general jurisdiction from refusing to exercise jurisdiction solely because a suit is brought under federal law. Because the state court had general jurisdiction of personal injury actions, the refusal to hear the FELA action constituted discrimination against rights arising under federal laws, in violation of the Supremacy Clause.[322]

The Supremacy Clause prohibits state courts from refusing to apply federal law because of disagreement with its content. In *Mondou v. New York, New Haven, and Hartford Railroad*, for example, the state courts declined to recognize FELA actions, finding that FELA was against state policy and that application of federal law was "inconvenient and confusing." The Supreme Court held that FELA may be enforced of right, in state courts, when their jurisdiction is "adequate to the occasion." The Supreme Court found that the court's jurisdiction was "adequate to the occasion," because the state court was a court of general jurisdiction with cognizance over wrongful death actions.[323]

## § 15.24 STATE COURTS MAY REFUSE JURISDICTION OVER FEDERAL CLAIMS UNDER NEUTRAL STATE PROCEDURAL RULES

States may apply their own neutral procedural rules to federal claims, unless federal law preempts those rules because application of the state rules would defeat federal substantive rights.[324] A state court may refuse jurisdiction over a federal claim because of a neutral state rule regarding court administration.[325]. In three cases, the Supreme Court has upheld a state court's dismissal of a federal claim based on a state procedural rule. In *Douglas v. New York, New Haven and Hartford Railroad*, the Court upheld the dismissal of a FELA action under a state statute that permitted dismissal of both federal and state claims when neither the plaintiff

---

[321] Howlett v. Rose, 496 U.S. 356, 381–382 (1990) (state law granting sovereign immunity to school board was not jurisdictional rule).

[322] McKnett v. St. Louis & San Francisco Ry. Co., 292 U.S. 230, 233–234 (1934); *see* 45 U.S.C. § 51 *et seq.* (FELA).

[323] Mondou v. New York, New Haven & Hartford R.R., 223 U.S. 1, 55–57 (1912); *see* 45 U.S.C. § 51 *et seq.* (FELA).

[324] *See* Felder v. Casey, 487 U.S. 131, 143 (1988).

[325] *See* Missouri *ex rel.* Southern Ry. v. Mayfield, 340 U.S. 1, 2–5 (1950); Herb v. Pitcairn, 324 U.S. 117, 123 (1945).

nor the defendant was a forum state resident.[326] In *Herb v. Pitcairn*, a city court denied jurisdiction over a FELA action because the action arose outside its territorial jurisdiction. Although the state court was not free to dismiss the federal claim "because it is a federal one," the Court found no evidence that the state court "construed the state jurisdiction and venue laws in a discriminatory fashion."[327] Finally, in *Missouri ex rel. Southern Ry. v. Mayfield*, the Court held that a state court could apply the doctrine of forum non conveniens to bar adjudication of a FELA case if the state "enforces its policy impartially so as not to involve a discrimination against Employers' Liability Act suits."[328]

## § 15.25 STATE COURTS MAY NOT APPLY STATE LAW IN FEDERAL CLAIMS TO DEFEAT FEDERAL RIGHTS

Federal law defines the elements and defenses even when the federal action is brought in state court. For example, in a FELA action brought in state court, federal law controls the proper measure of damages and the availability of prejudgment interest.[329] A state court may not apply a state law defense to a federal claim that the litigants could not raise in federal court. Federal rights could be defeated if states were permitted to determine what defenses could be raised in suits under federal statutes. Moreover, application of state defenses to federal claims would subvert national uniformity, thus thwarting the purpose of the federal legislation.[330] For example, a state court could not apply a state law defense of sovereign immunity to bar a Section 1983 claim against a school board because the school board could not have raised the defense in federal court.[331]

A state court may apply its own procedural rules to a federal action unless state law would frustrate congressionally-created substantive rights. In *Felder v. Casey*, the Supreme Court held that a state notice-of-claim statute that shortened the limitations period and imposed an exhaustion-of-remedies requirement on claims against public agencies did not apply to Section 1983 actions brought in state court. The Court concluded that application of the state procedural statute would frustrate congressionally-created substantive rights because Congress made the decision to subject state subdivisions to liability for violations of federal rights, and the state legislature had no authority to override this decision.[332]

---

[326] Douglas v. New York, New Haven & Hartford R.R., 279 U.S. 377, 387 (1929); *see* 45 U.S.C. § 51 *et seq.* (FELA).

[327] Herb v. Pitcairn, 324 U.S. 117, 123 (1945); *see* 45 U.S.C. § 51 *et seq.* (FELA).

[328] Missouri *ex rel.* Southern Ry. v. Mayfield, 340 U.S. 1, 4–5 (1950); *see* 45 U.S.C. § 51 *et seq.* (FELA).

[329] Monessen Southwestern R.R. Co. v. Morgan, 486 U.S. 330, 335 (1988) (state rule that damages did not have to be reduced to present value was inapplicable in FELA action); *see* 45 U.S.C. § 51 *et seq.* (FELA).

[330] Howlett v. Rose, 496 U.S. 356 (1990); Dice v. Akron, Canton & Youngstown R.R., 342 U.S. 359, 361 (1952).

[331] *See, e.g.*, Howlett v. Rose, 496 U.S. 356 (1990).

[332] Felder v. Casey, 487 U.S. 131, 143 (1988).

# Appendix

# SELECTED PROVISIONS OF THE UNITED STATES CONSTITUTION, THE FEDERAL RULES OF CIVIL PROCEDURE, AND TITLE 28, UNITED STATES CODE

## (Effective as of January 2015)

### ARTICLE III, UNITED STATES CONSTITUTION

#### Section 1.

The judicial Power of the United States, shall be vested in one supreme Court, and in such inferior Courts as the Congress may from time to time ordain and establish. The Judges, both of the supreme and inferior Courts, shall hold their Offices during good Behaviour, and shall, at stated Times, receive for their Services, a Compensation, which shall not be diminished during their Continuance in Office.

#### Section 2.

The judicial Power shall extend to all Cases, in Law and Equity, arising under this Constitution, the Laws of the United States, and Treaties made, or which shall be made, under their Authority; — to all Cases affecting Ambassadors, other public Ministers and Consuls; — To all Cases of admiralty and maritime Jurisdiction; — to Controversies to which the United States shall be a Party; — to Controversies between two or more States; — between a State and Citizens of another State; — between Citizens of different States; — between Citizens of the same State claiming Lands under Grants of different States, and between a State, or the Citizens thereof, and foreign States, Citizens or Subjects.

In all Cases affecting Ambassadors, other public Ministers and Consuls, and those in which a State shall be Party, the supreme Court shall have original Jurisdiction. In all the other Cases before mentioned, the supreme Court shall have appellate Jurisdiction, both as to Law and Fact, with such Exceptions, and under such Regulations as the Congress shall make.

The Trial of all Crimes, except in Cases of Impeachment, shall be by Jury; and such Trial shall be held in the State where the said Crimes shall have been committed; but when not committed within any State, the Trial shall be at such Place or Places as the Congress may by Law have directed.

#### Section 3.

Treason against the United States, shall consist only in levying War against them, or in adhering to their Enemies, giving them Aid and Comfort. No Person shall be convicted of Treason unless on the Testimony of two Witnesses to the same overt Act, or on Confession in open Court.

The Congress shall have Power to declare the Punishment of Treason, but no Attainder of Treason shall work Corruption of Blood, or Forfeiture except during the Life of the Person attainted.

## ELEVENTH AMENDMENT, UNITED STATES CONSTITUTION

### Amendment XI. Suits Against States.

The Judicial power of the United States shall not be construed to extend to any suit in law or equity, commenced or prosecuted against one of the United States by Citizens of another State, or by Citizens or Subjects of any Foreign State.

## FEDERAL RULES OF CIVIL PROCEDURE

### Rule 4. Summons.

* * * *

**(k)** Territorial Limits of Effective Service.

**(1)** ***In General.*** Serving a summons or filing a waiver of service establishes personal jurisdiction over a defendant:

**(A)** who is subject to the jurisdiction of a court of general jurisdiction in the state where the district court is located;

**(B)** who is a party joined under Rule 14 or 19 and is served within a judicial district of the United States and not more than 100 miles from where the summons was issued; or

**(C)** when authorized by a federal statute.

**(2)** ***Federal Claim Outside State — Court Jurisdiction.*** For a claim that arises under federal law, serving a summons or filing a waiver of service establishes personal jurisdiction over a defendant if:

**(A)** the defendant is not subject to jurisdiction in any state's courts of general jurisdiction; and

**(B)** exercising jurisdiction is consistent with the United States Constitution and laws.

* * * *

**(n)** Asserting Jurisdiction over Property or Assets.

**(1)** ***Federal Law.*** The court may assert jurisdiction over property if authorized by a federal statute. Notice to claimants of the property must be given as provided in the statute or by serving a summons under this rule.

**(2)** ***State Law.*** On a showing that personal jurisdiction over a defendant cannot be obtained in the district where the action is brought by reasonable efforts to serve a summons under this rule, the court may assert jurisdiction over the defendant's assets found in the district. Jurisdiction is acquired by seizing the assets under the circumstances and in the manner provided by state law in that district.

**History**

(Amended July 1, 1963; July 1, 1966; Aug. 1, 1980; Jan. 12, 1983,P.L. 97–462, § 2, 96 Stat. 2527; Aug. 1, 1987; Dec. 1, 1993; Dec. 1, 2000.)

(As amended Dec. 1, 2007.)

## SELECTED PROVISIONS OF TITLE 28, UNITED STATES CODE

### § 1331. Federal Question.

The district courts shall have original jurisdiction of all civil actions arising under the Constitution, laws, or treaties of the United States.

(Added June 25, 1948, ch. 646, 62 Stat. 930; amended July 25, 1958, Pub. L. 85–554, § 1, 72 Stat. 415; Oct. 21, 1976, Pub. L. 94–574, § 2, 90 Stat. 2721; Dec. 1, 1980, Pub. L. 96–486, § 2(a), 94 Stat. 2369.)

### § 1332. Diversity of Citizenship; Amount in Controversy; Costs.

**(a)** The district courts shall have original jurisdiction of all civil actions where the matter in controversy exceeds the sum or value of $75,000, exclusive of interest and costs, and is between—

**(1)** Citizens of different States;

**(2)** citizens of a State and citizens or subjects of a foreign state, except that the district courts shall not have original jurisdiction under this subsection of an action between citizens of a State and citizens or subjects of a foreign state who are lawfully admitted for permanent residence in the United States and are domiciled in the same State;

**(3)** citizens of different States and in which citizens or subjects of a foreign state are additional parties; and

**(4)** a foreign state, defined in section 1603(a) of this title [28 USCS § 1603(a)], as plaintiff and citizens of a State or of different States.

**(b)** Except when express provision therefor is otherwise made in a statute of the United States, where the plaintiff who files the case originally in the Federal courts is finally adjudged to be entitled to recover less than the sum or value of $75,000, computed without regard to any setoff or counterclaim to which the defendant may be adjudged to be entitled, and exclusive of interest and costs, the district court may deny costs to the plaintiff and, in addition, may impose costs on the plaintiff.

**(c)** For the purposes of this section and section 1441 of this title [28 USCS § 1441]—

**(1)** a corporation shall be deemed to be a citizen of every State and foreign state by which it has been incorporated and of the State or foreign state where it has its principal place of business, except that in any direct action against the insurer of a policy or contract of liability insurance, whether incorporated or unincorporated, to which action the insured is not joined as a party-defendant, such insurer shall be deemed a citizen of—

**(A)** every State and foreign state of which the insured is a citizen;

**(B)** every State and foreign state by which the insurer has been incorporated; and

**(C)** the State or foreign state where the insurer has its principal place of business; and

**(2)** the legal representative of the estate of a decedent shall be deemed to be a citizen only of the same State as the decedent, and the legal representative of an infant or incompetent shall be deemed to be a citizen only of the same State as the infant or incompetent.

**(d)** (1) In this subsection—

**(A)** the term "class" means all of the class members in a class action;

**(B)** the term "class action" means any civil action filed under rule 23 of the Federal Rules of Civil Procedure or similar State statute or rule of judicial procedure authorizing an action to be brought by 1 or more representative persons as a class action;

**(C)** the term "class certification order" means an order issued by a court approving the treatment of some or all aspects of a civil action as a class action; and

**(D)** the term "class members" means the persons (named or unnamed) who fall within the definition of the proposed or certified class in a class action.

(2) The district courts shall have original jurisdiction of any civil action in which the matter in controversy exceeds the sum or value of $5,000,000, exclusive of interest and costs, and is a class action in which—

**(A)** any member of a class of plaintiffs is a citizen of a State different from any defendant;

**(B)** any member of a class of plaintiffs is a foreign state or a citizen or subject of a foreign state and any defendant is a citizen of a State; or

**(C)** any member of a class of plaintiffs is a citizen of a State and any defendant is a foreign state or a citizen or subject of a foreign state.

(3) A district court may, in the interests of justice and looking at the totality of the circumstances, decline to exercise jurisdiction under paragraph (2) over a class action in which greater than one-third but less than two-thirds of the members of all proposed plaintiff classes in the aggregate and the primary defendants are citizens of the State in which the action was originally filed based on consideration of—

**(A)** whether the claims asserted involve matters of national or interstate interest;

**(B)** whether the claims asserted will be governed by laws of the State in which the action was originally filed or by the laws of other States;

**(C)** whether the class action has been pleaded in a manner that seeks to avoid Federal jurisdiction;

**(D)** whether the action was brought in a forum with a distinct nexus with the class members, the alleged harm, or the defendants;

**(E)** whether the number of citizens of the State in which the action was originally filed in all proposed plaintiff classes in the aggregate is substantially larger than the number of citizens from any other State, and the citizenship of the other members of the proposed class is dispersed among a substantial number of States; and

**(F)** whether, during the 3-year period preceding the filing of that class action, 1 or more other class actions asserting the same or similar claims on behalf of the same or other persons have been filed.

**(4)** A district court shall decline to exercise jurisdiction under paragraph (2)—

**(A)** (i) over a class action in which—

**(I)** greater than two-thirds of the members of all proposed plaintiff classes in the aggregate are citizens of the State in which the action was originally filed;

**(II)** at least 1 defendant is a defendant—

(aa) from whom significant relief is sought by members of the plaintiff class;

(bb) whose alleged conduct forms a significant basis for the claims asserted by the proposed plaintiff class; and

(cc) who is a citizen of the State in which the action was originally filed; and

**(III)** principal injuries resulting from the alleged conduct or any related conduct of each defendant were incurred in the State in which the action was originally filed; and

**(ii)** during the 3-year period preceding the filing of that class action, no other class action has been filed asserting the same or similar factual allegations against any of the defendants on behalf of the same or other persons; or

**(B)** two-thirds or more of the members of all proposed plaintiff classes in the aggregate, and the primary defendants, are citizens of the State in which the action was originally filed.

**(5)** Paragraphs (2) through (4) shall not apply to any class action in which—

**(A)** the primary defendants are States, State officials, or other governmental entities against whom the district court may be foreclosed from ordering relief; or

**(B)** the number of members of all proposed plaintiff classes in the aggregate is less than 100.

**(6)** In any class action, the claims of the individual class members shall be aggregated to determine whether the matter in controversy exceeds the sum or value of $5,000,000, exclusive of interest and costs.

**(7)** Citizenship of the members of the proposed plaintiff classes shall be determined for purposes of paragraphs (2) through (6) as of the date of filing of the complaint or amended complaint, or, if the case stated by the initial pleading is not subject to Federal jurisdiction, as of the date of service by plaintiffs of an amended pleading, motion, or other paper, indicating the existence of Federal jurisdiction.

**(8)** This subsection shall apply to any class action before or after the entry of a class certification order by the court with respect to that action.

**(9)** Paragraph (2) shall not apply to any class action that solely involves a claim—

**(A)** concerning a covered security as defined under 16(f)(3) of the Securities Act of 1933 (15 U.S.C. 78p(f)(3)) and section 28(f)(5)(E) of the Securities Exchange Act of 1934 (15 U.S.C. 78bb(f)(5)(E));

**(B)** that relates to the internal affairs or governance of a corporation or other form of business enterprise and that arises under or by virtue of the laws of the State in which such corporation or business enterprise is incorporated or organized; or

**(C)** that relates to the rights, duties (including fiduciary duties), and obligations relating to or created by or pursuant to any security (as defined under section 2(a)(1) of the Securities Act of 1933 (15 U.S.C. 77b(a)(1)) and the regulations issued thereunder).

**(10)** For purposes of this subsection and section 1453 [28 USCS § 1453], an unincorporated association shall be deemed to be a citizen of the State where it has its principal place of business and the State under whose laws it is organized.

**(11)** (A) For purposes of this subsection and section 1453 [28 USCS § 1453], a mass action shall be deemed to be a class action removable under paragraphs (2) through (10) if it otherwise meets the provisions of those paragraphs.

**(B)**

**(i)** As used in subparagraph (A), the term "mass action" means any civil action (except a civil action within the scope of section 1711(2) [28 USCS § 1711(2)]) in which monetary relief claims of 100 or more persons are proposed to be tried jointly on the ground that the plaintiffs' claims involve common questions of law or fact, except that jurisdiction shall exist only over those plaintiffs whose claims in a mass action satisfy the jurisdictional amount requirements under subsection (a).

**(ii)** As used in subparagraph (A), the term "mass action" shall not include any civil action in which—

**(I)** all of the claims in the action arise from an event or occurrence in the State in which the action was filed, and that allegedly resulted in injuries in that State or in States contiguous to that State;

**(II)** the claims are joined upon motion of a defendant;

**(III)** all of the claims in the action are asserted on behalf of the general public (and not on behalf of individual claimants or members of a purported class) pursuant to a State statute specifically authorizing such action; or

**(IV)** the claims have been consolidated or coordinated solely for pretrial proceedings.

**(C)**

**(i)** Any action(s) removed to Federal court pursuant to this subsection shall not thereafter be transferred to any other court pursuant to section 1407 [28 USCS § 1407], or the rules promulgated thereunder, unless a majority of the plaintiffs in the action request transfer pursuant to section 1407 [28 USCS § 1407].

**(ii)** This subparagraph will not apply—

**(I)** to cases certified pursuant to rule 23 of the Federal Rules of Civil Procedure; or

**(II)** if plaintiffs propose that the action proceed as a class action pursuant to rule 23 of the Federal Rules of Civil Procedure.

**(D)** The limitations periods on any claims asserted in a mass action that is removed to Federal court pursuant to this subsection shall be deemed tolled during the period that the action is pending in Federal court.

**(e)** The word "States", as used in this section, includes the Territories, the District of Columbia, and the Commonwealth of Puerto Rico.

### History

(June 25, 1948, ch 646,62 Stat. 930; July 26, 1956, ch 740, 70 Stat. 658; July 25, 1958, P.L. 85–554, § 2, 72 Stat. 415; Aug. 14, 1964, P.L. 88–439, § 1, 78 Stat. 445; Oct. 21, 1976, P.L. 94–583, § 3, 90 Stat. 2891; Nov. 19, 1988, P.L. 100–702, Title II, §§ 201(a), 202(a), 203(a), 102 Stat. 4646; Oct. 19, 1996, P.L. 104–317, Title II, § 205(a), 110 Stat. 3850.)

(As amended Feb. 18, 2005, P.L. 109–2, § 4(a), 119 Stat. 9; Dec. 7, 2011, P.L. 112–63, Title I, §§ 101, 102, 125 Stat. 758.)

### § 1341. Taxes by States.

The district courts shall not enjoin, suspend or restrain the assessment, levy or collection of any tax under State law where a plain, speedy and efficient remedy may be had in the courts of such State.

(Added June 25, 1948, ch. 646, 62 Stat. 932.)

**§ 1359. Parties Collusively Joined or Made.**

A district court shall not have jurisdiction of a civil action in which any party, by assignment or otherwise, has been improperly or collusively made or joined to invoke the jurisdiction of such court.

**§ 1367. Supplemental Jurisdiction.**

**(a)** Except as provided in subsections (b) and (c) or as expressly provided otherwise by Federal statute, in any civil action of which the district courts have original jurisdiction, the district courts shall have supplemental jurisdiction over all other claims that are so related to claims in the action within such original jurisdiction that they form part of the same case or controversy under Article III of the United States Constitution. Such supplemental jurisdiction shall include claims that involve the joinder or intervention of additional parties.

**(b)** In any civil action of which the district courts have original jurisdiction founded solely on section 1332 of this title, the district courts shall not have supplemental jurisdiction under subsection (a) over claims by plaintiffs against persons made parties under Rule 14, 19, 20, or 24 of the Federal Rules of Civil Procedure, or over claims by persons proposed to be joined as plaintiffs under Rule 19 of such rules, or seeking to intervene as plaintiffs under Rule 24 of such rules, when exercising supplemental jurisdiction over such claims would be inconsistent with the jurisdictional requirements of section 1332.

**(c)** The district courts may decline to exercise supplemental jurisdiction over a claim under subsection (a) if—

**(1)** the claim raises a novel or complex issue of State law,

**(2)** the claim substantially predominates over the claim or claims over which the district court has original jurisdiction,

**(3)** the district court has dismissed all claims over which it has original jurisdiction, or

**(4)** in exceptional circumstances, there are other compelling reasons for declining jurisdiction.

**(d)** The period of limitations for any claim asserted under subsection (a), and for any other claim in the same action that is voluntarily dismissed at the same time as or after the dismissal of the claim under subsection (a), shall be tolled while the claim is pending and for a period of 30 days after it is dismissed unless State law provides for a longer tolling period.

**(e)** As used in this section, the term "State" includes the District of Columbia, the Commonwealth of Puerto Rico, and any territory or possession of the United States.

(Added Dec. 1, 1990, Pub. L. 101–650, § 310(a), 104 Stat. 5113.)

**§ 1390. Scope.**

**(a)** Venue defined. As used in this chapter [28 USCS §§ 1390 et seq.], the term "venue" refers to the geographic specification of the proper court or courts for the litigation of a civil action that is within the subject-matter jurisdiction of the district courts in general, and does not refer to any grant or restriction of subject-matter jurisdiction providing for a civil action to be adjudicated only by the district court for a particular district or districts.

**(b)** Exclusion of certain cases. Except as otherwise provided by law, this chapter [28 USCS §§ 1390 et seq.] shall not govern the venue of a civil action in which the district court exercises the jurisdiction conferred by section 1333 [28 USCS § 1333], except that such civil actions may be transferred between district courts as provided in this chapter [28 USCS §§ 1390 et seq.].

**(c)** Clarification regarding cases removed from State courts. This chapter [28 USCS §§ 1390 et seq.] shall not determine the district court to which a civil action pending in a State court may be removed, but shall govern the transfer of an action so removed as between districts and divisions of the United States district courts.

**History**

(Added Dec. 7, 2011,P.L. 112–63, Title II, § 201(a), 125 Stat. 762.)

### § 1391. Venue Generally.

**(a)** Applicability of section. Except as otherwise provided by law—

**(1)** this section shall govern the venue of all civil actions brought in district courts of the United States; and

**(2)** the proper venue for a civil action shall be determined without regard to whether the action is local or transitory in nature.

**(b)** Venue in general. A civil action may be brought in—

**(1)** a judicial district in which any defendant resides, if all defendants are residents of the State in which the district is located;

**(2)** a judicial district in which a substantial part of the events or omissions giving rise to the claim occurred, or a substantial part of property that is the subject of the action is situated; or

**(3)** if there is no district in which an action may otherwise be brought as provided in this section, any judicial district in which any defendant is subject to the court's personal jurisdiction with respect to such action.

**(c)** Residency. For all venue purposes—

**(1)** a natural person, including an alien lawfully admitted for permanent residence in the United States, shall be deemed to reside in the judicial district in which that person is domiciled;a natural person, including an alien lawfully admitted for permanent residence in the United States, shall be deemed to reside in the judicial district in which that person is domiciled;

**(2)** an entity with the capacity to sue and be sued in its common name under applicable law, whether or not incorporated, shall be deemed to reside, if a defendant, in any judicial district in which such defendant is subject to the court's personal jurisdiction with respect to the civil action in question and, if a plaintiff, only in the judicial district in which it maintains its principal place of business; and

**(3)** a defendant not resident in the United States may be sued in any judicial district, and the joinder of such a defendant shall be disregarded in determining where the action may be brought with respect to other defendants.

**(d)** Residency of corporations in States with multiple districts. For purposes of venue under this chapter, in a State which has more than one judicial district and in which a defendant that is a corporation is subject to personal jurisdiction at the time an action is commenced, such corporation shall be deemed to reside in any district in that State within which its contacts would be sufficient to subject it to personal jurisdiction if that district were a separate State, and, if there is no such district, the corporation shall be deemed to reside in the district within which it has the most significant contacts.

**(e)** Actions where defendant is officer or employee of the United States.

**(1)** In general. A civil action in which a defendant is an officer or employee of the United States or any agency thereof acting in his official capacity or under color of legal authority, or an agency of the United States, or the United States, may, except as otherwise provided by law, be brought in any judicial district in which (A) a defendant in the action resides, (B) a substantial part of the events or omissions giving rise to the claim occurred, or a substantial part of property that is the subject of the action is situated, or (C) the plaintiff resides if no real property is involved in the action. Additional persons may be joined as parties to any such action in accordance with the Federal Rules of Civil Procedure and with such other venue requirements as would be applicable if the United States or one of its officers, employees, or agencies were not a party.

**(2)** Service. The summons and complaint in such an action shall be served as provided by the Federal Rules of Civil Procedure except that the delivery of the summons and complaint to the officer or agency as required by the rules may be made by certified mail beyond the territorial limits of the district in which the action is brought.

**(f)** Civil actions against a foreign state. A civil action against a foreign state as defined in section 1603(a) of this title [28 USCS § 1603(a)] may be brought—

**(1)** in any judicial district in which a substantial part of the events or omissions giving rise to the claim occurred, or a substantial part of property that is the subject of the action is situated;

**(2)** in any judicial district in which the vessel or cargo of a foreign state is situated, if the claim is asserted under section 1605(b) of this title [28 USCS § 1605(b)];

**(3)** in any judicial district in which the agency or instrumentality is licensed to do business or is doing business, if the action is brought against an agency or instrumentality of a foreign state as defined in section 1603(b) of this title [28 USCS § 1603(b)]; or

**(4)** in the United States District Court for the District of Columbia if the action is brought against a foreign state or political subdivision thereof.

**(g)** Multiparty, multiforum litigation. A civil action in which jurisdiction of the district court is based upon section 1369 of this title [28 USCS § 1369] may be brought in any district in which any defendant resides or in which a substantial part of the accident giving rise to the action took place.

**History**

(June 25, 1948, ch. 646,62 Stat. 935; Oct. 5, 1962, P.L. 87–748, § 2, 76 Stat. 744; Dec. 23, 1963, P.L. 88–234, 77 Stat. 473; Nov. 2, 1966, P.L. 89–714, §§ 1, 2, 80 Stat. 1111; Oct. 21, 1976, P.L. 94–583, §§ 3, 5, 90 Stat. 2721, 2897; Nov. 19, 1988, P.L. 100–702, Title X, § 1013(a), 102 Stat. 4669; Dec. 1, 1990, P.L. 101–650, Title III, § 311, 104 Stat. 5114; Dec. 9, 1991, P.L. 102–198, § 3, 105 Stat. 1623; Oct. 29, 1992, P.L. 102–572, Title V, § 504, 106 Stat. 4513; Oct. 3, 1995, P.L. 104–34, § 1, 109 Stat. 293; Nov. 2, 2002, P.L. 107–273, Div C, Title I, Subtitle A, § 11020(b)(2), 116 Stat. 1827; Dec. 7, 2011, P.L. 112–63, Title II, § 202, 125 Stat. 763.)

**§ 1404. Change of Venue.**

**(a)** For the convenience of parties and witnesses, in the interest of justice, a district court may transfer any civil action to any other district or division where it might have been brought or to any district or division to which all parties have consented.

**(b)** Upon motion, consent or stipulation of all parties, any action, suit or proceeding of a civil nature or any motion or hearing thereof, may be transferred, in the discretion of the court, from the division in which pending to any other division in the same district. Transfer of proceedings in rem brought by or on behalf of the United States may be transferred under this section without the consent of the United States where all other parties request transfer.

**(c)** A district court may order any civil action to be tried at any place within the division in which it is pending.

**(d)** Transfers from a district court of the United States to the District Court of Guam, the District Court for the Northern Mariana Islands, or the District Court of the Virgin Islands shall not be permitted under this section. As otherwise used in this section, the term "district court" includes the District Court of Guam, the District Court for the Northern Mariana Islands, and the District Court of the Virgin Islands, and the term "district" includes the territorial jurisdiction of each such court.

**History**

(June 25, 1948, ch. 646,62 Stat. 937; Oct. 18, 1962, P.L. 87–845, § 9, 76A Stat. 699; Oct. 19, 1996, P.L. 104–317, Title VI, § 610(a), 110 Stat. 3860; Dec. 7, 2011, P.L. 112–63, Title II, § 204, 125 Stat. 764.)

**§ 1406. Cure or Waiver of Defects.**

**(a)** The district court of a district in which is filed a case laying venue in the wrong division or district shall dismiss, or if it be in the interest of justice, transfer such case to any district or division in which it could have been brought.

**(b)** Nothing in this chapter shall impair the jurisdiction of a district court of any matter involving a party who does not interpose timely and sufficient objection to the venue.

**(c)** As used in this section, the term "district court" includes the District Court of Guam, the District Court for the Northern Mariana Islands, and the District Court of the Virgin Islands, and the term "district" includes the territorial jurisdiction of each such court.

(Added June 25, 1948, ch. 646, 62 Stat. 937; amended May 24, 1949, ch. 139, § 81, 63 Stat. 101; Sept. 13, 1960, Pub. L. 86–770, § 1, 74 Stat. 912; Oct. 18, 1962, Pub. L. 87–845, § 10, 76A Stat. 699; April 2, 1982, Pub. L. 97–164, § 132, 96 Stat. 39; Oct. 19, 1996, Pub. L. 104–317, § 610, 110 Stat. 3860.)

### § 1407. Multidistrict Litigation.

**(a)** When civil actions involving one or more common questions of fact are pending in different districts, such actions may be transferred to any district for coordinated or consolidated pretrial proceedings. Such transfers shall be made by the judicial panel on multidistrict litigation authorized by this section upon its determination that transfers for such proceedings will be for the convenience of parties and witnesses and will promote the just and efficient conduct of such actions. Each action so transferred shall be remanded by the panel at or before the conclusion of such pretrial proceedings to the district from which it was transferred unless it shall have been previously terminated: *Provided, however,* That the panel may separate any claim, cross-claim, counter-claim, or third-party claim and remand any of such claims before the remainder of the action is remanded.

**(b)** Such coordinated or consolidated pretrial proceedings shall be conducted by a judge or judges to whom such actions are assigned by the judicial panel on multidistrict litigation. For this purpose, upon request of the panel, a circuit judge or a district judge may be designated and assigned temporarily for service in the transferee district by the Chief Justice of the United States or the chief judge of the circuit, as may be required, in accordance with the provisions of chapter 13 of this title. With the consent of the transferee district court, such actions may be assigned by the panel to a judge or judges of such district. The judge or judges to whom such actions are assigned, the members of the judicial panel on multidistrict litigation, and other circuit and district judges designated when needed by the panel may exercise the powers of a district judge in any district for the purpose of conducting pretrial depositions in such coordinated or consolidated pretrial proceedings.

**(c)** Proceedings for the transfer of an action under this section may be initiated by—

**(i)** the judicial panel on multidistrict litigation upon its own initiative, or

**(ii)** motion filed with the panel by a party in any action in which transfer for coordinated or consolidated pretrial proceedings under this section may be appropriate. A copy of such motion shall be filed in the district court in which the moving party's action is pending.

The panel shall give notice to the parties in all actions in which transfers for coordinated or consolidated pretrial proceedings are contemplated, and such notice shall specify the time and place of any hearing to determine whether such transfer shall be made. Orders of the panel to set a hearing and other orders of the panel issued prior to the order either directing or denying transfer shall be filed in the office of the clerk of the district court in which a transfer hearing is to be or has been held. The panel's order of transfer shall be based upon a record of such hearing at which material evidence may be offered by any party to an action pending in any district that would be affected by the proceedings under this section, and shall be supported by findings of fact and conclusions of law based upon such record. Orders of transfer and such other orders as the panel may make thereafter shall be filed in the office of the clerk of the district court of the transferee district and shall be effective when thus filed. The clerk of the transferee district court shall forthwith transmit a certified copy of the panel's order to transfer to the clerk of the district court from which the action is being transferred. An order denying transfer shall be filed in each district wherein there is a case pending in which the motion for transfer has been made.

**(d)** The judicial panel on multidistrict litigation shall consist of seven circuit and district judges designated from time to time by the Chief Justice of the United States, no two of whom shall be from the same circuit. The concurrence of four members shall be necessary to any action by the panel.

**(e)** No proceedings for review of any order of the panel may be permitted except by extraordinary writ pursuant to the provisions of title 28, section 1651, United States Code. Petitions for an extraordinary writ to review an order of the panel to set a transfer hearing and other orders of the panel issued prior to the order either directing or denying transfer shall be filed only in the court of appeals having jurisdiction over the district in which a hearing is to be or has been held. Petitions for an extraordinary writ to review an order to transfer or orders subsequent to transfer shall be filed only in the court of appeals having jurisdiction over the transferee district. There shall be no appeal or review of an order of the panel denying a motion to transfer for consolidated or coordinated proceedings.

**(f)** The panel may prescribe rules for the conduct of its business not inconsistent with Acts of Congress and the Federal Rules of Civil Procedure.

**(g)** Nothing in this section shall apply to any action in which the United States is a complainant arising under the antitrust laws. "Antitrust laws" as used herein include those acts referred to in the Act of October 15, 1914, as amended (38 Stat. 730; 15 U.S.C. 12), and also include the Act of June 19, 1936 (49 Stat. 1526; 15 U.S.C. 13, 13a, and 13b) and the Act of September 26, 1914, as added March 21, 1938 (52 Stat. 116, 117; 15 U.S.C. 56); but shall not include section 4A of the Act of October 15, 1914, as added July 7, 1955 (69 Stat. 282; 15 U.S.C. 15a).

**(h)** Notwithstanding the provisions of section 1404 or subsection (f) of this section, the judicial panel on multidistrict litigation may consolidate and transfer with or without the consent of the parties, for both pretrial purposes and for trial, any action brought under section 4C of the Clayton Act.

(Added April 29, 1968, Pub. L. 90–296, § 1, 82 Stat. 109; amended September 30,

1976, Pub. L. 94–435, § 303, 90 Stat. 1396.)

**§ 1441. Removal of Civil Actions.**

**(a)** Generally. Except as otherwise expressly provided by Act of Congress, any civil action brought in a State court of which the district courts of the United States have original jurisdiction, may be removed by the defendant or the defendants, to the district court of the United States for the district and division embracing the place where such action is pending.

**(b)** Removal based on diversity of citizenship.

**(1)** In determining whether a civil action is removable on the basis of the jurisdiction under section 1332(a) of this title [28 USCS § 1332(a)], the citizenship of defendants sued under fictitious names shall be disregarded.

**(2)** A civil action otherwise removable solely on the basis of the jurisdiction under section 1332(a) of this title [28 USCS § 1332(a)] may not be removed if any of the parties in interest properly joined and served as defendants is a citizen of the State in which such action is brought.

**(c)** Joinder of Federal law claims and State law claims.

**(1)** If a civil action includes—

**(A)** a claim arising under the Constitution, laws, or treaties of the United States (within the meaning of section 1331 of this title [28 USCS § 1331]), and

**(B)** a claim not within the original or supplemental jurisdiction of the district court or a claim that has been made nonremovable by statute, the entire action may be removed if the action would be removable without the inclusion of the claim described in subparagraph (B).

**(2)** Upon removal of an action described in paragraph (1), the district court shall sever from the action all claims described in paragraph (1)(B) and shall remand the severed claims to the State court from which the action was removed. Only defendants against whom a claim described in paragraph (1)(A) has been asserted are required to join in or consent to the removal under paragraph (1).

**(d)** Actions against foreign states. Any civil action brought in a State court against a foreign state as defined in section 1603(a) of this title [28 USCS § 1603(a)] may be removed by the foreign state to the district court of the United States for the district and division embracing the place where such action is pending. Upon removal the action shall be tried by the court without jury. Where removal is based upon this subsection, the time limitations of section 1446(b) of this chapter [28 USCS § 1446(b)] may be enlarged at any time for cause shown.

**(e)** Multiparty, multiforum jurisdiction.

**(1)** Notwithstanding the provisions of subsection (b) of this section, a defendant in a civil action in a State court may remove the action to the district court of the United States for the district and division embracing the place where the action is pending if—

**(A)** the action could have been brought in a United States district court under section 1369 of this title [28 USCS § 1369]; or

**(B)** the defendant is a party to an action which is or could have been brought, in whole or in part, under section 1369 [28 USCS § 1369] in a United States district court and arises from the same accident as the action in State court, even if the action to be removed could not have been brought in a district court as an original matter.

The removal of an action under this subsection shall be made in accordance with section 1446 of this title [28 USCS § 1446], except that a notice of removal may also be filed before trial of the action in State court within 30 days after the date on which the defendant first becomes a party to an action under section 1369 [28 USCS § 1369] in a United States district court that arises from the same accident as the action in State court, or at a later time with leave of the district court.

**(2)** Whenever an action is removed under this subsection and the district court to which it is removed or transferred under section 1407(j) [28 USCS § 1407(j)] has made a liability determination requiring further proceedings as to damages, the district court shall remand the action to the State court from which it had been removed for the determination of damages, unless the court finds that, for the convenience of parties and witnesses and in the interest of justice, the action should be retained for the determination of damages.

**(3)** Any remand under paragraph (2) shall not be effective until 60 days after the district court has issued an order determining liability and has certified its intention to remand the removed action for the determination of damages. An appeal with respect to the liability determination of the district court may be taken during that 60-day period to the court of appeals with appellate jurisdiction over the district court. In the event a party files such an appeal, the remand shall not be effective until the appeal has been finally disposed of. Once the remand has become effective, the liability determination shall not be subject to further review by appeal or otherwise.

**(4)** Any decision under this subsection concerning remand for the determination of damages shall not be reviewable by appeal or otherwise.

**(5)** An action removed under this subsection shall be deemed to be an action under section 1369 [28 USCS § 1369] and an action in which jurisdiction is based on section 1369 of this title [28 USCS § 1369] for purposes of this section and sections 1407, 1697, and 1785 of this title [28 USCS §§ 1407, 1697, and 1785].

**(6)** Nothing in this subsection shall restrict the authority of the district court to transfer or dismiss an action on the ground of inconvenient forum.

**(f)** Derivative removal jurisdiction. The court to which a civil action is removed under this section is not precluded from hearing and determining any claim in such civil action because the State court from which such civil action is removed did not have jurisdiction over that claim.

### History

(June 25, 1948, ch 646,62 Stat. 937; Oct. 21, 1976, P.L. 94–583, § 6, 90 Stat. 2898; June 19, 1986, P.L. 99–336, § 3(a), 100 Stat. 637; Nov. 19, 1988, P.L. 100–702, Title

X, § 1016(a), 102 Stat. 4669 Dec. 1, 1990, P.L. 101–650, Title III, § 312, 104 Stat. 5114; Dec. 9, 1991, P.L. 102–198, § 4, 105 Stat. 1623; Nov. 2, 2002, P.L. 107–273, Div C, Title I, Subtitle A, § 11020(b)(3), 116 Stat. 1827.)

(As amended Dec. 7, 2011,P.L. 112–63, Title I, § 103(a), 125 Stat. 759.)

**§ 1446. Procedure for Removal of Civil Actions.**

**(a)** Generally. Except as otherwise expressly provided by Act of Congress, any civil action brought in a State court of which the district courts of the United States have original jurisdiction, may be removed by the defendant or the defendants, to the district court of the United States for the district and division embracing the place where such action is pending.

**(b)** Removal based on diversity of citizenship.

**(1)** In determining whether a civil action is removable on the basis of the jurisdiction under section 1332(a) of this title [28 USCS § 1332(a)], the citizenship of defendants sued under fictitious names shall be disregarded.

**(2)** A civil action otherwise removable solely on the basis of the jurisdiction under section 1332(a) of this title [28 USCS § 1332(a)] may not be removed if any of the parties in interest properly joined and served as defendants is a citizen of the State in which such action is brought.

**(c)** Joinder of Federal law claims and State law claims.

(1) If a civil action includes—

**(A)** a claim arising under the Constitution, laws, or treaties of the United States (within the meaning of section 1331 of this title [28 USCS § 1331]), and

**(B)** a claim not within the original or supplemental jurisdiction of the district court or a claim that has been made nonremovable by statute, the entire action may be removed if the action would be removable without the inclusion of the claim described in subparagraph (B).

**(2)** Upon removal of an action described in paragraph (1), the district court shall sever from the action all claims described in paragraph (1)(B) and shall remand the severed claims to the State court from which the action was removed. Only defendants against whom a claim described in paragraph (1)(A) has been asserted are required to join in or consent to the removal under paragraph (1).

**(d)** Actions against foreign states. Any civil action brought in a State court against a foreign state as defined in section 1603(a) of this title [28 USCS § 1603(a)] may be removed by the foreign state to the district court of the United States for the district and division embracing the place where such action is pending. Upon removal the action shall be tried by the court without jury. Where removal is based upon this subsection, the time limitations of section 1446(b) of this chapter [28 USCS § 1446(b)] may be enlarged at any time for cause shown.

**(e)** Multiparty, multiforum jurisdiction.

**(1)** Notwithstanding the provisions of subsection (b) of this section, a defendant in a civil action in a State court may remove the action to the district court of the United States for the district and division embracing the place where the action is pending if—

**(A)** the action could have been brought in a United States district court under section 1369 of this title [28 USCS § 1369]; or

**(B)** the defendant is a party to an action which is or could have been brought, in whole or in part, under section 1369 [28 USCS § 1369] in a United States district court and arises from the same accident as the action in State court, even if the action to be removed could not have been brought in a district court as an original matter.

The removal of an action under this subsection shall be made in accordance with section 1446 of this title [28 USCS § 1446], except that a notice of removal may also be filed before trial of the action in State court within 30 days after the date on which the defendant first becomes a party to an action under section 1369 [28 USCS § 1369] in a United States district court that arises from the same accident as the action in State court, or at a later time with leave of the district court.

**(2)** Whenever an action is removed under this subsection and the district court to which it is removed or transferred under section 1407(j) [28 USCS § 1407(j)] has made a liability determination requiring further proceedings as to damages, the district court shall remand the action to the State court from which it had been removed for the determination of damages, unless the court finds that, for the convenience of parties and witnesses and in the interest of justice, the action should be retained for the determination of damages.

**(3)** Any remand under paragraph (2) shall not be effective until 60 days after the district court has issued an order determining liability and has certified its intention to remand the removed action for the determination of damages. An appeal with respect to the liability determination of the district court may be taken during that 60-day period to the court of appeals with appellate jurisdiction over the district court. In the event a party files such an appeal, the remand shall not be effective until the appeal has been finally disposed of. Once the remand has become effective, the liability determination shall not be subject to further review by appeal or otherwise.

**(4)** Any decision under this subsection concerning remand for the determination of damages shall not be reviewable by appeal or otherwise.

**(5)** An action removed under this subsection shall be deemed to be an action under section 1369 [28 USCS § 1369] and an action in which jurisdiction is based on section 1369 of this title [28 USCS § 1369] for purposes of this section and sections 1407, 1697, and 1785 of this title [28 USCS §§ 1407, 1697, and 1785].

**(6)** Nothing in this subsection shall restrict the authority of the district court to transfer or dismiss an action on the ground of inconvenient forum.

**(f)** Derivative removal jurisdiction. The court to which a civil action is removed under this section is not precluded from hearing and determining any claim in such civil action because the State court from which such civil action is removed did not have jurisdiction over that claim.

### History

(June 25, 1948, ch 646,62 Stat. 937; Oct. 21, 1976, P.L. 94–583, § 6, 90 Stat. 2898; June 19, 1986, P.L. 99–336, § 3(a), 100 Stat. 637; Nov. 19, 1988, P.L. 100–702, Title X, § 1016(a), 102 Stat. 4669 Dec. 1, 1990, P.L. 101–650, Title III, § 312, 104 Stat. 5114; Dec. 9, 1991, P.L. 102–198, § 4, 105 Stat. 1623; Nov. 2, 2002, P.L. 107–273, Div C, Title I, Subtitle A, § 11020(b)(3), 116 Stat. 1827.)

(As amended Dec. 7, 2011,P.L. 112–63, Title I, § 103(a), 125 Stat. 759.)

### § 1447. Procedure After Removal Generally.

**(a)** In any case removed from a State court, the district court may issue all necessary orders and process to bring before it all proper parties whether served by process issued by the State court or otherwise.

**(b)** It may require the removing party to file with its clerk copies of all records and proceedings in such State court or may cause the same to be brought before it by writ of certiorari issued to such State court.

**(c)** A motion to remand the case on the basis of any defect other than lack of subject matter jurisdiction must be made within 30 days after the filing of the notice of removal under section 1446(a) [28 USCS § 1446(a)]. If at any time before final judgment it appears that the district court lacks subject matter jurisdiction, the case shall be remanded. An order remanding the case may require payment of just costs and any actual expenses, including attorney fees, incurred as a result of the removal. A certified copy of the order of remand shall be mailed by the clerk to the clerk of the State court. The State court may thereupon proceed with such case.

**(d)** An order remanding a case to the State court from which it was removed is not reviewable on appeal or otherwise, except that an order remanding a case to the State court from which it was removed pursuant to section 1442 or 1443 of this title [28 USCS § 1442 or 1443] shall be reviewable by appeal or otherwise.

**(e)** If after removal the plaintiff seeks to join additional defendants whose joinder would destroy subject matter jurisdiction, the court may deny joinder, or permit joinder and remand the action to the State court.

### History

(June 25, 1948, ch 646,62 Stat. 939; May 24, 1949, ch 139, § 84, 63 Stat. 102; July 2, 1964, P.L. 88–352, Title IX, § 901, 78 Stat. 266; Nov. 19, 1988, P.L. 100–702, Title X, § 1016(c), 102 Stat. 4670; Dec. 9, 1991, P.L. 102–198, § 10(b), 105 Stat. 1626; Oct. 1, 1996, P.L. 104–219, § 1, 110 Stat. 3022.)

(As amended Nov. 9, 2011,P.L. 112–51, § 2(d), 125 Stat. 546.)

### § 1453. Removal of class actions

**(a)** Definitions. In this section, the terms "class", "class action", "class certification order", and "class member" shall have the meanings given such terms under section 1332(d)(1) [28 USCS § 1332(d)(1)].

**(b)** In general. A class action may be removed to a district court of the United States in accordance with section 1446 [28 USCS § 1446] (except that the 1-year limitation under section 1446(c)(1) [28 USCS § 1446(c)(1)] shall not apply), without regard to whether any defendant is a citizen of the State in which the action is brought, except that such action may be removed by any defendant without the consent of all defendants.

**(c)** Review of remand orders.

**(1)** In general. Section 1447 [28 USCS § 1447] shall apply to any removal of a case under this section, except that notwithstanding section 1447(d) [28 USCS § 1447(d)], a court of appeals may accept an appeal from an order of a district court granting or denying a motion to remand a class action to the State court from which it was removed if application is made to the court of appeals not more than 10 days after entry of the order.

**(2)** Time period for judgment. If the court of appeals accepts an appeal under paragraph (1), the court shall complete all action on such appeal, including rendering judgment, not later than 60 days after the date on which such appeal was filed, unless an extension is granted under paragraph (3).

**(3)** Extension of time period. The court of appeals may grant an extension of the 60-day period described in paragraph (2) if—

**(A)** such extension is for good cause shown and in the interests of justice, for a period not to exceed 10 days.all parties to the proceeding agree to such extension, for any period of time; or

**(B)** such extension is for good cause shown and in the interests of justice, for a period not to exceed 10 days.

**(4)** Denial of appeal. If a final judgment on the appeal under paragraph (1) is not issued before the end of the period described in paragraph (2), including any extension under paragraph (3), the appeal shall be denied.

**(d)** Exception. This section shall not apply to any class action that solely involves—

**(1)** a claim concerning a covered security as defined under section 16(f)(3) of the Securities Act of 1933 (15 U.S.C. 78p(f)(3) [77p(f)(3)]) and section 28(f)(5)(E) of the Securities Exchange Act of 1934 (15 U.S.C. 78bb(f)(5)(E));

**(2)** a claim that relates to the internal affairs or governance of a corporation or other form of business enterprise and arises under or by virtue of the laws of the State in which such corporation or business enterprise is incorporated or organized; or

**(3)** a claim that relates to the rights, duties (including fiduciary duties), and obligations relating to or created by or pursuant to any security (as defined under section 2(a)(1) of the Securities Act of 1933 (15 U.S.C. 77b(a)(1)) and the regulations issued thereunder).

### History

(Added Feb. 18, 2005,P.L. 109–2, § 5(a), 119 Stat. 12; May 7, 2009, P.L. 111–16, § 6(2), 123 Stat. 1608.)

(As amended Dec. 7, 2011,P.L. 112–63, Title I, § 103(d)(2), 125 Stat. 762.)

### § 1631. Transfer to Cure Want of Jurisdiction.

Whenever a civil action is filed in a court as defined in section 610 of this title or an appeal, including a petition for review of administrative action, is noticed for or filed with such a court and that court finds that there is a want of jurisdiction, the court shall, if it is in the interest of justice, transfer such action or appeal to any other such court in which the action or appeal could have been brought at the time it was filed or noticed, and the action or appeal shall proceed as if it had been filed in or noticed for the court to which it is transferred on the date upon which it was actually filed in or noticed for the court from which it is transferred.

(Added Apr. 2, 1982, Pub. L. 97–164, § 301(a), 96 Stat. 55.)

### § 1651. Writs.

**(a)** The Supreme Court and all courts established by Act of Congress may issue all writs necessary or appropriate in aid of their respective jurisdictions and agreeable to the usages and principles of law.

**(b)** An alternative writ or rule nisi may be issued by a justice or judge of a court which has jurisdiction.

(Added June 25, 1948, ch. 646, 62 Stat. 944; amended May 24, 1949, ch. 139, § 90, 63 Stat. 102.)

### § 2283. Stay of State Court Proceedings.

A court of the United States may not grant an injunction to stay proceedings in a State court except as expressly authorized by Act of Congress, or where necessary in aid of its jurisdiction, or to protect or effectuate its judgments.

(Added June 25, 1948, ch. 646, 62 Stat. 968.)

# INDEX

[References are to sections.]

## A

[References are to sections.]



## B

# C

[References are to sections.]



## F

[References are to sections.]

[References are to sections.]



## R

## T



## V

[References are to sections.]

# TABLE OF CASES

[References are to pages]

## A

[References are to pages]

[References are to pages]

[References are to pages]

[References are to pages]



## C

[References are to pages]

[References are to pages]

[References are to pages]



# D

## E

[References are to pages]



# F

[References are to pages]



# G

[References are to pages]



## H

[References are to pages]

[References are to pages]



## I

## J



## K

[References are to pages]

[References are to pages]



## L

[References are to pages]



## M

[References are to pages]

[References are to pages]

[References are to pages]

## N

[References are to pages]

[References are to pages]



# O

## P

[References are to pages]

[References are to pages]



## Q



## R

[References are to pages]

[References are to pages]

## S

[References are to pages]

[References are to pages]

[References are to pages]



## T

[References are to pages]



## U

[References are to pages]

[References are to pages]

[References are to pages]

[References are to pages]



## Y



## Z

# TABLE OF STATUTES

[References are to pages]

## United States Constitution—Cont.



## United States Code

[References are to pages]

**United States Code**—Cont.



**United States Code**—Cont.

[References are to pages]

**United States Code**—Cont.



**United States Code**—Cont.

[References are to pages]

**United States Code—Cont.**



**United States Code—Cont.**

[References are to pages]

### United States Code—Cont.



### Code of Federal Regulations



### Federal Rules of Appellate Procedure



### Federal Rules of Civil Procedure



### Federal Rules of Civil Procedure —Cont.

[References are to pages]

### Federal Rules of Civil Procedure —Cont.



### Federal Rules of Evidence



### Federal Rules of Bankruptcy Procedure